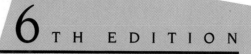

6TH EDITION

Development Through Life
A Psychosocial
Approach

6TH EDITION

Development Through Life
A Psychosocial Approach

Barbara M. Newman
Philip R. Newman
The Ohio State University

ITP™ **Brooks/Cole Publishing Company**
An International Thomson Publishing Company

Pacific Grove • Albany • Bonn • Boston • Cincinnati • Detroit • London • Madrid • Melbourne
Mexico City • New York • Paris • San Francisco • Singapore • Tokyo • Toronto • Washington

Sponsoring Editor: Jim Brace-Thompson
Marketing Team: Carolyn Crockett, Jean Thompson
Editorial Associates: Cathleen S. Collins,
   Patsy Vienneau
Production Editor: Kirk Bomont
Production Assistant: Tessa McGlasson
Manuscript Editor: Margaret Ritchie
Permissions Editor: Linda Rill
Interior and Cover Design: Roy R. Neuhaus

Art Coordinator: Lisa Torri
Interior Illustration: Precision Graphics,
   Judith Macdonald
Photo Editor: Kathleen Olson
Photo Researcher: Sue C. Howard
Indexer: Do Mi Stauber
Typesetting: Weimer Graphics
Cover Printing: Phoenix Color Corporation, Inc.
Printing and Binding: Quebecor Printing Hawkins

Cover: Detail from Pablo Picasso, Ronde des Enfants, 1959. Museo de la Abadia, Montserrat,
   Catalonia/Index/Bridgeman Art Library, London/Superstock.

Credits continue on p. 759.

Brooks/Cole Publishing Company
A division of International Thomson Publishing Inc.
I(T)P The ITP logo is a trademark under license.

Copyright © 1995, 1991, 1987, 1984, 1979, 1975 by Barbara M. Newman and Philip R. Newman

For more information, contact:

BROOKS/COLE PUBLISHING COMPANY
511 Forest Lodge Road
Pacific Grove, CA 93950
USA

International Thomson Publishing Europe
Berkshire House 168-173
High Holborn
London WC1V 7AA
England

Thomas Nelson Australia
102 Dodds Street
South Melbourne, 3205
Victoria, Australia

Nelson Canada
1120 Birchmount Road
Scarborough, Ontario
Canada M1K 5G4

International Thomson Editores
Campos Eliseos 385, Piso 7
Col. Polanco
11560 México D. F. México

International Thomson Publishing GmbH
Königswinterer Strasse 418
53227 Bonn
Germany

International Thomson Publishing Asia
221 Henderson Road
#05-10 Henderson Building
Singapore 0315

International Thomson Publishing Japan
Hirakawacho Kyowa Building, 3F
2-2-1 Hirakawacho
Chiyoda-ku, Tokyo 102
Japan

Printed in the United States of America

10   9   8   7   6   5

Library of Congress Cataloging-in-Publication Data
Newman, Barbara M.
   Development through life : a psychosocial approach / Barbara M.
  Newman, Philip R. Newman. — 6th ed.
     p.   cm.
   Includes bibliographical references and index.
   ISBN 0–534–23334–1
   1. Developmental psychology.   I. Newman Philip R.   II. Title.
BF713.N48   1995
155—dc20   94-38712
                                                                  CIP

To Erik H. Erikson and Robert J. Havighurst

Brief Contents

Contents

3   *Theories of Change*   68

4   *The Period of Pregnancy and Prenatal Development*   130

5   Infancy (Birth to 2 Years)   188

6 *Toddlerhood (2–4 Years)*   248

Early School Age (4–6 Years)

7

8   *Middle School Age* (6–12 Years)   352

9 *Early Adolescence* (12–18 Years)   404

10 Later Adolescence (18–22 Years) 468

12 Middle Adulthood (34–60 Years)   570

Preface

Twenty years have gone by since the first edition of *Development Through Life* was published. It's almost time for this book to vote. Two editions of the book have been translated into Japanese, and in 1994 we had a chance to spend several months with our Japanese translator, Professor Mamoru Fukutomi, who visited with us at Ohio State. One of our most admired doctoral students, Dr. James Kuo, translated the text into Chinese, and the Chinese edition has been divided into two volumes to make it more affordable to a wide audience. It seems as if *Development Through Life* has found a life of its own, a life that brings us in contact with scholars, students, and practitioners from around the world. We are pleased to discover that people in many parts of the world recognize and relate to the ideas and themes of the text.

We started this book in our own early adulthood and have continued to work on it through our middle adulthood. It has been a constant orienting framework for our scholarly work through the birth and parenting of our three children, the death of our parents, the successes and disappointments of our work lives, and the delights and conflicts of our relationship as husband and wife. The themes of this book have allowed us to anticipate and cope with many of the normative challenges of adult life, as well as to maintain a hopeful outlook in the face of unanticipated crises. We hope that the orientation of this text will provide these same benefits for you. The life-span perspective is a means of understanding the challenges, conflicts, and achievements that are central to people living through stages other than our own. In this respect, it challenges our egocentrism. It assumes an interconnectedness among people at various periods of life and helps guide one's interactions with others so that they are optimally sensitive, supportive, and facilitative to the forces for growth at each life stage.

Perspective

Development Through Life is a general introduction to the study of human development from conception through very old age. The text treats physical, intellectual, social, and emotional growth in each of 11 stages and emphasizes that development results from the interdependence of these areas at every stage. We also give special attention to the conditions that promote optimal development throughout life. Psychosocial theory provides a conceptual framework for the text as we highlight the continuous interaction of individual competencies with the demands and resources of culture. Development is viewed as a product of genetic, maturational, societal, and self-directed factors.

Applying this integrating perspective to an analysis of human development has several advantages. First, although the subject matter is potentially overwhelming, the psychosocial framework helps to identify meaningful directions of growth across the life span. Second, the framework helps readers to assess the influence of experiences during earlier life stages on later development, as well as the impact of later development on the course of earlier stages. It also helps readers to understand some of the ways that their own past, present, and future expectations are systematically connected to the lives of those older and younger than they. Third, the framework offers a hopeful outlook on the total life course: The promise of continuous growth validates many of the struggles of adolescence, early adulthood, and middle adulthood.

Organization

We have retained the basic focus and organization of the text in this edition. However, we have thoroughly updated the material and added new sections. The first chapter establishes the orientation and assumptions of the text and introduces the scientific process through which a systematic study of development becomes possible. Chapter 2 presents a detailed discussion of the basic concepts of psychosocial theory, including an analysis of its strengths and weaknesses. Proponents of psychosocial theory argue that human development can be conceptualized as a sequence of stages from conception through very old age. At each stage, several major tasks require new kinds of learning; further, at each stage there arises a major developmental conflict, or psychosocial crisis. This conflict results from a discrepancy between our competencies as we enter a particular stage and the demands of our environment—family, school, or community. We can resolve the conflict either gradually or suddenly, but in any case, it must be resolved. Development occurs in an ever-changing social context; successfully resolving conflicts and accomplishing tasks at one stage of our lives allows us to cope with new demands our culture and members of our immediate social groups impose at the next stage. At each stage, we redefine ourselves and our relationships with others. Continuity and change, whether in response to internal pressures and environmental demands or as a result of our own choices and commitments, are both products of development.

Chapter 3 outlines significant ideas about change and growth from other theoretical perspectives. In this edition, Vygotsky's contextual theory and Bronfenbrenner's ecological systems theory have been added. The broad range of theoretical concepts provides the intellectual structure for later discussions of physical, cognitive, social, and emotional development. These theories help readers analyze apparent conflicts among the maturational, societal, and individual forces toward growth. In presenting a variety of theoretical perspectives, we also offer a multidimensional source of information about individual behaviors and patterns of change.

In Chapter 4, fetal development is studied in relation to the pregnant woman and her social environment. Continued discoveries in the field of behavioral genetics have been included in this revision. We have given new emphasis to research on the risks to fetal development associated with a pregnant woman's exposure to a wide range of substances, especially nicotine, alcohol, caffeine, other drugs, and environmental toxins. The ways in which poverty adds to the risks to which fetuses may be exposed are highlighted in this chapter. The topic of abortion is also examined in this chapter, and, in this edition, the legal issues surrounding abortion are presented in new detail.

Chapters 5 through 14 trace basic patterns of normal growth and development in the remaining stages of human life: infancy, toddlerhood, early school age, middle school age, early adolescence, later adolescence, early adulthood, middle adulthood, later adulthood, and very old age. In these chapters we consider how individuals organize and interpret their experience, noting changes both in their behavior and in the environmental demands they face. Each chapter begins with an examination of four or five of the critical developmental tasks of the stage. These tasks reflect global aspects of development, including physical growth and sensory and motor competence, cognitive maturation, social relationships, and self-understanding. We consider the psychosocial crisis of each stage in some detail. We also show how successfully resolving a crisis helps individuals develop a prime adaptive ego quality and how unsuccessful resolution leads to a core pathology. Although most people grow developmentally—albeit with pain and struggle—others do not. People who acquire core pathologies lead withdrawn, guarded lives; for the most part, they become psychologically unhealthy and, often, physically unhealthy as well.

We conclude each chapter by applying research and theory to a topic of societal importance at the given life stage. These seemingly controversial discussions often provide a productive transition from the gathering of new ideas and information to the more active practice of applying these ideas to difficult social issues. Table 2.7 contains an overview of the basic tasks, crises, and applied topics.

The Sixth Edition

The changes in the sixth edition do not affect the basic structure of the book. We hope that many new sections bring greater clarity, elaboration, or a fresh way of thinking to a topic. We have increased our presentation of information about development in cultures outside the United States and expanded the picture of how the wide variety of ethnic subcultures in the United States influences the processes and directions of development. The notion that development is a product of the continuous interaction between individuals' genetically guided characteristics and cultural resources, beliefs, and values is illustrated time and again in the discussion of cultural and subcultural comparisons. This edition introduces numerous examples of the ways that poverty, discrimination, and various forms of societal oppression affect individual development. These revisions help to raise questions about which aspects of development are universal and which are shaped by society. They help us appreciate the wide range of contexts in which development takes place and the remarkable capacities for growth and adaptation that are evidenced at every period of life.

In this edition, we have continued to emphasize the theme of genetic and environmental interaction. Research in human development continues to reveal the dynamic interplay between genetically based human capacities and the sociocultural context in which they are nurtured and expanded. We have tried to reflect this in many of the developmental tasks discussed, including language, self-regulation, emotional development, motor development, the elaboration of cognitive skills, orientation toward parenting, the formation of intimate relationships, the development of capacities necessary to carry out productive work, and the ability to cope with the physical changes of aging.

Since the time of the fifth edition, the field has experienced the death of both Erik Erikson and Robert Havighurst, two wonderful scholars whose writing and outlook have guided and inspired our own intellectual development. The combined contributions of these scholars have shaped the basic direction of psychosocial theory and have guided an enormous amount of research in human development. They directed us to look at the process of growth and change across the life span. They recognized the intimate interweaving of the individual's life story with the sociohistorical context, emphasizing societal pressures that call for new levels of functioning at each life stage. In their writing, they communicated an underlying optimism about each person's resilience, adaptability, and immense capacity for growth. At the same time, they wrote with a moral passion of our responsibility as teachers, therapists, parents, scholars, and citizens to create a caring society. We celebrate these ideas in the sixth edition.

Acknowledgments

We express our appreciation to many students, colleagues, and friends who shared their ideas with us. Our children, Sam, Abe, and Rachel, made constructive comments about the content, appearance, and tone of the book. To each new edition, our children bring new talents and perspectives that enrich our efforts. Two special friends, Kirk Bloir and Dana McCormick, helped us prepare the manuscript. The sixth edition was produced under the guidance of a wonderful editor, Jim Brace-Thompson. Other staff at Brooks/Cole who helped bring this edition to life include Kirk Bomont, Sue Howard, Roy Neuhaus, Kathleen Olson, and Patsy Vienneau. We were very lucky to have had the benefit of their creative energy. Finally, we acknowledge the thoughtful, constructive comments and suggestions of the following reviewers: Mary Ann Bush, Western Michigan University; Roger DeWitt, Aims Community College; Ken Elliott, University of Maine at Augusta; Russell Isabella, University of Utah; Chuck Joiner, Arkansas State University; Anthony King, Case Western Reserve University; Joe Kishton, University of North Carolina at Wilmington; John McAdoo, Michigan State University; Leon Rappaport, Kansas State University; Emily Scott-Lowe, Pepperdine University; and Susan Zuravin, University of Maryland.

Barbara M. Newman
Philip R. Newman

6TH EDITION

Development Through Life
A Psychosocial Approach

The integrating theme for our analysis of life-span development is psychosocial theory. Each life story is a product of the dynamic interaction between the person and his or her significant social relationships. It is a story of continuity and change, a dance of movement and growth.

The Development Through Life Perspective

In this book, we attempt to bring you the most accurate information and the newest, most thought-provoking ideas about human development so that you will be able to continue to chart your own course as you travel through life. Human development is very puzzling and relatively unexplored. If we are to understand it, we must explore how people integrate beliefs and experiences at each stage of development in their efforts to make sense of their lives. This process is as individual as each person's life story. Yet common threads of organization and understanding allow us to know one another, care for one another, and contribute to one another's well-being.

In this chapter, we give you a brief introduction to four central issues in the study of the life span. First, we outline our assumptions about the study of human development that have guided the orientation of the text. Second, we introduce the broad concept of a psychosocial approach to development. Third, we highlight basic principles of the scientific process on which much of our knowledge about development is based. Finally, we introduce data about life expectancy in order to start you thinking in a very concrete way about the course of your own life and the decisions you make that may have a direct impact on your own life story.

Assumptions of the Text

Our perspective on development through life embraces four assumptions that are critical to the organization and focus of this book. They are a product of our psychosocial orientation and our awareness of the significance of the societal and historical contexts in which behavior occurs.

The life story is one of continuity and change. As individuals in the Emmons family grow, the family changes. New relationships form and yet certain patterns of self and connection to others remain constant.

1. *Growth occurs at every period of life, from conception through very old age.*
2. *Individual lives show continuity and change as they progress through time.* An awareness of the processes that contribute to both continuity and change is central to an understanding of human development.
3. *We need to understand the whole person, because we function in an integrated manner.* To achieve such an understanding we need to study the major internal developments in physical, social, emotional, and cognitive capacities and their interrelationships. We also need to study actions, the many forms of observable behavior.

4. *Every person's behavior must be analyzed in the context of relevant settings and personal relationships.* Human beings are highly skilled in adapting to their environment. The meaning of a given behavior pattern or change must be interpreted in light of the significant physical and social environments in which it occurs.

A Psychosocial Approach: The Interaction of the Biological, Psychological, and Societal Systems

Erik Erikson (1963, p. 37) wrote that human life as the individual experiences it is produced by the interaction and modification of three major systems: the biological system, the psychological system, and the societal system.

The *biological system* includes all those processes necessary for the physical functioning of the organism (Figure 1.1). Our sensory capacities, our motor responses, and the workings of our respiratory, endocrine, and circulatory systems are all biological processes. They develop and change as a consequence of genetically guided maturation, environmental resources such as nutrition and sunlight, exposure to environmental toxins, encounters with accidents and diseases, and life habits related to daily exercise, eating, sleeping, and the use of drugs.

The *psychological system* includes those processes central to thinking, reasoning, and making meaning of experiences (Figure 1.2). Our memory and perception; our problem-solving, language, and symbolic abilities; and our orientation to the future—all require the use of psychological processes. The psychological system provides the resources for processing information and navigating reality. Like the biological processes, the psychological processes develop and change over one's life span. Change is guided in part by genetic information. The maturation of intellectual functioning, for example, appears to be directed by a genetic plan. A number of genetically transmitted diseases result in intellectual impairment and a reduced capacity for learning. Change also results from the accumulation of experiences and from encounters with various educational settings. The psychological

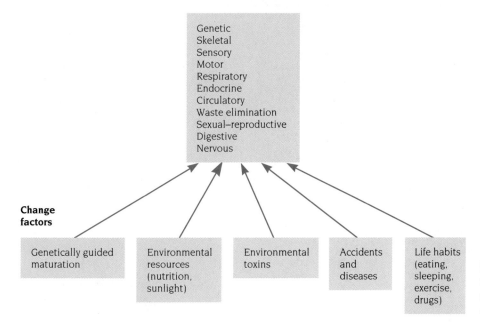

FIGURE 1.1
Some elements of the biological system

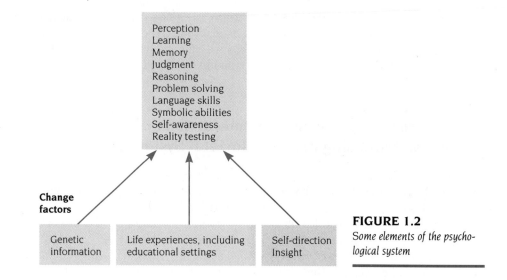

FIGURE 1.2

Some elements of the psycho-logical system

processes are further enhanced by numerous other life experiences, such as sports, camping, travel, reading, and talking with people. Finally, change can be self-directed. A person can decide to pursue a new interest, for example, or to learn another language, or to adopt a new set of ideas. Through self-insight or perhaps psychotherapy, one can begin to think about oneself and others in a new light.

The *societal system* includes those processes through which a person becomes integrated into society (Figure 1.3). Societal influences include social roles, rituals, cultural myths, social expectations, leadership styles, communication patterns, family organization, ethnic and subcultural influences, political and religious ideologies, patterns of economic prosperity or poverty and war or peace,

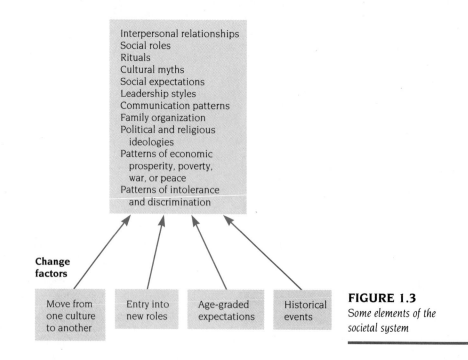

FIGURE 1.3

Some elements of the societal system

Immigration brings dramatic change in the societal process. This Hmong mother, newly settled in California, is going to try to raise an "All-American Kid."

and exposure to racism, sexism, and other forms of discrimination, intolerance, or intergroup hostility. Much of the impact of the societal system on psychosocial development results from interpersonal relationships, often relationships with close or significant others.

The societal processes, too, can change over one's life span. One of the most striking instances of such changes occurs when a person moves from one culture to another. In this case, many of one's fundamental assumptions about oneself and one's social relationships are modified.

Historical events—conditions of war or peace, being the victor or the vanquished, living in prosperity or poverty—influence how people in a given culture perceive themselves. For example, the conditions of World War II—forced military service, decreases in the availability of resources and the resulting system of rationing, the increased involvement of women in the labor market, the bombing of European cities, the unveiling of unprecedented human atrocities, the explosion of the first nuclear bomb over Japan—had a lasting impact on the values and ideology of the people who lived through that period, even if they took no part in the war itself.

Even in less extreme cases, the influence of society on an individual can change over the life course. Entry into new roles brings new demands and behaviors. Most societies have expectations of competence and participation of members that change for each stage of life. These expectations may be in harmony or in conflict with the maturation of the biological and psychological processes.

The *psychosocial approach* focuses on the internal experiences that are the products of interactions among the biological, psychological, and societal processes. When we consider biological processes, we focus on the effects of physical attributes and physical changes on our personal sense of self and our relationships. When we focus on psychological processes, we examine our internal representations of information and relationships—how we categorize and interpret experience. When we focus on societal processes, we examine how our membership in one kind of group rather than another affects our thoughts, feelings, and actions. Changes in one of the three systems—biological, psychological, or societal—generally bring about changes in the others.

A Case Example

We can see how the three systems interact in the case of Rose, a 60-year-old woman who has been having serious attacks of dizziness and shortness of breath as Thanksgiving approaches. Rose is normally active and energetic. Usually she looks forward to entertaining her family, which includes three married daughters, one married son, and their children. However, her son has recently been divorced. Feelings between him and his ex-wife are bitter. Any attempts on Rose's part to communicate with her daughter-in-law or her granddaughter meet with outbursts of hostility from her son. Rose knows she cannot invite her former daughter-in-law and her granddaughter to a family gathering that includes her son.

Rose's daughters suggest having the dinner at one of their homes in order to prevent further conflict. They hope this solution will take some of the pressure off their mother and ease the attacks. Rose agrees, but her attacks continue.

All three systems are involved in Rose's situation. The biological system is expressing the conflict through the symptoms of dizziness and shortness of breath. We must recognize that the psychological and societal demands may elicit responses from the biological system, as they commonly do in people under stress. Although the solution to the problem must be found in the psychological system, the biological system often alerts the person to the severity of the problem through the development of physical symptoms.

Rose's psychological system is involved in interpreting her son's behavior, which she views as forcing her to choose between him and her daughter-in-law and granddaughter. She might also use psychological processes to try to arrive at a solution to the conflict. So far, Rose has not identified any satisfactory solution. Although she can avoid the conflict most of the time, the impending Thanksgiving dinner is forcing her to confront it directly.

The psychological system contributes to Rose's self-concept as well as how she views her role within her family. Through memory, Rose retains a sense of her family at earlier periods, when they enjoyed greater closeness. Having to face a Thanksgiving dinner at which she will feel angry at her son or guilty about excluding her daughter-in-law and her granddaughter places her in a fundamental conflict. The Thanksgiving meal is also a symbolic event, representing Rose's idea of family unity, which she cannot achieve.

The societal system influences the situation at several levels. First, there are the societal expectations regarding the mother role: Mother is nurturing, loving, and protecting. But Rose cannot be nurturing without sending messages of rejection either to her son or to her daughter-in-law and granddaughter.

Second, our society has no clear norms for relating to various family members after a divorce. How should one behave toward the former spouse, the noncustodial parent, the child, and the extended-family members, especially the grandparents? Rose is confused about what to do.

Third, the Thanksgiving celebration has social, religious, and cultural significance. This family ritual was performed in Rose's home when she was a child, and she has carried it through in her own home as an adult. Now, however, she is being forced to pass the responsibility for this festival to her daughter before she is ready to do so and, as a result, Rose is likely to feel a special sense of loss. She will also lose the sense of family unity that she has tried to preserve.

To grasp the importance of the cultural component of the societal process, think how a Japanese person might react to being unable to celebrate Thanksgiving. Thanksgiving is not a Japanese holiday and has no particular emotional or historical significance within the Japanese culture. The importance of Thanksgiving to Rose is linked to her cultural identity. Throughout the world, individuals define their cultural identities in part by the rituals associated wtih specific holidays and life transitions. These culturally determined events have real meaning in the development of the hearts and minds of the culture's members. Even within a country, subcultures may observe certain holidays and rituals that are distinctly different from those of other subcultures and from the society at large.

Fourth, specific interpersonal dynamics are at work here. Rose and her son have a history of conflict that continues to interfere in her other family relationships.

This case illustrates how conflict in the psychological and societal systems can result in symptoms in the biological system. Ordinarily, a person uses the psychological system to create a solution to the conflict. Perhaps because of Rose's past socialization, her age, and her personality, she is expressing the conflict biologically and is unable to use psychological processes to resolve it.

The psychosocial approach highlights the continuous interaction of the individual and the social environment. At each period of their lives, people spend much of their time mastering a relatively small group of psychological tasks that are essential for social adaptation within their society. Each life stage brings a normative crisis, which can be viewed as a tension between one's competencies and the new demands of society. The resolution of each crisis provides a new set of social abilities that influences the person's general orientation to the next stage and the succeeding stages.

Throughout our lives, several personal relationships occupy our attention. Some of these relationships are more important than others, but their quality and diversity provide a basis for the study of one's psychosocial development. As we progress through the stages of life, most of us develop an increasing capacity to initiate new relationships and to innovate in our thoughts and actions so as to direct the course of our lives.

We strive to make sense of our experiences. The meaning we derive depends on our beliefs about ourselves, about our relationships with others, and about the world as our society defines it. This meaning changes over our lives as a result of the maturation of our biological and psychological systems and as we increase our participation in our societal system.

Pablo Picasso, Picasso's Stage, 1970. *Toward the end of his life, Picasso used the metaphor of the stage to summarize the conflicts and relationships that were important to him. In order to see the ongoing action, we have to take into account characters from the past, characters waiting in the wings, and the audience out front. Reality is constructed from many social perspectives.*

Take the concept of love. In infancy, love is almost entirely physical. It is the pervasive sense of comfort and security that we feel in the presence of our caregivers. By adolescence, our idea of love includes loyalty, emotional closeness, and sexuality. In adulthood, our concept of love may expand to include a new emphasis on companionship and open communication. The need to be loved and to give love remains important throughout life, but the self we bring to a loving relationship and the signs of love change with age.

We humans struggle to define ourselves through a sense of connectedness with certain other people and groups and through feelings of distinctiveness from others. We establish categories that define whom we are connected to, whom we care about, and which of our own qualities we admire. We also establish categories that define those to whom we are not connected, those whom we do not care about, and those qualities of our own that we reject or deny. These categories provide us with an orientation toward certain kinds of people and away from others and toward certain life choices and away from others. It is important to be sensitive to the existence of these categories in your own mind and to be aware that they can change.

The Scientific Process

The *scientific process* allows us to create a body of knowledge. Essentially it is a method for developing information that contains within it procedures for ensuring that the information will be correct. In this section, we describe the process through which scientific knowledge is achieved (Figure 1.4) and then discuss the fundamental components of research design, including selecting a sample, a

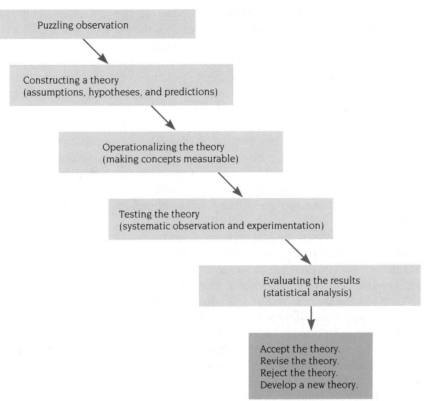

FIGURE 1.4
The scientific process

method, and an approach to data collection; evaluating the existing research; and conducting research according to ethical principles.

Scientific thinking usually begins when one attempts to reason systematically about a puzzling idea or observation. The observer tries to figure out how the observation may be explained and thinks about what leads to what and which things cause other things to happen. As a result, one develops a set of interrelated ideas to account for the observation. These ideas, often referred to as *assumptions*, *hypotheses*, and *predictions*, constitute a theory. The theory is not an end in itself; it is a way to get going.

The next step of the scientific process is to test the theory through experimentation and observation. A good theory contains specific predictions about cause and effect. After the predictions are stated, one must figure out how to test whether they are accurate.

One must *operationalize* the concepts of a theory in order to test them. That is, one must translate an abstract concept into something that can be observed and measured. Consider the concept of personal attraction. One who decided to measure personal attraction, for example, could think about the various ways in which people show they are attracted to each other. One might observe that people who are mutually attracted tend to look into each other's eyes rather than off to the side. The amount of eye contact is a way of defining the concept of attraction so that it can be observed and measured. Eye contact thus becomes an *operational definition* of personal attraction.

Often the theory is not tested by the same person who develops it, and who may therefore have some personal investment in demonstrating that the theory is correct. The scientific process usually involves the ideas of more than one person.

Sometimes people with different points of view engage in a debate as they try to refute positions they find flawed. At other times two or more people work on different phases of theory building, experimentation, and evaluation.

If a theory is fruitful, many researchers working in independent groups will devise ways of extending and clarifying it. Working in this way, as a community of scholars, helps to ensure that a theory will not be confirmed simply because of the theorist's personal biases. For example, Erik Erikson was not the person who tested his psychosocial theory. Researchers such as James Marcia, Ruthellen Josselson, Alan Waterman, and Jacob Orlofsky pursued some of Erikson's hypotheses about identity development and developed strategies for operationalizing Erikson's concepts, especially the psychosocial crisis of personal identity versus identity confusion. Their work clarified Erikson's concepts and supported many of his views about the relation of personal identity to subsequent development.

The final phase of the scientific process involves an evaluation of the observations. Statistical techniques help determine whether the results of a series of observations could have happened by chance, in which case we have no reason to assume that any systematic causal mechanism was operating. Such results will not confirm the theory, and we may decide to test it further and perhaps modify it. If the observations have a low probability of having occurred by chance, we may assume that something other than chance factors caused what we have observed. If our results support the theory's predictions, we are likely to accept them as providing evidence for the theoretical explanation. We may still be skeptical, though, and go on to test the theory through further experimentation.

What if the results do not fit the theory's predictions? One response is to re-examine the methods and design of the study. Perhaps the key concepts were not measured appropriately or the sample was biased in some way. When the results are inconclusive or contrary to the predictions, scholars may try another research approach before revising the theory. But when several different studies fail to support the hypotheses, we tend to lose confidence in the entire structure of the theory. We may revise the theory, or we may discard the theory and begin to develop an alternative explanation for our observations.

In summary, the scientific process consists of creating a theory, testing it through experimentation, and modifying, rejecting, or accepting it. To the extent that it is confirmed by the scientific process, a theory helps us interpret many of our observations about reality.

The sections that follow provide an overview of the basic principles of the research process as it is applied to the study of human development. In reviewing these principles, you will begin to grasp the challenge of trying to arrive at a systematic body of knowledge about the patterns of continuity and change in the human life course. At the same time you will encounter concepts that will improve your ability to ask critical, analytic questions about the research discussed in subsequent chapters and elsewhere.

Scientific Observation

Scientific observation is somewhat different from personal observation. Scientific observation in human development, as in other areas of social science, is characterized by three essential qualities. It must be objective, repeatable, and systematic. These qualities may or may not be characteristic of the way you use observation to test your own personal theories.

Objectivity means that the observations accurately reflect the events that are taking place and are not unduly influenced by what the observer expects or hopes to see. Suppose that you want an objective assessment of your physical attractiveness. You cannot just go up to some friends or relatives and ask them to tell you whether they find you attractive. Because they know you and presumably would not like to insult you, they may slant their answers.

A more objective approach might be to include your photograph with those of 100 other people chosen at random. You would then ask another student to give the photographs to ten people who do not know you and to have each of them rate the photographs for physical attractiveness. You might or might not like the outcome, but at least your method would be objective! It would reveal what other people thought of your attractiveness, without their being biased by any feelings about you.

Repeatability means that someone else who approaches the same task of research will observe the same things as the original investigator. To satisfy this requirement, the investigator must carefully define all procedures used in the research study, describe all the essential characteristics of the subjects (such as age, sex, and social class), and describe the setting or situation where the observations were made.

Systematic means comprehensive and orderly. Systematic observation requires focusing on behaviors that are relevant to a basic relationship, not poking here and there at unrelated events. Scientists have a framework of essential questions that they strive to answer thoughtfully, in a logical order.

Theory and scientific observation are intimately connected in the scientific process. Theories guide research in areas that are important to study. They generate hypotheses that can be tested or evaluated by means of systematic observation. Research can both support theories and produce observations that challenge theories. As we noted earlier, the outcome of research efforts sometimes leads scholars to revise a theory or to formulate a new theory.

Research Design

Numerous methods are used to carry out research in human development. Research investigations are designed just as cars, bridges, and buildings are designed. How should you go about designing a research study to answer a question you have?

In formal scientific work, small groups of highly trained professionals often meet to try to identify the most foolproof methods available for finding answers to a question. Scientists know that the information they gain from conducting research will be heavily influenced by the way they gather their data and by the characteristics of the subjects involved in their study. Just as theories are formulated to draw our attention to essential concepts and causal relationships, research is designed to build a body of objective and readily interpreted evidence.

A research design includes: the sample to be selected for the study; the method to be used to gather information; the frequency with which data are to be gathered; and the statistical techniques to be used to analyze the data.

Selecting a Sample

Sampling is the method of choosing subjects for a study. The choice of the subjects for a study will influence the results. Just like studies in any other area of social science, studies of human development are vulnerable to problems of sampling. The investigator's selection of subjects is related to the kinds of questions being asked. Ideally, a study of some universal principle of development will include as wide a range of subjects as possible. Studies of normal language development, for example, might include children from various ethnic, racial, social-class, and cultural groups. If a pattern of growth is hypothesized to be universal, it should apply to children from a wide variety of family and societal backgrounds.

A study intended to focus on the effects of certain life conditions on development should compare people who have experienced those conditions with people who have not experienced those conditions. Sometimes it is hard to decide on the most appropriate comparison groups. If you wanted to understand the impact of divorce on young couples, what would be a good comparison group? Older adults who have divorced? Young adults who have not divorced? Young adults who have lost a spouse through death? Each of these comparisons would allow you to answer a slightly different question.

Children and adolescents are typically embedded in at least two settings: family and school. When researchers study children in the school, they may capture something about the school environment that influences how children respond. Similarly, if researchers study children in the home, they may capture something about the home environment that influences the children's responses. One cannot assume that behavior observed in one context, whether it is school, home, playground, or laboratory, will also be observed in the others.

The sample and the larger population from which the sample is taken determine which generalizations may be made from the research findings. If the sample for a study is selected from only middle- and upper-middle-class male college students, can the findings of the research be applied to women, to people who are not college students, to younger or older people, or to people of lower or higher social classes? Strictly speaking, we cannot generalize beyond the population from which a sample was selected. Nevertheless, we often do generalize, and the validity of such a generalization depends partly on the type of research question investigated.

Some research questions, such as those involving some physiological issues, require relatively little attention to the character of the sample. If we were interested in the firing of neurons in the cortex, for example, we might assume that any human subjects who were not brain-damaged would give us comparable information. Even here, however, the age of the subject may influence the firing time, so the sample should probably include subjects of various ages. Then we would be more confident in generalizing the results to all people.

Research questions that focus on attitudes, motives, or beliefs must include a consideration of the background of the subjects. We simply cannot assume that all subjects will bring the same basic attitudes or values to the research question. Attitudes are shaped by a wide range of socialization and sociohistorical factors, and it would be unwise to assume, for example, that the attitudes of members of racial and ethnic minorities are the same as the attitudes of white subjects.

How, then, is sampling done? Four methods are frequently used:

Random sampling: Each person has an equal chance of being included. The researcher may ensure equal opportunity by putting everyone's name on a slip of paper and then choosing some of the slips blindly, or by selecting names from a list based on a table of random numbers.

Stratified sampling: Subjects are deliberately selected from a variety of levels or types (strata) of people in the population. For example, the proportions of upper-, middle-, and lower-income groups in the sample may be selected to correspond with their proportions in the population. Within each level, however, the subjects are selected at random.

Matched groups: The researcher selects two or more groups of subjects who are similar on many dimensions.

Volunteer sampling: Subjects are selected from among people who volunteer.

Random sampling and stratified sampling are used to ensure that a sample will be representative of the population chosen for the research. Then we can be confident in generalizing from the sample to the population. The ratio of men to women, for example, should be approximately the same in the sample as in the population from which it is drawn. Either method ensures representativeness in regard to any characteristic of the subjects, such as race, income, or educational background. Matched groups are sometimes used in experiments when the purpose is to administer different conditions to similar groups of people.

The method that most limits generalization is volunteer sampling. One never knows what type of person will volunteer for a study, and, as a result, the researcher cannot tell how far to generalize the results. Reliance on volunteers may also produce special problems. The kind of person who volunteers for a study on obedience, for example, may be especially obedient, so that the results will be slanted. Nevertheless, volunteer samples are used frequently. Often they are the only source of information on the attitudes and behavior of a particular group. People who are in treatment for a certain kind of problem, for example, are often asked to volunteer for research on that problem. Without their voluntary cooperation, a researcher could not begin to document the background characteristics, attitudes, coping strategies, or course of recovery related to the problem.

You will undoubtedly read some studies referred to as *clinical studies*. The term usually indicates that some of the participants or an entire family has been involved in some type of treatment program or is on a waiting list to receive clinical treatment. This treatment may be related to (1) health, as in studies of low-birth-weight infants, asthmatic or diabetic adolescents, or older adults who have Alzheimer's disease; (2) mental health, as in studies of child abuse, autism, schizophrenia, or suicide; (3) physically challenging conditions, such as blindness or deafness; or (4) developmental delay resulting from genetically transmitted diseases or from abusive or negligent family environments.

These studies are especially important in understanding the causes of clinical conditions, the developmental path along which they travel, the effects of certain interventions, and the long-term consequences of these conditions for adaptation. At the same time, one must be careful not to generalize findings from clinical studies to the population as a whole. Theories that are developed from clinical studies to account for the causes of these conditions or to propose treatments for them cannot necessarily be applied to individuals and families that are not seeking treatment. Interventions that might make sense and be effective in working with clinical populations are not necessarily appropriate for or relevant to other groups.

Research Methods

A variety of methods have been used to study development. Each has its strengths and weaknesses, allowing the investigator to focus on some set of behaviors at the expense of others. The choice of method must fit the problem under

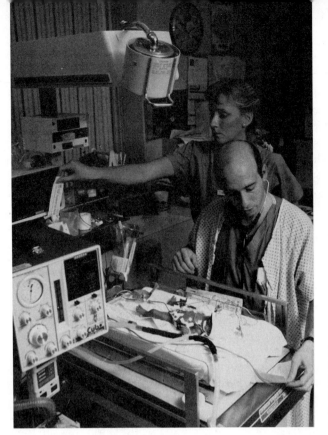

Data gathered by monitoring this very low birth-weight infant can be used to identify the impact of various treatment strategies.

study. Five general categories of developmental research are described here: observation, case studies, interviews, surveys and tests, and experimentation.

Observation   Direct observation of children in the home and at school is one of the oldest methods of studying development. Researchers have used mothers' diaries and observation logs to gather information about intimate settings that could not be discovered in any other way. Jean Piaget was guided by naturalistic observations of his own children in the formulation of his theory of cognition. Today some researchers conduct observations in homes, schools, day-care centers, and nursing homes. Others bring individuals—and sometimes friends or whole families—into homelike laboratory settings where they can watch behavior under somewhat more constant and controlled physical conditions (Kochanska, Kuczynski & Radke-Yarrow, 1989).

Naturalistic observation, or the careful monitoring of subjects' behavior without any kind of manipulation, provides insight into how things occur in the real world. Sometimes, researchers go into a setting to observe the full range of interactions and behavior patterns. On the basis of their field notes, they begin to develop hypotheses about important relationships. Then they may test these hypotheses through more focused observation or through more controlled experimentation.

In other instances, researchers use naturalistic observation to examine a specific behavior or relationship. They may be looking for various forms of peer aggression, patterns of social cooperation, or conditions that promote cross-gender interaction. In these cases, the observers have a predefined focus and limit the scope of their observations to the behavior relevant to their concern.

One strength of naturalistic observation is that it allows one to capture naturally occurring responses as they take place. Another strength is that the actual behavior may guide the researcher's conceptualization. In this case, rather than setting up a specific task or a group of questions and asking individuals to respond, the observer examines the full range of relevant behaviors.

Naturalistic observation also has some limitations as a research method. First, it is often difficult for observers to agree on exactly what occurred. Often the researcher compares two or more observers' codings of the same situation in an effort to determine whether they rated the same behaviors in the same way. This is called *interobserver reliability*. When interobserver reliability is high, several people can agree about what they saw and how to code or categorize it. When interobserver reliability is low, the researcher must determine why and correct the differences found in the observation techniques, usually through training the observers.

A second difficulty in the observational method is that some settings contain so much activity that it may be difficult to observe it all accurately. Finally, one who is studying a particular behavior or sequence of behaviors is never assured that this target behavior will occur within the limitations of a realistic period of observation.

The technology of videotaping is a powerful tool for naturalistic observation as well as for experimentation. A videotape can be reviewed over and over again. Several observers can watch a tape, stop it, and discuss what they saw. The same events can be observed from several points of view. Researchers interested in children's play, for example, may videotape a child's free play in three or four settings—perhaps at a preschool, at a park, at home, and at a friend's house. Several observers may then review the tapes, each looking for a different aspect of behavior, such as creativity, peer interaction, complex motor skills, or language use. Without interfering with the child's behavior, the videotaped record offers a vehicle for detailed and repeated analysis.

Observational studies lend themselves to an examination of correlation rather than causation. *Correlation* refers to the degree to which knowing the value of one variable, such as age, allows one to predict something about another variable, such as helpfulness. Observational researchers can ask many types of questions: Do children who play alone show more creativity in their play? Do the adolescents who are most aggressive with others have parents who use a lot of physical discipline? Do older adults who receive a lot of help and support from their children have higher self-esteem than those who do not receive much help from their children?

A statistic called a *correlation coefficient* is calculated. A correlation coefficient tells whether there is a mathematical relationship between the variables and what that relationship is. Many of the research findings reported in studies of development are reports of correlations. A correlation coefficient can range from a value of +1.0 to −1.0.

Let us take the correlation between the variables aggression and school performance. If higher levels of aggression are associated with better school performance, the correlation between the two variables is positive (toward +1.0); that is, as one increases, so does the other. If higher levels of aggression are associated with lower school performance, the correlation is negative (toward −1.0); that is, as one increases, the other declines. If there is no systematic relationship between aggression and school performance, the correlation will be close to 0. The strength of the association between the variables is reflected in whether the correlation is closer to 0 or closer to +1.0 or −1.0. Figure 1.5 shows a perfect positive, a zero, and a perfect negative correlation.

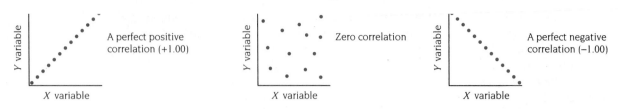

Note: Each point represents one person measured on both variables.

FIGURE 1.5

Positive, zero, and negative correlations between X *and* Y

A high positive or negative correlation between two variables shows only that there is an association between them. It indicates nothing about causation. A strong association between aggression and low grades in school does not mean that being aggressive causes children to get poor grades. Perhaps low grades cause children to be aggressive. Or perhaps some other factor, such as a short attention span or low motivation for school success, accounts for both the aggression and the low grades.

Case Studies   A case study is an in-depth description of a single person, family, or social group. The purpose of a case study is to describe the behavior of only that person or group. Case studies usually describe in detail the experiences of a single person or examine a phenomenon that does not conform to theoretical predictions. Case studies have been used to examine the sequence of life events that has led up to a certain crisis or major decision. They have been used to document the course of mental disorder and treatment. In some instances, they have been used to illustrate a theoretical construct (Runyan, 1982).

Case studies may be based on a variety of sources of information, including interviews, therapy sessions, prolonged observation, logs, letters, diaries, remembrances, historical documents, and talks with people who know the person or the group under study.

Some case studies document the lives of great individuals. In *Gandhi's Truth,* Erik Erikson (1969) analyzed the life of Mohandas Gandhi. Erikson considered Gandhi's childhood, adolescence, and young adulthood as they contributed to Gandhi's personality, to his moral philosophy, and to his behavior as a powerful social leader.

Other case studies describe clinical problems. Sigmund Freud used cases to clarify the origins of some mental disorders. He showed through his cases how the method of psychoanalysis could be used to identify the conflicts that were at the base of the patient's symptoms. In one of his classic cases, Freud analyzed a strong irrational fear of horses in a 5-year-old boy he called Little Hans (Freud, 1909/1955). The boy's fear was so strong that he refused to go out of his house because he thought that a horse in the street would bite him. Freud reasoned that Hans's fear was actually an indirect way of expressing strong psychological conflicts about sex and aggression that the child could not admit to his conscious mind. Freud worked from careful notes kept by the boy's father, who was a physician. Many of these notes are published in the case. Little Hans was treated by his father under Freud's guidance.

Case studies may also focus on social groups, families, or organizations. One of Anna Freud's most famous cases described the attachments that developed among a group of orphans who had lived together in a concentration camp during World War II (Freud & Dann, 1951). The study focused on the children's attachment to one another and their strategies for maintaining their sense of connectedness once they were placed in a more normal social environment.

Case studies have the advantage of illustrating the complexity and unique-ness of individual lives. Studies of large samples often identify general relation-ships. Case studies provide concrete examples of how these relationships are experienced by specific individuals. Some cases give the details of an experience that is rare or unusual and therefore might not lend itself to a large-scale study. Sometimes the case study brings a problem to the attention of researchers, who then pursue it through other methods.

Case studies have been criticized as unscientific. They are obviously not rep-resentative of large groups of individuals, and one must be cautious about gener-alizing the conclusions drawn from a case study to other individuals or groups. If the gathering of information in the case study has been biased or subjective, the results or conclusions of the study may be of little worth. Finally, critics argue that case studies lack reliability. Two people who do case studies of the same individ-ual may come up with very different views of the events and their significance.

These limitations suggest that one must have a very clear idea of one's pur-pose and a systematic approach to gathering information in order to conduct a case study that meets the standards of scientific observation. At the same time, vividly written, compelling case material has consistently stimulated theory and research in the field of human development.

Interviews Many case studies are based largely on face-to-face interviews. This method may also be used to gather data from large numbers of individuals and from people in clinical settings.

Interviews may be highly structured, almost like a verbal survey, or very open-ended, allowing the subject to respond freely to a series of general ques-tions. The success of the interview method depends heavily on the skill of the

Case studies, such as the his-torical biography "Schindler's List," provide an in-depth analysis of human behavior. In this instance, the case explores the forces that bring a successful, respected German industrialist to risk his life and fortune to save thousands of Jews.

Piaget's use of the interview method to elicit a young child's cognitive reasoning can be seen in two excerpts from his works. In the first, Piaget (1929) was exploring a 5-year-old child's understanding of dreams:

> *Where does the dream come from?*—I think you sleep so well that you dream.—*Does it come from us or from outside?*—From outside.—*What do we dream with?*—I don't know.—*With the hands? . . . With nothing?*—Yes, with nothing.—*When you are in bed and you dream, where is the dream?*—In my bed, under the blanket. I don't really know. If it was in my stomach(!) the bones would be in the way and I shouldn't see it.—*Is the dream in your head?*—It is I that am in the dream: it isn't in my head(!) When you dream, you don't know you are in the bed. You know you are walking. You are in the dream. You are in bed, but you don't know you are. (pp. 97–98)

Here Piaget (1963) was describing a 7-year-old child's understanding of class inclusion:

> You present the child with an open box that contains wooden beads. The child knows they are all wooden because he handles them, touching each and finding that it is made of wood. Most of these beads are brown, but a few are white. The problem we pose is simply this: are there more brown beads or more wooden beads? Let us call A the brown beads, B the wooden beads: then the problem is simply that of the inclusion of A in B. This is a very difficult problem before the age of 7 years. The child states that all the beads are wooden, states that most of them are brown and a few are white, but if you ask him if there are more brown beads or more wooden beads he immediately answers: "There are more brown ones because there are only two or three white ones." So you say: "Listen, this is not what I am asking. I don't want to know whether there are more brown beads or more white beads, I want to know whether there are more

BOX 1.1

Piaget's Interview Method

In studies using a Piagetian-style interview, children explain how they reached an answer and why they think their answer is correct. This provides insight into the reasoning behind correct and incorrect responses.

brown beads or more wooden beads." And, in order to make it easier, I take an empty box and place it next to the one with the beads and I ask: "If I were to put the wooden beads into that box would any remain in this one?" The child answers: "No, none would be left because they are all wooden." Then I say: "If I were to take the brown beads and put them into that box, would any be left in this one?" The child replies: "Of course, two or three white ones would remain." Apparently he has now understood the situation, the fact that all the beads are wooden and that some are not brown. So I ask him once more: "Are there more brown beads or more wooden beads?" Now it is evident that the child begins to understand the problem, sees that there is indeed a problem, that matters are not as simple as they seemed at first. As we watch him we observe that he is thinking very hard. Finally he concludes, "But there are still more brown beads; if you take the brown ones away, only two or three white beads remain."

interviewer. Interviewers are trained to be nonjudgmental as they listen to a person's re-sponses, and they try to create rapport with the person by conveying a feeling of trustworthiness and acceptance. In an unstructured interview, the interviewer must make use of this rapport to encourage the person to say more in answer to a question and to share thoughts that may be private or personal.

The interview method has traditionally been associated with clinical research, and it is becoming a major method in the study of cognition and language as well. Piaget's structured interview technique (Piaget, 1929) provides a model for the investigation of conceptual development (see Box 1.1). The researcher who uses this technique asks a child a question (say, "Are clouds living or dead?") and then follows up on the answer with questions about how the child arrived at his or her conclusion. In other studies, Piaget asked children to solve a problem and then asked them to explain how they had arrived at the solution. The child becomes an informant about his or her own conceptual capacities. This approach has been adapted to the study of moral development, interpersonal development, and prosocial behavior. The interview method has the advantage of allowing individuals to contribute their own views on the topic being studied. They can tell the interviewer what is important to them, why they might choose one alternative over another, or what they think is wrong with the investigator's view of the situation. People may also, of course, present themselves as they want the interviewer to see them; when they do, they are said to be exhibiting a *self-presentation bias*.

An interviewee's responses are vulnerable to influence by the interviewer. By smiling, nodding, frowning, or looking away, the interviewer can deliberately or inadvertently communicate approval or disapproval. There is a fine line between establishing rapport and influencing responses.

Surveys and Tests   Survey research is a means of collecting specific information from a large number of participants. If people are to respond directly to surveys, they must be able to read and write, unless the survey questions are read to them. The survey method is most commonly used with middle-school children, adolescents, and adults. Survey information about infants and toddlers is often collected from parents, child-care workers, physicians, nurses, and others who are responsible for meeting the needs of these young children. Thus surveys have contributed a great deal to our knowledge about how adults perceive the behavior and needs of young children.

Surveys may be used to collect information about attitudes ("Do you believe teachers should be permitted to use corporal punishment in disciplining their students?"); about current behavior and practices ("How many hours per day do you watch television?"); about aspirations ("What do you hope to do when you graduate from high school?"); and about perceptions ("How well does your mother/father or son/daughter understand your views?").

Survey questions are prepared in a standard form, and the responses are usually coded according to a prearranged set of categories. In well-designed surveys, the questions are stated clearly and offer response choices that are not ambiguous or overlapping. In the most powerful surveys, the sample of subjects is carefully selected to be representative of the population under study. Surveys may be conducted by telephone, through the mail, in classrooms, at work, or in the participants' homes.

Tests are often similar in form to surveys. They consist of groups of questions or problems that the person is expected to answer. Tests are usually designed to measure a specific ability or characteristic. You are no doubt familiar with the kinds of tests typically given in schools. You are presented with a group of items and asked to produce the correct answer or to select the correct answer from among several choices, as in intelligence tests and achievement tests. A researcher may use these tests along with some other measures to learn how intelligence relates to social life, emotions, or self-understanding.

Other tests are designed to measure a variety of psychological constructs, such as creativity, conformity, depression, and extroversion. Some tests assess whether a person has some form of mental illness, learning disorder, developmental disability, or physical challenge.

In order to be of use, psychological tests must be reliable and valid. Tests are *reliable* when they provide approximately the same score or the same diagnosis each time the same person takes the test. This is not to say that the test should not indicate change when change has occurred. But a person who takes a reliable test on two consecutive days should get approximately the same score on both days unless some deliberate training or intervention has been introduced in the meantime. There ought to be a positive correlation (toward +1.0) between the two scores.

Tests are *valid* when they measure what they claim to measure. The people who design the tests must define the construct they are trying to measure. They must also provide evidence that their test really measures this construct (Messick, 1989). Consider the various tests that have been designed to measure intelligence in infants and very young children. The results of these tests are not very closely related to the results of tests of intelligence given to the same people in adolescence and adulthood (Bayley, 1970). In other words, the correlations between the test results for infants and those for the same subjects when they are older tend to be low (nearer to 0.0 than to −1.0 or +1.0). Perhaps the underlying components of intelligence differ in babies and in adolescents and adults. Perhaps intelligence evolves in so many ways that one's measured intelligence as an infant and as an adult have little in common. Or perhaps the infant tests are measures of sensory processing and central nervous system coordination rather than measures of broad, adaptive intelligence.

Certain advantages of surveys and tests make them widely useful in developmental research: They allow us to compare the responses of large groups of respondents; they have been designed to address a wide variety of topics; and, with a prearranged coding or scoring system, many of them can be easily administered and evaluated.

This method also has limitations. Some surveys create attitudes where none existed before. For example, you might ask sixth-grade children questions about their satisfaction with their school curriculum. They may answer a lot of questions on this topic, but they may not have given much thought to the issue before. Another problem is the gap between the answers to survey questions or scores on tests and actual behavior. Children may say they would rather read than watch television, but in real life they may watch television most of the time and rarely read. Similarly, parents may say that they allow their children to participate in family decisions but may actually not give their children much voice.

The use of tests in the United States to determine school admissions and placement has come under serious attack (Weinberg, 1989). Some tests have been criticized for putting an unfair emphasis on knowledge derived from a white, middle-class, Eurocentric cultural perspective. Some tests have been criticized for putting at a disadvantage children whose first language is not English. Some tests have been criticized for being insensitive to different learning styles and modes of synthesizing information.

Intelligence tests in particular have been criticized because they are used to decide children's educational placement, but they do not encompass the full array of psychological factors associated with social competence and adaptive behavior. Psychological tests continue to be used in research to explore the relationship among developmental domains. Their use in such settings as schools and treatment facilities is becoming increasingly controversial.

Experimentation   Experimentation is a method best suited to examining unidirectional causal relationships. In an experiment, some variable or group of variables is systematically manipulated while others are held constant. The variable that is manipulated by the experimenter is called the *independent variable*. The variable defined by the subjects' responses or reactions is the *dependent variable*.

In some experiments, one group of subjects has a certain set of experiences or receives information (usually referred to as a *treatment*) that is not provided to another group. The group that experiences the experimenter's manipulation is called the *experimental group*. The group that does not experience the treatment or manipulation is called the *control group*. Differences in behavior between the two groups are then attributed to the treatment. In other experiments, the behavior of a single group of subjects is compared before and after the treatment or across several treatments. Once again, systematic differences in behavior before and after the treatment are attributed to the experimental manipulation. In this case, each subject serves as his or her own "control."

Control is the key to successful experimentation. The experimenter must exercise control in selecting the individuals or groups who will participate in a study. The participants must be able to bring equivalent competences to the situation. If this condition is not met, one cannot assume that the differences in behavior between the groups are due to the treatment.

The experimenters must control the way a task is presented to the participants so that such factors as the ability to understand the instructions, the order of events, and the degree of comfort and familiarity with the setting do not interfere with the subjects' behavior. Control ensures that changes in the subjects' behaviors have in fact resulted from the experimental manipulation.

Suppose we are interested in the impact of unemployment on children and adults at various ages. We cannot (nor do we want to) cause some people to lose their jobs and others to be retained in their jobs. We can, however, compare children of about the same age and social class whose parents have experienced unemployment with children whose parents have not. We can also compare adolescents and adults who are unemployed with those who are working.

Assignment to a "treatment" occurs as a result of real-world events. It is the task of the scientist to compare some of the consequences of this treatment—in this case, the experience of unemployment—and to deal with the limitations imposed on the results by how the individuals arrived in one treatment group or the other to begin with. The researcher can compare children, adolescents, and adults who have experienced unemployment with those who have not but cannot say that unemployment is the only factor that may account for the differences observed.

The *experimental method* has the advantage of providing conclusions about causal relationships. If we can show that subjects' behavior changes only when

The visual cliff apparatus was designed as part of an experimental research program to study the relationship of depth perception and motor development. Once babies can crawl, they will not venture onto the "deep" part of the cliff.

something in the experimental situation changes, we can conclude that the manipulation has caused the changes in behavior.

Experiments also have limitations. We cannot be certain about how applicable a controlled laboratory situation is to the real world: Would the behaviors that are observed in the laboratory also be observed at home, at school, or at work? Through studies of attachment (which is discussed in Chapter 5), we have learned that infants and young children do not behave the same way in the presence of their mothers as they do when their mothers are absent. This research makes us aware that experimental research with young children that does not allow their mothers to be present may produce behavior that differs in quantity, quality, and sequence from the behavior that would be observed under more normal conditions, when the mothers were present.

Experimental studies tend to suggest that Event A causes Response B. In many domains of development, however, a multifaceted reciprocal process promotes change. Just think for a moment about the development of romantic relationships among college students. Falling in love depends on many domains and on the two partners' fit or lack of fit in each domain. Romantic attachments may be influenced by physical appearance, shared values, capacity for emotional expressiveness, abilities, temperaments, intelligence, and the reactions of parents and friends, to name just a few factors. Each person reacts to the other, building toward or pulling away from new levels of affection and closeness. This is

TABLE 1.1   Advantages and Disadvantages of Five Methods of Developmental Research

Method	*Definition*	*Advantages*	*Disadvantages*
Observation	Systematic description of behavior	Documents the variety of ongoing behavior; captures what happens naturally, without experimental intervention	Time-consuming; requires careful training of observers; observer may interfere with what would normally occur
Case studies	In-depth description of a single person, family, or group	Focuses on complexity and unique experiences of individual; permits analysis of unusual cases	Lacks generalizability; conclusions may reflect bias of investigator; hard to replicate
Interviews	Face-to-face interaction in which each person can give a full account of his or her views	Provides complex first-person account	Vulnerable to investigator bias
Surveys and tests	Standard questions administered to large groups	Permits data collection from large samples; requires little training; very flexible	Wording and way of presenting questions may influence responses; response may not be closely related to behavior; tests may not be appropriate for use in schools or clinical settings
Experimentation	Analysis of cause-effect relations by manipulation of some conditions while others are held constant	Permits testing of causal hypotheses; permits control and isolation of specific variables	Laboratory findings may not be applicable to other settings; focuses on a unidirectional model of causality

reality. The development of a romantic bond is a complex process because a love relationship is a system; that is, it is sustained and promoted by continuous feedback and interaction between the partners as well as by many other factors, not by one or two external factors that can be said to promote or inhibit romantic attachments.

The advantages and disadvantages of the five research methods are summarized in Table 1.1.

Designs for Studying Development

The primary concern of developmental research is to describe and account for patterns of continuity and change. Four major research approaches have been created for examining development: retrospective studies, cross-sectional studies, longitudinal studies, and cohort sequential studies.

Retrospective Studies   A researcher engaged in a retrospective study asks the participants to report on experiences from an earlier time in their lives. Many early studies of child-rearing used parents' recollections of their parenting techniques to evaluate their patterns of child care. Researchers who studied the effects of stress during pregnancy often asked women to recall their emotional state before, during, and after their child was born. Investigators of personality development use retrospective data by asking adolescent or adult subjects to recall important events of their childhood.

This approach produces a record of what a person has retained of past events. We cannot be certain that these events really occurred as they are remembered. For that matter, we cannot be certain that they occurred at all. Piaget (1951) described a vivid memory from his second year of life:

> I was sitting in my pram, which my nurse was pushing in the Champs Elysées, when a man tried to kidnap me. I was held in by the strap fastened around me while my nurse bravely tried to stand between me and the thief. She received various scratches, and I can still see vaguely those on her face. (p. 188)

Thirteen years later, when Piaget was 15, the nurse joined a religious order. She wrote to his parents and returned a watch they had given her for protecting Jean from the kidnapper. She confessed that she had made up the story even to the point of scratching her own face. Piaget believed he had created the visual memory from the story his parents had told him about the incident.

The passage of time may change the significance of certain past events in a person's memory. As we gain new levels of cognitive complexity or change our attitudes, we reorganize our memories of the past so as to bring them into line with our current level of understanding. Sometimes events of the past that have been long forgotten or "repressed" suddenly surface. It is extremely difficult to determine the accuracy of these memories (Loftus, 1993). They may be entangled with current experiences or with ideas taken from books, movies, or conversations with others. They may be altered by the suggestion that something happened that did not, or by the suggestion that something did not happen that actually did. Because memory is so easily modified by suggestion, its usefulness in uncovering systematic data about the past is limited.

Cross-Sectional Studies   Studies that compare simultaneously people of different ages or of different social backgrounds or from different school or community settings are called *cross-sectional studies*. Such studies are quite commonly used in research on child development. Investigators may compare children of different levels of biological maturity or of different chronological ages to learn how a particular developmental domain changes with age.

One such study explored differences in how children aged 7, 9, and 12 were able to reason about problems to which there was more than one solution (Horobin & Acredolo, 1989). Even though the younger children were aware that there were multiple solutions, they were more likely than the older children to settle on one solution and insist that it was correct.

The limitation of the cross-sectional method is that it blurs the pattern of individual development. With respect to the study on reasoning, the cross-sectional approach tells us that most 12-year-olds are more flexible in their reasoning than most 7-year-olds. It does not tell us how the children who were the most flexible at age 7 would have performed at age 12 in comparison with those who were the least flexible.

Longitudinal Studies   A longitudinal study involves repeated observations of the same subjects at different times. The time between observations may be brief, as from immediately after birth to two or three days after birth. Or observations may be repeated over the entire life course, as in Leo Terman's longitudinal

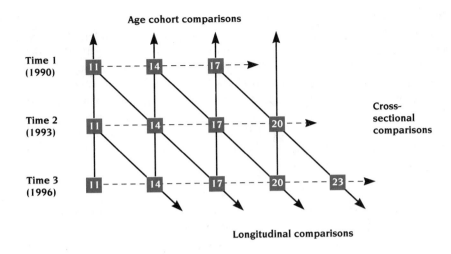

Age cohort comparisons

FIGURE 1.6
*Elements of a cohort
sequential design*

study of gifted children (Sears, 1977; Sears & Barbee, 1978; Terman, 1925; Terman & Oden, 1947, 1959).

Longitudinal studies have the advantage of allowing us to consider the course of development of a particular group of individuals. We can discover how certain characteristics of children in infancy or toddlerhood relate to those same characteristics when the individuals reach adolescence or adulthood. We can also learn whether certain qualities of childhood, such as intelligence or outgoingness, are relevant to overall social adjustment or life satisfaction in later years.

Longitudinal studies may be very difficult to complete, especially if they are intended to cover a significant age period, such as the years from childhood into adulthood. Over this span of time, participants may drop out of the study, the investigators may lose funding or interest in the project, and the methods may become outdated. Questions that once seemed important may no longer be seen as vital. One of the greatest limitations of these studies is that they focus on only one generation of subjects. Historical and social factors that may influence the course of this group's development will be inextricably intertwined in the observations. One cannot tell if all people growing up at all times in history would exhibit the pattern of changes that characterize this particular group.

Cohort Sequential Studies A cohort sequential design combines the cross-sectional and the longitudinal approaches into one method of study (Schaie, 1965). Groups of participants, called *cohorts*, are selected because they are a certain number of years apart in age. For example, we might begin with a group of adolescents who are 11, 14, and 17. Every three years, this group would be interviewed until the 11-year-olds have turned 17. In addition, every three years, a new group of 11-year-olds would be added to the study.

This combination of a longitudinal and a cross-sectional design is a very powerful developmental research method. It produces immediate cross-sectional data, longitudinal data after three and six years, and a comparison of children who were the same age (11, 14, or 17) at three different times. This third comparison permits us to identify social and historical factors that may influence age-related differences. The elements of a cohort sequential design are seen in Figure 1.6.

Evaluating Existing Research

In addition to collecting new data, social scientists give considerable scholarly effort to reviewing and evaluating the existing research. Statistical techniques allow us to compare the findings of a variety of studies so that we may identify patterns of results. As a student, you may be asked to review research findings on some topic that is of interest to you. Most researchers use this method to keep well informed on the research being reported in their subject area and analyze the work of others to generate well-founded conclusions about areas of study that interest them. The study, analysis, and evaluation of the current research literature constitute a special skill in their own right.

Ethics

In conducting research with living beings, and especially with children, social scientists continually confront ethical questions. *Ethics* refers to principles of conduct that are founded on a society's moral code. As part of their professional socialization, researchers are obligated to maintain humane, morally acceptable treatment of all living subjects (American Psychological Association, 1992).

The ethical guidelines for research with human subjects encompass a variety of considerations. Because we are concerned about subjects' right to privacy, the identities of individual subjects must be kept confidential. The subjects must not be coerced into participating in a research project, and a refusal to participate should have no negative consequences. If children in a classroom, for example, decide that they do not want to participate in a research project, or if their parents do not give permission for them to participate, these children should not be shamed, given an undesirable alternate assignment, or given a lower grade.

Researchers must protect subjects from unnecessary painful physical and emotional experiences, including shame, failure, and social rejection. Researchers must weigh the benefits of the new information they may discover in a particular study against the potential risks or harm to the subjects. Two questions must guide the researcher's decisions:

1. How would you feel if you, or one of your family members, were a subject in this study?
2. Can the problem be studied in ways that do not involve pain, deception, or emotional or physical stress?

The American Psychological Association has published a guide for researchers titled *Ethical Principles in the Conduct of Research with Human Participants* (1982). This guide requires that human subjects be told about all aspects of the research that may influence their decision to participate. They must be free to withdraw from the study at any time. They are entitled to a full explanation of the study once it has been completed. When the subjects are children, their parents must be given this information and must approve their children's participation. Most schools, day-care centers, hospitals, nursing homes, and other treatment centers also have their own review procedures for determining whether they will permit research to be carried out with the people in their programs.

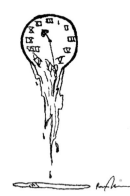

How much thought have you given to your projected life expectancy? The more you know about your anticipated future, the more informed your decisions can be concerning important life events.

The Life Span

The task of mapping one's future depends on how long one expects to live. Naturally, we can make only rough predictions. We know that our lives may

The social world of older adults is composed of about two-thirds women and one-third men.

be cut short by a disaster, an accident, or an illness. However, our best guess about how long we will live is based on the average life expectancy of others in our group.

Table 1.2 presents data on the average life span of people in the United States during seven time periods. Look first at the top row of the table, labeled "At birth." The average life expectancy of people born at the turn of the 19th century was about 49 years. For people born at the time of the stock market crash and the beginning of the Great Depression, the average life expectancy was about 59 years. The average life expectancy of people born at the beginning of World War II was around 64. The average life expectancy of people born in 1978 was approximately 73 years and rose to 75 years for those born in 1989. As we look across these generations, it is quite clear that the length of life has been increasing for more and more people.

The next few lines in Table 1.2 show us something else. People who had reached advanced ages (65, 75, and 80) in each of the time periods (1900–1902,

TABLE 1.2	**Average Remaining Lifetime at Various Ages, 1900–1989**						
Age	**1989**	**1978**	**1968**	**1954**	**1939–1941**	**1929–1931**	**1900–1902**
At birth	75.3	73.3	70.2	69.6	63.6	59.3	49.2
65 years	17.2	16.3	14.6	14.4	12.8	12.3	11.9
75 years	10.9	10.4	9.1	9.0	7.6	7.3	7.1
80 years	8.3	8.1	6.8	6.9	5.7	5.4	5.3

Source: U.S. Bureau of the Census, 1984, 1992.

TABLE 1.3   Projections of Life Expectation at Birth for 1980, 1990, 2000, and 2050, by Sex

					Increase	
Sex	**1980***	**1990***	**2000***	**2050†**	**1990–2000**	**1990–2050**
Male	70.0	72.1	73.5	75.0	1.4	2.9
Female	77.4	79.0	80.4	83.6	1.4	4.6
Difference	7.4	6.9	6.9	8.6	0.0	1.7

*Source: U.S. Bureau of the Census, 1991.
†*Source*: U.S. Social Security Administration, 1981.

1929–1931, 1939–1941, 1954, 1968, 1978, and 1989) had a much longer life expectancy than people who were born in those time periods. Thus someone who was 65 at the turn of the century (born in 1835) was expected to live to be 76.9; someone who was 75 at that time (born in 1825) was expected to live to be 82.1; and someone who was 80 years old during that period (born in 1820) was expected to live to be 85.3. These figures suggest that hazards during the early and middle years of life shorten the average life expectancy at birth. Infant mortality was a major factor in limiting life expectancy at the turn of the century. Many women in their early adult years died in childbirth, and respiratory diseases were a serious threat to life during the middle adult years. If one survived these common killers, one's chance for a long later life increased.

Using these kinds of statistics to estimate the life span, we are able to compute rather accurate projections of changes in its length. The average person born in 1989 can expect to live 25 years longer than one who was born in 1900. The average life expectancy of people born in 1989 is 75.3. At the extreme end of the life span, however, we find a much less dramatic increase in life expectancy. People who were 65 in 1989 (born in 1924) could be expected to live to be about 82; people who were 75 in 1989 (born in 1914) could be expected to live to be 86; and people who were 80 in 1989 (born in 1909) could be expected to live to be 88.3.

The Social Security Administration makes projections of life expectations that are quite reliable. These data, showing the life expectations of men and women separately, are seen in Table 1.3. They show that, overall, men do not live as long as women. They die younger around the world as well as in various regions of the United States. However, based on the data for 1990, we can see that the gap in life expectancy for U.S. males and females has closed somewhat since 1980. We might wonder whether projections about the year 2050 may also be modified as a result of the increased exposure to health risks experienced by many adult women in the labor force and because of new advances in the treatment of cardiac diseases in men. In the Appendix, you will find data on national patterns of life expectancy by race and sex as well as regional patterns within the United States and international comparisons. Here you will note significant racial differences in life expectancy, differences that show an advantage for whites in the early years of life, but an advantage for blacks in the later years after 65. The observation of racial differences in life expectancy at advanced ages has not been fully explained. One speculation is that those African-Americans who survive the stresses and hardships of childhood, adolescence, and adult life must be especially hardy and resistent to the effects of biological aging in later life. These data provide very concrete evidence of the impact of the societal system on the biological system. Medical advances, knowledge about the impact of lifestyle choices, access to health care services, and success in coping with life stresses or protection from life stresses can all contribute to a longer and healthier adulthood.

You can see that, according to the government statistics, the life span of both men and women is expected to increase from 1980 to 2050. The question arises whether this increase will continue or whether there is an upper limit to the length of the life span. There are theories supporting both sides. Bernice Neugarten (1981), a noted human development scholar, argued that, if the rates of advance in such fields as medicine and nutrition proceed for the next 40 years at the rate at which they have progressed for the last 60, by 2020 many people may be living to be 120 years old. Others have pointed out that the primary killers of infants, adults, and aging persons have already been brought under control and that there is little room left for expansion in the human life span, which they view as genetically limited. They have argued that the best we can hope for is a healthier, rather than a longer, period of life.

When you try to estimate your own life expectancy, you must consider projections for people in your country, region, and state and in your age, educational, racial, and sex groups. The more careful your comparisons are, the more accurate your estimate is likely to be. Individual lifestyle factors are also associated with longevity. A group of adults born between 1895 and 1919 were studied in 1965 and again in 1984 (Guralnick & Kaplan, 1989). A variety of demographic, health, and lifestyle factors were associated with a high level of functioning for the group in 1984, when they ranged in age from 65 to 89. These factors included having a fairly high family income; having no hypertension, arthritis, or back pain; being a nonsmoker; having normal weight; and consuming a moderate amount of alcohol. The last three factors in particular are influenced largely by personal decisions, and even hypertension and back pain are linked in part to lifestyle factors that are under a person's control.

Many of our most important life decisions are made with either an implicit or an explicit assumption about how long we expect to live. Our perception of our life expectancy has an impact on our behavior, self-concept, attitudes, and outlook on the future. The way we feel about ourselves, our activities, and our relationships are often guided by underlying assumptions about the point we have reached in life. Consider an African-American male born in 1989; he can expect to live to age 65. A white American female born in 1989 can expect to live to age 79. The black male will grow up looking at the years after about age 55 or 60 as old age. The white female will probably not consider herself old until she reaches about 70. These differences in outlook, coupled with actual differences in health and resources, will affect the way these two people regard themselves and go about their daily activities in middle and later life. The best advice to be given here is to make as accurate an estimate as possible while you explore the implications of various possibilities.

Chapter Summary

Psychosocial theory emphasizes interaction among the biological, psychological, and societal systems. As a result of maturation and change in each of these systems, individuals' beliefs about themselves and their relationships are modified. Although each life story is unique, we can identify important common patterns, allowing us to anticipate the future and to understand one another.

The scientific process results in a body of knowledge that informs our understanding of human development. Scientific observation must be objective, repeatable, and systematic. Five principal research methods are: naturalistic observation, case studies, interviews, surveys and tests, and experimentation. Each has its advantages and disadvantages, but all provide insights into continuity and change over the life span. Research design is also important in the study of change. Four significant designs are: retrospective studies, cross-sectional studies, longitudinal studies, and cohort sequential designs. The method and design of research have a powerful effect on how the findings may be interpreted.

Demographic information about the life span stimulates thought about one's own life expectancy. In the United States, the average life expectancy has increased by almost 50% in this century. This dramatic change affects how each of us views our own future. We need to study human development within a constantly changing context. We can never be satisfied that the information from earlier periods will hold true for future generations.

References

American Psychological Association. (1982). *Ethical principles in the conduct of research with human participants.* Washington, DC: Author.

American Psychological Association. (1992). Ethical principles of psychologists and code of conduct. *American Psychologist, 47,* 1597–1611.

Bayley, N. (1970). Development of mental abilities. In P. H. Mussen (Ed.), *Carmichael's manual of child psychol-ogy* (3rd ed., Vol. 1). New York: Wiley.

Erikson, E. H. (1963). *Childhood and society* (2nd ed.). New York: Norton.

Erikson, E. H. (1969). *Gandhi's truth: On the origins of militant nonviolence.* New York: Norton.

Freud, A., & Dann, S. (1951). An experiment in group upbringing. In R. Eissler, A. Freud, H. Hartmann, & E. Kris (Eds.), *The psychoanalytic study of the child* (Vol. 6). New York: International Universities Press.

Freud, S. (1909/1955). An analysis of a phobia in a five-year-old boy. In J. Strachey (Ed.), *The standard edition of the complete psychological works of Sigmund Freud* (Vol. 10). London: Hogarth. (First German edition 1909)

Guralnick, J. M. & Kaplan, G. A. (1989). Predictors of healthy aging: Prospective evidence from the Alameda County study. *American Journal of Public Health, 79,* 703–708.

Horobin, K., & Acredolo, C. (1989). The impact of probability judgments on reasoning about multiple possibilities. *Child Development, 60*(1), 183–200.

Kochanska, G., Kuczynski, L. & Radke-Yarrow, M. (1989). Correspondence between mothers' self-reported and observed child-rearing practices. *Child Development, 60*(1), 56–63.

Loftus, E. F. (1993). The reality of repressed memories. *American Psychologist, 48,* 518–537.

Messick, S. (1989). Meaning and values in test validation: The science and ethics of assessment. *Educational Researcher, 18,* 5–11.

Neugarten, B. L. (1981). Growing old in 2020: How will it be different? *National Forum, 61*(3), 28–30.

Piaget, J. (1929). *The child's conception of physical causality.* New York: Harcourt, Brace. (Originally published in French 1926)

Piaget, J. (1951). *Play, dreams, and imitation in childhood.* New York: Norton.

Piaget, J. (1963). The attainment of invariants and reversible operations in the development of thinking. *Social Research, 30,* 283–299.

Runyan, W. M. (1982). *Life histories and psychobiography: Explorations in theory and method.* New York: Oxford University Press.

Schaie, K. W. (1965). A general model for the study of developmental problems. *Psychological Bulletin, 64,* 92–107.

Sears, P. S., & Barbee, A. H. (1978). Career and life satisfaction among Terman's gifted women. In J. Stanley, W. George, & C. Solano (Eds.), *The gifted and the creative: Fifty year perspective.* Baltimore: Johns Hopkins University Press.

Sears, R. R. (1977). Sources of life satisfactions of the Terman gifted men. *American Psychologist, 32,* 119–128.

Terman, L. M. (1925). *Genetic studies of genius.* Stanford, CA: Stanford University Press.

Terman, L. M., & Oden, M. H. (1947). *The gifted child grows up: Twenty-five years' follow-up of a superior group.* Stanford, CA: Stanford University Press.

Terman, L. M., & Oden, M. H. (1959). *The gifted group at mid-life: Thirty-five years' follow-up of the superior child.* Stanford, CA: Stanford University Press.

Weinberg, R. A. (1989). Intelligence and IQ: Landmark issues and great debates. [Special issue]. *American Psychologist, 44*(2), 98–104.

CHAPTER 2

Psychosocial theory emphasizes the interaction between the
developing person and the complex social environment.
The direction of development for this lovely child is shaped
by the expectations, ambitions, and cultural beliefs of
those who surround her, as well as by her own talents,
temperament, and vision of the future.

Psychosocial Theory

I n this chapter, we will define the concept of theory and introduce the basic concepts of psychosocial theory, which provides the integrating framework for our analysis of human development.

What Is a Theory?

A *theory* is a logical system of general concepts that underlies the organization and understanding of observations. The sciences have their formal theories, and we all have our informal, intuitive theories about our social lives. A formal scientific theory is a set of interconnected statements, including assumptions, definitions, axioms, postulates, hypothetical constructs, intervening variables, laws, and hypotheses. Some of the statements follow logically from certain other statements.

The function of this set of interconnected statements is to describe unobservable structures, mechanisms, or processes and to relate them to each other and to observable events. For example, in learning, the information that has been learned is not observable. However, according to certain principles of learning theory, we infer that new learning has taken place when some responses or behaviors become more likely and others become less likely under particular conditions.

A formal theory should meet certain requirements. It should be logical and internally consistent; that is, its statements should not contradict each other. The theory should be testable; that is, its hypothetical constructs should be translatable into testable hypotheses. The theory should be parsimonious, relying on as few assumptions, constructs, and propositions as possible. Finally, a theory should integrate previous research, and it should deal with a relatively large area of science (Miller, 1993).

Theories are constructed to organize and interpret observations that we want to know more about. Theories help us identify orderly relationships among many diverse events, guide us to those factors that have explanatory power, and identify those that do not. In the area of personality development, for example, one theory may point to dreams and slips of the tongue as data worth observing, while another may direct our attention to goals and aspirations. Different theories are likely to address the same observation from different perspectives. For instance, some theories about development emphasize social roles, some emphasize cognition, and others emphasize motivation.

Individuals experience life as an integration of biological, psychological, and societal factors, which are discussed in Chapter 1. An adequate theory of human development should interrelate all three systems because the way they function together exerts the greatest influence on human behavior. To evaluate a theory we must answer three questions:

1. *Which phenomena is the theory trying to explain?* A theory used to explain intellectual development may include hypotheses about the evolution of the brain, the growth of logical thinking, or the capacity to use symbolism. Such a theory is less likely to explain fears, motives, or friendship.

As an example, Jean Piaget (1950) offered a developmental theory of the origins of logical thought. In his view, every organism strives to attain equilibrium with its environment, and equilibrium among the cognitive elements within itself. He hypothesized (a) that thought is organized in order to achieve equilibrium; (b) that development takes place in a predictable sequence of naturally occurring stages, each with unique strategies for making meaning out of experiences; and (c) that children are active agents in constructing knowledge. His theory has been useful in helping us understand how children differ from adults and how they interpret and explain events. Piaget's theory does not, for example, direct our attention to how children learn and remember specific facts, why certain fears persist, or how children and parents achieve a sense of attachment.

Understanding the focus of the theory helps us to identify its *range of applicability*. Although principles from one theory may have relevance to another area of knowledge, we usually begin to evaluate a theory in terms of the events it is intended to explain.

2. *What assumptions does the theory make?* Assumptions are the guiding premises underlying the logic of a theory. In order to evaluate a theory, you must first understand what its assumptions are. Charles Darwin assumed that lower life forms "progress" to higher forms in the process of evolution. Freud assumed that all behavior is motivated and that the unconscious is a "storehouse" of motives and wishes.

The assumptions of any theory may or may not be correct. If we assume that the sun is the center of the solar system, we will come to other conclusions than if we assume that the earth is the center of the universe. Assumptions may be influenced by their cultural context, by the sample of observations from which the theorist has drawn inferences, by the current knowledge base of the field, and by the intellectual capacities of the theorist.

3. *What does the theory predict?* Theories add new levels of understanding by suggesting causal relationships, by unifying diverse observations, and by identifying the importance of events that may have gone unnoticed. Theories of human development offer explanations regarding the origins and functions of human behavior and the changes that can be expected in it from one period of life to the next.

We expect a theory of human development to provide explanations about four issues:

1. What are the mechanisms that account for growth from conception through old age, and to what extent do these mechanisms vary across the life span?
2. What factors underlie stability and change across the life span?
3. How do physical, cognitive, emotional, and social functions interact? How do these interactions account for mixtures of thoughts, feelings, health states, and social relationships?
4. How does the social context affect individual development?

The Psychosocial Perspective

Although psychosocial theory is not the only or the most widely accepted framework for studying human development, it provides a rich, thought-provoking structure within which to explore the major issues of growth and development across the life span. In Chapter 3, you will review seven other theoretical perspectives on human development, each offering valuable insights into the process of growth and change, and each with a history of having guided a productive line of scholarly inquiry. We have selected psychosocial theory as an organizing framework for this text because it allows us to identify and integrate information from a wide range of disciplines covering a diversity of topics, and because it combines three features that are not as clearly articulated or integrated in other analyses of development.

First, psychosocial theory addresses growth across the life span, identifying and differentiating central issues from infancy through old age.

Second, the theory assumes that we are not totally at the mercy of biological and environmental influences. At every stage of life, we have the capacity to contribute to our own psychological development and to integrate, organize, and conceptualize our own experiences so as to protect ourselves and to direct the course of our lives.

Third, the theory takes into consideration the active contribution of one's culture to one's individual growth. At each life stage, cultural goals and aspirations, social expectations and requirements, and the opportunities that the culture provides make demands on us that draw forth reactions. These reactions influence which of a person's capabilities will be developed further. This vital link between the individual and the world is a key mechanism of development.

In order to preserve and protect its culture, each society encourages patterns of parenting, provides unique opportunities for education, and communicates

BIOGRAPHICAL SKETCH

**Erik H. Erikson
1902–1994**

(continued)

Erik Erikson was born in Frankfurt, Germany, in 1902. His Danish parents were divorced before his birth, and his mother married his pediatrician, Dr. Homburger, before Erikson was 5. In early adulthood, after growing up in the home of this prosperous physician, Erikson would serve as teacher, student, and patient in the household of another physician, Sigmund Freud.

At age 18, after completing gymnasium (a German secondary school that prepares students to study at a university), Erikson traveled around Europe for a year, spending several months on the shores of Lake Constance reading, writing, and enjoying the beauty of the setting. When he returned home, he enrolled in art school and pursued this study for the next few years. After traveling to Florence, Italy, where he concluded that he was not going to succeed as an artist, he and some of his friends, including Peter Blos, wandered around for a time, searching for a sense of themselves and their personal resources (Coles, 1970).

Erikson and Blos accepted an invitation to teach in a private school that had been founded by Anna Freud for the children of students at the Vienna Psychoanalytic Society. In Vienna, Erikson studied the techniques of psychoanalysis and underwent a training analysis with Anna Freud. His decision to become an analyst was encouraged by the supportive, influential analysts of the Psychoanalytic Society, who were eager to help promising people enter the field they had created. Erikson's admission to training

was unusual in that he had neither a university nor a medical degree.

After analytic training and marriage, Erikson set off for the United States and became a child analyst on the faculty of the Harvard Medical School. Three years later, he went to Yale, and two years after that, he went off to study the Sioux in South Dakota. After completing his research observations on the Sioux, he opened a clinical practice in San Francisco. During this time, he also conducted a study of the Yuroks. In 1942, he became a faculty member at the University of California at Berkeley.

In 1950, Erikson left Berkeley and became an analyst on the staff of the Austen Riggs Center in Stockbridge, Massachusetts. In the late 1950s, he became a professor of human development at Harvard. He retained this position until his retirement. Until recently, he and his wife, Joan, continued to expand their analysis of human development. Their book *Vital Involvement in Old Age* (1986) probes the life histories of a number of octogenarians and examines the achievement of a fully developed humanness in old age.

Erikson's major theoretical work, *Childhood and Society*, was synthesized while he was at Berkeley and published in 1950, when he was 48. In this work, Erikson presents a psychosocial theory of development. A revised edition was published in 1963, and he expanded and revised his theory in many other books and papers. In two biographies, he applied the principles of psychosocial theory to analyses of the lives

values and attitudes toward basic domains of behavior, including sexuality, intimacy, and work. Each society has its own view of the qualities that enter into maturity, qualities that are infused into the lives of individuals and help determine the direction of human growth within the society.

One of the great theorists who identified and developed psychosocial theory was Erik H. Erikson. Erikson initially was trained as a psychosexual theorist. His interest in the effects of sexuality on functioning and in the ideas of the biologist Julian Huxley led Erikson to focus on the influence of social instincts on functioning.

Basic Concepts of Psychosocial Theory

Psychosocial theory represents human development as a product of the interaction between individual (*psycho*) needs and abilities and societal (*social*)

of Martin Luther and Mohandas Gandhi (Erikson, 1958, 1969).

It is clear that Erikson took a personal route to realizing his potential. His writings blend compassion, keen observational skills, a poetic synthesis of ideas and experiences, and a persistent inquiry into the interrelationships of individual lives and societies. In the course of his own intellectual development, he mastered several disciplines, including psychoanalysis, cultural anthropology, psychology, theology, and history. In his search for deeper understanding, he remained open to all human behavior that would inform his questioning mind, drawing on life histories, clinical cases, and fictional characters.

As observations from his clinical practice raised questions that the research literature was unable to answer, he turned to a study of traditional cultures and historical figures, pursuing ideas that would help him clarify his analysis of human development. Through his clinical and theoretical writings, he demonstrated that the evolved structure of each individual, although very complex, can be studied and understood. Among his other discoveries, he identified a process, the psychosocial crisis, that links individuals and the societies they create in a fundamental way that produces development.

Erikson won the Pulitzer Prize and the National Book Award. In 1984 he received the G. Stanley Hall Award from the Division of Developmental Psychology of the American Psychological Association for distinguished contributions to developmental psychology.

(*continued*)

Joan Erikson

Sigmund Freud

Anna Freud

Pablo Picasso, First Communion, *1895-1896. Religious ceremonies often mark critical transitions and define the path toward moral and spiritual maturity. Picasso portrays the earnestness with which this young child experiences her first communion. She is taking part in an ancient ritual that will shape her self-concept and guide her ethical decision making.*

expectations and demands. The theory accounts for the patterns of individual development that emerge from the more global process of psychosocial evolution.

Julian Huxley (1941, 1942) used the term *psychosocial evolution* to refer to those human abilities that have allowed us to gather knowledge from our ancestors and transmit it to our descendants. Child-rearing practices, education, and modes of communication transmit information and ways of thinking from one generation to the next. At the same time, people learn how to develop new information, new ways of thinking, and new ways of teaching their discoveries to others. Through this process, according to Huxley, psychosocial evolution has proceeded at a rapid pace, bringing with it changes in technology and ideology that have allowed us to create and modify the physical and social environments in which we live.

Our theory of psychosocial development offers an organizational framework for considering individual development in psychosocial evolution. The transmission of values and knowledge across generations requires the maturation of individuals who are capable of internalizing knowledge, adapting it, and transferring it to others. People change and grow systematically, enhancing their potential for carrying their own and succeeding generations forward.

As we view it, psychosocial theory is based on six organizing concepts: (1) the stages of development, (2) developmental tasks, (3) the psychosocial crisis, (4) a central process for resolving the crisis of each stage, (5) a radiating network of significant relationships, and (6) coping—that is, the new behavior people generate to meet the challenges and build the relationships of their lives. Figure 2.1 shows development as a building process. The structure grows larger as the radius of

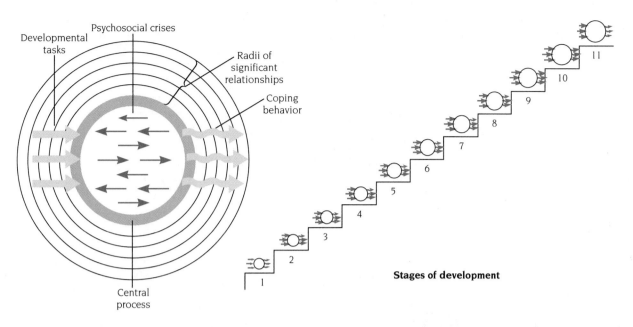

Stages of development

significant relationships expands and as the achievements of earlier stages are integrated into the behavior of the next stage of development.

At each stage, the accomplishments from the previous stages are applied toward mastery of the next challenges presented by a mixture of developmental tasks, psychosocial crisis, central process, and significant relationships. The interplay of these factors provides the experiential base for new psychosocial learning, and therefore for development. Each stage is unique and leads to the acquisition of new skills related to new capabilities.

FIGURE 2.1
Six basic concepts of psychosocial theory

Stages of Development

A *stage of development* is a period of life that is characterized by a specific underlying organization. A wide variety of behaviors can be viewed as expressing the underlying structure of each stage. At every stage, some characteristics differentiate it from the preceding and succeeding stages. Stage theories propose a specific direction for development, and each new stage incorporates the gains made during earlier stages (Davison et al., 1980; Fischer & Silvern, 1985; Flavell, 1982; Levin, 1986; Miller, 1993).

The stage concept suggests areas of emerging competence or conflict that may explain a range of behaviors. To some extent, you can verify the stage concept through your analysis of your own past. You can probably recall earlier periods when you were very preoccupied by efforts first to gain your parents' approval, then to win acceptance by your peers, and later to understand yourself. Each of these concerns may have appeared all-encompassing at the time, but eventually it gave way to a new preoccupation. At each stage, you were confronted with a unique problem that required the integration of your personal needs and skills with the social demands of your culture. The end product was a new orienting mode and a new set of capabilities for engaging in interactions with others.

Erikson (1950/1963) proposed eight stages of psychosocial development. The conception of these stages can be traced in part to the stages of psychosexual development proposed by Freud and in part to Erikson's own observations and rich mode of thinking.

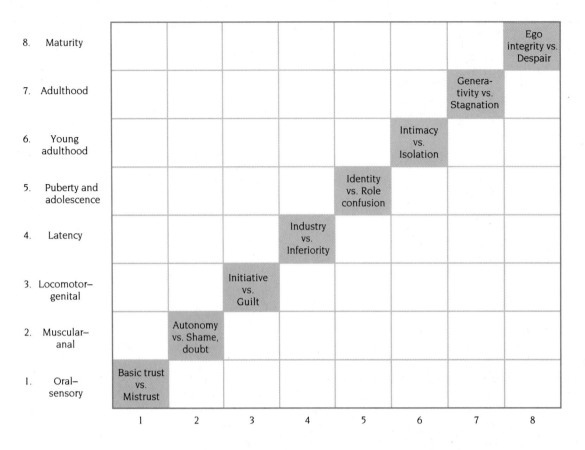

FIGURE 2.2

Erikson's psychosocial stages
Source: Erikson, 1963.

Figure 2.2 is the chart Erikson produced in *Childhood and Society* to describe the stages of psychosocial development. The boxes identify the main psychosocial ego conflicts of the various stages. These ego conflicts produce new ego skills.

The concept of the psychosocial stages of development is very good as far as it goes, but Erikson's road map seems incomplete. If the idea of psychosocial evolution has any validity—and we believe it does—new stages can be expected to develop as a culture evolves.

We have identified 11 stages of psychosocial development, each associated with an approximate age range: (1) prenatal, from conception to birth; (2) infancy, from birth to 2 years; (3) toddlerhood, from 2 to 4 years; (4) early school age, 4 to 6 years; (5) middle school age, 6 to 12 years; (6) early adolescence, 12 to 18 years; (7) later adolescence, 18 to 22 years; (8) early adulthood, 22 to 34 years; (9) middle adulthood, 34 to 60 years; (10) later adulthood, 60 to 75 years; and (11) very old age, 75 until death.

By discussing a prenatal stage, a second stage of adolescent development, and very old age, we are adding three stages to the ones Erikson proposed. This revision is a product of our analysis of the research literature, our observations through research and practice, discussions with colleagues, and suggestions from other stage theorists.

The elaboration of psychosocial theory by the addition of these three new stages provides a good demonstration of the process of theory construction. Theories of human development emerge and change within a cultural and historical context. Patterns of biological evolution and psychosocial evolution occur within a cultural frame of reference. The extension of the adolescent period, for

Prenatal	Conception to birth	
Infancy	Birth to 2 years	
Toddlerhood	2 to 4 years	
Early school age	4 to 6 years	
Middle school age	6 to 12 years	
Early adolescence	12 to 18 years	
Later adolescence	18 to 22 years	
Early adulthood	22 to 34 years	
Middle adulthood	34 to 60 years	
Later adulthood	60 to 75 years	
Very old age	75 until death	

FIGURE 2.3

Eleven stages of the life span and approximate ages

example, is a product of changes in the timing of onset of puberty in modern society, the expanding need for education and training before entry into the world of work, related changes in the structure of the educational system, and the variety of the available life choices in work, marriage, parenting, and ideology. Our observations relating to the life circumstances and preoccupations of certain age groups have led to the addition of new stages of development.

Figure 2.3 shows the 11 stages of psychosocial development we have identified. Because a person moves from one stage to another after psychosocial events have occurred rather than because of chronological age, the age range given for each stage is only an approximation. Each person has his or her own timetable for growth.

An assumption of this and other stage theories is that the psychological development that takes place at each stage will have a significant effect on all subsequent stages; that is, the stages are viewed as a sequence. Although one can anticipate challenges that will occur at a later stage, one passes through the stages in an orderly pattern of growth.

Erikson (1950/1963) proposed that the stages of development follow the *epigenetic principle*; that is, a biological plan for growth allows each function to emerge systematically until the fully functioning organism has developed. There is no going back to an earlier stage because experience makes retreat impossible. In the logic of psychosocial theory, the entire life span is required for all the functions of psychosocial development to appear and become integrated.

The concept of life stages permits us to consider the various aspects of development at a given period of life and to speculate about their interrelation. It also encourages us to focus on the experiences that are unique to each life period—

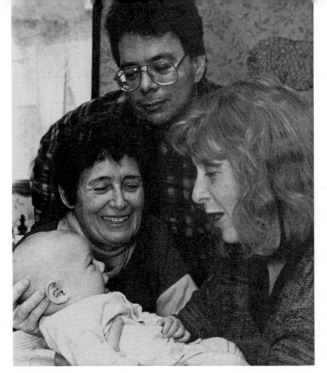

A unique feature of families, as compared to work groups, is that they typically include people at several different life stages, who have to function together as members move from one stage to the next.

experiences that deserve to be understood both in their own right and in terms of their contribution to subsequent development.

When programs and services are designed to address critical needs in such areas as education, health care, housing, and social welfare, the developmental stage approach allows the designers to focus on the needs and resources of the particular population to be served.

The main caution we would offer is to avoid thinking of stages as pigeonholes. Just because a person is described as being at a given stage does not mean that he or she cannot function at other levels. It is not unusual for people to anticipate later challenges before they become dominant. Many children of toddler and preschool age, for example, play "house," envisioning having a husband or a wife and children. You might say that, in this play, they are anticipating the issues of intimacy and generativity that lie ahead. While some elements of the central psychosocial skills can be observed at all ages, the intensity with which they are expressed at certain times marks their importance in the definition of a developmental stage. Erikson et al. (1986) put it this way:

> The epigenetic chart also rightly suggests that the individual is never struggling only with the tension that is focal at the time. Rather, at every successive developmental stage, the individual is also increasingly engaged in the anticipation of tensions that have yet to become focal and in reexperiencing those tensions that were inadequately integrated when they were focal; similarly engaged are those whose age-appropriate integration was then, but is no longer, adequate. (p. 39)

As one leaves a stage, the achievements of that stage are neither lost nor irrelevant to later stages. Erikson (1950/1963) warns us to take care not to become too structural in our thinking. Although the theory suggests that important ego strengths emerge from the successful resolution of conflicts at every stage, we should not assume that these strengths, once established, are never challenged or shaken. Events may take place later in life that call into question the essential beliefs established in an earlier period.

For example, the psychosocial conflict during early school age is initiative versus guilt. Its positive outcome, a sense of initiative, is a joy in innovation and experimentation and a willingness to take risks in order to learn more about the world. Once achieved, the sense of initiative provides a positive platform for the formation of social relationships as well as for further creative intellectual inquiry and discovery. However, experiences in a highly authoritarian school environment or in a very judgmental, shaming personal relationship may cause one to inhibit this sense of initiative or to mask it with a facade of indifference.

The idea of life stages should be used to highlight the changing orientations toward oneself and others that dominate periods of the life span. The essential idea is that how one perceives and experiences one's life varies qualitatively from stage to stage.

An alternative approach in the study of human development is to trace single processes or systems throughout life. We might, for instance, consider changes in emotional functioning across the life span, from infancy through later life. This approach may provide greater detail regarding the emergence and modification of each system. It would not, however, contribute as much to an understanding of the interaction of the systems within the person or of the ways in which inte-grated individuals experience their lives. If you wish to study the continuity and change within a particular system throughout life, you may wish to refer to the sections of each chapter that deal with the theme of interest to you.

To our minds, movement from one stage to the next is the result of changes in several major systems at approximately the same time. The new mixture of needs, capabilities, and expectations is what produces the new orientation toward experience at each new stage. In our view, one can identify the important systems of each stage by looking at what researchers have identified as the major unique preoccupations of each period. Generally, these developmental tasks reflect areas of accomplishment in physical, cognitive, social, and emotional development, as well as development of the self-concept.

Developmental Tasks

Developmental tasks, the second organizing concept of psychosocial theory, consist of a set of skills and competencies that contribute to increased mastery over one's environment and that define what is healthy, normal development at each age in a particular society. The tasks form a sequence: Success in learning the tasks of one stage leads to development and a greater chance of success in learning the tasks of later stages. Failure at the tasks of one stage leads to greater difficulty with later tasks or may even make later tasks impossible to master.

Robert J. Havighurst believed that human development is a process in which people attempt to learn the tasks required of them by the society to which they are adapting. These tasks change with age because each society has *age-graded expectations* for behavior. "Living in a modern society is a long series of tasks to learn" (Havighurst, 1972, p. 2). The person who learns well receives satisfaction and reward; the person who does not suffers unhappiness and social disapproval.

Although Havighurst's view of development emphasizes the guiding role of society in determining which skills need to be acquired at a certain age, it does not totally ignore the role of physical maturation. Havighurst believed that there are *sensitive periods* for learning developmental tasks—that is, times when the person is most ready to acquire a new ability. Havighurst called these periods *teachable moments*. Most people learn developmental tasks at the time and in the sequence appropriate in their society. If a particular task is not learned during the sensitive period, learning it may be much more difficult later on.

Learning that occurs during a sensitive period may enhance learning and performance in this task later in life. Initially, skills are learned in the sensitive period, when much is happening both internally and externally to stimulate that area of growth. Once the sensitive period has passed, however, learning may still continue. Language skills, for example, do not cease to develop after toddlerhood. New and more complex ways of using language are learned throughout life. Much of the elementary and high school curriculum focuses on developing language, including expanding one's vocabulary, developing skills in oral and written communication, and learning new languages. Gerontologists are discovering that motivation plays a great role in increasing the linguistic skills of elderly people who wish to learn a new language before taking a trip to Europe.

The basic tasks we identify differ from Havighurst's. Our choice of tasks is based on the general areas of accomplishment that have been identified by researchers as critical to psychological and social growth at each stage of life in a modern, technological culture.

We recognize that the demands for growth may differ according to the orientation and complexity of a particular society. The tasks we present as central to successful adaptation for children growing up in a postindustrial society such as that of the United States are not necessarily the appropriate standard for maturation and growth in a developing country or in a more traditional tribal culture. As we discuss specific life stages, we will highlight some of the differences in developmental tasks that may be influenced by culture or subculture.

We believe that a relatively small number of major psychosocial tasks dominate a person's problem-solving efforts and learning during a given stage. As these tasks are mastered, new competencies enhance the person's ability to engage in more complex social relationships. To our way of thinking, a successful culture stimulates behavior that helps its members learn what they need to know for both their own survival and that of the group.

The tasks may reflect gains in physical skills, cognitive skills, social skills, emotional skills, and elaboration of the self-concept. One of the developmental tasks of infancy, for example, is the formation of a bond of attachment to the caregiver. A person's ability to form close friendships in childhood and intimate relationships in adolescence and adult life builds on the capacity for attachment that is established with a caregiver during infancy.

Keep in mind that one is changing on several major levels during each period of life. Tasks involving physical, emotional, intellectual, and social growth, as well as growth in the self-concept, all contribute to one's resources for coping with the challenges of life. Table 2.1 shows the developmental tasks we have identified as having major effects on the life experiences of most people in modern society and the stages during which each set of tasks is of primary learning value. There are 42 developmental tasks in the list. Whereas the infant is learning orientations and skills related to the first 5, the young adult has already acquired skills related to the 27 tasks from the previous stages. New learning may continue in these areas as well as in the 4 new developmental tasks faced by the young adult. The very old person has all the areas of previous learning to draw from while working on 3 tasks and the crisis of the final stage.

TABLE 2.1 Developmental Tasks Associated with Life Stages

Life Stage*	Developmental Tasks
Infancy (birth to 2 years)	Social attachment Maturation of sensory, perceptual, and motor functions Sensorimotor intelligence and primitive causality Understanding the nature of objects and the creation of categories Emotional development
Toddlerhood (2 to 4)	Elaboration of locomotion Fantasy play Language development Self-control
Early school age (4 to 6)	Sex-role identification Early moral development Self-theory Group play
Middle school age (6 to 12)	Friendship Concrete operations Skill learning Self-evaluation Team play
Early adolescence (12 to 18)	Physical maturation Formal operations Emotional development Membership in the peer group Sexual relationships
Later adolescence (18 to 22)	Autonomy from parents Gender identity Internalized morality Career choice
Early adulthood (22 to 34)	Exploring intimate relationships Childbearing Work Lifestyle
Middle adulthood (34 to 60)	Management of career Nurturing of the marital relationship Expanding caring relationships Management of the household
Later adulthood (60 to 75)	Promotion of intellectual vigor Redirection of energy toward new roles and activities Acceptance of one's life Development of a point of view about death
Very old age (75 until death)	Coping with physical changes of aging Development of a psychohistorical perspective Travel through uncharted terrain

*We do not consider the concept of developmental tasks appropriate to the prenatal stage.

Mastery of the developmental tasks is influenced by the resolution of the psychosocial crisis of the previous stage, and it is this resolution that leads to the development of new social capabilities. These capabilities orient the person toward new experiences, a new aptitude for relationships, and new feelings of personal worth as he or she confronts the challenges of the developmental tasks

BIOGRAPHICAL SKETCH

Robert J. Havighurst
1900–1991

Robert J. Havighurst was born on June 5, 1900. In 1924, he received his Ph.D. in chemistry from Ohio State University and then did postdoctoral study in physics and chemistry at Harvard University. In 1930, he married Edythe McNeely, and together they had five children. After teaching science at the high school and college levels for a few years, he made a major shift in career direction, focusing his interest on problems of adolescent development and the educational process. From 1934 to 1941, he worked for the General Education Board of the Rockefeller Foundation, where he became a leader in sponsoring research programs in child development and innovative educational programs. Through his efforts during World War II, resources were directed to the relocation of European scholars, especially psychodynamic scholars who were interested in child development, including Bruno Bettelheim, Peter Blos, Erik Erikson, and Fritz Redl. In 1941, he became a professor of education at the University of Chicago, where he eventually led in the formation of the Committee on Human Development. At his retirement in 1974, he was named Professor Emeritus in Development and Education.

Havighurst is known for many contributions to the fields of psychology, sociology, and education. In the 1950s, he guided a major research project demonstrating that children who are unsuccessful in school become socially alienated. At that time, he and his colleagues estimated that about 30% of adolescents were drifters and socially alienated young people of all social classes, though their backgrounds were predominantly lower middle class and working class (Havighurst et al., 1962). This is one of the few estimates ever offered of the number of disaffected youth in American society.

Havighurst proposed the concept of developmental tasks in his book *Developmental Tasks and Education*, which was first published for his students in 1948. Later, he applied this concept to a life-span analysis of development in *Human Development and Education*, published in 1953. Many theoretical systems have been built around this idea because of its relevance to understanding the basic process of human development. Havighurst also proposed the idea of the "teachable moment," the time when a person is most sensitive to the learning related to a particular task. In collaboration with several anthropologists, Havighurst studied child-rearing practices across race and social class in the United States; the emotional, social, and moral development of children in six Native American cultures; and retirement in six European countries. His research repeatedly clarified the significant contributions of social class and culture to development as well as highlighting the theme of various paths for healthy development in adolescence and adult life. Havighurst was actually one of the very first to initiate coursework on and systematic research into the normal processes of adult development and aging, thus establishing the full life course as the appropriate domain for the study of human development. Over his life he authored or co-authored more than 50 books and hundreds of articles, chapters, and monographs (Neugarten, 1993).

In 1969, Havighurst received the Thorndike Award in Educational Psychology from the American Psychological Association, and in 1977, he received the award for Distinguished Scientific Contributions from the Society for Research in Child Development.

of the next stage. In turn, the skills learned during a particular stage as a result of work on its developmental tasks provide the tools for the resolution of the psychosocial crisis of that stage. Task accomplishment and crisis resolution interact to produce individual life stories.

Psychosocial Crisis

A *psychosocial crisis*, the third organizing concept of psychosocial theory (Erikson, 1950/1963), arises when one must make psychological efforts to adjust to the demands of one's social environment at each stage of development. The word *crisis* in this context refers to a normal set of stresses and strains rather than to an extraordinary set of events.

Societal demands vary from stage to stage. The individual experiences these demands as mild but persistent guidelines for and expectations of behavior. They may be demands for greater self-control, a further development of skills, or a stronger commitment to goals. Before the end of each stage of development, the individual tries to achieve a resolution, to adjust to society's demands, and at the same time to translate those demands into personal terms. This process produces a *state of tension* that the individual must reduce in order to proceed to the next stage. It is this tension state that produces the psychosocial crisis.

A Typical Psychosocial Crisis

The psychosocial crisis with which you are probably most familiar is identity versus identity confusion, which is associated with later adolescence. An *identity crisis* is a sudden disintegration or deterioration of the framework of values and goals that a person relies on to give meaning and purpose to daily life.

An identity crisis usually involves strong feelings of anxiety and depression. The anxiety occurs because the person fears that without the structure of a clear value system, unacceptable impulses will break through and he or she will behave in ways that may be harmful or immoral. The depression occurs because the person suddenly feels worthless. When our previously established goals come to seem meaningless, we are likely to be overwhelmed by a feeling that our actions have no purpose or value.

A college student's identity crisis may be intensified under two conditions, both of which demand a rapid, intense examination of one's values. First, the identity crisis may be heightened when students attend a college where the value orientation departs significantly from their own and where they interact frequently with faculty members. These students believe they should admire and respect adults, especially their professors, and they suddenly feel at a loss when significant adults challenge their values. Yet they may try desperately to sustain their old value system in order to maintain a sense of control. This kind of conflict may also occur when students who have very traditional values and a clear career agenda attend a highly selective and prestigious private college. A student may want to attend Harvard or Yale, say, because of its status and reputation and yet may be totally unprepared for the strong socialization pressures that such schools exert—pressures to examine ideas objectively, to open oneself up to new views, and to experiment with many roles. Going to a prestigious liberal arts college is not the same as buying a Mercedes Benz or a Brooks Brothers suit. It is more than a status symbol; it is a life experience that can create intense conflict in students who are not prepared for it.

Second, the identity crisis may be heightened in students who are exploring and experimenting when external demands force them to make a value commit-

TABLE 2.2 Psychosocial Crises of the Life Stages	
Life Stage*	***Psychosocial Crisis***
Infancy (birth to 2 years)	Trust versus mistrust
Toddlerhood (2 to 4)	Autonomy versus shame and doubt
Early school age (4 to 6)	Initiative versus guilt
Middle school age (6 to 12)	Industry versus Inferiority
Early adolescence (12 to 18)	Group identity versus alienation
Later adolescence (18 to 22)	Individual identity versus identity confusion
Early adulthood (22 to 34)	Intimacy versus isolation
Middle adulthood (34 to 60)	Generativity versus stagnation
Later adulthood (60 to 75)	Integrity versus despair
Very old age (75 until death)	Immortality versus extinction

*We do not consider the concept of psychosocial crisis appropriate to the prenatal stage.

ment while they are still uncertain or confused. For some students, the need to decide on a major, to make a commitment to a love relationship, or to take a stand on a campus controversy will reveal that they do indeed know what they want, and they will be reassured that their values are more fully shaped than they had realized. Students who make this happy discovery will move in the direction of identity achievement. Other students, however, who are uncertain about which values and goals are best, may feel overwhelmed when sudden demands for commitment send their existing tentative value structure into disorganization.

Psychosocial Crises of the Life Stages

Table 2.2 lists the psychosocial crisis at each stage of development from infancy through very old age. This scheme, derived from Erikson's model shown in Figure 2.2, expresses the crises as polarities—for example, trust versus mistrust, and autonomy versus shame and doubt. These contrasting conditions suggest the underlying dimensions along which each psychosocial crisis is resolved. According to psychosocial theory, most people experience both ends of the continuum. The inevitable discrepancy between one's level of development at the beginning of a stage and society's push for a new level of functioning by the end of it creates at least a mild degree of the negative condition. Even within a loving, caring social environment that promotes trust, an infant will experience some moments of frustration or disappointment that result in mistrust, and even the most industrious, skillful child of middle school age will encounter some tasks that are too difficult or some feelings of inferiority in comparison with a more talented peer.

The outcome of the crisis at each stage is a balance or integration of the two opposing forces. For each person, the relative frequency and significance of positive and negative experiences will contribute to a resolution of the crisis that lies at some point along a continuum from extremely positive to extremely negative.

It should be noted that the likelihood of a completely positive or a completely negative resolution is small. Most individuals resolve the crisis in the direction of the positive pole. That is, for most people the weight of experience combined with their natural maturational tendencies supports a positive resolution of the crisis. At each successive stage, however, the likelihood of a negative resolution increases as the developmental tasks become more complex and the chances of encountering societal barriers to development rise. A positive resolution of each crisis provides new ego strengths that help the person meet the demands of the next stage.

If we are to understand the process of growth at each life stage, we have to consider the negative as well as the positive pole of each crisis. The negative poles offer an insight into basic areas of human vulnerability. Experienced in moderation, the negatives foster a clarification of ego positions, individuation, and moral integrity. While a steady diet of mistrust is undesirable, for example, it is important that a trusting person be able to evaluate situations and people for their trustworthiness and to discern the cues that are being sent about safety or danger in any encounter. Recognizing those who may not be concerned about one's needs or welfare is certainly advantageous. However, mistrusting others and being overly careful in all relationships may lead to hopelessness. In every psychosocial crisis, the experiences at both the positive and the negative poles contribute to the total range of a person's adaptive capacities.

Why conceptualize life in terms of crises? Does this idea adequately portray the experience of the individual, or does it overemphasize conflict and abnormality? The term *crisis* implies that normal development does not proceed smoothly. The theory hypothesizes that tension and conflict are necessary elements in the developmental process and that crisis and its resolution are basic, biologically based components of life experience at every stage; in fact, they are what drive the ego system to develop new capacities. "Growing pains" occur at every stage of life. Those who expect their problems to be over after adolescence will be sorely disappointed.

The term *psychosocial* draws our attention to the fact that these developmental crises are the result of cultural pressures and expectations. The theory suggests that, in the process of normal development, individuals will experience tension regardless of their culture because of the culture's need to socialize and integrate its members. Although the tension itself is not a result of personal inadequacies, failure to resolve it can seriously limit future growth. To some extent, psychosocial theory attempts to account for failures in development that appear at every stage in life. The concept of crisis implies that at any stage something can interfere with growth and reduce one's opportunities to experience personal fulfillment.

The exact nature of the conflict is not the same at all stages. Few cultural limits are placed on infants, for example; the outcome of the infancy stage depends greatly on the skill of the caregiver. At early school age, the culture stands in fairly direct opposition to the child's initiative in some matters and offers abundant encouragement to initiative in others. In young adulthood, the dominant cultural push is toward the establishment of intimate relationships; yet an individual may be unable to attain intimacy because of cultural norms set against certain forms of interaction.

Psychosocial theory suggests that crises are a predictable part of growth. At every life stage, we can anticipate that there will be some discrepancy between the skills that have been developed before it begins and the expectations for growth during the stage. As reflected in the epigenetic principle, the succession of crises occurs in a predictable sequence over the life course. Although Erikson did not specify the exact ages for each crisis, the theory hypothesizes an age-related progression in which each crisis has its time of special ascendancy. The combination

Some environments call forth a cautious or mistrustful response. If you walk down this alley every day to school or work, you may be very comfortable here. If you have never been in this alley before, you might approach it with wariness.

Earthquakes, floods, and hurricanes often produce major unforeseen crises for vast numbers of people. Homes and communities are destroyed. People at different psychosocial stages will adapt in very different ways. Children, for example, may experience a terrible loss of confidence in their parents' ability to protect them. Older adults may lose a lifetime of treasures and memories, as well as a sense of social support.

of biological, psychological, and societal forces that operate to bring about change has a degree of regularity that places each psychosocial crisis at a particular period of life.

In addition to these predictable crises, any number of unforeseen stresses may arise. Parents' divorce, the death of a sibling, victimization by violence, the loss of a job, and widowhood are examples of unforseen life crises. The need to cope with them may overwhelm a person, particularly if several occur at the same time. The picture of predictable developmental stress that is emphasized in psychosocial theory must be expanded to include the possibility of unanticipated crises. Although these chance events may foster growth and new competencies, they may also result in defensiveness, regression, or dread. The impact of an unpredictable crisis will depend on whether the person is in a state of psychosocial crisis at the time (Cummings, Greene & Karraker, 1991; Larson & Ham, 1993).

The combination of predictable crises, unpredictable crises, and unique historical pressures may bring to light prior crises that require reorganization. For example, during early adulthood, when issues of intimacy versus isolation are salient, it is common to find a reworking of industry versus inferiority as well (Whitbourne et al., 1992). Young adults encounter the very concrete challenges of establishing themselves in the labor market and achieving self-sufficiency through paid employment. The intensity of this additional crisis will depend in part on historical factors, such as the economic and materialistic orientation of the society as a specific age group enters early adulthood. It will also depend on individual factors, especially whether the young adult has developed a clear commitment to occupational values during the earlier period of identity versus identity confusion. Thus, the crises are not resolved and put to rest once and for all: Each crisis is played and replayed both during ongoing developmental changes and when life events challenge the balance that was achieved earlier.

Pablo Picasso, Paulo
Drawing, *1923. Paulo,
Picasso's son, is shown in deep
concentration as he sketches
at his desk. Through imitation,
a child takes ownership of
actions and skills that he or
she has observed in the adult
world. It is little wonder that
Paulo, surrounded by the
actions and products of artistic
creation, is drawn to imitate
those behaviors. And it is
clearly with great delight that
Picasso chose to immortalize
this behavior, revealing the
etiology of the creative process
in the child.*

The Central Process for Resolving the Psychosocial Crisis

Every psychosocial crisis reflects some discrepancy between the person's developmental competencies at the beginning of the stage and societal pressures for more effective, integrated functioning. Under normal circumstances, the person is ready with certain new skills and capacities for social relationships. Our society is organized in such a way that age-related demands on individuals are communicated through their significant social relationships. For example, the law requires that all 6-year-olds go to school, but it is parents who actually send them there. The law requires that people remain in school until they are 16, but it is peers, teachers, parents, and adolescents' own aspirations that encourage their continued attendance.

The demands exerted on a person by all elements of the social world make up what Erikson (1982) refers to as the *social system*. A person's ego includes a social processing system that is sensitive to social expectations, which serve as natural stimulators of one's social processing mechanisms.

We have offered an extension of psychosocial theory by identifying a central process through which each psychosocial crisis is resolved. The *central process*, the fourth organizing concept of psychosocial theory, links the individual's needs with the requirements of the culture at each life stage. Significant relationships and relevant competencies change at every life stage. Specific modes of psychological work and of social interaction must occur if a person is to continue to grow.

TABLE 2.3	The Central Process for Resolution of the Psychosocial Crisis	
Life Stage*	***Central Process***
Infancy (birth to 2 years)	Mutuality with caregiver
Toddlerhood (2 to 4)	Imitation
Early school age (4 to 6)	Identification
Middle school age (6 to 12)	Education
Early adolescence (12 to 18)	Peer pressure
Later adolescence (18 to 22)	Role experimentation
Early adulthood (22 to 34)	Mutuality among peers
Middle adulthood (34 to 60)	Person-environment fit and creativity
Later adulthood (60 to 75)	Introspection
Very old age (75 until death)	Social support

*We do not consider the concept of central process appropriate to the prenatal stage.

For example, imitation is viewed as the central process for psychosocial growth during toddlerhood (2 to 4 years), when children expand their range of skills by imitating adults, siblings, television models, playmates, and even animals. Imitation appears to provide toddlers with enormous satisfaction. As they increase the similarity between themselves and admired members of their social groups, through imitation, they begin to experience the world as other people and animals experience it. They exercise some control over potentially frightening or confusing events by imitating elements of those occurrences in their play.

The movement toward a sense of autonomy in toddlerhood is facilitated by the child's readiness to imitate and by the variety of models available for observation. Imitation expands children's range of behavior, and through persistent imitative activity, children expand their sense of self-initiated behavior and control over their actions. Repetitive experiences of this kind lead to the development of a sense of personal autonomy.

Imitation is more dominant in the behavioral repertoire during toddlerhood than at any other time in life, although it is often used as a learning and social strategy at other stages. Also, the society—in this case, through the significant relationship with the parents—tells the child, "That's good, Robbie. Now watch Daddy, and do it just the way he does." Not only are this child's tendencies toward imitation internally motivated, but his society is telling him, "Imitate! It will help you learn."

Table 2.3 shows the central processes that lead to the acquisition of new skills, the resolution of the psychosocial crisis, and successful coping at each life stage. Each of these processes appears to take on heightened significance during a particular stage, and each can be encouraged through the organization of significant social relationships.

The central process for coping with the challenges of each life stage provides both personal and societal mechanisms for taking in new information and reorganizing existing information. It also suggests the means that are most likely to lead to a revision of the psychological system so that the crisis of the particular stage may be resolved. Children of age 5 or 6, for example, incorporate many of

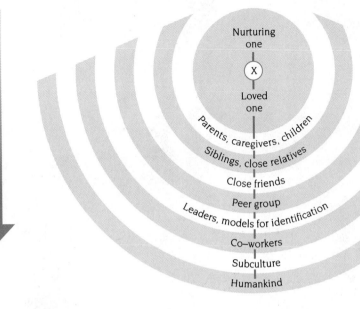

Degree of closeness

Nurturing
one

X

Loved
one

Parents, caregivers, children

Siblings, close relatives

Close friends

Peer group

Leaders, models for identification

Co-workers

Subculture

Humankind

FIGURE 2.4

Radius of significant relationships

their parents' beliefs into their own worldview through the process of identification. They begin to value many of the same goals and behaviors that their parents do. Thus, their psychological system is reorganized in a way that emphasizes the importance of some goals over others, and their images of an ideal self take shape in relation to newly internalized values. Each central process results in an intensive reworking of the psychological system, including a reorganization of boundaries, values, and images of oneself and others.

Radius of Significant Relationships

The fifth organizing principle of psychosocial theory is the *radius of significant relationships* (Erikson, 1982, p. 31) (see Figure 2.4). Initially, a person focuses on a small number of relationships. During childhood, adolescence, and early adulthood, the number of relationships expands and takes on greater variety in depth and in intensity. In middle and later adulthood, the person often returns to a small number of extremely important relationships that provide opportunities for great depth and intimacy. Most of the demands made on a person are made by people in these significant relationships.

In infancy, the significant social relationship is with a maternal or nurturing person. Most often, the mother is the significant other. However, the father, the siblings, a grandparent, or a substitute caregiver may also provide this significant relationship. One significant relationship is necessary, but it is possible for an infant to have more than one.

Most toddlers establish relationships with a widening circle of caregivers. At early school age, relationships with family members, including siblings and grandparents as well as parents, become stronger and deeper, and more relationships with friends and teachers become important.

At middle school age, significant relationships are found with a widening circle of people, including acquaintances in the neighborhood and at school. In early adolescence, the peer group, clubs and organizations, work, and religious groups provide new relationships that help people define themselves.

At each stage of development we have a radius of significant relationships. Those closest to us are the people who stand out in our thoughts, toward whom we experience intense emotions, and with whom we enjoy a sense of understanding, companionship, and loyalty.

In later adolescence, the radius of significant relations expands to include mentors, leaders, and models for leadership as people struggle to create an integrated personal identity. In early adulthood, partners in friendship, sex, competition, and cooperation provide significant relationships, and there is a new focus on the depth of relationships. In addition, for most people, children emerge as significant relations at this time.

In middle adulthood, significant relations are based on family, work, and/or community. Relationships may also extend to friendships established in other cities and countries. Adults are influenced by social relationships that have an impact on the lives of their children and their parents as well as on their own lives. In later adulthood and very old age, the significant relationships become more abstract, as one develops a more general relation to humanity, and at the same time more focused, as one develops a new level of caring for the few close relatives and friends who are still living. These are the relationships that transmit the messages of society and that produce states of tension.

According to Erikson's formulation, readiness to engage in this ever-changing network is a result of the epigenetic plan. At each stage of life, this network determines the demands that will be made on the person, the way he or she will be taken care of, and the meaning that the person will derive from the relationships. The relationship network varies from person to person, but each person has a network of significant relationships and an increasing readiness to enter into a widening social arena (Duck, 1988; Grusec & Lytton, 1988; Higgins, Ruble & Hartup, 1985).

Coping Behavior

Coping behavior, the sixth organizing concept of psychosocial theory, consists of active efforts to resolve stress and create new solutions to the challenges of each developmental stage. Robert White (1974) identified three components of the coping process: (1) the ability to gain and process new information, (2) the ability to maintain control over one's emotional state, and (3) the ability to move freely within one's environment.

Coping behavior is an important concept in psychosocial theory because it explains how new, original, creative, unique, and inventive behavior occurs. In addition, it lets us predict that individuals will behave in original, spontaneous, and successful ways in their active social lives. In the face of threat, coping behavior allows for the individual to develop and grow, rather than merely maintain equilibrium or become disorganized.

White illustrated the coping process by describing high school seniors' strategies for coping with the challenge of college. Those who go to the campus, talk to the students there, start reading for courses they will take, or take summer jobs in which they will be interacting with college students are doing more than maintaining their current level of functioning or equilibrium. They are devising coping strategies that will lead to increased information about their future setting and increased competence in it.

In coping with life challenges, individuals create their own strategies, which reflect their talents and motives. Think of the first day of kindergarten for a group of 5-year-olds. Some children are just sitting, shyly watching the teacher and the other children. Others are climbing all over the equipment and eagerly exploring the new toys. Still others are talking to the teacher or the other children, finding out names, making friends, or telling about the bus ride to school. Each of these strategies can be understood as a way of gathering information while preserving a degree of autonomy and integrity in a new and potentially threatening environment. No one way is right or even best, except as it serves the person by allowing access to information, freedom of movement, and some control over the emotions evoked by the new challenge.

An individual's characteristic style of coping appears to be influenced by a variety of factors, including gender, the available resources, the nature of interpersonal relationships, and the accumulation of life experiences. In addition, personality provides some consistency to the person's coping style. Children who are temperamentally difficult, for example—that is, children who are irritable and fearful; who have difficulty establishing regular eating, sleeping, and toileting patterns; and who have high activity levels—have been found to adapt less readily to change and are more vulnerable when they encounter such a misfortune as divorce or family economic hardship (Hetherington, 1989; Rutter, 1987).

Everyone's coping style undergoes some developmental transformations. With increased maturity, people approach stressful events more philosophically and are less likely than the young to use simplistic forms of coping, such as escape, denial, and blaming others for their misfortunes. They are able to reconceptualize negative events, finding some positive consequences in them or redefining them in a more positive light. Adults who have reached a high level of maturity seem to be able to determine when it is best to try to take action and

TABLE 2.4	**The Prime Adaptive Ego Quality at Each Psychosocial Stage**	
Stage	**Ego Quality**	**Definition**
Infancy	Hope	An enduring belief that one can attain one's deep and essential wishes
Toddlerhood	Will	A determination to exercise free choice and self-control
Early school age	Purpose	The courage to imagine and pursue valued goals
Middle school age	Competence	The free exercise of skill and intelligence in the completion of tasks
Early adolescence	Fidelity (I)	The ability to freely pledge and sustain loyalty to individuals and groups
Later adolescence	Fidelity (II)	The ability to freely pledge and sustain loyalty to values and ideologies
Early adulthood	Love	A capacity for mutuality that transcends childhood dependency
Middle adulthood	Care	A commitment to concern about what has been generated
Later adulthood	Wisdom	A detached yet active concern with life itself in the face of death
Very old age	Confidence	A conscious trust in oneself and assurance about the meaningfulness of life

Source: Based on Erikson, 1978.

when it is best to accommodate to the situation (Folkman et al., 1987; Labouvie-Vief, Hakim-Larson & Hobart, 1987).

Prime Adaptive Ego Qualities

Erikson (1978) postulated *prime adaptive ego qualities* that develop from the positive resolution of the psychosocial crisis of a given stage and provide resources for coping with the next. He described these qualities as mental states that form a basic orientation toward the interpretation of life experiences. A sense of competence, for example, permits a person to feel free to exercise his or her wits to solve problems without being weighed down by a sense of inferiority.

The prime adaptive ego qualities and their definitions are listed in Table 2.4. These ego qualities contribute to the person's dominant worldview, which throughout life must be reformulated to accommodate new ego qualities.

Core Pathologies

Although most people develop the prime adaptive ego qualities, a potential core pathology or destructive force may also develop as a result of ineffective, negatively balanced crisis resolution at each stage (Erikson, 1982) (Table 2.5). The core pathologies also serve as guiding orientations for behavior. These pathologies move people away from others, tend to prevent further exploration of interpersonal relations, and obstruct the resolution of subsequent psychosocial crises.

TABLE 2.5   Core Pathology at Each Life Stage

Life Stage*	Core Pathology	Definition
Infancy	Withdrawal	Social and emotional detachment
Toddlerhood	Compulsion	Repetitive behaviors motivated by impulse or by restrictions against the expression of impulse
Early school age	Inhibition	A psychological restraint that prevents freedom of thought, expression, and activity
Middle school age	Inertia	A paralysis of action and thought that prevents productive work
Early adolescence	Isolation	Lack of companions
Later adolescence	Repudiation	Rejection of roles and values that are viewed as alien to oneself
Early adulthood	Exclusivity	An elitist shutting out of others
Middle adulthood	Rejectivity	Unwillingness to include certain others or groups of others in one's generative concern
Later adulthood	Disdain	A feeling of scorn for the weakness and frailty of oneself and others
Very old age	Difference	An inability to act because of overwhelming self-doubt

Source: Based on Erikson, 1982.

The energy that would normally be directed toward mastering the developmental tasks of a stage is directed instead toward resisting or avoiding change. The core pathologies are not simply passive limitations or barriers to growth. They are energized worldviews leading to strategies that protect people from further, unwanted association with the social system and its persistent, tension-producing demands.

Evaluation of Psychosocial Theory

Although we believe that psychosocial theory provides a useful theoretical framework for organizing the vast array of observations in the field of human development, we recognize that it has weaknesses as well as strengths. We must not lose sight of either its strengths or its weaknesses if we are to be sensitive to how the theory itself may influence our thinking. The strengths and weaknesses of psychosocial theory are listed in Table 2.6.

Strengths

Psychosocial theory provides a very broad context within which to study development. The theory links the process of child development to the later stages of adult life, to the needs of society, and to the ability of societies to interact with one another. Although many scholars agree that such a broad perspective is

TABLE 2.6   Evaluation of Psychosocial Theory

Strengths	*Weaknesses*
The theory provides a broad context, linking development in various stages of life to the resources and demands of society.	The basic concepts of the theory are abstract and difficult to operationalize.
It emphasizes ego development and directions for healthy development across the life span.	Explanations of the mechanisms for resolving crisis and moving from one stage to the next are not well developed.
It provides a useful framework for psychotherapy.	The specific number of stages and their link to a genetic plan for development have not been adequately demonstrated, especially in adulthood.
It emphasizes the dynamic interplay between a genetic plan and the forces of culture and society in guiding individual development.	The theory is dominated by a male, Eurocentric perspective that gives too much emphasis to the emergence of individuality and not enough emphasis to social competence and social needs.
The concept of normative psychosocial crises provides an effective set of constructs for examining the tension between the individual and society.	The specific way in which culture encourages or inhibits development at each life stage is not clearly elaborated.

necessary, few other theories attempt to address the dynamic interplay between individual development and society.

The emphasis of psychosocial theory on ego development and ego processes provides insight into the directions of healthy development throughout life. At the same time, the theory is useful as a framework for approaching psychotherapy and counseling in that it provides a guide to the tensions that may disrupt development at each life stage. It also recognizes the contributions that individuals make to their own well-being.

The theory offers a dynamic picture of the interplay between a genetically guided plan for development and the powerful forces of culture and society in shaping the course of development at every life stage.

The concept of normative psychosocial crises is a creative contribution that identifies predictable tensions between socialization and maturation throughout life. Societies, with their structures, laws, roles, rituals, and sanctions, are organized to guide individual growth toward a particular ideal of mature adulthood. If individuals grew in that direction naturally, as a result of an unfolding, genetically guided plan, presumably there would be no need for these elaborate social structures. But every society faces problems when it attempts to balance the needs of the individual with the needs of the group. All individuals face problems when they attempt to experience their individuality while still maintaining the support of their group. Psychosocial theory gives us concepts for exploring these natural tensions.

Weaknesses

One weakness of psychosocial theory is that its basic concepts are presented in language that is abstract and difficult to examine empirically (Crain, 1985; Miller, 1993). Such terms as *initiative*, *personal identity*, *intimacy*, *generativity*, and *integrity*—

concepts included in the psychosocial crises—are hard to define and even more difficult to translate into objective measures. Nonetheless, efforts have been made along this line. James Marcia, Alan Waterman, Anne Constantinople, and others have contributed to a rather extensive literature that examines the construct of personal identity. Other researchers have tackled the concept of intimacy, and still others have tried to operationalize the concepts of generativity and integrity. A questionnaire measure based on Erikson's psychosocial theory, the Inventory of Psychosocial Development, has been used to trace the emergence of psychosocial crises and their resolution in samples varying in age from adolescence to later adulthood (Walasky, Whitbourne & Nehrke, 1983–1984; Waterman & Whitbourne, 1981; Whitbourne et al., 1992; Constantinople, 1969).

In addition to studies meant to test psychosocial theory, many others have a bearing on its constructs. In each of the stages of life that we will be examining, you will find an analysis of research that has a clear link to the constructs of psychosocial theory.

Another weakness of the theory is that explanations of the mechanisms for resolving crises and moving from one stage to the next are not well developed. Erikson has not offered a universal mechanism for crisis resolution, nor has he detailed the kinds of experiences that are necessary at each stage if one is to cope successfully with the crisis of that stage. We have addressed this weakness by introducing the concepts of developmental tasks and central process for each stage. The developmental tasks suggest some of the major achievements that permit a person to meet the social expectations of each stage. The central process identifies the primary social context within which the crisis is resolved. Using these two vehicles, we are beginning to glimpse the answers to many questions about how development takes place.

The specific number of stages and their link to a biologically based plan for development has been criticized, most notably in discussions of the stages of adulthood (Crain, 1985). Other human development theorists, such as Robert Peck, Robert Gould, Daniel Levinson, and Marjorie Lowenthal, have taken a more differentiated view of the stages of adulthood and later life. We have responded to these criticisms by treating adolescence as two distinct stages and by adding a stage of adulthood: very old age. You will also read about the important developmental issues of the prenatal period, a stage that Erikson's theory does not consider, but one that clearly plays a central role in setting the stage for a lifetime of vulnerabilities and competences. In our view, these revisions present no threat to the usefulness of the theory. Rather, they demonstrate the natural evolution of a theoretical framework as it continues to encounter new observations.

Finally, the theory has been criticized as being dominated by a male, Eurocentric, individualistic perspective (Gilligan, 1982). The themes of autonomy, initiative, industry, and personal identity all emphasize the process of individuation. In this and other theories of development, ego development, separateness from family, autonomy, and self-directed goal attainment have been equated with psychological maturity. Relatively little attention has been given to themes that have been identified as central to the developmental experiences of girls and young women—themes of interpersonal competence, connection, and affiliation (Josselson, 1987). These themes also seem to be emerging within more collectively oriented ethnic subcultures, cultures in which maturity is equated with one's ability to support and sustain the success of the family or the extended-family group rather than with one's own achievement of status, wealth, or recognition. Within the framework of psychosocial theory, the theme of connection is

At the Quinciniera, a 15-year-old Mexican-American girl celebrates mass with her family. Within the Mexican-American tradition, family bonds remain central to identity formation throughout the adolescent and young adult years, carrying with them a special sense of obligation and loyalty as well as personal pride and protectiveness.

addressed directly through the first psychosocial crisis of trust versus mistrust in infancy, but then the thread is lost until early adolescence and early and middle adulthood, when group identity, intimacy, and generativity direct our focus back to the critical links that individuals build with others. Indirectly, the concept of the radius of significant relationships is present at every phase of life, suggesting that how one defines oneself is always intimately linked to one's meaningful social connections. We use this construct throughout the text to maintain the perspective of the person interwoven in a tapestry of relationships, focusing especially on family and friends in childhood; on the family, the peer group, love relationships, and close friends in early and later adolescence; and on intimate partners, family, friends, and co-workers in various phases of adult life.

Chapter Summary

Psychosocial theory offers a life-span view of development, which is a product of the interactions between individuals and their social environments. The needs and goals of both the individual and society must be considered in conceptualizing human development. Predictability is found in the sequence of psychosocial stages, in the central process involved in the resolution of the crisis at each stage, and in the radius of significant relationships. Individuality is expressed in the achievement of the developmental tasks, in the development of a worldview, and in the style and resources for coping that a person brings to each new life challenge.

At the beginning of this chapter we discussed the three questions you must ask in order to evaluate a theory. Let us now answer these questions with respect to psychosocial theory:

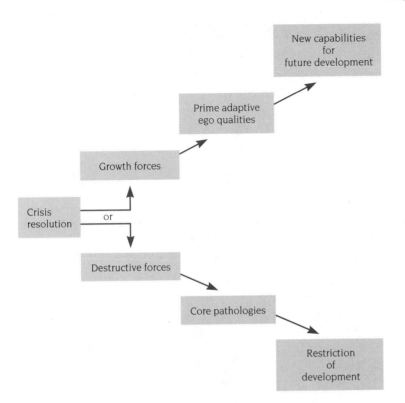

FIGURE 2.5

Mechanism for positive and negative psychosocial development

1. *Which phenomena is the theory trying to explain?* The theory attempts to explain human development across the life span, especially patterned changes in self-understanding, social relationships, and worldview.

2. *What assumptions does the theory make?* Human development is a product of three factors: biological evolution, the interaction between individuals and social groups, and the contributions that individuals make to their own psychological growth.

3. *What does the theory predict?* There are 11 distinct stages of development. Developmental tasks are dictated by the interaction of the biological, psychological, and societal systems during each stage. A normal crisis arises at each stage of development, and a central process operates to resolve it. Each person is part of an expanding network of significant relationships that convey society's expectations and demands. These relationships also provide encouragement in the face of challenges. New behaviors continue to be possible throughout life.

Development will be optimal if a person can create new behavior and relationships as a result of skill acquisition and successful crisis resolution during each stage of growth. Lack of development and core pathologies result from tendencies that restrict behavior in general and new behavior in particular (especially social behavior). The mechanism for positive and negative development is diagrammed in Figure 2.5.

The basic concepts of psychosocial theory provide the framework for analyzing development across 11 life stages. Each chapter from 4 through 14 is devoted to one life stage. With the exception of Chapter 4, on pregnancy and prenatal development, each starts with a discussion of the developmental tasks of that

TABLE 2.7   **Organization of the Stages**

Life Stage	Developmental Tasks	Psychosocial Crisis
Prenatal (conception to (birth)		
Infancy (birth to 2 years)	Social attachment Maturation of sensory, perceptual, and motor functions Sensorimotor intelligence and primitive causality Understanding the nature of objects and creation of categories Emotional development	Basic trust versus basic mistrust
Toddlerhood (2 to 4)	Elaboration of locomotion Fantasy play Language development Self-control	Autonomy versus shame and doubt
Early school age (4 to 6)	Sex-role identification Early moral development Self-theory Group play	Initiative versus guilt
Middle school age (6 to 12)	Friendship Concrete operations Skill learning Self-evaluation Team play	Industry versus inferiority
Early adolescence (12 to 18)	Physical maturation Formal operations Emotional development Membership in the peer group Sexual relationships	Group identity versus alienation
Later adolescence (18 to 22)	Autonomy from parents Gender identity Internalized morality Career choice	Individual identity versus identity confusion
Early adulthood (22 to 34)	Exploring intimate relationships Childbearing Work Lifestyle	Intimacy versus isolation
Middle adulthood (34 to 60)	Management of a career Nurturing the marital relationship Expanding caring relationships Management of the household	Generativity versus stagnation
Later adulthood (60 to 75)	Promotion of intellectual vigor Redirection of energy toward new roles Acceptance of one's life Development of a point of view about death	Integrity versus despair
Very old age (75 until death)	Coping with the physical changes of aging Development of a psychohistorical perspective Travel through uncharted terrain	Immortality versus extinction

(continued)

TABLE 2.7   (continued)

Central Process	Prime Adaptive Ego Quality	Core Pathology	Applied Topic
Mutuality with caregiver	Hope	Withdrawal	Abortion The role of the parents
Imitation	Will	Compulsion	Discipline Day care
Identification	Purpose	Inhibition	The impact of television
Education	Competence	Inertia	Sex education
Peer pressure	Fidelity (I)	Isolation	Adolescent alcohol use
Role experimentation	Fidelity (II)	Repudiation	Career decision-making
Mutuality among peers	Love	Exclusivity	Divorce
Person-environment fit and creativity	Care	Rejectivity	Discrimination in the workplace
Introspection	Wisdom	Disdain	Retirement
Social support	Confidence	Diffidence	Meeting the needs of the frail elderly

life stage. As we trace developments in physical growth, emotional growth, intel-lectual skills, social relationships, and self-understanding, you can begin to appreciate that development is simultaneous and interrelated in all of these dimensions during each period of life.

In the second section of each chapter, we describe the psychosocial crisis of the stage under discussion, accounting for the tension by examining the individ-ual's needs and personal resources in light of the dominant societal expectations. In addition to defining the crisis, we conceptualize the central process by which it is resolved. Some crises involve interaction with significant others, as in the case of trust versus mistrust or intimacy versus isolation. Others involve private, inter-nal reorganization, such as the crisis of individual identity versus identity confu-sion, or integrity versus despair. The resolution of the crisis at each stage devel-ops either new ego strengths or new core pathologies.

At the end of each chapter, we use the material we have discussed to analyze a selected topic that is of persistent concern to our society. These topics are con-troversial, and they may generate sentiment as they deepen understanding. We intend these sections to stimulate the application of developmental principles to other real-world concerns.

Take a moment to study Table 2.7. You can use this table as a guide to the major themes of the text. It may help you to see the connections among the top-ics within a chapter, or to trace threads of continuity over several periods of life. You may also use this table in constructing a life map for yourself, which will reveal the levels of tension and the major psychosocial factors that are currently affecting your self-concept and your relationships with others.

References

Coles, R. (1970). *Erik H. Erikson: The growth of his work.* Boston: Atlantic-Little, Brown.

Constantinople, A. (1969). An Eriksonian measure of personality development in college students. *Developmental Psychology, 1,* 357–372.

Crain, W. C. (1985). *Theories of development: Concepts and applications* (2nd ed.). Englewood Cliffs, NJ: Prentice-Hall.

Cummings, E. M., Greene, A-L. & Karraker, K. H. (Eds). (1991). *Lifespan perspectives on stress and coping.* Hillsdale, NJ: Erlbaum.

Davison, M. L., King, P. M., Kitchener, K. S. & Parker, C. A. (1980). The stage sequence concept in cognitive and social development. *Developmental Psychology, 16,* 121–131.

Duck, S. (1988). *Handbook of personal relationships: Theory, research, and interventions.* New York: Wiley.

Erikson, E. H. (1950/1963). *Childhood and society.* New York: Norton.

Erikson, E. H. (1958). *Young man Luther.* New York: Norton.

Erikson, E. H. (1969). *Gandhi's truth.* New York: Norton.

Erikson, E. H. (1978). Reflections on Dr. Borg's life cycle. In E. H. Erikson (Ed.), *Adulthood* (pp. 1–31). New York: Norton.

Erikson, E. H. (1982). *The life cycle completed: A review.* New York: Norton.

Erikson, E. H., Erikson, J. M. & Kivnick, H. Q. (1986). *Vital involvement in old age.* New York: Norton.

Fischer, K. W. & Silvern, L. (1985). Stages and individual differences in cognitive development. *Annual Review of Psychology, 36,* 613–648.

Flavell, J. H. (1982). Structures, stages, and sequences in cognitive development. In W. A. Collins (Ed.), *The concept of development* (pp. 1–28). Hillsdale, NJ: Erlbaum.

Folkman, S., Lazarus, R. S., Pimley, S. & Novacek, J. (1987). Age differences in stress and coping process. *Psychology and Aging, 2,* 171–184.

Gilligan, C. (1982). *In a different voice.* Cambridge: Harvard University Press.

Grusec, J. E. & Lytton, H. (1988). *Social development: History, theory, and research.* New York: Springer-Verlag.

Havighurst, R. J. (1948). *Developmental tasks and education.* Chicago: University of Chicago Press.

Havighurst, R. J. (1953). *Human development and education.* New York: Longmans, Green.

Havighurst, R. J. (1972). *Developmental tasks and education* (3rd ed.). New York: David McKay.

Havighurst, R. J., Bowman, P. H., Liddle, J. P., Mathews, Ch. V. & Pierce, J. V. (1962). *Growing up in River City.* New York: Wiley.

Hetherington, E. M. (1989). Coping with family transitions: Winners, losers, and survivors. *Child Development,* 60, 1–14.

Higgins, E. T., Ruble, D. N. & Hartup, W. W. (1985). *Social cognition and social development: A sociocultural perspective.* New York: Cambridge University Press.

Huxley, J. (1941). *The uniqueness of man.* London: Chatto & Windus.

Huxley, J. (1942). *Evolution: The magic synthesis.* New York: Harper.

Josselson, R. (1987). *Finding herself: Pathways to identity development in women.* San Francisco: Jossey-Bass.

Labouvie-Vief, G., Hakim-Larson, J. & Hobart, C. J. (1987). Age, ego level, and the life-span development of coping and defense processes. *Psychology and Aging,* 2, 286–293.

Larson, R. & Ham, M. (1993). Stress and "Storm and Stress" in early adolescence: The relationship of negative events with dysphoric affect. *Developmental Psychology,* 29, 130–140.

Levin, I. (1986). *Stage and structure: Reopening the debate.* Norwood, NJ: Ablex.

Miller, P. H. (1993). *Theories of developmental psychology* (3rd ed.). New York: W. H. Freeman.

Neugarten, B. L. (1993). Obituaries: Robert J. Havighurst (1900–1991). *American Psychologist,* 48, 1290–1291.

Piaget, J. (1950). *The psychology of intelligence.* New York: Harcourt Brace; London: Routledge & Kegan Paul.

Rutter, M. (1987). Psychosocial resilience and protective mechanisms. *American Journal of Orthopsychiatry,* 57, 316–331.

Walaskay, M., Whitbourne, S. K. & Nehrke, M. F. (1983–1984). Construction and validation of an ego-integrity status interview. *International Journal of Aging and Human Development,* 18, 61–72.

Waterman, A. S. & Whitbourne, S. K. (1981). The inventory of psychosocial development. *Journal Supplement Abstract Service: Catalog of Selected Documents in Psychology,* 11, (Ms. No. 2179).

Whitbourne, S. K., Zuschlag, M. K., Elliot, L. B. & Waterman, A. S. (1992). Psychosocial development in adulthood: A 22-year sequential study. *Journal of Personality and Social Psychology,* 63, 260–271.

White, R. W. (1974). Strategies of adaptation: An attempt at systematic description. In G. V. Coelho, D. A. Hamburg & J. E. Adams (Eds.), *Coping and adaptation* (pp. 47–68). New York: Basic Books.

CHAPTER 3

Theories guide our inquiry much as this child guides the blind minotaur. Theories help us begin to make sense of a multitude of observations and give us a structure around which knowledge can be built.

Theories of Change

When we study human development through life, we must move from an overview of development to a detailed explanation of the specific processes. Psychosocial theory provides the conceptual umbrella for our approach to human development, but we need other theories to explain behavior at different levels of analysis. In accounting for both stability and change through life, we need theoretical constructs that will help us to account for global evolutionary change, societal and cultural change, and individual change. In addition, we need concepts that help explain the contributions of life experiences, maturational factors, and one's own constructions of experience to physical, cognitive, social, emotional, and self development.

This chapter introduces the basic concepts of seven major theories: evolutionary theory, cultural theory, psychosexual theory, cognitive developmental theory, learning theory, social role theory, and systems theory. Knowledge of several theoretical perspectives will help us maintain flexibility in interpreting behavior and will facilitate our understanding of the integration of individuals and social systems.

Biological Evolution

The theory of evolution explains how diverse and increasingly more complex life-forms have come to exist. Evolutionary theory assumes that the natural laws that apply to plant and other animal life also apply to humans. This theory is important to the study of human development because it integrates human beings into the vast array of life-forms. Evolutionary theory emphasizes the importance of biological forces in directing growth and the gradual modification of species as they adapt to specific environments.

Natural Selection

Although the theory of evolution existed before his work, Charles Darwin has been credited with the discovery of natural selection, the basic mechanism that could account for the transformation of species over long periods and in many different environments. Darwin believed that unchanging laws of nature apply uniformly throughout time. This assumption, called *uniformitarianism*, had been advanced by Charles Lyell (1830/1833). The challenge that this belief posed was to discover the basic mechanism that accounts for species change from the beginnings of life to the present, and the mechanism that Darwin (1859/1979) discovered is natural selection. Natural selection operates at the level of the genes that are passed from one generation to the next in individual organisms that are reproductively successful. Reproductive success, sometimes called *fitness*, varies among the members of a species (Archer, 1991).

Every species produces more offspring than can survive to reproduce because of a limited food supply and natural dangers. Darwin observed quite a bit of *variability* among members of the same species in any given location, a variability due to genetic differences. Because of these varying patterns of genetic makeup, some individuals were better suited than others to the immediate environment and were more likely to survive, mate, and produce offspring. These offspring were also more likely to have characteristics appropriate to that location. Eventually, the species would change genetically to become more successful, or it would evolve into a new species. If the environment changed (in climate, for example), only certain variations of organisms would survive, and again species would evolve. Forms

As their environment became increasingly polluted, the silvery peppered moths were more readily seen and eaten, but the dark peppered moths survived.

of life that failed to adapt would become extinct. It is important to understand that it is the variability within a species that ensures the species' continuation or its development into new forms.

The law of natural selection has been referred to (first by Herbert Spencer, 1864) as the principle of "survival of the fittest." This phrase often calls up images of head-to-head combat between the members of a species, but Darwin (1859/1979) described the process in the following way:

> It may metaphorically be said that natural selection is daily and hourly scrutinizing, throughout the world, the slightest variation; rejecting those that are bad, preserving and adding up all that are good; silently and insensibly working, whenever and wherever opportunity offers, at the improvement of each organic being in relation to its conditions of life. We see nothing of these slow changes in progress, until the hand of time has marked the lapse of ages, and then so imperfect is our view into long-past geological ages, that we see only that the forms of life are now different from what they formerly were. (p. 77)

Adaptation

Adaptation is the process that underlies evolutionary change—the process by which living things develop characteristics that enable them to thrive in a particular environment. Adaptation can operate at the biological level, as a change in some physical characteristic over generations; it can also operate at the behavioral level, as a change in some pattern of behavior.

Biological Adaptation

Biological adaptation can be seen in the coloration of the peppered moth. Because of genetic variation, some peppered moths have a very light, silvery color, while others are characterized by dark black patches. The silvery-flecked moths have excellent camouflage when they are at rest on lichen, a simple plant form that grows on rocks and trees. In areas where air pollution has killed lichen and blackened tree trunks, however, the black variety of peppered moth has an adaptive advantage. The black variety almost totally replaced the silver form in many industrial areas. In communities that have succeeded in reducing air pollution by controlling factory emissions and reducing automobile traffic, the silvery peppered moth is making a comeback.

Behavioral Adaptation

Behavioral adaptations are learned, not transmitted through genetic information that offspring inherit from their parents. However, if behavioral adaptations increase fitness, the genes of those who have adopted these behaviors are more likely to survive into future generations than the genes of those who do not practice these behavioral strategies. We humans pass on our behavioral adaptations through child-rearing practices, schools, and other culture bearers. With our remarkable capacity to develop behavioral adaptations, we can survive and thrive under quite varied environmental conditions.

One example of behavioral adaptation is the patterns of dress seen in the world's various climates. We do not wear the same kinds of clothing in a hot tropical climate, a hot dry climate, a temperate climate, and an arctic climate. This type of behavioral adaptation is essential to the survival of the individual. Other behavioral adaptations, such as courtship rituals and rules that determine who is a permissible marriage partner, influence an individual's opportunities to reproduce.

Evolution and the Human Species

"If one sets January 1 as the origin of life on earth, marine vertebrates would then first appear on November 24, dinosaurs on December 16, and man at 10:15 P.M. on December 31" (Lerner & Libby, 1976). The evolution of the family of humans began

BIOGRAPHICAL SKETCH

Charles Darwin
1809–1882

1881

Charles Darwin was born in 1809 into an educated family with a long-standing tradition of belief in the theory of evolution. Darwin's grandfather Erasmus Darwin was one of the pioneers in the development of evolutionary theory. As a schoolboy, Darwin rebelled against the classical pattern of learning by rote memorization. He preferred to spend long periods of time outdoors, exploring nature and puzzling over its mysteries.

As a young man, Darwin was sent to study medicine. He found the lectures boring and the work distasteful so he left medical school, gravely disappointing his father. Darwin was then sent to Cambridge to study theology in preparation to enter the clergy, but he found this study even less interest-

1854   1840

ing than medicine. He continued to spend much of his time outdoors, exploring nature.

In 1831, an opportunity arose that allowed Darwin to indulge his passion for the outdoors in a professionally acceptable way: He became the resident naturalist on the HMS *Beagle.* The crew's mission was to sail to South America, to survey its coast and the islands of the Pacific, to map this region, and to document its plant and animal life. The voyage lasted from 1831 to 1836. During those years, Darwin demonstrated unbounded energy in his exploration of the natural phenomena that he encountered.

Returning to England, Darwin settled down to work on the samples he had collected and to reflect on his observations. With painstaking attention to detail, over a period of 20 years he developed his theory of how species change and evolve into new plant or animal forms. However, he postponed writing about his views while he searched for examples that would support his argument. Not until 1859, when he learned that another naturalist, Alfred Russell Wallace, was about to introduce a very similar argument, was Darwin compelled to publish *The Origin of Species.*

only about 2 million years ago with the species *Homo habilis* and *Homo erectus*. Anthropologists have two opposing views of the origin of modern humans, *Homo sapiens*, which can be described very roughly as the "candelabra" model of evolution and the "Noah's ark" model of evolution. The *candelabra model* suggests that modern humans evolved simultaneously in several parts of the world and therefore argues for continuity in evolution from ancient *Homo erectus* ancestors to modern *Homo sapiens*, with a gradual transformation of features and characteristics. Differences among Asian, African, European, and Australian people are considered very ancient, having arisen early in the transformation from *Homo erectus* to *Homo sapiens* in each geographic area.

The *Noah's ark theory* suggests that modern humans have evolved from a group of common ancestors, *Homo sapiens*, who most likely had their origins in Africa about 200,000 years ago. This group of advanced humans then dispersed throughout the Old World and replaced the more primitive populations. In this view, there was no continuity from ancient to modern humans, but a rapid extinction (*rapid* meaning somewhere between 1000 and 13,000 years) of one group and expansion of the other. This theory leads to the conclusion that the racial differences we observe today are not based in very ancient local differences but evolved after the establishment of *Homo sapiens* in many parts of the world.

A combination of fossil evidence and genetic evidence provides strong support for the Noah's ark theory (Lewin, 1987; Tattersall, Delson & Van Couvering, 1988). The similarities in features of fossil evidence found in many parts of the world are so great that it seems unlikely that these humans could have evolved independently, without having had a recent common ancestor. In addition, with techniques from molecular biology, it is possible to trace characteristics of mitochondrial DNA showing that the modern humans found in various areas of Europe, Asia, and America are quite similar and suggesting a common genetic ancestry. The DNA would not be so similar if these humans had evolved independently from local primitive ancestors.

Thus, the picture that is taking shape is that the offspring of a common modern ancestor migrated throughout the world and dominated the other human species. This domination was comparatively rapid, fueled by enormously powerful mental evolution and the accompanying forms of cultural evolution, such as complex tool development, advanced techniques for hunting and gathering, the invention of agriculture, and the eventual growth of tribes, chiefdoms, and political states. Wilson (1975) termed the process through which humans achieved such a rapid and advanced level of functioning the *autocatalysis model*:

> When the earliest hominids became bipedal as part of their terrestrial adaptation, their hands were freed, the manufacture and handling of artifacts was made easier, and intelligence grew as part of the improvement of the tool-using habit. With mental capacity and the tendency to use artifacts increasing through mutual reinforcement, the entire materials-based culture expanded. Cooperation during hunting was perfected, providing a new impetus for the evolution of intelligence, which in turn permitted still more sophistication in tool using, and so on through cycles of causation. . . . The autocatalysis model usually includes the proposition that the shift to big game accelerated the process of mental evolution. (pp. 567–568)

The domination by modern humans was probably achieved subtly, rather than by open warfare or competition. Their superiority in hunting skills, toolmaking, and planning probably gave the modern species an evolutionary advantage by enabling them to establish dependable sources of high-quality food (Simons, 1989). Assuming that the two forms of humans, modern and archaic *Homo sapiens*,

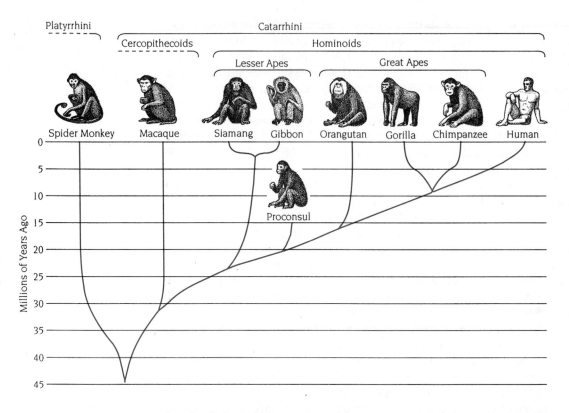

FIGURE 3.1

Evolutionary tree of hominoids. Hominoids are the superfamily of primates that includes the lesser apes (siamangs and gibbons), great apes (chimpanzees, gorillas, and orangutans), and humans.
Source: *Walker & Teaford, 1989.*

lived side by side for a time in the same geographic area, one analysis suggests that a 2% increase in the mortality rate of the more ancient species could have led that species to be replaced by the more modern form in as few as 30 generations (Zubrow, cited in Lewin, 1987).

Humans have characteristics that link them to the larger group of *mammals* from which they descended: They produce live young; the mothers feed their young on milk produced by the mammary glands; and the human body is covered with skin, which is protected by hair. Humans also have some characteristics that link them to other *primates*, the class of mammals that includes humans, apes, monkeys, lemurs, and tarsiers (see Figure 3.1). Primates share ten major characteristics:

1. Progressive movement of the eyes toward the midline of the head and consequent development of stereoscopic (three-dimensional) vision.
2. Retention of five-digit extremities and of the major bones of the arms and legs: clavicle, radius, and fibula.
3. Progressive development of the digits, particularly the thumb and big toe, which allows increased dexterity.
4. Development of flattened nails, instead of claws, and also of sensitive pads on the tips of the digits.
5. Progressive shortening of the snout, reduction in the size of the apparatus for smell, and consequent reduction in olfactory acuity.
6. Great increase in the size of the brain.
7. Prolongation of prenatal and postnatal development.
8. Decrease in the number of teeth and retention of a simple molar system.
9. Overall increase in body size, progressive development toward upright stature, and increased dependence on the hind limbs for locomotion.
10. Development of complex social organizations.

Through his study of the links between human behavior and the behavior of related animal species, Darwin (1872/1965) became interested in the adaptive functions of emotions. He suggested that emotional expressions were originally a form of preparation for such critical survival behaviors as attack, locomotion, defense, breathing, and vision. Through evolution, these expressions have become part of our system of communication. Emotional expressions, especially facial ones, reveal the inner state of the individual to others in the social group.

The frown is an expression with clearly adaptive origins. It originated as an intense stare directed at an object close to the face. Many species—including dogs, Capuchin monkeys, and humans—typically lower their eyebrows when they frown, a move that helps focus the eyes on the object,

BOX 3.1

Evolutionary Theory and Emotions

reduces glare, and protects the eyes should the object's position suddenly change. In most animals, a direct stare is a good indication of concentrated interest and little or no fear. Often, a stare and a frown immediately precede an attack. The frown has become an expression of confidence and assertive threat in monkeys, apes, and humans.

Some of the basic emotions are innate patterns, emitted without need of practice or the imitation of others, as can be seen in the emotional development of infants. The startle, the grimace, the smile, and the expression of disgust are all reflexive responses that have been observed in early infancy. Of course, the interpretation and expression or inhibition of emotions in childhood and adulthood depend on the cultural context and the individual's cognitive capacity.

Each of these characteristics contributes to the essential quality of human behavior. The structure of our hands permits the flexible manipulation of objects as tools. Reduced reliance on smell and relatively greater reliance on vision influence our mode of exploring the environment. Perhaps the most critical item on the list for human beings is the size, structure, and complexity of the brain. The prolonged period of prenatal and postnatal development characteristic of human infants provides the evolutionary basis for our work in the study of development.

All human beings, regardless of culture, share characteristics that tie them together as a species. They can mate and produce living children who in turn are capable of reproducing. They produce spoken symbolic language. They store information and pass it on from one generation to the next. They are self-conscious; that is, they raise questions about their origin and anticipate their death.

Ethology

Ethology is the comparative study of the biological bases of behavior from an evolutionary perspective. Ethology uses observation, experimentation, and the comparative method to investigate (1) the proximal causes of behavioral acts, (2) the relative contribution of inheritance and learning to these acts, and (3) the adaptive significance and evolutionary history of various patterns of behavior within and across species. Ethologists emphasize the importance of studying behavior in natural settings (Blurton-Jones, 1972; Eibl-Eibesfeldt, 1975). Laboratory experiments are used to discover answers to questions derived from these observations.

Evolutionary theory focuses our attention on those capacities and behavior patterns that contribute to long-term survival and continued adaptation. Therefore, the study of individual behavior and development focuses on how a

From an evolutionary perspective, the future of a species depends on the ability of individual members of the species to mate, reproduce, and rear their young to the age when they can mate and reproduce. The attachment behavioral system is central to the offspring's survival.

particular behavior contributes not just to the future growth and development of the individual but to the adaptation and continuation of the species.

The future of a species depends on the capacity of its individual members to survive, mate, reproduce, and rear their young. Some of the factors that contribute to the vigor and continuity of a species are the health of the individuals when they attain reproductive capacity, the characteristics of the environment that promote or inhibit procreation, and the capacity of sexually mature partners to rear their offspring.

From Darwin's interest in the evolution of species grew the biologist's interest in those behaviors that are central to the species' survival, including feeding efficiency, competition among males for breeding females, and cooperation among males in warding off predators and competing primates. The field of ethology has emerged as the study of evolutionarily significant behaviors that appear to be innate and specific to a particular species, behaviors that are commonly associated with eating, mating, and protecting a species from harm.

Two early contributors to the field of ethology, Konrad Lorenz (1935/1981) and Niko Tinbergen (1951), focused on *innate behaviors* and how they are expressed under natural conditions. Innate behaviors are present in some standard or shared form in all members of a species. They are expressed without previous learning, remaining relatively unchanged by experience. Innate behaviors include *reflexes*, which are simple responses to simple stimuli. A baby's grasp of a finger or other object that is placed in its palm is a reflex. Although many infant reflexes disappear by the end of the first year, some reflexes, including sucking, creeping, stepping, and grasping, are replaced by very similar behaviors that come under voluntary control.

Table 3.1 lists three kinds of infant reflexes: (1) reflexes that serve some adaptive function for the survival of the newborn; (2) reflexes that have been adaptive for the survival of genetically related species over the period of evolution; and (3) reflexes whose functions are not known. The third group includes patterned behaviors that are either remnants of more complex patterns in other species or perhaps latent resources for future adaptations of which we are not yet aware.

Some innate behaviors, called *fixed* or *model action patterns*, are more complex than reflexes. Birds build nests, squirrels bury nuts, and goslings follow their mothers. These behaviors are genetically guided sequences that are prompted by a particular stimulus pattern that releases or signals the behavior. The *releasing stimulus* may be a certain odor, color, movement, sound, or shape, or it may require a special relation between stimuli.

In recent years, some ethologists have turned their attention to the study of human behavior. Lorenz (1943) first hypothesized that certain aspects of an infant's appearance stimulate positive emotional responses in adult caregivers. The quality of "cuteness" or "babyness" that Lorenz identified includes a head that is large in proportion to the body, large eyes, and round, pudgy cheeks.

John Bowlby (1958, 1988) has been influential in bringing the ethological perspective to bear on development through the study of attachment. Bowlby describes the *attachment behavioral system* as a complex set of reflexes and signaling behaviors that bring about caregiving responses from adults. These responses in turn shape an infant's expectations and help to create an inner representation of the parent as a caring, comforting person.

The infant's innate capacities for smiling, cooing, grasping, and crying draw the adult's attention and provoke a sympathetic response. The adult's gentle cuddling, soothing, and smiling establish a sense of security in the child. Viewed in

TABLE 3.1	Some Reflexes of the Human Infant	
Reflex	*Evoking Stimulus*	*Response*
Reflexes That Facilitate Adaptation and Survival		
Sucking reflex	Pressure on lips and tongue	Suction produced by movement of lips and tongue
Pupillary reflex	Weak or bright light	Dilation or constriction of pupil
Rooting reflex	Light touch to cheek	Head movement in direction of touch
Startle reflex	Loud noise	Similar to Moro reflex (below), with elbows flexed and fingers closed
Swimming reflex	Neonate placed prone in water	Arm and leg movement
Reflexes Linked to Competences of Related Species		
Creeping reflex	Feet pushed against a surface	Arms and legs drawn under, head lifted
Flexion reflex	Pressure on sole of foot	Involuntary bending of leg
Grasp reflex	Pressure on fingers or palm	Closing and tightening of fingers
Moro reflex	Infant lying on back with head raised—rapidly release head	Extension of arms, head thrown back, spreading of fingers, crossing arms across body
Springing reflex	Infant held upright and slightly forward	Arms extend forward and legs drawn up
Stepping reflex	Infant supported under the arms above a flat surface	Rhythmical stepping movement
Abdominal reflex	Tactile stimulation	Involuntary contraction of abdominal muscles
Reflexes of Unknown Function		
Achilles tendon reflex	Blow to Achilles tendon	Contraction of calf muscles and downward bending of foot
Babinski reflex	Mild stroke on sole of foot	Fanning and extension of toes
Tonic neck reflex	Infant on back with head turned to one side	Arm and leg on side toward which head is facing are extended, other arm and leg flexed

this light, attachment is an innate behavior system that promotes the safety of off-spring in infancy and provides the basis for the trusting social relationships that are necessary for mating and parenting in adulthood.

Bowlby (1988) argues that attachment behavior serves the basic survival function of protection:

> Whilst attachment behaviour is at its most obvious in early childhood, it can be observed throughout the life cycle, especially in emergencies. Since it is seen in virtually all human beings (though in varying patterns), it is regarded as an integral part of human nature and one we share (to a varying extent) with members of other species. The biological function attributed to it is that of protection. To remain within easy access of a familiar individual known to be ready and willing to come to our aid in an emergency is clearly a good insurance policy—whatever our age. (p. 27)

Mary Ainsworth extended the research on attachment by developing a research paradigm in which the infant-mother attachment system can be observed systematically. Her work is discussed in some detail in Chapter 5 as it relates to the developmental task of forming social attachments. In psychoanalytic theory, Bowlby's notion that attachment behavior can be observed throughout life is extended by the notion of the anaclitic relationship. Freud argued that a positive mother-infant dyad establishes the inital prototype for a supportive, protective relationship and that the choice of subsequent object relationships is influenced by their resemblance to this early attachment system.

Focusing on a different behavioral system, William Charlesworth (1988) studied the importance of social interaction as a mechanism that allows humans to *obtain resources from the environment* at any point in the life span. He suggested that the resources required to resolve the crises of the psychosocial stages vary with the stage. For example, the infant requires protection, food, and attention; the toddler may require a toy or someone to talk to; the child of middle school age may need tools and materials for work; and the early adult may need a mate. Strategies for obtaining these resources change with development. Infants learn to signal their needs by crying or fussing. As they get older, children acquire an increasingly diverse set of strategies to use in their efforts to get the resources they need. Both aggressive and help-giving behaviors are designed to elicit the needed resources.

Other areas of interest in the ethological study of development include family development and child-rearing behaviors; peer-group behaviors; play behaviors; altruism; aggression and dominance; language; the communication of emotions, especially through facial expressions; mating and reproductive behaviors; and naturally occurring problem solving.

Implications for Human Development

With its focus on reproductive success, evolutionary theory highlights three phases of the life history: healthy growth and development leading up to the reproductive period; success in mating and the conception of offspring; and the ability to parent offspring so they can reach reproductive age and bear offspring of their own (Charlesworth, 1992). An organism is most vulnerable during childhood; children require care if they are to survive to reproductive age. It is important to understand that biological capacities and the environments in which they can be expressed operate together to produce behavior. A genetic plan, shaped through hundreds of generations, guides infants' predispositions, capacities, and sensitivities. Evolutionary theory points out that infants come into the world with a range of innate capacities and potentials. They have competences that permit them to establish social contact, to organize information, and to recognize and communicate their needs. At the same time, these innate capacities are expressed within specific contexts. The quality of parenting, the adequacy of resources, and the

Pablo Picasso, Bernard Picasso with His Mother, 1959. *Evolutionary theory emphasizes the link between genetically based capacities, such as the sucking reflex, and the relevant characteristics of the environment—the presence of a nurturing, responsive mother, for example.*

competition for resources with other siblings are examples of environmental factors to which infants must adapt. Childhood experiences shape the future of the human species by providing the context for the establishment of attachments, meaningful social competences, and problem-solving capacities, all of which have a bearing on individuals' behavior in adulthood, particularly their ability to form intimate relationships and to parent their offspring.

During adolescence, when sexual activity emerges and attitudes about marriage and parenting are being formulated, the quality of life for young people is critical to the future of human beings of every cultural group.

The evolutionary perspective draws attention to the interconnection between an individual's life history and the long-range history of the species. Principles of natural selection operate slowly over generations. However, the reproductive success of individuals over the course of their own lives will determine whether their genetic material will continue to be represented in the larger population. Many general areas of human behavior are relevant to the successful survival and fitness of individuals and groups (Charlesworth, 1992):

Reproductive strategies, such as having few or many sex partners, or entering into sexual activity early or late

Infant immaturity requiring prolonged care

Infant-caregiver attachment

Parent-child conflicts and sibling rivalry

Peer-group formation and functions, especially cooperation, competition, dominance, and submission

Pair bonding and mate selection

Helping behavior and altruism

Learning as an adaptive behavior

Individual creation and modification of the environment

Social evolution and the elaboration of rites, rituals, and religions

The evolutionary perspective directs attention to the importance of variability for a species' survival. Individual differences contribute to the vigor of the species. Human beings are genetically designed to permit wide variations in size, body shape, coloration, strength, talent, intelligence, and personality. This variability contributes to our capacity to adapt successfully to a wide variety of environmental conditions and therefore to protect the species as a whole from extinction.

One unique aspect of the human species is our ability to modify the environment in significant ways; we not only adapt to the environment but alter it to suit our needs. We all hope that we will alter the environment in ways that will enhance our species' survival. However, some of the environmental risks to which pregnant women, young children, and the rest of us are exposed make us aware that not all human modifications of the environment are beneficial to everyone. We all face a grave responsibility to ensure that the species will not become a victim of its own inventiveness.

Cultural Theory

In comparison with evolutionary theory, which places great emphasis on the role of the genotype in providing the mechanisms for development, cultural theory places its primary emphasis on the environment, particularly on the broad, far-ranging context of culture for shaping and guiding development. The term *culture* as used in this text refers to the learned systems of meanings and patterns of behavior that are shared by a group of people and transmitted from one generation to the next. *Physical culture* encompasses the objects, technologies, structures, tools, and other artifacts of a culture. *Social culture* encompasses norms, roles, beliefs, values, rites, and customs (Herkovits, 1948; Triandis et al., 1980; Rohner, 1984; Betancourt & Lopez, 1993).

On a more general level, culture has been described as a *worldview*, a way of making meaning of the relationships, situations, and objects encountered in daily life. Basic ideas concerning whether people are in control of nature or a part of nature, who is included in the definition of family, what characteristics indicate mental health or mental illness, which acts are hostile and which are nurturing, and which aspects of the environment are dangerous and which are valued—all these and many other mental constructions are shaped by the culture into which one is born (Kagitcibasi, 1990).Culture guides development not only through encounters with certain objects, roles, and settings, but through the meanings linked to actions.

Cross-cultural theory has tended to analyze the patterns of behavior shared by groups of individuals rather than the development of individuals within groups. Although attention has been given to differences in roles and relationships among group members based on such basic categories as gender, age, and kinship relations, the primary focus has been on understanding how these roles and relationships preserve the broad fabric of the culture and promote the group's continuation and survival. Although scholars recognize that culture is created by humans and is learned rather than inherited, they tend to study how culture shapes and gives meaning to human behavior rather than how individuals alter or redirect the patterns of culture. In fact, we are often not conscious of the variety of ways in which culture shapes our behavior. Especially when people have lived in only one cultural environment, many of the behaviors that a student of culture would call customs or rituals are thought of as simply the natural way of doing things. Standing a particular distance from another person during an informal conversation, making direct eye contact with another person, extending one's hand in greeting, and thinking of certain people as members of one's family and others as outside the family—these are a small sample of the many practices shaped by culture.

One of the values of a cross-cultural approach to human development is to increase our awareness of how culture shapes our own behavior as well as to understand the practices of members of other cultural groups (Dundes, 1968; Triandis, 1989). In fact, Michael Cole (1989) argues that the study of culture is intricately interwoven with the study of human behavior. Since humans as a species are able to modify and, in many instances, create their environments, and since they have the capacity to transmit knowledge about these modifications from one generation to the next, the human experience is in many ways uniquely embedded in the historical framework of culture. Culture both guides and limits our ways of knowing.

Cultural Determinism

Ruth Benedict was one of the first cultural anthropologists to argue for a diversified view of human development. There are many cultures on the earth, each one celebrating its own holidays, following its own religion, defining its own version of family, and prescribing its own pattern of roles and role expectations. According to Benedict (1934/1950), the course of individual development is predominantly a product of cultural expectations.

Cultural determinism refers to the power of culture to shape individual experience, a perspective in striking contrast to the evolutionary view. Biological factors are considered relatively insignificant in comparison with the role of culture in governing patterns of personality development:

> Insect society takes no chances; the pattern of the entire social structure is carried in the cell structure of each individual ant, so that one isolated individual can automatically reproduce the entire social order of its own colony just as it reproduces the shape of antennae or of abdomen. For better or worse, man's solution has been at the opposite pole. Not one item of his tribal social organization, of language, or his local religion, is carried in his germcell. His whole centuries-evolved civilization is at the mercy of any accident of time and space. If he is taken at birth to another continent, it will be the entire set of cultural traits of the adoptive society that he will learn, and the set that was his by heredity will play no part. (Benedict, 1929/1968, p. 183)

Benedict recognized that some experiences are universal. One major common thread is the transformation of a person from a dependent child into a relatively independent, responsible adult. But Benedict observed that the path one follows in changing from a child to an adult varies from one culture to another. The degree to which the transitions are experienced as emotionally stressful or smooth depends on whether the cultural conditioning is continuous or discontinuous.

Continuity is found when a child is given information and responsibilities that apply directly to his or her adult behavior. For example, Margaret Mead (1928/1950) observed that in Samoan society, girls 6 or 7 years old commonly took care of their younger siblings, and that as they grew older, their involvement in this caregiving role increased. The *role expectations*, however, were not substantially changed.

Discontinuity is found when a child is either barred from activities that are open only to adults or forced to "unlearn" information or behavior that is accepted in children but considered inappropriate for adults. The change from expectations of virginity before marriage to expectations of sexual responsiveness after marriage

BIOGRAPHICAL SKETCH

**Ruth Benedict
1887–1948**

Ruth Fulton Benedict was born in New York City in 1887. Her father died very suddenly when Ruth was 21 months old. Her mother, now responsible for Ruth and a younger sister, Margery, returned for a while to live with her parents on a farm in central New York State. Mrs. Fulton taught school and then, in 1899, became a staff member of the Buffalo Public Library at a salary of $60 per month.

Ruth suffered from two major childhood crises: a hearing loss due to a severe attack of measles and the emotional trauma associated with her father's death and her mother's extreme, prolonged grief. Ruth withdrew into an elaborate private world populated by beautiful dead people, like her father and Christ, and an imaginary companion. In her real world, she was very uninvolved, even alienated from others.

Fortunately, her intellectual abilities resulted in her gaining a scholarship to a preparatory school in Buffalo, and then to Vassar, where she studied English literature and graduated as a Phi Beta Kappa in 1909. Her early adult years were a period of confusion and depression. She worked as a social worker and a teacher and then began an ambitious writing project that she never finished. In 1914 she married Stanley Benedict, who became a professor of biochemistry at Cornell University Medical School in New York City. After a brief period of happiness in this marriage, Benedict became frustrated by the lack of meaning and direction in her life. In 1919, she enrolled in the New School for Social Research in New York City and discovered the field of anthropology. She later studied anthropology at Columbia University under Franz Boas and completed her Ph.D. in 1923. Her dissertation focused on the concept of the guardian spirit among North American Indians. Benedict maintained a

strong interest in the contributions of a culture's literature, religions, language, and aesthetic dimensions to the overall impact of the culture on its members, and she expressed her interest in the religious and aesthetic dimensions of life through her poetry, which she wrote under a pseudonym until the early 1930s.

Benedict served as an assistant to Boas on a year-to-year appointment from 1923 to 1931, when Boas finally arranged for her to become an assistant professor at Columbia University. At that point, her own theoretical analysis of patterns of culture and the ways in which different cultures define and value certain personality types began to take shape. *Patterns of Culture* was published in 1934 and served as the primary introduction to the field of cultural anthropology for the the next 25 years.

During World War II, Benedict wrote a widely distributed pamphlet, *The Races of Mankind* (1943). She conducted extensive research on contemporary cultures, including those of Romania, Thailand, and Japan, while she worked for the Office of War Information. After the war, she extended this research into a powerful book on Japanese culture, *The Chrysanthemum and the Sword* (1946). This achievement was followed by her receipt of a large grant from the Office of Naval Research to study contemporary cultures. In the 1920s, Benedict had hardly been able to get a salary or a faculty appointment, but in the 1940s, she was the director of one of the largest projects that American anthropologists had ever undertaken. In 1947–1948, she was president of the American Anthropological Association, becoming the first woman to serve as the leading figure in an American learned society. In 1948, Columbia made her a full professor. She died that fall of heart disease.

Pablo Picasso, Two Brothers, *1905. This painting of two brothers suggests the theme of cultural continuity. The older brother assumes responsibility for the protection and care of his younger sibling. We can imagine that when he is mature he will extend this love toward his own children.*

in American society is an example of discontinuity. Sexuality and sex play are viewed as inappropriate behavior for young children but appropriate for adults.

Benedict suggested that the degree to which behaviors appear to occur in stages depends on the degree of discontinuity in cultural conditioning. Cultures that have discrete, age-graded expectations for individuals at different periods in life produce a developmental pattern of different age groups' having distinct characteristics and appearing to function at different skill levels. These societies are marked by public ceremonies, graduations, and other rites of passage from one stage to the next. Cultures that are permissive and open and that recognize few distinctions between the responsibilities of children and those of adults do not produce age-graded stages of development. In those societies, development is a much more gradual, fluid transformation in which adult competences are built directly on childhood accomplishments.

The idea of cultural determinism has been critical in guiding cross-cultural research on the basic issues of human development, especially on questions about the universality of certain characteristics of individual development, family life, and gender-role differences. In one of the most ambitious cross-cultural studies of child development, Beatrice Whiting and Carolyn Edwards (1988) drew on systematic observations of 12 cultural communities to examine "the processes by which the culturally determined environment affects the development of sex-differentiated behavior during the childhood years" (p. 3). These investigators linked the development of male and female children to the status of men and women, the division of labor among men and women, the extent of the mother's

The Kwanza celebration was developed to provide African Americans with an annual ritual that highlights aspects of their common ancestry and shared cultural heritage.

daily work load, and the amount of social support available to the mother during the child's early years. In societies where men have much higher status than women, boys begin to distance themselves from women, including their mothers, between the ages of 5 and 10.

Ethnic Subcultures

Although societies may be characterized by certain shared cultural characteristics, most modern societies are made up of a large number of subcultures. Because of its relative youth among the nations of the world, and because of the way it has been and is being populated, the United States is especially rich in ethnic subcultures.

An ethnic group has been defined as "a collectivity within a larger society having real or common ancestry, memories of a shared historical past, and a cultural focus on one or more symbolic elements defined as the epitome of their peoplehood" (Schermerhorn, 1978, p. 12). Individual members of an ethnic group differ in the intensity with which they identify with this subculture, but they generally share some common values, beliefs, preferences or tastes, and norms of behavior. They also share a sense of loyalty to the ethnic group, which is likely to become heightened if the security of the group is threatened. Some ethnic groups are defined in part by a common racial ancestry and therefore may be referred to as racial subcultures. Ethnicity, however, is the more general concept because it encompasses the many aspects of shared experience, including racial similarities, that contribute to a sense of group identity (See & Wilson, 1988).

Identification with an ethnic subculture introduces another layer of influence in the process of cultural determinism. Ethnic subcultural values shape one's outlook on such critical areas of life as marriage, child-rearing practices, educational aspirations, and gender-role definitions. These aspects of one's worldview can be in conflict or in harmony with values held in the workplace, school, and the larger political community (Horowitz, 1985). In the United States, the dominant ethnic group is Anglo-Saxon Protestant. All other groups experience some tension between pressures toward *assimilation*, a process through which unique cultural patterns are relinquished or modified in order to conform to the dominant culture, and pressures toward ethnic identification. At the same time, there are broad values for *pluralism*, an appreciation for and encouragement of cultural differences.

Persistent negative ethnic stereotypes may influence the self-concept of members of an oppressed ethnic subculture. What is more, in many communities racism and ethnic prejudices result in the separation of ethnic groups, reducing the amount and type of contact members of one group have with members of the others. One result is heightened *ethnocentrism*, a belief in the inherent superiority of one's own ethnic group, and a lack of understanding about the values and worldview of members of other subcultures.

Implications for Human Development

According to the concept of cultural determinism, the events of the various stages of development will be experienced as stressful or calm depending on how they are treated by the culture. This contrast is seen in the ways in which different cultures mark an adolescent girl's first menstruation (Mead, 1949/1955). In some societies, people fear menstruation and treat the girl as if she were dangerous to others. In other societies, she is viewed as having powerful magic that will affect her own future and that of the tribe. In still others, the perceived shamefulness of sex requires that the menstruation be kept as secret as possible. The culture thus determines how a biological change is marked and how the transition will be perceived.

Societies vary in the extent to which they expect people to make significant life decisions at each age and in the range of choices they make available. American adolescents are asked to make decisions regarding sex, work, politics, religion, marriage, and education. In each of these areas, the alternatives are complex and varied. As a result, adolescence is prolonged, and the risk of leaving this period without having found solutions to these problems is great. In cultures that allow fewer choices and provide a clearer path from childhood to adulthood, adolescence may be brief and relatively free of psychological stress.

Human development must be approached with an appreciation of the cultural context. Cultural expectations concerning the timing of certain life events, such as schooling, work, marriage, childbearing, and political and religious leadership, influence the tempo and tone of one's life history. Cultures also vary in the personal qualities they admire and those they consider inappropriate or shameful. A society's standards of beauty, leadership, and talent determine how easily an individual can achieve status within it.

One of the criticisms of our scientific knowledge about human development is that it lacks the diversity of cultural contexts. If we accept the idea of cultural determinism, we must agree that development can be fully understood only if we consider the particular ecological and cultural context in which it occurs. Much of what we know about development is based on a very small sample of the peoples of the world. In particular, the social sciences have studied development in the United States, Canada, and Europe more than they have studied development in the variety of Third World nations of Africa, Latin America, and Asia. Thus, attempts to identify and establish universal principles of development must always be tempered by the realization that our scientific observations have been limited (Nsamenang, 1992).

An individual's life course is influenced by his or her identification with subcultural norms and values, as well as by the overarching norms and values of the dominant culture. The relative contribution of subcultural influences to people's development depends on the intensity of their loyalty to the subcultural group, on the amount of time they spend with members of their own subcultural group and with members of other subcultural groups, and on how the group is viewed or treated within the larger society. As we consider the dynamics of normative development through life, we must keep in mind that people of various ethnic sub-cultures may have unique views on such issues as the definition of successful maturity, the value of marriage and childbearing, and the proper balance between individual achievement and one's responsibility to family and community.

BIOGRAPHICAL SKETCH

Sigmund Freud
1856–1939

(continued)

Sigmund Freud was born in Freiberg, Moravia (now Pribor, Czech Republic), in 1856. Both his grandfather and his great-grandfather had been rabbis. One of Freud's early memories was of his strong resentment of his baby brother, who had been born when Freud was 19 months old. Freud was filled with guilt over his angry feelings when the infant died at 8 months.

Freud was trained as a neurologist in Vienna during the 1870s. His early research focused on the functions of the medulla, the conduction of nerve impulses in the brain and spinal cord, and the anesthetic properties of cocaine (Freud, 1963). In 1882, Freud's interest turned from physiology to psychology because of his association with Josef Breuer. Breuer and Freud developed a theory of hysteria that attributed certain forms of paralysis to psychological conflict rather than to physiological damage (Breuer & Freud, 1895/1955).

As a physician, Freud continued his scientific interest in psychology by keeping careful notes on his patients. In many of his writings, he presents the actual cases from which he derived his theory of psychological functioning.

In 1905, Freud published his theory of infantile sexuality and its relation to adult life, ideas that produced a fury of insults and criticism. His medical colleagues could not accept the idea of childhood sexuality and considered his public lectures on the topic crude and distasteful. Primarily because of these lectures and writings, Freud was denied a professorial appointment at the University of Vienna. Even Breuer, his longtime colleague and collaborator, found Freud's preoccupation with sexual motives offensive and terminated their association.

In response to his exclusion from the medical community, Freud helped to form the International Congress on Psychoanalysis. There, he developed his psychosexual theory and taught the principles of psychoanalysis to his followers. Freud was very intolerant of any questioning of or deviation from his views. Alfred Adler and Carl Jung broke away from the congress to establish their own schools of thought after repeated unsuccessful attempts to get Freud to modify his theory in the direction of their ideas.

Toward the end of his life, Freud, like Albert Einstein in Germany, was forced to leave Austria to protect himself and his family from the threat of extermination by the Nazis. In the 1930s, Freud and Einstein corresponded regarding their perceptions

Psychosexual Development

Freud's (1933/1964) psychoanalytic psychosexual theory focuses on the development of an individual's emotional and social life. Although much of his theory has been revised, refuted, or repressed, many contributions of psychosexual theory continue to influence contemporary personality theories and the study of human development. Freud focused on the impact of sexual and aggressive drives on the individual's psychological functioning, distinguishing between the impact of sexual drives on mental activity and their effect on reproductive functions. Based largely on material from therapeutic sessions with his patients, Freud's theory recognized the profound influence of sexuality on mental activity. In addition, he came to believe that very young children have strong sexual drives. He argued that, although children are incapable of reproduction, their sexual drives operate to direct aspects of their fantasies, problem solving, and social interactions.

(continued)

Freud's patients visited him in his office in Vienna surrounded by cultural artifacts that were sources of stimulation to his own thinking. Central to the office was the famous couch. Freud sat behind the patient to avoid influencing the direction of the patient's free association through inadvertent eye contact and facial expressions.

of anti-Semitism, sharing their experiences as men of science who had been subjected to the same form of bitter attack (Einstein & Freud, 1933/1964).

Freud died of cancer in England in 1939. He devoted the last years of his life to extensive writing that furthered the pursuit of his theory by other analysts and scholars.

Freud suggested that all behavior (except that resulting from fatigue) is motivated. This is a profound assumption. It carries with it an implicit need for a psychology of behavior. Behavior has meaning; it does not occur randomly or without purpose. Much of Freud's work was an attempt to describe the processes by which motives, especially sexual and aggressive motives, prompt behavior. His interpretation of all psychological events is based on this hypothesis.

A second hypothesis of psychoanalytic theory is that there is an area of the psyche called the *unconscious*, which is a storehouse of powerful, primitive motives of which the person is unaware. Unconscious as well as conscious motives may motivate behavior simultaneously. Thus, behavior that may appear to be somewhat unusual or extremely intense is described as *multiply determined*; that is, this single behavior expresses many motives, some of which the person can recognize and control and others of which operate unguided by conscious thought. Freud's analysis of normal development as well as his explanations for specific forms of mental illness are derived from how sexual and aggressive drives press for expression and are inhibited or given various outlets in thoughts, dreams, behavior, and symptoms.

Four basic contributions of psychosexual theory are discussed in the following sections: domains of consciousness, three basic structures of personality, defense mechanisms, and five stages of psychosexual development.

Domains of Consciousness

One of Freud's most enduring contributions was his analysis of the topography of mental activity. In Freud's theory, the human mind is like an iceberg. *Conscious processes* are like the tip that protrudes out of the water; they make up only a small part of the mind. Our conscious thoughts are fleeting. We can have only a few of them at any one time, and as soon as energy is diverted from a thought or image, it disappears from consciousness.

A second area, the *preconscious*, is analogous to the part of the iceberg near the waterline. Preconscious thoughts are readily accessible to consciousness through focused attention. You may not be thinking about your hometown or your favorite desserts right now, but if someone were to ask you about either of them, you could readily recall and discuss them.

The *unconscious*, like the rest of the iceberg, is hidden from view. It is a vast network of content and processes that are actively barred from consciousness. Freud hypothesized that the content of the unconscious, a storehouse of wishes, fears, impulses, and repressed memories, plays a major role in guiding behavior even though we cannot account for it consciously. Behaviors that are unusual or extremely intense may not make sense if they are explained only in terms of conscious motives.

A young patient of Freud's who had recently been married sometimes forgot his wife's name, evidence that Freud used as a clue to the content of the man's unconscious. Freud hypothesized that consciously the man felt he loved his wife and thought they were happy together, but that in his unconscious, the man had strong, negative feelings about his wife, feelings that were so unacceptable that they could not be allowed expression. By forgetting his wife's name, Freud reasoned, the young man could express some level of hostility toward his wife and, at the same time, punish himself (with embarrassment and social censure) for his unconscious anger toward her.

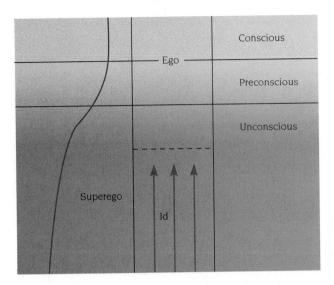

FIGURE 3.2
Freud's model of the structure of personality

Three Structures of Personality

Freud (1933/1964) described three components of personality: the id, the ego, and the superego (see Figure 3.2). Although it sometimes seems as if these structures are like three little cartoon characters battling things out inside the mind, they are actually more accurately components of a general process of adaptation very similar to the process of adaptation described in evolutionary theory. The *id* is the source of instincts and impulses. It is the primary source of psychic energy, and it exists from birth. The id expresses its demands according to the *pleasure principle*: We are motivated to seek pleasure and avoid pain. The pleasure principle does not take into account the feelings of others, society's norms, or agreements between people. Its rule is to achieve the immediate discharge of impulses. When you lie to a friend to protect your own image, or when you cut ahead of people in line so you won't have to wait, you are operating according to the pleasure principle.

The logic of the id is also the logic of dreams. This kind of thinking is called *primary process thought*. It is characterized by a lack of concern about the constraints of reality. In primary process thought there are no negatives. Everything is yes. There is no time. Nothing happens in the past or in the future. Everything is now. Symbolism becomes flexible. One object may symbolize many things, and many different objects may mean the same thing. Many male faces can all represent the father. A house may be a symbol for one's mother, a lover, or the female genitals as well as for a house.

Ego is the term for all mental functions that have to do with a person's relation to the environment. When you read the term *ego*, you should think of it as shorthand for a multitude of cognitive processes, such as perception, learning, memory, judgment, self-awareness, and language skills. Freud thought the ego begins to develop in the first six or eight months of life and is well established by the age of 2 or 3. Of course, much change and growth occur after this time as well. The ego responds to the demands of the environment and helps a person function effectively in the world. The ego also responds to the demands of the id and the superego and helps the person satisfy needs, live up to ideals and standards, and establish a healthy emotional balance.

BOX 3.2

The Cognitive Unconscious

Since the early 1960s, scholarly interest in cognitive processes has resulted in renewed attention to the notion of the *cognitive unconscious*, the range of mental structures and processes that operate outside awareness but play a significant role in conscious thought and action (Kihlstrom, 1987). Just as Freud argued, it is becoming evident that conscious thought accounts for only a small proportion of our capacities to identify, analyze, recall, and synthesize information.

One model of how humans process information suggests that there are a large number of processing units or modules, each devoted to a specific task or category (Rumelhart & McClelland, 1986; Gazzaniga, 1989). The activation of one unit may excite some units and inhibit others. Information about an object may be found in a number of units. For instance, the concept of an apple may be represented in units related to things that are red, fruits, teachers, health ("An apple a day keeps the doctor away"), and other, more idiosyncratic units (such as a fear of bees that swarm around rotting apples or a pleasant memory of the family picking apples or the smell of apple-sauce cooking in Mother's kitchen). Many mental functions, including language, memory, and planning, may respond to the presentation of an apple as a stimulus, although most of them would respond unconsciously. This view of how the brain is organized gives a major role to unconscious processing, which accompanies all types of conscious activities.

One of the goals of psychotherapy is to help people recognize and admit into consciousness deeply troubling fantasies, beliefs, wishes, or impulses that are blocked from consciousness. Often, these unconscious thoughts are linked to strong feelings of shame, guilt, humiliation, or fear of loss of love. During psychotherapy, the patient gradually tests the therapist in order to determine whether these unconscious thoughts can be expressed without getting a negative reaction from the therapist. At the same time, the analyst helps the patient move closer and closer to pulling these thoughts into consciousness (Weiss, 1990). Once the patient can bring this blocked material into consciousness, he or she can begin to understand and manage both the thoughts and the anxiety they produce, and the material gradually becomes less troubling.

One of the major controversies facing psychoanalytic psychotherapy is how real the "repressed" memories are that are recalled in therapy (Jaroff, 1993). Critics argue that these memories are actually a product of repeated suggestions by the psychotherapist, who has a preconceived idea of what must be at the basis of the client's conflicts. Others suggest that the details of one very traumatic event may be blocked from conscious memory or distorted in the process of recollection, but that repeated exposure to an aversive experience, such as sexual abuse by a parent or a relative, is unlikely to be totally forgotten. Further research on long-term memory and its storage and retrieval processes, especially the memory of emotionally charged experiences, is likely to shed additional light on this process (Doris, 1991).

The ego operates according to the *reality principle*. Under this principle, the ego protects the person by waiting to gratify id impulses until a socially acceptable form of expression or gratification can be found. In the ego, primary process thought becomes subordinated to a more reality-oriented process called *secondary process thought*, which begins to dominate as the ego matures.

Secondary process thought is the kind of logical, sequential thinking that we usually mean when we discuss thinking. It allows people to plan and act in order to engage the world and achieve gratification in personally and socially acceptable ways. It enables people to delay gratification. It helps people test plans by examining whether they will really work. This last process is called *reality testing*.

Pablo Picasso, Caricature of the Artist, 1903. *In each of us, the id is the source of instincts and impulses. At age 22, Picasso drew this devilish caricature of himself, suggesting his impulsive, primate nature.*

The *superego* includes moral precepts (the *conscience*) and one's ideals about being a moral person (the *ego ideal*). Freud's work led him to conclude that the superego does not begin to develop until the age of 5 or 6 and probably is not firmly established until several years later. The superego determines many of one's ideas about which behaviors are proper, acceptable, and admirable, and which behaviors are improper and unacceptable. It also defines one's aspirations and goals as a "good" person.

The superego psychologically punishes a person for unacceptable behavior and rewards a person for acceptable behavior. Because it is formed during early childhood, the superego tends to be harsh and unrealistic in its demands. It is often just as illogical and unrelenting in its search for proper behavior as the id is in its search for pleasure. When a child thinks about behaving in a morally unacceptable way, the superego sends a warning by producing feelings of anxiety and guilt.

The superego is developed through a process called *identification*. Motivated by love, fear, and admiration, children actively imitate characteristics of their parents and internalize their parents' values. Through identification, the parents' values become the ideals and aspirations of their children. Parents and others in the environment may, however, make demands that a child does not internalize as part of the superego. The ego deals with these demands as well as with the superego's internalized demands.

Ego processes work toward satisfying id impulses through thoughts and actions without generating strong feelings of guilt in the superego. In one sense, the ego processes serve both the id and the superego, striving to provide gratification, but in morally and socially acceptable ways. In another sense, the ego is the executive of the personality. The strength of the ego determines the person's effectiveness in meeting his or her needs, in handling the demands of the superego, and in dealing with the demands of reality. If the ego is strong and can establish a good balance among the id, the superego, and the environmental demands, the person is satisfied and free of immobilizing guilt and feelings of worthlessness.

When the id and the superego are stronger than the ego, the person may be tossed and turned psychologically by strong desires for pleasure and strong constraints against attaining those desires. When environmental demands are strong and the ego is weak—for example, when an adolescent is confronted by strong pressures for peer conformity and the threat of peer rejection—a person may also be overwhelmed. In Freud's psychoanalytic theory, it is the breakdown of the ego that leads to mental disorder.

Much of the relationship of the id, the ego, and the superego is played out at an unconscious level. In the early years, aspects of basic drives and primary process thought are noticeable in a child's consciousness, indicating the conscious presence of the id. As the ego grows stronger, it is able to push the id's desires and fantasies into the unconscious, so that the person can attend to the exploration and demands of the external world. Freud thought that the superego also operated mostly at the unconscious level. He thought the ego, however, functioned at both the conscious and the unconscious levels.

Defense Mechanisms

Much of the ego's work involves mediating the conflicts between the id's demands for gratification and the superego's demands for good behavior. This work is conducted outside the person's awareness. When unconscious conflicts threaten to break through into consciousness, the person experiences anxiety. If the ego functions effectively, it pushes these conflicts into the unconscious and thereby protects the person from unpleasant emotion. The ego proceeds to satisfy desires in acceptable ways by directing behavior and social interaction.

Strong unresolvable conflicts may cause constant anxiety, and symptoms may emerge. A person who desires what she or he feels to be very "bad," such as an unconscious wish to harm a parent or to be sexually intimate with a sibling, may experience anxiety without recognizing its source. The ungratified impulse continues to seek gratification, the superego continues to find the impulse unacceptable, and the conflict continues to produce anxiety in the person's conscious experience. The unpleasant emotional state may preoccupy the person and make it difficult to handle normal day-to-day demands.

Defense mechanisms protect the person from anxiety. They distort, substitute something else for, or completely block out the source of the conflict. They are usually initiated unconsciously. Often, the defense mechanism used depends on a person's age and the intensity of the perceived threat. Young children tend to use denial and repression (pushing thoughts from awareness). A more diverse set of defenses, requiring greater cognitive complexity, becomes available in the course of development. In situations of the greatest threat, denial is often the initial defense used, regardless of age.

Freud thought the basic defense mechanism was *repression*, a process that pushes unacceptable impulses into the unconscious. It is as if a wall were constructed between the unconscious and the conscious mind so that anxiety-provoking thoughts and feelings cannot enter consciousness. With unacceptable thoughts and impulses far from awareness, the person is protected from uncomfortable feelings of anxiety and may devote his or her remaining psychic energy to interchange with the interpersonal and physical environments. This defensive strategy has two major costs. First, the energy required to continue to protect the conscious mind from these thoughts reduces the amount of mental energy available to cope with other daily demands. Second, if too many thoughts and feelings are relegated to repression, the person loses the use of his or her emotional system to monitor and evaluate reality.

The following are defense mechanisms:

Repression: Unacceptable wishes are barred from conscious thought.

Projection: Unacceptable wishes are attributed to someone else.

Reaction formation: Unacceptable feelings are expressed as the opposite feelings.

Regression: One avoids confronting conflicts and stresses by reverting to behaviors that were effective and comforting at an earlier life stage.

Displacement: Unacceptable impulses are expressed toward a substitute target.

Rationalization: Unacceptable feelings and actions are justified by logical or pseudological explanations.

Isolation: Feelings are separated from thoughts.

Denial: Parts of external reality are denied.

Sublimation: Unacceptable wishes are channeled into socially acceptable behaviors.

According to Freud, all normal people resort to defense mechanisms at various times in their lives. These mechanisms not only reduce anxiety but also may lead to positive social outcomes. Physicians who use isolation may be able to function effectively because they can use their knowledge without being hindered by their feelings. Children who rationalize defeat may be able to protect their self-esteem by viewing themselves favorably. The child who projects angry feelings onto someone else may find that this technique stimulates a competitive orientation that enhances his or her performance.

Some people rely more on one or two defensive techniques than on the others. The resultant *defensive style* becomes part of an overall personality pattern that permits one to regulate the impact of the environment and to perceive experiences in ways that are compatible with one's needs.

The excessive use of defense mechanisms, however, may indicate a deeper psychological problem. Defense mechanisms draw psychological energy from the ego. Energy that is used to prevent certain wishes from entering conscious thought is not available for other life activities. A person whose energy is devoted to defensive strategies may be unable to develop other ego functions and to use those functions adequately.

Psychosexual Stages

Freud assumed that the most significant developments in personality take place during five life stages from infancy through adolescence, the primary emphasis being given to the first five or six years of life. After that, according to Freud, the essential pattern for expressing and controlling impulses has been established. Later life serves only to uncover new modes of gratification and new sources of frustration.

The stages Freud described reflect his emphasis on sexuality as a driving force. Freud used the term *sexuality* quite broadly, referring to the full range of physical pleasure, from sucking to sexual intercourse. He also attached a positive life-force symbolism to the concept of sexuality, suggesting that sexual impulses provide a

Pablo Picasso, Silenius Dancing, 1933. *Freud emphasized the role of sexual impulses in directing and shaping personality and interpersonal life.*

thrust toward growth and renewal. At each stage, a particular body zone is of heightened sexual importance. The shift in focus from one body zone to the next is due largely to the biologically based unfolding of physical maturation. The five stages Freud identified are the oral, the anal, the phallic, the latent, and the genital.

During the *oral stage*, in the first year of life, the mouth is the site of sexual and aggressive gratification. Freud characterized infants as dependent, incorporative, and little able to differentiate themselves from others. As infants learn to delay gratification, the ego becomes more clearly differentiated, and they become aware of the distinction between themselves and others.

In the *anal stage*, during the second year of life, the anus is the most sexualized body part. With the development of the sphincter muscles, a child learns to expel or withhold feces at will. The conflict at this stage focuses on the subordination of the child's will to the demands of the culture (via the parents) for appropriate toilet habits.

The *phallic stage* begins during the third year of life and may last until the child is 6. It is a period of heightened genital sensitivity, but without the hormonal changes that accompany puberty. Freud described the behavior of children at this stage as bisexual: They direct sexualized activity toward both sexes and engage in self-stimulation. This is the stage during which the Oedipal or Electra complex is observed.

The *Oedipal complex* in boys and the *Electra complex* in girls result from ambivalence surrounding their heightened sexuality. The child has a strong, sexualized attraction to the parent of the opposite sex, may desire to have the exclusive attention of that parent, and may fantasize that the other parent will leave, or perhaps die. At the same time, the child fears that amorous overtures to the desired parent may result in hostility or retribution by the parent of the same sex, or in the withdrawal of that parent's love. Parental threats intended to prevent the child from masturbating add to the child's fears that sexualized fantasies will result in punishment or the withdrawal of love.

Freud believed that once the Oedipal or Electra conflict is resolved, the child enters a period of *latency*. During this period, which lasts from about age 7 to puberty, no new significant conflicts or impulses arise. The primary personality development during this period is the maturation of the superego.

The final stage of development, the *genital stage*, begins with the onset of puberty, when the person directs her or his sexual impulses toward someone of the opposite sex. Adolescence brings about a reawakening of the Oedipal or Electra conflicts and a reworking of earlier childhood identifications. Freud explained the tension of adolescence as the result of the sexual threat that the mature adolescent poses to the family unit. In an effort to avoid this threat, adolescents may withdraw from their families or temporarily devalue their parents. With the selection of a permanent sex partner, the threat of intimacy between young people and their parents diminishes, and a more autonomous relationship with the parents becomes possible.

Freud believed that the psychological conflicts that arise during adolescence and adulthood result from a failure to satisfy or express specific childhood wishes. At any of the childhood stages, the sexualized impulses may have been so frustrated or overindulged that the person continues to seek their gratification at later stages of life. Freud used the term *fixation* to refer to continued use of pleasure-seeking or anxiety-reducing behavior appropriate to an earlier stage of development. Since no person can possibly satisfy all wishes at every life stage, normal development depends on the ability to channel the energy from those impulses into activities that either symbolize the impulses or express them in a socially acceptable form. This process is called *sublimation*.

During adolescence and early adulthood, patterns of impulse expression, fixation, and sublimation crystallize into a life orientation. From this point on, the content of the id, the regulating functions of the superego, and the executive functions of the ego rework the struggles of childhood through repeated episodes of engagement, conflict, and impulse gratification or frustration.

Freud's psychoanalytic emphasis on early childhood gave an enormous boost to the study of young children. Unfortunately, this much-needed focus on the early years of development may have distracted psychoanalytically oriented psychologists from considering the relevance of later development.

Modern scholars in the psychoanalytic tradition have begun to direct their attention to development during adulthood (Greenspan & Pollack, 1980). Of particular relevance to life-span development is the expanded interest in ego development as expressed in the focus on the self, self-understanding, and self-other relationships, referred to as *object relations* (Goldberg, 1988; Stern, 1987; Gardner, 1983). These theorists study how ego strengths and cognitive capacities contribute to the formation of meaningful interpersonal relationships, and how the quality of interpersonal relationships contributes to the further expansion and maturity of the ego. The focus on early object relations has been expanded to an examination of experiences of bereavement and loss in adult life (Parkes, 1987; Viorst, 1986) and disorders in the development of the self-concept during childhood and adolescence (Cicchetti & Toth, 1993).

Feminist criticism of Freud's analysis of the psychosexual development of women, especially his view of the Electra complex and his obviously sexist perspective on the female body, led to a new psychoanalytic approach to issues of gender and the psychology of women (Fast, 1984; Westkott, 1986; Alpert, 1986).

Implications for Human Development

Psychoanalytic theory emphasizes the tension between interpersonal demands and intrapsychic demands in the shaping of personality. The ego develops skills for dealing with the realities of the interpersonal world, for satisfying personal needs, and for imposing personal standards and aspirations on how these needs are satisfied. The expectations of others, particularly parents, are internalized and given personal meaning in the formation of the superego. By developing this idea, Freud was able to show how a person translates the demands of the interpersonal world into his or her own personal way of functioning and, at the same time, incorporates new demands and experiences into the development of personality. Freud focused particularly on the effects of sexual impulses on personal and interpersonal life.

One of the major early contributions of psychoanalytic theory was the identification of the influence of childhood experiences on adult behavior. Psychoanalytic theory was unique in its focus on stages of development, family interactions, and unresolved family conflicts as explanations for adult behavior. The emphasis Freud gave to the importance of parenting practices and their implications for psychosexual development provides one of the few theoretical frameworks for examining parent-child relationships. Many of the early empirical studies in developmental psychology focused on issues derived from his theory, such as child-rearing and discipline practices, moral development, and childhood aggression.

The psychoanalytic approach recognizes the importance of motives, emotions, and fantasies to human behavior. Within this framework, human behavior springs at least as much from emotional needs as from reason. The theory suggests that underlying motives and wishes explain behaviors that otherwise might not make sense. Psychoanalytic theory recognizes domains of thought that may not appear to be logical to the observer, but that make sense from the point of view of the individual. Many domains of mental activity, including fantasies, dreams, primary process thoughts and symbols, and defense mechanisms, influence how people derive meaning from their experiences. Through the construct of the unconscious, Freud provided a means of explaining thoughts and behavior that appear irrational, self-destructive, or contradictory. The idea that development involves efforts to find acceptable outlets for strong, often socially unacceptable impulses still guides therapeutic intervention with children, adolescents, and adults.

Another critical point is Freud's recognition of the role of sexual impulses during childhood. Whereas Freud believed that a sexual relationship with a loving partner is important in a healthy adulthood, when sexual impulses have a direct outlet, he also recognized that children have sensual needs for stimulation and satisfaction, which they seem to have no acceptable means of satisfying. Today, we are more aware of a child's need for hugging, snuggling, and physical warmth with loving caregivers, but most adults in our society still find it difficult to permit young children the direct expression of sexual impulses. Childhood wishes and needs, bottled up in the unconscious by defense mechanisms, guide behavior indirectly through symbolic expression, dreams, or, in some cases, the symptoms of mental disorders. We need only look at a daily newspaper to recognize that the acceptance and expression of sexual impulses continues to be a point of conflict in modern society. Controversies over sexual dysfunction, sexual abuse, rape by strangers and acquaintances, sexual harassment in the workplace, sexually transmitted diseases, contraception, abortion, infidelity, and homophobia reveal how difficult Americans find dealing with the expression of sexual impulses. The relationship between changing sexual needs and behavior during adulthood and aging still requires research in the study of development throughout life.

Cognitive Development

Cognition is the process of organizing and making meaning of experience. Interpreting a statement, solving a problem, synthesizing information, and critically analyzing a complex task—all are cognitive activities. Perhaps the most widely known and influential of the modern cognitive theorists is Jean Piaget. His concepts provide the initial focus of this section. Recent interest in the social framework within which cognition develops has been stimulated by the work of L. S. Vygotsky. Several of his important contributions, introduced toward the end of this section, complement and expand the developmental perspective on how logical thought emerges and changes over the life course.

Basic Concepts in Piaget's Theory

According to Piaget, every organism strives to achieve equilibrium. *Equilibrium* is a balance of organized structures, whether motor, sensory, or cognitive. When structures are in equilibrium, they provide effective ways of interacting with the environment. Whenever changes in the organism or in the environment require a revision of the basic structures, they are thrown into disequilibrium (Piaget, 1978/1985). Piaget focused both on equilibrium with the environment, achieved through the formation of schemes and operations that form systematic, logical structures for comprehending and analyzing experience, and on equilibrium within the schemes and operations themselves.

In this theory, knowing is an active process of achieving and reachieving equilibrium, not a constant state (Miller, 1993). Knowledge is discovered and rediscovered in the continuous interaction of the person and the environment. We approach new situations with expectations that we have developed in the past, and each new experience changes those expectations somewhat. Our ability to understand and interpret experience is constantly changing as we encounter diversity and novelty in the environment.

Piaget assumed that the roots of cognition lie in the infant's biological capacities. He posited that intelligence unfolds systematically when the environment offers adequate diversity and support for exploration. Among the concepts that inform Piaget's theory, three are of special relevance here: scheme, adaptation, and stages of development.

Scheme

Piaget and Inhelder (1969) defined a *scheme* as "the structure or organization of actions as they are transferred or generalized by repetition in similar or analogous circumstances" (p. 4). Piaget preferred the term *scheme* to the term *concept* to describe coordinated patterns of action, since the term *concept* connotes coordinated mental representations and words. He used *scheme* to discuss what he thought of as the counterpart of concepts and conceptual networks during the period of infancy, before language and other symbolic systems are developed.

Two kinds of schemes begin to form during infancy through the repetition of regular sequences of actions. The first guides a particular action, such as grasping a rattle or sucking on a bottle. The second links sequences of actions, such as climbing into the high chair in order to eat breakfast or crawling to the door to greet Daddy when he comes home (Uzgiris, 1976). Infants behave differently with people who are familiar and those who are unfamiliar. They differentiate between playful sounds, such as cooing and babbling, and sounds that will bring

Self-Portrait, 1896

Yo Picasso, 1901

Self-Portrait with a Palette, 1906

Self-Portrait, 1907

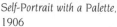

The self-concept is a complex scheme that undergoes continuous revision. In these four self-portraits, completed at ages 15, 20, 25, and 26, Picasso shapes and revises not only his artistic techniques but his self-image as well.

a caregiver, such as crying and screeching. They differentiate between the foods they will eat readily and those they reject. Such groupings suggest schemes, developed by a mental coordination that evolves with an infant's repeated transactions with aspects of the environment. Schemes are created and modified continuously throughout life. For our purposes here, a scheme is any organized, meaningful grouping of events, feelings, and related images, actions, or ideas.

Adaptation

Piaget (1936/1952) viewed cognition as continuously evolving as the content and diversity of experiences stimulate the formation of new schemes. People are constantly striving to attain equilibrium, both with the environment and with the cognitive components of their mental structures. According to Piaget, knowledge is the result of *adaptation*, or the gradual modification of existing schemes to take into account the novelty or uniqueness of each experience. You can see the similarity between this use of the term *adaptation* and its use in evolutionary theory. Piaget (1936/1952) extended the concept of adaptation, suggesting that it works to produce modifications in the capacity for logical thought: "It is by adapting to things that thought organizes itself, and it is by organizing itself that it structures things" (pp. 7–8).

Adaptation is a two-part process in which the continuity of existing schemes and the possibility of altering schemes interact. One part of the adaptation process is *assimilation*, the interpretation of new experiences in terms of an existing scheme. Assimilation contributes to the continuity of knowing. For example, Karen thinks that anyone who goes to the private high school in her city is a snob, so when she meets Gail, who attends the private school, she expects Gail to be a snob. After talking with Gail for five minutes, she concludes that Gail really *is* a snob. Here we see assimilation: Karen interprets her interactions with Gail in light of her existing scheme concerning the kinds of students who attend the private school.

The second part of the adaptation process is *accommodation*, the modification of familiar schemes to account for new dimensions of the object or event that are revealed through experience. For example, Karen and Gail spend a little more time together, and Karen discovers that Gail is not rich and is attending the private high school on a scholarship. She and Karen actually have a lot of common interests. Gail is quite friendly and wants to see Karen again. Karen decides that not everyone who goes to the private school is a snob and realizes that she has to

Pablo Picasso, Maya Sleeping, 1938. *Adaptation involves two complementary processes, assimilation and accommodation. Babies use the sucking scheme to assimilate new objects. They accommodate by modifying the sucking scheme to provide comfort as well as nutrition.*

postpone her judgment of people until she gets to know them a little better. Here we see accommodation: Karen has modified her scheme concerning the private school's students in order to integrate the new information she has received.

Throughout life, we gain knowledge gradually through the related processes of assimilation and accommodation. In order to have a new idea, we must be able to relate a new experience, thought, or event to some already-existing scheme. We must also be able to modify our schemes in order to differentiate the novel from the familiar. On the one hand, we distort reality to make it fit our existing cognitive structures. On the other hand, when our current cognitive structures cannot account for the new experiences, we adjust the structures to the demands of reality.

According to Piaget, cognitive development proceeds in small steps. Moderately discrepant experiences can be accommodated, but if the discrepancies are too different from our current level of understanding, we will gain no new understanding.

Stages of Development

Piaget was interested in *knowing* as an active process, a means of constructing meaning, rather than in the specific content of our knowledge. He therefore focused on the abstract structures that underlie how children approach experiences. As he worked with children, he was more interested in how they arrived at the answers to the problems they were solving than in the answers themselves.

Working with these observations, Piaget developed the theory that there are four basic stages of cognitive development, which encompass abstract processes that can be applied to many content areas and can be observed at roughly the same chronological age periods across cultures. These stages show a fundamental pattern of cognitive maturation, a universal path along which the human capacity for logical reasoning unfolds. Piaget was not trying to explain why some children know more about mathematics and others know more about history, or why some children learn more readily through talking and listening (auditory modes) while others learn more readily by reading (visual mode), or why some children can solve a problem at age 8 years and others cannot solve that same

BIOGRAPHICAL SKETCH

**Jean Piaget
1896–1980**

Jean Piaget was born in Switzerland in 1896. Like Darwin, he showed talent as a naturalist early in childhood. He observed and studied birds, fossils, and sea shells and, at the age of 10, contributed a note on the albino sparrow to a scientific journal. While in high school, he began to publish papers describing the characteristics of mollusks. His work in this area was so impressive that he was invited to become the curator of the mollusk collection at the Geneva Museum. He earned his doctorate at the University of Neuchatel in 1918 with a dissertation on the mollusks of Vallais. For cognitive psychology, the most direct consequence of Piaget's training as a naturalist was his sense that the principles of biology could be used to explain the evolution of knowledge. In addition, the observational skills he had honed served him well as he developed his theory.

After several years of research, Piaget was able to define a set of problems and methods that would guide his program of research and theory building. Between 1918 and 1921, he worked in the laboratory of Theodore Lipps, whose research focused on the study of empathy and aesthetics. Piaget also spent some time working at Eugene Bleuler's psychiatric clinic near Zurich, where he learned the techniques of psychiatric interviewing. Then, he went to the Sorbonne in Paris, where he had the opportunity to work in the laboratory of Alfred Binet. Binet's laboratory was actually an elementary school in which studies on the nature of intelligence were being conducted. There, Piaget investigated children's responses to reasoning tests and became interested in the patterns of thought revealed by their incorrect answers. The clinical interview technique he devised to determine how children arrive at their answers to reasoning problems focused on how children think rather than on how much they know.

Piaget's observations provided the basis for his first articles on the characteristics of children's thought processes. One of these articles brought him to the attention of the editor of *Psychological Archives*, who offered him the job of director of studies at the Institut Jean-Jacques Rousseau in Geneva. There, Piaget began to investigate children's moral judgments, theories about everyday events, and language. It was not until the period from 1923 to 1929, when Piaget conducted experiments with and systematic observations of preverbal infants, that he began to unravel the basic mysteries of the growth of logical thought. This work was significantly enriched by his observations of his own children.

Piaget produced a massive quantity of research and theory about cognitive development, logic, the history of thought, education, and the theory of knowledge (epistemology). In 1969, the American Psychological Association gave Piaget the Distinguished Scientific Contribution Award for the work that had revolutionized our understanding of the nature of human knowledge and the development of intelligence. He continued his work on cognitive development until his death in 1980, at the age of 83.

problem until 8 years, 6 months. He was trying to explain the epigenesis of logical thought—the development of new structures for thought—not individual differences in knowledge and reasoning or differences that result from cultural and subcultural experiences.

In his four stages of cognitive development, Piaget viewed intelligence as following regular, predictable patterns of change. At each new stage, the competences of the earlier stages are integrated into a qualitatively new approach to thinking and knowing.

The first stage, *sensorimotor intelligence*, begins at birth and lasts until approximately 18 months of age. This stage is characterized by the formation of increasingly complex sensory and motor schemes that allow infants to organize and exercise some control over their environment.

The second stage, *preoperational thought*, begins when the child learns a language and ends at about age 5 or 6. During this stage, children develop the tools for representing schemes symbolically through language, imitation, imagery, symbolic play, and symbolic drawing. Their knowledge is still very much tied to their own perceptions.

The outdoor environment is a rich source of stimulation for sensorimotor exploration.

The third stage, *concrete operational thought*, begins at about age 6 or 7 and ends in early adolescence, at around 11 or 12. During this stage, children begin to appreciate the logical necessity of certain causal relationships. They can manipulate categories, classification systems, and hierarchies into groups. They are more successful in solving problems that are clearly tied to physical reality than in generating hypotheses about purely philosophical or abstract concepts.

The final stage of cognitive development, *formal operational thought*, begins in adolescence and persists through adulthood. This level of thinking permits a person to grasp many simultaneously interacting variables and to create systems of laws or rules that can be used for problem solving. Formal operational thought reflects the quality of intelligence on which science and philosophy are built.

In later chapters, when we explore these stages in greater depth, we will find that some evidence supports and some conflicts with Piaget's cognitive developmental theory. Because the importance of understanding the development of the human capacity for reasoning and knowing has understandably led to an enormous amount of scholarly research, we now have an extensive literature that examines many of Piaget's conclusions and another body of literature that extends his theory in new directions. The evidence supporting qualitatively unique developmental levels of the sort Piaget described is quite impressive. At the same time, the evidence that culture, experience, and conditions of learning affect one's performance at each stage is also compelling. Individual factors, too, introduce variations in timing, sequence, and performance (Fischer & Silvern, 1985).

Implications for Human Development

Piaget's theory has had an enormous influence on research in the field of human cognition. At the risk of oversimplifying, let us give a few of the implications of the theory for the study of human development. First, the theory suggests that cognition has its base in the sensory and motor capacities of the human infant—knowledge is derived from action. Second, discrepancies between existing schemes or concepts and current experiences promote cognitive development. Encounters with all types of novelty, especially experiences that are moderately distinct from rather than widely different from what is already known, advance new ideas and new ways of organizing thought. In adolescence and adulthood, encounters with differences in opinion through discussion and through reading are just as important as encounters with different types of sensory materials in infancy and toddlerhood. Third, infants do have the capacity for thinking and problem solving. Although infants cannot use symbolic strategies, they can establish certain logical connections between means and ends that guide their problem-solving efforts. Fourth, infants, toddlers, and school-age children think in different ways, and the ways they think are different from the ways adults think. Although their thinking is organized and logical, the same principles of logic that typically govern adult thought do not govern the thinking of young children. Fifth, beginning with the period of concrete operations, children can use many of the principles that are fundamental to scientific reasoning. They can also begin to reason about their reasoning; that is, they are capable of metacognition, or the many strategies we use to organize and prepare ourselves to think more clearly and effectively. Sixth, thinking about the social world is regulated by many of the same principles as thinking about objects in the physical world. As children learn about the principles that govern objects and physical relationships, they are also learning about themselves and others.

Vygotsky's Concepts of Cognitive Development

Piaget focused on children's cognitive development as they investigate, explore, discover, and rediscover meaning in their world. Although he acknowledged the significance of social factors in the cognitive process, especially parents and peers, his theory emphasizes individuals in interaction with their environment. In contrast, L. S. Vygotsky, often referred to as a *contextualist*, argued that development can be understood only within a social framework. Vygotsky (1962, 1978) proposed that the study of cognitive development must take as its unit of analysis *the child in activity in a setting*. Rather than thinking of individuals interacting with their environments, he suggested that meaning derives from the child's social, historical, and cultural contexts as well as from the child's biological maturation. The child and the culture are intricately interwoven through the process of social interaction. New levels of understanding begin at an interpersonal level as two individuals, initially an infant and an adult, coordinate their interactions. Eventually, interpersonal collaboration becomes internalized to make up the child's internal mental framework. Through continuous interaction with others, especially adults and older children, a child revises and advances his or her levels of understanding:

> New understanding, gained through collaboration, is a product of the child's original understanding, the partner's different understanding, the child's difficulties with the task and the ways they are expressed in the course of their interaction, the partner's response to those difficulties, and so on. Since this process evolves over time, and each person's responses depend on what the other has previously done or said, the outcome is one that cannot be attributed to either one or the other. The unit of analysis extends beyond the individual. (Tudge & Winterhoff, 1993, p. 76)

Three of the central concepts in Vygotsky's theory are introduced here: culture as a mediator of cognitive structuring, movement from the intermental to the intramental, and the zone of proximal development.

Culture as a Mediator of Cognitive Structuring

Culture, as we discussed earlier in the chapter, consists of physical settings, tools and technologies, and a patterned system of customs, beliefs, information, and social relationships. Within broad cultural groups, subcultures also exist with unique but shared patterns of behavior, values, and goals. When Vygotsky argued that cognitive development can be understood only in the context of culture, he brought our attention to this pervasive sense of culture. Think for a moment about the many ways that culture shapes the content of thought and the processes through which ideas are developed. A simple conversation between a mother and a child or a situation in which an older sibling is trying to instruct a younger sibling includes layers of cultural beliefs and strategies—beliefs about what children think about; the skills they are encouraged to attain; the sources of information that are available to them; the ways that information is shared; the kinds of activities that children, adolescents, and adults are permitted to engage in; and the limits that are placed on participation in certain settings or certain forms of interaction (Miller, 1993).

Of the many elements of culture that shape cognition, Vygotsky had a special interest in tools and signs as human inventions that shape thought. Technical *tools*, like plows, cars, and weapons, and *signs*, sometimes referred to as *psychological tools*, like symbolic systems, counting systems, and strategies for remembering, modify the child's relationship to the environment. Through the use of tools, humans change how they organize and think about the world. Vygotsky viewed tools as a means by which the human mind has been shaped and modified over the course of history.

In particular, Vygotsky emphasized language as a sign system that dramatically alters human cognition. Language, which begins as a primarily social process linking individuals, ultimately guides mental functioning. Through language, children can recall the past, create problem-solving strategies, organize and categorize their experiences, and talk about and plan for the future: "The most significant moment in the course of intellectual development, which gives birth to the purely human forms of practical and abstract intelligence, occurs when speech and practical activity, two previously completely independent lines of development, converge" (Vygotsky, 1978, p. 24).

Movement from the Intermental to the Intramental

Perhaps contrary to common sense, Vygotsky argued that high-level mental functions begin in external activity that is gradually reconstructed and internalized. Using the example of pointing, Vygotsky claimed that initially an infant will reach toward an object that is out of reach, stretching the hand in the direction of the object and making grasping motions with the fingers. This is a movement directed to the object, but as soon as the mother recognizes that the child wants the object and is able to satisfy the child's request, the child begins to modify the reaching and grasping motion into a socially meaningful gesture: pointing. The mother's understanding of the gesture and the intermental coordination between mother and infant result in an intramental process for the infant, an understanding of the special relationship, in this case, between the desired goal, the mother as mediator, and the pointing as a meaningful sign. According to Vygotsky (1978):

> Every function in the child's cultural development appears twice: first on the social level, and later, on the individual level; first, between people (interpsychological), and then inside the child (intrapsychological). This applies equally to voluntary attention, to logical memory, and to the formation of concepts. All the higher functions originate as actual relations between human individuals. (p. 57)

The Zone of Proximal Development

Taking the idea of internalization a step further, Vygotsky (1978) offered the concept of the *zone of proximal development* as the immediate framework through which learning and development converge. The zone is "the distance between the

Children can reach higher levels of functioning when they have guidance from older children in performing a new task.

actual developmental level as determined by independent problem solving and the level of potential development as determined through problem solving under adult guidance or in collaboration with more capable peers" (p. 86).

We have all had the experience of being unable to solve a task by ourselves, but being successful with the assistance and advice of someone else. The typical efforts of parents to help a child put together a jigsaw puzzle by suggesting strategies, like selecting all the straight-edged pieces first to make the border or sorting the many pieces into those of a similar color, are examples of how learning takes place within the zone. Children watch older children perform a task, and they copy the strategy; children ask their parents or teachers for help when they get stuck in a task; parents give children suggestions about how to organize a task or how to use resources that will help them complete an assignment. In these and many other instances, children expand the level of their independent problem-solving capacities by drawing on the expertise of others. Vygotsky suggested that the level of functioning a child can reach when taking advantage of the guidance of others reflects the cognitive capacities that are in the process of maturing, as compared to those that have already matured. What is more, cognitive development grows in the direction of the intellectual characteristics of those who people the child's world. In a very immediate and direct way, the culture and the social context guide the direction of new learning and promote development. Learning within the zone of proximal development sets into motion the reorganization and internalization of existing developmental competences, which then become synthesized at a new and higher intramental level.

Implications for Human Development

Vygotsky's theory suggests that the boundaries between the individual and the environment are much less clear than one might infer from most other theories of human development. In fact, he directed attention to the guiding role of social interaction and culture in shaping and orienting cognition, thus bringing the study of cognitive development into much greater harmony with many of the concepts of psychosocial theory than does Piaget's framework.

Several specific implications of Vygotsky's work can be inferred. First, the mental structures and functioning of people raised in different cultures will be different, just as the thinking of a toddler is different from the thinking of an adult. Second, because intermental experiences and networks structure intramental events, one's family and others who influence and control the structure of one's early learning and problem-solving experiences will have a strong influence on the structure of one's thinking. Third, individuals can promote their own cognitive development by seeking interactions with others who can help draw them to higher levels of functioning within their zone of proximal development.

Theories of Learning

Learning theorists have proposed mechanisms to account for the relatively permanent changes in behavior that occur as a result of experience. Humans have such an extensive capacity to adapt to changes in their environment because they are so well equipped to learn. Four theories of learning that have made significant contributions to the study of human development are reviewed in the following section: (1) classical conditioning, (2) operant conditioning, (3) social learning, and (4) cognitive behaviorism. Reading about these theories, you will begin to appreciate that *learning* encompasses a wide variety of processes.

Classical Conditioning

The principles of classical conditioning, sometimes referred to as *Pavlovian conditioning*, were developed by Ivan Pavlov (1927/1960). Pavlov's work focused on how the control of a response can be shifted from one stimulus to another. In much of his work, he used the salivary reflex as the response system, and he carried out extensive research in an effort to understand the conditions under which stimuli in the environment other than food would elicit or inhibit salivation.

The model for classical conditioning is seen in Figure 3.3. The four basic elements in a classical conditioning experiment are the neutral stimulus (NS), the unconditioned stimulus (US), the unconditioned response (UR), and the conditioned response (CR). Before conditioning, the bell is a *neutral stimulus* (NS). It elicits a response of interest or attention, but nothing more. The sight and smell of food are the *unconditioned stimuli* (US) that elicit salivation, the *unconditioned response* (UR). During conditioning trials, the bell is rung shortly before the food appears. The dog is said to have been conditioned when it salivates to the sound of the bell, even before the food is presented. The bell, therefore, comes to control the salivation response. Salivation that occurs in response to the bell alone is called the *conditioned response* (CR). You may be able to understand this form of learning by thinking of your own reaction when you look at your watch and realize that dinnertime is approaching. Often, just knowing that the time when you usually eat is near is a stimulus for hunger pangs.

Modern research on Pavlovian conditioning has demonstrated that conditioning is a means by which the learner identifies structure in the environment (Davey, 1987; Rescorla, 1988). The pairing of two events, such as the sound of a bell and the presentation of food, becomes significant because one stimulus becomes a signal for the other. The CS does not always have to occur before the US. If a CS occurs frequently along with a US, but there is no systematic relationship between the two, conditioning will not take place. The light may be on in the kitchen whenever the telephone rings, for example, but since there is no

Before conditioning

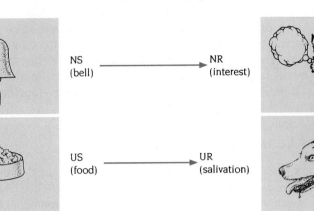

NS
(bell) → NR
(interest)

US
(food) → UR
(salivation)

During conditioning

NS

US

→ UR

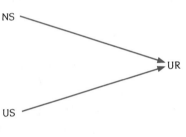

After conditioning

CS → CR

NS = Neutral stimulus   UR = Unconditioned response
NR = Neutral response   CS = Conditioned stimulus
US = Unconditioned stimulus   CR = Conditioned response

FIGURE 3.3
Classical conditioning

Before conditioning, the bell is a neutral stimulus that evokes interest but no other response. With several pairings of the bell and food, the bell becomes a conditioned stimulus that evokes the conditioned salivation response.

predictable relationship between the light and the telephone, the light does not become a signal that the telephone is going to ring. Conditioning is not an artificial paradigm; it is an actual process by which one stimulus provides information about another. Through conditioning, we learn to anticipate and prepare for coming events.

As we have just said, conditioning does not take place randomly between any two events linked in time. A conditioned response is established to the degree that there is a "meaningful" relationship between the CS and the US. Usually, they must occur together many times before conditioning is established. Furthermore, the CS itself is not totally neutral. A visual stimulus such as a colored light will prompt visual orienting, for instance, whereas an auditory stimulus may simply increase attention or arousal. In a conditioning experiment, the learner builds many associations simultaneously. Although the focus of a particular experiment may be establishing a link between one CS and one US, the learner will build links among many elements of the environment—for example, its visual, auditory, and olfactory components—including the US. Pavlovian conditioning provides a model for understanding how multiple associations, sometimes stored at the unconscious level, can be established and triggered in the processes of concept formation, memory, and problem solving (McClelland & Rumelhart, 1986; Rumelhart & McClelland, 1986).

Implications for Human Development

Classical conditioning accounts for a great deal of the associational learning that occurs throughout life. When a specific symbol is paired with an image, an emotional reaction, or an object, that symbol takes on new meaning. The associations made through classical conditioning may involve labels and concepts, but they do not necessarily require language skills. During infancy and toddlerhood, a variety of positive and negative emotional reactions are conditioned to people, objects, and environments as the child develops attachments. Our reactions to the taste of a certain type of food or the feel of a particular material may be the result of conditioned learning that has persisted into adulthood. Similarly, fears may be the result of classical conditioning. Many people recall at least one frightening experience, such as nearly drowning, being beaten, or falling from the top of a slide. The association of fear or pain with a specific stimulus may lead to a systematic avoidance of that object for the rest of one's life.

Operant Conditioning

E. L. Thorndike (1898) studied a different type of learning, called *operant conditioning*, by observing cats as they figured out how to escape from a cage. Thorndike described a process of trial-and-error learning in which the cats made fewer and fewer random movements and increasingly directed their behavior to the correct solution (pulling a string to release a latch). Operant conditioning emphasizes the role of repetition and the consequences of behavior in learning.

One of the best-known American psychologists is B. F. Skinner. Skinner had the benefit of reviewing Pavlov's work on classical conditioning and Thorndike's work on trial-and-error learning. In an early paper, Skinner (1935) summarized the essential differences between the two kinds of learning:

1. In classical conditioning, the conditioned response can begin at zero level; that is, it may not be present at all. In trial-and-error learning, a response must be made if it is to be reinforced or strengthened.
2. In classical conditioning, the response is controlled by what precedes it. In trial-and-error learning, the response is controlled by what follows it.
3. Classical conditioning is most suitable for internal responses (emotional and glandular reactions). Trial-and-error learning is most suitable for external responses (muscle movements and verbal responses).

Skinner's work followed the lines of Thorndike's. His focus was on the modification of voluntary behaviors through the consequences of those behaviors.

In the traditional operant conditioning experiment, the researcher selects a response in advance and then waits for the subject to make the desired response (or at least a partial response). Then, the experimenter presents a reinforcement. A *reinforcement* is operationally defined as any stimulus that makes a repetition of the response more likely.

There are two kinds of reinforcers. Some, such as food and smiles, increase the rate of response when they are present. These are called *positive reinforcers*. Others, such as electric shock, increase the rate of the response when they are removed. These are called *negative reinforcers*.

In one such experiment, a researcher places a rat in a cage. An electric grid in the floor of the cage is activated. As soon as the rat presses a bar, the electric shock is turned off. Soon the rat learns to press the bar quickly in order to turn off the shock. The shock is a negative reinforcer because its removal strengthens the response of bar pressing.

Suppose a mother gets upset whenever she hears her baby cry. She may try a number of things to stop the crying: rocking, feeding, talking, or changing the baby's diapers. If one of these behaviors makes the baby stop crying, it is reinforced; that is, the mother is more likely to try that behavior the next time. The baby's cry is a negative reinforcer because when it stops, the specific caregiving response is strengthened.

A stimulus can be considered a positive reinforcement only if it, in fact, makes some behavior more likely to occur. In the process of socialization, parents may offer a reward that fails to strengthen a response because it has no reinforcing properties for the child. For example, a parent may offer a new bicycle if the child can stay dry during the night for two weeks. If bed-wetting is an expression of the child's persistent wish to be babied and protected, the bicycle, which would permit greater mobility and distance from the parent, may fail to serve as a reinforcement for staying dry.

Operant conditioning develops behavior patterns that are under the learner's voluntary control (Davey & Cullen, 1988). The person can choose to make a response or not, depending on the consequences associated with the behavior. In many instances, however, the behavior to be learned has never occurred before. How can one be reinforced for making a complex response if one has never made it?

Shaping

One means of developing a new complex response is *shaping*. Here, the response is broken down into its major components. At first, a response that is only an approximation of one element of the behavior is reinforced. Gradually, new elements of the behavior are added, and a reinforcement is given only when two or three components of the response are linked together. Once the person makes the complete response, the approximations are no longer reinforced.

Parents often use the shaping process to teach their young children such complicated behaviors as using the toilet, observing table manners, and caring for their belongings. Parents may begin toilet training, for example, by reinforcing children when they behave partially in the desired way, such as telling the parents that they have to go to the bathroom. Eventually, the children receive rewards only when they have completed the entire behavior sequence (including wiping themselves, flushing the toilet, adjusting their clothing, and washing their hands).

Schedules of Reinforcement

Since Ferster and Skinner first addressed the topic in 1957, much research has been devoted to establishing which conditions of learning result in the strongest, longest-lasting habits. *Schedule of reinforcement* refers to the frequency and regularity with which reinforcements are given. A new response is conditioned rapidly if reinforcement is given on every learning trial. This schedule is called *continuous reinforcement*. Responses that are established under conditions of continuous reinforcement are very vulnerable to *extinction*; that is, if the reinforcement is removed for several trials, the performance deteriorates rapidly (see Figure 3.4).

Some schedules vary the amount of time or the number of trials between reinforcements. This procedure is called *intermittent reinforcement*. The learner responds on many occasions when no reinforcement is provided but does receive rein-

BIOGRAPHICAL SKETCH

Burrhus Frederic Skinner was born in 1904 in Susquehanna, Pennsylvania. As a child, he liked to build such mechanical creations as roller-skate scooters, steerable wagons, and rafts. He was an eager explorer and enjoyed biking and canoeing with his friends along the Susquehanna River.

Skinner studied English literature at Hamilton College and graduated in 1926, after which he tried a writing career. Despite a letter of encouragement from Robert Frost, Skinner came to the conclusion that he had nothing important to say.

In 1928, Skinner enrolled in the graduate program in psychology at Harvard, where he studied animal behavior. He described his life as a graduate student as highly focused:

> I would rise at six, study until breakfast, go to classes, laboratories, and libraries with no more than fifteen minutes unscheduled during the day, study until exactly nine o'clock at night and go to bed. I saw no movies or plays, seldom went to concerts, had scarcely any dates, and read nothing but psychology and physiology. (1967, p. 398)

Skinner received his Ph.D. in 1931 and stayed at Harvard as a research fellow for five more years. He began his faculty career at the University of Minnesota, where he wrote *The Behavior of Organisms* (1938). During World War II, he was a research scientist, working on a project to train pigeons to pilot torpedoes and bombs. Although this project was never implemented, Skinner continued to conduct much of his research with pigeons, creating unique experimental equipment that allowed pigeons to make complex responses. He even taught pigeons to play table tennis! After two years as a Guggenheim fellow, Skinner became chairman of the psychology department at Indiana University. In 1947, he returned to Harvard, where he remained until his retirement.

A major emphasis of Skinner's work was his empirical approach to understanding behavior. He searched for explanations that were tied to observed relationships between behaviors and their consequences. In the process, he devised a number of remarkable inventions, including the Skinner box, an apparatus in which animal behaviors could be modified, monitored, and recorded; a temperature-controlled mechanical crib that was intended to provide the ideal environment for an infant; and the teaching machine, which provided step-by-step instructions and immediate feedback. In addition to his experimental contributions to the field of learning, his utopian novel, *Walden Two* (1948), and his extension of behaviorist principles to social criticism in *Beyond Freedom and Dignity* (1971) provided strong arguments for the powerful role of the environment in determining and controlling behavior.

B. F. *Skinner*
1904–1990

Do you have a "lucky" shirt? Do you avoid walking under ladders? Have you ever noticed that some baseball players talk to the ball before they pitch or take a certain kind of practice swing before they bat? All these oddities are instances of superstitious behavior. We can usually see a logical connection between a behavior and its intended consequence: We wash our hands in order to remove dirt, or we put on a jacket in order to stay warm on a chilly day. Some behavior, however, is repeated even though it is not clearly tied to any observable consequence.

According to the operant conditioning view, superstitious behavior is the result of the accidental pairing of a behavior and a reinforcement. Suppose that just before a batter gets up to bat, he knocks the mud from his cleats. On this at-bat, he hits a triple and scores the winning runs for his team. The next time he gets up to bat, he knocks the mud from his cleats on the chance that he may hit a triple again. If a positive consequence follows every once in a while, it will be enough to maintain the behavior. Here, we see an intermittent reinforcement schedule in action.

BOX 3.3

Operant Conditioning and Superstitions

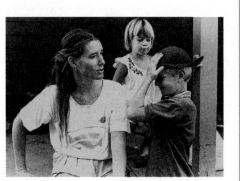

If you have ever known a child who has a lucky hat, you know there is no point in arguing: the hat is going to stay put.

Some people fear that something undesirable will happen if they do *not* perform some behavior—that they will have bad luck, say, if they fail to hold their breath as they pass a cemetery. They reduce the fear by performing the ritual. The fear reduction in itself is reinforcing, and the ritual continues to be performed. Behavior that appears illogical to an observer may be tied to a reinforcement history that maintains it.

forcement every once in a while. Such schedules result in the most durable learning. Intermittent reinforcement lengthens the time that an operant behavior remains in the learner's repertoire after reinforcement has been permanently discontinued (Ferster & Culbertson, 1982).

A variable reinforcement schedule (intermittent reinforcement) is probably truer to real life. It would be very difficult for anyone to learn a behavior if every instance of it had to be reinforced. A person often makes a new response when no observers are present, when teachers are attending to other matters, or in the context of other behaviors that are followed by a negative consequence. Research on operant conditioning demonstrates that the conditions of intermittent reinforcement are precisely those under which the longest-lasting habits are formed.

Implications for Human Development

The principles of operant conditioning apply whenever the environment sets up priorities for behavior and conditional rewards or punishments for approximating a desired behavior. People change whenever their operant behaviors adapt to changes in environmental contingencies. The environment controls the process of adaptation by establishing and modifying contingencies (Skinner, 1987).

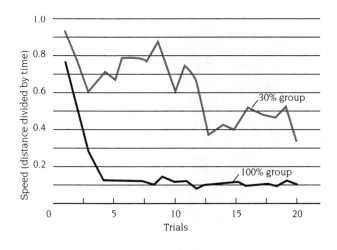

FIGURE 3.4
Continuous versus intermittent reinforcement. This figure shows runway speeds for two groups of rats once reinforcement has been discontinued. One group has previously been reinforced on every trial; the other has been reinforced on only 30% of the trials. Running speed declines rapidly for the group trained under continuous reinforcement. The group that has been trained under intermittent reinforcement continues to run quickly for the first 10 trials and remains above the 100% group for all 20 trials.
Source: Gleitman, 1986.

Behavior can be modified in the desired direction as long as the person who is guiding the conditioning has control over the distribution of valued rewards. We believe that these principles are especially applicable to the learning that takes place during toddlerhood (2 to 4 years) and early school age (4 to 6). Children of these ages are unlikely to be able to identify the existing framework of reinforcement. Once they can identify a reinforcement schedule, they may choose to adapt to it, to resist it, or to redefine the environment in order to discover new sources of reinforcement.

There is no doubt that operant conditioning occurs often throughout life. Reinforcement schedules set by one's work, one's spouse, and oneself operate on much of one's behavior as an adult. Reinforcement conditions determine the behavior that will be performed, and how long a behavior will persist once the reinforcement for it is removed.

Social Learning

Social learning theory differs from both classical conditioning and operant conditioning in two important respects. First, it focuses largely on learning in a social context. Rather than stripping away the social meaning that surrounds much of human learning, it acknowledges the social environment as a stimulus for learning. Second, it introduces imitation and direct instruction as additional means of acquiring new behavior. In its more recent expression, social learning theory also gives a much greater role to cognitive processes, including the knowledge the learner already has, the influence of one's expectations about how one's behavior is evaluated, and anticipation of the probable outcomes of success and failure.

The concept of *social learning* evolved from an awareness that much learning is based on observing and imitating other people's behavior (Bandura & Walters, 1963). Changes in behavior can occur without a specific pattern of positive or negative reinforcement. They can also occur without numerous opportunities for trial-and-error practice. A child can observe someone perform a task or hear someone say a new expression and imitate that behavior accurately on the first try.

We have emphasized the role of *imitation* as the central process in resolving the crisis of autonomy versus shame and doubt in toddlerhood. At that age, imi-

Pablo Picasso, Courtesan with Jeweled Collar, 1901. *Imitation is the process through which most social learning occurs. Imitation is a common strategy in the training of young artists. This painting of a courtesan, done when Picasso was 21 years old, shows the strong influence of Toulouse-Lautrec.*

tation provides a mechanism for the rapid acquisition of new behavior. Think about all the things a child of 4 can say or do. It would be impossible for parents to deliberately teach a child every single behavior; they would have no time left to eat, sleep, or work. Instead, adults provide the *models* for many activities. They express feelings, voice attitudes, perform tasks, and enact their moral values. By observing and imitating many of these behaviors, children become socialized into their family's and their community's way of life.

A great deal of early research in social learning theory was devoted to identifying the conditions in which a child will imitate a model (Bandura, 1971, 1977, 1986). Children have been found to imitate aggressive, altruistic, helping, and stingy models. They are most likely to imitate models who are prestigious, who control resources, or who themselves are rewarded. Bandura and Walters (1963) suggested that children not only observe the behavior of a model but watch what happens to the model. When the model's behavior is rewarded, the behavior is more likely to be imitated; when the model's behavior is punished, the behavior is more likely to be avoided. When naughty behavior goes unpunished, it too is likely to be imitated. This process is called *vicarious reinforcement*. Through observational learning, a child can learn a behavior and also acquire the motivation to perform the behavior or resist performing that behavior depending on what is learned about the consequences of the behavior. Thus, observational learning encourages self-regulation and the internalization of standards for resisting certain behavior as well as for enacting other behavior (Grusec, 1992).

Recent directions in social learning theory have taken an increasingly cognitive orientation (Bandura, 1989b). That is, through observational learning, the child becomes acquainted with the general concepts of the situation as well as the specific behavior. Direct reinforcement or nonreinforcement provides one type of information about how to behave in a certain situation. In addition, we watch others, learn about the consequences of their actions, and remember what others have told or shown us and what we have read or learned about the situation. Over time, a person begins to form a mental representation for the situation, the required behavior, and the expected outcome. A child may learn that, in one teacher's classroom, it is appropriate to ask lots of questions and offer suggestions for ways of solving problems, while in another teacher's classroom, it is better to remain quiet, take notes, and not try to engage the teacher. The rules for behavior in each setting are abstracted from what has been observed in watching others, what has happened following one's own behavior in the past, and what one understands about the demands of the immediate situation.

People's judgments about how well they expect to perform, or whether they expect to improve their skill level through training, have a clear impact on their performance. Bandura (1982, 1989a) identified self-efficacy as a key element in the cognitive basis of behavior. *Self-efficacy* is defined as the sense of confidence that one can perform the behavior demanded by a situation. According to Bandura (1989a), the decision to engage in a situation, as well as the intensity of effort expended in the situation, depends on a person's confidence of success:

> Those who have a high sense of efficacy visualize success scenarios that provide positive guides for performance and they cognitively rehearse good solutions to potential problems. Those who judge themselves as inefficacious are more inclined to visualize failure scenarios and to dwell on how things will go wrong. Such inefficacious thinking weakens motivation and undermines performance. (p. 729)

Bandura points out that adjustment depends on one's judgment about the outcome of a situation. If a woman with a strong sense of self-efficacy is in an environment that is responsive and rewards good performance, she is likely to behave in a self-assured, competent way. If this same woman is in an environment that is unresponsive and does not reward accomplishment, she is likely to increase her effort and even to try to change the environment. People who judge their efficacy to be low give up and become apathetic in unresponsive environments. In responsive environments, they may become more depressed and self-critical when they see others who appear to be similar succeeding.

The concept of self-efficacy clarifies how people adapt when they enter new roles or new situations. The successes and failures we observe in others and the encouragement we receive from others influence our expectations. Coping behavior can also be influenced by a history of prior efficacy.

Implications for Human Development

The principles of social learning theory are assumed to operate in the same way throughout life. The concept of social learning highlights the relevance of models' behavior in guiding the behavior of others. These models may be parents, older siblings, peers, entertainment stars, or sports heroes. Insofar as new role models may be encountered at any life stage, new observational learning is always possible. Exposure to a certain array of models and a certain pattern of rewards or punishments results in the encouragement to imitate some behaviors and to inhibit the performance of others. The similarity in behavior among people of the same age reflects their exposure to a common history of models, rewards, and

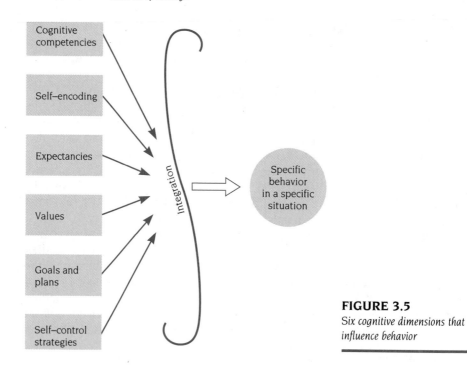

FIGURE 3.5
Six cognitive dimensions that influence behavior

punishments. Recognition of one's potential impact as a model for others, especially in the role of parent, teacher, clinician, counselor, or supervisor, ought to result in self-conscious monitoring of one's behavior in the presence of those who may be using one as a model for new learning.

Cognitive Behaviorism

One objection raised frequently against classical and operant conditioning as theories of learning is that they have no language or concepts that describe events that occur in the learner's mind. Learning is described as a relationship between environmental events and individual responses. In discussing the intervening set of responses that influence learning, Edward Tolman (1932/1967, 1948) said that the learner develops a *cognitive map*, which is an internal mental representation of the learning environment. Individuals who perform a specific task in a certain environment attend primarily to that task, but they also form a representation of the rest of the setting—that is, a cognitive map. The map includes expectations about the setting's reward system, its spatial relationships, and the kind of behavior accorded the highest priority. An individual's performance in a situation represents only part of what she or he has learned. The fact that people respond to changes in the environment indicates the existence of a complex mental map.

Cognitive behaviorists study the many internal mental activities that influence behavior. According to Walter Mischel (1973, 1979), at least six cognitive factors must be taken into account if a person's behavior is to be understood: cognitive competencies, self-encoding, expectancies, values, goals and plans, and self-control strategies (see Figure 3.5). *Cognitive competencies* consist of knowledge, skills, and abilities. *Self-encoding* is one's self-evaluation and self-conceptualization. An interesting finding in this area is that depressed people tend to evaluate themselves more realistically than those who are not depressed. Mischel (1979) argued that "to feel good about ourselves we may have to judge

TABLE 3.2	**Four Learning Processes**		
Classical Conditioning	*Operant Conditioning*	*Social Learning*	*Cognitive Behaviorism*
When two events occur very close together in time, they acquire similar meanings and produce similar responses	Responses that are under voluntary control can be strengthened or eliminated, depending on the consequences associated with them.	New responses can be acquired through the observation and imitation of models.	In addition to new responses, the learner acquires a mental representation of the situation, including expectations about rewards and punishments, the kinds of responses that are appropriate, and the physical and social settings in which they occur.

ourselves more kindly than we are judged" (p. 752). In other words, most people who are not chronically depressed may bias their evaluations of themselves toward self-enhancement.

Here, *expectancies* refers to our expectations about our ability to perform, the consequences of our behavior, and the meaning of the events in our environment. *Values* consist of the relative importance we place on the outcomes of situations. One person may value high levels of task performance, while another may value success in social situations. Our behavior in a situation is influenced by how we value its possible outcome. *Goals and plans* are our personal standards of performance and the strategies we develop for achieving them. Obviously, we all differ in our goals and plans; these differences will lead to considerable variations in behavior. *Self-control strategies* are our techniques for regulating our own behavior. With *self-control*, we can learn how to leave the realm of stimulus control in order to gain control over our behavior. The more aware we are of the effects of stimuli on our behavior, the more effectively we may overcome, channel, or eliminate their influence. Of these six areas, the one that has received the most attention among those interested in learning and performance is expectancies.

Implications for Human Development

Cognitive behaviorism suggests that, through the full range of learning processes, including classical conditioning, operant conditioning, and observational learning, the learner acquires cognitive structures that influence subsequent learning and performance. We might say that the learner acquires an outlook on the learning situation. This outlook may influence his or her feeling of familiarity with the task, motivation to undertake the task, optimism about performing the task successfully, and strategies for approaching the task. In addition to everything a parent, a teacher, or a supervisor might do to structure a learning environment, we must always take into account the outlook the learner brings to the task. Differences in judgments of self-efficacy, self-control strategies, values, and goals influence the way people approach a learning situation.

Summary of Learning Theories

All four of the learning theories contribute insights into human behavior (see Table 3.2).

Classical conditioning focuses on the extensive network of associations that are formed between symbols and stimuli, enduring emotional reactions to one's environment, and the organization of learning associated with reflexive patterns.

Operant conditioning emphasizes the acquisition of behavioral patterns on the basis of their consequences. Social learning theory adds the important element of imitation: People learn new behaviors by watching others. Through social learning, individuals develop an understanding of the social consequences of behavior that leads to new patterns of behavioral expression and self-regulation. Finally, cognitive behaviorism suggests that a complex set of expectations, goals, and values can be treated as behavior and influences performance. Although information or skills can be learned, they will not be expressed in behavior unless expectations about oneself and the environment justify their use. This perspective highlights the capacity to guide the performance of one's own new learning.

Social Roles

Another conceptualization of the environment's effect on development has been suggested by such social psychologists as Orville Brim (1966) and such sociologists as Talcott Parsons (Parsons & Bales, 1955). They trace socialization and personality development through a person's participation in increasingly diverse and complex social roles. A *role* is any set of behaviors that has a socially agreed-on function and an accepted code of norms (Biddle, 1979; Biddle & Thomas, 1966; Brown, 1965). The term *role* was taken from the theater, where the actor's behavior is distinct and predictable because she or he has a part to play and follows a script. You may recall this metaphor from Shakespeare's analysis in *As You Like It*: "All the world's a stage, / and all the men and women merely players; / They have their exits and their entrances; / And one man in his time plays many parts" (act 2, scene 7).

Role theory applies this same framework to social life (Biddle, 1986). The three elements of concern in role theory are the patterned characteristics of social behavior (*role enactment*), the parts or identities a person assumes (*social roles*), and the scripts or shared expectations of behavior that are linked to each part (*role expectations*).

Social roles serve as a bridge between the individual and the society. Every society has a range of roles, and individuals learn about their associated expectations. As people enter new roles, they modify their behavior to conform to these role expectations.

An infant has few roles that have socially agreed-on functions. In our own culture, the roles of an infant may include child, sibling, and grandchild, but at successive life stages, the person plays a variety of roles within the family as well as within other social institutions, such as school, business, and community.

The concept of roles highlights the social context of the developmental process. Although individuals bring their unique temperaments, skills, and values to the interpretation and enactment of the roles they play, most roles exist independently of the people who play them. Thus, knowledge of the functions and norms associated with any given role influences both the performance of the role and the responses of a whole network of people associated with the performer (Goffman, 1959; Biddle, 1979). For example, our expectations about the role of a teacher guide our evaluation of each new teacher we meet, and the same expectations influence how each teacher actually behaves in this role. Each role is usually linked to one or more related, or *reciprocal*, roles. The student and the teacher, the parent and the child, and the salesperson and the customer are in reciprocal roles. Each role is partly defined by the other roles that support it.

Four Dimensions of Social Roles

Social roles have four dimensions: number, intensity of involvement, amount of time required, and degree of structure.

First, as the *number of roles* increases, one's cognitive complexity, social perspective taking, and interpersonal problem-solving ability can be expected to increase. In fact, Parsons (Parsons & Bales, 1955) argued that socialization can best be understood as an outcome of participation in a growing number of increasingly diverse and complex social roles. People who resist taking on new roles can be viewed as forestalling their development by closing off access to new responsibilities and demands.

Social roles can provide both structure and meaning to one's life. When asked, "Who are you?" most people list their social roles. For example, you might say you are a college student, a son or daughter, a brother or sister, a worker, a citizen of the United States, a mother or father, and so on. Even though multiple roles involve conflicting demands for time and attention, they provide structure for one's daily behavior and, at the same time, enhance feelings of well-being (Thoits, 1986).

The more the *intensity of involvement* in a role, the greater the investment of attention and energy, the greater the emotional commitment to the role, and perhaps the greater the anxiety about failure to meet role expectations. As a person becomes fused with a role, his or her personality is increasingly influenced by its socialization pressures. Sarbin and Allen (1968) offered an 8-point scale of role involvement, from 0, or noninvolvement, to 7, where the self is indistinguishable from the role. At the low end, Sarbin and Allen give the example of a person whose membership in a club has lapsed for a number of years; no role behavior is expected of this person, although he or she may resume involvement at any time. At the high end of the scale, Sarbin and Allen's example is a person who believes he or she is the object of witchcraft; the total being is so involved in the role that death can result.

The *amount of time the role demands* is important because a time-consuming role sets up the basic structure for many daily interactions. The role of gas station attendant, for example, may not involve high intensity, but it may require so many hours each day that the person has few opportunities to enact other roles. In fact, a low-intensity role may be a source of constant personal frustration if it continues to demand a large number of hours.

Social roles vary in their *degree of structure*—that is, the extent to which role expectations are specified and the degree of consensus about how they should be performed. There are written criteria for some social roles, such as member of Congress, police officer, and college president, so that the role performer and the audience agree on the behavior appropriate to the role. Such public figures are generally held accountable for their performance of the services they were elected, hired, or appointed to provide. Even less public roles, such as secretary, bookkeeper, and salesperson, have a specified degree of structure, and like public figures, these workers are expected to perform the services for which they were hired.

When roles are highly structured, *person-role fit* comes into question. When there is lack of fit, a role occupant is continually frustrated by demands for behavior that is not compatible with his or her temperament, talents, or motives. In contrast, when the fit is comfortable, a highly structured role may provide the reassurance and support that come from knowing what is expected. When person

The role of close friend is an example of a social role that usually has high emotional intensity and low structure. Friends establish whatever role expectations they wish in order to ensure a satisfying intimate relationship.

and role are compatible, a highly structured role may encourage the development of new competences that will contribute to a person's maturation and growth.

Some roles are much less clearly articulated. They may be defined by cultural myths (for example, the role of explorer) or by community norms (such as the role of neighbor). The enactment of some roles is quite private and is viewed only by members of the immediate family or a few close friends. In these instances, one is free to define the role as it suits the few people who are involved. Lovers, siblings, close friends, and marriage partners can develop their relationship along a variety of paths without scrutiny and elaborate socialization pressures for specific role performances. This does not mean that no expectations accompany these roles; rather, they provide room for individual agreements and improvisation. However, privately defined roles can generate considerable conflict if the people in reciprocal roles cannot agree on how a role should be played. For example, if a husband and wife cannot agree on the expectations that accompany these roles, the marriage will suffer from continual conflict and uncertainty.

Implications for Human Development

In all cultures, new roles await individuals as they move from one life stage to another. These roles may be directly associated with age, such as the role of "elder" or the role of "high school student." Other roles may be accessible only to those of a certain age who demonstrate other relevant skills, traits, or personal preferences. The role of baby-sitter generally does not begin until adolescence; the role of dentist does not become available until young adulthood; the role of full professor is usually not possible until middle adulthood. The culture's implicit theory of development determines the positions open to each age group.

Some of the most important life roles persist across several stages. For example, we are someone's child from infancy until death, and we may be a partner in an intimate sexual relationship from adolescence through later adulthood. In each of these roles, there is both continuity and change (Feldman & Feldman, 1975). The expectations about the role performance remain the same in some

BOX 3.4

Role Strain and Parenthood

A recurring theme in the literature on parenthood is *role strain*, a sense of overload that results when too many expectations are associated with a role (Biddle, 1986). Each of the four dimensions of social roles may contribute to strain in the parental role.

When parenting is added to other adult roles, especially those of worker and spouse, the demands of the new role may seem overwhelming. Because the parent role has great intensity, the sense of involvement in all the behaviors associated with the role intensifies, and so does anxiety about failing to meet the expectations of the role. First-time parents, especially, may have little confidence in their ability to fulfill their role, and the level of anxiety associated with the role and its expectations rises accordingly.

The parental role also takes a lot of time, which is underestimated by most first-time parents. When new parents, especially mothers, reflect on the time they spend in a variety of social roles, they find the parental role more time-consuming than any other, and more time-consuming than any role they have played in the past.

Role strain linked with parenting is also related to the structure of the role. Some adults have a very clear set of ideas about how they should enact their parental role, but many are unsure. Husbands and wives are likely to differ in their views on child-rearing techniques, and these differences require time to resolve. Because of the hardships or distress they recall from their own childhood, many adults do not want to raise their children as they were raised, so they have to learn a new script for this role.

There are at least four ways to minimize the role strain associated with the parental role (Rollins & Galligan, 1978; Bahr, Chappell & Leigh, 1983; Cowan & Cowan, 1988):

1. When the rewards for role enactment are frequent, the demands of the role seem less onerous. Adults who have a lot of encouragement from family, friends, and community for their active involvement in parenting will probably feel less stress from the amount of time and effort they invest in it.

2. The delegation of role responsibilities can reduce role strain. Adults who can hire others to help with some of their parenting responsibilities or who can turn to family members for help will experience less role strain than those who are solely responsible for parenting. Couples flexible enough to alter and share household responsibilities in response to the demands of parenting will also experience more satisfaction and less strain.

3. The integration of several aspects of the role into one activity can reduce role strain. Some parents become quite inventive in finding ways to maintain contact with their infant, carry out their household chores and other work, and still have time with each other.

4. Role strain is reduced when marriage partners reach a consensus about their parental roles. New parents who have resolved their differences regarding their child-rearing philosophy, child-care activities, and the division of household responsibilities experience less role strain and a higher level of marital satisfaction than those who continue to have opposing views.

respects but change in others. We can begin to see how social roles provide consistency to life experiences and how they prompt new learning.

In the following chapters, we describe a number of life roles, including kinship roles, sex roles, age roles, and occupational roles. As the number of roles that people fill simultaneously increases, individuals must learn some of the skills of role playing, role differentiation, and role integration. Resolving the developmental crisis of later adolescence (individual identity versus identity confusion) demands the integration of several diverse roles so that one may maintain a sense of personal continuity. With each new role, one's self-definition changes and one's potential for influencing the world increases.

Throughout life, we also lose roles. The most dramatic instance is the death of a reciprocal role partner. When a parent, sibling, or spouse dies, we lose an important reciprocal role. Graduation from school, divorce, loss of employment, and retirement are other transitions that result in role loss. Social role theory helps us to understand the stress of these changes by recognizing the time, emotional intensity, structure, and culturally shared meaning that are bound up in a single life role and the disorientation that is likely to follow its loss.

Systems

Up to this point, we have been shifting from one way of viewing individual behavior to another. Whether the behavior we scrutinize is associated with the survival of the species or with the survival of the social organization, our attention is repeatedly drawn to the ongoing interaction of the individual and the environment. We cannot make sense of individual elements of thought or behavior without relating them to one another and to the context in which they occur. In its own way, each of the theories we have surveyed draws our attention to the fact that individuals develop within complex systems.

In attempting to describe and account for the characteristics of systems and to view individuals as interconnected elements (Sameroff, 1982), *systems theories* take the position that the whole is more than the sum of its parts. Any system, whether it is a cell, an organ, an individual, a family, or a corporation, is comprised of *interdependent elements* that share some common goals, interrelated functions, boundaries, and an identity. We cannot wholly understand the system by identifying each of the component parts because the processes and relationships of those parts result in a larger, coherent entity. The language system, for example, is more than the capacity to make vocal utterances, to use grammar, and to acquire vocabulary. It is also the coordination of these elements within a context of shared meaning.

Similarly, a family system is more than the sum of the characteristics and competences of the individual family members. Families are a composite of many factors, including a sense of having a common destiny, as well as the genetic heritage of the two spouses and then of their developing children. As spouses develop or create their own composite heritage, this "we-ness" of communication patterns and reciprocal role relationships also identifies the family. All of these elements may be modified and elaborated as a family undergoes transformations in attempting to survive. An open or permeable family boundary is responsive to stimulation and information from both within and outside the family, which the family can use for healthy, adaptive growth and change. A closed family boundary does not allow for interchange and adaptive responses to the environment.

A system cannot violate the laws that govern the functioning of its parts, and at the same time, it cannot be explained solely by those laws. For example, biological functioning cannot violate the laws of physics and chemistry, but the laws of physics and chemistry cannot fully explain biological functioning. Similarly, children's capacities for cognitive growth cannot violate the laws of biological functioning, but biological growth does not fully explain children's quality of thought.

Children's play can be understood from a systems perspective by thinking about the child's embeddedness in family, peer group, neighborhood, and culture. This scene of children at play in the streets of Ghana is similar in many ways to scenes one might imagine on the streets of New York City or Los Angeles. But in certain ways, the meaning and rhythm of the play is unique to these children on this street with this particular group of friends.

Individuals, families, communities, schools, and societies are *open systems*. Ludwig von Bertalanffy (1950, 1968) defined open systems as structures that maintain their organization even though their parts constantly change. Just as the water in a river is constantly changing while the river itself retains its boundaries and course, so the molecules of human cells are constantly changing while the various biological systems retain their coordinated functions.

Open systems share certain properties: They take in energy from the environment, they transform this energy into some type of product that is characteristic of the system, they export the product into the environment, and they draw on new sources of energy from the environment to continue to thrive (Katz & Kahn, 1966). As we have noted, this process requires an open boundary. The more open the boundary, the more vigorously the process operates. Each system has a unique set of processes appropriate to the particular forms of energy, product, and transformations relevant to that system. In the analysis of systems, one focuses more on the processes and the relationships among the parts that permit a system to survive and grow than on the characteristics of the parts themselves.

Systems move in the direction of adapting to or incorporating more and more of the environment into themselves in order to prevent the disorganization that environmental fluctuations may cause (Sameroff, 1982). Adaptation, whether the concept is articulated by Darwin, Piaget, Skinner, or Bandura, seems to be a fundamental process. Ervin Laszlo (1972) described this property of an open system as *adaptive self-regulation*. A system uses *feedback mechanisms* to identify and respond to environmental changes. The more information about the environment the system is capable of detecting, the more complex these feedback mechanisms must be. When the oxygen level of the environment is reduced, for example, you tend to grow sleepy. While you sleep, your breathing slows and you use less oxygen.

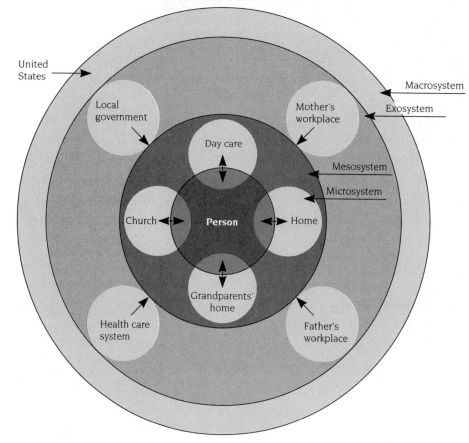

FIGURE 3.6

A *topography of the relationship among systems. Specific
examples of microsystems and
systems in the exosystem are
given, but many other systems
could be shown. Arrows in the
mesosystem show a two-way,
or bidirectional influence;
arrows in the exosystem are
undirectional, since the developing person does not participate
in those settings.*
Source: Based on Bronfenbrenner,
1979.

Some of these adjustments are managed unconsciously by the organization of
biological systems. Others are managed more deliberately by efforts to minimize
the effects of environmental changes. Most systems can store or save resources so
that temporary shortages do not disrupt their operation.

When open systems are confronted by new environmental conditions, they
have the capacity for *adaptive self-organization*. The system retains its essential
identity by creating new substructures, by revising the relationships among its
components, or by creating new, higher levels of organization that coordinate
its existing substructures.

In the systems perspective, the components and the whole are always in tension, and what one understands and observes about the system depends on
where one stands in this complex set of interrelationships. All living entities are
parts and wholes. A person is a part of a family, a classroom or work group, a
friendship group, and a society. A person is also a whole: a coordinated, complex
system composed of physical, cognitive, emotional, social, and self-concept subsystems. Part of the story of human development is told through an analysis of the
adaptive regulation and organization of those subsystems. Simultaneously, the
story is told through the way larger systems fluctuate and impinge on individuals,
forcing adaptive regulation and reorganization as a means of achieving stability.

In an effort to elaborate and clarify the interlocking system of systems in
which human behavior takes place, Urie Bronfenbrenner (1979) offered the following topography of the environmental structure (see Figure 3.6):

A *microsystem* is a pattern of activities, roles, and interpersonal relations experienced by the developing person in a given setting with particular physical and material characteristics.

A *mesosystem* comprises the interrelations among two or more settings in which the developing person actively participates (such as, for a child, the relations among home, school, and neighborhood peer group; for an adult, among family, work, and social life).

An *exosystem* refers to one or more settings that do not involve the developing person as an active participant, but in which events occur that affect, or are affected by, what happens in the setting containing the developing person.

The *macrosystem* refers to consistencies in the form and content of lower-order systems (micro-, meso-, and exo-) that exist, or could exist, at the level of the subculture or the culture as a whole, along with any belief systems of ideology underlying such consistencies. (pp. 22, 25, 26)

Thus, Bronfenbrenner argues that development is influenced directly by the interactions that take place within a single microsystem, such as the family, and by the similarities and differences in patterns of interaction that occur across the various systems in which the person functions (the mesosystem). In addition, events in other, adjoining systems, such as decisions in the workplace that affect a parent's work schedule or decisions in city government that affect the resources for local schools, influence development even though the child does not participate directly in these systems. Further, the roles, norms, and resources within each system, as well as the interrelationships among systems, have a unique pattern of organization and reflect an underlying set of beliefs and values that are different from one culture or subculture to the next; these cultural characteristics are also transmitted to the developing person.

Implications for Human Development

The relevance of systems theory to human development can be most readily appreciated in its application to families. In family system theories, which focus on how families establish and maintain stable patterns of functioning, families are viewed as emotional units identifiable by certain *boundaries* and *rules* (Kantor & Lehr, 1975; Giles-Sims, 1983). The boundaries of the family determine who is considered a family member and who an outsider. They influence how information, support, and validation of the family unit are sought and how new members are admitted into the family. Some families have very strict rules that maintain a narrow boundary around the family, and they admit few sources of information or contact. Other families extend the sense of belonging to a wide range of people, who bring ideas and resources to the family system.

Family systems are maintained by patterns of communication. *Positive* and *negative feedback loops* stabilize, diminish, or increase certain types of interactions. A feedback loop is positive when a child offers a suggestion and a parent recognizes and compliments the child on that suggestion. In such a pattern, the child is encouraged to continue to offer suggestions, and the parent comes to view the child as having valuable suggestions to offer. A feedback loop is negative if a parent ignores the child's suggestion or scolds the child for making it. The child is less likely to make further suggestions, and the parent is likely to view the child as having no valuable ideas to offer. Many positive and negative feedback loops operate in all families to sustain certain underlying qualities of the system, such as the power hierarchy, the level of conflict, and the balance between autonomy and dependence among the members.

One of the most commonly noted characteristics of family systems is the interdependence of the family members. Changes in one family member are accompanied by changes in the others. Imagine for a moment that a family's members are standing in a circle and holding a rope. As each person tries to exert enough tension on the rope to keep it tight and preserve the circular shape, the amount of tension he or she must exert depends on what every other person is doing. Now imagine that one member of the family lets go of the rope and steps away. In order to retain the shape and tension of the rope, everyone else has to adjust his or her grip. Letting go of the rope is an analogy for many kinds of changes that may occur in a family: A parent becomes ill, a child goes off to college, or a parent takes on a demanding job outside the home. The system adjusts by redefining the family's relationships, modifying its patterns of communication, and adjusting its boundaries; that is, the members and their interdependencies change. Similar adjustments must be made if a member is added to the family system, or when the system undergoes some other major transition.

The systems perspective offers an especially productive approach to clinical problems. A person who has been identified as dysfunctional is treated not as a lone individual but as part of a family system. The assumption is that the person's problems are a result of how the person—whether a child, a parent, or a grandparent—is treated by other family members, and that the only way to bring about changes in the person's functioning is to alter the functioning of the other members of the system as well. If the person is "underfunctioning" (for example, acting irresponsibly, not communicating, not performing at his or her level of capability, withdrawing, or acting impulsively), one assumes that others in the family are "overfunctioning" (that is, assuming many of the person's roles and responsibilities in order to "take up the slack"). The dysfunctional behavior is maintained because it is part of an emotional unit. In other words, the dysfunction belongs neither to the person nor to the other family members but to the particular interdependence of the family members that appears to be necessary to preserve the viability of the family system as a whole (Bowen, 1978).

By definition, family systems are also interdependent with adjacent systems. Thus, the understanding of families requires an analysis of the resources and demands of other social systems that impinge on families, as well as of the opportunities families have for influencing the adjoining systems. A woman who is in an extremely demanding, stressful, and sexist work environment, for example, may be constantly tired, tense, and irritable in her behavior toward her family members. She may duplicate her resentments from her work in how she treats and expects to be treated by her family. If the job is important to her and to her family, no one may be willing to acknowledge the bizarre impact her work is having on the family's life. Family violence, the effects of unemployment on families, the participation of mothers in the labor force, day care, and the role of parents in their children's schooling are all being examined from a systems perspective.

Chapter Summary

The seven theoretical perspectives we have reviewed take distinct approaches to continuity and change across the life span.

Evolutionary theory provides an overall temporal framework for understanding individual development. Although a life span of 85 or 90 years may seem long, it is only a flicker in the 1 to 2 million years of human biological adaptation.

Evolutionary theory highlights the biologically and especially the genetically governed aspects of growth and development. This perspective does not ignore the environment; rather, it proposes that the environment provides the specific conditions that require adaptation. However, adaptive change can occur only if it is supported by the genetically based characteristics of the organism. The tempo and pattern of human development are governed by a genetic plan.

Cultural theory takes almost the opposite view. Within this framework, the significance of biological maturation depends on how it is treated by the culture. The possibilities for cultural variation in the life span are enormous. What we understand to be the normal or natural pattern and tempo of change in competence, roles, and status depends heavily on what a society expects of individuals of different ages, gender, and degree of kinship.

Psychosexual theory links the evolutionary and cultural perspectives. Human development is seen as following a biologically determined path. The changing patterns of social relationships are a result of the unfolding of sexual impulses and the sexualization of body zones. Sexual impulses, wishes, and fears, many of which are unconscious, guide behavior and give it meaning. Culture plays a major role in establishing the taboos on and the acceptable patterns of sexual gratification, which lead to conflicts, fixations, and the strategies used for sublimation. According to psychosexual theory, basic personality patterns are established in infancy and childhood. This theory also identifies the family, especially the parent-child relationship, as the primary context within which conflicts related to the socialization of sexual impulses are resolved.

Cognitive theories focus on the origins of rational thought and the capacity for scientific reasoning. Piaget's cognitive theory, like psychosexual theory, views development as a product of a biologically guided plan for growth and change; that is, the elements that make cognitive growth possible are all present in the genetic information that governs the growth of the brain and the rest of the nervous system. However, the process of intellectual growth requires interaction with a diverse and responsive environment. Cognitive development is fostered by a recognition of discrepancies between existing schemes and new experiences. Through the reciprocal processes of assimilation and accommodation, schemes are modified and integrated to form the basis for organizing and explaining experience. Vygotsky's contribution places the development of the higher mental processes in a dynamic social context. Although thinking and reasoning depend on biologically based capacities, how mental activity is organized reflects the unique characteristics of the culture, especially as they are transmitted through language, tools, and social relationships.

Learning theories focus on the mechanisms that permit individuals to respond to their diverse environments and on the permanent changes in thought and behavior that accompany changes in the environment. Behavior can be shaped and modified by systematic changes in environmental conditions. According to learning theorists, human beings have an especially flexible behavioral system. No assumptions are made in this theory about universal stages of growth; growth occurs as conditions in the environment change, requiring changes in response patterns. The similarity among individuals at a particular stage in life is explained by their being exposed to similar environmental conditions, patterns of reinforcement, and models.

Instead of looking at the environment at the microscopic level of the learning theories and considering every unique stimulus and its corresponding response, social role theory suggests that learning is organized around key social functions called *roles*. As people attempt to enact roles, they integrate their behavior into meaningful units. Meaning is provided by the definition of the role and the expectations of those in reciprocal roles. Human development is a product of entry into an increasing number of complex roles over the life span. As people acquire and lose roles, they change their self-definitions and their relationships with social groups. Most societies define roles that are linked with gender, age, marital status, and kinship. These roles provide patterning to the life course. However, the patterns are understood to be products of the structures and functions of the society rather than of genetic information.

Systems theory takes a unique scientific perspective. Rather than seeking to analyze causal relationships, systems theory emphasizes the multidimensional sources of influence on individuals and the simultaneous influence of individuals on the systems of which they are a part. Each person is at once a component of one or more larger systems and a system unto herself or himself. One must approach the study of human development from many angles, identifying the critical resources, the flow of resources, and the transformation of resources that underlie the adaptive process of reorganization and growth.

References

Alpert, J. L. (1986). *Psychoanalysis and women: Contemporary reappraisals.* Hillsdale, NJ: Analytic Press.

Archer, J. (1991). Human sociobiology: Basic concepts and limitations. *Journal of Social Issues, 47,* 11–26.

Bahr, S. J., Chappell, C. K. & Leigh, G. K. (1983). Age at marriage, role enactment, role consensus, and marital satisfaction. *Journal of Marriage and the Family, 45,* 795–804.

Bandura, A. (Ed.). (1971). *Psychological modeling.* Chicago: Aldine-Atherton.

Bandura, A. (1977). *Social learning theory.* Englewood Cliffs, NJ: Prentice-Hall.

Bandura, A. (1982). Self-efficacy mechanism in human agency. *American Psychologist, 37,* 122–147.

Bandura, A. (1986). *Social foundations of thought and action: A social cognitive theory.* Englewood Cliffs, NJ: Prentice-Hall.

Bandura, A. (1989a). Regulation of cognitive processes through perceived self-efficacy. *Developmental Psychology, 25,* 729–735.

Bandura, A. (1989b). Social cognitive theory. *Annals of Child Development, 6,* 1–60.

Bandura, A. & Walters, R. H. (1963). *Social learning and personality development.* New York: Holt, Rinehart & Winston.

Benedict, R. (1929/1968). The science of custom. In A. Dundes (Ed.), *Every man his way* (pp. 180–188). Englewood Cliffs, NJ: Prentice-Hall.

Benedict, R. (1934/1950). *Patterns of culture.* New York: New American Library.

Benedict, R. (1946). *The chrysanthemum and the sword.* Boston: Houghton Mifflin.

Benedict, R. & Weltfish, G. (1943). *The races of mankind.* New York: Public Affairs Committee, Inc.

Bertalanffy, L. von. (1950). The theory of open systems in physics and biology. *Science, 111,* 23–28.

Bertalanffy, L. von (1968). *General systems theory* (rev. ed.). New York: Braziller.

Betancourt, H. & Lopez, S. R. (1993). The study of culture, ethnicity, and race in American psychology. *American Psychologist, 48,* 629–637.

Biddle, B. J. (1979). *Role theory: Expectations, identities, and behaviors.* New York: Academic Press.

Biddle, B. J. (1986). Recent developments in role theory. In R. H. Turner & S. F. Short, Jr. (Eds.), *Annual Review of Sociology, 12,* 67–92.

Biddle, B. J. & Thomas, E. J. (1966). *Role theory: Concepts and research.* New York: Wiley.

Blurton-Jones, N. (1972). *Ethological studies of child behavior.* Cambridge: Cambridge University Press.

Bowen, M. (1978). *Family therapy and clinical practice.* New York: Aronson.

Bowlby, J. (1958). The nature of the child's tie to his mother. *International Journal of Psychoanalysis, 39,* 350–373.

Bowlby, J. (1988). *A secure base: Parent-child attachment and healthy human development.* New York: Basic Books.

Breuer, J. & Freud, S. (1895/1955). Studies on hysteria. In J. Strachey (Ed.), *The standard edition of the complete psychological works of Sigmund Freud* (Vol. 2). London: Hogarth.

Brim, O. G., Jr. (1966). Socialization through the life cycle. In O. G. Brim, Jr., & S. Wheeler (Eds.), *Socialization after childhood.* New York: Wiley.

Bronfenbrenner, U. (1979). *The ecology of human development.* Cambridge, MA: Harvard University Press.

Brown, R. (1965). *Social psychology.* New York: Free Press.

Charlesworth, W. (1988). Resources and resource acquisition during ontogeny. In K. B. McDonald (Ed.), *Sociobiological perspectives on human behavior.* New York: Springer-Verlag.

Charlesworth, W. R. (1992). Darwin and developmental psychology: Past and present. *Developmental Psychology, 28,* 5–16.

Cicchetti, D. & Toth, S. L. (Eds.). (1993). *Rochester Symposium on Developmental Psychopathology: Vol. 5. Disorders and dysfunctions of the self.* Rochester, NY: University of Rochester Press.

Cole, M. (1989). Cultural psychology: A once and future discipline? In J. J. Berman (Ed.), *Nebraska Symposium on Motivation, 1989: Cross-cultural perspectives* (pp. 279–335). Lincoln: University of Nebraska Press.

Cowan, C. P. & Cowan, P. A. (1988). Who does what when partners become parents: Implications for men, women, and marriage. In R. Palkovitz & M. B. Sussman (Eds.), *Transitions to parenthood* (pp. 105–132). New York: Hawthorn Press.

Darwin, C. (1859/1979). *The illustrated "Origin of Species."* Abridged and introduced by Richard E. Leakey. New York: Hill & Wang.

Darwin, C. (1872/1965). *The expression of the emotions in man and animals* (2nd authorized ed.). Chicago: University of Chicago Press.

Davey, G. (1987). *Cognitive processes and Pavlovian conditioning in humans.* New York: Wiley.

Davey, G. & Cullen, C. (1988). *Human operant conditioning and behavior modification.* New York: Wiley.

Doris, J. (1991). *The suggestibility of children's recollections: Implications for eyewitness testimony.* Washington, DC: American Psychological Association.

Dundes, A. (1968). *Every man his way.* Englewood Cliffs, NJ: Prentice-Hall.

Eibl-Eibesfeldt, I. (1975). *Ethology: The biology of behavior* (2nd ed.). New York: Holt, Rinehart & Winston.

Einstein, A. & Freud, S. (1933/1964). Why war? In J. Strachey (Ed.), *The standard edition of the complete psychological works of Sigmund Freud* (Vol. 22, pp. 195–218). London: Hogarth.

Fast, I. (1984). *Gender identity: A differentiation model.* Hillsdale, NJ: Analytic Press.

Feldman, H. & Feldman, M. (1975). The family life cycle: Some suggestions for recycling. *Journal of Marriage and the Family, 37,* 277–284.

Ferster, C. B., & Culbertson, S. A. (1982). *Behavior principles* (3rd ed.). Englewood Cliffs, NJ: Prentice-Hall.

Ferster, C. B. & Skinner, B. F. (1957). *Schedules of reinforcement.* New York: Appleton-Century-Crofts.

Fischer, K. W. & Silvern, L. (1985). Stages and individual differences in cognitive development. In M. R. Rosenzweig & L. W. Porter (Eds.), *Annual Review of Psychology, 36,* 613–648.

Freud, S. (1933/1964). New introductory lectures on psychoanalysis. In J. Strachey (Ed.), *The standard edition of the complete psychological works of Sigmund Freud* (Vol. 22). London: Hogarth.

Freud, S. (1963). *The cocaine papers.* Vienna and Zurich: Dunquin Press.

Gardner, M. R. (1983). *Self inquiry.* Hillsdale, NJ: Analytic Press.

Gazzaniga, M. S. (1989). Organization of the human brain. *Science, 245,* 947–952.

Giles-Sims, J. (1983). *Wife battering: A systems theory approach.* New York: Guilford Press.

Goffman, E. (1959). *The presentation of self in everyday life.* Garden City, NY: Doubleday.

Goldberg, A. (1988). *A fresh look at psychoanalysis: The view from self psychology.* Hillsdale, NJ: Analytic Press.

Greenspan, S. I. & Pollack, G. H. (1980). *The course of life: Vol. 3. Adulthood and the aging process: Psychoanalytic contributions toward understanding personality development.* DHHS Publication no. ADM 81-1000. Washington, DC: U.S. Government Printing Office.

Grusec, J. E. (1992). Social learning theory and developmental psychology: The legacies of Robert Sears and Albert Bandura. *Developmental Psychology, 28,* 776–786.

Herkovits, M. (1948). *Man and his works.* New York: Knopf.

Horowitz, D. (1985). *Ethnic groups in conflict.* Berkeley: University of California Press.

Jaroff, L. (1993). Lies of the mind. *Time, 142,* pp. 52–59.

Kagitcibasi, C. (1990). Family and socialization in cross-cultural perspective: A model of change. In J. J. Berman (Ed.), *Nebraska Symposium on Motivation, 1989: Cross-cultural perspectives.* Lincoln: University of Nebraska Press.

Kantor, D. & Lehr, W. (1975). *Inside the family.* San Francisco: Jossey-Bass.

Katz, D. & Kahn, R. L. (1966). *The social psychology of organizations.* New York: Wiley.

Kihlstrom, J. F. (1987). The cognitive unconscious. *Science, 237,* 1445–1452.

Laszlo, E. (1972). *Introduction to systems philosophy: Toward a new paradigm of contemporary thought.* New York: Harper & Row.

Lerner, I. M. & Libby, W. J. (1976). *Heredity, evolution, and society* (2nd ed.). San Francisco: W. H. Freeman.

Lewin, R. (1987). Africa: Cradle of modern humans. *Science, 237,* 1292–1295.

Lorenz, K. Z. (1935/1981). *The foundations of ethology* (Trans. K. Z. Lorenz and R. W. Kickert). New York: Springer-Verlag.

Lorenz, K. Z. (1943). Die angeborenen Formen möglicher Erfahrung. *Zeitschrift für Tierpsychologie, 5,* 235–409.

Lyell, C. (1830/1833). *Principles of geology* (3 vols.). London: J. Murray.

McClelland, J. L. & Rumelhart, D. E. (1986). *Parallel distributed processing* (Vol. 2). Cambridge: MIT Press.

Mead, M. (1928/1950). *Coming of age in Samoa*. New York: New American Library.

Mead, M. (1949/1955). *Male and female: A study of the sexes in a changing world*. New York: Mentor.

Miller, P. H. (1993). *Theories of developmental psychology* (3rd ed.). New York: W. H. Freeman.

Mischel, W. (1973). Toward a cognitive social learning reconceptualization of personality. *Psychological Review, 80,* 252–283.

Mischel, W. (1979). On the interface of cognition and personality: Beyond the person-situation debate. *American Psychologist, 34,* 740–754.

Nsamenang, A. B. (1992). *Human development in cultural context: A Third World perspective*. Cross-cultural Research and Methodology Series, Vol. 16. Newbury Park, CA: Sage.

Parkes, C. M. (1987). *Bereavement: Studies of grief in adult life* (2nd ed.). Madison, CT: International Universities Press.

Parsons, T. & Bales, R. F. (Eds.). (1955). *Family socialization and interaction process*. New York: Free Press.

Pavlov, I. P. (1927/1960). *Conditioned reflexes*. New York: Dover Press.

Piaget, J. (1924/1952). *Judgment and reasoning in the child*. New York: Humanities Press.

Piaget, J. (1926/1951). *The child's conception of the world*. New York: International Universities Press.

Piaget, J. (1936/1952). *The origins of intelligence in children*. New York: Humanities Press.

Piaget, J. (1941/1952). *The child's conception of number*. New York: Humanities Press.

Piaget, J. (1950). *The psychology of intelligence*. New York: Harcourt, Brace; London: Routledge & Kegan Paul.

Piaget, J. (1954). *The construction of reality in the child*. New York: Basic Books.

Piaget, J. (1978/1985). *The equilibration of cognitive structures*. Chicago: University of Chicago Press.

Piaget, J. & Inhelder, B. (1969). *The psychology of the child*. New York: Basic Books.

Rescorla, R. A. (1988). Pavlovian conditioning: It's not what you think it is. *American Psychologist, 43,* 151–160.

Rohner, R. P. (1984). Toward a conception of culture for cross-cultural psychology. *Journal of Cross-Cultural Psychology, 15,* 111–138.

Rollins, B. C. & Galligan, R. (1978). The developing child and marital satisfaction of parents. In R. M. Lerner & G. B. Spanier (Eds.), *Child influences on marital and family interaction: A life-span perspective*. New York: Academic Press.

Rumelhart, D. E. & McClelland, J. L. (1986). *Parallel distributed processing* (Vol. 1). Cambridge: MIT Press.

Sameroff, A. J. (1982). Development and the dialectic: The need for a systems approach. In W. A. Collins (Ed.), *The concept of development: The Minnesota Symposia on Child Psychology* (Vol. 15). Hillsdale, NJ: Erlbaum.

Sarbin, T. R. & Allen, V. L. (1968). Role theory. In G. Lindzey & E. Aronson (Eds.), *The handbook of social psychology* (2nd ed., Vol. 1). Reading, MA: Addison-Wesley.

Schermerhorn, R. A. (1978). *Comparative ethnic relations: A framework for theory and research*. Chicago: University of Chicago Press.

See, K. O. & Wilson, W. J. (1988). Race and ethnicity. In N. J. Smelser (Ed.), *Handbook of sociology* (pp. 223–242). Newbury Park, CA: Sage.

Simons, E. L. (1989). Human origins. *Science, 245,* 1343–1350.

Skinner, B. F. (1935). The generic nature of the concepts of stimulus and response. *Journal of Genetic Psychology, 12,* 40–65.

Skinner, B. F. (1938). *The behavior of organisms*. New York: Appleton-Century-Crofts.

Skinner, B. F. (1948). *Walden two*. New York: Macmillan.

Skinner, B. F. (1967). Autobiography of B. F. Skinner. In E. Boring & G. Lindzey (Eds.), *History of psychology in autobiography* (Vol. 5, pp. 387–413). New York: Appleton-Century-Crofts.

Skinner, B. F. (1971). *Beyond freedom and dignity*. New York: Knopf.

Skinner, B. F. (1987). Whatever happened to psychology as the science of behavior? *American Psychologist, 42,* 780–786.

Spencer, H. (1864). *Principles of biology* (Vol. 1). London: William & Norgate.

Stern, R. (1987). *Theories of the unconscious and theories of the self*. Hillsdale, NJ: Analytic Press.

Tattersall, I., Delson, E. & Van Couvering, J. (1988). *Encyclopedia of human evolution and prehistory* (pp. 267–274). New York: Garland.

Thoits, P. A. (1986). Multiple identities: Examining gender and marital status differences in distress. *American Sociological Review, 51,* 259–272.

Thorndike, E. L. (1898). Animal intelligence: An experimental study of the associative processes in animals. *Psychological Review, 2*(Monograph Suppl. 8).

Tinbergen, N. (1951). *The study of instinct*. Oxford: Clarendon Press.

Tolman, E. C. (1932/1967). *Purposive behavior in rats and men*. New York: Appleton-Century-Crofts.

Tolman, E. C. (1948). Cognitive maps in rats and men. *Psychological Review, 55,* 189–208.

Triandis, H. (1989). The self and social behavior in differing cultural contexts. *Psychology Review, 96,* 506-520.

Triandis, H., Lambert, W., Berry, J., Lonner, W., Heron, A., Brislin, R. & Draguns, J. (Eds.). (1980). *Handbook of cross-cultural psychology*. (Vols. 1–6). Boston: Allyn & Bacon.

Tudge, J. R. H. & Winterhoff, P. A. (1993). Vygotsky, Piaget, and Bandura: Perspectives on the relations between the social world and cognitive development. *Human Development, 36,* 61–81.

Uzgiris, I. C. (1976). The organization of sensorimotor intelligence. In M. Lewis (Ed.), *Origins of intelligence: Infancy and early childhood* (pp. 123–164). New York: Plenum Press.

Viorst, J. (1986). *Necessary losses*. New York: Simon & Schuster.

Vygotsky, L. S. (1962). *Thought and language*. Cambridge: MIT Press.

Vygotsky, L. S. (1978). *Mind in society*. Cambridge: Harvard University Press.

Walker, A. & Teaford, M. (1989, January). The hunt for *Proconsul*. *Scientific American*, pp. 76–82.

Weiss, J. (1990). Unconscious mental functioning. *Scientific American, 262*, 103–109.

Westkott, M. (1986). *The feminist legacy of Karen Horney*. New Haven, CT: Yale University Press.

Whiting, B. B. & Edwards, C. P. (1988). *Children of different worlds: The formation of social behavior*. Cambridge: Harvard University Press.

Wilson, E. O. (1975). *Sociobiology: The new synthesis*. Cambridge: Belknap Press.

CHAPTER 4

The fetus develops within the context of the pregnant woman's body, her family, and her culture. The path of development is guided largely by genetic information, but the outcome of the pregnancy and the robustness or vulnerability of the newborn is influenced as well by the kind of environment the pregnant woman provides.

The Period of Pregnancy and Prenatal Development

Our analysis of psychosocial development begins with the period of pregnancy and prenatal growth. Actually, you could take your personal life story back much further than that. You might ask how your parents met, what socialization each had for the parental role, and what the cultural contexts were of their infancy and childhood. You might ask about the environmental factors that may have influenced your prenatal development, such as your mother's nutritional status, exposure to environmental hazards, or use of drugs during labor and delivery. You might ask those same questions regarding your grandparents, great-grandparents, and earlier ancestors. Each past generation has contributed in some significant ways to your life story.

In this chapter, we take the perspective of both the developing fetus and the expectant parents. For the parents, the parental role begins with the decision to have children, the experiences of pregnancy, and the events of childbirth. For the child, the process of growth begins with the moment of fertilization.

During the prenatal period, genetic factors guide the tempo of growth and the emergence of individual characteristics. As the human fetus grows, sensory and motor competencies emerge. The psychosocial environment provides resources for and challenges to healthy development. Cultural attitudes toward pregnancy and childbirth, maternal nutrition, poverty and the associated stresses, and the use of obstetric drugs are among the factors that may affect growth.

Genetics and Development

From the time of fertilization, genetic information provides a set of guidelines for the individual's development. It determines the nature of a person's resources and may, in some cases, place severe constraints on development. Given one's genetically based potential, a wide range of individual variation is possible, depending on the quality of the environment, the degree of fit between the person and the environment, and the person's unique resources for coping with the world.

Genes and Chromosomes as Sources of Genetic Information

When we talk about inherited characteristics, we are really referring to two different kinds of heredity. The first kind includes all the genetic information that comes to us as members of the human species. We inherit genetic information that is shared by all human beings, such as patterns of motor behavior (walking upright, for instance), brain size, and body structure, including the proportional size of the head, torso, and limbs. Two of the most relevant of these species-related characteristics are the readiness to learn and the inclination to participate in social interaction. All humans share these attributes.

The second kind of heredity consists of characteristics that have been transmitted through a specific *gene pool*. Such traits as hair color, skin color, blood group, and height result from the genetic information passed on from one generation to the next. The principles of genetics that we describe here refer primarily to this second group of inherited characteristics, the products of a specific gene pool (Thompson, McInnes & Willard, 1991). Genetic information links each new person to the human species in general and to a specific genetic ancestry.

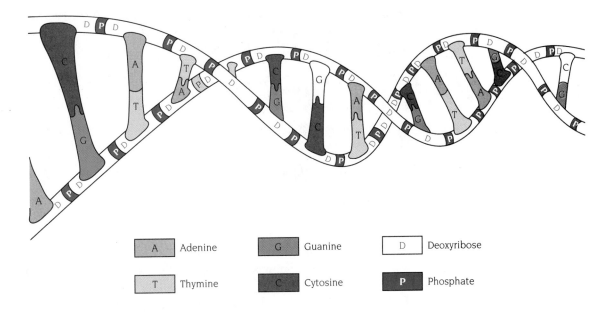

| | A | Adenine | | G | Guanine | | D | Deoxyribose |
| | T | Thymine | | C | Cytosine | | P | Phosphate |

FIGURE 4.1

Diagram of a small part of a DNA molecule

The biochemical basis of genetic information is the DNA (*deoxyribonucleic acid*) molecule, which has the shape of a double helix (see Figure 4.1), looking something like a twisted rope ladder. The sides of this genetic ladder are composed of alternating units of sugar (deoxyribose) and phosphate, and the rungs are made up of pairs of nitrogen bases. Nitrogen bases are so named because they include the element nitrogen as well as the elements hydrogen and carbon. Four nitrogen bases are involved: *adenine* (A), *guanine* (G), *cytosine* (C), and *thymine* (T). These bases are often referred to by their initial letters, and A, G, C, and T are called the genetic alphabet.

Adenine (A) and guanine (G) are *purine* bases. Cytosine (C) and thymine (T) are *pyrimidine* bases. The purine bases are smaller than the pyrimidine bases. Only combinations of adenine and thymine or guanine and cytosine are the right size to fit into the space between the sides of the genetic ladder. Thus C-G, G-C, A-T, and T-A are the only pairs of bases that are possible in DNA molecules. Figure 4.1 shows the shape and composition of DNA. The order of the base pairs and the accompanying side material of sugar and phosphate determine the meaning of the genetic message.

Chromosomes—long, thin strands located in the cell nucleus—are formed from chains of DNA molecules. Late in the 19th century, cell biologists learned how to stain the chromosomes. In fact, the word *chromosome* means "colored body." After it was discovered that chromosomes could be stained, biologists could count and study them and learned that the chromosomes in each cell occur in pairs. They also learned that the cells of the body of each species contain a specific number of chromosomes. It was not until the 1950s that Joe Hin Tjio and Albert Levan of the Institute of Genetics in Lund, Sweden, determined that human cells contain 46 chromosomes, in 23 pairs. The common fruit fly, which is used in much genetic research, has only 8 chromosomes.

A *gene* is a portion of DNA that codes for one hereditary characteristic and occupies a specific place on a chromosome. Human beings have about 100,000 functional genes distributed along the 23 pairs of chromosomes (Figure 4.2).

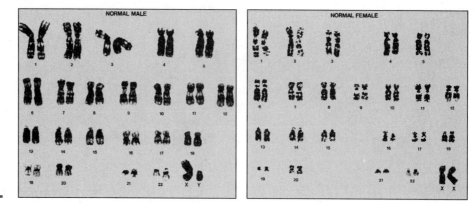

FIGURE 4.2

The 23 pairs of chromosomes in a human male and a human female. The 23rd pair determines the individual's sex—males have an X and a Y; females have two X's.

Genetic mapping involves identifying the specific location of each gene on a specific chromosome, which is an enormous task: The smallest human chromosome bands that can be recognized under the microscope contain from 2 to 5 million base pairs of DNA and many genes (Patterson, 1987; NIH/CEPH Collaborative Mapping Group, 1992).

One chromosome in each chromosome pair comes from the father and one from the mother. The chromosome pairs differ in size, some containing over 1000 genes and others containing 2000. In 22 pairs of chromosomes, both members are similar in shape and size. They also contain the same kinds of genes. The 23rd pair of chromosomes is a different story: Females have two X chromosomes, and males have one X and one Y chromosome. The X and Y notation is used because these chromosomes differ in shape and size (the X chromosome is longer than the Y chromosome: see the last pair in Figure 4.2). There are very few similarities in the genes present on the X and Y chromosomes.

It is important to note here that the same group of chromosomes does not appear in each *gamete* (egg or sperm cell). When the cells divide, the chromosomes separate independently. There are 2^{23} possible combinations of chromosome separation in any individual's gametes.

Additional variability in the pattern of genetic information results from *crossing over*. When the cells divide during *meiosis*, some of the material from the paternal and maternal chromosome strands may cross over and exchange places on the strand. The resulting sequence of specific genetic information on a chromosome is unlike that in either the original maternal or the original paternal code.

Through crossing over, new arrangements of genetic information may be passed on to offspring. This variation in the patterning of genetic information adds to the diversity of offspring possible for any single couple. When one considers the fertilization process and the chance meeting of one sperm and one egg cell, the number of different individuals that might be produced by two adults is $2^{23} \times 2^{23}$, or 64 trillion, even without any crossing over.

The Laws of Heredity

The laws that govern the process by which genetic information is transmitted from parent to offspring were discovered by Gregor Mendel (1866), a monk who studied the inherited characteristics of plants, particularly garden peas. His laws were formulated long before the discovery of the biochemical materials that compose genes and chromosomes.

Alleles

In the 22 pairs of identical chromosomes, each gene has at least two states or conditions, one on each chromosome strand in the pair. These alternative states are called *alleles*. Whatever the allelic state of the gene from one parent, the other parent's allele for that gene may be either the same or different. If both alleles are the same, the gene is said to be *homozygous*. If the alleles are different, the gene is *heterozygous*.

Genotype and Phenotype

The genetic information about a trait is called the *genotype*. The observed characteristic is called the *phenotype*. Genotype influences phenotype in three ways. First, the differences in the allelic states of a gene sometimes result in a *cumulative relation*, in which more than one pair of genes influences the trait. An example of this kind of relation is the genetic contribution to height. A person who receives mostly "tall" genes will be tall; a person who receives mostly "short" genes will be short. Most people receive a mix of "tall" and "short" genes and are of average height.

Second, the differences between alleles may result in *codominance*, a state in which both genes are expressed in the new cell. An example of codominance is the AB blood type, which results from the joining of an A blood-type allele and a B blood-type allele. This blood type is not a mixture of A and B, nor is A subordinated to B or B to A; instead, a new blood type, AB, is formed.

Third, the differences in the allele states of a gene may result in a dominance relation. *Dominance* means that, if one allele is present, its characteristic is always observed whether or not the other allele of the allelic pair is the same. The allele that dominates is called the *dominant gene*. The allele that is present, but whose characteristic is masked by the dominant gene, is called the *recessive gene*. Eye color is the result of a dominance relation. The gene for brown eyes (B) is dominant over the gene for blue eyes (b). The probability that the recessive trait of blue eyes will emerge in the offspring of two heterozygous parents is illustrated in Figure 4.3. The possible combinations of the gene related to brown or blue eye color are BB, Bb, bB, and bb. Only if both parents carry the b allele and that allele is present in each of the gametes that form the offspring will the child have blue eyes. As the figure shows, on the average only 25% of the offspring of heterozygous parents have blue eyes.

In the case of a dominance relation, genetic information is not always observed in some outward characteristic. For example, people with alleles BB and Bb may both have brown eyes, even though they have different genetic information. For brown and blue eye color, there are two phenotypes (brown and blue) but three genotypes—two dominant alleles (BB), two recessive alleles (bb), or one dominant and one recessive allele (Bb or bB).

Sex-Linked Characteristics

Certain genetic information is said to be *sex-linked* because the gene for the specific characteristic is found on the sex chromosomes. The female ova carry only X chromosomes. Half of the male sperm carry Y chromosomes, and half carry X chromosomes. Male children can be produced only when a sperm carrying a

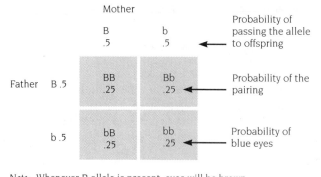

FIGURE 4.3

Probability of heterozygous parents' producing a blue-eyed offspring

Note: Whenever B allele is present, eyes will be brown.

Y chromosome fertilizes an egg, and the result is an XY combination in the 23rd chromosome pair. All sperm carrying X chromosomes will produce female children.

Sex-linked traits are more likely to be observed in males, even though they are present in the genotype of females. You will understand this more readily if you visualize the XY chromosome pair. When a trait is carried on the Y chromosome, it will be inherited and transmitted only by males, since only males have the Y chromosome.

Interestingly, the Y chromosome is quite small, and very few exclusively Y-linked traits have been identified. One of the key genes that has been identified on the Y chromosome is referred to as *testis-determining factor* (TDF). This gene (or genes) is responsible for setting into motion the differentiation of the testes during embryonic development. Once the testes are formed, they begin to produce hormones that account for the further differentiation of the male reproductive system.

In addition to the Y-linked genes, sex-linked traits that are carried on the X chromosome are more likely to be observed in males than in females, because males do not have a second X chromosome with which to offset the effects of an X-linked trait. Currently, a map of the human X chromosome is being constructed through a coordinated, international research effort. The X chromosome comprises about 160 million base pairs. Roughly 40% of the X chromosome has been identified. Genes associated with 26 inherited diseases have already been reproduced, and the location of genes associated with 50 others has been identified (Mandel et al., 1992).

Hemophilia is an example of a sex-linked trait. *Hemophiliacs* lack a specific blood protein that causes blood to clot after a wound (Lawn & Vehar, 1986). The allele for hemophilia is carried on the X chromosome. If the allele is either heterozygous or homozygous for the dominant characteristic (normal clotting), a female child will have normal blood-clotting capability. Only if she is homozygous for the recessive characteristic (a very rare occurrence) will she be hemophilic. The male, on the other hand, has only one allele for the blood-clotting gene, which he inherits from his mother. If that allele is dominant, his blood will clot normally; if it is recessive, he will be hemophilic (see Figure 4.4).

There are other genes that are expressed exclusively in one sex but are not found on the sex chromosomes per se. For example, the genes for male beard development and female breast development are not located on the sex chromo-

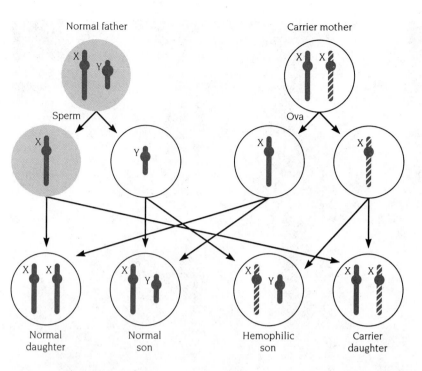

Normal father

Carrier mother

Sperm

Ova

Normal daughter

Normal son

Hemophilic son

Carrier daughter

FIGURE 4.4
Sex-linked inheritance of hemophilia. Sex-linked inheritance of hemophilia results from the location of the factor VIII gene on the X chromosome. A male carrying a mutant factor VIII gene lacks normal factor VIII and is hemophilic. A female carrier is protected by the normal gene on her second X chromosome, but half of her daughters will be carriers and half of her sons will be hemophilic. When a father is hemophilic (not shown), his sons will not be hemophilic, because they receive his Y (not his X) chromosome, but his daughters will be carriers.
Source: Lawn & Vehar, 1986.

somes. However, these characteristics will emerge only in the presence of the appropriate hormonal environment, which *is* directed by the sex chromosomes.

Genetic Sources of Individuality

The study of genetics reveals that individual variability is due to more than the many variations in environment and experience that confront a growing person. Variability is built into the mechanisms of heredity. Each adult couple has the potential for producing a variety of genetically distinct children. Four areas in which genetic determinants contribute to individual variability are rate of development, individual traits, abnormal development, and psychosocial evolution.

Genetic Determinants of Rate of Development

Genes regulate the rate and sequence of maturation. The concept of an epigenetic plan for growth and development is based on the assumption that a genetically guided system promotes or restricts the growth of cells over the life span. Genetic factors have been found to play a role in behavioral development, including the onset of various levels of reasoning, language, and social orientation.

Considerable evidence of the role of genetics in guiding the rate and sequence of development has been provided by studies of identical twins (who have the same genetic structure). The rates at which identical twins develop are highly correlated, even when those twins are reared apart. A number of characteristics, including the timing of the acquisition of motor skills, personality development, changes in intellectual capacity among aged twins, and the timing of physical maturation, show a strong genetic influence (Holden, 1987).

Genes can be viewed as internal regulators that set the pace for maturation. They signal the onset of significant developmental changes throughout life, such

Baldness is a sex-linked trait, carried on the X chromosome and observed primarily in men. In this family portrait, the grandmother sitting in the middle of the front row is celebrating her 95th birthday. She still has a full head of hair, but she is surrounded by her bald sons.

as growth spurts, the eruption of teeth, puberty, and menopause. They also appear to set the limits of the life span. A small number of genes influences how many times the cells of a specific organism can divide and replicate (Marx, 1988). Research on three different animal species—fruit flies, worms, and mice—shows that when the most long-lived of a species are bred, the offspring have a longer life than average (Barinaga, 1991).

Differences in the rate of development contribute to our understanding of psychosocial growth. These differences bring different children into contact with new aspects of their environments and provide them with changing capacities at different chronological ages. Thus, the genetic processes that regulate readiness for certain kinds of growth and vulnerabilities to particular kinds of stress contribute to systematic differences among individuals. For example, adult expectations for the accomplishment of such specific tasks as toilet training, getting dressed without help, and learning to write interact with the child's developmental level. Disappointment may be conveyed to developmentally "late" children, and pride and approval may be conveyed to developmentally "accelerated" children.

Genetic Determinants of Individual Traits

Genes contain specific information about a wide range of human characteristics, from eye color and height to the ability to taste a particular substance called *phenylthiocarbamide* (which to tasters is bitter but to nontasters has no taste at all). Some characteristics are controlled by a single gene. However, most significant characteristics, such as height, weight, blood group, skin color, and intelligence, are controlled by the combined action of several genes. When multiple genes are involved in the regulation of a trait, the possibilities for individual differences in that trait increase. Since many characteristics are regulated by multiple genes, the variety of human genotypes is enormous.

Pablo Picasso, Three Women, 1933. *The many possible combinations of genetic information produce tremendous individual variation. In this drawing, Picasso shows us how basic geometric shapes can be combined in a variety of ways to produce humanlike figures, similar and yet each unique.*

Genetic factors also play a substantial role in individual differences in personality (Plomin, 1990, 1994; Loehlin, 1992; Holden, 1987). Personality traits such as sociability (a tendency to be sociable and outgoing), inhibition (a tendency to be cautious and socially shy or withdrawn), and neuroticism (a tendency to be anxious and emotionally sensitive) are pervasive dimensions of personality that appear to have strong genetic components. Even in rather specific areas of personality, such as political attitudes, aesthetic preferences, and sense of humor, identical twins show greater similarity than fraternal twins, even when the identical twins are reared apart from each other.

Extending the analysis of the impact of genetics on individual differences, Sandra Scarr (1992) suggested at least three ways in which genetic factors influence the environments of individuals, thus increasing the impact of genetics on the expression and elaboration of individual differences. First, most children are raised by their parents in environments created by their parents. Thus, children receive both their genes and their environment from a common genetic source— their parents. As an example, a parent who is temperamentally sociable is more likely than a withdrawn or timid parent to have lots of people at the house, to enjoy the companionship of others, and therefore to expose his or her children to more companionate adults. Second, people draw out responses from others that are related to their own personality characteristics. Thus, broad, genetically based aspects of one's individuality will affect the kinds of social responses one receives from others, including one's parents. Third, as people mature and become increasingly assertive in selecting certain experiences and rejecting others, their own temperaments, talents, intelligence, and level of sociability will guide the kinds of environments they select and will strengthen certain genetic predispositions, while dampening others.

Genetic Determinants of Abnormal Development

In addition to characteristics such as physical appearance, temperament, talent, and intellectual capacity, a wide variety of abnormalities, or *anomalies*, have a genetic cause. The most dramatic anomalies result in an abortion of the fetus early in the pregnancy. It is estimated that a majority of the spontaneous abortions that occur early in pregnancy are the results of chromosomal abnormalities

TABLE 4.1	Estimated Incidence of Causes of Major Congenital Malformations
Cause	**Incidence (%)**
Chromosomal aberrations	6
Environmental factors	7
Single gene defects	8
Multifactorial inheritance*	25
Unknown	54

*Multiple genes at different loci on chromosomes interact with environmental factors to product malformations.
Source: Moore, 1988.

in the fertilized zygotes (the developing organism formed from the father's sperm and the mother's egg) (Clayman, 1989).

Of those infants who survive the neonatal period, an estimated 3%–5% of newborns have one or more major recognizable anomalies (Cunningham, MacDonald & Gant, 1989). The incidence of anomalies increases to 6% or 7% as some disorders are diagnosed later in childhood. The causes of these malformations and disorders are listed in Table 4.1, along with an estimate of the incidence of each type of cause. Some birth defects are linked to a specific chromosome (6%) or a single gene (8%). Similarly, some are linked solely to environmental factors, such as drugs, medications, and fetal and maternal infections. The majority of malformations are products of the interaction of genetic vulnerabilities in the presence of certain environmental hazards or are of unknown origin (Moore, 1988).

Some genetic and chromosomal disorders are listed in Table 4.2 (Clayman, 1989). The disorders are presented in two broad categories: those that are associated with specific genes and those that are associated with chromosomal abnormalities. Within those categories, some disorders are found on 1 of the 22 pairs of autosomal chromosomes (chromosomes other than the sex chromosomes), and others are on one of the sex chromosomes. Among the genetic disorders that result from a dominant gene, about 300 have been identified; among those that result from a recessive gene, about 250 have been identified. The chromosomal site of a number of genetic disorders has been identified through molecular biology techniques, work that will lead eventually to a clearer understanding of the molecular mechanisms that account for these disorders (Anderson, 1992).

The variety of genetic abnormalities serves to broaden the range of individual variability. Many of the irregularities pose a challenge both to the adaptive capacities of the afflicted person and to the caregiving capacities of the adults involved. Certain genetic diseases are linked directly to our ancestry; therefore the incidence of some genetic diseases is higher in certain populations than in others (Thompson et al., 1991). Even relatively mild irregularities, such as a shock of white hair, a birthmark, an elongated middle toe, or a long nose, may become significant in the person's psychological functioning. Sometimes such irregularities carry negative connotations or block the person's level of functioning. Although many of these irregularities may not be of medical concern or require treatment, they are relevant to a person's evolving sense of self.

TABLE 4.2   Genetic and Chromosomal Disorders

I. Genetic disorders
   A. Autosomal dominant gene
      1. *Achondroplasia (dwarfism)*: Abnormal bone growth, especially in the arms and legs, results in short stature, short limbs, a well-developed trunk, and a head of normal size except for a somewhat protruding forehead.
      2. *Huntington's chorea*: rapid jerky, involuntary movements; deterioration of muscle coordination and mental functioning. Symptoms usually do not appear until age 35–50. Results from genetic defect on chromosome 4.
      3. *Marfan's syndrome*: Elongated fingers; deformed chest and spine; abnormal heart. Tendons, ligaments, and joint capsules are weak.
   B. Autosomal recessive gene
      1. *Albinism*: Hair, skin, and eyes lack the pigment melanin. Often accompanied by visual problems and a tendency to skin cancer.
      2. *Cystic fibrosis*: Certain glands do not function properly. The glands in the lining of the bronchial tubes produce excessive amounts of thick mucus, which lead to chronic lung infections. Failure of the pancreas to produce enzymes necessary for the breakdown of fats and their absorption from the intestines leads to malnutrition. Sweat glands are also affected. Often fatal by age 30. Missing base pairs on chromosome 7.
      3. *Sickle-cell anemia*: Malformation of red blood cells reduces the amount of oxygen they can carry. Results in fatigue, headaches, shortness of breath on exertion, pallor, jaundice, pain, and damage to kidneys, lungs, intestine, and brain.
      4. *Tay-Sachs disease*: Absence of a certain enzyme results in the buildup of harmful chemicals in the brain. Results in death before age 3.
   C. X-linked recessive
      1. *Color blindness*: Defect of light-sensitive pigment in one or more classes of cone cells in the retina of the eye and/or an abnormality in or reduced number of cone cells themselves. The two common types are reduced discrimination of light wavelengths within the middle (green) and long (red) parts of the visible spectrum.
      2. *Hemophilia*: Absence of a blood protein (factor VIII) reduces effectiveness of blood clotting. Severity of disorder varies. Bleeding episodes likely to begin in toddlerhood.
      3. *Duchenne muscular dystrophy*: Progressive degeneration of muscle fibers. Most common form of childhood dystrophies. Muscle weakness early in life. Few survive teen years. Thirty percent of affected males are also mentally retarded.

(continued)

Genetic Technology and Psychosocial Evolution

The products of psychosocial evolution, including behavioral adaptations, the transfer of knowledge, new inventions, and new forms of social organization, were once believed to be carried by social mechanisms rather than to be incorporated in the genetic structure. As a result of scientific knowledge, however, we are entering an era when it is possible to intervene to influence the genotype. One such intervention is *genetic counseling*. Individuals and couples whose families have a history of a genetic disease, or who for some other reason worry about the possibility of transmitting a genetic disease to their children, can have a blood test for genes that may result in the inherited disorder. The location of the genes that account for such abnormalities as Tay-Sachs disease, sickle-cell anemia, Duchenne

TABLE 4.2   *(continued)*

II. Chromosomal disorders
  A. Autosomal abnormality
    1. *Down syndrome*: Usually three rather than two chromosomes 21. The excess chromosome results in physical and intellectual abnormalities, including IQ in the range of 30–80; distinctive facial features, heart defects, intestinal problems, hearing defects; susceptibility to repeated ear infections. Tendency to develop narrowing of the arteries in adulthood, with attendant increase in risk of heart disease. Such people tend to be affectionate and friendly, and to get along well with other family members. Most are capable of at least some learning.
  B. Sex-chromosome abnormalities
    1. *Turner's syndrome*: Usually caused by a lack of one X chromosome in a girl; sometimes one of two X chromosomes is defective; occasionally some cells are missing on an X chromosome. These abnormalities result in defective sexual development and infertility, short stature, absence or retarded development of secondary sex characteristics, absence of menstruation, narrowing of the aorta, and a degree of mental retardation.
    2. *Klinefelter's syndrome*: One or more extra X chromosomes in a boy. This abnormality results in defective sexual development, including enlarged breasts and small testes, infertility, and often mental retardation.
    3. *Fragile X syndrome*: A small portion of the tip of the X chromosome is susceptible to breakage under certain conditions. The damage results in mental retardation, learning disabilities, and abnormalities in growth regulation, such as a big head, higher than normal birth weight, large or protruding ears, and a long face. Behavior problems include hand flapping, hand biting, hyperactivity, poor eye contact, autism, social withdrawal, and shyness. More boys are affected than girls, and boys' problems tend to be more severe.

Source: Based on Clayman, 1989.

muscular dystrophy, and cystic fibrosis have been identified. Couples who carry genes for one of these diseases can be advised about the probability of having children who may be afflicted so that they can decide whether they want to reproduce. If significant numbers of the carriers of genetic diseases decided not to reproduce, the incidence of these diseases in the population would decline significantly over time. Thus, a psychosocial intervention would indeed modify the gene pool.

In the years ahead, genetic technology promises to take us even further than genetic counseling through the direct modification of the genetic structure of an individual. In January 1989, the National Institutes of Health (NIH) launched a project to map the *human genome*—that is, to identify and list in order all of the genome's (the full set of chromosomes that carries all the inherited traits of an organism) approximately 3 billion base pairs. Once completed, this map may permit us to predict an individual's vulnerability to genetic diseases, to treat genetically caused diseases, and possibly to "enhance" a person's genetic potential through the introduction of gene modifications (Jaroff, 1989; NIH/CEPH Collaborative Mapping Group, 1992). As an example, the gene that is defective in patients with *cystic fibrosis*, a condition common in children and young adults in which a thick, sticky mucus obstructs the airways and increases vulnerability to infection, has recently been identified (Collins, 1992). Cystic fibrosis is the most common and potentially lethal of the autosomal recessive diseases among

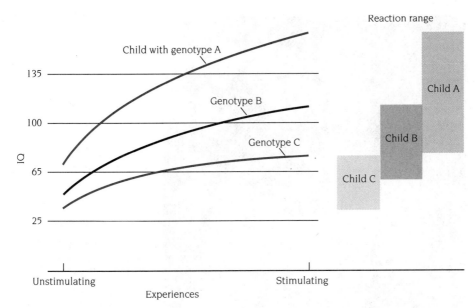

FIGURE 4.5
Hypothetical reaction ranges of intelligence
Source: Gottesman, 1963.

Caucasians. Now that the biochemical process associated with the defective gene has been analyzed, a wide variety of therapeutic techniques are being developed, including both drug therapy and gene therapy.

Toward the end of 1988, the United States government scrutinized and then approved the first transfer of a foreign gene into humans, in an experiment being conducted at the National Institutes of Health. The initial gene-transfer experiment was limited to ten cancer patients who were not expected to live more than 90 days. In this first test, the transplanted gene served as a marker to help track the progress of an experimental cancer treatment. This experiment was not considered *gene therapy* because the transplanted gene was not expected to produce a therapeutic benefit (Roberts, 1989). As of 1992, 11 active clinical procedures were being carried out that involved gene marking or gene therapy, and 9 others had been approved for implementation (Anderson, 1992).

Gene transfer, the patenting of new life forms created through genetic engineering, and the new technique of genetic fingerprinting, which is used to help identify criminal suspects, are just some of the topics that are raising new ethical concerns. There is a general consensus that gene therapy used to treat serious diseases such as cystic fibrosis or cancer is ethical. However, there is much less agreement about the use of intervention to alter the genetic code at the level of the zygote or to attempt to introduce genes that are intended to enhance aspects of normal development in humans. Through discussion, debate, research, observation of events, and court cases, we are hammering out a set of ethics that not only deals with specific issues but sets the tone for the way we conceptualize life itself.

Evaluating the Impact of Heredity on Behavior

One way to summarize the influences of genetics on behavior is to view the genotype as establishing a *reaction range*—that is, a range of possible responses to environmental conditions, the limits of which are determined by one's genotype. Under similar environmental conditions, genetic differences are most likely to be expressed. However, when environmental conditions vary, the advantages of one genotype over another may be masked by the adversities or opportunities of the situation. Figure 4.5 shows the hypothetical reaction ranges of three children with

The concept of reaction range is illustrated in the very high level of functioning evidenced by this girl with Down syndrome who is learning to perform job-related tasks in the bakery of her supportive residence.

respect to intelligence. Child A has greater genetic potential for intelligence than Child B, who has greater potential than Child C. When all three children are in unstimulating environments, their IQs develop at the lower end of their potential range. When all three children are in stimulating environments, their IQs develop toward the upper end of their potential range. If the three children are in different environments, the differences in genetic potential may be masked by the way the environments act on this potential. If Child B and Child C are in stimulating envi-

---

A question of interest to developmental psychologists, educators, and parents is the relative contribution of genetic and environmental factors to intelligence. In fact, intelligent behavior requires the successful integration of both. Although it relies on the structure of the central nervous system and the sense receptors, which are products of genetically guided information, the healthy functioning of these systems requires adequate nutrition, rest, and

BOX 4.1

Hereditary Influences on Intelligence

(continued)

freedom from disease, conditions that vary with the environment. Intelligent behavior also relies on experiences with diverse stimuli, appropriate social interactions, and the cultivation of problem-solving strategies—all elements of the physical and social environment.

The influence of genetic factors on intelligence may be observed in two ways. First, we know that specific genetic irregularities can cause degrees of mental retardation. Two examples are Down syndrome and phenylketonuria (PKU). The Down syndrome child has three chromosomes at chromosome 21 rather than the normal two. The additional chromosome leads to an overproduction of enzymes, which results in both intellectual and physical abnormalities. PKU is a condition that results from a certain recessive gene (p). When a child is homozygous for p, a specific enzyme is not produced. The outcome is that an amino acid, phenylalanine, which is normally transformed into another amino acid, does not change. Phenylalanine accumulates in the body and damages the brain. If PKU is diagnosed within the first week of life, a reduction in the intake of phenylalanine in milk and other foods will minimize the negative effects. Many other genetic diseases have some negative effects on intellectual growth. Thus, genetic diseases play an indisputable role in restricting intellectual potential.

A second approach to understanding the influence of genetics on intelligence is through the study of family relationships. Family members may be related closely or distantly. The closer the relatives, the more similar their genetic makeup. If intelligence is influenced by genetics, close relatives should be more similar in intelligence than distant relatives.

The figure opposite shows the degree of similarity found in more than 100 studies of intelligence in siblings of four degrees of relationship. Similarity in intelligence increases with the degree of genetic relatedness. The similarity in intelligence of identical, or monozygotic (MZ), twins gives striking evidence of the contribution of genetics to intelligence. Fraternal, or dizygotic (DZ), twins who share the same prenatal, home, and child-rearing environments show much less similarity than do identical twins and not much more than "ordinary" siblings.

Many studies that supply evidence of genetic contributions to intelligence highlight the role of the environment as well. For example, the Texas Adoption Project (Horn, 1983, 1985) compared IQ data on more than 400 adopted children, their

BOX 4.1

(continued)

adoptive mothers, and their biological mothers. The IQs of the adopted children and their biological mothers were more highly correlated than the IQs of the children and their adoptive mothers: The brighter adopted children were the offspring of the brighter biological mothers, clear evidence of genetic influence. This pattern demonstrates that genetic factors continue to play an important role in the development of individual differences.

Evidence of environmental influences on intelligence was found in the fact that the average IQ of the adopted children as a group was significantly higher than that of their biological mothers, but quite similar to that of their adoptive mothers. This pattern demonstrates that the adoptive environment had an enriching effect on the children, raising the IQ level of the group as a whole. The positive influence of the adoptive environment on the children's measured IQ illustrates the notion of the reaction range to which we referred earlier.

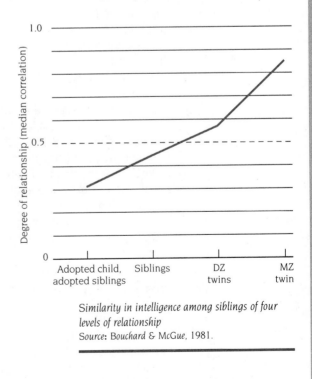

Similarity in intelligence among siblings of four levels of relationship
Source: *Bouchard & McGue, 1981.*

Identical twins continue to exhibit similarities in appearance, talents, and lifestyle preferences into adulthood.

ronments and Child A is in an unstimulating environment, Child B may have the highest measured IQ, and the IQs of Children C and A may be lower and very similar. Each child's intellectual ability can be expressed as a range that is a product of the interaction of genetic potential and environment.

The concept of the reaction range can be seen clearly in the outlook for children with Down syndrome (Patterson, 1987). This condition, which occurs in 1 of every 700 live births, is the most common genetic cause of mental retardation in the United States. In the early part of this century, children born with Down syndrome had a life expectancy of 9 years. Today, the life expectancy of a Down syndrome child is 30 years, and 25% of these children live to age 50. Medical care, early and constant educational intervention, physical therapy, and a nurturing home environment have significant, positive results for children with Down syndrome. Under optimal conditions, these children, whose IQs range from 30 to 80, are able to achieve a moderate degree of independence and to participate actively in the life of their families.

Let us now explore the physical process through which genetic information is actually transmitted and see how the early phases of development unfold.

Normal Fetal Development

Fertilization

One normal ejaculation contains several hundred million sperm. This large number is necessary to ensure fertilization, because most sperm die on the path through the vagina and the uterus. Each microscopic sperm is composed of a pointed head and a tail. The head contains the genetic material necessary for reproduction. The tail moves like a whip as the sperm swims through the cervix and uterus and into the fallopian tubes. Swimming at a rate of an inch in 8 minutes, sperm may reach the egg in as little as 30 minutes. The journey usually takes about 6 hours, and sperm can stay alive in the uterus for up to 5 days.

During most of the menstrual cycle, the plug of mucus in the cervix is thick and difficult to traverse. At the middle of the cycle, when an ovum is about ready to be released, the mucus thins out, allowing more sperm to pass through the cervix and travel farther into the uterus in search of an ovum. The change in the mucus also lessens the vagina's natural acidity, making it a more hospitable environment for sperm cells.

In contrast to the male, who produces billions of sperm in a lifetime, the female ordinarily releases just one ovum, or egg, each month, midway through the menstrual cycle. In a lifetime of approximately 40 fertile years, during which she can be expected to have two children, the average woman releases approximately 450 eggs. Each girl is born with her complete supply of eggs.

Like the sperm, the ovum is a single cell that contains genetic material. In comparison with body cells, the egg cell is quite large (0.12 millimeters), about the size of the period at the end of this sentence. When the ovum is mature, it is encased in a sac of fluid and floats to the surface of the ovary. The sac ruptures and releases the ovum into one of the two fallopian tubes. Millions of feathery hairs in the fallopian tube sweep around the ovum and gently move it toward the uterus.

The ovum may be fertilized at any point as it moves through the fallopian tube, but usually fertilization occurs in the outer third of the tube, close to the uterus. Only one sperm can enter the egg. As the first sperm passes through the cell membrane, a rapid change in the membrane's chemistry effectively locks out other sperm. If the ovum is not fertilized within the first 24 hours of its maturity, it begins to disintegrate and is shed along with the lining of the uterus in the next menstrual period.

Once inside the egg cell, the sperm loses its tail, and the head becomes a normal cell nucleus. The egg cell also goes through a final change in preparation for fertilization. The two nuclei meet in the egg cytoplasm, lose their nuclear membranes, and integrate their separate chromosomal material into a single set of 23 pairs of chromosomes. At this moment, all the information necessary to activate growth and produce a new, unique individual is contained in a single cell.

Twins

The cell produced when the sperm fertilizes the egg is referred to as a *zygote*. The zygote travels down the fallopian tube and divides as it travels toward the uterus without growing larger. After about a week, this mass of cells implants in the uterus. Occasionally, a zygote divides in two and separates. Then two individuals with the same chromosomal composition begin to form. These individuals are referred to as *monozygotic* (MZ) *twins* because they come from a single zygote. These twins are always of the same sex, and they are strikingly similar in physical appearance, a characteristic leading to the term *identical twins*. Much research has been done on identical twins who have been raised together and identical twins who have been raised apart to reveal the relative contributions of heredity and environment to intellectual, emotional, social, and physical development.

Fraternal twins occur as a result of multiple ovulations in the same cycle. Each egg develops separately in the ovary, is shed and fertilized individually, and develops separately in the uterus. The result is *dizygotic* (DZ) *twins*—that is, two-egg twins. Actually, they are littermates and may be of different sexes. Genetically, they bear no more resemblance to one another than other children of the same parents. However, they do share a more common parenting environment than do most siblings who are born one or more years apart. Approximately 1 in 90 pregnancies results in twins, most commonly dizygotic twins (Clayman, 1989).

Infertility and Alternative Means of Reproduction

For approximately 1 married couple out of 12 of child-bearing age in the United States, the normal process of fertilization does not occur. Infertility, or the inability to conceive, may result from problems in the reproductive system of either the man or the woman, or in the systems of both. The limited research literature on the emotional impact of infertility suggests that it is a major source of stress. The discovery of infertility forces a couple to reassess the meaning and purpose of their marriage. It raises doubts about self-worth in the man and woman; it often disrupts the couple's satisfaction with their sexual relationship; and it often isolates the couple because of the difficulty of discussing this very personal family problem with others (Sabatelli, Meth & Gavazzi, 1988; Jarboe, 1986).

A woman who had tried unsuccessfully to conceive for eight years put it this way:

> "I can tell you that everyone who faces this is extremely vulnerable and will pretty much try anything . . . because we're desperate. . . .
>
>   I felt like the fact that I couldn't do the very thing that my body was designed to do—to conceive and carry a child—must mean that I wasn't fully a woman. And all my other accomplishments seemed to fade into the background in the face of this failure." (Sperling, 1989, p. 1D)

Some remarkable alternatives are being developed for couples who are unable to conceive. In 1990, an estimated 1 million new patients sought treatment for infertility (Elmer-Dewitt, 1991). With each of these alternatives comes new challenges in the ways we define families and in the meanings we give to men's and women's reproductive functions (Robison, 1989; Silverman, 1989).

Artificial insemination is probably the best-developed alternative to natural fertilization. A woman who wants to conceive goes to a clinic every month and has sperm injected into her vagina. These sperm have been donated and frozen. Some sperm banks keep the donors' characteristics on file. This procedure enables the couple to select the sperm of a donor who closely resembles the husband. A single woman can select features she desires in her offspring. Other banks blend sperm so that the recipient cannot trace the donor's identity. The Office of Technology Assessment reported that approximately 172,000 women in the United States undergo artificial insemination each year, and that about 65,000 babies are conceived annually by this procedure (Byrne, 1988).

Another alternative to natural fertilization is *in vitro fertilization* (fertilization in an artificial environment). In this process, an egg is removed from the ovary and placed in a petri dish inside an incubator. Then, a few drops of sperm are added to the dish. If the egg is fertilized and the cell begins to divide, the fertilized egg is replanted in the uterus for subsequent development. A survey of 146 clinics that perform in vitro fertilization found that the procedure is successful in about 9% of cases (Sperling, 1989). A recent version of this procedure is called *sperm injection*. A single sperm is injected into an egg. Several eggs fertilized in this manner are implanted in the mother's uterus. One Belgian physician reported 100 births associated with this new method (Associated Press, 1993).

In a third procedure, *gamete intrafallopian transfer* (GIFT), eggs and sperm are transferred into a woman's fallopian tubes. Fertilization takes place as it

Baby M (pictured here at age 8) and her birth mother enjoy the comfort of their enduring relationship.

normally would, within the woman's reproductive system. These eggs and sperm may come from a husband and a wife or from other donors. Thus, the fetus may be genetically related to the husband, to the wife, to both, or to neither.

A fourth alternative is *in vivo fertilization* (fertilization in a living body). In this procedure, a husband and wife involve another woman in the conception. The other woman, who has demonstrated her fertility, is artificially inseminated with the husband's sperm. Once an embryo has formed, it is transferred to the wife's uterus, which becomes the gestational environment. The child is therefore genetically related to the husband, but not to the wife.

A fifth alternative involves a *surrogate mother*. Sperm from an infertile woman's husband are injected into the surrogate mother during the time of her monthly ovulation. The surrogate bears the child and returns it to the parents at birth. About 100 babies per year are born to surrogate mothers (Byrne, 1988). In one remarkable case of this type, a woman agreed to be the surrogate mother for her own daughter who wanted a child but was born without a uterus. At age 42, this mother gave birth to her own twin grandchildren (Elmer-Dewitt, 1991).

All these alternatives have raised legal and ethical questions (Andrews, 1984; Elson, 1989; Elmer-Dewitt, 1991). The husband of a woman who is planning to be artificially inseminated must consent to the procedure and agree to assume legal guardianship of the offspring. The lack of official guidelines for screening donors raises the issue of who should be responsible if a child resulting from artificial insemination has a severe genetic anomaly. Another concern being raised is what the sperm donor's rights are to a relationship with his offspring. In 1983, a California man was granted weekly visitation rights to a child who had been conceived with his sperm.

In the widely publicized case of Baby M., William and Elizabeth Stern paid Mary Beth Whitehead $10,000 to be a surrogate mother. After the birth, Mrs. Whitehead decided that she wanted to keep the baby. In ensuing court battles, the

New Jersey Supreme Court decided that the contract between the couple and Mrs. Whitehead was void and that it was illegal to pay a woman to bear a child for someone else. Nonetheless, the court granted custody of the child to the Sterns, arguing that they could provide the child a more stable home environment. The court rejected the right of Elizabeth Stern to adopt the baby and supported Mrs. Whitehead's right of continued visitation. This complex pattern of decisions creates a precedent that other states may follow. Surrogate parenting may be made illegal or may be so tightly regulated that it becomes an underground practice, although it is currently endorsed by the medical community (Lacayo, 1988; Silverman, 1989).

Finally, what limits should be placed on the production of embryos in vitro? Should we permit scientists to produce embryos from frozen sperm and egg cells for purposes other than implantation? In a troubling case, conflict arose between a couple, Risa and Steven York, and the Jones Institute for Reproductive Medicine in Norfolk, Virginia. The Yorks, who lived in New Jersey, began to participate in an in vitro fertilization program at the Jones Institute in 1986. Three implant attempts failed. Then the Yorks decided to move to California, and they asked the Jones Institute to send their frozen embryo to a comparable medical facility in Los Angeles. The institute refused. According to the Jones Institute, the Yorks must have the embryo implanted at their facility. Otherwise, the Yorks could donate it to the institute to be used by another couple or for experimentation, or they could have it destroyed (Elson, 1989).

Thousands of frozen embryos are held in various medical and laboratory facilities in the United States (Elson, 1989). State laws governing their use as well as their rights are often conflicting and confusing. Questions are raised about the rights of parents to determine the fate of these embryos, the embryos' rights to protection and inheritance, and the responsibility of institutes and laboratories to ensure the proper use of the embryos. A disturbing element here is the obvious detachment of the embryo from its parental origins, which tends to encourage a view of embryos as products rather than as emerging beings.

Development in the First Trimester

The period of pregnancy, typically 40 weeks after the last menstrual period or 38 weeks from ovulation, is often conceptualized in three 3-month periods called *trimesters*. Each trimester brings changes in the status of the developing fetus and its supporting systems. These changes are summarized briefly in Table 4.3. (Major directions in fetal development are described in greater detail in Moore, 1988.)

The pregnant woman also experiences changes during the trimesters. In the first trimester, many women are not certain that they are pregnant. By the last trimester, not only is the woman certain, but so is everyone else!

After fertilization, the egg begins to divide. The first series of cell divisions does not increase the mass of the cells, nor do the cells take on specialized functions; rather, the cell material is redistributed among several parts. When implantation is successful, by the sixth day after fertilization the egg makes contact with the lining of the uterus and begins to attach itself there. Sometimes the egg does not reach the uterus but attaches itself to the fallopian tube or even some area of the intestine. The embryo may grow in these locations until the organ ruptures.

The three weeks following implantation are devoted primarily to elaboration of the supportive elements that will house the embryo. An *amniotic sac* surrounds the embryo and fills with a clear, watery fluid. This fluid acts as a cushion that buffers the embryo and permits it to move about and change position.

TABLE 4.3   Major Developments in Fetal Growth During the Three Trimesters

First Trimester	Second Trimester	Third Trimester
Fertilization	Suckling and swallowing	Nervous system matures
Growth of the amniotic sac	Preference for sweet taste	Coordination of sucking and swallowing
Growth of the placenta	Skin ridges on fingers and toes	Mechanisms for regulating body temperature
Emergence of body parts	Hair on scalp, eyebrows, back, arms, legs	More efficient digestion and excretion
Differentiation of sex organs	Sensitivity to touch, taste, light	Degeneration of the the placenta toward the end of the ninth month
Initial formation of central nervous system	Sucks thumb	9-month average size: 20 inches, 7 to 7½ pounds
Movement	6-month average size: 10 inches, 2 pounds	
Grasp reflex		
Babinski reflex		
Heartbeat		
3-month average size: 3 inches, about ⅖ ounce		

It is at this point—about three weeks after implantation, when the woman's menstrual period is about two weeks overdue—that the first reliable tests can determine if she is pregnant. Once the embryo is firmly implanted in the uterus, special cells in the placenta produce a hormone that maintains the uterine lining. This hormone is excreted through the kidneys, so a urine sample can be evaluated to determine its presence.

The *placenta* is an organ that is newly formed with each pregnancy and is expelled at birth. The nutrients necessary for the embryo's growth pass through the placenta; the embryo's waste passes through the placenta and into the mother's blood. Thus, the placenta is an exchange station at which adult material is synthesized for the embryo's use and intruders harmful to the embryo's development can be screened out. However, the screening is imperfect. Even though the mother's blood and the embryo's blood are contained in independent systems, the placenta permits the mother's blood and the baby's blood to come close enough so that oxygen and nutrients from the mother's blood can enter the fetal system, and waste products from the fetal system can be removed. In the process, certain substances in the mother's system may affect the fetal system. Agents that can produce malformations while the tissues and organs are forming are referred to as *teratogens*. Teratogens take a wide variety of forms, such as viruses, medicines that a pregnant woman ingests, alcohol and other drugs, and environmental toxins. During the first trimester—especially Weeks 3 through 9—the embryo is particularly sensitive to the disruptive influences of teratogens (see Figure 4.6).

In the third and fourth weeks, the embryo's cells differentiate rapidly, taking on the specialized structures that will permit them to carry out unique functions in the body. Similar cells are grouped into tissues that gradually emerge as body organs. The first essential changes include the establishment of the body form as an elongated cylinder and the formation of precursors of the brain and the heart. The central nervous system begins to develop very early in the prenatal period and continues to develop throughout childhood and adolescence. The *neural tube*, which is the first structural basis of the central nervous system, begins to take shape at the end of the third week after conception. By the end of the fifth week,

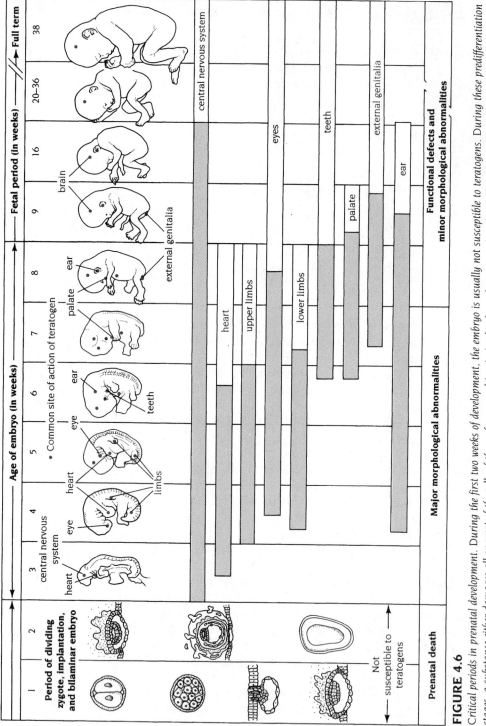

FIGURE 4.6

Critical periods in prenatal development. During the first two weeks of development, the embryo is usually not susceptible to teratogens. During these predifferentiation stages, a substance either damages all or most of the cells of the embryo, resulting in its death, or damages only a few cells, allowing the embryo to recover without developing defects. Dark denotes highly sensitive periods; light indicates stages that are less sensitive to teratogens. Severe mental retardation may result from the exposure of the embryo/fetus to certain teratogenic agents, such as high levels of radiation, from the 8th to 16th weeks.
Source: Moore, 1988.

the tube is differentiated into five bulges that are the forerunners of the major subdivisions of the brain. Most of the neurons that make up the cerebral cortex are produced by the end of the second trimester. However, regions of the cortex continue to mature over the first four years of life (Greenough, Black & Wallace, 1987; Nowakowski, 1987; Aoki & Siekevitz, 1988).

By the end of the fourth week, the head, the upper trunk, and the lower trunk are visible, as are limb buds and forerunners of the forebrain, the midbrain, the hindbrain, the eyes, and the ears. The embryo will have increased 50 times in length and 40,000 times in weight since the moment of fertilization.

By the end of the second month, the embryo looks quite human. It weighs about 2.25 grams and is about 28 millimeters (1 inch) long. Almost all the internal organs are formed, as well as the external features of the face, the limbs, the fingers, and the toes. At eight weeks, the embryo will respond to mild stimulation. The embryonic period ends at about ten weeks after the last menstrual period. Most of the essential structures are formed by this time. The term *fetus* is used from this point until birth.

In the third month, the fetus grows to 3 inches and its weight increases to 14 grams. The head is about one-third of the total body length. During this month the fetus assumes the "fetal position": arms curled up toward the face and knees bent in to the stomach. The eyelids are fused.

A dramatic change takes place in the sex organs. All embryos go through a bisexual stage during which no sex-linked characteristics can be discerned. Both females and males have a surface mass that becomes the testes in males and eventually degenerates in females. In females, new sex cells grow to form the ovaries. Both males and females have two sets of sex ducts. In males, the sperm ducts develop and the female ducts degenerate. In females, the fallopian tubes, the uterus, and the vagina develop, and the other ducts degenerate. Finally, both males and females have a conical area that is the outlet for the bladder duct. When the male testes develop, this area forms into the penis and scrotum. In females it remains to form the clitoris, which is surrounded by the genital swellings of the labia majora. Differentiation of the male genitalia requires the release of the hormone testosterone. The "fallback" position in fetal development is to develop the female genital structures. In other words, if testosterone is not produced, the baby will develop the reproductive structures of a female even though the chromosomal sex is male (Stechler & Halton, 1982; Kimura, 1992).

The genetic factors that produce the differentiation of the fetus as male or female appear to influence more than the formation of the reproductive organs and the production of hormones. Research on the organization and structure of the brain suggests that, during fetal and early postnatal development, sex hormones direct male and female brains along slightly different paths (Kimura, 1992). Three areas of the brain—the hypothalamus, the amygdala, and the hippocampus—have been studied as potential sites for sex differences in structure that may relate to some of the functional areas in which men's and women's problem-solving and cognitive skills differ.

The 3-month-old fetus moves spontaneously and has both a grasp reflex and a Babinski reflex, in which the toes extend and fan out in response to a mild stroke on the sole of the foot. When an amplified stethoscope, called a *Doppler*, is applied to the mother's stomach, the fetal heartbeat can be heard through the uterine wall by the expectant parents as well as the physician. When we were expectant parents, we were unbelievably thrilled to hear those first faint heartbeats of a life still strangely remote!

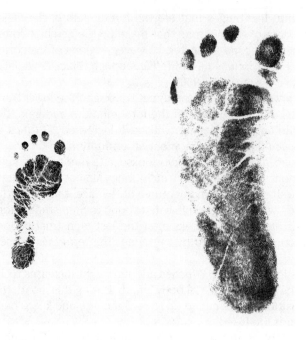

These are the birth footprints of a baby born prematurely at 23 weeks and one born at a full 40-week gestational age.

Development in the Second Trimester

During the second trimester, the average fetus grows to 10 inches and increases in weight to almost 2 pounds. The fetus continues to grow at the rate of about an inch every ten days from the fifth month until the end of the pregnancy. During this trimester, the uterus itself begins to stretch and grow. It rises into the mother's abdominal cavity and expands until, by the end of the ninth month, it is pushing against the ribs and diaphragm. The reality of a growing life becomes more evident to the pregnant woman during this trimester as she observes the change in her profile and experiences the early fetal movements called *quickening*. These movements are first experienced as light bubbles or twitches; later, they can be identified as the foot, elbow, or fist of the restless resident.

During the fourth month, the fetus begins to suck and swallow. Whenever it opens its mouth, amniotic fluid enters and cycles through the system. The amniotic fluid provides some nutrients in addition to those absorbed through the placenta. The 4-month-old fetus shows some preference for a sweet taste: If sugar is introduced into the amniotic fluid, it will swallow the fluid faster.

In the fifth month, the skin begins to thicken, and a cheesy coating of dead cells and oil, the vernix caseosa, covers the skin. The individuality of the fetus is marked by the pattern of skin ridges on the fingers and toes. Hair covers the scalp, eyebrows, back, arms, and legs.

The sensory receptors of the fetus are well established by the end of the sixth month. The fetus is sensitive to touch and may react to it with a muscle movement. It will also stick out its tongue in response to a bitter taste. Throughout the sixth month, the nostrils are plugged by skin cells. When these cells dissolve, the nose fills with amniotic fluid; thus, smell is probably not possible until birth.

The external ear canal is filled with fluid, and the fetus does not tend to respond to sound until the eighth or ninth month; however, the semicircular canals of the inner ear are sensitive to stimulation. The nerve fibers that connect the retina to the brain are developed by six months; infants born prematurely at this time respond to light.

BOX 4.2

*Looking In on
the Fetus*

Most expectant parents worry about whether their baby is developing normally. Today, many of these worries can be minimized through technologies that allow us to evaluate fetal development during the early months of pregnancy. Several of these techniques are associated with some risk and should not be used without ample justification. However, especially in high-risk pregnancies, monitoring fetal development may lead to interventions that will save lives when problems do exist, and that will reduce the stress associated with unfound worry. Four monitoring strategies are described here (Cunningham et al., 1989).

Electronic fetal-heart-rate monitoring: Rather than listen to the fetal heart rate periodically by stethoscope, birth attendants can monitor it continuously through electronic equipment that is painlessly attached to the pregnant woman's abdomen. This technique is especially useful in detecting any disruption in the fetal oxygen supply during labor.

Ultrasound: Based on submarine sonar technology from World War II, ultrasound uses reflected sound waves to produce a visual image of the fetus. Ultrasound can be used to date the pregnancy more precisely, to diagnose multiple pregnancies, and to detect certain structural defects in the fetus.

Amniocentesis: About 20 cubic centimeters of amniotic fluid are withdrawn from the uterus, as in the figure at the right.

When this procedure is carried out in the 16th week of pregnancy, fetal cells can be evaluated for chromosomal or enzyme disorders. Later in pregnancy, fetal cells can be evaluated for the maturation of the lungs. Serious respiratory disorders can be prevented when cesarean deliveries are delayed until the lungs are adequately developed.

Fetoscopy: The fetus can be examined directly and its blood sampled through a fiber-optic lens inserted into the uterus. This technique permits the diagnosis of genetic disorders, especially blood diseases that cannot be detected in amniotic fluid, so that disorders can be treated surgically and medically before birth.

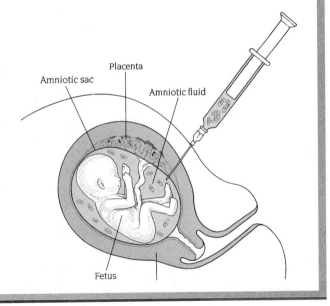

At 25 weeks, the fetus functions well within its uterine environment. It swallows, digests, excretes, moves about, sucks its thumb, rests, and grows. However, the nervous system, which begins to develop at 3 weeks, is still not mature enough to coordinate the many systems that must function simultaneously to ensure survival. With advances in medical technology, a 25-week-old fetus weighing roughly 1000 grams has about a 70% chance of survival if it is placed in an intensive-care neonatal nursery. By 30 weeks, survival outside the uterus is almost certain (Usher, 1987).

Development in the Third Trimester

In the last trimester, the average fetus grows from 10 to 20 inches and increases in weight from 2 to 7 or 7 1/2 pounds. These increases in body size and weight are paralleled by a maturation of the central nervous system. Studies of infants' responses to maternal speech suggest that a fetus experiences its mother's speech sounds during the third trimester and becomes familiar with the sound of her voice (DeCasper & Spence, 1986; Spence & DeCasper, 1987).

The advantages that a full-term fetus has over a premature 28-week-old fetus include (1) the ability to begin and maintain regular breathing, (2) a stronger sucking response, (3) well-coordinated swallowing movements, (4) stronger peristalsis and therefore more efficient digestion and waste excretion, and (5) a more fully balanced control of body temperature.

The full-term infant has been able to take advantage of minerals in the mother's diet for the formation of tooth enamel. As the placenta begins to degenerate in the last month of pregnancy, antibodies against various diseases that have been formed in the mother's blood pass into the fetal bloodstream. They provide the fetus with immunity to many diseases during the first few months of life.

The uterus cannot serve indefinitely as the home of the fetus. Several factors necessitate the eventual termination of the fetal-uterine relationship. First, as the placenta degenerates, antibodies that form in the mother's and the fetus's blood would destroy the blood of the other. Second, because the placenta does not grow much larger than 2 pounds, the fetus, as it reaches its maximum size, cannot obtain enough nutrients to sustain life. Third, the fetal head cannot grow much larger than the pelvic opening without endangering the brain in the birth process. Even though soft connecting membranes permit the skull plates to overlap, head size is a factor that limits fetal growth.

We do not know the exact set of factors that signals the onset of uterine contractions and the birth process. The approximate time from conception to birth is 38 weeks. However, there is a great deal of variability in the duration of pregnancies and in the size of full-term infants, even infants born to the same mother.

The Birth Process

Birth is initiated by involuntary contractions of the uterine muscles referred to as *labor*. The length of time from the beginning of labor to the birth of the infant is highly variable. The average time is 14 hours for women undergoing their first labor (primiparas) and 8 hours for women undergoing later labors (multiparas).

The uterine contractions serve two central functions: effacement and dilation. *Effacement* is the shortening of the cervical canal. *Dilation* is the gradual enlargement of the cervix from an opening only millimeters wide to one of about 10 centimeters—large enough for the baby to pass through. Effacement and dilation occur without deliberate effort by the mother.

Once the cervix is fully enlarged, the mother can assist in the birth by exerting pressure on the abdominal walls of the uterus. The baby, too, helps in the birth process by squirming, turning its head, and pushing against the birth canal.

Stages of Labor

The medical profession describes three stages of labor, two of which are illustrated in Figure 4.7. The first stage begins with the onset of uterine contractions and ends with the full dilation of the cervix; this is the longest stage. The second stage involves the expulsion of the fetus. It begins at full dilation and ends with

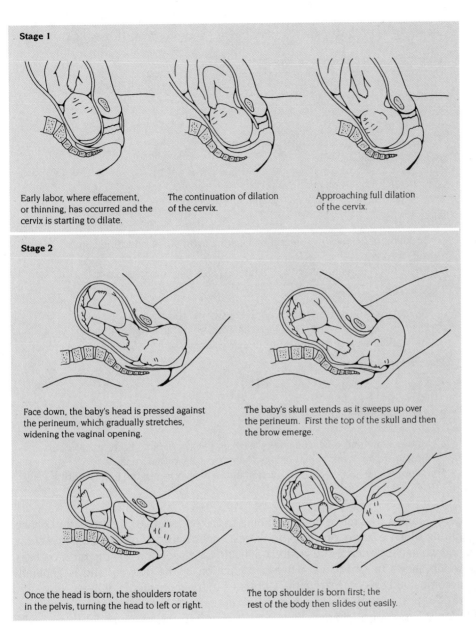

Stage 1

Early labor, where effacement, or thinning, has occurred and the cervix is starting to dilate.

The continuation of dilation of the cervix.

Approaching full dilation of the cervix.

Stage 2

Face down, the baby's head is pressed against the perineum, which gradually stretches, widening the vaginal opening.

The baby's skull extends as it sweeps up over the perineum. First the top of the skull and then the brow emerge.

Once the head is born, the shoulders rotate in the pelvis, turning the head to left or right.

The top shoulder is born first; the rest of the body then slides out easily.

FIGURE 4.7
The first two stages of labor
Source: *Clarke-Stewart & Koch, 1983.*

the delivery of the baby. The third stage begins with delivery and ends with the expulsion of the placenta. This stage usually lasts five to ten minutes.

These three stages of labor do not precisely parallel the personal experience of childbirth. For example, while the birth of the placenta is considered a unique stage of labor in the medical model, it is rarely mentioned in women's accounts of their birth experiences. On the other hand, many of the signs of impending labor that occur in the last weeks of pregnancy may well be viewed as the experiential beginning of labor.

In terms of the psychological adaptation to the birth process, labor can be viewed as having five phases: (1) early signs that labor is approaching; (2) strong, regular uterine contractions signaling that labor has begun and generally

TABLE 4.4   Significant Events of Five Psychological Stages of Labor

Phase 1: Early signs that labor is approaching

1. Lightening (about 10 to 14 days before delivery). The baby's head drops into the pelvic area.
2. Release of the plug that has kept the cervix closed.
3. Discharge of amniotic fluid.
4. False labor: irregular uterine contractions.

Phase 2: Onset of labor

1. Transition from home to hospital or birthing center.
2. Strong, regular contractions 3–5 minutes apart.

Phase 3: Transition

1. Accelerated labor, with contractions lasting up to 90 seconds and coming 2 or 3 minutes apart.
2. Some sense of disorientation, heightened arousal, or loss of control.

Phase 4: Birth

1. The baby's head presses down on the bottom of the birth canal.
2. The mother experiences a strong, reflexive urge to push to expel the baby.
3. The mother typically is moved from a labor area to a more sterile delivery room.

Phase 5: Postpartum period

1. Mother and infant have initial contact.
2. Placenta is expelled.
3. Rapid alteration of the hormone system to stimulate lactation and shrink the uterus.
4. Mother and infant engage in early learning behaviors; infant attempts to nurse; mother explores infant and begins to interpret his or her needs.
5. Return to the home and introduction of the newborn into the family setting.

accompanied by a move from the home to the hospital; (3) the transition phase, during which contractions are strong, rest times between contractions are short, and women experience the greatest difficulty or discomfort; (4) the birth process, which allows the mother's active participation in the delivery and is generally accompanied by a move from the labor area to the more sterile delivery room; and (5) the postpartum period, which involves the initial interactions with the newborn, physiological changes that mark a return to the prepregnant state, and a return home. The significant events of these phases are summarized in Table 4.4.

Cesarean Delivery

Sometimes a normal, spontaneous vaginal delivery is dangerous to the mother or the newborn (Cunningham et al., 1989). One alternative is to remove the baby surgically through an incision in the uterine wall. The procedure is named after the Roman emperor Julius Caesar, who, legend has it, was delivered this way. The likelihood that he was actually delivered surgically is questionable, since until as late as the 17th century the operation was usually fatal to mothers.

The incidence of cesarean deliveries in the United States increased from 5.5% of births in 1970 to 24% in 1990 (Burt, Vaughan & Daling, 1988; *Healthy People* 2000, 1990). The procedure may be used if labor is severely prolonged and the fetus appears to be at risk for lack of oxygen. It may also be used when the infant is in the breech position (feet or buttocks first rather than head first) or if the mother's pelvis is too small for the infant's head to pass through.

It is still standard procedure to deliver a baby by cesarean if the mother has had such an operation before. However, this practice may vary by region. With the physician's approval, some women do have vaginal deliveries after they have had a cesarean delivery.

The cesarean delivery makes childbirth a surgical procedure, requiring anesthetics, intravenous feeding of the mother, and a prolonged recovery period. Although the procedure undoubtedly saves many infants and mothers who would not survive vaginal childbirth, there is concern that it is being misused for the convenience of health professionals, or of busy mothers who want to be able to schedule deliveries and thus avoid waiting for the unpredictable onset of labor. The U.S. Public Health Service goal statement *Healthy People* 2000 (1990) calls for a reduction of the national cesarean rate to 15%, a goal implying that a substantial number of the current cesarean procedures are not required.

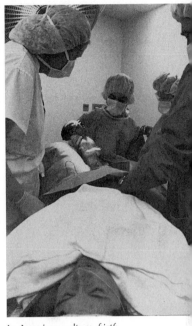

In American culture, birth usually takes place in a specially equipped delivery room and includes the use of certain technologies, like the forceps, which is used to aid in difficult deliveries. You can see the forceps' marks on the baby's head.

Some scholars have begun to examine the impact of the cesarean delivery on both the newborn and the parents. At this point, it appears that in the short run—that is, within five minutes after birth—babies delivered by cesarean are more likely to show signs of risk than babies delivered vaginally. This difference holds for babies who are delivered by repeat cesarean section, and who therefore are not at risk in other ways (Burt et al., 1988). However, long-term follow-ups of babies delivered by cesarean section find no effects on the child's IQ or standardized math and verbal test scores (Entwisle & Alexander, 1987).

The effects of cesarean delivery on parents can be seen in the findings of two studies. In one, mothers whose children had been delivered by cesarean section expressed greater dissatisfaction with the childbirth experience itself than mothers whose children had been born vaginally. However, they did not show more problems in postpartum adjustment. Their levels of anxiety, depression, and perceptions of their competence as mothers were about the same as those of mothers who had had a more normal delivery. Both the mothers and the fathers of babies delivered by cesarean section tended to be more involved in the parental role. They viewed their children in a more positive light and had higher expectations of their children's school success than other parents (Padawer et al., 1988).

The other study showed that parents' expectations concerning a child's academic ability and school success appear to be a long-term outcome of the birth experience and have a significant influence on the child's own expectations of school performance in the first and second grades (Entwisle & Alexander, 1987). One explanation suggested for these findings is that the special difficulties associated with childbirth increase the commitment the parents make to their child. We must be careful not to overgeneralize the results of the research, but the implication that involvement in parenting is related to difficulties associated with childbirth deserves further study.

Infant Mortality

The *infant mortality rate* is the number of infants who die during the first year of life per 1000 live births during that year. In 1991, the U.S. rate was estimated at 10.3 deaths per 1000 live births, a mortality rate that was equaled only by that of the 55-to-64-year-old age group and older. Although the infant mortality rate has declined for both the white and the black populations, the rate for black babies was just about as high in 1989 (17.7 deaths per 1000 live births) as that for white babies in 1970 (17.8 deaths per 1000; U.S. Bureau of the Census, 1992). Roughly two-thirds of infant deaths occur during the first month after birth. Most of those who die have severe birth defects, are very premature, or experience *sudden infant death syndrome* in which apparently healthy babies are put to bed and are later found dead with no clear explanation, even after autopsy (Clayman, 1989).

Infant mortality rates are influenced by many factors, including (1) the frequency of birth complications; (2) the robustness of the infants who are being born, which is influenced by their prenatal nutrition and degree of exposure to viruses or bacteria, damaging X rays, drugs, and other teratogens; (3) the mother's age; and (4) the facilities that are available for prenatal and newborn care. One-fourth of infant deaths result from complications associated with low birth weight. If the conditions leading to prematurity could be altered, our infant mortality rate would be significantly improved (Wilcox & Skjoerven, 1992).

Infant mortality rates vary from one country and region of the world to another. In 1991, the infant mortality rate in Japan was 4.4, but in that same year, the mortality rate in 13 countries of the world was over 120. The United States, with all its resources and advanced technology, in fact, ranks behind 21 other industrialized countries, including Australia, Austria, Canada, Denmark, France, Israel, Spain, Hong Kong, and Japan. Within the United States, regional infant mortality rates range from a low of 6.8 per 1000 in Vermont to a high of 23.2 per 1000 in the District of Columbia (U.S. Bureau of the Census, 1992).

The density of low-income population, the availability of educational materials on the impact of diet and drugs on the developing fetus, and the adequacy of the medical facilities for high-risk newborns all contribute to the regional variations in infant death rates among populations of different incomes. Children conceived in poverty are at the greatest risk. Their mothers receive poorer quality prenatal care, and as we will see in the sections to follow, they are exposed to more factors during the prenatal period that jeopardize their survival than are children conceived in more advantaged families. The chances that any one infant will survive the stresses of birth depend on the convergence of biological, environmental, cultural, and economic influences on his or her intrauterine growth, delivery, and postnatal care (Polednak, 1991).

The Mother, the Fetus, and the Psychosocial Environment

The course and pattern of prenatal development are directly guided by genetic information. Yet we cannot ignore the psychosocial environment in which pregnant women are embedded. A woman's attitudes toward pregnancy and childbirth, her lifestyle, the resources available to her during her pregnancy, and the behavior demanded of her by her culture all influence her sense of well-being. Many of these same factors may directly affect the health and growth of the fetus.

The Impact of the Fetus on the Pregnant Woman

Consider some of the ways in which a fetus influences a pregnant woman. Being pregnant alters a woman's body image and her sense of well-being. Some women feel especially vigorous and energetic during much of their pregnancy. Other women experience distressing symptoms such as nausea, backache, swelling, headache, and irritability. In some cases, pregnancy is accompanied by serious illnesses that threaten the mother's health.

Changes in Roles and Social Status

Women who become pregnant may be treated in new ways by their significant partners. Usually, fathers become more concerned for and supportive of their pregnant partners, and pregnant women may also be viewed in a new light by their peers. In some communities, adolescent girls who become pregnant feel ashamed or guilty. In others, becoming pregnant during adolescence is viewed by the peer group as an accomplishment—a sign of maturity. In the world of work, women who become pregnant may be given fewer responsibilities or may be passed over for promotions. In business settings, pregnancy may be viewed as an annoyance, something that is likely to interfere with productivity and is at best to be tolerated.

Within the family, a pregnant woman is likely to be treated with new levels of concern and care. Her pregnancy affects her spouse, her parents, her siblings, and her in-laws. By giving birth to a first child, a woman transforms her husband into a father, her mother and father into grandparents, and her brothers and sisters into uncles and aunts. Being pregnant may alter the gender identity of the baby's mother and/or father: Becoming pregnant may be viewed as confirmation of a woman's femininity, impregnating a woman may represent confirmation of a man's virility (Heitlinger, 1989).

In some societies, pregnancy and childbirth confer special status on a woman. In Japan, for example, traditional values place motherhood above all other women's roles: "Only after giving birth to a child did a woman become a fully tenured person in the family" (Bankart, 1989). When they become mothers, Japanese women begin to have an impact on government, community, and public life as the people who are specially responsible for molding and shaping the next generation. For Mexican-American women, childbearing is likely to be viewed within a broad religious context: "It is considered the privilege and essential obligation of a married woman to bear children. But children come 'when God is willing'" (Hahn & Muecke, 1987).

Changes in the Mother's Emotional State

Women have emotional as well as physical reactions to pregnancy. Pregnancy is listed as the 12th most stressful life change in a list of 43 life events in the Social Readjustment Rating Scale (Holmes & Rahe, 1967). The woman's attitude toward her unborn child may be pride, acceptance, rejection, or—as is usually the case—ambivalence. In most normal pregnancies, women experience anxiety and depression as well as positive feelings of excitement and hopefulness. The normal physical changes during the gestational period include symptoms that are often associated with depression, such as fatigue, sleeplessness, slowed physical movement, preoccupation with one's physical state, and moodiness (Kaplan, 1986). In addition, throughout the pregnancy, the woman has recurring worries about whether the baby will be healthy and whether the delivery will go smoothly.

Certain psychosocial factors are associated with increased anxiety and depression during pregnancy. Women who are having marital difficulties, who do not have adequate social support during pregnancy, and who have conflict about their own personal identity are likely to experience greater emotional stress (Fleming et al., 1988). It is possible that strong emotional reactions, such as prolonged anxiety or depression, may influence the fetal environment directly through the secretion of maternal hormones that cross the placental barrier.

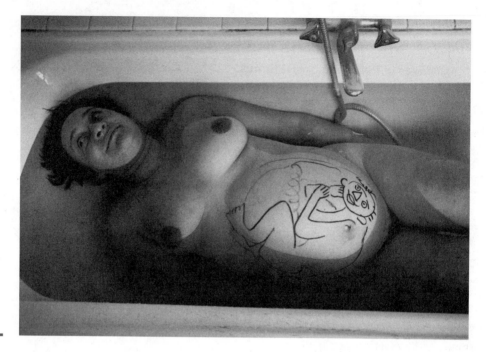

Sometimes, being pregnant brings out a woman's special sense of humor. It looks as if Florence just couldn't wait to get a glimpse of baby Theo.

However, evidence in this regard is mixed (Sameroff & Chandler, 1975/1992; Vaughn et al., 1987). The evidence is much clearer that the mother's emotional state during pregnancy is related to her experiences during labor and to her subsequent parenting behaviors.

A woman's feelings about her femininity, her attitudes toward the unborn child, and her psychological stability are associated with difficulties experienced during pregnancy and labor. Women who have more stable personalities and a positive orientation toward pregnancy react more favorably to the stresses of labor than do anxious, irritable women, who are more likely to have longer labors and more labor or delivery room complications. During delivery, women who are very anxious tend to request and receive more medication, which may influence the responsiveness of their newborn infants (Yang et al., 1976; Standley, Soule & Copans, 1979).

The contribution of maternal anxiety to complications during labor and delivery was studied with a group of Guatemalan women (Sosa et al., 1980). The hospital normally did not permit any visitors to remain with an expectant woman on the maternity ward. Each woman in this study, however, was assigned a companion who stayed with her until delivery, talking to the woman, holding her hand, rubbing her back, and providing emotional support during labor. These mothers had fewer complications during labor than a group of women who had no companion, and their babies showed fewer signs of fetal distress. The mean length of labor was more than ten hours shorter for those women who had a companion than for those who were alone during labor.

The mother's emotional state during pregnancy has an impact beyond the events of childbirth. Women who experience notable depression during pregnancy are more likely to continue feeling depressed in the months after giving birth. Studies of these mothers show that they have difficulty feeling attached to their babies, they are more likely to feel out of control or incompetent in their parenting, and they exhibit fewer affectionate behaviors toward their infants (Fleming et al., 1988; Field et al., 1985).

In interaction with depressed mothers, infants are less playful, show less

---

BOX 4.3

Couvade

Some cultures observe the formal practice of *couvade*, in which the expectant father takes to his bed and observes very specific taboos during the period shortly before birth. Among the Arapesh of New Guinea, childbearing is believed to place as heavy a burden and drain of energy on the father as on the mother. Some cultures believe that by following the ritual couvade, the fathers distract the attention of evil spirits so that the mother and the baby can pass through the childbirth transition more safely (Helman, 1990).

Even in groups that do not practice the ritual couvade, it is common to find men experiencing some couvade symptoms, such as general fatigue, stomach cramps, nausea, dizziness, or backache. Trethowan (1972), one of the first to document the nature and extent of couvade symptoms in the normal population, suggested that these physical symptoms are a product of a man's emotional ambivalence toward his wife. The expectant father may experience empathy and identify with his wife's pregnant state. At the same time, he may experience some jealousy of his wife, resentment of the loss or potential loss of intimacy in their relationship, repulsion by his wife's physical appearance, or some envy of his wife's ability to bear a child. These psychological conflicts, many of which are probably unconscious or unexpressed, are amplified by an expectant father's conscious worries about the health and well-being of his wife and their baby. The combination of these stresses may produce the couvade syndrome.

---

activity, and express fewer signs of contentment, fewer face-to-face interactions, and less imitation of their mothers than do babies of nondepressed mothers (Field et al., 1985). At 3 months, infants of depressed mothers show similar characteristics even in interaction with nondepressed adults, a finding suggesting that a "depressed" temperamental social style has developed (Field et al., 1988). This research still leaves the question of causality unanswered. Is the impact of maternal depression on the infant the result of genetic influences, the presence of hormones associated with the mother's depression in the prenatal environment, the style of mothering characteristic of depressed women, or some cumulative effect of these factors?

Fathers' Involvement in Childbirth

Trends in the United States have leaned dramatically toward greater involvement of the father during labor and delivery. Husbands often attend childbirth classes with their wives to learn to assist them during the delivery.

The father's presence is clearly a great comfort to the pregnant woman during delivery. When the father is present, women tend to have shorter labors, report experiencing less pain, use less medication, and feel more positive about themselves and their childbirth experience (Grossman et al., 1980). Fathers also describe their participation in the birth as a peak experience. However, research does not permit us to conclude that fathers who participate in the birth experience have a more intimate relationship with their children than fathers who are not present at the birth (Palkovitz, 1985; Palm & Palkovitz, 1988).

The Impact of the Pregnant Woman on the Fetus

Among the factors that influence the fetus's development are the mother's age, her use of drugs during pregnancy and delivery, her exposure to environmental toxins, and her diet. The quality of a pregnant woman's physical and emotional health before and during pregnancy is linked to her own knowledge about and

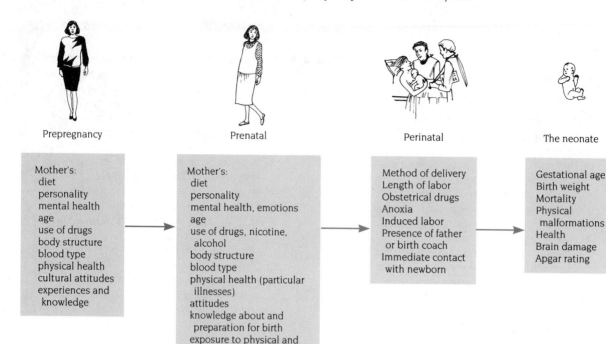

FIGURE 4.8

Factors that influence prenatal development and the status of the neonate
Source: Clarke-Stewart & Koch, 1983.

preparation for pregnancy, as well as to her culture's attitudes and practices associated with childbearing. These factors are summarized in Figure 4.8. One of the most powerful, overarching influences of the psychosocial environment on fetal development is poverty. Embedded in the conditions of poverty are many of the individual factors associated with suboptimal prenatal development.

Mother's Age

The capacity for childbearing begins about 1 year to 1 1/2 years after the beginning of menarche (the beginning of regular menstrual periods) and ends at the end of the climacteric (the ending of regular menstrual periods). Thus, a woman is potentially fertile for about 35 years during her lifetime. Pregnancy and childbirth may occur at any or many points during this period. The effects of childbirth on the physical and psychological well-being of a mother vary with her age and her emotional commitment to the mother role. Similarly, these factors contribute significantly to the survival and well-being of her infant.

Women between the ages of 16 and 35 tend to provide a better uterine environment and to give birth with fewer complications than do women under 16 or over 35. Particularly when it is their first pregnancy, women over 35 are likely to have a longer labor than younger women, and labor is more likely to result in the death of either the infant or the mother. The two groups with the highest probability of giving birth to premature babies are women over 35 and those under 16 (Schuster, 1986).

Premature children of teenage mothers are more likely than those of older mothers to have neurological defects that will influence their coping capacities. Also, mothers under 16 tend to receive less adequate prenatal care and to be less biologically mature. Consequently, adolescent mothers are more likely to experience complications during pregnancy that may endanger their infants and

TABLE 4.5	Live Birthrates by Age of Mother, 1960–1989 (Births per 1000 Women)						
Year	10–14	15–19	20–24	25–29	30–34	35–39	40–44
1960	0.8	89.1	258.1	197.4	112.7	56.2	15.5
1965	0.8	70.5	195.3	161.6	94.4	46.2	12.8
1970	1.2	68.3	167.8	145.1	73.3	31.7	8.1
1975	1.3	56.3	114.7	110.3	53.1	19.4	4.6
1980	1.1	53.0	115.1	112.9	61.9	19.8	3.9
1986	1.3	50.6	108.2	109.2	69.3	24.3	4.1
1989	1.4	58.1	115.4	116.6	76.2	29.7	5.2

Source: U.S. Bureau of the Census, 1986, 1989, 1992.

themselves. Evidence suggests that good medical care, nutrition, and social support improve the childbirth experiences of adolescent mothers who are *over* 16. However, the physical immaturity of those under 16 puts the mother and the infant at greater risk (Quilligan, 1983; Roosa, 1984).

A primary risk for infants of mothers who are over 40 is Down syndrome (Moore, 1988). It is hypothesized that some part of the high incidence of Down syndrome among older women is the result of deteriorating ova. However, older women are also likely to have male partners who are their age or older. Even though the male's sperm are produced anew daily, some evidence suggests that among older men the rate of genetically defective sperm increases. Thus, aging in one or both partners may contribute to the increased incidence of Down syndrome babies born to older women. These explanations are not entirely satisfactory, since older women who have had multiple births are not as likely to have a Down syndrome child as are women who are having their first child at an older age. What is more, many Down syndrome babies are born to women who are under 35. It is likely that in some cases the syndrome is a result of errors that occur during cell division, and that in others it is a result of a genetically transmitted condition.

Adolescents do not appear to be as aware as older women of the risks inherent in early childbirth. In 1989, about 518,000 babies were born to women under 20. Over 400,000 legal abortions were performed for women under 20, accounting for 26% of all induced abortions (U.S. Bureau of the Census, 1992).

Table 4.5 shows the rate of live births to women across the age range 10–44 from 1960 through 1989. There were declines over this 29-year period in every age range except the youngest. However, from 1986 to 1989, there was an increase in the birthrates for all age groups. Two other observations about the data presented in Table 4.5 are relevant to our understanding of adult life. First, since 1960 the trend has shifted from a higher birthrate at the ages 20–24 to a slightly higher birth rate at ages 25–29. Second, the decline in the overall birthrate is also expressed in a reduction of the childbearing period: In 1989, far fewer children were being born to women 30 years and older than was the case in 1960. From 1980 to 1989, the number of children born to each 1000 women 30 years old and over rose. However, this increase does not come close to returning to the levels of childbearing in the older age ranges that was characteristic of the early 1960s.

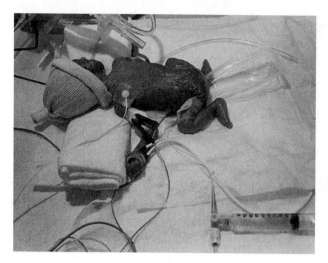

This premature, cocaine-addicted infant will struggle to survive the negative effects of the prenatal environment.

In later chapters, we will discuss the psychosocial consequences of childbearing for adolescents and adults. Here, we want to emphasize that the pattern of fetal development, the quality of prenatal care, and the degree of risk during childbirth are all associated with the age of the mother during pregnancy.

Maternal Drug Use

The range of drugs used by pregnant women is enormous. Iron, diuretics, antibiotics, hormones, tranquilizers, appetite suppressants, and other drugs are being either prescribed or taken voluntarily by pregnant women. In addition, women influence the fetal environment through their voluntary use of such drugs as alcohol, nicotine, caffeine, marijuana, cocaine, and other narcotics (Chasnoff, 1988). Studies of the effects of specific drugs on fetal growth suggest that many drugs ingested by pregnant women are in fact metabolized in the placenta and transmitted to the fetus. What is more, although the impact of a specific dosage of a drug on the pregnant woman may be minimal, the impact on the fetus may be quite dramatic.

In reviewing the following sections on the impact of drugs on fetal development, two principles must be considered. First, evidence suggests that genetic predisposition may make some developing fetuses more vulnerable than others to the negative effects of certain drugs or toxins. Data on this point are clear in animal studies because animals are more likely to have litters of offspring, some of which show greater resilience to the presence of prenatal teratogens than others (Vorhees & Mollnow, 1987). Second, especially when we consider disruption to the central nervous system, most teratogens do not have an all-or-none impact. The consequence of exposure varies by the dosage, the duration of exposure, and the timing of exposure.

Nicotine   Babies born to women who smoke during pregnancy weigh less than those born to nonsmoking mothers. A review of 45 studies on this relationship reported that babies born to smokers weighed an average of 200 grams less than babies born to nonsmokers (U.S. Department of Heath, Education, and Welfare, 1979). Women who smoke are at greater risk for miscarriages and stillbirths (Streissguth et al., 1989; Armstrong, McDonald & Sloan, 1992). Neurological examinations of babies exposed to nicotine during the prenatal period showed decreased levels of arousal and responsiveness at 9 and 30 days after birth (Fried et al., 1987).

Alcohol   The evidence is conclusive that alcohol is a teratogen. Prenatal exposure to alcohol can influence brain development, interfere with cell development and organization, and modify the production of neurotransmitters, which are critical to the maturation of the central nervous system (West, 1986). The complex impact of alcohol on fetal development has been given the name *fetal alcohol syndrome* (Jones et al., 1973; Clarren & Smith, 1978; Abel, 1984). Fetal alcohol syndrome is associated with disorders of the central nervous system, low birth weight, and malformations of the face, eyes, ears, and mouth. The risk of fetal alcohol syndrome for infants born to women who drink heavily—that is, about 1.5 ounces or more of alcohol a day—is 30%–50%. Even moderate daily alcohol use can produce some of these symptoms, especially if the drinking is combined with malnutrition. At a rate of 1 to 3 infants affected per 1000 live births, fetal alcohol syndrome is the greatest source of environmentally caused disruption to the prenatal central nervous system (Voorhees & Mollnow, 1987).

In a longitudinal study of the effects of prenatal exposure to alcohol, children born to mothers who consumed 1.5 ounces of alcohol (one average-strength drink) daily during pregnancy showed significantly lower IQ scores at age 4 than did children whose mothers used little or no alcohol (Streissguth et al., 1989). Alcohol use was a significant predictor of reduced IQ scores, even when many other factors—the mother's educational level, the child's birth order, the family's socioeconomic level, the child's involvement in preschool, and the quality of the mother-child interaction—were taken into account. In other words, the many environmental variables that are known to have a positive effect on a young child's intellectual functioning did not compensate for the insult to the central nervous system associated with exposure to alcohol during gestation. We emphasize the risks associated with prenatal exposure to alcohol because alcohol is so widely used in American society, and what many adults consider to be a "safe" or socially acceptable amount of alcohol can have a negative effect on the fetus.

Caffeine   Caffeine freely crosses the placenta. Caffeine is commonly consumed in coffee, certain sodas, and tea. Heavy caffeine consumption—defined in one study as more than 300 milligrams, or roughly three cups of coffee per day or more—is associated with an increased risk of low birth weight, and there is a modest relationship to prematurity. Infants born to women who reduced the amount of caffeine they drank after the sixth week of pregnancy showed no ill effects associated with early caffeine consumption (Fenster et al., 1991; McDonald, Armstrong & Sloan, 1992).

Narcotics   The use of narcotics, especially heroin and cocaine, as well as methadone (a drug used in the treatment of heroin addiction), has been linked to increased risks of birth defects and low birth weight and to higher rates of infant mortality (Dinges, Davis & Glass, 1980; Zuckerman et al., 1989). Infants who have been prenatally exposed to opiates, cocaine, and methadone show a pattern of extreme irritability, high-pitched crying that is evidence of neurological disorganization, fever, sleep disturbances, feeding problems, muscle spasms, and tremors (Hans, 1987). These babies are at high risk for *sudden infant death syndrome*. Longer-range studies find that children who were exposed to addictive drugs in the prenatal period continue to show problems in fine-motor coordination, have difficulty focusing and sustaining their attention, and, perhaps as a result, have more school adjustment problems. Of course, it is difficult to separate the direct prenatal effects of these drugs on the nervous system from effects after birth associated with being parented by a drug-using mother or the effects on parenting of the social and educational environment in which the mother herself may have developed.

In the 1980s, the widespread use of crack, an inexpensive, smokable form of cocaine, dramatically increased the number of cases of cocaine-exposed babies, especially in major cities such as New York, Los Angeles, Detroit, and Washington, D.C. In a survey, 18 large hospitals in 15 large cities reported increases in the numbers of cocaine-exposed babies during the second half of the 1980s. Estimates range from 30,000 to 100,000 crack-exposed babies born annually (Gittler & McPherson, 1991).

Because of the widespread abuse of cocaine, some law-enforcement officials are arresting and charging women who have exposed their unborn infants to these harmful and illegal substances (Sachs, 1989). A woman who gave birth to her second cocaine-addicted infant in Hollywood, Florida, was arrested and charged with child abuse, and her baby was placed in foster care. Prosecutors want to hold pregnant women responsible for behavior that jeopardizes their infants' health. In 19 states, laws have been passed that allow criminal charges to be filed against women who give birth to babies who have illegal substances in their blood. Several states have tried taking babies away from these mothers. This action poses an extremely difficult moral dilemma. Those who oppose such actions argue that alcohol use, smoking, and other forms of maternal behavior also have known negative effects on the developing fetus. Should women who use these substances be charged with child abuse? What is more, can we ensure that the babies taken from these mothers and placed in foster care will do better than they would have done in the care of their birth mothers (Willwerth, 1991; Feinman, 1992)?

A concern associated with intravenous drug use is the spread of the human immunodeficiency virus (HIV) and the acquired immunodeficiency syndrome (AIDS) from pregnant women to their unborn children. About 70% of women with HIV infection have been infected through their own drug use or that of a sex partner. The relationship of cocaine use, prostitution, and sexually transmitted diseases, including AIDS, is posing a growing health risk to unborn children, especially among poor urban minorities (Judson, 1989; Darney et al., 1989). Children born to mothers who have the HIV virus have about a 50% chance of developing the disease, and 95% of those infected die within the first three years of life. At present, there is no way to treat babies infected with AIDS. Because their immune system is deficient or inoperative, they cannot fight off the many infections that babies typically encounter (Seabrook, 1987).

Prescription Drugs   Other drugs are administered to women during pregnancy as part of the treatment for a medical condition. The tragic outcome of the use of thalidomide for the treatment of morning sickness in the 1960s alerted us to the potential danger of certain chemicals to the fetus, particularly during the period of fetal differentiation and growth in the first trimester. Thalidomide taken

Pregnancy and the Prenatal Period

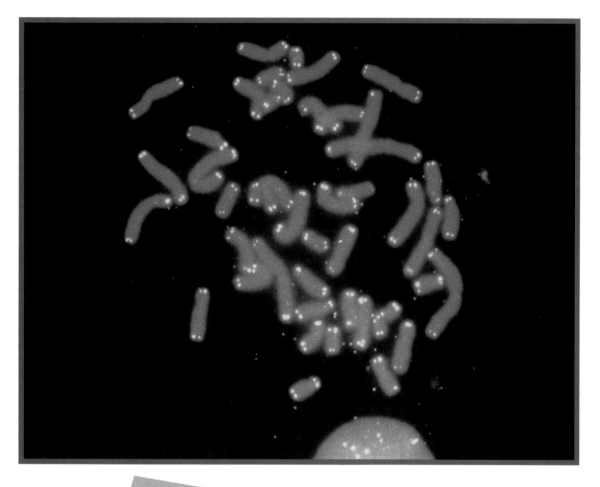

The chromosomes shown are in metaphase, each having replicated but not yet divided. The bright yellow spots at the ends of each chromosome are the telomeres. These end segments do not carry genes but help preserve the integrity of the chromosome as it is duplicated again and again.

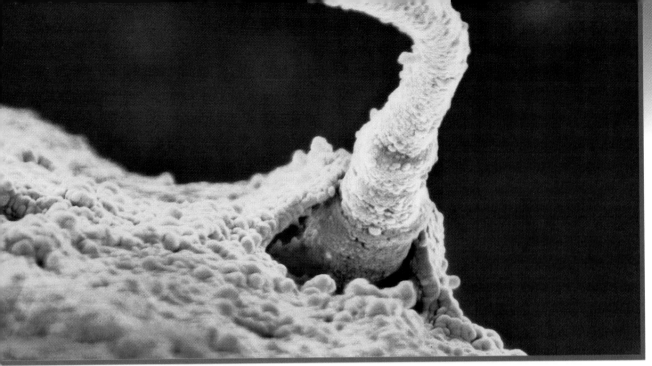

At the moment of conception, the sperm breaks through the lining of the egg and the genetic material from the two gametes combines.

As the fertilized egg begins to divide, it travels along the fallopian tube toward the uterus.

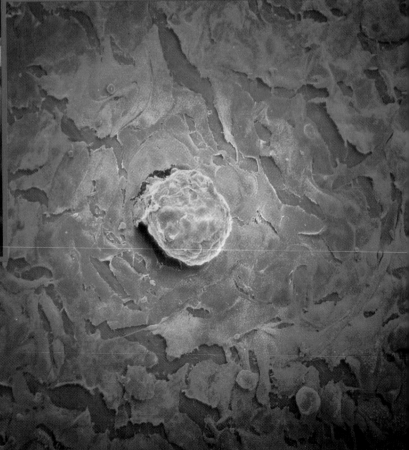

By the sixth day after fertilization, the zygote begins to implant in the thickened lining of the uterine wall. Once the zygote is implanted, the amniotic sac and the placenta begin to form.

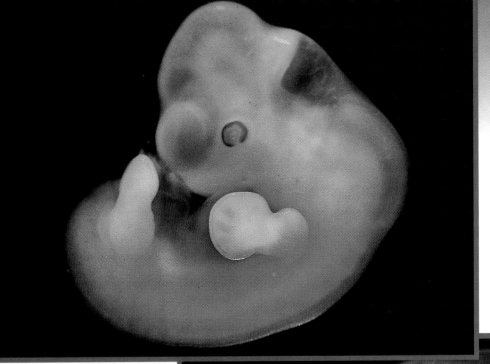

At 5½ weeks, cell differentiation has resulted in an embryo that is about 0.4 inch (1 cm) long. You can identify the emerging shapes of the head, arm, and fingers. At this stage, the human embryo is similar in many ways to other embryonic vertebrates.

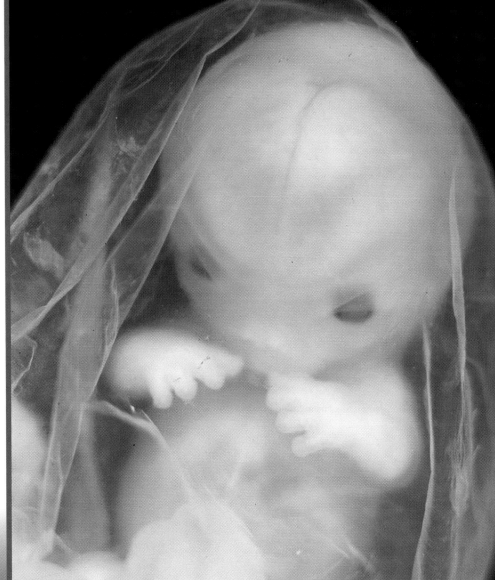

At 8 weeks, the fingers are clearly differentiated and the hand is distinct from the forearm. Reflexes sometimes guide the hand toward the face.

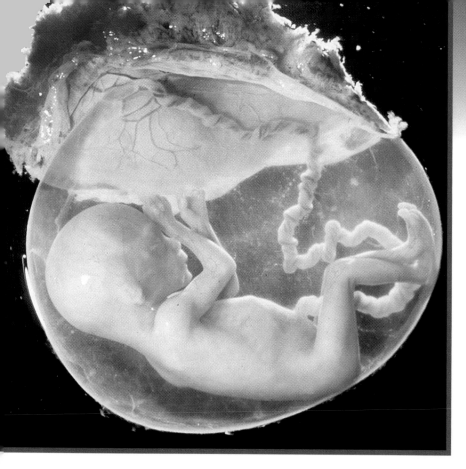

At 16 weeks, the fetus is about 6.4 inches (16 cm) long and is clearly recognizable as a human child. The fetus has assumed what is known as the "fetal position"—arms curled up near the head and legs bent in toward the stomach—a position that remains part of the human behavioral repertoire throughout life.

At 23 weeks, the fetus is about 12 inches (30 cm) long, still small enough to have room to swim about in the expanding uterus. As any pregnant woman will tell you, the fetus is active at this stage, kicking, grasping, waving its arms, and turning over.

during the 21st to 36th days after conception can cause gross deformities of the baby's limbs.

Some drugs are administered to help sustain the pregnancy. In one case, a group of boys whose mothers had been treated during pregnancy with estrogen and progesterone were studied when they were 6 and 16 years old. At both ages, the boys showed lower ratings in aggressiveness and athletic ability than a matched sample of boys whose mothers had not been treated with these female hormones (Yalom, Green & Fisk, 1973). In another case, a sample of 119 women were treated with prednisone, first to alleviate infertility and then to maintain their pregnancies. The birth weight of their babies was significantly lower than that of the babies of a control group. Both male and female children who are exposed to testosterone-type hormones prenatally show more masculine-style behavior and respond in a more masculine way on tests of personality, gender role, and work and family values (Reinisch & Karow, 1977; Reinisch & Sanders, 1984). The effects of some kinds of drugs may persist for a long time after birth, either by directly altering the central nervous system or by influencing the pattern of caregiver-infant interactions.

Environmental Toxins

As more and more women enter the work force and assume nontraditional work roles, concern about the hazards of work settings for fetal development continues to grow. In an Allied Chemical plant, fear that fluorocarbon 22 might cause fetal damage led to the layoff of five women workers. Two of those women chose to be sterilized in order to hold their jobs (Bronson, 1979). Wives of men who are employed in hazardous environments may also experience higher rates of miscarriage, sterility, and birth defects in their babies (Howes & Krakow, 1977). In one study, fathers' exposure to specific solvents and chemicals at work was linked to higher rates of spontaneous abortions among their wives (Lindbohm et al., 1991).

The workplace is not the only setting in which pregnant women may be exposed to environmental toxins. Women who regularly ate a large amount of polluted Lake Michigan fish for six years before they became pregnant had infants who showed certain memory deficits at 7 months of age (Jacobson et al., 1985). Although the level of these toxins—industrial waste products found in air, water, and soil—had no measurable effects on the mothers, it was high enough to influence central nervous system functioning in the fetuses. This finding makes it clear that all communities must be sensitive to the quality of their water, air, and soil. Each unborn generation depends on its predecessors for protection from these environmental hazards.

Research must continue on the effects of substances that are potentially toxic to fetuses. Although the danger to young children of exposure to lead is well documented, the effects of various levels of exposure on infants and young children are still ill defined (Schroeder, 1987). The potential harm to developing fetuses by herbicides and pesticides used in forests and farmlands is also arousing concern (Morris, 1987). Many of these products are discovered to be teratogens only after abnormal reproductive outcomes have been systematically documented over several years.

Obstetric Anesthetics

The study of the effects on the newborn of drugs used during delivery provides further evidence of the infant's dependence on the immediate environment. Initially, pain-relieving drugs were used for the benefit and convenience of mother and physician, and their effects on the newborn were not noticed. However, evidence suggests that the kind, amount, and timing of anesthetic use in delivery are all factors that may induce neonatal depression and affect the coping capacities of newborns (Stechler & Halton, 1982; Naulty, 1987). When babies whose mothers had received medication during labor were compared with babies whose mothers had not, the first group was observed to perform less well on measures of perception, motor skills, and attentiveness (Brackbill et al., 1974).

There appear to be two points of view about the seriousness of this problem. Research has shown that a range of drugs, including tranquilizers, local anesthetics, and general anesthetics administered by inhalation, may interfere with the baby's behavior. The use of anesthetic drugs during delivery has been found to interfere with the infant's ability to habituate to a stimulus (that is, to stop responding after repeated presentations of the stimulus); to reduce the infant's smiling and cuddliness; and to reduce alert responses to new stimuli. Furthermore, the relationship between drug use and some infant behavior has been observed to last as long as 28 days (Aleksandrowicz & Aleksandrowicz, 1974; Brackbill, 1977; Murray et al., 1981).

Some researchers, on the other hand, view the relationship of drug use in delivery to newborn behavior as minimal. In one study, three aspects of the pregnancy—maternal attitudes about the pregnancy, the length of labor, and the use of medication—were related to infant behavior (Yang et al., 1976). The more irritable or depressed the mother was, the more drugs she used. The more drugs used, and the earlier they were used, the longer was the first stage of labor, and the greater was the drugs' influence on the newborn's behavior, although this influence did not have strong or long-lasting effects. It may not be the drugs themselves that have a lasting impact on the newborn; rather, the behavioral effects of the drugs may influence the mother's perceptions of the newborn, which may alter the quality of the early infant-caregiver relationship (Lester, Als & Brazelton, 1982).

Research on the susceptibility of newborns to drugs alerts us to the potential impact of a wide range of substances on an immature and rapidly changing infant. Evidence of the effects of food additives on newborns and of chemical pollutants on both fetuses and newborns warns us that infants may have unique sensitivities to the environment that may not be observed in older children or adults (Giacoia & Yaffe, 1987).

Mother's Diet

The notion that no matter what the pregnant woman eats, the fetus will get what it needs for growth is simply not true. Providing adequate nutrition for fetal development requires both a balanced diet and the capacity to transform nutrients into a form that the fetus can ingest. The placenta takes care of the latter process. The mother must take care of the former (Lindblad, 1987).

Experimental research on the effects of maternal malnutrition on fetal development has been conducted primarily with rats. Fetal rats exposed to a low-protein diet had lower body and brain weights, fewer cerebral cells, and less cerebral protein than rats whose mothers received a normal diet. In most of these experimental studies, few of the offspring survived birth or lived to adulthood, and the reproductive behavior of those that did survive was greatly reduced. Thus, the experimental evidence suggests that severe malnutrition interferes with normal fetal and postnatal development (Coursin, 1974).

The effects of maternal malnutrition on the developing human fetus remain a topic of scientific controversy. Some experts suggest that birth weight is affected only when the mother experiences starvation or dramatically inadequate nutrition during the last trimester of pregnancy (Cassady & Strange, 1987). Others argue that malnutrition during the phase of cell division results in smaller organ size that cannot be reversed by later dietary supplements (Brazelton, 1987).

Most of the data on the effects of malnutrition on human fetal growth have come from the impact of disasters and crises, such as famines, wars, and extreme poverty, that prevent access to adequate diets. Malnutrition is inferred from the baby's low birth weight in comparison with his or her *gestational age* (the age of the fetus from the time of conception until birth). Babies who are small for their gestational age have a higher mortality rate, more complications during post-delivery care, and a higher risk of mental or motor impairment than do babies who are of average weight for their gestational age (Cassady & Strange, 1987). The relative contribution of malnutrition to these outcomes is difficult to assess. Women who experience these conditions encounter other stresses—increased exposure to disease, anxiety, and exposure to environmental toxins—that may also affect fetal growth.

A child may be malnourished during pregnancy, after birth, or both. Although some degree of growth retardation is hypothesized to occur if a fetus is malnourished, the most severe impact on growth occurs when resources are inadequate both before and after the child is born (Brasel, 1974). This is the case in many poverty-stricken areas of the world. When prenatal malnutrition is followed by postnatal malnutrition and disease, it is impossible to study the effects of prenatal malnutrition alone.

Studies that have been designed to intervene by supplementing diet during pregnancy have provided mixed evidence that a pregnant woman's diet can be successfully modified to increase the newborn's weight. When Guatemalan mothers were able to consume 20,000 additional calories during the nine months of pregnancy, their babies were an average of 0.2 kilograms (7 ounces) heavier than the babies born to mothers whose diets had not been supplemented (Habicht et al., 1974). However, controlled studies involving samples in the United States have not found meaningful improvement in the birth weights of babies born to mothers who were receiving dietary supplements (Cassady & Strange, 1987).

Some effects of malnutrition can be offset after birth. Infants' growth potential allows those who have access to food to make up for their slowed prenatal growth (Tanner, 1990). With access to an adequate diet after birth, infants who were malnourished at birth show increased activity, make greater demands on the environment, and prompt more active caregiving responses (Brazelton, 1987). This pattern of interaction may offset the initial deficits brought about by an inadequate prenatal nutritional environment.

The Impact of Poverty

Perhaps the most powerful psychosocial factor that influences the life chances of the developing fetus is poverty. Poor women are likely to experience the cumulative effects of many of the factors associated with infant mortality and developmental vulnerabilities (Swyer, 1987): Poverty is linked to poor prenatal care. Poor women are likely to begin having babies at an earlier age and to have repeated pregnancies into their later adult years, both practices that are associated with low-birth-weight infants. Women who have had little education are less likely to be aware of the risks of smoking, alcohol, and drug use for their babies and are more likely to use or abuse these substances. Poor women are less likely to have been vaccinated against some of the infectious diseases, such as rubella, that can harm the developing fetus. Poverty is linked with malnutrition, higher instances of infection, and higher rates of diabetes and cardiovascular disease, which are all linked to low birth weight and physical vulnerability (Cassady & Strange, 1987).

Many of the risks that face infants born to poor women are preventable. A well-organized, accessible system of regional medical-care facilities combined with an effective educational program on pregnancy and nutritional support can improve significantly the health and vigor of babies born to poor women (Swyer, 1987). A systematic evaluation of a program of coordinated maternity care for women on Medicaid in North Carolina demonstrated that a comprehensive prenatal care program improves birth outcomes, even in a high-risk population (Buescher et al., 1991). This kind of coordination involves more than prenatal visits. It includes nonmedical support services, such as making sure the woman has access to food stamps, is part of the Women, Infants, and Children (WIC) food program, has the transportation needed for prenatal and postnatal health appointments, and receives housing assistance or job training when necessary.

Resources must be provided to care for, educate, and support children whose intellectual, physical, and emotional capabilities have been restricted before birth by their mothers' poverty. The life chances and quality of survival of infants born to the poor are a reflection of the value that a society places on social justice.

The Impact of Culture

In order to appreciate the events surrounding the birth of a child, one must understand some of the idiosyncrasies in a culture's approach to birth. The beliefs, values, and guidelines for behavior regarding pregnancy and childbirth have been referred to as the *birth culture* (Jordan, 1983; Hahn & Muecke, 1987). The decision to have a child, the social and physical experiences of pregnancy, the particular style of help that is available for the delivery of the child, and the care and attitudes toward both mother and baby after delivery are all components of the birth culture. One cannot assume that everyone in a cultural group adheres to the full script of the birth culture, but at the very least, these guidelines are part of the mythology or lore that surfaces as a woman and her partner experience the events of pregnancy.

Data on the approaches to pregnancy and childbirth in traditional cultures are drawn primarily from the Human Relations Areas Files (Murdock & White, 1969) and from Ford's (1945) comparison of reproductive behavior in 64 cultures. In most traditional societies, men and nontribal women are not allowed to observe delivery. Further, many of the events related to conception and delivery are considered too personal or private to discuss with outsiders. Thus, the data on childbearing practices are not complete. Comparisons across cultures serve only to place the American system in a cultural context.

Reactions to Pregnancy

Many cultures share a strong assumption that the behavior of expectant parents will influence the developing fetus and the ease or difficulty of childbirth. Of the 64 cultures studied by Ford (1945), 42 prescribed certain behaviors for expectant parents and prohibited others.

Adolescent pregnancy has a different meaning in different subcultures. This young Hispanic mother-to-be appears to be greeted with mixed reactions as friends express interest, admiration, and perhaps a measure of disapproval.

Many such restrictions are dietary:

> Among the Pomeroon Arawaks, though the killing and eating of a snake during the woman's pregnancy is forbidden to both father and mother, the husband is allowed to kill and eat any other animal. The cause assigned for the taboo of the snake is that the little infant might be similar, that is, able neither to talk nor to walk. (Roth, 1953, p. 122)

In many Asian, Mediterranean, and Central and South American cultures, pregnancy is believed to be affected by the balance of what are considered "hot" and "cold" foods in a woman's diet. Pregnant women are advised to avoid both very "hot" foods, such as chili peppers and salty or fatty foods, and very "cold" foods, such as acidic, sour, or cold, fresh foods (Hahn & Muecke, 1987).

Attitudes toward pregnant women can be characterized along two dimensions: (1) solicitude versus shame and (2) adequacy versus vulnerability (Mead & Newton, 1967).

Solicitude Versus Shame   Solicitude toward the pregnant woman is shown in the care, interest, and help of others. For example,

> It is said among Jordon villagers that "as people are careful of a chicken in the egg, all the more so should they be of a child in its mother's womb." (Grandquist, 1950)

> As the Chagga in Africa say, "Pay attention to the pregnant woman! There is no one more important than she." (Guttmann, 1932)

At the other end of this dimension are the cultures that keep pregnancy a secret as long as possible. This custom may stem from a fear that damage will come to the fetus through supernatural demons, or it may result from shyness about the sexual implications of pregnancy.

Societies that demonstrate solicitude increase the care given to the pregnant woman and fetus. These attitudes emphasize the importance of birth as a mechanism for replenishing the group, and additional resources are likely to be provided to the pregnant woman. By keeping the pregnancy a secret, cultures that instill a sense of shame in the woman do not promote the health of the mother or the fetus and may not encourage a desire to have children.

Adequacy Versus Vulnerability   In many societies, pregnancy is a sign of sexual prowess and a means of entrance into social status. Some cultures do not arrange a wedding until after the woman has become pregnant. In a *polygynous* family, one in which a man has more than one wife, the pregnant wife receives the bulk of her husband's attention and may prevent her husband from taking an additional wife (Grandquist, 1950). In some cultures, women are considered more attractive after they have borne children: "Thus, the Aymara widow of South America with many children is regarded as a desirable bride" (Tichauer, 1963); "Lepcha men consider that copulation with women who have borne more than one child is more enjoyable and less exhausting than with other adult women" (Gorer, 1938).

The other end of this continuum is the view that child-making is exhausting, that pregnant women are vulnerable, and that women grow more frail with each pregnancy. Among the Arapesh of New Guinea (Mead, 1935), pregnancy is tiring for both men and women! Once menstruation stops, the husband and the wife believe that they must copulate repeatedly in order to provide the building materials for the fetus's semen and blood.

Many cultures teach that during pregnancy the woman and the fetus are more readily exposed to evil spirits. According to several records, the forces of life and death are engaged in a particularly intense competition for the mother and the fetus around the time of delivery.

One can think of solicitude and shame, and adequacy and vulnerability, as two dimensions that create a matrix within which the birth culture of any society or subculture can be located. One might describe the U.S. medical birth culture, for example, as being characterized by solicitude and vulnerability. Pregnant women are usually treated with increased concern and care, and they are often placed within a medical system that increases their sense of dependency. Attitudes in the workplace also contribute to the sense of vulnerability because pregnancy is often viewed as incompatible with serious dedication to the job.

Within this framework, pregnancy may be viewed as a time of great rejoicing or extreme shame, and of feeling sexually powerful or extremely vulnerable. One may expect that the view taken toward pregnancy in the culture as a whole determines the kinds and severity of the symptoms associated with pregnancy, the types of treatment or medical assistance sought during pregnancy, and the degree to which pregnancy itself is responded to as a life stress. A culture's attitudes toward pregnancy and birth also influence parenting attitudes and behavior. For example, in attitudes of solicitude or shame, one finds notions of the value of children and fears about whether the child will be a good or evil force in the family or community. In attitudes of adequacy versus vulnerability, one finds ideas about whether children bring resources or drain the family of resources, and whether children are an extension of the family's power or a new source of vulnerability and risk.

Reactions to Childbirth

Childbirth is an important event in traditional cultures. The delivery is usually attended by two or more assistants with specific assigned roles. Traditional birth attendants are found in all areas of the world. They are usually women who have had children themselves and who are respected members of their community. In Jamaica, the *nana*, or midwife, is one of the key figures in the village. She is called on to assist in many family crises. During pregnancy and childbirth, the *nana* provides assistance in the many rituals and taboos that mark the rebirth of the woman as a mother, and she usually cares for the mother and the infant throughout the pregnancy and until the ninth day after birth (Kitzinger, 1982).

In most traditional cultures, childbirth takes place in a familiar setting— either at home or in a nearby birthing hut. If the birth takes place at home, a woman may be separated from others by a curtain for privacy, but she knows that her family members are close at hand. Women typically give birth standing, squatting, or sitting and reclining against something or someone. The Western custom of lying on one's back with one's feet in the air has no counterpart in traditional birth cultures (Helman, 1990). Nor are women expected to be moved from one setting or room to another during the phases of labor. That appears to be a ritual reserved for women in modern, industrialized societies.

Views about the birth itself range from an extreme negative pole, at which birth is seen as dirty and defiling, to an extreme positive pole, at which it is seen as a personal achievement. The view of childbirth as a normal physical event is the midpoint on this continuum.

When birth is viewed as dirty, as it is by the Arapesh of New Guinea and the Kadu Gollas of India, the woman must go to an area away from the village to deliver her child. Many cultures, such as that of the ancient Hebrews, require extensive purification rituals after childbirth. Vietnamese villagers believe that mothers should not bathe or shampoo their hair for a month after giving birth so that the baby will not "fall apart," and that the new mother must not have sexual intercourse for 100 days (Stringfellow, 1978). A slightly more positive orientation toward childbirth is to identify it as a sickness. This view takes the pregnant Cuna Indian woman to her medicine man for daily medication. The midpoint of this spectrum—what we might most appropriately describe as "natural childbirth"— finds the mother delivering her baby in the presence of many members of the community, without much expression of pain and little magic or obstetrical mechanics.

Clark and Howland (1978) described childbirth for Samoan women:

> The process of labor is viewed by Samoan women as a necessary part of their role and a part of the life experience. Since the baby she is producing is highly valued by her culture, the mother's delivery is also commendable and therefore ego-satisfying. Pain relief for labor may well present the patient with a conflict. She obviously experiences pain as demonstrated by skeletal muscle response, tossing and turning, and fixed body positions, but her culture tells her that she does not need medication. It is the "spoiled" palagi [Caucasian] woman who needs pain-relieving drugs. Moreover, the culture clearly dictates that control is expected of a Samoan woman, and no overt expressions of pain are permissible. (p. 166)

At the most positive end of the scale, birth is seen as a proud achievement:

> Among the Ila of Northern Zimbabwe, women attending at birth were observed to shout praises of the woman who had a baby. They all thanked her, saying, "I give thanks to you today that you have given birth to a child." (Mead & Newton, 1967, p. 174)

A similar sentiment is expressed in Marjorie Karmel's (1983) description of the Lamaze method of childbirth:

From the moment I began to push, the atmosphere of the delivery room underwent a radical transformation. Where previously everyone had spoken in soft and moderate tones in deference to my state of concentration, now there was a wild encouraging cheering section, dedicated to spurring me on. I felt like a football star, headed for a touchdown. (pp. 93–94)

The American view of childbirth seems to be evolving toward an emphasis on safety for mother and child, and toward building a sense of competence in the mother and the father as they approach the care of their newborn (Sameroff, 1987). In comparison with the medical practices of the 1940s and 1950s, we are seeing less use of obstetrical medication during childbirth, greater involvement of fathers or other birth coaches during labor and delivery, more immediate contact between infants and their parents, more opportunities for the baby to spend much of the day with the mother, opportunities for siblings to visit, and shorter hospital stays.

At the same time, women are taught that the best way to promote the healthy development and safe delivery of their child is to make early and regular visits to their obstetrician during the prenatal period, and to observe restrictions in diet, the use of drugs, and exposure to certain environmental hazards that may harm the fetus. In some instances, a woman may feel that she is an active member of a team who will participate in the delivery of her baby, but often she does not know the physicians, nurses, or other medical professionals who are actually present when the baby is born. Midwifery and birthing centers have been slow to develop in the United States, and most physicians strongly urge their patients to deliver their children in a hospital. What is more, the steady increase in the use of cesarean deliveries contradicts the view of childbirth as a natural event that is well within the control and competence of mothers and their family support systems.

It is reasonable to speculate that events at the time of the birth influence the mother's feelings about herself and her parenting ability. Efforts by the community, especially family members, close friends, and health-care professionals, to foster a woman's competence in and control of the situation, as well as to express caring and support for her, seem to promote a woman's positive orientation toward herself and her mothering role. Messages of social rejection, doubts about a woman's competence, and attempts to take away control or to isolate the mother from her infant or her social support system may undermine the woman's self-esteem and interfere with her effectiveness as she approaches the demanding and exhausting task at hand.

The population of the United States is increasingly diverse, with immigrants from over 60 countries in a single year. Attention must be given to understanding the cultural norms of the pregnant woman and her family support system. In addition, efforts are needed to interpret the key elements of the U.S. birth culture for women who are not familiar with it, so that they may understand and possibly reinterpret those aspects that may appear disrespectful or threatening (Hahn & Muecke, 1987).

Applied Topic
Abortion

Abortion is the termination of pregnancy before the fetus is able to live outside the uterus. Each year, thousands of pregnancies are terminated through spontaneous abortion, usually referred to as *miscarriage*. However, the focus of this section is on the voluntary termination of pregnancy. In obstetrical practice, abortions are induced differently before and after 12 weeks of gestation. Before 12 weeks, the pregnancy is aborted by dilating the cervix and then either removing the contents of the uterus by suction with a vacuum aspirator or scraping out the uterus. After 12 weeks, abortion can be induced by the injection of a saline solution or prostaglandin, which stimulates labor. The fetus may be removed surgically by a procedure similar to a cesarean section (Cunningham et al., 1989).

Research in France resulted in the development of a drug, RU 486, that interrupts pregnancy by interfering with the synthesis and circulation of progesterone (Baulieu, 1989). The drug is most effective if it is taken within the first seven to nine weeks after the last menstrual period. It results in a shedding of the lining of the uterus, so there is no need for vacuum aspiration or surgical intervention. From January through September 1989, more than 2000 French women per month used RU 486, with a success rate of over 95% when it was used within the first seven weeks of pregnancy. At present, the drug is being evaluated in the United States. Should it become available, it would bring the decision about abortion more directly under a woman's personal control.

In 1920, after the Russian Revolution, the USSR was one of the first countries to permit abortion at the mother's request. Although the legalization of abortion is a modern phenomenon, abortion as a means of birth control has been practiced, along with infanticide, throughout history and across cultures (Krannich, 1980). Both the Aranda of central Australia and the Hopi of Arizona, for example, have been known to induce abortions by tying a belt very tightly around the mother's abdomen (Murdock, 1934). In modern China, official policy permits each married couple to have only one child. Many pregnant women who already have a child are forced to have an abortion.

The Legal Context of Abortion in the United States

At the heart of the abortion controversy in the United States is the conflict between society's responsibility to protect the rights of a woman and to protect the rights of an unborn child. On the one side are those who insist that a woman has a right to privacy and an absolute right to choose or reject motherhood. On the other side are those who seek to protect the rights of the unborn fetus, which is incapable of protecting its own interests.

A main point requiring definition in the abortion controversy is the developmental age at which the embryo is so far individualized as to be entitled to protection by the state. In 1973, in the case of *Roe v. Wade*, the U.S. Supreme Court proposed a developmental model to address that issue. The Court supported the division of pregnancy into three trimesters and considered abortion a woman's right in the first trimester, guarded by the Constitution's protection of privacy. The Court said that, in the second trimester, some restrictions could be placed on access to abortion because of its risk to the mother; the fetus's rights were still not an issue during this period. In the final trimester, when the fetus was regarded as having a good chance of surviving outside the uterus, states could choose not to permit abortion. This ruling endorsed a woman's right to full control over the abortion decision until the fetus reaches a point of developmental viability. At that point, the Court ruled, the society's responsibility to the unborn child outweighs the woman's right to freedom and privacy.

For some years since that decision, the Supreme Court has ruled unconstitutional state laws that tried to regulate abortions. But in July 1989, the Supreme

Court upheld a Missouri law that makes it illegal for any public institution or any public employee to perform an abortion. In addition, the Missouri law defines an individual life as beginning at conception, implying the state's responsibility to protect the fetus from that time. Finally, the law requires physicians who perform abortions after 20 weeks of pregnancy to test first to determine whether the fetus is capable of independent survival. If it is, abortion is illegal (*Economist*, 1989). The upholding of the Missouri law did not overturn *Roe v. Wade*, but it gave the states new freedom to impose restrictions on the accessibility of abortions.

In a decision reached in June 1992, the Supreme Court reviewed a set of laws passed by the Pennsylvania legislature. In its decision, it confirmed that *Roe v. Wade* "established a rule of law and component of liberty we cannot renounce" (Greenhouse, 1992). The Court argued that state laws ought not to impose an *undue burden* on a woman by placing major obstacles in her way if she seeks an abortion before the fetus has reached viability. However, of five sections of the Pennsylvania law, the Court considered four acceptable and agreed that they did not represent an undue burden. These restrictions were:

1. Requiring a woman to wait for 24 hours after hearing a presentation at the physician's office intended to persuade her to change her mind.
2. Requiring teenagers to have the consent of one parent or a judge before having an abortion.
3. Requiring the physician to specify any medical emergency that would justify waiving requirements 1 or 2.
4. Requiring the physician or clinic to make regular reports to the state.

A fifth provision, requiring a married woman to tell her husband of her intention to have an abortion, was rejected. Thus, states are defining in their own ways the degree to which they will make resources available for abortions and the extent to which they will try to direct the abortion-making decision through the presentation of certain types of information and the exclusion of others. Figure 4.9 provides a state-by-state overview of the laws related to abortion. You can see that the legal climate regarding this issue varies widely from one region of the country to another.

The Incidence of Legal Abortions

The number of reported legal abortions increased dramatically after the *Roe v. Wade* decision, from 745,000 in 1973 to 1,591,000 in 1989. Some of the characteristics of U.S. women who had legal abortions in 1989 are summarized in Table 4.6. The data suggest that women having abortions came from a great diversity of backgrounds and family and cultural contexts and had different reasons for wanting abortions. The *abortion ratio*—that is, the number of abortions per 1000 combined abortions and live births—increased from 193 in 1973 to 300 in 1980 and declined to 286 in 1989. The age group 20–24 years old had the highest rate of abortions (33% of all abortions), followed by those 15–19 (25% of all abortions) and those 25–29 (22% of all abortions). White women had two-thirds of all reported abortions. Most of the abortions were performed on unmarried women. The majority had had no prior births and no prior abortions.

The Impact of Abortion on Women

What do we know about the impact of abortions on women? Are abortions medically risky? How do women cope emotionally with the experience of abortion?

	Virtually all abortions prohibited	Health-care providers prohibited from abortion counseling	Woman required to notify husband	Parental consent required for minors	Counseling required for women; often a 24-hour minimum delay	Abortion prohibited in public facilities; public employees may not participate	Medicaid funding unavailable unless a woman's life is in danger
Alabama	■			■	■		■
Alaska					■		
Arizona	■					■	■
Arkansas	■			■			■
California	■						
Colorado	■		■				■
Connecticut							
Delaware	■				■		■
D.C.	■						■
Florida			■		■		■
Georgia				■			■
Hawaii							
Idaho					■		
Illinois			■				■
Indiana				■			■
Iowa							
Kansas	■			■	■		■
Kentucky			■		■	■	■
Louisiana	■	■		■	■	■	■
Maine					■		■
Maryland	■				■		
Massachusetts	■			■	■		
Michigan	■			■			■
Minnesota				■			
Mississippi	■				■		■
Missouri		■		■	■	■	■
Montana			■		■		■
Nebraska				■	■		■
Nevada					■		■
New Hampshire	■						■
New Jersey							
New Mexico	■						■
New York							
N. Carolina							
N. Dakota		■	■	■	■	■	■
Ohio				■	■		■
Oklahoma	■						■
Oregon							
Pennsylvania			■		■	■	
Rhode Island			■	■	■		■
S. Carolina			■	■			■
S. Dakota							■
Tennessee							■
Texas	■						■
Utah	■		■	■	■		■
Vermont	■						
Virginia					■		
Washington							
W. Virginia	■			■			
Wisconsin	■				■		
Wyoming				■			

FIGURE 4.9

A *state-by-state overview of abortion-related laws*

Source: *Based on Lacayo, 1992.*

TABLE 4.6   Legal Abortions: Selected Characteristics, 1989

Total legal abortions	1,591,000
Abortion Ratio (number of abortions per 1000 abortions and live births)	286
Age of women (%)	
Under 15	1
15–19	25
20–24	33
25–29	22
30–34	12
35–39	6
40 and over	2
Race (%)	
White	65
Black and other	36
Marital status (%)	
Married	17
Unmarried	83
Number of prior live births (%)	
None	51
1	24
2	17
3	6
4 or more	3
Number of prior induced abortions (%)	
None	57
1	27
2 or more	16
Weeks of gestation (%)	
Less than 9 weeks	50
9–10 weeks	27
11–12 weeks	12
13 weeks or more	11

Source: U.S. Bureau of the Census, 1992.

In 1965, 20% of all deaths associated with pregnancy and childbirth were linked to abortion. Since the legalization of abortion, related deaths have decreased by over 50%. In 1989, maternal deaths associated with legal abortions were 0.8 per 100,000; maternal deaths associated with pregnancy and childbirth were 8 per 100,000 (U.S. Bureau of the Census, 1992). Legal abortion, especially before 12 weeks, was ten times safer physically than carrying a pregnancy to term. In 1989, after an extensive evaluation of the existing research, the then U.S. surgeon general, C. Everett Koop, reported that "the scientific studies do not provide conclusive data about the health effects of abortion on women" (Holden, 1989, p. 730). Of the 250 studies included in Koop's review, which focused on the psychological impact of abortion, most were so seriously flawed methodologically that their results could not be used to support either side of the abortion debate (Wilmoth, 1992).

The typical psychological experience of women who have abortions is relief (Lemkau, 1988). Especially when the pregnancy is unwanted and the abortion is performed within the first 12 weeks, women generally resolve any negative feelings and thoughts they may have had soon after the abortion (Adler et al., 1990). However, many women do experience some ambivalence while making their decision.

Several factors are associated with a positive abortion outcome (Alter, 1984; Miller, 1992). Women who have an androgynous gender identity—that is, women who have flexible access to both masculine and feminine characteristics—report less sense of loss, less anxiety, fewer physical symptoms, and fewer thoughts about death than other women (androgyny is discussed further in Chapter 10). These women tend to have a less traditional gender-role orientation and expect to find a variety of sources of satisfaction in their lives in addition to or instead of child-rearing.

Another factor related to postabortion adjustment is a woman's views about the acceptability of abortion. Not surprisingly, women who believe that abortion is an acceptable solution to an unwanted pregnancy and that abortion is also acceptable to their friends, family, and partner are less likely to experience strong feelings of regret or emotional upset following an abortion (Miller, 1992).

In some instances, abortion is associated with lingering negative feelings. Lemkau (1988) reviewed clinical cases in which abortion produced strong, unresolved negative emotions. Sometimes, when a genetic anomaly is discovered in the fetus, abortion is performed late in pregnancy. A woman who has already become attached to the fetus grieves for her loss. In other second-trimester abortions, the ambivalence that caused the delay in the decision to have an abortion is exaggerated by the physical discomfort associated with a later abortion. Finally, some women discover that they are unable to conceive after an abortion, and guilt, anger, and regret surface. Women who are divorced, separated, or widowed at the time of an abortion appear to be more vulnerable to strong negative emotional reactions (Speckhard & Rue, 1992). Even though most abortions are associated with positive feelings of having taken control of one's destiny, we should not dismiss the emotional risks that some women face.

Women and their unborn babies are not the only persons affected by the abortion decision. In 1976, the Supreme Court ruled that a woman did not need the consent of her husband or the child's father to have an abortion, overruling a requirement of the father's consent that had been legislated in 12 states (Etzioni, 1976). This opinion was confirmed again in the 1992 Pennsylvania ruling cited above. The Supreme Court has supported a woman's independence from her husband or a child's father with regard to reproductive decision making. However, questions about the legal rights of fathers to determine the fate of their unborn children are still being raised, and the laws will probably continue to be challenged as fathers become increasingly committed to participation in parenting.

Not much is known about men's reactions to their partners' abortions. Shostak and McLouth (1985) interviewed 1000 men who had accompanied women to abortion clinics across the United States. Of these men, 93% said they would alter their birth-control methods as a result of the experience; 83% believed that abortion was a desirable way of resolving the pregnancy problem. Many of these men expressed anxiety, frustration, and guilt in relation to the unwanted pregnancy and the abortion. Clearly, more research is needed into how fathers' reactions to and attitudes about abortion contribute to the abortion decision.

The debate surrounding the legalization and availability of abortion services is an excellent example of a psychosocial controversy. On one side are those who insist on a woman's right to privacy and her absolute right to choose or reject motherhood. On the other side are those who seek to protect the rights of the unborn fetus, which is incapable of protecting its own interests. Embedded in this controversy are key human development issues: When does human life begin? When is a fetus viable—that is, capable of life outside the uterus? What is the impact of an abortion on a woman's physical health and psychological well-being? What is the impact of bearing and rearing an unwanted child on a woman's physical health and psychological well-being? What is the impact of being an unwanted child? What are the rights of fathers with respect to a woman's decision to have an abortion? What are the rights and responsibilities of parents in regard to an adolescent's abortion? In much the same way that the society is struggling to define death and to resolve the ethical issues surrounding the technological interventions that prolong the lives of people who have been severely brain-damaged or who are terminally ill, the society is struggling to define the beginnings of life and to resolve the ethical issues surrounding society's responsibilities to adult women and their unborn children.

Chapter Summary

A fetus develops in a psychosocial context. Genetic inheritance links each new infant to both a specific ancestry and the evolutionary history of the species. Genetic factors contribute to the rate of development as well as to the pattern of individual characteristics. Many personal competencies and abnormalities have their origins in the pattern of genetic information provided at fertilization. Our understanding of the biochemical basis of genetics is leading to the development of new technologies that may one day result in the ability to correct genetic abnormalities or to modify the genotype. These advances pose new psychosocial dilemmas and call for a public well educated in science, human development, and ethics.

The nine months of fetal development involve a rapid differentiation of body organs and a gradual integration of survival functions, especially the ability to suck and swallow, the regulation of breathing and body temperature, and the maturation of the digestive system. Sense receptors are prepared to respond to stimulation long before they are put into use. The central nervous system, which begins to take shape in the third and fourth weeks after conception, continues to develop and change throughout the prenatal period and into childhood and adolescence.

The birth process itself has five phases. The early signs that birth is approaching orient the parents and ready the birth canal for the baby's passage. Labor and delivery involve involuntary uterine contractions. The length of labor is quite variable, although it is usually shorter for women who have already had a child. The most difficult phase of delivery is the transition to full labor, when the contractions become strongest and last the longest.

The mother and the fetus are interdependent. Pregnancy affects a woman's social roles and social status and influences how people treat her and what resources become available to her, along with her physical well-being and her emotional state. A mother's attitude toward her pregnancy and her developing attachment to her unborn child set the stage for the quality of her parenting after the child is born.

Characteristics of the mother, her lifestyle, and her physical and cultural environment all influence fetal development. Of special note are the mother's age, any drugs she takes during her pregnancy, her exposure to certain diseases and environmental toxins, the use of anesthetic drugs during delivery, and her diet. Of specific social concern is the impact of poverty on fetal development; infants conceived by very poor women are exposed to the cumulative effects of many of the environmental hazards that are known to result in low birth weight and congenital abnormalities.

The experiences of pregnancy and childbirth are embedded in a cultural context. The birth culture provides a set of guidelines for behavior and attitudes toward and beliefs about restrictions on the woman's activities, the availability of resources, and the treatment of a pregnant woman by others. A matrix of orientations toward pregnancy reflects solicitude versus shame, and adequacy versus vulnerability. Most birth cultures can be located within this matrix.

Several factors involved in the prenatal period converge in the issue of abortion. The decision to abort reflects the mother's attitude toward childbirth; her criteria for a healthy, normal child; her age and economic resources; and her access to a safe means of ending the pregnancy. The decision about abortion also reflects the culture's attitudes about the moral implications of ending a life after conception and legal principles about when the fetus itself has a right to society's protection. Finally, the decision to abort is related to the safety, accessibility, and expense of the procedure.

The stage is now set to consider the remaining life stages in a psychosocial context. We have a sense of a child emerging into an existing family, community, and cultural network. The challenges to growth at every life stage reflect the balance between the unique talents and resources that a person offers and the barriers, expectations, and resources that he or she confronts in the environment.

References

Abel, E. L. (1984). *Fetal alcohol syndrome and fetal alcohol effects*. New York: Plenum.

Adler, N. E., David, H. P., Major, B. N., Roth, S. H., Russo, N. F. & Wyatt, G. (1990). Psychological responses after abortion. *Science*, 248, 41–44.

Aleksandrowicz, M. K. & Aleksandrowicz, D. R. (1974). Obstetrical pain-relieving drugs as predictors of infant behavior variability. *Child Development*, 45, 935–945.

Alter, R. C. (1984). Abortion outcome as a function of sex-role identification. *Psychology of Women Quarterly*, 8, 211–233.

Anderson, W. F. (1992). Human gene therapy. *Science*, 256, 808–813.

Andrews, L. B. (1984). Yours, mine and theirs. *Psychology Today*, 18, 20–29.

Aoki, C. & Siekevitz, P. (1988). Plasticity in brain development. *Scientific American*, 259, 56–64.

Armstrong, B. G., McDonald, A. D. & Sloan, M. (1992). Cigarette, alcohol, and coffee consumption and spontaneous abortion. *American Journal of Public Health*, 82, 85–87.

Associated Press. (1993). Baby on the way through new technique. *Columbus Dispatch* (August 15), p. 5A.

Bankart, B. (1989). Japanese perceptions of motherhood. *Psychology of Women Quarterly*, 13, 59–76.

Barinaga, M. (1991). How long is the human life-span? *Science*, 254, 936–938.

Baulieu, E. (1989). Contragestion and other clinical applications of RU 486, an antiprogesterone at the receptor. *Science*, 245, 1351–1357.

Bouchard, T. J. & McGue, M. (1981). Familial studies of intelligence: A review. *Science*, 212, 1055–1059.

Brackbill, Y. (1977). Long-term effects of obstetrical anesthesia on infant autonomic function. *Developmental Psychology*, 10, 529–535.

Brackbill, Y., Kane, J., Manniello, R. L. & Abramson, D. (1974). Obstetric premedication and infant outcome. *American Journal of Obstetrics and Gynecology*, 118, 377–384.

Brasel, J. (1974). Cellular changes in intrauterine malnutrition. In M. Winick (Ed.), *Nutrition and fetal development*. New York: Wiley.

Brazelton, T. B. (1987). Behavioral competence of the newborn infant. In G. B. Avery (Ed.), *Neonatology: Pathophysiology and management of the newborn* (pp. 379–399). Philadelphia: Lippincott.

Bronson, G. (1979). Issue of fetal damage stirs women workers at chemical plants. *Wall Street Journal* (February 9).

Buescher, P. A., Roth, M. S., Williams, D. & Goforth, C. M. (1991). An evaluation of the impact of maternity care coordination on Medicaid birth outcomes in North Carolina. *American Journal of Public Health*, 81, 1625–1629.

Burt, R. D., Vaughan, T. L. & Daling, J. R. (1988). Evaluating the risks of cesarean section: Low Apgar score in repeat C-section and vaginal deliveries. *American Journal of Public Health*, 78, 1312–1314.

Byrne, G. (1988). Artificial insemination report prompts call for regulation. *Science*, 241, 895.

Cassady, G. & Strange, M. (1987). The small-for-gestational-age (SGA) infant. In G. B. Avery (Ed.), *Neonatology: Pathophysiology and management of the newborn* (pp. 299–331). Philadelphia: Lippincott.

Chasnoff, I. J. (1988). *Drugs, alcohol, pregnancy, and parenting*. Hingham, MA: Kluwer.

Clark, A. L. & Howland, R. I. (1978). The American Samoan. In A. L. Clark (Ed.), *Culture, childbearing, and the health professionals* (pp. 154–172). Philadelphia: F. A. Davis.

Clarren, S. K. & Smith, D. W. (1978). The fetal alcohol syndrome. *New England Journal of Medicine*, 298, 1063–1067.

Clayman, C. B. (1989). *The American Medical Association encyclopedia of medicine*. New York: Random House.

Collins, F. S. (1992). Cystic fibrosis: Molecular biology and therapeutic implications. *Science*, 256, 774–779.

Coursin, D. B. (1974). Overview of the problem. In M. Winick (Ed.), *Nutrition and fetal development*. New York: Wiley.

Cunningham, F. G., MacDonald, P. C. & Gant, N. F. (1989). *Williams' obstetrics* (18th ed.). Norwalk, CT: Appleton & Lange.

Darney, P. D., Myhra, W., Atkinson, E. S. & Meier, J. (1989). Sero survey of human immunodeficiency virus infection in women at a family planning clinic: Absence of infection in an indigent population in San Francisco. *American Journal of Public Health*, 79, 883–885.

DeCasper, A. J. & Spence, M. J. (1986). Prenatal maternal speech influences newborns' perceptions of speech sounds. *Infant Behavior and Development*, 9, 133–150.

Dinges, D. F., Davis, M. M. & Glass, P. (1980). Fetal exposure to narcotics: Neonatal sleep as a measure of nervous system disturbance. *Science*, 209, 619–621.

Economist. (1989). The fearful politics of abortion (July 8), pp. 21–23.

Elmer-Dewitt, P. (1991). Making babies. *Time*, 138, 56–63.

Elson, J. (1989). The rights of frozen embryos. *Time* (July 24), p. 63.

Entwisle, D. R. & Alexander, K. L. (1987). Long-term effects of cesarean delivery on parents' beliefs and children's schooling. *Developmental Psychology*, 23, 676–682.

Etzioni, A. (1976, November). The husband's rights in abortion. *Trial*.

Feinman, C. F. (1992). *The criminalization of a woman's body*. Binghamton, NY: Hawthorn Press.

Fenster, L., Eskenazi, B., Windham, G. C. & Swan, S. H. (1991). Caffeine consumption during pregnancy and fetal growth. *American Journal of Public Health*, 81, 458–461.

Field, R., Healy, B., Goldstein, S., Perry, S., Bendell, D., Schanberg, S., Zimmerman, E. A. & Kuhn, C. (1988). Infants of depressed mothers show "depressed" behavior even with nondepressed adults. *Child Development*, 59, 1569–1579.

Field, R., Sandberg, D., Garcia, R., Vega-Lahr, N., Goldstein, S. & Guy, L. (1985). Pregnancy problems, postpartum depression, and early mother-infant interactions. *Developmental Psychology*, 21, 1152–1156.

Fleming, A. S., Ruble, D. N., Flett, G. L. & Shaul, D. L. (1988). Postpartum adjustment in first-time mothers: Relations between mood, maternal attitudes, and mother-infant interactions. *Developmental Psychology*, 24, 71–81.

Ford, C. S. (1945). *A comparative study of human reproduction*. New Haven, CT: Yale University Publications in Anthropology, No. 32.

Fried, P. A., Watkinson, B., Dillon, R. F. & Dulberg, C. S. (1987). Neonatal neurological status in a low-risk population after prenatal exposure to cigarettes, marijuana, and alcohol. *Journal of Developmental and Behavioral Pediatrics*, 8, 318–326.

Giacoia, G. P. & Yaffe, S. J. (1987). Drugs and the perinatal patient. In G. B. Avery (Ed.), *Neonatology: Pathophysiology and management of the newborn* (pp. 1317–1348). Philadelphia: Lippincott.

Gittler, J. & McPherson, M. (1991). Drugs and drug abuse. In *Information Please Almanac*, 1992, (45th ed.). Boston: Houghton Mifflin.

Gorer, G. (1938). *Himalayan village: An account of the Lepchas of Sikkim*. London: Michael Joseph.

Grandquist, H. (1950). *Child problems among the Arabs*. Helsinki: Soderstrom.

Greenhouse, L. (1992). Surprising decision: Majority issues warning on White House effort to overturn Roe. *The New York Times* (June 30), pp. A1 & A7.

Greenough, W. T., Black, J. E. & Wallace, C. S. (1987). Experience and brain development. *Child Development*, 58, 539–559.

Grossman, F. K., Eichler, L. S. & Winickoff, S. A. (1980). *Pregnancy, birth, and parenthood.* San Francisco: Jossey-Bass.

Guttmann, B. (1932). *Die Stammeslehvender des Chagga* (Vol. 1). Munich: C. H. Beck.

Habicht, J. P., Yarbrough, C., Lechtig, A. & Klein, R. E. (1974). Relation of maternal supplementary feeding during pregnancy to birth weight and other sociological factors. In M. Winick (Ed.), *Nutrition and fetal development.* New York: Wiley.

Hahn, R. A. & Muecke, M. A. (1987). The anthropology of birth in five U.S. ethnic populations: Implications for obstetrical practice. *Current Problems in Obstetrics, Gynecology, and Fertility*, 10, 133–171.

Hans, S. L. (1987). Maternal drug addiction and young children. *Division of Child, Youth, and Family Services Newsletter*, 10, 5, 15.

Healthy People 2000: National Health Promotion and Disease Prevention Objectives. (1990). Washington, DC: U.S. Department of Health and Human Services, Public Health Service, DHHS publication PHS 91-50212.

Heitlinger, A. (1989). Current medical, legal, and demographic perspectives on artificial reproduction in Czechoslovakia. *American Journal of Public Health*, 79, 57–61.

Helman, C. G. (1990). *Culture, health, and illness* (2nd ed.). London: Wright.

Holden, C. (1987). The genetics of personality. *Science*, 237, 598–601.

Holden, C. (1989). Koop finds abortion evidence "inconclusive." *Science*, 243, 730–731.

Holmes, T. H. & Rahe, R. H. (1967). The social readjustment rating scale. *Journal of Psychosomatic Research*, 11, 213–218.

Horn, J. M. (1983). The Texas Adoption Project: Adopted children and their intellectual resemblance to biological and adoptive parents. *Child Development*, 54, 268–275.

Horn, J. M. (1985). Bias? Indeed! *Child Development*, 56, 779–780.

Howes, C. & Krakow, J. (1977). Effects of inevitable environmental pollutants. In F. Rebelsky (Chair), *Pollution of the fetus.* Symposium conducted at the annual convention of the American Psychological Association, San Francisco.

Jacobson, S. W., Fein, G. G., Jacobson, J. L., Schwartz, P. M. & Dowler, J. K. (1985). The effect of intrauterine PCB exposure on visual recognition memory. *Child Development*, 56, 853–860.

Jarboe, P. J. (1986). A comparison study of distress and marital adjustment in infertile and expectant couples. Ph.D. dissertation, Ohio State University.

Jaroff, L. (1989). The gene hunt. *Time* (Mar. 20), pp. 62–67.

Jones, K. L., Smith, D. W., Ulleland, C. N. & Streissguth, A. P. (1973). Patterns of malformation in offspring of chronic alcoholic mothers. *Lancet*, 1, 1267–1271.

Jordan, B. (1983). *Birth in four cultures: A crosscultural investigation of childbirth in Yucatan, Holland, Sweden and the United States* (3rd ed.). Montreal: Eden Press.

Judson, F. N. (1989). What do we really know about AIDS control? *American Journal of Public Health*, 79, 878–882.

Kaplan, B. J. (1986). A psychobiological review of depression during pregnancy. *Psychology of Women Quarterly*, 10, 35–48.

Karmel, M. (1983). *Thank you, Dr. Lamaze.* Philadelphia: Lippincott.

Kimura, D. (1992). Sex differences in the brain. *Scientific American*, 267, 119–125.

Kitzinger, S. (1982). The social context of birth: Some comparisons between childbirth in Jamaica and Britain. In C. P. MacCormack (Ed.), *Ethnography of fertility and birth* (pp. 181–203). London: Academic Press.

Kliman, D. G. & Kohl, R. (1984). *Fatherhood USA.* New York: Garland Press.

Krannich, R. S. (1980). Abortion in the United States: Past, present, and future trends. *Family Relations*, 29, 365–374.

Lacayo, R. (1988). Baby M. meets Solomon's sword. *Time* (Feb. 15), p. 97.

Lacayo, R. (1992). Abortion: The future is already here. *Time* (May 4), p. 97.

Lawn, R. M. & Vehar, G. A. (1986). The molecular genetics of hemophilia. *Scientific American*, 254, 48–56.

Lemkau, J. R. (1988). Emotional sequelae of abortion: Implications for clinical practice. *Psychology of Women Quarterly*, 12, 461–472.

Lester, B. M., Als, H. & Brazelton, T. B. (1982). Regional obstetric anesthesia and newborn behavior: A reanalysis toward synergistic effects. *Child Development*, 53, 687–692.

Lindblad, B. S. (1987). *Perinatal nutrition.* San Diego: Academic Press.

Lindbohm, M., Hemminki, K., Bonhomme, M. G., Anttila, A., Rantala, K., Heikkilä, P. & Rosenberg, M.J. (1991). Effects of paternal occupational exposure on spontaneous abortions. *American Journal of Public Health*, 81, 1029–1033.

Loehlin, J. C. (1992). *Genes and environment in personality development*, Thousand Oaks, CA: Sage.

Mandel, J. L., Monaco, A. P., Nelson, D. L., Schlessinger, D. & Willard, H. (1992). Genome analysis and the human X chromosome. *Science*, 258, 103–109.

Marx, J. (1988). Are aging and death programmed in our genes? *Science*, 242, 33.

McDonald, A. D., Armstrong, B. G. & Sloan, M. (1992). Cigarette, alcohol, and coffee consumption and prematurity. *American Journal of Public Health, 82,* 87–90.

Mead, M. (1935). *Sex and temperament in three primitive societies.* New York: Morrow.

Mead, M. & Newton, N. (1967). Cultural patterning of perinatal behavior. In S. A. Richardson & A. F. Guttmacher (Eds.), *Childbearing—its social and psychological aspects.* Baltimore: Williams & Wilkins.

Mendel, G. (1866). Experiments with plant hybrids. *Proceedings of the Brunn Natural History Society.*

Miller, W. B. (1992). An empirical study of the psychological antecedents and consequences of induced abortion. *Journal of Social Issues, 48,* 67–93.

Moore, K. L. (1988). *The developing human: Clinically oriented embryology* (4th ed.). Philadelphia: Saunders.

Morris, R. A. (1987). The use of legislatively mandated birth registries in conducting research on behavioral teratology/toxicology. *Division of Child, Youth, and Family Services Newsletter, 10*(4), 12.

Murdock, G. P. (1934). *Our primitive contemporaries.* New York: Macmillan.

Murdock, G. P. & White, D. R. (1969). Standard cross-cultural sample. *Ethnology, 8,* 329–369.

Murray, A. D., Dolby, R. M., Nation, R. L. & Thomas, D. B. (1981). Effects of epidural anesthesia on newborns and their mothers. *Child Development, 52,* 71–82.

Naulty, J. S. (1987). Obstetric anesthesia. In G. B. Avery (Ed.), *Neonatology: Pathophysiology and management of the newborn.* Philadelphia: Lippincott.

Newsweek. (1989). The future of abortion (July 17), pp. 14–26.

NIH/CEPH Collaborative Mapping Group. (1992). A comprehensive genetic linkage map of the human genome. *Science, 258,* 67–86.

Nilsson, L. (1977). *A child is born.* New York: Delacorte Press/F. Lawrence.

Nowakowski, R. S. (1987). Basic concepts of CNS development. *Child Development, 58,* 568–595.

Padawer, J. A., Fagan, C., Janoff-Bulman, R., Strickland, B. R. & Chorowski, M. (1988). Women's psychological adjustment following emergency cesarean versus vaginal delivery. *Psychology of Women Quarterly, 12,* 25–34.

Palkovitz, R. (1985). Fathers' attendance, early contact, and extended care with their newborns: A critical review. *Child Development, 56,* 392–406.

Palm, G. F. & Palkovitz, R. (1988). The challenge of working with new fathers: Implications for support providers. In R. Palkovitz & M. B. Sussman (Eds.), *Transitions to parenthood* (pp. 357–376). New York: Haworth.

Patterson, D. (1987). The causes of Down's syndrome. *Scientific American, 257*(2), 52–61.

Plomin, R. (1990). *Nature and nurture: An introduction to human behavioral genetics.* Pacific Grove, CA: Brooks/Cole.

Plomin, R. (Ed.). (1994). *Individual differences and development* (Vol. 6). Thousand Oaks, CA: Sage.

Polednak, A. P. (1991). Black-white differences in infant mortality in 38 standard metropolitan statistical areas. *American Journal of Public Health, 81,* 1480–1482.

Quilligan, E. J. (1983). *Pregnancy, birth, and the infant.* NIH publication no. 82-2304. U.S. Department of Health and Human Services. Washington, DC: U.S. Government Printing Office.

Reinisch, J. M. & Karow, W. G. (1977). Prenatal exposure to synthetic progestins and estrogens: Effects on human development. *Archives of Sexual Behavior, 6,* 257–288.

Reinisch, J. M. & Sanders, S. A. (1984). Prenatal gonadal steroidal influences on gender-related behavior. In G. D. DeVries, J. P. C. DeBruin, H. B. M. Uylings & M. A. Corher (Eds.), *Sex differences in the brain: The relation between structure and function: Vol. 61. Progress in Brain Research.* Amsterdam: Elsevier.

Roberts, L. (1989). Human gene transfer approved. *Science, 243,* 473.

Robison, J. T. (1989). Noncoital reproduction. *Psychology of Women: Newsletter of Division 35, American Psychological Association, 16*(1), 3–5.

Roosa, M. W. (1984). Maternal age, social class, and the obstetric performance of teenagers. *Journal of Youth and Adolescence, 13,* 365–374.

Roth, W. E. (1953). Precautions during pregnancy in New Guinea. In M. Mead & N. Calas (Eds.), *Primitive heritage.* New York: Random House.

Sabatelli, R. M., Meth, R. L. & Gavazzi, S. M. (1988). Factors mediating the adjustment to involuntary childlessness. *Family Relations, 37,* 338–343.

Sachs, A. (1989). Here come the pregnancy police. *Time* (May 22), pp. 104–105.

Sameroff, A. J. (1987). Psychologic needs of the parent in infant development. In G. B. Avery (Ed.), *Neonatology: Pathophysiology and management of the newborn* (pp. 358–378). Philadelphia: Lippincott.

Sameroff, A. J. & Chandler, M. J. (1975/1992). Reproductive risk and the continuum of caretaking casualty. In F. D. Horowitz, M. Hetherington & S. Scarr, Developmental theories for the 1990s: Development and individual differences. *Child Development, 63,* 1–19.

Scarr, S. (1992). Developmental theories for the 1990s: Development and individual differences. *Child Development, 63,* 1–19.

Schroeder, S. R. (1987). Behavioral toxicology: Assessment technology for neurotoxic effects of lead exposure in humans. *Division of Child, Youth, and Family Services Newsletter, 10*(1), 14–15.

Schuster, C. S. (1986). Intrauterine development. In C. S. Schuster & S. S. Ashburn (Eds.), *The process of human development* (pp. 67–94). Boston: Little, Brown.

Seabrook, C. (1987). Children—"Third wave" of AIDS victims. *Atlanta Journal* (February 19), pp. 1A, 12A.

Shostak, A. & McLouth, G. (1985). *Men and abortion.* New York: Praeger.

Silverman, P. R. (1989). Deconstructing motherhood. *Readings: A Journal of Reviews and Commentary in Mental Health,* 4, 14–18.

Sosa, R., Kennell, J., Klaus, M., Robertson, S. & Urrutia, J. (1980). The effect of a supportive companion on perinatal problems, length of labor, and mother-infant interaction. *New England Journal of Medicine,* 303, 597–600.

Speckhard, A. C. & Rue, V. M. (1992). Postabortion syndrome: An emerging public health concern. *Journal of Social Issues,* 48, 95–119.

Spence, M. J. & DeCasper, A. J. (1987). Prenatal experience with low-frequency maternal-voice sounds influence neonatal perception of maternal voice samples. *Infant Behavior and Development,* 10, 133–142.

Sperling, D. (1989). Success rate for in vitro is only 9%. *USA Today* (March 10), p. 1D.

Standley, K., Soule, B. & Copans, S. A. (1979). Dimensions of prenatal anxiety and their influence on pregnancy outcome. *American Journal of Obstetrics and Gynecology,* 135, 22–26.

Stechler, G. & Halton, A. (1982). Prenatal influences on human development. In B. B. Wolman (Ed.), *Handbook of developmental psychology* (pp. 175–189). Englewood Cliffs, NJ: Prentice-Hall.

Streissguth, A. P., Barr, H. M., Sampson, P. D., Darby, B. L. & Martin, D. C. (1989). IQ at age 4 in relation to maternal alcohol use and smoking during pregnancy. *Developmental Psychology,* 25, 3–11.

Stringfellow, L. (1978). The Vietnamese. In A. L. Clark (Ed.), *Culture, childbearing, and the health professionals* (pp. 174–182). Philadelphia: F. A. Davis.

Swyer, P. R. (1987). The organization of perinatal care with particular reference to the newborn. In G. B. Avery (Ed.), *Neonatology: Pathophysiology and management of the newborn* (pp. 13–44). Philadelphia: Lippincott.

Tanner, J. M. (1990). *Foetus into man: Physical growth from conception to maturity,* (rev. ed.). Cambridge: Harvard University Press.

Thompson, M. W., McInnes, R. R. & Willard, H. F. (1991). *Genetics in medicine* (5th ed.). Philadelphia: Saunders

Tichauer, R. (1963). The Aymara children of Bolivia. *Journal of Pediatrics,* 62, 399–412.

Trethowan, W. (1972). The couvade syndrome. In J. Howells (Ed.). *Modern perspectives in psycho-obstetrics.* New York: Brunner/Mazel.

U. S. Bureau of the Census. (1992). *Statistical Abstract of the United States: 1992.* (112th ed.). Washington, DC: U.S. Government Printing Office.

U.S. Department of Health, Education, and Welfare. (1979). *Smoking and health: A report of the surgeon general.* Washington, DC: U.S. Government Printing Office.

Usher, R. (1987). Extreme prematurity. In G. B. Avery (Ed.), *Neonatology: Pathophysiology and management of the newborn* (3rd ed., pp. 264–298). Philadelphia: Lippincott.

Vaughn, B. E., Bradley, C. F., Joffe, L. S., Seifer, R. & Barglow, P. (1987). Maternal characteristics measured prenatally are predictive of ratings of temperamental "difficulty" on the Carey Infant Temperament Questionnaire. *Developmental Psychology,* 23, 152–161.

Vorhees, C. V. & Mollnow, E. (1987). Behavioral teratogenesis: Long-term influences on behavior from early exposure to environmental agents. In J. D. Osofsky (Ed.), *Handbook of infant development* (pp. 913–971). New York: Wiley.

West, J. R. (1986). *Alcohol and brain development.* London: Oxford University Press.

Wilcox, A. J. & Skjoerven, R. (1992). Birth weight and perinatal mortality: The effect of gestational age. *American Journal of Public Health,* 82, 378–382.

Wilmoth, G. H. (1992). Abortion, public health policy, and informed consent legislation. *Journal of Social Issues,* 48, 1–17.

Willwerth, J. (1991). Should we take away their kids? *Time* (May 13), pp. 62–63.

Yalom, I. D., Green, R. & Fisk, N. (1973). Prenatal exposure to female hormones. *Archives of General Psychiatry,* 28, 554–561.

Yang, R. K., Zweig, A. R., Douthitt, T. C. & Federman, E. J. (1976). Successive relationships between maternal attitudes during pregnancy, analgesic medication during labor and delivery, and newborn behavior. *Developmental Psychology,* 12, 6–14.

Zuckerman, B., Frank, D. A. & Hingson, R. (1989). Effects of maternal marijuana and cocaine use on fetal growth. *New England Journal of Medicine,* 320, 762–768.

CHAPTER 5

Through a process of mutual adaptation, mother and
infant establish a pattern of meaningful interactions and
build the foundation for trust.

INFANCY
(Birth to 2 Years)

Infancy is a period of dramatically rapid growth. During the first year of life, the infant's birth weight almost triples. By the age of 2, the fundamentals of voluntary movement, language, and concept formation can be observed. The global behaviors of early infancy become well-differentiated requests for the satisfaction of specific needs. The outstanding feature of infancy is the integration of simple responses into increasingly coordinated, meaningful patterns of behavior. This direction of development can be seen in each of the areas to be discussed in the chapter: the establishment of social attachments, the maturation of sensory and motor functions, the formation of cognitive schemes related to causality and the nature of objects, and the expression, interpretation, and regulation of emotions.

Infants are far more competent than they were once believed to be. A burgeoning literature documents many perceptual, cognitive, and social capacities that appear to be guided by genetic information. We can systematically observe individual differences in temperament and intellectual ability even within the first six months of life (Mandler, 1990). We now appreciate the degree to which infants actively select and organize information and contribute to their own care (Belsky & Tolan, 1981; Osofsky, 1987; Bower, 1989).

The role of genetics in guiding infant development is becoming increasingly well documented as the methods of studying infant behavior reach new levels of sophistication (Plomin, 1990, 1994). At the same time, longitudinal and cross-cultural studies reveal the significant impact of the child's early environment on her or his development. The mother's personality, the father's involvement in child care, cultural beliefs surrounding child-rearing practices, and poverty are all factors that add to a child's vulnerability or resilience (Plomin & McClearn, 1993).

In recent years, as American families have become smaller, we have seen a change in the emphasis society places on infancy: Each child is taken much more seriously. The medical community is devising complex technologies for saving the lives of babies born at 1200 grams (39 ounces) and 1000 grams (32 ounces). The psychological community is studying infant temperament and the early origins of personality, focusing on individual differences among infants from the very first weeks of life. A growing "baby industry" produces special equipment, foods, toys, books, and other paraphernalia. Many parents take classes, read books and magazines, and join support groups so that they can "get it right the first time."

The impact of the birth cohort on the lives of individual children is just beginning to be documented—that is, how children born in the same historical period experience certain common patterns of opportunities and challenges. For example, we are learning how the baby-boom generation has collided with the social institutions of our society, including the schools, the labor market, marriage, and housing. Now we have a baby bust, and we are beginning to appreciate the special attention that these precious new lives attract.

Developmental Tasks

Five areas of development are very important during infancy: (1) social attachment; (2) sensory-perceptual and motor functions (e.g., seeing, hearing, eye-hand coordination, reaching, crawling, and walking); (3) understanding the relation between actions and their consequences at a behavioral rather than a conceptual level; (4) understanding the nature of objects and creating categories that link objects, people, and events in groups; and (5) emotional development (happiness, sadness, and anger). Maturation and growth in each area provides the foundation

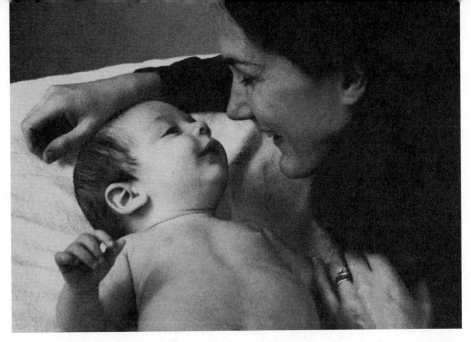

At ten days old, this infant and his mother are forming the first phase of an attachment as they gaze, smile, and coo at each other.

for subsequent development in social relationships, intellectual accomplishments, self-understanding, and mastery of the physical challenges required for autonomous functioning.

Social Attachment

Social attachment is the process through which people develop specific, positive emotional bonds with others. As we saw in Chapter 3, John Bowlby (1958) introduced the concept of the attachment behavior system as an organized pattern of infant signals and adult responses that lead to a protective, trusting relationship during the very earliest stage of development. Recent work has begun to consider the formation of attachments at later points in life, but the original interest in this behavioral system was in how it kept the infant close to the caregiver and thus ensured the infant's protection against possible harm.

The nurturing responses of the caregiver constitute a complementary behavioral system that we often refer to as *parenting*, or *caregiving* (Bowlby, 1988; Ainsworth, 1985). Certain patterns of caregiver–infant interaction in the first months of life contribute to the formation of attachment. One of the most significant of these is *synchrony* of interactions (Isabella & Belsky, 1991). Parent-infant dyads that show positive attachment relations within one year are characterized in the early months by interactions that are rhythmic, well timed, and mutually rewarding. Dyads in which the caregiver is unresponsive to the infant's signals of distress, overly intrusive when the infant is calm, or underinvolved have less positive attachments.

At least three behaviors form the evidence that an attachment has been formed. First, infants try to maintain contact with the object of attachment (Ainsworth, 1973). Second, infants show distress when the object of attachment is absent (Schaffer & Emerson, 1964). Third, infants are more relaxed and comfortable with the object of attachment and more fretful with other people (Bronson, 1973).

Stages of Attachment

Ainsworth (1973, 1985) described five sequential stages in the development of social attachment (see Table 5.1). In the first stage, during the first three months of life, infants engage in a variety of behaviors, including sucking, rooting, grasping,

TABLE 5.1	Five Stages in the Formation of Attachment	
Stage	**Age**	**Characteristics**
1	Birth to 3 months	Infant uses sucking, rooting, grasping, smiling, gazing, cuddling, and visual tracking to maintain closeness with caregivers.
2	3–6 months	Infant is more responsive to familiar figures than to strangers.
3	6–9 months	Infant seeks physical proximity and contact with object(s) of attachment.
4	9–12 months	Infant forms internal mental representation of object of attachment, including expectations about the caregiver's typical responses to signals of distress.
5	12 months and beyond	Child uses a variety of behaviors to influence the behavior of the objects of attachment in ways that will satisfy needs for safety and closeness.

smiling, gazing, cuddling, and visual tracking, that serve to maintain closeness with a caregiver or to bring the caregiver to the infant. However, these behaviors do not appear to be aimed at a specific person. Through contacts these behaviors produce, babies learn about the unique features of their caregivers.

In the second stage, from about 3 months to about 6 months of age, an infant's attachment is expressed through preferential responsiveness to a few familiar figures. Infants smile more at the familiar person than at a stranger, show more excitement at that person's arrival, and appear to be upset when he or she leaves.

In the third stage, from about 6 to 9 months, babies actively seek physical proximity to the objects of attachment. The ability to crawl and the ability to coordinate reaching and grasping contribute to greater control over their actions.

In the fourth stage, from about 9 to 12 months, babies form the first internal representation of their caregivers, which provides the first, working model of an attachment relationship. Specific characteristics of a caregiver and expectations about how a caregiver will respond to the infant's actions are organized into a complex attachment scheme: the internal, mental representation of the anticipated responses of a caregiver.

In the fifth stage, in toddlerhood and later, young children use a variety of behaviors to influence the behavior of their parents and other objects of attachment in order to satisfy their own needs for closeness. Children may ask to be read to, to be cuddled at bedtime, and to be taken along on errands. They devise these strategies to produce caregiver behaviors that will satisfy their continuing needs for physical contact, closeness, and love.

As children mature from toddlerhood to the early and middle school years, they begin to conceptualize new risks and threats to their security and may initiate new strategies for maintaining closeness to the objects of their attachment. Especially when they are undergoing unusual stress, as in times of illness, divorce, or rejection, children of any age who have a secure attachment may try to activate the attachment system by sending signals that will result in comforting and closeness.

Stranger Anxiety   During the second half of the first year, two signs of the child's growing attachment to a specific other person are observed: stranger anxiety and separation anxiety. *Stranger anxiety* is the baby's discomfort or tension in the presence of unfamiliar adults. Babies vary in how they express their protest to strangers and in how intensely they react. They may cling to their parents, refuse to be held, stiffen at the stranger's touch, or merely avert their eyes from the stranger's face.

The baby's response to a stranger depends on the specifics of the situation, including how close the mother is, how the stranger approaches the baby, and how the mother responds to the stranger (Keltenbach, Weinraub & Fullard, 1980). For example, if a mother speaks in a positive tone of voice to her baby about a stranger, the baby's response to the stranger is likely to be positive (Feinman & Lewis, 1983). The baby's response is also influenced by the amount of prior experience with unfamiliar adults. Normally, we take wariness of strangers as a positive sign—that is, that babies are able to detect the differences between their parents and adults they do not know. Of course, wariness of strangers continues to be expressed throughout life. In fact, we often see more distinct expressions of suspiciousness or fear among adults encountering strangers than we do among babies.

Separation Anxiety   At about 9 months, infants give another indication of the intensity of their attachment to their parents by expressing rage and despair when the parents leave. This reaction is called *separation anxiety*. Separation may evoke two different kinds of behavior. Sometimes, separation from the caregiver will stimulate attachment behaviors, especially efforts to find the caregiver and regain physical contact (Ainsworth, Bell & Stayton, 1971). Separation may also evoke protest, despair, or detachment, depending on the length of the separation (Bowlby, 1960; Robertson & Robertson, 1989).

The baby's response to separation also depends on the conditions of separation. Babies 9 months old and over show physical signs of separation-related distress after about 30 minutes of separation. The distress is more evident when the substitute caregiver is passive than when he or she interacts with the baby warmly and playfully (Larson, Gunnar & Hertsgaard, 1991; Gunnar et al., 1992).

Infants are less distressed about separation when their mothers leave them alone in a room at home than when they do so in a laboratory (Ross et al., 1975). They are less likely to protest if the mother leaves the door to the room open than if she closes the door as she leaves. The protest response to separation seems to express the baby's strong desire to maintain contact with the object of attachment. The importance of contact may be to (1) meet physical needs, (2) help the child overcome physical barriers, (3) provide protection or comfort, or (4) provide novel and stimulating interactions (Hay, 1980). When high levels of responsiveness and warmth characterize the parent-infant relationship, the infant has many reasons to want to maintain access to the caregiver.

We expect babies eventually to become more flexible about their parents' temporary departures and to learn to tolerate brief separations. At age 2 years, children are able to use a photograph of their mothers to help sustain their adaptation to a new setting in the mothers' absence (Passman & Longeway, 1982). By the age of 3, children may even look forward to a night with a baby-sitter or an afternoon at Grandfather's house. Once the primary attachment is fully established, children can comfort themselves by creating mental images of their parents and by remembering their parents' love for them. During infancy, however,

Children who have a secure attachment can use their object of attachment as a secure base in times of uncertainty. Here, a child looks openly at an unfamiliar photographer while she holds tightly to her mother's knee.

the parents' physical presence remains a focal point of babies' attention and concern. Parents who, for one reason or another, are forced to leave their children for a long time may return to discover that the children are temporarily withdrawn and cold to them, and that their previously loving and affectionate children have sudden outbursts of rage. Infants, who have no adequate language, use such behaviors to communicate anger and frustration at their abandonment.

Objects of Attachment

An infant may establish an early, positive emotional relationship with both the mother and the father, and with any other person who is performing many child-care activities and expresses warmth and affection for the child, such as an older sibling or a child-care professional. However, the quality of attachment is not necessarily identical in each relationship (Bretherton, 1985; Bridges, Connell & Belsky, 1988). For example, when Lamb (1976) studied the attachment of infants to their mothers and fathers, he found that the babies tended to have playful interactions with their fathers—smiling, laughing, and looking—and comforting, stress-reducing interactions with their mothers. When only one parent was present, the babies showed attachment to that parent. When both parents were present, the babies had a different pattern of interaction with each.

In a study conducted in Israel, kibbutz-reared infants showed great similarity in their attachment to their fathers and to their specially trained caregivers (called *metapelets*) (Sagi et al., 1985). However, there was no consistent similarity in the quality of their attachments to their mothers and fathers or to their mothers and *metapelets*. In subsequent research, when these kibbutz children had reached age 5, the quality of their infant attachment to the *metapelet* was a significant predictor of their socioemotional development in school and at free play in their children's house (Oppenheim, Sagi & Lamb, 1988). This research suggests that infants are able to have a variety of attachment relationships. Exactly how the infant synthesizes the internal representations of various attachments is not well understood. It does not appear that the primary attachment model simply generalizes to all other significant relationships. Rather, distinct attachments are formed based on the time spent together and on the quality of the interactions with each object of attachment (Fox, Kimmerly & Schafer, 1991).

TABLE 5.2		The Strange-Situation Laboratory Procedure		
Episode	**Duration**	**Participants***	**Events**
1	30 sec	M, B, O	O shows M and B into the room, instructs M on where to put B down and where to sit, O leaves.
2	3 min.	M, B	M puts B down close to her chair, at a distance from the toys. She responds to B's social bids but does not initiate interaction. B is free to explore. If B does not move after 2 minutes, M may take B to the toy area.
3	3 min.	M, B, S	This episode has three parts. S enters, greets M and B, and sits down opposite M without talking for 1 minute. During the 2nd minute, S engages M in conversation. S then joins B on the floor, attempting to engage B in play for 1 minute. At the end of this episode, M leaves "unobtrusively" (B usually notices).
4	3 min.	B, S	S sits on her chair. She responds to B's social bids but does not initiate social interaction. If B becomes distressed, S attempts to comfort B. If this is not effective, M returns before 3 minutes are up.
5	3 min.	M, B	M calls B's name outside the door and enters (S leaves unobtrusively). If B is distressed, M comforts B and tries to reengage B in play. If B is not distressed, M goes to sit on her chair, taking a responsive, noninitiating role. At the end of the episode, M leaves, saying, "Bye-bye; I'll be back."
6	3 min.	B	B remains alone. If B becomes distressed, the episode is curtailed and S enters.
7	3 min.	B, S	S enters, comforting B if required. If she cannot comfort B, the episode is curtailed. If B calms down or is not distressed, S sits on her chair, taking a responsive role as before.
8	3 min.	M, B	M returns (S leaves unobtrusively). M behaves as in episode 5.

*O = observer; M = mother; B = baby; S = stranger.
Source: Bretherton, 1988.

Quality of Attachment

The quality of attachment varies from family to family and from one parent-child dyad to another. The adults' acceptance of the infant and their ability to respond to the infant's varying communications are important to a secure attachment. The parents' ways of expressing affection and rejection influence how well they meet their babies' strong needs for reassurance and comfort (Tracy & Ainsworth, 1981).

Differences in the quality of attachment of babies and their caregivers have been observed in a standard laboratory procedure called the *strange situation* (Ainsworth et al., 1978; Bretherton, 1990). Over 20 minutes, the child is exposed to a sequence of events that is likely to stimulate the attachment system (see Table 5.2). The infant and the caregiver enter an unfamiliar laboratory environment, a stranger enters, the caregiver leaves briefly, and the caregiver and the infant experience opportunities for reunion. During this experiment, researchers have the opportunity to make systematic observations of the child's behavior, the caregiver's behavior, and characteristics of their interactions as well as to compare this behavior across segments of the situation.

Four Patterns of Attachment   Originally, three major patterns of attachment behavior were identified through the strange-situation methodology: (1) secure attachment, (2) anxious-avoidant attachment, and (3) anxious-resistant attachment. In American samples, about two-thirds of the children tested were characterized as securely attached. However, we will see that this percentage varies considerably from subgroup to subgroup, depending on socioeconomic status and subcultural context. Of the remaining third of the children, sometimes referred to as insecurely attached, more children fell into the anxious-avoidant category than into the anxious-resistant category (Ainsworth et al., 1978).

More recently, a fourth form of attachment behavior has been described in studies of clinically depressed mothers and high-risk populations, such as infants who have been abused. This attachment behavior has been described by some as a combination of avoidant and resistant (Radke-Yarrow et al., 1985; Crittenden, 1985), and by others as insecure-disorganized, disorganized-disoriented, or disorganized attachment (Main & Solomon, 1986, 1990; Carlson et al., 1989a; van Ijzendoorn et al., 1992). Only a small percentage of infants from normal families show this pattern. For example, Main and Solomon (1990) found that 13% of 268 attachment classifications of middle-class mothers and infants were categorized as disorganized. The frequency of the disorganized pattern increased as the severity of social risk factors increased (Lyons-Ruth, Alpern & Repacholi, 1993). Among infants from multiproblem families receiving supportive services, 28% were described as showing disorganized attachment behavior (Spiker & Booth, 1988). Of infants of low-income mothers with serious depression who were not receiving support services, 54% showed the disorganized pattern (Lyons-Ruth et al., 1990), and of infants from maltreating families, 82% were found to have disorganized attachments (Carlson, Cicchetti, Barnett & Braunwald, 1989b).

Infants showing a disorganized attachment appear to have serious behavior problems in the preschool period. In one study of 62 low-income families, 71% of the preschoolers who were characterized as showing deviant levels of hostility had been evaluated in infancy as having disorganized attachments (Lyons-Ruth et al., 1993). Not all the infants who were classified as disorganized in infancy were rated as excessively hostile, and not all mothers whose children developed a disorganized attachment had severe psychosocial problems themselves. However, when the mother did have serious psychosocial problems and the baby developed a disorganized attachment, the likelihood of showing hostility and aggression in the preschool period increased markedly. More research is needed to identify further developmental outcomes linked to disorganized attachment. This pattern is likely to be found to be associated with very serious mental health problems later in childhood and beyond.

The attachment patterns reflect different approaches to coping with the stresses induced in the strange situation. Infants who have a *secure attachment* actively explore their environment and interact with strangers while their mothers are present. After a brief separation, the mothers' return reduces their separation distress and permits them to return to exploration of the environment. Infants who show an *anxious-avoidant attachment* avoid contact with their mothers after separation or ignore the mothers' efforts to interact. They show less distress at being alone than other babies. Infants who have an *anxious-resistant attachment* are very cautious in the presence of the stranger. Their exploratory behavior is noticeably disrupted by the caregiver's departure. When the caregiver returns, these infants appear to want to be close to the caregiver, but they are also angry and so are very hard to comfort or soothe. The behavior of babies who have *disorganized attachment* is especially noticeable in the reunion period. The disorganized babies have no consistent strategy for managing the stress of being separated from and then reunited with their attachment figure. They behave in contradictory, unpredictable ways that seem to convey extreme fear or utter confusion. A fearful response would make sense if an abused child is reacting to the return of the abuser.

The validity of the attachment categorizations based on observations in the strange situation is bolstered in part by observations of the mother and the infant at home (Tracy & Ainsworth, 1981; Ainsworth, 1985; Sroufe, 1985). When observed at home, babies who have a secure attachment cry less than other babies. They greet their mothers more positively on reunion after everyday separations and appear to respond more cooperatively to their mothers' requests. Securely attached babies seem to expect their caregiver to be accessible and responsive, and this confidence permits them to explore the environment and to accept brief separations with little protest.

The mothers of babies who are characterized as anxious-avoidant seem to reject their babies, almost as if they were angry at their babies. These mothers spend less time holding and cuddling their babies than other mothers, and more of their interactions appear to be unpleasant or even hurtful. At home, these babies cry a lot, are not readily soothed by contact with the caregiver, and yet appear to be quite distressed by separations. These babies have strong needs for security, but their internal representation of the caregiver seems to predict that their requests for comfort will be rejected. Thus, in the laboratory situation, they defend themselves against rejection by avoiding contact with the caregiver.

The third group, infants who are characterized as anxious-resistant, have mothers who are inconsistent in their responsiveness. Sometimes these mothers ignore clear signals of distress. At other times, they interfere with their infants in order to make contact. Although these mothers appear to enjoy close physical contact with their babies, they do not necessarily make this contact in ways appropriate to the baby's needs. As a result, the infants form an internal representation of attachment as being highly unpredictable. These babies try to maintain proximity and to avoid unfamiliar situations that will heighten the uncertainty of their accessibility to their caregiver. Their responses reflect frustration by their inability to predict or control the responsiveness of their caregiver.

Within the fourth group, characterized as having disorganized-disoriented attachment responses, some, but not all, infants encounter a variety of very unusual parental behaviors, such as physical abuse, sexual manipulation, prolonged lack of responsiveness, intense irritability, alcohol- and/or drug-induced rages or stupors, or psychotic delusions or other psychotic symptoms. In some cases, infants experience prolonged maternal absences due to institutionalization or incarceration. This is the group at greatest risk for subsequent social and cognitive dysfunction.

Is the Strange-Situation Procedure Valid Across Cultures?   Questions have been raised about the validity of the strange situation in assessing attachment across cultures. Generally, researchers have found the procedure to be useful and manageable in cross-cultural studies. Other good measures of attachment correlate well with the strange-situation classifications. Assuming that it is a valid measure and that attachment behavior is an ethologically adaptive behavioral system, we would expect to observe it in all societies and cultures.

In an analysis of 32 studies of attachment in eight countries—the United States, Germany, Great Britain, the Netherlands, Sweden, Israel, Japan, and

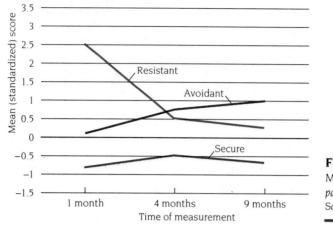

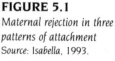

FIGURE 5.1

Maternal rejection in three patterns of attachment
Source: Isabella, 1993.

China—secure attachment was found to be the modal pattern (van Ijzendoorn & Kroonenberg, 1988). What is more, the proportions of children categorized as anxious-avoidant and anxious-resistant varied more in studies carried out within countries than in those that compared children of different countries. One of two studies conducted in Japan, for example, found that 32% of the children were anxious-resistant; the other study found only 19% in this category. Similarly, studies of different populations of children in the United States have found very different patterns of attachment. For example, many studies conducted in the United States have found that roughly 67% of mother-infant dyads show a secure attachment. However, in a careful study of the precursors of attachment within a sample that was predominantly Mormon, only 44% of the infants had developed a secure attachment by age 12 months.

Two conclusions can be drawn from these cross-cultural and subcultural comparisons. First, the strange situation does appear to be valid in exploring the attachment system in a variety of countries and ethnic populations. Second, the differences that are linked to subcultural or ethnic differences within a society are greater than the differences among countries, especially the United States and the countries of Western Europe. These differences suggest a normal range of variability in attachment history, as well as a link to one's ethnic or subcultural identity.

Factors That Account for Differences in Attachment Patterns

How can we account for the differences in the quality of attachment from one caregiver-infant dyad to another? In general, we know that high levels of caregiver sensitivity and low levels of rejection or hostility toward the infant in the first nine months are associated with the formation of a secure attachment. Isabella (1993) found that the mothers of infants who are insecurely attached at 12 months have been consistently more rejecting and less sensitive during the first year than the mothers of securely attached infants. Figure 5.1 illustrates the level of caregiver rejection in the three attachment groups over the first nine months. The pattern of rejection in the avoidant group increases steadily, whereas the pattern of rejection in the resistant group starts out very high and declines. Still, both groups experience more maternal rejection at every period than do the securely attached babies.

Three general factors appear to produce the kind of sensitivity and synchrony that underlies the establishment of a secure attachment. First, one may ask what mental representation of a parental or caregiving person do caregivers bring to this role. Adults who recall their own parents as accepting, responsive, and available are more likely to enact those qualities as caregivers. Adults who experienced early loss or disruption of an attachment relationship have more difficulty providing a secure base for their offspring (Ricks, 1985; Fonagy, Steele & Steele, 1991).

Cultural and subcultural differences are likely to be integrated into one's mental representation of a parental or caregiving person. The culture's beliefs about an infant, including how fragile or vulnerable infants are, how best to respond to their signals of distress, and what skills or temperamental qualities are most valued, are likely to shape a caregiver's practices (Coll, 1990). The study of attachment-related responses across American ethnic subgroups is grossly incomplete. However, some examples suggest how a cultural worldview influences the pattern of parental responsiveness and sensitivity. In a comparison of working-class African-American, Chicano, and Anglo parents, the African-American and Chicano parents valued moving beyond the dependency of infancy as soon as possible (Bartz & Levine, 1978). Thus, they expected their children to show earlier autonomy and responsibility for their behavior than the Anglo group. This difference translated into earlier weaning and toileting, as well as the expectation of earlier walking and gaining control over the expression of feelings. Another study compared Anglo, African-American, and Cuban-American mothers' perceptions of infant crying and related responses (Zeskind, 1983). The African-American mothers were least likely to perceive their babies' cries as urgent or distressing, and in line with this perception, they were least likely to cuddle their babies. The Cuban-American mothers were most likely to soothe their babies with a pacifier and by cuddling and responding quickly to their babies' cries. These comparisons suggest distinct normative patterns of caregiving from one ethnic group to the next.

Second, contemporary factors may influence an adult's ability to provide a secure base for attachment. What immediate conditions may detract from the caregiver's ability to be psychologically available to, responsive to, and accepting of the infant's needs? Among them are the caregiver's self-esteem, the degree of control the caregiver believes he or she should have over the infant's behavior, the quality of the marital relationship both before and after the child is born, the presence of a supportive social network that validates the person's caregiving efforts, and the person's involvement in the labor market (Chase-Lansdale & Owen, 1987; Donovan & Leavitt, 1989; Howes & Markman, 1989). The parent's mental health is another very significant consideration (Lyons-Ruth et al., 1993). All these factors may influence a caregiver's sensitivity to an infant's signals.

Third, the quality of the attachment may be influenced by characteristics of the infant. Certain aspects of the infant's temperament, especially fearfulness, sociability, and the intensity of negative emotions, influence how the attachment relationship is established (Izard et al., 1991). In the strange situation these temperamental qualities can be identified as children are observed in the exploratory phase, in their response to the stranger, and in the intensity of their distress both when the caregiver leaves and when he or she returns. Some research shows that infants who are especially irritable and who react with distress to moderate levels of stimulation are more likely to develop the resistant behavior characteristic of an anxious-resistant attachment (Goldsmith & Alansky, 1987; Belsky & Rovine, 1987). Most studies have shown, however, that temperament per se does not determine whether a secure attachment will be established. Rather, it influences the kinds of parental responses that are needed to help the infant form an internal

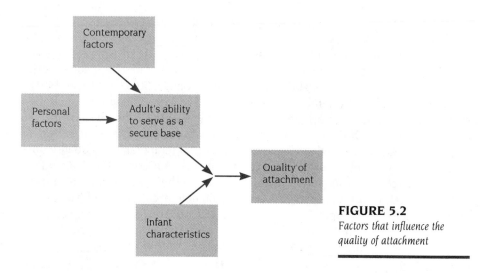

FIGURE 5.2

Factors that influence the quality of attachment

representation of a secure base (Thompson, Connell & Bridges, 1988; Vaughn et al., 1989).

Figure 5.2 shows the elements that are central to the establishment of a secure attachment relationship. They include experiences in the adult's family of origin and early life, experiences in the adult's contemporary situation, and characteristics of the infant that evoke certain patterns of caregiving.

Maternal Employment and Infant Attachment

The impact of employment on infants' overall emotional development has been studied within the framework of attachment theory. In the combined results of a large number of studies that compared the attachment relationships of

---

BOX 5.1

Is There a Critical Period for Attachment?

A *critical period* is a time of maximal sensitivity to or readiness for the development of certain skills or behavior patterns. The particular skill or behavior pattern is not likely to emerge before the onset of the critical period, and it is extremely difficult, if not impossible, to establish once the critical period has passed. The successful emergence of any behavior that has a critical period for development depends on the coordination of the biological readiness of the organism and environmental supports (Scott, 1987).

The earliest work to suggest a critical period for development was done in the field of embryology. Stockard (1907, 1921) found that when certain chemicals were added to the water where fish eggs were developing, the eggs produced deformed embryos. This effect depended on when the chemicals were introduced. Examples of critical periods in human fetal development were provided in Chapter 4. The exposure of a human embryo to the rubella virus during the first trimester of gestation may cause massive disruption in the formation of body organs. The third month of gestation is a critical period for sexual development. In the presence of the hormone testosterone, the bisexual fetus becomes an anatomical male. In the absence of that hormone, the fetus becomes an anatomical female.

Konrad Lorenz (1935, 1937/1961) was one of the first ethologists to compare the critical periods in physical development and behavioral development. Lorenz described a process of social attachment among birds that he called *imprinting*. In this process, the young bird establishes a

(continued)

comparatively permanent bond with its mother. In her absence, the young bird imprints on other available targets, including a model of its mother or a human being. For birds, the onset of the critical period coincides with the time at which they are able to walk. The critical period ends when they begin to fear strangers. After this point, no new model or species can be substituted as a target for imprinting. The long-lasting results of imprinting include not only the early maintenance of contact with the mother bird but the adult bird's focus of courting and mating behaviors on other members of the species during the reproductive period.

The question raised about a critical period for attachment is whether there is a specific time during infancy when the child develops a strong, well-differentiated preference for one person. It is fairly obvious that soon after a child's birth the parent's attachment to the child becomes quite specific; that is, the parent would not be willing to replace his or her own child with any other child of similar age. At what point does the child make this kind of commitment to the parent?

Yarrow (1963, 1964, 1970) observed 100 infants who were shifted from foster mothers to adoptive mothers. The infants who were separated from their foster mothers at 6 months or earlier showed minimal distress. They did not tend to express prolonged anger or depression over separation if their physical and emotional needs continued to be met. If one recalls that separation anxiety is not usually observed before the age of about 9 months, it is not surprising that these infants adapted so well to longer separations before this age.

All the infants who were transferred from foster mothers to adoptive mothers at 8 months or older showed strong negative reactions, including angry protest and withdrawal. These infants found the disruption of their earlier relationships very stressful. One cannot, however, infer from these observations that new attachments to the adoptive parents would not eventually form.

BOX 5.1

(continued)

Konrad Lorenz inadvertently became the target of imprinting for these geese. They followed him as if he were their mother.

Later research by Bowlby (1980) described the emotional development of adolescents who had been moved repeatedly from one foster home or institution to another. These youngsters had never had any opportunity to form an enduring, stable, loving relationship with a caring adult. As adolescents, they were found to be *affectionless*, unable to form mutually trusting or close relationships with others.

Based on these observations of disruption in naturally occurring mother-infant relationships, we can say that the onset of a critical period for attachment must begin some time after the age of about 6 months. This does not mean that the first six months play no role in the establishment of a strong bond between the child and the caregiver. On the contrary, these early months provide the background experiences of consistency, warmth, and familiarity upon which the specific attachment is built.

If the critical period for attachment begins at about age 6 months, when does this period end? This question is more difficult to answer. Longitudinal studies have reported consistency in the quality of attachment from ages 12 to 18 months, from 12 to 20 months, and from 12 months to 6 years. Barring prolonged separation, it appears that the mental representation of the attachment starts to take shape around 6 months and is established by the end of the first year of life (Main, Kaplan & Cassidy, 1985).

infants whose mothers were employed full time with infants whose mothers were employed part time or who were not employed, 36% of the infants of full-time working mothers were classified as having an insecure attachment compared to 29% of the part-time or nonemployed mothers (Clarke-Stewart, 1989; Belsky, 1988, 1990). This observation has led to an active debate about the risks associated with infant care. Jay Belsky (1988, 1990) has argued that, based on the research findings, for infants who experience 20 hours per week or more of some type of alternative child care during the first year of life, there is greater risk of insecurity in their maternal attachment and of later disruption in social adjustment.

Other scholars have countered that the studies do not provide a sound basis for this conclusion (Clarke-Stewart, 1989; Fox & Fein, 1990; Zigler & Lang, 1991). Margaret Owen and her colleagues (1984) hypothesized that perhaps the instability of the employment situation rather than the employment itself caused disruption in the attachment relationship. They assessed attachment to mother and father in a sample of 59 middle-class children at ages 12 months and 20 months. The families were divided into four maternal employment groups; full time, part time, nonemployed, and one group that changed employment status between the 12-month and the 20-month observation. Overall, 85% of the infants were securely attached to their mothers at 12 months, and 77% were securely attached to their fathers. At 20 months, 86% were securely attached to their mothers, and 64% were securely attached to their fathers. Thus, in this sample, maternal employment was not associated with a high rate of insecure attachments, and there was no evidence that mothers who were employed full or part time had less secure attachments with their infants than the nonemployed mothers. The attachment patterns were quite stable over the two measurement periods. What is more, the attachment patterns of the mothers who had changed employment status were just as stable as were those of mothers who had had the same employment status during the two-year study. Going back to work after 12 months did not alter the quality of the mother-child attachment. The study did, however, find greater instability in the infants' attachment to their fathers when their mothers changed employment status after 12 months. Of 13 infants whose mothers' employment status changed, 6 showed a change of attachment with their fathers between ages 12 months and 20 months: 4 from secure to insecure, and 2 from insecure to secure. The authors suggested that these changes reflect adjustments that are required by fathers when the mothers modify their employment status.

In studies of attachment, it is not uncommon for about one-third of the samples to be evaluated as insecurely attached. The percentage of insecure attachments in this composite analysis does not differ substantially from the findings in many studies of nonemployed mothers. Insecurity in attachment may result from exposure to poor-quality infant care, or from stress on mothers who are working full time. These two factors may be compounded in that mothers who are highly stressed may make hasty decisions about infant care, failing to take the time to evaluate the quality of care their babies are receiving. Some scholars have suggested that the strange situation itself is not an appropriate measure of the attachment of babies who are accustomed to frequent separations from their mothers. These babies may be able to handle their mothers' departure more easily and may not seek proximity upon reunion, both of which behaviors are typically considered evidence of anxious-avoidant attachment.

Many mothers of infants go to work having made careful arrangements for alternative child care and still feeling guilty that they may be harming their infants

Many of the same physical cues that indicate the formation of an attachment between infant and caregiver can be seen in the love relationships of adolescents and adults— gazing, touching, snuggling, and affectionate "cooing."

because they really believe that mothers should stay home with their babies. Many fathers share this belief and are uncomfortable about the amount of time their children spend in the care of others. It may take many years to disabuse parents of these concerns even if solid evidence is eventually available about the conditions of employment, child care, and family roles that support optimal development.

The Relevance of Attachment to Later Development

An attachment is more than the expression of behavior; it is an internal representation of the characteristics of a specific relationship (Main et al., 1985). This representation provides the infant with a set of rules with which to organize information and to interpret experiences related to the relationship. The representation takes shape as a product of the infant's efforts to maintain contact with the caregiver and the caregiver's customary responses to these attempts. In a secure attachment, the representation is based on the infant's confidence that his or her attempts to make contact with the caregiver will be accepted.

From ages 12 to 18 months, the quality of infant-mother attachment appears to remain quite stable. Secure attachments in infancy have been associated with positive adaptive capacities when the child is 3½ to 5 years old. Securely attached infants become preschoolers who show greater resilience, self-control, and curiosity (Vaughn et al., 1979). As we discussed earlier, a subgroup of the infants who have a disorganized attachment are very hostile, aggressive preschoolers.

Adolescents and adults can reflect on the nature of their early attachments and the mental representations they have produced and can reinterpret their meaning. For example, a boy who, during his infancy and toddler years, viewed his mother as rejecting because she was often unavailable for comfort and contact may, as an adolescent, realize that his mother was often away because she was working. He may understand that his mother was doing everything she could to provide for her family and that she was really too exhausted to respond to him when she was at home. This insight may modify the nature of the boy's attachment representation and allow him to approach new relationships more confidently.

From a life-span perspective, the quality of the attachment formed in infancy influences the formation of later relationships (Ainsworth, 1989). Children who have formed secure attachments are likely to find more enjoyment in close peer friendships during their preschool years (Park & Waters, 1989). It makes sense that

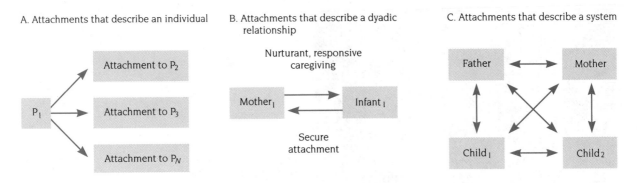

A. Attachments that describe an individual

B. Attachments that describe a dyadic relationship

C. Attachments that describe a system

FIGURE 5.3

Three levels of attachment
Source: Newman & Newman, 1988.

the cognitive representation one forms of an attachment relationship influences one's expectations of an intimate partner. Adult love relationships can be characterized along many of the same dimensions as infant attachments, including the desire to maintain physical contact with the loved one, increased disclosure and responsiveness to the loved one, the effectiveness of the loved one in providing comfort and reassurance that reduce distress, and an element of exclusiveness or preferential response in comparison with that to other friends, relatives, and acquaintances.

The parenting relationship can also be understood as an elaboration of the attachment representation. Adults who have experienced a secure attachment in their own infancy are more likely to be able to comfort and respond to their children. Adults whose childhood attachments were unpredictable or even hostile are more likely to have difficulty coping successfully with young infants' needs (Ricks, 1985).

We do not mean to imply that the quality of adult love relationships or parental behavior is determined solely by the quality of childhood attachments. Many experiences and concepts intervene to modify the attachment representation and to expand one's capacity to love another person after infancy. However, attachment is a construct that may help to describe three levels of lifetime behavior: individual, dyadic, and systemic (see Figure 5.3).

Maturation of Sensory-Perceptual and Motor Functions

The Physical Status of the Newborn

The average full-term baby born in the United States weighs 3300 grams (7 to 7.5 pounds) and is 51 centimeters (20 inches) long. Boys are slightly heavier and longer than girls. At birth, girls' nervous systems and bones are about two weeks more mature than boys'.

In the first minute after birth, and then again at five minutes, the newborn's life signs are evaluated by the *Apgar scoring method*, named for its originator, Virginia Apgar (1953; see Table 5.3). Five life signs are scored on a scale from 0 to 2: heart rate, respiratory effort, muscle tone, reflex irritability, and body color. A score of 7–10 means the infant is in good condition. Scores of 4–6 mean fair condition and indicate a need to administer supplemental oxygen. Scores of 0–3 suggest extremely poor condition and the need for resuscitation. Even among the highest group, who score 7–10, those with scores of 7 or 8 show less efficient attention and less habituation to stimuli than the higher scoring infants. The most important use of the Apgar is to evaluate the need for

TABLE 5.3   The Apgar Scoring Chart

Sign	Score		
	0	**1**	**2**
Heart rate	Absent	Slow (less than 100 beats/minute)	Over 100 beats/minute
Respiratory effort	Absent	Slow or irregular breathing	Good crying, strong breathing
Muscle tone	Flaccid or limp	Weak; some flexion of extremities	Active motion; strong flexion of extremities
Reflex irritability	No response	Weak cry, grimace, cough, or sneeze	Vigorous cry, grimace, cough, or sneeze
Color	Blue, pale	Body pink; extremities blue	Completely pink

Source: Apgar, 1953.

immediate intervention; it does not predict subsequent development (Francis, Self & Horowitz, 1987).

Babies vary a great deal in their degree of physical maturity at birth. These differences influence their capacity to regulate such survival functions as breathing, digesting, waking, and sleeping. Infants who weigh less than 2500 grams (about 5 pounds, 8 ounces) are called *low-birth-weight babies*. Low birth weight may result from being born before the full period of gestation; from the mother's inadequate diet, smoking, or use of drugs; or from genetic disorders, as discussed in Chapter 4. These factors tend to lower the fetus's weight at any given gestational age. Babies who are light for their gestational age are at greater *risk*. They are more likely to experience problems at birth and after than those who are born prematurely but are of average weight for their gestational age (Cassady & Strange, 1987). Box 5.2 discusses some of what is known about the development of very small babies.

At birth, the genetic program that has been carried out during the gestation period provides most newborn infants with intact sensory organs and a well-formed brain. The infant brain contains an estimated 100 to 300 billion neurons, or nerve cells, that are already linked in pathways designed to perform specific functions. The basic organization of the brain does not change after birth, but details of its structure seem to demonstrate *plasticity* for some time, particularly in the cerebral cortex (the tissue that forms the folded ridges on the brain's surface). Experience appears to place its own imprint on the establishment of neural connections: Sights, smells, sounds, tastes, touches, and posture activate and, with time, strengthen specific neural pathways, while others fall into disuse. For example, a childhood imbalance in the use of both eyes will cause permanent deficits in the visual perception of the underused eye. It appears that, in the neural network of the brain, less-used pathways may be abandoned, well-used pathways broadened, and new pathways added where they are needed (Aoki & Siekevitz, 1988). The infant's interaction with the immediate stimulus environment shapes the organization of neural connections, creating very early patterns of familiarity and meaning.

BOX 5.2

Very Small Babies

In our culture, we count our age from the date of our birth. But today many babies are born before they are fully developed. Modern technology has pushed back the limits of fetal viability to about 24 weeks of gestational age, or a weight of about 500 grams (slightly over 1 pound). These tiny babies, not much bigger than the palm of your hand, go through weeks of round-the-clock care in a struggle to survive. About 17,000 infants who weigh less than 2 pounds are cared for in the nation's intensive care nurseries. These babies have about a 70% chance of survival; the smallest babies have only a 20% chance (Kantrowitz, 1988).

What do we know about the developmental progress of these very small babies? What is the quality of their relationship with their parents, modified by their prolonged hospitalization and their obvious vulnerability and risk? How do parents cope with the anxieties and frustrations of caring for their very tiny baby? What are the effects on the child's cognitive capacities and later intellectual development? Because this is a group that has survived in appreciable numbers only in recent decades, many of these questions are still unanswered, but we are beginning to have a picture of the psychosocial development of very small babies.

In the formation of an attachment between parent and infant, very low birth-weight preterm babies are clearly different from full-term babies. They are less physically attractive; they have higher-pitched, unpleasant cries; they are more easily over-stimulated and more difficult to soothe; and they are less able to establish rhythmic patterns of social interaction. What is more, the early weeks and months of parental contact with these babies takes place in the intimidating environment of the hospital, where the babies are usually hooked up to monitors, have one or more tubes in their bodies, and are going through periodic physical crises in the struggle for survival. In this situation, it is a wonder that any kind of attachment develops at all.

When the parents have opportunities to interact with and care for their infants during the hospital stay, they often develop an almost irresistible tendency to become absorbed in their child, just as parents of full-term babies do. The process of attachment, however, appears to face greater challenges. These parents find it harder to synchronize their parenting activities with the activities of their babies. They perceive their babies as being difficult and as giving few cues of satisfaction or responsiveness. In other words, a sense of reciprocity between parent and infant is more difficult to establish in the early months of life (Levy-Shiff, Sharir & Mogilner, 1989). Nonetheless, in assessments of attachment at age 2, very low birth-weight babies were just as likely as full-term babies to have formed secure attachments to both their mothers and their fathers, depending on the health and robustness of the infants (Easterbrooks, 1989).

Extremely low birth-weight infants appear to be at risk for problems in subse-

(continued)

Sensory and Perceptual Systems

During the first months of life, the sensory and perceptual systems—vision, hearing, taste, smell, touch, motion sensitivity, and responsiveness to internal cues (proprioception)—develop rapidly and appear to function at a more advanced level than the motor system. Since voluntary muscle movements are not yet under the infant's control in the early days and months of life, researchers have to employ considerable ingenuity to gauge infants' sensory and perceptual competencies. Current work uses behaviors such as gazing time, changes in heart rate, sucking, facial action, and head turning as indicators of infants' responses to sensory stimulation. Infants appear to be quite sensitive to internal and environmental stimuli. In the first months of life, genetic programs and experience combine to construct neural networks, and before very long, sensations appear to be

BOX 5.2

(continued)

quent cognitive development. Infants born weighing less than 1500 grams are likely to suffer serious brain hemorrhages. In addition, their underdeveloped lungs cannot deliver an adequate supply of oxygen to the brain. Severe respiratory distress during the early months of life is associated with cognitive deficits in the first year of life, and with learning and language deficits during the preschool years and into the early school years (Rose, Feldman & Wallace, 1992; Rose et al., 1988; Field, Dempsey & Shuman, 1983). The babies at greatest risk for cognitive delays are those born before 30 weeks of gestation to parents who have very limited educational and financial resources.

Because of the great risk of cognitive deficits in babies with both low birth weight and preterm status, intervention programs have been designed for working with mothers and their low-birth-weight preterm infants. One such intervention, the Infant Health and Development program, involved 935 mother-infant pairs at eight sites (Brooks-Gunn et al., 1993). One-third of the infants and their mothers were involved in intervention over the first three years, and the other two-thirds received periodic pediatric follow-up visits and referral to other services. The intervention included home visits, center-based infant programming after 12 months, and involving the mothers in parent group meetings. All the children showed declines in measured IQ from 12 to 24 and 36 months. However, the groups that participated in the intervention showed less

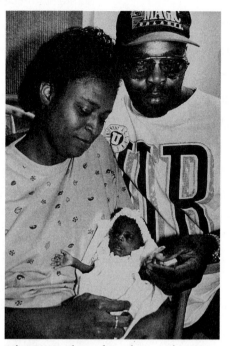

When Caci Burke was born, three months prematurely, she weighed 12.9 ounces. After four months in the hospital, her mother and father finally got to take her home.

decline. The intervention was most beneficial for the heavier babies (birth weights of over 2000 grams) and least effective for the lightest babies (birth weights under 1500 grams).

organized and represented as meaningful perceptions in the infant's brain. One thing is becoming increasingly clear: Infants' sensory and perceptual capabilities provide the basis for establishing effective interactive relationships with their caregivers.

Vision Infants respond to a variety of visual dimensions, including movement, color, brightness, complexity, light-dark contrast, contours, depth, and distance (Hickey & Peduzzi, 1987; Banks & Dannemiller, 1987). In the early postnatal weeks, infants focus optimally on objects that are about 20 centimeters away, about the distance of a mother's face if she were cradling her baby in her arms. Newborns can shift focus to scan and keep track of a moving target, but not as easily and smoothly as older babies. Young infants appear to focus their attention on the contours or outer borders of objects rather than on the inner details. Thus, if you are holding a young baby, the child may appear to be staring at your hairline or your chin rather than at your mouth.

Visual acuity improves rapidly during the first four months. Pattern perception and movement perception mature as well. By 2 months, infants appear to have formed an expectation of a visual sequence; as they watch a pattern of events, they show evidence of anticipating the next event in the sequence (Canfield & Haith, 1991; Aslin, 1987). Four-month-old babies perceive objects much as adults would, although they do not have the same set of cognitive associations with objects that imply specific functions or categories. They recognize shapes and they detect complex patterns of motion like human walking. Three-month-old infants respond to wavelengths of light as though they perceive distinct hues of blue, green, yellow, and red (Bornstein, Kessen & Weiskopf, 1976; Teller & Bornstein, 1987; Aslin, 1987).

The human face and "faceness" appear to have special appeal to newborns. In addition to their response to the form, shape, and movement of human facial features, infants 1 to 2 days old can discriminate and imitate the happy, sad, and surprised expressions of a live model (Field et al., 1982). This very early capacity for imitation wanes and is replaced by a voluntary capacity to imitate facial expressions during the second year of life. Some 2-day-old infants discriminate between their mother's face and the face of a stranger (Field et al., 1984). By 3 months, almost all infants distinguish a parent's face from that of a stranger (Zucker, 1985).

Hearing   Hearing is the earliest link between the newborn and the mother. The fetus is sensitive and responsive to auditory stimuli in the uterus (DeCasper & Spence, 1986; Aslin, 1987). Before birth, infants hear their mother's heartbeat, and this sound continues to have soothing properties for the infant in the days and weeks after birth. Newborns can distinguish their mother's voice from another female voice (DeCasper & Fifer, 1980).

Young infants perceive changes in loudness, pitch, duration, and location of sounds (Kuhl, 1987). They use sounds to localize objects in space even without the aid of visual cues (Clifton, Perris & Bullinger, 1991). One of the earliest stimuli to evoke a smile is the sound of the human voice. Infants appear to be capable of making most of the basic sound distinctions used in human speech throughout the world. Sound sensitivity becomes more focused as infants become more reliant on language-specific sounds, indicating a reorganization of sensory capabilities as the child listens to people speaking a particular language (Werker, 1989). Here we see another example of the plasticity referred to earlier: the fine-tuning of a neural network as a result of experience.

Taste and Smell   The sense of taste is at least partially functional in utero (Mistretta & Bradley, 1977). From the observation of facial expressions, one can detect differences in infants' ability to differentiate among various tastes, especially sweet, sour, bitter, and salty. Two hours after birth, an infant's facial responses to a sweet taste (sucrose) are characterized primarily by relaxation and sucking. Sucrose has an especially calming effect on newborns and appears to reduce pain (Blass & Smith, 1992). Salty, sour, and bitter solutions produce the same negative upper- and mid-face responses, but different accompanying lower-face actions: the lips purse in response to a sour taste; the mouth gapes in response to a bitter taste; and no distinctive lower facial reaction is seen in response to a salty taste (Rosenstein & Oster, 1988).

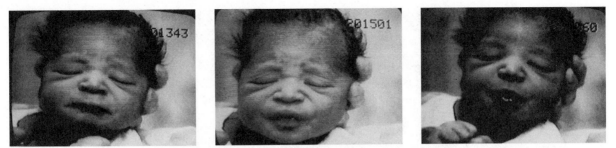

This sequence of facial expressions was elicited by a sweet solution. The initial negative grimace is followed by relaxation and sucking.

Breast-fed infants are particularly sensitive to their mothers' body odors (Cernoch & Porter, 1985). One study showed that, by their sense of smell, 7-day-old babies could distinguish their own mothers' nursing pads from those of other mothers (MacFarlane, 1975). The mother's odor may play an important role in stimulating early mother-infant interactions (Porter, Balogh & Makin, 1988).

Touch   The skin is the largest sensory organ and the earliest to develop in utero. Evidence from animal and human research suggests that touch plays a central role in development. Gentle handling, including rocking, stroking, and cuddling a baby, has soothing effects. Controlled laboratory experiments indicate that mothers of newborn infants can successfully identify their own babies by touch if they have been with the infant for one hour or more since childbirth; the recognition was not based on olfactory or other nontactile cues (Kaitz et al., 1992). In many cultures, *swaddling*, or wrapping a baby snugly in a soft blanket, is commonly used to sooth a newborn. One of the effective techniques of caring for low-birth-weight babies is regular, gentle stroking, rocking, and other forms of soothing touch.

Kinesthetic stimulation may arouse as well as sooth an infant. Many caregivers attempt to get their babies' attention by jiggling or bouncing them. Some theorists state that caregivers often use kinesthetic stimulation to maintain optimal responses, employing soothing techniques when the baby is upset or stressed and more vigorous arousing techniques to engage the baby in social interaction or to get the baby's attention (Yarrow, Pedersen & Rubenstein, 1977). In many cultures, babies are carried on the mother's back, in a side sling, or in a front pouch so they have continuous physical contact with the caregiver as well as opportunities to encounter a wide range of visual, auditory, and olfactory stimuli as they move about the house or through the community.

Touch is an active as well as a passive sense; babies use touch to explore objects and people, including their own bodies. Sucking and mouthing are early forms of exploratory touch. Babies recognize qualities of objects from how the objects feel in their mouths: nubby, smooth, chewy, flexible, or rigid (Rose & Ruff, 1987). Of course, in older infants, most tactile information comes through touching with the hands and bringing objects to the face in order to take a closer look or to explore with the mouth. By the age of 5 or 6 months, infants can use their hands for the controlled examination of objects, fingering the surface to explore small details and transferring the object from hand to hand to detect corners, shapes, and the flexibility of surfaces as well as the overall size of the object (Gibson, 1962; Ruff, 1984).

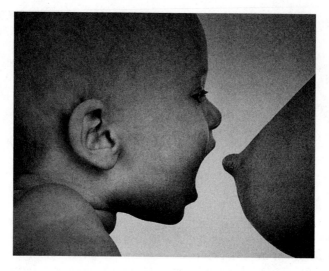

"First meal"

The Interconnectedness of Sensory and Perceptual Capacities Even though the sensory and perceptual capacities evolve independently, they function simultaneously, in an interconnected system, to provide a variety of information about the environment. For example, when an infant is being nursed, the mother at first guides the baby toward her breast, but the baby also uses visual, tactile, olfactory, and kinesthetic cues to find and grab hold of the nipple. A baby who is very hungry may close her eyes to concentrate exclusively on bursts of sucking behavior, coordinating sucking and swallowing as efficiently as possible. But as the initial swallows of milk satisfy the strong hunger pangs, the baby pauses to take in other aspects of the situation. She may gaze at the contours of her mother's face, playfully lick the milk dripping from her mother's breast, smell its fragrance and taste its special sweet taste, and listen to the sounds of her mother's voice offering comfort or inviting conversation. The baby may reach up to explore her mother's skin or relax in the comfort of her mother's gentle embrace. All the sensory information becomes integrated to create familiarity with this scenario, including a growing recognition of the mother and a rich mixture of sensory impressions associated with this special situation in which hunger is satisfied.

Motor Development

At birth, one reason that infants appear to be so helpless is that their voluntary muscle responses are poorly coordinated. They do not have the strength and coordination in their head and neck, arms, and legs that would allow them to initiate smooth, purposeful actions. Development in the brain and the spinal cord, along with increases in muscle strength and coordination, lead to extraordinary changes in motor behavior over the first two years of life. Motor development follows two fundamental directions: from the head, neck, and shoulders to the legs and feet (*cephalocaudal*), and from the center, including the shoulders and trunk, to the extremities, the hands and fingers (*proximodistal*). In addition, motor behavior shifts from being largely reflexive to being purposeful and voluntary. In Table 3.1 in Chapter 3, you saw several common infant reflexes, including the evoking stimulus and the response. Infant reflexes include sucking, grasping, rooting (turning the head in the direction of the cheek that is stroked), coughing, and stepping. Many of these built-in responses help infants survive and lead them on to

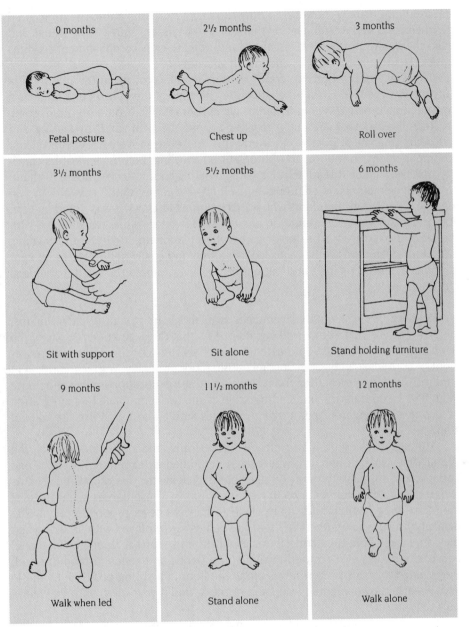

FIGURE 5.4

Sequence of motor development and locomotion in infants
Note: *The age at which 50% of babies mastered each skill is indicated. These norms were established in the 1960s by means of the Denver Developmental Screening Test.*
Source: *Based on Frankenberg & Dodds, 1967.*

develop more complicated sequences of voluntary behavior. The sucking reflex is a good example. At birth, inserting something in an infant's mouth produces the sucking reflex. This reflex helps infants gain nourishment relatively easily before sucking behavior is under voluntary control. Before long, however, infants become skillful in controlling the strength and sensitivity of their sucking behavior. They begin exploring their hands and other objects with their mouths as well as efficiently ingesting nourishment.

Motor skills develop as a result of physical growth, maturation of the bones and muscles, and maturation of the nervous system. Figure 5.4 shows the normal sequence of development of motor and movement skills during the first year of life. Babies vary in the sequence of these skills and in the rate at which they acquire them. Usually, however, during the first 12 months babies begin to hold their heads up and to roll over by themselves; they learn to reach for things and grasp them; and they sit, crawl, stand, and walk. Each accomplishment requires practice, refinement, struggle, and, finally, mastery.

Consider Brad's efforts to crawl. He is placed face down in the middle of a gaily colored blanket. His mother kneels at the edge of the blanket and dangles a favorite stuffed bear. She smiles and says encouragingly, "Come on, Brad; come get Teddy." Brad looks intently, reaches toward the bear, and, by kicking and squirming, manages to move forward. This snakelike movement is Brad's first accomplishment on the way to well-organized crawling. Before he masters crawling, however, he must learn to raise himself on his knees, to coordinate his hand and leg movements, and to propel himself forward rather than backward. In systematic observations of infants who were beginning to crawl, it was noted that the ability to maintain one's weight on one arm and two legs while reaching out with the second hand was a precursor to crawling (Goldfield, 1989). Thus, crawling behavior, which tends to be regarded as natural and easily performed in infancy, is in fact achieved by long and patient effort to coordinate the head, shoulders, arms, and legs.

Walking   A similar pattern emerges as infants learn to walk (Clark & Phillips, 1993). In the early phases of walking, it appears that the segmental motion of the thigh and the shank must be mastered as well as the coordination of the movement of both legs. Walking is unstable at first, but gradually, with a great deal of hard work and repetition over about three months, infants appear to develop both thigh-shank coordination and coordination of the two legs. Once this integration of movement is established, walking becomes stable and much like the walk of adults.

Although walking upright is clearly a genetically guided human capacity, the age at which infants begin to walk may be modified by experience. On the one hand, lack of stimulation or encouragement may delay the age of walking. Dennis (1960) observed orphans in two Iranian institutions. These babies spent most of their time lying on their backs in their cribs and were never propped upright. The institutions were so understaffed that the babies rarely played with adults. When they were taken from their cribs, it was usually to be set on the floor and left alone. Few of the babies ever crawled in the typical hands-and-knees fashion; instead, they tended to scootch themselves along the floor in a sitting position. Of the 1- and 2-year-olds, none could walk, and of the 3- and 4-year-olds, only 15% could walk unassisted.

On the other hand, some experiences advance the age at which walking begins. Infants who were given practice in strengthening the stepping reflex when they were 2–8 weeks old walked at an earlier age than babies who had not had this kind of practice (Zelazo, Zelazo & Kolb, 1972). In cross-cultural observations of African and West Indian child-rearing practices, babies spent much more time in a vertical position than do most U.S. infants. Mothers propped the babies up with pillows, carried them upright in a sling, and gently stretched and massaged the babies' back, arms, and legs, all of which helped to strengthen head and neck control and to orient the babies to upright locomotion (Super, 1981; Hopkins & Westra, 1988).

The achievement of competence in each of the sensory-perceptual and motor tasks depends on a child's maturational level, on environmental conditions, and on the strength of the child's desire for mastery. The sensory-perceptual and motor systems interact to produce more complex, fine-tuned behavior. For example, evidence suggests that infants learn to perceive in new ways to accomplish locomotion over slopes. Older infants, aged 14 months, investigated the slopes by touching, gently stepping, and swaying at the top of the slope before descending. They tended to invent a special strategy for descending, such as scooting down backward, sliding down while sitting, or crawling. Younger infants, aged 8 months, did not seem to appreciate the steepness of the slopes, and they approached the descent as they would a flat surface, often sliding off the ramp. Learning to evaluate and navigate a slope appears to require the fine-tuning of exploratory behavior (Adolph, Eppler & Gibson, 1993).

Reaching and Grasping   Reaching, grasping, and manipulating objects illustrate the maturation of the motor system from relatively gross, uncoordinated movements to finely tuned, purposeful actions. Both grasping and reaching have their origins in reflexive behaviors (Fentress & McLeod, 1986). Very young infants can support their full weight through the strength of their grasping reflex. When propped in an infant seat, they will reach and grasp reflexively at an object—and reach their target about 40% of the time. At age 4 weeks, this reflexive reaching behavior seems to disappear, and by 5 months, it is replaced by voluntary reaching, accurate grasping, clutching, and letting go (Bower, 1987).

The transition from involuntary to voluntary reaching and grasping results from genetically guided maturation coupled with repeated discovery, exploration, and practice of controlled, coordinated muscle movements. Here a 2½-month-old girl gains control of her hands and fingers:

> She has discovered her hands, stares at them many times a day for three or four minutes at a time, watches them as she wiggles fingers, extends and flexes them, rotates wrists. She also clasps her hands together and stares at them out in front of her at arm's length. (Church, 1966, p. 7)

Voluntary reaching begins as the child tries to make contact with objects on the same side of the body as the outstretched hand. By 4½ months, babies will reach for objects placed on the same side, the opposite side, or in the middle of the body. By this age, babies have also become skilled in using both hands to hold an object, so they are more able to keep the object close enough to investigate. They may shift from exploring with their fingers to sucking and biting to find out more about the object (Rochat, 1989). By 12 months, babies can use their index finger and thumb to pick up tiny things, such as clots of dust, little threads, pieces of dry cereal, and spaghetti noodles. With this advance, they can also manipulate things by lifting latches, turning knobs, and placing small things inside bigger things and trying to get them out. These activities bring the baby new information about how obects work and how they relate to one another. At the same time, they bring the baby into new conflicts with a caregiver who knows that tiny things that shouldn't are going to go into the mouth and objects that need to be left alone are going to be picked and pried at.

Infants advance socially, intellectually, and emotionally as they achieve sensory-perceptual and motor skills. Sensory and motor accomplishments allow them to gain access to and awareness of their environment. Increases in motor control permit infants to experience more varied stimulation, to explore objects more deliberately, and to pursue goals voluntarily. Motor development may play a role in determining developmental sequences or "timetables" in domains such as touch and depth perception. If so, motor behavior may be more important and

The combination of reaching and crawling gives infants access to new objects in their environment, like a cat's tail!

influential than it has been thought to be in accounting for progress in cognitive development (Bushnell & Boudreau, 1993). An increased sense of control is usually associated with positive emotions, such as joy, confidence, and delight. Changes in the process of social attachment also rely on changes in sensory-perceptual and motor skills. Creeping, crawling, and walking give children increased control over making and maintaining contact with their caregivers and thus enhance their feelings of effectiveness, security, and well-being.

Sensorimotor Intelligence and Primitive Causality

How do infants organize their experiences? Piaget (1970) suggested that the primary mechanism underlying the growth of intelligence during infancy is *sensorimotor adaptation*. In this process, infants actively engage the environment. Initially, they use their instinctive reflex responses, such as sucking, grasping, rooting, and gazing, to explore their world. Gradually, as they gain voluntary control over their behavior, infants alter their responses to explore the unique properties of the objects around them. Infants do not use the conventional symbolic system of language to organize experience. Rather, they form schemes based on perception and direct investigation of the environment. The notion of sensorimotor intelligence, then, encompasses the emergence and elaboration of simple and complex schemes for the patterns of movement and the sensory experiences that are associated with specific environmental events.

BOX 5.3

Temperament

In a child's temperament, we can see how genetic determinants of individuality influence the process of adaptation to the family group. *Temperament* is a theoretical construct that refers to relatively stable characteristics of response to the environment that can be observed during the first months of life (Thomas & Chess, 1980; Hubert et al., 1982; Lerner & Lerner, 1983). In early work on this construct, Escalona (1968) found that infants differed in their sensitivity to various sensory modalities, some being easily irritated by noises, others showing sensitivity to touch. She also found consistent differences in how easy or difficult it was for babies to shut out the stimulus environment and how readily upset or easily soothed they were. Thomas, Chess, and Birch (1970) rated newborns on nine dimensions: activity level, rhythmicity, approach-withdrawal, adaptability, intensity of reaction, threshold of responsiveness, quality of mood, distractibility, and attention span and persistence. As you can see, many of these dimensions are related to the sensory-perceptual and motor systems and to the adaptive strategies infants use to orient to or withdraw from stimulation. From these ratings, Thomas et al. classified babies into three temperamental groups: easy, difficult, and slow-to-warm-up. As shown in Table 5.4, roughly 40% of babies are characterized as easy, and 35% were of mixed characteristics that could not be classified.

There is considerable evidence that

(continued)

some aspects of temperament, including activity level, sociability, and emotionality, are influenced by a person's genetic make-up (Thomas & Chess, 1977, 1986; Buss & Plomin, 1984, 1986; Goldsmith et al., 1987; Goldsmith & Campos, 1986; Wilson & Matheney, 1986; Braungart et al., 1992). In addition, some dimensions of temperament, especially emotionality and activity level, show a modest stability over the adjacent periods of infancy and toddlerhood (Bates, 1987). In one study, infants were seen at age 2 days, and then at 5, 14, and 25 months (Calkins & Fox, 1992). Measures of infant distress and reactivity to frustration at 2 days and at 5 months were associated with a temperamental category referred to as *inhibition* at 24 months. Inhibited children show a pattern of restraint, avoidance, wariness of unfamiliar people, objects, and events (Robinson et al., 1992). In contrast, *uninhibited* children show a comparatively rapid and fearless approach to novelty. There is considerable interest in linking these temperamental characteristics to personality traits that in adulthood are described as introversion and extroversion.

The stability of temperament from infancy into later childhood and into adulthood is still a matter of question. Measures of temperament in infancy do not correlate highly with measures in the early and middle school years. In all likelihood, temperamental characteristics can be modified as the child reacts to socialization pressures at home and at school and develops new inner

---

Think for a moment of a familiar experience, such as tying a shoelace. Learning to tie a shoelace requires little, if any, language. In fact, explaining to a young child how to tie a shoelace is particularly difficult because very few words or concepts are part of the process. This kind of motor routine is a use of sensorimotor intelligence that continues into adulthood. When infants begin to adapt their sucking reflex to make it more effective, or when they use different techniques of sucking for the breast and the bottle, they are demonstrating sensorimotor intelligence. The familiar scheme for sucking is modified so that it takes into account the special properties of the breast and the bottle.

One of the most important components of sensorimotor intelligence is the capacity to anticipate that certain actions will have specific effects on objects in the environment. Babies learn to associate specific actions with regularly occurring results. In other words, infants develop a scheme for *causality* based solely on

capacities to regulate his or her behavior. Thomas and Chess (1977, 1986) found that when parents were calm and allowed their children to adapt to novelty at a leisurely pace, difficult children grew more comfortable and accepted new routines more easily. However, when their parents were impatient and demanding, difficult children remained difficult and had a hard time adjusting to new situations as they grew older.

Children's temperament influences the tone of their interactions, the frequency of their interactions, the way others react to them, and the way they react to the reactions of others. The fit between parents' temperament and their children's temperament plays an important part in the quality of the parent-child relationship (Plomin,

BOX 5.3

(continued)

1990). An active, socially outgoing parent may feel some disappointment with a baby who does not respond eagerly to social interaction. The home environment, including the quality of parent-child interactions and the resources that are made available to children, is, to a degree, the product of certain inherited characteristics of both parents and children. An adult's warmth, sociability, intelligence, and activity level, which are genetically guided, will be expressed in her or his parenting behaviors. Similarly, infants' characteristics, such as their physical appearance, sensitivity to stimulation, sociability, and intelligence, which are genetically guided, will call forth certain parental responses and will shape the direction of parenting.

TABLE 5.4　Three Types of Infant Temperament

Type	Description	% of Total Sample
Easy	Positive mood, regular body functions, low or moderate intensity of reaction, adaptability, positive approach to rather than withdrawal from new situations	40
Slow to warm up	Low activity level, tendency to withdraw on first exposure to new stimuli, slow to adapt, somewhat negative in mood, low intensity of reaction	15
Difficult	Irregular body functions, unusually intense reactions, tendency to withdraw from new situations, slow to adapt to change, generally negative mood	10

Source: Based on Thomas et al., 1970.

---

sensory and motor experience. For example, they discover that if they cry, Mama will come to them; if they kick a chair, it will move; and if they let go of a spoon, it will fall to the floor. These predictable sequences are learned through repetition and experimentation. The predictability of the events depends on their consistency, as well as on the child's initiation of the action. Infants also experiment to determine the variety of results that a single action may cause (Keil, 1975; Rovee & Rovee, 1969). Eventually, they can work backward, selecting a desirable outcome and then performing the behavior that will produce it.

In an intriguing six-month analysis, researchers videotaped infants who were learning to use a spoon for eating (Connolly & Dalgleish, 1989). At first, the actions appeared to focus on exploration of the spoon itself. The infants banged the spoon, sucked it, or rubbed it in their hair. Then, they showed an understanding of the purpose of the spoon as a tool by repeating the action sequence of dipping the spoon in a dish and bringing it to the mouth. However, no food was on the spoon. In the third phase, the babies began to incorporate the function and the action by loading the spoon with food and then bringing it to the mouth. During this phase, they made so many errors that very little food actually got to the mouth via the spoon. Finally, the babies were able to coordinate the action and the function by using the other hand to steady the bowl, by altering the angle of the spoon, by picking up food they had dropped, and by devising other strategies to enhance the function, depending on the type of food involved. Here, we see a demonstration of how one rather complex motor behavior becomes part of a problem-solving action sequence during the sensorimotor period of development.

Schemes for complex, purposeful causal behavior develop gradually during the first two years of life. This achievement requires that infants understand the properties of the objects in their environment. They must also find a variety of strategies for manipulating objects. Finally, they must be able to select the most effective strategies for coordinating their actions to achieve specific goals. For example, one does not use the same strategies to reach a ball that has rolled under the couch and to tape a new drawing to the wall.

Six Phases in the Development of Causal Schemes

Piaget and Inhelder (1966/1969) described the development of causal schemes in six phases (see Table 5.5) Subsequent research and related theoretical revisions have confirmed these levels of cognitive development (Fischer & Silvern, 1985). In the first phase (*reflexes*), cause and effect are linked through involuntary reflexive responses. Babies suck, grasp, and root in response to specific types of stimulation. These built-in responses are the genetic origins of intelligence.

In the second phase (*first habits*), the reflexive responses are used to explore a wider range of stimuli. For example, babies explore toys, fingers, parents' noses, and blankets by sucking on them. Gradually, they discover the unique properties of objects and modify their responses according to the demands of those objects. The act of satisfying the need to suck by bringing an object to the mouth is an early form of purposeful, causal behavior.

The third and fourth phases involve the coordination of means and ends, at first in familiar situations and then in new ones. In the third phase (*circular reactions*), babies connect an action with an expected outcome: They shake a rattle and expect to hear a noise; they drop a spoon and expect to hear a crash; they pull Daddy's beard and expect to hear an "ouch." They do not yet understand why the specific action leads to the expected outcome, but they will signal surprise when the expected outcome does not follow (Wentworth & Haith, 1992).

In the fourth phase (*coordination of means and ends*), infants use familiar actions or means to achieve new outcomes. They may shake a rattle to startle Mommy or pull Daddy's beard to force him to look away from the television set. The means and the ends have become quite distinct, and there can be no doubt that the behavior is purposeful at this point.

The fifth phase (*experimentation with new means*) begins with experimentation with familiar means to achieve new goals (the fourth phase). When familiar strategies do not work, children will modify them through sensorimotor problem solving. For instance, children will try to reach a drawer by standing on a box, to fix a broken toy with a string, or to make a gift by wrapping a toy in a piece of tissue.

TABLE 5.5	Six Phases in the Development of Causal Schemes	
Period	**Approximate Age**	***Characteristic***
1. Reflexes	From birth	Reflexive responses to specific stimuli
2. First habits	From 2nd week	Use of reflexive responses to explore new stimuli
3. Circular reactions	From 4th month	Use of familiar actions to achieve familiar results
4. Coordination of means and ends	From 8th month	Deliberate use of actions to achieve new goals
5. Experimentation with new means	From 11th month	Modification of actions to reach goals
6. Insight	From 18th month	Mental recombination of means and ends

Source: Based on Piaget & Inhelder, 1969.

The last phase in the development of sensorimotor causality (*insight*) involves mental manipulations of means-ends relationships. Children carry out trial-and-error problem-solving activities and planning in their minds. Instead of actually going through a variety of physical manipulations, they anticipate the outcomes of some actions in their minds. Thus, they can sort out possible solutions and reject some without having to try them out. The result is insight, in which mental, rather than physical, experimentation brings the child to the best solution.

The capacity to perceive oneself as a causal agent and to predict the outcome of one's actions is essential to all subsequent experiences of mastery. This capacity is the cornerstone of the development of a sense of competence. It involves investigation of the environment, directed problem solving, and persistence in working toward a goal (Yarrow et al., 1983; MacTurk et al., 1987). Adults' abilities to formulate a plan, execute it, and evaluate its outcome depend on this skill.

Understanding the Nature of Objects and Creating Categories

When infants are given the freedom, they show a remarkable propensity for exploration. From birth, they try to make direct sensory contact with objects in their environment. They reach for, grasp, and mouth objects. They track objects visually and alter their gaze to maintain visual contact with the objects. Rather than being passive spectators, babies are active explorers of their environment (Rochat, 1989; Ruff et al., 1992). As products of this active engagement with the object world, two related but independent aspects of infant intelligence develop: an understanding of the nature of objects and the ability to categorize similar objects.

The Nature of Objects

Through repeated gazing, manipulating, and examining, infants establish that objects have basic properties: boundaries, size, weight, color, malleability, texture, the capacity to contain something else or not, and the capacity to occupy space. All of these properties influence how infants explore objects and how they eventually weave objects into other actions or causal schemes (Sera, Troyer & Smith, 1988; MacLean & Schuler, 1989; Palmer, 1989; Spelke, von Hofsten & Kestenbaum, 1989).

Pablo Picasso, Little Girl with Boat, 1938. *Children learn a lot about the properties of objects through play with their favorite toys.*

One of the most carefully documented of object properties is *object permanence* (Wellman, Cross & Bartsch, 1986). Piaget (1954) argued that understanding the properties of objects is fundamental to logical thought. He discussed the scheme for object permanence as a gradual process through which infants develop the concept that objects in the environment are permanent and do not cease to exist when they are out of reach or view; the same physical laws that govern objects in full view are expected to govern objects that are hidden or covered. For example, if a toy truck bounces up against a wooden block in full view and cannot pass through the wooden block, then it would bounce up against the wooden block even if the truck and the block were hidden behind a screen.

Progress in developing the concept of object permanence can be traced through a child's reactions when objects are removed from her or his perceptual field or are moved from one place to another (Harris, 1975; Bertenthal & Fischer, 1983; Sophian & Yengo, 1985). Initially, infants are aware of only those objects that are in their immediate perceptual field. If a 6-month-old girl is playing with a rattle, it exists for her. If the rattle drops out of her sight or is taken away, she may show some immediate distress, but she will not pursue the object. In a very real sense, out of sight is out of mind. However, by 9 months, babies can watch an object being moved from one location to another, and they will begin to search for a hidden object after it has been moved. By 17 months, infants can pursue an object from one hiding place to the next even when they have not seen where the object has been hidden. However, even 2-year-olds may get confused if the object is displaced more than two or three times (Gopnik & Meltzoff, 1987).

The concept of object permanence can be easily understood by anyone who has observed the excitement and delight of a young boy engaged in a game of peek-a-boo. When he covers his eyes, what he has been looking at no longer exists. When he uncovers his eyes, he is thrilled and somewhat surprised to see the object again. The game is the most fun for those children who have not developed the concept of object permanence because, for them, the object's reappearance is not totally predictable.

Certain experiences appear to help build the scheme for object permanence. Babies who are adept at crawling or who have mobility in an infant walker seem to have more effective search strategies when objects are hidden from their view (Benson & Uzgiris, 1985; Kermoian & Campos, 1988). As babies gain greater control over their movement through the environment, they are better able to use landmarks other than their own bodies to locate objects. They can also experiment with the notion of leaving and retrieving objects and are discovering familiar objects in novel locations. Even at very early ages, before infants can search for and retrieve objects, they appear to have a memory of the locations of objects and to be aware that objects take up space (Baillargeon, 1987; Baillargeon & Graber, 1988). If babies of 8 or 9 months are permitted to search for an object immediately after it is hidden, they are very effective in finding it. However, if they have to wait for 5 or 10 seconds before they can search, or if the object has been moved from one container to a very similar container, they may become confused.

The attainment of the concept of object permanence frees children from total reliance on what they can see. The ability to hold the image of an object in the mind is the first step in the emergence of complex representational thinking (Ramsay & Campos, 1978).

The achievement of object permanence and the establishment of social attachment are interrelated because the scheme for object permanence is applied to both humans and inanimate objects. One reason babies experience separation anxiety is that they are not certain that a person to whom they are attached will continue to exist when that person is out of sight or inaccessible. Once the infant has a clear understanding of object permanence, the fear that a loved caregiver may vanish when he or she leaves is reduced. Interestingly, some qualities of maternal care are associated with the emergence of object permanence during the first seven months of life. Babies whose mothers communicate with them frequently, express positive feelings toward them, and actively stimulate achievement are more likely to apply the scheme of permanence to people as well as things (Chazan, 1981). The growth of social attachment and the achievement of object permanence may thus be mutually enhancing.

The Categorization of Objects

Objects have both properties and functions. As infants explore and experiment with objects, they begin to devise schemes for grouping objects together. They modify these schemes to add new items to the category and to differentiate one category from another. Categories may consist of the physical properties of objects, such as "smooth" and "rough"; or they may consist of the functions of objects, such as "something to sit on" and "something to dig with."

We have known for some time that infants are capable of forming visual categories. Early work on babies' preference for "faceness" in a visual presentation suggested that very young infants are able to see regularity in certain stimuli and to differentiate those stimuli from others that may be comparably complex but have no resemblance to a face. Infants 3–5 months old can differentiate abstract stimuli, such as patterns of dots, and can distinguish those that fit the category from those that do not (Hayne, Rovee-Collier & Perris, 1987; Younger & Gotlieb, 1988). One may wonder, however, whether these observations reflect more of a capacity for visual memory than a capacity to create an internal representation of a category of objects or events.

One of the most robust categories that appears early in infancy is the distinction between persons and objects (Ellsworth, Muir & Hains, 1993). Infants smile, vocalize, and become more active in interaction with people than with objects. By age 3 months, infants already show an ability to categorize stimuli as people or objects by smiling almost exclusively at people; they may look with equal interest at objects, especially novel objects, but their smiles are reserved for people. This distinction between the social and the nonsocial realm can be considered a foundational category. It provides a basis for our emphasis on the unique role of social relationships in the process of adaptation and growth. From this basic distinction between person and object, further categories emerge that serve to differentiate the infant's social and physical environments.

A common experiment used to determine whether children can form and use categories is to ask children to sort objects. By age 12 months, babies can select objects that form a single category from among a larger selection of objects. For example, they can pull all the orange rubber ducks from a group and put them in a basket. By 18 months, children can perform multidimensional sorting tasks. They can, for example, sort eight objects, such as four brightly colored yellow rectangles and four human-shaped plastic figures, into two distinct groups (Gopnik & Meltzoff, 1987, 1992). This kind of sorting does not require naming the objects. However, shortly after children become capable of two-group sorting, they often very quickly learn to name objects (Gopnik & Meltzoff, 1992). Thus, categorizing and naming appear to be closely linked. By the end of the second year of life, babies know that objects have certain stable properties, that some objects "belong" with others, and that objects have names. With these achievements, infants impose a new degree of order and predictability on their daily experiences.

Emotional Development

Emotions provide an organizing framework for communication during infancy (Campos & Barrett, 1984). An infant can produce a range of emotional expressions, including fear, distress, disgust, surprise, excitement, interest, joy, anger, and sadness. The most readily recognized of infant facial expressions are joy, interest, surprise, and distress. Even adults who have had little experience with infants can identify these expressions from slides taken of babies' faces (Oster, Hegley & Nagel, 1992). Parents and other caregivers rely on the facial, vocal, and behavioral cues related to these emotions to determine an infant's inner states and goals (Malatesta & Izard, 1984). In cycles of interaction, responsive caregivers also monitor changes in a baby's *affect*, or emotional state, to determine whether their interventions are effective.

When interactions go astray and an adult cannot understand what a baby needs, the adult tries to repair or revise the communication (Tronick, 1989). Think of a 6-month-old baby who wants a toy that is out of reach. The baby waves her arms in the direction of the toy, makes fussy noises, and looks distressed. As her father tries to figure out what the baby wants, he watches the baby's expressions to discover whether he is on the right track. Parents who are attuned to this form of communication are more likely to help babies achieve their goals, and the

TABLE 5.6	**States of Arousal in Newborns**
Regular sleep (RS)	Full rest; low muscle tonus; low motor activity; eyelids firmly closed and still; even, regular respiratory rhythm, about 36 breaths per minute.
Irregular sleep (IS)	Slightly greater muscle tonus; gentle motor activity; frequent facial grimaces and smiles; occasional rapid eye movement; irregular respiration, about 48 breaths per minute.
Periodic sleep (PS)	Intermediate between RS and IS; bursts of rapid, shallow breathing alternating with bursts of deep, slow breathing.
Drowsiness (D)	More activity than in RS but less activity than in IS or PS; eyes opened and closed; eyes, when open, dull and glazed and may roll upward; respiration variable but of higher frequency than during RS.
Alert inactivity (AI)	Slight activity; face relaxed; eyes open and "bright"; respiration constant and more rapid than in RS.
Waking activity (WA)	Frequent, diffuse motor activity; vocalizations; skin flushed when active; irregular respiration.
Crying (C)	Vigorous, diffuse motor activity; facial grimaces; skin red; eyes open or partially closed; crying vocalization.

Source: Based on Wolff, 1966.

babies are more likely to persist in attempts to communicate because they have succeeded before in such interactions.

Babies can also recognize and discriminate the affective expressions of others. Very young infants can differentiate facial expressions of fear, anger, happiness, sadness, and surprise (Walker-Andrews, 1986; Hornik, Risenhoover & Gunnar, 1987; Caron, Caron & MacLean, 1988; Ludemann & Nelson, 1988). They use both visual and auditory information to make these distinctions. Under certain circumstances, infants use the emotional responses of others to guide their own behavior. They often use their mothers as a *social reference*, but other adults may serve this function as well (Klinnert et al., 1986; Hornik & Gunnar, 1988; Walden & Ogan, 1988). As infants approach an unfamiliar adult or an ambiguous situation, they look to their mother and use her facial and/or verbal expressions as a source of information about the situation. If the mother expresses wariness or a negative emotion, the infant is more likely to withdraw or to explore with caution. If the mother expresses a positive emotion, the infant is more likely to approach the situation or the unfamiliar person with confidence. By age 12 months, infants consistently use this mechanism to try to appraise an ambiguous situation (Rosen, Adamson & Bakeman, 1992).

The domain of emotions is a two-way channel through which infants and their caregivers establish *intersubjectivity*, a state in which both partners have the same understanding and take the same meaning from a situation. Babies and caregivers are able to engage in reciprocal, rhythmic interactions; to appreciate state changes in one another; and to modify their actions according to information being sent by the other. Through a shared repertoire of emotions, babies and their caregivers can understand one another and create shared meanings. Thus, emotional expression becomes a building block of trust.

TABLE 5.7	Age-Related Changes in Three Dimensions of Emotions		
Month	*Pleasure-Joy*	*Wariness-Fear*	*Rage-Anger*
0–3	Endogenous smile; turning toward	Startle/pain; obligatory attention	Distress due to covering the face, physical restraint, extreme discomfort
3	Pleasure		Rage (disappointment)
4-5	Delight; active laughter	Wariness	
7	Joy		Anger
9		Fear (stranger aversion)	
12	Elation	Anxiety; immediate fear	Angry mood, petulance
18	Positive valuation of self	Shame	Defiance
24	Affection		Intentional hurting
36	Pride, love		Guilt

Note: The age specified is that of neither the first appearance of the affect in question nor its peak occurrence; it is the age at which the literature suggests the reaction is common.

Source: Sroufe, 1979.

In the sections that follow, we discuss three facets of emotional development during infancy. First, new emotions emerge. Second, with cognitive maturation, a child interprets events differently, and new emotions may be attached to familiar situations. An experience that may once have caused wariness, such as seeing a new toy or hearing a loud noise, becomes a source of excitement or joy as the child gains mastery over the situation. Third, children develop strategies for regulating their emotions so that they are not overwhelmed by emotional intensity.

Emotional Differentiation

Emotions gradually become differentiated during the first two years of life. Peter Wolff (1966) described seven states of arousal in newborn infants, each of which is characterized by a distinctive pattern of respiration, muscle tone, motor activity, and alertness (see Table 5.6). In these states, we see the earliest distinctions among distress (crying), interest (alert inactivity), and excitement (waking activity). A newborn's state of arousal influences his or her capacity to respond to the environment.

Changes in state also serve to cue responses from caregivers. Crying usually brings some effort to comfort or soothe. Visual alertness is likely to prompt social interactions. Parents try to interact with their infants, achieve eye contact, and initiate nonverbal exchanges during the alert phases (Tronick, Als & Brazelton, 1979).

The broad range of emotions unfolds gradually from the basic states of arousal and distress. The differentiation of emotions follows a regular pattern, as Table 5.7 suggests. This table describes age-related changes in three dimensions of emotion: pleasure-joy, wariness-fear, and rage-anger. Emotional responses

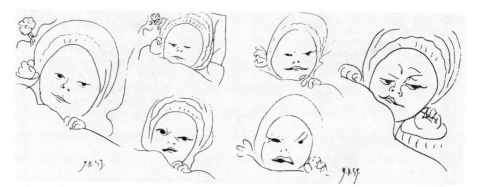

Pablo Picasso, Six Sketches of a Baby's Face, *1959. Fascinated with his grandson, Bernard, Picasso drew him almost as an animated cartoon. We see the range of emotional expressions of a very young infant, from pleasure to intense anger.*

during the first month are closely tied to the internal state of the infant. Physical discomfort, arousal, pain, and changing tension in the central nervous system are the major sources of emotions. During the ages from 1 to 6 months, emotions begin to be tied more to a separation of the self and the environment. Babies smile at familiar faces, show interest in and curiosity about novel stimuli, and show rage when nursing is disrupted or when they are prevented from viewing an activity that they have been intently watching.

The period from 6 to 12 months reflects a greater awareness of the context of events. Emotions of joy, anger, and fear are tied to a baby's ability to recall previous experiences and to compare them with a current event. These emotions also reflect a baby's ability to exercise some control over the environment and his or her frustration when goals are blocked.

Emotions that are observed during the second year of life—especially anxiety, pride, defiance, and shame—suggest an emerging sense of self. These infants recognize that they can operate as causal agents. They also begin to respond to the emotions of others and give love to others through hugs, kisses, and tender pats. They can share toys, comfort another distressed infant, and imitate another person's excitement. In becoming a more distinct being, an infant achieves a new awareness of the capacity to give and receive pleasure as well as of the vulnerability of the self and others.

Emotional Interpretation

Observations of the facial expressions of emotions provide a key to the meaning of significant events. In one study, when babies were videotaped after an inoculation at 2 and 4 months of age, their emotional reactions included closed-eye expressions of physical distress and anger. However, when they were filmed at 19 months, their expressions involved more open-eyed anger, suggesting greater awareness of the source of their discomfort (Izard et al., 1983).

Emotional expression following a brief separation from the mother gives another clue to the development of attachment as well as to the quality of the attachment in mother-infant pairs (Hyson & Izard, 1985). Interest, anger, and sadness, as well as blends of these emotions, were all seen in babies observed during brief separations from their mothers at age 13 months and again at 18 months. Some emotions were highly stable from one age to the next. Infants who reacted to separation with expressions of interest at 13 months were likely to show the same emotion at 18 months, and infants who reacted with anger at 13 months were also likely to show anger at 18 months. Expressions of sadness, however, did not show continuity. Over time, there was an increase in the expression

The infant's smile is a social treasure, and parents and grandparents may go to great lengths to bring out this sweet expression. Yet researchers have discovered that an infant's smile has a wide variety of meanings and is produced in response to many stimuli.

The very earliest smiles, observed during the first month of life, may occur spontaneously during sleep or in response to a high-pitched human voice. Gentle tactile stimulation—touching, tickling, and rocking—may also produce these early smiles. A baby's first smiles are not a true form of social communication, although they are likely to produce positive feelings in the adult caregiver (Wolff, 1963, 1987).

Social smiles begin to be observed at the age of about 5 weeks. These smiles are first produced in response to a wide range of stimuli: familiar faces and voices (especially the mother's), strangers, and non-human objects. After about 20 weeks, the smiling response becomes differentiated. Infants continue to smile broadly and frequently at familiar people and objects, but they no longer smile readily at strangers or unfamiliar objects. The social smile conveys both a recognition of familiarity and an invitation to further communication or interaction (Ambrose, 1963; Sroufe et al., 1984).

The cognitive smile seems to develop alongside the social smile. Infants smile in

BOX 5.4

What Is in a Smile?

response to their own behavior, as if they were expressing satisfaction with their accomplishments (Papousek & Bernstein, 1969; Watson, 1970). At 3 months, babies smile in response to events that are moderately familiar, as if expressing pleasure in understanding the situation (Kagan, 1984). Infants smile elaborately when they are able to make something happen, as when they wiggle a mobile or hear a bell jangle when they kick their feet (Cicchetti & Schneider-Rosen, 1984). These "mastery" smiles do not appear to have a social intention. By 8 months, infants smile when they are able to resolve uncertainty or when they are able to grasp a new concept (Kagan, 1984).

In the second year of life, smiling is associated with a primitive form of humor. Babies smile when they recognize incongruity, such as a picture of a mother drinking from a baby bottle or crawling on her hands and knees. These smiles suggest that the baby appreciates something about the discrepancy between what is being presented and what the baby normally observes (Cicchetti & Schneider-Rosen, 1984).

Babies smile in a variety of contexts. The conditions that evoke smiles change as the baby matures. Thus, smiles, like other emotional expressions, should be interpreted in relation to the infant's existing schemes and goals.

Boy, these cubes are slippery.

The mastery smile!

of sadness, either alone or blended with other emotions. This change suggests that many babies give a new meaning to separation during the second year of life—a meaning that reflects a greater capacity to separate themselves and others, and therefore a more complex appreciation of loss.

Emotional Regulation

Infants develop strategies for coping with intense emotions, both positive and negative. Most of the research in this area has focused on how children deal with distress (Dodge, 1989). Even newborns have some strategies for reducing the intensity of distress, such as turning the head away, sucking on the hands, or closing the eyes. As infants gain new motor coordination and control, they can move away, distract themselves with other objects, or soothe themselves by rocking, stroking themselves, or thumb-sucking (Kopp, 1989). However, in many instances, babies cannot regulate the intensity of their emotions. Any parent, child-care provider, or infant researcher can describe times when a baby's emotions became so intense that his or her normal capacity for self-comforting simply did not work. We sometimes call these periods of intense emotionality *tantrums*.

One of the most important elements in the development of emotional regulation is how caregivers assist infants in this effort (Kopp, 1989; Tronick, 1989). Caregivers may provide direct support when they observe that a child is distressed. They may cuddle, hug, rock, or swaddle a baby, or they may offer food, a pacifier, or some other form of comfort. Through words and actions, they may help a child interpret the source of the stress or may suggest ways to reduce the distress.

Caregivers' approaches to emotional regulation vary with the culture. Some cultures regulate emotions by protecting a child from certain arousing situations. Japanese mothers, for example, try hard to prevent their children from being exposed to anger. They avoid frustrating young children so that the children do not experience anger. Parents rarely express anger to their young children, especially in public. Thus, Japanese parents try to regulate anger by minimizing the child's experience of it (Miyake et al., 1986).

In another example, Anglo and Puerto Rican mothers were compared with respect to what they considered ideal and negative behavior in the strange situation (Harwood, 1992). Anglo mothers thought it undesirable for a baby to cling to the mother during the initial phase and to cry the whole time when the mother left the room. They also thought it undesirable for the baby to be unhappy when the mother returned and to come to her for comfort or to express anger at her. The Puerto Rican mothers thought it undesirable for the baby to be extremely active and to ignore the mother during the initial phase, to ignore the mother when she left the room, and to continue to play actively when the mother returned, without acknowledging her. The implication is that the Puerto Rican mothers were more accepting of the clinging, distressed emotional expressions of their children, valuing babies who were loving and quiet, and who remained close to them. The Anglo mothers placed greater value on control of the expression of negative emotions and on their infant's ability to become engaged in active exploration. Cultural values concerning the expression and control of distress influence how mothers respond to distress signals and what they teach their babies about how to regulate feelings of wariness, fear, and anxiety.

Emotions may also be regulated through experiences with the emotions themselves (Campos, Campos & Barrett, 1989). Children observe anger, pride, shame, or sadness in their parents in response to their own emotional expressions. As we pointed out in discussing social referencing, a child's uncertainty and fear may be strengthened if the social reference also expresses fear, but fear may be dissipated if the social reference expresses enthusiasm and confidence. Parents may interrupt their child's anger by expressing disapproval. Children may be distracted from sadness by seeing laughter and joy in someone else. Through empathy, children may reduce their angry feelings toward someone else by seeing how sad or frightened the other person is.

As children come to understand the consequences or implications of a situation, they have new motives for regulating or failing to regulate their emotions. Children may extend or expand their signals of distress if they think these signals will help them achieve their goals, such as special attention or nurturing. Children may try to disguise their distress if they think that signals of distress will provoke additional pain. Emotional regulation, just like emotional signaling, takes place within an interpersonal context. The degree to which an infant devises effective strategies for reducing distress depends on how his or her signals of distress are treated by others, on his or her goals in the situation, and on his or her ability to synchronize the cognitive, physical, and affective elements of the situation.

The Psychosocial Crisis: Trust Versus Mistrust

The term *psychosocial crisis* refers to a state of tension that results from discrepancies between the developmental needs and competencies of the individual at the beginning of a stage of life and the culture's expectations concerning the individual's level of functioning. In infancy, the specific nature of this crisis is described as a tension between trust (infants' confidence in their caregivers) and mistrust (a sense of wariness, withdrawal, and worthlessness).

Trust

In adult relationships, *trust* refers to an appraisal of the predictability, dependability, and genuineness of another person (Rempel, Holmes & Zanna, 1985). Trust emerges as one person discovers that another is honest, understanding, and dependable. As the level of trust grows, the partners may take new risks by disclosing information or feelings that may lead to rejection. Relationships that survive these risks increase the trust. However, trust is more than a summary of the past; it is a faith that the relationship will weather the uncertainties of an unpredictable future. A trusting relationship links confidence based on the past with faith about the future.

For infants, trust is an emotion, a state of confidence that they are valued and that their needs will be met. Infants seek warmth, nurturance, comfort, and stimulation from their parents (Erikson, 1950, 1963). Trust is inferred from the infant's increasing capacity to delay gratification and from the warmth and delight that are evident in interactions with family members. The infant's sense of trust is an emotional state that provides an undifferentiated feeling of oneness with the world.

Erikson (1978) tied the capacity for trust with the basic human strength of hope: "Hope is the enduring belief in the attainability of primal wishes, in spite of the dark urges and rages which mark the beginnings of existence and leave a lasting residue of threatening estrangement" (p. 26). The hope that is born during infancy provides optimism in the face of risk. Throughout life, the capacity for trust and a sense of trustworthiness give one the energy to seek new solutions and the hope of resolving difficult challenges.

Mistrust

Experiences of mistrust during infancy may arise from at least three sources. First, wariness is one of the earliest infant emotions, linked initially to at least two infant reflexes; the startle response in reaction to loud noises and the Moro reflex in response to sudden loss of support. One might say that all infants are "prewired" to be alert to certain environmental dangers. One of the caregiver's functions is to minimize the infant's exposure to stimuli that evoke these reflexes and, over time, to comfort and reassure babies when they encounter stimuli that are interpreted as threatening.

Second, babies may lack confidence in the good intentions of others. If the caregiver is unable to differentiate the infant's needs and respond appropriately to them, or if the caregiver is unusually harsh while meeting the infant's needs, the infant may begin to doubt the trustworthiness of the environment. Third, babies experience the power of their own rage. When intense feelings of anger or distress exceed the infant's capacity for self-regulation, infants experience periods of disorganization and may doubt their own lovableness as they encounter the violence of their own capacity for anger.

Parents play a central role in helping infants resolve the conflict between trust and mistrust. Most parents make some mistakes in responding to their infant's signs of distress, particularly when the baby is very small. They try the bottle and, if crying continues, may change diapers, give water, move the child to another room, or put the child to bed, until something "works." Over time, however, they learn to interpret their child's signals correctly and to respond appropriately (Kropp & Haynes, 1987).

It appears that doubt or anxiety about the bond of trust is more common than we may have expected. About one-third of American infant-mother pairs that have been systematically observed show evidence of an insecure attachment. Cross-cultural research provides further evidence that a significant proportion of infants have difficulty deriving emotional comfort and security from their attachment relationships.

In extreme cases, parents grossly neglect their infants. They leave the baby alone without anyone to care for his or her needs. They refuse to change or bathe the baby. They do not treat the baby's wounds or protect the baby from danger. They may consistently express hostility to the infant or may not communicate at all (Lyons-Ruth et al., 1987). In such circumstances, infants discover that their parents are physically and psychologically unavailable (Egeland & Sroufe, 1981), and mistrust results from their inability to gain physical or psychological comfort. This mistrust may manifest itself in withdrawal from interaction and in symptoms of depression and grief, such as sobbing, lack of emotion, lethargy, and loss of appetite (Field et al., 1988).

The Central Process: Mutuality with the Caregiver

Underlying the resolution of the crisis of trust versus mistrust is the process through which a child and a caregiver establish *mutuality*, a relationship in which each partner modifies and regulates his or her behavior in response to the other. Parental sensitivity and intersubjectivity, discussed earlier in this chapter, are both elements in the establishment of mutuality. Initially, mutuality is built on the consistency with which the caregiver responds appropriately to the child's needs. When a child cries because of thirst, the caregiver becomes able to interpret

Pablo Picasso, Inez and Child, 1947. *In the process of achieving mutuality, caregivers must learn how to balance the encouragement of exploration and the use of constraint. Using the safety of his mother's lap as a secure base, this baby is ready to squiggle free and begin to explore. If it's safe and appropriate, the mother will probably let him down; if it's not, she will have to find some new strategy for keeping him confined.*

that cry and gives the child water rather than changing the child's diaper. The caregiver comes to appreciate the variety of needs expressed by a child, and the child learns to expect that her or his personal needs will be met.

An infant influences the responses of a caregiver in many ways. Infants' irritability and soothability contribute to adults' responses to them. Infants may reject or end an interaction by fussing, becoming tense, crying, or falling asleep. They may maintain an interaction by smiling, cooing, snuggling comfortably, or maintaining eye contact. Techniques of comforting do not call forth the same responses from all babies (Campos, 1989). A pacifier helps comfort some babies; others respond to being wrapped snugly in a warm blanket. Bringing an infant up to one's shoulder may be more effective in reducing crying than cradling the baby from side to side or comforting a baby who remains lying down. These different responses are evidence of the infant's active role in establishing the bond of mutuality.

An infant and a caregiver learn to regulate the amount of time that passes between the expression of a need and its satisfaction. In a study of mother-infant interactions, Bell and Ainsworth (1972) observed mothers' responses to infant crying during the first year of life. Over the course of the year, the infants' crying decreased, and the mothers tended to respond more quickly to their cries. This finding suggests a process of mutual adaptation by mothers and infants. The mothers were more consistent in their responses than were the infants. Some mothers came quickly and ignored few cries. Other mothers waited a long time and ignored much of the crying. A striking finding was that the longer mothers delayed in responding to their infants' cries, the more crying the infants did in later months. Babies whose mothers responded promptly in the first six months of life cried less often in the second six months.

Coordinating Social Interactions

The study of mutuality of the infant and the caregiver has focused in some detail on the coordination of social interaction. Infants and their caregivers develop a cycle of interaction (Brazelton et al., 1974; Tronick & Cohn, 1989). *Coordination* refers to two related characteristics of interaction: matching and synchrony. *Matching* means that the infant and the caregiver are involved in similar behaviors or states at the same time. They may be playing together with an object, cooing and smiling at each other, or fussing and angry at each other. *Synchrony* means that the infant and the caregiver move from one state to the next in a fluid pattern. When infants are paying attention to their caregivers, the caregivers attempt to stimulate them. As they withdraw attention, the caregivers learn to reduce stimulation and wait until the infants are ready to interact again.

In normal development, mother-infant interactions become increasingly coordinated (Tronick & Cohn, 1989; Bernieri, Reznick & Rosenthal, 1988). This does not mean that most of the interactions are coordinated. In fact, especially when babies are very young, matched interactions appear to become mismatched rather quickly. The explanation may lie partly in the infant's inability to sustain coordinated communication, partly in a rapid shift of need states, and partly in the adult's inability to sustain nonverbal communication for lengthy periods. In normal dyads, however, mismatches are usually followed by *communication repairs*, so that infants and mothers cycle again through points of coordination in their interactions.

At a theoretical level, we can view this process of coordination, mismatch, and repair as a fundamental building block of mutuality. Infants and caregivers gain confidence in their ability to communicate. Infants have many opportunities to experience the satisfaction of shared communication and a sense of being embedded in a responsive social environment. They also experience frequent recovery from a mismatched state to a state of effective communication, so that they can be hopeful about their ability to make these repairs in the future.

The importance of reciprocal interactions in building trust and hope during infancy is highlighted by studies of parents with psychological problems. Sensitivity to an infant's emotional states, the ability to respond appropriately to an infant's needs, and the quality of common, daily interactions may all be impaired by *family risk factors*. Studies of parents who are experiencing marital discord, who have been victims of child abuse or neglect, who are depressed, or who are mentally ill suggest that the interaction cycles of these parents and their children lack synchrony (Rutter, 1990). For example, in a comparison of mothers who had been maltreated as children and mothers who had not, the maltreated mothers were less involved with their children during play, used fewer strategies to direct their children's activities, and used a more negative tone toward their children (Alessandri, 1992).

When depressed and nondepressed mothers and their 3-month-old infants were filmed in face-to-face interactions, the depressed mothers and their infants were found to spend less time in matched behavior states than the nondepressed mothers and their infants (Field et al., 1990). What is more, the quality of their interactions was different. As Figure 5.5 indicates, depressed mothers and their infants spent more of their matched time in states of anger-protest or

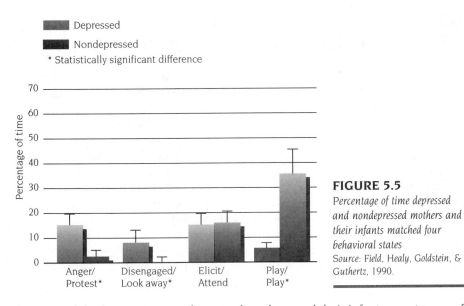

FIGURE 5.5

Percentage of time depressed and nondepressed mothers and their infants matched four behavioral states

Source: *Field, Healy, Goldstein, & Guthertz, 1990.*

disengaged–looking-away. Nondepressed mothers and their infants spent more of their matched time in play.

We cannot be certain of the influence of this pattern of interaction on the long-term psychosocial development of the infants. For some, the effect seems to be depression and mistrust. If the mothers recover from their depression, or if the infants have opportunities to interact with other, nondepressed adults, the dyad may establish more positive social interaction patterns. The Field et al. study, as well as others, suggests that, even at very early ages, infants are sensitive and responsive to the content and mood of their mothers' interactive style.

Coordinating Family Patterns

The initial formation of mutuality seems to rely heavily on the parents' ability to respond appropriately and in the "right" amount of time to a child's behavior. Soon, children are expected to wait until the caregiver is ready to attend to them. They are expected to remain calm and preoccupied while a parent leaves the room for a short time, trusting that the parent will return. In our culture, they are also expected to modify their schedule of needs so that, by the end of their first year, they sleep when the rest of the family sleeps, play when the rest of the family is awake, and eat three or, at most, four times a day, generally when the other family members eat.

The match or mismatch between an infant's rhythms and the family's rhythms affects the overall adjustment of a family to a new baby (Sprunger, Boyce & Gaines, 1985). Some babies are quite predictable; the timing of their sleeping, eating, playtime, and even fussy periods follows a clear pattern. Other babies are much less regular. Families also vary in the regularity of their daily schedules. Some families have consistent mealtime hours, rather strict bedtime and waking hours, and a predictable pattern of work and leisure activities. Other families are more erratic. When the rhythmicity of infant and family are similar, whether consistent or erratic, little additional adjustment is required to integrate the infant into the family. However, when there is a mismatch in rhythmicity, the parents and the infant must undergo a mutual regulation to achieve a comfortable balance. Both the child and the parents must be willing to modify their behavior. When this happens, the product is a rhythmic, interdependent system (Osofsky & Connors, 1979).

Applied Topic
The Role of Parents

Parents have an enormous responsibility for maintaining and promoting the psychological growth of their children. We have portrayed infants as active, adaptive, and eager to master the environment. At the same time, we have pointed to a number of examples of the need for environmental support to facilitate growth. The immaturity of human infants at birth necessitates a long period of dependence on adults. The few instinctive behaviors of human infants in comparison with the infants of other species is compensated for by an enormous capacity to learn. For this potential to be realized, infants must rely on their parents to maintain their health, provide stimulation, and protect them from danger. During the long period of dependence, infants become entwined in complex social systems and develop strong emotional bonds to their caregivers. The quality of these early relationships provides infants a mental representation that guides their later development of friendships, intimacy, and relationships to their own children.

Safety in the Physical Environment

One of the central responsibilities that parents face is to ensure infants' survival by protecting them from environmental dangers. The ecology of home and neighborhood, including the society's degree of modernization, influences the kinds of dangers to which infants are exposed and the kinds of practices families and cultures invent to protect their offspring. In addition to physical risks, some dangers are linked to superstitions, religious beliefs, and matters of the spirit world.

The presence of dangers or risks in the environment usually elicits some effort to restrict a child's movement through swaddling, carrying the baby in a sling, or placing the baby in a playpen. Because of concern about dangers, caregivers also invoke certain prohibitions, such as telling the child, "No, don't touch that," or pulling the child away from something dangerous. As children become more mobile in the second half of the first year, the need to introduce prohibitions and to monitor the child's exploratory activities increases. Depending on the cultural values concerning independent exploration, caregivers may heighten their restrictions and prohibitions or may try to modify the environment to permit safe, unrestricted exploration.

Certain child-rearing practices arise from a desire to protect young children from known dangers. For example, Robert LeVine (1977) described the practice of many African cultures of carrying infants 18 months and older on the back, even though they were able to walk around. He learned that this practice was used to prevent toddlers from getting burned on the open cooking fires at an age when they were mobile enough to walk or stumble into the fire and not old enough to know how to inhibit their movements. Seeing the pain inflicted by accidental burns, parents took special precautions to prevent their children from wandering too close to the fire. Other hazards in the neighborhood, such as falling off steep cliffs or into lakes, rivers, or wells, prompted this same carrying behavior.

In societies with high infant mortality rates, infants are more likely to be carried for long periods of the day and for a longer part of their infancy (Goldberg, 1977). This custom promotes continuous monitoring of the infant's needs and

The particular risks in an environment introduce specific needs for constraining an infant's exploration. Without supervision, this infant may begin eating the lead-based paint she is peeling off the wall.

protection from harmful agents in the home. Practices such as swaddling and carrying may severely limit a child's exploratory behavior. They discourage activities in which infants act as causal agents, discovering the multiple consequences of their actions. Very close, prolonged swaddling actually places infants at high risk of developing serious respiratory infections (Yurdakok, Yavuz & Taylor, 1990). However, if a caregiver's primary concern is the baby's survival, that goal will dominate the caregiver's orientation toward child care.

In industrialized countries, infants face different types of hazards, such as electrical outlets, steep stairs, and open containers of insecticides, cleaning agents, and other poisons. Many American families protect babies from these dangers by putting up gates at a doorway or at the top of a stairway, or by placing an infant in a crib or playpen to restrict her or his exploration. In other homes, the strategy is to "baby-proof" the home by removing as many known dangers as possible so that the baby has maximum freedom for exploration. These two different strategies reflect two different values concerning child rearing, both with the same goal of providing maximum safety and protection from danger. In the former case, parents try to preserve their adult environment. Children must modify their behavior in order to fit into the home. In the latter case, parents modify their adult environment to accommodate the baby's developmental needs.

A strong cultural value in the United States for nurturing independence during infancy has led to the adoption of devices that promote early motor competence, such as jumpers, climbers, and walkers. Just as swaddling is associated with some risks, so walkers, in particular, have been associated with many accidents. With a walker, infants can move about before they can walk independently or can judge distance and depth accurately. Infants may become so confident of their ability to move around in the home that they tumble down stairs.

These examples related to protecting infants from dangers in the physical environment illustrate the dynamic interaction between the universal need for safety and the changing and varied cultural contexts in which this need is met. Infant-care practices are guided largely by parental beliefs. In some societies, these beliefs may be supported in part by scientific research, but they are formed mostly by the transmission of family and community wisdom from one parental generation to the next. Layered on top of these wisdoms are contemporary responses to newly emergent dangers. As a community becomes more modernized, for example, new diseases and new threats to safety emerge, and strategies evolve to prevent or guard against them.

Fostering Emotional and Cognitive Development

Another component of the parents' role during infancy is their ability to promote emotional and cognitive development. As we see it, much of the behavior that appears to be important in the development of strong emotional bonds between infants and parents is also central to the fostering of intellectual growth.

Let us look at some examples. Social attachment and understanding the nature of objects were discussed earlier. What do parents do to encourage attachment? They respond consistently and appropriately to their infants' needs. They maintain contact with their infants by holding, cuddling, looking at, and speaking to them. They smile at their infants, and they expend energy to make the infants smile. All of this behavior helps infants achieve a well-differentiated image of the parents, as well as positive feelings of warmth and a wish to stay close to them.

The vividness of the parents' image is enhanced through a variety of sensory experiences and by repeated contact. We get clues to the richness of infants' images of their parents from their preferential smiling at them and from their distress when they are left in the care of strangers.

Once specific attachments have been formed, children pursue their parents all around the house. When their parents leave the room, infants cry out to them, crawl after them, or gaze intently in the direction in which they left. All of this behavior is evidence of attachment, and it also signals the emergence of the concept of the permanent object. The fact that children pursue their parents when the parents are out of sight means that the children have an image of the parents in their minds that is more permanent than merely their visual perception of them. Here we have an exciting example of the parents' dual function: In maintaining a close bond with the child, the parents nurture emotional attachment and provide a basis for conceptual growth (Jackson, Campos & Fischer, 1978).

If you have ever observed a child and a parent in a novel environment, such as a doctor's office, you may have seen another example of this dual function. The parent serves as an island of safety and reassurance from which the child can explore (Ainsworth, 1979; Bowlby, 1988). The child first moves out into the environment and returns to the parent. The next time, the child may wander a bit farther, poking at magazines, couches, or other children before once again returning to the parent. One may even see the child leave the room and wander into the hallway or into an empty examining room, eventually to return (if not first retrieved by a watchful nurse) to the parent's side. Parents can use the trust and confidence they have built with their infants to encourage exploration, to introduce their infants to new and unfamiliar objects, and to support the infants' efforts to master difficult motor tasks. The image comes to mind of a smiling mother with outstretched arms bending toward her child and saying, "Walk to Mommy." Trust in a human relationship serves to generate trust in the environment as a whole. Once children trust the bond between themselves and their parents, the parents can use that confidence to encourage an open, exploring attitude toward the unfamiliar (Zahn-Waxler, Radke-Yarrow & King, 1977; Heckhausen, 1987).

Another way that parents foster both emotional and intellectual growth is by structuring the stimulus environment to suit the infant's developmental level (Yarrow & Goodwin, 1965; Bornstein, 1985; Stevens & Bakeman, 1985; Bradley, Caldwell & Rock, 1988). The central idea is that parents should recognize the infant's perspective in providing toys, sounds, and visual stimulation. Part of the parents' function is to initiate interactions and not just to respond to their infants' demands for attention. Parents need to create what they perceive to be a suitable environment: one that allows a variety of experiences, a reasonable amount of frustration, and adequate opportunities to experience success. Furthermore, parents should be attuned to their infants' developing skills and alter the environment appropriately. As their children mature, the parents must provide more complex stimuli, more opportunities for autonomy, and more encouragement for tolerating frustration.

In one interesting study that demonstrated this process, mothers and fathers were videotaped as they played with their 7-, 10-, and 13-month-old babies. Their toy play changed with the developmental competences of the infants. The parents of the younger babies were likely to demonstrate or direct their infants' play. The parents of the older babies were more likely to encourage turn-taking, pretend play, and play involving the coordination of several toys. Parents of older babies were more likely to use words rather than actions in guiding the play. Their babies showed greater competence in exploring the toys, and the parents demonstrated developmentally appropriate strategies as play companions (Power, 1985).

Fathers' and Mothers' Parental Behavior

Questions have been raised about the roles of the father and the mother in child rearing. As we noted earlier, babies form strong attachments to their fathers as well as to their mothers. Fathers may be just as involved in and sensitive to their babies' needs as mothers. However, the daily interactions between mothers and babies and those between fathers and babies are distinct (Belsky, Gilstrap & Rovine, 1984; Power, 1985). A greater proportion of the time mothers spend with their babies is devoted to caregiving. Fathers, who spend less time overall with their babies, tend to focus more on play, especially physical play. When mothers play with their babies, the play tends to be with words or with toys, as opposed to rough-and-tumble activity (Power, 1985).

Mothers more frequently respond to their babies, express affection, and follow up on behavior their babies initiate. Mothers are also likely to be more accepting of their child's behavior and to emphasize and value emotional expressiveness. Fathers are more likely to disregard babies' cues and to direct their attention to new targets. They are more likely to emphasize control and

Not all fathers play their role from the wings. Robert Meyer is a single parent who adopted his daughter, Juliet, at birth. "Juliet and I have created a bonding with each other that is stronger than any I ever had with either of my parents, as well as a friendship. The type of parenting that I practice is that of learning by experiment and experience." (Nestor, 1992, p. 102)

discipline (Rosen & Rothbaum, 1993). At home, fathers are likely to continue their leisure activity, such as reading or watching television, in the presence of their babies, whereas mothers are likely to interact with their babies.

One implication of these differences is that fathers and mothers probably view their parental roles differently. American mothers tend to emphasize the *process* of development: They use parenting techniques that focus on enhancing their children's comfort, trust, and curiosity. American fathers tend to emphasize *product*: They use parenting techniques to strengthen their children's bodies and to direct their behavior toward correct solutions to problems.

Evidence also suggests that mothers and fathers view their infants differently. Fathers tend to consider infants less cognitively and socially competent than mothers do. The more involved a father is in infant care, however, the less difference there is between his and the mother's conception of the infant's competence (Ninio & Rinott, 1988). These differences in perception may help explain why fathers pay less attention to infants, engage them in rough-and-tumble play, and disregard babies' cues in playful interchanges. This style of play may underestimate the infant's need for and capability of engaging in more demanding and stimulating activities. Fathers may become more effective parents if they are helped to understand the complexity and sophistication of infant competences. They may then see their efforts with their children as more valuable and may learn to interact with their infants more appropriately.

The love that parents feel for each other is a key to building a warm, supportive, and reassuring environment for rearing young children.

Parents as Advocates

In addition to providing care, more and more parents are becoming responsible for arranging alternative care for their infants. In this case, the parents become advocates for their child. Parents must review the alternatives available to them and select a setting that will meet their infant's needs as well as accommodate their work requirements and their economic resources. Family day care, in-home baby-sitting, and day care at a center are three common alternatives for the single-parent or two-earner family.

To function as advocates for their children, parents may have to engage in an unfamiliar kind of thinking. They may even feel unqualified to make the kinds of judgments required. For example, parents must evaluate the competence and motivation of the adults who will care for their children. They must estimate how successful these caregivers will be in meeting their child's needs for security and stimulation. They must consider the degree to which alternative caregivers will reflect their own parental philosophy and how the caregiver's philosophy will influence their child.

Even when pressures to continue a caregiving arrangement are very strong, parents must be able to assess its impact on their children. They must try to judge whether their children are in the kind of responsive, stimulating environment that will enhance development. In the best situations, alternative care settings actually complement a parent-infant relationship. In the worst settings, infants may be neglected and abused. It is essential for parents to maintain communication with the alternative caregivers, to assess the quality of the care, and to intervene promptly when necessary to ensure their infant's well-being.

A variety of contextual factors play their part in parents' ability to promote their child's optimal development. Adults who themselves have had difficult experiences with a caregiver come to the parental role with special challenges.

237

They may not have experienced the comfort, responsiveness, or appropriate stimulation that we have learned are essential for effective parenting. Some factors, however, help to make up for these deficits. The quality of one's marriage and the emotional support one receives from one's spouse are important in sustaining positive parent-child relationships (Cox et al., 1989; Dickstein & Parke, 1988; Egeland, Jacobvitz & Sroufe, 1988; Simons et al., 1993). Couples who experience mutuality and trust in their own relationship are better able to create a predictable, supportive, and caring family environment for their children.

Sources of social support beyond the marriage partner may also enhance one's effectiveness as a parent. This support may come from the child's grandparents and other family members, from health and mental health professionals, and from friends (Levitt, Weber & Clark, 1986; Stevens, 1988). The effective use of a social support network ensures that adults will not be isolated as parents, and that other people will be available to help the parents identify and interpret child-rearing problems. Often, the help is very direct—for example, child care or sharing of clothes, playthings, and furniture. Support may also come in the form of companionship and validation of the importance of the parenting role. However, evidence suggests that support from one's social network cannot fully compensate for the lack of spousal support or for the stresses on parenting caused by economic pressures that prevent parents from meeting basic life needs (Simons et al., 1993).

A third contextual factor that influences effective parenting is the adult's prior experience with child rearing and child care. Adults who have had previous child-rearing experiences are likely to be more efficient and accurate in solving child-rearing problems (Holden, 1988). They are more likely to recognize and differentiate infants' signals as meaningful, and they are more likely to consider the infant's developmental level a relevant factor in interpreting the child's behavior (Adamson et al., 1987).

In reviewing the material in this chapter, you can begin to appreciate the demanding nature of the parents' role in promoting optimal development during infancy. The elements of effective parenting that we have identified or implied are listed in Table 5.8. As a parent, one must rely heavily on one's own psychological well-being and on the loving support of caring friends and family to sustain the ego strengths and emotional resources necessary to the task.

How parents conceive of their role has a major influence on the direction and rate of their infants' development. Parenting also allows adults opportunities for creative problem solving, empathy, physical closeness, and self-insight. The role of parent makes considerable cognitive and emotional demands, but attachment to a child also promotes the parent's own psychological development. These contributions to adult development will be described further in Chapters 11 and 12.

Chapter Summary

During infancy, a child rapidly develops sensory and motor skills, social relationships, and conceptual skills. Infants are born with the capacity to perceive their environment and to evoke responses from their caregivers. In this sense, they are not helpless. During the first year, voluntary motor functions mature rapidly. A social attachment forms between the infant and the primary caregiver, forming the basic mental representation for subsequent intimate relationships. Sensorimotor

TABLE 5.8	Optimizing an Infant's Development

Provide stimulation.

Provide warmth and affection; express positive feelings toward the baby in many ways—verbally, through touching and hugging, and through playful interactions.

Encourage the child's active engagement in and exploration of the environment; encourage the child's mobility.

Try not to control the child's behavior too much.

Help the child understand that he or she causes things to happen.

Help the child engage in directed problem solving.

Encourage the child to persist in efforts to reach a goal.

Keep things predictable, especially when the infant is very young.

Spend time with the child; be available when the child needs you.

Communicate often directly with the child; engage the child in verbal interaction.

Guide language development by using words to name, sort, and categorize objects and events.

Accept the child's efforts to achieve closeness.

Be responsive; be sensitive to the child's state; learn to interpret the child's signals accurately; time your responses appropriately.

Find effective ways to soothe and comfort the child in times of distress.

Help the child interpret sources of distress and find ways to regulate distress.

To the extent possible, prevent the child from being exposed to intensely negative, hostile, and frightening events.

Be aware of the visual and auditory cues you send when you interact with the child.

Pay attention to how the child is changing over time.

Monitor the child's emotional expressions to evaluate the success of specific actions and interventions.

intelligence begins with the use of motor and sensory capacities to explore and understand the environment. Of the many schemes that are established during this period, the emergence of an increasingly complex sense of causal relationships, the establishment of the concept of object permanence, and the formation of categories of objects are achievements that impose order and predictability on experience. Emotions are an early and continuous means of achieving intersubjectivity between infants and their caregivers.

The establishment of trust between the infant and the caregiver is significant in both intellectual and social development. Through repeated interaction with the caregiver, the infant develops a concept of the adult as both separate and permanent. Social attachment is closely tied to the infant's recognition of her or his parents as separate beings. Once established, the trusting relationship between the infant and the caregiver becomes a source of security for the infant's further explorations of the environment.

Infants are skilled in adapting to their environment, but they cannot bring about gross changes in that environment. Parents and other caregivers are ultimately responsible for structuring the environment so that it is maximally suited to the infant. These adults are also the sources of the responsiveness, sensitivity, acceptance, and warmth that create an atmosphere conducive to the establishment of trust.

References

Adamson, L. B., Bakeman, R., Smith, C. B. & Walters, A. S. (1987). Adults' interpretation of infants' acts. *Developmental Psychology*, 23, 383–387.

Adolph, K. E., Eppler, M. A. & Gibson, E. J. (1993). Crawling versus walking infants' perception of affordances for locomotion over sloping surfaces. *Child Development*, 64, 1158–174.

Ainsworth, M. D. S. (1973). The development of infant-mother attachment. In B. M. Caldwell & H. N. Ricciuti (Eds.), *Review of child development research* (Vol. 3). Chicago: University of Chicago Press.

Ainsworth, M. D. S. (1979) Infant-mother attachment. *American Psychologist*, 34, 932–937.

Ainsworth, M. D. S. (1985). Patterns of infant-mother attachments: Antecedents and effects on development. *Bulletin of the New York Academy of Medicine*, 61, 771–791.

Ainsworth, M. D. S. (1989). Attachments beyond infancy. *American Psychologist*, 44, 709–716.

Ainsworth, M. D. S., Bell, S. M. V. & Stayton, D. J. (1971). Individual differences in strange-situational behavior of one-year-olds. In H. A. Schaffer (Ed.), *The origins of human social relations*. London: Academic Press.

Ainsworth, M. D. S., Blehar, M. C., Waters, E. & Wall, S. (1978). *Patterns of attachment: A psychological study of the strange situation*. Hillsdale, NJ: Erlbaum.

Alessandri, S. M. (1992). Mother-child interactional correlates of maltreated and nonmaltreated children's play behavior. *Development and Psychopathology*, 4, 257–270.

Ambrose, J. A. (1963). The concept of a critical period in the development of social responsiveness. In B. M. Foss (Ed.), *Determinants of infant behavior* (Vol. 2). New York: Wiley.

Aoki, C. & Siekevitz, P. (1988). Plasticity in brain development. *Scientific American*, 259, 56–64.

Apgar, V. (1953). Proposal for a new method of evaluating the newborn infant. *Anesthesia and Analgesia*, 32, 260–267.

Aslin, R. N. (1987). Visual and auditory development in infancy. In J. D. Osofsky (Ed.), *Handbook of infant development* (2nd ed., pp. 5–97). New York: Wiley.

Baillargeon, R. (1987). Object permanence in 3½ and 4½ -month-old infants. *Developmental Psychology*, 23, 655–664.

Baillargeon, R. & Graber, M. (1988). Evidence of location memory in 8-month-old infants in a nonsearch AB task. *Developmental Psychology*, 24, 502–511.

Banks, M. S. & Dannemiller, J. L. (1987). Infant visual psychophysics. In P. Salapatek & L. Cohen (Eds.), *Handbook of infant perception* (Vol. 1). Orlando, FL: Academic Press.

Bartz, K. W. & Levine, E. S. (1978, November). Child rearing by black parents: A description and comparison to Anglo and Chicano parents. *Journal of Marriage and the Family*, 40, 709–719.

Bates, J. E. (1987). Temperament in infancy. In J. D. Osofsky (Ed.), *Handbook of infant development*, (2nd ed., pp. 1101–1149). New York: Wiley.

Bell, S. M. & Ainsworth, M. D. S. (1972). Infant crying and maternal responsiveness. *Child Development*, 43, 1171–1190.

Belsky, J. (1988). The "effects" of infant day care reconsidered. *Early Childhood Research Quarterly*, 3, 235–272.

Belsky, J. (1990). Parental and nonparental child care and children's socioemotional development: A decade in review. *Journal of Marriage and the Family*, 52, 885–903.

Belsky, J., Gilstrap, B. & Rovine, M. (1984). The Pennsylvania infant and family development project: Vol. 1. Stability and change in mother-infant and father-infant interaction in a family setting at one, three, and nine months. *Child Development* 55, 692–705.

Belsky, J. & Rovine, M. (1987). Temperament and attachment security in the strange situation: An empirical rapprochement. *Child Development*, 58, 787–795.

Belsky, J. & Tolan, W. (1981). The infant as producer of his development: An ecological analysis. In R. Lerner & N. Busch-Rossnagel (Eds.), *The child as producer of its own development*: A life-span perspective. New York: Academic Press.

Benson, J. B. & Uzgiris, I. C. (1985). Effect of self-initiated locomotion on infant search activity. *Developmental Psychology*, 21, 923–931.

Bernieri, F. J., Reznick, J. S. & Rosenthal, R. (1988). Synchrony, pseudosynchrony, and dissynchrony: Measuring the entrainment process in mother-infant interactions. *Journal of Personality and Social Psychology*, 54, 243–253.

Bertenthal, B. I. & Fischer, K. W. (1983). The development of representation in search: A social-cognitive analysis. *Child Development*, 54, 846–857.

Blass, E. M. & Smith, B. A. (1992). Differential effects of sucrose, fructose, glucose, and lactose on crying in 1- to 3-day-old human infants: Qualitative and quantitative considerations. *Developmental Psychology*, 28, 804–810

Bornstein, M. H. (1985). How infant and mother jointly contribute to developing cognitive competence in the child. *Proceedings of the National Academy of Science*, USA, 82, 7470–7473.

Bornstein, M. H., Kessen, W. & Weiskopf, S. (1976). The categories of hue in infancy. *Science*, 191, 201–202.

Bower, T. G. R. (1987). *Development in infancy* (2nd ed.). New York: W. H. Freeman.

Bower, T. G. R. (1989). *The rational infant: Learning in infancy*. New York: W. H. Freeman.

Bowlby, J. (1960). Separation anxiety. *International Journal of Psychoanalysis*, 41, 69–113.

Bowlby, J. (1980). *Attachment and loss: Vol. 3. Loss, sadness, and depression*. New York: Basic Books.

Bowlby, J. (1988). *A secure base: Parent-child attachment and healthy human development*. New York: Basic Books.

Bradley, R. H., Caldwell, B. M. & Rock, S. L. (1988). Home environment and school performance: A ten-year follow-up and examination of three models of environmental action. *Child Development*, 59, 852–867.

Braungart, J. M., Plomin, R., Defries, J. C. & Fulker, D. W. (1992). Genetic influence on tester-rated infant temperament as assessed by Bayley's Infant Behavior Record: Nonadoptive and adoptive siblings and twins. *Developmental Psychology*, 28 (1), 40–47.

Bretherton, I. (1985). Attachment theory: Retrospect and prospect. In I. Bretherton & E. Everett (Eds.), *Growing points of attachment theory and research* (pp. 3–35). *Monographs of the Society for Research in Child Development*, 50 (1–2, Serial No. 209).

Bretherton, I. (1990). Open communication and internal working models: Their role in the development of attachment relationships. In R. Dienstbier & R. A. Thompson (Eds.), *Nebraska Symposium on Motivation 1988: Socioemotional Development*, 36, 57–113: Lincoln:University of Nebraska Press.

Bridges, L. J., Connell, J. P. & Belsky, J. (1988). Similarities and differences in infant-mother and infant-father interaction in the strange situation: A component process analysis. *Developmental Psychology*, 24, 92–100.

Bronson, G. W. (1973). Infants' reactions to an unfamiliar person. In L. J. Stone, H. T. Smith & L. B. Murphy (Eds.), *The competent infant*. New York: Basic Books.

Brooks-Gunn, J., Klebanov, P. K., Liaw, F. & Spiker, D. (1993). Enhancing the development of low-birth-weight, premature infants: Changes in cognition and behavior over the first three years. *Child Development*, 64, 736–753.

Bushnell, E. W. & Boudreau, J. P. (1993). Motor development and the mind: The potential role of motor abilities as a determinant of aspects of perceptual development. *Child Development*, 64, 1005–1021.

Buss, A. H. & Plomin, R. (1984). *Temperament: Early developing personality traits*. Hillsdale, NJ: Erlbaum.

Buss, A. H. & Plomin, R. (1986). The EAS approach to temperament. In R. Plomin & J. Dunn (Eds.), *The study of temperament: Changes, continuities, and challenges*. Hillsdale, NJ: Erlbaum.

Calkins, S. D. & Fox, N. A. (1992). The relations among infant temperament, security of attachment, and behavioral inhibition at twenty-four months. *Child Development*, 63, 1456–1472.

Campos, J. J. & Barrett, K. C. (1984). Toward a new understanding of emotions and their development. In C. E. Izard, J. Kagan & R. B. Zajonc (Eds.), *Emotions, cognition, and behavior* (pp. 229–263). Cambridge: Cambridge University Press.

Campos, J. J., Campos, R. G. & Barrett, K. C. (1989). Emergent themes in the study of emotional development and emotion regulation. *Developmental Psychology*, 25, 394–402.

Campos, R. G. (1989). Soothing pain-elicited distress in infants with swaddling and pacifiers. *Child Development*, 60, 781–792.

Canfield, R. L. & Haith, M. M. (1991). Young infants' visual expectations for symmetric and asymmetric stimulus sequences. *Developmental Psychology*, 27, 198–208.

Carlson, V., Cicchetti, D., Barnett, D. & Braunwald, K. (1989a). Disorganized/disoriented attachment relationships in maltreated infants. *Developmental Psychology*, 25, 525–531.

Carlson, V., Cicchetti, D., Barnett, D. & Braunwald, K. (1989b). Finding order in disorganization: Lessons from research on maltreated infants' attachment to their caregivers. In D. Cicchetti & V. Carlson (Eds.), *Child maltreatment: Theory and research on the causes and consequences of maltreatment* (pp. 494–528). New York: Cambridge University Press.

Caron, A. J., Caron, R. F. & MacLean, D. J. (1988). Infant discrimination of naturalistic emotional expressions: The role of face and voice. *Child Development*, 59, 604–616.

Cassady, G. & Strange, M. (1987). The small-for-gestational-age (SGA) infant. In G. B. Avery (Ed.), *Neonatology: Pathophysiology and management of the newborn* (pp. 299–331). Philadelphia: Lippincott.

Cernoch, J. M. & Porter, R. H. (1985). Recognition of maternal axillary odors by infants. *Child Development*, 56, 1593–1598.

Chase-Lansdale, P. L. & Owen, M. T. (1987). Maternal employment in a family context: Effects on infant-mother and infant-father attachments. *Child Development*, 58, 1505–1512.

Chazan, S. E. (1981). Development of object permanence as a correlate of dimensions of maternal care. *Developmental Psychology*, 17, 79–81.

Church, J. (1966). *Three babies: Biographies of cognitive development*. New York: Random House.

Cicchetti, D. & Schneider-Rosen, K. (1984). Theoretical and empirical considerations in the investigation of the relationship between affect and cognition in atypical populations of infants. In C. E. Izard, J. Kagan & R. B. Zajonc (Eds.), *Emotions, cognition, and behavior* (pp. 366–408). Cambridge: Cambridge University Press.

Clark, J. E. & Phillips, S. J. (1993). A longitudinal study of intralimb coordination in the first year of independent walking: A dynamical systems analysis. *Child Development*, 64, 1143–1157.

Clarke-Stewart, K. A. (1989). Infant day care: Maligned or malignant? *American Psychologist*, 44, 266–273.

Clifton, R., Perris, E. & Bullinger, A. (1991). Infants' perception of auditory space. *Developmental Psychology*, 27, 187–197.

Coll, C. T. G. (1990). Developmental outcome of minority infants: A process-oriented look into our beginnings. *Child Development*, 61, 270–289.

Connolly, K. & Dalgleish, M. (1989). The emergence of a tool-using skill in infancy. *Developmental Psychology*, 25, 894–912.

Cox, M. J., Owen, M. T., Lewis, J. M. & Henderson, V. K. (1989). Marriage, adult adjustment, and early parenting. *Child Development*, 60, 1015–1024.

Crittenden, P. M. (1985). Maltreated infants: Vulnerability and resilience. *Journal of Child Psychology and Psychiatry*, 26, 85–96.

DeCasper, A. & Fifer, W. (1980). Of human bonding: Newborns prefer their mothers' voices. *Science*, 208, 1174–1176.

DeCasper, A. J. & Spence, M. J. (1986). Prenatal maternal speech influences newborns' perception of speech sounds. *Infant Behavior and Development*, 9, 133–150.

Dennis, W. (1960). Causes of retardation among institutionalized children: Iran. *Journal of Genetic Psychology*, 96, 47–59.

Dickstein, S. & Parke, R. D. (1988). Social referencing in infancy: A glance at fathers and marriage. *Child Development*, 59, 506–511.

Dodge, K. A. (1989). Coordinating responses to aversive stimuli: Introduction to a special section on the development of emotion regulation. *Developmental Psychology*, 25, 339–342.

Donovan, W. L. & Leavitt, L. A. (1989). Maternal self-efficacy and infant attachment: Integrating physiology, perceptions, and behavior. *Child Development*, 60, 460–472.

Easterbrooks, M. A. (1989). Quality of attachment to mother and to father: Effects of perinatal risk status. *Child Development*, 60, 825–830.

Egeland, B., Jacobvitz, D. & Sroufe, L. A. (1988). Breaking the cycle of abuse. *Child Development*, 59, 1080–1088.

Egeland, B. & Sroufe, L. A. (1981). Attachment and early maltreatment. *Child Development*, 52, 44–52.

Ellsworth, C. P., Muir, C. P. & Hains, S. M. J. (1993). Social competence and person-object differentiation: An analysis of the still-face effect. *Developmental Psychology*, 29, 63–73.

Erikson, E. H. (1950). *Childhood and society*. New York: Norton.

Erikson, E. H. (1963). *Childhood and society* (rev. ed.). New York: Norton.

Erikson, E. H. (1978). Reflections on Dr. Borg's life cycle. In E. H. Erikson (Ed.), *Adulthood* (pp. 1–31). New York: Norton.

Escalona, S. K. (1968). *The roots of individuality*. Chicago: Aldine.

Feinman, S. & Lewis, M. (1983). Social referencing at ten months: A second-order effect on infants' responses to strangers. *Child Development*, 54, 878–887.

Fentress, J. C. & McLeod, P. J. (1986). Motor patterns in development. In E. M. Blass (Ed.), *Handbook of behavioral neurobiology: Vol. 8. Developmental psychobiology and developmental neurobiology*. New York: Plenum.

Field, R. M., Cohen, D., Garcia, R. & Greenberg, R. (1984). Mother-stranger face discrimination by the newborn. *Infant Behavior and Development*, 7, 19–25.

Field, R. M., Woodson, R. W., Greenberg, R. & Cohen, C. (1982). Discrimination and imitation of facial expressions by neonates. *Science*, 218, 179–181.

Field, T., Dempsey, J. & Shuman, H. H. (1983). Five-year follow-up of preterm respiratory distress syndrome and postterm postmaturity syndrome in infants. In T. Field & A. Sostek (Eds.), *Infants born at risk: Physiological, perceptual, and cognitive processes* (pp. 317–335). New York: Grune & Stratton.

Field, T., Healy, B., Goldstein, S. & Guthertz, M. (1990). Behavior-state matching and synchrony in mother-infant interactions of nondepressed versus depressed dyads. *Developmental Psychology*, 26, 7–14.

Field, T., Healy, B., Goldstein, S., Perry, S., Bendell, D., Schanberg, S., Zimmerman, E. A. & Kuhn C. (1988). Infants of depressed mothers show "depressed" behavior even with nondepressed adults. *Child Development*, 59, 1569–1579.

Fischer, K. W. & Silvern, L. (1985). Stages and individual differences in cognitive development. *Annual Review of Psychology*, 36, 613–648.

Fonagy, P., Steele, H. & Steele, M. (1991). Maternal representations of attachment during pregnancy predict the organization of infant-mother attachment at one year of age. *Child Development*, 62, 891–905.

Fox, N. & Fein, G. G. (1990). *Infant day care: The current debate*. Norwood, NJ: Ablex.

Fox, N. A., Kimmerly, N. L. & Schafer, W. D. (1991). Attachment to mother/attachment to father. *Child Development*, 62, 210–225.

Francis, P. L., Self, P. A. & Horowitz, F. D. (1987). The behavioral assessment of the neonate: An overview. In J. D. Osofsky (Ed.), *Handbook of infant development* (2nd ed., pp. 723–779). New York: Wiley.

Gibson, J. J. (1962). Observations on active touch. *Psychological Review*, 69, 477–491.

Goldberg, S. (1977). Infant development and mother-infant interaction in urban Zambia. In P. H. Leiderman, S. R. Tulkin & A. Rosenfeld (Eds.), *Culture and infancy: Variations in the human experience* (pp. 211–244). New York: Academic Press.

Goldfield, E. C. (1989). Transition from rocking to crawling: Postural constraints on infant movement. *Developmental Psychology, 25*, 913–919.

Goldsmith, H. H. & Alansky, J. A. (1987). Maternal and infant temperamental predictors of attachment: A meta-analytic view. *Journal of Consulting and Clinical Psychology, 55*, 805–816.

Goldsmith, H. H., Buss, A. H., Plomin, R., Rothbart, M. K., Thomas, A., Chess, S., Hinde, R. A. & McCall, R. B. (1987). Roundtable: What is temperament? Four approaches. *Child Development, 58*, 505–529.

Goldsmith, H. H. & Campos, J. J. (1986). Fundamental issues in the study of early development: The Denver twin temperament study. In M. E. Lamb & A. Brown (Eds.), *Advances in developmental psychology* (pp. 231–283). Hillsdale, NJ: Erlbaum.

Gopnik, A. & Meltzoff, A. (1987). The development of categorization in the second year and its relation to other cognitive and linguistic developments. *Child Development, 58*, 1523–1531.

Gopnik, A. & Meltzoff, A. N. (1992). Categorization and naming: Basic-level sorting in eighteen-month-olds and its relation to language. *Child Development, 63*, 1091–1103.

Gunnar, M. R., Larson, M. C., Hertsgaard, L., Harris, M. L. & Brodersen, L. (1992). The stressfulness of separation among nine-month-old infants: Effects of social context variables and infant temperament. *Child Development, 63*, 290–303.

Harris, P. (1975). Development of search and object permanence during infancy. *Psychological Bulletin, 82*, 332–334.

Harwood, R. L. (1992). The influence of culturally derived values on Anglo and Puerta Rican mothers' perceptions of attachment behavior. *Child Development, 63*, 822–839.

Hay, D. F. (1980). Multiple functions of proximity seeking in infancy. *Child Development, 52*, 636–645.

Hayne, H., Rovee-Collier, C. & Perris, E. E. (1987). Categorization and memory retrieval by three-month-olds. *Child Development, 58*, 750–767.

Heckhausen, J. (1987). Balancing for weaknesses and challenging developmental potential: A longitudinal study of mother-infant dyads in apprenticeship interactions. *Developmental Psychology, 23*, 762–770.

Hickey, T. L. & Peduzzi, J. D. (1987). Structure and development of the visual system. In P. Salapatek & L. Cohen (Eds.), *Handbook of infant perception* (Vol. 1). Orlando, FL: Academic Press.

Holden, G. W. (1988). Adults' thinking about a child-rearing problem: Effects of experience, parental status, and gender. *Child Development, 59*, 1623–1632.

Hopkins, B. & Westra, T. (1988). Maternal handling and motor development: An intracultural study. *Genetic, Social and General Psychology Monographs, 14*, 377–420.

Hornik, R. & Gunnar, M. R. (1988). A descriptive analysis of infant social referencing. *Child Development, 59*, 626–634.

Hornik, R., Risenhoover, N. & Gunnar, M. (1987). The effects of maternal positive, neutral, and negative affective communications on infant responses to new toys. *Child Development, 58*, 937–944.

Howes, P. & Markman, H. J. (1989). Marital quality and child functioning: A longitudinal investigation. *Child Development, 60*, 1044–1051.

Hubert, N. C., Wachs, T. D., Peters-Martin, P. & Gandour, M. J. (1982). The study of early temperament: Measurement and conceptual issues. *Child Development, 53*, 571–600.

Hyson, M. C. & Izard, C. E. (1985). Continuities and changes in emotion expressions during brief separation at 13 and 18 months. *Developmental Psychology, 21*, 1165–1170.

Isabella, R. A. (1993). Origins of attachment: Maternal interactive behavior across the first year. *Child Development, 64*, 605–621.

Isabella, R. A. & Belsky, J. (1991). Interactional synchrony and the origins of infant-mother attachment: A replication study. *Child Development, 62*, 373–384.

Izard, C. E., Haynes, O. M., Chisholm, G. & Baak, K. (1991). Emotional determinants of infant-mother attachment. *Child Development, 62*, 906–917.

Izard, C. E., Hembree, E., Dougherty, L. & Spizziri, C. (1983). Changes in two-to-nineteen-month-old infants' facial expression following acute pain. *Developmental Psychology, 19*, 418–426.

Jackson, E., Campos, J. J. & Fischer, K. W. (1978). The question of decalage between object permanence and person permanence. *Developmental Psychology, 14*, 1–10.

Kagan, J. (1984). The idea of emotion in human development. In C. E. Izard, J. Kagan & R. B. Zajonc (Eds.), *Emotions, cognition, and behavior* (pp. 38–72). Cambridge: Cambridge University Press.

Kaitz, M., Lapidot, P., Bronner, R. & Eidelman, A. I. (1992). Parturient women can recognize their infants by touch. *Developmental Psychology, 28*, 35–39.

Kantrowitz, B. (1988, May 16). Preemies. *Newsweek*, pp. 62–70.

Keil, P. F. (1975). The development of the young child's ability to anticipate the outcome of simple causal events. Paper presented at the meeting of the Society for Research in Child Development, Denver.

Keltenbach, K., Weinraub, M. & Fullard, W. (1980). Infant wariness toward strangers reconsidered: Infants' and mothers' reactions to unfamiliar persons. *Child Development, 51*, 1197–1202.

Kermoian, R. & Campos, J. J. (1988). Locomotor experience: A facilitator of spatial cognitive development. *Child Development, 59*, 908–917.

Klinnert, M. D., Emde, R. N., Butterfield, P. & Campos, J. J. (1986). Social referencing: The infant's use of emotional signals from a friendly adult with mother present. *Developmental Psychology, 22,* 427–432.

Kopp, C. B. (1989). Regulation of distress and negative emotions: A developmental view. *Developmental Psychology, 25,* 343–354.

Kropp, J. P. & Haynes, O. M. (1987). Abusive and nonabusive mothers' ability to identify general and specific emotion signals of infants. *Child Development, 58,* 187–190.

Kuhl, P. K. (1987). Perception of speech and sound in early infancy. In P. Salapatek & L. Cohen (Eds.), *Handbook of infant perception* (Vol. 1). Orlando, FL: Academic Press.

Lamb, M. E. (1976). Twelve-month-olds and their parents: Interaction in a laboratory playroom. *Developmental Psychology, 12,* 237–244.

Larson, M. C., Gunnar, M. R. & Hertsgaard, L. (1991). The effects of morning naps, car trips, and maternal separation on adrenocortical activity in human infants. *Child Development, 62,* 362–372.

Lerner, J. V. & Lerner, R. M. (1983). Temperament and adaptation across life: Theoretical and empirical issues. In P. B. Baltes & O. G. Brim (Eds.), *Life span development and behavior* (Vol. 5, pp. 197–231). New York: Academic Press.

LeVine, R. A. (1977). Child rearing as cultural adaptation. In P. H. Leiderman, S. R. Tulkin & A. Rosenfeld (Eds.), *Culture and infancy: Variations in the human experience* (pp. 15–28) New York: Academic Press.

Levitt, M. J., Weber, R. A. & Clark, M. C. (1986). Social network relationships as sources of maternal support and well-being. *Developmental Psychology, 22,* 310–316.

Levy-Shiff, R., Sharir, H. & Mogilner, M. B. (1989). Mother– and father–preterm infant relationship in the hospital preterm nursery. *Child Development, 60,* 93–102.

Lorenz, K. F. (1935). Der Kumpan in der Urwelt des Vogels. *Journal Ornithologie, 83,* 137.

Lorenz, K. F. (1937/1961). Imprinting. In R. C. Birney & R. C. Teevan (Eds.), *Instinct.* Princeton, NJ: Van Nostrand.

Ludemann, P. M. & Nelson, C. A. (1988). Categorical representation of facial expressions by 7-month-old infants. *Developmental Psychology, 24,* 492–501.

Lyons-Ruth, K., Alpern, L. & Repacholi, B. (1993). Disorganized infant attachment classification and maternal psychosocial problems as predictors of hostile-aggressive behavior in the preschool classroom. *Child Development, 64,* 572–585.

Lyons-Ruth, K., Connell, D. B., Grunebaum, H. & Botein, S. (1990). Infants at social risk: Maternal depression and family support services as mediators of infant development and security of attachment. *Child Development, 61,* 85–98.

Lyons-Ruth, K., Connell, D. B., Zoll, D. & Stahl, J. (1987). Infants at social risk: Relations among infant maltreatment, maternal behavior, and infant attachment behavior. *Developmental Psychology, 23,* 223–232.

MacFarlane, J. A. (1975). Olfaction in the development of social preferences in the human neonate. In *Parent-infant interaction.* Ciba Foundation Symposium, 33, pp. 103–113.

MacLean, D. J. & Schuler, M. (1989). Conceptual development in infancy: The understanding of containment. *Child Development, 60,* 1126–1137.

MacTurk, R. H., McCarthy, M. E., Vietze, P. M. & Yarrow, L. J. (1987). Sequential analysis of mastery behavior in 6- and 12-month-old infants. *Developmental Psychology, 23,* 199–203.

Main, M., Kaplan, N. & Cassidy, J. (1985). Security in infancy, childhood, and adulthood: A move to the level of representation. In I. Bretherton & E. Everett (Eds.), *Growing points of attachment theory and research* (pp. 66–104). *Monographs of the Society for Research in Child Development, 50* (1–2, Serial No. 209).

Main, M. & Solomon, J. (1986). Discovery of insecure-disorganized/disoriented attachment pattern. In T. B. Brazelton and M. W. Yogman (Eds.), *Affective development in infancy* (pp. 95–124). Norwood, NJ: Ablex.

Main, M. & Solomon, J. (1990). Procedures for identifying infants as disorganized/disoriented during the Ainsworth Strange Situation. In M. Greenberg, D. Cicchetti & E. M. Cummings (Eds.), *Attachment in the preschool years: Theory, research and intervention* (pp. 121–160). Chicago: University of Chicago Press.

Malatesta, C. A. & Izard, C. E. (1984). The ontogenesis of human social signals: From biological imperative to symbol utilization. In N. A. Fox & R. J. Davidson (Eds.), *The psychobiology of affective development* (pp. 161–206). Hillsdale, NJ: Erlbaum.

Mandler, J. (1990). A new perspective on cognitive development in infancy. *American Scientist, 28,* 236–243.

Mistretta, C. M. & Bradley, R. M. (1977). Taste in utero: Theoretical considerations. In J. M. Weiffenbach (Ed.), *Taste and development* (pp. 279–291). DHEW Publication no. NIH 77-1068. Bethesda, MD: U.S. Department of Health, Education, and Welfare.

Miyake, K., Campos, J., Kagan, J. & Bradshaw, D. (1986). Issues in socioemotional development in Japan. In H. Azuma, I. Hakuta & H. Stevenson (Eds.), *Kodomo: Child development and education in Japan* (pp. 239–261). New York: W. H. Freeman.

Ninio, A. & Rinott, N. (1988). Fathers' involvement in the care of their infants and their attributions of cognitive competence to infants. *Child Development, 59,* 652–663.

Oppenheim, D., Sagi, A. & Lamb, M. E. (1988). Infant-adult attachments on the kibbutz and their relation to socioemotional development four years later. *Developmental Psychology, 24,* 427–433.

Osofsky, J. D. (1987). *Handbook of infant development* (2nd ed.). New York: Wiley.

Osofsky, J. D. & Connors, K. (1979). Mother-infant interaction: An integrative view of a complex system. In J. D. Osofsky (Ed.), *Handbook of infant development* (pp. 519–548). New York: Wiley.

Oster, H., Hegley, D. & Nagel, L. (1992). Adult judgments and fine-grained analysis of infant facial expressions: Testing the validity of a priori coding formulas. *Developmental Psychology, 28,* 1115–1131.

Owen, M. T., Easterbrooks, M. A., Chase-Landsdale, L. & Goldberg, W. A. (1984). The relation between maternal employment status and the stability of attachments to mother and to father. *Child Development, 55,* 1894–1901.

Palmer, C. F. (1989). The discriminating nature of infants' exploratory actions. *Developmental Psychology, 25,* 885–893.

Papousek, H. & Bernstein, P. (1969). The functioning of conditioning stimulation in human neonates and infants. In A. Ambrose (Ed.), *Stimulation in early infancy.* London: Academic Press.

Park, K. A. & Waters, E. (1989). Security of attachment and preschool friendships. *Child Development, 60,* 1076–1081.

Passman, R. H. & Longeway, K. P. (1982). The role of vision in maternal attachment: Giving 2-year-olds a photograph of their mother during separation. *Developmental Psychology, 18,* 530–533.

Piaget, J. (1954). *The construction of reality in the child.* New York: Basic Books.

Piaget, J. (1970). Piaget's theory. In P. H. Mussen (Ed.), *Carmichael's manual of child psychology* (3rd ed.). New York: Wiley.

Piaget, J. & Inhelder, B. (1966/1969). *The psychology of the child.* New York: Basic Books.

Plomin, R. (1990). *Nature and nurture: An introduction to human behavioral genetics.* Pacific Grove, CA: Brooks/Cole.

Plomin, R. (1994). *Genetics and experience.* Thousand Oaks, CA.: Sage.

Plomin, R. & McClearn, G. E. (1993). *Nature, nurture, and psychology.* Hyattsville, MD: American Psychological Association.

Porter, R. H., Balogh, R. D. & Makin, J. W. (1988). Olfactory influences on mother-infant interactions. In C. Rovee-Collier & L. Lipsitt (Eds.), *Advances in infancy research* (Vol. 5, pp. 39–68). Norwood, NJ: Albex.

Power, T. G. (1985). Mother- and father-infant play: A developmental analysis. *Child Development, 56,* 1514–1524.

Radke-Yarrow, M., Cummings, E. M., Kuczynski, L. & Chapman, M. (1985). Patterns of attachment in two- and three-year-olds in normal families and families with parental depression. *Child Development, 56,* 591–615.

Ramsay, D. S. & Campos, J. J. (1978). The onset of representation and entry into stage six of object permanence development. *Developmental Psychology, 14,* 79–86.

Rempel, J. K., Holmes, J. G. & Zanna, M. P. (1985). Trust in close relationships. *Journal of Personality and Social Psychology, 49,* 95–112.

Ricks, M. H. (1985). The social transmission of parental behavior: Attachment across generations. In I. Bretherton & E. Waters (Eds.), *Growing points of attachment: Theory and research* (pp. 211–227). *Monographs of the Society for Research in Child Development, 50* (1–2, Serial No. 209).

Robertson, J. & Robertson, J. (1989). *Separation and the very young.* New York: Free Association Books.

Robinson, J. L., Kagan, J., Reznick, J. S. & Corley, R. (1992). The heritability of inhibited and uninhibited behavior: A twin study. *Developmental Psychology, 28* (6), 1030–1037.

Rochat, P. (1989). Object manipulation and exploration in 2- to 5-month-old infants. *Developmental Psychology, 25,* 871–884.

Rose, S. A., Feldman, J. F., McCarton, C. M. & Wolfson, J. (1988). Information processing in seven-month-old infants as a function of risk status. *Child Development, 59,* 589–603.

Rose, S. A., Feldman, J. F. & Wallace, I. F. (1992). Infant information processing in relation to six-year cognitive outcomes. *Child Development, 63,* 1126–1141.

Rose, S. A. & Ruff, H. A. (1987). Cross-modal abilities in human infants. In J. D. Osofsky (Ed.), *Handbook of infant development* (2nd ed., pp. 318–362). New York: Wiley.

Rosen, K. S. & Rothbaum, F. (1993). Quality of parental caregiving and security of attachment. *Developmental Psychology, 29,* 358–367.

Rosen, W. D., Adamson, L. B. & Bakeman, R. (1992). An experimental investigation of infant social referencing: Mothers' messages and gender differences. *Developmental Psychology, 28,* 1172–1178.

Rosenstein, D. & Oster, H. (1988). Differential facial responses to four basic tastes in newborns. *Child Development, 59,* 1555–1568.

Ross, G., Kagan, J., Zelazo, P. & Kotelchuck, M. (1975). Separation protest in infants in home and laboratory. *Developmental Psychology, 11,* 256–257.

Rovee, C. K. & Rovee, D. T. (1969). Conjugate reinforcement of infant exploratory behavior. *Journal of Experimental Child Psychology, 8,* 33–39.

Ruff, H. A. (1984). Infants' manipulative exploration of objects: The effects of age and object characteristics. *Developmental Psychology, 20,* 9–20.

Ruff, H. A., Saltarelli, L. M., Capozzoli, M. & Dubiner, K. (1992). The differentiation of activity in infants' exploration of objects. *Developmental Psychology, 28,* 851–861.

Rutter, M. (1990). Commentary: Some focus and process considerations regarding effects of parental depression on children. *Developmental Psychology, 26,* 60–67.

Sagi, A., Lamb, M. E., Lewkowicz, K. S., Shoham, R., Dvir, R. & Estes, D. (1985). Security of infant-mother, -father, and -metapelet attachments among kibbutz-reared Israeli children. In I. Bretherton & E. Everett (Eds.), *Growing points of attachment theory and research* (pp. 257-275). *Monographs of the Society for Research in Child Development, 50* (1–2, Serial No. 209).

Schaffer, H. R. & Emerson, P. E. (1964). *The development of social attachments in infancy. Monographs of the Society for Research in Child Development, 29* (Whole No. 94).

Scott, J. P. (1987). Critical periods in processes of social organization. In M. H. Bornstein (Ed.), *Sensitive periods in development: Interdisciplinary perspectives* (pp. 247–268). Hillsdale, NJ: Erlbaum.

Sera, M. D., Troyer, D. & Smith, L. B. (1988). What do two-year-olds know about the sizes of things? *Child Development, 59,* 1489–1496.

Simons, R. L., Lorenz, F. O., Wu, C. & Conger, R. D. (1993). Social network and marital support as mediators and moderators of the impact of stress and depression on parental behaviors. *Developmental Psychology, 29,* 368–381.

Sophian, C. & Yengo, L. (1985). Infants' understanding of visible displacements. *Developmental Psychology, 21,* 932–941.

Spelke, E. S., von Hofsten, C. & Kestenbaum, R. (1989). Object perception in infancy: Interaction of spatial and kinetic information for object boundaries. *Developmental Psychology, 25,* 185–186.

Spiker, S. J. & Booth, C. (1988). Maternal antecedents of attachment quality. In J. Belsky & T. Nezworksi (Eds.), *Clinical implications of attachment* (pp. 300–323). Hillsdale, NJ: Erlbaum.

Sprunger, L. W., Boyce, W. T. & Gaines, J. A. (1985). Family-infant congruence: Routines and rhythmicity in family adaptations to a young infant. *Child Development, 56,* 564–572.

Sroufe, L. A. (1985). Attachment classification from the perspective of infant-caregiver relationships and infant temperament. *Child Development, 56,* 1–14.

Sroufe, L. A., Schork, E., Motti, F., Lawroski, N. & La Freniere, P. (1984). The role of affect in social competence. In C. E. Izard, J. Kagan & R. B. Zajonc (Eds.), *Emotions, cognition, and behavior* (pp. 38–72). Cambridge: Cambridge University Press.

Stevens, J. H., Jr. (1988). Social support, locus of control, and parenting in three low-income groups of mothers: Black teenagers, black adults, and white adults. *Child Development, 59,* 635–642.

Stevens, J. H., Jr. & Bakeman, R. (1985). A factor analytic study of the HOME scale for infants. *Developmental Psychology, 21,* 1196–1203.

Stockard, C. R. (1907). The artificial production of a single median cyclopian eye in the frog embryo by means of sea water solutions of magnesium chloride. *Archiv für Entwicklungs Mechanik der Organismen, 23,* 249.

Stockard, C. R. (1921). Developmental rate and structural expression. *American Journal of Anatomy, 28,* 115.

Super, C. M. (1981). Cross-cultural research on infancy. In H. C. Triandis & A. Heron (Eds.). *Handbook of cross-cultural psychology: Vol. 4. Developmental psychology.* London: Allyn & Bacon.

Teller, D. Y. & Bornstein, M. H. (1987). Infant color vision and color perception. In P. Salapatek & L. Cohen (Eds.), *Handbook of infant perception* (Vol. 1). Orlando, FL: Academic Press.

Thomas, A. & Chess, S. (1977). *Temperament and development.* New York: Brunner/Mazel.

Thomas, A. & Chess, S. (1980). *The dynamics of psychological development.* New York: Brunner/Mazel.

Thomas, A. & Chess, S. (1986). The New York longitudinal study: From infancy to early adult life. In R. Plomin & J. Dunn (Eds.), *The study of temperament: Changes, continuities, and challenges.* Hillsdale, NJ: Erlbaum.

Thomas, A., Chess, S. & Birch, H. (1970). The origin of personality. *Scientific American, 223,* 102–109.

Thompson, R. A., Connell, J. P. & Bridges, L. J. (1988). Temperament, emotion, and social interactive behavior in the strange situation: A component process analysis of attachment system functioning. *Child Development, 59,* 1102–1110.

Tracy, R. L. & Ainsworth, M. D. S. (1981). Maternal affectionate behavior and infant-mother attachment patterns. *Child Development, 52,* 1341–1343.

Tronick, E. Z. (1989). Emotions and emotional communication in infants. *American Psychologist, 44,* 112–119.

Tronick, E. Z., Als, H. & Brazelton, R. B. (1979). Early development of neonatal and infant behavior. In F. Falkner & J. M. Tanner (Eds.), *Human growth: Vol. 3. Neurobiology and nutrition* (pp. 305–328). New York: Plenum.

Tronick, E. Z. & Cohn, J. F. (1989). Infant-mother face-to-face interaction: Age and gender differences in coordination and the occurrence of miscoordination. *Child Development, 60,* 85–92.

van Ijzendoorn, M. H., Goldberg, S., Kroonenberg, P. M. & Frenkel, O. J. (1992). The relative effects of maternal and child problems on the quality of attachment: A meta-analysis of attachment in clinical samples. *Child Development, 63,* 840–858.

van Ijzendoorn, M. H. & Kroonenberg, P. M. (1988). Cross-cultural patterns of attachment: A meta-analysis of the strange situation. *Child Development, 59,* 147–156.

Vaughn, B., Egeland, B., Sroufe, L. A. & Waters, E. (1979). Individual differences in infant-mother attachment at twelve and eighteen months: Stability and change in families under stress. *Child Development, 50,* 971–975.

Vaughn, B. E., Lefever, G. B., Seifer, R. & Barglow, P. (1989). Attachment behavior, attachment security, and temperament during infancy. *Child Development, 60,* 728–737.

Walden, T. A. & Ogan, T. A. (1988). The development of social referencing. *Child Development, 59,* 1230–1240.

Walker-Andrews, A. S. (1986). Intermodal perception of expressive behaviors: Relation of eye and voice? *Developmental Psychology, 22,* 373–377.

Watson, J. S. (1970). Smiling, cooing, and "the game." Paper presented at the annual meeting of the American Psychological Association, Miami, FL.

Wellman, H. M., Cross, D. & Bartsch, K. (1986). *Infant search and object permanence: A meta-analysis of the A-not-B error. Monographs of the Society for Research in Child Development,* 51 (3, Whole No. 214).

Werker, J. F. (1989). Becoming a native listener. *American Scientist, 77,* 54–59.

Wilson, R. S. & Matheny, A. P., Jr. (1986). Behavior genetics research in infant temperament: The Louisville twin study. In R. Plomin & J. Dunn (Eds.), *The study of temperament: Changes, continuities, and challenges.* Hillsdale, NJ: Erlbaum.

Wolff, P. H. (1963). Observations on the early development of smiling. In B. M. Foss (Ed.), *Determinants of infant behavior* (Vol. 2). New York: Wiley.

Wolff, P. H. (1966). Causes, controls, and organization of behavior in the neonate. *Psychological Issues, 5* (1, Whole No. 17).

Wolff, P. H. (1987). *The development of behavioral states and the expression of emotions in early infancy.* Chicago: University of Chicago Press.

Yarrow, L. J. (1963). Research in dimensions of early maternal care. *Merrill-Palmer Quarterly, 9,* 101–114.

Yarrow, L. J. (1964). Separation from parents in early childhood. In M. L. Hoffman & L. W. Hoffman (Eds.), *Review of child development research* (Vol. 1). New York: Sage.

Yarrow, L. J. (1970). The development of focused relationships during infancy. In J. Hellmuth (Ed.), *Exceptional infant* (Vol. 1.). New York: Brunner/Mazel.

Yarrow, L. J. & Goodwin, M. S. (1965). Some conceptual issues in the study of mother-infant interaction. *American Journal of Orthopsychiatry, 35.* 21–33.

Yarrow, L. J., McQuiston, S., MacTurk, R. H., McCarthy, M. E., Klein, R. P. & Vietze, P. M. (1983). The assessment of mastery motivation during the first year of life. *Developmental Psychology, 19,* 159–171.

Yarrow, L. J., Pedersen, F. A. & Rubenstein, J. (1977). Mother-infant interaction and development in in-fancy. In P. H. Leiderman, S. R. Tulkin & A. Rosenfeld (Eds.), *Culture and infancy: Variations in the human experience* (pp. 539–564). New York: Academic Press.

Younger, B. & Gotlieb, S. (1988). Development of categorization skills: Changes in the nature or structure of infant form categories? *Developmental Psychology, 24,* 611–619.

Yurdakok, K., Yavuz, T. & Taylor, C. E. (1990). Swaddling and acute respiratory infections. *American Journal of Public Health, 80,* 873–875.

Zahn-Waxler, C., Radke-Yarrow, M. & King, R. A. (1977). The impact of the affective environment on young children. Paper presented at the biennial meeting of the Society for Research in Child Development, New Orleans.

Zelazo, P. R., Zelazo, N. A. & Kolb, S. (1972). "Walking" in the newborn. *Science, 176,* 314–315.

Zeskind, P. S. (1983). Cross-cultural differences in maternal perceptions of cries of low- and high-risk infants. *Child Development, 54,* 1119–1128.

Zigler, E. F. & Lang, M. E. (1991). *Child care choices: Balancing the needs of children, families, and society.* New York: Free Press.

Zucker, K. J. (1985). The infant's construction of his parents in the first six months of life. In T. M. Field & N. A. Fox (Eds.), *Social perception in infants.* Norwood, NJ: Ablex.

CHAPTER 6

Toddlerhood is sometimes referred to as the play age.
During this period, the capacity for symbolic thought
combines with a strong motivation for mastery to transform daily life into endless opportunities for fantasy play.

Toddlerhood (2–4 Years)

The dominant characteristic of the stage of life called *toddlerhood* is activity. The toddler is extremely busy—talking, moving, fantasizing, and planning all the time. The outpouring of physical activity—its vigor, constancy, and complexity—is remarkable. Equally impressive is the flood of cognitive accomplishments, especially language production and unique forms of playful fantasy. Toddlers seem to bubble with unpredictable, startling thoughts and actions that keep adults in a state of puzzled amazement.

The motivation for this abundance of activity appears to be a need for self-assertion and mastery. During the years from 2 through 4, children grow increasingly aware of their individuality and are driven to test it out. The familiar negativism of 2-year-olds, which evolves into a more mature willfulness by age 3, is evidence of a powerful need to define and assert the self.

New motor and cognitive capacities give toddlers new abilities to move around freely in their environment and to accept the challenges of a wide variety of exploratory activities. The delight of stacking colored circles on a post changes to the glee of stacking pots and pans in the kitchen and, further, to stacking boxes or blocks for a fantasy spacecraft. Each new accomplishment is accompanied by the pride and pleasure of having mastered an activity at a new level of complexity.

Another characteristic of this life stage is a readiness to learn to limit and regulate one's actions. Once children learn to run, they take great pleasure in chasing madly around the room, pretending to be a wild stallion or a racing car. This new skill is a delight to them, and they eagerly try it out. Before long, however, they also have to control their running behavior to avoid injury or the wrath of their parents or other caregivers. The control of action requires considerable responsiveness to one's physical and social environment, and makes use of such cognitive skills as information processing and decision making (Pick, 1989). In their self-discovery, toddlers must also learn to take the needs of others and their own needs into account.

Between the ages of 2 and 4, toddlers change dramatically from egocentric children who are unaware of their interdependence with others to more self-conscious individuals. At the beginning of the stage, toddlers assert themselves in what appear to be very independent ways. By the end of the stage, this pseudoindependence has been transformed into a more realistic assessment of how they are dependent on others and how they are independent. In sum, toddlerhood is a period of activity and mastery, self-regulation, and an increasing awareness of dependence and independence.

Developmental Tasks

Elaboration of Locomotion

The use of the word *toddler* to describe the life stage from 2 to 4 is in itself a clue to the important part that locomotion plays. In fact, it is only during the first year of this stage that the child actually toddles. By age 3, the child's walk has changed from the precarious, determined, half-humorous waddle known as the *toddle* to a more graceful, continuous, effective stride (Clark & Phillips, 1993).

Difficulties encountered by engineers and inventors in trying to duplicate human locomotor skills in robots have illustrated just how intricate and exquisite the toddler's locomotor accomplishments are (Pick, 1989). The possibility that lifelong movement patterns are acquired during these two years extends our

Pablo Picasso, First Steps, *1943. A child's first steps are a major symbol of the movement toward autonomy. In this painting, the child relies on the mother for stability and guidance but with the clear purpose of taking leave of her.*

appreciation of toddlers' efforts. Renewed interest in motor development suggests that qualitative changes in locomotive behavior are not simply a result of maturation of the cerebral cortex (Kalverboer, Hopkins & Geuze, 1993). Changes in body weight and muscle mass, combined with new capacities to coordinate feedback from the limbs and to judge the amount of effort needed to achieve a motoric goal, are all components in what appears to be a regular progression in motor behavior (Getchell & Robertson, 1989).

As walking becomes a more comfortable form of locomotion, new skills are added to the repertoire. Children learn to negotiate the stairs and to walk along sloping planes. They test these skills by trying to balance as they walk along the edge of a curb or along the top of a concrete ledge. Running and jumping are the next elaborations to emerge. By the age of 4, children are likely to leap from stairways, tables, porch railings, or ladders. They have begun to imagine what it might be like to fly. Jumping is their closest approximation to flying. Evidence suggests that the underlying structure of the jumping pattern remains stable throughout childhood and into adulthood (Clark, Phillips & Peterson, 1989). The child's delight in exploring jumping behavior may result from the acquisition of a fundamental movement pattern that fills the child with a basic sense of mastery as well as a sense of lifelong possibilities.

Children's running abilities become more elaborated all through toddlerhood. At first, youngsters may run for the sake of running. They practice the art over and over again for a long time. Later in toddlerhood, running changes from a kind of game in itself to a valuable component of many other games. The absolute speed of toddlers is limited by somewhat precarious balance and short legs.

However, this limitation does not discourage them from devoting a great deal of time and energy to running. The goals of mastery and getting to new places for exploration are too strong to dampen their enthusiasm.

Toddlers are often exposed to a wide variety of other forms of locomotion, such as swimming, skiing, skating, sledding, and dancing. They seem eager to use their bodies in a variety of ways, and they learn quickly (Ridenour, 1978). As their physical coordination improves, children engage in a new repertoire of large-muscle activities: climbing, sliding, swinging, pounding, digging, and rough-and-tumble play. These forms of physical activity provide an important source of information about the physical self. They offer a key avenue to experiencing mastery, and they are the basis for a lot of fun. Toddlers enjoy their bodies and are generally joyful when in the midst of physical play. Thus, physical activity contributes in an essential way to the toddler's self-concept. Children who lack muscle strength or coordination experience strong feelings of frustration as they struggle to keep their balance, to throw or catch a ball, or to use their hands and feet to perform new tasks.

One of the vehicles of locomotion that has special meaning for the American toddler is the tricycle. The tricycle provides enormous pleasure because of its potential speed, reversibility, turning capability, and horn. It is also an object through which the toddler can identify with other children and with adults. The connection of tricycle, bicycle, and car is quickly and easily made by the toddler. The tricycle combines the joys of physical movement, the thrill of danger and independence, and the social significance of mechanized transportation. Usually, a tricycle (or a comparable pedal toy) has a great deal of psychological significance for the child. It is the first in a chain of objects that will symbolize the child's increased independence from the family and heightened identification with her or his peer group.

One might conclude that, when taken literally, *toddler* is a poor word to apply to these youngsters. Children actually leave toddling early in this stage of life and acquire a range of locomotive skills that they can use with speed and precision. Large-muscle movement and control are great sources of pleasure to a child, confirming feelings of competence and selfhood. All the same, the connotations of the word *toddler*—a short, cherubic, smiling, uncertain little person with an overhanging belly and a bulging behind, who lurches on tiptoe from place to place—are too accurate in the figurative sense for the term to be abandoned.

Fantasy Play

Jean Piaget (1970) described the years from about 2 to 5 or 6 as the stage of *preoperational thought*. This is a transitional period during which the schemes that were developed during infancy are represented internally. The most significant achievement of this new stage of cognitive development is the capacity for *semiotic* thinking, the understanding that one thing can stand for another (Miller, 1993). In semiotic thinking, children learn to recognize and use symbols and signs. *Symbols* are usually related in some way to the object for which they stand. The cross, for example, is a symbol of Christianity. In pretend play, a scarf or a blanket may be a symbol for a pillow or a dress. *Signs* stand for things in a more abstract, arbitrary way. Words are signs; there is no direct relation between the word *dog* and the animal to which the word refers, yet the word stands for the object. For adults, it seems natural to use matchsticks or little squares of cardboard to represent people or buildings, but for children, the idea that a stick may be a car or a horse is a dramatic change in thinking that emerges gradually during the preoperational period.

Vygotsky (1978) emphasized the critically new capacity for thought that is reflected in imaginary play. In play, the meaning of objects and actions is derived from the ideas children have about the pretend situation. For example, when a child plays house, he or she applies all that is known about the mother role in taking on that role. The child has encountered many, many examples of behavior that are associated with being a mother. To fit together the pieces of the puzzle about what it takes to be a mother, the young player now attempts to try out as much of this behavior as possible in whatever ways will work.

Children acquire five representational skills that allow them to manipulate objects mentally rather than by actual behavior: imitation in the absence of the model, mental images, symbolic drawing, symbolic play, and language. Each of these skills frees children from real events. Children can express relationships they may have known in the past by imitating them, drawing them, or acting them out in fantasy. They can also portray events and relationships that they wish would occur or that they wish to alter.

The Capacity for Pretense

Pretense, whether through symbolic play, symbolic drawing, or telling make-believe stories, requires that children understand the difference between pretend and real. Sometimes, adults wonder whether children can in fact distinguish between what is real and what is pretend. The line between make-believe and reality may become blurred for all of us. We encounter such confusion frequently when we watch television. Which of the things we see on television are pretend and which are real? Are commercials advertising products real or pretend? Is a television news story real or pretend? Are dramatic reenactments of historical events real or pretend?

In very simplified situations, children as young as 2 can tell when someone is pretending and can follow the transformations in a pretend sequence (Walker-Andrews & Harris, 1993). For example, an investigator might tell a child that she is going to fill two bowls with cereal, and pretend to fill the bowls. Then the investigator pretends to eat all of her cereal, saying something at the end to indicate that the cereal is all gone. She then asks the child to feed a doll its cereal. Many 2-year-olds and most 3-year-olds can follow this type of scenario, selecting the bowl that is still full of pretend cereal and feeding it to the doll. Toddlers know the difference between what an object really is and what someone is pretending that it is (Flavell, Flavell & Green, 1987). For example, 3-year-olds understand that a sponge is really a sponge, but they can pretend it is a boat floating in the water or a car driving along the road. Three-year-olds also understand the difference between knowing something and pretending something. If they see a rabbit, they know it is real, but they also know that they do not have to have seen a rabbit in order to imagine one. However, compared with older children, 3-year-olds are more convinced that imagination reflects reality. For example, if they imagine something, like a fire-breathing dragon or a horse with wings, they think it may actually exist. In contrast, 4-year-olds understand that something that is imagined may not have a counterpart in reality (Woolley & Wellman, 1993).

Fantasy play and language are contrasting forms of representation. In acquiring language, children learn to translate their thoughts into a commonly shared system of signs and rules. For language to be effective, children must use the same words and grammar as the older members of the family, discovering how to translate their thoughts into existing words and categories. Fantasy serves almost the opposite function. In fantasy, children create characters and situations that may have a very private meaning. There is no need to make the fantasy comprehensible to an audience. There are probably many times when children have strong feelings but lack the words to express them. They may be frustrated by their helplessness or angry at being overlooked. They can express and soothe these feelings in the world of imagination, even though the feelings may never become part of a shared conversation (Erikson, 1972).

During infancy, play often consists of the repetition of a motor activity. Infants delight in sucking their toes or dropping a spoon from the high chair. These are typical *sensorimotor play* activities. Toward the end of infancy, sensorimotor play includes the deliberate imitation of parental acts. Children who see their mothers washing the dishes may enjoy climbing up on a chair and getting their hands wet, too. At first, these imitations occur only when they are stimulated by the sight of the parent's activity. As children enter toddlerhood, they begin to imitate parental activities when they are alone. A vivid mental image of an action permits them to copy what they recall instead of what they see. This is the beginning of *symbolic play*. Before the period of preoperational thought, children do not really pretend because they cannot let one thing stand for something else. Once the capacity for symbolic thought emerges, children become increasingly flexible in allowing an object to take on a wide variety of pretend identities.

Young 2-year-olds appear to be able to understand the context of a pretend situation. Using pretend props, they can pretend to feed a hungry animal or to give a thirsty animal a drink. They can assign a pretend function to a substitute prop, treating a wooden block as if it were a banana or a piece of cake. And they can follow through with the consequences of a pretend situation, like pretending to wipe up pretend spilled tea with a towel (Harris & Kavanaugh, 1993). These very young children can construct a make-believe world in which objects are assigned a pretend meaning (toy blocks can be bananas) and words are used in pretend ways ("feed the monkey a banana" is acted out by putting a toy block up to the mouth of a toy monkey).

Changes in Fantasy Play During Toddlerhood

Toddlers can direct their play in response to mental images that they have generated by themselves. At first, their symbolic play is characterized by the simple repetition of very familiar activities. Pretending to sweep the floor, to be asleep, to be a dog or cat, and to drive a car are some of the early play activities of toddlers.

Fantasy play changes in four ways during toddlerhood (Lucariello, 1987):

1. The action component becomes more complex as children integrate a sequence of actions.
2. Children's focus shifts from the self to fantasies that involve others and the creation of multiple roles.
3. The play involves the use of substitute objects, including objects children only pretend to have, and eventually the invention of complex characters and situations.
4. The play becomes more organized and planned, and play leaders emerge.

First, children combine a number of actions in a play sequence. From pretending to sweep the floor or pretending to take a nap, they devise strings of activities that are part of a complex play sequence. While playing fire fighter, children may pretend to be the fire truck, the hose, the ladder, the engine, the siren, the

In social pretense, children coordinate their roles and behaviors to sustain the fantasy.

people being rescued, and the fire fighters. All the elements of the situation are brought under the children's control through this fantasy enactment.

Second, children become increasingly able to include others in their play and to shift the focus of the play from the self to the others (Howes, 1987; Howes, Unger & Seidner, 1989). One can see a distinction here between solitary pretense, social play, and social pretend play. Children engaged in *solitary pretense* are involved in their own fantasy activities, such as pretending that they are driving a car or giving a baby a bath. Children engaged in *social play* join with other children in some activity. They may dig together in the sand, build with blocks, or imitate each other's silly noises. In *social pretend play*, children have to coordinate their pretense. They establish a fantasy structure, take roles, agree on the make-believe meaning of props, and solve pretend problems. That 2- and 3-year-olds can participate in this type of coordinated fantasy play is quite remarkable, especially given their very limited use of language to establish and sustain coordination.

Third, fantasy play changes as children become more flexible in their use of substitute objects in their play. Fantasy play begins in the areas closest to children's daily experience. They use real objects or play versions of those objects as props in their pretense. For example, they pick up a toy telephone and pretend to make a call to Grandma or pretend to have a picnic with toy cups and plates and plastic foods. But as they develop their fantasy skills, these props are no longer essential. Children can invent objects, create novel uses for common objects, and sometimes pretend to have an object when they have nothing (Boyatzis & Watson, 1993).

The play moves away from common daily experiences to invented worlds based on stories, on television programs, or on purely imagined characters and situations. Children may take the roles of characters with extraordinary powers. They may pretend to fly, to become invisible, or to transform themselves into other shapes with the aid of a few secret words or gestures. Their identification with a particular fantasy hero or heroine may last for days or even weeks as they involve the characters of the story in a variety of fantasy situations.

Fourth, fantasy play becomes more planned and organized. The planning emerges as children try to coordinate their pretend play with other players. It is also a product of a new realization of what makes pretend play most fun, and of the desire to make sure that those components are included in the play. In a preschool or day-care group, certain children are likely to take the lead in organizing the direction of fantasy play. They may set the play in motion or give it direction by suggesting the use of certain props, by assigning roles, or by working out the context of the play. Here we see a child demonstrating this kind of leadership:

Stuart (climbing up on a tractor tire): This will be our shark ship, OK? Get on quick, Jeremy! The sharks will eat you!

Jeremy: No! This is my police helicopter!

Stuart: Well, OK. We're police. But we need to chase the sharks, OK? I see the sharks way down there! Come on!

Jeremy: OK. Let's get 'em! (They both make helicopter noises and swat at make-believe sharks with plastic garden tools.) (Trawick-Smith, 1988, p. 53)

Some people distinguish symbolic role playing from games with rules, implying that the latter are guided by a formal set of mental operations that constrain play, while the former is open and flexible. However, it is clear that pretend play operates within a rule-bound structure (Vygotsky, 1978; Harris & Kavanaugh, 1993). In order to coordinate symbolic play with a partner, children have to come to some mutual understanding about the situation, the props, the characters, and the plot. The players have to limit their behavior in ways that conform to the unspoken or latent rules of the pretense. For example, if the children decide that certain leaves are the pretend food, then no one can use the leaves as bricks to build a house or as weapons to shoot someone. If one player is supposed to be the mommy, that player has to act like the mommy and not like the baby. In games with rules, the rules are more readily spelled out, but in both types of play, a part of what makes it fun is to function within the boundaries of certain kinds of constraints.

Dramatic role playing, in which a child takes on the role of another person or creates a fantasy situation, increases steadily from the ages of 3 through 5. By the age of 6, however, children become involved in games with rules. They may use their fantasy skills during play by making up new games or new rules rather than by engaging in pretend play. If you are looking for the experts in diversified, elaborated fantasy, observe 4- and 5-year-olds (Cole & La Voie, 1985).

Fantasy play is not simply a diversion. Children use fantasy to experiment with and understand their social and physical environments and to expand their thinking (Piers & Landau, 1980; Hutt et al., 1988). Views of the importance and value of fantasy play vary widely. Piaget (1962) emphasized the assimilative value of play. Through fantasy and symbolic play, he believed, children are able to make meaning of experiences and events that are beyond their full comprehension. Fantasy play is a private world to which the rules of social convention and the logic of the physical world do not necessarily apply. From this perspective, fantasy play frees the child from the immediacy of reality, permitting mental manipulations and modifications of objects and events.

Erikson (1972) considered play vital in promoting personality and social development. He valued play as a mechanism for dramatizing the psychological conflicts that children are struggling with, such as angry feelings toward their siblings or parents or jealousy over a friend's new toys. Often, according to Erikson, the play not only represents the problem but offers a solution so that children experience some new sense of resolution and a reduction in the tension associated with the conflict. Symbolic play provides a certain flexibility or leeway in structuring the situation and, at the same time, imposes some limits so that children may experience a new mastery of issues that are perplexing or overwhelming in real life.

Researchers who have studied children who do not engage in much pretend play and other researchers who have tried to increase the level of pretend play among toddlers have found that pretend play actually fosters cognitive and social development (Rubin, 1980; Saltz & Saltz, 1986). Children who have well-developed pretending skills tend to be well liked by their peers and to be viewed as peer leaders (Ladd, Price & Hart, 1988). This is a result of their advanced communication skills, their greater ability to take the point of view of others, and their ability to reason about social situations. Children who have been encouraged in a playful, imaginative approach to the manipulation and exploration of materials and objects through fantasy show more complex language use and more flexible approaches to problem solving (Burke, 1987). Clearly, the importance of fantasy play in the full social, intellectual, and emotional development of young children cannot be underestimated. Some parents and teachers want to define a young child's cognitive growth in terms of the acquisition of words and concepts that seem relevant to the "real world." They emphasize the importance of learning numbers and letters, memorizing facts, and learning to read. However, research on cognitive development suggests that gains in the capacity for symbolic thought provide the essential underpinnings of subsequent intellectual abilities, such as abstract reasoning and inventive problem solving.

The Role of Play Companions

Cognitive developmental theory emphasizes the normal emergence of representational thought and symbolic play as the natural outcome of cognitive maturation during toddlerhood. However, the quality of that play as well as its content depends in part on the behavior of a child's play companions. Consider the following incident. In a university preschool where college students were having their first supervised experience as teachers of young children, a child of 3 made a bid for some pretend play with a student teacher. The child picked up the toy telephone and made ringing noises. The student teacher picked up another phone and said, "Hello." The child asked, "Is Milly there?" The student teacher said, "No," and hung up the phone. Rather than extending the pretense into a more elaborate social pretend situation by saying something like "Who is calling?" or pretending to put Milly on the phone, the student teacher brought the scenario to a close.

As play companions, parents, siblings, peers, and child-care professionals can significantly enrich a child's fantasy play. Play companions can elaborate a child's capacity for fantasy, legitimize fantasy play, and help the child to explore new domains of fantasy. Research has shown that when mothers are available as play companions, the symbolic play of their 2-year-old children is more complex and lasts for a longer time (Slade, 1987). When adults are trained to engage in and encourage pretend play with toddlers, the toddlers show a higher level of ability to coordinate their responses with those of the adults. From the ages of 16–32 months, toddlers become increasingly skillful in directing an adult's behavior and negotiating changes in kinds of play (Eckerman & Didow, 1989).

In child-care settings, the availability of a stable group of age-mates results in more complex, coordinated play. Children who have had many changes in their

Within the day-care setting, skilled adults and a stable group of playmates help to extend and enhance pretense.

child-care arrangements are less likely to engage in complex social pretend play with other children (Howes & Stewart, 1987). Since toddlers rely so heavily on imitation and nonverbal signals to initiate and develop their social pretend play, the more time they have together, the more complex their fantasy play will be.

Imaginary Companions

Probably the most sophisticated form of symbolic play is the creation of an imaginary friend (Singer, 1975). An imaginary friend, which may be an animal, a child, or some other creature, springs, complete in concept, from the mind of the child. It occupies space. It has its own personality, which is consistent from day to day. It has its own likes and dislikes, which are not necessarily the same as those of its creator. Although not all children who have imaginary companions disclose this information to adults, some studies have shown that as many as 65% of toddlers have imaginary companions, and some children have more than one (Singer & Singer, 1990).

In one study, investigators invited children who had imaginary companions to come to the laboratory and play with their companions (Taylor, Cartwright & Carlson, 1993). The children seemed willing to talk about their companions, and they thought the investigators would be able to see and touch their companions just as they could. For most of the children, the companions remained consistent for six months and retained an active role in the child's fantasy life.

Several functions are served by an imaginary friend: It takes the place of other children when there are none around; it serves as a play companion for pretend play; it serves as a confidant for children's private expression; and it is often involved in their efforts to differentiate between right and wrong. Sometimes, toddlers do things they know are wrong because they cannot stop themselves, and they find it difficult to accept responsibility for their misdeeds. They did not wish to be bad; they do not want to displease their parents; and the imaginary friend becomes a convenient scapegoat. Toddlers report that, although they tried very hard to stop their friend, it went right ahead and did the "bad" thing anyway. When children use an excuse of this kind, they are communicating that they understand the difference between right and wrong but are unwilling or unable to assume total responsibility for their misconduct. In general, imaginary friends can be seen as evidence of toddlers' ability to differentiate themselves from others and of their attempts to gain control over their impulses.

Language Development

In the process of language development, children acquire *communicative competence*: They become adept at using all the aspects of language that a child must master (Harris, 1992). They learn the sound system (phonology), the system of meanings (semantics), the rules of word formation (morphology), the rules of sentence formation (syntax; morphology and syntax combine to make up the grammar of a language), and the adjustments to the social setting that are necessary to produce and interpret communication (pragmatics). Communicative competence begins during infancy and develops throughout the life span. Vocabulary, grammar, and pragmatics continue to be expanded and refined as one engages in formal schooling, and as one enters a wider range of social settings where specific words, expressions, and styles of interaction are used. But toddlerhood appears to be the time of a dramatic explosion in verbal competence over a relatively brief period.

Prelinguistic Accomplishments

Thought and language seem to travel independent courses that intersect during the second year of life (Molfese, Molfese & Carrell, 1982). Before that time, we observe vocalization without meaning—that is, cooing (mostly vowel sounds, noticeable at 1 to 2 months) and babbling (consonant-vowel sounds repeated over and over, which begin at about 4 months). We also observe thoughtful action patterns without verbal labels—reaching and grasping, for example, or retrieving a toy that has rolled under a table. (This is the type of behavior we referred to as *sensorimotor intelligence* in Chapter 5.)

In addition, we observe *language perception*. Infants are able to recognize sounds and differentiate between sound combinations before they understand the meanings of the sounds (Bates, O'Connell & Shore, 1987). Very young infants can hear and distinguish among the major sounds used in all human languages.

Babies also respond to the rhythmic manner of adult talking that is characteristic of the ways adults interact with preverbal babies. Anne Fernald (1985, 1993) called this talk "parentese," but you might call it baby talk. She analyzed the speech patterns of adults who were talking to 5-month-old English-learning babies in English, German, Italian, and Japanese. The infant-directed vocalizations involved a raised pitch, exaggerated intonation, shortened phrases, and a slower pace of speech. Babies seemed to catch the emotional tone of these communications, responding more positively to approval, like "Good," and more negatively to prohibitions, like "Don't" or "No."

Babbling

By approximately 10–12 months, infants produce the sounds of their native language, as distinct from the full range of sounds of human language that is evident in their earlier cooing and babbling (Best, McRoberts & Sithole, 1988; Werker & Lalonde, 1988). Babbling, initially characterized by sounds used in many languages, begins to reflect the sounds and intonations infants are most likely to hear. Sounds they do not hear drop out of their babbling.

Infants of this age also use sounds, like grunting and whining, in combination with gestures to achieve a goal, such as getting their mother to reach something for them. Sounds may also be used to express emotion or to get someone's attention (Dore, 1978; Bates et al., 1987). These vocalizations before language are early forms of purposeful communication. Other communication strategies emerge at about 9–11 months. Infants begin to seek adult interest and attention by *showing* them objects and thereby initiating interactions. Soon after showing, infants begin to *give* objects. Adults who are willing to engage in this type of exchange find the baby bringing them a whole variety of toys, utensils, and scraps of dust for their inspection. Following giving, the next significant gesture is *pointing*. Through pointing, infants and adults establish a shared reference point with respect to some object in the environment.

Around this time, it becomes clear that infants understand the meanings of some individual words (Huttenlocher, 1974; Oviatt, 1980). This ability to understand words, called *receptive language*, precedes the ability to produce spoken words and phrases. According to one analysis, middle-class infants have a receptive language of between 17 and 97 words by age 13 months (Bates et al., 1987).

Words with Meaning

One of the first significant events in the development of *language production* is the naming of objects. With repetition, a sound or word becomes associated with a specific object or a set of related objects. For example, a child may say *ba* whenever she sees her bottle. If she is thirsty and wants her bottle, she may try saying *ba* in order to influence her mother to produce the bottle. Gestures, actions, and facial expressions often accompany the "word" and help establish its meaning in the caregiver's mind. If the baby's "word" has meaning to the mother and serves to satisfy the baby's needs, it will probably be retained as a meaningful sign. B*a* may come to mean "bottle" and other liquids the child wishes to drink, such as juice, water, or soda.

The important characteristic of first words is their shared meaning. Even though *ba* is not a real word, it functions in the same way that any noun does: It names a person, place, or thing (Greenfield & Smith, 1976). These single-word utterances accompanied by gestures, actions, vocal intonation, and emotion are called *holophrases*, which convey the meaning of an entire sentence. For example, saying *ba, ba* in a pleading tone while pointing to the refrigerator and jumping up and down conveys the meaning "I need a bottle" or "Get me the bottle." Gradually, the child discovers that every object, action, and relationship has a name (Waxman & Hall, 1993).

Young children first talk about what they know and what they are interested in. Common first words include important people (*Mamma, Dadda,* and names of siblings), foods, pets, toys, body parts (*eye, nose*), clothes (*shoe, sock*), vehicles (*car*), favorite objects (*bottle, blanket*), other objects in the environment (*keys, trees*), actions (*up, bye-bye*), pronouns (*you, me*), and states (*hot, hungry*), and a few key commands (*no, please, down, more*). From 15 to 18 months, the infant makes significant progress in learning the names of objects and applying those names to pictures or real examples of them (Oviatt, 1982). During the second year, the child's vocabulary increases from about 10 words to almost 300.

Sometime around 18 months, the child quickly acquires a large number of new words, and the rapid rate at which the vocabulary grows continues throughout the toddler and early school years (Rice, 1989). One researcher found that during this period children learn about 14,000 new words (Templin, 1957). In order to accomplish this feat, children seem to "fast-map" new meanings as they experience words in conversation. To fast-map is to form quickly an initial, partial understanding of a word's meaning. A child fast-maps by relating the word to the known vocabulary and restructuring the known-word storage space and its related conceptual categories (Carey, 1978). The child has to hear the new word only once or a very few times in a context that makes its meaning clear (Rice & Woodsmall,

The toy telephone is an effective vehicle for stimulating language development in the context of pretense.

1988). Thus, without direct word-by-word tutoring, children accumulate numerous samples of their culture's language from the speech they hear and attach a minimally satisfactory definition to each word or phrase. During the early and middle school years, children devote considerable time and attention to exploring vocabulary, correcting some meanings that were incorrectly learned, and expanding the full range of meanings and underlying concepts that are linked to the many words they acquired so rapidly.

Two-Word Sentences

The second year is marked by the second important stage of language development: the formation of two-word sentences. These two-word sentences are referred to as *telegraphic speech*. Children link two words that are essential to communicate what they intend to say. Just as in a telegram, however, other words—verbs, articles, prepositions, pronouns, conjunctions—are left out. A child will say, "Big ball," "More juice," or "No bed." Before this point, children tend to utter single words accompanied by gestures and actions. When they string two words together, they convey more meaning, and they rely less heavily on gestures and actions to communicate their intentions. The acquisition of telegraphic speech allows a child to make fuller use of the symbolism inherent in language to communicate meaning.

Children are quite innovative in using two-word sentences. They continue to understand more than they are able to say, but they appear to use their limited number of words and their newfound ability to combine words to get their point across. Children may convey different meanings with the same sentence. "Daddy go," for example, may be used either to tell someone that Daddy has left or to tell Daddy to leave. Children often indicate their meanings by their tone of voice or by the words they stress. The use of two-word sentences is characteristic of toddler-age language learners in many cultures (Slobin, 1985).

Early two-word combinations are guided by the meanings that the child wishes to express and by the variety of objects, people, and interactions in the immediate environment (Braine, 1976; Bloom, 1993). One finds considerable variability in the word combinations used by children within one culture. The patterns of word combinations used by some children do not overlap at all with the patterns used by other children. The objects and actions children talk about may be similar, but the word patterns they use to talk about them are their own (Bloom, Lightbown & Hood, 1975). Children also vary widely in the rate at which they

TABLE 6.1 Basic Sequence in Acquiring Grammatical Inflections	
Inflection	**Example**
-ing	Puppy is runn*ing*
in	*In* the pot.
on	I am *on* the bed.
Plural: -*s*	Apple*s*
Past irregular	*Fell, hit, ran*
Possessive: -'*s*	Baby'*s* toy.
Use of *to be* as main verb without contraction	The boys *are* home.
Articles	I want *a* bottle.
Past regular	You walk*ed* too fast.
Third-person regular	He walk*s*
Third-person irregular	She *has*, he *does*
Uncontractible progressive auxiliary	This *is* going fast.
Use of *to be* as main verb with contraction	That'*s* Bill.
Contractible progressive auxiliary	I'*m* talk*ing*.

Source: Based on Brown, 1973.

acquire language, in the way they master specific aspects of language, and in their patterns of combining words (Ferguson, 1989). They also vary in their preference for the use of nounlike words (Nelson, 1973). Children who prefer to use nounlike words and then extend their use of language to verbs and other words begin to master grammar earlier and more effectively than children who begin with another pattern of usage (Bates, Bretherton & Snyder, 1988).

Early language appears to be closely tied to the representation of sensorimotor schemes. It expresses the properties and relationships of objects and people that are important in a child's life. Language use emerges within a larger communication system and reflects a child's cognitive capacities. At the same time, it reflects the perceptual and functional characteristics of the environment, so that the kinds of objects and relationships that are central to daily life influence the content and complexity of a child's early language (Nelson, 1981).

Grammatical Transformations

The grammar of a particular language provides a set of rules that permit the complexity and variety of one person's thinking to be readily understood by someone else. Consider the difference in meaning between "The boy hit the ball" and "The ball hit the boy." The simple matter of word order in a sentence is critical in preserving meaning. The basic format of an English sentence—noun phrase followed by verb phrase—is a central part of its grammar. In order to ask a question or to produce a negative sentence, the speaker *transforms* this word order according to a specific set of rules. The addition of certain inflections and modifiers transforms sentences further to convey complexities of time, possession, number, and relation. Examples of common inflections and the typical order in which they are learned are shown in Table 6.1. When Brown (1973) analyzed the developing grammar of three children, he found that although the rate of acquiring these inflections varied, the order was surprisingly consistent. As children learn the grammatical transformations of their language, they become much more effective in expressing exactly what they have in mind.

A surprising observation is that children use correct transformations for the past tenses of irregular verbs (*went, gave, ran*) before they use correct inflections of regular verbs (*talked, walked, jumped*). It appears that, at first, children learn the past tenses of irregular verbs through rote memory. Once they learn the rule for expressing the past tense by adding *-ed*, they *overgeneralize* this rule and begin making errors in the use of the past tense. So while a 2-year-old is likely to say, "I ran fast," a 3-year-old may say, "I runned fast."

The errors young children make alert us that they are working out a system of rules to use in communicating meaning. It is unlikely that these errors result from imitation of adult speech. Children say such things as "What dat feeled like?" or "Dose are mines." They have certainly not copied these expressions from adults; rather, these errors suggest the beginning of a grammar that becomes more specialized and accurate as children have the opportunity to match their speech to that of others (Schatz, 1983).

Milestones and Limitations

The milestones in language development during the first four years of life, as described by Eric Lenneberg (1967), are seen in Table 6.2. During the first year of life, babies are highly sensitive to spoken language. They use vocalization playfully as a source of sensory stimulation. Gradually, babies produce vocalizations that imitate spoken language. In the second year, babies understand words and phrases. They develop a vocabulary and begin to form two-word phrases. During the third year, language is definitely used to communicate ideas, observations, and needs. Comprehension of spoken language seems almost complete. Some of children's speech may not be easily understood by people outside the family, partly because they are unable to produce clear phonetic sounds and partly because their knowledge of adult grammar is limited. During the fourth year, most children acquire an extensive vocabulary. They can create sentences that reflect most of the basic rules of grammar. Their language is now a vehicle for communicating complex thoughts that are usually understood by children and adults outside the family.

Although the fundamentals of language are well established by age 4, there are still some things that toddlers cannot achieve with language. For example, if you ask a 4-year-old boy to go upstairs and find an orange towel, he may be able to repeat your instructions exactly and still not be able to follow them. He will go upstairs and forget what it is that he is looking for, or he may return with a pillow instead of a towel. You may find him trying to wheel the TV set to the stairs. The child is not deliberately trying to violate your instructions; he is merely unable to use verbal instructions effectively to guide his own behavior (Tinsley & Waters, 1982). As another example, Mary may raise a fuss about wanting the biggest piece of cake. If you allow her to make a choice, she selects a piece with lots of frosting. Clearly, the word *biggest* is not being used correctly. Even though Mary is able to memorize and repeat the words *big, bigger,* and *biggest,* she does not yet understand the concept to which they refer.

Both of these examples demonstrate that toddlers' language development is somewhat misleading. One may assume that children fully understand the more abstract meanings of the words they use, but in fact, their language continues to be very idiosyncratic throughout toddlerhood. Children are developing the skills

TABLE 6.2	**Milestones in Language Development**
At the Completion of:	*Vocalization and Language*
12 weeks	Markedly less crying than at 8 weeks; when talked to and nodded at, smiles, followed by squealing-gurgling sounds usually called cooing, that is, vowel-like in character and pitch-modulated; sustains cooing for 15–20 seconds.
16 weeks	Responds to human sounds more definitely; turns head; eyes seem to search for speaker; occasionally some chuckling sounds.
20 weeks	The vowel-like cooing sounds begin to be interspersed with more consonantal sounds; acoustically, all vocalizations are very different from the sounds of the mature language of the environment.
6 months	Cooing changing into babbling resembling one-syllable utterances; neither vowels nor consonants have very fixed recurrences; most common utterances sound somewhat like *ma, mu, da,* or *di.*
8 months	Reduplication (or more continuous repetition) becomes frequent; intonation patterns become distinct; utterances can signal emphasis and emotions.
10 months	Vocalizations are mixed with sound play such as gurgling or bubble-blowing; appears to wish to imitate sounds, but the imitations are never quite successful; beginning to differentiate between words heard by making differential adjustment.
12 months	Identical sound sequences are replicated with higher relative frequency of occurrence and words (*mama* or *dadda*) are emerging; definite signs of understanding some words and simple commands ("Show me your eyes").
18 months	Has a definite repertoire of words—more than 3 but fewer than 50; still much babbling but now of several syllables with intricate intonation pattern; no attempt at communicating information and no frustration at not being understood; words may include items such as *thank you* and *come here,* but there is little ability to join any of the lexical items into spontaneous two-item phrases; understanding is progressing rapidly.
24 months	Vocabulary of more than 50 items (some children seem to be able to name everything in environment); begins spontaneously to join vocabulary items into two-word phrases; all phrases appear to be own creations; definite increase in communicative behavior and interest in language.
30 months	Fastest increase in vocabulary with many new additions every day; no babbling at all; utterances have communicative intent; frustrated if not understood by adults; utterances consist of at least two words, many have three or even five words; sentences and phrases have characteristic child grammar, that is, they are rarely verbatim repetitions of an adult utterance; intelligibility is not very good yet, though there is great variation among children; some seem to understand everything that is said to them.
3 years	Vocabulary of some 1,999 words; about 80% of utterances are intelligible even to strangers; grammatical complexity of utterances is roughly that of colloquial adult language, although mistakes still occur.
4 years	Language is well established; deviations from the adult norm tend to be more in style than in grammar.

Source: Lenneberg, 1967.

Reading together is one of the ways parents help elaborate their children's language skills.

of language by acquiring the building blocks; fancy, subtle, complex verbal skills will come only after they have learned the fundamentals.

Interaction and Language Development

Probably the most important contribution of caregivers to cognitive growth is the opportunity for interactions. An interactive human being responds often to a child's questions, provides information, reacts in unexpected ways to surprise the child, explains plans or strategies, or offers praise.

Burton White and colleagues compared the child-rearing practices of mothers whose children were judged to be socially and intellectually competent with the practices of mothers whose children were judged to be below average (White & Watts, 1973; White, Kaban & Attanucci, 1979). The mothers of the competent children spent more time in interaction with them than did the mothers of the below-average children. This was true at every age period from 12 to 33 months. "The amount of live language directed to a child was perhaps the strongest single indicator of later intellectual and linguistic and social achievement" (White et al., 1979). This does not mean that it is necessary to be with a child continuously. One implication is that children benefit from frequent opportunities for interaction. Another is that competent children generate more interaction than below-average children.

Certain characteristics of a language partner have been shown to facilitate a child's language acquisition and communication skills (Snow, 1984). Language learning involves mutual regulation and upward scaffolding. *Scaffolding* is a process through which a child and an adult attempt to arrive at a shared understanding about a communication, at which point the adult interacts so as to expand or enrich the child's communicative competence (Nelson, 1973). Children may try to match the verbal expressions used by adults, both in pronunciation and in the selection of words. However, the child is often misunderstood because his or her pronunciation is so discrepant from that of the real word (*ambiance* for *ambulance*, *snuffin' cake* for *stomach ache*). Adults may use parentese or some other strategy to make sure they are being understood. Through frequent interactions, adults encourage language development by establishing a good balance between modifying their own speech somewhat and modeling more elaborated, accurate expressions for their children.

In trying to understand the relationship of the child's verbal expression to its cognitive meaning, adults use several strategies to learn the meaning. One is *expansion*, or the elaboration of the child's expression:

Child: Doggie wag
Parent: Yes, the dog is wagging her tail.

Another strategy is *prompting*, often in the form of a question. Here the parent urges the child to say more:

Child: More crackel.
Parent: You want more what?

The immediate matching of the adult utterance to the content or topic of the child's verbalization is called *semantic contingency*, which is effective in facilitating language acquisition. The kinds of sentences parents use help children to see how they can produce new sentences that are more grammatically correct and therefore more meaningful to others.

Socially interactive rituals such as telling stories, playing word games, verbal joking and teasing, and reading books together also seem to enhance language development, especially by building vocabulary and preparing children to use language comfortably in social situations. Reading aloud has been identified as an especially important language activity, not only to prepare children for literacy, but to expand children's language skills (Crain-Thoreson & Dale, 1992; Valdez-Menchaca & Whitehurst, 1992). During toddlerhood, adults may start out by reading picture books and asking children questions about the pictures. Some books are read aloud so often that toddlers begin to "read" them from memory or retell the story from the pictures. As children enter early school age, this type of ritualized reading activity provides a framework for their concept of what it means to be a reader, including the ideas that the printed letters make up words; that stories usually have a beginning, a middle, and an end; and that printed words and spoken words are similar. They also discover that you can learn some things from the pictures and other things from the printed words (Schickedanz, 1986).

Children and parents often engage in language games that expand the child's use of words and phrases. These games are usually part of ongoing family life, not as separate activities, but as an extension of related activities. In an observational study, Fernald and Morikawa (1993) analyzed the quality of talk that accompanied play of Japanese and American mothers and their babies. The babies were 6, 12, and 19 months old. Both the Japanese and the American mothers used a simplified form of speech—often single words, nonsense words, and repetition—when playing with their babies. With the younger babies, both sets of mothers often used language to get the child's attention, whereas, with the 12-month-olds, the mothers often made sounds as if the toy itself were making them (a pig oinking or a dog barking).

The two groups of mothers differed in how they introduced language into the play. The American mothers used many more nouns and tended to use the same noun repeatedly to refer to the object. The Japanese mothers were less likely to label the object and more likely to use sounds that were something like the sound the object might make (*oink oink* for the pig or *vroom vroom* for the car or truck). The American mothers tended to play with their children by calling attention to the toy, naming some of its parts, and asking the children questions about the toy: "See the car? You like it? It's got nice wheels." Japanese mothers were more likely to involve the toy in some form of social exchange: "Here! It's a vroom vroom. I give it to you. Now give this to me. Yes! Thank you." The name of the object is less important in this exchange than the involvement of mother and child in a reciprocal interaction: "The Japanese mothers typically explained that their goals were to talk gently and to use sounds the infant could imitate easily. American mothers were more likely to report that their goals were to attract the infant's attention and to teach the infant words" (Fernald & Morikawa, 1993, p. 653).

Most of the research on communication partners has focused on mothers and their infants or toddlers. But what about fathers and siblings as language partners? How do these interactions influence language development? Very little research has been done on the patterns of verbal interaction among different members of the same family. In a study of low-income African-American families, the contributions of siblings to toddlers' language skills were observed (Norman-Jackson, 1982). Preschoolers whose older siblings were successful readers showed greater language competence. The older siblings were a significant source of verbal stimulation for their younger brothers and sisters. These findings suggest that parents and siblings make distinct contributions to the child's language environment. What is more, children may learn to interact in different ways with their mothers, fathers, and siblings.

The Language Environment

Language is a cultural tool in socializing and educating young children; it is one of the many inventions that create a sense of group identity and that pass the mythology, wisdom, and values of the culture from one generation to the next. Because language is a part of the psychosocial environment, competence in its use solidifies the young child's membership in the immediate family and in the larger cultural group (Rogoff & Morelli, 1989).

Of course, children grow up in a wide range of language environments. Subgroups and families vary not only in the language or dialect they speak but in their reliance on verbal or nonverbal expression, their typical patterns of communication, and the importance they place on language as a means to help children achieve competence in various domains (Bernstein, 1972; Hess & Shipman, 1965; Wertsch, 1978).

At the present time, the United States faces critical challenges in the education of young children. Many of these challenges are related to the quality of the young child's language environment, its correspondence to the language environment of the schools, and the relevance of the schools' approach to the requirements of the workplace in oral and written communication. The concept of multicultural education suggests that we must begin to recognize and value differences in the context and style of language use in various subcultures as one component of intellectual development, and that we must introduce opportunities for children with different language competencies to build on their strengths in the educational environment.

There is considerable evidence that children develop problem-solving strategies and verbal responses in specific social environments (Miller-Jones, 1989). Language proficiency has at least two components (Snow, 1987). One is the use of language in face-to-face interactions—language used specifically for social situations. The other is language removed from any specific context—language knowledge as it is usually measured by tests of vocabulary, verbal reasoning, and writing. Proficiency in one area may not predict proficiency in another.

Consider *bilingualism*. Bilingualism is a social as well as a linguistic character-istic, and children who are proficient in two or more languages are also embedded in a complex sociocultural environment (Hakuta & Garcia, 1989). In many areas of Europe, in sections of Canada, and in some parts of the United States, bilingual-ism is the norm. People who cannot speak more than one language are left out of important community transactions. Research has found that learning two lan-guages does not generally hamper children's cognitive development, especially if being a native speaker of one language rather than another has no stigmatizing consequences (Diaz, 1983). It appears that young bilingual children are adept at switching from one language to another as the conversational situation demands. Observations of a 2-year-old girl learning both Norwegian and English provided evidence that even at that very young age she could use her two languages in ways that were appropriate to the context (Lanza, 1992). In fact, children may use their different languages as a way to impose boundaries on social interactions and to add clarity to social relationships.

In the United States, however, the schools assign a high priority to profi-ciency in English. Even at a time when educators bemoan American schoolchil-dren's ignorance of foreign languages, the criteria for success in bilingual educa-tion is proficiency in the abstract, academic English-language skills. Some people contend that one of the strengths of the United States as a nation is that it has had one shared language throughout such a large territory. The United States, populated as it has been by many waves of immigration from many different lands, has relied on English as one means of linking its citizens to its political, economic, and educational processes. Nonetheless, many language groups sur-vive within their neighborhoods and communities, and many citizens speak a lan-guage other than English within their homes. The challenge we are facing now is making use of the language proficiencies that children have and building on them, rather than creating a conflict between proficiency in English and proficiency in the native language, a conflict that may impede the child's language competence as well as disrupt the child's social identification with her or his non-English-language environment (Olsen, 1988).

The development of language skills is by no means complete at the close of toddlerhood. Important language functions develop more fully during early and middle school age. Older children can use language to plan a problem-solving strategy, guide a complex series of motor activities, or identify the relationships among objects. Vocabulary expands, and words are used more and more in the ways they are used in adult speech. Sentences become more complex and include conditional and descriptive clauses. The irregular verbs and nouns are learned and used correctly (Moskowitz, 1978). As children attend school, they learn to conceptualize the grammatical structure of their language. Beyond the formal elements of vocabulary, grammar, reading, and writing, language development plays a critical role in subsequent psychosocial crises, especially the establish-ment of group identity, intimacy, and generativity. It is impossible to think of the elaboration of adult thinking and reasoning or the elaboration of adult social relationships without language as a means of accumulating new ideas and information, and as a means of expressing one's thoughts and feelings to others. It is primarily through the quality of one's spoken language that one achieves the levels of disclosure that sustain significant personal relationships. Language is also the most common channel through which conflicts are resolved and cohesiveness is formed within groups, whether of friends, co-workers, or family members.

By refusing to eat, this baby exercises his own self-regulatory ability.

Self-Control

Self-control has been defined as the ability to comply with a request, to modify behavior according to the situation, to postpone action, and to behave in a socially acceptable way without having to be guided or directed by someone else (Kopp, 1982). These abilities reflect a growing sense of selfhood. They also reflect the cognitive ability to assess a situation and to compare it with previously learned guidelines on how to behave. Finally, they reflect the ability to express or redirect impulses in order to reduce their intensity.

Early in infancy, self-control is usually understood as the infant's ability to prevent disorganization brought on by overstimulation and to recover from emotional distress. In addition to the many strategies that caregivers use to try to arouse infants when they are not paying attention and to soothe or calm infants when they are overaroused, babies have their own internal regulating strategies (Kopp, 1982). For example, by sucking or rocking, babies can soothe themselves. They can also resist overstimulation by turning away, crying, or going to sleep. Further maturation in the ability to "override" negative emotions and to regulate or reduce the intensity of emotional responses is noted at about 9–10 months. These gains have been linked to maturation of the frontal cortex and to an increased interconnection of the right and left frontal lobes. In the face of emotionally arousing situations, these advances in cerebral maturation permit infants to override habitual responses with a more reasoned, problem-solving orientation. In addition, the left frontal lobe may play a role in modifying the intensity of negative emotional reactions in the right frontal lobe (Fox & Davidson, 1984, 1987; Thompson, 1990).

Control of Impulses

During toddlerhood, self-control develops in two directions: control of impulses and self-regulated goal attainment. First, children improve their ability to modify and control their impulses. The case of Colin illustrates how toddlers may fall prey to their impulses. Sometimes, they simply cannot interrupt an ongoing action, even one they know is inappropriate. Colin, aged 2 years, 9 months, is just starting nursery school:

> In his relations with children, Colin progressed quickly from a quiet, friendly, watching relationship on the first few days to actively hugging the other children. The hugging seemed to be in an excess of friendliness and was only mildly aggressive. Having started hugging he didn't know how to stop, and usually just held on until he pulled the child down to the floor. This was followed very closely by hair pulling. He didn't pull viciously, but still held on long enough to get a good resistance from the child. He grabbed toys from others. When stopped by an adult from any of these acts, he was very responsive to reason, would say, smiling, "I won't do it any more," would tear around the room in disorganized activity, and then return to hugging or pulling hair. (Murphy, 1956, pp. 11–12)

From ages 2 to 4, children are increasingly able to modify and control their impulses and to withstand delays in the gratification of their impulses. They also become more willing to modify their behavior because they do not wish to cause distress to others. The ability to regulate or restrain behavior is a product of changing cognitive, social, and emotional competencies. Children become increasingly sensitive to the negative consequences of impulsive acts. At the same time, they develop new strategies to help them manage feelings of frustration (Vaughn, Kopp & Krakow, 1984; Zahn-Waxler, Radke-Yarrow, Wagner & Chapman, 1992).

Increasing Sensitivity to the Distress of Others   Toddlers can observe and empathize with distress expressed in others, both children and adults. In addition, they begin to understand when they have been the cause of someone else's distress (Zahn-Waxler et al., 1992; Zahn-Waxler, Robinson & Emde, 1992). Often, the socialization environment helps focus toddlers' attention on these instances when parents or teachers point out their actions and the consequences. The following observation from a study of family interaction shows how a conversation about negative consequences and a child's concern over his mother's distress contributed to the self-regulation of impulses:

> Danny is 33 months old. He and his mother are at the sink washing dishes. Danny blows a handful of suds at his mother and some gets in her eyes. Danny is laughing at this new game.
>
> **M**: No! Nuh uh, Danny.
> Danny you got it in my eye. (mild negative affect)
> Danny stops laughing.
> **M:** Don't do that in my eye, ok?
> It hurts to get soap in your eye.
> **D:** (very serious) I won't. (Brown & Dunn, 1992, pp. 347–348)

A New Sense of Time   During toddlerhood, children gain in self-control as they begin to develop a rudimentary sense of time, including some appreciation of the future. Toddlers repeatedly discover and then learn to trust that, although what they want is not available to them at the moment, it will often be available after a brief delay. As they become aware that after a period of delay their needs will very likely be met, the delay itself becomes less frustrating. This sequence depends heavily on the caregivers' responsiveness and on their ability to provide the gratifications that they have asked the children to delay. As children learn that they can trust their caregivers to keep promises, it becomes easier to wait for what has been promised.

Strategies That Help Children Manage Their Impulses   Of course, some events challenge even the most patient child's limits. Children must learn techniques for managing their emotions when they are aroused. One of the first tactics toddlers use to inhibit an impulse is to divert their attention from a forbidden object. In a study of the ability to delay behavior, an adult showed 2-year-olds an unusual telephone and asked them not to touch it, then stepped out of the room for a few moments (Vaughn et al., 1986). In the experimenter's absence, the children's behavior was observed, and the time that elapsed before they touched the phone was measured. The experimenter returned as soon as a child had touched the phone, or within 2½ minutes. Behaviors associated with an ability to delay touching the phone included looking away from the phone, playing with their hands or covering their faces with their hands, and talking about something other than the telephone.

Language and fantasy are children's most useful tools for managing impulses. Talking about feelings and needs enables adults to help children understand more about their emotions and to help them devise strategies for self-regulation. Thompson (1990) suggested four ways that caregivers use talking about emotions to help young children gain control. First, parents articulate what might be thought of as the family or cultural rules of emotional expression: "Don't get so excited; calm down!" or "Stop that fussing; big boys don't whine and cry!" These lessons give young children an idea about the acceptable levels of impulses or emotional intensity and about the types of emotions that need to be regulated.

Second, adults help modify the intensity of emotions through reassuring or distracting talk. They may try to distract a child who is worried about getting an injection, or try to convince the child that the shot won't hurt or that it will be just a little sting. Or they may try to comfort a sobbing child by talking about some happy event that will distract the child from his or her troubles.

Third, adults may give children ideas for ways to manage their impulses. They might help a child by suggesting that the child think of pleasant times from the past or by laughing out loud when they are very frightened. Adults teach children superstitions, rituals, and stories about how people handle their strong feelings.

Fourth, children listen to adults talking about their own strong emotions and impulses. Thus, through imitation, they discover strategies for expressing or inhibiting their strong impulses. Through this means, they also gain additional information about the kinds of impulses and emotional expressions that are acceptable or even desirable in the broader culture and those that are not acceptable.

The more articulately children can express their wishes, the better the chances that their needs will be met. When their needs cannot be met, they can use language to express how they feel. Feelings that are expressed are easier for children to control than those that are not. Children can also learn to use language to interrupt their own impulsive acts. For example, when young children were exposed to a clown box, they were able to resist the distraction and return to their work by saying such things as "I'm not going to look at Mr. Clown Box" or "Don't bother me" (Mischel & Patterson, 1976; Patterson & Mischel, 1976).

It takes a lot of self-control for this older sister to cope with the baby's wailing. She holds her ears and grits her teeth rather than giving the baby a wallop or a shake.

When children are asked to resist temptation, they use a variety of verbal strategies, including talking quietly to themselves and singing songs to distract themselves (Mischel, Shoda & Rodriguez, 1989). Toddlers who can talk to themselves may be able to control their fears, modify their anger, and soften their disappointments. They may repeat their parents' comforting words, or they may develop their own verbal strategies for reducing pain and suffering. When a boy who feels bad about something says, "Superheroes don't cry," he is making an effort to control his emotional state.

The development of symbolic imagery allows children to create imaginary situations in which disturbing problems can be expressed and resolved. Through fantasy play, toddlers can control situations that are far beyond their real-world capacities (Singer & Singer, 1990). They can punish and forgive, harm and heal, fear and conquer fear, all within the boundaries of their own imagination.

Children can dissipate some of the intensity of their impulses by talking about them and weaving them into fantasy situations. They gradually become more masters than slaves of their emotional needs. Children enter the stage of toddlerhood on the tail end of the whip of emotional impulses. They seem easily frustrated, impatient, and demanding. Their feelings may quickly gain momentum until they are beyond control. By the end of toddlerhood, children have moved into the pivot position in the whip. They are better able to control how fast their emotions build up and how their emotions are expressed. Just as the pivot person in the whip is occasionally pulled off stride, so may children lose control from time to time. In general, however, toddlers begin to regulate their own impulses effectively as their understanding of time, their use of language, and their capacity for fantasy expression develop.

Individual Differences in the Ability to Control Impulses   The ability to delay gratification varies with the individual. At least three factors are associated with differences in the ease or difficulty children have in controlling their impulses (see Figure 6.1). First, toddlers differ in their capacity to empathize with the distress of others. Empathy itself appears to have a genetic as well as an environmental basis. In a study of monozygotic and dizygotic twins who were 2 years old, the monozygotic twins showed greater similarity in their emotional concern about

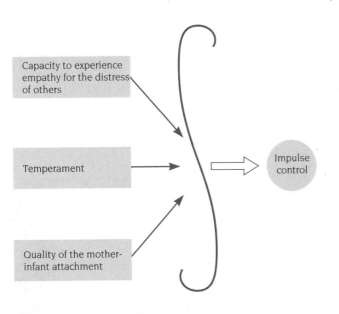

FIGURE 6.1

Factors associated with the ease or difficulty toddlers have in controlling their impulses

and response to others' distress than did the dizygotic twins. In addition, mothers who showed a stronger concern for others in their child-rearing strategies had children whose empathy was more fully developed. Further, girls were observed to be more empathic than boys (Zahn-Waxler, Robinson & Emde, 1992). Individual differences in sensitivity to the distress of others lead to differences in how upset a child may be by finding that his or her behavior has caused someone suffering and in how willing the child may be to curb that behavior in the future.

Second, differences in temperament affect self-control. Children who are more aggressive, active, or socially outgoing may experience more situations in which their actions are viewed as disruptive or in need of control. Children who are more socially inhibited, withdrawn, or passive may encounter fewer expectations to curb or restrict their behavior (Kochanska & Radke-Yarrow, 1992). In a study of preschool children's social skills and popularity, those children who were described as showing high levels of emotional intensity and who had poor self-regulatory coping skills were less well liked by their peers (Eisenberg et al., 1993). A recent analysis of a family history of aggressive behavior suggested that a genetic deficiency carried on the X chromosome may account for the difficulties that some males have in controlling their aggressive impulses (Brunner et al., 1993)

Third, some evidence supports the idea that the capacity for self-regulation may depend on the quality of the mother-infant attachment. Children who lack attachment security are more likely to exhibit irritability, avoidance, resistance, and aggressiveness as preschoolers (Teti et al., 1991). These toddlers will have more difficulty calming themselves and reducing the intensity of their impulses. Put in a more positive way, one of the benefits of a secure attachment is children's capacity over time to internalize many of the soothing, reassuring strategies that their mothers have used to comfort and protect them, and to apply these strategies to their own intense emotional states.

Since the early 1960s, Walter Mischel and his colleagues have investigated the process by which children delay gratification. One of their consistent findings has been that the ability to delay gratification varies with the individual. At age 4, children who tend to delay gratification longer tend to be more intelligent, to be more

The expression of anger, which is important to the child's development of a sense of autonomy, typically generates tension between parents and children (Wenar, 1982). Toddlers get angry for many reasons, including inability to perform a task, parental restrictions on behavior, and peer or sibling rivalry. As toddlers become increasingly involved in directing the outcomes of their activities, they get angry when someone interrupts them or offers unrequested assistance (Bullock & Lutkenhaus, 1988). In addition, it appears that some children are temperamentally more aggressive than others.

Children rely heavily on their parents as models for learning how to express and control anger. The times when parents are angry are very important. Children learn as much or more about the expression of anger from watching their parents when they are angry as they do from verbal explanations or punishment (Bandura, 1977). Children are sensitive to anger between their parents, even when it is not directed at them. Parents' hostility to each other, expressed through quarrels, sarcasm, and physical abuse, increases children's sensitivity to anger and is closely related to disturbances in development (J. S. Cummings et al., 1989).

In an ethnographic study of the socialization of anger and aggression, three 2½-year-old girls and their mothers from a working-class neighborhood of Baltimore were studied in detail. The mothers of these girls considered assertiveness and self-defense essential to survival in their neighborhood. Along with socialization strategies that focused on controlling

BOX 6.1

The Control of Angry Feelings

aggression when it was inappropriate, the mothers found many ways to model aggressiveness as they talked to others in the girls' presence and to reward certain displays of toughness and assertiveness in the girls' behavior (Miller & Sperry, 1987).

Pablo Picasso, Child with Lobster, *1941. We sense the young boy's greed, the feeling that he should be able to have everything he wants. It is the frustration of this greed that often produces children's angry feelings. As we nurture autonomy in children, we also have to teach them acceptable ways of expressing anger when their will is blocked.*

(continued)

likely to resist temptation, to demonstrate greater social responsibility, and to have higher achievement strivings (Mischel et al., 1989). According to Mischel's research, a 4-year-old's ability to use self-regulatory strategies to delay gratification seems to have enduring effects. More than ten years later, children who had waited longer in the experimental situation that required self-imposed delay of gratification at age 4 were described by their parents as socially and academically more competent than their peers. Their parents rated these children as more verbally fluent and able to express ideas, as using and responding to reason, and as being more competent and skillful. These children were more attentive and able to concentrate, to plan, and to think ahead, and they were also seen as better able to cope with frustration and to resist temptation.

BOX 6.1

(continued)

The child who can express anger and not lose control makes tremendous gains in the development of autonomy. Anger at and conflict with parents give toddlers evidence that they are indeed very separate from their parents, and that the separateness, although painful, is legitimate. Children who are severely punished or ridiculed for their anger are left in a state of doubt. They see models for the expression of anger in the way their parents respond to them and yet are told that anger is not appropriate for them.

Several strategies help young children to manage or reduce the intensity of their anger (Berkowitz, 1973; Thompson, 1990). These include ignoring aggression; providing brief "time-out" periods in a nearby quiet area until the emotion has subsided; arousing feelings that are incompatible with the anger, especially empathy for the victim; minimizing exposure to stimuli that arouse aggressive impulses; explaining the consequences of aggressive actions for the other person; and explaining the circumstances that may have led to the initial feelings of anger or frustration.

For the sake of the child's emerging self-concept, angry feelings must be allowed some form of legitimate expression. In the process of expressing angry feelings, children learn to control themselves and to channel these emotions into constructive rather than destructive activity. Between ages 2 and 5, the frequency of angry, aggressive behaviors declines as children develop effective strategies for self-control (Cummings, Iannotti & Zahn-Waxler, 1989).

As Freud hypothesized, the ability to delay gratification seems to be an important component of ego development. The work of Mischel and his colleagues suggests that toddlers who are able to delay gratification make greater strides in ego development throughout childhood. Even though most children acquire the skills needed for more successful delays as they get older, the ones who demonstrate these skills earliest seem to gain an advantage by elaborating the growing network of ego skills more effectively.

Self-Regulated Goal Attainment

The second sense in which self-control develops has to do with toddlers' feelings that they can direct their behavior and the behavior of others to achieve intended outcomes (Messer et al., 1987). During infancy, children become increasingly aware of themselves as causal agents. They make things happen. In toddlerhood, children become much more assertive about their desire to initiate actions, to persist in activities, and to determine when these activities should stop. Their sense of *agency*—their view of themselves as the originators of action—expands to include a broad array of behaviors. Children want to participate in decisions about bedtime, the clothes they wear, the kinds of foods they eat, and family activities. They want to do things they see their parents and their older siblings doing. Their confidence in their own ability to handle very difficult tasks is not modified by a realistic assessment of their own skills. According to toddlers, "Anything you can do, I can do better." When they have opportunities to do some of these new and complex things and they succeed, they gain confidence in themselves and their abilities. They feel themselves to be valuable members of the family as they contribute to routine household tasks. Their feelings of confidence and value are matched by the acquisition of a wide variety of complex, coordinated skills.

A number of abilities must come together before toddlers can engage in these self-regulated, goal-directed behaviors.

First, the actor must be able to anticipate a not-yet-attained goal state and must understand that this goal can be reached through some specific activity. Second, the actor must represent the means-end relation between activities and their outcomes. . . . Beyond such representational abilities, however, additional skills, that we will label volitional skills, are necessary for translating knowledge into successful action. Generally, volitional skills involve remaining task oriented, that is, keeping the antici- pated goal in mind, and monitoring progress toward an anticipated goal state. This includes waiting or searching for appropriate opportunities to act, resisting distrac- tions, overcoming obstacles, correcting actions, and stopping acting when a goal is reached. (Bullock & Lutkenhaus, 1988, p. 664)

Speech and Goal Attainment   Vygotsky (1978) argued for an especially cen- tral role for speech in self-directed goal attainment and practical problem solving. Summarizing his own research observations and those of others, he described the problem-solving behaviors of toddlers as involving both speech and action. Toddlers use what was described by Piaget (1952) as "egocentric speech" to con- trol and direct their behavior. The speech is considered egocentric because it is not intended to communicate with anyone else and often doesn't make sense to anyone else. Vygotsky (1978) suggested that egocentric speech, or speech turned toward the self, and actions are part of the same problem-solving function. The more difficult the problem, the more speech is necessary for the child to find a solution: "Children solve practical tasks with the help of their speech, as well as their eyes and hands" (p. 26).

Speech gives children a new degree of freedom, flexibility, and control in approaching tasks and working toward a goal. They can use words to call to mind tools that are not visible. They can plan steps toward a goal and repeat these steps to guide their actions. They can use words like *slowly* or *be careful* or *hold tight* to con- trol their behavior as they work on a task.

The kind of speech that guides problem solving emerges from the social speech that characterizes children's interactions with adults. Often, when young children try to figure out how to work something or how to get something that is out of reach, they turn to adults for help. Vygotsky suggested that the kinds of talk that adults use as they guide young children is then used by the children themselves to support and guide their own behavior. He referred to this process as the "internalization of social speech" and suggested that through this mecha- nism children's social environment shapes their thinking, planning, and problem solving. In a sense, a child's capacity for self-directed goal attainment depends largely on what he or she has taken in of the spoken, practical advice and guid- ance given by adults and older peers who have tried to help the child solve prob- lems in the past.

Sometimes, toddlers' enthusiasm and self-confidence go beyond their poten- tial for performance. They watch their parents easily managing a task and think they can do it just as easily. If left to try the task on their own, they fail. They become discouraged and frustrated because they expected success. If their par- ents tell them not to try, they are also frustrated, because they are certain that they would do a good job. Probably, the best solution to this problem is to co- operate with toddlers, allowing them to do what they can and giving assistance when they need it. As children engage in tasks that are somewhat beyond their capacity, they learn to evaluate their strength and skill more realistically without feeling humiliated by failure. By the end of toddlerhood, children are better able to evaluate the requirements of a wide variety of tasks and can judge whether they can accomplish a task by themselves.

Pablo Picasso, Paulo on a Donkey, *1923. By fostering autonomy, children grow in their self-confidence and their desire for mastery. You can probably recall what Picasso has captured here in your own memory of your first pony ride. Timid, drawn to the small creature with the big ears, Paulo takes the reins and attempts to assert his mastery over the donkey.*

We have considered two rather different phenomena under the developmental task of self-control. Children's ability to control their impulses is closely linked to the psychoanalytic concept of delay of gratification, as Freud (1905/1953) used it to describe development during the oral and anal stages. Mastery is a general motivation that accounts for children's efforts to increase their competence through persistent investigation and skillful problem solving (White, 1960; Harter, 1982). Both abilities foster toddlers' growing awareness of themselves. To function effectively as family members, toddlers must feel confident in their ability to control the inner world of their feelings and the outer world of decisions and tasks. As toddlers discover that they can tolerate stress, express or withhold their anger as appropriate, and approach difficult tasks and succeed at them, they also lay claim to a growing definition of selfhood. Toddlerhood is an important time in the development of a person's sense of self-efficacy, the conviction that one can perform the behaviors demanded by a specific situation (Bandura, 1989). The more toddlers can do by themselves, the more confidence they will have in their ability to control the outcomes of their actions and to achieve their goals.

The Psychosocial Crisis: Autonomy Versus Shame and Doubt

During toddlerhood, children become aware of their separateness. Through a variety of experiences, they discover that their parents do not always know what they want and do not always understand their feelings. In early toddlerhood, children use rather primitive devices to explore their independence. They may say "no" to everything offered to them whether they want it or not. This is the period that people often refer to as the *terrible twos*. Toddlers seem very demanding and insist on having things done their own way. It is difficult to reason with 2-year-olds.

Autonomy

The positive pole of the psychosocial crisis of toddlerhood is autonomy. During this period of life, *autonomy* refers to the ability to behave independently, to perform actions on one's own. The unique characteristics of growth toward autonomy are its energy and its persistence. Children do not just prefer to do most things on their own; they *insist* on it. Once children begin to work on a task, such as putting on pajamas or tying shoelaces, they will struggle along time after time until they have mastered it. They may adamantly reject help and insist that they can manage on their own. They will allow someone else to help them only when they are sure that they can progress no further by themselves.

The establishment of a sense of autonomy requires not only tremendous effort by the child but extreme patience and support from the parents. Toddlers' demands for autonomy are often exasperating. They challenge their parents' good sense, goodwill, and good intentions. Parents must learn to teach, cajole, absorb insults, wait, and praise. Sometimes, they must allow their children to try things that the children may not be able to do. By encouraging their children to engage in new tasks, parents hope to promote their sense of competence.

In the development of autonomy, toddlers shift from a somewhat rigid nay-saying, ritualized, unreasonable style to an independent, energetic, persistent one (Erikson, 1963). The behavior of older toddlers is characterized by the phrase "I can do it myself." They are less concerned about doing things their own way and more concerned with doing them on their own. Toddlers demonstrate an increasing variety of skills. Each new accomplishment gives them great pride. When doing things independently leads to positive results, the sense of autonomy grows. Toddlers begin to create an image of themselves as people who can manage situations competently and who can satisfy many of their own needs. Children who have been allowed to experience autonomy should, by the end of toddlerhood, have a strong foundation of self-confidence and feelings of delight in behaving independently.

Shame and Doubt

Some children fail to emerge from toddlerhood with a sense of mastery. Because of their failure at most attempted tasks or continual discouragement and criticism from parents—or, most likely, because of both—some children develop an overwhelming sense of shame and self-doubt. This is the negative resolution of the psychosocial crisis of toddlerhood (Erikson, 1963). *Shame* is an intense emotion that can result from two different types of experiences (Morrison, 1989).

One source of shame is social ridicule or criticism. You can probably reconstruct feelings of shame by imagining being scolded for having spilled your milk or for having lost your jacket. Shame generally originates in an interpersonal interaction in which you feel that you have violated a valued social standard or in which you have been embarrassed or ridiculed for behaving in a stupid, thoughtless, or clumsy way (Tangney et al., 1992). When you are shamed, you feel small, ridiculous, and humiliated. Some cultures rely heavily on public humiliation as a means of social control. Adults in these cultures grow up with a strong concern about "saving face." One of their greatest fears is to be publicly accused of immoral or dishonorable actions. In some instances, such shame can lead to suicide.

The other source of shame is internal conflict. As children construct an understanding of what it means to be a good, decent, capable person, they build a mental image of an ideal person, the *ego ideal*. Children feel shame when they see their behavior as not meeting the standards of their ideal, even though they have not broken a rule or done anything naughty.

The experience of shame is extremely unpleasant. In order to avoid it, children may refrain from all kinds of new activities. Children who feel shame lack confidence in their abilities and expect to fail at what they do. Thus, the acquisition of new skills becomes slow and painful, and feelings of self-confidence and worth are replaced by constant doubt. Children who have a pervasive sense of *doubt* feel comfortable only in highly structured and familiar situations in which the risk of failure is minimal. As college students, young people who have high levels of shame were also characterized by high levels of resentment, irritability, anger, suspiciousness, and a tendency to blame others (Lewis, 1987; Kaufman, 1989).

Under normal conditions, all children experience some failures amid their many successes. Even the most patient parent may occasionally shame a child for making a mess or disturbing others. Such occurrences help children make a more realistic assessment of their independence and skills. Children who resolve the crisis in favor of autonomy will still question whether they can succeed, and they may still experience shame when they fail, but they will usually be predisposed toward trying many activities. The children who resolve the crisis in favor of shame and doubt will avoid new activities and cling to what they already know.

Toilet Training

Within Freud's psychoanalytic theory, the classic psychological conflict between individual autonomy and social demands for conformity is toilet training. As Robert White (1960) pointed out, in this particular conflict children are destined to lose. They must subordinate their autonomy to expectations for a specific routine regarding elimination. Toddlers must master a number of skills in order to succeed at toilet training. They must have some word or signal to use to communicate their need to go to the bathroom. They must be able to get to the bathroom, either by finding their own way or by finding someone to direct them. They must be able to delay elimination until they have arrived at the bathroom and removed their clothes.

Children cannot control elimination until their musculature is sufficiently developed. This is an obvious but extremely important point. On average, the sphincter muscles, which control the ability to hold onto and let go of fecal material, do not become fully mature and workable until the child is between 1½ and 2 years old. Before the sphincters have attained this maturation, children will be unable to control their bowel movements

For the child to experience a sense of competence during the toilet-training period, a number of things must occur: (1) The body must be ready; (2) the child must be able to give a signal when it is time to go; and (3) the child must be able to respond to an internal cue and anticipate the necessary action. There is some

"O.K., I'm done now. Can you get me down from here?"

evidence that girls achieve bladder control earlier than boys. Problems with bed wetting are somewhat more common for boys than for girls. This difference in bladder control is probably due to a difference in muscle development rather than a difference in motivation, frustration, or activity level.

If parents wait to begin toilet training until their children show signs of readiness in all areas, the children are likely to see this task as a source of pride and accomplishment rather than as a struggle of wills. They will be happy to be able to accomplish something that is so important to their parents. Their success will increase their self-confidence.

Classic psychoanalytic theory (Freud, 1905/1953, 1913/1958) considers the ages of 2–4 to be a period of obsessive-compulsive characteristics and neuroses. *Obsessions* are persistent, repetitive thoughts that serve to limit the spread of anxiety by focusing it on a very specific set of thoughts. *Compulsions* are repetitive, ritualized actions that serve the same function. The sources of anxiety that motivate obsessive thought and compulsive behavior, according to psychoanalytic theory, are unconscious conflicts related to the anal region of the body and the process of bowel control. Obsessive-compulsive behaviors are observable in the normal person's concern about order, cleanliness, and planning. These behaviors are usually under the person's control and can be useful tools for personal organization. In the neurotic individual, however, such thoughts and behaviors are beyond personal control and often impede effectiveness.

Although toilet training is an interesting paradigm that highlights the issues of willfulness, body control, and parental authority, the concept of autonomy encompasses a much broader spectrum of behavior. The historical emphasis on toilet training in the development of personality seems to have been too narrow and restrictive. Bowel control is only one of a variety of skills that are mastered during a healthy toddlerhood and that are channeled into the development of autonomy and competence.

To a Maasai warrior, the spear is a precious possession.

As Maasai girls play follow-the-leader in the background, a little boy wields a large pretend spear. In every culture, imitation is a powerful mechanism for transmitting customs and skills.

The Central Process: Imitation

The primary mechanism by which toddlers emerge as autonomous individuals is *imitation*. Although imitation requires the presence of active models, its outcome is a shift of the action from the model to the imitator. In other words, once toddlers succeed in imitating a certain skill, that skill belongs to them and they can use it for any purpose they like. Toddlers seem driven to imitate almost everything they observe, including their parents' positions at the toilet. Toddlers' vocabularies expand markedly through their imitation of the words they hear in adult conversations, on television, and in stories. Their interest in dancing, music, and other activities stems from imitation of their parents and peers. As soon as one child in a play group makes a funny noise or performs a daring act, the other children appear to be compelled to re-create this novel behavior.

The imitative behavior of toddlers is very different from the socially induced conformity observed in older children. Toddlers are not aware of a great many social norms and therefore feel little pressure to conform to them. Their imitative behavior is really a vehicle for learning. Every act becomes their own, even if it has been inspired by others. The primary motivation for imitation during toddlerhood is the drive for mastery and competence.

In studies of imitation in the home environment, toddlers show an impressive pattern of imitating their parents' household, self-care, and caretaking activities. They show increasing interest in imitating behaviors that are socially meaningful and valued. These observations have led researchers to suggest that imitation is critical in satisfying toddlers' need for social competence (Kuczynski, Zahn-Waxler & Radke-Yarrow, 1987). Through imitation, they may also derive pleasure from the similarity they perceive between themselves and their model. This perceived similarity is a secondary benefit of the imitative process (Kagan, 1958).

Imitation is also a means of participating in and sustaining social interactions (Grusec & Abramovitch, 1982). Within a peer setting, imitation emerges as a dominant strategy whereby children coordinate their behaviors with those of other toddlers. Before verbal communication becomes a truly useful tool for establishing or maintaining social contact, toddlers imitate one another. Through imitation, toddlers can feel connected to one another and begin to invent coordinated games (Eckerman, Davis & Didow, 1989). With increasing cognitive maturity, children select for imitation behaviors that have relevance to their own needs for mastery, for nurturance, and for social interaction.

The emphasis on imitation highlights the central role of culture at this period of life. Children are surrounded by daily events that provide models for imitation, which reflect the culture of their families and communities. Without evaluating this array, toddlers rapidly accumulate the vocabulary of speech and action that belongs to their cultural group. How visitors are greeted when they arrive at the home; how adults groom themselves, dress, and speak to one another; how household tasks and chores are performed; how older children amuse themselves; how young people and older people treat each other—the thousands of words, gestures, and rituals of daily life make up the culture absorbed by watchful toddlers as they arm themselves with the resources to press toward autonomy.

Applied Topics
Discipline *and* Day Care
Discipline

Discipline is a process for shaping the child to the parents' expectations of what is culturally acceptable or valued. The content of the discipline (the kinds of acts that are prohibited) and the techniques that are used (the methods of control) bring the child's behavior within culturally shared norms. Most parents "inherit" their approach to discipline from their own family of origin and from the culture in which they were reared. Discipline is also necessary to protect a child from harm. Some activities of inquisitive and active toddlers are dangerous and must be restrained or redirected. Thus, the need for discipline may change as children are exposed to new technologies and unfamiliar situations. When it is used effectively, discipline gives children some techniques for controlling their own behavior.

Toddlers' naive egocentrism and physical exuberance frequently bring them into conflict with their parents, siblings, and peers. Negativism, or the clear refusal to comply with the requests of others, is a hallmark of toddlerhood (Wenar, 1982; Haswell, Hock & Wenar, 1981). Eventually, the child's refusal to comply will conflict with a parent's insistence on a particular behavior. Thus, we can expect occasions for discipline to be inevitable in parent-child interactions during toddlerhood. Ideally, parental discipline will build toddlers' ability to impose limits on their own behavior without feeling extremely inhibited by fear of their parents' scorn.

Disciplinary practices have been divided into three general categories (Hoffman, 1977):

1. *Power assertion*: Physical punishment, shouting, attempts to physically move a child or inhibit behavior, taking away privileges or resources, or threatening any of these things.
2. *Love withdrawal*: Expressing anger, disappointment, or disapproval; refusing to communicate; walking out or turning away.
3. *Inductions*: Explaining why the behavior was wrong; pointing out the consequences of the behavior for others; redirecting the behavior by appealing to the child's sense of mastery, fair play, or love of another person.

In addition to these three general categories of discipline techniques, parental modeling and reinforcement of acceptable behavior are significant in the development of internal control (Maccoby, 1992). If children are to correct their own behavior, they must know what acts are considered appropriate as well as how to inhibit their inappropriate acts. Modeling and reinforcement aid children in directing their own behavior, while discipline inhibits or redirects children's behavior.

Early research on parental discipline focused on children's internalization of moral prohibitions. To what extent do children raised by one primary mode of discipline succeed in controlling their own behavior and in confessing when they fail? Hoffman (1970) summarized the findings as follows:

> The frequent use of power assertion by the mother is associated with weak moral development to a highly consistent degree. Induction discipline and affection, on the other hand, are associated with advanced moral development, although these relationships are not quite as strong and consistent across the various age levels as the negative ones for power assertion.... In contrast to induction, love withdrawal relates infrequently to the moral indices and the few significant findings obtained do not fit any apparent pattern. (p. 292)

Studies have consistently reported that children of parents who frequently use power-assertive techniques tend to show high levels of aggression themselves (Anthony, 1970; Chwast, 1972). Several hypotheses have been raised to explain this relationship. First, physical punishment may serve to frustrate the child and create further aggressive impulses. Second, parents who discipline a child with physical punishment may provide a model of aggressive behavior. Third, parents who punish aggression toward themselves may also encourage or reward aggression toward others, causing the child to be aggressive. Finally, aggressive children may provoke parents into using power-assertive strategies. For example, Buss (1981) reported that there was more conflict in parent-child interactions when the child had a very high activity level. The parents of very active children were more likely to use physical control and to become involved in power struggles with their children than were the parents of less active children.

Some laboratory studies, however, suggest that physical punishment may succeed in inhibiting undesirable behavior if it is used just at the onset of the undesired behavior (Aronfreed & Reber, 1965; Walters, Parke & Cane, 1965). This use of punishment may be more appropriately described as *avoidance conditioning*. In these situations, children were prevented from touching a preferred toy just before they were going to handle it. When left alone with the toy, children who had been thus punished directed their attention to another toy. We suggest that when punishment is used in a natural setting, it is probably used after the misdeed has occurred. Under these conditions, physical punishment tends to heighten rather than inhibit aggressive impulses.

Love withdrawal has little, if any, positive effect on the internalization of moral prohibitions, although it may be effective in bringing about compliance with adult expectations (Forehand et al., 1976). The effect of love withdrawal is to stimulate children's need for approval and to increase their anxiety about expressing hostility. Children whose parents use love withdrawal as a primary discipline technique tend to be anxious about expressing their impulses and are willing to conform to the wishes of adult authorities (Hoffman, 1980). These characteristics are differentiated from morality because they have a minimal conceptual component (children do not know why they should refrain from some activity) and produce a high level of anxiety about external consequences (parents may withdraw their love).

Inductions succeed when the other two techniques fail because they provide children with a conceptual framework that guides their behavior, and because

TABLE 6.3	Discipline Techniques and Their Consequences for Personality and Moral Development	

Discipline Technique	*Personality Correlates*	*Moral Behaviors*
Power assertion	Aggressive behavior and fantasy	Minimal internalization of moral prohibitions
Love withdrawal	Anxiety and dependence	No clear relationship to moral behavior
Inductions	Autonomy and concern for others	Advanced moral development

they arouse children's empathy by pointing out the consequences of their behavior for others (Leizer & Rogers, 1974). Families that use inductions as their primary discipline technique may be described as democratic rather than authoritarian. Such families are characterized by a warm, accepting atmosphere, a high degree of communication among family members, and an orientation of concern for and tolerance of others (Odom, Seeman & Newbrough, 1971). Children of parents who set firm, age-appropriate standards for behavior are generally sociable, responsible, self-confident, and considerate of others (Baumrind, 1971). In addition to their effectiveness in producing compliance with parental wishes, inductions involve more elaborate parent-child communication than do the other techniques. Thus, inductions have the effect of promoting verbal skills as well as "good" behavior (Lytton, 1976).

Table 6.3 summarizes the three discipline techniques that we have discussed. Each of the three orientations toward control of the child—power assertion, love withdrawal, and induction—has implications for personality development and for the child's capacity to internalize moral controls. The use of these discipline techniques reflects more global parental orientations and values, such as the desire to promote a child's autonomy, the need to ensure conformity to social norms and expectations, concerns about safety, and respect for authority.

The Discipline Context

In the current perspective on discipline and socialization, parents and children influence one another interactively through a continuous stream of behaviors. Rather than seeing socialization as unidirectional, with the parents' actions directing child outcomes, scholars now treat socialization as a *co-constructed* process. Parents and children "develop coherent expectations concerning each other's behavior, joint goals, shared scripts from which each acts, and shared meanings that make fuller coordination of their activity possible" (Maccoby, 1992, p. 1014). Three elements interact to form a comprehensive picture of discipline as a co-constructed process: the parents' beliefs, the situation in which the discipline takes place, and the child's responses.

Parents' Beliefs   An adult's personal theory about the appropriate role of parents in guiding the behavior of their children at various ages influences how that person interprets and reacts to a child's actions. This theory is shaped by that person's own level of psychosocial maturity, by cultural assumptions regarding children and how they should be treated, and by the person's earlier experiences in observing and interacting with young children. When Mondell and Tyler (1981) investigated the relationship between parents' psychosocial maturity and parent-child interactions, they found that parents with a high degree of competence and trust were more likely to perceive their children as capable and resourceful than were parents with a low degree of these qualities. Such parents were also more likely to approach a joint problem-solving task with warm, positive, and helpful interactions.

An adult's approach to discipline is guided by a subjective assessment of a child's actions. Parents' views of their child's competence and their perception of whether the action was intentional influence the type and severity of the discipline they apply (Dix, Ruble & Zambarano, 1989). That is, parents tend to take a child's age and relevant skills into account as they assess the seriousness of a misdeed. They may be less stern in punishing an action if they think the child did not understand that what he or she was doing was wrong. They feel angrier and tend to be more stern when they conclude that a child was in fact deliberately responsible for the misdeed.

Another element in parents' assessment of misconduct is whether they believe a child's behavior is the product of a personal trait or of the situation (Mills & Rubin, 1990). Parents who conclude that a child is "naturally" aggressive and boisterous may react calmly to an aggressive outburst, whereas parents who believe the child is being purposefully defiant may react with greater force.

The parents' reaction depends heavily on their cultural outlook and values. Some parents believe it is important to be very firm with a child who is temperamentally aggressive in order to help the child develop self-control. They may be more understanding of a child who is usually very easygoing and suddenly becomes aggressive. Cultural and child-rearing values influence parents' interpretation of a child's behavior and thus their course of action (Kochanska, Kuczynski & Radke-Yarrow, 1989).

The Discipline Situation   The situation may influence both whether and how a child is disciplined. We all know that loud singing or asking Mom to play house may be acceptable when everyone is relaxed. The same behavior may not be acceptable, however, when Mom is trying to pay the bills or get dinner ready. In a laboratory simulation of this phenomenon, parents were in a room with their two children, one in the 3- to 5-year-old range and one under 3 (Zussman, 1980). Parental behavior toward the children was observed in two conditions: when the parents could play with the children and when they were preoccupied with a task that competed with the children for their attention. When the parents were involved in the competing task, they had fewer positive interactions with their older child and more frequent critical or punishing interactions with their younger one. Here, we see that the circumstances that lead to discipline may reflect the parents' agenda as well as the child's.

The Child's Response   Because a disciplinary situation is interactive, the child's response to a parent's initial request for compliance may influence the parent's subsequent actions. Very young children often comply with a parent's request or command: The father says, "No, don't touch!" and the baby withdraws her hand. In other instances, an adult may redirect a young child's misbehavior by distracting the child and offering some alternative activity or object. As children reach the age of 3 or 4, however, they become more active advocates for their own wishes and may resist a command by negotiating: "I do it later," "I already tried some," or "Just a little more." When parents point out a mistake or a misdeed, a 3-year-old may offer a justification and try to avoid punishment: "Baby did it,"

Many of these facts were gathered by the National Commission on Children and reported in a summary of its research, *Just the Facts*, published in 1993. The term *poverty* as it is used in these facts refers to the federal guidelines for the poverty level.

BOX 6.2

Facts Regarding Children in Poverty in the United States

- In constant 1991 dollars, the median family income for families with children ($34,990) was *lower* that the median family income for families without children ($36,943).
- Children are the poorest age group today in America: 20% of children under the age of 18 live in poverty; 25% of infants and toddlers under 3 live in poverty; 24% of children under age 6 live in poverty; 12.4% of the elderly live in poverty.
- Roughly 14 million children live in poverty. Over half these children (about 7.5 million) are white. Minorities are disproportionately represented among the poor: 46% of all black children and 40% of all Hispanic children are poor, compared to 17% of all white children.
- Children living in poverty are about equally divided between those who live in urban areas and those who live in rural and suburban areas.
- Children living in a single-parent home are at greater risk of living in poverty; for children under age 6, the poverty rate in a single-parent family is 57% (about 3 million children). However, a large number of children in two-parent families also grow up in poverty; the poverty rate for children under 6 in married-couple families is 12% (about 2 million children).

"I'm tired," "I need it," or "It's mine." These justifications may lead to new negotiations. In some instances, parents may change their minds on hearing a child's reasoning and may allow the child to continue the behavior. In general, toddlers are more effective in offering reasonable justifications and negotiating alternative behavior when their parents engage in these types of interactions than when parents issue stern commands and apply physical punishment (Dunn & Munn, 1987; Kuczynski, Kochanska, Radke-Yarrow & Girnius-Brown, 1987).

Generally, toddlers are very sensitive to expressions of parental disapproval. As they move through toddlerhood, they begin to appreciate the extent of their dependence on their parents. They want to please their parents, and they want to feel a sense of pride, not shame or doubt. Most of children's behavior can be regulated with minimal adult intensity. Often, children know immediately after a misdeed that they have done the wrong thing. Extensive punishment or shaming at that point serves only to generate anxiety rather than to reinforce the child's internal recognition of an inappropriate act.

Poverty and Discipline

Poverty is both an economic and a psychological condition. Each year the federal government establishes a poverty level for families of varying sizes. In 1991, the official poverty threshold for a family of three was $10,860; for a family of four, it was $13,924. The psychology of poverty is more difficult to define. It is not so directly linked to absolute financial resources as to perceptions that one is consistently unable to meet basic needs and an associated anxiety about the inadequacy of one's resources. Thus, as a result of unemployment or divorce, a sudden loss of income may result in a sense of poverty even if the actual income is above the level designated by the federal guidelines. Facts regarding children in poverty in the United States are summarized in Box 6.2.

The Influence of Poverty on Child Development   Poverty in and of itself does not place inevitable limits on a child's development. There are many instances, both famous and less well-known, of children who have grown up in poverty and who have achieved eminence. However, it is well documented that poverty increases the risks children face, including malnourishment, poor-quality health care, living in a hazardous physical environment, living in a dangerous neighborhood, receiving poor-quality or inadequate child care, and participating in an ineffective school system. Thus, poverty is linked to reduced access to the basic resources associated with survival.

In a review of the relationship of economic hardship and parenting practices, Vonnie McLoyd (1990) argued that economic hardship also results in emotional distress that disrupts the parents' marital relationship and then both directly and indirectly disrupts their relationship to the child. Frustration and anger at the conditions of poverty may give way to feelings of weakness, victimization, and loss of control. These many factors often cause both physical and mental health problems that may be expressed in pessimism, loss of hope, depression, drug and alcohol abuse, and psychosomatic ailments.

Because of the parents' high levels of emotional distress, economic hardship is likely to produce parent-child interactions that do not support the child's intellectual or emotional development (McLoyd, 1990). Poor mothers are more likely than more affluent mothers to use power assertion and physical punishment as a form of discipline. In one national study of poverty, parenting practices, and

Poverty exposes young children to high levels of risk and stress in day-to-day life.

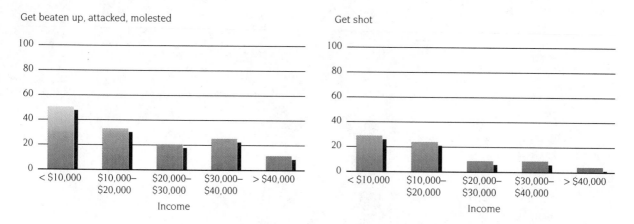

FIGURE 6.2

Percentage of parents, by family income, who worry "a lot" that their child will get attacked or get shot.
Source: National Commission on Children, 1991.

children's mental health, the amount that parents used spanking was directly related to their current level of poverty. This pattern was the same for black, Hispanic, and non-Hispanic white families. The more likely parents were to use spanking and harsh discipline, the greater the level of their children's emotional symptoms, both internal distress characterized by depression, fearfulness, and crying and externally directed behavior such as arguing, disobedience, destructiveness, and impulsiveness (McLeod & Shannon, 1993).

Poor parents emphasize obedience and are less likely to use reasons and explanations in their discipline practices. They are less likely to reward their children through praise and encouragement and less likely to ask their children for their ideas and opinions. In general, poor parents have been characterized as less sensitive to their child's needs and less emotionally supportive. Some of these parenting practices may be reflective of the fact that these parents worry more about the risks to which their children are exposed (see Figure 6.2).

Factors That Mediate the Impact of Poverty   Like every other environmental factor, poverty has varied impacts on children and families. Although we are still a very long way from fully understanding how some children escape its negative effects, we do know that many children who live in poverty continue to develop optimally. Some scholars have emphasized the notion of resilience as a characteristic of children. These children appear to have inner strengths that permit them to get the resources they need, to define their situation positively, and to transcend the challenges of their lives (Garmezy, 1991). These children also have an easy, sociable temperament. They are active, seeking out stimulation and evoking responses from others. They are bright and can solve problems readily. They usually have at least one supportive, loving relationship with a family member as well as access to supportive contacts outside the family.

Some parents also have resources that appear to buffer the impact of poverty. Among single, low-income, African-American mothers, for example, level of education, the presence of an emotionally supportive social network, and strong religious beliefs all help to reduce the negative effects of poverty (Kelly, Power & Wimbush, 1992; McLoyd, 1990; Jayakody, Chatters & Taylor, 1993). We also suspect that persistent poverty has more detrimental effects on development than transitory poverty. Persistent poverty in the life of a small child is a strong predictor of a wide variety of physical and mental health problems. Parents who can see their poverty as transitory and can take steps to move out of it may also differ in their supportiveness and responsiveness to their children.

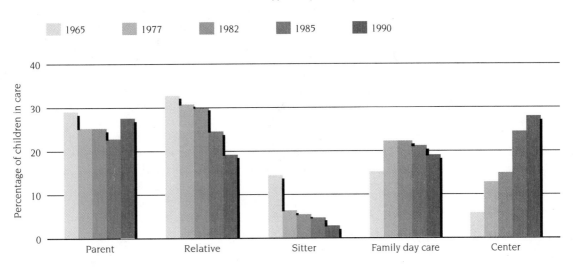

Day Care

Child-care arrangements for toddlers vary with the presence of a father in the family, the child's age, and the employment of the mother, either full or part time. Figure 6.3 illustrates changes from 1965 to 1990 in the patterns of child care for preschool-age children whose mothers were employed. You can see the steady increase in the use of centers, so that in 1990 about the same percentage of toddlers were cared for in centers as were cared for by their parents. Family members, especially fathers and grandparents, were responsible for about a third of the children who were cared for in their own homes or in someone else's home. More than one child-care arrangement was made for about 13% of the children. A child may have been in a half-day nursery and then have a baby-sitter for the rest of the day, or a child may have been in day care all day and then have a relative baby-sitting in the early evening (National Commission on Children, 1993; U.S. Bureau of the Census, 1991).

In addition to the great variety of child-care arrangements, children are increasingly (or perhaps we are increasingly aware that they are) being left at home alone. In numerous examples, young children, including toddlers, have been left home alone for extended periods. In some cases, toddlers are left in the care of brothers or sisters who are only slightly older than they are. According to a U.S. Census Bureau (1991) report, in 1987 an estimated 7736 three- and four-year-old children of working mothers cared for themselves. In our view, no one can argue that leaving a toddler alone constitutes adequate child care.

What happens during the waking hours and in the transitions from naps to waking or from waking to sleep is what toddler care is all about. Toddlers seek out time to elaborate their locomotion, to engage in fantasy play, to interact verbally so as to developed effective language skills, and to learn self-control. Psychosocial development will occur to the extent that the mix of the child's time includes opportunities to engage in and continuously extend these abilities with supportive adults and other children as well as during time alone. There must be numerous opportunities to explore their individuality and self-directed action, as well as experiences of reassurance, connection, and support.

In the United States, child-care arrangements constitute a highly diverse "market," especially when compared with kindergarten through 12th grade public education (Holloway & Fuller, 1992). Child care in America is covered by minimal

FIGURE 6.3
Primary care arrangements for preschool children of employed mothers, 1965–1990
Source: *National Commission on Children*, 1993

federal and state regulation. Children are in the care of a wide range of caregivers with varying types of education and training, from no specific background and training at all to bachelor's and master's degrees. Child-care arrangements reflect a variety of philosophies about the care of young children, wide differences in curriculum, and a great range in the physical settings where young children spend time. The laissez-faire approach to the care of toddlers seems to reflect a cultural belief that the nurturance and socialization of young children is primarily the responsibility of the family, while the schooling of children over the age of 5 is a public concern.

Because of the growing national need for child care and a wide choice of child-care arrangements, parents, educators, and policymakers are asking critical questions: How does day care influence the development of young children? What is our obligation to ensure quality day care for the children of working parents? What is our obligation as a society to meet the health, nutrition, and safety needs of the children of poor parents?

The Impact of Day Care

Early-childhood programs have arisen from two rather distinct historical sources. One source was university laboratory programs set up to promote optimal development in young children by creating a nursery school cirriculum that focused on health care, nutrition, and early peer socialization. These programs and related activities carried on in churches and community centers usually focused on enriching the lives of middle- and upper-middle-class children. The other source was child-welfare programs set up to protect poor, abused, and immigrant children and to bring them services that their parents could not afford or did not know about (Holloway & Fuller, 1992).

This second kind of child care evolved into the federally funded Head Start program, whose primary purpose is to prevent school failure by preparing children to enter school ready to learn. Head Start is a comprehensive early childhood program designed for low-income children and their families. Ideally, in addition to an academic curriculum, Head Start programs provide medical, dental, nutritional, and mental health care for young children and serve as a focal point for parent education and family support (Shore, 1993; Zigler & Muenchow, 1992). As you read about the effects of day care on young children, it is important to try to distinguish the type of program being evaluated. Many reports that appear to evaluate Head Start, for example, actually use data from model preschool programs that are not part of the broad federal Head Start program. Not all day-care programs have the same comprehensive mission as Head Start, and Head Start programs themselves are of varying quality.

Assessments of day care's effects on young children generally focus on intellectual abilities, socioemotional development, and peer relations. Research has tended to emphasize the impact of day care on the children of very poor families, children who are at special risk for school failure, illiteracy, and subsequent minimal employment or unemployment. Although the mission of Head Start programs includes health, mental health, and family support, evaluations of day care do not usually include data on these variables.

Increasingly, researchers are agreeing that the effect of quality day care on toddlers is positive. The research literature is still developing, and many questions are still unanswered, but data from model programs show that quality day care contributes to intellectual achievement, as reflected in higher IQ scores, both during the preschool years and during the first grade (Burchinal, Lee & Ramey,

Quality day care fosters autonomy through contact with skilled adults who can expand a child's repertoire of skills and ideas, in a setting designed to promote a child's sense of mastery.

1989). Achievement in specific areas such as mathematics is also higher in the early elementary grades. However, both IQ and achievement test advantages dissipate, so that by the later elementary grades children who attended early daycare programs do not score significantly higher than control subjects who did not attend early-childhood programs. Similar patterns of initial IQ advantages that last for a few years have also been found in studies of Head Start children (McKey et al., 1985).

In addition to test score benefits, children who have participated in model programs and Head Start are less likely to be placed in special education classrooms and are less likely to be held back a grade. These advantages are of significance in thinking about the trade-off in costs and benefits of providing early educational experiences to children at risk of school failure (Haskins, 1989).

The Perry Preschool Project, a model program that has carried out extensive longitudinal research on its participants, has seen a number of indications of academic success. At age 19, children who had attended a quality child-care program had higher grades, fewer failing grades, a more positive attitude toward school, and a higher literacy rate than a comparable group of very poor young adults who had not participated in a quality child-care program (Schweinhart & Weikart, 1988).

In studies of the impact of day care on intelligence and school achievement, researchers in the United States have tended to study how quality child care modifies the negative effects of poverty. This focus leaves open the question of whether early day care is enriching for the children of middle-class parents, whose resources and educational backgrounds are likely to be more supportive of a child's intellectual achievement. A study of Swedish child care showed positive effects of early day care (beginning sometime after age 6 or 7 months) on the cognitive performance and teacher ratings of children of both low- and middle-income parents with varying educational backgrounds (Andersson, 1989). The children who entered day care during their first year of life were described as "more persistent and independent and more verbally facile than other children, and they were less anxious and more socially confident" (Andersson, 1992, p. 20). Advantages of early day care that transcended the family's socioeconomic status continued to be observed when the children were 13 years old. Similar research is needed in the United States to understand the relative benefits of early-childhood education for children in middle- and upper-middle-class families as well as for children in poor families.

Quality day care is also associated with higher levels of social competence, self-esteem, and empathy. Children who interact positively with adults in their day-care settings are more likely to continue to interact positively and comfortably with their teachers and classmates in the elementary grades (Vandell, Henderson & Wilson, 1988). Some studies have found that children with day-care experience are less compliant with their parents' wishes and more aggressive with their peers than children who have not been in day care (Clarke-Stewart & Fein, 1983). This willfulness may result from the greater need to assert oneself in a group to have one's needs met. It may also reflect an advanced level of independence that results from functioning in more than one socialization setting (Clark-Stewart, 1989). Whether these qualities of noncompliance and aggressiveness lead to long-term problems in social adjustment has not been determined.

Few of the evaluations of model programs or Head Start have reported on long-term social consequences. However, results from the Perry Preschool Project showed that, by age 19, fewer of the children studied had committed delinquent acts or had been processed by the courts; fewer had been on welfare; and more had been employed (Berrueta-Clement et al., 1984; Haskins, 1989). There are no comparable data to indicate this type of long-term social benefit from Head Start.

Quality day care also has an impact on peer relations. Children benefit from opportunities to interact with a variety of peers in settings where adults are readily available to help them make choices and resolve differences. The quality and complexity of social play are especially enhanced when children remain in the same child-care setting rather than moving from one arrangement to another. In stable conditions, toddlers, whose verbal skills are limited, expand their strategies for coordinating their play with others and for exploring shared fantasies (Clarke-Stewart, 1989; Howes & Stewart, 1987). By the time they reached age 8, children who had experienced quality care at age 4 were more likely to engage in friendly interactions with their age-mates, were less likely to play alone, and were less likely to be described as shy than children who had had low-quality day-care experiences (Vandell et al., 1988). At age 19, students who had been in the Perry Preschool Project were more likely to report that they provided help to their friends and family than were comparison subjects, but they were less likely to volunteer without pay for community service.

Since Head Start is a more comprehensive program, it is worthwhile to consider its additional benefits for children. In 30 studies that reported on the health impact of Head Start, the data show that participating children are more likely to get a wide variety of examinations and assessments covering medical and dental health, speech and hearing, vision, and nutrition. All of these opportunities allow a direct response to young children's physical needs when their parents may not be aware of emerging problems or are not sure how to address these problems.

Because Head Start provides meals, young children in the program have a much higher daily nutritional intake than similar children who are not in the program. Thus, Head Start succeeds in bringing to very young children essential benefits that they are not receiving through their families.

As an additional benefit, Head Start has had a positive impact on families and communities. An estimated 30,000 parents and community members have been involved in some form of training and career development. Head Start has created an estimated 76,000 jobs, the majority of which are held by minority members in the communities where the programs are located. These benefits empower adults to influence the quality of education in their communities and broaden their understanding of the educational process (Holloway & Fuller, 1992; Haskins, 1989).

In his effort to evaluate the critical features of programs that will have a long-term impact, David Weikart found three factors (Berrueta-Clement et al., 1984) to be associated with effectiveness. Program effectiveness depends on the *style of program operation*, that is, a commitment to high quality and a special blending of various elements such as curriculum, parent involvement, supervision and training of the staff, fostering positive relationships among the staff, and ongoing opportunities for staff development and evaluation.

Program quality is also influenced by the *leadership* of the program. Effective leaders must be in touch with the needs and concerns of the families in the community. They must be regarded with trust and confidence by parents, staff, and other members of the community. And they must be able to provide the kind of supervision of staff and guidance for program development that fosters an ongoing air of enthusiasm and optimism about the importance of the program in the lives of children.

Finally, Weikart emphasized *parent involvement*. Without support to parents and other family members, the impact of the program on young children is unlikely to endure. Through their increased understanding of the educational process and their positive attitude toward education, parents help sustain a child's motivation, encourage new activities, and seek out resources, such as tutoring, summer enrichment programs, and after-school activities, that will supplement a child's education. Supportive family members encourage young children through the difficult times and keep trying to find solutions that will help children overcome barriers to academic achievement.

Directions for the Future

We face a critical gap between the demand for *affordable, quality* day care and its availability. Although the supply of child-care settings appears to be ample, settings that meet the standards of high quality are comparatively scarce. In addition, services for certain groups, including children with disabilities, children whose parents have evening work schedules, children who are ill, and children who need year-round programs, are in short supply (National Commission on Children, 1993).

Concern about the need for affordable, quality day care is expressed by parents who are in the labor market as well as by those who would like to be in the labor market. We now have a national parental leave policy, so that parents can take time off to care for their newborns without risking the loss of their jobs. But concerns about child care continue throughout toddlerhood and well into the elementary-school years, when children need adult supervision before and after school hours. Policies and resources are needed to improve the training and upgrade the salaries of child-care professionals, to provide subsidies to help cover the cost of child care, and to improve the licensing regulations for people who provide day care in their homes (Buie, 1988).

Corporations are recognizing the need to address their employees' child-care needs. Worries about their children and the difficulty of making adequate child-care arrangements result in parental anxiety, missed workdays, and decreased productivity. Companies are addressing this issue in several ways (Quinn, 1988):

Emergency care: The company provides temporary care on those days when an employee's regular arrangement fails.

Discounts: The company arranges for a 10% discount with a national child-care chain or picks up 10% of the fee.

Vouchers: The company makes payments toward whatever child-care arrangement a parent selects. One company gives special assistance to all employees who earn less than $30,000 a year. Another provides a subsidy during a child's first year of life.

Referral services: The company identifies and lists good day-care centers it can recommend to its employees.

On-site day care: Day-care centers are created at the workplace. The U.S. Senate and House of Representatives provide on-site day care for their members and employees.

Flexible benefits: Employees arrange to have the money they pay for child care deducted from their salaries; this money does not count as taxable income.

A comprehensive national policy that places quality child care high on the list of priorities is evolving slowly. Some people are still reluctant to accept the participation of women, especially mothers of young children, in the labor force. In addition, the public tends to underestimate and devalue the training and expertise necessary to provide quality care, an attitude that leads to low salaries and very difficult working conditions for child-care professionals. Furthermore, most adults, having had little or no formal training in child development and parenting, are poorly informed about the characteristics of quality care. They do not know what to look for or what questions to ask. As a result, they may place their child in a setting that meets their own requirements for cost and convenience but does not contribute optimally to their child's development.

Day care is clearly not the right choice for all families. If parents devote enough time and attention to care for their toddlers at home, and if they approach this responsibility with enthusiasm, patience, and an understanding of their role in promoting optimal development, the result can be wonderful. Toddlers bring a playfulness and freshness to day-to-day life that is uplifting and eye-opening for their parents. And parents can extend toddlers' sense of excitement about learning through almost any task, from sweeping the dust from under the bed to taking a walk to the neighborhood library. Through daily care, closeness and affection grow as parents watch and share with their children hundreds of moments of discovery—discovery of new words, new motor activities, new delight in a sensation or a sound, new pride in solving a jigsaw puzzle or building a high tower of blocks. There may be nothing more intimate than watching someone you love come to understand a new idea or achieve a new level of competence.

But for many families, some kind of child-care arrangement is not only necessary, but desirable, and the toddlers in these families have a right to quality care. If day-care settings and Head Start programs are to have the desired beneficial impact, they must be adequately funded. By the end of the 1980s, Head Start budgets had been so reduced that over half the centers were described as marginal or poor (Zigler, 1993). Before Head Start can expand to serve more children, the centers that currently exist must be adequately staffed and funded. The comprehensive services that such a program promises require a highly trained staff, professionals who can coordinate social service programs and resources, a fully developed family involvement component, and a developmentally appropriate curriculum that is adequately linked to the cultural strengths and resources of the children and their community. Although there is still plenty of room for diversity and innovation in early-childhood education programs, we know enough about standards of quality to be able to hold all preschool and day-care centers to these standards.

As we consider policies for the education of children from poor families, we must sustain the gains made during the preschool Head Start years. Most poor children are not just poor when they are toddlers. They remain poor throughout their elementary- and middle-school years. Research has shown that, beginning in the early elementary grades, poor children lose ground during the summers in comparison to their more affluent peers, who are exposed to new experiences and new resources when school is out (Entwistle & Alexander, 1990). Poor children may require access to additional educational and cultural experiences throughout the elementary- and middle-school years in order to maintain pace with their wealthier age-mates. Extra involvement in intellectually stimulating activities, whether through summer activities, after-school programs, weekend workshops, or talent clubs, may be necessary to sustain academic motivation and bring more poor children into the work force with the required skills and a positive orientation toward learning and problem solving.

Chapter Summary

The developmental tasks of toddlerhood improve children's ability to find order and consistency in their world and to express the self. Locomotive skills heighten toddlers' sense of mastery and expand their boundaries of experience. The emergence of fantasy provides them with an internal, personal form of symbolic representation. In areas in which control is very difficult or impossible, fantasy allows a pseudomastery in which barriers are overcome and limitations of reality are of less importance. Conflicts can be acted out, and pretend solutions can be found. Fantasy may be enhanced by language, but it most certainly thrives even in the absence of words. Language is both a tool for the expression of feelings and concepts and a primary mechanism of socialization. Toddlers' use of language gives us clues to their cognitive development and their needs. Through language, children influence others, gain access to worlds of information, and learn new strategies for the control and expression of their impulses. Efforts at self-control, both impulse regulation and self-directed goal attainment, begin in toddlerhood and continue through life.

The psychosocial crisis of autonomy versus shame and doubt reflects the child's persistent needs for self-expression and mastery. Young children develop individuality by exercising the skills that develop during toddlerhood. Self-doubts result from repeated ridicule, shaming, and failure.

Autonomy and individuation ordinarily emerge in the context of the parent-child relationship. Toddlers are avid observers, imitating and incorporating parental behaviors and values into their own routines. Parental interaction, acceptance, and discipline all contribute to a child's emerging sense of individuality. However, living in poverty increases the likelihood that parents will be psychologically unavailable or will use harsh, restrictive disciplinary strategies that produce shame or unexpressed rage in their young children.

Increasing numbers of young children are being cared for in group settings. The impact of day care depends heavily on the quality of the personnel, the nature of the program, and an appropriate physical environment. Many studies suggest that quality child care contributes to the toddler's optimal development. A major concern, however, is the availability of affordable, quality care to all those families that need it.

References

Andersson, B. (1989). Effects of public day care: A longitudinal study. *Child Development, 60,* 857–866.

Andersson, B. (1992). Effects of day-care on cognitive and socioemotional competence of thirteen-year-old Swedish schoolchildren. *Child Development, 63,* 20–63.

Anthony, E. J. (1970). The behavior disorders of children. In P. H. Mussen (Ed.), *Carmichael's manual of child psychology* (3rd ed., Vol. 2). New York: Wiley.

Aronfreed, J. & Reber, A. (1965). Internalized behavioral suppression and the timing of social punishment. *Journal of Personality and Social Psychology, 1,* 3–16.

Bandura, A. (1977). *Social learning theory.* Englewood Cliffs, NJ: Prentice-Hall.

Bandura, A. (1989). Regulation of cognitive processes through perceived self-efficacy. *Developmental Psychology, 25,* 729–735.

Bates, E., Bretherton, I. & Snyder, L. (1988). *From first words to grammar.* Cambridge: Cambridge University Press.

Bates, E., O'Connell, B. & Shore, C. (1987). Language and communication in infancy. In J. Osofsky (Ed.), *Handbook of infant development* (2nd ed., pp. 149–203). New York: Wiley.

Baumrind, D. (1971). Current patterns of parental authority. *Developmental Psychology Monographs, 4,* 99–103.

Berkowitz, L. (1973). Control of aggression. In B. M. Caldwell & H. N. Ricciuti (Eds.), *Review of child development research* (Vol. 3). Chicago: University of Chicago Press.

Bernstein, B. (1972). Social class, language, and socialization. In P. P. Giglioli (Ed.), *Language and social context.* Harmondsworth, England: Penguin.

Berrueta-Clement, J. R., Schweinhart, L. J., Barnett, W. S., Epstein, A. S. & Weikart, D. P. (1984). *Changed lives: The effects of the Perry Preschool Program on youths through age* 19. Ypsilanti, MI: High/Scope Press.

Best, C. T., McRoberts, G. W. & Sithole, N. M. (1988). Examination of perceptual reorganization for nonnative speech contrasts: Zulu click discrimination by English-speaking adults and infants. *Journal of Experimental Psychology: Human Perception and Performance, 14,* 345–360.

Bloom, L. (1993). Word learning. *Society for Research in Child Development Newsletter,* Winter, pp. 1, 9, 13.

Bloom, L., Lightbown, P. & Hood, B. (1975). *Structure and variation in child language. Monographs of the Society for Research in Child Development, 40*(2, Serial No. 160).

Boyatzis, C. J. & Watson, M. W. (1993). Preschool children's symbolic representation of objects through gestures. *Child Development, 64,* 729–735.

Braine, M. D. S. (1976). *Children's first word combinations.* Monographs of the Society for Research in Child Development, 41(1).

Brown, J. R. & Dunn, J. (1992). Talk with your mother or your sibling? Developmental changes in early family conversations about feelings. *Child Development, 63,* 336–349.

Brown, R. (1973). *A first language: The early stages.* Cambridge: Harvard University Press.

Brunner, H. G., Breakerfield, M. N. X. O., Ropers, H. H. & van Dost, B. A. (1993). Abnormal behavior associated with a point notation in the structure gene for mono-amine oxidase A. *Science, 262,* 578–580.

Bullock, M. & Lutkenhaus, P. (1988). The development of volitional behavior in the toddler years. *Child Development, 59,* 664–674.

Buie, J. (1988). Efforts for better child care increase. APA *Monitor, 19,* 28.

Burchinal, M., Lee, M. & Ramey, C. (1989). Type of day-care and preschool intellectual development in disadvantaged children. *Child Development, 60,* 128–137.

Burke, B. (1987). The role of playfulness in developing thinking skills: A review with implementation strategies. In S. Moore & K. Kolb (Eds.), *Reviews of research for practitioners and parents* (No. 3, pp. 3–8). Minneapolis: Center for Early Education and Development.

Buss, D. M. (1981). Predicting parent-child interactions from children's activity level. *Developmental Psychology, 17,* 59–65.

Carey, S. (1978). The child as word learner. In M. Halle, G. Miller & J. Bresnan (Eds.), *Linguistic theory and psychological reality* (pp. 264–293). Cambridge: MIT Press.

Chwast, J. (1972). Sociopathic behavior in children. In B. B. Wolman (Ed.), *Manual of child psychopathology*. New York: McGraw-Hill.

Clark, J. E. & Phillips, S. J. (1993). A longitudinal study of intralimb coordination in the first year of independent walking: A dynamical systems analysis. *Child Development*, 64, 1143–1157.

Clark, J. E., Phillips, S. J. & Petersen, R. (1989). Developmental stability in jumping. *Developmental Psychology*, 25, 929–935.

Clarke-Stewart, K. A. (1989). Infant day care: Maligned or malignant? *American Psychologist*, 44, 266–273.

Clarke-Stewart, K. A. & Fein, G. G. (1983). Early childhood programs. In P. H. Mussen (Ed.), *Handbook of child psychology*; Vol. 2, *Infancy and developmental psychobiology* (pp. 917–1000). New York: Wiley.

Cole, D. & La Voie, J. C. (1985). Fantasy play and related cognitive development in 2 to 6 year olds. *Developmental Psychology*, 21, 233–240.

Crain-Thoreson, C. & Dale, P. S. (1992). Do early talkers become early readers? Linguistic precocity, preschool language, and emergent literacy. *Developmental Psychology*, 28, 421–429.

Cummings, E. M., Iannotti, R. J. & Zahn-Waxler, C. (1989). Aggression between peers in early childhood: Individual continuity and developmental change. *Child Development*, 60, 887–895.

Cummings, J. S., Pellegrini, D. S., Notarius, C. I. & Cummings, E. M. (1989). Children's responses to angry adult behavior as a function of marital distress and history of interparent hostility. *Child Development*, 60, 1035–1043.

Diaz, R. M. (1983). Thought and two languages: The impact of bilingualism on cognitive development. *Review of Research in Education*, 10, 23–54.

Dix, T., Ruble, D. N. & Zambarano, R. J. (1989). Mothers' implicit theories of discipline: Child effects, parent effects, and the attribution process. *Child Development*, 60, 1373–1391.

Dore, J. (1978). Conditions for the acquisition of speech acts. In I. Markova (Ed.), *The social context of language*. New York: Wiley.

Dunn, J. & Munn, P. (1987). Development of justification in disputes with mother and sibling. *Developmental Psychology*, 23, 791–798.

Eckerman, C. O., Davis, C. C. & Didow, S. M. (1989). Toddlers' emerging ways of achieving social coordinations with a peer. *Child Development*, 60, 440–453.

Eckerman, C. O. & Didow, S. M. (1989). Toddlers' social coordinations: Changing responses to another's invitation to play. *Developmental Psychology*, 25, 794–804.

Eisenberg, N., Fabes, R. A., Bernzweig, J., Karbon, M., Poulin, R. & Hanish, L. (1993). The relations of emotionality and regulation to preschoolers' social skills and sociometric status. *Child Development*, 64, 1418–1438.

Entwisle, D. R. & Alexander, K. L. (1990). Summer setback: Race, poverty, school composition, and achievement. *American Sociological Review*, 57, 72–84.

Erikson, E. H. (1963). *Childhood and society* (2nd ed.). New York: Norton.

Erikson, E. H. (1972). Play and actuality. In M. W. Piers (Ed.), *Play and development* (pp. 127–167). New York: Norton.

Ferguson, C. (1989). Individual differences in language learning. In M. L. Rice & R. L. Schiefelbusch (Eds.), *Teachability of language*. Baltimore: Brookes.

Fernald, A. (1985). Four-month-old infants prefer to listen to motherese. *Infant Behavior and Development*, 8, 181–195.

Fernald, A. (1993). Approval and disapproval: Infant responsiveness to vocal affect in familiar and unfamiliar languages. *Child Development*, 64, 657–674.

Fernald, A. & Morikawa, H. (1993). Common themes and cultural variations in Japanese and American mothers' speech to infants. *Child Development*, 64, 637–656.

Flavell, J. H., Flavell, E. R. & Green, F. L. (1987). Young children's knowledge about the apparent-real and pretend-real distinctions. *Developmental Psychology*, 23, 816–822.

Forehand, R., Roberts, M. W., Doleys, D.M., Hobbs, S. A. & Resick, P. A. (1976). An examination of disciplinary procedures with children. *Journal of Experimental Child Psychology*, 21, 109–120.

Fox, N. A. & Davidson, R. J. (1984). Hemispheric substrates of affect: A developmental model. In N. A. Fox & R. J. Davidson (Eds.), *The psychobiology of affective development* (pp. 353–381). Hillsdale, NJ: Erlbaum.

Fox, N. A. & Davidson, R. J. (1987). Electroencephalogram asymmetry in response to the approach of a stranger and maternal separation in 10-month-old infants. *Developmental Psychology*, 23, 233–240.

Freud, S. (1905/1953). Three essays on the theory of sexuality. In J. Strachey (Ed.), *The standard edition of the complete psychological works of Sigmund Freud* (Vol. 7). London: Hogarth Press.

Freud, S. (1913/1958). The disposition to obsessional neurosis: A contribution to the problem of choice of neurosis. In J. Strachey (Ed.), *The standard edition of the complete psychological works of Sigmund Freud* (Vol. 2). London: Hogarth Press.

Garmezy, N. (1991). Resilience in children's adaptation to negative life events and stressed environments. *Pediatric Annals*, 20, 459–466.

Getchell, N. & Robertson, M. A. (1989). Whole body stiffness as a function of developmental level in children's hopping. *Developmental Psychology, 25,* 920–928.

Greenfield, P. M. & Smith, J. H. (1976). *The structure of communication in early language development.* New York: Academic Press.

Grusec, J. E. & Abramovitch, R. (1982). Imitation of peers and adults in a natural setting: A functional analysis. *Child Development, 53,* 636–642.

Hakuta, K. & Garcia, E. E. (1989). Bilingualism and education. *American Psychologist, 44,* 374–379.

Harris, M. (1992). *Language experience and early language development: From input to uptake.* Hillsdale, NJ: Erlbaum.

Harris, P. L. & Kavanaugh, R. D. (1993). *Young children's understanding of pretense. Monographs of the Society for Research in Child Development, 58(1).*

Harter, S. (1982). The perceived competence scale for children. *Child Development, 53,* 87–97.

Haskins, R. (1989). Beyond metaphor: The efficacy of early childhood education. *American Psychologist, 44,* 274–282.

Haswell, K., Hock, E. & Wenar, C. (1981). Oppositional behavior of preschool children: Theory and intervention. *Family Relations, 30,* 440–446.

Hess, R. D. & Shipman, V. C. (1965). Early experiences and the socialization of cognitive modes in children. *Child Development, 36,* 869–886.

Hoffman, M. L. (1970). Moral development. In P. H. Mussen (Ed.), *Carmichael's manual of child psychology* (3rd ed., Vol. 2). New York: Wiley.

Hoffman, M. L. (1977). Moral internalization: Current theory and research. In L. Berkowitz (Ed.), *Advances in experimental social psychology* (Vol. 10). New York: Academic Press.

Hoffman, M. L. (1980). Moral development in adolescence. In J. Adelson (Ed.), *Handbook of adolescent psychology.* New York: Wiley.

Holloway, S. D. & Fuller, B. (1992). The great child-care experiment: What are the lessons for school improvement? *Educational Researcher, 21,* 12–19.

Howe, N. (1991). Sibling-directed internal state language, perspective taking, and affective behavior. *Child Development, 62,* 1503–1512.

Howes, C. (1987). *Peer interaction of young children. Monographs of the Society for Research in Child Development,* 53(1, Serial No. 217).

Howes, C. & Stewart, P. (1987). Child's play with adults, toys, and peers: An examination of family and child-care influences. *Developmental Psychology, 23,* 423–430.

Howes, C., Unger, O. & Seidner, L. B. (1989). Social pretend play in toddlers: Parallels with social play and with solitary pretend. *Child Development, 60,* 77–84.

Hutt, S. J., Tyler, S., Hutt, C. & Foy, H. (1988). *Play exploration and learning: A natural history of the preschool.* New York: Routledge.

Huttenlocher, J. (1974). The origins of language comprehension. In R. L. Solso (Ed.), *Theories in cognitive psychology.* Potomac, MD: Erlbaum.

Jayakody, R., Chatters, L. M. & Taylor, R. J. (1993). Family support to single and married African American mothers: The provision of financial, emotional, and child care assistance. *Journal of Marriage and the Family, 55,* 261–276.

Kagan, J. (1958). The concept of identification. *Psychological Review, 65,* 296–305.

Kalverboer, A. F., Hopkins, B. & Geuze, R. (1993). *Motor development in early and later childhood: Longitudinal approaches.* New York: Cambridge University Press.

Kaufman, G. (1989). *The psychology of shame.* New York: Springer.

Kelly, M. L., Power, T. G. & Wimbush, D. D. (1992). Determinants of disciplinary practices in low-income black mothers. *Child Development, 63,* 573–582.

Kochanska, G., Kuczynski, L. & Radke-Yarrow, M. (1989). Correspondence between mothers' self-reported and observed child-rearing practices. *Child Development, 60,* 56–63.

Kochanska, G. & Radke-Yarrow, M. (1992). Inhibition in toddlerhood and the dynamics of the child's interactions with an unfamiliar peer at age 5. *Child Development, 63,* 325–335.

Kopp, C. B. (1982). Antecedents of self-regulation: A developmental perspective. *Developmental Psychology, 18,* 199–214.

Kuczynski, L., Kochanska, G., Radke-Yarrow, M. & Girnius-Brown, O. (1987). A developmental interpretation of young children's noncompliance. *Developmental Psychology, 23,* 799–806.

Kuczynski, L., Zahn-Waxler, C. & Radke-Yarrow, M. (1987). Development and content of imitation in the second and third years of life: A socialization perspective. *Developmental Psychology, 23,* 276–282.

Ladd, G. W., Price, J. M. & Hart, C. H. (1988). Predicting preschoolers' peer status from their playground behaviors. *Child Development, 59,* 986–992.

Lanza, E. (1992). Can bilingual two-year-olds code-switch? *Journal of Child Language, 19,* 633–658.

Leizer, J. I. & Rogers, R. W. (1974). Effects of method of discipline, timing of punishment, and timing of test on resistance to temptation. *Child Development, 45,* 790–793.

Lenneberg, E. H. (1967). *Biological foundations of language.* New York: Wiley.

Lewis, H. B. (1987). Shame and the narcissistic personality. In D. L. Nathanson (Ed.), *The many faces of shame* (pp. 93–132). New York: Guilford Press.

Lucariello, J. (1987). Spinning fantasy: Themes, structure, and the knowledge base. *Child Development, 58,* 434–442.

Lytton, H. (1976). The socialization of two-year-old boys: Ecological findings. *Journal of Child Psychology and Psychiatry, 17,* 287–304.

Maccoby, E. E. (1992). The role of parents in the socialization of children: An historical overview. *Developmental Psychology*, 28, 1006–1017.

McKey, R. H., Condelli, L., Ganson, H., Barrett, B. J., McConkey, C. & Plantz, M. C. (1985). *The impact of Head Start on children, families, and communities*. (DHHS Publication No. OHDS 85-31193). Washington, DC: U.S. Government Printing Office.

McLeod, J. D. & Shanahan, M. J. (1993). Poverty, parenting, and children's mental health. *American Sociological Review*, 58, 351–366.

McLoyd, V. C. (1990). The impact of economic hardship on black families and children: Psychological distress, parenting, and socioemotional development. *Child Development*, 61, 311–346.

Messer, D. J., Rachford, D., McCarthy, M. E. & Yarrow, L. J. (1987). Assessment of mastery behavior at 30 months: Analysis of task-directed activities. *Developmental Psychology*, 23, 771–781.

Miller, P. H. (1993). *Theories of developmental psychology* (2nd ed.). New York: W. H. Freeman.

Miller, P. J. & Sperry, L. L. (1987). The socialization of anger and aggression. *Merrill-Palmer Quarterly*, 34, 217–222.

Miller-Jones, D. (1989). Culture and testing. *American Psychologist*, 44, 360–366.

Mills, R. S. L. & Rubin, K. H. (1990). Parental beliefs about problematic social behaviors in early childhood. *Child Development*, 61, 138–151.

Mischel, W. & Patterson, C. J. (1976). Substantive and structural elements of effective plans. *Journal of Personality and Social Psychology*, 34, 942–950.

Mischel, W., Shoda, Y. & Rodriguez, M. L. (1989). Delay of gratification in children. *Science*, 244, 933–938.

Molfese, D. L., Molfese, V. J. & Carrell, P. L. (1982). Early language development. In B. B. Wolman (Ed.), *Handbook of developmental psychology* (pp. 301–322). Englewood Cliffs, NJ: Prentice-Hall.

Mondell, S. & Tyler, F. B. (1981). Parental competence and styles of problem-solving/play behavior with children. *Developmental Psychology*, 17, 73–78.

Morrison, A. P. (1989). *Shame: The underside of narcissism*. Hillsdale, NJ: Analytic Press.

Moskowitz, B. A. (1978). The acquisition of language. *Scientific American*, 239, 92–108.

Murphy, L. (1956). *Personality in young children: Vol. 2. Colin, a normal child*. New York: Basic Books.

National Commission on Children. (1993). *Just the facts: A summary of recent information on America's children and their families*. Washington, DC: Author.

Nelson, K. (1973). *Structure and strategy in learning to talk. Monographs of the Society for Research in Child Development*, 38(1–2).

Nelson, K. (1981). Individual differences in language development: Implications for development and language. *Developmental Psychology*, 17, 170–187.

Norman-Jackson, J. (1982). Family interactions, language development, and primary reading achievement of black children in families of low income. *Child Development*, 53, 349–358.

Odom, L., Seeman, J. & Newbrough, J. R. (1971). A study of family communication patterns and personality integration in children. *Child Psychiatry and Human Development*, 1, 275–285.

Olsen, L. (1988). *Crossing the schoolhouse border: Immigrant students and the California public schools*. San Francisco: California Tomorrow.

Oviatt, S. L. (1980). The emerging ability to comprehend language: An experimental approach. *Child Development*, 51, 97–106.

Oviatt, S. L. (1982). Inferring what words mean: Early development in infants' comprehension of common objects' names. *Child Development*, 53, 274–277.

Patterson, C. J. & Mischel, W. (1976). Effects of temptation-inhibiting and task-facilitating plans on self-control. *Journal of Personality and Social Psychology*, 33, 209–217.

Piaget, J. (1952). *The language and thought of the child*. London: Routledge & Kegan Paul.

Piaget, J. (1962). *Play, dreams, and imitation in childhood*. New York: Norton.

Piaget, J. (1970). Piaget's theory. In P. H. Mussen (Ed.), *Carmichael's manual of child psychology* (3rd ed., Vol. 1). New York: Wiley.

Pick, H. L. (1989). Motor development: The control of action. *Developmental Psychology*, 25, 867–870.

Piers, M. W. & Landau, G. M. (1980). *The gift of play*. New York: Walker.

Quinn, J. B. (1988). A crisis in child care. *Newsweek* (February 15), p. 57.

Rice, M. L. (1989). Children's language acquisition. *American Psychologist*, 44, 149–156.

Rice, M. L. & Woodsmall, L. (1988). Lessons from television: Children's word learning when viewing. *Child Development*, 59, 420–429.

Ridenour, M. V. (Ed.). (1978). *Motor development: Issues and applications*. Princeton, NJ: Princeton Books.

Rogoff, B. & Morelli, G. (1989). Perspectives on children's development from cultural psychology. *American Psychologist*, 44, 343–348.

Rubin, K. H. (1980). Fantasy play: Its role in the development of social skills and social cognition. *New Directions in Child Development*, 9, 69–84.

Saltz, R. & Saltz, E. (1986). Pretend play training and its outcomes. In G. Fein & M. Rivkin (Eds.), *The young child at play: Reviews of research* (Vol. 4, pp. 155–173). Washington, DC: National Association for the Education of Young Children.

Schatz, M. (1983). Communication. In J. H. Flavell & E. M. Markman (Eds.), *Handbook of child psychology* (Vol. 3, pp. 841–889). New York: Wiley.

Schickedanz, J. A. (1986). *More than the ABCs: The early stages of reading and writing.* Washington, DC: National Association for the Education of Young People.

Schweinhart, L. J. & Weikart, D. P. (1988). The High/Scope Perry Preschool Program. In R. H. Price, E. L. Cowen, R. P. Lorion & J. Ramos-McKay (Eds.), *Fourteen ounces of prevention* (pp. 53–66). Washington, DC: American Psychological Association.

Shore, M. F. (1993). Doing the right thing. *Readings*, 8, 4–7.

Singer, D. G. & Singer, J. L. (1990). *The house of make-believe: Children's play and developing imagination.* Cambridge: Harvard University Press.

Singer, J. L. (1975). *The inner world of daydreaming.* New York: Colophon Books.

Slade, A. (1987). A longitudinal study of maternal involvement and symbolic play during the toddler period. *Child Development*, 58, 367–375.

Slobin, D. I. (1985). *The cross-linguistic study of language acquisition* (Vols. 1, 2). Hillsdale, NJ: Erlbaum.

Snow, C. E. (1984). Parent-child interaction and the development of communicative ability. In R. L. Schiefelbusch & J. Pickar (Eds.), *Communicative competence: Acquisition and intervention* (pp. 69–108). Baltimore: University Park Press.

Snow, C. E. (1987). Beyond conversation: Second language learners' acquisition of description and explanation. In J. P. Lantolf & A. Labarca (Eds.), *Research in second language learning: Focus on the classroom* (pp. 3–16). Norwood, NJ: Ablex.

Tangney, J. P., Wagner, P., Fletcher, C. & Gramzow, R. (1992). Shamed into anger? The relation of shame and guilt to anger and self-reported aggression. *Journal of Personality and Social Psychology*, 62, 669–675.

Taylor, M., Cartwright, B. S. & Carlson, S. M. (1993). A developmental investigation of children's imaginary companions. *Developmental Psychology*, 29, 276–285.

Templin, M. C. (1957). *Certain language skills in children.* Minneapolis: University of Minnesota Press.

Teti, D. M., Nakagawa, M., Das, R. & Wirth, O. (1991). Security of attachment between preschoolers and their mothers: Relations among social interaction, parenting stress, and mothers' sorts of the attachment Q-set. *Developmental Psychology*, 27, 440–447.

Thompson, R. A. (1990). Emotion and self-regulation. In R. A. Thompson (Ed.), *Nebraska Symposium on Motivation, 1988* (Vol. 36, pp. 367–467). Lincoln: University of Nebraska Press,

Tinsley, V. S. & Waters, H. S. (1982). The development of verbal control over motor behavior: A replication and extension of Luria's findings. *Child Development*, 53, 746–753.

Trawick-Smith, J. (1988). "Let's say you're the baby, OK?": Play leadership and following behavior of young children. *Young Children*, 43, 51–59.

U.S. Bureau of the Census. (1991). *Statistical abstract of the United States: 1991* (111th ed.). Washington, DC: U. S. Government Printing Office.

Valdez-Menchaca, M. S. & Whitehurst, G. J. (1992). Accelerating language development through picture book reading: A systematic extension to Mexican day care. *Developmental Psychology*, 28, 1106–1114.

Vandell, D. L., Henderson, V. K. & Wilson, K. S. (1988). A longitudinal study of children with day-care experiences of varying quality. *Child Development*, 59, 1286–1292.

Vaughn, B. E., Kopp, C. B. & Krakow, J. B. (1984). The emergence and consolidation of self-control from 18 to 30 months of age: Normative trends and individual differences. *Child Development*, 55, 990–1004.

Vaughn, B. E., Kopp, C. B., Krakow, J. B., Johnson, K. & Schwartz, S. S. (1986). Process analyses of the behavior of very young children in delay tasks. *Developmental Psychology*, 22, 752–759.

Vygotsky, L. S. (1978). *Mind in society.* Cambridge: Harvard University Press.

Walker-Andrews, A. S. & Harris, P. L. (1993). Young children's comprehension of pretend causal sequences. *Developmental Psychology*, 29, 915–921.

Walters, R. H., Parke, R. D. & Cane, V. A. (1965). Timing of punishment and the observation of consequences to others as determinants of response inhibition. *Journal of Experimental Child Psychology*, 2, 10–30.

Waxman, S. R. & Hall, D. G. (1993). The development of a linkage between count nouns and object categories: Evidence from fifteen- to twenty-one-month-old infants. *Child Development*, 64, 1224–1241.

Wenar, C. (1982). On negativism. *Human Development*, 25, 1–23.

Werker, J. F. & Lalonde, C. E. (1988). Cross-language speech perception: Initial capabilities and developmental change. *Developmental Psychology*, 24, 672–683.

Wertsch, J. V. (1978). Adult-child interaction and the roots of metacognition. *Quarterly Newsletter of the Institute for Comparative Human Development*, 2, 15–18.

White, B. L., Kaban, B. T. & Attanucci, J. S. (1979). *The origins of human competence.* Lexington, MA: D. C. Heath.

White, B. L. & Watts, J. C. (1973). *Experience and environment* (Vol. 1). Englewood Cliffs, NJ: Prentice-Hall.

White, R. W. (1960). Competence and the psychosexual stages of development. In M. R. Jones (Ed.), *Nebraska Symposium on Motivation* (Vol. 8). Lincoln: University of Nebraska Press.

Woolley, J. D. & Wellman, H. M. (1993). Origin and truth: Young children's understanding of imaginary mental representations. *Child Development*, 64, 1–17.

Zahn-Waxler, C., Radke-Yarrow, M., Wagner, E. & Chapman M. (1992). Development of concern for others. *Developmental Psychology*, 28, 126–136.

Zahn-Waxler, C., Robinson, J. L. & Emde, R.N. (1992). The development of empathy in twins. *Developmental Psychology, 28,* 1038–1047.

Zigler, E. (1993). *Head Start and beyond: A national plan for extended childhood intervention.* New Haven, CT: Yale University Press.

Zigler, E. & Muenchow, S. (1992). *Head Start: The inside story of America's most successful educational experiment.* New York: Basic Books.

Zussman, J. V. (1980). Situational determinants of parental behavior: Effects of competing cognitive activity. *Child Development, 51,* 792–800.

CHAPTER 7

Starting school is more than a symbol of growing up. It represents an expansion of the child's social world, bringing numerous encounters with societal norms, higher expectations, and new information, each having an effect on the child's self-concept.

Early School Age
(4–6 Years)

From a psychosocial perspective, the *early school age* brings with it increasingly complex social influences. By the age of 6, virtually all American children are enrolled in school. Children today are encountering school or school-like experiences at earlier ages than they have in the past. In 1991, 40% of 3- and 4-year-olds were enrolled in school, an increase from 20% in 1970 (U.S. Bureau of the Census, 1992). School brings external evaluation, new opportunities for success and failure, settings for peer-group formation and social evaluation, and the initiation of a set of experiences that may lead to advancement of socioeconomic status in adulthood. At a more immediate level, school is a new source of influence on the child beyond the family. Beliefs and practices followed at home will come under scrutiny and may be challenged by community norms and values. Parents' personal hopes and aspirations for their children may be tempered by the reality of the children's school performance. In addition to family and school, the peer group, the neighborhood, and television all influence children's self-concept during early school age.

Most early-school-age children exhibit wide-ranging curiosity about all facets of life. Once they become aware of alternatives to their own families' philosophies and lifestyles, they begin to question familiar notions. The independence of action seen in the toddler is replaced by independence of thought in the early-school-age child.

Developmental Tasks

Sex-Role Identification

Every human society has patterns of organization based partially on gender. Males and females are often assigned different roles, engage in different tasks, have access to different resources, and are viewed as having different powers and attributes. The specific content of these gender roles varies widely from one culture to another. For example, in contrast to the many societies in which males appear to have a favored and dominant position, several cultures give special priority to girls and women. Among the Kanjar of Pakistan and northern India, girls and women provide more than half the family income through the sale of ceramic and papier-mâché toys; through dancing, begging, and giving carnival rides; and through prostitution (Cronk, 1993). Kanjar men are described as "passive, cooperative and subordinate to females, whereas Kanjar women dominate public and private affairs and are socialized to be aggressive and independent" (p. 279).

The current debate about gender is not whether gender differences exist. The question is where to locate the explanation for gender differences (Bohan, 1993; Thompson, 1993). The *individual-differences* perspective suggests that gender differences reside within the individual as persistent, internal attributes. Whether the differences are a result of biology, socialization, or an interaction between the two, this perspective suggests that differences between males and females are stable characteristics that individuals bring to various situations.

The *constructivist* perspective suggests that gender differences are a product of particular interactions that have a certain socially agreed-upon, gender-related meaning. In this view, the specific behaviors that are described as masculine or feminine depend largely on the situation, including expectations that people will behave in gender-appropriate ways. For example, in a study of social interaction between pairs of toddlers (Jacklin & Maccoby, 1978; Maccoby, 1990), one variable

measured was the amount of time one partner stood watching while the other child played with the toys, a behavior called *passive*. No sex differences were observed overall in the frequency of passive behavior. In same-sex pairs, girls were rarely passive, but in mixed-sex pairs, the girl frequently stood watching while the boy played with the toys. This kind of finding is replicated at older ages, showing that girls and boys, men and women, interact in stereotypically gender-defined ways, particularly when they are observed in public settings and in mixed-sex groups.

We cannot resolve this debate. Our goal in the discussion that follows is to understand how children begin to conceptualize gender as a dimension of their self-concept, as an organizing principle of social life, and as a guide to their behavior.

We do not expect a lifetime's work on gender identity to have been completed by the end of early school age. During this period, however, significant conceptual and emotional changes give the sex role greater clarity and highlight the relevance of one's sex in the overall self-concept.

The women of the Hopi, a Native American tribe of the southwestern United States, enjoy comparatively high status, because the land, house, and household furnishings belong to the wife and are passed from mother to daughter. Even though men function as village chiefs, the title of chief follows the female's line. In the traditional Hopi culture, the woman initiated a marriage proposal, and either the husband or the wife could initiate a divorce. To divorce her husband, a woman could simply pack up his belongings and leave them outside the door to the pueblo.

FIGURE 7.1

The development of the gender concept

1. Correct use of the gender labels.
2. Gender is stable.
3. Gender is constant.
4. Gender has a genital basis.

Understanding Gender

Understanding one's gender involves four components that emerge in a developmental sequence from toddlerhood through early school age (Kohlberg, 1966): using the correct gender label, understanding that gender is stable, understanding gender constancy, and understanding the genital basis of gender (see Figure 7.1).

The correct use of the appropriate gender label is the earliest component of sex-role identification to be achieved. The categorization of people as male and female is a natural category, much like the distinction between the familiar object and the stranger or between people and inanimate objects, which we discussed in Chapter 5. Even before the abstract categories *male* and *female* are understood, children learn by imitating their parents to refer to themselves as boys or girls. From infancy, parents make continual reference to a child's gender in such sentences as "That's a good boy" or "That's a good girl."

By the age of 2 1/2, children can accurately label other children as boys or girls, and by the age of 3, they can sort photographs of boys and girls. They can also apply gender labels such as *Mommy* and *Daddy, brother* and *sister,* and *boy* and *girl* accurately (Thompson, 1975; Leinbach & Fagot, 1986). Once they know these sex-related labels, children seek out cues that will help them make these distinctions correctly. Thus, their attention is directed to the differences between males and females.

Understanding gender constancy appears to emerge somewhat later, usually between ages 4 and 7 (Serbin, Powlishta & Gulko, 1993). There appears to be a relationship between understanding the genital basis of gender and understanding that gender is constant. In research involving 3-, 4-, and 5-year-olds, the majority of children who understood the genital differences between the sexes could also tell that a child's sex did not change simply because the child was dressed up to look like a member of the opposite sex. These young children understood that sex is a constant feature of a person, no matter how the person is dressed or whether the hair is long or short. The majority of the children who had no knowledge of genital differences were also unable to respond correctly to questions about constancy (Bem, 1989).

Sex-Role Standards

Sex-role standards are cultural expectations about appropriate behavior for boys and girls, and for men and women. What are the sex-role standards in American culture? In research on sex-role standards, one normally asks children to identify whether certain activities, occupations, or traits are more frequently associated with males, females, or both. For example, in the Sex-Role Learning Index, children are shown drawings of 20 objects traditionally associated with sex roles, 10 for the male sex role (such as a hammer, a shovel, and a fire helmet) and 10 for the female sex role (such as an iron, a stove, and dishes). By age 7, most children make a perfect score on this type of test, illustrating that they know how their society links gender and activities or occupations (Edelbrock & Sugawara, 1978; Beere, 1990; Serbin et al., 1993). Knowledge of sex-typed personality traits, such as gentle and affectionate or adventurous and self-confident, emerges somewhat later. In one study of over 550 children, sixth-graders answered about 90% of these types of questions correctly (Serbin et al., 1993).

The significance of an early-school-age child's knowledge about sex-role standards is the implication that these standards will shape the child's preferences and behaviors. Accompanying these expectations are conditional rewards, incentives, and sanctions. Adults not only expect things of a child in relation to the child's gender but also do things in order to produce compliance with these expectations. Some parents believe that boys should be assertive and fight for their rights. Others believe that boys should think carefully about what is right and wrong and guide their actions by reason rather than impulsive aggression. Each of these sets of parents has a conception of male attributes that they communicate to their sons by a variety of means over a long period of time. The toys parents give their children, the experiences to which they expose their children, and the activities in which they encourage their children's participation all reflect the parents' sex-role standards. By the time children reach early school age, they have been encouraged to adopt those standards and have been punished for what their parents have viewed as sex-inappropriate behavior. For example, young girls may be shamed for assertiveness by being told that they are acting "bossy," and young boys may be warned to "stop acting like a sissy."

Langlois and Downs (1980) compared the reactions of mothers, fathers, and peers to a child who was playing with same-sex and opposite-sex toys. Opposite-sex toy choices had different consequences for boys and girls. A girl was likely to be rewarded for playing with same-sex toys and punished for playing with opposite-sex toys, whether she was with her mother, her father, or a peer. Boys received more punishment from their peers for playing with same-sex toys than for playing with opposite-sex toys. Mothers were actually likely to *reward* boys more for opposite-sex play than for same-sex play. Fathers, however, were likely to punish boys for opposite-sex toy choices. The picture we get from this study is that girls experience more consistent sex-role socialization from their parents and their peers than do boys. Boys encounter more diverse and contradictory socialization pressures. In addition, fathers appear to be more consistent than mothers in guiding girls and boys toward traditional play behavior. Mothers seem to direct both boys and girls toward female-sex-typed activities.

Recent work on gender-role development suggests that, as the cognitive underpinnings related to the concept of gender mature, children form *gender schemes*, or personal theories about cultural expectations and stereotypes related to gender. Children tend to organize their perceptions, focus their attention, and

Pablo Picasso, Paulo as Torero, 1925. *Every culture has its own sex-role standards. For Spanish children, the matador is a standard of masculinity, combining bravery, grace, and skill.*

interpret information in such as way as to be consistent with their gender scheme (Levy & Carter, 1989; Bem, 1981; Martin & Halverson, 1987). Evidence suggests that, for boys, gender schemes play a role in the recollection of behavior from as early as age 2 (Bauer, 1993). By the kindergarten years, both boys and girls recall information that is consistent with their gender stereotypes better than information that is counter to the stereotype or that is more relevant to the opposite sex (Liben & Signorella, 1993). Among children aged 5–12, the greater their knowledge of sex-role standards, the greater their preference for same-sex peers and for sex-typed adult activities and occupations (Serbin et al., 1993).

Not all children are equally rigid in applying sex-role standards to themselves or to others. Flexibility in the application of sex-role standards to oneself and others appears to be influenced by both cognitive factors and socialization. Children appear to learn the stereotypes and expectations related to their own gender before learning the expectations for the opposite gender (Martin, Wood & Little, 1990). Preschool-age children are more likely to see gender-role transgressions (e.g., boys playing with dolls or girls pretending to be fire fighters) as more permissible than are older children, aged 6 and 7 (Smetana, 1986; Lobel & Menashri, 1993). In particular, young children who have more advanced abilities

TABLE 7.1	**Four Motives for Parental Identification**
Motive	*Definition*
Fear of loss of love	A child behaves like a parent in order to ensure a continued positive love relationship.
Identification with the aggressor	A child behaves like a parent in order to protect himself or herself from the parent's anger.
Identification to satisfy needs for power	A child behaves like a parent in order to achieve a vicarious sense of the power associated with the parent.
Identification to increase perceived similarity	A child behaves like a parent to increase his or her perceived similarity to the parent and thereby to share in the parents' positive attributes

to differentiate between moral norms (like telling the truth) and social norms (like saying "please" and "thank you") are also less stereotyped in their play activities and toy choices (Lobel & Menashri, 1993). Among 5- to 10-year-olds, training in multiple-classification skills (sorting objects into more than one category) is associated with more egalitarian, less stereotyped responses to gender-related tasks (Bigler & Liben, 1992).

Girls are generally more flexible about sex roles than boys. Young boys whose fathers live in the home typically have an earlier knowledge of sex-typed roles. However, if these fathers participate in nontraditional activities in the home, the boys' sex-role knowledge is delayed. Children whose mothers do nontraditional tasks develop a more flexible attitude, seeing more activities and occupations as appropriate for both males and females, and they themselves are more flexible in their preferences for activities, occupations, and friends (Serbin et al., 1993).

Identification with Parents

The third component of sex-role identification involves parental identification. *Identification* is the process through which one person incorporates the values and beliefs of another. To identify with someone is not to become exactly identical to that person, but to increase one's sense of allegiance and closeness to that person. Through the process of identification, ideals, values, and standards of the family and community are internalized so that they become a part of the individual's own belief system. During early school age, most children admire and emulate their parents. They begin to internalize their parents' values, attitudes, and worldviews. We emphasize identification as a major mechanism of socialization in childhood, but it can occur at any point in the life span.

Identification has received a great deal of attention in the psychological literature. The most persistent question raised is why children alter their behavior in the direction of becoming more like one parent or the other. What motives are satisfied in this process? There appear to be four substantially different theories about the motives for identification (see Table 7.1). Two of these processes are suggested by psychoanalytic theory: fear of loss of love and identification with the aggressor.

The *fear of loss of love* is a very primitive motive. It is founded on a child's initial realization of dependence on the parents. A child behaves like a parent in order to ensure a continued positive relationship. Eventually, the child incorporates

Identification is strengthened as a child tries to increase the actual physical similarities between himself and his father.

aspects of the loved one's personality into his or her own self-concept. The child can then feel close to the loved person even when they are not physically together (Jacobson, 1964). If a child can be like a loved parent, the parent's continuous presence is not required to reassure the child about that parent's love.

Identification with the aggressor was described in detail by Anna Freud (1936). This motive is aroused when children experience some degree of fear of their parents. In order to protect themselves from harm, they perform behaviors that are similar to those they fear. This kind of identification may give children a magical feeling of power as well as decrease the parents' tendency to aggress against them. Parents who see a great deal of similarity between themselves and their children are less likely to threaten or harm them.

Social learning theory focuses attention on a third motive for identification, the need for *status and power* (Mischel, 1966; Bandura, 1977, 1986). Studies of modeling show that children are more likely to imitate the behavior of a model who controls resources than they are the behavior of a model who is rewarded. The imitative behavior is motivated by a vicarious feeling of power experienced when they behave in the same way as the powerful model. Within a family, children are likely to have personality characteristics similar to those of the more dominant parent (Hetherington, 1967).

Kagan (1958) contributed a fourth motive for identification by suggesting that children behave as their parents do to increase the *perceived similarity* between them. Children attribute a number of valued characteristics to their parents, including physical size, good looks, special competencies, power, success, and respect. Children more readily share these positive attributes when they perceive a similarity between themselves and their parents. Children experience this sense of similarity in three principal ways: (1) by perceiving actual physical and psychological similarities, (2) by adopting parental behaviors, and (3) by being told about similarities by others. Increasing perceptions of similarity promote stronger identifications.

These motives apply to the process of identification at all ages and regardless of the sex of the identifier or the model. How do these motives influence the specific task of developing sex-role identification? For a particular child, one or another of these motives may dominate the dynamics of sex-role identification, but all four motives are involved in the process. The most obvious motive is perceived similarity (Heilbrun, 1974). At age 5 or 6, children recognize the similarity in gender with their same-sex parent. This perception is often enhanced by comments like "When you're a daddy, you'll do this, too" or "You have your mother's patience." As a result of the formation of the gender scheme, children pay close attention to behaviors of their same-sex parent and to references to expectations for children or adults of their sex.

As predicted by social learning theory, individual differences in sex-typed preferences in toys and play activities as well as in sex-role knowledge are linked to parental attitudes and behaviors. Parents who have more traditional sex-typed attitudes tend to have children who are more sex-typed in their play preferences and whose knowledge of sex-typed stereotypes develops at a younger age (Fagot & Leinbach, 1989; Weinraub et al., 1984). When mothers work outside the home, the children tend to form more flexible cognitions and less sex-typed preferences for activities and adult occupations. Evidence related to specific efforts to reduce gender-related stereotypes and to increase nontraditional preferences suggests that vicarious reinforcement of nontraditional or countertraditional behaviors may be effective with children, especially children in the age range of 4–10 (Katz & Walsh, 1991). Thus, parents can make deliberate efforts to encourage more flexibility in gender-role conceptualization and preferences by deliberately modeling atypical activities or by reading or devising stories that involve counterstereotypical situations.

Sex-Role Preference

The fourth component of sex-role identification is the development of a personal preference for the kinds of activities and attitudes associated with the masculine or feminine sex role. Preferences for sex-typed play activities and same-sex play companions have been observed among preschoolers as well as older children (Caldera, Huston & O'Brien, 1989; Maccoby, 1988). The attainment of these preferences is a more complex accomplishment than might be imagined. In fact, one's sex-role preference may fluctuate considerably throughout life.

One's *sex-role preference* depends primarily on three factors. First, the more closely one's own strengths and competencies approximate the sex-role standard, the more one will prefer being a member of that sex. Second, the more one likes the same-sex parent, the more one will prefer being a member of that sex. These two factors begin to have a significant impact on a child's sex-role preference as his or her self-concept becomes more clearly differentiated. As children enter school and are exposed to the process of evaluation, they begin to have a more realistic sense of their unique qualities. As they acquire this self-reflective ability, they can appreciate the similarities and discrepancies between (1) self and the sex-role standard and (2) self and the same-sex parent.

The third determinant of sex-role preference consists of environmental cues as to the value of one sex or the other. The cues may emanate from the family, ethnic and religious groups, the media, social institutions (such as the schools), and other culture carriers. Many cultures have traditionally valued males more than females and have given males higher status (Huber, 1990). To the extent that such culturally determined values are communicated to children, males are likely to establish a firmer preference for their sex group, and females are likely to experience some ambivalence toward, if not rejection of, their sex group. In other words, it is easier to be happy and content with oneself if one feels highly valued and more difficult if one feels less valued.

Some families develop a strong preference regarding the sex of an expected child. In a sample of over 6000 married women in the United States, 63% of those who had never had children expressed a preference that their first child be a male

TABLE 7.2   Dimensions of Sex-Role Identification

Dimension	Sex-Role Outcome
Developing an understanding of gender	I am a boy; I will grow up to be a man.
	I am a girl; I will grow up to be a woman.
Acquiring sex-role standards	Boys are independent; they play with trucks.
	Girls are interpersonal; they play with dolls.
Identifying with the same-sex parent	I am a lot like Daddy. I want to be like him when I grow up.
	I am a lot like Mommy. I want to be like her when I grow up.
Establishing a sex-role preference	I like being a boy. I'd rather be a boy than a girl.
	I like being a girl. I'd rather be a girl than a boy.

and their second a female. Women who considered an even number of children ideal wanted to have an equal number of boys and girls. Women who preferred an uneven number of children wanted more sons than daughters (Westoff & Rindfuss, 1974). If the wish for a child of a particular sex is not fulfilled and the parents do not shed their commitment to the "missed" sex, the family may present obstacles to sex-role preference.

In a longitudinal study of Swedish children from birth to age 25, the parents' prenatal preferences for a son or daughter were related to perceived problems in the mother-child and father-child relationships (Stattin & Klackenberg-Larsson, 1991). Mothers' perceptions of problems in the parent-child relationship, especially the relationship between fathers and their nonpreferred daughters, were significantly related to the fathers' disappointed hopes for a son. Looking back on their relationship with their parents at age 25, nonpreferred daughters were especially likely to note problems in their relationship with their parents, saying that their mothers did not have time for them, that their fathers were stricter with them and had less time for them, and that their relationships with their fathers were, in general, worse than the relationships described by preferred daughters.

Thus, it is possible to know what sex one is and what behaviors are expected of members of that sex and yet wish one were a member of the opposite sex. In our own experience, if groups of men and women are asked whether they ever wished to be of the opposite sex, many more women than men will admit to having wished to be of the opposite sex. This finding may reflect some perceived advantages of the male role in our culture. It may reflect the more serious sanctions against men who value or exhibit behaviors defined as feminine. And it may reflect the greater flexibility that girls and women exhibit in their gender schemes, which permits them access to a wider range of behaviors as desirable and possible.

The four components of the acquisition of sex-role identification—(1) developing an understanding of gender, (2) learning sex-role standards, (3) identifying with parents, and (4) establishing a sex-role preference—are summarized in Table 7.2. The outcome of the process for an individual child depends greatly on the characteristics of his or her parents and their approach to sex-role socialization, the child's personal capacities and preferences, and the cultural and familial values placed on one gender or the other.

A child's sex-role identity becomes a basic cognitive scheme that influences the interpretation of experiences (Bem, 1981; Martin, 1989). Children learn that people are grouped into two sexes; males and females. In our society, this dichotomy tends to impose itself on a wide array of social situations, even situations like work, play, and politics, where one's genital sex is not especially relevant. Once children have this powerful category, they go about the business of figuring out how to apply it. They recognize people as men and women, boys and girls, and they identify themselves as members of one of these two groups. They form expectations based on this categorization that certain toys, interests, and behaviors are appropriate for boys and others are appropriate for girls; certain activities, dispositions, and occupations are appropriate for men and women. These expectations are generally reinforced by the beliefs of the older children and adults with whom the children interact. Thus, the gender schemes that are conceived during childhood play a significant role in shaping the direction of a child's daily activities and in formulating a preliminary vision of the future.

Early Moral Development

Early moral development involves a process of taking parental standards and values as one's own. This process is called *internalization*, and it takes place gradually over the early-school-age years. During toddlerhood, a child's attention is focused on limits of and standards for behavior. Children feel that demands for proper behavior do not come from within themselves but emanate from the external world. During early school age, standards and limits become part of a child's self-concept. Specific values are acquired from parents, but they become integrated elements of the child's worldview.

A 3-year-old boy, for example, may take great delight in hitting his dog with a stick. In the midst of one of these attacks, his mother scolds him. She insists that he stop and explains that it is cruel to hurt the dog. If her punishment is not very harsh, she may have to remind the boy on several other occasions that hitting the dog is not permitted. As the boy internalizes this standard, he begins to experience internal control over his own behavior. He may see the dog lying calmly in the sun and, with a gleam in his eye, begins to pick up a stick. At that moment, his behavior is interrupted by a feeling of tension, which is accompanied by the thought that it is wrong to hit the dog. If the standard has been successfully internalized, the emotional tension and the thought will be sufficient to inhibit the boy from hitting the dog.

For early school-age children, achievements in moral development include changes in three interrelated domains:

1. Learning the moral code of one's community and making judgments about whether something is good or bad, right or wrong.
2. Experiencing the array of emotions that foster caring about others and that produce anxiety, guilt, and remorse when a moral standard has been violated.
3. Taking appropriate actions to inhibit negative impulses or to give help and act in a caring, helpful manner, depending on the situation.

A variety of theories explain how these domains of knowledge, emotion, and action evolve to produce the internalized moral behavior we consider appropriate for the early-school-age child.

Learning Theory

Behavioral learning theory provides explanations for shaping moral behavior. Within this theoretical perspective, moral behavior and the process of internalization are viewed as a response to environmental reinforcements and punishments

Scolding is a negative consequence that should reduce the likelihood of an undesired behavior.

(Aronfreed, 1969). Moral behaviors, just like other operant responses, can be shaped by the consequences that follow the behavior. A positive, prosocial behavior, like offering to help put the toys away or comforting another child who is distressed, is likely to be repeated if it is rewarded. If a behavior is ignored or punished, it is less likely to occur. If a child performs a misdeed or defies an authority and suffers negative consequences, these consequences ought to reduce the likelihood that such behavior will recur. If a child is in an unpleasant or painful environment and performs a behavior that reduces or eliminates the unpleasantness, he or she is more likely to perform this same behavior again in similar situations. For example, if a child says, "I'm sorry; I'll try to do better next time," and this apology reduces the parent's anger or irritability, this behavior is likely to be repeated at other times when the parent is angry at the child. Internalization may result, therefore, as the behaviors that lead to a more comfortable, less unpleasant or threatening environment become more common and the behaviors that produce parental anger or conflict drop away.

The special case of *avoidance conditioning* is often viewed as a paradigm for understanding internalization in behavioral terms. Having been punished in the past for wrongdoings, a child contemplating a misdeed should feel tension. Avoiding or inhibiting the impulse to misbehave reduces the tension and is therefore reinforcing. This process may occur even when the person who has been involved in administering the punishments is absent. In other words, the scenario of thinking about a wrong or naughty action, feeling the anxiety that is associated with past punishments, and reducing that anxiety by exercising restraint may take place mentally, without any observable behavior. Over time, the reinforcement of tension reduction that is linked to controlling a wrongful impulse strengthens the tendency to inhibit the impulse, and the child's behavior becomes less and less impulsive.

Social learning theory offers another source of moral learning: the observation of models. By observing and imitating helpful models, children can learn prosocial behavior. By observing the negative consequences that follow the misdeeds of models, children also can learn to inhibit their own misbehavior. Their moral behavior is not limited to the actions they have performed. It may be based on expectations formulated from observations of how the conduct of relevant models has been rewarded or punished (Bandura, 1977). Children may even formulate abstract rules, concepts, and sets of propositions about moral behavior by extracting meaningful elements from several incidents of observational learning. In the process, children form a mental representation by selecting and organizing observed responses and use this mental model to guide, compare, and modify their own moral behavior (Bandura, 1991).

Finally, cognitive learning theory describes how moral behavior is influenced by the interaction of situational factors and expectations, values, and goals that have been derived from earlier learning (Mischel, 1973). For example, some people place great value on success in athletics and may be more tempted to violate norms in order to succeed in such a milieu than in an academic setting. The expectation that a misdeed will be observed and punished leads to greater resistance to temptation than does the expectation that a misdeed will go unnoticed. Similarly, the belief that positive, prosocial behaviors are expected and will be noticed influences a child's generosity and helpfulness (Froming, Allen & Jensen, 1985). These factors suggest that, although enduring moral qualities may be developed through the consistent reinforcement of empathetic, sensitive, and just responses, the specific situation will also influence the extent to which moral behavior is displayed (Carroll & Rest, 1982).

Cognitive-Developmental Theory

Cognitive-developmental theorists have focused on the orderly sequence of development of the child's thoughts about moral issues. Piaget (1932/1948) described the major transition in moral judgment as a shift from heteronomous to autonomous morality. In *heteronomous morality*, rules are understood as fixed, unchangeable aspects of social reality. Children's moral judgments reflect a sense of subordination to authority figures. An act is judged as right or wrong depending on the letter of the law, the amount of damage that was done, and whether or not the act was punished. In *autonomous morality*, children see rules as products of cooperative agreements. Moral judgments reflect a child's participation in a variety of social roles and in egalitarian relationships with friends. Give-and-take with peers highlights mutual respect and mutual benefit as rewards for holding to the terms of agreement or abiding by the law.

Expanding on this view, cognitive-developmental theorists have described a sequence of stages of moral thought (Kohlberg, 1976; Gibbs, 1979; Damon, 1980). As children become increasingly skillful in evaluating the abstract and logical components of a moral dilemma, their moral judgments change. At the core of this change is the mechanism called *equilibration*. Stage changes in moral reasoning are associated with efforts to reconcile new perspectives and ideas about basic moral concepts, such as justice, intentionality, and social responsibility, with existing views about what is right and wrong. Children's reasoning may be thrown into disequilibrium by external sources, such as their parents' use of explanations and inductions regarding a moral dilemma or encounters with friends who reason differently about a moral conflict. In addition, children's own cognitive maturation, especially the ability to think abstractly and hypothetically about interrelated

TABLE 7.3   Stages of Moral Judgment

Level I: Preconventional

Stage 1	Judgments are based on whether behavior is rewarded or punished.
Stage 2	Judgments are based on whether the consequences result in benefits for self or loved ones.

Level II: Conventional

Stage 3	Judgments are based on whether authorities approve or disapprove.
Stage 4	Judgments are based on whether the behavior upholds or violates the laws of society.

Level III: Postconventional

Stage 5	Judgments are based on preserving social contracts based on cooperative collaboration.
Stage 6	Judgments are based on ethical principles that apply across time and cultures.

Source: Based on Goslin (Ed.), 1969, and Lickona (Ed.), 1976.

variables, determines how their reasoning about moral dilemmas will be structured (Piaget, 1975/1985; Walker, 1988).

Kohlberg (1969, 1976) described three levels of moral thought, each characterized by two stages of moral judgment (see Table 7.3). At Level I, *preconventional morality*, Stage 1 judgments of justice are based on whether a behavior is rewarded or punished. Stage 2 judgments are based on an instrumental view of whether the consequences will be good for "me and my family." The first, and to some degree the second, stages of Level I characterize children of early school age. Level II, *conventional morality*, is concerned with maintaining the approval of authorities at Stage 3 and with upholding the social order at Stage 4. Level III, *postconventional morality*, brings an acceptance of moral principles that are viewed as part of a person's own ideology rather than simply being imposed by the social order. At Stage 5, justice and morality are determined by a democratically derived social contract. At Stage 6, a person develops a sense of universal ethical principles that apply across history and cultural contexts. We will consider Levels II and III in greater depth in Chapter 10.

Research indicates that Stage 6 reasoning is rarely achieved, and very few people function at this level consistently. One can think of a few individuals, such as Gandhi, Mother Teresa, and Martin Luther King, Jr., whose moral judgments were based on ethical principles that apply across time and culture, transcending the laws and conventions of a specific society. Kohlberg (1978) admitted the rarity of this type of thinking and argued that Stage 6 reasoning is more of a hypothetical construct to which moral reasoning may progress. Most of the research has included children, adolescents, and young adults as subjects. From the point of view of our psychosocial perspective, it is reasonable to conclude that Stage 6 reasoning is most likely to be observed beginning in middle adulthood, when people become preoccupied with issues of generativity and concerns that transcend their own lifetime.

When children argue about how a game should be played, they introduce new points of view and create cognitive disequilibrium. This is a positive process that fosters new levels of reasoning.

Research on movement through the stages suggests that they reflect a developmental sequence. People do not necessarily use only one level of moral reasoning at a time. Over time, however, one finds a gradual shift toward the maximum use of one perspective and the decreasing use of less mature views (Carroll & Rest, 1982; Kohlberg, 1979; Rest, 1983). The process of movement from one stage to the next appears to involve a period of consolidation followed by a period of transition (Snyder & Feldman, 1984; Walker & Taylor, 1991b). During consolidation, most people use one modal stage of reasoning, along with some reasoning at one stage below and very little at one stage above the mode. However, in a period of transition, reasoning is expanded in the direction of the next more advanced stage and becomes more evenly divided between two adjacent stages with more and more reasoning occurring at the more advanced stage over time.

This theory of moral development leads one to expect the moral reasoning of early-school-age children to be dominated by concerns about the consequences of their behavior. At Stage 1, children's judgments of good and bad, right and wrong, are based on whether a behavior has been rewarded or punished. At Stage 2, children's moral judgments are based on whether the behavior will bring about benefits for them or for other people they care about. Thus, young children's moral outlook has a utilitarian orientation (Kohlberg, 1976). Research with first-graders confirms that this outlook is quite common, whether children are discussing hypothetical or real-life moral dilemmas (Walker, 1989).

The preoccupation with consequences highlights the significance of the home and school environments in establishing and supporting young children's moral code. To build a basis for making moral judgments, children need to understand the consequences of their behaviors for others. Thus, we can appreciate clearly why inductions—explanations that emphasize the effects of one's actions on others—are such a key disciplinary method for young children. In addition, the moral climate of home and school provide the early structure for the content of the moral code. Behaviors that are linked to moral principles, such as telling the truth, being generous, respecting the feelings of others, and being respectful of authority figures, become woven into children's concepts of right and wrong. The clarity of this moral code depends on the consistency with which positive examples lead to positive outcomes and negative examples lead to negative outcomes (Garrod, 1993).

Not all rules or prohibitions have to do with moral concerns. There is a difference between morality, which usually involves the rights, dignity, and welfare of others, and *social convention*, which involves socially accepted norms and regulations (Turiel, 1983). For example, in the preschool context, stealing another child's toy would be a moral transgression; a transgression of social convention would be getting up and wandering away during large-group time. Preschool-age children are consistently able to differentiate between moral and social-convention transgressions. They understand that moral transgressions are wrong because they affect the welfare of others and that social-convention transgressions are wrong because they are disruptive or create disorder (Smetana, 1985). Social-convention transgressions depend on the situation. At home, it may be permissible to get up from the table during dinnertime before everyone has finished and go somewhere to play, whereas it is not permissible to get up from the snack table at preschool until the teacher says everyone may leave. Moral transgressions apply more consistently across settings: It is morally wrong to steal at home, at preschool, or at a friend's house. It is significant that children as young as 3 and 4 make this distinction when they evaluate transgressions. In addition, in contrast to social-convention transgressions, young children tend to judge moral transgressions to be more serious, deserving of greater punishment, and independent of the rules or authority in a situation (Smetana, Schlagman & Adams, 1993).

Psychoanalytic Theory

The psychoanalytic theorists suggest that a moral sense develops as a result of strong parental identification. The focus of the psychoanalytic theory of moral development is on the internalization of values and the factors that sustain impulse control under conditions of temptation. The earlier discussion of identification with parents and the discussion of superego development in Chapter 3 provide the basis for understanding the psychoanalytic treatment of moral development. Classical psychoanalytic theory views a child's conscience, or superego, as an internalization of parental values and moral standards. It holds that the superego is formed during the phallic stage, between the ages of about 4 and 7, as a result of the conflict between internal sexual and aggressive impulses and the ways in which the parents deal with the behavioral manifestations of those impulses.

According to psychoanalytic theory, the more severely a parent forces a child to inhibit her or his impulses, the stronger the child's superego will be. Freud (1925/1961) assumed that males would develop more highly differentiated and punitive superegos than females because he believed that males' impulses are

Pablo Picasso, Four Girls with Chimera, 1934. *The child's conscience develops out of the tension between strong id impulses and the need for parental love. In this etching, the innocence of the four young girls is contrasted with a terrible monster. According to psychoanalytic theory, the monster is actually within each of us, making demands and wanting its needs satisfied.*

more intense. He also believed that because of the greater impulsive energy demonstrated by males, boys are treated more harshly by their parents than are girls. Finally, Freud suggested that males identify with their fathers for two reasons: fear of losing the father's love and fear of the father as an aggressor. This identification with the father is an intense one and should lead to a fully incorporated set of moral standards. According to Freud, a female identifies with her mother for a single reason: fear of loss of love. Since Freud considered this motivation for identification less intense than that of the male, he believed that the female's superego would be correspondingly weaker.

Research on the Development of Conscience   Research on the development of conscience has failed to support Freud's hypotheses. Studies that have investigated the ability to resist temptation or to confess after wrongdoing have found that young girls are better able to resist temptation than boys and show a pattern of decreasing moral transgressions over the toddlerhood and early school years (Mischel, Shoda & Rodriguez, 1989). Studies that have attempted to assess the relative contributions of mothers and fathers to children's moral behavior have found that mothers' values and attitudes are strongly related to the moral behavior of their children, whereas the values and attitudes of fathers have little relationship to their children's moral behavior (Hoffman, 1970). Finally, research has found that the children of parents who use harsh physical punishment do not have higher levels of internalization. They are likely to inhibit impulsive behaviors in the presence of their parents, but when they are observed with their peers away from home, they tend to be physically aggressive and do not control their behavior well (Hart, Ladd & Burleson, 1990; Pettit, Dodge & Brown, 1988). Parental warmth, deemphasis on power assertion, democratic decision making, and modeling of resistance to temptation appear to contribute to high levels of prosocial behavior and social responsibility (Maccoby, 1992; Kochanska, 1991).

Neopsychoanalytic Theory   These findings raise doubts about Freud's views on the formation of conscience and the relative strength of the superego in males and females. In fact, psychoanalytic theory now tends to view the critical time for moral development as coming earlier in life, in infancy (Mahler, 1963; Kohut, 1971). Infants develop an awareness of three domains: the body and its physical experiences and needs; the existence of others; and the relations between the self and others (Beit-Hallahmi, 1987). All subsequent psychological growth must be assimilated into these three domains. Thus, according to this view, the origins of moral reasoning and behavior have links to very early feelings about the self and its needs, especially the feelings of pleasure and pain. Morality has a basis in a young child's awareness of others who are valued, and on behaviors that strengthen or threaten the bonds between the self and these others. This view suggests that some basis of early morality lies in the child's own sense of self-love, a wish to enhance and not to harm or violate the self. Another basis is the extension of this self-love to the other and the wish to preserve the feelings of connection, trust, and security that have been established in the early parent-infant relationship. The moral aspect of the self is built on the close, affectional bond with the caregiver, including the positive feelings of empathy and connectedness that emerge in this early relationship and the internalization of early prohibitions that are accompanied by emotional signals such as anger and disapproval (Emde, Johnson & Easterbrooks, 1987; Emde et al., 1991).

Freud's work remains a significant contribution to the area of moral development because he drew attention to the powerful role of the superego and the ego ideal in motivating and inhibiting behavior. He also created interest in the origins of moral beliefs in early childhood. However, his description of the process by which parental values are incorporated into a child's moral code appears to be faulty. Most likely, Freud underestimated the power of the need to reassure oneself about parental love. The strong affectional bonds between a parent and a child are the most effective forces in promoting positive moral behavior. Freud's analysis of gender differences in morality reflect a cultural stereotype that characterizes men as more rational, logical, and in control of their emotions and impulses than women. Women, in contrast, are portrayed as temptresses, distracting men from their responsibilities and luring them into immoral behaviors.

Research on Empathy and Perspective Taking

Empathy has been defined as sharing the perceived emotion of another—"feeling with another" (Eisenberg & Strayer, 1987, p. 5). This definition emphasizes one's emotional reaction to the observation of another person's emotional condition. By merely observing the facial expressions, body attitudes, and vocalizations of another person, a child can identify that person's emotion and feel it personally. The range of emotions with which one can empathize depends on the clarity of the cues the other person sends and on one's own prior experiences.

The capacity for empathy changes with development. Hoffman (1987) described four levels of empathy, especially in reference to the perception of another person's distress:

Global empathy: You experience and express distress as a result of witnessing someone else in distress. Example: A baby cries upon hearing the cries of other infants.

Egocentric empathy: You recognize distress in another person and respond to it in the same way you would respond if the distress were your own. Example: A toddler offers his own cuddle blanket to another child who is crying.

Empathy for another's feelings: You show empathy for a wide range of feelings and anticipate the kinds of reactions that might really comfort someone else.

Empathy for another's life conditions: You experience empathy when you understand the life conditions or personal circumstances of a person or group.

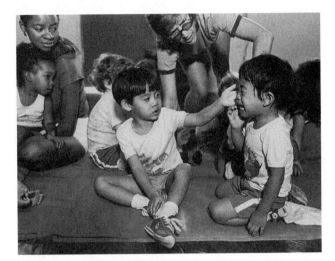

Empathy and perspective taking contribute to the development of prosocial behavior. Young children are able to respond to the distress of others and offer consolation.

The capacity for empathy begins in infancy and evolves as children achieve new levels of understanding about the self and others, as well as a greater capacity to use language to describe their emotions. Very young children appear to be able to recognize and interpret auditory and facial cues that suggest emotional expressions in others. In the newborn nursery, when one infant starts to wail, the other infants begin to cry (Martin & Clark, 1982; Sagi & Hoffman, 1976). Three- and four-year-olds can recognize the emotional reactions of other children to specific problems. Both American and Chinese children were able to recognize "happy" and "unhappy" reactions by age 3. The differentiation among "afraid," "sad," and "angry" developed slightly later. The specific cues for these feelings were linked to cultural patterns of expressing emotions. Nevertheless, it was clear that the youngest children in both cultural groups could recognize emotional states in another person (Borke, 1973). In addition to being able to correctly recognize another's emotions, early-school-age children can usually identify the circumstances that may have produced another child's emotional response, especially responses of anger and distress, and can understand and empathize with another child's feelings. Children are most likely to think that external events produce emotional reactions: "The teacher made her put her toys away," or "He tripped over the blocks." But they can also think about internal states that may produce strong emotions: "He's mad because he didn't get a turn," or "She's sad because her stomach hurts" (Hoffner & Badzinski, 1989; Fabes et al., 1988, 1991).

The ability to identify pleasurable and unpleasurable emotions in others and to empathize with those emotions makes the child receptive to moral teachings. Empathy can serve a proactive function by enlisting a child's efforts to help another person. It can also serve a reactive function by generating remorse for having caused an emotional state in another person. In either case, the child is able to experience how the other person feels and therefore to modify his or her own behavior (Hoffman, 1987).

Another element in the development of a conceptualization of morality is the child's appreciation of the other person (Chandler & Boyes, 1982). *Perspective taking* refers to a person's ability to consider a situation from the point of view of another person. This faculty requires a recognition that someone else's point of view may differ from one's own. It also requires the ability to analyze the factors that may account for these differences. When children can assess these factors, they can begin to transcend the personal perspective and attempt to look at a situation from another person's point of view.

Imagine a child who wants to play with another child's toy. If the first child thinks, "If I had that toy, I would be happy, and if I am happy, everyone is happy," then she or he may take the toy without anticipating that the other child will be disappointed. Although empathy provides an emotional bridge that enables children to discover the similarities between self and others, it does not teach them about differences. Learning about differences requires perspective taking. In fact, several psychologists have argued that the capacity to take another person's perspective is achieved only gradually through peer interaction and peer conflict (Flavell, 1974; Piaget, 1932/1948; Selman, 1971).

Children of 4 and 5 frequently exhibit prosocial behaviors that evidence an understanding of others' needs. The most common of these behaviors are sharing, cooperating, and helping. Two examples illustrate the nature of this kind of social perspective taking:

> The path of a child with an armload of Playdough was blocked by two chairs. Another child stopped her ongoing activity and moved the chair before the approaching child reached it.
> A boy saw another child spill a puzzle on the floor and assisted him in picking it up. (Iannotti, 1985, p. 53)

Interestingly, the young children who score highest in formal measures of perspective taking do not necessarily exhibit high levels of prosocial behavior in preschool settings. At this early age, an important determinant of whether children will spontaneously offer help is whether they can pinpoint others' emotional states in real-life situations.

Robert Selman (1980) studied the process of social perspective taking by analyzing children's responses to a structured interview. Children see audiovisual filmstrips that depict interpersonal conflicts. They are then asked to describe the motivation of each actor and the relationships among the various performers. Four levels of social perspective taking are described. At Level 1, the youngest children (4–6 years old) recognize different emotions in the various actors, but they assume that all the actors view the situation much as they do. The children at Level 4 (about 10–12 years old) realize that two people are able to take each other's perspective into account before deciding how to act. Furthermore, they realize that each of those people may view the situation differently from the way they do.

Many moral dilemmas require that children subordinate their personal needs for someone else's sake. To resolve such situations, children must be able to separate their personal wants from the other person's. Selman's research suggests that children under 10 can rarely approach interpersonal conflicts with this kind of objectivity.

Evidence of the gradual change in perspective-taking abilities can be seen in a study of how young children evaluated the emotional reactions of children who were categorized as victims and victimizers (Arsenio & Kramer, 1992). Children aged 4, 6, and 8 were shown pictures and told an accompanying story (see Figure 7.2):

> Two children were at their coat lockers in school, and one child showed the other child some candies that he or she (two sets of drawings with female and male characters depending on sex of child) had received. The child who had been shown the candies saw that the locker room was empty, and that child (the victimizer) took the candies out of the victim's coat and put them into his or her own pocket. (p. 917)

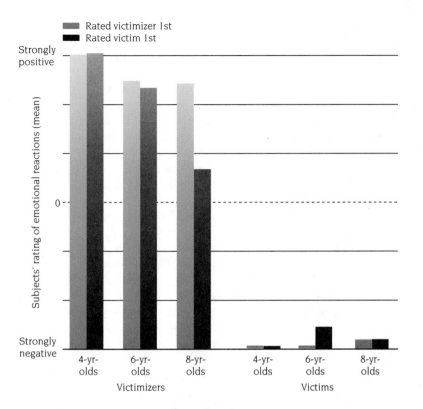

Rated victimizer 1st
Rated victim 1st

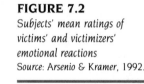

FIGURE 7.2

Subjects' mean ratings of victims' and victimizers' emotional reactions
Source: *Arsenio & Kramer, 1992.*

After seeing the pictures and hearing the story, the children were asked to tell and then rate how the two children felt at the end of the story. The responses were categorized by whether the children described the victim or the victimizer first. All the children identified the victim as having strong negative feelings, regardless of whether they described the victim first or second. Most of the children at each age level evaluated the victimizer as having happy or good feelings. Only the oldest children attributed some mixed emotions to the victimizer, and then only when they described the victim first. These older children could see that there might be some negative emotional consequence to victimizing someone, although the predominant view, based on the positive consequences of the actions, was to assume that the victimizer would be basically happy. The results of this research suggest that the young child's ability to understand the negative emotions of the victim will not necessarily outweigh the anticipated positive emotions of being the victimizer.

Research on Parental Discipline

The last contribution to a theory of moral development that we will consider comes from the research on parental discipline, which was discussed in detail in Chapter 6. When disciplining a child, the parent emphasizes that certain behaviors are really wrong and should be inhibited while other behaviors are positive and should be repeated. This distinction between good and bad behaviors and the accompanying parental approval or disapproval begins to form the content of the child's moral code.

In addition, the parent uses some specific techniques of discipline. Four elements seem to be important in determining the impact of these techniques on the child's future behavior. First, the discipline should help the child interrupt or inhibit the forbidden action. Second, the discipline should point out a more acceptable form of behavior so that the child will know what is right in a future instance. Third, the discipline should provide some reason, understandable to the child, why one action is inappropriate and the other more desirable. Fourth, the discipline should stimulate the child's ability to empathize with the victim of his or her misdeeds. In other words, children are asked to put themselves in their victim's place and to see how much they dislike the feelings they caused in the other person.

In considering discipline as a mechanism for teaching morality, one becomes aware of the many interacting and interrelated components of a moral act. The discipline techniques that are most effective in teaching morality to children are those that help them to control their own behavior, to understand the meaning of their behavior for others, and to expand their feelings of empathy. Discipline techniques that do not include these characteristics may succeed in inhibiting undesired behavior but may fail to achieve the long-term goal of incorporating moral values into future behavior. Kochanska (1991, 1993) argued strongly that the child's temperament is often overlooked in determining the likely effectiveness of certain disciplinary techniques. In particular, children who are temperamentally fearful, who are inhibited in response to novel stimuli, and who choose to retain close proximity to their mothers as young children are especially sensitive to messages of disapproval. For these children, just a small dose of parental criticism is adequate to promote moral internalization, and too much power assertion appears to be counterproductive. In contrast, children who are highly active and who are insensitive to messages of disapproval appear to require much more focused and directive discipline, especially a consistent program of recognizing and rewarding good behaviors while minimizing the situations and stimuli that may provoke impulsive or aggressive actions.

In addition to using approval or disapproval, parents guide moral development by modeling positive, prosocial behaviors and by talking with their children about moral issues. In Chapter 6, we discussed the use of scaffolding to promote more effective communicative competence. In much the same way, parents can scaffold their child's moral reasoning by raising questions about moral decisions their children are facing and introducing new arguments or alternative points of view as their children think about moral conflicts (Walker & Taylor, 1991a).

Review

The child of early school age is in the process of developing an initial moral code. The five approaches to this issue are summarized in Table 7.4. Each highlights an essential element of the larger, more complex phenomenon. Learning theory points out that an external reward structure inhibits or reinforces behavior. Cognitive theory suggests that conceptual immaturity characterizes this early phase of moral development. Psychoanalytic theory is especially concerned with the relationship between parental identification and the development of conscience. The work on empathy and perspective taking shows that moral behavior requires an emotional and cognitive understanding of the needs of others. These prosocial skills help children to appreciate how other children or adults may be experiencing reality. With this insight, children can modify their own actions to benefit others. Theory and research on parental discipline suggest that parents promote moral development when they try to increase children's understanding of the effects of their behavior on others. It seems reasonable to conclude that moral behavior involves an integration of moral judgments, understanding of the reward structure, parental identification, and empathy for others.

TABLE 7.4   Contributions to the Study of Moral Development

Conceptual Source	Significant Contributions	Consequences for a Particular Aspect of Moral Development
Learning theory	Relevance of an external system of rewards and punishments Imitation of models Formation of expectations about the reward structure	Moral behavior Internalization of a moral code
Cognitive theory	Conceptual development of notions of intentionality, rules, justice, and authority Stages of moral judgment	Moral judgments Distinction between moral transgression and social-convention transgressions
Psychoanalytic theory	Parental identification Formation of the superego	Internalization of parental values Experience of guilt
Research on empathy and perspective taking	Ability to experience another's feelings begins very early and changes with age Ability to recognize differences in point of view emerges slowly during the early and middle school years Peer conflict, peer interactions, and specific role-taking training all increase perspective-taking skills	Empathy heightens concern for others; helps inhibit actions that might cause distress Perspective taking can foster helping and altruism
Research on parental discipline	Parents define moral content Parents point out the implications of a child's behavior for others Creation of a reward structure Differential impact of power, love withdrawal, warmth, and inductions	Moral behavior Moral reasoning Internalization of moral values Empathy and guilt

Self-Theory

We can think of the self-concept as a theory that links a person's understanding of the nature of the world, the nature of the self, and the meaning of interactions between the self and the environment (Epstein, 1973, 1991; Epstein et al., 1993). In general, the orientation of the self-theory is to make transactions between the self and the world turn out as positively and beneficially for the person as possible. One's theory about oneself draws on such inner phenomena as dreams, emotions, thoughts, fantasies, and feelings of pleasure or pain. It is also based on the consequences of transactions with the environment. As with any set of concepts, the complexity and logic of the self-theory depend on the maturation of cognitive functions. Further, since the self-theory is based on personal experiences and observations, one would expect it to be modified over the life course by changing physical and socio-emotional competencies as well as by participation in new roles.

One of the earliest psychological analyses of self-theory was provided by William James (1961/1892). He described two elements of the self, the "me" and the "I." The "me" is the element that we are most familiar with in developmental research. It is the self as object, the self one can describe, including physical

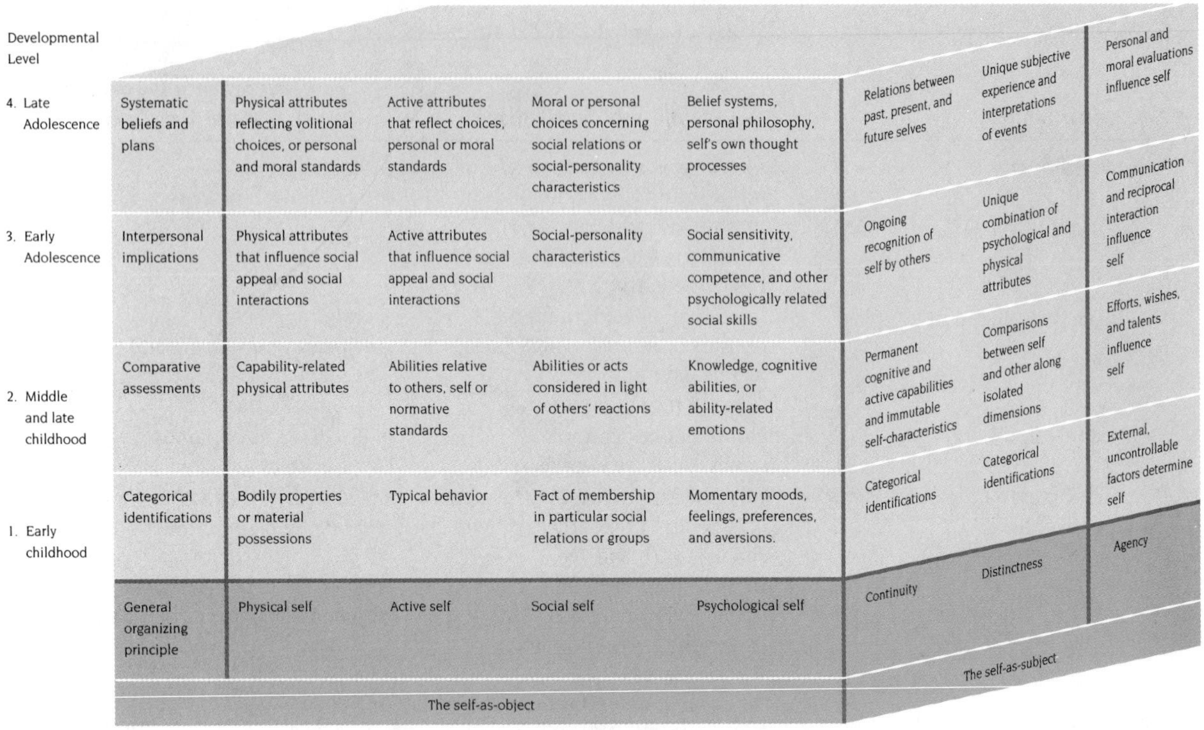

Developmental Level	General organizing principle	Physical self	Active self	Social self	Psychological self	Continuity	Distinctness	Agency
4. Late Adolescence	Systematic beliefs and plans	Physical attributes reflecting volitional choices, or personal and moral standards	Active attributes that reflect choices, personal or moral standards	Moral or personal choices concerning social relations or social-personality characteristics	Belief systems, personal philosophy, self's own thought processes	Relations between past, present, and future selves	Unique subjective experience and interpretations of events	Personal and moral evaluations influence self
3. Early Adolescence	Interpersonal implications	Physical attributes that influence social appeal and social interactions	Active attributes that influence social appeal and social interactions	Social-personality characteristics	Social sensitivity, communicative competence, and other psychologically related social skills	Ongoing recognition of self by others	Unique combination of psychological and physical attributes	Communication and reciprocal interaction influence self
2. Middle and late childhood	Comparative assessments	Capability-related physical attributes	Abilities relative to others, self or normative standards	Abilities or acts considered in light of others' reactions	Knowledge, cognitive abilities, or ability-related emotions	Permanent cognitive and active capabilities and immutable self-characteristics	Comparisons between self and other along isolated dimensions	Efforts, wishes, and talents influence self
1. Early childhood	Categorical identifications	Bodily properties or material possessions	Typical behavior	Fact of membership in particular social relations or groups	Momentary moods, feelings, preferences, and aversions.	Categorical identifications	Categorical identifications	External, uncontrollable factors determine self
General organizing principle		Physical self	Active self	Social self	Psychological self	Continuity	Distinctness	Agency

The self-as-object

The self-as-subject

FIGURE 7.3

A developmental model of self-understanding
Source: Damon and Hart, 1988.

characteristics, personality traits, social roles and relationships, thoughts, and feelings. The "I" is more subjective. It is the self as one who is aware of one's own actions. It can be characterized by four fundamental features: a sense of agency or initiation of behaviors, a sense of uniqueness, a sense of continuity from moment to moment and day to day, and an awareness of one's own awareness—metacognition (Damon & Hart, 1988).

James thought of the "I" as the essential domain through which one experiences a vivid, compelling sense of self-sameness and meaning from day to day. Yet, he thought of it as largely unmeasurable. However, building on these ideas and more contemporary research and theory, Damon and Hart (1988) devised a model of self-understanding that includes both the me (self-as-object) and the I (self-as-subject) (see Figure 7.3). Along the front face of the cube, the self-as-object, Damon and Hart identified four domains of the "me": physical self, active self, social self, and psychological self. Along the side face of the cube, self-as-subject, they identified three domains of the "I": continuity, distinctiveness, and agency. Development, shown by the vertical changes in each of these seven domains, is traced from early childhood through late adolescence. According to Damon and Hart, one can recognize evidence of self-understanding in each domain even in early childhood. Rather than seeing development as movement from an awareness of physical properties and behaviors at an early age to an awareness of social relationships and psychological traits at a later age, they provided evidence that what changes is the general organizing principle around which all aspects of the "me" and the "I" are synthesized.

Developmental Changes in the Self-Theory

At each stage, the self-theory is the result of a person's cognitive capacities and dominant motives as they come in contact with the stage-related expectations of the culture (Stipek, Recchia & McClintic, 1992). In infancy, the self consists primarily of an awareness of one's independent existence. The infant discovers body boundaries, learns to identify recurring need states, and feels the comfort of loving contact with caregivers. During the second year of life, self-recognition and the evolving sense of the self as a causal agent add new dimensions to the self-theory. Gradually, these experiences are integrated into a sense of the self as a permanent being who has an impact on the environment, existing in the context of a group of other permanent beings who either do or do not respond adequately to the infant's internal states.

In toddlerhood, the self-theory grows through an active process of self-differentiation. Children explore the limits of their capacities and the nature of their impact on others. Because of toddlers' inability to entertain abstract concepts and their tendency toward egocentrism (the perception of oneself as the center of the world), their self-theories are likely to depend on being competent and being loved. There is little recognition of social comparisons (being better or worse than someone else), but an increasing sensitivity to the positive and negative reactions of others. By the age of 3½ or 4, toddlers seem to understand the idea of competition in a game, and they seem to take pleasure in winning as well as some disappointment in losing. However, it is unclear to what extent they actually reflect on the self, making judgments of their strengths and weaknesses or distinguishing their various arenas of competence (Emde & Buchsbaum, 1990).

During early and middle school age, the self-theory becomes more differentiated. Children can distinguish between the real self (how one actually is) and the ideal self (how one would like to be). They can recognize some discrepancies between how they describe themselves and how their parents or friends may describe them (Oosterwegel & Oppenheimer, 1993). And they can differentiate among various areas of activities like math, reading, and music, indicating perceptions of strength in certain areas and weakness in others (Eccles et al., 1993).

According to Damon and Hart (1988), in early childhood, the self is understood as an accumulation of *categorical identifications*. No additional linkage or significance is taken from these categorical statements, simply a recognition that they exist.

> Examples: What kind of person are you? *I have blue eyes.* Why is that important? *It just is.*
> What kind of a person are you? *I'm Catholic.* What does that say about you? *I'm Catholic, and my mother is, and my father is, and my grandmother, and my grandfather, and I'm Catholic too.* (pp. 59–60)

In middle and late childhood, the organizing principle shifts to *comparative assessments*. Self-understanding relies on comparisons of oneself with social norms and standards or of oneself with specific other people.

> Examples: What are you like? *I'm bigger than most kids.* Why is that important? *I can run faster than everybody.*
> What are you like? *I'm not as smart as most kids.* Why is that important? *It takes me longer to do my homework.* (pp. 62–63)

From ages 4 to 6, children become more aware that people have different points of view. An understanding of logical relations contributes to an appreciation of the concept of cultural norms: If one is in a certain role, one is expected to act in a certain way. Sex-role standards are especially important in this regard. Children are very sensitive to any implication that they are not living up to the expectations of how a boy or girl ought to act. Children are also aware of moral imperatives that define good and evil. All these cognitive gains make a child more sensitive to social pressure, more likely to experience feelings of guilt or failure,

The pleasure associated with achieving competence in a valued skill boosts self-esteem.

and more preoccupied with issues of social comparison, self-criticism, and self-evaluation. At the same time, the child remains largely dependent on adults for material and emotional resources and is therefore highly attuned to positive and negative parental feedback. For these reasons, the issue of self-esteem becomes especially salient during the early- and middle-school-age periods.

Self-Esteem

For every component of the self—the physical self, the self as reflected in others' behavior, and the array of personal aspirations and goals—a person makes an evaluation of worthiness. This self-evaluation, or *self-esteem*, is based on three essential sources: (1) messages of love, support, and approval from others; (2) specific attributes and competencies; and (3) the way one regards these specific aspects of the self, both in comparison with others and in relation to one's ideal self (Pelham & Swann, 1989). Feelings of being loved, valued, admired, and successful contribute to a sense of worth. Feelings of being ignored, rejected, scorned, and inadequate contribute to a sense of worthlessness. These very early affective experiences contribute to a general sense of pride or shame, worthiness or worthlessness, that is captured in the global statements children make about themselves even as early as age 3 or 4 (Eder, 1989; Eder, Gerlach & Perlmutter, 1987).

Information about specific aspects of the self is accumulated through experiences of success and failure in daily tasks or when particular aspects of one's competence are challenged. A young child may develop a positive sense of self in athletics, problem solving, or social skills through the encouraging reactions of others as well as through the pleasure associated with succeeding in each of these areas (Harter, 1985).

With experience in a variety of roles and settings, each specific ability takes on a certain level of importance for a person. Not all abilities are equally valued at home, at school, and by friends. People may believe they have abilities in some areas but not in those they consider highly important. Others may believe they have only one or two areas of strength, but they may highly value those areas and believe them to be critically important to overall success. Self-esteem is influenced by the value one assigns to specific competencies in relation to one's overall life goals and personal ideals. Thus, it is possible to be a success in the eyes of others and still feel a nagging sense of worthlessness. Similarly, it is possible

Play and the Child's Environment

In war-torn Somalia, children watched as warlords and armed gangs terrorized the people, destroyed buildings, and extorted money from relief workers. This bizarre violence can be seen reflected in play, as children imitate the thieves and thugs with "guns" made of scraps of wire, string, and cloth.

After a decade of fighting, the Soviet military finally withdrew from Afghanistan, leaving reminders like this tank (as well as an estimated ten million land mines). The adults look with dismay at the destruction of their farmland, but the children turn the remnants of war into novel pieces of play equipment.

Some places are designed to support children's play. In some communities, only one or two children would play on this equipment at a time, but it seems the more the merrier for these Navajo boys.

The street is an important play space in many neighborhoods—for skateboarding, rollerblading, bike riding, baseball, or stickball.

A friendly game of hockey takes shape on this Newfoundland street.

In Philadelphia, the street is a good place to go to cool off in the spray of a water hydrant.

Of course, the sidewalk is a favorite spot for play. It doesn't take much equipment to get a fast-paced game of jump rope going.

A front yard can quickly become the site of a small business. These girls are selling homegrown fruit in Berkeley, California. Those of us who didn't have lemon trees in our yard as children might remember selling lemonade or fresh-picked berries.

Where there are no streets or sidewalks or playgrounds nearby, the open fields provide plenty of room for play. This young New Zealander runs with her pet sheep through the high country near Canterbury.

to feel proud and confident even though others may not value the activities and traits in which one takes great satisfaction.

By adulthood, one has a pervasive sentiment about one's worth that sets a tone of either optimism or pessimism about the future. One's level of self-esteem contributes to one's willingness to take risks, expectations of success or failure, and expectations that one will have a meaningful impact on others.

Rosenberg (1979) considered the impact on self-esteem of what he described as *contextual dissonance*. Children are influenced by the social groups that immediately surround them. During early school age, children emerge from the continuity of their families and neighborhoods into the more diverse context of school. This new context may complement or contrast with the major social characteristics of the family, specifically religion, race, and social class. Rosenberg cited evidence of the negative effects of a dissonant environment in all three of these areas. Catholics who had been raised in a non-Catholic neighborhood were likely to have lower self-esteem than those raised in a Catholic one. Similar findings were observed among Protestants and Jews raised in dissonant neighborhoods. Racial dissonance and economic dissonance have also been found to be related to low self-esteem. For example, black preschool-age children in an all-black Mississippi rural town reportedly had higher self-esteem than did those in a racially mixed Michigan urban area (McAdoo, 1985). The implication of these studies is that self-esteem is bolstered by a feeling of continuity and belongingness. Conversely, experiences of dissonance and lack of fit between one's personal values or qualities and the qualities valued by the community may result in lowered self-esteem.

Many people are thrust into situations that undermine their basically positive self-esteem (Setterlund & Niedenthal, 1993). Circumstances that may lead to disruption in a basic sense of self-worth include adolescents' moving to a new high school where peers' values are discrepant from their home and personal values, immigrants' being viewed as outsiders by the members of their new community, or individuals' being hired to perform an important leadership role in an organization where the other employees have a very different background and training. Finding oneself the only female in a classroom of male students or the only male in an office of female workers may have similar undermining effects on self-esteem.

Feelings of positive self-worth provide a protective shield around the self. If a person has a positive, optimistic self-evaluation, then messages that are negative and incongruent with that self-evaluation will be deflected. A person with high self-esteem will explain a failure by examining the task, the amount of time needed for its completion, the other people involved, or the criteria for evaluating success and failure. People with high self-esteem use a variety of strategies to minimize the importance of negative feedback. They do not permit a failure to increase doubt about their basic worth. By contrast, people with low self-esteem will see any failure as new evidence of their lack of worth (Brown & Mankowski, 1993; Brown & Gallagher, 1992).

Low self-esteem appears to be associated with a lack of clarity about one's essential characteristics. For example, a person with low self-esteem may endorse contradictory pairs of descriptive terms, seeing the self as both timid and bold or flexible and rigid. This confusion is linked to inconsistency, instability, and a lack of confidence in one's essential nature. Because of this confusion, people with low self-esteem are likely to have difficulty deciding what social situations to participate in. They are likely to place themselves in situations where they receive

Early-school-age children know how to make one another look ridiculous. Sometimes the line between playful goofing around and hurtful teasing is hard to distinguish.

contradictory or negative social messages about their worth and thereby expose themselves to even greater confusion (Brockner, 1984; Swann, 1990). Over time, lack of certainty about oneself is likely to be related to problems with identity achievement and to greater vulnerability to negative feedback that increases confusion and produces negative emotions (Campbell, 1990; Baumgardner, 1990; Setterlund & Niedenthal, 1993).

Some scholars have speculated about the possible negative consequences of an unrealistically positive self-esteem. For example, people with high self-esteem seem to deflect failure messages in one area by exaggerating their abilities in another area (Brown & Smart, 1991). This strategy may be viewed as producing an inappropriately grandiose assessment of the self that is not validated by the views of others. Others suggest that parents and teachers may be so intent on providing self-enhancing strategies for their children, focusing on building up the "me," that the children become indifferent to the plight of others and lose sight of the kinds of positive feelings associated with helping others (Burr & Christensen, 1992). We speculate that it may be very important to develop strategies to enhance self-esteem in children who have low self-esteem or whose self-esteem has declined because of current experiences of failure or loss. This type of intervention may help prevent serious episodes of depression (Pelham, 1991). However, it is not clear whether it is advisable to take active steps toward self-esteem enhancement for children who already have a healthy, positive sense of self-worth.

Self-Esteem and the Early-School-Age Child

At each life stage, as individuals set new goals for themselves or as discrepancies in competence become apparent, temporary periods of lowered self-esteem may be anticipated. Research on self-esteem suggests that early-school-age children may be especially vulnerable to fluctuations in feelings of self-worth (Kegan, 1982; Cicirelli, 1976; Long, Henderson & Ziller, 1967). Preschool- and kindergarten-age children assess their own competencies to be significantly higher than do children in Grades 1–4. In addition, girls in the early school grades are more critical of their abilities than are boys and have lower expectations of success (Frey & Ruble, 1987; Butler, 1990).

Toddlers have been described as highly egocentric. In general, they feel good about themselves and do not differentiate between competence and social approval; rather, they respond to all positive experiences as evidence of their ultimate importance and value. They are much more likely to react to positive feedback after a success than to react to negative feedback after a failure (Stipek et al., 1992). They also use imitation to build a greater sense of their own mastery (Butler, 1989).

Early-school-age children, by comparison, are increasingly aware of the discrepancy between their own competencies and what they recognize as the skills expected of them by their teachers and parents or the skills exhibited by older children. They are able to view themselves as objects of the evaluations of others. They are also aware of the importance of acceptance by adults and peers outside the family, especially their teachers and classmates (Weinstein et al., 1987). These newly valued others may not be as proud of their skills or as understanding about their limitations as their family members are. In peer competition, they begin to feel anxiety about their performance and about how their abilities will be evaluated in comparison with those of others (Butler, 1989). At school, for example, young children often make critical comments about one another's work. Criticisms tend to outnumber compliments, and boys tend to be more critical than girls of their peers' work (Frey & Ruble, 1987). The combination of open peer criticism and a heightened emphasis on peer competition may make the school an environment in which one's self-esteem is frequently challenged.

Finally, early-school-age children are beginning to achieve a degree of internalization of social norms, including ideals to be attained as well as prohibitions, which they apply in a rather strict, rule-bound way. They are highly critical of rule violations, whether committed by themselves or by others. Intentions, motives, and special circumstances are less salient to early-school-age children than the overt consequences of behavior. Thus, their newly formed capacity for guilt may lead to a heightened anxiety over failure to live up to their own moral code.

For all these reasons, the early-school-age child is likely to experience feelings of depression and worthlessness. This decrease in self-esteem may be seen as a temporary fluctuation. Young children need frequent reassurance from adults that they are competent and that they are loved. They need numerous opportunities to discover that their unique talents and abilities are useful and important, and that they can have a positive impact on others. As competencies increase, as thought becomes more flexible, and as the child makes meaningful friendships, we expect self-esteem to rise.

Group Play

Group Games

The early-school-age child continues to use vivid fantasies in play. During this period, a new form of play emerges. Children show interest in group games that are more structured and somewhat more oriented to reality than play that is based primarily on imagination. Ring-around-the-rosie, London Bridge, and farmer-in-the-dell are examples of early group play. Hide-and-seek and statue-maker are more complex games of early school age. They involve more cognitive complexity, physical skill, and ritual. These games combine fantasy with an emphasis on peer cooperation. Group play is a transitional form of play between the fantasy play of the toddler and the team sports and other games with rules of the middle-school-age child (Erikson, 1977).

The few rules of group games are simple enough so that a child can use them effectively to begin a game and determine a winner without the help of an adult.

Usually, no team concept is involved in these games. A game is played repeatedly, so that many children have an opportunity to win. The particular pleasure that children derive from these games seems to result more from peer cooperation and interaction than from the possibility of being a winner (Garvey, 1977).

Many of these games permit children to shift roles. A child is the hider and then the seeker, the catcher and then the thrower, the statue-maker and then the statue. Through group play, children experience the reciprocal nature of role relationships. Whereas many of their social roles are fixed—son or daughter, sibling, student—in play with peers, children have opportunities to experience a variety of perspectives (Lee, 1975; Sutton-Smith, 1972).

Friendship Groups

Friendship relations in early school age are based on the exchange of concrete goods and the mutual enjoyment of activities. Friendships are maintained through acts of affection, sharing, or collaboration in fantasy or constructive play. By the age of 4 or 5, children who have stable friendships become skilled in coordinating their interactions with their friends, creating elaborate pretend games and being willing to modify their play preferences so that both members in the friendship have a chance to enjoy the kinds of play they like best (Park, Lay & Ramsay, 1993). Children build a snow fort together, play space adventure with one another, or sleep over at one another's houses. Friendships may be broken by the taking of a toy, hitting, or name-calling (Damon, 1977).

Young children tend to evaluate situations on the basis of outcomes rather than intentions. Therefore, they are often harsh in assigning blame in the case of negative outcomes. For example, children were asked how much they should be blamed for another child's getting hurt. The "injury" took place in six different hypothetical situations. In the case of lowest level of responsibility, the child was accidentally hurt by someone's toy, but the owner did not actually cause the injury. At this level, 6-year-olds were more likely than older children or adults to blame themselves for the outcome (Fincham & Jaspars, 1979). Because of this rigid approach to social responsibility, peer play is frequently disrupted by quarrels, "tattling" on others, and hard feelings about injustices.

Even though children appear to be drawn into the active world of peer friendships, this is an uneven, difficult, and often extremely frustrating terrain for many early-school-age children. For example, many 5- and 6-year-olds participate in play fighting. In a study of children's perceptions of play fighting, Italian and British children of ages 5, 8, and 11 were surveyed about the differences between real fighting and play fighting (Smith et al., 1992). About half the children liked play fighting, somewhat more boys than girls. But about 80% thought that there was a risk that play fighting could lead to a serious, "real" fight. This might happen if there was an accidental injury, if the play fighting got carried away into mean name-calling, or if, when one child accidentally hurt the other, the second child mistook the injury as purposeful and hurt the first child back. Five-year-olds said that if play fighting turned into real fighting they would tell an adult. No matter whether the other child was a friend or not, they believed that such a transgression had to be handled with a serious intervention by a grown-up. The older children were more likely to forget about it, especially if the other person was a friend.

One of the most notable characteristics of young children's friendship groups is that they are likely to be segregated by sex. When boys and girls are free to choose play companions, they tend to choose others of their own sex. This pattern

Pablo Picasso, Circle of Children, 1952. *Little children typically grow up within the supportive companionship of same-sex friendship groups.*

of same-sex social groupings among children is found not only in the United States but in most other cultures (Edwards & Whiting, 1988). In one longitudinal study, children aged 4½ were found playing with same-sex friends about three times more often than with opposite-sex friends. By age 6½, they were 11 times more likely to be playing with same-sex friends (Maccoby & Jacklin, 1987).

The significance of the formation of same-sex social groups is that boys and girls grow up in quite distinct peer environments (Maccoby, 1988, 1990). Boys and girls tend to use different strategies to achieve dominance or leadership in their groups. Boys are more likely to use physical assertiveness and direct demands; girls are more likely to use verbal persuasiveness and polite suggestions. The verbal exchanges in all-boy groups are apt to include frequent boasts, commands, interruptions, heckling, and generally playful teasing. Boys try to top one another's stories and to establish dominance through verbal threats. The interactions in all-girl groups tend to include agreeing with and acknowledging the others' comments, listening carefully to one another's statements, and talking about things that bind the group together in a shared sentiment or experience. In mixed-sex groups, girls discover that the leadership and interpersonal skills they have developed in their all-girl groups are not very effective in controlling the behaviors of boys. As a result, their negative views of boys are reinforced and their tendency to seek all-girl peer interactions increases.

Of course, many young children do form friendships with children of the opposite sex. These friendships may begin as early as infancy or toddlerhood between children who live in the same neighborhood or attend the same day-care center. These friendships seem to be sustained by a compatibility of interests and play preferences and may survive the trend toward seeking same-sex friendships, even during the early and middle school years (Howes & Phillipsen, 1992). However, the general tendency to form same-sex friendship groups is an important aspect of social development that is established during the early childhood years and continues into adolescence (Bukowski et al., 1993). Even though a boy and a girl grow up in the same culture, in the same neighborhood, and even in the same family, the tendency to establish separate play and friendship groups fosters the development of distinctive gender-linked communication strategies and makes the achievement of mutual understanding between boys and girls difficult.

In addition to the preference for same-sex friends, boys and girls tend to prefer to interact in different-size groups. Early-school-age girls seem to enjoy dyadic interactions over larger group situations, whereas boys seem to enjoy the larger group settings (Benenson, 1993). This is not to say that boys and girls cannot function effectively in both dyadic and larger peer-group situations, but when given their choice, boys tend to prefer the group and girls the dyad. These two configurations, the group and the dyad, provide different opportunities for intimacy, different needs to exercise dominance and control, and different problems in the coordination of action. They provide models for somewhat different forms of adult social relationships, the dyad being associated with intimacy between partners or in parent-child relationships, and the peer group being associated with sports teams, work groups, and families.

The Psychosocial Crisis: Initiative Versus Guilt

As children resolve positively the toddlerhood crisis of autonomy versus shame and doubt, they emerge from that stage with a very strong sense of themselves as unique individuals. During early school age, they shift their attention toward investigation of the external environment. They attempt to discover the same kind of stability, strength, and regularity in the external world that they have discovered within themselves.

Initiative

Initiative is the active, conceptual investigation of the world in much the same sense that autonomy is the active, physical manipulation of it (Erikson, 1963). The child's motivation for and skill in investigation depends on the successful development of a strong sense of autonomy. When children have acquired self-control and confidence in themselves, they can perform a variety of actions and observe the consequences. They discover, for example, what things make parents or teachers angry and what things please them. They may deliberately perform a hostile act in order to evoke a hostile response. Children's curiosity about the order of the universe ranges from the physical to the metaphysical. They may ask questions about the color of the sky, the purpose of hair, the nature of God, the origin of babies, or the speed at which fingernails grow. They take things apart, explore the alleys and dark corners of their neighborhood, and invent toys and games out of odds and ends.

Initiative, like autonomy, is an expression of the "I," the executive branch of the self (Damon & Hart, 1988). Initiative is an expression of agency, an outgrowth of early experiences of the self as a causal agent which continues to find expression as children impose themselves and their ideas and questions onto their social world.

One expression of initiative is children's playful exploration of their own bodies and sometimes their friends'. It is not uncommon to find 5- and 6-year-olds intently involved in a game of "doctor" in which both "doctor" and "patient" have their pants off. Boys of this age may occasionally be observed in a game that is won by the individual who can achieve the longest urine trajectory. Girls report occasions on which they have attempted to urinate from a standing position "in the same way a boy does." Both boys and girls engage in some form of masturbation. These behaviors are evidence of children's growing curiosity about and pleasure in their bodies and their physical functioning.

Children may express initiative in isolation, by attempting to discover how things work and by building or inventing novel devices. They may also express initiative in social situations by asking questions, asserting their presence, and taking leadership. In one study of social competence, children described the strategies they used to enter a peer-group play situation (Dodge et al., 1986). Two children were playing a game (they were referred to as the hosts), and a third child was asked to enter the room and try to initiate play with the others. The entry episode was videotaped and coded. In addition, both the child who tried to initiate play and the two hosts were interviewed about the episode and asked to evaluate how successful the entry child had been. Three strategies for initiating interaction were judged to be effective and were associated with other evidence of social competence:

1. Children established common ground by giving meaningful information in response to questions.
2. Children engaged in a positive, friendly interchange with the others.
3. Children did not show evidence of negative, irritable behaviors. The children who were least successful in initiating entry into the play "were disruptive, . . . made nagging, weak demands, . . . engaged in incoherent behaviors, or . . . disagreed with hosts without citing a rule or reason" (Dodge et al., 1986, p. 25).

Guilt

Guilt is an emotion that accompanies the sense that one has been responsible for an unacceptable thought, fantasy, or action (Izard, 1977). Guilt is recognized as a fundamental emotion that usually is accompanied by remorse and a desire to make reparation for real or imagined wrong-doing. It has the adaptive function of promoting social harmony because it disrupts or inhibits aggressive actions and leads people to ask for forgiveness or to try to compensate for wrongs they may have done.

Three theories offer slightly distinct explanations for the dynamics that underlie feelings of guilt (Zahn-Waxler & Kochanska, 1990). The psychoanalytic perspective views guilt as an emotional reaction to one's unacceptable sexual and aggressive impulses. These impulses are especially threatening during the phallic stage, when hostility and feelings of sexuality toward one's parents become a focus of the child's wishes and must be repressed.

Work on empathy, guided by Martin Hoffman (1982), suggests that guilt may be awakened at a very early age through emotional arousal and sensitivity to another person's emotional distress. This view of guilt based on empathy is not defensive; it is closely linked to prosocial feelings and the basic emotional ties between infants and their caregivers.

The third, more cognitive, perspective suggests that guilt occurs when one fails to act in accord with one's own personal standards and beliefs. This view supposes a more advanced level of self-reflection and the ability to compare one's

Occasionally, a child experiences an increasingly burdensome amount of guilt rather than the usual sense of initiative. One expression of overwhelming guilt is a strong, irrational fear of some object or situation. This fear is called a *phobia*. Some common phobias of early childhood are a fear of going to school, of the dark, and of some kind of animal. These fears preoccupy the child's fantasies and limit his or her ability to explore the environment. The child thinks a lot about the object of fear and experiences a great deal of anxiety in connection with these thoughts.

The case of school phobia is an interesting example. An estimated 17 children per 1000 experience school phobia each year (Davison & Neale, 1990). The phobia consists of a dread of some aspect of the school situation, such as a teacher, another child, a janitor, or even eating school food. As the time to go to school arrives each morning, the child's anxiety increases. The child may complain of nausea or stomach pain and may even vomit. Once parents agree to let the child stay home, the anxiety and symptoms fade quickly—until the next morning (Coolidge, 1979).

In the psychoanalytic perspective, school phobia is a conflict related more closely to separation from the parents—usually the mother—than to a fear of school itself (Phelps, Cox & Bajorek, 1992). The initial fear of some event at school is echoed in the parents' reluctance to separate from the child. At a symbolic level, the child senses that his or her mother is in danger of serious illness or death. These fears are a projection of the child's unacceptable hostile feelings toward the mother. This threat to the mother can be averted only if the child stays home to protect her. Thus, going to school is equated with losing mother, childhood, and safety. When the actual fears of school are not confronted and the unconscious hostility toward the mother is not expressed, the idea of going to school becomes more and more frightening.

A phobia may also be understood as a means of directing anxiety and guilt over unacceptable thoughts, behaviors, or fantasies to a specific target. Rather than

BOX 7.1

Childhood Phobias

Pablo Picasso, Little Girl Standing, *1945. For some children, an overburdening sense of guilt makes the world appear to be a fearsome place rather than an invitation to experimentation.*

accept personal responsibility for inappropriate behavior, the child projects the unacceptable impulses onto an element of the environment, such as a horse or a dog. The child is not doing fearful and harmful things; they are being done by something out there that evokes the child's fear.

Through the phobia, the child expresses guilty feelings without having to take personal blame. In that sense, the phobia serves as a temporary protective device until the child can identify and control those impulses that are specifically linked to social disapproval. For the child who cannot take responsibility for socially devalued impulses or who experiences a great deal of anxiety in many areas, the range of feared objects and settings may grow rather than diminish. The extremely phobic child fears danger in most of the environment and cannot distinguish between fears that emanate from personal impulses and those that are realistic appraisals of external danger.

behaviors against personal standards. In this theory, guilt begins to be experienced in early and middle school age as children begin to be more comparative in their organization and evaluation of self.

Every culture imposes some limits on legitimate experimentation and investigation. Some questions may not be asked; some acts may not be performed. Adults' reactions determine whether the child will learn to view specific behaviors, such as aggressiveness, sexual play, or masturbation, as wrong or as acceptable. Children gradually internalize cultural prohibitions and learn to inhibit their curiosity in the taboo areas. One taboo shared by most cultures is the prohibition of incest (Gagnon, 1977; McCary, 1978). Most children learn that any behavior that suggests sexual intimacy between family members is absolutely forbidden. Even the thought of such a relationship comes to generate feelings of anxiety and guilt. The child's curiosity in other domains is limited to the extent that the family and the school impose restrictions on certain areas of inquiry or action. The psychosocial crisis of initiative versus guilt is resolved positively when children develop the sense that an active, questioning investigation of the environment is informative and pleasurable. Inquiry is tempered by a respect for personal privacy and cultural values. However, the preponderant psychological state of mind is curiosity and experimentation. The child learns that, even though certain areas are off limits, efforts to understand most aspects of the world are appropriate.

Guilt, like other negative poles of the psychosocial crises, can have an adaptive function. As children grow in their sense of empathy and in their ability to take responsibility for their actions, they are able to acknowledge when their actions may have caused harm or when their words may have been hurtful to someone else. Normal levels of guilt have been associated with positive levels of prosocial behavior and high levels of empathy (Tangney, 1991). Feelings of guilt generally lead to remorse and some attempt to set things right again, to restore the positive feelings in a relationship.

At the extreme, however, some children suffer from overwhelming guilt. These children feel that each of their questions or doubts about the world is inappropriate. They frequently experience guilt about their own impulses and fantasies, even when they have taken no actions and no negative consequences have resulted. They begin to believe that their thoughts and actions are responsible for much of the misfortune or unhappiness of others. For example, young children of depressed mothers express unusually high levels of distress, concern, and feelings of responsibility for others' unhappiness. Mothers who are consistently sad set an example of blaming themselves for most of the bad things that happen. In addition, depressed mothers are likely to withdraw love when the child has misbehaved, a discipline technique associated with high levels of guilt and anxiety (Zahn-Waxler et al., 1990). In this kind of environment, a child learns to restrict new behaviors out of fear that they may cause harm or unhappiness to someone else. In effect, the child comes to feel that curiosity itself is taboo and feels guilty whenever it is aroused. The child who resolves the initiative-guilt crisis in the direction of guilt is left to rely almost totally on his or her parents or on other authorities for directions on how to operate in the world.

The psychosocial crisis of initiative versus guilt highlights the intimate relationship between intellectual curiosity and emotional development. During this stage, the parents and the school transmit the cultural attitudes toward experimentation, curiosity, and investigation. They also make demands that direct the child's curiosity away from familial, subgroup, and cultural areas of taboo. Children are expected to develop the ability to control their own questions and behavior. Whereas violations may bring disapproval and punishment, successful

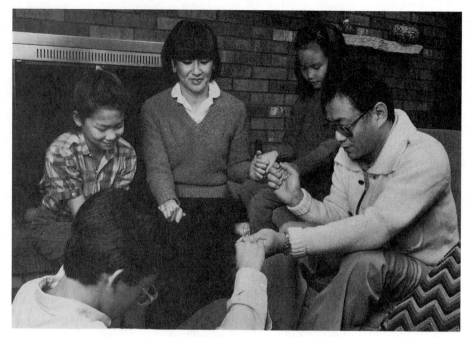

In a shared moment of family prayer, children identify with their parents' ethical and moral values and strengthen their ego ideal.

self-control may attract no notice whatsoever. Children must develop a strong internal moral code that will help them avoid punishment. They must also develop the ability to reward themselves for correct behavior. The more areas of restriction that are imposed on children's thinking, the more difficult it will be for children to distinguish between legitimate and inappropriate areas of investigation. The only way that children have of coping with this problem is to develop a rigid moral code that restricts many aspects of thought and action.

The Central Process: Identification

The discussion of the developmental tasks during early school age points directly to identification as the central process in the resolution of the conflict between initiative and guilt. Children at this age actively strive to enhance their self-concepts by incorporating into their own behavior some of the valued characteristics of their parents. Identification is one mechanism that children use to maintain connection with their parents. Children identify even with parents who are extremely brutal. Since most of the behaviors that these children incorporate are aggressive ones, the children of aggressive parents often tend to be aggressive toward others. Parental identification allows children to feel that their parents are with them even when they are not physically present. This feeling of connection with parents provides an underlying sense of security for children in a wide variety of situations.

Viewed from another perspective, identification allows children a growing sense of independence from their parents (Jacobson, 1964). Children who know how their parents would respond in a given situation no longer need the parents' physical presence to direct their behavior. Children who can praise or punish themselves for their actions are less dependent on their parents to perform these functions.

Parental identification affects children's development in two rather different ways. On the one hand, the closeness with parents provides the basis for the incorporation of parental sanctions and prohibitions. Once children have integrated these guidelines for behavior, they are bound to feel guilty whenever they anticipate abandoning them. On the other hand, the security that results from strong parental identification allows children increased freedom when they are away from their parents. The child whose parental identification is strong is more likely to question the environment, take risks, and initiate action.

Identification with parents results in a strengthening of the child's personality. An important outcome of early-school-age identification is the formation of an ideal self-image, which psychoanalytic theorists sometimes refer to as the *ego ideal* (Freud, 1929/1955; Sandler et al., 1963). The conscience not only punishes misdeeds but also rewards actions that bring children closer to some aspect of their ideal self-image. The ideal self is a complex view of the self as it may be in the future, including skills, profession, values, and personal relationships. The ideal self is a fantasy, a goal that is unlikely to be attained even in adulthood. Nonetheless, the discrepancy between the real self and the ideal self is a strong motivator. As children strive to achieve their ideal, they attempt new activities, plan things that strain the limits of their abilities, take risks, and resist temptations that might interfere with their desired goals.

The ego ideal is more unrealistic during early school age than it is at later stages. Children fantasize anything they wish about themselves in the future. They take their parents' values very literally and use them to project an ideal person of mythic proportions. The ideal self may include the strength of Hercules, the wealth of Queen Elizabeth II, the wisdom of Confucius, and the compassion of Jesus. The lack of realistic constraints on the ego ideal allows children to investigate and experience vicariously certain human qualities that may always be beyond their reach. As people grow older, it is important that the fantasy of the ideal self-image become increasingly attainable, although still beyond what has been attained. People who find it difficult to modify their ideal self-images become vulnerable to personal frustration and psychological despair because they are unable to be what they wish. Many 6-year-old children may wish to become president of the United States. This largely unrealistic fantasy is very exciting and, for some, ennobling. However, very few people actually achieve this position. By the time one reaches early adulthood, it is important to have developed an occupational ideal that is closer to what is actually attainable.

Identification with parents is the process by which the ideal self-image and moral prescriptions are blended into the child's personality. To the extent that children are unable to control their behavior so that it corresponds to the sanctions and ideals that they have internalized, they will experience guilt. To the extent that children's behavior approaches their ideals and conforms to internalized sanctions, they will experience feelings of self-confidence that will allow them to take initiative. The balance between guilt and self-confidence determines the eventual resolution of the psychosocial crisis of initiative versus guilt.

The crisis of initiative versus guilt captures the child's need to question existing norms and the emerging feelings of moral concern when these norms are violated. This crisis does not focus specifically on intellectual development; rather, one must assume that the level of questioning that takes place during this stage is possible only because of an increase in cognitive complexity. The process of positive parental identification promotes the incorporation of cultural norms and strengthens the child's sense of competence. Socialization during this stage may foster a creative openness or an anxious dread of novelty.

Applied Topic
The Impact of Television

If you were to look around the homes of American families in the early 1940s, you would find that only a few of the most wealthy families had televisions. Today over 90% of American families have at least one TV set, and many families have more than one. College students have television sets in their dormitory rooms, hospitals provide televisions in the rooms, motels and hotels have televisions with additional pay channels for viewing movies, there are televisions that can be plugged into the cigarette lighter of the car for "on-the-road viewing," and there are hand-held televisions that children can carry with them just like small radios and tape players. The centrality of television as a force in daily life was vividly portrayed in the movie *Rain Man*, in which the main character becomes intensely anxious if he thinks he is going to miss his regular, daytime television programs.

Televisions are operated an average of about 7 hours per day in American homes (Steinberg, 1985). Studies of the viewing time of individuals of different ages suggest that even infants are exposed to about half an hour of television daily. The pattern of hours of viewing is shown in Figure 7.4. On average, children in the age range 4–6 watch about 2½ hours of television daily (Liebert & Sprafkin, 1988). This average, of course, gives no indication of the wide variation of TV watching by children in this age range. Some children watch as much as 6 or 8 hours of television a day on the weekends. A study of first-graders found that about one-third watched 4 or more hours of television daily and about one-tenth watched none (Lyle & Hoffman, 1972).

Since television is so pervasive in our lives, it makes sense to ask about its impact on development. How do the amount of time spent watching television and the content of the programs that are watched influence the cognitive and socioemotional development of young children? To what extent is television a stimulus for optimal development? Can we draw any implications that might be useful to parents and teachers who have responsibility for guiding young children's choices in regard to television viewing?

Cognitive Consequences

Many parents and educators worry that television is turning our children into a generation of couch potatoes who are lulled into a life of mental and physical passivity. A review of over 200 studies of the impact of television on children's cognitive development concluded that the evidence was mixed (Landers, 1989b). Television viewing does appear to replace certain other activities, such as going to the movies, reading comic books, listening to the radio, and participating in organized sports. Williams and Handford (1986) compared the daily activities of adults and children in three Canadian towns: one that had no television (NOTEL), one that had only one television channel (UNITEL), and one that had four channels (MULTITEL). Data were collected before television came to NOTEL and then again four years later. Before television, the children and youths in NOTEL were significantly more involved in community and sports activities than youths in the other two towns. Once NOTEL had television reception, participation in these activities dropped dramatically.

Television does not appear to reduce time spent doing homework, although, to the distress of many adults, children often have the television on when they do their homework (Sheehan, 1983). Even when the television is on, however,

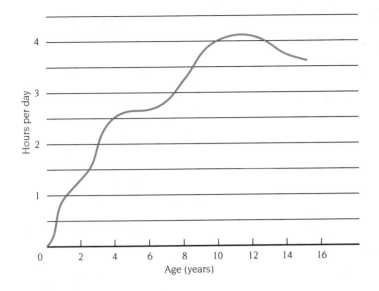

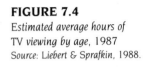

FIGURE 7.4

Estimated average hours of
TV *viewing by age, 1987*
Source: Liebert & Sprafkin, 1988.

children are not really glued to the tube. Preschool-age children are observed to tune out frequently while they watch television. They often ignore long portions of the audio component of programs (Hayes & Birnbaum, 1980). They are especially distracted by the presence of toys, by parts of programs that seem lifeless or boring, and by the mere fact of having already watched television for a while (Anderson, 1977). A study of 5-year-old children in their own homes found that the children were looking at the television only 67% of the time they were in the room while it was on (Anderson et al., 1985). Visual attention to the television appears to peak at about age 9 and then declines slightly to an adult rate of about 60% of the time (Huston et al., 1992). In any attempt to assess the impact of television, it is important to determine whether heavy viewers are actually focusing their attention on the television or treating it as background for other activities.

Research on cognitive development suggests that social interaction is an important stimulus for cognitive growth. Children benefit by interacting with others who express ideas and opinions that differ from their own. Day-to-day exchanges with adults and peers force children to examine their own point of view and to "decenter" as they seek solutions to problems or make plans as members of a group. From this perspective, television has a negative effect on cognitive development insofar as it reduces social interaction. We have already seen that the mere presence of television in a community reduces participation in community activities. Even within the family, when the television is on, conversation dwindles. An observational study of family television viewing found that children interacted less both with each other and with their fathers during viewing than during nonviewing periods (Brody, Stoneman & Sanders, 1980).

The need for peer-group interaction is certainly not met during the hours when the child watches television (Gadberry, 1974). For many young children, watching television is a solitary activity. This is a time when they are interacting neither with peers nor with adults. The noninteractive aspect of television does not reduce the young child's egocentrism. Without interaction, children cannot discover whether their interpretation of what they are viewing is the same as or different from what was intended.

Many studies have been focused on the potential relationship between television viewing and specific cognitive processes. The results of these studies have shown limited effects (Huston et al., 1992). Television viewing in and of itself is not related to reduced attention span, reduced academic achievement, reduced reading time, reduced creativity and imagination. Similarly, claims that television viewing enhances cognitive functioning have had little support (Anderson & Collins, 1988). The effects of television are mediated by the child's intelligence, the other activities and stimuli in the environment, and the kind and amount of viewing. For example, in a synthesis of 23 studies of television viewing, academic achievement was highest among children who viewed about 10–15 hours of television per week and then declined sharply as viewing hours increased from 20 to 40 hours (Williams et al., 1982). The lack of clear evidence of negative or positive consequences of television viewing is somewhat counterintuitive. If one compared children who spend time watching television with children who spend time playing video games and computer games, one wonders whether the two forms of leisure activity would be associated with different patterns of mental activity and different levels of cognitive functioning.

One aspect of watching television that has received attention is the impact of televised advertising on the attitudes and buying preferences of children (Liebert & Sprafkin, 1988; Comstock & Paik, 1991). Children as young as 3 and 4 can usually tell the difference between programs and commercials. Under the age of 8, however, children are not clearly aware of the marketing intention of the advertisement. Young children tend to trust that what is said or shown about a product during a commercial as accurate and true. They do not understand disclaimers ("some assembly required"), and they do not understand the company's motivation for presenting the commercial. From age 8 up to age 12, there is a marked increase in children's understanding of the profit motive associated with advertising and an accompanying decline in trust in commercial messages.

Advertisements aimed at young viewers have at least two negative consequences. First, children are likely to have conflicts with their parents when they want to buy products that they have seen advertised on television. Since young children are more gullible than adults, they find it hard to accept their parents' judgment about the actual worth of the advertised product. Parents and children are very likely to differ on whether the product will really be as much fun as the child has been led to believe. The only way some children can learn to be more discerning is to buy something and be disappointed.

The second negative consequence relates specifically to highly sugared food products, such as candies, sweet fruit-flavored drinks, and sugared cereals. Advertisements for these products make up about 80% of children's television advertising (Liebert & Sprafkin, 1988). Exposure to these advertisements is likely to influence young children's beliefs about nutrition as well as their selection of foods and snacks. When children are exposed to commercials for these sugary snacks, they are much more likely to select them when they have a choice, even when they know that fruits and vegetables are healthier snacks than candies (Gorn & Goldberg, 1982).

Socio-emotional Consequences

The dominant focus of research on the socio-emotional impact of television viewing has been on the role of televised *violence* on the beliefs and behaviors of young children. Concern about television violence is particularly meaningful within the context of the child's growing moral consciousness. More than 20 years of laboratory experiments, field experiments, and analyses of naturally occurring behaviors

Watching televised violence adds new violent behaviors to the child's repertoire and increases the level of aggression in a child's play.

have led to the conclusion that televised violence has definite negative consequences for young children's behaviors and beliefs.

Studies of children in the United States and in other countries provide evidence that at least three processes are at work that may increase the level of aggressiveness in children who watch televised violence (see Table 7.5) (Comstock & Paik, 1991; Huston et al., 1992; Huesmann & Eron, 1986; Huesmann & Malamuth, 1986; Josephson, 1987; Liebert & Sprafkin, 1988). First, children observe televised role models who perform aggressive actions. Especially when

TABLE 7.5 Three Processes That May Increase the Level of Aggression in Children Who Watch Televised Violence

Process	Possible Consequence
Observing role models who engage in aggressive actions	Imitation of violent action likely when 1. hero is provoked and retaliates with aggression. 2. hero is rewarded for violent actions. New violent behaviors added to repertoire.
Viewing aggressive actions leads to heightened level of arousal	Brings network of aggressive thoughts, feelings, memories, and action tendencies into consciousness. Repeated stimulation strengthens this network. Stimulation interacts with aggressive temperament to increase the likelihood of aggressive action.
Viewing aggression affects beliefs and values	Aggressive behavior is seen as acceptable way to resolve conflicts. Viewers are hardened to use of aggression in peer interactions. Aggression is used as a response to frustration. Viewers expect others to be aggressive toward them. Viewers worry about being victims of aggression. Viewers see the world as a dangerous place.

the hero is provoked and retaliates with aggression, the child is likely to imitate the aggressive actions. Thus, the viewing of televised violence adds new violent behaviors to the child's repertoire. In addition, when the hero is rewarded or viewed as successful because of his or her violent actions, children's tendencies to express aggression are increased (Bandura, 1973).

The second process linked to the impact of televised violence is a heightening of arousal. The fast action that usually accompanies televised violence captures the viewer's attention. The violent incident raises the child's level of emotionality, bringing to the fore other aggressive feelings, thoughts, memories, and action tendencies. The more frequently this network of elements is activated, the stronger will be their association. Thus, children who have seen a lot of televised violence and are temperamentally aggressive are likely to engage in overt acts of aggression because of the strength of arousal prompted by the televised stimulus (Berkowitz, 1984, 1986).

Finally, exposure to televised violence affects a young child's beliefs and values. Children who are exposed to frequent episodes of televised violence are more likely to believe that aggressive behavior is an acceptable way to resolve conflicts, and they become hardened to the use of aggression in peer interactions. They are also more accepting of the use of aggression as a response to frustration. In addition, children (and adults) who are exposed to televised violence are more likely to expect that others will be aggressive toward them; they are more likely to worry about being victims of aggression; and they are more likely to see the world as a dangerous place (Bryant, Carveth & Brown, 1981; Gerbner et al., 1980; Thomas & Drabman, 1977).

Television as a Stimulus for Optimal Development

Researchers have barely begun to scratch the surface of television's uses to promote optimal development. There is clear evidence that children who are exposed to prosocial programming are influenced toward more positive social behavior (Hearold, 1986). Many programs, some developed for children and others intended for a broader viewing audience, convey positive ethical messages about the value of family life, the need to work hard and sacrifice in order to achieve important goals, the value of friendship, the importance of loyalty and commitment in relationships, and many other cultural values. A number of contemporary programs include characters of many races and ethnic backgrounds. Many feature women in positions of authority or performing acts of heroism. Through exposure to these programs, children learn to challenge racial and gender stereotypes and develop positive images of people of other racial and cultural groups (Liebert & Sprafkin, 1988).

Public television has succeeded in developing programs that directly address the educational needs of young children. *Sesame Street* is the best known and most well documented of these efforts. It is clear that young children who consistently watch *Sesame Street* benefit in a variety of intellectual tasks, such as recognizing letters, numbers, and shapes; sorting objects into groups; and recognizing relationships among objects. Children who watched *Sesame Street* regularly between the ages of 3 and 5 showed measurable improvement in vocabulary. These gains have been documented for boys and girls from a variety of socio-economic backgrounds (Rice et al., 1990).

After the success of *Sesame Street*, other programs directed at the development of literacy, science education, and mathematical skill appeared. Professionals are confident that we can introduce ideas and information to children and have the technology to produce quality public television to supplement instruction and improve literacy for a broad range of children. However, relatively few resources are directed toward this activity. Japan, Great Britain, and Australia all invest significantly more in the development of public television programming for children than the United States does: "In 1985, the British Broadcasting Corp. carried 590 hours of newly produced TV programs for children compared to 87.5 hours in the United States" (Landers, 1989a).

Advice to Parents and Teachers

Many families find that they end up arguing about the amount of television their children are watching. The withdrawal of television becomes a punishment for a wide range of misbehaviors, from telling a lie to getting in trouble in school. Parents and children may argue about which programs to watch or about turning off the television at bedtime. Children may find that their parents are so involved in television that they cannot get their attention, and when parents are not home, they may use the television as a substitute companion for their children. Since television is a component of contemporary life, it makes sense to help children get the most out of it. Making it the focus of conflicts and battles over control does not seem to be very productive. Parents and teachers need to be actively involved in planning and guiding a child's experiences with television (Tangney, 1987; Huston et al., 1992). They should emphasize more do's than don'ts:

1. Do watch television with young children when you can, and talk about the stories and information presented. Talk about how situations that are presented on television may or may not be similar to real life.
2. As appropriate, follow up ideas and suggestions presented in educational programming with activities at home or in the classroom. Such activities give children ideas about how to respond more actively to the information being presented on television.
3. Encourage children to sample a wide variety of television programs. Introduce them to news specials, science programs, opera, concerts, classic movies, and coverage of special events as well as children's programming.
4. Talk with children about what the purpose of commercials is, how they are made, how they intend to influence children's behaviors, and what children should listen for in evaluating televised commercials.
5. Limit young children's exposure to television violence. It will probably not be possible to eliminate it entirely, but special efforts should be made to reduce the early-school-age child's exposure to violent programming before bedtime, and to talk about how and why violence is used.
6. Talk about the other activities children can participate in instead of watching television. Help children choose among the many possible uses of their time.
7. Use the VCR to tape programs that are developmentally appropriate for children. These tapes may be shown when children are home because of illness, or when the regular evening programming is unsuitable for a child of a certain temperament or developmental level.

Chapter Summary

Early school age marks the beginning of work on developmental tasks that will persist well into adulthood. The four tasks of early school age are closely interrelated. The complex process of sex-role identification has cognitive, affective, physical, and interpersonal elements. As young children clarify the content of their sex-role identity, they create a set of beliefs about the self including their self-worth, their relationships with other children, and the kinds of activities and interests that are appropriate for them, not only in the present but in the future. The sex-role identity of the early-school-age child will be revised and reintegrated as it becomes a core element of personal identity in adolescence.

The development of conscience, with its capacity to reward and punish, brings an internalization of moral standards. Moral development is accompanied by a heightened sensitivity to violating basic cultural standards, many of which relate to interpersonal behavior, especially behavior toward adults and toward peers. The child's experiences with transgressions, guilt, or praise for prosocial behavior have implications for the elaboration of the self-theory and particularly for the establishment of self-esteem.

Although the self-theory is continuously revised with entry into new roles and new cognitive capacities, the establishment of a positive sense of worth in early school age brings an important tone of optimism as the child faces new challenges. Competence and social acceptance are the essential antecedents of self-esteem. The increased involvement with peers in play brings about an appreciation of others' perspectives, social acceptance, and delight in the intimacy of friends.

The psychosocial crisis of initiative versus guilt has direct implications for such essential personality characteristics as self-esteem, creativity, curiosity, and risk taking. The child who resolves this crisis positively will be fortified with an active, exploratory approach to the environment. Guilt plays an important role in orienting children toward the implications of their actions for others. In moderation, it appears to be an essential ingredient in preserving social bonds. In the extreme, however, excessive guilt restricts creative thought and limits action.

The impact of television on the early-school-age child highlights the interconnectedness of emotional and cognitive development. The potential for television to contribute to the optimal development of young children has only begun to be realized.

References

Anderson, D. R. (1977). *Children's attention to television*. Paper presented at the biennial meeting of the Society for Research in Child Development, New Orleans.

Anderson, D. R. & Collins, P. A. (1988). *The impact on children's education: Television's impact on cognitive development*. Washington, DC: U.S. Department of Education.

Anderson, D. R., Field, D. E., Collins, E. P. L. & Nathan, J. G. (1985). Estimates of young children's time with television: A methodological comparison of parent reports with time-lapse video home observation. *Child Development, 56*, 1345–1357.

Aronfreed, J. (1969). The concept of internalization. In D. A. Goslin (Ed.), *Handbook of socialization theory and research*. Chicago: Rand McNally.

Arsenio, W. F. & Kramer, R. (1992). Victimizers and their victims: Children's conceptions of the mixed emotional consequences of moral transgressions. *Child Development, 63*, 915–927.

Bandura, A. (1973). *Aggression: A social learning analysis*. Englewood Cliffs, NJ: Prentice-Hall.

Bandura, A. (1977). *Social learning theory*. Englewood Cliffs, N.J.: Prentice-Hall.

Bandura, A. (1986). *Social foundations of thought and action*. Englewood Cliffs, NJ: Prentice-Hall.

Bandura, A. (1991). Social cognitive theory of moral thought and action. In W. M. Kurtines & J. L. Gewirtz (Eds.), *Handbook of moral behavior and development: Vol. 1. Theory* (pp. 45–103). Hillsdale, NJ: Erlbaum.

Bauer, P. J. (1993). Memory for gender-consistent and gender-inconsistent event sequences by twenty-five-month-old children. *Child Development, 64*, 285–297.

Baumgardner, A. H. (1990). To know oneself is to like oneself: Self-certainty and self-affect. *Journal of Personality and Social Psychology, 58*, 1062–1072.

Beere, C. A. (1990). *Gender roles: A handbook of tests and measures*. New York: Greenwood.

Beit-Hallahmi, B. (1987). Critical periods in psycho-analytic theories of personality development. In M. H. Bornstein (Ed.), *Sensitive periods in development: Interdisciplinary perspectives* (pp. 211–221). Hillsdale, NJ: Erlbaum.

Bem, S. L. (1981). Gender schema theory: A cognitive account of sex-typing. *Psychological Review, 88,* 354–364.

Bem, S. L. (1989). Genital knowledge and gender constancy in preschool children. *Child Development, 60,* 649–662.

Benenson, J. F. (1993). Greater preference among females than males for dyadic interaction in early childhood. *Child Development, 64,* 544–555.

Berkowitz, L. (1984). Some effects of thoughts on anti- and prosocial influences of media events: A cognitive-neoassociation analysis. *Psychological Bulletin, 95,* 419–427.

Berkowitz, L. (1986). Situational influences on reactions to observed violence. *Journal of Social Issues, 42,* 93–103.

Bigler, R. S. & Liben, L. S. (1992). Cognitive mechanisms in children's gender stereotyping: Theoretical and educational implications of a cognitive based intervention. *Child Development, 63,* 1351–1363.

Bohan, J. S. (1993). Regarding gender. *Psychology of Women Quarterly, 17,* 5–21.

Borke, H. (1973). The development of empathy in Chinese and American children between 3 and 6 years of age: A cross-cultural study. *Developmental Psychology, 9,* 102–108.

Brockner, J. (1984). Low self-esteem and behavioral plasticity. In L. Wheeler (Ed.), *Review of personality and social psychology* (Vol. 4, pp. 237–271). Beverly Hills, CA: Sage.

Brody, G. H., Stoneman, Z. & Sanders, A. K. (1980). Effects of television viewing on family interactions: An observational study. *Family Relations, 29,* 216–220.

Brown, J. D. & Gallagher, F. M. (1992). Coming to terms with failure: Private self-enhancement and public self-effacement. *Journal of Experimental Social Psychology, 28,* 3–22.

Brown, J. D. & Mankowski, T. A. (1993). Self-esteem, mood, and self-evaluation: Changes in mood and the way you see you. *Journal of Personality and Social Psychology, 64,* 421–430.

Brown, J. D. & Smart, S. A. (1991). The self and social conduct: Linking self-representation to prosocial behavior. *Journal of Personality and Social Psychology, 60,* 368–375.

Bryant, J., Carveth, R. A. & Brown, D. (1981). Television viewing and anxiety: An experimental examination. *Journal of Communication, 31,* 106–119.

Bukowski, W. M., Gauze, C., Hoza, B. & Newcomb, A. F. (1993). Differences and consistency between same-sex and other-sex peer relationships during early adolescence. *Developmental Psychology, 29,* 255–263.

Burr, W. R. & Christensen, C. (1992). Undesireable side effects of enhancing self-esteem. *Family Relations, 41,* 480–484.

Butler, R. (1989). Mastery versus ability appraisal: A developmental study of children's observations of peers' work. *Child Development, 60,* 1350–1361.

Butler, R. (1990). The effects of mastery and competitive conditions on self-assessment at different ages. *Child Development, 61,* 201–210.

Caldera, Y. M., Huston, A. C. & O'Brien, M. (1989). Social interactions and play patterns of parents and toddlers with feminine, masculine, and neutral toys. *Child Development, 60,* 70–76.

Campbell, J. (1990). Self-esteem and clarity of the self-concept. *Journal of Personality and Social Psychology, 59,* 538–549.

Carroll, J. L. & Rest, J. R. (1982). Moral development. In B. B. Wolman (Ed.), *Handbook of developmental psychology* (pp. 434–451). Englewood Cliffs, NJ: Prentice-Hall.

Chandler, M. & Boyes, M. (1982). Social-cognitive development. In B. B. Wolman (Ed.), *Handbook of developmental psychology* (pp. 387–402). Englewood Cliffs, NJ: Prentice-Hall.

Cicirelli, V. G. (1976). Effects of evaluating task competence on the self-concept of children from different socioeconomic status levels. *Journal of Psychology, 94,* 217–223.

Comstock, G. A. (with Haejung Paik). (1991). *Television and the American child.* San Diego: Academic Press.

Coolidge, J. C. (1979). School phobia. In J. D. Noshpitz (Ed.), *Basic handbook of child psychiatry* (pp. 453–463). New York: Basic Books.

Cronk, L. (1993). Parental favoritism toward daughters. *American Scientist, 81,* 272–279.

Damon, W. (1977). *The social world of the child.* San Francisco: Jossey-Bass.

Damon, W. (1980). Patterns of change in children's social reasoning: A two-year longitudinal study. *Child Development, 51,* 1010–1017.

Damon, W. & Hart, D. (1988). *Self-understanding in childhood and adolescence.* New York: Cambridge University Press.

Davison, G. C. & Neale, J. M. (1990). *Abnormal psychology: An experimental clinical approach* (5th ed.). New York: Wiley.

Dodge, K. A., Pettit, G. S., McClaskey, C. L. & Brown, M. M. (1986). Social competence in children. *Monographs of the Society for Research in Child Development, 51*(2, Serial No. 213).

Eccles, J., Wigfield, A., Harold, R. D. & Blumenfeld, P. (1993). Age and gender differences in children's self- and task perceptions during elementary school. *Child Development 64,* 830–847.

Edelbrock, C. & Sugawara, A. I. (1978). Acquisition of sex-typed preferences in pre-school-aged children. *Developmental Psychology, 14,* 614–623.

Eder, R. A. (1989). The emergent personologist: The structure and content of 3½, 5½, and 7½-year-olds' concepts of themselves and other persons. *Child Development, 60,* 1218–1228.

Eder, R. A., Gerlach, S. G. & Perlmutter, M. (1987). In search of children's selves: Development of the specific and general components of the self-concept. *Child Development, 58,* 1044–1050.

Edwards, C. P. & Whiting, B. B. (1988). *Children of different worlds.* Cambridge: Harvard University Press.

Eisenberg, N. & Strayer, J. (1987). Critical issues in the study of empathy. In N. Eisenberg & J. Strayer (Eds.), *Empathy and its development* (pp. 3–13). Cambridge: Cambridge University Press.

Emde, R. N., Biringen, Z., Clyman, R. B. & Oppenheim, D. (1991). The moral self of infancy: Affective core and procedural knowledge. *Developmental Review, 11,* 51–270.

Emde, R. N. & Buchsbaum, H. K. (1990). "Didn't you hear my mommy?" Autonomy *with* connectedness in moral self-emergence. In D. Cicchetti & M. Beeghly (Eds.), *The self in transition: Infancy to childhood* (pp. 35–60). Chicago: University of Chicago Press.

Emde, R. N., Johnson, W. F. & Easterbrooks, A. (1987). The do's and don'ts of early moral development: Psychoanalytic tradition and current research. In J. Kagan & S. Lamb (Eds.), *The emergence of morality in young children* (pp. 245–276). Chicago: University of Chicago Press.

Epstein, S. (1973). The self-concept revisited; or, a theory of a theory. *American Psychologist, 28,* 404–416.

Epstein, S. (1991). Cognitive-experiential self-theory: An integrative theory of personality. In R. Cutis (Ed.), *The self with others: Convergences in psychoanalytic, social, and personality psychology* (pp. 111–137). New York: Guilford.

Epstein, S., Lipson, A., Holstein, C. & Huh, E. (1993). Irrational reactions to negative outcomes: Evidence for two conceptual systems. *Journal of Personality and Social Psychology, 62,* 328–339.

Erikson, E. H. (1963). *Childhood and society* (2nd ed.). New York: Norton.

Erikson, E. H. (1977). *Toys and reasons.* New York: Norton.

Fabes, R. A., Eisenberg, N., McCormick, S. E. & Wilson, M. S. (1988). Preschoolers' attributions of the situational determinants of others' naturally occurring emotions. *Developmental Psychology, 24,* 376–385.

Fabes, R. A., Eisenberg, N., Nyman, M. & Michealieu, Q. (1991). Young children's appraisals of others' spontaneous emotional reactions. *Developmental Psychology, 27,* 858–866.

Fagot, B. I. & Leinbach, M. D. (1989). The young child's gender schema: Environmental input, internal organization. *Child Development, 60,* 663–672.

Fincham, F. & Jaspars, J. (1979). Attribution of responsibility to the self and other in children and adults. *Journal of Personality and Social Psychology, 37,* 1589–1602.

Flavell, J. H. (1974). The development of inferences about others. In W. Mischel (Ed.), *Understanding other persons.* Oxford: Blackwell, Basil & Mott.

Freud, A. (1936). *The ego and mechanisms of defense.* New York: International Universities Press.

Freud, S. (1925/1961). Some psychical consequences of the anatomical distinction between the sexes. In J. Strachey (Ed.), *The standard edition of the complete psychological works of Sigmund Freud* (Vol. 19). London: Hogarth Press.

Freud, S. (1929/1955). Three essays on the theory of sexuality. In J. Strachey (Ed.), *The standard edition of the complete psychological works of Sigmund Freud* (Vol. 7). London: Hogarth Press.

Frey, K. S. & Ruble, D. N. (1987). What children say about classroom performance: Sex and grade differences in perceived competence. *Child Development, 58,* 1066–1078.

Froming, W. J., Allen, L. & Jensen, R. (1985). Altruism, role-taking, and self-awareness: The acquisition of norms governing altruistic behavior. *Child Development, 56,* 1123–1228.

Gadberry, S. (1974). Television as baby-sitter: A field comparison of preschoolers' behavior during playtime and during television viewing. *Child Development, 45,* 1132–1136.

Gagnon, J. H. (1977). *Human sexualities.* Glenview, IL: Scott, Foresman.

Garrod, A. (1993). *Approaches to moral development: New research and emerging themes.* New York: Teachers College Press.

Garvey, C. (1977). *Play.* Cambridge: Harvard University Press.

Gerbner, G., Gross, L., Morgan, M. & Signorelli, N. (1980). The "mainstreaming" of America: Violence profile no. 11. *Journal of Communication, 30,* 10–29.

Gibbs, J. C. (1979). Kohlberg's moral stage theory: A Piagetian revision. *Human Development, 22,* 89–112.

Gorn, G. J. & Goldberg, M. E. (1982). Behavioral evidence of the effects of televised food messages on children. *Journal of Consumer Research, 9,* 200–205.

Hart, C. H., Ladd, G. W. & Burleson, B. R. (1990). Children's expectations of the outcomes of social strategies: Relations with sociometric status and maternal disciplinary styles. *Child Development, 61,* 127–137.

Harter, S. (1985). Competence as a dimension of self-evaluation: Towards a comprehensive model of self-worth. In R. Leahy (Ed.), *The development of the self* (pp. 55–121). New York: Academic Press.

Hayes, D. S. & Birnbaum, D. W. (1980). Preschoolers' retention of televised events: Is a picture worth a thousand words? *Developmental Psychology, 16,* 410–416.

Hearold, S. (1986). A synthesis of 1043 effects of television on social behavior. In G. Comstock (Ed.), *Public communications and behavior* (Vol. 1, pp. 65–133). New York: Academic Press.

Heilbrun, A. B., Jr. (1974). Parent-identification and filial sex role behavior: The importance of biological context. In J. K. Cole & R. Dienstbier (Eds.), *Nebraska Symposium on Motivation* (pp. 125–194). Lincoln: University of Nebraska Press.

Hetherington, E. M. (1967). The effects of familial variables on sex typing, on parent-child similarity, and on imitation in children. In J. P. Hill (Ed.), *Minnesota Symposium on Child Psychology* (Vol. 1, pp. 82–107). Minneapolis: University of Minnesota Press.

Hoffman, M. L. (1970). Moral development. In P. H. Mussen (Ed.), *Carmichael's manual of child psychology* (3rd ed., Vol. 2). New York: Wiley.

Hoffman, M. L. (1982). Development of prosocial motivation: Empathy and guilt. In N. Eisenberg (Ed.), *The development of prosocial behavior* (281–313). New York: Academic Press.

Hoffman, M. L. (1987). The contribution of empathy to justice and moral judgment. In N. Eisenberg & J. Strayer (Eds.), *Empathy and its development* (pp. 47–80). Cambridge: Cambridge University Press.

Hoffner, C. & Badzinski, D. M. (1989). Children's integration of facial and situational cues to emotion. *Child Development, 60,* 411–422.

Howes, C. & Phillipsen, L. (1992). Gender and friendship: Relationships within peer groups of young children. *Social Development, 1,* 230–242.

Huber, J. (1990). Macro-micro links in gender stratification. *American Sociological Review, 55,* 1–10.

Huesmann, L. R. & Eron, L. D. (1986). *Television and the aggressive child: A cross-national comparison.* Hillsdale, NJ: Erlbaum.

Huesmann, L. R. & Malamuth, N. M. (1986). Media violence and antisocial behavior: An overview. *Journal of Social Issues, 42,* 1–6.

Huston, A. C., Donnerstein, E., Fairchild, H., Feshbach, N. D., Katz, P. A., Murray, J. P., Rubinstein, E. A., Wilcox, B. L. & Zuckerman, D. (1992). *Big world, small screen: The role of television in American society.* Lincoln: University of Nebraska Press.

Iannotti, R. J. (1985). Naturalistic and structured assessments of prosocial behavior in preschool children: The influence of empathy and perspective taking. *Developmental Psychology, 21,* 46–55.

Izard, C. E. (1977). *Human emotion.* New York: Plenum.

Jacklin, C. N. & Maccoby, E. E. (1978). Social behavior at 33 months in same-sex and mixed-sex dyads. *Child Development, 49,* 557–569.

Jacobson, E. (1964). *The self and the object world.* New York: International Universities Press.

James, W. (1892/1961). *Psychology: The briefer course.* New York: Harper & Row.

Josephson, W. L. (1987). Television violence and children's aggression: Testing the priming, social script, and disinhibition predictions. *Journal of Personality and Social Psychology, 53,* 882–890.

Kagan, J. (1958). The concept of identification. *Psychological Review, 65,* 296–305.

Katz, P. A. & Walsh, P. V. (1991). Modification of children's gender-stereotyped behavior. *Child Development, 62,* 338–351.

Kegan, R. (1982). *The evolving self: Problems and process in human development.* Cambridge: Harvard University Press.

Kochanska, G. (1991). Socialization and temperament in the development of guilt and conscience. *Child Development, 62,* 1379–1392.

Kochanska, G. (1993). Toward a synthesis of parental socialization and child temperament in early development of conscience. *Child Development, 64,* 325–347.

Kohlberg, L. (1966). A cognitive-developmental analysis of children's sex-role concepts and attitudes. In E. E. Maccoby (Ed.), *The development of sex differences.* Stanford, CA: Stanford University Press.

Kohlberg, L. (1969). Stage and sequence: The cognitive-developmental approach to socialization. In D. A. Goslin (Ed.), *Handbook of socialization theory and research.* Chicago: Rand McNally.

Kohlberg, L. (1976). Moral stages and moralization: The cognitive-developmental approach. In T. Lickona (Ed.), *Moral development and behavior.* New York: Holt, Rinehart & Winston.

Kohlberg, L. (1978). Revisions in the theory and practice of moral development. In W. Damon (Ed.), *Moral development: New directions for child development* (Vol. 2, pp. 83–88). San Francisco: Jossey-Bass.

Kohlberg, L. (1979). *The meaning and measurement of moral development.* Worcester, MA: Clark Lectures, Clark University.

Kohut, H. (1971). *The analysis of the self.* New York: International Universities Press.

Landers, S. (1989a). Big Bird, experts sing praises of kids' shows. *APA Monitor, 20*(7), 32.

Landers, S. (1989b). Watching TV, children *do* learn. *APA Monitor, 20*(3), 25.

Langlois, J. H. & Downs, A. C. (1980). Mothers, fathers, and peers as socialization agents of sex-typed play behaviors in young children. *Child Development, 51,* 1217–1247.

Lee, L. C. (1975). Toward a cognitive theory of interpersonal development: Importance of peers. In M. Lewis & L. A. Rosenblum (Eds.), *Friendship and peer relations.* New York: Wiley.

Leinbach, M. D. & Fagot, B. I. (1986). Acquisition of gender labels: A test for toddlers. *Sex Roles, 15,* 655–667.

Levy, G. D. & Carter, D. B. (1989). Gender schema, gender constancy, and gender-role knowledge: The roles of cognitive factors in preschoolers' gender-role stereotype attributions. *Developmental Psychology, 25,* 444–449.

Liben, L. S. & Signorella, M. L. (1993). Gender-schematic processing in children: The role of initial interpretations of stimuli. *Developmental Psychology, 29,* 141–149.

Liebert, R. M. & Sprafkin, J. (1988). *The early window: Effects of television on children and youth* (3rd ed.). New York: Pergamon Press.

Lobel, T. E. & Menashri, J. (1993). Relations of conceptions of gender-role transgressions and gender constancy to gender-typed toy preferences. *Developmental Psychology, 29,* 150–155.

Long, B. H., Henderson, E. H. & Ziller, R. C. (1967). Developmental changes in the self-concept during middle childhood. *Merrill-Palmer Quarterly, 13,* 201–215.

Lyle, J. & Hoffman, H. R. (1972). Children's use of television and other media. In E. A. Rubinstein, G. A. Comstock & J. P. Murray (Eds.), *Television in day-to-day life: Patterns of use* (pp. 129–256). Washington, DC: U.S. Government Printing Office.

Maccoby, E. E. (1988). Gender as a social category. *Developmental Psychology, 24,* 755–765.

Maccoby, E. E. (1990). Gender and relationships: A developmental account. *American Psychologist, 45,* 513–520.

Maccoby, E. E. (1992). The role of parents in the socialization of children: An historical overview. *Developmental Psychology, 28,* 1006–1017

Maccoby, E. E. & Jacklin, C. N. (1987). Gender segregation in childhood. In E. H. Reese (Ed.), *Advances in child development and behavior* (Vol. 20, pp. 239–287). New York: Academic Press.

Mahler, M. S. (1963). Thoughts about development and individuation. *Psychoanalytic Study of the Child, 18,* 307–324.

Martin, C. L. (1989). Children's use of gender-related information in making social judgments. *Developmental Psychology, 25,* 80–88.

Martin, C. L. & Halverson, C. F. (1987). The roles of cognition in sex roles acquisition. In D. B. Carter (Ed.), *Current conceptions of sex roles and sex typing: Theory and research* (pp. 123–137). New York: Praeger.

Martin, C. L., Wood, C. H. & Little, J. K. (1990). The development of gender stereotype components. *Child Development, 61,* 1891–1904.

Martin, G. B. & Clark, R. D. III. (1982). Distress crying in neonates: Species and peer specificity. *Developmental Psychology, 18,* 3–9.

McAdoo, H. P. (1985). Racial attitude and self-concept of young black children over time. In H. P. McAdoo & J. L. McAdoo (Eds.), *Black children: Social, educational, and parental environments* (pp. 213–242). Newbury Park, CA: Sage.

McCary, J. L. (1978). *McCary's human sexuality* (3rd ed.). New York: Van Nostrand.

Mischel, W. (1966). Theory and research on the antecedents of self-imposed delay of reward. In B. A. Maher (Ed.), *Progress in experimental personality research* (Vol. 3, pp. 81–132). New York: Academic Press.

Mischel, W. (1973). Toward a cognitive social learning reconceptualization of personality. *Psychological Review, 80,* 252–283.

Mischel, W., Shoda, Y. & Rodriguez, M. L. (1989). Delay of gratification in children. *Science, 244,* 933–938.

Oosterwegel, A. & Oppenheimer, L. (1993). *The self-system: Developmental changes between and within self-concepts.* Hillsdale, NJ: Erlbaum.

Park, K. A., Lay, K. & Ramsay, L. (1993). Individual differences and developmental changes in preschoolers' friendships. *Developmental Psychology, 29,* 264–270.

Pelham, B. W. (1991). On the benefits of misery: Self-serving biases in the depressive self-concept. *Journal of Personality and Social Psychology, 61,* 670–681.

Pelham, B. W. & Swann, W. B., Jr. (1989). From self-conceptions to self-worth: On the sources and structure of global self-esteem. *Journal of Personality and Social Psychology, 57,* 672–680.

Pettit, G. S., Dodge, K. A. & Brown, M. M. (1988). Early family experience, social problem-solving patterns, and children's social competence. *Child Development, 59,* 107–120.

Phelps, L., Cox, D. & Bajorek, E. (1992). School phobia and separation anxiety: Diagnostic and treatment comparisons. *Psychology in the Schools, 29,* 384–394.

Piaget, J. (1932/1948). *The moral judgment of the child.* Glencoe, IL: Free Press.

Piaget, J. (1975/1985). *The equilibration of cognitive structures: The central problem of intellectual development* (T. Brown & K. Thampy, Trans.). Chicago: University of Chicago Press.

Rest, J. R. (1983). Morality. In J. H. Flavell & E. M. Markman (Eds.), *Handbook of child psychology: Cognitive development* (Vol. 3). New York: Wiley.

Rice, M. L., Huston, A. C., Truglio, R. & Wright, J. C. (1990). Words from Sesame Street: Learning vocabulary while viewing. *Developmental Psychology, 26,* 421–428.

Rosenberg, M. (1979). *Conceiving the self.* New York: Basic Books.

Sagi, A. & Hoffman, M. L. (1976). Empathic distress in the newborn. *Developmental Psychology, 12,* 175–176.

Sandler, J., Holder, A. & Meers, P. M. (1963). The ego ideal and the ideal self. *Psychoanalytic Study of the Child, 18,* 139–158.

Selman, R. (1980). *The growth of interpersonal understanding: Developmental and clinical analysis.* New York: Academic Press.

Selman, R. L. (1971). Taking another's perspective: Role-taking development in early childhood. *Child Development, 42,* 1721–1734.

Serbin, L. A., Powlishta, K. K. & Gulko, J. (1993). The development of sex typing in middle childhood. *Monographs of the Society for Research in Child Development,* 58 (Whole No. 232).

Setterlund, M. B. & Niedenthal, P. M. (1993). "Who am I? Why am I here?": Self-esteem, self-clarity, and prototype matching. *Journal of Personality and Social Psychology, 65,* 769–780.

Sheehan, P. W. (1983). Age trends and the correlates of children's television viewing. *Australian Journal of Psychology, 35,* 417–431.

Smetana, J. G. (1985). Preschool children's conceptions of transgressions: Effects of varying moral and conventional domain-related attributes. *Developmental Psychology, 21,* 18–29.

Smetana, J. G. (1986). Preschool children's conceptions of sex-role transgressions. *Child Development, 57,* 862–871.

Smetana, J. G., Schlagman, N. & Adams, P. W. (1993). Preschool children's judgments about hypothetical and actual transgressions. *Child Development, 64,* 202–214.

Smith, P. K., Hunter, T., Carvalho, A. M. A. & Costabile, A. (1992). Children's perceptions of playfighting, play-chasing and real fighting: A cross-national interview study. *Social Development, 1,* 211–221.

Snyder, S. S. & Feldman, D. H. (1984). Phases of transition in moral development: Evidence from the domain of spatial representation. *Child Development, 55,* 981–989.

Stattin, H. & Klackenberg-Larsson, I. (1991). The short- and long-term implications for parent-child relations of parents' prenatal preferences for their child's gender. *Developmental Psychology, 27,* 141–147.

Steinberg, C. (1985). *TV facts.* New York: Facts on File.

Stipek, D., Recchia, S. & McClintic, S. (1992). Self-evaluation in young children. *Monographs of the Society for Research in Child Development,* 57(1, Serial No. 226).

Sutton-Smith, B. A. (1972). Syntax for play and games. In R. E. Herron & B. Sutton-Smith (Eds.), *Child's play.* New York: Wiley.

Swann, W. B., Jr. (1990). To be known or be adored? The interplay of self-enhancement and self-verification. In E. T. Higgins & R. M. Sorrentino (Eds.), *Handbook of motivation and cognition: Foundations of social behavior* (pp. 404–448). New York: Guilford.

Tangney, J. P. (1987). TV in the family. *Bryn Mawr Now, 14,* 1, 14.

Tangney, J. P. (1991). Moral affect: The good, the bad, and the ugly. *Journal of Personality and Social Psychology, 61,* 598–607.

Thomas, M. H. & Drabman, R. S. (1977). *Effects of television violence on expectations of others' aggression.* Paper presented at the annual convention of the American Psychological Association, San Francisco.

Thompson, L. (1993). Conceptualizing gender in marriage: The case of marital care. *Journal of Marriage and the Family, 55,* 557–569.

Thompson, S. K. (1975). Gender labels and early sex role development. *Child Development, 46,* 339–347.

Turiel, E. (1983). *The development of social knowledge: Morality and convention.* Cambridge: Cambridge University Press.

U.S. Bureau of the Census. (1992). *Statistical Abstract of the United States,* 1992. Washington, DC: U.S. Government Printing Office.

Walker, L. J. (1988). The development of moral reasoning. *Annals of Child Development, 5,* 33–78.

Walker, L. J. (1989). A longitudinal study of moral reasoning. *Child Development, 60,* 157–166.

Walker, L. J. & Taylor, J. H. (1991a). Family interactions and the development of moral reasoning. *Child Development, 62,* 262–283.

Walker, L. & Taylor, J. H. (1991b). Stage transitions in moral reasoning: A longitudinal study of developmental processes. *Developmental Psychology, 27,* 330–337.

Weinraub, M., Clemens, L. P., Sockloff, A., Ethridge, T., Gracely, E. & Meyers, B. (1984). The development of sex role stereotypes in the third year: Relationship to gender labeling, identity, sex-typed toy preference, and family characteristics. *Child Development, 55,* 1493–1503.

Weinstein, R. S., Marshall, H. H., Sharp, L. & Botkin, M. (1987). Pygmalion and the student: Age and classroom differences in children's awareness of teacher expectations. *Child Development, 58,* 1079–1093.

Westoff, C. F. & Rindfuss, R. R. (1974). Sex preselection in the United States: Some implications. *Science, 184,* 633–636.

Williams, P. A., Haertel, E. H., Walberg, H. J. & Haertel, G. D. (1982). The impact of leisure-time television on school learning: A research synthesis. *American Educational Research Journal, 19,* 19–50.

Williams, T. H. & Handford, A. G. (1986). Television and other leisure activities. In T. H. Williams (Ed.), *The impact of television: A natural experiment in three communities* (pp. 143–213). Orlando, FL: Academic Press.

Zahn-Waxler, C. & Kochanska, G. (1990). The origins of guilt. In R. A. Thompson (Ed.), *Nebraska Symposium on Motivation,* 1988 (Vol. 36, pp. 183–258). Lincoln: University of Nebraska Press.

Zahn-Waxler, C., Kochanska, G., Krupnick, J. & McKnew, D. (1990). Patterns of guilt in children of depressed and well mothers. *Developmental Psychology, 26,* 51–59.

CHAPTER 8

Children struggle to increase their competence in the
shadow of a culture, teacher, or mother who urges,
instructs, compliments, and criticizes.

Middle School Age (6–12 Years)

Historically, the *middle-school-age* period, which covers the ages from about 6 to 12, was not considered of major importance to an understanding of development. Freud's psychoanalytic theory treated the years following the resolution of the Oedipal conflict as a time when sexual and aggressive impulses are repressed and active only in the unconscious. He called this period the *latency stage*, a term that suggests that no significant contributions to personality formation can be traced to it. For a long time, psychologists tended not to study the psychological development of the middle-school-age years.

More recent interest in the theories of Erik Erikson and Jean Piaget has stimulated developmental research focusing on children who are between the ages of 6 and 12. These theories emphasize intellectual growth, competence, and a growing investment in work. During this time, children are learning the fundamental skills of their culture. They spend a great deal of their time every day learning the skills that are valued by their society, whether these skills be reading, writing, and arithmetic or hunting, fishing, and weaving. As children gain confidence in their skills, they begin to have more realistic images of their potential contributions to the larger community.

The competence that develops during the middle school years applies to social as well as work-related skills. This is a time when parent-child relationships, peer friendships, and participation in meaningful interpersonal communication provide children with the social skills they will need if they are to cope with the upcoming challenges of adolescence. Children's cognitive accomplishments appear to develop in conjunction with their achievements in the social and emotional domains.

For many middle-school-age children, this is a joyful, vigorous time. The fears and vulnerabilities of their early school days are behind them. Energized by ego qualities of hope, will, and purpose, most middle-school-age children are able to enjoy many of the resources and opportunities of their communities. Even as the presence of their family members continues to be a comfort to them, they begin to explore more complex social relationships with their peers and other significant adults (Galbo, 1983).

In those children who develop core pathologies, we find withdrawal, a compulsion to perform repetitive behaviors, and inhibition of thought, expression, and activity. These children often come to the attention of school officials when they demonstrate a paralysis of action and thought that prevents productive work or a pattern of overt aggression that results in peer rejection and persistent disruption in the classroom.

In some parts of the world, the lives of children aged 6–12 are marked by extreme disorganization and exploitation. For example, during the fighting in Sarajevo, Bosnia-Herzegovina, hundreds of children, many without their mothers or fathers, escaped the war on buses to be relocated in Russia and other parts of Europe (*Columbus Dispatch*, 1992). Firsthand accounts of children growing up in the midst of war illustrate the psychological and physiological consequences of daily exposure to violence, suffering, and threats of destruction that are out of their control (Garbarino, Kostelny & Dubrow, 1991). In some parts of the world, slavers travel through impoverished areas kidnapping, buying, or luring children into forms of slavelike labor where they are often beaten, sexually abused, and degraded. Children as young as 6 are being sold or given away by poor families as slaves or bonded laborers: "In Haiti, more than 100,000 children, sold or given away by poor families, toil as domestic servants . . . in Pakistan as many as 20 million people, 7.5 million of them children, are working as bonded laborers in factories, on farms and on construction projects, unable to pay off employer advances" (*Time*, 1993). In such circumstances, the opportunity for young children to work on the developmental tasks of friendship formation, concrete operational reasoning, skill learning, self-evaluation, and team play may be viewed as a great societal luxury; having the time, resources, and security to promote areas of cognitive, social, and emotional development is only possible within the context of a society that is economically and politically stable and ideologically committed to the intellectual and interpersonal future of its children.

Developmental Tasks

Friendship

Can you remember some things about a friend you had when you were 10 years old? Friendships of the middle school years are not likely to be as enduring as the attachment relationships of infancy. Yet, some of these friendships are quite memorable; they may have many of the elements of a close affectional bond. At this age, children describe close friends as people who like the same activities, share common interests, enjoy each other's company, and can count on each other for help (Youniss, 1980; Ainsworth, 1989).

Friendships may not be as essential to survival as attachment relations, but they clearly provide social and developmental advantages (Ainsworth, 1989; Hartup, 1989). According to ethological theory, being a member of a group has protective advantages. Group cooperation gives a selective advantage to many social species, especially in tracking and hunting for food. Therefore, the skills of cooperation and sociability may advance the species as a whole as well as the individual. On an individual level, children who are able to participate in positive peer friendships are embedded in an intellectually and socially stimulating environment.

Family Influences on Social Competence

Not all children enter the middle school years with the same capacity to make friends and to enjoy the benefits of close peer relations. Early family experiences contribute to a child's sociability and social competence. The process of becoming ready for friendship may begin in infancy. Children who have secure attachments in infancy are more popular in preschool and engage more freely in social interactions. They are perceived as more helpful and better able to consider the needs of others (Sroufe & Fleeson, 1986; Park & Waters, 1989).

A mother's discipline techniques, the way she speaks to her child, and her parenting values are all linked to a child's social competence and popularity. Children whose mothers interact with them in positive, agreeable ways and openly express their feelings are likely to have more positive friendship relations. These patterns are observable as early as preschool and continue to be found in the elementary grades (Youngblade & Belsky, 1992). Mothers who use power-assertive discipline techniques and who believe that aggression is an acceptable way of resolving conflicts have children who expect to get their way by asserting power in peer conflicts (Dishion et al., 1991; Haskett & Kistner, 1991). In observations of the social relationships of 8- to 12-year-old children who had been physically abused, the abused children had lower ratings of social status among their peers, they were described by their peers as being aggressive and uncooperative,

These children, playing the Hebrew version of Scrabble, learn to work out disagreements, admire one another's skill, and compete while remaining friends.

and their teachers described them as showing noticeable behavior problems (Salzinger et al., 1993).

The family environment influences a child's social competence in at least three ways. First, children may directly imitate their parents' positive or aggressive behaviors. If parents ask a lot of questions and invite their child's opinions, for example, the child may be more likely to show interest in the ideas and opinions of others. Second, a parent's disciplinary technique may influence what a child expects in a social interaction. Children who have been exposed to aggressive parental techniques believe that these same strategies will work with their peers. As a result, these children are more likely to experience social rejection. Third, parents who are highly restrictive and who try to control their children's behavior are less likely to permit their young children to have many peer social interactions. These children arrive at the middle school years with less experience in peer play (Putallaz, 1987; Pettit, Dodge & Brown, 1988; Hart, Ladd & Burleson, 1990).

Three Lessons of Friendship

Children learn at least three lessons from daily interactions with their peers. The first lesson is an increasing appreciation of the many points of view that are represented in the peer group. As children play together, they discover that there may be several versions of the same song, differing sets of rules for the same game, and different customs for the same holiday. The second lesson teaches children to be increasingly sensitive to the social norms and pressures of their peer group. The third lesson is closeness to a same-sex peer.

Perspective Taking and Cognitive Flexibility   As children interact with peers who see the world differently than they do, they begin to understand the limits of their own points of view. Piaget (1932/1948) suggested that peers have an important influence in diminishing one another's self-centered outlook precisely because they interact as equals. Children are not forced to accept one another's ideas in quite the same way as they feel forced to accept the ideas of adults. They argue, bargain, and eventually compromise in order to maintain friendships. The opportunity to function in social peer groups for problem solving and for play leads children away from the egocentrism of early childhood and closer to the eventual flexibility of adult thought. The benefit of these interactions is most likely to occur when peers have differences in perspective that result in conflicts that must be resolved. The benefits are especially positive for children who interact with slightly more competent peers who can introduce more advanced or flexible approaches to problem solving (Tudge, 1992).

A substantial body of evidence demonstrates that the behavior of well-adjusted, competent children is maintained in part by a number of social-cognitive abilities, including social perspective taking, interpersonal problem solving, and information processing (Dodge et al., 1986; Elias, Beier & Gara, 1989; Downey & Walker, 1989; Carlo et al., 1991). These cognitive abilities appear to foster a child's entry into successful peer interactions. At the same time, active participation with peers tends to promote the development of these social-cognitive abilities.

Perspective-taking ability relates to other social skills that contribute to the quality of a child's social relationships. Such skills include the ability to analyze social problems, the ability to empathize with the emotional state of another person, the ability to understand that others may construe a situation differently because of their own information or beliefs, and a willingness to accept individual differences in personality or abilities (Chalmers & Townsend, 1990; Wellman, 1990; Pillow, 1991; Montgomery, 1993). Children who are sensitive to the variety of perspectives that coexist in a social situation are also likely to be more positively evaluated by their peers (Pellegrini, 1985). Rejected and withdrawn children often lack the social skills that would win them acceptance by their age-mates (Patterson, 1982; French, 1988).

An interactive process is set in motion. Children who have opportunities to participate in peer friendships make progress in achieving new levels of interpersonal understanding. As interpersonal understanding grows, children acquire the skills and sensitivity with which to be more effective with—and usually more valued by—their peers. Rejected children come to expect negative behaviors from others. A vicious cycle develops between the rejected child and her or his peers, each having negative expectations of the other. As this cycle continues, the rejected child's reputation becomes increasingly negative, and the child has little opportunity to develop positive relationship skills (Waas, 1988).

Acceptance and Rejection   The peer group evolves norms for acceptance and rejection. As children become aware of these social norms, they begin to experience pressures to conform. Adults, particularly teachers, lose some of their power to influence children's behavior. In the classroom, the early-school-age child focuses primarily on the teacher as a source of approval and acceptance, whereas the middle-school-age child perceives the peer group as an equally significant *— MoRe* audience. Children often play to the class instead of responding to the teacher. The roles of class joker, class snob, and class hero or heroine emerge during the middle-school-age years and serve as ways of gaining approval from the peer group.

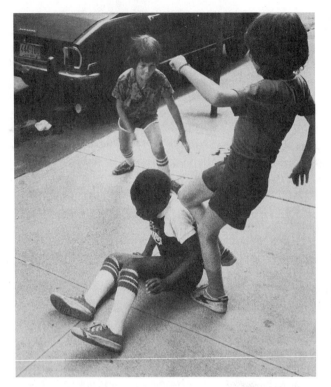

Some children are known as "bullies." They are quick to use aggressive strategies in peer interactions, they attribute hostile intentions to others, and they have an exaggerated idea about their own importance in comparison to others.

The need for peer approval becomes a powerful force toward conformity (Pepitone, Loeb & Murdock, 1977). Children learn to dress, talk, and joke in ways that are acceptable to their peers. From Grades 3 through 9, they become increasingly willing to conform to peer behaviors that might be considered antisocial. For example, it has been reported that ninth-graders are more willing than third-graders to go along with peer cheating, stealing, and trespassing (Berndt, 1979). Heterosexual antagonism, which is very common at this stage, is perpetuated by pressures toward conformity. If all the fifth-grade boys hate girls, Johnny is not very likely to admit openly that he likes to play with Mary. There are indications that perceived pressures to conform are stronger in the fifth and sixth grades than at later times, even though the importance of specific peer groups has not yet peaked (Gavin & Furman, 1989).

With the increased emphasis on peer acceptance and conformity comes the risk of peer rejection and feelings of loneliness. In a study of over 500 children between the ages of 8 and 11, more than 10% expressed feelings of loneliness and social dissatisfaction (Asher, Hymel & Renshaw, 1984). A significant proportion of the children had trouble making friends (17%), felt left out (18%), and agreed that they felt alone (14%). Not surprisingly, children who were infrequently mentioned as a best friend by others were more lonely than those who were mentioned as a best friend by three or more other children. Four social characteristics appear to combine to increase a child's experiences of loneliness. First, children who are withdrawn and who tend to be alone or who prefer to be involved in isolated activities even when other children are present tend to form a negative view of themselves as socially incompetent. Second, children who have trouble forming any kind of close friendship that provides emotional closeness and support are more likely to feel lonely. Third, peer rejection is especially powerful in producing feelings of loneliness. Children who experience a generally positive level of peer acceptance feel less alone than those who are rejected by their peers (Crick & Ladd, 1993). Finally, children who tend to blame themselves for their lack of social acceptance feel more lonely and are possibly less likely to believe that they can do anything to improve their situation (Renshaw & Brown, 1993; Cassidy & Asher, 1992; Rubin, LeMare & Lollis, 1990).

Some children who are rejected are disruptive and aggressive with their peers; others are socially withdrawn but do not exhibit aggressive tendencies; a third group has been described as both aggressive and withdrawn (French, 1988, 1990; Hymel, Bowker & Woody, 1993). All these groups tend to have multiple problems. Children in the *aggressive-rejected* group are more likely than nonaggressive children to attribute hostile intentions to others. They tend to see peer interactions as threatening, and they also say they would be likely to use aggressive strategies in response to negative peer behaviors (Sancilio, Plumert & Hartup, 1989; Quiggle et al., 1992). The aggressive children also tend to have a somewhat exaggerated idea of their competences.

Children in the *withdrawn* group tend to be inhibited, anxious, and interpersonally reserved. They have a negative self-concept and tend to interpret negative peer reactions as resulting from their own personal failings (Hymel et al., 1993). They have difficulty dealing with stress. These children also exhibit inappropriate affect and display various unusual behavioral mannerisms that are likely to draw ridicule from their peers (French, 1988). Some withdrawn children report close relationships with a favorite sibling. However, having this kind of sibling support does not appear to protect these children entirely from the negative consequences of peer rejection (East & Rook, 1992). The withdrawn-rejected children are more likely to experience high levels of loneliness and to worry about the quality of their relationships with peers (Parkhurst & Asher, 1992).

Children in the *aggressive-withdrawn* group tend to be the least well liked of all three types of rejected children. They exhibit anxiety, poor self-control, and social withdrawal in addition to aggressive behavior. They are rated by other children as incompetent in school ability; unattractive; showing the poorest skills in leadership, cooperation, or sense of humor; and the most likely to behave inappropriately in school. Despite high levels of peer rejection, however, they do not have the same low self-concept and negative view of their abilities as the withdrawn children.

Rejected children tend to retain this status throughout elementary school. They are likely to have future adjustment problems and often require psychiatric treatment in adolescence or adulthood (Coie & Krehbiel, 1984; Hymel et al., 1990).

Close Friends   The opportunity for peer-group interaction usually leads to the formation of dyadic same-sex friendships that may become quite intimate (Berndt, 1981). These are the years in which children have "best friends." In the course of these friendships, children share private jokes, develop secret codes, tell family secrets, set out on "dangerous" adventures, and help each other in times of trouble. They also fight, threaten, break up, and reunite. Sullivan (1949) pointed out the significance of these early same-sex friendships as building blocks for adult relationships. It is significant that the child experiences love for and closeness to a peer rather than an adult. The relationship is more likely to allow for mutuality of power, status, and access to resources (French, 1984). Conflicts in a relationship may be worked out in terms that the children control rather than escalating into dimensions having adult significance. One child cannot take away another child's allowance or send the other child out of the room when a conflict arises. The children must resolve their differences within the framework of their commitment to each other.

The structure of a school or classroom influences friendship formation. Close friends often see each other during the school day in classes and extracurricular activities (Hallinan, 1979; Epstein, 1983b). Close friendships appear to be influenced by attractiveness, intelligence, classroom social status, and satisfaction with and commitment to the best friend (Clark & Ayers, 1988). In a study of over 800 children in Grades 3–5, 78% had at least one reciprocating best friend (one child named another as one of his or her three best friends, and that other child named the first child on his or her list as well), and 55% had a *very* best friend. More girls than boys had best friends, and the quality of best friendships was somewhat different for girls and boys. Girls and boys described their best friend relationships quite similarly with respect to having low levels of conflict or betrayal and high levels of companionship and shared recreational activities. However, girls described their best friend relationships as having higher levels of caring and personal validation ("makes me feel good about my ideas"), intimacy ("we always tell each other our problems"), help and guidance ("help each other with schoolwork a lot"), and conflict resolution ("we make up easily when we have a fight") (Parker & Asher, 1993).

In addition to differences in the quality of best friendships, the friendship structures of boys differ somewhat from those of girls. Boys' friendship networks are somewhat larger and looser (Karweit & Hansell, 1983). The number of reciprocated female friendships increases with age (Epstein, 1983a). Middle-school-age girls spend more time each day than boys talking on the phone to their best friends, and their time spent talking to friends increases from sixth to eighth grade (Crockett, Losoff & Petersen, 1984). Girls have more in-school contact in service clubs and student government, while boys have their greatest contact with close friends in athletics (Karweit, 1983). Boys come into more contact with their best friends at nonschool functions and make more out-of-school friends than girls. Boys are more concerned than girls about status in selecting friends, and they make more unreciprocated friendship choices as a result (Karweit & Hansell, 1983; Clark & Ayers, 1988).

Children's need for the friendship of peers brings them into an increasingly complex social system. They learn that approval is conditional on conformity to certain norms, that other children do not necessarily share their view of the world, and that there are opportunities for unique emotional experiences that cannot be duplicated in the home. The friendship group is a transitional allegiance between commitment to the family and commitment to the larger social community.

Concrete Operations

We have described intelligence during infancy as consisting of sensory and motor patterns used to explore the environment and to gain specific ends. During toddlerhood, children develop a variety of representational skills. These skills free them from complete reliance on their immediate physical environment. They create novel situations and solve problems by using thought, fantasy, and language. Piaget (Piaget & Inhelder, 1969) suggested that at about age 6 or 7 a qualitatively new form of thinking develops. He described this new stage of intellectual development as *concrete operational thought*.

Before beginning our account of concrete operational thought, let us discuss the Piagetian notion of mental operations. The word *operation* suggests an action that is performed on an object or a set of objects. A mental operation is a

BOX 8.1

When Friends Disagree

We have argued that peer interaction fosters cognitive growth because peers are free both to share and to disagree with others' points of view. But does this really happen? Are children more open to and honest with their friends than they are with children who are not their friends? Will children change their views when friends disagree with them?

A study of boys and girls aged 8–10 approached the question of how friends and nonfriends handle conflict (Nelson & Aboud, 1985). Pairs of children who were friends and pairs who were not friends were asked to resolve their differences about a social-ethical problem. Among the problems they had to discuss were "What should you do if you get home and find that you accidentally picked up something at a store and forgot to pay for it?" and "What is the thing to do if a boy (girl) much smaller than you starts a fight with you?" In describing the interactions among the pairs, three differences were observed:

1. Friends offered each other more explanations than did nonfriends.
2. Friends criticized each other more than did nonfriends.
3. Friends who disagreed changed their opinions following discussions more readily than did nonfriends. Further, such changes were likely to be in the direction of a higher level of social responsibility.

Other research supports the finding that good friends do not avoid conflict and seem able to resolve conflicts relatively easily. Their disagreements do not last long, and they remain positive in their assessment of their relationship even when they disagree (Parker & Asher, 1993). Although close friends may not seek out conflict and criticism in their friendship, its presence appears to play a valuable role in promoting moral reasoning and social cognition.

transformation that is carried out in thought rather than in action. Piaget argued that such transformations are built on some physical relationship that the younger child can perform but cannot articulate. For example, a toddler can arrange a graduated set of circles on a stick so that the largest circle is at the bottom of the stick and the smallest circle is at the top. The child does not have a verbal label for the ordering operation but can perform the action. During concrete operations, children begin to appreciate a large group of actions that can be performed on objects and can perform them mentally without having to do so behaviorally. Thus, a mental operation is an internal representation of an alteration in the relationships among objects.

During the stage of concrete operations, a number of conceptual skills are gradually achieved. The ones that have received the most attention are (1) conservation skills, (2) classification skills, and (3) combinatorial skills. Each one comprises a group of interrelated operations. These skills bring children in touch with the logic and order of the physical world. They allow children to experience the predictability of physical events. As children take a new approach to problem solving through the use of the logical principles associated with concrete operational thought, they generalize these principles to their thinking about friendships, team play and other games with rules, and their own self-evaluation. As the order of the physical world becomes more apparent, children begin to seek logic and order in the social and personal domains as well. Sometimes, this search for order is frustrated by the unpredictability of the social world. At other times, children find that they can use their enhanced capacities for reasoning to solve interpersonal problems and to arrange their daily life so that it better meets their interests and needs.

Identity:
It's the same clay.

Reversibility:
You can roll it back
into a ball.

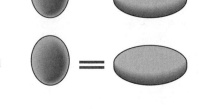

FIGURE 8.1

*Three concepts that contribute
to conservation*

Reciprocity:
The ball is small and
thick; the pancake
is large and thin.

Conservation

The basic meaning of *conservation* is that physical matter does not magically appear or disappear despite changes in form or container. The concept of conservation can be applied to a variety of dimensions, including mass, weight, number, length, and volume. The child who "conserves" is able to resist perceptual cues that alter the form of an object, insisting that the quantity remains the same despite the change in form. One of the most common problems of this type that Piaget investigated involves conservation of mass. The child is presented with two clay balls and asked to tell whether or not they are equal. Once the child is satisfied that the balls are equal, one of them is flattened out into a pancake. The child is then asked, "Which has more—this one [the pancake] or this one [the ball]?" Sometimes, the child is also asked whether the clay pieces are still the same. The child who does not conserve says the pancake has more clay because it is a lot wider than the ball. This child is still in the preoperational stage of thought. He or she is using personal perceptions to make judgments. The child who conserves knows that the two pieces of clay are still identical in mass and can explain why.

Children eventually use three concepts to ascertain that equality in any physical dimension has not been altered (see Figure 8.1). First, the child may explain that the pancake has the same amount of clay as the ball; no clay has been added or taken away. This is an example of the concept of *identity*: The pancake is still the *same* clay, and nothing has been changed except its shape. Second, the child may point out that the experimenter can turn the pancake back into a ball. This is an example of the concept of *reversibility*: The child becomes aware that operations can be reversed, so that their effects are nullified. Third, the child may notice that, although the pancake has a larger circumference, the ball is much thicker. When the child can simultaneously manipulate two dimensions, such as circumference and thickness, we observe the concept of *reciprocity*. In the clay ball example, change in one dimension is compensated for by change in another; the total mass remains the same. With consolidation of the concepts of identity, reversibility, and reciprocity, the child is able to conserve in any physical dimension.

There appears to be a developmental sequence in the capacity to conserve. Children generally conserve mass and number earliest, weight later, and volume last. Piaget also noted that the development of conservation does not proceed evenly across all of the physical modes. Research has shown that children who are unable to conserve quantity in an unfamiliar object, such as poker chips, can do so with a more familiar substance, such as M & M's (Lovell, 1961; Uzgiris, 1964; Goodnow, 1969; Gulko et al., 1988). Differences are not only seen when contrasting familiar and unfamiliar materials. For example, in one set of experiments, girls from low socioeconomic backgrounds were able to perform conservation of liquid tasks when the task was presented in the standard manner of comparing the experimenter's glass and their own. However, when the task was embedded in a story where juice had to be divided between two dolls, their performance declined. One interpretation of this difference in performance is that the girls identified the correct principles when the task was framed as a scientific exploration and where the experimenter served as an authority figure who expected a certain type of response. But in a pretense context, the principles of conservation were not salient to these girls. Evidence of a lack of generalizability of knowledge from in-school to out-of-school contexts is found in other areas of reasoning, especially mathematical codes and scientific principles (Perret-Clermont, Perret & Bell, 1991).

Questions have been raised about the meaning of conservation tasks, the timing of the emergence of conservation, and the possibility of teaching children to conserve. The way the task is presented and the kinds of questions asked may influence a child's responses. For example, the task may emphasize identity or equivalence. In an identity task, the child is asked to judge whether a single clay ball (V) has the same amount of clay after it has been rolled into a sausage (V_1). In an equivalence task, there are two balls of clay. The child is asked to judge whether the ball that is rolled into a sausage has the same amount of clay as the standard, comparison ball. Some studies have shown that children can perform the identity task earlier than the equivalence task; some have shown just the opposite; and some have argued that identity and equivalence are achieved at the same time (Brainerd & Hooper, 1978; Miller, 1978; Silverstein et al., 1982). In a study of 5- to 7-year-olds, children were asked to say how the materials looked, and then to say how they really were. Giving the child this distinction between appearance and reality resulted in more correct answers than the standard procedure, in which this distinction was not made (Bijstra, Van Geert & Jackson, 1989).

Some studies have demonstrated that it is possible to train young children of preschool age to conserve (Brainerd, 1977). These training studies have both theoretical and practical implications. Theoretically, Piaget's view of development suggests that there is a period of maturational readiness for the application of logical operations to physical objects. Thus, explanations of rules and relationships ought not to be relevant to a child who is not cognitively ready to understand them. The training studies suggest that it is possible to introduce such concepts as identity and reversibility so that children as young as 4 can achieve conservation. Further, they transfer conservation from the tasks involved in training to other materials and dimensions (Field, 1981; May & Norton, 1981). Apparently, the most important element in modifying a child's approach to conservation is being confronted by someone else's reasoning that contradicts one's own. For this contradiction to be effective, however, the child must be approaching a level of readiness to reorganize his or her thinking, and the gap between the current level of reasoning and the new ideas must not be too great. The implication here is that entry into a new stage of thought may emerge earlier and may be more readily influenced by the social environment than Piaget's cognitive developmental theory predicts.

In fact, contemporary work on cognition emphasizes the idea of the *social construction of meaning*. This notion, extended from Vygotsky's theory, emphasizes that, in most learning situations, the child not only is trying to understand the logical or symbolic features of the problem but is also trying to understand the social meaning of the situation. For example, in one study of 6- to 10-year-olds, the children were given a task with incomplete instructions. The focus of the study was on how children would handle the task and the extent to which they would ask for information from the experimenter to fill in the gaps in the instructions. Most of the children tried to complete the task on their own, without asking any questions to clarify the instructions. Even older children who were clearly aware that the instructions were inadequate did not ask for clarification. Most of the questions that were asked seemed to be directed toward confirming that they were doing the right thing—that is, questions directed toward gaining social approval from the experimenter rather than questions directed toward revealing more about the logic of the task. The idea is that learning is embedded in the social norms for interactions between adult authority figures and children. Transactions such as question asking, which adults may construe as a means of gaining information, are often constructed by children as a means of reassuring themselves that they are behaving appropriately and meeting the adults' expectations (Perret-Clermont et al., 1991).

Practically speaking, the implication is that preschool- and kindergarten-age children can integrate and apply more abstract concepts than educators once believed they could. For example, studies of children as young as 3 and 4 have shown that they understand the idea that materials are made of tiny particles that retain their properties even when they are invisible. They can use this notion of particles to explain how a substance, such as sugar, continues to exist in a solution and retains its sweetness even when it is invisible (Au, Sidle & Rollins, 1993; Rosen & Rozin, 1993). Early-childhood educators have found that, through a planned program of exploring, experimenting, and describing the transformation of materials, young children can be guided to conceptualize the physical world in a systematic, logical manner.

Classification Skills

Classification was first discussed in Chapter 5, where we described basic categorization skills. *Classification* is the ability to identify properties of categories, to relate categories or classes to one another, and to use categorical information to solve problems. One of the adaptive benefits of categorization is that one can assume that whatever holds true for one member of a category is likely to hold true for other members of a category. If water and juice are both liquids, then if you can pour water, you can pour juice. Other substances classified as liquids should also have this property, even substances one has never seen. In the middle-school-age years, children's knowledge of categories and of the information associated with various categories expands dramatically. What is more, children have a broad range of categories available into which to incorporate a novel observation. The value of classification skills is not purely to organize objects or experiences into classes, but to take advantage of what is known about these categories to make inferences about the characteristics and dynamics of members of the same categories, members of hierarchically related categories, and objects that are not members of a specific category (Kalish & Gelman, 1992; Lopez et al., 1992; Farrar, Raney & Boyer, 1992).

One component of classification skills is the ability to group objects according to some dimension that they share. The other component is the ability to order subgroups hierarchically, so that each new grouping will include all previous subgroups. Vygotsky (1932/1962) suggested a method for studying classification in young children. Children are presented with a variety of wooden blocks

Classification skills provide a basic cognitive building block for many hobbies. In baseball card collecting, for example, one can sort by team, by position, by year, by player, by recognition (Rookie of the Year), and so on. Every so often, you have to bring all the cards out and go through them to reclassify, meld in new acquisitions, and refine the collection.

that differ in shape, size, and color. Under each block is a nonsense syllable. The children are instructed to select, one at a time, all the blocks that have the same syllable. The youngest children, who would be characterized as preoperational in Piaget's stage theory, tend to select blocks by their color. Their technique for grouping is highly associative (Nelson, 1974). They choose each new block to match some characteristic of the previous selection, but they do not hold in mind a single concept that guides their choices.

Older children who have entered the stage of concrete operations tend to focus on one dimension at first, perhaps shape, and to continue to select blocks until they discover that they have made an incorrect choice. They use this discovery to change their hypothesis about which characteristics of the blocks are associated with the nonsense syllable. This classification task demonstrates the concrete operational child's ability to hold a concept in mind and to make a series of decisions on the basis of that concept. It also demonstrates that, during the stage of concrete operations, children can use mistakes to reorient their problem-solving strategy.

Piaget studied reasoning about class hierarchies or class inclusion by asking questions about whether a group of objects included more members of one subtype than of the group as a whole (Piaget, 1941/1952; Chapman & McBride, 1992). Thus, when a set of pictures shows three ducks, six sparrows, and two robins, one might ask, "Are there more sparrows or more birds in these pictures?" This is an unusual kind of question, one that children are probably rarely asked. By the age of 8 or 9, however, many children can respond correctly because they recognize the distinction between classes and subclasses. In order to handle such problems, children have to inhibit their tendency to reinterpret the question in line with a more common comparison, such as "Are there more sparrows than ducks?"

In one study of class inclusion reasoning, an intriguing pattern was found. Children aged 3 and 4, who could not repeat the question and who clearly had not learned any rules about classes, were more likely to answer correctly than children of 5 and 6. Children aged 7 and 8 performed better than any of the younger children. The 5- and 6-year-olds, who answered quickly and confidently, were consistently incorrect. They seemed unable to inhibit the more obvious comparison in order to consider the actual question (McCabe et al., 1982).

The capacity for classifying and categorizing has been explored in relation to specific domains such as health and illness concepts or concepts of the family. For example, children were told about 21 different human groupings and asked to say whether these groupings were a family: "Here are Mr. Mead and his son Tom. They live together, just the two of them. Are they a family?" The youngest subjects (4- to 6-year-olds) had trouble accepting examples involving single parents or biologically related people who do not live in the same home as instances of a family. Principles of biological relatedness and shared physical residence were both important to these youngest children's view of a family. By middle school age, the children were able to accept a wider variety of groups as meeting certain essential criteria of a family, usually biological relatedness and emotional closeness. Emotional closeness was endorsed by 80% of the subjects as a defining feature of a family and was used repeatedly as a basis for judging whether a specific instance of a grouping could be considered a family or not (Newman, Roberts & Syre, 1993).

Combinatorial Skills

A third characteristic of concrete operational thought is the development of *combinatorial skills*. Once they have acquired the scheme for conservation of number, children understand that certain physical transformations will not alter the number of units in a set. If ten poker chips are lined up in a row, there will still be ten chips whether they are spread out, squeezed tightly together, or stacked up. Children begin counting and can use counting to answer a "how many" question sometime between the ages of 3 and 4. For example, they can assign one number to each item in a set of four poker chips and tell you that there are four chips in all. However, young children have more difficulty selecting a set of six chips from a larger pile of chips, or establishing that two sets of chips are equal in number. They also have trouble solving verbal story problems when no concrete objects are present (Jordan, Huttenlocher & Levine, 1992; Sophian, 1988). Conservation of number is achieved around age 6 or 7 (Halford & Boyle, 1985). Addition, subtraction, multiplication, and division are all learned at this stage. Children learn to apply the same operations no matter what specific objects or quantities are involved. Piaget claimed that it is no coincidence that schools begin to instruct children in the basic skills of arithmetic at age 6. It is probably a strength of our schools that they meet an important aspect of intellectual readiness at the appropriate time.

The stage we have identified as early school age marks the beginnings of concrete operational thought. At this age, children's performance on tests of cognitive maturity is likely to be inconsistent. For example, children can conserve quantity but may make errors in conservation of weight, volume, or space. They

TABLE 8.1   Components of Concrete Operational Thought

Component	*New Abilities*
Conservation	Ability to perceive identity
	Ability to perceive reversibility
	Ability to manipulate two dimensions simultaneously in reciprocity
Classification	Ability to group objects according to some common dimension
	Ability to order subgroups in a hierarchy
Combinatorial skills	Ablility to manipulate numbers in addition, subtraction, multiplication, and division

may be able to perform a classification task correctly when they sort by one dimension, such as color, but may make errors when asked to sort objects that have more than one dimension in common. The process of classifying objects and the logic of conservation are not fully integrated until sometime during middle school age and may not reach peak performance until later adolescence or adulthood (Flavell, 1982).

As concrete operational intelligence develops, the child gains insight into the regularities of the physical world and the principles that govern relationships among objects. Table 8.1 summarizes the components of concrete operational thought. Perceptions of reality become less convincing than a logical understanding of how the world is organized. For example, even though it looks as if the sun sinks into the water, we know that what we see is a result of the earth's rotation on its axis. However, experiences in the grocery store with large, partially filled cereal boxes and attractively shaped bottles of shampoo attest to the occasional failure of the cognitive system to dominate perceptual experience.

Metacognition

As Piaget began his method of inquiry into concrete operational thought, he pointed the way to the study of metacognition. Rather than being concerned with the exact answers children gave to the questions he asked, he was concerned about how they explained their answers. How do children know what they know? What reasons can they give to justify or support their answers? *Metacognition* refers to a whole range of processes and strategies we use to assess and monitor our knowledge. It includes the "feeling of knowing" that accompanies problem solving, the ability to distinguish those answers about which we are confident from those answers about which we have doubts (Butterfield, Nelson & Peck, 1988). One element of this "feeling of knowing" is understanding the source of one's beliefs. For example, we can be told about something, we can see it for ourselves, or we can feel and touch something. All three of these sources of information may coincide to create a single belief, or we may discover that there are inconsistencies between what someone says is true and what we perceive through sight or touch. By the ages of 4 and 5, children are able to understand how all three sources of information have contributed to their understanding of an experience (O'Neill & Gopnik, 1991).

Metacognition includes the ability to review various strategies for approaching a problem in order to choose the one that is most likely to result in a solution

Higher-order problem solving of the type involved in strategic games requires metacognitive skills.

(Carr et al., 1989). It includes the ability to monitor one's comprehension of the material one has just read and to select strategies for increasing one's comprehension (Cross & Paris, 1988).

Metacognition develops in parallel with other cognitive capacities. As children develop in their ability to attend to more variables in their approach to problems, they simultaneously increase their capacity to take an "executive" posture in relation to cognitive tasks. They can detect uncertainty and introduce strategies to reduce it. They can learn study techniques that will enhance their ability to organize and recall information. These capacities continue to develop as the child becomes a more sophisticated learner. They are also quite amenable to training, both at home and at school. Metacognition appears to be a natural component of cognitive development. However, just like first-level cognitive capacities, it is constructed in a social context. Interactions between children and adults or peers nurture and stimulate metacognition by helping children to identify sources of information, to talk about and recognize the differences between feelings of certainty and uncertainty in their knowledge, and to devise effective strategies for increasing their feelings of knowing.

Skill Learning

Perhaps the area in which growth is most impressive during middle school age is the acquisition of skills. Science, history, and mathematics are accessible to children who can master the principles of classification and causality. Middle-school-age children have a growing appreciation of time as a nonsubjective unit. Because of the maturation of concrete operational thought, they can manipulate techniques of measurement. They can entertain an explanatory hypothesis and evaluate evidence that supports or disproves it. All of these cognitive skills allow children to move rapidly beyond the limits of their own experience into a consideration of events that happened long ago, that may happen in the future, or that are hypothesized to be happening all the time.

Children vary widely in their rate of intellectual development and in their capacities to perform skills. For example, by the first or second grade, children have been identified as mathematically gifted, normal, or mathematically "disabled" (Geary, Brown & Samaranayake, 1991; Geary & Brown, 1991). These designations relate to children's abilities to perform relatively simple mathematical operations such as addition. Differences in early mathematical ability relate to children's capacity to use a variety of counting strategies as well as to their ability to retain and recall math facts from memory. In a longitudinal study of cognitive growth, Klausmeier (1977) reported an enormous variability in the attainment of all concepts. For example, 17% of the 4th-graders in the study understood supraordinate-subordinate relations, a concept that 30% of the 12th-graders did not understand. By age 11 or 12, some children were using such strategies as hypothesizing, inferring, organizing, and generalizing, while some slowly developing children did not attain this range of skills until age 17 or 18.

Reading

In some ways, reading is the most significant intellectual skill that develops during middle school age because it opens the door to all the others. Reading provides access to new information, new uses of language, and new forms of thinking. Children are limited in their ability to learn mathematics, social studies, and science if they cannot read. Once a child can read fluently, the possibilities for independent inquiry expand significantly.

Children probably begin to read in a variety of ways. As David and his mother drove from home to preschool every day, they used a game with street signs along the road to build the bridge from language to literacy. At first, David would ask his mother to tell him what every sign said. After a while, David began to "read" the signs by memorizing words and phrases that were linked to certain shapes and patterns in the signs. Other children begin to read by learning letters and the sounds linked to them, and by experimenting with sounding out the letters when they are strung together. At first, most children are bewildered and confused by these experiences. This is a time when they require a good deal of support and encouragement for their efforts. Gradually, through a process of trial, feedback, and repetition, children learn to read simple words and simple sentences (Knight & Fischer, 1992).

Early in the process of learning to read, children understand and communicate orally a great deal more than they can read by themselves. They must learn how to use these oral communication skills in the comprehension of written language (Carroll, 1986). At some point, a child begins to articulate the concept "I can read" or "I am a reader." Once this idea is part of the self-concept, efforts to read increase and are energized by a confidence in one's potential for success.

Reading is a complex skill and involves the acquisition of many new techniques over the middle-school-age years. Box 8.2 helps us to understand the complexity of skilled reading. Children do not have to score extremely high in intelligence tests to make substantial progress in learning to read (Share, McGee & Silva, 1989). Most children, unfortunately, spend little or no time reading books outside school; over time, those who do some book reading show the greatest gains in reading achievement between the second and fifth grades (Anderson, Wilson & Fielding, 1988).

Parents' influence on children's reading achievement has been consistently documented. Parents affect their children's reading in at least five ways: in the value they place on literacy, in the emphasis they place on academic achievement, in the reading materials they make available at home, in the time they spend reading with their children, and in the opportunities they provide for verbal interaction in the home (Hess & Holloway, 1984; Schickedanz, 1986). Parents who value the ability to read, who urge their children to do well in school, who provide resources

Four basic assumptions about the characteristics of skilled reading have been described and appear to have received research support (Spiro, Bruce & Brewer, 1980; Hall, 1989):

1. Skilled reading depends on perceptual, cognitive, and linguistic processes.

2. Skilled readers obtain information from many levels simultaneously by synthesizing information derived from graphophonemes (the shapes of letters associated with sounds), morphemes (basic units that make up words), semantics (meanings), syntax (rules of grammar that dictate word order), pragmatics (cues provided by the context and past experience), schematics (construction and use of conceptual schemes to account for how information is arranged; prior knowledge about story structure), and interpretation. Thus, reading may be viewed as a process of simultaneous interactions that do not proceed in a strict sequence from basic perceptual units to a general interpretation of the text.

3. The capacity of the human information-processing system limits the amount that a person can perceive in a single fixation on a text, the speed of eye movement, the number of chunks of information that can be held in short-term memory, and the speed with which information can be retrieved from long-term memory. It appears that in the skilled reader, lower-level processes, such as decoding, function automatically. This allows the reader to attend to higher-order comprehension processes.

4. Reading involves the use of strategies. Skilled readers read with a purpose and continuously monitor their comprehension. Skilled readers perceive breakdowns in understanding, are selective in focusing their attention on various aspects of what they are reading, and refine their interpretation of the text as they read.

BOX 8.2

Characteristics of Skilled Reading

Much research still remains to be done before we will be able to explain how these processes work and to identify other processes that are essential for skilled reading. Still, the characteristics that have been identified give us a sense of just how complex the reading process is. The array of skills that middle-school-age children acquire as they learn to be skillful readers is marvelous indeed.

Pablo Picasso, The Reading of the Letter, *1921. Reading opens up a vast world of new ideas and information. Two friends sharing the same written material can elaborate their friendship by talking about what they have read.*

for reading, who read with them, and who talk with them produce children who are more skilled readers than parents who don't.

Parents may also have an indirect effect on how well a child will learn to read by influencing the child's placement in a school reading group (Goldenberg, 1989). They may do so by helping a child understand his or her school's reading curriculum (schools differ in their approaches to teaching reading), and by encouraging good work habits and appropriate classroom behavior. Parents who do these things may influence a teacher's perception of their child and, as a result, the child's assignment to a reading-level group. Ability grouping for reading instruction is practically universal in elementary schools (Slavin, 1987). Teachers depend on their perceptions of a child's ability, work habits, and behavior when they assign students to reading groups (Haller & Waterman, 1985). The higher the level of the children's reading group, the better they learn how to read.

The rudiments of a wide range of other skills may also be acquired during the middle school age:

mathematics	theater	art
music	dance	crafts
mechanics	sports	science
sewing	cooking	
writing	computer operation	

Using the information provided in Box 8.2 concerning the characteristics of skilled reading, we can construct a more general model that helps us understand what is being accomplished in building complex behavioral skills.

First, the development of skill depends on a combination of sensory, motor, perceptual, cognitive, linguistic, emotional, and social processes.

Second, skills are attained through the simultaneous integration of many levels of the component elements of skilled behavior. Skills are not acquired in strict sequence, from simple to complex. Simple and more complex components of skilled behavior are worked on at the same time.

Third, limits of the human system place constraints on an individual's capacity to perform skilled behavior. With practice, lower-level processes begin to function automatically, so a person can attend to higher-order processes. A skilled writer, for example, may write or type words automatically while attending to plot or character development.

Fourth, skilled behavior requires the use of strategies. Skillful people operate with purpose and continuously monitor their performance. They perceive breakdowns in performance, are selective in focusing attention on various aspects of what they are working on, and refine higher-order processes as they perform the skill. This model of skill development focuses on the elements that are necessary to move from what might be considered a novice level to a more advanced level in skill performance.

A Model of the Developing Mind

Think about the skill development that takes place in so many domains from about age 6 to about age 12. We observe children reaching high levels of functioning in such diverse areas as sports, reading, writing and story making, mathematical problem solving, art, and science. One is led to marvel at the complexity of the expansion of human thought processes needed to support such advanced functioning. Demetriou, Efklides, and Platsidou (1993) presented a general model of the developing mind that brings some of this complexity to light (see Figure 8.2). In their model, intellectual development is a product of the ongoing interactions among three structural systems: the processing system, the hypercognitive system, and the specialized structural systems (SSSs). The *processing system* (the inner circle in Figure 8.2) is composed of the elements of thinking that enter into every form of intellectual endeavor. It includes the speed of processing information, the control of processing information, and the storage and retrieval of information. According to the model, these processing systems respond to whatever task activates them, whether the stimuli are musical, verbal, or mathematical symbols.

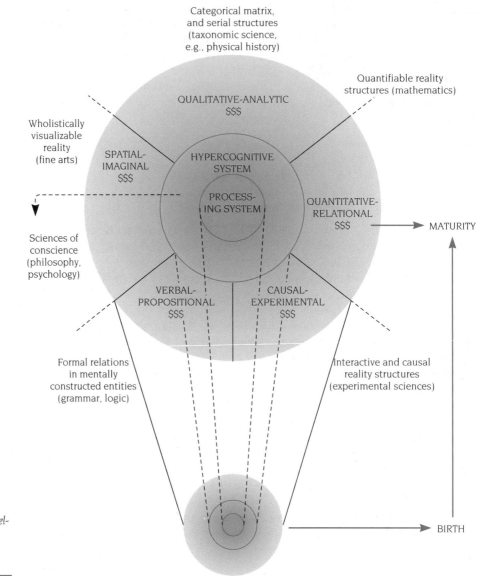

FIGURE 8.2

The general model of the developing mind

Source: Demetriou, Efklides, & Platsidou, 1993.

The *hypercognitive system* (the circle surrounding the processing system in Figure 8.2) is composed of all the functions that make meaning of something. In this model, the hypercognitive system tries to interpret a particular task or problem, evaluating what is required to solve it, and then assigning the problem to the one or more specialized systems that are best equipped to solve it. As new skill areas are established, more alternative strategies are available to approach the solution of particular tasks or problems.

The *specialized structural systems* (areas labeled SSS in the outer circle of Figure 8.2) are viewed as modular rather than generally available across all cognitive domains. In their model, Demetriou et al. identified five SSSs, each of them best suited to a particular family of problems and associated with a unique profile of mental abilities. In this model, each of the five SSSs can be brought into action to apply its own unique set of concepts or schemes, operations, or strategies to the task at hand. The more familiar the task and the more fully developed the SSS, the less likely it is that any other SSS will be recruited to aid in the problem-solving process.

According to this model, development can occur in all three components. The processing system can become more efficient, attention can be improved to control the input of information, and storage and retrieval can become more effective. The hypercognitive system can develop as metacognitive capacities mature, allowing the person to make finer and more accurate assessments of the nature of problems being encountered and the kinds of skills that are most appropriate to their solution. Within each SSS, new subcapacities may be acquired. For example, in the causal-experimental domain, the achievement of schemes for conservation are elaborated into the more formal scientific hypothesis-raising and hypothesis-testing strategies of scientific research. Developmental changes may result from the maturation of the central nervous system and the perceptual-motor capacities. They may arise from an individually guided motivation to increase one's skill level in a particular SSS. And they may arise from external sources such as participation in peer interactions that model new approaches to problem solving or from direct instruction or intervention, both at the hypercognitive level (teaching new approaches to recognizing and analyzing problems) and at the SSS level (teaching new techniques for representing and solving specific kinds of problems). Over time, and especially from about the ages of 10–12, we see a fantastic synergy of maturation, motivation, and external stimulation that seems to accelerate the growth process so that 11- and 12-year-olds appear qualitatively different in their approach to solving problems and enormously more skillful in their day-to-day functioning than younger children.

The Social Context of Skill Development

Recent attention has been given to the social and cultural context in which many skills, especially school-related abilities, emerge (Eccles, 1993). Progress in skill development is influenced by parental and school expectations regarding levels of performance. It is also influenced by a child's motivation to want to achieve new levels of ability and to direct her or his attention and energy to practice, problem solving, and the formulation of new strategies within a particular domain. Skill development may be enriched by interactions with skillful peers as well as by the appropriate intervention of teachers, coaches, and guides.

Consider the ongoing concern regarding mathematics ability among American students, especially in comparison to their Japanese and Chinese counterparts. In 1980, comparative studies showed that 1st- and 5th-grade American children in Minneapolis were substantially behind their age-mates in Sendai, Japan, and Taipei, Taiwan, in tests of mathematics achievement. In a ten-year follow-up, American children still lagged behind, and by the 11th grade, the gap in achievement had widened (Stevenson, Chen & Lee, 1993). Even the top 10% of the Minneapolis students scored at about the average level of the Taipei and Sendai students. It is difficult to account for these cross-national comparisons on the basis of ability. All three countries have practically universal enrollment of school-age children. What is more, when children were compared in their knowledge of general information of the type not included in the school curriculum, the American children in 1st and 5th grades scored higher than the Japanese and Chinese children.

At least four sociocultural factors interact to contribute to the advantage that Japanese and Chinese children show in mathematical skill development. First,

Chinese children use the abacus in their math lessons.

there is a difference in parents' views about what they should expect of their children. American parents appear to be satisfied with their children's level of mathematics performance and do not expect their children to do better than they are doing. In contrast, Japanese and Chinese parents have high expectations for their children's performance. Second, there is a difference in how parents evaluate their children's schools. American parents are generally satisfied with the school curriculum and think that the schools are doing a good job. Far fewer Japanese and Chinese parents view the schools as good or excellent. The public pressure in these cultures is for greater and greater improvement in the quality of education. They are more critical of their schools, and even though Japanese and Chinese children spend more time on homework than American children, these parents are more likely to encourage their children to spend even more time on homework.

Third, there are cultural differences in the emphasis given to ability as compared to effort. American parents and teachers highlight the importance of natural ability as a major factor in accounting for individual differences in mathematical ability. Japanese and Chinese parents and teachers are more likely to see outstanding performance as being a result of studying hard. If you believe that skill depends on natural ability, you might conclude that not much can be done to improve performance. If you believe that skill depends on effort, you may be more inclined to devote additional time and focused application to reach a new level of performance.

Finally, in contrast to what might be expected, by 11th grade American children are more stressed by school than Chinese or Japanese children. American students in the 11th grade reported frequent experiences of stress, anxiety about school, and aggression. They were less clear about the central role of school achievement in their lives. They had more competing demands on their time from after-school jobs, sports, and dating than the Japanese or Chinese adolescents. One interpretation of this difference is that American families and children set a greater value on freedom of choice and individuality than the Japanese or Chinese families. As a result, there is less consistency in the priority that American schoolchildren, their parents, and their teachers place on academic achievement in relation to the many other activities that claim time and attention.

The emphasis on skill building and the energy that middle-school-age children bring to the acquisition of new skills suggest a strong parallel to toddlerhood. At both stages, children's motives for competence and mastery are directed outward to the environment. At both stages, children appear to be delighted by the potential for learning that almost every new encounter offers. However, as a result of their cognitive capacities and their awareness of social expectations, skill learning at middle school age is embedded in a much more complex framework of continuous monitoring and self-assessment. In addition, children's beliefs and attitudes about which skills are important, what they should expect of themselves, what others expect of them, and what kinds of competing demands should influence their dedication to skill development all contribute to the levels of performance they are likely to achieve.

Self-Evaluation

During the middle-school-age years, the emphasis on skill building is accompanied by a new focus on self-evaluation. Children strive to match their achievements to internalized goals and external standards. Simultaneously, they receive feedback from others about the quality of their performance. In early school age, children begin to receive messages about how well they are accomplishing tasks set before them. They may be designated as "Red Group" readers, or they may see a long line of stars after their names on the bulletin board. They may be asked to sit in the left-hand row to receive "special" help or may be told to go down the hall for tutoring. These and many other signs are sources of social evaluation that children incorporate into their own self-evaluations.

During middle school age, the process of self-evaluation is further complicated because the peer group joins the adult world as a source of social comparison, criticism, and approval. In toddlerhood and early school age, children are likely to observe and imitate their peers in order to learn new strategies for approaching a task or out of curiosity to see how their peers are doing a particular project. But in middle school age, pressures toward conformity, competition, and the need for approval feed into the self-evaluation process. Children begin to pay attention to the work of others in order to assess their own abilities (Butler & Ruzany, 1993). The child's athletic skills, intellectual abilities, and artistic talents are no longer matters to which only teachers and parents respond. Peers also identify others' skills and begin to generate profiles of one another: "Oh, Rafael is good in math, but he runs like a girl"; "Jane is kind of fat, but she writes great stories"; "I like Rashidah best because she's good at everything." Depending on their resolution of the crises of toddlerhood and early school age, children approach the process of self-evaluation from a framework of either self-confidence or self-doubt. They may expect to find tasks easy to accomplish and approach them vigorously, or they may anticipate failure and approach tasks with hesitation.

In research involving children in the age range 8–13, Susan Harter (1985, 1993) devised a method for assessing children's perceptions of competence in five specific domains: scholastic competence, athletic competence, likability by peers, physical appearance, and behavioral conduct. In addition, she measured general or global self-esteem. Her research was guided by the idea that by the age of 8 children not only would be able to differentiate specific areas of competence but would view certain areas as more important than others. She found that self-esteem is highest in those children who view themselves as competent in domains that they judge to be important. Competence in relatively unimportant domains is not especially strongly related to overall self-esteem.

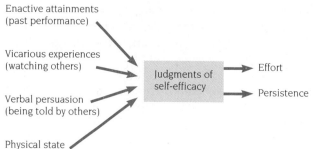

FIGURE 8.3

Four components of self-efficacy

Self-Efficacy

How do children assess their competence in a specific ability area? Albert Bandura (1982) theorized that judgments of self-efficacy are crucial to understanding this process. *Self-efficacy* is defined as the person's sense of confidence that he or she can perform the behaviors demanded in a specific situation. Expectations of efficacy vary with the specific ability. In other words, a child may view efficacy in one way in a situation requiring mathematical ability and in another way in one requiring physical strength.

Bandura has suggested that four sources of information contribute to judgments of self-efficacy (see Figure 8.3). The first source is *enactive attainments*, or prior experiences of mastery in the kinds of tasks that are being confronted. Children's general assessment of their ability in any area (e.g., mathematics, writing, or gymnastics) is based on their past accomplishments in that area (Skaalvik & Hagtvet, 1990). Successful experiences increase their perceived self-efficacy, whereas repeated failures diminish it. Failure experiences are especially detrimental when they occur early in the process of trying to master a task. Many boys and girls are diverted from mastering such sports as tennis and baseball because they have made mistakes early in their participation. They develop doubts about their abilities that prevent them from persisting in the task.

The second source is *vicarious experience*. Seeing a person similar to oneself perform a task successfully may raise one's sense of self-efficacy; seeing a person similar to oneself fail at a task may lower it (Brown & Inouye, 1978).

Verbal persuasion is the third source. Children can be encouraged to believe in themselves and to try a new task. Persuasion is likely to be most effective with children who already have confidence in their abilities. The persuasion helps to boost their performance level.

The fourth source is *physical state*. People monitor their body states in making judgments about whether or not they can do well. When children feel too anxious or frightened, they are likely to anticipate failure. Children who are excited and interested but not overly tense are more likely to perceive themselves as capable of succeeding.

Self-efficacy judgments are related to children's perceptions of their likelihood of success. These judgments also determine the factors to which children attribute their success or failure (McAuley, Duncan & McElroy, 1989). In the face of difficulty or failure, children who have confidence in their abilities and high self-efficacy will work harder to master challenges. They will attribute their difficulties to a failure to try hard enough, and they will redouble their efforts. Children who have a low sense of self-efficacy tend to give up in the face of difficulty because they attribute their failure to a basic lack of ability (Bandura & Schunck, 1981). The

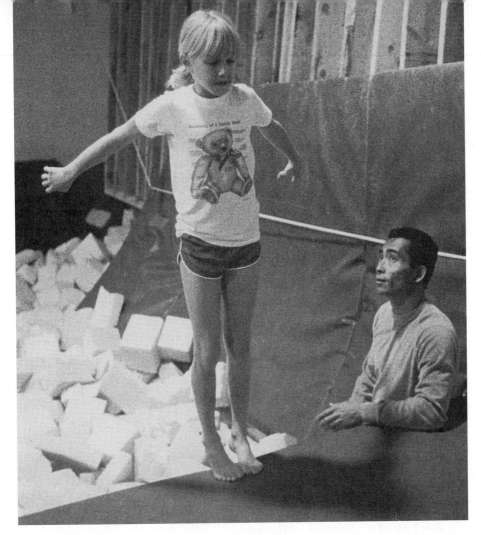

Past successes, the success or failure of the other children who are learning this skill, the encouragement of the coach, and internal feelings of anxiety or calm all contribute to this girl's sense of self-efficacy as she tries to learn how to perform a back flip.

level of self-efficacy also affects how children prepare to handle new challenges. In their thoughts, emotions, and preparation for action, those who are preoccupied by self-doubts differ from those who believe in themselves.

Social Expectations

In our society, it is extremely difficult for children to develop independent, internal criteria by which to judge their abilities. If the skills of the culture were more manual, perhaps it would be easier for children to make such judgments. In learning to plow a field, for example, one can look back over the land and see whether the furrows are deep enough and the rows straight. Many important areas of accomplishment, however, have no clear, objective standards with which children can readily compare their performance. In writing an English composition, how can one judge whether one has done an adequate job? How, indeed, can a child evaluate improvement?

Several theories of the self suggest that the appraisals and expectations of others become incorporated into one's own self-evaluation. Self-esteem is based on the general positive regard and approval of others, and on the specific expectations they have for one's ability and achievement in certain areas of performance (Harter, 1993; Jussim, 1990a). In attempting to assess their own abilities, children tend to rely on many external sources of evaluation, including grades, teachers' comments, parental approval, and peer approval (Crooks, 1988).

If feedback from important adults suggests to children that they are cooperative, intelligent, and creative, these attributes are likely to be incorporated into their self-evaluations. Children who see themselves as cooperative and intelligent are likely to approach social and intellectual tasks with optimistic expectations about their performance. Conversely, feedback suggesting lack of competitiveness, intelligence, and creativity can produce a pessimistic or antagonistic approach to the challenges of skill development.

Social expectations contribute to children's expectations about their own abilities and behavior (Harris & Rosenthal, 1985). Evaluative feedback that is associated with intellectual ability or skill feeds into children's conceptualization of their own competence. Repeated failure information or remarks that imply lack of ability tend to make children less confident of success in subsequent tasks. The pattern of expectations appears to crystallize during the second and third grades. Preschoolers do not make systematic use of success or failure feedback in predicting their next success (Parsons & Ruble, 1977). Even in the first grade, children's expectations about the grades they will receive on their first report cards are not clearly related to their IQs or to parents' or teachers' expectations, nor are they closely related to children's later estimates of their grades. By the end of the first grade, however, children begin to be more accurate predictors of their performance (Entwisle et al., 1987; Alexander & Entwisle, 1988). By fifth grade, children are very aware of their teachers' expectations for their performance, and they are likely to mirror those expectations in their own academic achievement (Weinstein et al., 1987).

The Self-Fulfilling Prophecy   The feedback students receive from their teachers is not wholly objective. Teachers' expectations about their students' abilities may be based on objective assessments, but they may also be derived from stereotypes about certain types of children or biases based on prior experiences, like having a child's older siblings in class in prior years or hearing unfavorable comments from other teachers. Merton (1948) suggested that problems may arise through a process that he called the *self-fulfilling prophecy*. This concept refers to the idea that false or inaccurate beliefs can produce a reality that corresponds with these beliefs.

In the original study on the effect of teacher expectations on student performance, teachers were led to believe that certain students were "late bloomers" who would show major gains in IQ later on in the school year. These children, chosen at random from among first- and second-graders, actually did show increases in IQ of 10–15 points in comparison to the control group (Rosenthal & Jacobson, 1968). The effect did not continue into the third and fourth grades, and overall, the correlation between teachers' expectations and students' measured IQ was modest.

Subsequent naturalistic studies of the self-fulfilling prophecy in classroom settings have shown that it has a consistent, but comparatively small, effect on student performance. One way of expressing the size of the effect is that if one could control for actual ability and prior achievement, the teachers' erroneous expectations might lead to increases in performance among about 10% of children who were targets of high expectations and decreases in performance among about 10% of children who were targets of low expectations (Jussim, 1990b). The impact of these erroneous perceptions is likely to be increased when the person making the judgments is especially rigid or highly motivated to maintain and confirm his or her negative views of a certain group. Thus, one might expect a stronger impact

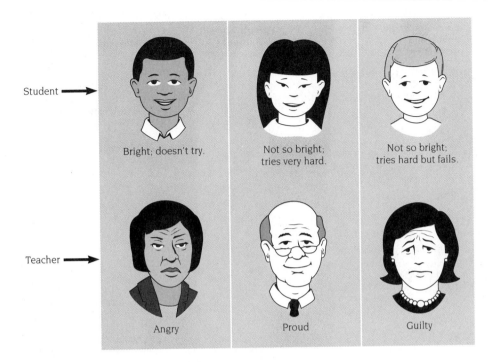

Student →

Bright; doesn't try.   Not so bright; tries very hard.   Not so bright; tries hard but fails.

Teacher →

Angry   Proud   Guilty

FIGURE 8.4
Student's ability and effort, teacher's reactions

of biased perceptions and the self-fulfilling prophecy among teachers who endorse prejudiced views, whether the target of prejudice is race, gender, social class, religion, or some other classification.

Certain conditions make children more or less vulnerable to internalizing false expectations. Children who are unsure about their abilities and those who are learning something for the first time may be more likely to rely on the information they receive from others to assess their abilities. Being in a new situation, like moving to a new school or changing from elementary to middle school, may increase a child's dependence on social expectations for performance. Middle-school-age children, to whom many new domains of skill development are just being introduced, may be more vulnerable to the effects of biased perceptions and erroneous expectations than are older children (Jussim, 1990b).

In addition, some children appear to monitor their social environment more self-consciously than others (Musser & Browne, 1991). High self-monitoring children are more aware of the emotional and nonverbal behavior of others and make more use of social information to evaluate and regulate their own behavior. These children are more responsive to subtle forms of feedback about their performance, taking in more information about social expectations for their performance than do the children who are comparatively oblivious of the intricacies of the social environment.

Teachers' expectations for a student's performance are influenced by their assessments of both the student's ability and the student's effort. In a study of elementary-school teachers, a relationship was found between the teachers' explanations for students' success and failure and the emotions they felt under the various conditions (see Figure 8.4). It was presumed that these emotional reactions were among the major cues that teachers sent to students about their performances. When teachers believed that students' poor performances were due to a lack of effort, they were likely to feel angry toward the students, particularly if

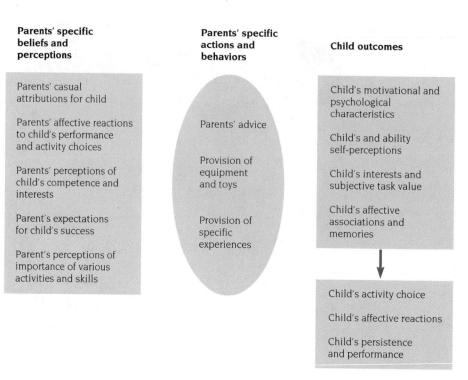

FIGURE 8.5

The relationship of parents' gender-role-stereotype beliefs and perceptions to parental actions and behaviors and child outcomes
Source: Adapted from Eccles, 1993.

they believed the students were capable of very good work. When children of low ability suddenly began putting forth a great deal of effort, teachers were likely to take pride in their own accomplishments, believing they had really helped these children become more motivated. If low-ability students who were trying very hard failed, teachers felt a sense of guilt. Teachers were more willing to accept personal responsibility for certain configurations of student success and failure than for others. The students who made teachers the angriest were the bright ones who did not try hard. The research on teacher expectations illustrates how social expectations influence both perceptions of other people and the quality of interpersonal communication (Prawat, Byers & Anderson, 1983).

Parents' Expectations   Parents' as well as teachers' expectations influence children's perceptions of their abilities. This process is demonstrated in a study of parents' and children's attitudes toward mathematical aptitude (Parsons, Adler & Kaczala, 1982). Children in Grades 5–11 and their parents were asked about their attitudes toward the children's mathematics achievement. Parents had lower expectations for their daughters' math achievement than for their sons'. They believed that mathematics is more difficult for girls than for boys and requires more effort. Their expectations about their children's aptitude were better predictors of the children's self-assessments than were the children's own past performances in mathematics.

Continuing to focus on the relationship between gender-role bias and the socialization of children's competencies and interests, Eccles (1993) proposed the following model (see Figure 8.5):

The evidence suggests that general (parental) gender-role-beliefs influence perceptions of individual children's competencies and interests, which in turn affect the kinds of experiences parents provide. . . . Essentially, we believe that parents' gender-role stereotypes, in interaction with their children's sex, affect the following mediators:

1) parents' causal attributions for the children's performance; 2) parents' emotional reaction to their children's performance in various activities; 3) the importance parents attach to their children's acquiring various skills; 4) the advice parents provide their children regarding involvement in various skills; and 5) the activities and toys parents provide. In turn, we predict that these subtle and explicit mediators influence the development of the following child outcomes across the various gender-role-stereotyped activity domains: 1) children's confidence in their ability; 2) children's interest in mastering various skills; 3) children's affective reaction to participating in various activities; and as a consequence of these self and task perceptions, 4) the amount of time and type of effort the children end up devoting to mastering and demonstrating various skills. (p. 170)

A number of studies support the underlying dynamics of this model. Independent of actual gender differences in specific domains including math, sports, and English, parents' stereotypes about which gender is more talented in a particular area influence their perceptions of their own child's competence in that area. Parents' perceptions of competence are directly related to their children's perception of competence (Eccles, Jacobs & Harold, 1990).

Other studies have examined the impact of parents' expectations on the judgments that academically capable children make about their abilities. In a phenomenon described as the *illusion of incompetence*, some children who perform well on tests of academic achievement (at the 90th percentile or above) perceive themselves as below average in academic ability. These children expect lower levels of success, are less confident, attempt less challenging tasks, and say that their schoolwork is more demanding than peers of similar high ability who have more positive self-evaluations. It appears that parents play a central role in establishing these children's low assessments of themselves. Children who have an illusion of incompetence think that their parents have a low opinion of their abilities and expect little of them. They see their fathers, in particular, as holding to very rigorous standards that they are not expected to meet (Phillips, 1984, 1987). The parent-child dynamics that are likely to underlie this negative assessment were observed in a study involving children with high academic ability and varying levels of perceived academic competence. Children worked with their mothers and fathers on solvable and unsolvable tasks. The fathers of children who had low perceptions of their academic competence were found to interact with their children in more critical or unsupportive ways than did the fathers of children who had high perceptions of their academic competence. Further, the children who had illusions of incompetence were more emotionally upset and dependent when they approached the unsolvable tasks (Wagner & Phillips, 1992).

The discussion of self-evaluation highlights children's sensitivity to their social environment. They become aware of existing roles and norms and of the sanctions for norm violation. Direct experiences with success and failure are important, but they are embedded in a context of social expectations. Messages of reassurance and encouragement from parents and teachers can play a key role in establishing a positive sense of competence and in motivating children to persist in the face of difficult challenges. The negative effects of false or erroneous teacher expectations can be combated through techniques directed at giving children many opportunities for success in a particular domain so that they come to trust their own judgments about their abilities. In addition, parents can advise children that some teachers have prejudiced attitudes and help them identify the signs that such attitudes are operating unfairly in the classroom. By the end of the middle school years, children have had enough school experience so that they can detect favoritism, bias, and unfair treatment and can devise strategies to protect themselves from the impact of negative biases. The more children are embedded in strong, supportive social relationships, the more confidence they will have in their general worth and the more likely they will be to arrive at accurate assessments of their abilities.

Team Play

During middle school age, a new dimension is added to the quality of a child's play. Children begin to participate in team sports, and as a result, they gain a sense of team success as well as personal success. Team sports are generally more complicated than the kinds of games described as group play in Chapter 7. The rules are so complex that they may require a referee or an umpire if they are to be followed accurately. In these sports, children join together into teams that remain together for the duration of the game. Some children join teams that play together for an entire season, such as Little League. Through participation in team play, one can see a "preworking" of the skills and orientations that will apply to the world of work and to the functioning of the family group. Three significant characteristics of the experience of team membership are relevant to development during this stage: (1) interdependence; (2) the division of labor; and (3) competition.

Interdependence

Team membership carries with it an awareness that one's acts may affect the success or failure of the entire group. There is a definite emphasis on winning and losing. Children may be ostracized or ridiculed if they contribute to a team loss. Although team sports do provide opportunities for individual recognition, it is quite clear that team success casts a halo over even the poorest players and team failure a shadow over even the best. In this sense, participation in team sports is an early lesson in *interdependence*. All of the team members rely on one another, and ideally, it will be to everyone's advantage to assist the weaker members in improving the quality of their play. The best coaches are noted for inspiring this sense of interdependence and mutual support among team members. They urge team members to work together to improve their skills. What often happens, however, is that the poorest players are scorned and scapegoated, particularly if the team loses.

Division of Labor

The *division of labor* as an effective strategy for attaining a goal is experienced through participation with peers on teams. Children learn that each position on a team has a unique function and that the team has the best chance of winning if each player performs a specific function rather than trying to do the work of all the other players. The concept of the team encompasses the variety of activities in which each of the team members actually engages. A complementary concept is cooperation. Team members learn that if the team as a whole is to do its best, the members must help one another. Rather than playing all the roles, a team member tries to help each other member play his or her role as well as possible. Cooperation takes many forms: Members share resources, take time to help other team members improve their skills, plan strategies together, work together on the field, cheer each other up, bring out the equipment, or clean up after the game. In many sports, there is a dynamic tension between competition and cooperation.

As they take their positions in the field, these children learn the importance of the division of labor. Each position has a special function and is important to the success of the team as a whole.

Team members may compete with each other for a more desirable position or for the status of being the top player. At the same time, the team members know that they have to support each other, especially when they play against another team.

The team may well become an experiential model for approaching other complex organizations (Shears & Bower, 1974). Once children learn that certain goals can best be attained when tasks are divided among a group of people, they begin to conceptualize the principles behind the organization of social communities. They recognize that some children are better suited to handling one aspect of the task and others to handling another. Some children enjoy the skill development associated with team play, others enjoy learning the rules and devising strategies, others especially value peer companionship, and still others have a strong inner motive to compete and to try to win (Klint & Weiss, 1987). The distribution of roles to fit the children's individual skills and preferences is a subtle element of the learning that is acquired through team play.

Competition

Finally, team play teaches children about *competition* and the importance of winning. In team sports, both sides cannot win; success for one side must result in failure for the other. If the team experience is a laboratory for learning lessons about the larger social community, this characteristic promotes a view of social situations in competitive terms. Some children come to think of business, politics, popularity, and even interpersonal conflicts as win-lose situations in which the primary goal is to beat one's opponents. The idea of a win-win strategy to resolve conflict is very foreign in this context.

Winning is a great "high." Many young adults have fond memories associated with winning an important game or a big match. They hope to reexperience the energy that occurs as a result of winning as they approach their adult activities. The metaphor of playing on a winning team is deeply interwoven into the world of work, helping to give focus and drive to day-to-day work-related obligations and tasks. When adults look back on their childhood play experiences, many recall the excitement associated with competition and continue to long for this excitement in their daily life. In one study of women in traditional and nontraditional professions, for example, more professional businesswomen and other women in nontraditional fields remembered experiences playing in competitive sports and being on teams with both males and females during their childhood (Coats & Overman, 1992).

In contrast to those who are energized by the challenges of competition, some children are especially sensitive to the pain of failure. The public embarrassment and private shame that accompany failure are powerful emotions. Some children will go to remarkable extremes to avoid failing. In team sports, each game ends with a winning and a losing side. Children who have a low sense of self-esteem are more likely to experience intense anxiety about losing in a competitive situation (Brustad, 1988). One can claim that losing is an important kind of learning for children, but as Vince Lombardi said, "Show me a good loser, and I'll show you a loser." Involvement in team sports is guaranteed to bring with it the bitterness of losing and the commitment to avoid losing, experiences that drive some children away from sports and into other domains of competence.

Team play has implications for both intellectual and social development. Children who play team sports learn to see themselves as contributors to a larger effort and learn to anticipate the consequences of their behavior for the group. Games that involve teams are generally so complex that children are called on to learn many rules, make judgments about those rules, plan strategies, and assess the strengths and weaknesses of the other players. All of these characteristics of participation in team sports can stimulate cognitive growth (Smith, 1986). In one study, for example, children were divided into soccer "experts" and soccer "novices" (Schneider & Bjorklund, 1992). The experts had an impressive depth of knowledge about the game of soccer and, when given a memory task involving soccer-related items, were able to use their expertise to perform the task at a high level. Interest in sports and competitive team play has been used as a motivational "hook" to interest children in other areas of school ability. For example, in Columbus, Ohio, a former Ohio State University football player who also played professional football organized a summer camp for 5th- through 12th-graders. The focus of the camp was to combine sports with math and science education. The curriculum was developed to teach math and science for 2 1/2 hours each day and to spend the remainder of the day in practical applications in the area of sports. For example, the students might learn the principles of physics that account for why a baseball travels faster than a football and might then experiment with these principles on the ball field (Beaulieu, 1992).

In-Group and Out-Group Attitudes

The social consequences of team play can be divided into in-group and out-group attitudes. With regard to the in-group, the child learns to value team goals and to contribute to them. Identification with team goals may require a child to relinquish a personal goal, such as being first at bat, for the good of the team. The child receives feedback from the other team members about skills and may be helped to improve by other team members. Children learn to value their roles as elements in the larger system and to see their interdependence with the other players. They learn that team victories give them great personal satisfaction and that team defeats can be a source of frustration and depression.

The child learns to see the outcome of competition as a win-or-lose situation. The other team is the "enemy," and there is no alternative to trying one's hardest

TABLE 8.2	Development of Attitudes as a Result of Team Play Experiences	
In-Group Attitudes	**Out-Group Attitudes**
The child learns:	The child learns:
1. To value and contribute to team goals.	1. That the outcome of competition is win or lose.
2. To relinquish personal goals for team goals.	2. That the other team is the "enemy."
3. To receive and use feedback and help from team members.	3. That one must try one's hardest to defeat the other team.
4. To value her or his role as an element in a larger system and to perceive interdependence.	4. That there is and should be antagonism between teams.
5. That team victories give personal satisfaction and team defeats bring frustration and depression.	5. That assisting the other team is unethical

to defeat it. Antagonism toward the out-group is valued in team sports, and any attempt to assist the other team is seen as unethical.

Many older adolescents recall that in-group and out-group attitudes were formed even within their team. Although this may appear contradictory to the concepts of interdependence and group cooperation, it clearly happens. Certain children are "earmarked" as the true athletes of the team, and the others may feel like outsiders. Sometimes, parents who are influential in a community take steps behind the scenes to make sure their children are given special treatment. In these instances, the out-group children may feel that they not only are competing with members of the opposing team but have to protect themselves from insults, pranks, and other efforts by their own team members to ostracize them.

The expression of in-group and out-group boundaries was observed in a study of sharing among middle-school-age children (Dickstein, 1979). Children shared more with a friend than with a disliked peer. With friends, children always preferred a norm of equal treatment. With nonfriends, children always preferred a norm of rivalry. Even those children who were quite skillful in perspective taking were not likely to apply this ability to disliked peers.

Children may belong to more than one in-group, and the people who are categorized as members of an out-group may change according to the situation. For example, Ryan and his friend Tom were on the school soccer team together, but they belonged to different summer baseball leagues. During the summer, they had to compete against each other, so it usually turned out that they spent more time together and were closer friends during the school year than they were during the summers. Table 8.2 shows the in-group and out-group attitudes that result from experiences in team play.

All human societies observe distinctions between in-group and out-group attitudes and behaviors. The *in-group* is a group whose members share common norms, goals, and values. The in-group members also share a common fate; in sports, for example, the team wins or loses as a team. Feelings of cohesiveness with and similarity to members of an in-group prompt behaviors supportive of that group's survival. The *out-group* is any group whose goals are either in opposition to or inconsistent with the goals of the in-group. Any group may be perceived as an out-group, even though it does not actually pose any physical threat to members of the in-group. For sports teams, the out-group's goal of winning is directly in competition with the in-group's similar goal (Triandis, 1990). We learn that moral principles that apply to members of the in-group do not necessarily apply to members of the out-group. In the extreme, adults may justify killing a member of an out-group under conditions of declared war.

Team experiences that elaborate in-group and out-group attitudes are socialization experiences that have both positive and negative consequences. For most children, belonging to a team, making friends, learning new skills, and enjoying the sense of success associated with a collaborative effort are very positive experiences of middle school age. However, we all know of instances where rivalries escalate into peer hatreds, children from neighboring schools turn against each other, and coaches humiliate and degrade children in order to instill a commitment to the team and a determination to win. Perhaps the question is whether, particularly in team sports, the focal point of the activity is to enhance children's natural impulses for competence and skill elaboration, or whether the team activity becomes a way for adults to vent their own frustrated needs for domination and power.

The Psychosocial Crisis: Industry Versus Inferiority

According to psychosocial theory (Erikson, 1963), the person's fundamental attitude toward work is established during the middle-school-age period. As children develop skills and acquire personal standards of evaluation, they make an initial assessment of whether or not they will be able to make a contribution to the social community. They also make an inner commitment to strive for success. Some children are keenly motivated to compete against a standard of excellence and to achieve success. Others have low expectations about the possibility of success and are not motivated by achievement situations. The strength of a child's need to achieve success is well established by the end of this stage (Atkinson & Birch, 1978).

Industry

Industry is an eagerness to acquire skills and to perform meaningful work. During middle school age, many aspects of work are intrinsically motivating. The skills are new. They bring the child closer to the capacities of adults. Each new skill allows the child some degree of independence and may even bring new responsibilities that heighten his or her sense of worth. In addition to the self-motivating factors associated with increased competence, external sources of reward promote skill development. Parents and teachers encourage children to "get better" at what they do through grades, material rewards, additional privileges, and praise. Peers also encourage the acquisition of some skills, though they may have some negative input with regard to others. Certain youth organizations, such as Scouting and 4-H, make the acquisition of skills a very specific route to success and higher status.

In an effort to develop a measure of industry, Kowaz and Marcia (1991) described the construct as comprising three dimensions. One dimension was viewed as the cognitive component of industry and was defined as the acquisition

In every culture, it is essential to nurture a sense of industry. Children are urged to develop new skills and to feel a sense of pride in new accomplishments. This Afghan boy is learning the techniques of metalcraft.

of the basic skills and knowledge valued by the culture. The second dimension was considered the behavioral component of industry and was defined as the ability to apply the skills and knowledge effectively through characteristics such as concentration, perseverance, work habits, and goal-directedness. The third dimension, the affective component, was defined as a positive emotional orientation toward the acquisition and application of skills and knowledge, such as a general curiosity and desire to know, a pride in one's efforts, and an ability to handle the distresses of failure as well as the joys of success.

Inferiority

Given the internal thrust toward skill building that is generated by motives for competence and external rewards for mastery, it may appear that there should be no real conflict at this stage. One might think that everyone is united in a commitment to the joy and fulfillment that accrue from experiences of competence.

What experiences of middle school age, then, might generate a sense of inferiority? Feelings of worthlessness and inadequacy come from two sources: the self and the social environment. Alfred Adler (1935) directed our attention to the central role that organ inferiority may play in shaping a person's perceptions of his or her abilities. *Organ inferiority* is any physical or mental limitation that prevents the acquisition of certain skills. Children who cannot master certain skills experience some feelings of inferiority. Individual differences in aptitude, physical development, and prior experience result in experiences of inadequacy in some domain. No one can do everything well. Children discover that they cannot master every skill they attempt. Even the child who feels quite positive toward work and finds new challenges invigorating will experience some degree of inferiority in a specific skill that he or she cannot master.

If we assumed that success in one area could compensate for failure in another, we would be safe in minimizing the effect of individual areas of inadequacy on the overall resolution of the psychosocial conflict of industry versus inferiority. However, the social environment does not reinforce success in all areas equally. During the middle-school-age years, success in reading is much more highly rewarded than success in tinkering with broken automobile engines. Success in team sports is more highly valued than success in operating a ham radio. It is extremely difficult for a child who does not excel in the culturally valued skills to compensate through the mastery of others.

The social environment also generates feelings of inferiority through the process of social comparison. Particularly in the school setting, but even in the home, children are confronted by statements suggesting that they are not as "good" as some peer, sibling, or cultural subgroup. Children are grouped, graded, and publicly criticized on the basis of how their efforts compare with someone else's. The intrinsic pleasure of engaging in a task for the challenge it presents conflicts with messages that stimulate feelings of self-consciousness, competitiveness, and doubt: "I like playing ball, but I'm not as good as Ted, so I don't think I'll play." During middle school age, children may refuse to try a new activity because they fear the possibility of being bettered by their peers (Crooks, 1988).

Finally, the social environment stimulates feelings of inferiority through the negative value it places on any kind of failure. Two types of failure messages that may contribute to feelings of inferiority have been described. One type consists of criticisms of the child's motivation. Such criticisms imply that, if the child had really tried, she or he could have avoided failure. The other type refers more specifically to a lack of ability. Here, the implication is that the child does not have the competence to succeed. This type of failure message is associated with a pattern of attitudes about the self that has been described as learned helplessness.

Learned helplessness is a belief that one's efforts have little to do with success or failure and that the outcome of task situations is largely outside one's control (Seligman, 1975; Nelson, 1987). In a study of fourth-, fifth-, and sixth-graders, children were asked to verbalize their thoughts as they worked on various tasks. The children's verbalizations following failure showed a clear difference between the mastery-oriented and the helpless children. The mastery-oriented children were able to keep a positive attitude, to increase their problem-solving efforts, and to use their past mistakes to correct their approach. The helpless children began to blame themselves ("I never did have a good memory"). They emphasized the negative aspects of the task or criticized their own abilities and tried to find ways to escape from the situation (Diener & Dweck, 1980). Helpless children tend to discount their successes, and in response to even a few remarks about their lack of ability, they generate a self-definition that leads them to take a pessimistic view of their future success (Phillips, 1984; Holloway, 1988).

Middle-school-age children are often shamed for failure just as toddlers are shamed when they wet their pants. Earlier themes of doubt and guilt are intimately associated with feelings of inferiority. Messages about failure usually suggest that there is an external standard of perfection, an ideal, that the child did not meet. A few failure experiences may generate such strong negative feelings that the child will avoid engaging in new tasks in order to preclude failure.

Failure in school and the public ridicule that it brings have been shown to play a central role in the establishment of a negative self-image. This is especially the case when the initial self-concept is negative (Calhoun & Morse, 1977). The school represents the voice of the larger society. Children who continually fail to meet the standards set by school adults are likely to incorporate a view of themselves as failures. Sometimes, children defend themselves against the threat of failure messages by blaming others for their failures or by bragging to others that they can succeed in other ways. Much as it may appear that these children do not care about school or scorn school goals, the school remains a symbol of cultural authority. Failure in school can easily lead a child to feel locked out of the larger social community.

In extreme cases, we see the reluctance, the self-doubt, and the withdrawal of children who feel very inferior. The resolution of the crisis in the direction of inferiority suggests that these children cannot conceive of themselves as having the potential to contribute to the welfare of the larger community. This is a very serious consequence. It makes the gradual incorporation of the individual into a meaningful social group very difficult. The irony of the crisis at this stage is that the social community, which depends on the individual's motives for mastery for its survival, is itself such a powerful force in negating those motives by communicating messages of inferiority.

The Central Process: Education

Every culture must devise ways of passing on the wisdom and skills of past generations to its young. This is the meaning of education in its broadest sense. Education is different from schooling. The practice of separating formal educational experiences from the direct, intimate hands-on activities of home and community is only about 100 years old. Before the industrial revolution, most children became educated by participating with their parents in the tasks of home life, farming, commerce with neighbors, and participation in religious life (Coleman, 1987). In the case of the nobility, children often had tutors who supervised their education at home.

Today, however, schools bear the primary responsibility for education. Teaching, which began as an extension of the parental role, has become a distinct profession. In our culture, education is not the kind of continuous interplay between the skilled and the unskilled that it is in more traditional cultures. Formal learning takes place in a special building during certain hours of the day. To be sure, the success of that experience in building a child's skills and a sense of the self as a learner depends heavily on the ongoing involvement and commitment of family members (Coleman, 1987; Stevenson & Baker, 1987). For today's children, however, school plays a key role in the formation of a personal sense of industry.

During the elementary-school years, the goal of education is to help children develop the basic tools of learning. Central to this process is an introduction to the language of concepts, theories, and relationships that will allow them to organize their experiences (Cole & D'Andrade, 1982). Schools strive to develop verbal and analytic problem solving. Instruction focuses on rules, descriptions, and abstract concepts (Tharp, 1989). Children are exposed to a range of disciplines and to methods of inquiry for dealing with complex problems. Throughout the educational process, children are presented with problems of increasing difficulty. They are given many opportunities to practice their newly developing skills. The practice offers children continuous feedback about their level of competence.

In addition to the acquisition of skills and knowledge, schools emphasize an approach to behavior that can be described as a combination of "citizenship" and

The process of formal education has changed dramatically over this century. The design of the classroom, the roles of teacher and student, and the methods of instruction have all been targets for experimentation and modification. Yet the essential objectives—to impart skills, values, and information from one generation to the next—remain basically unchanged.

"study habits." Schools impart a code of conduct that is intended to facilitate the teacher's ability to guide students' attention, to help children organize and focus on the tasks at hand, and to foster a respectful, cooperative attitude toward adults and peers. Much of the literature that addresses the problems of teacher bias or the self-fulfilling prophecy in teachers' evaluations of children from low-income or minority families implicates the lack of fit between the students' cultural resources regarding study skills, work habits, and demeanor (for example, disruptive behaviors, manner of speech, or style of dress) and the teachers' expectations.

In general, the students' experiences of academic success are a product of the interaction between the teachers' background and ability to relate to students of various cultural backgrounds, and the students' cognitive and noncognitive resources, especially their "citizenship" and "study habit" behaviors (Alexander, Entwisle & Thompson, 1987). In a test of this notion, students' background characteristics, such as gender, race, and family income, and students' basic skills, absenteeism, study habits, and appearance were related to their coursework mastery and grades (Farkas et al., 1990). It was clear that teachers' evaluations of coursework mastery and actual course grades were significantly related to their assessment of the students' study habits, in addition to their basic skills. In this particular analysis, it was the Asian-American students who benefited most by being rewarded for what teachers perceived to be high levels of class participation, effort, organization, and good-quality homework. As part of the school-based educational process, children are exposed to a combined agenda, focusing both on the elaboration of skills and on the acquisition of behaviors that are associated with success within the school culture.

Going to school results in exposure to adults who provide models for commitment to learning (Rutter, 1983). These adults generally have skills of their own that give children some sense of how much more there is to learn. Schooling, therefore, provides opportunities not only to gain mastery but to acquire goals and standards for the development of more advanced skills.

Middle-school-age children are at a stage of cognitive development that permits them to grasp the fundamental principles of the problems that the school poses for them. The art of teaching lies in presenting problems at a level of complexity that will be meaningful to children but just a step beyond their present ability level. As a result, learning becomes a tantalizing process in which the problems themselves lure the children into expending effort to solve them. The sense of this process is captured in an adult's reminiscences about his music teacher from high school:

> Beyond anything else, Griff wanted you to love and be as deeply affected by music as he was. His daughter, Ann, recently reminded me that when he was sometimes criticized for the problems students experienced with the difficult music he assigned, Griff would respond: "I don't care what a kid does to music. I care what the music does to the kid." Ever since he first convinced me to take voice lessons and seriously consider a career in music, Griff's visions have been a daily realization, as my life's work has, happily, been devoted to the arts. (Mosel, 1992, p. 12)

However, not all children approach schooling with the same expectations of success or the same trust in adults or in the formal education process. Some groups view education as the means to economic security, intellectual development, and political empowerment. Others are skeptical of teachers, schools, and education. They expect to be alienated from the learning process by a devaluing of their basic language, heritage, and beliefs. They believe that the only way to improve their condition is through major political and economic change. In their view, education per se will not empower them or their children. Children in these groups may conclude that the only way to retain their basic sense of self-confidence is to withdraw from school and try to establish their competence among their peers (Spencer, 1985; Ogbu, 1987).

An integral approach to providing a successful educational environment for all children is contextualization of the learning process. To *contextualize* instruction is to carry it out in ways that first draw on a child's existing experiences, previous knowledge, and concepts, and then to expand that understanding in new directions. Contextualizing calls for a recognition that the classroom may be organized in a variety of ways: Children may engage in private study and small-group problem solving, for instance, as well as form a large group that listens and responds to the teacher. Contextualization may require the teacher to draw on the heroes and heroines, stories, songs, and myths of a cultural group in order to help children feel comfortable with more abstract concepts. It may require the acknowledgment of different modes of expression, patterns of social conversation, and language. Finally, contextualizing may call for parents and other important community figures to become involved in the learning process so that the children are not isolated from their social community (Tharp, 1989; Tharp & Gallimore, 1988).

All these efforts may be particularly beneficial to groups that have been alienated from schooling or that approach schooling with mistrust. When the educational process is contextualized, children are strengthened in their own cultural identity. When their strivings for personal and cultural achievement are validated, the conflict that often develops between school professionals and members of minority cultures need not arise. Teachers and school administrators become more confident in the school abilities of children, and children become more willing to persist in order to build competence in school-related tasks (Comer, 1985).

In recent years, the problem of violence in the schools has threatened to undermine the quality of the educational experience for children in many American communities (see Box 8.3). Because of all the concern that has been expressed about the high rates of illiteracy in the United States, and the poor performance of American children in math and science in comparison to children in other nations, the current secretary of education has sent two bills to Congress: one that provides funding for schools to increase their security and one that

Times have really changed in America's schools. Consider the comparison presented in Table 8.3 showing the kinds of problems public school teachers worried about in the 1940s and the kinds of problems they worry about now. The statistics cited in this discussion were taken from an article by T. Toch in the U.S. *News & World Report* of November 8, 1993. In 1993, an estimated 3 million crimes were committed in or near public school buildings across the United States. In a national survey, 16% of eighth-graders said they feared for their safety when they were at school. Such fears may be stimulated in part by exposure to violence in the media, but they are also associated with real and increased levels of violence among children in schools. The New York City schools reported 5,761 violent incidents in 1992, and the mayor of New York announced a plan to station police officers in all of the city's public schools. Of the nation's eighth-graders, 9% had carried some type of weapon to school in the past month, and one estimate was that about 270,000 guns were in the nation's schools each day.

Many people focus on the availability of guns to children and youth as one source of the problem. Children are lured into a cycle of fear: In order to protect themselves from becoming victims, children decide that they need to be armed; the presence of weapons increases the likelihood of violence. Most children, whether inner-city or suburban, say they would have little difficulty obtaining a gun. Stolen guns are available for about $50. The government is having trouble restricting access to guns

BOX 8.3

Violence in American Schools

TABLE 8.3 Public-School Teachers' Perceptions of Top Disciplinary Problems

1940	1990
Talking out of turn	Drug abuse
Chewing gum	Alcohol abuse
Making noise	Pregnancy
Running in the halls	Suicide
Cutting in line	Rape
Dress-code violations	Robbery
Littering	Assault

Source: Toch, 1993.

for minors. For example, Congress passed a Gun Free School Zones Act in 1990, but the law was declared unconstitutional. Meanwhile, school systems are spending scarce resources on security systems. In at least 45 urban school districts, children are screened by metal detectors. Some schools are installing bulletproof window glass. Like those in New York City, many school districts are increasing the number of police in and around their schools. In one elementary school in Connecticut, children saw two fellow students gunned down outside the school. The school principal explained, "Kids didn't want to go to class, they couldn't eat or sleep, they burst out crying. . . . We couldn't think about teaching reading, writing and arithmetic until we dealt with these problems" (Toch, 1993, p. 34).

provides resources for violence-prevention programming, including dealing with anger and conflict resolution, reducing racial stereotypes, and training students in peer mediation (Toch, 1993). We are dealing with very basic needs: safety and security. When children are threatened, very little higher-order thinking goes on. The quality of life within the school, the emotional climate, and the interactions between children and adults as well as among the children themselves—all contribute to children's openness to learning. Children who are relaxed, who are having a good time, and who feel acknowledged and involved in the teaching-learning process are likely to be more attentive, to try harder, and to take pleasure and pride in their achievements (Stevenson, 1992).

Applied Topic
Sex Education

Why should sex education be considered an issue of middle childhood? No developmental theory suggests that this is a stage of heightened sexuality. In fact, most people who work with children of this age report frequent expressions of antagonism between males and females. However, the life-span approach is encouraging about the possibility of preparing oneself during an earlier stage for events anticipated during a later one. We know that the next stage of development, early adolescence, arouses both anxiety and excitement about sexual encounters. Many girls experience the transitions of puberty at age 11 or 12. Boys follow soon after at ages 13–15. The United States has one of the highest rates of births to adolescent girls of any industrialized nation. (This problem is discussed in greater detail in Chapter 9.) Becoming a parent at an early age introduces critical developmental risks for young mothers and fathers as well as for their babies. To delay sex education until most children have already entered puberty and take the chance of their engaging in sexual activity without having had the opportunity to discuss and anticipate its possible consequences seems to be a serious societal mistake.

What is more, the transition into middle school or junior high school is a very stressful event for many children. This school change is often accompanied by a drop in self-esteem and in school performance. Without appropriate support, young adolescents are likely to experience a decline in their academic aspirations and an increase in their willingness to explore sexual activity (Brooks-Gunn & Furstenberg, 1989). Early sexual activity is often associated with other problem behaviors, such as drug use, theft, violence, and school problems. Especially for boys, entry into sexual intercourse before age 14 is associated with involvement in several of these other problem areas, a finding suggesting a special need to provide early sex education that is meaningful and relevant to boys as well as girls (Ketterlinus et al., 1992).

Sex education is relatively new in American schools. At present, the programs tend to be inserted into courses in biology, health science, family life, or physical education. In the middle school or junior high school, the curriculum of these "sex-ed" units focuses on "sexual anatomy, the physical and psychological changes in puberty, reproduction, dating, and sexually transmitted diseases" (Katchadourian, 1990, p. 346). Usually, these courses are not comprehensive, and

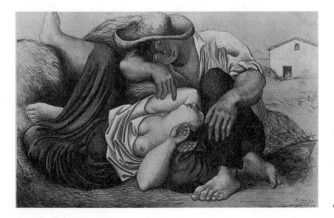

Pablo Picasso, Sleeping Peasants, *1919. Sex education is most appropriate before the intense sexual drives of adolescence are fully awakened. For these two peasants, sexuality does not seem to pose a barrier to a relaxed, uninhibited relationship.*

the quality and scope of sex education vary widely by school, school district, and state (Muraskin, 1986; Caldas, 1993). There are differences of opinion about how well informed American adolescents are about sex. One source suggests that 88% of American adolescents understand about effective contraception, for example, and another survey concludes that most teens are not even knowledgeable about the basic facts (Mullener, 1987; Coles & Stokes, 1985). It seems to us that a comprehensive introduction to sex education during the middle school years is critical to the health and well-being of American youth. It has the potential to reduce the high-risk sexual practices that are often linked to unwanted adolescent pregnancies and to provide a new level of emotional support that will help sustain self-esteem and continued cognitive growth during the early adolescent years.

The usefulness of information about sexuality and the reproductive process can be measured by the extent to which such information minimizes a child's uncertainty, embarrassment, and feelings of isolation during the actual events of puberty. In addition, it can be evaluated in light of the sexual decisions young adolescents make. Sex education ought to address the motivational factors associated with sexual activity and childbirth as well as the biological and anatomical realities. It ought to place sexual activity and childbearing within the larger context of a young person's life roles, goals for the future, and connection with family and community. In a comprehensive sex-education curriculum, sexual behavior should be linked to the other domains of health-promoting behaviors, communication skills, relationship development, and the expression of emotions.

How might such a program be structured so that it would be readily integrated into children's understanding of their world? The developmental tasks of the middle-school-age years are useful in designing an approach to the problem. The child's involvement in skill learning, increased capacity for logical reasoning, investment in the social group, and growing ability to set standards and evaluate personal performance all suggest that a relatively structured group-learning situation would be a successful format for the discussion of sexuality.

Three sex-education themes are particularly important at this age. First, sexuality must be discussed within the context of its role as a central mechanism for evolution and for the survival of the culture. With this orientation, children can approach the topic logically, as an element of a larger natural system. They can begin to ask questions about the mechanisms of reproduction as part of an investigation of the more complex matter of species survival. The facts of sexual maturation can then be presented as a natural necessity. The children can begin to appreciate that their own maturity allows them to participate in a kind of activity that has meaning at a biological, anthropological, and historical level as well as at a personal level. Sex education becomes a vehicle for introducing the biological facts of sexuality and reproduction within a larger intellectual examination of such topics as the evolution of humans, the adaptive nature of social living units, the roles of males and females in a society, the factors that promote reproductive success, and the contributions of males and females to the survival of children.

The presentation of facts about sexuality in this context has several consequences. It allows children to approach the matter as an intellectual subject that requires an extension of skills and information to be well-understood. It also expands children's view of their own development as an expression of a much larger evolutionary process. Children are challenged to abandon their somewhat egocentric view of their behavior by seeing the link between their own body functions and impulses and the survival of a species. Finally, children are made aware of the norms that have been established for the expression of sexual impulses in their own and other cultures. They learn to appreciate the meaning of their own cultural identity as they become acquainted with the rituals, ceremonies, and practices of other cultural groups.

Second, the child must learn to see sexual intimacy within the context of intimate personal relationships as well as in relation to human survival. Here, we emphasize the distinction between sex as a biological dimension and love as a psychological one. Knowing the facts about sexual reproduction does not help most children to accept the reality that their parents have had sexual intercourse. It does not help them to manage the expression of their impulses or to assess the emotional costs of sexuality. There is a gap between children's ability to process information about sexual matters and their ability to apply that information to real-life events.

Teachers must help children to expand their understanding of intimacy in order to enhance their appreciation of the role of sexuality in adolescent and adult relationships. Children must understand that sexual closeness is a means of communicating love as well as of making babies. This type of sex-education curriculum would examine the range of human efforts to communicate feelings of love and to come to terms with the expression of sexual impulses. Painting, sculpture, literature, drama, poetry, movies, and songs are examples of media through which people have attempted to share their confusion, delight, and sorrow about love. Children can learn to see the beauty that has been captured in these artistic expressions as well as the exploitation of this theme. Through an analysis of the arts, and through their own artistic expressions, children can begin to share some of their own feelings about love. The goal is to increase children's feelings of competence in the expression of personal emotions and to aid them in valuing their emotional life as a part of their character.

The capacity to love does not become fully mature until adulthood. Nonetheless, during the middle-school-age years, children can learn that the feelings they experience toward others are emotions with which people have struggled for centuries. Hidden in those feelings is the possibility of great personal joy. Children can learn that the feelings of love that they now share with friends, parents, and boyfriends or girlfriends, and that they may later share with husbands or wives and their own children, bring them closer to an ultimate personal fulfillment.

Third, sexuality must be studied within the interpersonal contexts that adolescents are likely to experience (Juhasz & Sonnenshein-Schneider, 1987; Boltan & MacEachron, 1988; Marsiglio, 1988). Students must be helped to locate the place of sexuality in their definitions of masculinity and femininity. It is likely that girls and boys approach the whole notion of sexual intimacy differently. Boys who are involved in early sexual activity are more likely to see it as evidence of their independence and transition into adult status. Girls are more likely to be aware of the costs and risks associated with early sexual activity and may be more oriented to seeing sex as a way to establish or preserve a relationship (Small, Silverberg & Kerns, 1993). These ideas and assumptions should be examined critically in the context of a larger picture of interpersonal relationships.

Family and cultural factors that shape the definitions of gender and sexuality should be explored. Children need to raise questions about the responsibility of men and women in the procreation and nurturance of infants, including cultural

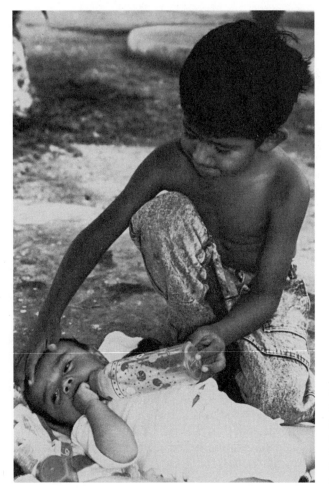

Giving middle-school-age boys experiences and responsibility for the care of infants might help them appreciate the possible consequences of adolescent sexual activity.

norms about their respective responsibilities for preventing unwanted pregnancies. This curriculum may include an exploration of family and community attitudes and values in regard to contraception, as well as those factors that prevent the consistent use of contraceptives. Through role playing and problem solving, children could assess the consequences of early pregnancy in the light of their goals for personal freedom, academic achievement, and a career. At the interpersonal level, they need to practice assertiveness strategies as well as alternative strategies for satisfying their needs for intimacy and sexuality. Ideally, such a curriculum would help young people build a peer culture in which they supported the values of postponing entry into sexual activity and preventing unwanted pregnancy.

This description of the focus of a sex-education course clearly expands the concept as it is currently approached. Sex education can be seen as an exciting invitation to teach children about their bodies, their function in the history of evolution, and their potential for creative expression. This version of a sex-education program would be a legitimate school-centered function that would fulfill a spirit of what we described earlier as the process of education. Such a program would be an intellectually stimulating process rather than the embarrassing, bothersome chore that is currently associated with the traditional "health class." Here is an opportunity to take a topic in which children are already intensely interested and to expand that naive curiosity into a full view of one of the most powerful themes in human history.

Chapter Summary

The middle-school-age child develops work and social skills that are crucial to later life stages. During this period, a remarkable synergy occurs across the cognitive domains, bringing new levels of skill development, expanded information, and elaborate cognitive strategies for approaching and solving problems. Children apply their cognitive abilities not only in the academic, school-related domains, but in an increased capacity for social cooperation, self-evaluation, and peer-group participation. As a result of the combination of cognitive and social skill development, middle-school-age children are able to make significant contributions to the social groups to which they belong. They are also likely to seek approval and acceptance from these groups.

Industry, as we have discussed it, focuses primarily on building competence. It is quite clear that the family, peer group, and school all play their part in support of feelings of mastery or failure. However, in our society, school is the environment in which continuous attention is given to the child's success or failure in basic skill areas. The child's emerging sense of industry is closely interwoven with the quality of the school environment and the extent to which the child encounters experiences that both foster enthusiasm for new learning and provide objective feedback about levels of mastery. An understanding of skill development must combine an appreciation of the child's intellectual maturity with a sense of the significant motives that may influence his or her willingness to learn.

Although earlier psychological theories have not considered middle school age very influential in the process of psychological development, the events of this stage play an extremely important part in the psychology of the person. Issues of industry, mastery, achievement, success, social skills, cooperativeness, and interpersonal sensitivity are all salient in the events of middle school age. A person's orientation to friendship and work, two essential aspects of adult life, begin to take shape during this stage.

References

Adler, A. (1935). The fundamental views of individual psychology. *International Journal of Individual Psychology*, 1, 5–8.

Ainsworth, M. D. S. (1989). Attachments beyond infancy. *American Psychologist*, 44, 709–716.

Alexander, K. L. & Entwisle, D. R. (1988). Achievement in the first two years of school: Patterns and processes. *Monographs of the Society for Research in Child Development*, 53(2, Serial No. 218).

Alexander, K. L., Entwisle, D. R. & Thompson, M. S. (1987). School performance, status relations, and the structure of sentiment: Bringing the teacher back in. *American Sociological Review*, 52, 655–682.

Anderson, R. C., Wilson, P. T. & Fielding, L. G. (1988). Growth in reading and how children spend their time outside of school. *Reading Research Quarterly*, 23, 285–303.

Asher, S. R., Hymel, S. & Renshaw, P. D. (1984). Loneliness in children. *Child Development*, 55, 1456–1464.

Atkinson, J. W. & Birch, D. (1978). *Introduction to motivation* (2nd ed.). New York: Van Nostrand.

Au, T. K., Sidle, A. L. & Rollins, K. B. (1993). Developing an intuitive understanding of conservation: Invisible particles as a plausible mechanism. *Developmental Psychology*, 29, 286–299.

Bandura, A. (1982). Self-efficacy mechanism in human agency. *American Psychologist*, 37, 122–147.

Bandura, A. & Schunck, D. H. (1981). Cultivating competence, self-efficacy, and intrinsic interest through proximal self-motivation. *Journal of Personality and Social Psychology*, 41, 586–598.

Beaulieu, L. (1992). Teaching more than just sports. *Columbus Dispatch* (June 28), p. 6D.

Berndt, T. J. (1979). Development changes in conformity to peers and parents. *Developmental Psychology*, 15, 608–616.

Berndt, T. J. (1981). Relations between social cognition, nonsocial cognition, and social behavior: The case of friendship. In J. H. Flavell & L. D. Ross (Eds.), *Social cognitive development: Frontiers and possible futures.* Cambridge: Cambridge University Press.

Bijstra, J., Van Geert, P. & Jackson, S. (1989). Conservation and the appearance-reality distinction: What do children really know and what do they answer? *British Journal of Developmental Psychology*, 7, 43–53.

Bolton, F. G., Jr., & MacEachron, A. E. (1988). Adolescent male sexuality: A developmental perspective. *Journal of Adolescent Research*, 3, 259–273.

Brainerd, C. J. (1977). Cognitive development and concept learning: An interpretive review. *Psychological Bulletin*, 84, 919–939.

Brainerd, C. J. & Hooper, F. H. (1978). More on the identity equivalence sequence: An update and some replies to Miller. *Psychological Bulletin*, 85, 70–75.

Brooks-Gunn, J. & Furstenberg, F. F., Jr. (1989). Adolescent sexual behavior. *American Psychologist*, 44, 249–257.

Brown, I., Jr., & Inouye, D. K. (1978). Learned helplessness through modeling: The role of perceived similarity in competence. *Journal of Personality and Social Psychology*, 36, 900–908.

Brustad, R. J. (1988). Affective outcomes in competitive youth sport: The influence of intrapersonal and socialization factors. *Journal of Sport and Exercise Psychology*, 10, 307–321.

Butler, R. & Ruzany, N. (1993). Age and socialization effects on the development of social comparison motives and normative ability assessment in kibbutz and urban children. *Child Development*, 64, 532–543.

Butterfield, E. C., Nelson, T. O. & Peck, V. (1988). Developmental aspects of the feeling of knowing. *Developmental Psychology*, 24, 654–663.

Caldas, S. J. (1993). Current theoretical perspectives on adolescent pregnancy and childbearing in the United States. *Journal of Adolescent Research*, 8, 4–20.

Calhoun, G., Jr. & Morse, W. C. (1977). Self-concept and self-esteem: Another perspective. *Psychology in the Schools*, 14, 318–322.

Carlo, G., Knight, G. P., Eisenberg, N. & Rotenberg, K. J. (1991). Cognitive processes and prosocial behaviors among children: The role of affective attributions and reconciliations. *Developmental Psychology*, 27, 456–461.

Carr, M., Kurtz, B. E., Schneider, W., Turner, L. A. & Borkowski, J. G. (1989). Strategy acquisition and transfer among American and German children: Environmental influences on metacognitive development. *Developmental Psychology*, 25, 765–771.

Carroll, D. W. (1986). *Psychology of language.* Pacific Grove, CA: Brooks/Cole.

Cassidy, J. & Asher, S. R. (1992). Loneliness and peer relations in young children. *Child Development*, 63, 350–365.

Chalmers, J. B. & Townsend, M. A. R. (1990). The effects of training in social perspective taking on socially maladjusted girls. *Child Development*, 61, 178–190.

Chapman, M. & McBride, M. L. (1992). Beyond competence and performance: Children's class inclusion strategies, superordinate class cues, and verbal justifications. *Developmental Psychology*, 28, 319–327.

Clark, M. L. & Ayers, M. (1988). The role of reciprocity and proximity in junior high school friendships. *Journal of Youth and Adolescence*, 17, 403–411.

Coats, P. B. & Overman, S. J. (1992). Childhood play experiences of women in traditional and nontraditional professions. *Sex Roles*, 26, 261–271.

Coie, J. D. & Krehbiel, G. (1984). Effects of academic tutoring on the social status of low-achieving, socially rejected children. *Child Development*, 55, 1465–1478.

Cole, M. & D'Andrade, R. (1982). The influence of schooling on concept formation: Some preliminary conclusions. *Quarterly Newsletter of the Laboratory of Comparative Cognition*, 4, 19–26.

Coleman, J. S. (1987). Families and schools. *Educational Researcher*, 16, 32–38.

Coles, R. & Stokes, G. (1985). *Sex and the American teenager.* New York: Harper & Row.

Columbus Dispatch. (1992). War chases children out of Sarajevo. (Associated Press) (May 11), p. 3A.

Comer, J. P. (1985). Empowering black children's educational environments. In H. P. McAdoo & J. L. McAdoo (Eds.), *Black children: Social, educational, and parental environments* (pp. 123–138). Newbury Park, CA: Sage.

Crick, N. R. & Ladd, G. W. (1993). Children's perceptions of their peer experiences: Attributions, loneliness, social anxiety, and social avoidance. *Developmental Psychology*, 29, 244–254.

Crockett, L., Losoff, M. & Petersen, A. (1984). Perceptions of the peer group and friendship in early adolescence. *Journal of Early Adolescence*, 4, 155–181.

Crooks, T. J. (1988). The impact of classroom evaluation practices on students. *Review of Educational Research, 58*, 438–481.

Cross, D. R. & Paris, S. G. (1988). Developmental and instructional analyses of children's metacognition and reading comprehension. *Journal of Educational Psychology, 80*, 131–142.

Demetriou, A., Efklides, A. & Platsidou, M. (1993). The architecture and dynamics of developing mind: Experiential structuralism as a frame for unifying cognitive developmental theories. *Monographs of the Society for Research in Child Development, 58*(5–6, Serial No. 234).

Dickstein, E. B. (1979). Biological and cognitive bases of moral functioning. *Human Development, 22*, 37–59.

Diener, C. I. & Dweck, C. S. (1980). An analysis of learned helplessness: 2. The processing of success. *Journal of Personality and Social Psychology, 39*, 940–952.

Dishion, T. J., Patterson, G. R., Stoolmiller, M. & Skinner, M. L. (1991). Family, school, and behavioral antecedents to early adolescent involvement with antisocial peers. *Developmental Psychology, 27*, 172–180.

Dodge, K. A., Petit, G. S., McClaskey, C. L. & Brown, M. M. (1986). Social competence in children. *Monographs of the Society for Research in Child Development, 51*(2, Serial No. 213).

Downey, G. & Walker, E. (1989). Social cognition and adjustment in children at risk for psychopathology. *Developmental Psychology, 25*, 835–845.

East, P. L. & Rook, K. S. (1992). Compensatory patterns of support among children's peer relationships: A test using school friends, nonschool friends, and siblings. *Developmental Psychology, 28*, 163–172.

Eccles, J. S. (1993). School and family effects on the ontogeny of children's interests, self-perceptions, and activity choices. In J. E. Jacobs (Ed.), *Nebraska Symposium on Motivation: 1992* (Vol. 40, pp. 145–208). Lincoln: University of Nebraska Press.

Eccles, J. S., Jacobs, J. E. & Harold, R. D. (1990). Gender-role stereotypes, expectancy effects, and parents' role in the socialization of gender differences in self perceptions and skill acquisition. *Journal of Social Issues, 46*, 182–201.

Elias, M. J., Beier, J. J. & Gara, M. A. (1989). Children's responses to interpersonal obstacles as a predictor of social competence. *Journal of Youth and Adolescence, 18*, 451–465.

Entwisle, D. R., Alexander, K. L., Pallas, A. M. & Cadigan, D. (1987). The emergent academic self-image of first-graders: Its response to social structure. *Child Development, 58*, 1190–1206.

Epstein, J. (1983a). Examining theories of adolescent friendships. In J. Epstein & N. Karweit (Eds.), *Friends in school: Patterns of selection and influence in secondary schools.* New York: Academic Press.

Epstein, J. (1983b). Selection of friends in differently organized schools and classrooms. In J. Epstein & N. Karweit (Eds.), *Friends in school: Patterns of selection and influence in secondary schools.* New York: Academic Press.

Erikson, E. H. (1963). *Childhood and society* (2nd ed.). New York: Norton.

Farkas, G., Grobe, R. P., Sheehan, D. & Shuan, Y. (1990). Cultural resources and school success: Gender, ethnicity, and poverty groups. *American Sociological Review, 55*, 127–142.

Farrar, M. J., Raney, G. E. & Boyer, M. E. (1992). Knowledge, concepts, and inferences in childhood. *Child Development, 63*, 673–691.

Field, D. (1981). Can preschool children really learn to conserve? *Child Development, 52*, 326–334.

Fischer, K. & Bidell, T. R. (1993, Fall). Beyond the stage debate: Keeping the constructor in constructivism. *Newsletter of the Society for Research in Child Development, 5*, 11.

Flavell, J. H. (1982). On cognitive development. *Child Development, 53*, 1–10.

French, D. C. (1984). Children's knowledge of the social functions of younger, older and same-age peers. *Child Development, 55*, 1429–1433.

French, D. C. (1988). Heterogeneity of peer-rejected boys: Aggressive and nonaggressive subtypes. *Child Development, 59*, 976–985.

French, D. C. (1990). Heterogeneity of peer rejected girls. *Child Development, 61*, 2028–2031.

Galbo, J. J. (1983). Adolescents' perceptions of significant adults. *Adolescence, 18*, 417–428.

Garbarino, J., Kostelny, K. & Dubrow, N. (1991). *No place to be a child: Growing up in a war zone.* Lexington, MA: Lexington Books.

Gavin, L. A. & Furman, W. (1989). Age differences in adolescents' perceptions of their peer groups. *Developmental Psychology, 25*, 827–834.

Geary, D. C. & Brown, S. C. (1991). Cognitive addition: Strategy choice and speed of processing differences in gifted, normal, and mathematically disabled children. *Developmental Psychology, 27*, 398–406.

Geary, D. C., Brown, S. C. & Samaranayake, V. A. (1991). Cognitive addition: A short longitudinal study of strategy choice and speed-of-processing differences in normal and mathematically disabled children. *Developmental Psychology, 27*, 787–797.

Goldenberg, C. N. (1989). Parents' effects on academic grouping for reading: Three case studies. *American Educational Research Journal, 26*, 329–352.

Goodnow, J. J. (1969). Problems in research on culture and thought. In D. Elkind & J. H. Flavell (Eds.), *Studies in cognitive development: Essays in honor of Jean Piaget.* New York: Oxford University Press.

Gulko, J., Doyle, A., Serbin, L. A. & White, D. R. (1988). Conservation skills: A replicated study of order of acquisition across tasks. *Journal of Genetic Psychology, 149,* 425–439.

Halford, G. S. & Boyle, F. M. (1985). Do young children understand conservation of number? *Child Development, 56,* 165–176.

Hall, W. S. (1989). Reading comprehension. *American Psychologist, 44,* 157–161.

Haller, E. & Waterman, M. (1985). The criteria of reading group assignments. *Reading Teacher, 38,* 772–782.

Hallinan, M. (1979). Structural effects on children's friendships and cliques. *Social Psychological Quarterly, 42,* 43–54.

Harris, M. J. & Rosenthal, R. (1985). Mediation of interpersonal expectancy effects: 31 meta-analyses. *Psychological Bulletin, 97,* 363–386.

Hart, C. H., Ladd, G. W. & Burleson, B. R. (1990). Children's expectations of the outcomes of social strategies: Relations with sociometric status and maternal disciplinary styles. *Child Development, 61,* 127–137.

Harter, S. (1985). *The Self-Perception Profile for Children.* (Manual), University of Denver.

Harter, S. (1993). Visions of self: Beyond the me in the mirror. In J. E. Jacobs (Ed.), *Nebraska Symposium on Motivation: 1992* (Vol. 40, pp. 99–144). Lincoln: University of Nebraska Press.

Hartup, W. W. (1989). Social relationships and their developmental significance. *American Psychologist, 44,* 120–126.

Haskett, M. E. & Kistner, J. A. (1991). Social interactions and peer perceptions of young physically abused children. *Child Development, 62,* 979–990.

Hess, R. & Holloway, S. (1984). Family and school as educational institutions. *Review of Child Development Research: Vol. 7. The Family* (pp. 179–222). Chicago: University of Chicago Press.

Holloway, S. D. (1988). Concepts of ability and effort in Japan and the United States. *Review of Educational Research, 58,* 327–345.

Hymel, S., Bowker, A. & Woody, E. (1993). Aggressive versus withdrawn unpopular children: Variations in peer and self-perceptions of multiple domains. *Child Development, 64,* 879–896.

Hymel, S., Rubin, K. H., Rowden, L. & LeMare, L. (1990). Children's peer relationships: Longitudinal predictions of internalizing and externalizing problems from middle to late childhood. *Child Development, 61,* 2004–2021.

Jordan, N. C., Huttenlocher, J. & Levine, S. C. (1992). Differential calculation abilities in young children from middle- and low-income families. *Developmental Psychology, 28,* 644–653.

Juhasz, A. M. & Sonnenshein-Schneider, M. (1987). Adolescent sexuality: Values, morality, and decision making. *Adolescence, 22,* 579–590.

Jussim, L. (1990a). Expectancies and social issues: Introduction. *Journal of Social Issues, 46,* 1-8.

Jussim, L. (1990b). Social realities and social problems: The role of expectancies. *Journal of Social Issues, 46,* 9–34.

Kalish, C. W. & Gelman, S. A. (1992). On wooden pillows: Multiple classification and children's category-based inductions. *Child Development, 63,* 1536–1557.

Karweit, N. (1983). Extracurricular activities and friendship selection. In J. Epstein & N. Karweit (Eds.), *Friends in school: Patterns of selection and influence in secondary schools.* New York: Academic Press.

Karweit, N. & Hansell, S. (1983). Sex differences in adolescent relationships: Friendships and status. In J. Epstein & N. Karweit (Eds.), *Friends in school: Patterns of selection and influence in secondary schools.* New York: Academic Press.

Katchadourian, H. (1990). Sexuality. In S. S. Feldman & G. R. Elliot (Eds.), *At the threshold: The developing adolescent* (pp. 330–351). Cambridge: Harvard University Press.

Ketterlinus, R. D., Lamb, M. E., Nitz, K. & Elster, A. B. (1992). Adolescent nonsexual and sex-related problem behaviors. *Journal of Adolescent Research, 7,* 431–456.

Klausmeier, H. J. (1977). *Individual differences in cognitive development during the school years.* Paper presented at the annual convention of the American Psychological Association, San Francisco.

Klint, K. A. & Weiss, M. R. (1987). Perceived competence and motives for participating in youth sports: A test of Harter's competence motivation theory. *Journal of Sport Psychology, 9,* 55–65.

Knight, C. C. & Fischer, K. W. (1992). Learning to read words: Individual differences in developmental sequences. *Journal of Applied Developmental Psychology, 13,* 377–404.

Kowaz, A. M. & Marcia, J. E. (1991). Development and validation of a measure of Eriksonian industry. *Journal of Personality and Social Psychology, 60,* 390–397.

Lopez, A., Gelman, S. A., Gutheil, G. & Smith, E. (1992). The development of category-based inductions. *Child Development, 63,* 1070–1090.

Lovell, K. (1961). *The growth of basic mathematical and scientific concepts in children.* New York: Philosophical Library.

Marsiglio, W. (1988). Adolescent male sexuality and heterosexual masculinity: A conceptual model and review. *Journal of Adolescent Research, 3,* 285–303.

May, R. B. & Norton, J. M. (1981). Training-task orders and transfer in conservation. *Child Development, 52,* 904–913.

McAuley, E., Duncan, T. E. & McElroy, M. (1989). Self-efficacy cognitions and causal attributions for children's motor performance: An exploratory investigation. *Journal of Genetic Psychology, 150*, 65–73.

McCabe, A. E., Siegel, L. S., Spence, I. & Wilkinson, A. (1982). Class-inclusion reasoning: Patterns of performance from three to eight years. *Child Development, 53*, 780–785.

Merton, R. K. (1948). The self-fulfilling prophecy. *Antioch Review, 8*, 193–210.

Miller, S. A. (1978). Identity conservation and equivalence conservation: A critique of Brainerd and Hooper's analysis. *Psychological Bulletin, 85*, 58–69.

Montgomery, D. E. (1993). Young children's understanding of interpretive diversity between different-age listeners. *Developmental Psychology, 29*, 337–345.

Mosel, S. (1992, Fall). Remembering great teachers at Parker: Chauncey Griffith. *Parker Magazine*, p. 12.

Mullener, E. (1987). Poverty's children. *New Orleans Times-Picayune* (October 6), p. 6.

Muraskin, L. (1986). Sex education mandates: Are they the answer? *Family Planning Perspectives, 18*, 171–174.

Musser, L. M. & Browne, B. A. (1991). Self-monitoring in middle childhood: Personality and social correlates. *Developmental Psychology, 27*, 994–999.

Nelson, E. (1987). Learned helplessness and children's achievement. In S. Moore & K. Kolb (Eds.), *Reviews of research for practitioners and parents* (No. 3, pp. 11–22). Minneapolis: Center for Early Education and Development.

Nelson, J. & Aboud, F. E. (1985). The resolution of social conflict between friends. *Child Development, 56*, 1009–1017.

Nelson, K. (1974). Variations in children's concepts by age and category. *Child Development, 45*, 577–584.

Newman J. L., Roberts, L. R. & Syre, C. R. (1993). Concepts of family among children and adolescents: Effect of cognitive level, gender, and family structure. *Developmental Psychology, 29*, 951–962.

Ogbu, J. U. (1987). Variability in minority school performance: A problem in search of an explanation. *Anthropology and Education Quarterly, 18*, 312–334.

O'Neill, D. K. & Gopnik, A. (1991). Young children's ability to identify the sources of their beliefs. *Developmental Psychology, 27*, 390–397.

Park, K. A. & Waters, E. (1989). Security of attachment and preschool friendships. *Child Development, 60*, 1076–1081.

Parker, J. G. & Asher, S. R. (1993). Friendship and friendship quality in middle childhood: Links with peer group acceptance and feelings of loneliness and social dissatisfaction. *Developmental Psychology, 29*, 611–621.

Parkhurst, J. T. & Asher, S. R. (1992). Peer rejection in middle school: Subgroup differences in behavior, loneliness, and interpersonal concerns. *Developmental Psychology, 28*, 231–241.

Parsons, J. E., Adler, T. F. & Kaczala, C. M. (1982). Socialization of achievement attitudes and beliefs: Parental influences. *Child Development, 53*, 310–321.

Parsons, J. E. & Ruble, D. N. (1977). The development of achievement-related expectancies. *Child Development, 48*, 1075–1079.

Patterson, G. R. (1982). *Coercive family processes.* Eugene, OR: Castalia.

Pellegrini, D. S. (1985). Social cognition and competence in middle childhood. *Child Development, 56*, 253–264.

Pepitone, E. A., Loeb, H. W. & Murdock, E. M. (1977). *Social comparison and similarity of children's performance in competitive situations.* Paper presented at the annual convention of the American Psychological Association, San Francisco.

Perret-Clermont, A., Perret, J. & Bell, N. (1991). The social construction of meaning and cognitive activity in elementary school children. In L. B. Resnick, J. M. Levine & S. D. Teasley (Eds.), *Perspectives on socially shared cognition* (pp. 41–62). Washington, DC: American Psychological Association.

Pettit, G. S., Dodge, K. A. & Brown, M. M. (1988). Early family experience, social problem-solving patterns, and children's social competence. *Child Development, 59*, 107–120.

Phillips, D. A. (1984). The illusion of incompetence among academically competent children. *Child Development, 55*, 2000–2016.

Phillips, D. A. (1987). Socialization of perceived academic competence among highly competent children. *Child Development, 58*, 1308–1320.

Piaget, J. (1932/1948). *The moral judgment of the child.* Glencoe, IL: Free Press.

Piaget, J. (1941/1952). *The child's conception of number.* London: Kegan Paul, Trench & Trubner.

Piaget, J. & Inhelder, B. (1969). *The psychology of the child.* New York: Basic Books.

Pillow, B. H. (1991). Children's understanding of biased social cognition. *Developmental Psychology, 27*, 539–551.

Prawat, R. S., Byers, J. L. & Anderson, A. H. (1983). An attributional analysis of teachers' affective reactions to student success and failure. *American Educational Research Journal, 20*, 137–152.

Putallaz, M. (1987). Maternal behavior and children's sociometric status. *Child Development, 58*, 324–340.

Quiggle, N. L., Garber, J., Panak, W. F. & Dodge, K. A. (1992). Social information processing in aggressive and depressed children. *Child Development, 63*, 1305–1320.

Renshaw, P. D. & Brown, P. J. (1993). Loneliness in middle childhood: Concurrent and longitudinal predictors. *Child Development, 64,* 1271–1284.

Rosen, A. B. & Rozin, P. (1993). Now you see it, now you don't: The preschool child's conception of invisible particles in the context of dissolving. *Developmental Psychology, 29,* 300–311.

Rosenthal, R. & Jacobson, L. (1968). *Pygmalion in the classroom: Teacher expectations and student intellectual development.* New York: Holt, Rinehart & Winston.

Rubin, K. H., LeMare, L. J. & Lollis, S. (1990). Social withdrawal in children: Developmental pathways to peer rejection. In S. R. Asher & J. D. Coie (Eds.), *Peer rejection in childhood* (pp. 217–252). Cambridge: Cambridge University Press.

Rutter, M. (1983). School effects on pupil progress: Research findings and policy implications. *Child Development, 54,* 1–29.

Salzinger, S., Feldman, R. S., Hammer, M. & Rosario, M. (1993). The effects of physical abuse on children's social relationships. *Child Development, 64,* 168–187.

Sancilio, M. F. M., Plumert, J. M. & Hartup, W. W. (1989). Friendship and aggressiveness as determinants of conflict outcomes in middle childhood. *Developmental Psychology, 25,* 812–819.

Schickedanz, J. A. (1986). *More than the ABCs: The early stages of reading and writing.* Washington, DC: National Association for the Advancement of Young Children.

Schneider, W. & Bjorklund, D. F. (1992). Expertise, aptitude, and strategic remembering. *Child Development, 63,* 461–473.

Seligman, M. E. P. (1975). *Helplessness.* San Francisco: W. H. Freeman.

Share, D. L., McGee, R. & Silva, P. A. (1989). IQ and reading progress: A test of the capacity notion of IQ. *Journal of the American Academy of Child and Adolescent Psychiatry, 28,* 97–100.

Shears, L. M. & Bower, E. M. (1974). *Games in education and development.* Springfield, IL: Charles C Thomas.

Silverstein, A. B., Pearson, L. B., Aguinaldo, N. E., Friedman, S. L., Tokayama, D. L. & Weiss, Z. T. (1982). Identity conservation and equivalence conservation: A question of developmental priority. *Child Development, 53,* 819–821.

Skaalvik, E. M. & Hagtvet, K. A. (1990). Academic achievement and self-concept: An analysis of causal predominance in a developmental perspective. *Journal of Personality and Social Psychology, 58,* 292–307.

Slavin, R. E. (1987). Grouping for instruction in the elementary school. *Educational Psychologist, 22,* 109–127.

Small, S. A., Silverberg, S. B. & Kerns, D. (1993). Adolescents' perceptions of the costs and benefits of engaging in health-comprising behaviors. *Journal of Youth and Adolescence, 22,* 73–87.

Smith, T. L. (1986). Self-concepts of youth sport participants and nonparticipants in grades 3 and 6. *Perceptual and Motor Skills, 62,* 863–866.

Sophian, C. (1988). Limitations on preschool children's knowledge about counting: Using counting to compare two sets. *Developmental Psychology, 24,* 634–640.

Spencer, M. B. (1985). Racial variations in achievement prediction: The school as a conduit for macrostructural cultural tension. In H. P. McAdoo & J. L. McAdoo (Eds.), *Black children: Social, educational, and parental environments* (pp. 85–111). Newbury Park, CA: Sage.

Spiro, R. J., Bruce, B. C. & Brewer, W. F. (Eds.). (1980). *Theoretical issues in reading comprehension.* Hillsdale, NJ: Erlbaum.

Sroufe, L. A. & Fleeson, J. (1986). Attachment and the construction of relationships. In W. W. Hartup & Z. Rubin (Eds.), *Relationships and development* (pp. 51–72). Hillsdale, NJ: Erlbaum.

Stevenson, D. L. & Baker, D. P. (1987). The family-school relation and the child's school performance. *Child Development, 58,* 1348–1357.

Stevenson, H. W. (1992, December). Learning from Asian schools. *Scientific American, 267*(6), 70–77.

Stevenson, H. W., Chen, C. & Lee, S. (1993). Mathematics achievement of Chinese, Japanese, and American children: Ten years later. *Science, 259,* 53–58.

Sullivan, H. S. (1949). *The collected works of Harry Stack Sullivan* (Vols. 1, 2). New York: Norton.

Tharp, R. G. (1989). Psychocultural variables and constants: Effects on teaching and learning in schools. *American Psychologist, 44,* 349–359.

Tharp, R. G. & Gallimore, R. (1988). *Rousing minds to life: Teaching, learning, and schooling in social context.* Cambridge: Cambridge University Press.

Time. (1993). Alas, slavery lives: A new report details a world still plagued by human bondage. March 22, p. 26.

Toch, T. (with T. Gest & M. Guttman). (1993). Violence in schools: When killers come to class. *U.S. News & World Report* (November 8), pp. 30–37.

Triandis, H. C. (1990). Cross-cultural studies of individualism and collectivism. In J. J. Berman (Ed.), *Nebraska Symposium on Motivation: 1989* (Vol. 37, pp. 41–134). Lincoln: University of Nebraska Press.

Tudge, J. R. H. (1992). Processes and consequences of peer collaboration: A Vygotskian analysis. *Child Development, 63,* 1364–1379.

Uzgiris, I. C. (1964). Situational generality of conservation. *Child Development, 35,* 831–841.

Vygotsky, L. S. (1932/1962). *Thought and language.* Cambridge: MIT Press; New York: Wiley.

Waas, G. A (1988). Social attributional biases of peer-rejected and aggressive children. *Child Development, 59,* 969–975.

Wagner, B. M. & Phillips, D. A. (1992). Beyond beliefs: Parent and child behaviors and children's perceived academic competence. *Child Development, 63,* 1380–1391.

Weinstein, R. S., Marshall, H. H., Sharp, L. & Botkin, M. (1987). Pygmalion and the student: Age and classroom differences in children's awareness of teacher expectations. *Child Development, 58,* 1079–1093.

Wellman, H. M. (1990). *The child's theory of mind.* Cambridge: MIT Press.

Youngblade, L. M. & Belsky, J. (1992). Parent-child antecedents of 5-year-olds' close friendships: A longitudinal analysis. *Developmental Psychology, 28,* 700–713.

Youniss, J. (1980). *Parents and peers in social development: A Sullivan-Piaget perspective.* Chicago: University of Chicago Press.

CHAPTER 9

Rapid physical changes, self-consciousness, and a need for peer approval are all characteristics of early adolescence. Here Picasso shows us the delicacy of youth, the boy taking on a contemplative pose and emerging, almost as a work of art, into young manhood.

Early Adolescence (12–18 Years)

At this point in our discussion of life stages, we depart once again from Erikson's conceptualization. His psychosocial theory views adolescence as a single stage unified by the resolution of the central conflict of identity versus identity confusion. Erikson's approach attempts to address the tasks and needs of children and youth ranging in age from about 11 to 21 within one developmental stage. From our own research on adolescents and our assessment of the research literature, we have come to the conclusion that two distinct periods of psychosocial development occur during these years. This chapter discusses the stage of early adolescence. Chapter 10 discusses later adolescence.

We have identified *early adolescence* as a period that begins with the onset of puberty and ends with graduation from high school (or roughly age 18). This stage is characterized by rapid physical changes, significant cognitive and emotional maturation, sexual awakening, and a heightened sensitivity to peer relations. We have called the psychosocial crisis of this stage *group identity versus alienation*. The second stage, *later adolescence*, begins at approximately age 18 and continues for about three or four years. This stage is characterized by new advances in the establishment of autonomy from the family and the development of a personal identity. The psychosocial crisis of this period is *individual identity versus identity confusion*. The second adolescent stage closely parallels Erikson's conceptualization of the entire period of adolescence.

Although we agree that the crisis of individual identity accurately reflects the concerns of the college-age adolescent, we have found that this conceptualization is inadequate for understanding the concerns of younger adolescents. Young adolescents must resolve questions about their connections, especially their relationships with their peer groups, before they can create individual identities. It seems crucial that high-school-age adolescents develop a sense of group identity as a prelude to a sense of individual identity. Of course, elements of personal identity are forged at this stage, as are elements of other subsequent psychosocial orientations, including intimacy, generativity, integrity, and immortality. In addition, early adolescents may rework and synthesize their earlier psychosocial orientations as they engage in a more complex and demanding sociocultural environment.

Developmental Tasks

Physical Maturation

The onset of early adolescence is marked by rapid physical changes. The changes associated with puberty—a "height spurt," the maturation of the reproductive system, the appearance of secondary sex characteristics, and the redistribution of body weight—generally begin at age 11 in females and at age 13 in males. Variability in the rate of development is well documented (Faust, 1977; Brooks-Gunn & Reiter, 1990; Tanner, 1978/1990). The time from the appearance of breast buds to full maturity may range from 1½ to 6 years for girls; the male genitalia may take from 2 to 5 years to reach adult size. These individual differences in maturation suggest that during early adolescence the chronological peer group is biologically far more diverse than it was during early and middle school age.

Pubertal development influences psychological and social development in at least three ways (Clausen, 1975). First, physical growth alters a person's actual *ability to perform tasks*. Early adolescents are taller and stronger than younger children and have greater coordination and endurance. Second, physical growth can

The increase in muscle strength that takes place during puberty allows young people to reach new levels of competence in performing the physical tasks of adulthood.

alter how *one is perceived by others*. For example, early adolescents may be viewed as less cuddly or more threatening than younger children. Third, physical growth influences *how adolescents perceive themselves*. The physical changes may make them feel more like adults or, if the results are disappointing, may make adulthood harder to accept. Of course, the direction of influence depends largely on how the changes of puberty are viewed and marked by the society.

The degree to which one's body matches the desired or socially valued body build of the culture influences social acceptance by peers and adults. This match between body shape and cultural values also influences the future course of psychosocial development. Our culture gives some special self-esteem advantages to muscular, well-developed males and petite, shapely females. In contrast, it detracts from the self-esteem of thin, gangling boys and overweight males and females.

Physical Changes in Boys

Physical maturation poses different problems for males and females. Although both sexes must adjust to a changing body image, the culture places distinct values and taboos on the kinds of changes experienced by each.

Boys generally welcome the changes involving increased height and muscle mass that bring them one step closer to adult maturity. On the one hand, a mature physique usually brings well-developed physical skills that are highly valued by peers and adults alike. On the other hand, the period of rapid growth may leave a boy awkward and uncoordinated for a time. This awkwardness results because growth does not take place at the same rate in all parts of the body. One particular discrepancy is the time lag between the height spurt and the increase in muscle strength. For boys, the peak increase in muscle strength usually occurs about 12–14 months after the peak height spurt (Carron & Bailey, 1974). This time lag results in a temporary period during which a boy simply cannot accomplish what he might expect, given his height. Psychologically, this awkward period

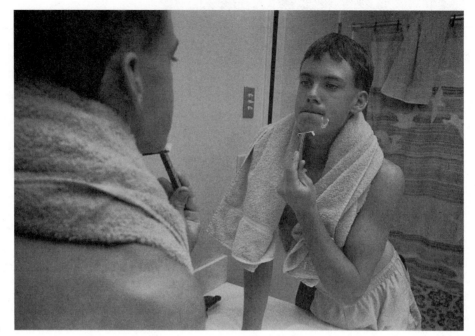

Shaving is one of the positive rituals marking a boy's transition into adolescence.

poses some strong challenges to the boy's self-esteem. He simply looks funny and out of shape. He may be easily embarrassed by this condition. He cannot fully accept his new body image at first, and he doubts whether others can.

The onset of the growth of the testes and the penis also poses important problems for early adolescent males. Testicular growth is one of the first signs of puberty in boys. Boys are generally not well prepared by their parents for the maturation of their reproductive organs (Bolton & MacEachron, 1988). Specifically, they are not taught about spontaneous ejaculation and may be surprised, scared, or embarrassed by it. The sexual connotation of the event may make it difficult for boys to seek an explanation from their parents. They are left to gain information from friends and reading material or to worry in private about its meaning. For many boys, spontaneous ejaculation provides an important clue to the way in which physical adult sexuality and reproduction are accomplished. The pleasure of the ejaculation and the positive value of the new information that it provides are counterbalanced by a mild anxiety (Gaddis & Brooks-Gunn, 1985; Marsiglio, 1988). This is only one of the developments that arouse ambivalence in many boys during early adolescence.

In a study of first ejaculation among Nigerian boys, many of the same patterns were found as have been reported in American samples. The main difference was that the Nigerian boys were about two years older at the time of their first ejaculation. Most of the boys had not been prepared for this experience; however, those who had been prepared had received their information largely from male sources, especially older brothers. The experience itself was associated with mild to strong feelings of pride and pleasure, and it made the boys feel grown-up. Many boys expressed some mild feelings of upset, embarrassment, and shame. There was no difference in reactions between the boys who had been well prepared for their experience and those who had not been prepared (Adegoke, 1993).

A third area of physical development that has psychological and social meaning for the boy is the development of secondary sex characteristics, particularly the growth of facial and body hair. The equipment and the ritual behaviors

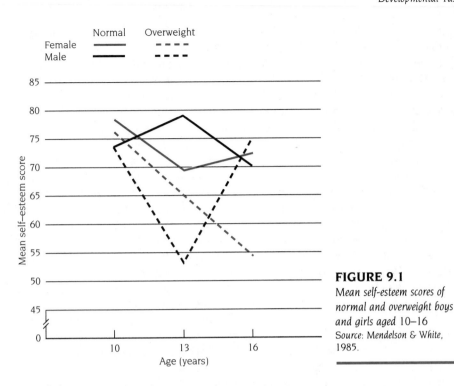

FIGURE 9.1

Mean self-esteem scores of normal and overweight boys and girls aged 10–16
Source: Mendelson & White, 1985.

associated with shaving are closely linked to the masculine sex role. Most boys are eager to express their identification with this role by shaving, and they use the slightest evidence of facial hair as an excuse to take razor in hand. The ritual of shaving not only provides some affirmation of the boy's masculinity but also allows him an acceptable outlet for his narcissism. As he shaves, it is legitimate for him to gaze at and admire his changing image. In some subcultures, a mustache is an important symbol of manliness. Thus some young men cultivate and admire their mustaches as evidence of their enhanced male status.

Physical Changes in Girls

For girls the onset of puberty occurs at approximately age 11—almost two years sooner than the parallel experience for boys. The height spurt is one of the earliest of the pubertal changes. Initially, the increase in height may be embarrassing as a girl finds herself towering above her male classmates. Girls often slouch in an attempt to disguise their increased height.

Girls' predominant concern about their changing physique is obesity. When the growth spurt begins, most girls notice a plumping of their features. In an attempt to ward off what they perceive as a tendency toward obesity, many early adolescent girls begin a process of strict and often faddish dieting. This strategy is ill timed since their bodies require well-balanced diets and increased caloric intake during the period of rapid growth.

During early adolescence, obesity is associated with negative feelings about one's appearance and one's body. This association is closely tied to our cultural preference for the slender female body shape, a preference that results in the perception by a majority of adult women that they are overweight and leads almost half of adult women to some type of weight-loss diet (Thornberry, Wilson & Golden, 1986). Research suggests that being overweight has little relation to self-esteem in middle school age but does begin to have a negative relation to self-esteem during early adolescence (see Figure 9.1). At age 10, self-esteem did not differ significantly for normal and overweight boys and girls. Overweight boys had lower self-esteem than boys of normal weight at age 13 but not at younger or older ages. Overweight girls had lower self-esteem than girls of normal weight at 16 (Mendelson & White, 1985; Martin et al., 1988). The impact of obesity on self-esteem illustrates the effect of physical development and body shape on self-evaluation and self-acceptance during this stage.

Obesity is related to activity level. One of the compounding factors in obesity among many adolescent girls is that, even though they want to be slender, they also tend to reduce their activity level with age. In an ethnically diverse sample of over 550 girls in Grades 5–12, only 36% met the national goal for strenuous activity: 15 minutes of strenuous activity at least three times per week (Wolf et al., 1993). The amount of overall activity and strenuous activity decreased with age, and obesity was negatively correlated with activity. The study also revealed differences in exercise patterns across ethnic groups. Hispanic and Asian-American girls had significantly lower scores on activity level than African-American and white girls. Two cultural hypotheses were formulated to explain this pattern, but neither one has been tested. First, it is possible that strenuous physical activity is viewed as especially unfeminine by Asian-Americans and Hispanics. Second, it is possible that the slender body type is not seen as desirable by these ethnic groups; thus, there is less motivation to do strenuous exercise. We do not know much about ethnic differences in adolescence, especially as they relate to preferences for body type and standards of physical attractiveness.

In girls, the development of primary sex characteristics includes the development of breast buds and the onset of the menstrual cycle. To the average girl, the development of breast buds is a welcome sign of her growing maturity and femininity (Brooks-Gunn & Warren, 1988). Some girls begin to wear brassieres in anticipation of the onset of breast development. Most girls are prepared by their mothers for menstruation. However, menstruation is often handled as a matter of hygiene rather than as a sexual transition (Logan, 1980). Many girls do not understand the relation of menstruation to reproduction. They simply accept their monthly periods as another sign of their femininity.

At the age when most girls begin to menstruate (approximately 12), their male peers may still be ignorant of this phenomenon. The girl is often put in a position of having to explain or hide the facts of her growth. Girls rarely tell their male peers or their fathers about the onset of menarche, but they do discuss it with their female friends and their mothers. The discrepancy in the onset of puberty in boys and girls and the uneven dissemination of information about it may make it difficult for a girl to fully accept the changes she is experiencing. The memoirs of Simone de Beauvoir (1959) reflect this ambivalence:

> We were staying with friends. . . . I awoke horror-stricken one morning: I had soiled my nightdress. I washed it and got dressed: again I soiled my underclothes. I had forgotten Madeleine's vague prophecies, and I wondered what shameful malady I was suffering from. Worried and feeling somehow guilty, I had to take my mother into my confidence: she explained to me that I had now become "a big girl," and bundled me up in a very inconvenient manner. I felt a strong sense of relief when I learned that it had happened through no fault of my own; and as always when something important happened to me, I even felt my heart swell with a sort of pride. (p. 101)

Most girls seem to react to menstruation with a mix of positive and negative feelings. The positive feelings reflect a pride in maturing and in the confirmation of their womanliness. The negative feelings reflect the inconvenience, some unpleasant symptoms, and the possible embarrassment of menstruation (Brooks-Gunn & Reiter, 1990).

The development of secondary sex characteristics, especially the growth of body hair, may be a greater burden for girls than it is for boys. The cultural preference for smooth-skinned females requires regular shaving of underarms and legs. This shaving ritual, however, is not filled with the same positive sex-role validation as is face shaving for adolescent boys. The adolescent girl learns that she must make certain alterations in her physical appearance in order to meet the cultural standards for femininity.

Generally, girls are more dissatisfied than boys with their physical appearance and their overall body image. This pattern was found among Finns as well as Americans (Petersen et al., 1984; Rauste-von Wright, 1989). For girls, self-consciousness and dissatisfaction with their appearance reach their peak between the ages of 13 and 15. By 18, the more satisfied a young woman is with her body image, the more likely she is to have a positive outlook on social relationships with her family, her peers, and people in general.

The Secular Trend

Along with the genetic influence on growth and sexual maturation, the environment plays an important role in the eventual attainment of one's growth potential. A *secular growth trend* is a decrease over time in the average age at which physical maturation takes place (Van Wieringen, 1978). Changes in hygiene, nutrition, and health care have contributed to an earlier growth spurt over the past century. Children aged 10–14 increased in height by an average of 2 to 3 centimeters every decade from 1900 to 1960. Adult height is not necessarily greater; it is simply attained earlier.

Other evidence of a secular trend is the shift in age at menarche. There is some controversy about the extent of this shift. Data reported by Tanner (1978/1990) show a decrease in the average age at menarche from 13.5 to 14 in 1950 to 12.5 to 13 in 1970. At present, the mean age at menarche is 12.3, but the range is from 9 to 17. Age at menarche varies among countries and even among socioeconomic groups within a country. Sources based on Roman, Islamic, and medieval writings suggest that females have matured in the age range of 12–14 for many centuries (Bullough, 1981). Lack of precise records and the confounding of health and social class with age at menarche make it difficult to confirm long-term historical trends. Lower age at the onset of menarche is associated with an improved standard of living, including health, diet, and social class (Tanner, 1981). The secular trend has been documented across ethnic group samples that have had comparable access to adequate nutrition (Brooks-Gunn & Reiter, 1990).

Individual Differences in Maturation Rate

The rate of physical maturation varies in boys just as it does in girls. It has been noted that boys who mature later than their age-mates experience considerable psychological stress and develop a negative self-image (Clausen, 1975; Mussen & Jones, 1957). Late-maturing boys are treated as if they were younger than they really are. They may become isolated from their peers and may behave in a silly, childish manner in order to gain attention.

Boys who mature earlier than their age-mates tend to have an advantage. They develop a positive self-image, in part because they are likely to be given increased responsibility by their parents and teachers. They are generally more satisfied with their bodies; they feel more positive about being boys; and they are likely to be more involved in school activities by the tenth grade than are late-maturing boys (Blyth, Bulcroft & Simmons, 1981). Fifth- and sixth-grade boys who are more physically mature report more positive daily emotions, better attention, more feelings of being strong, and some greater awareness of states of tension (Richards & Larson, 1993). In general, early-maturing boys experience the kinds of positive mood and sense of centeredness that are reflected in the social qualities of leadership and personal confidence.

The consequences of early and late maturation differ for girls and boys (Dwyer & Mayer, 1971). Both early- and late-maturing girls experience some tension with regard to their physical development. Since girls mature about two years earlier than boys, the early-maturing girl stands out among all her male and female age-mates. Her stature and breast development violate the cultural equation of femininity with petiteness. Early onset of menstruation is especially stressful, resulting in heightened self-consciousness and anxiety (Hill, 1988). Early maturers are less likely to have been prepared for the onset of menstruation, and they are less likely to have close friends with whom they can discuss it. For a time, at least, early-maturing girls may be embarrassed by their femininity. Not only do they look very different from their peers, but they are experiencing significant physical changes that they cannot discuss readily with their age-mates.

Several studies suggest that early pubertal onset is a source of stress for girls (Kornfield, 1990; Caspi & Moffitt, 1991). They experience higher levels of conflict with their parents and are more likely to report depression and anxiety (Wierson, Long & Forehand, 1993). There is some evidence that early-maturing girls earn lower grades and lower scores on academic achievement tests. They are also more likely to be identified as behavior problems in school (Blyth et al., 1981). Early-maturing girls tend to start dating earlier and to perceive themselves as more popular with boys than do late-maturing girls. Some studies report that early-maturing girls are more likely to engage in high-risk, promiscuous sexual behavior. In general, however, the timing of the transition to puberty in and of itself is not a strong predictor of a girl's emotional well-being. Rather, timing interacts with other events, such as school transition, family conflict, or peer acceptance, to influence how a girl will construct the meaning of this physical transition (Brooks-Gunn & Reiter, 1990; Richards & Larson, 1993).

These examples of the psychological impact of the timing of physical maturation highlight the interaction between the biological and the social systems in development. Early-maturing girls and late-maturing boys may become isolated from their peers. Individuals who deviate from the normal physical growth pattern may be rejected by the group because they look different and are experiencing different psychological events than are most of the group members. Similarly, the advantages of early maturation for boys are primarily a product of the admiration and leadership role attributed to them by their parents and peers. Being off-time, either early or late, with respect to physical maturation may result in negative perceptions of one's body image and dissatisfaction with one's physical appearance that persist well beyond adolescence (Rauste-von Wright, 1989).

Review of Major Trends in Physical Development

Both boys and girls experience parallel phases of physical maturation during early adolescence. Although girls experience these changes somewhat earlier, both sexes must adapt to increases in height and weight and to the maturation of primary and secondary sex characteristics. As a result of earlier maturation of their reproductive systems, girls often introduce dating, "going together," and romance

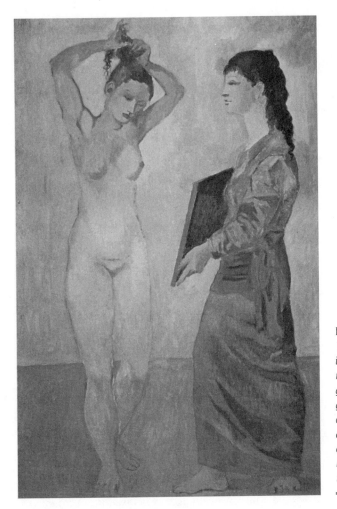

Pablo Picasso, Toilette, *1906. Narcissism is expressed in a preoccupation with one's mirror image. Most adolescent girls and boys take longer in grooming and are more self-conscious about their physical appearance than younger children. Their rooms may be a mess, but their hair is styled to perfection.*

into the peer culture. Biological changes in the girls energize the social system to incorporate and evolve rituals to deal with reproductive and sexual topics. This is a good example of how changes in the biological system may modify the social system.

Four points have been made about the psychological meaning of these body changes for males and females:

1. The physical changes enable adolescents to think of themselves as approaching adulthood.
2. The changes influence a young person's identification with the role of man or woman.
3. The person becomes more egocentric and self-involved.
4. The changes produce ambivalence about new aspects of the self. If the family and peer group are not supportive of these changes, negative feelings and conflicts are likely to result.

The timing of physical growth may determine whether the changes of puberty are experienced as positive or negative. Acceptance of these physical changes seems to require adequate information about their meaning, a positive identification with one's sex role, and an atmosphere of family and peer support.

One of the stereotypes of adolescence is that it is a time of risk taking. Of course, not all youth expose themselves to risks, and youth are not alone in taking risks. However, some disturbing data suggest that contemporary youth do indeed expose themselves to high rates of preventable injuries. The leading cause of death among U.S. adolescents is accidents, especially motor vehicle accidents, and the second most common cause of death in this group is homicides (U.S. Bureau of the Census, 1992). The death rate by homicides is higher for adolescents than for any other age group.

In addition to risk behaviors that are associated with mortality, adolescents are known for their rejection of safety precautions. The age range 16–18 is the peak period for the initiation of smoking, drinking, and the use of illicit drugs. One estimate found that one in seven adolescents in the United States has a sexually transmitted disease; 47% of American youth are sexually active and they or their partner do not always use a contraceptive. About 26% of eighth-graders and 38% of tenth-graders reported riding in a car with a driver who was intoxicated or using drugs (Quadrel, Fischhoff & Davis, 1993; Benson, 1992).

Weapon carrying has also increased dramatically since the middle 1980s. A study of weapon carrying in two junior high

BOX 9.1

Safety and Risk Behaviors in Adolescence

schools in Washington, D.C., found that, among males, 47% had carried knives and 25% had carried guns over the prior two weeks. Among females, 37% had carried knives and 4% had carried guns (Webster, Gainer & Champion, 1993). This problem has become so serious that reducing weapon carrying among adolescents has been formally included as one of the national health objectives for the year 2000.

Adolescents appear to expose themselves to a wider range of high-risk behaviors between the ages of 12 and 17, and during that same time, they use fewer safety precautions. In a study of over 2000 junior high and high school students in rural and urban areas of Iowa, four areas of safety behavior were assessed. The percentage of adolescents who used a safety belt while riding in the front or back seat of a car, or who used any type of helmet while riding a bicycle, moped, skateboard, or snowmobile, decreased with age. Similarly, safety strategies associated with swimming, such as checking the depth of the water before diving or always swimming with a partner, decreased with age. At the same time, the percentage who drove a car while drunk or high on drugs increased with age, even when opportunities to drive, which normally increase with age, were taken into account (Schootman et al., 1993).

The concept of the secular trend alerts us to the importance of the psychosocial context of physical development. Not only are peers experiencing diverse patterns of growth, but parents and grandparents may be reacting to a discrepancy between their children's development and their own timetable for growth. What is more, because the period of reproductive capacity starts earlier than it did 50 years ago, young people must cope with special challenges in the expression and regulation of their sexual impulses. One consequence of the earlier onset of puberty is that adolescents may find themselves in potentially high-risk situations at a relatively young age. Given the kinds of risks inherent in a technological society, it is no wonder that adolescent exposure to risk behaviors is a major contemporary health concern (see Box 9.1).

Formal Operations

Early adolescents begin to think about the world in new ways. From early adolescence on into adulthood, the quality of thought changes in some very significant directions. Thought becomes more abstract. Young people are able to think about

Scientific problem solving requires the ability to raise hypotheses, to manipulate several variables at once, and to reason about the logical outcomes of various procedures. Experience with scientific experimentation probably improves the flexibility and clarity of formal operational thought.

several dimensions at once rather than focusing on just one domain or issue at a time. Thinking becomes more reflective, and adolescents are increasingly aware of their own thoughts as well as of the accuracy or inaccuracy of their knowledge. Adolescents are able to generate hypotheses about events that they have never perceived (Keating, 1990). These complex cognitive capacities were described by Jean Piaget as *formal operations* (Inhelder & Piaget, 1958; Piaget, 1970, 1972; Chapman, 1988).

It is important to recognize that these qualities of thought reflect what is possible for adolescents rather than what is typical. Most adolescents, and older adults as well, approach problem solving in a practical, concrete way in their typical everyday functioning. However, under the most supportive conditions, more abstract, systematic, and self-reflective qualities of thought can be observed and bring a new perspective to how adolescents approach the analysis of information and the acquisition of knowledge (Fischer, 1980; Eckstein & Shemesh, 1992; Fischer et al., 1993).

Piaget proposed that, in the transition from concrete to formal operational thought, thoughts are governed more by logical principles than by perceptions and experiences. In the period of concrete operational thought, children use mental operations to explain changes in tangible objects and events. In the period of formal operational thought, young people use mental operations to manipulate and modify thoughts and other mental processes. An important feature of formal operational thought is the ability to formulate hypotheses to explain an event, and then to follow the logic that a particular hypothesis implies: "Hypothetical reasoning implies the subordination of the real to the realm of the possible, and consequently the linking of all possibilities to one another by necessary implications that encompass the real, but at the same time go beyond it" (Piaget, 1972, p. 3).

One of the classic experiments that Piaget and Inhelder designed to demonstrate the development of hypothetico-deductive reasoning involves the explanation of the swing of a pendulum. The task is to find out what variable or combination of variables controls the speed of the swing. Four factors can be varied: the mass of the object; the height from which the pendulum is pushed; the force with which it is pushed; and the length of the string. To investigate this problem, it is necessary to isolate the separate factors and then to vary only one factor at a time, while keeping the others constant. As it happens, only the length of the string influences the speed of the pendulum. The challenge is to demonstrate that the length of the string accounts for the speed and that the other factors do not. Children in the stage of concrete operational thought have difficulty coordinating the interaction of four separate variables and may lose track of what is being varied and what is being held constant. After trying one or two strategies, the child may simply give up. Using formal operational thought, a child can create a matrix of variables and test each factor separately to evaluate its contribution (Inhelder & Piaget, 1958; Flavell, 1963).

Several skills are involved in problem solving of this kind. First, one must be able to identify the separate factors and the possible effect of each. Second, one must be able to consider the possible interactions among the factors. Third, one must be able to develop a systematic method of testing each factor in combination with each other factor. The conceptual system of possible solutions guides problem solving (Neimark, 1975; Siegler, Liebert & Liebert, 1973).

Six new conceptual skills emerge during the stage of formal operations (Neimark, 1982; Demetriou & Efklides, 1985). Each of these skills has implications for how adolescents approach interpersonal relationships and the formulation of personal plans and goals, as well as for how they analyze scientific and mathematical information. First, adolescents are able to manipulate mentally more than two categories of variables at the same time; for example, they can consider the relationship of speed, distance, and time in planning a trip (Acredolo, Adams & Schmid, 1984). They can draw on many variables to explain their behavior as well as the behavior of others. Second, they are able to think about things changing in the future; they can realize, for instance, that their relationship with their parents will be very different in ten years' time. Third, they can hypothesize about a logical sequence of possible events; for example, they can predict the college and occupational options that may be open to them, depending on how well they do in certain academic coursework in high school. Fourth, they can anticipate the consequences of their actions. For instance, they realize that if they drop out of school, certain career possibilities will be closed to them. The fact that they can anticipate consequences enables them to achieve a prior knowledge of the possible outcomes of doing something and allows them to decide on that basis whether they wish to do it.

Fifth, they can detect the logical consistency or inconsistency in a set of statements. They can test the truth of a statement by finding evidence that supports or disproves the statement. They are troubled, for example, by the apparent contradiction of the statement "All men are equal before the law" and the possibility of a presidential pardon for certain high-status lawbreakers.

Sixth, they can think in a relativistic way about themselves, other individuals, and their world. They know that they are expected to act in a particular way because of the norms of their community and culture. They also know that, in other families, communities, and cultures, different norms govern the same behavior. As a result, the decision to behave in a culturally accepted manner

TABLE 9.1	**New Conceptual Skills That Emerge During the Stage of Formal Operational Thought**

1. Ability to manipulate mentally more than two categories of variables simultaneously.
2. Ability to think about the changes that come with time.
3. Ability to hypothesize logical sequences of events.
4. Ability to foresee consequences of actions.
5. Ability to detect logical consistency or inconsistency in a set of statements.
6. Ability to think in relativistic ways about self, others, and the world.

becomes a more conscious commitment to the society. At the same time, it is easier for them to accept members of other cultures because they realize that these people are the products of societies with different sets of rules and norms (O'Mahoney, 1989).

Table 9.1 gives a synopsis of the conceptual skills associated with formal operational reasoning.

In general, the changes in conceptual development that occur during early adolescence result in a more flexible, critical, and abstract view of the world. The abilities to hypothesize logical sequences of action, to conceptualize change, and to anticipate the consequences of actions all contribute to a more realistic sense of the future (Klineberg, 1967; Lessing, 1972). The view of the future includes both hopes, such as career goals, educational attainment, and beginning a family, and fears, such as concerns about unemployment or the possibility of war (Nurmi, 1987; Gillies, 1989).

Criticism of the Concept of Formal Operations

In Piaget's theory of cognitive development, formal operational reasoning is viewed as the final stage in the maturing of logical thought. A number of scholars have pointed to limitations in this construction. First, questions have been raised about the extent to which there is a stagelike consolidation in the use of formal reasoning. Many studies show that most adolescents and adults do not function at the formal operational level, and that their use of formal reasoning is inconsistent across problem areas. For example, Neimark (1975) followed changes in problem-solving strategies over 3½ years. Even the oldest subjects in her study, who were 15, did not apply formal operational strategies to all problems. Although performance across problems was not consistent, there did appear to be a progression through levels of problem-solving approaches during the years from 11 to 15. Neimark (1982) described these levels as (1) no rule, (2) limited rules, (3) a collection of rules or unelaborated principles, and (4) general principles. In another study of formal operational thinking among 13-year-olds, few significant correlations were found in performance across six different measures (Overton & Meehan, 1982). In other words, children at this age did not consistently apply a formal operational reasoning approach to problems across various specific content areas.

A second criticism of formal reasoning as a construct is that it is not broad enough to encompass the many dimensions along which cognitive functioning matures. Referring back to the model of the developing mind presented in Chapter 8, one recognizes at least two other domains in which growth takes place:

the information-processing system and the hypercognitive system. Increases in the speed, efficiency, and capacity of information storage have been documented during the period from 11 to 14 (Thatcher, Walker & Giudice, 1987). It is quite likely that improvements in logical reasoning are in part a result of being able to handle greater quantities of information more quickly and efficiently. In addition to development in basic processing, there is evidence of gains in information and knowledge about a number of topics, as a result of both schooling and increased mastery in specific areas of expertise. One consequence of the combination of greater information-processing capacity and a broader knowledge base is that hypercognitive processing improves. Adolescents can hold a problem in mind and approach it from several different angles, assessing which one offers the most promising avenue to a solution (Keating, 1990).

Egocentrism

The term *egocentrism* refers to the child's limited perspective at the beginning of each new phase of cognitive development (Piaget, 1926; Inhelder & Piaget, 1958). In the sensorimotor phase, egocentrism appears as an inability to separate one's actions from their effects on specific objects or people. As the scheme for causality is developed, the first process of decentering occurs. Infants recognize that certain actions have predictable consequences and that novel situations call for new, relevant behaviors; for example, one cannot turn the light on by turning the knob on the radio.

In the phase of preoperational thought, egocentrism is manifested in an ability to separate one's own perspective from that of the listener. When a 4-year-old girl tells you about something that happened to her at the zoo, she may explain events as if you had seen them, too. When a 3-year-old boy is explaining something to his grandmother over the phone, he may point to objects in the room, unaware that his grandmother cannot *see* over the phone lines.

The third phase of heightened egocentrism occurs in the transition from concrete to formal operational thought. As children develop the capacity to formulate hypothetical systems, they begin to generate assumptions about their own and others' behavior that will fit into these abstract formulations. For example, an early adolescent boy may insist that cooperation is a more desirable mode of interaction than competition. He believes that, in theory, cooperation will benefit each participant and provide more resources for the group as a whole. This boy may become angry or disillusioned on discovering that his teachers, parents, and even peers seek competitive experiences and appear to enjoy them. He may think, "If the cooperative system is so superior, why do people persist in their illogical joy in triumphing over an opponent?" This kind of egocentrism reflects an inability to recognize that others may not share one's own hypothetical system.

In early adolescence, decentering requires an ability to realize that one's ideals are not shared by all others. We live in a pluralistic society, in which each person is likely to have distinct goals and aspirations. Early adolescents gradually discover that their neat, logical life plans must be constantly adapted to the expectations and needs of relevant others. As they develop the flexibility of thought that accompanies formal operational perspective taking, their egocentrism should decline. Social acceptance also reduces egocentrism. Early adolescents who are confident of their parents' emotional support are less self-conscious than those who experience parental rejection or overcontrol (Riley, Adams & Nielsen, 1984).

Early adolescent egocentrism has two characteristics that may affect social interaction as well as problem solving. First, early adolescents are preoccupied by their own thoughts. They may become somewhat withdrawn and isolated as their consciousness expands. Thoughts about the possible and the probable, the near and the distant future, and the logical extension of contemporary events to future consequences flood their minds. David Elkind (1967) described one aspect of this process as the formation of a *personal fable*, an intense investment in one's own thoughts and feelings and a belief that these thoughts are unique. Adolescents may conclude that they alone are having certain insights or certain difficulties and that no one else can understand or sympathize with their thoughts. This tendency to withdraw into their own speculations may cut off their access to new information or ideas and may inhibit their social interaction.

Second, early adolescents may assume that others share their preoccupations. Elkind (1967) referred to this assumption as the *imaginary audience*. Instead of recognizing that everyone is equally wrapped up in his or her own concerns and plans, early adolescents envision their own thoughts as being the focus of other people's attention. This subjectivity generates an uncomfortable self-consciousness that makes interaction awkward. There is some question about the cognitive processes involved in this heightened self-consciousness. On the one hand, a preoccupation with the idea that others are watching one's every move may be an important element in decentering, which directs attention to others and to how one may be viewed by them. The concern about others' perceptions thus stimulates cognitive maturation. On the other hand, self-consciousness may be an outcome of an increased ability to consider the point of view of others and their expectations for one's behavior.

As a result of changes in cognitive functioning, adolescents become more aware of their own mental activity. They may become intensely preoccupied with their thoughts and fantasies, seeking opportunities for solitude so that they have time to think.

We begin to understand early adolescence as a time when young people's ideas of reality take on convincing intensity. Early adolescents are likely to believe that their interpretations of interactions are correct and, therefore, they are less flexible in considering alternative possibilities. Needless to say, egocentrism remains a problem well past adolescence. At each new phase of expanding awareness, people tend to rely heavily on their own experiences and perceptions in order to minimize the anxiety associated with uncertainty. Part of the progress of formal thought implies a reliance on reason over experience. We have more confidence in what we know than in what we can see or hear. Thus, we can find ourselves trapped in an egocentric perspective. We may interpret new experiences as examples of familiar concepts rather than as novel events. We may reject evidence for an argument because it does not support an already carefully developed explanation. Casting around for new evidence and new explanations is a lifelong challenge. It is much easier to rely on earlier assumptions than to continually call our perspective into question.

Factors That Promote Formal Operational Thought

Several environmental conditions facilitate the development of formal operational thought and reduce egocentrism. First, early adolescents begin to function in a variety of role relationships that place both compatible and conflicting demands on them. Among these role relationships are son or daughter, worker, student, friend, dating partner, religious believer, and citizen. Early adolescents experience firsthand the pressures of multiple expectations for their behavior. At times, for example, expectations for the student role may be at odds with those for the child or the friend role.

Early adolescents must learn to manipulate and balance these demands. In order to do so successfully, they must learn to manipulate mentally more than two variables at any one time. The experience of participating in a variety of roles also facilitates relativistic thinking by demonstrating that what is acceptable and valued in one situation may not be acceptable or valued in another (Chandler & Boyes, 1982).

Ongoing interactions with parents may provide a powerful, second stimulus to cognitive development, especially when parents encourage their children to examine their assumptions, to find evidence to support their arguments, and to evaluate their sources of information as they approach problems in daily life (Dunham, Kidwell & Portes, 1988).

The third environmental condition that facilitates the development of the cognitive skills of early adolescence is the adolescent's participation in a more heterogeneous peer group (Looft, 1971). When children move from their community elementary school to a more centralized junior high and high school, they are likely to become acquainted with other students whose family backgrounds and social class are different from their own. In working and playing with these friends, they realize the extent to which their expectations of the future differ from those of their new acquaintances and the extent to which their present values are shaped by the families and neighborhood from which they come.

The use of formal operational skills may be observed in adolescent discussions of peer-related issues and in the formation of boyfriend-girlfriend relationships, a domain that is new and requires a wide range of hypothesis-formulating and hypothesis-testing mental activities. We have observed our own children as they talk back and forth to friends in person, over the phone, and through notes, helping each other to answer questions and generate alternative explanations in

Although formal schooling may play a central role in fostering advanced forms of reasoning and problem solving, many students experience long periods of boredom at school.

order to put themselves in favorable or desirable positions and to wiggle out of uncomfortable circumstances. Here is an example of a conversation between a 15-year-old girl and her best friend:

C: I'm so frustrated, I can't stand it. Before S and I started to date, he was nice to me. I enjoyed being with him. He said hello to me in the halls; we'd walk along together. We talked about all kinds of things. Now that we're going out, he seems rude and uncaring. When we're with other people, he jumps in when I start to talk, and his eyes say, "Be quiet." He breezes by me in the halls sometimes, and when we talk about things (if we talk), he acts as if he is always right. I don't think he cares about me anymore. What's going on?

D: I know he likes you because he tells me. Maybe you should talk to him and tell him what he does and how it makes you feel.

C: No. If I do that, he'll get mad and he won't like me anymore. Why don't you talk to him?

D: No. That wouldn't do any good because then he would know you talked to me about this, and he would not like it or he would just say what he thinks would make him look good.

This conversation goes on. Many possible scenarios are developed about why this behavior is occurring and many hypotheses are raised about what can be done. The girls project the likely outcomes of each set of possible actions and attempt to evaluate the results of each. Finally, a tentative conclusion is reached: Boys treat girls differently when they are involved in a boyfriend-girlfriend relationship than when they are not. In the "just friends" situation, the boy tends to treat the girl as an equal; in the boyfriend-girlfriend situation, the boy tends to expect to dominate the girl. A solution is derived: C must shape S up. Because she still likes him very much and wants to go out with him, she must change his behavior so that it is supportive and comfortable for her. She must be the one to do this. Because S really does like her and because he may not realize how his behavior is affecting her, chances are good that he will respond to C's approach rather than lose her as a girlfriend.

The context of the friendship between C and D allows C to trust discussing her problem with D so that they can examine it fully. It also allows D to disagree with C without terminating the conversation. Thus, C can get a somewhat different point of view about her situation, and the two friends can explore a very personal problem more objectively and rationally than C probably can on her own.

The fourth condition that fosters the development of the cognitive skills of early adolescence is the content of the high school curriculum. Courses in science, mathematics, and language formally expose the student to the logical relationships inherent in the world. The student is also formally introduced to the hypothetico-deductive style of reasoning. The fine arts and the humanities foster conceptions of how the world has been or might be. They expand the repertoire of representational thought. In sum, the gains in conceptual skill made during early adolescence may be facilitated by the person's active involvement in a more complex and differentiated academic environment (Kuhn, Amsel & O'Loughlin, 1988; Rabinowitz, 1988; Linn et al., 1989).

We must interject a caveat about our emphasis on schooling as a vehicle that promotes formal operational reasoning. All school experiences are not equally effective in promoting abstract, hypothetical reasoning. Keating (1990) described the characteristics that are important in creating a cognitively stimulating school experience:

> Students need to be engaged with meaningful material; training of thinking skills must be embedded in a knowledge of subject matter, for acquisition of isolated content knowledge is likely to be unproductive; serious engagement with real problems has to occur in depth and over time; students need experiences that lead to placing a high value on critical thinking, to acquiring it as a disposition, not just as a skill; and many of these factors occur most readily, and perhaps exclusively, when students have the opportunity for real, ongoing discourse with teachers who have reasonably expert command of the material to be taught. (p. 77)

The key factors necessary for stimulating abstract reasoning and critical thinking may not be present in much of what students encounter in the high school classroom.

We do not expect to see a mature scientist or a profound philosopher by the end of early adolescence. Formal operational thought still has to be brought to bear on the reality of significant problems. There is a process of rejecting or building on strategies that have been acquired earlier. However, the opportunity for cognitive growth during this period is extensive. Adolescents are capable of generating novel solutions and applying them to current life challenges. They can also be objective about the problem-solving process and can gain insight into their own mental activity.

Emotional Development

Descriptions of adolescence often refer to new levels of emotional variability, moodiness, and emotional outbursts. Clearly, adolescents are more aware than younger children of gradations in their emotional states and are able to attribute their emotions to a wider range of causes. However, some researchers have questioned whether adolescence really brings the peaks and valleys of emotional intensity that are stereotypically linked to this time of life.

In an attempt to assess this question, researchers gave an electronic paging device to children and adolescents aged 9–15 and asked them to describe their emotional state every time they were paged (Larson & Lampman-Petraitis, 1989). Over one week, each participant responded about 37 times. The variability of emotions was not found to increase with age. However, both the boys and the girls in the older group expressed fewer extremely positive emotions and more mildly negative emotions than did the children in the younger group. In a subsequent study using similar methods, daily emotions were monitored in relation to children's pubertal status (Richards & Larson, 1993). Both boys and girls with a more mature body shape at each age reported more frequent thoughts and feelings about love. Pubertal development was slightly related to increased feelings of anger in girls, but in general, physical maturation was not closely linked to patterns of specific emotions in girls. In boys, the relationships between pubertal development and emotions were much stronger. Those boys who were more mature reported more experiences of feeling frustrated, tense, and "hyper." They also reported a more positive mood, a greater ability to focus their attention, and more feelings of strength. Thus, in boys, pubertal changes were associated with both positive moods and a restless irritability.

Adolescents are aware of a more differentiated palette of emotions. Among the more troublesome of these emotions are anxiety, shame, embarrassment, guilt, shyness, depression, and anger (Adelson & Doehrman, 1980). Adolescent girls are likely to have a heightened awareness of new levels of negative emotions that focus inward, such as shame, guilt, and depression; boys are likely to have a heightened awareness of new levels of negative emotions that focus on others, such as contempt and aggression (Stapley & Haviland, 1989; Ostrov, Offer & Howard, 1989).

Given the likelihood of a more differentiated range of emotions during adolescence, a major task is to gain a tolerance of one's emotionality. This means accepting one's feelings and not interpreting them as a sign of "going crazy" or "being strange." Adolescents who are highly sensitive to social expectations or overly controlled about expressing or accepting their feelings probably experience a sense of shame about their emotional states. Attempts to rigidly control or defend oneself against feelings are likely to result in social alienation or maladaptive behaviors.

In a study of the coping style of adolescents, Moriarty and Toussieng (1976) summarized the basic orientation to emotions that is achieved during this life stage. The subjects were described as either *sensers* or *censors*. The sensers were willing to be influenced by new experiences. They preferred to seek out new activities, engage people, and question inconsistencies. They accepted their emotions and sought out experiences that would modify their values. The censors preferred to limit their sensory experiences. They tried to clarify their parents' values by discovering what was acceptable in society. They had limited peer interaction and were uninvolved in school. They rejected experiences or ideas that did not confirm their traditional views. Both sensers and censors are normal, healthy adolescents whose coping styles will work in our society. However, the two orientations reflect rather distinct solutions to the challenge of integrating emotional experiences into the self-concept.

Eating Disorders

One consequence of anxiety and overcontrol of emotions is a disorder known as *anorexia nervosa* (Yates, 1989). Anorexia is found primarily in girls, and the symptoms usually begin shortly after the weight spurt that accompanies puberty. Adolescents with this condition focus their behavior on weight loss. They take an obsessive, determined position in rejecting most foods. They may experience intense eating binges, followed by prolonged avoidance of food. During the latter phase, they are continuously nauseous and have trouble holding food down. In addition, they tend to have a distorted perception of their body image, seeing themselves as much fatter than they really are. The outcome of this condition is a potentially life-threatening loss of weight.

The origins of anorexia nervosa are not fully understood. Many authors implicate the cultural infatuation with thinness as a stimulus of this condition. In addition, a preoccupation with body appearance may be provoked by the relatively rapid physical changes associated with puberty. However, in addition to these factors, which all adolescents have to deal with, the adolescents who suffer from anorexia tend to have difficulty accepting and expressing their emotions. Compared with adolescents who have other types of emotional disorders, anorexics show less emotional expressivity, greater timidity, and more submissiveness. Anorexics have been described as "duty bound, rigidly disciplined, and moralistic with underlying doubts and anxious hesitancy" (Strober, 1981, pp. 289–290).

Another, more common eating disorder in adolescence is *bulimia*, which involves spurts of binging and overeating followed by the use of different strategies to prevent the absorption of food, such as induced vomiting, the use of laxatives, or strenuous exercise. Bulimia has an incidence of between 5% and 18% in the adolescent population and is experienced somewhat more evenly by males and females. Although both bulimia and anorexia produce serious health risks, anorexia appears to be more likely to lead to death from the complications of starvation (Millstein & Litt, 1990).

Delinquency

In contrast to adolescents whose overcontrol of emotions causes problems, others are impulsive and react strongly to any emotionally arousing environmental stimulus. They seem to be unable to modify the intensity of their reactions. A consequence of this impulsiveness for a large proportion of normal adolescents is involvement in delinquent acts: "Over 80 percent of American adolescents admit to committing one or more delinquent acts, most of these minor, in the course of a few years of adolescence" (Gold & Petronio, 1980, p. 523). The inability to exert intellectual control over their impulses is probably a passing experience for most young people. The fear and guilt that follow a delinquent act are usually enough punishment to prevent further violations.

In some adolescents, however, committing several delinquent acts weakens the ability to impose social constraints on such behavior, and the involvement in delinquency intensifies. One national survey categorized about 30% of males and 10% of females as serious violent offenders. These adolescents had committed three or more violent crimes in a one-year period sometime before their 18th birthday. The boys committed more crimes than the girls, and their crimes tended to be more serious (McCord, 1990; Elliott, Huizinga & Menard, 1989; Blumenstein et al., 1986). In 1990, roughly 16% of the total arrests involved people aged 15–18, but this age group accounted for 28% of the serious crimes, such as motor vehicle thefts, arson, burglary, and murder (U.S. Bureau of the Census, 1992).

Since so many young people now carry some type of weapon with them, especially knives and guns, one question that arises is about the emotional correlates of this type of behavior. Are children who carry weapons primarily preoccupied with fear and motivated by self-defense, or are the weapons an extension of their aggressive motives? In one analysis, teens who carried guns were found to differ from those who carried knives (Webster et al., 1993). For females, the more people a female knew who had been victims of violence, the more likely she was to carry a knife. For males, two strong predictors of carrying a knife were having been threatened with a knife and having been frequently involved in fights, although not usually being the one who started the fights. It appears from these findings that carrying a knife is linked to self-protective motives. Too few females carried guns for the researchers to identify predictors for that group. For the males, however, correlates of carrying a gun included having been arrested before, having been involved in many fights and being one of the people who started fights, and believing that shooting people was justifiable in certain circumstances. It appeared that gun carrying was linked to a much more violent, aggressive orientation and could not really be construed as a strategy for self-protection.

Depression

One of the emotions that has received considerable attention in the recent literature is depression (Garrison et al., 1989; Robertson & Simons, 1989). *Depression* is used in at least three different contexts (Petersen et al., 1993). First, one can speak of *depressed mood*, which refers to feelings of sadness, a loss of hope, a sense of being overwhelmed by the demands of the world, and general unhappiness. Almost everyone experiences depression at some time or another, describing it as the "blues," feeling "down in the dumps," or feeling "low." People who suffer from depression may experience other symptoms, including worrying, moodiness, crying, loss of appetite, difficulty sleeping, tiredness, loss of interest in or enjoyment of activities, and difficulty concentrating. Depression may range from mild, short-lived periods of feeling sad and discouraged to severe feelings of guilt and worthlessness. A depressed mood may be predictive of more serious emotional disorders, but it is not in itself a clinical diagnosis. One estimate is that about 35% of adolescents, a higher percentage for girls than for boys, have experienced a depressed mood in the previous six months.

The second use of the concept of depression is the notion of a *depressive syndrome*. This term refers to a constellation of behaviors and emotions that occur together. The syndrome usually includes complaints about feeling depressed, anxious, fearful, worried, guilty, and worthless. Roughly 5% of the normal population experiences this syndrome.

The third use of the concept of depression is its central role in clinical diagnosis. For a diagnosis of *major depressive disorder*, the adolescent will have experienced five or more symptoms for at least two weeks:

> Depressed mood or irritable mood most of the day; decreased interest in pleasurable activities; changes in weight or perhaps failure to make necessary weight gains in adolescence; sleep problems; psychomotor agitation or retardation; fatigue or loss of energy; feelings of worthlessness or abnormal amounts of guilt; reduced concentration and decision-making ability; and repeated suicidal ideation, attempts, or plans of suicide. (Petersen et al., 1993, p. 156)

Depressed mood is of special concern during early adolescence for several reasons (Maag, Rutherford & Parks, 1988; Brooks-Gunn & Petersen, 1991). First, it is associated with adolescent suicide (see Box 9.2). Although depression is not always a precursor of suicide, there is some link between depression and thoughts of suicide. Second, depression is linked to alcohol and drug abuse. Adolescents who are struggling with strong feelings of depression may turn to alcohol or other drugs to try to alleviate or escape from these feelings. Third, adolescents who are depressed may be unable to participate effectively in the classroom, so that their academic performance deteriorates. Finally, depression during adolescence may be a forerunner of severe depression later in adulthood.

A number of challenges that adolescents face make them vulnerable to depression. At present, no single theory is accepted as the explanation for depression. Certain factors appear to increase the likelihood of depression, and others

Suicide at any age is deeply troubling. But adolescent suicide is cause for special anguish and soul searching. Why would a young person, with all of adult life ahead with its endless possibilities and opportunities, choose death? Is it possible that the prospect of becoming an adult is becoming so threatening and terrifying that some young people would rather die than grow up?

Public concern over adolescent suicide has been increasing in response to the change in the suicide rate among adolescents since the early 1960s. Suicide, which is the third leading cause of death among adolescents aged 15–19, rose from 3.6 per 100,000 in 1960 to 11.3 per 100,000 in 1989 (Garland & Zigler, 1993). Over this period, the suicide rate for the total population stayed relatively constant. In a comparison of racial and ethnic groups, Native Americans had the highest rate, with an especially high rate among Apaches (Berlin, 1987). White males were more likely to commit suicide than African-Americans. Some claim that the rate of 11.3 per 100,000 is an underestimate, since there is a social stigma to reporting a death as suicide and there are financial consequences to identifying a death as a suicide rather than as an accident. It is suspected that a significant number of adolescent deaths involving automobile accidents are actually suicides.

The number of completed suicides among adolescents is still relatively small, but an additional large number of adolescents have attempted suicide. Males are four times as likely as females to complete a suicide; females are three times as likely as males to attempt a suicide. National surveys find that from 6% to 13% of adolescents say they have attempted suicide at least once; however, very few have actually received any medical treatment or mental health care following the attempt (Garland & Zigler, 1993). And beyond suicide attempts, a national Gallup survey found that 15%

BOX 9.2

Suicide in Adolescence

Pablo Picasso, The Death of Casagemas, 1901.

had considered suicide (Ackerman, 1993). Instances of suicides prompted by widely publicized suicides, copycat suicides, and clusters of friends who commit suicide as part of a pact suggest that suicidal ideation can be triggered by a variety of external events as well as by internal depression or as a reaction to humiliation or loss.

In attempting to understand the causes of suicide, primary risk factors have been identified (Garland & Zigler, 1993). These factors were reconstructed by studying the lives of adolescents who committed suicide. They may not be very useful in predicting whether a particular individual will commit or attempt suicide. These risk factors include:

Drug and alcohol abuse
A prior suicide attempt
A history of psychiatric illness
A history of antisocial, aggressive behavior
A family history of suicidal behavior
The availability of a firearm

In addition to these factors, there is usually some precipitating event. A shameful or humiliating experience, a notable failure, and rejection by a parent or a romantic partner are all examples. Use of drugs that alter cognitive functioning and decrease inhibitions, coupled with easy access to a gun, suggest one likely path from suicidal ideation to suicidal action.

seem to buffer adolescents from these feelings. Some research points to genetic factors associated with the clinical diagnosis of depression. However, if we think back to the research on the interaction between depressed mothers and their infants discussed in Chapter 5, it is hard to separate genetic and environmental factors in the etiology of clinical depression.

Parental loss or parental rejection has been found to increase an adolescent's vulnerability to depression (Robertson & Simons, 1989). In one longitudinal study of the consequences of economic pressures on families, a path was shown from the family's economic stresses to increased parental depression, which produced heightened marital conflict, increased hostility and less nurturance toward the children, and subsequent adjustment problems in adolescent daughters, especially problems with hostility and depression (Conger et al., 1993).

In addition, adolescence is a time of life when one is likely to encounter loss, failure, and rejection as well as a pileup of negative events and hassles. Even though we no longer view adolescence as a unique period of emotional turmoil, it is pretty clear that adolescents are exposed to more negative events than are younger children, perhaps in part because they are more aware of what other people are experiencing. In part, more is expected of adolescents, so there is more to worry about. And, of course, adolescents have a wider circle of relationships, through which they are exposed to more problems, expectations, and disappointments. Adolescents report experiencing hassles in the following domains: social alienation (disagreements with teachers, disliking other students); excessive demands (not enough time to meet responsibilities, not enough time for sleep); romantic concerns (dissatisfaction in a romantic relationship); decisions about one's personal future (important decisions about a future career); loneliness and unpopularity (being ignored); assorted annoyances and concerns (money problems, disagreement with a boyfriend or girlfriend); social mistreatment (being taken advantage of, having one's trust betrayed); and academic challenge (struggling to meet other people's standards of performance at school) (Kohn & Milrose, 1993). Within this list, peer relations, including boyfriend-girlfriend relations and the many elements of interpersonal experience that are part of being a member of a friendship group, play a very central role. Poor peer relationships in early adolescence are a significant risk factor for depression (Petersen, Sarigiani & Kennedy, 1991).

Adolescents are relatively inexperienced in coping with these kinds of stressors. They may not have developed strategies for interrupting or reducing the feelings of grief or discouragement that are likely to accompany stressful life events. The combination of pressures on parents, especially marital conflicts and economic pressures, plus exposure to failures, disappointments, and loss of relationships with peers and in school, are clearly linked to a negative mood, especially sadness and depression (Larson & Ham, 1993). Feelings of depression may also be intensified by accompanying hormonal changes (Susman, Dorn & Chrousos, 1991). Young people may become convinced of their worthlessness, and this distortion of thought may lead them toward social withdrawal or self-destructive actions.

Experiences of depression appear to be more common in adolescent girls than boys. This gender difference has been found in comparisons of the depression scores of Anglo, black, and Mexican-American and other Hispanic adolescents (Roberts & Sobhan, 1992). In addition, Mexican-American adolescents appear to have a higher incidence of depression than Anglos, blacks, or other Hispanic ethnic groups. Evidence of a greater risk for depression among females continues to be found in studies of adults (Jones-Webb & Snowden, 1993).

Although prepubescent boys are somewhat more likely to show signs of depression than prepubescent girls, this pattern reverses during adolescence (Nolen-Hoeksema, Girgus & Seligman, 1991; Petersen et al., 1991). Several ideas have been offered to explain this reversal. First, at puberty, girls become critical of their bodies, especially in their concern about being overweight and being unattractive. This attitude may lead to prolonged feelings of dissatisfaction with the self and a consequent depression. Second, girls tend to look within for explanations of their failures, blaming failures and problems on their own lack of ability, where boys tend to focus on factors outside the self, blaming other people or unfair conditions for their failures.

Third, although girls tend to receive strong social support from their parents and friends, they are also somewhat more sensitive to the problems that people in their support network are having. Girls who have higher levels of caring and who are likely to become involved in the problems of their close friends are more vulnerable to depression (Gore, Aseltine & Colten, 1993). The negative experiences that a girl's best friend or members of her friendship group are going through tend to add to her own negative mood. Fourth, girls tend to persist in trying to account for negative events or to explain them, so that these events have more time to disturb them. Boys tend to distract themselves with other thoughts or just to "put them out of their mind" (Nolen-Hoeksema, 1987). Fifth, in adolescence, girls begin to experience numerous microaggressions spawned by the sexist views of their teachers, their male peers, and even their parents. These negative messages create a picture of a world in which the adolescent girl is viewed as less important, less competent, and less entitled to her own independent views than her male peers. The result is increased feelings of insecurity, lack of confidence, and new feelings of worthlessness.

Membership in the Peer Group

We pointed out the importance of peer interaction in psychological development in Chapters 7 and 8. During early adolescence, the peer group becomes more structured and organized than it was previously (Newman, 1982). The implications of the individual's relation to the peer group become more clearly defined. Before the adolescent period, it is important to have friends but not so important to be a member of a definable group. The child's friends are often found in the neighborhood, local clubs and sports teams, community centers, or classrooms. Friendship groups are homogeneous. They are the product of informal associations, residential area, and convenience. In early adolescence, young people spend more time away from home. Dyadic friendships become an increasingly important source of social support, and the quality of these friendships changes (Levitt, Guacci-Franco & Levitt, 1993).

Adolescent friendships provide opportunities for emotional intimacy, support, and understanding as well as companionship and fun. Talking with friends, either in person or on the telephone, becomes a dominant daily activity, especially for girls (Raffaelli & Duckett, 1989). Early adolescents have the cognitive skills to consider the needs and feelings of others. The qualities of self-disclosure and intimate knowledge of the other become more central to the formation and maintenance of adolescent friendships (Berndt, 1982; Tedesco & Gaier, 1988). Friendships become more intimate and more selective than they were during the middle-school-age period. One adolescent boy whose friendship had ended described the process as follows:

> [My friend] is trying to single out his friends now. At the beginning of the year, he was friends with almost everybody because he wanted to be friends over the school year with a lot of kids. Now he's singling out best friends. (Berndt & Hoyle, 1985, p. 1013)

In addition to changes in friendships and in the quality and functions associated with close friends, new layers of peer relationships, sometimes known as the

A peer group can often be recognized by a shared style of dress. Here we see the "preppy" look, the studied combination of fashionable and comfortable.

clique and the crowd, begin to take shape. *Cliques* are small friendship groups of five to ten friends. Usually these groups provide the framework for frequent interactions both within school and in the neighborhood. Adolescents usually do not refer to their group of friends as a clique, but the term is used to connote a certain "tightness" among the members. These are the kids who hang out together, who know about each others' families, who plan activities together, and who stay in touch with each other from day to day. In the transition from middle school or junior high school to the larger, more heterogeneous environment of the high school, there is a reordering of students according to a variety of abilities and a corresponding reordering of friendship groups. It may take some time for adolescents to find their clique, and the members of this group may change from time to time over the first year or two of high school.

Crowd refers to a large group that is usually recognized by a few predominant characteristics, such as their orientation toward academics, involvement in athletics, use of drugs, or involvement in deviant behavior. When the "leading crowd" of a particular neighborhood elementary or middle school goes off to a more centralized high school, the members of that group find that they are, to some degree, competing with the "leading crowds" of the other neighborhood schools from which the high school draws its students. After some contact at the high school, the several "leading crowds" are reordered into a single "leading crowd." Some students find that their social positions have been maintained or enhanced, whereas others find them to have deteriorated somewhat as a result of a reevaluation of their abilities, skills, or traits.

Popularity and acceptance into a peer group at the high school may be based on one or more of the following characteristics: good looks; athletic ability; social class; academic performance; future goals; affiliation with a religious, racial, or ethnic group; special talents; involvement with drugs or deviant behavior; or general alienation from school. Although the criteria for membership may not be publicly articulated, the groups tend to include or exclude members according to consistent standards. Physical attractiveness continues to be a powerful force in determining popularity. Especially for very attractive and unattractive adolescents, physical appearance may be a primary determinant of social acceptance or rejection (Cavior & Dokecki, 1973; Musa & Roach, 1973).

Some of the well-known crowds present in American high schools today are affectionately called *populars, gangsters* or *hoods, punkers, jocks, druggies,* and *nerds.* A new group, called the *mods* or *progressives,* expressly rejects this traditional social stratification. The progressives emphasize individuality and the value of forming a personal identity. In setting themselves apart from the other groups, however, they form a new one (Stevenson et al., 1987). In racially diverse schools, it is not uncommon for students to identify peer groups based specifically on ethnic categories, such as the Asian group, the Mexican-Americans, and the African-Americans. Each of the crowds can be identified within a school setting by their dress, their language, the activities in which they participate, and the school settings in which they are most likely to congregate. The peer culture in any high school is determined largely by the nature of the peer groups that exist in that school and their characteristic patterns of interaction (Brown, 1990). These large, visible groups provide an array of prototypical identities. Although many adolescents resist being labeled as part of one crowd or another, they usually recognize that these categories of students exist in their school.

In one analysis of over 3000 students in Grades 9–12, drawn from nine high schools in two different states, nine crowd types were identified with a high degree of regularity across the schools. These crowds were labeled by the students as jocks, populars, popular nice, average-normal, brains, partyers, druggies, loners, and nerds (Durbin et al., 1993). These crowds had distinct profiles with respect to their school grades, their use of alcohol and drugs, their involvement in delinquent acts, their involvement in fights and carrying weapons to school, and their perceptions of how involved they were in the social life at the school. Thus, the youth culture, as it is sometimes called, actually comprises a number of subcultures, each endorsing somewhat different attitudes toward adults and other authority figures, school and academic goals, and drugs and deviant behavior, and expressing different orientations toward partying and social life (Brown et al., 1993).

Individual adolescents are faced with a variety of choices for peer-group membership. On entering high school, adolescents establish a reputation based on how they act, what they seem interested in, and what their friends and acquaintances say about them. They come in contact with a number of people who may offer their friendship. This is the informal route to membership in a peer group. The adolescent learns to look beyond the initial offer of friendship and to assess the group from which the potential friend comes. The person may decide to accept the friendship or reject it on the basis of the reputation of the potential friend's peer-group association (see Box 9.3). While some adolescents accept one of the crowd categories as their appropriate group, others claim that they are friends with people from several different crowds, and still others do not believe that they are a part of any crowd. These adolescents may have a small group of friends with

BOX 9.3

Interracial Friendships Among High School Students

One of the anticipated outcomes of the movement to desegregate America's schools was that, through opportunities for daily cross-race interactions, children would form interracial friendships and thereby reduce the level of racism in our society. To what extent are black-white friendships being formed during the high school years?

Drawing on a national sample of over 58,000 sophomores and seniors at more than 1000 public and private high schools in the United States, researchers attempted to address this question (Hallinan & Williams, 1989). They considered the possible dyadic (two-person) groups that could be formed among students and then asked whether a friendship existed in these dyads. In other words, of all the two-person groups in a school, how many were friendships in which Person A said that Person B was a friend? The results showed that cross-race friendships were quite rare. When all factors were taken into account, such as a school's size and the proportion of black students in a school, same-race friendships were six times more likely than cross-race friendships. However, cross-race friendships were more likely to be reciprocated than same-race friendships. If Student A named someone of another race as a friend, that person was very likely to name Student A as a friend as well.

The results of this analysis are disappointing. Of more than 18,000 friendships identified by students, only about 350 involved black and white friends. There was no relationship between the proportion of black students in a school and the likelihood of interracial friendships. The data do not address the possibility that racial attitudes are influenced by participation in racially diverse schools. They do, however, alert us to the fact that the natural process of friendship formation will not lead to greater levels of interracial interaction without some additional structural or curricular intervention.

whom they interact, but they reject identifying with any of the stereotypical groups that exist in their school.

Peer groups have boundaries. Membership in cliques is relatively stable, but always vulnerable to change. One description suggests that these groups have some very central members who serve as leaders, others who are regularly included in the activities of the clique, and others on the periphery. At the same time, there are those labeled "wannabe's" who would like to be part of the clique but for one reason or another are never fully included (Hansell, 1985). Some students try to push their way into a certain group. Others may fall out of a group. Dating someone who is a member of the clique or getting involved in a school activity (such as athletics or cheerleading) may be a way of moving into a new peer group. What is more likely is that through gossip, refusal to adhere to group norms, or failure in heterosexual relationships, individuals may slip outside the boundaries of their clique. Changing one's crowd identity may be even more difficult than changing from one clique to another. When the school population is relatively stable, it is very difficult to lose the reputational identity one has already established (Jones, 1976).

Important skills that are learned by becoming a member of a peer group are the assessment of group structure and the selection of the particular group or groups with which one would like to affiliate. As one begins to develop a focused peer-group affiliation, one becomes aware of that group's internal structure and norms (Dunphy, 1963). In adolescence, the structure may include patterns of dominance, dating, and relationships with others outside the group. Associated with each of these dimensions of social structure are sets of norms or expectations for the behavior of the peer-group members. As adolescents discover their positions in the dominance hierarchy of the group, they learn how they may advance within it and what behaviors are expected of members at various levels. On the basis of all this information, they must decide whether their personal growth is compatible with the peer-group affiliation they have made. There is some evidence that being a member of a peer group is linked to well-being. The peer group serves as a source of social support and helps to buffer stress. As time goes along, however, many eleventh- and twelfth-graders perceive the close connections with a single clique as less important or central to their social life. Close dyadic friendships and love relationships begin to play a greater role, and especially for girls, the time and energy that used to be focused on preserving the friendship group is redirected to these more intimate relationships (Smith, 1987).

We suggest that membership in an adolescent peer group is a forerunner of membership in an adult social group. Adolescent peer groups are somewhat less organized than their adult counterparts, but they are considerably more structured than childhood friendship groups. Through peer-group membership, adolescents begin to learn techniques for assessing the organization of social groups and their own position within them. They develop aspirations for advancing their own social standing. In addition, they gain some insight into the rewards and costs of extensive group identification. Although the actual friends made during adolescence may change as one grows older, the social skills learned at this time provide a long-lasting basis for functioning in a mature social group.

Parents and Peers

How does involvement with peers during early adolescence relate to closeness to family members? Do adolescents abandon family interactions and values for peer interaction and peer values? Can closeness to peers compensate for a lack of closeness to parents, or does the intimacy achieved with parents extend outward to a circle of friends? To what extent do parents continue to have an influence on adolescent peer relationships?

In the transition from childhood to adolescence, the child's radius of significant relationships changes. One study that looked at the structure and function of social support involved African-American, Anglo, and Hispanic children in three age groups: 7, 10, and 14 (Levitt et al., 1993). In the transition from 7 to 10, extended-family members become increasingly important to children as a source of support. This pattern was found in all three ethnic groups, but the African-American and Hispanic children were more likely to identify extended-family members as sources of support than were the Anglo children. From 10 to 14, friends become an increasingly important source of support. In addition, the number of people mentioned as friends increased notably from age 7 to age 14. However, at all three ages and in all three ethnic groups, family members continue to be mentioned as the most central in these children's lives, "the people who are the most close and important to you—people you love the most and who love you the most." What is more, at each age, support from the close, inner circle made up largely of family members was an important correlate of well-being and sociability.

As we consider the increasingly important role of peer relationships in early adolescence, we must keep in mind that under optimal conditions this process takes place against a background of continuing close, supportive relationships with family members. Adolescents describe a variety of overt signs of independence from their families. They may make decisions about clothes, dating, and so

Opportunities for adolescents and parents to interact at home are very important for the adolescent's sense of well-being and connection to family. The quality of these interactions is often characterized by a new level of openness and collaboration, with parents and children exchanging ideas and points of view.

on; they may have cars; they may stay out late; and they may earn their own money. However, they maintain an emotional attachment to their families and to the value orientations of their families.

What is the nature of parent-adolescent interaction? How do differences in its quality influence the adolescent's well-being? These questions have been addressed in a variety of ways. One approach has been to investigate the amount and quality of time adolescents spend with their parents. In one study, more than 400 students in grades 10–12 were asked to tell how many times they interacted with a variety of people during a day when they were not in school (Newman, 1979). These adolescents reported an average of 13.5 daily interactions with their parents and about the same number with close friends. In another study, adolescents were given an electronic paging device. From 8 A.M. to 11 P.M., they were paged five to seven times. Each time they were paged, they were to write down what they were doing, why they were doing it, and how they were feeling. Only about 6% of the total number of observations involved interactions with adults. These adolescents reported feeling more excited when they interacted with adults but also more constrained, passive, and weak than when they interacted with peers (Csikszentmihalyi, Larson & Prescott, 1977).

Montemayor (1982) interviewed tenth-graders about how they spent time during the day. They spent most of their free time with peers, less with parents, and least alone. They spent most of their task time alone, less with parents, and least with peers. Boys spent more time with their fathers and girls more time with their mothers. Boys and girls spent about the same amount of time with both parents together. The interactions with parents were not especially conflictual. Over a three-day period, male adolescents reported an average of 0.85 conflicts with their parents and females 1.21 conflicts. Conflicts between girls and their mothers were the most frequent and the most intense.

Time spent at home in positive interactions with adults appears to have positive consequences for adolescents. In a study of eighth-graders, time spent at home was positively related to perceptions of the family environment as intellectually and culturally stimulating. There was a strong relationship between time spent at home in leisure and recreational activity and a sense of well-being (McMillan & Hiltonsmith, 1982). At the opposite end of the continuum, experiences of parental rejection or neglect were found to be closely linked to low self-esteem and depression (Robertson & Simons, 1989; Rosenberg, Schooler & Schoenbach, 1989).

Time spent in public with adults appeared to be more conflictual. Adolescents who reported a high level of parental companionship also reported feeling self-conscious about and preoccupied with the evaluations of others (Adams & Jones, 1982). Although adolescents may feel good about being affectionate with and close to their parents, they are also sensitive to perceived expectations that adolescents and parents should not be too chummy. Although frequent open communication between adolescents and their parents contributes to a positive relationship, it is misleading to assume that these interactions are always positive in tone. It is hard work for parents and adolescents to keep the channels of communication open.

As adolescents go through puberty, conflicts with their parents increase. Conversations are marked by new levels of assertiveness on both sides (Papini & Sebby, 1988; Papini, Datan & McCluskey-Fawcett, 1988). These conflicts tend to be about rather mundane issues like household chores, how money will be spent, whether the child is spending enough time on schoolwork, or curfews, rather than on basic value issues like political ideology or religious beliefs (Montemayor, 1983; Steinberg, 1990). Resolutions of these family conflicts lead to the establishment of a new balance of power or control within the family (Feldman & Gehring, 1988). This balance appears to be negotiated somewhat differently by males and females.

Steinberg (1981) described parent-child interactions among boys aged 11–14 and their parents. As boys proceed through puberty, the parents increasingly interrupt their sons and the boys increasingly interrupt their mothers. The parents' explanations decline, and family interactions become more rigid. After the period of rapid pubertal growth, adolescent-parent conflicts subside somewhat. Mothers interrupt their sons less, and sons become increasingly deferential to their fathers.

The pattern for girls is a bit different (Hill, 1988). In the months following menarche, parents interrupt their daughters more during conversations. Girls are more likely to yield to the interruptions of their mothers, but they do not tend to yield to their fathers' interruptions. Daughters assert themselves with their mothers through a high frequency of interruptions and with their fathers by an unwillingness to yield the conversation when their fathers interrupt them. Over time, parents notably increase their explanations when their opinions differ from their daughter's, suggesting a new respect for the daughter's independent views and indicating a new definition of her power in the family.

Membership in the "druggie" crowd appears to be linked to parental neglect and low parental expectations for academic achievement.

A consequence of frequent, reasonable interactions and a family norm that allows the expression of conflict is that parents can be more effective in communicating their expectations and learning about their child's point of view. Parents and adolescents are quite familiar with each other's views. In one study, parents and adolescents completed the Offer Self-Image Questionnaire (OSIQ) (Offer, Ostrov & Howard, 1982). Out of 38 items, there were only 12 on which the parents' and the adolescents' endorsements differed by more than 10%. Parents tended to underestimate the importance of their children's having girlfriends or boyfriends. They also underestimated the extent to which their children found dirty jokes amusing. Parents thought that peers found their children more attractive than the children believed they did. Parents thought that their sons' feelings were more easily hurt than the sons thought they were. Parents thought that their daughters were more confident and more ready to enter the competition of adult life than the daughters thought they were. Parents thought that both their sons and their daughters were less able to take criticism and learn from others than the children thought they were. This discrepancy may have resulted from the children's being more willing to take criticism and learn from others than they were from their parents.

This picture of parent-adolescent views was confirmed by a study describing adolescents' discussions with their parents and peers (Hunter, 1985). Over the age ranges 12–13 and 14–15, adolescents discussed academic-vocational, social-ethical, and family relations topics more often with their parents than with their friends. However, they discussed peer relations more with their friends. This finding suggests that parents really may not have as much information about their children's peer relations as about other important topics. Although adolescents generally perceive their parents as willing to explain their opinions and as understanding the adolescents' points of view, in the domain of peer relations there is a noticeable contrast. In this one area, adolescents are likely to perceive low levels of understanding on the part of parents.

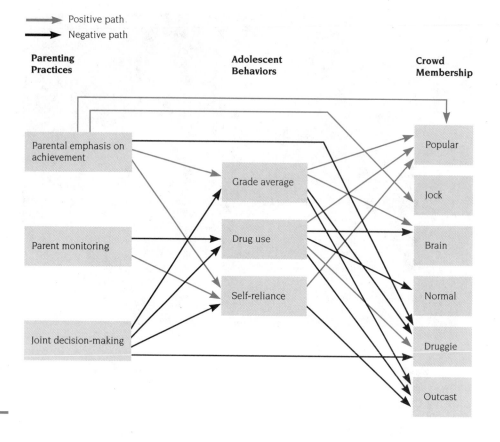

FIGURE 9.2

Parenting practices, adolescent behaviors, and crowd membership
Source: Brown, Mounts, Lamborn & Steinberg, 1993.

It is important to recognize that early adolescence comes close on the heels of middle childhood. It does not make sense to assume that shortly after a period of intense socialization and dependence a child will be eager to reject most of what she or he has learned at home. Young adolescents are still very attached to their parents. It is unlikely that they will feel prepared to face life without their parents' emotional support and approval. Thus, the parent-child conflict of early adolescence is about achieving autonomy while preserving the bonds of affection and goodwill that were formed earlier. There is a dynamic tension between remaining a valued, loved member of the family group and having the freedom to explore new relationships and new visions of the self.

The quality of the home environment, especially the parenting practices, has implications for the adolescent's peer relationships as well as for the quality of parent-child interactions. You will recall from the discussion in Chapter 8 that high levels of power assertion by parents are associated with a greater likelihood of peer rejection during the middle school years. Studies of the relationship of parenting practices to adolescent peer-group membership are extending this analysis. A model was proposed that linked parenting practices to adolescent behaviors and ultimately to crowd affiliation (see Figure 9.2) (Brown et al., 1993; Durbin et al., 1993). Parenting practices, listed in the left-hand column, were evaluated on three dimensions: the extent to which parents emphasized academic achievement, parental monitoring of adolescent behaviors, and the degree to which parents involved adolescents in decision-making. Adolescent behaviors, listed in the center column, were evaluated by examining the students' grade point averages, drug use, and self-reliance. Finally, the students were characterized by one of six crowd affiliations, listed in the right-hand column. Parenting practices were significantly linked to the children's behavior, which in turn was a strong predictor of their crowd affiliation. A positive (+) path indicates a positive correlation between a parenting practice and an adolescent behavior or a particular crowd membership. A negative (–) path indicates an inverse relationship between a parenting practice and an adolescent behavior or a crowd membership. The pattern was especially clear for the positive linking of parental emphasis on academic achievement, the child's high grades, and association with the "brain" crowd, and for the linking of low parental monitoring, little joint decision-making, little emphasis on academic achievement, and the high likelihood of adolescents' use of drugs and identification with the "druggie" crowd. One implication of this study is that, even though adolescents may perceive their involvement with their peers as a domain separate and distinct from their family life, the thread of parental socialization practices and their consequences for adolescent behavior continue to influence peer relations.

Sexual Relationships

During adolescence, peer relationships are modified by the introduction of sexual interests and behavior. This increased interest in sexual relationships stems from social expectations as well as sexual maturation and related desires for romance as well as for physical intimacy. In many cultures, the act of first intercourse, sometimes referred to as *defloration* for girls, is a significant marker of the transition from adolescence to adulthood. In our own society, the norms for engaging in sexual activity differ by ethnic group and gender. In general, sexual activity has been disengaged from marriage and childbearing. Most adolescents and adults do not believe, nor do they behave as if, sex ought to be reserved for married couples, but in some subcultures, this is still held as the ideal. And although males and females are becoming more alike in their patterns of sexual activity, most subcultures continue to endorse a pattern that promotes earlier entry into sexual activity for males and a more restrained, reluctant posture regarding sexual activity for females.

The sexual transition may take place in very different contexts for adolescents. It may be a planned event, or it may be an unplanned impulse, often combined with alcohol use or a drug high. It may be viewed as a marker of independence or as an act of rebellion against and defiance of the family. It may take place in the context of an ongoing close relationship or as part of a casual encounter. Usually, the earlier the entry into sexual activity and intercourse, the more likely the act is to be part of a profile of high-risk behaviors, including alcohol use, drug use, and delinquent activity. The later the entry, the more likely it is to be seen as a marker of the transition into adulthood or as a planned aspect of the deepening commitment in an ongoing relationship (Flannery, Rowe & Gulley, 1993; Ketterlinus et al., 1992).

The Transition to Coitus

Udry and Billy (1987) devised a model to explain the transition to coitus in early adolescence (see Figure 9.3). In that model, three basic dimensions account for the adolescent's initiation of sexual activity: motivation, social controls, and attractiveness. Motivation can be accounted for by biological factors, especially new levels of hormone production; by a new level of desire to achieve

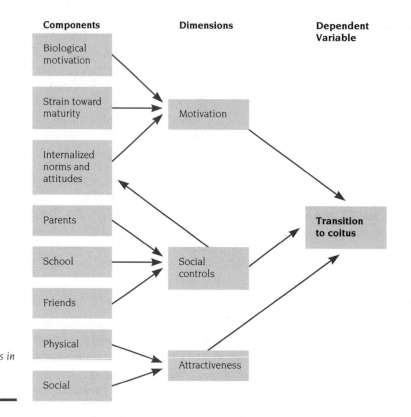

FIGURE 9.3

Model of transition to coitus in early adolescence
Source: Udry & Billy, 1987.

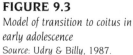

independence and to engage in adult behaviors; and by certain internalized norms and attitudes that may either encourage or reduce the motivation for sexual activity. The social controls provide the normative environment within which sexual activity is embedded. According to the model, these controls are a product of parental socialization and practices, school achievement and educational aspirations, and the attitudes and sexual experiences of friends. We may add here the influence of religious beliefs and values. The third dimension, attractiveness, influences the availability of partners. Attractiveness is defined in part by pubertal maturation, in part by social acceptance or popularity, and in part by whether one is judged to be pretty or handsome.

In an effort to assess this model, the researchers found that the transition to sexual intercourse for white boys was most strongly predicted by hormonal levels and by popularity with the opposite sex. Other studies confirm that hormone levels are related to boys' sexual behavior (Udry, 1988; Susman et al., 1985). The norms and expectations encouraging the transition to sexual activity may be so clear for males that it is difficult to find many factors other than pubertal maturation that can account for the transition.

There is no clear relationship between hormone levels or pubertal maturation and girls' sexual activity (Udry et al., 1985; Katchadourian, 1990). For girls, the various social controls, including parents, school achievement, friends' attitudes and behaviors, and religious values, all play an important part in predicting sexual intercourse. Girls must reach some level of pubertal maturation before the decision about voluntary entry into sexual activity becomes an issue. Beyond that point, however, a girl's decision to become sexually active is influenced by her own self-esteem, her personal aspirations, her parents' values, her educational

The expression of sexual attraction and physical intimacy can be one of the most pleasurable yet conflict-ridden areas of adolescent development.

expectations, the capacity of her parents to exercise appropriate control over their child's social and school activities, and the norms of her peer group (Brooks-Gunn & Furstenberg, 1989; Newcomer & Udry, 1987; Hanson, Myers & Ginsburg, 1987).

One of the clearest cultural influences on adolescent sexual behavior is religious participation. Adolescents who attend religious services frequently and who value religion as an important aspect of their lives have less permissive attitudes toward premarital sex. This finding applies equally to Catholic, Protestant, and Jewish young people. The relationship is accentuated in adolescents who describe themselves as Fundamentalist Protestant or Baptist. However, an adolescent's attitudes toward premarital sex are shaped by many factors in addition to their religious socialization. By the time young people are making independent decisions about religious participation, they also have opinions on whether or not they believe in premarital sex. Thus, those young people who have more permissive views on sex are less likely to attend religious services and find less satisfaction in religious participation (Thornton & Camburn, 1989).

Dating relationships during early adolescence provide the initial context for sexual activity. Pubertal changes may increase a young person's interest in sexual ideation, but the timing of dating per se depends heavily on the norms of the peer group and the community (Garguilo et al., 1987). One of the strongest predictors of early sexual activity is dating at an early age. Adolescents who "go steady" are much more likely to be sexually active than are those who do not (Hanson et al., 1987).

In the United States, the historical trend has been toward earlier involvement in sexual intercourse for both boys and girls, and greater sexual activity for girls (Dreyer, 1982). The percentage of boys and girls at the high school level reporting sexual intercourse increased consistently after 1925. In the period 1974–1979, more than half the senior boys and a bit less than half the senior girls had experienced intercourse. Recent studies suggest that "by age 15, about 17% of boys and 6% of girls are no longer virgins; at age 18, 67% of boys and 44% of girls are sexually experienced; by age 20, the figures go up to 80% for males and 70% for females" (Katchadourian, 1990, p. 336).

The timing of the transition to first intercourse varies by ethnic group, and within ethnic groups, variations can be seen between males and females as well as between urban and rural populations (Day, 1992). In a national sample, 18- to 25-year-olds were asked about the age at which they had first had sexual

TABLE 9.2	Mean Age at First Intercourse by Ethnicity and Age	
	Males	*Females*
Mexican-American	16.3	17.6
Latino	15.4	17.8
African-American	14.3	16.8
White	16.3	17.4

Source: Day, 1992.

intercourse. The modal ages were 18 for women and 16 for men. Table 9.2 shows the average age by ethnicity and gender. African-American males reported the youngest age, and there was more than a two-year difference between African-American males and females. Latino males reported the next youngest age, and there was a two-year difference between Latino males and females. Mexican-American males and white males reported the oldest ages. The age differences among the four groups of females were small. African-American females report the youngest age, but it was only one year different from the Latino females, who report the oldest age.

Within ethnic groups, different family and community factors were associated with early or later age of sexual transition. For example, for Chicano males and females, having a biological father in the home was associated with a later age of sexual intercourse. For Latino females, having a stepfather in the home increased the likelihood of an early entry into sexual activity. For both Chicano and Latino females, low self-esteem was associated with an earlier age of sexual activity. Among African-American females, living in a rural community was associated with earlier entry into sexual activity. For African-American males, especially those under age 18, attending a predominantly African-American high school was associated with earlier entry into sexual activity. Conservative family values tended to delay sexual activity for African-American males. Among white females, a strong occupational desire and parents' higher levels of education were associated with delayed sexual activity. In this group, high self-esteem was associated with sexual activity at a younger age. All these intergroup differences illustrate that the sexual transition is embedded in a complex psychosocial context and that generalizations about adolescent sexual behavior are likely to miss the mark when differences in gender, ethnicity, and community values are not taken into consideration.

Any data regarding entry into sexual activity and age at first intercourse must be interpreted with caution. First, the data reported by ethnicity are often confounded by social class. Second, the differences between rural and urban communities, such as those noted by Day in the study discussed above, are not often included in the analyses. Third, the reporting is retrospective (asking adolescents to think back to when they first engaged in sexual activities) and is vulnerable to inconsistencies and memory errors (Alexander et al., 1993).

Of course, sexual relationships do not necessarily involve intercourse. Many levels of sexual activity, from autoerotic sexual fantasies and masturbation to dyadic behaviors that may include handholding, kissing and hugging, and heavy petting, are involved in becoming a sexual adult. What is more, initial experiences with sexual intercourse do not necessarily result in frequent sexual activity. For example, boys who experience an early-pubertal sexual initiation may not have another sexual experience for a year or more (Brooks-Gunn & Furstenberg, 1989).

Orientation to Sexuality

Most young people are involved in a variety of romantic relationships during adolescence (Levesque, 1993). Components of both gender identity and sexual orientation are formulated during this period of life. Recall the study that monitored emotions during puberty and showed that both boys and girls had increased thoughts and feelings about love as they became physically mature (Richards & Larson, 1993). Some early adolescents are sexually permissive and are regularly active in sex play, from petting to intercourse. Other early adolescents are much less physically active. Some of these people may remain relatively uninterested in sexual relationships; others think about sexual relationships a good deal. The manner in which early adolescents think about sexual relationships varies. Some are preoccupied by thoughts of very romantic, beautiful relationships. Some become infatuated with rock stars, athletes, movie stars, or other sex symbols. Others manifest rather perverse obsessions with sexual material. Whatever the resulting adult sexual orientation, it can be assumed that the early adolescent's sexual awakenings represent a system that is just being started up and tested out. As a result of sexual experiences, adolescents begin to think of themselves as sexual, develop scripts and schemes for how to act sexually with others, and begin to formulate ideas about the kinds of people they find sexually attractive.

Although one might assume that sexual orientation—heterosexual, homosexual, or bisexual—begins to take shape in early adolescence, the research literature on this point is sparse. Many adolescents report some kind of homosexual experience, such as arousal at the sight of a member of the same sex or a transient infatuation with a same-sex peer. Many adult homosexuals recall that their sexual orientation took shape in adolescence, but exactly how sexual encounters that take place in early adolescence contribute to a homosexual orientation is not well understood.

The paths to a gay sexual identity vary widely. In one study of a volunteer sample of 77 gay males, most recalled having an awareness of gay feelings as early as middle school or early adolescence but did not label themselves gay until later adolescence (D'Augelli, 1991). The majority (75%) knew they were gay *before* their first sexual experience. And once they had labeled themselves gay, they waited an average of eight years to disclose their homosexuality to someone else. The reports of adolescents who are openly gay suggest that this is a very stressful realization, one that is commonly accompanied by negative reactions from parents and friends, and by open acts of hostility from school peers (Remafedi, 1987). Anticipating the strong social censure attached to an unconventional sexual orientation, adolescents are likely to deny it to or try to function as heterosexuals during this period of life.

Problems and Conflicts Associated with Sexuality

The sexual system is one of the most problematic components of psychosocial development for young people in the United States. Most parents do not feel comfortable discussing sexuality with their children. In addition to private thoughts, impulses, and fantasies, which may result in feelings of guilt or confusion, young people confront conflicting messages about sexual behavior from their peers, the mass media, and the religious community. New risks of sexually transmitted diseases, especially AIDS, introduce anxiety about the expression of sexual impulses. In a sample of over 1000 students from 13 urban and rural California high schools, only 20% of the students thought they had some chance of getting AIDS. However, among those who claimed to be sexually active, 60% had done something to try to avoid exposure to AIDS, most commonly using a condom or having their boyfriend use a condom and having fewer sex partners (Leland & Barth, 1993). The threat of exposure to AIDS is clearly having an impact on how young people think about sexual activity and its associated risks.

On television and in films, young people see numerous examples of sexual intimacy suggesting that sexual gratification ought to be more immediate and more satisfying than it is likely to be in real life. Often, they do not find the emotional closeness and understanding they may seek in a sexually intimate relationship. What is more, many adolescents, especially females, are exposed to unwanted sexual activity. In a sample of seventh-, ninth-, and eleventh-grade girls, 21% reported unwanted sexual contact ranging from unwanted touching and fondling to unwanted or forced intercourse (Small & Kerns, 1993). In many of these instances, unwanted sexual intercourse occurred on the first date, or in a dating relationship. This pattern illustrates the problematic nature of sexual contact in early adolescence. The boundaries around acceptable sexual contact are unclear, the sexual agenda for males and females is likely to be very different, and other risk-taking behaviors, including alcohol and drug use, may create an unwanted sexual encounter. The lack of supervision and monitoring by adults, as well as the lack of opportunity to talk about sexuality with caring adults, may place adolescents at risk for early sexual experiences that are abusive. The sex-linked problems that many people encounter—unintended pregnancy, marital infidelity, rape, sexual child abuse, pornography, and sexually transmitted diseases—are evidence that the socialization process is failing to promote mature sexuality in significant numbers of adolescents and adults in the United States.

Parenthood in Early Adolescence

One of the consequences of early entry into sexual activity may be adolescent pregnancy. To get a sense of the magnitude of this issue, consider the following data. In 1989, 518,000 live infants were born to women aged 19 or younger, and 407,000 legal abortions were performed on women in this age group. Close to a million adolescent girls in that year became pregnant, and almost half terminated the pregnancy through abortion, a good indicator that the pregnancy was unwanted. After several years of a steady birthrate for adolescents, the years from 1980 to 1989 saw a new increase. The birthrate (the number of births to women per 100,000 women in the age group) for mothers aged 10–14 increased from 1.1 in 1980 to 1.4 in 1989, and for mothers aged 15–19, the rate increased from 53 in 1980 to 58.1 in 1989 (U.S. Bureau of the Census, 1992).

Social policies advocating the prevention of early pregnancy and public programs for family planning and abortion tend to emphasize the negative consequences of pregnancy for adolescent girls and their babies. However, studies of pregnant adolescents generally find that these girls do not differ much in attitudes, mental health, or cognitive abilities from those who are sexually active but did not become pregnant. We must be careful not to label a group of adolescents deviant simply because they are pregnant.

Contraception　　A critical factor in explaining the high rate of adolescent pregnancy is the ambivalence of American parents, teachers, and teens toward contraception. In comparison with adolescents in many European countries, the majority of American adolescents do not integrate contraception into their view of natural sexual activity. American adolescents are largely uninformed about the variety of methods of contraception and their relation to the biological factors that prevent pregnancy (Morrison, 1985). One study of sexually active adolescent girls reported that only 35% consistently used contraceptives, 27% never used them, and 39% were inconsistent in their use. The result of this inconsistent use or rejection of contraception was that 32% became pregnant (Zelnik & Kantner, 1980).

The use or nonuse of contraceptives is associated with religious beliefs, family attitudes and behaviors, and peer norms. For example, low-income African-American female adolescents have more negative attitudes toward birth control than white adolescents, and they value fertility more. Thus, African-American females who are sexually active are less likely to use contraceptives (Edelman & Pittman, 1986; Pete & DeSantis, 1990; Zabin, Astone & Emerson, 1993). However, African-American adolescent males tend to be more consistent in their use of condoms than other groups (Pleck, Sonenstein & Ku, 1991). About 40% of adolescent girls believe contraception is the responsibility of the male, but most males are ineffective or inconsistent in their use of contraceptives (Franklin, 1988).

In one national survey of adolescent males aged 15–19, 30% reported using condoms all the time, including with their recent partners and with their last partner, and 57% reported using a condom in their last intercourse. These rates are higher than those observed in the early 1980s (Pleck et al., 1991). However, this still leaves 70% of adolescent males who are inconsistent in their use of condoms or who do not use condoms at all. The view that males have a responsibility to prevent pregnancy, concern about the partner's wishes, and concern about AIDS were all positively related to adolescent males' consistent condom use. Concerns about reduced sexual pleasure and the embarrassment of using a condom, coupled with the pattern of having a number of sexual partners, were related to inconsistent condom use. Variations in attitudes about the costs and benefits of contraception, religious beliefs about contraception, and lack of concrete knowledge about how to use contraceptives help us understand why the technology of contraception is not as successful among sexually active American youth as it might be.

Consequences of Teenage Pregnancy   The phenomenon of teenage parenthood is a complex one that touches the lives of the adolescent mother and father, the child or children born to them, their parents, and the schools, counseling services, and family-planning services that have been created to help very young parents cope with parenthood (Franklin, 1988; Caldas, 1993). The consequences of teenage pregnancy and parenthood for the young mother and her infant depend on the psychosocial context of the pregnancy. Within the time period of early adolescence, there is a big difference between becoming a mother at age 14 or at age 18. There is a strong relationship between age at first birth and one's family income at age 27 (Moore et al., 1993). This effect is mediated through a number of other personal and family factors that appear to unfold following the first birth, such as continuing in school, chances of getting married, the kind of work one does and one's personal earnings, and the earning capacity of other family members. For African-American females, the poverty level is high regardless of age at first birth. However, the earlier African-American females begin childbearing, the more children they are likely to have, a factor that increases the level of poverty. For Hispanic females, delaying childbearing resulted in higher educational attainment, a factor that predicts higher personal income by age 27. For white females, delaying the age of childbearing was associated with older age at first marriage, fewer children, and higher personal earnings. For all three ethnic groups, but especially for whites and Hispanics, each year of delayed childbearing had a substantial impact on reducing the chances of ending up in poverty by age 27.

One of the great paradoxes of adolescent parenthood is the contrast between young girls' aspirations about mothering and the actual experience of child-rearing. Here are the comments of two young mothers:

> Ann (14): When I got pregnant, my parents wanted me to have an abortion, but I'm an only child, and it's a lonely feeling when you're an only child. I just said, "Well, I'm going to keep the baby because now I'll have somebody I'll feel close to, instead of being lonely all the time." (Fosburgh, 1977, p. 34)

Some what selfish attitudes ? !

> Mary (17): It was great, 'cause now I got him and nobody can take him away from me. He's mine, I made him, he's great. Something real can give me happiness. He can make me laugh and he can make me cry and he can make me mad. (Konopka, 1976, p. 39)

Many adolescents do not have the emotional, social, or financial resources to sustain the kind of caring relationship they envision with their children. They may be unable to anticipate that their own needs must often be sacrificed to their babies' needs. One outcome of this discrepancy between aspirations and reality is an outpouring of the young mother's hostility toward her baby. The risk of child abuse is great in families with teen parents, especially when the factors of poverty and single-parent family structure converge with early childbearing (Gelles, 1989; Zuravin, 1988).

Complications during labor and delivery may be devastating to the newborn's health. Are young mothers more likely than older ones to experience such complications? Mothers under 19 are less likely than older mothers to initiate prenatal care during the first trimester of pregnancy. Infants born to mothers under 17 are at greater risk than those born to women in their 20s and 30s. They have a higher risk of dying during the first year, of being born prematurely or at a low birth weight, and of suffering neurological damage as a result of complications associated with delivery (McCarthy & Hardy, 1993). Thus, young parents are more likely to have to cope with the special needs of a developmentally handicapped child. However, these risks arise from converging socioeconomic factors rather than from biological inadequacies of being young. Studies involving large numbers of births at urban hospitals tend to find that younger mothers in general (those under 20) are actually *less likely* to experience complications of pregnancy and negative birth outcomes than older mothers, particularly when factors associated with poverty are taken into account (Roosa, 1984; McCarthy & Hardy, 1993).

Is a pregnant adolescent who marries better off than one who does not? Adolescent pregnancy and adolescent marriage have separate consequences for future educational attainment, occupational achievement, and marital stability. Having a baby in adolescence is associated with lower educational and occupational levels, whether or not the young woman gets married. Getting married in adolescence is associated with a greater chance of divorce or separation than getting married at age 20 or older. Somewhat surprisingly, however, adolescent marriage without children is somewhat more likely to be associated with later marital instability than is adolescent marriage accompanied by adolescent childbirth (Teti & Lamb, 1989). With respect to financial resources, adolescents who are

What lies in the future for this couple and for their marital relationship? Divorce rates are especially high among those who marry before age 20, but if the woman is already pregnant, the couple has a better chance of staying together than if she is not.

married at the time of their first birth have a higher household income than do those who are single at the time of their first birth (Astone, 1993).

In an attempt to get a bit closer to the factors that lead to certain sexual decisions, including the decision to have a child, Pete and DeSantis (1990) conducted a case study of five African-American girls who were pregnant or had recently delivered a child. One must be cautious about generalizing these observations to all African-American adolescent mothers or to adolescent mothers as a whole. All five were 14 years old and in the eighth grade. They were from low-income families in Miami, Florida. Despite the very small sample size, the focus of this study is especially relevant because it considers the point of view of a critical group. Less than 15% of all adolescents are African-American, yet 47% of births to unmarried teens are to African-American girls. What is more, poor African-American adolescents are likely to have babies at a very young age, and the risks of their early childbearing contribute to the significantly higher incidence of morbidity and mortality among African-American babies.

Several factors that emerged from the interviews with these very young mothers challenge some of our beliefs about adolescent pregnancy and confirm others.

First, the girls had all passed up other opportunities to become sexually active. They said that they had waited to become sexually active until they had established a relationship that they believed was based on trust and love. They had not delayed sexual activity in order to avoid pregnancy. They had assumed that the person with whom they had sex would not abandon them.

Second, they had not used contraceptives for a variety of reasons. Some had believed that they could not get pregnant ("I thought I was too young to get pregnant"). Some had relied on their boyfriends to use contraception, but the methods used had been inconsistent or nonexistent. Most of the girls were confused about the use of contraceptives or lacked the means to obtain them.

Third, the girls all described a daily life in which they had a large amount of unsupervised free time. They all lived with adults who did not or were not able to supervise their behaviors effectively. One girl had moved out of the house when her mother became hooked on crack. Another girl lived with her grandmother, who could never talk with her about sex or her social life. Although the girls all said they felt close to their parent or guardian, the adults did not monitor these girls' social lives or talk about sexual decisions.

Fourth, the girls had denied that they were pregnant as long as they could:

> However, even though Deb had missed several periods, was sick every morning, and had fainted several times, she vehemently denied she was pregnant for seven months. . . . As Deb so clearly put it, "as long as I did not tell anyone I was pregnant, as far as I was concerned, I wasn't pregnant." (Pete & DeSantis, 1990, p. 151)

Finally, the girls all believed that, once a person became pregnant, it was her responsibility to have and keep the baby. Since they had waited so long to admit the pregnancy, abortion was out of the question. Adoption was also never considered. None of the parents or guardians thought the girls should get married because they were too young. All the fathers who continued to maintain contact with the mother and baby were involved in the care and provided some financial support for the baby. Three of the fathers took their babies to their homes every other weekend. Even though the girls' parents or guardians were disappointed by the pregnancy, they had not rejected these young mothers. Several had even accepted some responsibility themselves for the pregnancy. The pregnancy and childbirth had not resulted in a deterioration of the girls' support systems.

Adolescent Fathers   Although the focus on adolescent pregnancy has been on girls, there is growing concern about adolescent fathers. It is difficult to determine the number of teenage fathers. Many young mothers will not reveal the name of their baby's father. Many of these fathers are not adolescents but older men. National data from 1984 reported that of 479,647 infants born to teenage mothers, only 19% also had teenage fathers (Hardy & Duggan, 1988). According to census data, 120,000 males between the ages of 15 and 19 were named as the fathers in live births for the year 1989 (U.S. Bureau of the Census, 1992). This is a decline from 189,000 in 1970, but an increase from 105,000 in 1986.

Most studies of adolescent pregnancy find that, contrary to the stereotype, many of the fathers remain in contact with the mother and the child. Some adolescent fathers marry the mother; others live with her for a while. It is less common for African-American adolescent fathers to live with their child shortly after the infant's birth than it is for white and Hispanic fathers (Marsiglio, 1987). Often, the couple continues to date. In some instances, the couple actually marry several years after the child is born. In many cases, the father contributes financial support to the mother and child, even when the couple do not marry. Many fathers, however, have little education and are minimally employed, so the material support they can provide is very limited (Robinson, 1988; Hardy & Duggan, 1988).

William Marsiglio (1989) compared African-American and white male adolescents' preferences about pregnancy resolution and family formation. These data were gathered from responses to a hypothetical question: "Please imagine that you have been dating the same girl who is about your age for the past year and that she told you last week that she was 2 months pregnant with your child. For the purpose of this survey assume that your girlfriend wants you to live with her and your child." Beginning with this premise, the boys in the survey were asked

Most African-American adolescent fathers have a positive attitude about staying connected to their baby and the baby's mother.

about how likely they would be to live with the child, their attitudes about doing this, their evaluation of what might be the positive and negative consequences of this decision, and their overall preference of how they would like to see the pregnancy resolved if it were entirely their decision.

African-American adolescents were significantly less likely to endorse abortion as the solution to this situation. This was true even when the adolescent's parents' education was taken into account. For example, none of the African-American males whose parents were college graduates selected abortion as a solution, while 40% of the white males whose parents were college graduates would have preferred abortion. African-American and white males were about equally likely to endorse the idea of living with the child and the baby's mother (45% of both groups selected this option). African-American males were more likely than white males to see an advantage to living with the baby as providing a chance to care for the baby's daily physical needs and to enable them to assume greater financial responsibility for the situation. In other respects, African-American and white males viewed the positive consequences of the situation quite similarly. White males were more likely than African-American males to see the situation as reducing their chances of pursuing further education and limiting their chances to spend time with their friends. In other respects, African-American and white males evaluated the negative consequences of the situation quite similarly. African-American males were more likely to agree that living with the child and the mother would require having a steady job. The study illustrates that African-American adolescents have a positive attitude toward continuing their relationship with the baby and the baby's mother, even though the actual patterns of real-life behavior do not provide evidence of this intention, perhaps because African-American males are younger when they father their first child and are therefore less likely to be able to leave their own homes. It may be that African-American adolescents have less chance to find a good, steady job, so they do not have the resources to support their baby. And it may be that, in the African-American community, the mother's family is more willing to have the mother and baby live with them, so there is no real place or urgent need for the unwed father.

Fathering a child is bound to stimulate conflicting feelings of pride, guilt, and anxiety in the adolescent boy. He must struggle with the fact that his sexual adventures have resulted in a pregnancy that may bring conflict and pain to someone for whom he cares. He must confront the choices he and his girlfriend have in coping with an unplanned pregnancy. He may feel shut out from the birth of a child he has fathered. Feeling obligated to provide financial support for his girlfriend and child may lead him to drop out of school and enter the labor market even though he can hope to be only minimally employed (Hendricks & Fullilove, 1983).

Not much systematic research has been done on the attitudes, knowledge, or behaviors of adolescent fathers or the impact of fatherhood on a teenage boy's subsequent development (Robinson, 1988). Few adolescent pregnancy programs consider the needs of adolescent fathers. Limited evidence suggests, however, that many fathers experience stress related to the pregnancy and could benefit from some kind of counseling (Lamb & Elster, 1985). Those who have studied the problem of unwed fathers argue that much stronger emphasis should be placed on the father's responsibility, not only for financial support of the mother and child but for continued interaction with the baby. Efforts to include young fathers in family-planning programs, parent education, and employment-training initiatives would help strengthen the social context for the young mother and her child and would contribute to the young man's psychosocial development.

There is no question that early entry into parenthood creates problems for both girls and boys. Early entry into parenthood threatens to propel girls into adult responsibilities and, at the same time, to derail their educational experiences and thereby reduce their occupational choices. When adolescent pregnancy is followed by disruption of education, loss of family and peer support, and poverty, the life chances for the young girl and her child are severely reduced. However, these consequences do not necessarily occur. Much depends on the response of family members, schools, community agencies, and peers. Further, some young parents have greater personal resources than others to bring to their new parental role. Differences in how adolescent pregnancy is construed in various ethnic and social-class communities must be taken into account in the design of prevention and intervention programs.

For both girls and boys, a key to the prevention of early pregnancy requires building greater confidence and commitment to the consistent use of contraception as part of any sexual relationship. For girls, fostering a sense of academic self-efficacy and investment in academic goals leading to postsecondary education and/or professional training is an especially important area for intervention (Plotnick, 1992; Ohannessian & Crockett, 1993). For boys, building greater social expectations and commitment to assuming the financial and social responsibilities associated with fatherhood, including sending clearer messages from family and community that boys do have responsibilities in these areas and devising specific opportunities for boys to enact these responsibilities, seem promising directions for intervention (National Urban League, 1987; Olds et al., 1988).

The Psychosocial Crisis: Group Identity Versus Alienation

Group Identity

We are positing an additional psychosocial conflict that confronts individuals as they make the transition from childhood to adolescence. We call this conflict *group identity versus alienation. Group identity* refers to the aspect of an individual's self-theory that focuses on membership in and connection with social groups. It is an extension of the ego system's sense of "we," which is first formed in the attachment relationship of infancy. It is an elaboration of the very early sense of trust, in which an infant establishes a foundation of social connection through which both self and other are defined.

The *we* includes those elements of the mind that are associated with the very deep desire to be connected to others and with the underlying sense that one is connected to others. The *we* can be compared to the I, which includes those elements of the mind associated with the very deep desire to be an independent individual with an underlying sense that one's life has meaning and value. The *we* and the I are complementary aspects of the ego system, although at times they may be in conflict. Throughout life, there may be tension between desires for individuality and desires for connection. Certain cultures emphasize connection over individuality, while others put individuality ahead of connection. However, all societies must deal with both aspects of the ego: the I as agent, originator, and executive of one's individual thoughts and actions, and the *we* as agent, originator, and executive of collective, cooperative enterprises that preserve and further the survival of the group (Triandis, 1990).

Early adolescents experience a search for membership, an internal questioning about the groups of which they are most naturally a part. They ask themselves, "Who am I, and with whom do I belong?" Although membership in a peer group may be the most pressing concern, questions about other group identifications also arise. Adolescents may seek commitment to a religious organization; they may evaluate the nature of their ties to the immediate or extended family; and they begin to understand the unique characteristics of their racial, ethnic, or cultural identity. Research confirms that, in the most positive pattern, peer-group membership does not replace attachment to parents or closeness to the family. Rather, the adolescent's network of supportive relations extends beyond the family and into the domain of meaningful peer relationships. Typically, those adolescents who show strong signs of mental health and adaptive coping strategies may be described as having positive communication and trusting relationships with their parents or other close family members as well as strong feelings of trust and security among their friends (Raja, McGee & Stanton, 1992; Levitt et al., 1993).

In the process of seeking group affiliation, adolescents are confronted by the fit or lack of fit between their personal needs and values and the values held by relevant social groups in the environment. Self-evaluation takes place within the context of the meaningful groups that are available for identification. Individual needs for social approval, affiliation, leadership, power, and status are expressed in the kinds of group identifications that are made and rejected during early adolescence.

In a positive resolution of the conflict of group identity versus alienation, adolescents perceive an existing group that meets their social needs and provides them with a sense of group belonging. It is this sense of group belonging that facilitates psychological growth and helps integrate the developmental tasks of early adolescence. In one attempt to measure this concept, Luhtanen and Crocker (1992) devised a measure of *collective self-esteem*, defined as the relatively stable evaluation of the value of one's group membership. In this approach, they included several dimensions of group belonging: one's enactment of the roles prescribed by the group; one's feelings of comfort and belonging with other group members; one's appraisal of the group's status in the eyes of others; and the salience of the group in one's life. All four dimensions contribute to the formation of a positive group identification.

Pablo Picasso, Girl in a Chemise, 1905. *The tendency to withdraw into one's own thoughts and feelings, combined with the possibilities of parental neglect and peer rejection, produces strong sentiments of alienation.*

Alienation

A negative resolution of the conflict leaves adolescents with a pervasive sense of alienation from their peers. *Alienation* refers to social estrangement; that is, an absence of social support or meaningful social connection (Mau, 1992). The alienated adolescent does not experience a sense of belonging to a group; rather, he or she is continually uneasy in the presence of peers. Parents may cause the negative outcome by pressing adolescents to restrict their association to a particular peer group, which in turn does not offer the adolescent membership. Alienation may also result if the adolescent looks over the existing groups and does not find one that really meets his or her personal needs. In this case, the adolescent may never become a member of a peer group. A third basis for the negative outcome is the possibility that no peer group will offer acceptance or friendship, in which case the adolescent is gradually shut out of all the existing groups in the social environment. For example, some young people ascribe too avidly to adult values and norms. Their peers see them as goodie-goodies or nerds and do not welcome them into the peer culture (Allen, Weissberg & Hawkins, 1989). Other adolescents have poor social skills, being either overly aggressive and domineering or overly withdrawn and socially inept. It is not unusual for adolescents to identify certain students in their high school as "loners" or "outcasts" (Brown et al., 1993).

During early adolescence, it is common for young people to become preoccupied with their own feelings and thoughts. They may withdraw from social interactions, unwilling to share the vulnerability and confusion that accompany physical, intellectual, and social growth. In this sense, most adolescents feel some of the loneliness and isolation that are implied by the term *alienation*. Even with their peers, they feel they must exercise caution in sharing their most troublesome concerns for fear of rejection or ridicule. The maintenance of an interpersonal "cool"—a desire to be perceived as someone who is competent rather than vulnerable—may stand in the way of building strong bonds of commitment to social groups.

The tension between expectations for group affiliation and barriers to group commitment is a product of the self-consciousness and egocentrism of this life stage and of the potential for rejection by existing groups. The lack of peer social support that may result from a negative resolution of this crisis may have significant implications for adjustment in school, self-esteem, and subsequent psychosocial development. Chronic conflict about one's integration into a meaningful reference group may lead to lifelong difficulties in the areas of personal health, work, and the formation of intimate family bonds (East, Hess & Lerner, 1987; Spencer, 1982, 1988).

The Central Process: Peer Pressure

Adolescents' circles of friends, their interests, and their styles of dress quickly link them to subgroups that give them continuity and meaning within the context of their neighborhoods or schools. These groups demand conformity to their norms and a demonstration of commitment and loyalty to their members. At the same time, young people outside the groups form expectations that reinforce adolescents' connections to specific peer groups and prohibit their movement to others. The peer-group social structure is usually well established in most high schools, and members of that structure exert pressure on newcomers to join one peer group or another. An individual who becomes a member of any group is more acceptable to the social system as a whole than one who tries to remain unaffiliated and aloof.

School adults both passively accept and actively encourage the organization of students into peer groupings. In the passive mode, they accept the friendship groups as they exist in the school and do little, if anything, to bring members of different peer groups into a working relationship with one another. They allow students to establish boundaries, rivalries, and areas of cooperation in their relationships. In the active mode, they reinforce some characteristics of the peer groups by selecting certain students for particular kinds of tasks. In most schools, for example, members of one peer group monitor the halls and assist in record keeping, while members of another fix the teachers' cars and operate equipment.

There is an implicit acceptance by school adults of the peer-group structure as it exists. They make almost no effort to alter this structure, which they may remember from their own high school days. Explicitly, school adults rely on members of specific peer groups to perform certain functions and to act along particular lines. Teachers as well as students appear to expect that individuals who dress in a certain way will be members of one peer group and that students who have a particular level of intellectual skill will belong to another. School adults often rely on the leaders of the various peer groups to convey and enforce the school's norms for acceptable behavior within their own groups. The peer-group structure, then, is an important vehicle for the maintenance of order and predictability in the school. Far from challenging this arrangement, school adults count on it to facilitate their jobs.

The process of affiliating with a peer group requires one to open up to the pressures and social influences it imposes. This pressure provides the context within which the crisis of group identity versus alienation is resolved. Adolescents are at the point in their intellectual development where they can conceptualize themselves as objects of expectations. They may perceive these expectations as forces urging them to be more than they think they are: braver, more outgoing, more confident, and so forth. Peer pressure may have a positive effect on the adolescent's self-image and may serve as a motive for group identification. Those dimensions of the self that are valued by the peer group become especially salient in each young person's self-assessment (Hoge & McCarthy, 1984).

As members of peer groups, adolescents have more influence than they would have as single individuals. They begin to understand the value of collective enterprise. In offering membership, peer groups expand adolescents' feelings of self-worth and protect them from loneliness. When family conflicts develop, adolescents can seek comfort and intimacy among their peers. For adolescents to benefit in these ways from affiliation with a peer group, they must be willing to suppress some of their individuality and find pleasure in focusing on those attributes that they share with peers.

Peer pressure may be exercised in a variety of areas, including involvement with other adolescents, school, and family; drug use; engaging in misconduct; sexual activity; and conformity in preferences in dress, music, or entertainment. Within a particular group, pressures may be strong in one or two areas but not in the others. For example, in a comparison of three peer groups—the jock-populars, the druggie-toughs, and the loners—the druggie-toughs perceived the strongest peer pressure toward misconduct. Jock-populars perceived greater pressure toward school involvement than the druggie-toughs. However, pressure toward peer involvement (spending free time with peers) was equally high in all three groups (Clasen & Brown, 1985). The norms for cigarette smoking have been studied as another example of a voluntary behavior that may be influenced by peer pressure. For example, in one study of sources of peer influence on cigarette smoking, the crowd identified as the "burnouts" (combination of druggies, radicals, and punks) smoked four times as many cigarettes per week as the average students and ten times as many cigarettes as the jock-preps (Urberg, 1992). One might expect that the pressure to conform to this behavior would be exceedingly strong within the burnouts crowd, whereas other groups might show much more variability in their norms related to smoking.

Peer groups do not command total conformity. In fact, most peer groups depend on the unique characteristics of their members to lend definition and vigor to the roles that emerge within them. However, the peer group places considerable importance on some maximally adaptive level of conformity in order to bolster its structure and strengthen its effectiveness in satisfying its members' needs; indeed, most adolescents find some security in peer-group demands to conform. The few well-defined characteristics of the group lend stability and substance to adolescents' views of themselves. In complying with group pressure, adolescents have an opportunity to state unambiguously that they are someone and that they belong somewhere.

Adolescents may also perceive some peer expectations as being in conflict with their personal values or needs. For example, they may feel that intellectual skills are devalued by the peer group, that they are expected to participate in social functions they do not enjoy, or that they are encouraged to be more independent from their families than they prefer to be. In most cases, adolescents' personal values are altered and shaped by peer-group pressure to increase their similarity to the other group members. If, however, the peer group's expectations are too distant from the adolescents' own values, establishing a satisfying group identification will become much more difficult. In this case, adolescents will continuously experience tension and conflict as they try to balance the allure of peer-group membership with the cost of abandoning their personal beliefs.

This persistent conflict and the accompanying tension are painful and confusing to adolescents. If they move closer to the peer group, they find the tension increasing, perhaps to an uncomfortable level. They must therefore pull back from the group to a safer level of tension. As they do so, their own values dominate, and they return to a level of emotional arousal that is tolerable for them. During the years from 12 to 16, adolescents become more adept in resisting peer pressure. Susceptibility to peer pressure seems to peak at about 13 or 14, when adolescents are most sensitive to peer approval and are making the initial transition toward new levels of behavioral autonomy and emotional independence from their parents (Urberg et al., 1990; Lamborn & Steinberg, 1993). Through encounters with peer pressure and opportunities to see how it feels to conform or resist, they develop a growing appreciation of the content of their personal values against the backdrop of peer expectations. However, if the emotional costs of approaching the peer group become too great, adolescents may not truly open themselves up to group pressures. Therefore, they will be unable to establish the sense of group identity that is so central to psychosocial growth during this period of life. An inability to reduce the tension and conflict between group pressure and personal values produces a state of alienation, in which the individual is unable either to identify with social groups or to develop personal friendships.

Ethnic-Group Identity

One of the most challenging aspects of establishing group identity facing minority adolescents is the formation of an ethnic-group identity (Spencer & Markstrom-Adams, 1990). Ethnic identity is not merely knowing that one is a member of a certain ethnic group, but recognizing that some aspects of one's thoughts, feelings, and actions are influenced by one's ethnic identity. One's ethnic group becomes a significant reference group whose values, outlook, and goals are taken into account as one makes important life choices.

In the United States, a history of negative imagery, violence, discrimination, and invisibility has been linked to African-Americans, Native Americans, Asian-Americans, and Hispanics. Young people in each of these groups encounter conflicting values as they consider the larger society and their own ethnic identity. They must struggle with the negative or ambivalent feelings that are linked with their own ethnic group because of the cultural stereotypes that have been conveyed to them through the media and the schools, and because of the absence of role models from their own group who are in positions of leadership and authority.

Issues of ethnic-group identity may not become salient until early adolescence. As minority children grow up, they tend to incorporate many of the ideals and values of the Anglo culture. Suddenly, in adolescence, they may find

Peers can help one another resolve issues of ethnic identity by forming organized groups that focus on racial and ethnic heritage. Adolescents can achieve a sense of pride in their unique ethnic heritage and still embrace their identity as Americans.

themselves excluded from it. At that time, peer groups become more structured. Sanctions against cross-race friendships and dating relationships become more intense. Minority adolescents may encounter more overt rejection and failure in academic achievement, employment, and school leadership. They may find that their family and ethnic-group values are actually in conflict with the values of the majority culture. They may feel that they have to choose between their ethnic-group identity and membership in a nonminority group. In some cases, commitment to an ethnic-group identity takes the place of membership in a peer group. In other instances, minority youths are rejected by their Anglo peers. They may flounder, not having established a clear ethnic identity, and may struggle through a period of bitter rejection. In still other instances, youths create peer groups within their own ethnic group.

The salience of peer-group membership may not be as great for the adaptation of minority youth as it has been described as being for white adolescents. In one study of family and peer relations, after taking social class into account, African-American adolescents reported both higher levels of parental control and higher levels of family intimacy than white subjects (Giordano, Cernkovich & DeMaris, 1993). In addition, African-American adolescents reported that they perceived less peer pressure, less need for peer approval, and somewhat lower levels of intimacy in their friendships. One ought not interpret this pattern as indicating that friendship relationships are unimportant to African-American adolescents; rather, friendships may be less intense for African-American than for white adolescents. African-American adolescents may be socialized to function more independently, to be more flexible in accepting their friends, and to be less dependent on their friends than on their family for feelings of self-worth and emotional security. We do not really know much about intragroup differences in sources and quality of social support among minority youth and how these patterns are associated with well-being.

Applied Topic
Adolescent Alcohol Use

American high-school-age youth have a higher level of illicit drug use than those of any other industrialized nation. By their senior year in high school, roughly 40% of American high school students have tried an illegal drug, whether marijuana, amphetamines, heroin or other opiates, cocaine, or barbiturates. However, the use of most of these drugs has been declining since 1975. Figure 9.4 shows the lifetime use of illicit drugs by U.S. twelfth-graders. The downward trend has shifted in the most recent report finding a new increase in marijuana use by the 12th-graders in 1993. In contrast to the overall decline in illicit drug use, alcohol use has remained at a stable and relatively high level since 1975. An ongoing national study of high school seniors' drug use and related attitudes shows a widespread use of alcohol from 1975 to 1992 (Johnston, O'Malley & Bachman, 1993). Among high school seniors, nearly all the students (87.5%) had tried alcohol at least once; 69% of eighth-graders had already tried alcohol. Recent trends in alcohol use provide a mixed picture. Among high school seniors, those who drank monthly declined from 72% in 1980 to 51% in 1992, and daily drinking dropped from 7% in 1979 to 3.4% in 1992. However, initiation into alcohol use appeared to be starting at an earlier age. Among eighth-graders surveyed in 1991 and 1992, 27% reported having been drunk at least once, and 8% said they had been drunk in the past 30 days. In a rural sample of seventh-graders, about 60% had used alcohol in the past year, and about 8% had used it four or five times a month (Sarvela & McClendon, 1988).

Alcohol depresses the central nervous system. Although many people think that alcohol makes one "high," at its greatest levels of concentration in the body it can cause death by suppressing breathing. Although this outcome is extremely rare, it may occur after "chugging" large quantities of alcohol, a practice that is sometimes included in certain adolescent initiation rites and demonstrations of manliness. There are two other situations in which alcohol use has potentially lethal consequences. One is the use of alcohol in combination with other drugs, especially barbiturates. The other is its use in combination with driving. One study of tenth-, eleventh-, and twelfth-graders found that 57% had driven while intoxicated and 78% had ridden in a car while the driver was drinking (DiBlasio, 1986).

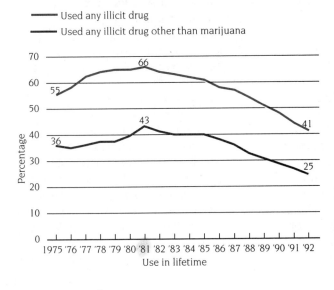

— Used any illicit drug

— Used any illicit drug other than marijuana

FIGURE 9.4

Lifetime use of illicit drugs by twelfth-graders

Source: Johnston, O'Malley & Bachman, 1993.

TABLE 9.3   Effects Associated with Various Amounts of Alcohol in a 150-Pound Person

Amount of Beverage	Alcohol Concentration in Blood (Percentage)	Effects
1 highball 5½ ounces of wine 1 bottle of beer	0.03	Slight changes in feeling
2 highballs 11 ounces of wine 3 bottles of beer	0.06	Feelings of warmth, relaxation
3 highballs 16½ ounces of wine 5 bottles of beer	0.09	Exaggerated emotion and behavior—noisy, talkative, or morose
4 highballs 22 ounces of wine 7 bottles of beer	0.12	Clumsiness—unsteady in standing and walking
5 highballs 27½ ounces of wine ½ pint of whiskey	0.15	Gross intoxication

Source: Coleman, 1976.

Table 9.3 shows the effects associated with various concentrations of alcohol in the blood. These effects depend on body weight and the amount of food consumed during drinking. However, it is clear that even three beers or two cocktails can alter behavior so as to produce feelings of warmth, relaxation, and some increase in sociability (Coleman, 1980).

Let us look at some of the factors associated with the use of alcohol and the part alcohol use plays in the adolescent's life. We are especially concerned about understanding the relationship between alcohol use and the major themes of early adolescence: physical development, cognitive development, peer relations, and parent-child relationships.

The physical development accompanying puberty leads to a heightened awareness of body sensations. In small quantities, alcohol has a relaxing effect that may accentuate pleasurable bodily sensations. Adolescents may use alcohol in an attempt to increase their sense of physical arousal, to reduce sexual inhibitions, and to minimize the self-consciousness that is a barrier to social interactions. In larger quantities, alcohol may alter reality testing in such a way that adolescents are willing to take risks or ignore certain physical limitations. While adolescents are intoxicated, the barriers of physical appearance, height, weight, or sexual immaturity may be minimized. Thus, dissatisfaction with one's body image may contribute to an inclination to drink heavily in social situations.

Growth in cognitive development during adolescence suggests that young people are increasingly able to anticipate the consequences of their actions. They can hypothesize about events that have not yet occurred and reason about their possible outcomes. Adolescents should be able to manipulate several variables at one time in order to solve a problem or make a decision. These skills suggest that adolescents can use information about the impact or risk of alcohol to guide their drinking behavior. However, many adolescents do not view alcohol consumption as terribly risky. In a national survey, 30% of high school seniors saw daily drinking as involving great risk, and 49% of high school seniors saw binge drinking (five or more drinks once or twice over a weekend) as involving great risk (Johnston et al., 1993). Students who drink alcohol frequently are less likely to see a great deal of risk in drinking, while those who drink little or not at all are more likely to see a great deal of risk (Small, Silverberg & Kerns, 1993). This pattern suggests cognitive consistency; in other words, adolescents who view a certain level of drinking behavior as highly risky are less likely to engage in that behavior. But what factors influence whether one views drinking as risky?

The two reference groups that influence the acceptability of drinking and the manner in which alcohol is consumed are the family and the peer group (Brook, Whiteman & Gordon, 1983). There appear to be many similarities between the ways in which students and adults in a community think about and use alcohol. Barnes (1981) surveyed students and adults in the same community to assess the similarity in their respective patterns of use. Adults and students showed similar patterns of use of beer, wine, and other liquors. They described similar patterns of alcohol use in the home on special occasions or at mealtimes. Three basic reasons for drinking were described by the two groups: conforming functions ("So I won't be different from my friends"); social, festive functions ("It's a good way to celebrate"); and personal effects ("It helps relieve pressure"). The first reason was somewhat more important to adolescents than to adults. The second was most important to both groups. The third was somewhat more important to adolescents than to adults. Neither the first nor the third reason helps to predict if a person will be a heavy drinker, whether student or adult. Barnes concluded that the drinking patterns of students and adults are extremely similar. The adult members of a community set the attitudinal and behavioral tone with regard to alcohol use, and adolescents are socialized to internalize that position.

A somewhat different view is seen if one asks adolescents about parental approval of drinking patterns. Adolescents perceive their parents as disapproving of almost any drug use. With respect to alcohol use, over 90% perceive their parents to be disapproving of having one or two drinks a day, and almost all high school seniors see their parents as disapproving of binge drinking (Johnston et al., 1993).

The impact of parental sanctions against alcohol use depends heavily on the quality of the parent-child relationship:

> Compared to users, nonusers feel closer to both parents, consider it important to get along well with them, and want to be like them when they grow up. Nonusers' parents more typically provide praise and encouragement, develop feelings of interpersonal trust, and help with personal problems. Perceived as stricter, nonusers' parents more typically have rules about homework, television, curfew, and drugs and alcohol. Yet, they are not more punitive. Instead, parental control is enhanced by praise and encouragement and by an emotionally close relationship that encourages youngsters to seek parental advice and guidance. Young people who feel loved and trusted by parents want to emulate them, not bring embarrassment by inappropriate behavior. (Coombs & Landsverk, 1988, p. 480)

The peer group also contributes to the patterns of alcohol use in adolescence. Here, we see some explanation of the potential inconsistencies in alcohol use. The majority (53%) of high school seniors say that they are around peers who use alcohol to get high, and close to 30% say they are around friends who get drunk at least once a week (Johnston et al., 1993). Even among eighth-graders, about 75% say they are around friends who drink.

At 14, adolescents may already be quite skillful at getting beer. They may have older siblings, parents, or older friends who will buy for them. And they know the stores in town that don't check IDs too carefully.

Most adolescents do not drink every day. However, many do engage in binge drinking, which they perceive as risky but as somehow acceptable within the peer context. Binge drinking is more frequent among boys than among girls and more frequent among the non-college-bound than among the college-bound. Although adolescents say they perceive greater risk in binge drinking than in taking one or two drinks every day, they are less likely to disapprove of binge drinking than of daily drinking. Further, adolescents perceive their peers' attitudes as being much more similar to their own and much less disapproving of binge drinking than the attitudes of their parents (Johnston et al., 1987).

Alcohol is a part of the life experience of almost every adolescent. Drinking is something an adolescent can do that symbolizes celebration, adult status, and some degree of behavioral independence from parents. Since most adults also drink, adolescents may readily perceive their disapproval of adolescent drinking as hypocritical. In this way, drinking may become an avenue for testing the limits of adult authority or for expressing behavioral autonomy from parental control.

From our knowledge of the central role of the peer group during this stage of life, we must assume that alcohol use is influenced in part by peer pressure to conform to a group norm. Peer-group leaders who experiment with alcohol at a young age or who approve of binge drinking, alcohol use at parties, or driving while intoxicated are highly influential in encouraging other group members to share these experiences. Peer expectations for alcohol use may become one criterion for peer-group acceptance. On the other hand, if peer norms reject alcohol use, the peer group may serve to shield its members from alcohol use and to deny membership to those who drink. The social reference group's support of alcohol use during adolescence has long-term effects.

Several studies have attempted to assess the risk factors that influence early entry into alcohol and other drug use (Newcomb & Bentler, 1989). In one study of fourth- and fifth-graders, 15% reported alcohol use without their parents' knowledge (Iannotti & Bush, 1992). Both peer and family variables were significant predictors of the use of alcohol without parents' knowledge. Children who perceived that many of their friends had been drinking and who perceived peer pressure to drink were more likely to drink themselves. In addition, children who were in classrooms where a larger number of children reported drinking were at greater risk of drinking themselves. Perceptions of the amount of drinking that occurred in the family were also an important predictor of early alcohol use. Another study of alcohol and drug use among seventh-graders confirmed the importance of peer and family influences (Farrell, Danish & Howard, 1992). Significant predictors of alcohol use included several peer factors: friends' approving of alcohol and drugs; feeling pressure to use alcohol and drugs; and knowing friends who had an alcohol and drug problem. There were also two family factors: being home alone 20 or more times in the past 30 days after school, and reporting that half or more of the adults the adolescents knew had an alcohol or drug problem.

The risk factors associated with early alcohol use are linked to social class and culture. Control over the sale of alcohol to minors, the cost of alcohol, and the efforts of parents and other adults, including school officials and the police, to monitor the use of alcohol among adolescents are all community factors that influence the use of alcohol in early adolescence. In addition, alcohol plays a somewhat different role in various ethnic, cultural, and religious groups. For example, a comparative analysis of African-American, Cuban, other Hispanic, and non-Hispanic white sixth- and seventh-grade males in Dade County, Florida, found different rates of alcohol use and different patterns of risk factors that predicted early use in the four groups (Vega et al., 1993). In this particular study, non-Hispanic whites had the highest percentage of early alcohol users (48%), Cubans the next highest (41%), other Hispanics the next highest (31%), and African-Americans the lowest (25%). In all groups, low family pride and the willingness of the adolescent to participate in delinquent behavior or to break the law were significant predictors of early alcohol use. The full list of risk factors was best able to account for alcohol use among the non-Hispanic white sample. In that group, family substance-abuse problems and peer approval for substance use were two of the most powerful predictors. The risk factors measured in the study were least effective in predicting alcohol use by the African-American sample. In that group, low family pride and the willingness of the adolescent to engage in nonnormative behaviors were the two most powerful predictors. The Cubans and other Hispanics showed distinct patterns of risk. These two groups had the highest levels of family pride, and for them, low family pride was a very strong predictor of alcohol use. For the other Hispanics, who included many boys who were recent immigrants from Latin American countries, some indicators of worthlessness, especially low self-esteem and prior suicide attempts, were associated with early alcohol use, but these factors were not especially relevant for the Cuban teens.

We have tried to point out how alcohol may become a part of the life of normal adolescents during the high school years. Experimentation with alcohol is relatively easy to understand in the context of the adolescent's psychosocial needs and the modeling of alcohol use in the family, the peer group, and the community. Although illegal alcohol use may be considered a normative "rite of passage" for most adolescents, it appears that children who begin to drink early in the adolescent years—that is, before ninth grade—are especially vulnerable to more serious involvement with alcohol and drug use. These children experience some combination of family, peer, and psychosocial pressures that increase their willingness to engage in deviant behavior and to ignore or minimize the risks associated with drinking.

Chapter Summary

In the use of alcohol by high school students, we see all the central themes of early adolescence. First, the physical sensations associated with a drug high point to the adolescent's general sensitivity to sensuality and preoccupation with body changes. Second, the issue of perceived risks suggests the adolescent's growing cognitive capacities. The adolescent is capable of relating to a hypothetical situation as well as to a factual one. Third, the use of alcohol suggests the significance of the peer group and identification with it. Alcohol use is only one behavior that may be motivated primarily by a need for peer acceptance and a desire to conform to peer-group norms. At the same time, family bonds and a sense of family support continue to play a role in strengthening adolescents' ability to resist peer pressures and to sustain an underlying sense of their personal worth.

The crisis of group identity versus alienation involves a potential tension between individual and family values and peer pressures to violate them. In many cases, no deep contradiction exists. Adolescent resistance to parental values may be more realistically interpreted as a demonstration of personal independence rather than as a declaration of guerrilla warfare. On the other hand, the threat of peer rejection may push those adolescents who lack confidence in their own worth to violate very essential values in the pursuit of acceptance. Teenage pregnancy, drug addiction, drunken driving, and serious delinquent behavior all reflect adolescents' capacity to engage in high-risk behaviors that have a great potential for modifying the life course and exposing the person to new and serious physical and emotional hazards. The cultural climate in which adolescents work out peer-group relationships is of critical importance to success in this stage. Existing social expectations, stereotypical roles, and value orientations may either strengthen or undercut the adolescent's efforts to achieve personal satisfaction in the context of the peer group.

References

Ackerman, G. L. (1993). A congressional view of youth suicide. *American Psychologist, 48,* 183–184.

Acredolo, C., Adams, A. & Schmid, J. (1984). On the understanding of the relationships between speed, duration, and distance. *Child Development, 55,* 2151–2159.

Adams, G. R. & Jones, R. M. (1982). Adolescent egocentrism: Exploration into possible contributions of parent-child relations. *Journal of Youth and Adolescence, 11,* 25–31.

Adegoke, A. A. (1993). The experience of spermarche (the age of onset of sperm emission) among selected boys in Nigeria. *Journal of Youth and Adolescence, 22,* 201–209.

Adelson, J. & Doehrman, M. J. (1980). The psychodynamic approach to adolescence. In J. Adelson (Ed.), *Handbook of adolescent psychology* (pp. 99–116). New York: Wiley.

Alexander, C. S., Somerfield, M. R., Ensminger, M. E., Johnson, K. E. & Kim, Y. J. (1993). Consistency of adolescents' self-report of sexual behavior in a longitudinal study. *Journal of Youth and Adolescence, 22,* 455–473.

Allen, J. P., Weissberg, R. P. & Hawkins, J. A. (1989). The relation between values and social competence in early adolescence. *Developmental Psychology, 25,* 458–464.

Astone, N. M. (1993). Are adolescent mothers just single mothers? *Journal of Research on Adolescence, 3,* 353–372.

Barnes, G. M. (1981). Drinking among adolescents: A subcultural phenomenon or a model of adult behaviors? *Adolescence, 16,* 211–229.

Beauvoir, S. de. (1959). *Memoirs of a dutiful daughter.* New York: World.

Benson, P. L. (1992). *The troubled journey: A profile of American youth.* Minneapolis: RespecTeen/Lutheran Brotherhood.

Berlin, I. N. (1987). Suicide among American Indian adolescents: An overview. *Suicide and Life-Threatening Behavior,* 17, 218–232.

Berndt, T. J. (1982). The features and effects of friendship in early adolescence. *Child Development,* 53, 1447–1460.

Berndt, T. J. & Hoyle, S. G. (1985). Stability and change in childhood and adolescent friendships. *Developmental Psychology,* 21, 1007–1015.

Blumstein, A., Cohen, J., Roth, J. A. & Visher, C. A. (1986). *Criminal careers and career criminals* (Vol. 1). Washington, DC: National Academy Press.

Blyth, D. A., Bulcroft, R. & Simmons, R. G. (1981). *The impact of puberty on adolescents: A longitudinal study.* Paper presented at the annual convention of the American Psychological Association, Los Angeles.

Bolton, F. G., Jr., & MacEachron, A. E. (1988). Adolescent male sexuality: A developmental perspective. *Journal of Adolescent Research,* 3, 259–273.

Brook, J. S., Whiteman, M. & Gordon, A. S. (1983). Stages of drug use in adolescence: Personality, peer, and family correlates. *Developmental Psychology,* 19, 269–277.

Brooks-Gunn, J. & Furstenberg, F. F., Jr. (1989). Adolescent sexual behavior. *American Psychologist,* 44, 249–257.

Brooks-Gunn, J. & Petersen, A. C. (1991). Studying the emergence of depression and depressive symptoms during adolescence. *Journal of Youth and Adolescence,* 20, 115–120.

Brooks-Gunn, J. & Reiter, E. O. (1990). The role of pubertal processes. In S. S. Feldman & G. R. Elliott (Eds.), *At the threshold: The developing adolescent* (pp. 16–53). Cambridge: Harvard University Press.

Brooks-Gunn, J. & Warren, M. P. (1988). The psychological significance of secondary sexual characteristics in 9- to 11-year-old girls. *Child Development,* 59, 161–169.

Brown, B. B. (1990). Peer groups and peer cultures. In S. S. Feldman & G. R. Elliott (Eds.), *At the threshold: The developing adolescent* (pp. 171–196). Cambridge: Harvard University Press.

Brown, B. B., Mounts, N., Lamborn, S. D. & Steinberg, L. (1993). Parenting practices and peer group affiliation in adolescence. *Child Development,* 64, 467–482.

Bullough, V. L. (1981). Age at menarche: A misunderstanding. *Science,* 213, 365–366.

Caldas, S. J. (1993). Current theoretical perspectives on adolescent pregnancy and childbearing in the United States. *Journal of Adolescent Research,* 8, 4–20.

Carron, A. V. & Bailey, O. A. (1974). Strength development in boys from 10 through 16 years. *Monographs of the Society for Research in Child Development,* 39(4).

Caspi, A. & Moffitt, T. E. (1991). Individual differences are accentuated during periods of social change: The sample case of girls at puberty. *Journal of Personality and Social Psychology,* 61, 157–168.

Cavior, N. & Dokecki, P. R. (1973). Physical attractiveness, perceived attitude similarity, and academic achievement as contributors to interpersonal attractions among adolescents. *Developmental Psychology,* 9, 44–54.

Chandler, M. & Boyes, M. (1982). Social cognitive development. In B. B. Wolman (Ed.), *Handbook of developmental psychology* (pp. 387–402). Englewood Cliffs, NJ: Prentice-Hall.

Chapman, M. (1988). *Constructive evolution: Origin and development of Piaget's thought.* New York: Cambridge University Press.

Clasen, D. R. & Brown, B. B. (1985). The multidimensionality of peer pressure in adolescence. *Journal of Youth and Adolescence,* 14, 451–468.

Clausen, J. A. (1975). The social meaning of differential physical and sexual maturation. In S. E. Dragastin & G. H. Elder (Eds.), *Adolescence in the life cycle: Psychological change and social context.* Washington, DC: Hemisphere.

Coleman, J. C. (1980). *Abnormal psychology and modern life* (6th ed.). Glenview, IL: Scott, Foresman.

Conger, R. D., Conger, K. J., Elder, G. H., Lorenz, F. O., Simons, R. L. & Whitbeck, L. B. (1993). Family economic stress and adjustment of early adolescent girls. *Developmental Psychology,* 29, 206–219.

Coombs, R. H. & Landsverk, J. (1988). Parenting styles and substance use in childhood and adolescence. *Journal of Marriage and the Family,* 50, 473–482.

Csikszentmihalyi, M., Larson, R. & Prescott, S. (1977). The ecology of adolescent activity and experience. *Journal of Youth and Adolescence,* 6, 281–294.

D'Augelli, A. R. (1991). Gay men in college: Identity processes and adaptation. *Journal of College Student Development,* 32, 140–146.

Day, D. (1992). The transition to first intercourse among racially and culturally diverse youth. *Journal of Marriage and the Family,* 54, 749–763.

Demetriou, A. & Efklides, A. (1985). Structure and sequence of formal and postformal thought: General patterns and individual differences. *Child Development,* 56, 1062–1091.

DiBlasio, F. A. (1986). Drinking adolescents on the roads. *Journal of Youth and Adolescence,* 15, 173–188.

Dreyer, P. H. (1982). Sexuality during adolescence. In B. B. Wolman (Ed.), *Handbook of developmental psychology* (pp. 559–601). Englewood Cliffs, NJ: Prentice-Hall.

Dunham, R. M., Kidwell, J. S. & Portes, P. R. (1988). Effects of parent-adolescent interaction on the continuity of cognitive development from early childhood to early adolescence. *Journal of Early Adolescence,* 8, 297–310.

Dunphy, D. C. (1963). The social structure of urban adolescent peer groups. *Sociometry, 26,* 230–246.

Durbin, D. L., Darling, N., Steinberg, L. & Brown, B. B. (1993). Parenting style and peer group membership among European-American adolescents. *Journal of Research on Adolescence, 3,* 87–100.

Dwyer, J. & Mayer, J. (1971). Psychological effects of variations in physical appearance during adolescence. In R. E. Muuss (Ed.), *Adolescent behavior and society: A book of readings.* New York: Random House.

East, P. L., Hess, L. E. & Lerner, R. M. (1987). Peer social support and adjustment of early adolescent peer groups. *Journal of Early Adolescence, 7,* 153–163.

Eckstein, S. & Shemesh, M. (1992). The rate of acquisition of formal operational schemata in adolescence: A secondary analysis. *Journal of Research in Science Teaching, 29,* 441–451.

Edelman, M. W. & Pittman, K. J. (1986). Adolescent pregnancy: Black and white. *Journal of Community Health, 11,* 63–69.

Elkind, D. (1967). Egocentrism in adolescence. *Child Development, 38,* 1025–1034.

Elliott, D. S., Huizinga, D. & Menard, S. (1989). *Multiple problem youth: Delinquency, substance use, and mental health problems.* New York: Springer-Verlag.

Farrell, A. D., Danish, S. J. & Howard, C. W. (1992). Risk factors for drug use in urban adolescents: Identification and cross-validation. *American Journal of Community Psychology, 20,* 263–286.

Faust, M. S. (1977). Somatic development of adolescent girls. *Monographs of the Society for Research in Child Development, 42*(1, Serial No. 169).

Feldman, S. S. & Gehring, T. M. (1988). Changing perceptions of family cohesion and power across adolescence. *Child Development, 59,* 1034–1045.

Fischer, K. W. (1980). A theory of cognitive development: The control and construction of hierarchies of skills. *Psychological Review, 87,* 477–531.

Fischer, K. W., Bullock, D., Rotenberg, E. J. & Raya, P. (1993). The dynamics of competence: How context contributes directly to skill. In R. Wozniak & K. Fischer (Eds.), *Development in context: Acting and thinking in specific environments* (JPS Series on Knowledge and Development, Vol. 1, pp. 93–117). Hillsdale, NJ: Erlbaum.

Flannery, D. J., Rowe, D. C. & Gulley, B. L. (1993). Impact of pubertal status, timing, and age on adolescent sexual experience and delinquency. *Journal of Adolescent Research, 8,* 21–40.

Flavell, J. H. (1963). *The developmental psychology of Jean Piaget.* Princeton, NJ: Van Nostrand.

Fosburgh, L. (1977). The make-believe world of teenage maturity. *New York Times Magazine* (August 7), pp. 29–34.

Franklin, D. L. (1988). Race, class, and adolescent pregnancy: An ecological analysis. *American Journal of Orthopsychiatry, 58,* 339–355.

Gaddis, A. & Brooks-Gunn, J. (1985). The male experience of pubertal change. *Journal of Youth and Adolescence, 14,* 61–69.

Garguilo, J., Attie, I., Brooks-Gunn, J. & Warren, M. P. (1987). Dating in middle school girls: Effects of social context, maturation, and grade. *Developmental Psychology, 23,* 730–737.

Garland, A. F. & Zigler, E. (1993). Adolescent suicide prevention: Current research and social policy implications. *American Psychologist, 48,* 169–182.

Garrison, C. Z., Schluchter, M. D., Schoenbach, V. J. & Kaplan, B. K. (1989). Epidemiology of depressive symptoms in young adolescents. *Journal of the American Academy of Child and Adolescent Psychiatry, 28,* 343–351.

Gelles, R. J. (1989). Child abuse and violence in single-parent families: Parent absence and economic deprivation. *American Journal of Orthopsychiatry, 59,* 492–501.

Gillies, P. (1989). A longitudinal study of the hopes and worries of adolescents. *Journal of Adolescence, 12,* 69–81.

Giordano, P. C., Cernkovich, S. A. & DeMaris, A. (1993). The family and peer relations of black adolescents. *Journal of Marriage and the Family, 55,* 277–287.

Gold, M. & Petronio, R. J. (1980). Delinquent behavior in adolescence. In J. Adelson (Ed.), *Handbook of adolescent psychology* (pp. 495–535). New York: Wiley.

Gore, S., Aseltine, R. H. & Colten, M. E. (1993). Gender, social-relational involvement, and depression. *Journal of Research on Adolescence, 3,* 101–126.

Hallinan, M. T. & Williams, R. A. (1989). Interracial friendship choices in secondary schools. *American Sociological Review, 54,* 67–78.

Hansell, S. (1985). Adolescent friendship networks and distress in school. *Social Forces, 63,* 698–715.

Hanson, S. L., Myers, D. R. & Ginsburg, A. L. (1987). The role of responsibility and knowledge in reducing teenage out-of-wedlock childbearing. *Journal of Marriage and the Family, 49,* 241–256.

Hardy, J. B. & Duggan, A. K. (1988). Teenage fathers and the fathers of infants of urban teenage mothers. *American Journal of Public Health, 78,* 919–922.

Hendricks, L. E. & Fullilove, R. E. (1983). Locus of control and use of contraception among unmarried black adolescent fathers and their controls: A preliminary report. *Journal of Youth and Adolescence, 12,* 225–233.

Hill, J. P. (1988). Adapting to menarche: Familial control and conflict. In M. R. Gunnar & W. A. Collins (Eds.), *Development during the transition to adolescence. Minnesota Symposium on Child Psychology* (Vol. 21, pp. 43–77). Hillsdale, NJ: Erlbaum.

Hoge, D. R. & McCarthy, J. D. (1984). Influence of individual and group identity salience in the global self-esteem of youth. *Journal of Personality and Social Psychology*, 47, 403–414.

Hunter, F. T. (1985). Adolescents' perception of discussions with parents and friends. *Developmental Psychology*, 21, 433–440.

Iannotti, R. J. & Bush, P. J. (1992). Perceived versus actual friends' use of alcohol, cigarettes, marijuana, and cocaine: Which has the most influence? *Journal of Youth and Adolescence*, 21, 375–389.

Inhelder, B. & Piaget, J. (1958). *The growth of logical thinking from childhood to adolescence*. New York: Basic Books.

Johnston, L. D., O'Malley, P. M. & Bachman, J. G. (1987). *National trends in drug use and related factors among American high school students and young adults, 1975–1986*. Rockville, MD: National Institute on Drug Abuse.

Johnston, L. D., O'Malley, P. M. & Bachman, J. D. G. (1993). *National survey results on drug use from Monitoring the Future Study, 1975–1992: Vol. 1. Secondary school students*. Rockville, MD: National Institute on Drug Abuse.

Jones, S. S. (1976). High school status as a historical process. *Adolescence*, 11, 327–333.

Jones-Webb, R. J. & Snowden, L. R. (1993). Symptoms of depression among blacks and whites. *American Journal of Public Health*, 83, 240–244.

Katchadourian, H. (1990). Sexuality. In S. S. Feldman & G. R. Elliott (Eds.), *At the threshold: The developing adolescent* (pp. 330–351). Cambridge: Harvard University Press.

Keating, D. P. (1990). Adolescent thinking. In S. S. Feldman & G. R. Elliott (Eds.), *At the threshold: The developing adolescent* (pp. 54–90). Cambridge: Harvard University Press.

Ketterlinus, R. D., Lamb, M. E., Nitz, K. & Elster, A. B. (1992). Adolescent nonsexual and sex-related problem behaviors. *Journal of Adolescent Research*, 7, 431–456.

Klineberg, S. L. (1967). Changes in outlook on the future between childhood and adolescence. *Journal of Personality and Social Psychology*, 7, 185–193.

Kohn, P. M. & Milrose, J. A. (1993). The inventory of high-school students' recent life experiences: A decontaminated measure of adolescents' life hassles. *Journal of Youth and Adolescence*, 22, 43–55.

Konopka, G. (1976). *Young girls: A portrait of adolescence*. Englewood Cliffs, NJ: Prentice-Hall.

Kornfield, S. (1990). *Impact of parental marital status, gender, and pubertal development on adolescent*. Unpublished manuscript, University of Georgia.

Kuhn, D., Amsel, E. & O'Loughlin, M. (1988). *The development of scientific thinking skills*. New York: Academic Press.

Lamb, M. E. & Elster, A. B. (1985). Adolescent mother-infant-father relationships. *Developmental Psychology*, 21, 768–773.

Lamborn, S. D. & Steinberg, L. D. (1993). Emotional autonomy redux: Revisiting Ryan and Lynch. *Child Development*, 64, 483–499.

Larson, R. & Ham, M. (1993). Stress and "storm and stress" in early adolescence: The relationship of negative events with dysphoric affect. *Developmental Psychology*, 29, 130–140.

Larson, R. & Lampman-Petraitis, C. (1989). Daily emotional states as reported by children and adolescents. *Child Development*, 60, 1250–1260.

Leland, N. L. & Barth, R. P. (1993). Characteristics of adolescents who have attempted to avoid HIV and who have communicated with parents about sex. *Journal of Adolescent Research*, 8, 58–77.

Lessing, E. E. (1972). Extension of personal future time perspective, age, and life satisfaction of children and adolescents. *Developmental Psychology*, 6, 457–468.

Levesque, R. P. (1993). The romantic experience of adolescents in satisfying love relationships. *Journal of Youth and Adolescence*, 22, 219–252.

Levitt, M. J., Guacci-Franco, N. & Levitt, J. L. (1993). Convoys of social support in childhood and early adolescence: Structure and function. *Developmental Psychology*, 29, 811–818.

Linn, M. C., Clement, C., Pulos, S. & Sullivan, P. (1989). Scientific reasoning during adolescence: The influence of instruction in science knowledge and reasoning strategies. *Journal of Research in Science Teaching*, 26, 171–187.

Logan, D. D. (1980). The menarche experience in 23 foreign countries. *Adolescence*, 15, 247–256.

Looft, W. R. (1971). Egocentrism and social interaction in adolescence. *Adolescence*, 12, 485–495.

Luhtanen, R. & Crocker, J. (1992). A collective self-esteem scale: Self-evaluation of one's social identity. *Personality and Social Psychology Bulletin*, 18, 302–318.

Maag, J. W., Rutherford, R. B., Jr. & Parks, B. T. (1988). Secondary school professionals' ability to identify depression in adolescents. *Adolescence*, 23, 73–82.

Marsiglio, W. (1987). Adolescent fathers in the United States: Their initial living arrangements, marital experience, and educational outcomes. *Family Planning Perspectives*, 19, 240–251.

Marsiglio, W. (1988). Adolescent male sexuality and heterosexual masculinity: A conceptual model and review. *Journal of Adolescent Research*, 3, 285–303.

Marsiglio, W. (1989). Adolescent males' pregnancy resolution preferences and family formation intentions: Does family background make a difference for blacks and whites? *Journal of Adolescent Research*, 4, 214–237.

Martin, S., Houseley, K., McCoy, H., Greenhouse, P., Stigger, F., Kenney, M. A., Shoffner, S., Fu, V., Korslund, M., Ercanli-Huffman, F. G., Carter, E., Chopin, L., Hegsted, M., Clark, A. J., Disney, G., Moak, S., Wakefield, T. & Stallings, S. (1988). Self-esteem of adolescent girls as related to weight. *Perceptual and Motor Skills*, 67, 879–884.

Mau, R. Y. (1992). The validity and devolution of a concept: Student alienation. *Adolescence*, 27, 731–741.

McCarthy, J. & Hardy, J. (1993). Age at first birth and birth outcomes. *Journal of Research on Adolescence*, 3, 373–392.

McCord, J. (1990). Problem behaviors. In S. S. Feldman & G. R. Elliott (Eds.), *At the threshold: The developing adolescent* (pp. 414–430). Cambridge: Harvard University Press.

McMillan, D. W. & Hiltonsmith, R. W. (1982). Adolescents at home: An exploratory study of the relationship between perception of family social climate, general well-being, and actual behavior in the home setting. *Journal of Youth and Adolescence*, 11, 301–315.

Mendelson, B. K. & White, D. R. (1985). Development of self-body-esteem in overweight youngsters. *Developmental Psychology*, 21, 90–96.

Millstein, S. G. & Litt, I. F. (1990). Adolescent health. In S. S. Feldman & G. R. Elliott (Eds.), *At the threshold: The developing adolescent* (pp. 431–456). Cambridge: Harvard University Press.

Montemayor, R. (1982). The relationship between parent-adolescent conflict and the amount of time adolescents spend alone and with parents and peers. *Child Development*, 53, 1512–1519.

Montemayor, R. (1983). Parents and adolescents in conflict: All families some of the time and some families most of the time. *Journal of Early Adolescence*, 3, 83–103.

Moore, K. A., Myers, D. E., Morrison, D. R., Nord, C. W., Brown, B. & Edmonston, B. (1993). Age at first childbirth and later poverty. *Journal of Research on Adolescence*, 3, 393–422.

Moriarty, A. E. & Toussieng, P. W. (1976). *Adolescent coping*. New York: Grune & Stratton.

Morrison, D. M. (1985). Adolescent contraceptive behavior: A review. *Psychological Bulletin*, 98, 538–568.

Musa, K. E. & Roach, M. E. (1973). Adolescent appearance and self-concept. *Adolescence*, 8, 385–395.

Mussen, P. H. & Jones, M. C. (1957). Self-conceptions, motivations, and interpersonal attitudes of late and early maturing boys. *Child Development*, 28, 243–256.

National Urban League. (1987). *Adolescent male responsibility, pregnancy prevention, and parenting program: A program development guide*. New York: Author.

Neimark, E. D. (1975). Longitudinal development of formal operations thought. *Genetic Psychology Monographs*, 91, 171–225.

Neimark, E. D. (1982). Adolescent thought: Transition to formal operations. In B. B. Wolman (Ed.), *Handbook of developmental psychology* (pp. 486–499). Englewood Cliffs, NJ: Prentice-Hall.

Newcomb, M. D. & Bentler, P. M. (1989). Substance use and abuse among children and teenagers. *American Psychologist*, 44, 242–248.

Newcomer, S. & Udry, J. R. (1987). Parental marital status effects on adolescent sexual behavior. *Journal of Marriage and the Family*, 49, 235–240.

Newman, P. R. (1979). Persons and settings: A comparative analysis of the quality and range of social interaction in two suburban high schools. In J. G. Kelly (Ed.), *Adolescent boys in high school: A psychological study of coping and adaptation*. Hillsdale, NJ: Erlbaum.

Newman, P. R. (1982). The peer group. In B. B. Wolman (Ed.), *Handbook of developmental psychology* (pp. 526–535). Englewood Cliffs, NJ: Prentice-Hall.

Nolen-Hoeksema, S. (1987). Sex differences in unipolar depression: Evidence and theory. *Psychological Bulletin*, 101, 259–282.

Nolen-Hoeksema, S., Girgus, J. S. & Seligman, M. E. P. (1991). Sex differences in depression and explanatory style in children. *Journal of Youth and Adolescence*, 20, 233–246.

Nurmi, J. (1987). Age, sex, social class, and quality of family interaction as determinants of adolescents' future orientation: A developmental task interpretation. *Adolescence*, 22, 977–991.

Offer, D., Ostrov, E. & Howard, K. I. (1982). Family perceptions of adolescent self-image. *Journal of Youth and Adolescence*, 11, 281–291.

Ohannessian, C. M. & Crockett, L. J. (1993). A longitudinal investigation of the relationship between educational investment and adolescent sexual activity. *Journal of Adolescent Research*, 8, 167–182.

Olds, D. L., Henderson, C. R., Jr., Tatelbaum, R. & Chamberlin, R. (1988). Improving the life-course development of socially disadvantaged mothers: A randomized trial of nurse home visitation. *American Journal of Public Health*, 78, 1436–1445.

O'Mahoney, J. F. (1989). Development of thinking about things and people: Social and nonsocial cognition during adolescence. *Journal of Genetic Psychology*, 150, 217–224.

Ostrov, E., Offer, D. & Howard, K. I. (1989). Gender differences in adolescent symptomatology: A normative study. *Journal of the American Academy of Child and Adolescent Psychiatry*, 28, 394–398.

Overton, W. F. & Meehan, A. M. (1982). Individual differences in formal operational thought: Sex role and learned helplessness. *Child Development, 53,* 1536–1543.

Papini, D. R., Datan, N. & McCluskey-Fawcett, K. A. (1988). An observational study of affective and assertive family interactions during adolescence. *Journal of Youth and Adolescence, 17,* 477–492.

Papini, D. R. & Sebby, R. A. (1988). Variations in conflictual family issues by adolescent pubertal status, gender, and family member. *Journal of Early Adolescence, 8,* 1–15.

Pete, J. M. & DeSantis, L. (1990). Sexual decision making in young black adolescent females. *Adolescence, 25,* 145–154.

Petersen, A. C., Compas, B. E., Brooks-Gunn, J., Stemmler, M., Ey, S. & Grant, K. E. (1993). Depression in adolescence. *American Psychologist, 48,* 155–168.

Petersen, A. C., Sarigiani, P. A. & Kennedy, R. E. (1991). Adolescent depression: Why more girls? *Journal of Youth and Adolescence, 20,* 247–272.

Petersen, A. C., Schulenberg, J. E., Abramowitz, R. H., Offer, D. & Jarcho, H. D. (1984). A self-image questionnaire for young adolescents (SIQYA): Reliability and validity studies. *Journal of Youth and Adolescence, 13,* 93–111.

Piaget, J. (1926). *The language and thought of the child.* New York: Harcourt, Brace.

Piaget, J. (1970). Piaget's theory. In P. H. Mussen (Ed.), *Carmichael's manual of child psychology* (3rd ed., Vol. 1). New York: Wiley.

Piaget, J. (1972). Intellectual evolution from adolescence to adulthood. *Human Development, 15,* 1–12.

Pleck, J. H., Sonenstein, F. L. & Ku, L. C. (1991). Adolescent males' condom use: Relationships between perceived cost-benefits and consistency. *Journal of Marriage and the Family, 53,* 733–746.

Plotnick, R. D. (1992). The effects of attitudes on teenage premarital pregnancy and its resolution. *American Sociological Review, 57,* 800–811.

Quadrel, M. J., Fischhoff, B. & Davis, W. (1993). Adolescent (in)vulnerability. *American Psychologist, 48,* 102–116.

Rabinowitz, M. (1988). On teaching cognitive strategies: The influence of accessibility of conceptual knowledge. *Contemporary Educational Psychology, 13,* 229–235.

Raffaelli, M. & Duckett, E. (1989). "We were just talking . . .": Conversations in early adolescence. *Journal of Youth and Adolescence, 18,* 567–582.

Raja, S. N., McGee, R. & Stanton, W. R. (1992). Perceived attachment to parents and peers and psychological well-being in adolescence. *Journal of Youth and Adolescence, 21,* 471–486.

Rauste-von Wright, M. (1989). Body image satisfaction in adolescent girls and boys: A longitudinal study. *Journal of Youth and Adolescence, 18,* 71–83.

Remafedi, G. (1987). Adolescent sexuality: Psychosocial and medical implications. *Pediatrics, 79,* 326–330.

Richards, M. H. & Larson, R. (1993). Pubertal development and the daily subjective states of young adolescents. *Journal of Research on Adolescence, 3,* 145–169.

Riley, T., Adams, G. R. & Nielsen, E. (1984). Adolescent egocentrism: The association among imaginary audience behavior, cognitive development, and parental support and rejection. *Journal of Youth and Adolescence, 13,* 401–417.

Roberts, R. E. & Sobhan, M. (1992). Symptoms of depression in adolescents: A comparison of Anglo, African, and Hispanic Americans. *Journal of Youth and Adolescence, 21,* 639–652.

Robertson, J. F. & Simons, R. L. (1989). Family factors, self-esteem, and adolescent depression. *Journal of Marriage and the Family, 51,* 125–138.

Robinson, B. E. (1988). Teenage pregnancy from the father's perspective. *American Journal of Orthopsychiatry, 58,* 46–51.

Roosa, M. W. (1984). Maternal age, social class, and the obstetric performance of teenagers. *Journal of Youth and Adolescence, 13,* 365–374.

Rosenberg, M., Schooler, C. & Schoenbach, C. (1989). Self-esteem and adolescent problems: Modeling reciprocal effects. *American Sociological Review, 54,* 1004–1018.

Sarvela, P. D. & McClendon, E. J. (1988). Indicators of rural youth drug use. *Journal of Youth and Adolescence, 17,* 335–348.

Schootman, M., Fuortes, L. J., Zwerling, C., Albanese, M. A. & Watson, C. A. (1993). Safety behavior among Iowa junior high and high school students. *American Journal of Public Health, 83,* 1628–1629.

Siegler, R. S., Liebert, D. E. & Liebert, R. M. (1973). Inhelder and Piaget's pendulum problem: Teaching preadolescents to act as scientists. *Developmental Psychology, 9,* 97–101.

Small, S. A. & Kerns, D. (1993). Unwanted sexual activity among peers during early and middle adolescence: Incidence and risk factors. *Journal of Marriage and the Family, 55,* 941–952.

Small, S. A., Silverberg, S. B. & Kerns, D. (1993). Adolescents' perceptions of the costs and benefits of engaging in health-compromising behaviors. *Journal of Youth and Adolescence, 22,* 73–88.

Smith, D. M. (1987). Peers, subcultures, and schools. In D. Marsland (Ed.), *Education and youth* (pp. 41–64). London: Falmer Press.

Spencer, M. B. (1982). Personal and group identity of black children: An alternative synthesis. *Genetic Psychology Monographs, 103,* 59–84.

Spencer, M. B. (1988). Self-concept development. In D. T. Slaughter (Ed.), *Black children in poverty: Developmental perspectives* (pp. 59–72). San Francisco: Jossey-Bass.

Spencer, M. B. & Markstrom-Adams, C. (1990). Identity processes among racial and ethnic minority children in America. *Child Development, 61,* 290–310.

Stapley, J. C. & Haviland, J. M. (1989). Beyond depression: Gender differences in normal adolescents' emotional experiences. *Sex Roles, 20,* 295–308.

Steinberg, L. (1990). Autonomy, conflict, and harmony in the family relationship. In S. S. Feldman & G. R. Elliott (Eds.), *At the threshold: The developing adolescent* (pp. 255–277). Cambridge: Harvard University Press.

Steinberg, L. D. (1981). Transformations in family relations at puberty. *Developmental Psychology, 17,* 833–840.

Stevenson, B. W., Roscoe, B., Brooks II, R. H. & Kelsey, T. (1987). Profiles of mod revivalists: A case study of a reemerging adolescent group. *Adolescence, 22,* 393–404.

Strober, M. (1981). A comparative analysis of personality organization in juvenile anorexia nervosa. *Journal of Youth and Adolescence, 10,* 285–295.

Susman, E. J., Dorn, L. D. & Chrousos, G. P. (1991). Negative hormones and affect levels in young adolescents: Concurrent and predictive perspectives. *Journal of Youth and Adolescence, 20,* 167–190.

Susman, E. J., Nottelmann, E. D., Inoff, G. E., Dorn, L. D., Cutler, G. B., Jr., Loriaux, D. L. & Chrousos, G. P. (1985). The relationship of relative hormone levels and physical development and social-emotional behavior in young adolescents. *Journal of Youth and Adolescence, 14,* 245–264.

Tanner, J. M. (1981). *A history of the study of human growth.* Cambridge, England: Cambridge University Press.

Tanner, J. M. (1978/1990). *Fetus into man: Physical growth from conception to maturity.* Cambridge: Harvard University Press.

Tedesco, L. A. & Gaier, E. L. (1988). Friendship bonds in adolescence. *Adolescence, 23,* 127–136.

Teti, D. M. & Lamb, M. E. (1989). Outcomes of adolescent marriage and adolescent childbirth. *Journal of Marriage and the Family, 51,* 203–212.

Thatcher, R. W., Walker, R. A. & Giudice, S. (1987). Human cerebral hemispheres develop at different rates and ages. *Science, 236,* 1110–1113.

Thornberry, O. T., Wilson, R. W. & Golden, P. (1986). Health promotion and disease prevention provisional data from the National Health Interview Survey: United States, January–June 1985. *Vital and Health Statistics of the National Center for Health Statistics, 119,* 1–16.

Thornton, A. & Camburn, D. (1989). Religious participation and adolescent sexual behavior. *Journal of Marriage and the Family, 51,* 641–654.

Triandis, H. C. (1990). Cross-cultural studies of individualism and collectivism. In J. J. Berman (Ed.), *Nebraska Symposium on Motivation: 1989* (Vol. 37, pp. 41–134). Lincoln: University of Nebraska Press.

Udry, J. (1988). Biological predispositions and social control in adolescent sexual behavior. *American Sociological Review, 53,* 709–722.

Udry, J. R. & Billy, J. O. G. (1987). Initiation of coitus in early adolescence. *American Sociological Review, 52,* 841–855.

Udry, J. R., Billy, J. O., Morris, N. M., Groff, T. R. & Raj, M. S. (1985). Serum androgenic hormones motivate sexual behavior in adolescent boys. *Fertility and Sterility, 43,* 90–94.

U.S. Bureau of the Census. (1992). *Statistical abstract of the United States, 1992* (112th ed.). Washington, DC: U.S. Government Printing Office.

Urberg, K. A. (1992). Locus of peer influence: Social crowd and best friend. *Journal of Youth and Adolescence, 21,* 439–450.

Urberg, K. A., Shyu, S. J. & Liang, J. (1990). Peer influence in adolescent cigarette smoking. *Addictive Behavior, 115,* 247–255.

Van Wieringen, J. C. (1978). Secular growth changes. In F. Falkner & J. M. Tanner (Eds.), *Human growth* (Vol. 2, pp. 445–473). New York: Plenum.

Vega, W. A., Zimmerman, R. S., Warheit, G. J., Apospori, E. & Gil, A. G. (1993). Risk factors for adolescent drug use in four ethnic and racial groups. *American Journal of Public Health, 83,* 185–189.

Webster, D. W., Gainer, P. S. & Champion, H. R. (1993). Weapon carrying among inner-city junior high school students: Defensive behavior vs. aggressive delinquency. *American Journal of Public Health, 83,* 1604–1608.

Wierson, M., Long, P. J. & Forehand, R. L. (1993). Toward a new understanding of early menarche: The role of environmental stress in pubertal timing. *Adolescence, 28,* 912–924.

Wolf, A. M., Gortmaker, S. L., Cheung, L., Gray, H. M., Herzog, D. B. & Colditz, G. A. (1993). Activity, in activity, and obesity: Racial, ethnic, and age differences among schoolgirls. *American Journal of Public Health, 83,* 1625–1627.

Yates, A. (1989). Current perspectives on the eating disorders: 1. History, psychological, and biological aspects. *Journal of the American Academy of Child and Adolescent Psychiatry, 28,* 813–828.

Zabin, L. C., Astone, N. M. & Emerson, M. R. (1993). Do adolescents want babies? The relationship between attitudes and behavior. *Journal of Research on Adolescence, 3,* 67–86

Zelnik, M. & Kantner, J. F. (1980). Sexual activity, contraceptive use, and pregnancy among metropolitan area teenagers: 1971–1979. *Family Planning Perspectives, 12,* 230–237.

Zuravin, S. J. (1988). Child maltreatment and teenage first births: A relationship mediated by chronic sociodemographic stress? *American Journal of Orthopsychiatry, 58,* 91–103.

CHAPTER 10

Engaged in the active resolution of the identity crisis, young people begin to shape their adult psychology. In this portrait of a young woman, we sense the balance and focus that accompanies identity achievement.

Later Adolescence (18–22 Years)

The years from 18 to 24 are characterized by heightened sensitivity to the process of identity development. Personal identity is developed as an individual struggles to answer the questions: What is the meaning of my life? Who am I? And where am I headed? Most young people are cognitively complex enough to conjure up alternative scenarios about their own future, including various kinds of work and various meaningful relationships. They struggle with the uncertainty of having to choose many of their own life's directions. This period is often characterized by a high level of anxiety. Even though most young people are energetic and capable, they are also troubled by the lack of certainty about their future. Some may worry about whether they will be able to succeed in a chosen direction; others may be anxious because they don't even know what direction they wish to take.

The historical and social contexts play key roles in shaping an individual's work on identity. In any historical period, one's choices depend on economic realities. Generally, the range of choices increases with one's economic resources, perhaps being constrained at the very top of the continuum by the obligatory roles that must be filled by the members of royal families. In addition, the range of choices is affected by historical realities like war or political revolution. In many communities in the United States, opportunities for paid employment are very limited, and many young people in the stage of later adolescence are unemployed even though they seek work. Both the content of identity and the emotions surrounding identity formation, the sense of optimism and hopefulness or suspiciousness and resentment, may be influenced by the range and kinds of opportunities that exist for education, training, and paid employment. Similarly, social and economic factors influence basic decisions regarding family formation. Decisions about whether to remain single or to marry and about whether to parent, although viewed as individual decisions, are influenced by the economic conditions of the times.

Gender socialization and sex-role orientation are influenced by historical and social factors. Currently, many societies permit much more flexibility in gender norms for both women and men, and much more information is available about the range of sex-role orientations than in the past. Increased choices about one's gender identity introduce both greater freedom and greater uncertainty than later adolescents may have faced in the 1950s, when the scripts for men and women were more narrowly defined. Encounters with prejudice and societal discrimination may close off opportunities for certain groups or impose barriers in terms of occupational and educational attainment that may shape identity either in a positive sense, by increasing motivation toward a particular goal, or in a negative sense, by forcing the person to abandon important aspirations.

Identity development in the period from 18 to 24 is a cornerstone of the unique individuality of adulthood. The work adolescents do on identity during this period is central to personality development as it plays out in adulthood. With the increase in life choices and life roles in our contemporary society, it is probably more important today than it was in the past for young people to embrace particular values, goals, and life commitments as being central to their identity. What is more, they must recognize that the process of clarifying and evaluating their values and goals will continue to be a challenge. Identity is not a firm and fixed blueprint for the rest of life. Rather, it is an orienting framework, a guide that helps shape decision-making.

Throughout adulthood, there are many opportunities to revisit earlier identity commitments. Still, the vision you create for yourself during this period remains salient. People can recall these images as they begin evaluating their adult life.

They think back to what they may have hoped for or what they may have predicted for their future when they were 18 to 24. They may be surprised by how much more they have actually accomplished or how much more pleasure they have experienced in certain roles than they ever thought they might at that age. Or they may be discouraged and disappointed to realize that some of the hopes, dreams, and goals they had for themselves turned out to be unattainable. Whatever the adult life course, the orientation established by the identity formulations of later adolescence must be reworked and extended.

Although the theme of identity development is often conceptualized within the framework of the college experience, we suggest that this process is critical for all those in the 18- to 24-year-old transition from adolescence into adult life. In fact, in the United States in 1991, only 41% of high school graduates were enrolled in college (U.S. Bureau of the Census, 1992). The majority of young people go directly to work, join the military, or enter technical training programs after high school. Unfortunately, most research on later adolescence has been limited to college students, who are a captive target for scholars of human development. However, we argue that the construct of personal identity and the related themes of one's relationship with parents, the formulation of a moral ideology, a gender identity, and a set of behaviors and goals related to work are all equally relevant to those later adolescents who do not attend college.

Developmental Tasks

Autonomy from Parents

Achieving a psychological sense of autonomy from one's parents must be understood as a multidimensional task that is accomplished gradually over the course of later adolescence and early adulthood. Autonomy is an ability to regulate one's own behavior and to select and guide one's own decisions and actions without undue control from or dependence on one's parents (Steinberg & Silverberg, 1986; Ryan & Lynch, 1989). Autonomy is not the same as rejection, alienation, or physical separation from parents. It is an independent psychological status in which parents and children accept each others' individuality. Many areas of similarity between parents and children may very well provide bonds for a continued close, supportive relationship into adulthood. However, those bonds are discovered through a process of self-definition. Adolescents who achieve autonomy can recognize and accept both the similarities and the differences between themselves and their parents without feeling totally absorbed in their parents' identity or totally alienated from their parents' love.

Autonomy requires independence of thoughts, emotions, and actions. Much of the psychosocial development that has occurred before this stage can be seen as preparing the individual for independence from his or her parents. Such skills as dressing oneself, handling money, cooking, driving a car, reading, and writing have been mastered. Although we take these skills for granted, they are essential for someone who is living independently. The physical maturation that has taken place also contributes to the possibility of autonomy. Daily survival requires a certain amount of physical strength, coordination, and endurance, qualities that arrive with the physical maturity of adolescence.

The process of identification and the accompanying internalization of values allow the person to function autonomously with a sense of what is appropriate behavior. The person's ability to leave the intimacy of the family may also be promoted by a growing involvement with the peer group. As peer relations become more reciprocal, they begin to satisfy many of the needs for closeness and support that were initially satisfied only within the boundaries of the family. Finally, the young person's cognitive maturity provides a fund of information, a level of problem-solving ability, and a capacity to plan for the future that help sustain independent living.

Within the family context, identity exploration is facilitated by an open exchange of ideas and a certain level of challenge. Adolescents must have opportunities to express their separateness within the boundaries of the family. They must feel that their parents accept and understand their need to have distinct opinions and views. Separateness is achieved within a context of mutual caring and emotional support. A secure attachment to parents, based on a perception of the parents as committed to their child's well-being, is essential for growth toward independence (Hauser et al., 1984; Grotevant & Cooper, 1985; Armsden & Greenberg, 1987).

Adolescents tend to feel comfortably independent if their parents encourage them to share in decision-making and provide explanations for the limits they set (Baumrind, 1991; Kamptner, 1988). Parents who are able to combine authoritative control with reason and frequent communication are likely to have assertive, responsible, and independent children. Either too restrictive or too permissive a pattern of parental demands seems to interfere with adolescents' ability to differentiate their value system from the values held by their parents. The clear communication of limits and expectations gives adolescents a sense of stability and confidence that appears to encourage the internalization of morality and self-reliance. Adolescents whose parents proceed in this way are confident about their values, willing to discuss problems with their parents, and, at the same time, ready to disregard parental views that appear inappropriate.

Autonomy and Leaving Home

Many later adolescents live outside their parents' homes. Living away from one's parents' household has become a symbol of independence, not only in our society but in some other cultures as well (Mitchell, Wister & Burch, 1989; DeVos, 1989). Whether young people leave home to go to college, join the military, get married, or take a job in another community, they and their parents see this step as a critical transition to adulthood.

Before about 1960, marriage was the most traditional reason for moving to a new residence, other than leaving temporarily for college or the military. Since that time, however, it has become increasingly common for adolescents and young adults to expect to live in a separate residence for some time before marriage. A survey of high school seniors in 1980 found that three-fourths expected to live on their own before marriage (Goldscheider & Goldscheider, 1987).

Parents and adolescent children have different views about the age at which children are expected to leave home. Parents tend to expect children to leave home at an older age, more closely tied to the expected age of marriage, than do adolescent children. Parents with more resources are likely to accept an earlier age of home leaving than are low-income families. In addition, parents expect daughters to live at home longer than sons, but these differences are not reflected in the expectations of the adolescents themselves. This is a potential source of family conflict. In stepfamilies, neither parents nor children are likely to expect home leaving to be related to the age of marriage. Children in these families are more likely to view leaving home as a way of becoming independent of a family

Leaving home to go to college has become a common transition in the process of achieving autonomy from parents.

environment that is not entirely comfortable (Goldscheider & Goldscheider, 1989).

Economic factors and social norms play a significant role in the timing of leaving home. In 1970, 47% of those aged 18–24 were living as the child of a householder, including students who were living in college housing during most of the year but identified their permanent residence as that of their parents; 38% were married and living in their own household. In 1991, 54% of this age group were living as the child of a householder, and only 22% were married and living in their own household. In both years, a greater percentage of females than males were married and in their own households, while a greater percentage of males than females were living with their parents (U.S. Bureau of the Census, 1992). As norms for age at marriage change, and as the costs of living independently increase, the likelihood that later adolescents will actually establish an independent household declines.

Autonomy and the College Experience

Going away to college is an intermediate move between establishing a permanent residence before marriage and living at home. The mere act of going to college does not in itself bring a sense of leaving home or psychological autonomy from parents. In fact, most students do not go very far away from home when they enter college as freshmen: 81% attend college in their home state (*Chronicle of Higher Education*, 1993). Many students continue to live at home while they attend college. Freshmen express a variety of attitudes that suggest different views about their desire to be independent from their family. For students entering college in the fall of 1992, 15% said that a very important reason for deciding to go to college was to get away from home. On the other hand, when asked about reasons

Students who attend college away from home have to take responsibility for many adult tasks—grocery shopping, laundry, paying bills, balancing a checking account, cleaning the room, and so on.

that were very important in selecting the college that they ended up attending, 24% said they wanted to live near home. In fact, as they enter college, students differ markedly in how much work they have already done toward achieving autonomy from their parents, how much they desire such autonomy, and what evidence they use to determine whether they have achieved autonomy.

When asked to tell how they knew when they had left home, college students generated eight categories of explanations (Moore & Hotch, 1981), including physical separation (moved to an apartment), emotional separation (don't feel close to the family), and personal control (make own decisions). Some students viewed leaving home as a positive experience and tied it to a sense of increased personal control. Others linked leaving home to negative feelings of emotional separation or homesickness. For most adolescents, whether they are at college or not, the process of achieving a psychological sense of independence from home includes working through feelings of separation and the loss of emotional closeness that was characteristic of an earlier period of childhood, resolving uncertainties about economic independence, facing the challenges of independent decision-making, and taking responsibility for those decisions and their consequences.

The experience of entering college focuses new attention on one's attachment relationships. An area of special interest has been the changing quality of the attachment relationship between college students and their parents as the students leave home (Bloom, 1987). Students who are living at college are more likely to rely on the mental representations of their attachment figures, whereas students who live with their parents continue to be involved daily with very concrete interactions. The issues of autonomy and control, establishing new guidelines and limits related to participation in family life, involvement in relationships with peers, and management of time and money are resolved in the absence of direct input from parents for most students who live at college, but these issues continue to involve parental input for students who live at home.

For students who live on campus, preoccupation with thoughts and concerns about one's parents tends to diminish over the course of the first semester, while new relationships form and a new confidence in one's own independent decision-making builds. The attachment scheme or representation rather than actual interactions with parents is what becomes modified. Many students who attend college away from home begin to have more positive thoughts and feelings about their parents. At the same time, they begin to detect a new level of confidence and respect from their parents, who appreciate that their children are managing to take on new responsibilities and to make good decisions on their own. Students who live at home tend to continue to be preoccupied by concerns and thoughts about their parents based on actual daily interactions, and the quality of their relationships is viewed as more conflictual (Sullivan & Sullivan, 1980; Berman & Sperling, 1991).

In addition to overall patterns of change that are characteristic of students who live at home and those who live on campus, we find evidence of individual differences in the salience of attachment issues. For example, Berman and Sperling (1991) found that college-age females tended to have higher levels of concern about their parents and were more preoccupied by thoughts of their parents than were college-age males. However, those males who showed an especially high level of concern and preoccupation with thoughts of their parents at the beginning of their freshman year were most likely to be experiencing strong feelings of depression by the end of the term. For females, high levels of attachment to parents were not linked to depression. Perhaps the male students had not fully realized the extent to which their sense of independence was sustained or supported by their parents. Upon separation, they discovered that they had relied more upon their parents for affection and support during the high school years than they had appreciated. Based on many observations of college-age students, it is clear that some are much less ready than others to embrace the demands for new levels of independence and responsibility.

The developing sense of autonomy from parents has implications for young people's relationships with other authority figures. As they become more confident about their independence, later adolescents are better able to evaluate the judgments of other authority figures. They are less likely to transfer their dependent relationship with their parents to situations that involve other authority figures. Previous infantile conceptualizations of the legitimacy and adequacy of people in positions of authority no longer suffice. Young people begin to evaluate teachers, bosses, national leaders, and other authority figures in a more mature and independent manner.

Gender Identity

Gender is a biologically based and socially defined category. The notion of a developmental task focusing on gender identity in later adolescence suggests that at this time some new and important revisions and elaborations of the child's earlier work on sex-role identification are taking place (see Chapter 7). The developmental task of forming one's gender identity reflects the need to integrate and synthesize the three basic components of gender—its biological, psychological, and social meanings—into a view of oneself as a man or a woman entering into the complex social world of adult life. The formulation of *gender identity* refers to the acquisition of a set of beliefs, attitudes, and values about oneself as a man or a woman in many areas of social life, including intimate relations, family, work, community, and religion (Giele, 1988).

The Role of Culture

The social system exists outside the person and operates independently. As we saw in Chapter 3 when we discussed *social role theory*, roles are basic building blocks of social organizations. Every organization, including a family, a workplace, a community, and a culture, can be described by its roles. For example, when we speak of the role of president or the role of father, most Americans have a common understanding of what these terms mean. In these two instances, the role of president does not necessarily refer to a male or a female, but in our country's history no woman has held the role, and the first president, George Washington, is referred to as the "father" of our country. We do not really have a "mother" of our country, unless it was Martha Washington, since she was George's wife. In another culture, people may not understand the concept of *president* at all, or they may view a president as an elected official and may not attach the gender-linked connotations associated with the role in the United States. In most cultures, there is a term for "father" which is gender-based, but the people who are referred to as fathers may differ widely from one society to another.

Individuals learn the roles of their social system throughout their lives. Through the socialization process, individuals internalize the expectations associated with many life roles and apply the socially shared norms and standards linked to these roles to their own behaviors. This process occurs with respect to gender-related roles as well as to kinship, age, occupation, and other socially constructed roles. For example, when a person becomes a parent, a male is called a father and a female is called a mother. Both are parenting roles, but gender is identified, and each gender-linked parental role is associated with somewhat different role expectations.

All cultures construct gender-differentiated roles. People in each culture expect one another to behave in certain ways because they are male or female. Perhaps more important, they form expectations of how men and women ought to act when they are together so that the distinctions between the genders are demarcated (Freud, 1994). These expectations are taught and learned, beginning very early in life. A dominant cultural practice in the United States is the circumcision of male babies. Roughly 70% of U.S. male infants are circumcised (Turner & Rubinson, 1993). This practice reflects beliefs about health care, parental desires for a child to resemble his father, and, for some groups, a religious rite signifying the obligations of manhood. In other societies, practices involving female genital circumcision translate expectations regarding the appropriate and valued qualities of women into physical realities:

> A girl, sometimes as young as an infant, has all or part of her external genitalia removed. That can mean excision of the clitoris and the labia minora. Then the surgeon—who typically isn't a doctor—scrapes the sides of the labia majora and stitches together the vulva with a thread or thorns, all while the girls are awake or held down. The purpose, dating to ancient Egypt: to ensure virginity and eliminate sexual sensation, thereby making women marriageable. The procedure is widespread in Africa and practiced in the Middle East and Southeast Asia as well; estimates say 85 to 114 million women, mostly Muslim, have endured some form of it. With increased emigration from Africa, even some women in the United States have had the procedure; it's not illegal, though two congresswomen introduced legislation in October [1993] to ban it. (Kaplan, 1993, p. 124)

In the United States many people argue that gender-based role distinctions are inappropriate, at least as part of public life. Men and women should be considered equal and treated identically in all public matters. But in many cultures there are very extreme, agreed-upon norms prescribing differences between males and females. Often these norms establish specific power differences as part of the gender distinctions. Typically men have more power and women less, but this is not always the case.

Others argue that men and women should be considered equal, but that they should be treated in ways that take into account differences in their needs and capacities. For example, a recent bill introduced in Congress requires that all public places such as auditoriums, stadiums, and theaters have twice as many public bathroom facilities for women as for men to take into account the physiological differences in women's elimination practices.

In the United States, and in many other industrialized nations, we are currently engaged in a wide-ranging dialogue about the scientific, legal, and sociohistorical bases of gender roles that is leading to a revision, perhaps even a revolution, in how gender serves as an organizing social structure. While this dialogue takes place across many groups and in many contexts, there is still powerful pressure on young people to achieve their own personal gender identity. Although they may be influenced by certain voices and views in the larger society, later adolescents must decide for themselves about the meaning they will make of their own designation as a male or a female.

Gender-Linked Expectations

In later adolescence, biological, psychological, and social systems produce heightened activity in the area of gender identity formulations. The person is learning about bodily feelings and psychological states that are relevant to sexual activity.

Psychologically, a person wrestles with what it means in his or her culture and in general to be a man or a woman. The knowledge base regarding the implications and consequences of gender for each individual broadens as new understanding about adult roles is acquired. The person's specific social system or social convoy operates to engage the individual by making demands for various degrees and amounts of gender-linked behavior. Gender-role expectations exist at the cultural, institutional, interpersonal, and individual levels. Yet individuals play a part in learning and accepting these expectations and synthesizing them with their own private assessments of their personal needs and goals.

A Reevaluation of Gender Constancy

Each of the components of sex-role identification discussed in Chapter 7 undergoes some transformation as work on gender identity continues. First, later adolescents can appreciate that the use of gender labels is a social convention and that, apart from the genital basis of this label, there are wide individual differences within gender groups in most traits and abilities. What is more, information about genetic anomalies as well as medical technologies may lead later adolescents to realize that it is possible to have a conflict between one's genetic gender and one's external genitalia. The possibility of a sex-change operation provides an alternative to the notion of gender constancy. In other words, later adolescents may realize that gender is not quite as fixed and constant as they may have believed when they were children.

Learning New Sex-Role Standards and Reevaluating Old Ones

The content of sex-role standards—that is, the cultural and subcultural expectations concerning the appropriate behavior of males and females—is different for later adolescents than for young children. The content changes as a

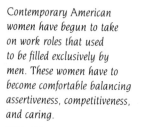

Contemporary American women have begun to take on work roles that used to be filled exclusively by men. These women have to become comfortable balancing assertiveness, competitiveness, and caring.

result of changing age-related expectations, and also as a result of social change. For a 6- or 7-year-old boy, it may have been important to learn to be independent, to stand up for himself, and not to hit little girls. For a later adolescent male, the sex-role expectations may include holding a steady job, demonstrating sexual prowess, or being competitive. For a 6- or 7-year-old girl, the emphasis may have been on taking turns, not being too bossy, and staying clean. For a later adolescent female, sex-role expectations may focus on being a caring, supportive friend; expressing maternal, nurturant behavior; or having an attractive figure and knowing how to dress well.

In later adolescence, both males and females begin to develop an analysis of what it takes to "get ahead" in their social world, whether success is defined as finding a mate, getting a good job, being a good parent, or being popular with and admired by the opposite sex. They may learn to be more flexible in their interpersonal behavior, modifying their strategy to suit their goals. They learn that traits such as assertiveness, goal-directed behavior, competitiveness, being a good communication partner, personal disclosure, and negotiation are all required in social situations, and they learn to develop and apply those traits as required. In previous generations, some of the traits mentioned above were considered masculine and some feminine. Today, they are perceived as traits that help both men and women succeed in work and family.

Sex-role standards may very well change over the 10-year period from a person's early-school-age years to his or her later adolescence. For example, mothers of daughters who were born in the 1970s may have emphasized early autonomy training and encouraged self-reliance, believing that their daughters were more likely to remain single longer and have nontraditional career expectations in which they would need to compete effectively with men. However, these girls, coming into their adulthood in the 1990s, are entering adulthood in a period when many of the "traditionally feminine" qualities, such as good interpersonal skills, the capacity for empathy, and the ability to build bonds of connection with others, are making a fashionable comeback, not just at home but in industry and global affairs, and not just for women but for men as well.

This change occurred as a result of the reexamination of socially imposed gender-role standards, leading to a reconfiguration of the traits and characteristics that are thought to be related to masculinity or femininity. Today, it is recognized that it benefits both male and female workers to be appropriately assertive, and that it benefits both male and female workers to be sensitive communicators.

Rigid expectations have been relaxed and replaced by a greater diversity of behavior that is considered acceptable for both men and women in our society. The greatest impact of this revision is on the later adolescent population as they formulate their gender identities. There are more options, choices, and goals, and there are fewer obstacles to expressing personal preferences. For some people, however, this lack of clarity about sex-role standards may lead to pathological, confused, or otherwise inappropriate behavior.

Revising One's Childhood Identifications

The component of parental identifications that contributes to gender identity is also reviewed and revised in later adolescence. During this time, young people begin to encounter a wide range of possible targets for identification. Within the college environment, students meet teachers, residence-hall counselors, and older students whose views and values may differ widely from those of their parents. Outside the college environment, workers meet supervisors, other workers, and social companions whose views and values differ widely from those of their parents. In addition, later adolescents may admire public figures, such as religious leaders, political leaders, artists, or scholars whose work and ideas are especially inspiring. In the process, later adolescents revisit the content of their parental identifications. They analyze those beliefs, attitudes, and values that they may have "swallowed whole" as children, evaluating which of their childhood beliefs are still relevant to their own personal vision of themselves functioning as a man or a woman in their current situation. They try to determine whether the lessons they learned as children about how husbands and wives, fathers and mothers, men and women, treat each other and think about each other remain applicable.

Adding a Sexual Dimension to Gender Identity

In addition to revisions in parental identifications, later adolescents must add a sexual dimension to their gender identity that did not play much of a part in their childhood gender-role identifications. The biological changes of puberty must be incorporated into one's gender identity. Adolescents must integrate an adult body into their self-concept. They become aware of their bodies as they experience changes in body shape, height, weight, and strength. Notions of physical attractiveness become more salient. Adolescents are aware that first impressions are based on physical appearance. Satisfaction with one's physical appearance provides an important basis for approaching social relations with a positive, optimistic outlook (Lerner, 1985; Rauste-von Wright, 1989). It may influence one's attractiveness or initial desirability as a sexual partner. Dissatisfaction with one's physical appearance, as integrated into the self-concept, may interfere with the formation of positive social relationships, causing the person to approach interpersonal contacts with self-consciousness and a pessimistic expectation that he or she will be rejected.

The hormonal changes of puberty bring new sexual impulses as well as the capacity for reproduction. Hormonal changes stimulate changes in the basis of relationships. These changes call attention to new emotions, such as jealousy, love, depression over loss of love, sexual arousal, and passion. Individual differences in hormone levels, especially testosterone, are linked to sex-role characteristics. In particular, high levels of testosterone production are associated with aggressiveness in males, with strong needs for achievement and independence in females, and with high levels of sexual energy in both males and females. Women

Pablo Picasso, Girl Before Mirror, 1932. *The crystallization of gender identity requires the integration of one's sexuality, including physical appearance, primary and secondary sex characteristics, and sexual drives and fantasies. One's sexual identity is as much a mental representation as a physical reality.*

who have high levels of testosterone describe themselves as robust, resourceful, impulsive, and unconventional (Baucom, Besch & Callahan, 1985). Maturation of the hormonal system, which influences emotional arousal as well as sexual urges, contributes to the development of one's gender identity.

Finalizing Gender-Role Preference

Finally, new work is done in the area of gender-role preference. Preference is based on an assessment of two factors: how well one can meet the cultural and social expectations associated with one's gender and how positively one views the status associated with one's gender. Think about what it means when white males make claims of "reverse discrimination." They are saying that the power differential between white males as members of a privileged, powerful group and women and minority males has been reversed. If later adolescents become aware that their gender prevents them from having access to resources, influence, and decision-making authority, they are likely to experience a decline in their gender-role preference. This could happen to males as well as females, depending on the paths they choose to pursue and the gender biases they encounter. For example, although we tend to think of career aspirations as being stifled for women as a result of attitudes on the part of men that women are simply not suited to a certain type of work, the reverse situation may apply to men who are interested in fields such as early-childhood education or nursing.

If later adolescents perceive that, apart from real differences in ability, one gender group is treated with greater respect, is given more opportunities, and is responded to with more attention or greater rewards, then their sex-role preferences are likely to be recalibrated. In our own experience, it appears that college students do not see much of this type of gender discrimination or gender prefer-ence. They tend to see the college environment as providing plenty of opportuni-ties and equal access to resources for males and females. What is more, both males and females feel equally oppressed by the stress of the demands and the uncertainty of the decisions they are trying to make. It is often not until they enter the world of adult employment that they begin to experience the power differen-tial that continues to operate to the benefit of white men in our society.

Those who enter the world of work at the end of high school are confronted by the power differential immediately. In addition, they may experience intimida-tion that forces them to accept the power differential. For example, a woman who makes two dollars per hour less than a male counterpart may be afraid to say any-thing because she needs the job. She will have to integrate the reality of what she experiences into the formulation of her gender identity. One strategy is to accept that this is the way things should be according to gender-role norms. Women should defer to men, and their contributions should be treated as less worthwhile. Another strategy may be to look for a different kind of work in a work setting where women and men are treated equally. While the college population tends to set the trends in according more variety and less rigidity to gender-linked role expecta-tions, the noncollege population has moved ahead in breaking down barriers in many male-dominated areas of work, such as construction, trucking, and public safety.

In the United States, there are currently wide variations in attitudes about gender-linked roles, and later adolescents are likely to encounter conflicting expectations regarding gender-role standards. The more diverse the community, the more likely the young person is to encounter contrasting views about what adult men and women ought to be like. The gender-linked expectations one expe-riences in face-to-face interactions provide a good deal of the content of sex-role standards. For later adolescents, a larger number of friends are available to help work out the conflicts related to sexual behavior and other gender issues (Levitt, Weber & Guacci, 1993). To an extent, individuals can shape and strengthen the nature of their gender identity by spending time with other people who support their views and values about how men and women ought to behave toward one another and what life paths are most desirable for males and females. Most stud-ies find that, during the college years, students become more flexible in their gen-der-role attitudes and more egalitarian in their views about how men and women ought to function in school, work, family, and community life (Pascarella & Terenzini, 1991).

Internalized Morality

The development of morality was introduced in Chapter 7, "Early School Age." At that stage, morality consists primarily of internalizing parental standards and val-ues, recognizing the difference between right and wrong, and learning to control one's behavior in anticipation of its moral consequences. As young people achieve a new level of autonomy from their parents and encounter new situations, they undoubtedly discover that some of the moral principles they learned as 6- or 7-year-olds neither apply to the new situations nor provide much of a rationale for why they should behave one way and not another. Later adolescents begin to clar-ify the distinction between social conventions and moral issues. Behaviors that may have been viewed as moral issues during childhood may be reevaluated as social conventions. As with some aspects of identification with parents or other

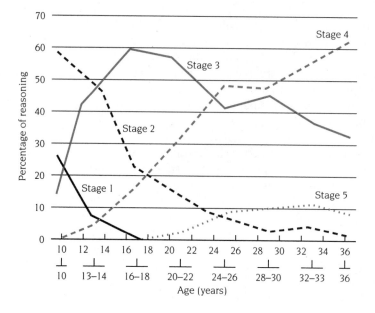

FIGURE 10.1

Mean percentage of male subjects in eight age groups who demonstrated five stages of moral reasoning
Source: *Colby, Kohlberg, Gibbs & Lieberman, 1983.*

authorities, some aspects of childhood morality must be dissolved and restructured to meet the impending demands of adulthood.

New Cognitive Capacities

Later adolescents bring new cognitive capacities to the arena of moral decision-making. They are more aware than younger children of the actual and possible consequences of their actions, both for themselves and for others. They are able to consider the multiple perspectives that are possible in a moral situation. They are increasingly aware of the rights and needs of others, and they are able to step outside the situation in order to examine how an action may satisfy their own needs but harm others. They are concerned about how principles of social responsibility, human rights, and justice can be preserved in a moral decision.

Lawrence Kohlberg (1964, 1969; Colby & Kohlberg, 1987) suggested that a qualitative change in a person's ability to identify moral issues and decide about moral behavior is expected from early school age to later adolescence. Kohlberg's theory of the development of moral thought includes three levels of moral reasoning, divided into six substages (see Chapter 7, Table 7.3).

At the preconventional level, from about ages 4 to 10, the child is concerned about the external consequences of behavior and about the power of those who represent authority. The conventional level, from about ages 10 to 18, represents a concern about the maintenance of the existing rule structure and a respect for authority. The postconventional level of moral reasoning includes an awareness of the social conventions that result in the formulation of rules and laws. From this perspective one can appreciate the cultural relativism of values and a commitment to either a personal or a universal set of moral principles including greater concern about matters of justice. The proportion of people who reach this level of moral reasoning is small, but it increases during early and middle adulthood.

Longitudinal data provide strong evidence of the sequential nature of these stages during childhood and adolescence. Figure 10.1 shows age trends in the use of moral reasoning among 58 male subjects who participated in a study for more than 20 years (Colby et al., 1983). Preconventional reasoning (Stages 1 and 2) was dominant in the youngest subjects, but it declined sharply between ages 10 and 14. Conventional reasoning (Stages 3 and 4) increased from age 10 on, became the dominant form of reasoning in early and later adolescence, and remained the dominant form of reasoning throughout the years of adulthood studied, with Stage 4 reasoning surpassing Stage 3 in the mid-20s. Postconventional reasoning (Stage 5) did not appear until age 18, then increased somewhat, but remained relatively rare in the period studied. These findings support the notion that the stages are reached in the sequence predicted. Other studies have confirmed the order of the stages and that subjects do not skip stages (Nisan & Kohlberg, 1982; Snarey, Reimer & Kohlberg, 1985; Colby & Kohlberg, 1987).

Individuals understand moral arguments at their own dominant level of reasoning or below, but not more than one step higher (Walker, 1982; Walker, de Vries & Bichard, 1984). Through participation in thought-provoking discussions, moral reasoning can advance to the next higher level (Berkowitz & Gibbs, 1983). Social and educational experiences tend to promote moral reasoning when they draw on existing constructs and also challenge those constructs by making their inadequacies clear (Gfellner, 1986). During later adolescence, young people are exposed to a broader social context at work, in their college courses, or through greater involvement in community and national affairs. To the extent that these experiences promote participation in open discussions about differing points of view and a more complex analysis of the many interdependent factors that contribute to the social order, young people are likely to have a new insight into moral situations (Mason & Gibbs, 1993).

The sequence of stages proposed by Kohlberg is noted in a variety of cultures outside the United States. Research has been done in Israel, Turkey, the Bahamas, Honduras, Mexico, India, Kenya, Nigeria, and Taiwan. The subjects in these studies used forms of reasoning similar to those used by American samples. The adults and adolescents in every culture used levels of reasoning that were higher than those used by the children (Nisan & Kohlberg, 1982; Rest, 1983; Snarey et al., 1985; Colby & Kohlberg, 1987). Although the sequence of stages appears to be well established, the level of moral reasoning that any individual actually attains depends on the kinds of moral challenges and situations the person encounters. For college students, encounters with the academic curriculum itself often create a degree of cognitive disequilibrium that promotes a revision in moral reasoning:

> "I was taking a theology class as a freshman in college and was presented with 'bold' alternatives to understand and interpret the creation story—primarily to understand it as a myth. My life up to that point was characterized by asking many questions but arriving at few answers. To those in my fundamentalist background, those questions were annoyances but not unsurmountable problems. In my shift to some answers to those questions, I moved away from fundamentalism to a more broadly based and responsible manner of critical thinking." [What happened?] "The professor was very bright and responsible, yet in a sophisticated way he was somewhat irreverent. I was troubled by the dilemmas that this posed for me in terms of my belief structures, but something about the information and the self-assurance of the professor encouraged me to embrace this new way of thinking." (Chickering & Reisser, 1993, p. 240)

Exposure to a diversity of information, relationships, and worldviews stimulates moral reasoning. The change from conventional to postconventional morality that begins during adolescence involves a rethinking of traditional moral principles. During this period, there may be a loosening of ties to the family of origin and an increase in encounters with an expanding network of friends, students,

Exposure to a diversity of opinions and values stimulates a new independence of thought that is sometimes expressed in protest against rules or administrative decisions that students consider unfair.

and co-workers. Through interactions with diverse reference groups, there is an increasing recognition of the subcultural relativity of one's moral code. There may also be a degree of conflict over which moral values have personal meaning.

Kohlberg's view of moral development has been challenged on a number of fronts. One criticism is that his picture of moral reasoning is based on a specific method, one in which individuals are asked to reach judgments about a particular type of moral dilemma. In Kohlberg's moral judgment interview, the dilemmas involve a *prohibitive moral judgment*, a decision about violating a law or breaking a promise in order to achieve some other goal. A typical example is the case of Heinz, a man who is placed in the dilemma of having to steal a drug from a pharmacist if he is to save his wife's life. *Prosocial moral judgments* involve a conflict between doing something helpful for someone else and meeting one's own needs. An example would be stopping to help a person whose car has stalled on the highway at the risk of being late for a very important job interview. People seem to be able to think more flexibly about a prosocial dilemma than about a prohibitive one. Moral decisions that draw on empathy and concern for the well-being of another person tend to evoke a higher level of moral reasoning than those that would require breaking a law (Kurdek, 1981; Eisenberg & Strayer, 1987).

Others point out that the level of moral reasoning is influenced largely by the situational context in which the dilemma is posed. For example, in one study, subjects were asked to resolve dilemmas involving situations related to the sale of a business and a community's position related to the free trade agreement between the United States and Canada (Carpendale & Krebs, 1992). Responses to these situations were compared to responses to the typical Kohlberg dilemmas. The responses to the Kohlberg dilemmas were more consistent, while the responses to the business dilemmas covered a wide range. The business dilemmas evoked a form of moral reasoning that was imbedded in a somewhat different ethic from the dilemmas focused on interpersonal conflicts or conflicts related to abstract situations in which a law might be broken. The business scenarios produced responses reflecting the profit motive and the need to protect one's business, one's employees, and one's power base. The implication is that mature moral reasoning takes into account the situational framework in which the dilemma is posed as well as the range of justifications available for taking one stance or another.

A third controversy in the field of moral reasoning focuses on whether women and men approach ethical decision-making differently. Carol Gilligan (1977, 1982) introduced a major challenge to Kohlberg's perspective, arguing that Kohlberg's description of the developmental course of reasoning about moral dilemmas is incomplete because it is based largely on the reasoning of male subjects about hypothetical rather than real-life situations. She claimed that men and women have distinctive orientations toward moral dilemmas. Women approach moral decisions with greater sensitivity to the context of the problem and a strong sense of caring, focusing on one's responsibility for others and one's feelings of connection to others. Men emphasize abstract principles, rules and laws, and the conflicts between the rights of the parties involved in the conflict. A woman, for example, might ask which outcome of a moral dilemma would result in the least harm for all concerned; a man might ask whether one person has the right to infringe on the rights of others (Friedman, Robinson & Friedman, 1987). These differences, according to Gilligan, are the product of different socialization patterns and result in different orientations to values, family life, and the basis of self-worth.

Several investigators have examined the claims of consistent differences between men and women in moral orientation. The literature is inconclusive regarding the strength and consistency with which men and women differ in their use of what have come to be called the *justice orientation* and the *caring orientation*. It appears that experiential and situational issues, as well as concerns about interpersonal obligations and caring, are more dominant in open-ended responses from both men and women than are issues of justice and individual rights (Ford & Lowery, 1986; Walker, de Vries & Trevethan, 1987; Galotti, 1989). Gilligan and Attanucci (1988) found that 53 of 80 subjects could be characterized by one orientation or the other, while the remaining subjects used both orientations, neither one playing a dominant role. However, males were more likely to use the justice orientation, and females dominated among those showing a caring orientation. The females were more varied in their moral orientations than the males. Walker (1989) devised a typology of four moral orientations: *normative*, stressing duty and adherence to rules and role expectations; *fairness*, emphasizing liberty, equity, equality, and reciprocity in relationships; *utilitarianism*, accentuating the relevance of one's actions to one's own happiness and to the welfare of others; and *perfectionism*, underscoring the principles of dignity, good conscience, and harmony between self and others. The first two were expected to be used more by males and the latter two by females. No gender differences were found in the use of these four themes; however, the older subjects showed a greater use of fairness and perfectionism, while their use of normative and utilitarian reasoning declined.

In a cross-sectional study of 8th-graders, 11th-graders, and college sophomores, students were asked to describe their moral reasoning strategies (Galotti, Kozberg & Farmer, 1991). The instructions were as follows: When faced with a moral dilemma, what issues or concerns influence your decision? In this context, a moral dilemma was defined as "a situation in which different things that you

TABLE 10.1   Themes That Guide Moral Decisions
Title and Description of Theme
What Others Would Think/Feel: Whether subject (S) consults others, or imagines others in a similar situation, to make a decision.
Effect on Others: Whether S considers the possible benefit or harm to other people in making the decision.
Situation Specifics: Whether S makes explicit references to the decision "depending on the situation."
Effect on Self: Whether S considers the possible benefit or harm to himself or herself in making the decision, including personal guilt, social reaction.
What I Feel: Whether S mentions "intuition" or "gut feeling" in making a decision or mentions "how I would feel." Emphasis on feeling.
Religious Teachings: Whether S considers formal religious teachings (e.g., the Bible, the Talmud) or reasons from experience in an organized religion (to be distinguished from "conscience" or "personal sense of right and wrong").
Greater Societal Good: Whether S refers explicitly to the concerns of society in general or to the "greatest good."
Legal Issues: Whether S refers to local, state, or federal laws.
Personal Code of Ethics: Whether S makes explicit references to a personal set of moral values or ethics, or to a personal sense of right and wrong, or to specific principles that are valued most highly; the values of the issues to S; the principles by which S was raised.
Systematic Reasoning: Whether S describes trying to reason logically, systematically, without being affected by mood or emotion. If S uses some of the following phrases: "weigh the pros and cons," "gathered all the facts," "think it through" "look at all the possibilities."
Rights of Others: Whether S explicitly mentions the (legal, personal, or moral) rights of other people (to be distinguished from the benefits or harm to people; see "Effect on Others," above).
Source: Galotti, Kozberg & Farmer, 1991.

value come into conflict." Eleven themes were identified from these essays (see Table 10.1). Females used more themes in their essays than did males, and the number of themes included in the essays increased with age. Only two themes showed a clear gender difference, females showing more use of "What Others Would Think" and "Effect on Self." The study found that reasoning based on the moral themes typically associated with a caring orientation was consistently more common than reasoning based on the themes associated with noncontextual, abstract reasoning at all ages, but that, with age, both males and females added more autonomous, justice-oriented reasoning to their repertoire.

Later adolescents must evolve an integrated, mature value system with which to guide their behavior, particularly in the face of strong pressures to violate their moral beliefs. Young people encounter situations that they have never faced before—situations that require moral evaluation, judgment, and decisions about action. A student may be asked by a college peer to lend a paper that he has written. A young woman may be invited to spend the weekend at a male friend's apartment. A young person may be asked to engage in direct and violent political acts to demonstrate acceptance of a cause. Decisions about maintaining religious traditions and practices may confront a young person who is away from home. In each of these situations, the person may not be aware of or may not be able to assess the immediate consequences of her or his behavior. Decisions must be based on an internalized set of moral principles and values that will help the person to evaluate the demands of the situation and plan the course of action that will be most congruent with her or his personal ideals.

Career Choice

The choice of occupation sets the tone for the early adult lifestyle. The world of work determines one's daily routine, including the time one wakes up, one's daily activities, expenditures of physical and mental energy, and conditions for both immediate and long-term rewards. Occupation confers social status and provides varying opportunities for advancement. Finally, occupation represents a direct or indirect expression of one's value system. In subsequent chapters, we will discuss socialization in the work setting and the management of a career. Here we focus on the process of career choice and its impact on development during later adolescence.

Work Experiences in Early Adolescence

Many adolescents hold part-time jobs while they attend high school. In 1991, roughly 40% of 16- and 17-year-olds were in the labor force (U.S. Bureau of the Census, 1992). By the time they have graduated from high school, only about 7% of high school seniors say they have never worked for pay (Bachman, Johnston & O'Malley, 1987). There is some controversy about the benefits of working during high school and the extent to which these work experiences actually make a positive contribution to the occupational component of identity development. Some find that adolescents who work long hours in stressful jobs are more likely to evidence increased cigarette smoking, marijuana and alcohol use, truancy, and poor academic performance in school (Steinberg & Dornbusch, 1991; Manning, 1990; Bachman, Bare & Frankie, 1986). Students who work long hours have less time for school activities, socialization with friends, or the development of other areas of interest. The kinds of work opportunities that are available to adolescents are usually minimally skilled jobs with high turnover, low pay, little decision-making responsibility, and little stimulation of skill development. These kinds of jobs are likely to produce depression and low self-esteem and may contribute to feelings of alienation from the school environment. For some adolescents, time spent in these kinds of work settings is associated with the development of cynical attitudes toward work and greater acceptance of unethical practices by workers.

Other researchers emphasize the diversity of work experiences and the potential benefits of certain kinds of work. Students who are able to find and keep a good job may feel more confident about themselves and their promise for future employment (Bachman et al., 1986). When the work does not involve too many hours, and when it involves skill development that young people see as related to their future career direction, the experience is likely to be associated with higher levels of well-being and less involvement in problem behaviors. For girls, the perception of continuity between school and work, feeling that work improves one's school performance, had an especially positive relationship with mental health and well-being (Mortimer et al., 1992).

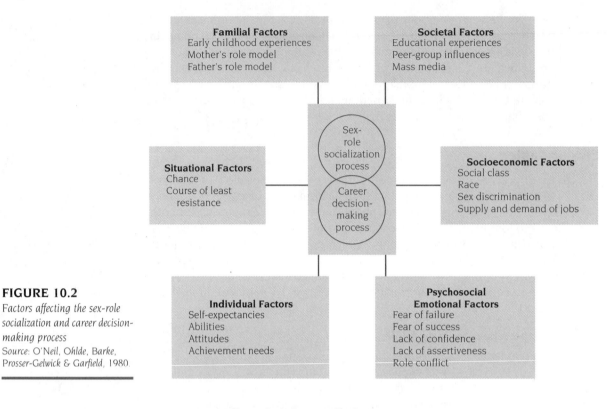

FIGURE 10.2

Factors affecting the sex-role socialization and career decision-making process

Source: O'Neil, Ohlde, Barke, Prosser-Gelwick & Garfield, 1980.

Factors Influencing Career Choice

As Figure 10.2 suggests, the process of career decision-making is influenced by six major factors: individual, psychosocial-emotional, socioeconomic, societal, familial, and situational (O'Neil et al., 1980). These same factors contribute to sex-role socialization. It is important to see the interrelationship of these two domains for young people in our culture. Sex-role socialization creates a powerful filter through which choices related to career development are made (Eccles, 1987).

Of the six types of factors described in Figure 10.2, high school and college students reported that the individual factors, such as abilities, interests, attitudes, and self-expectancies, most strongly affected their career decision-making. They perceived familial, societal, and socioeconomic factors as having little or no impact (O'Neil et al., 1980). This is contrary to the social science research, which provides extensive evidence that family factors play a key role in shaping educational aspirations and occupational goals, while societal and socioeconomic conditions are major factors influencing the job market and the chances of both employment and advancement.

Education and Career Choice   One of the major factors influencing career opportunities is education. It is well documented that career advancement and associated earnings are closely linked to levels of educational attainment. Table 10.2 shows the median earned income on the basis of educational level for men and women who were 25 years old or older in 1990. There is no question that continued education beyond high school is a key element in the career development process. As the data indicate, however, educational achievement does not result in the same economic advantages for men and women. Women with one to three years of college earned less than men who had only a high school diploma.

TABLE 10.2   Median Income of Men and Women 25 Years and Older, 1990, by Educational Attainment

Education	Median Annual Income ($)	
	Men	Women
1–3 years of high school: no diploma	20,902	14,429
High school graduate	26,653	18,319
1–3 years of college: no degree	31,734	22,227
5 years or more of college, college graduate— possible professional degree	49,304	33,750

Source: National Center for Education Statistics, 1992.

For youths who leave high school or who graduate from high school but do not go on to college, the job market has several unattractive features. Most of the jobs available at this level of educational attainment are

> routine, menial, temporary, more likely to be part time and to provide reduced monetary and nonmaterial rewards compared with jobs held by older workers. . . . Moreover, jobs within this sector are unusually unstable and may be supervised by rigid, autocratic employers, many of whom, particularly in the fast food industry, are not much older than the novice worker. (Borman & Hopkins, 1987, p. 136)

The impact of school experiences on subsequent career development goes beyond whether or not one plans to attend college. Vocational coursework of a specific nature, such as agricultural training, an emphasis on math and science courses, and frequent conversations with teachers about one's work-related decisions, are all associated with higher income and more stable work records after high school (Hubner-Funk, 1983; Griffin & Alexander, 1978).

For youths who do not go on to college, career development appears to have two phases (Freeman & Wise, 1982; West & Newton, 1983). Given the kinds of jobs that are available and the outlook on work that was developed during high school, many young people start out with a rather cavalier approach to work. They take whatever job is available, work without much intention of long-term commitment, and exhibit erratic work behavior. Most of these jobs do not require much training and do not lead to a career. Young people are likely to quit these jobs when they have earned enough money to pay for the things they want and then remain unemployed for a while until they need more money. During their 20s, the second phase begins as young adults become more serious about their work. They try to find a good job, they become more conscientious about their work performance, and they stay with the job for a longer period. This new seriousness about work is likely to be associated with other commitments, especially marriage, and is usually seen as a positive step in the transition to adulthood.

In modern, post-industrialized societies, the path toward occupational attainment is intimately linked to educational aspirations and achievements expressed in high school. In a longitudinal study of students who were high school seniors in 1980, 36% of those who said they hoped to earn a bachelor's degree had done so by 1986. In comparison, only 7% of those who expected to attend less than four years of college had earned a bachelor's degree by 1986 (National Center for Education Statistics, 1992). In a more detailed longitudinal study of Swedish

Job choices are quite restricted for young people who do not graduate from high school or who have no postsecondary technical training.

females, a similar pattern could be seen (Gustafson, Stattin & Magnusson, 1992). One group of young women, about 41% of the sample, had high educational motivation at age 15. After completing their compulsory secondary schooling, these women attended 2 to 5 years of advanced education leading to a career, and had no children by age 26. The other large group, 28% of the sample, had low educational motivation at age 15, did not go on to advanced education, and did have their own children by age 26. These groups did not differ by parental socioeconomic status or by measured IQ. The authors concluded that, even though women may say that they endorse the idea of combining work and family roles, most women begin to develop aspirations and attitudes during early adolescence that lead to the crystallization of a "homemaker" or "career" orientation that is played out in young adulthood.

Gender-Role Socialization and Career Choice   Gender-role socialization shapes career decisions through two significant psychological factors. First, as a result of socialization, men and women are likely to form different expectations about their ability to succeed in various career-related skills. Second, as a result of socialization, women and men are likely to establish different value hierarchies, reflecting different views of long-range life goals and their relative importance to one another (Eccles, 1987).

Self-expectancies about the ability to fulfill the educational requirements and the job duties of specific careers are a major factor in determining career choices (Bridges, 1988; Long, 1989). In studies of career choice or career aspirations among women, those with a strong sense of their own goals, an awareness of their personal needs, and an ability to cope realistically with stress have been more likely to adopt a nontraditional career choice (Nevill & Schlecker, 1988; Long, 1989). In one study, college students were asked to evaluate their ability to complete the educational requirements and fulfill the job duties of ten traditionally male occupations and ten traditionally female occupations (Betz & Hackett, 1981). Males reported higher self-efficacy on five "male" occupations: accountant, draftsman, engineer, highway patrol officer, and mathematician. Females reported higher self-efficacy on five "female" occupations: dental hygienist, elementary-school teacher, home economist, physical therapist, and secretary. Males thought that the most difficult job duties of the 20 occupations listed were those of art teacher. Females thought the most difficult duties were those of engineer. These differences in expectations about the ability to succeed were not paralleled by differences in the students' ability tests in math or English, which might have made certain career choices unrealistic. These data suggest that in the process of career decision making, strong sex-typed conceptualizations of the job demands of specific careers intervene to screen out some alternatives and highlight others.

Gender identity influences attitudes and values that determine one's career goals and related choices. In a study of the educational and occupational attainment of low-income, rural, Appalachian females, the importance of family socialization influences was highlighted (Wilson, Peterson & Wilson, 1993). Appalachian families living in rural areas tend to have strong family ties and high levels of consensus about norms for appropriate behaviors. Families tend to endorse what have been called traditional gender roles, in which the men are the dominant decision-makers and the women are expected to be homemakers while taking on low-paying jobs to help support the family. Educational and occupational aspirations are generally higher for male than for female children in these families, but both male and female children are encouraged to restrict their aspirations to career options that will keep them close to their childhood homes. In the study cited, one of the most important factors associated with a young Appalachian woman's educational and occupational attainment was her father's level of education. The more schooling the fathers had, the higher the family's expectations for their daughters' educational attainment, and the higher the daughters' own educational and occupational aspirations.

The consequences of gender-role socialization for career choice can be seen in the objectives that freshmen entering college in 1992 said were essential or very important in their lives (see Table 10.3). Although men and women shared many common objectives, about 11% more women than men endorsed social values, 20% more women emphasized helping others who were in difficulty, and 8% more women than men expressed concern about helping to promote racial understanding. About 5% more men than women endorsed being very well off financially, and 10% more men than women valued becoming successful in their own business (*Chronicle of Higher Education*, 1993). Values are likely to direct students toward majors and future careers that will help them experience a sense of personal integrity, a balance between what they say is important and what they do.

The impact of values is demonstrated by a study of the factors that are most salient to college men and women in choosing a major (Hearn, 1980; Hearn & Olzak, 1981). In their choice of major, men are less influenced by the supportive climate and quality of instruction. They tend to choose majors that appear to be linked with a high postgraduate payoff in career status or salary despite the less favorable atmosphere that may be associated with such majors. Women are more likely to consider the quality of the department's student-teacher interaction and student-centered orientation. The irony of this distinction is that internal supportiveness tends to be negatively related to high-status rewards. The decision of male students to choose high-status rewards and of female students to choose a

TABLE 10.3 Life Objectives Considered Essential or Very Important by College Freshmen		
Objective	**Men (%)**	**Women (%)**
Becoming accomplished in a performing art	10.3	10.7
Becoming an authority in own field	69.9	67.2
Obtaining recognition from colleagues for contributions to field	55.5	54.6
Influencing the political structure	21.9	18.5
Influencing social values	37.2	48.4
Raising a family	69.0	71.9
Having administrative responsibility for the work of others	42.2	40.4
Being very well off financially	75.8	70.7
Helping others who are in difficulty	52.3	71.9
Making a theoretical contribution to science	20.7	15.8
Writing original works	12.6	12.1
Creating artistic work	12.4	11.7
Becoming successful in own business	47.7	37.4
Becoming involved in programs to clean up environment	32.4	34.6
Developing a meaningful philosophy of life	44.0	46.8
Participating in a community-action prog4ram	22.0	29.6
Helping to promote racial understanding	37.5	45.8
Keeping up to date with political affairs	31.9	29.7

Source: Based on The Chronicle of Higher Education Almanac, 1993.

supportive climate tends to perpetuate sex differences in career building and occupational attainment.

Rethinking the Concept of Career Choice

The idea of career choice must be evaluated in light of rapid changes in the nature of work, the pervasiveness of the two-earner family lifestyle, the increased likelihood of multiple job and career changes over the life course, and the constant reconfiguration of the job market, especially the current trends toward "downsizing," "work force reductions" and "retraining" (Church, 1993). The labor market in the United States is undergoing a period of transformation. Large corporations and other major employers, especially the military and defense-related industries, are restructuring with a net loss of white-collar positions. Even though the United States has seen a net gain of about 2 million jobs per year, the kinds of jobs are changing, and many of the increases are in lower-paying jobs such as food service and retail sales.

Certain circumstances may severely restrict the notion of career choice. Many neighborhoods, especially in the inner city and in rural areas, are characterized by a combination of a small number of businesses and low-paying wages that produce chronic poverty. The small number of job opportunities results in an absence of part-time jobs that can help sustain educational advancement as well as in high levels of unemployment (W. T. Grant Foundation, 1988). Limitations in career choice may be self-imposed, especially if one is not willing to leave one's hometown when the industries in the local area are few or declining. High school dropouts may be forced to choose from among a limited set of alternatives. Without a high school diploma, the kinds of jobs that can be obtained and the amount of capital that can be accumulated are restricted. In 1991, 11% of those who did not have a high school diploma were unemployed (U.S. Bureau of the Census, 1992). Our society does provide some options, such as high-school-equivalency programs, military careers, military training in technical skills, and work-force training programs. However, these options are not well developed.

Projections for college graduates are also somewhat discouraging. Despite the importance that experts place on higher education and the development of higher-order cognitive problem-solving skills for the work force of the future, U.S. Labor Department estimates suggest that roughly 30% of each graduating class from now until 2005 will be underemployed or unemployed (Greenwald, 1993). Young people need to anticipate that their careers will change two or three times over their work life. Thus, it may be more adaptive to identify a range of jobs that are a good fit with one's talents and interests rather than to become narrowly focused on one occupational arena.

The idea of occupational choice ought not be confused with choice about labor-market participation. Today, most people do not have a choice about whether or not to work, but they may have a wide choice in the kind of work they will do. Before the 1970s, cultural norms tended to value the model in which women stayed at home while men functioned as the primary or only family participants in the labor market. However, even during this time, this model was applicable only to middle-income families—and primarily white middle-income families. Historically, African-American families have been two-earner families throughout the century, with African-American women having few options but to take the narrow range of occupations open to them. After the 1970s, many changes took place, not the least of which was the need for both partners to work in order to preserve the family's quality of life, changing attitudes toward participation of women in many occupational domains, and a liberalizing of views about the desirability for women to work. At the same time, enforcement of civil rights laws has opened up occupational opportunities so that the idea of career choice has become more of a reality for women as well as men, and for women of color as well as white women (Herring & Wilson-Sadberry, 1993). In the process, many more women have joined the labor force, both out of necessity and as a reflection of personal and professional aspirations. And more career paths are open to women, requiring more thought about finding the best match of personal interests, abilities, life goals and values to particular areas of work.

Career choice itself reflects a central component of the person's emerging identity. For some young people, occupational choice is a reflection of continued identification with their parents. They may select the same job or career as that of one of their parents, or they may select a career because it reflects their parents' aspirations for them. Little personal choice is involved. For some, primarily women, there continues to be a path of primary identification with the roles of wife and mother, with only secondary investment in the labor market. Many of these women, especially those who marry and have children after high school, return to school or to technical training in their 30s and 40s in order to pick up the thread of career development, either as a result of divorce or when their children get older. Increasing numbers of men realize that their occupational career will need to be coordinated and integrated with that of their spouse, so that there are new expectations for flexibility, for contributions to household tasks, and for active participation in child-rearing. These changes require new thinking by young

Pablo Picasso, Sailor, 1938. This image of the sailor captures a contemporary sense of the search for individual identity— a young man in the midst of a voyage with a broad-rimmed hat, an earring in one ear, one eye looking outward to the world and one turned inward on the self.

men about their own commitments to work and family life, as well as a new realization that they, too, need to screen their career aspirations through the lens of family values, just as women have done since the late 1960s.

Ideally, one's choice of occupation is the result of personal experimentation, introspection, self-evaluation, fact finding, and intuition. If so, this process becomes intimately interwoven with the individual's psychological development. In order to make a career choice, people may pose very difficult questions to themselves about their skills, temperament, values, and goals. When they make a decision after this kind of personal evaluation, they are likely to see their careers as a well-integrated part of their personal identities rather than as activities from which they are alienated or by which they are dominated.

The Psychosocial Crisis: Individual Identity Versus Identity Confusion

Erik Erikson provided a comprehensive treatment of the meaning and functions of individual identity, from his inclusion of this concept in the theory of psychosocial development in 1950 to his analysis of American identity in 1974. Erikson's notion of identity involves the merging of past identifications, future aspirations, and contemporary cultural issues. The major works in which he discussed identity are "The Problem of Ego Identity" (1959) and *Identity: Youth and Crisis* (1968). Our presentation of this concept is based on these works.

Later adolescents are preoccupied with questions about their essential character in much the same way that early-school-age children are preoccupied with questions about their origins. In their efforts to define themselves, later adolescents must take into account the bonds that have been built between them and others in the past as well as the direction that they hope to take in the future. Identity serves as an anchor point, providing the person an essential experience of continuity in social relationships.

> The young individual must learn to be most himself where he means the most to others—those others, to be sure, who have come to mean most to him. The term identity expresses such a mutual relation in that it connotes both a persistent sameness within oneself (self-sameness) and a persistent sharing of some kind of essential character with others. (Erikson, 1959, p. 102)

The Content Component of Identity

The structure of identity has two components: content and evaluation (Breakwell, 1986; Whitbourne, 1986). The *content*, what one thinks about, values, and believes in and the traits or characteristics by which one is recognized and known by others, may be further divided into the inner or private self and the public self. The *private self*, often described as a *sense of self*, refers to one's inner uniqueness and unity, a subjective experience of being the originator of one's thoughts and actions and of being self-reflective. Through the private self, one recognizes the range of values and beliefs to which one is committed, and one can assess the extent to which certain thoughts and actions are consistent with those beliefs. The private, subjective sense of self, which develops over the course of the life span, includes four basic elements:

- A sense of agency—being the originator of thoughts and actions.
- A sense of unity—sensing that one is the same basic self from one moment or one situation to the next.
- A sense of otherness—recognizing the boundaries between the self and others.
- A sense of decentering or distancing from oneself so that one can recognize and own one's thoughts and actions through self-reflection (Blasi, 1991; Glodis & Blasi, 1993).

The elements of the *public self* include the many roles one plays and the expectations of others. As young people move through the stage of later adolescence, they find that social reference groups, including family members, neighbors, teachers, friends, religious groups, ethnic groups, and even national leaders, have expectations in regard to their behavior. A young person may be expected to work, to attend college, to marry, to serve the country in the military, to attend religious services, to vote, and to provide economic support for family members. Persistent demands by meaningful others produce certain decisions that might have been made differently or not made at all if the individual were surrounded by a different configuration of social reference groups. In the process of achieving personal identity, one must synthesize the private sense of self with the public self derived from the many roles and relationships in which one is embedded.

The Evaluation Component of Identity

The second structural component of identity, *evaluation*, refers to the significance one places on various aspects of the identity content. Even though most people play many of the same roles, their identities differ, in part because they place different values on some of these roles. Some people are quite single-minded, setting great value on success in one domain, such as their vocational goals, and placing little stock in the others. Other people strive to maintain a balance of roles; they consider themselves successful if they can find enjoyment in a variety of relationships and activities.

This assessment of the importance of certain content areas in relation to others influences the use of resources, the direction of certain decisions, and the kinds of experiences that may be perceived as most personally rewarding or personally threatening. College students, for example, may differ in whether their academic success or their interpersonal success is most central to their sense of identity. Students who are more concerned about academic success take quite a different approach to the college environment, become involved in different kinds of activities, and have a different reaction to academic failure from students who are more concerned about interpersonal success (Reischl & Hirsch, 1989).

Both the content and the evaluation components of identity may change over the life course. In later adolescence, the focus is on integrating the various sources of content and determining which elements have the greatest salience. This is a major accomplishment that requires self-awareness, introspection, and the active exploration of a variety of roles and relationships. However, the individual identity that is formulated at the end of this period is often very abstract because later adolescents have not yet encountered many of the responsibilities, pressures, and conflicts of adult life. The ideological framework of identity has not yet been forged in the flames of reality.

The basic conflict of the psychosocial crisis of later adolescence is individual identity formation versus identity confusion. This conflict results from the enormous difficulty of pulling together the many components of the self, including changing perspectives on one's inner sense of beliefs and values as well as new and changing social demands, into a unified image that can propel the person toward positive, meaningful action. The process of identity formation is confounded by distractions of all sorts. Many young people find it very hard to sort out what they want to be from what their parents have urged them to become. Others have received little encouragement to become a separate person with independent feelings and views. Some are so beleaguered by feelings of inferiority and alienation that they do not have the optimism necessary to create a positive vision of their future. Still others find many paths appealing and have difficulty making a commitment to one above the others.

Identity Status

Identity formation is a dynamic process that unfolds as young people assess their competencies and aspirations within a changing social context of expectations, demands, and resources. A variety of potential resolutions of the psychosocial crisis of individual identity versus identity confusion have been described. At the positive pole is *identity achievement*; at the negative pole is *identity confusion*. Also discussed are a premature resolution, *identity foreclosure*; a postponement of resolution, *psychosocial moratorium*; and a *negative identity*.

One of the most widely used conceptual frameworks for assessing identity status was devised by James Marcia (1980; Waterman, 1982). Using Erikson's concepts, Marcia assessed identity status on the basis of two criteria: crisis and commitment. *Crisis* consists of a period of role experimentation and active decision-making among alternative choices. *Commitment* consists of a demonstration of personal involvement in the areas of occupational choice, religion, and

TABLE 10.4	Relationship of Identity Status, Crisis, and Commitment	
	Crisis	**Commitment**
Identity achievement	+	+
Foreclosure	–	+
Moratorium	+	–
Identity confusion	+/–	–

political ideology. On the basis of Marcia's interview, the status of subjects' identity development is assessed (see Table 10.4). People who are classified as *identity-achieved* have already experienced a crisis time and have made occupational and ideological commitments. People who are classified as *identity-foreclosed* have not experienced a crisis but demonstrate strong occupational and ideological commitments. Their occupational and ideological beliefs appear to be very close to those of their parents. The foreclosed identity is deceptive. A young person of 18 or 19 who can say exactly what he or she wants in life and who has selected an occupational goal may appear to be very mature. This kind of clarity of vision may impress peers and adults as evidence of a high level of self-insight. However, if this solution has been formulated through the wholesale adoption of a script that was devised by the young person's family, it may not actually reflect much depth of self-understanding.

People who are classified as being in a state of *psychosocial moratorium* are involved in an ongoing crisis. Their commitments are diffuse. People who are classified as *identity-confused* may or may not have experienced a crisis, and they demonstrate a complete lack of commitment. Marcia mentions that the identity-confused group has a rather cavalier, playboy quality that allows members to cope with the college environment. He suggests that the more seriously confused persons (such as those described by Erikson, 1959) may not appear in his sample because they are unable to cope with college.

Sometimes, cultural expectations and demands provide the young person with a clearly defined self-image that is completely contrary to the cultural values of the community. This is called a *negative identity* (Erikson, 1959). *Failure, good-for-nothing, juvenile delinquent, hood, gangster,* and *loser* are some of the labels that the adult society commonly applies to certain adolescents. In the absence of any indication of the possibilities of success or contribution to the society, the young person accepts such negative labels as a self-definition and proceeds to validate this identity by continuing to behave in ways that will strengthen it. Some young people grow up admiring people who have become very successful by following antisocial or criminal paths. Drug lords, gang leaders, leaders of groups that advocate hate, violence, and vengeance, and people who use elected political positions for personal gain are all examples of possible role models around which a negative identity may be formed.

A negative identity may also emerge as a result of a strong identification with someone who is devalued by the family or the community. A loving uncle who is an alcoholic or a clever, creative parent who commits suicide may stimulate a crystallization within the person as one who may share these undesirable characteristics.

A *negative identity can be formed around a philosophy of hatred.*

Linda, for example, established the negative identity of a person going crazy:

Her father was an alcoholic, physically abusive man, who terrified her when she was a child. . . . Linda, herself a bright child, became by turns the standard bearer for her father's proud aspirations and the target of his jealousy. Midway through grade school she began flunking all her courses and retreating to a private world of daydreams. . . . "I always expected hallucinations, being locked up, down the road coming toward me. . . . I always resisted seeing myself as an adult. I was afraid that at the point I stopped the tape [the years of wild experimentation] I'd become my parents. . . . My father was the closest person I knew to crazy." (Ochberg, 1986, pp. 296–297)

The foreclosed identity and the negative identity both resolve the identity crisis in ways that fall short of the goal of a positive personal identity. Yet both provide the person with a concrete identity. The more maladaptive resolution of the crisis is *identity confusion*. Young people in this state are unable to make a commitment to any single view of themselves. They may be unable to integrate the various roles they play. They may be confronted by opposing value systems or by a lack of confidence in their ability to make meaningful decisions. Within the private, subjective self, some young people may reach later adolescence having difficulty accepting or establishing clear ego boundaries, or they may not experience feelings of agency. At an unconscious level, they may have incorporated two or more conflicting ideas about the self—for example, an abusive, harsh, rejecting powerful father and a wise, loving, nurturant, powerful grandmother—that stand in opposition to one another. Under any of these conditions, the demands for integration and synthesis of a personal identity arouse anxiety, apathy, and hostility toward the existing roles, none of which they can successfully adopt.

In comparison to the moratorium group, young people in the confused status are less conscientious, more likely to experience negative emotions, and more disagreeable (Clancy & Dollinger, 1993). They are generally not outgoing; rather, they describe themselves as self-conscious and likely to feel depressed. Several studies have found that young people who are characterized as identity-confused have had a history of early and frequent involvement with drug use and abuse

(Jones, 1992). One might speculate that difficulties in resolving earlier psychosocial crises, especially conflicts related to autonomy versus shame and doubt, and initiative versus guilt, leave some young people with deficits in ego formation that interfere with the kind of energy and playful self-assertiveness that are necessary to the process of identity achievement.

Dolores, an unemployed college dropout, describes the feeling of meaningless drifting that is associated with identity confusion:

> "I have two sisters, and my father always told me I was the smartest of all, that I was smarter than he was, and that I could do anything I wanted to do . . . but somehow, I don't really know why, everything I turned to came to nothing. . . . I had every opportunity to find out what I really wanted to do. But . . . nothing I did satisfied me, and I would just stop. . . . Or turn away. . . . Or go on a trip. I worked for a big company for a while. . . . Then my parents went to Paris and I just went with them. . . . I came back . . . went to school . . . was a researcher at Time-Life . . . drifted . . . got married . . . divorced . . . drifted. [Her voice grew more halting.] I feel my life is such a waste. I'd like to write, I really would; but I don't know. I just can't get going." (Gornick, 1971)

The theoretical construct of identity status assumes a developmental progression. Identity confusion reflects the least defined status. Movement from confusion to foreclosure, moratorium, or achievement reflects a developmental progression. Movement from any other status to confusion suggests regression. A person who has achieved identity at one period may conceivably return to a crisis period of moratorium. However, those who are in a moratorium or achieved status can never be accurately described as foreclosed, since by definition they have already experienced some degree of crisis (Waterman, 1982).

In the process of evolving an individual identity, everyone experiences temporary periods of confusion and depression. The task of bringing together the many elements of one's experience into a coordinated, clear self-definition is difficult and time-consuming. Adolescents are likely to experience moments of self-preoccupation, isolation, and discouragement as the diverse pieces of the puzzle are shifted and reordered into the total picture. Thus, even the eventual positive identity formation will be the result of some degree of identity confusion. The negative outcome of identity confusion, however, suggests that the person is never able to formulate a satisfying identity that will provide for the convergence of multiple identifications, aspirations, and roles. Such individuals have the persistent fear that they are losing their hold on themselves and on their future.

Identity Formation for Males and Females

Questions have been raised about the process of identity formation and its outcome for young men and young women in our society. Some investigators have argued that the concept of identity as it has been formulated is a reflection of a male-oriented culture that focuses heavily on occupation and ideology rather than on interpersonal commitments. They suggest that the process of identity formation is different for young women, who must resolve issues of intimacy and interpersonal commitments before they can reach closure on commitments to the world of work. Women tend to be socialized to look to others to define their identity rather than to assume a proactive stance with respect to identity formation. All of these ideas reflect the impact of traditional distinctions in the male and female gender roles on identity formation.

From another perspective, however, one might assume that the kinds of ego strengths associated with identity achievement are equally important to the adaptive functioning of men and women (Ginsburg & Orlofsky, 1981). From this point of view, one might expect to find differences between males and females in the content of identity-related commitments and in the value placed on these content areas, but not in the process of crisis and commitment that leads to achieved identity.

Few sex differences in identity status have been discovered (Waterman, 1982). For both sexes, identity achievement is associated with positive ego qualities. "Identity achieved youths generally exhibit higher levels of self-esteem, greater cognitive and ego complexity, postconventional levels of moral reasoning, and a strong capacity for inner-directed behavior" (Craig-Bray, Adams & Dobson, 1988, p. 175).

In one analysis of the way older adolescents think about commitments, subjects were asked to define the concept of commitment (Galotti & Kozberg, 1987). Few gender differences were found in these definitions, except that women were more likely than men to mention the importance of keeping a promise or their word of honor. Other themes—mutual trust, expression of one's values, a social contract, ordering of priorities, perseverance, obligation, and dedication—were referred to equally often by men and women.

There is evidence that men and women handle the process of role experimentation and identity achievement somewhat differently. The uncertainty of the identity crisis is often accompanied by greater anxiety in women than in men. This anxiety may be linked to concerns about achievement strivings. Many women experience conflict between their image of femininity and their desire to set ambitious personal goals (Ginsburg & Orlofsky, 1981). Anxiety may also be a product of the general distress that women feel when they focus on their own agendas rather than on facilitating the agendas of others, as the society seems to expect them to do. In this context, the moratorium status, which is considered a positive interlude on the path toward achievement, has been found to be linked to higher levels of self-doubt in women than in men. This finding may result from the strong feelings of guilt women experience when they attempt to assert their self-sufficiency or when they try to disconnect from demanding relationships in order to focus on their own ideas and needs.

Other evidence of gender differences has been found in the content of the identity. Erikson's (1968, 1982) work suggests that ideological and vocational commitments are central to identity formation. Gilligan (1982) criticized this orientation, arguing that the interpersonal content may be more central for women, and that the clarification of interpersonal commitments opens the way for more advanced exploration of vocations and ideology. Research findings lend support to this concept (Mellor, 1989; Bilsker, Schiedel & Marcia, 1988; Schiedel & Marcia, 1985). The quality of interpersonal relations and the establishment of satisfying social commitments are more relevant to the development of a woman's identity than to the development of a man's. Measures of identity status that distinguish between interpersonal and ideological aspects of identity find that women score higher on interpersonal identity achievement than men (Benson, Harris & Rogers, 1992).

The Central Process: Role Experimentation

Later adolescents experiment with roles that represent the many possibilities for their future identities. They may think of themselves in a variety of careers in an effort to anticipate what it would be like to be members of specific occupational groups. They may take a variety of summer jobs, change their college major, read

Pablo Picasso, Harlequin, *1901. Young people experiment with roles that represent many possibilities for a mature identity. The Harlequin was Picasso's favorite masquerade, a mysterious identity that blends innocence, sensuality, and creativity.*

extensively, and daydream about success in several occupations. They consider whether or not to marry, and they begin to define the ideal qualities they are looking for in a long-term intimate partner. Dating is one form of role experimentation; it allows for a different self-presentation with each new date. Friendship is another important context within which young people begin to clarify their interpersonal commitments. In addition, they may evaluate their commitment to their religion, consider religious conversion, or experiment with different rationales for moral behavior. They may examine a variety of political theories, join groups that work for political causes, or campaign for candidates.

During later adolescence, people have few social obligations that require long-term role commitments. They are free to start and stop or to join and quit without serious repercussions to their reputations. As long as no laws are broken in the process of experimenting, young people have the opportunity to play as many roles as they wish in order to prepare themselves for the resolution of the identity crisis without risking serious social censure.

The process of *role experimentation* takes many forms. Erikson (1959) used the term *psychosocial moratorium* to describe a period of free experimentation before a final identity is achieved. Ideally, the moratorium allows individuals freedom from the daily expectations for role performance. Their experimentation with new roles, values, and belief systems results in a personal conception of how they can fit into society so as to maximize their personal strengths and gain positive recognition from the community. The idea of being able to disconnect from daily demands

The campus newspaper offers a context for role experimentation. As a reporter or editor, one has to be aware of the wide variety of issues and activities that take place on and around the campus. One can become deeply involved in an issue, then move on to something else.

and experiment with new roles may be more difficult for some later adolescents than for others. For example, young people who marry early and who go into the labor force right after high school may not have the luxury of a moratorium.

The concept of the psychosocial moratorium has been partially incorporated into those college programs that permit students to enroll in pass-fail courses before they select a major. The concern is to eliminate the problems of external evaluation during the decision-making process. Some high school students take a year for work, travel, or volunteer service before deciding about college or a career. College students often express a need for a moratorium by leaving school for a while (Ochberg, 1986). By leaving, they disrupt the expected path of educational and career development. They assert their autonomy by imposing their own timetable and agenda on a socially prescribed sequence. Travel abroad is another strategy for experiencing moratorium. The time in another culture can give students an opportunity to demonstrate their self-sufficiency, to examine many of their assumptions about values and goals, to express their individuality, and to break out of whatever social environment they may feel is constraining or overshadowing their sense of self. The moratorium offers temporary relief from external demands and an opportunity to establish their identity.

As parents observe the process of role experimentation, they may become concerned because an adolescent son or daughter appears to be abandoning the traditional family value orientation or lifestyle. The adolescent talks of changing religions, remaining single, or selecting a low-status career. The more vehemently the family responds to these propositions, the more likely the young person is to become locked into a position in order to demonstrate autonomy rather than being allowed to continue the experimentation until a more suitable personal alternative is discovered. Many adolescents seem to want to take a "shocking"

We tend to think of identity formation as a process that requires young people to distance themselves from the strong expectations and definitions imposed by parents and other family members. To achieve an individual identity, one must create a vision of the self that is authentic, a sense of having taken hold of one's destiny in an effort to reach goals that are personally meaningful. Yet recent research has demonstrated that the quality of family relationships contributes significantly to the young person's ability to achieve a personal identity (Kroger & Haslett, 1988; Kamptner, 1988; Papini, Sebby & Clark, 1989).

The relationship can be compared with the contribution of secure attachments in infancy to a subsequent willingness to explore the environment. Later adolescents who have a secure relationship with their parents and who are comfortable in loosening these ties can begin to explore the ideological, occupational, and interpersonal alternatives that will become their own identities. In particular, college students, both males and females, who have a positive attachment to their mothers are more likely to have an achieved identity and are less likely to be in the moratorium or identity-confused statuses than are students who have insecure, mistrustful relationships

BOX 10.1

Attachment and Identity Formation

with their mothers. Later adolescents who are still emotionally dependent on their parents and who require constant reassurance of their parents' affection show a greater tendency to experience identity confusion (Benson et al., 1992).

By the time individuals reach later adolescence, those who are securely attached to their parents are confident about their parents' affection and support. At the same time, they trust in their own worth, and in their ability to make decisions (Blain, Thompson & Whiffen, 1993). A sense of family security fosters identity formation in the following ways:

- It fosters confidence in the exploration of social relationships, ideologies, and settings.
- It establishes positive expectations in regard to interpersonal experiences outside the family.
- It fosters the formation of group identities apart from the family, thus providing a transitional context for work on individual identity.
- It provides a basic layer of self-acceptance, permitting the young person to approach the process of identity formation with optimism.

position or to question the "unquestionable" so that they have a feeling of control, a feeling that they have chosen their path rather than that they have simply followed the path that was carved out for them by their family, their culture, and their time in history. Parents are well advised to understand role experimentation as an expression of an appropriate developmental process in which a young person is trying on various roles, beliefs, and philosophies to see "how they fit." If at all possible, parents need to trust in this process, giving their opinions and reactions when appropriate, but encouraging the young person to find the combination of roles, values, goals, and commitments that bring the later adolescent the greatest feelings of enthusiasm and optimism about his or her own future.

Not all young people approach the process of role experimentation with the same degree of openness to new experiences and new information. You will recall the discussion of emotional style in Chapter 9, in which two types of individuals were described: the sensers and the censors. Extending this idea further, Michael Berzonsky (1989, 1993; Berzonsky & Sullivan, 1992) hypothesized that in later adolescence individuals differ in how they select, process, and apply self-relevant information. Three types of approaches to identity-information processing were described, each with a somewhat different implication for the place of role experimentation in the resolution of the identity search. The *informational* types "actively seek out and evaluate self-diagnostic information when negotiating identity issues and making decisions" (Berzonsky, 1993, p. 289). The *normative* types are "relatively more defensive and closed to feedback that may threaten hard core areas of the self" (Berzonsky, 1993, p. 290). The *diffuse-avoidant* types "procrastinate and delay dealing with self-relevant issues as long as possible. When push comes to shove, they tend to be influenced by immediate rewards and operate in a situation-sensitive fashion" (Berzonsky, 1993, p. 290). The implication is that the informational types are most likely to initiate role experimentation as a means of clarifying existing beliefs and values. The normative types have to process contradictions among the demands and expectations of the varying roles they play, but if possible they will probably avoid novel experiences that would challenge their views. The diffuse-avoidant types may engage in role experimentation if it is viewed as "cool" or is positively regarded among others in their peer group, but they probably would not take the initiative to seek out new experiences as a conscious, proactive strategy.

Role Experimentation and Ethnic Identity

In Chapter 9, we introduced the idea that group identity precedes individual identity. One component of group identity is an orientation toward one's ethnic group. Efforts to understand one's ethnic identity and to clarify one's commitment to a particular ethnic subculture lead to self-definition that facilitates work on personal identity as well. Part of forming a clear sense of one's personal identity requires an understanding of one's ancestry, especially one's cultural and ethnic heritage and the values, beliefs, and traditions that may have shaped one's child-rearing environment as well as one's vision of the future. Ethnic group identity typically involves an awareness of one's ethnic identity; the incorporation of certain ideals, values, and beliefs that are specific to that ethnic group; a sense of how this ethnic group is regarded by outsiders; and the way in which one orients oneself with respect to this group—that is, whether one seeks out other members of the group, feels proud of one's membership in the group, and has positive attitudes about the group (Cross, 1991).

As you might imagine, young people make the transition from early to later adolescence having done different amounts of work in exploring their ethnic group identity. One theory of ethnic minority identity development offers a five-stage model (Atkinson, Morten & Sue, 1983):

1. *Conformity.* Identification with the values, beliefs, and practices of the dominant culture.
2. *Dissonance.* Recognition and confusion about areas of conflict between the values, beliefs, and practices of the dominant culture and those of one's own ethnic group.
3. *Resistance and immersion.* Rejection of many elements of the dominant culture; education about and involvement in one's own ethnic group and its beliefs, values, and practices.
4. *Introspection.* Critical examination of the values, beliefs, and practices of both the dominant culture and one's own ethnic group's views.
5. *Articulation and awareness.* Identification of those values, beliefs, and practices from the dominant culture and one's own ethnic group that are combined into a unique synthesis that forms a personal, cultural identity.

In this model, one senses the interaction between ethnic identity and personal identity. Of course, not all young people experience all of these stages. For many, the stage of articulation and awareness may not occur until sometime later in adulthood. But for many later adolescents, the transitions from Stage 1, conformity, to Stages 2 and 3 are commonly stimulated by the college experience. The student body is usually much more diverse than one's high school. Young people of many racial, ethnic, social-class, regional, and religious backgrounds come together in college and are expected to live together in the residence halls, learn together in the classrooms, and collaborate in college organizations, social activities, sports, and cultural events. Exposure to this diversity often brings experiences of racial and ethnic prejudice, cultural ethnocentrism, and intergroup conflict. At the same time, exposure to the college curriculum offers an intellectual framework for understanding the historical, psychological, and sociological foundations of racism, prejudice, and cultural conflict.

Often, college students seek opportunities to learn more about their ethnic group identity. They may take courses that address the history, culture, and accomplishments of their group. They may become resentful about the lack of recognition that their group is given in the general operations of the university or in the broad spectrum of the curriculum. They may seek avenues for challenging the university, urging greater efforts to accept and celebrate their group's traditions, customs, and contributions. At the same time, they experience many pressures to function in accord with the values, beliefs, and practices of the dominant culture. As a result, they are propelled into an active process of role experimentation, looking at the world through multiple roles: as a member of their ethnic group on campus, as a member of the college community, as a member of a certain friendship group, as a major in some academic discipline or professional program, as a member of their family, and as a member of their neighborhood or ethnic community at home. Each of these social reference groups poses challenges to the formation of an ethnic identity, introducing areas of potential conflict as well as encouraging certain kinds of ideological commitment.

Eventually, a person has to improvise a solution to these multiple views of the self that works for him or her. This solution is usually supported by spending time with people who have arrived at a similar perspective, who understand and support one's beliefs and practices, who enjoy the same sense of celebration in one's ethnicity, and who make it possible to experience a basic sense of self-acceptance. Students who cannot find this support group, who continue to experience dissonance, or who do not encounter the intellectual and social supports necessary to move from questioning to articulation may become alienated from the college environment and are likely to leave.

Applied Topic
Career Decision-Making

One of the primary means by which identity is expressed in our society is commitment to an occupation. What is involved in reaching a decision about a career? How do later adolescents approach the task of career decision-making? What are some strategies that foster effective career decision-making?

Studies conducted in the United States, Canada, and Australia all confirm that concerns about future educational and career decisions constitute a major source of worry for adolescents (Violato & Holden, 1988). Seventy-six percent of women and seventy-four percent of men entering college as freshmen in 1989 said that they had worried about choosing a career during the past year (Dodge, 1989). Many people assume that the younger a person is when he or she makes a career choice, the better. Perhaps that is why so many high school students worry about their career choices.

Most career development professionals, however, advise that a decision about a career be delayed until later adolescence or early adulthood (Osipow, 1986). A person who delays the decision has a clearer sense of his or her adult interests and goals. And by delaying the career decision, one has more opportunities to explore alternative work scenarios and to understand more about the labor market. Nonetheless, high schools, colleges, and various industries urge young people to make these decisions as early as possible. Thus, some of the tension that later adolescents experience in connection with a choice of career is a product of the lack of fit between socialization pressures and their own developmental timetable. If a person is going to live to be 75 or 80 years old, there is no great rush to decide on a career by age 20. What is more, if one is likely to change careers two or three times over the life course, then selecting the first career ought to be viewed in a different light. This is not a decision that has to last a whole lifetime.

Career decision-making is linked to other aspects of identity development. In particular, later adolescents worry about the extent to which commitment to a career may conflict with other commitments to family roles or to values (Kram, 1985). Some young people struggle with the idea that success in a career may require them to sacrifice intimacy in family life. A young woman summarized this conflict when she described the advice she had received from her parents about her occupational future. Her mother had assured her that it was possible to combine work and family life, and that there are no greater satisfactions in life than those that come from raising a family. Her father had advised her that, if she hoped to compete and succeed in the world of work, she would have to devote herself entirely to that goal and should give up the idea of having a family (Eccles, 1987).

The process of career decision-making, then, requires a synthesis of self-concept, including an assessment of one's needs, interests, values, and abilities, with knowledge of the realities of the work environment, including the kinds of jobs and careers available, requirements for entry, and policies, regulations, and economic conditions influencing the job market. The choice of a career is actually subject to two influences at once: the education or training one chooses and the recruitment and selection policies of organizations and industries (Hall, 1976). A person has most control over the first of these factors, but the final outcome is surely influenced by the other as well. Box 10.2 provides some insight into the future of the American job market and its implications for job hopefuls.

Once a person begins to accept certain elements of her or his self-concept as they relate to the occupational aspect of identity, the process of career decision-making begins. Tiedeman (Tiedeman & O'Hara, 1963; Miller & Tiedeman, 1972) has developed a model of phases of career decision-making. The model illustrates how making career-related decisions helps to clarify one's occupational identity and, at the same time, uses the context of work to promote new learning about other aspects of the self (see Figure 10.3). A career decision depends on the outcomes of several tasks during adolescence and early adulthood. With effective problem solving, the person gains increased control over life events and is better prepared to meet the challenges of the next phase of decision-making. Tiedeman

The 1990s are bringing a new look to American business. Large companies are downsizing, reducing the numbers of white-collar employees, paying lower salaries, and using more contract services from smaller companies. These positions are not likely to be replaced in the near future; there is a mentality of doing more with less. These are long-term structural changes in the nature of large organizations (Church, 1993; Hage, Grant & Impoco, 1993). Manufacturing jobs continue to decline, while modest-paying jobs in sales and food service appear to be on the rise. The signing of the North American Fair Trade Agreement (NAFTA) and the opening of trade agreements with eastern European as well as Asian trading partners promises a much more internationalized business community. Even though unemployment rates are down, many people are working several part-time jobs because they cannot find full-time employment, and others who have been unemployed are returning to work in positions that pay much less than their previous jobs. Finally, the tremendous pace at which technologies transfer to the workplace means that most workers will need to have new skills to perform their jobs, if the jobs still exist, every five or six years.

Given these and many related changes in the U.S. labor market, experts make the following observations that have implications for career decision-making (Church, 1993):

Don't plan on a lifelong association with a large company. Most major corporations will have a relatively small central core and will contract out much of their work to smaller firms. Thus, many more people will work for fees, as consultants on one project and then another, rather than for salaries.

Small companies will be handling much of the work load. This means a need for each employee to be able to perform many tasks, to work effectively alone or in small groups, and to be good at hustling new assignments rather than merely showing up at work and performing the tasks at hand.

Be prepared for the likelihood of working for a foreign-owned business or for having business dealings with international clients, customers, or contractors. This means knowing about international business practices and cultures as well as international economics. The value of bilingualism as a credential of a prospective employee is increasing among U.S. employers.

Be prepared to function in a work setting in which women are increasingly likely to be the boss or the supervisor; in which the work force is racially diverse; and where customers, clients, and contractors expect employees to be effective in responding appropriately to differences in gender, race, and ethnicity.

Get as much education as possible in preparing for your job, and be prepared to keep improving your skills and knowledge base through continuing education, technical training, and personal study.

---

posits seven phases: The first four emphasize planning and clarification; the last three emphasize implementation.

In the *exploration phase*, the person realizes that a career decision must be made and therefore begins to learn more about those aspects of the self and the occupational world that are relevant to the impending decision. The person begins to generate alternatives for action. Uncertainty about the future and the many alternatives is accompanied by feelings of anxiety.

In the *crystallization phase*, the person becomes more aware of the alternatives for action and their consequences. Conflicts among alternatives are recognized and some alternatives are discarded. The person develops a strategy for making the decision, in part by weighing the costs and benefits of each alternative.

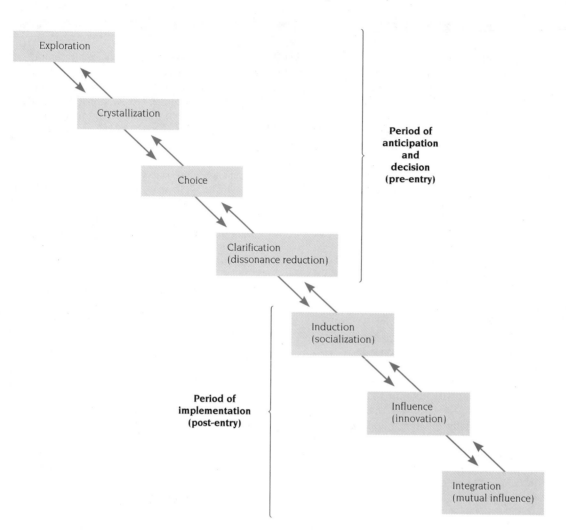

FIGURE 10.3

Seven phases of career decision-making

Source: Based on Tiedeman & O'Hara, 1963.

In the *choice phase*, the person decides which action alternative to follow. The decision is solidified in the person's mind as he or she elaborates the reasons why the decision is beneficial. There is a sense of relief and optimism as the person develops a commitment to executing the decision.

In the *clarification phase*, the person more fully understands the consequences of commitment to the decision that has been made. He or she plans definite steps to take and may actually take them in this phase or may delay them until a more appropriate time. The self-image is prepared to be modified by the decision.

During the *induction phase*, the person encounters the new environment for the first time. He or she wants to be accepted and looks to others for cues about how to behave. The person identifies with the new group and seeks recognition for his or her unique characteristics. Gradually the self-image is modified as the person begins to believe in the values and goals of the new group.

In the *influence phase*, the person is very much involved with the new group. He or she becomes more assertive in asking that the group perform better. The person also tries to influence the group to accommodate some of his or her values. The self is strongly committed to group goals. During this phase, the group's values and goals may be modified to include the orientation of the new member.

This student has a supervised field placement with an architect's firm. Fieldwork and internships provide important opportunities to gather more direct information about a particular career and to evaluate the fit between one's personal needs, interests, and talents and the demands of the work.

Finally, in the *integration phase*, group members react against the new member's attempts to influence them. The new member then compromises. In the process, he or she attains a more objective understanding of the self and the group. A true collaboration between the new member and the group is achieved. The new member feels satisfied and is evaluated as successful by the self and others.

This model emphasizes continuous interaction between the individual and the work context. At first, interaction is necessary to clarify the person's talents and choice of career. Later, it is necessary to achieve a satisfactory level of adaptation to the work environment. At each juncture, whether the decision relates to college major, occupation, job change, or career redirection, effective decision-making involves all seven phases.

Characteristics of the contemporary labor market may be contributing to new difficulties that later adolescents encounter as they attempt to move through the first four phases of Tiedeman's model:

• The increasing number of jobs and careers available make the *exploration* phase difficult.

• As a result of changes in technology as well as in organizational structure, some skills become obsolete and some job markets dry up. With the advent of desk-top publishing and computer composition, for example, jobs for typesetters are disappearing. A career may become obsolete in the time it takes a young person to prepare for it.

• As established firms lose their identities in corporate mergers, identification with a particular company ceases to be appropriate.

• As most large companies go through restructuring and downsizing, the people who are left are asked to do more tasks and a greater variety of them. In addition to one's special area of training, it is important to develop support skills, such as word processing, data management, literature search skills, and verbal as well as written communication skills.

• New careers emerge at a rapid pace. From the time one enters the *choice* phase to the time one enters the *influence* phase, new kinds of work roles may become available.

• Career paths are less clear than they once were. Young people are being advised to expect three or four career changes in their lifetime. One may move from the private to the nonprofit sector, from business to education, from service provider to entrepreneur.

• The cost of living, especially the costs of housing, health care, and education, introduces concerns about the amount of money that will be needed to live comfortably. Worries about making money may interfere with effective career decision-making.

As a result of the anxiety that attends career decision-making, career counseling has become a significant new career. Five suggestions from the career-counseling literature are helpful in developing an effective career decision-making process in later adolescence (Hall, 1976; Eccles, 1987):

1. *Gather information about various careers.* A career decision should be approached at least as systematically as the decision to buy a car. Know enough about your own interests, abilities, and values to select several appropriate occupations. Then find out as much as possible about the educational and training requirements, the future job market, the career ladder, and the various organizations where this kind of work is available.

2. *Engage in work-related tasks in which you experience success.* Success experiences are a critical element in judgments of self-efficacy. If you are to believe that you can succeed in a certain career, it is important to have experiences of success in demanding tasks that either approximate or are directly connected to the career in question.

3. *Recognize the needs relevant to each phase of career decision-making.* A person in the *crystallization* phase may need more specific information about the trade-offs of certain career paths. A person in the *choice* phase may need to develop a more personal relationship with someone in a particular career.

4. *Seek out a variety of sources of information.* Teachers may have one view of a career; managers and supervisors quite another. Talk to people who might be co-workers as well as those who would be bosses. Parents who have their children's long-range welfare at heart may be an important source of help in career decision-making. Friends are another important source, especially if they can engage in flexible fantasies about alternative futures.

5. *Build bridges between the abstract and the concrete.* Find opportunities to apply what you learn in the classroom to the work setting and to analyze observations from the work setting by reading, reflecting, and forming general principles about them. Ideally, one's career decisions will be a product of experiences and informed reflection about those experiences.

Chapter Summary

At the close of later adolescence, most young people have made the transition from childhood to adulthood. They are fully capable of surviving on their own in a complex culture. They have achieved a new level of independence from their parents, so that ties of love, trust, and support are expressed within a framework of mutual respect and autonomous decision-making. Those who have resolved the psychosocial crisis of this stage have an integrated identity that includes a definition of themselves as sexual, moral, political, and career participants. Identity achievement represents a private sense of unity and confidence in one's beliefs as well as a more public integration of roles and commitments to specific values.

The strain of this stage is felt in the tension between the person's need to question and experiment and the society's expectations for closure on significant themes, particularly occupation, gender identity, and political ideology. The expansion of roles and relationships exposes many young people to new views that require evaluation. The crisis of individual identity versus identity confusion suggests a new synthesis of earlier identifications, present values, and future goals into a consistent self-concept. This unity of self is achieved only after a period of uncertainty and open questioning. Role experimentation during this time is an essential strategy for coping with new information and new value orientations. Once young people know what they stand for, they can commit themselves more deeply to others.

References

Armsden, G. C. & Greenberg, M. T. (1987). The inventory of parent and peer attachment: Individual differences and their relationship to psychological well-being in adolescence. *Journal of Youth and Adolescence, 16,* 427–454.

Atkinson, D. R., Morten, G. & Sue, D. W. (1983). *Counseling American minorities: A cross-cultural perspective.* (2nd ed.). Dubuque, IA: William C. Brown.

Bachman, J. G., Bare, D. E. & Frankie, E. I. (1986). *Correlates of employment among high school seniors* (Monitoring the Future Occasional Paper 20). Ann Arbor, MI: Institute for Social Research.

Bachman, J. G., Johnston, L. D. & O'Malley, P. M. (1987). *Monitoring the future: Questionnaire responses from the nation's high school seniors,* 1986. Ann Arbor, MI: Survey Research Center, Institute for Social Research.

Baucom, D. H., Besch, P. K. & Callahan, S. (1985). Relation between testosterone concentrations, sex-role identity, and personality among females. *Journal of Personality and Social Psychology, 48,* 1218–1226.

Baumrind, D. (1991). Parenting styles and adolescent development. In R. M. Lerner, A. C. Petersen & J. Brooks-Gunn (Eds.), *The encyclopedia of adolescence* (pp. 746–758). New York: Garland.

Benson, M. J., Harris, P. B. & Rogers, C. S. (1992). Identity consequences of attachment to mothers and fathers among late adolescents. *Journal of Research on Adolescence, 2,* 187–204.

Berkowitz, M. W. & Gibbs, J. C. (1983). Measuring the developmental features of moral discussion. *Merrill-Palmer Quarterly, 29,* 399–410.

Berman, W. H. & Sperling, M. B. (1991). Parental attachment and emotional distress in the transition to college. *Journal of Youth and Adolescence, 20,* 427–440.

Berzonsky, M. D. (1989). Identity style: Conceptualization and measurement. *Journal of Adolescent Research, 4,* 267–281.

Berzonsky, M. D. (1993). Identity style, gender, and social-cognitive reasoning. *Journal of Adolescent Research, 8,* 289–296.

Berzonsky, M. D. & Sullivan, C. (1992). Social-cognitive aspects of identity style: Need for cognition, experiential openness, and introspection. *Journal of Adolescent Research, 7,* 140–155.

Betz, N. E. & Hackett, G. (1981). The relationship of career-related self-efficacy expectations to perceived career options in college women and men. *Journal of Counseling Psychology, 28,* 399–410.

Bilsker, D., Schiedel, D. & Marcia, J. (1988). Sex differences in identity status. *Sex Roles, 18,* 231–236.

Blain, M. D., Thompson, J. M. & Whiffen, V. E. (1993). Attachment and perceived social support in late adolescence: The interaction between working models of self and others. *Journal of Adolescent Research, 8,* 226–241.

Blasi, A. (1991). The self as subject in the study of personality. In D. Ozer, J. Healy & A. Stewart (Eds.), *Perspectives in personality* (Vol. 3, Part A, pp. 19–37). London: Kingsley.

Bloom, M. V. (1987). Leaving home: A family transition. In J. Bloom-Feshbach & S. Bloom-Feshbach (Eds.), *The psychology of separation and loss.* San Francisco: Jossey-Bass.

Borman, K. M. & Hopkins, M. (1987). Leaving school for work. *Research in the Sociology of Education and Socialization, 7,* 131–159.

Breakwell, G. M. (1986). *Coping with threatened identities.* London: Methuen.

Bridges, J. S. (1988). Sex differences in occupational performance expectations. *Psychology of Women Quarterly, 12,* 75–90.

Carpendale, J. I. M. & Krebs, D. L. (1992). Situational variation in moral judgment: In a stage or on a stage? *Journal of Youth and Adolescence, 21,* 203–224.

Chickering, A. W. & Reisser, L. (1993). *Education and identity* (2nd ed.). San Francisco: Jossey-Bass.

Chronicle of Higher Education. (1993, August 25). Almanac: Facts about the U.S., each of the 50 states, and D.C., 40, Washington, D.C.: Author.

Church, G. J. (1993, November 22). Jobs in an age of insecurity. *Time, 142* (22), 32–39.

Clancy, S. M. & Dollinger, S. J. (1993). Identity, self, and personality: 1. Identity status and the five-factor model of personality. *Journal of Research on Adolescence, 3,* 227–246.

Colby, A. & Kohlberg, L. (1987). *The measurement of moral judgment: Vol. 1. Theoretical foundations and research validation.* Cambridge: Cambridge University Press.

Colby, A., Kohlberg, L., Gibbs, J. & Lieberman, M. (1983). *A longitudinal study of moral judgment.* Monographs of the Society for Research in Child Development, 48(1, Serial No. 200).

Craig-Bray, L., Adams, G. R. & Dobson, W. R. (1988). Identity formation and social relations during late adolescence. *Journal of Youth and Adolescence, 17,* 173–188.

Cross, W. E., Jr. (1991). *Shades of black: Diversity in African-American identity.* Philadelphia: Temple University Press.

DeVos, S. (1989). Leaving the parental home in six Latin American countries. *Journal of Marriage and the Family, 51,* 615–626.

Dodge, S. (1989). More freshmen willing to work for social change and environmental issues, new survey finds. *Chronicle of Higher Education, 36,* A31–A35.

Eccles, J. S. (1987). Gender roles and women's achievement-related decisions. *Psychology of Women Quarterly, 11,* 135–171.

Eisenberg, N. & Strayer, J. (1987). *Empathy and its development* (pp. 3–13). Cambridge: Cambridge University Press.

Erikson, E. H. (1950). *Childhood and society.* New York: Norton.

Erikson, E. H. (1959). The problem of ego identity. *Psychological Issues, 1,* 101–164.

Erikson, E. H. (1968). *Identity: Youth and crisis.* New York: Norton.

Erikson, E. H. (1974). *Dimensions of a new identity.* New York: Norton.

Erikson, E. H. (1982). *The life cycle completed: A review.* New York: Norton.

Ford, M. R. & Lowery, C. R. (1986). Gender differences in moral reasoning: A comparison of the use of justice and care orientations. *Journal of Personality and Social Psychology, 50,* 777–783.

Freeman, R. B. & Wise, D. A. (1982). *The youth labor market: Problems in the United States.* Chicago: University of Chicago Press.

Freud, S. (1994). The social construction of gender. *Journal of Adult Development, 1,* 37–46.

Friedman, W. J., Robinson, A. B. & Friedman, B. L. (1987). Sex differences in moral judgments? A test of Gilligan's theory. *Psychology of Women Quarterly, 11,* 37–46.

Galotti, K. M. (1989). Gender differences in self-reported moral reasoning: A review of new evidence. *Journal of Youth and Adolescence, 18,* 475–488.

Galotti, K. M. & Kozberg, S. F. (1987). Older adolescents' thinking about academic/vocational and interpersonal commitments. *Journal of Youth and Adolescence, 15,* 147–163.

Galotti, K. M., Kozberg, S. F. & Farmer, M. C. (1991). Gender and developmental differences in adolescents' conceptions of moral reasoning. *Journal of Youth and Adolescence, 20,* 13–30.

Gfellner, B. M. (1986). Ego development and moral development in relation to age and grade level during adolescence. *Journal of Youth and Adolescence, 15,* 147–163.

Giele, J. Z. (1988). Gender and sex roles. In N. J. Smelser (Ed.), *Handbook of sociology* (pp. 291–326). Newbury Park, CA: Sage.

Gilligan, C. (1977). In a different voice: Women's conceptions of self and morality. *Harvard Educational Review, 47*, 481–517.

Gilligan, C. (1982). *In a different voice: Psychological theory and women's development*. Cambridge: Harvard University Press.

Gilligan, C. & Attanucci, J. (1988). Two moral orientations. In C. Gilligan, J. V. Ward, J. M. Taylor & B. Bardige, (Eds.), *Mapping the moral domain*. Cambridge: Harvard University Press.

Ginsburg, S. D. & Orlofsky, J. L. (1981). Ego identity status, ego development, and locus of control in college women. *Journal of Youth and Adolescence, 10*, 297–307.

Glodis, K. A. & Blasi, A. (1993). The sense of self and identity among adolescents and adults. *Journal of Adolescent Research, 8*, 356–380.

Goldscheider, C. & Goldscheider, F. (1987). Moving out and marriage: What do young adults expect? *American Sociological Review, 52*, 278–285.

Goldscheider, F. K. & Goldscheider, C. (1989). Family structure and conflict: Nest leaving expectations of young adults and their parents. *Journal of Marriage and the Family, 51*, 87–97.

Gornick, V. (1971). Consciousness. *New York Times Magazine*, January 10.

W. T. Grant Foundation. (1988). *The forgotten half: Non-college youth in America*. Washington, DC: William T. Grant Foundation Commission on Work, Family, and Citizenship.

Greenwald, J. (1993, November 22). Bellboys with B.A.s. *Time, 142*(22), 36–37.

Griffin, L. J. & Alexander, K. L. (1978). Schooling and socioeconomic attainments: High school and college influences. *American Journal of Sociology, 84*, 319–347.

Grotevant, H. D. & Cooper, C. R. (1985). Patterns of interaction in family relationships and the development of identity exploration in adolescence. *Child Development, 56*, 415–428.

Gustafson, S. B., Stattin, H. & Magnusson, D. (1992). Aspects of development of a career versus homemaking orientation among females: The longitudinal influence of educational motivation and peers. *Journal of Research on Adolescence, 2*, 241–259.

Hage, D., Grant, L. & Impoco, J. (1993, June 28). White collar wasteland: A hostile economy has cut short careers for many of America's best and brightest. *U.S. News & World Report, 114*(25), 42–52.

Hall, D. T. (1976). *Careers in organizations*. Santa Monica, CA: Goodyear.

Hauser, S. T., Powers, S. I., Noam, G., Jacobson, A. M., Weiss, B. & Follansbee, D. J. (1984). Familial contexts of adolescent ego development. *Child Development, 55*, 195–213.

Hearn, J. C. (1980). Major choice and the well-being of college men and women: An examination from developmental, structural, and organizational perspectives. *Sociology of Education, 53*, 164–178.

Hearn, J. C. & Olzak, S. (1981). The role of college major departments in the reproduction of sexual inequality. *Sociology of Education, 54*, 195–205.

Herring, C. & Wilson-Sadberry, K. R. (1993). Preference or necessity? Changing work roles of black and white women, 1973–1990. *Journal of Marriage and the Family, 55*, 315–325.

Hubner-Funk, S. (1983). Transition into occupational life: Environmental and sex differences regarding the status passage from school to work. *Adolescence, 18*, 709–723.

Jones, R. M. (1992). Ego identity and adolescent problem behavior. In G. R. Adams, T. P. Gullota & R. Montemayor (Eds.), *Adolescent identity formation* (pp. 216–233). Newbury Park, CA: Sage.

Kamptner, N. L. (1988). Identity development in late adolescence: Causal modeling of social and familial influences. *Journal of Youth and Adolescence, 17*, 493–514.

Kaplan, D. A. (1993, December 20). Is it torture or tradition? *Newsweek, 122*, p. 124.

Kohlberg, L. (1964). Development of moral character and moral ideology. In M. L. Hoffman & L. W. Hoffman (Eds.), *Review of child development research* (Vol. 1). New York: Sage.

Kohlberg, L. (1969). Stage and sequence: The cognitive-developmental approach to socialization. In D. A. Goslin (Ed.), *Handbook of socialization theory and research*. Chicago: Rand McNally.

Kram, K. E. (1985). *Mentoring at work: Developmental relationships in organizational life*. Glenview, IL: Scott, Foresman.

Kroger, J. & Haslett, S. J. (1988). Separation-individuation and ego identity status in late adolescence: A two-year longitudinal study. *Journal of Youth and Adolescence, 17*, 59–80.

Kurdek, L. A. (1981). Young adults' moral reasoning about prohibitive and prosocial dilemmas. *Journal of Youth and Adolescence, 10*, 263–272.

Lerner, R. M. (1985). Adolescent maturational changes and psychosocial development: A dynamic interactional perspective. *Journal of Youth and Adolescence, 14*, 355–372.

Levitt, M. J., Weber, R. A. & Guacci, N. (1993). Convoys of social support: An intergenerational analysis. *Psychology and Aging, 8*, 323–326.

Long, B. C. (1989). Sex-role orientation, coping strategies, and self-efficacy of women in traditional and nontraditional occupations. *Psychology of Women Quarterly*, 13, 307–324.

Manning, W. D. (1990). Parenting employed teenagers. *Youth and Society*, 22, 184–200.

Marcia, J. E. (1980). Identity in adolescence. In J. Adelson (Ed.), *Handbook of adolescent psychology* (pp. 159–187). New York: Wiley.

Mason, M. G. & Gibbs, J. C. (1993). Social perspective taking and moral judgment among college students. *Journal of Adolescent Research*, 8, 109–123.

Mellor, S. (1989). Gender differences in identity formation as a function of self-other relationships. *Journal of Youth and Adolescence*, 18, 361–375.

Miller, A. L. & Tiedeman, D. V. (1972). Decision making for the 70's: The cubing of the Tiedeman paradigm and its application in career education. *Focus on Guidance*, 5.

Mitchell, B. A., Wister, A. V. & Burch, T. K. (1989). The family environment and leaving the parental home. *Journal of Marriage and the Family*, 51, 605–614.

Moore, D. & Hotch, D. F. (1981). Late adolescents' conceptualizations of home-leaving. *Journal of Youth and Adolescence*, 10, 1–10.

Mortimer, J. T., Finch, M., Shanahan, M. & Ryu, S. (1992). Work experience, mental health, and behavioral adjustment in adolescence. *Journal of Research on Adolescence*, 2, 25–57.

National Center for Education Statistics. (1992). *Digest of education statistics*: 1992. Washington, DC: U.S. Government Printing Office.

Nevill, D. D. & Schlecker, D. I. (1988). The relation of self-efficacy and assertiveness to willingness to engage in traditional/nontraditional career activities. *Psychology of Women Quarterly*, 12, 91–98.

Nisan, M. & Kohlberg, L. (1982). Universality and variation in moral judgment: A longitudinal and cross-sectional study in Turkey. *Child Development*, 53, 865–876.

Ochberg, R. L. (1986). College dropouts: The developmental logic of psychosocial moratoria. *Journal of Youth and Adolescence*, 15, 287–302.

O'Neil, J. M., Ohlde, C., Tollefson, N., Barke, C., Piggott, T. & Watts, D. (1980). Factors, correlates, and problem areas affecting career decision making of a cross-sectional sample of students. *Journal of Counseling Psychology*, 27, 571–580.

Osipow, S. H. (1986). Career issues through the life span. In M. S. Pallack & R. Perloff (Eds.), *Psychology and work: Productivity, change, and employment* (pp. 137–168). Washington, DC: American Psychological Association.

Papini, D. R., Sebby, R. A. & Clark, S. (1989). Affective quality of family relations and adolescent identity exploration. *Adolescence*, 24, 457–466.

Pascarella, E. T. & Terenzini, P. T. (1991). *How college affects students: Findings and insights from twenty years of research*. San Francisco: Jossey-Bass.

Rauste-von Wright, M. (1989). Body image satisfaction in adolescent girls and boys: A longitudinal study. *Journal of Youth and Adolescence*, 18, 71–83.

Reischl, T. M. & Hirsch, B. J. (1989). Identity commitments and coping with a difficult developmental transition. *Journal of Youth and Adolescence*, 18, 55–70.

Rest, J. R. (1983). Morality. In P. H. Mussen (General Ed.), *Handbook of child psychology*: Vol. 3. *Cognitive development* (J. H. Flavell & E. M. Markman, Eds.). New York: Wiley.

Ryan, R. M. & Lynch, J. H. (1989). Emotional autonomy versus detachment: Revisiting the vicissitudes of adolescence and young adulthood. *Child Development*, 60, 340–356.

Schiedel, D. G. & Marcia, J. E. (1985). Ego identity, intimacy, sex-role orientation, and gender. *Developmental Psychology*, 21, 149–160.

Snarey, J. R., Reimer, J. & Kohlberg, L. (1985). Development of social-moral reasoning among kibbutz adolescents: A longitudinal cross-sectional study. *Developmental Psychology*, 21, 3–17.

Steinberg, L. & Dornbusch, S. M. (1991). Negative correlates of part-time employment during adolescence: Replication and elaboration. *Developmental Psychology*, 27, 304–313.

Steinberg, L. & Silverberg, S. (1986). The vicissitudes of autonomy in early adolescence. *Child Development*, 57, 841–851.

Sullivan, K. & Sullivan, A. (1980). Adolescent-parent separation. *Developmental Psychology*, 16, 93–104.

Tiedeman, D. V. & O'Hara, R. P. (1963). *Career development: Choice and adjustment*. New York: College Entrance Examination Board.

Turner, J. S. & Rubinson, L. (1993). *Contemporary human sexuality*. Englewood Cliffs, NJ: Prentice-Hall.

U.S. Bureau of the Census. (1992). *Statistical abstract of the United States*, 1992 (112th edition). Washington, DC: U. S. Government Printing Office.

Violato, C. & Holden, W. B. (1988). A confirmatory factor analysis of a four-factor model of adolescent concerns. *Journal of Youth and Adolescence*, 17, 101–113.

Walker, L. J. (1982). The sequentiality of Kohlberg's stages of moral development. *Child Development*, 53, 1330–1336.

Walker, L. J. (1989). A longitudinal study of moral reasoning. *Child Development*, 58, 157–166.

Walker, L. J., de Vries, B. & Bichard, S. L. (1984). The hierarchical nature of stages of moral development. *Developmental Psychology*, 20, 960–966.

Walker, L. J., de Vries, B. & Trevethan, S. D. (1987). Moral stages and moral orientations in real-life and hypothetical dilemmas. *Child Development*, 58, 842–858.

Waterman, A. S. (1982). Identity development from adolescence to adulthood: An extension of theory and a review of research. *Developmental Psychology*, 18, 341–358.

West, M. & Newton, P. (1983). *The transition from school to work*. London: Croom Helm.

Whitbourne, S. K. (1986). *The me I know: A study of adult identity*. New York: Springer-Verlag.

Wilson, S. M., Peterson, G. W. & Wilson, P. (1993). The process of educational and occupational attainment of adolescent females from low-income, rural families. *Journal of Marriage and the Family*, 55, 158–175.

CHAPTER 11

The major themes of early adulthood—work, intimacy, marriage, and parenting—are all captured in this image of the young Harlequin family.

Early Adulthood (22–34 Years)

TABLE 11.1	Major Concepts of Social Role Theory
Social role	Parts or identities a person assumes that are also social positions: kinship roles, age roles, sex roles, occupational roles
Role enactment	Patterned characteristics of social behavior generated by a social role
Role expectations	Scripts or shared expectations for behavior that are linked to each role
Role gain	Addition of roles
Role strain	Stress caused by too many expectations within a role
Role conflict	Conflict caused by competing demands of different roles
Role loss	Ending of a role; may result in stress and disorientation
Dimensions of life roles that vary from person to person	Number of roles Intensity of involvement in roles Time demands of each role Structure or flexibility of the role

Major Concepts in the Study of Adulthood

Welcome to adulthood. All that has gone before can be seen as preparation; all that follows can be viewed as actualization. We have considered psychosocial development through seven preparatory stages of life encompassing approximately 22 years. During these stages, one undergoes rapid physical, cognitive, social, and emotional development. In the United States, life expectancy is currently about 75 years. Thus, approximately 50 years remain after the seven preparatory stages. In our conceptual scheme, four stages of psychosocial development unfold during these 50 years. Let us briefly examine some of the concepts that are important to our discussion of adulthood.

Life Roles

Life role is one of the concepts most frequently used for understanding adulthood (Brim, 1966, 1968; Parsons, 1955). The major concepts of social role theory—introduced in Chapter 3—are summarized in Table 11.1. We considered this concept in Chapter 7 when we discussed sex-role identification, and again in Chapter 10 when we examined individual identity versus identity confusion. Clearly, roles are learned and enacted during childhood. In adulthood, however, people assume multiple roles that expand their opportunities for self-expression and bring them into contact with a great variety of social demands. The salient roles of adulthood, such as worker, spouse, parent, teacher, mentor, or community leader, give structure and meaning to life. Loss of or change in these roles is often associated with anxiety and emotional distress (Thoits, 1986).

Involvement in multiple roles not only contributes to personality development but also allows adults to help to socialize younger generations (Parsons, 1955). Adulthood can be seen as a series of increasingly differentiated and complex roles that the individual plays for substantial lengths of time. Only in adulthood do individuals experience the behavioral requirements of many of their roles, and these experiences provide a basis on which to train their children for the demands of life roles.

The expectations associated with adult roles provide a frame of reference within which individuals make their own personal decisions. For example, a woman may know what is expected of her in the worker role, but she may choose to ignore those expectations and strive for greater responsibilities, more power, or more autonomy. People may conform to role expectations, revise them, or reject them altogether. In addition to the tensions produced by role conflicts and role strain, some of the stresses of adulthood result from the need to redefine certain role expectations in order to preserve one's sense of self.

Social Clock

Bernice Neugarten and her colleagues (Neugarten, Moore & Lowe, 1965) proposed the concept of the *social clock* as a way of understanding adulthood. This term refers to "age norms and age expectations [that] operate as prods and brakes upon behavior, in some instances hastening behavior and in some instances delaying it" (p. 710). Neugarten and her associates suggested that social class groups tend to agree on the appropriate age for significant life events, such as marriage, child rearing, and retirement. This consensus exerts social pressure on individuals, pushing them to assume a particular role at an expected age. Age norms may also suppress behaviors that are considered inappropriate for one's age. Adults not only are aware of existing norms regarding the timing of certain behaviors but evaluate their own behaviors as being "on time" or "too soon" or "too late." The social clock is constantly being reset as people confront the challenges, demands, and new structures of modern society.

The social clock concept has been elaborated to include norms for the sequencing as well as the timing of transitions in social roles (Rindfuss, Swicegood & Rosenfeld, 1987). Earlier in the century, there was much more agreement about both the ideal timing of most transitions and the normative order. For example, if one thinks of the coordination of the occupational and family careers, then a normative path might be to finish school, enter the labor market, get married, and have children. However, beginning with adult cohorts surveyed in the 1970s, we have seen much less consensus about the best age to make these transitions and considerable diversity in patterns of change (Rosenfeld & Stark, 1987). For example, many men say that they started a full-time job before they graduated from high school. Many women return to school after marriage. Increasingly, young men and women who are not married have children. As a result of divorce, both men and women enter and then leave their marital role, and of course, this change influences the school, work, and parenting transitions as well.

Life Course

Life course refers to the integration and sequencing of phases of work and family life. Glen Elder (1985), who has been a leader in the elaboration of the life course perspective, describes the two central themes in this approach as trajectories and transitions. A *trajectory* is the path of one's life experiences in a specific domain, particularly work and family life. The family trajectory might include marriage, parenthood, grandparenthood, and widowhood. A *transition* is the beginning or close of an event or role relationship. In the work trajectory, for example, a transition

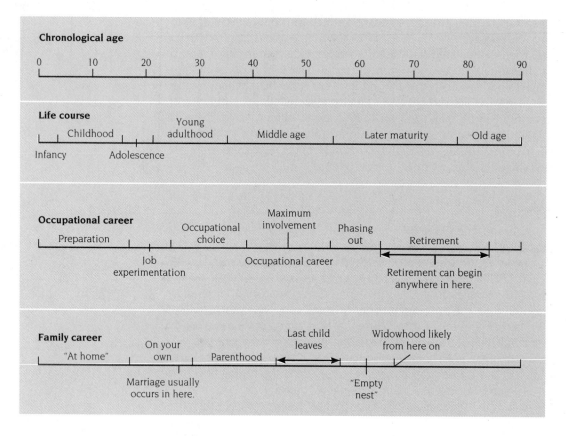

FIGURE 11.1

Relationships among age, life course, occupational career, and family career
Source: Atchley, 1975.

might be getting one's first job or being laid off or going back to school for an advanced degree. Transitions are the events that make up a lifelong trajectory.

The life course concept can be applied to the content of individual life histories as they are expressed in a social and historical time period (Atchley, 1975; Elder, 1975). Each person's life course can be thought of as a pattern of the adaptations that he or she has made to the configuration of cultural expectations, resources, and barriers experienced during a particular time period.

Figure 11.1 provides a view of the age-linked changes in occupational and family careers as they were perceived in the 1970s. The figure allows you to map the convergence of transitions across the occupational and family trajectories, illustrating periods of potential harmony and potential conflict between the demands in the two trajectories. Thinking about adult lives in the 1990s, you can see that this is just one possible map of the interconnections between work and family life in the course of a life. The occupational career and family careers look quite different for a woman who extends her educational preparation to include a professional degree, works before marriage, and delays childbearing into her middle to late 30s; a woman who remains single and dedicates her energy to excellence in a career; and a woman who marries out of high school, begins having children at 18, works during her childbearing years out of economic necessity, and then retires at 55 to enjoy her grandchildren and her personal freedom.

The pattern of the life course is influenced by the historical era. The life course of a person whose life began in 1900 and ended in 1975 might have looked quite different if that person's life had run from 1920 to 1995. The person would have gone through the same chronological phases during different periods of history

Work

This boy delivers flowers for a florist in Bogota, Colombia. He pedals his truck of freshly cut flowers to customers throughout the city. He may know little about the science of growing flowers, but he probably knows a lot about how to wind his way through the city streets to make his deliveries on time.

Women and men of the Tigray region of Ethiopia build an earthen dam to promote soil and water conservation. They work with rough shovels and baskets, struggling to protect their land from future devastations of drought and famine.

In a huge fish market in Tokyo, a man prepares fish filets for daily sale. He cuts slice after slice rapidly and evenly without injury.

In this Mexican family-run bakery, husband and wife work side-by-side. The bakery business turns one's life upside down. Bakers usually go to work in the evening and bake all night in order to have fresh goods in the morning.

Hospital workers stamp time cards at the start and end of a shift. Hospitals operate 24 hours a day, with shifts of employees coming and going at different times. Besides nurses and doctors, many kinds of employees are needed to keep these large, bureaucratic organizations running—from maintenance workers to data management specialists—all doing specialized work within a common setting.

Some kinds of work are learned through apprenticeships, with the skills and secrets of the trade passed from one generation to the next. This is a drum craftsman at work in his shop in Connecticut.

A single industry can involve people with very different specializations, as can be seen in these photographs. In the ocean off California, above, construction workers drive a pile that will help support an offshore mining platform.

In the protected setting of a scientific laboratory, a geologist for an Australian mining company uses a spectrometer, which provides a detailed analysis of the mineral content of ore samples.

At this banquet in Stockholm, Sweden, the guests of honor are the recipients of the 1992 Nobel Prize. It takes the combined efforts of hundreds of people to execute a banquet of this magnitude and elegance. Of these, the most conspicuous are food service personnel, but people in many other fields also contribute. For example, cab drivers bring the guests; clothiers and tailors sell and alter the guests' tuxedos and gowns; and manufacturers produce the silverware, glassware, china, and tablecloths.

The life stories of people in a similar cohort are often marked by common economic opportunities or misfortunes. For U.S. women in early adulthood during the World War II era, numerous employment opportunities opened up that had previously been filled almost exclusively by men.

Women entering early adulthood in the early 1990s found new opportunities for active military duty during the Gulf War, opening the way to many more leadership posts within the U.S. military than had been possible for women in the past.

with different opportunities, expectations, and challenges. The group of people who are roughly the same age during a particular historical period are referred to as a *cohort*. Differences in the occupational opportunities, educational resources, and number of people in the cohort are just three factors that may affect the pattern of life events. In addition, major crises, such as war, famine, and political unrest may alter a trajectory by introducing unanticipated transitions—for example, closing off certain activities, as when young men interrupt their education to go to war, and opening up new opportunities, as when women enter the labor market because many of the men are in the military (Elder, Caspi & van Nguyen, 1986; Elder, 1986).

In studying the life course, we are interested not only in the sequencing of events but in the psychological growth that occurs as adults strive to adjust to changing and sometimes conflicting role demands. People at different ages bring a distinct perspective to these events. For example, a crisis such as war may have a more direct impact on the behaviors of an adult coping with the events, whereas it may have a more direct impact on the values, fears, and beliefs of a child. We assume that the developmental level of the person and the particular developmental tasks and psychosocial crises that are most salient at the time will determine how a specific event will influence the life course (Stewart & Healy, 1989).

Functional Autonomy of Motives

A psychosocial conceptualization of the unique aspects of growth during adulthood requires a concept that frees the mind's energy to develop new motives, skills, interests, and goals. We find Gordon Allport's (1961) notion of the *functional autonomy of motives* most fruitful for explaining adult motivation. In this view, an individual's motive base is not fixed. A behavior is initially performed because of some need. The individual holds a job, for example, in order to earn enough money to support a family. The behavior itself becomes pleasurable and valued irrespective of its link to the original need. The person begins to enjoy work and to value it for its own sake. The valued behaviors—in this case, work behaviors—become functionally autonomous. The person engages in work because of the satisfactions it brings. The person may refuse a higher-paying job because the current work activities are so satisfying. This situation may also be reversed. The person works because of a need for money to support a family. He or she becomes good at making money and finds the process pleasurable. The pursuit of wealth becomes a functionally autonomous motive. The specific work becomes less valued than opportunities to earn money. The person may readily change jobs in order to receive a higher salary. He or she may begin to ignore the family in order to direct time and energy toward this newly established goal: accumulating wealth.

The concept of the functional autonomy of motives means that the individual's motive base is flexible and open to change. Stimulated by new experiences and new roles, the individual may uncover new motives that will press behavior in directions not taken earlier. The same behavior may be perpetuated by different motives in two individuals. Similar motives may perpetuate different kinds of behavior. One implication of this concept is that adulthood must be understood in terms not only of role learning and role change but also of the variety of individual motives that direct and sustain behavior.

Tendencies Toward Growth

Robert W. White (1966, pp. 374–405) identified five tendencies toward growth in adulthood: (1) stabilizing of ego identity, (2) freeing of personal relationships, (3) deepening of interests, (4) humanizing of values, and (5) expansion of caring. From his work on adult personality development, White found these to be the basic gains made during adulthood. They appear to be a mixture of the psychosocial crises of early and middle adulthood, suggesting a movement away from preoccupation with the self and an increasing investment in meaningful social relationships. Directions for change in personality development during adulthood are summarized in Table 11.2.

Erikson (1974) described the progression of developmental gains during adulthood in the following way. Notice the parallel to White's approach.

> In youth you find out what you **care to do** and who you **care to be**—even in changing roles. In young adulthood you learn whom you **care to be with**—at work and in private life, not only exchanging intimacies, but sharing intimacy. In adulthood, however, you learn to know what and whom you can **take care of**. (p. 124)

In summary, we find the concepts of life roles, the social clock, the life course, functionally autonomous motives, and human growth tendencies to be necessary to an understanding of the psychological development of the adult. Childhood is over. One addresses one's life with great expectations and exhilaration. After the initial excitement of the period subsides, one comes to realize that there is serious work to be done. Young adults are learning to engage in intense and meaningful relationships in marriage or with intimate partners, with friends, and with co-workers. At the same time, young adults are putting into action practices that express the values and beliefs to which they became committed at the close of later adolescence.

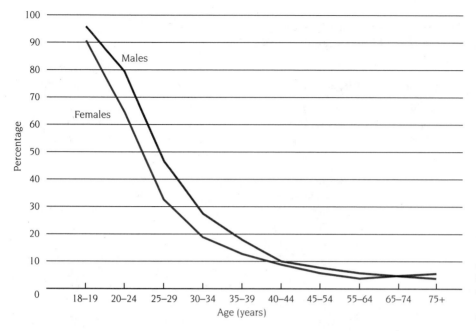

FIGURE 11.2
Never-married persons, by age and sex, 1991
Source: Based on Statistical Abstract of the United States, 1991.

Developmental Tasks

Young adults establish a style of life that will serve as a framework for the organization of experience during the rest of life. The *style of life* includes the tempo of activity, the balance of work and leisure, the establishment of a circle of friends of varying degrees of intimacy, and the selection of life activities that reflect the individual's value orientation. The most important social factors contributing to the creation of a lifestyle are whether one marries, the characteristics of one's marriage or intimate life partner, whether one has children and the characteristics of those children, and one's work. The extent to which one has a choice about each of these factors depends on cultural values and restrictions, societal norms and barriers, and socioeconomic factors, especially educational attainment. Each factor interacts with personality, interests, and life goals to shape a lifestyle.

Exploring Intimate Relationships

The period of early adulthood is a time when men and women explore the possibility of forming relationships that combine emotional closeness, shared interests and a shared vision of the future, and sexual intimacy. The nature of these relationships differ. Some young people engage in a form of "serial monogamy," a sequence of dyadic pairings with no commitment to marriage. Some young people find a same-sex partner with whom they make a long-term commitment even though formal marriage is not possible. Most young people are hoping to marry and become involved in dating relationships or friendship relationships, one of which is transformed into a more serious pattern of courtship and marriage.

Marriage is usually the central context within which work on intimate social relationships takes place. In 1991 only 10% of men and 9% of women ages 40–44 had never been married. Among those 65 years old and over in 1991, 4% of men and 5% of women had never been married (see Figure 11.2) (U.S. Bureau of the

TABLE 11.2	Tendencies for Change During Adulthood (based on Robert W. White's theory of adult maturity)			
Tendency	**Definition**	**Direction of Growth**	**Growth Trends**	**Situations That Produce Growth**
Stabilizing of ego identity	The self or the person one feels oneself to be	Increase of stability, sharper, clearer, more consistent, and free from transient influences; increasing independence from the daily impact of social judgments and experiences of success and failure	Placement in social roles; preferences for emphasis in role enactment; interests and initiatives the person brings to social roles; individuality; personal integration; sense of competence	Choices: Any incident that serves to heighten the efficacy of accumulated personal experiences as against new outside judgments; fresh experiences of success and failure; new objects of possible identification
Freeing of personal relationships	Responding to people in their own right as individuals	Human relationships that are increasingly responsive to the other person's real nature	Relationships with people who are important and with whom one has frequent and significant contact	Situations in which the other person behaves unexpectedly, thus disrupting one's habituated way of behaving; decreasing defensiveness against anxiety, allowing the person to observe and respond to others' behavior more openly
Deepening of interests	Interest always connected with an activity that wholly engages a person; progressive mastery of knowledge and skills relevant to a sphere of interest	Increasing identification of one's own satisfaction with development of objects of interest so that the inherent nature and possibilities for development of these interests increasingly guide the person's activity and become part of the satisfaction	As we come to live and act more fully on our interests, we increase both our knowledge and our capacity to influence what pertains to those interests	Action is undertaken and favorable consequences result; discovery; encouraging the interests of an older or younger person

(continued)

TABLE 11.2 (*continued*)

Tendency	Definition	Direction of Growth	Growth Trends	Situations That Produce Growth
Humanizing of values	Moral judgments	The person increasingly discovers the human meaning of values and their relation to the achievement of social purposes; increasingly brings to bear his or her own experiences and motives in affirming and promoting a value system	Values, whatever their content, become increasingly a reflection of one's own experiences and purposes	Situations in which existing values become a source of conflict; sudden empathic identification with some new aspect of value conflict
Expansion of caring	Transcendence of egocentrism; such deep concern for the welfare of someone or something that the meaning of one's own life is identified with the well-being of the object of care	Increased caring for the welfare of other persons and human concerns	Falling in love; taking care of the young; caring for cultural products and institutions	Situations that evoke the caring necessary to maintain civilized institutions and an environment suitable for raising the next generation; situations that evoke nurturant feelings and that offer an opportunity for nurture to be bestowed

Census, 1992). This pattern remained relatively constant from 1900 through the 1980s. Even though people today are more accepting of those who choose to remain single than they were in the 1960s, the number of young people who intend to remain single themselves has changed very little (Thornton, 1989). For most adults, happiness in life depends more on having a satisfying marriage than on any other domain of adult life, including work, friendships, hobbies, and community activities (Glenn & Weaver, 1981; Weingarten & Bryant, 1987; Broman, 1988).

The main change in the marriage pattern has been that more young adults postpone marriage until the end of their 20s. The percentage of single never-married women between the ages of 20 and 24 rose from 28% in 1960 to 64% in 1991. The comparable increase for single men was from 53% in 1960 to 80% in 1991 (U.S. Bureau of the Census, 1976, 1992; Stengel, 1985). It is currently normative for both men and women to be single during the years from 20 to 24.

Delaying the age at marriage is related to several other social trends, including having children at a later age, smaller projected family size, and therefore fewer years devoted to child rearing. Delaying age at marriage is also related to changing norms regarding sexual experimentation as a single person. The 1980s brought the uncoupling of sexual activity, marriage, and childbearing not only for adolescent girls, but for young adult women as well. Younger age at entry into sexual activity and increases in rates of cohabitation and of affairs between married men and single women suggest that even though many young women do not marry they become involved in intimate relationships during their 20s (Richardson, 1986). As we look to the future, it seems probable that an increasing proportion of men and women will remain single throughout their 20s, giving the domains of school and work greater influence in the early formulation of a lifestyle than the domains of marriage and family life.

Readiness to Marry

What determines whether or not the dating relationship will end in matrimony? A basic factor is the person's underlying desire to marry. In a national sample of unmarried people aged 19–25, the mean score on a 5-point scale (1 = strongly disagree, 5 = strongly agree) to the statement, "I would like to get married some day" was 4.3 (South, 1993). Only 12.6% of the respondents indicated that they did not want to marry. This analysis did reveal some differences among white, African-American, and Hispanic men and women. Given that all the groups held positive attitudes about marriage, the Hispanic men were the most enthusiastic about getting married and the African-American men were the least enthusiastic. Differences among the three ethnic groups of women were small and insignificant when factors of age, education, and employment were taken into account. Within racial groups, the African-American men and women differed more than did the men and women in the other two groups. On further analysis, it appeared that the reasons African-American men were somewhat less inclined toward marriage than white men were that they viewed marriage as having a potentially negative impact on their sex life and on their personal friendships.

Beyond desiring to marry, a very important factor is the readiness of the two individuals for a long-term commitment. Work on identity must be far enough along so that the possibility of a deep, emotional involvement with another person will be regarded as exciting rather than frightening. In studies of college students, a relationship has been found between identity status and the quality of intimacy. Those students who had achieved identity reported the most genuine intimate relationships. Those who were characterized as identity-confused were the least intimate and the most isolated (Orlofsky, Marcia & Lesser, 1973; Kacerguis & Adams, 1980; Craig-Bray, Adams & Dobson, 1988).

The developmental progression from identity achievement to intimacy is less clear-cut for women than it is for men. During later adolescence and early adulthood, women are likely to score higher than men on measures of intimacy. Further, it is not uncommon for some women to have high levels of intimacy even though they have foreclosed identities. Some research suggests that for women the issue of intimacy is resolved alongside work on identity, whereas for men identity resolution often precedes work on intimacy (Schiedel & Marcia, 1985).

For some young adults, readiness for marriage is a response to the social clock. Each social class has its own expectations about the best age for marriage. A group's ideal age at marriage is a good predictor of the actual age at which individuals in the group will marry (Teachman, Polonko & Scanzoni, 1987). For working-class groups, the ideal age for marriage is between 18 and 22. Adolescents who

The trend for college graduates to delay marriage is related to other lifestyle decisions, especially concerns about completing one's professional education and establishing a career. But for all their planning and preparation, older couples are just as caught up in the emotionality of the marriage ceremonies as are younger couples.

are dating seriously during high school are likely to marry soon after graduation. Once young working-class adults move past the age of 23 or 24, they find that the pool of eligible partners has been reduced significantly, and their anxiety about finding a mate increases. Young people who attend college tend to have a slightly later timetable for marriage. Participation in advanced education tends to delay marriage more for women than for men, perhaps because women who have had more education have alternative means to secure economic resources. For men, advanced education and higher earnings are likely to result in a somewhat earlier age at marriage, since men who have a more substantial income are more confident of being able to support a family (Teachman et al., 1987).

Readiness for marriage may be determined by some other personal agenda, such as completing work for an advanced degree, completing military service, or earning a certain income. In each case, the person with this kind of commitment is less receptive to expressions of love than he or she will be once the goal is achieved. In our culture, individuals have a great deal of freedom to choose their time of marriage and their marriage partner. Expectations that one will marry are strong, but young adults can at least follow their own timetables.

Selection of a Partner

Once a person is ready to consider marriage, the choice of partner and the decision to marry are influenced by a process of deepening attraction and commitment. Figure 11.3 provides a theoretical model of four phases of increasing involvement in the mate-selection process (Adams, 1986). At each phase, the relationship may be terminated if the key issues of that stage produce undesirable information or evaluation. The relationship may end if an alternative attraction

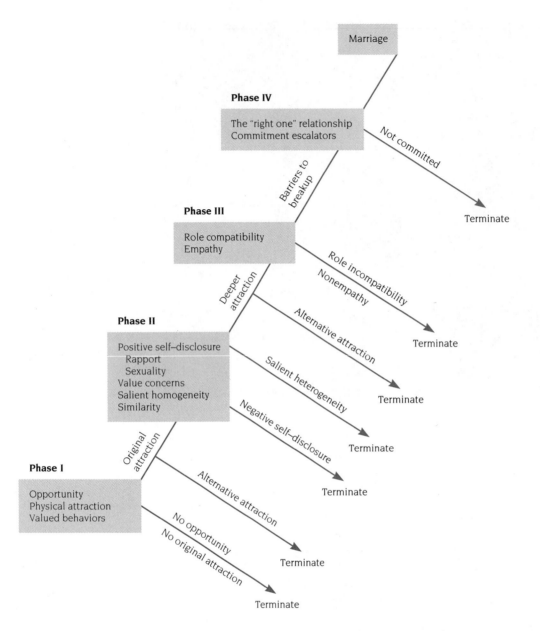

FIGURE 11.3

*The mate-selection process
in the United States*
Source: Based on Adams, 1986.

becomes so strong that it reduces investment in the first relationship. The alternative attraction may be another person, but it may also be a job, school, or the desire to achieve a personal goal.

In Phase I, partners are selected from among those who are available for interaction. Many of the choices one makes during adolescence and young adulthood, such as where to go to college, where to work, which parties to go to, and where to take a vacation, determine whom one meets. In each community, for each age group of women, the number of suitable available partners may differ depending on such characteristics as the educational level, employment opportunities, and racial composition of the men in that community (South & Lloyd, 1992). The number and characteristics of potential marriage partners differ if one lives in a metropolitan or a more rural community. In one analysis, the sex ratio of men to women was 119 unmarried men for every 100 unmarried women in rural communities and 106 unmarried men for every 100 unmarried women in metropolitan communities. Thus, earlier age at marriage for women in rural communities may be explained in part by a greater availability of male partners (McLaughlin, Lichter & Johnston, 1993).

Recent changes in the marriage patterns of African-Americans appear to be closely linked to the decline in the availability of appropriate African-American male partners. Single African-American women increased from 17% of the total African-American female population in 1970 to 34.5% in 1991 (U.S. Bureau of the Census, 1992). This decline in marriage is related in part to the shortage in the number of African-American men as a result of high mortality rates, and in part to the economic marginality of many African-American men, who have substantially higher rates of unemployment and imprisonment and lower educational attainment than white males (Taylor et al., 1990).

Even one's style of interaction—for example, whether one is shy and withdrawn or expressive and outgoing—influences the number and kinds of interactions that one has with others. In the most general sense, the choice of marriage partner depends on the network of interactions in which one is involved. Among those people one encounters, some attract attention and others do not. Physical appearance is a very important element in this initial attraction. In addition, people who are behaving in an admired, effective manner may be viewed as attractive or desirable.

Phase I, original attraction, moves on to Phase II as the partners begin to disclose information about themselves and interact in ways that deepen the relationship. In Phase II, the discovery of basic similarities and a feeling of rapport are central to continuing the relationship. Each person has key values and background characteristics that serve as a filter for assessing whether a person is an eligible partner. Of course, eligibility is defined differently by different people. For some, any person who is conscious is eligible. Others have criteria that limit the choice of a marriage partner to someone of a certain age range, religion, race, educational background, and family history. For example, some adults would not consider marriage to someone who does not share their religious faith. For these people, only members of their own religious group are perceived as eligible partners. If we look at trends in the United States from the 1920s to the 1980s, religion appeared to play a lesser role and educational level played a greater role in limiting one's choice of marriage partner. Young adults who were raised as Protestants and Catholics are more likely to marry one another today than in the past, whereas those whose highest educational level is a high school diploma and those who have attended college are less likely to intermarry (Kalmijn, 1991).

Many individuals may not even be aware of their own criteria for the eligibility of potential partners. For example, most women expect to marry men who are a few years older than they. Although they do not deliberately state this as a criterion for marriage, they simply do not interact with or feel drawn to a partner who is "too young" or "too old."

Similarity contributes to attractiveness. Most people seek marriage partners who will understand them and provide a sense of emotional support. They do not find attractive those who hold opposing views, come from quite different family backgrounds, or have temperamental qualities unlike their own. People of similar age and economic, religious, racial, and educational backgrounds marry each other in far greater proportions than would be expected by chance alone (Eshelman, 1985; Schoen & Wooldredge, 1989). For example, in 1991, only 0.4% of all married couples were made up of one African-American and one white partner (U.S. Bureau of the Census, 1992). Of course, there are many dimensions along which two people may recognize similarities or differences. They may seem quite different on some dimensions, such as religion and social class, yet discover that they are quite similar on others, such as life goals and political ideology. The more aware individuals are of the themes that are central to their own sense of personal identity, the better they can recognize the dimensions of similarity and difference in other people that will contribute to intimate relationships.

The relationship is likely to proceed from Phase II to Phase III if the partners extend the domains in which self-disclosure occurs, including sexual needs, personal fears, and fantasies. With each new risk taken, the discovery of a positive, supportive reaction in the partner deepens the level of trust in the relationship. Negative reactions following disclosures or the revelation of information that is viewed as undesirable may lead to the termination of the relationship. For instance, college students of both sexes consider a person much more desirable as a marriage partner if that person has had only light to moderate sexual experience. Students are especially rejecting of persons who have been involved in homosexual relationships (Williams & Jacoby, 1989). Thus, disclosures regarding prior sexual experiences may very well result in the termination of a relationship during Phase II.

In Phase III, the discovery of role compatibility and empathy begins to give the relationship a life of its own. Role compatibility is a sense that the two partners approach a situation in ways that work well together. Whether it is a visit to a relative's home, an office party, a casual evening with friends, or running out of gas on the highway, the two people discover that they like the way each behaves and that their combined behavior is effective. Empathy builds through these observations, enabling each partner to know how the other is responding and to anticipate the other's needs.

Once the partners are enjoying role compatibility and empathy, they move on to Phase IV, the "right one" relationship. In this phase, barriers to breaking up help consolidate the relationship. First, the partners have disclosed and taken risks with each other that they probably have not taken with others. Second, they have achieved comfortable feelings of predictability and empathy that make them more certain about each other than about possible alternative attractions. Third, through frequent role enactment together, they have been identified by others as a couple. There is usually social support for their remaining together. At this point, the costs of breaking up begin to be quite high, including loss of a confidant, a companion, and the social network in which the couple is embedded.

Cohabitation   In contemporary society, cohabitation rather than marriage may be the outcome of this process. In 1991 there were 3 million unmarried-couple households, an increase from 1.6 million such households in 1980 (U.S. Bureau of the Census, 1992). The probability of women entering a cohabiting relationship before marriage or before reaching the age of 35 increased from 2% for those born between 1928 and 1932 to 32% for those born between 1953 and 1957 (Schoen, 1992). In the youngest cohort, 63% married their first cohabitation partner before age 35.

The views expressed in the popular literature and among many couples are that cohabitation is a way of increasing marital stability by testing out couple compatibility before marriage. However, the research literature shows that those couples who have cohabited and then married are more likely to divorce than those who have not cohabited prior to their marriage (DeMaris & Rao, 1992). This pattern has been observed in studies in the United States, Sweden, and Canada. The exception to this pattern has been shown only in the most recent U.S. cohorts (those born 1948–1952 and 1953–1957). In these groups, couples who have married after cohabitation and those who never cohabited before marriage are equally stable or, perhaps one might say, equally unstable (Schoen, 1992).

A number of explanations have been offered to account for the greater instability of marriages following cohabitation. Because cohabitation has been comparatively nontraditional in the United States in the past, it has been suggested that people who cohabit have certain characteristics that may contribute to the formation of unstable marriages (Thomson & Colella, 1992). They may be more unconventional, adapting less well to some of the traditional role demands of marriage and holding to a more individualistic view of married life. They may have less commitment to the institution of marriage as a lifelong relationship. They may engage in more open conflict, leading over time to more negativity and hostility in the relationship. Although some of these hypotheses have received support, the changing social context of cohabitation and marriage makes it difficult to pin down the explanation.

One of the questions being raised about cohabitation is "What type of relationship is it?" Is it an informal alternative to marriage, or is it more like singlehood, except that it involves a bond of connection with a partner? In a comparison of women who have cohabited with those who have not, a significantly larger proportion of the cohabiting women want to get married. For these women, cohabitation is not a substitute for marriage but more like an element in the courtship process (Tanfer, 1987). In a 14-year longitudinal analysis of the white high school seniors of the class of 1972, subjects who were cohabiting were compared with those who were in a first marriage and with those who were single (Rindfuss & VandenHeuvel, 1990). In this comparison, cohabiting couples appeared to be more like singles than like married couples. The vast majority did not define themselves as married. They had employment and educational activities more similar to the single than to the married respondents. And they were more like the singles in saying that they did not plan to have children in the next two years. Other studies show a similar pattern in that cohabiting couples choose each other and exhibit a lifestyle more like that of singles than like that of married couples. Within this view, cohabitation is described as an "intimate relationship that maximizes individuation" (Landale & Fennelly, 1992).

However, in other samples, cohabitation appears to have a different meaning. In a study of Puerto Rican women who live on the mainland, primarily in New York, the nature of informal unions was studied (Landale & Fennelly, 1992). The sample ranged in age from 15 through 49. In the group aged 20–29, 16.5% said they were in an informal marriage. Only 8% described their relationship as cohabitation. *Consensual unions* without a civil or religious marriage has been practiced in Latin America for centuries and is regarded as a form of marital union. The practice is becoming less common on the island of Puerto Rico itself, but it is regarded as legitimate among mainland Puerto Rican women. Women who had a child within such a relationship were more likely to describe the relationship as informal marriage than as cohabitation. Women who had been married before were also more likely to describe their current relationship as informal marriage rather than cohabitation. In this sample, it appears that the informal unions were perceived by women to be more like marriage than like singlehood. This literature suggests that cohabitation embraces a continuum of meaning from short-term

The decision to adopt a child has added a new dimension of intimacy to this lesbian couple's relationship.

relationships to long-term commitments. In some subcultures, consensual unions without the formal rites of marriage are perceived as a very satisfactory, stable framework for personal and family relationships.

Relationships Between Partners of the Same Sex   The research on gay and lesbian couples is quite incomplete. What we present here is derived from research based on self-selected volunteer samples. Gay men and lesbians who would not volunteer to participate in research may be quite different in their outlook or adjustment from those who are comfortable enough to discuss the quality of their relationships. In addition, much of the literature is based on white middle-class participants. Gay men and lesbians are a diverse group with respect to their interests, talents, educational backgrounds, family backgrounds, careers, and other important aspects of adult roles. The description of gay and lesbian relationships that can be derived from the existing research misses much of the diversity that one would expect to uncover as this form of intimate relationship is studied in greater detail (Macklin, 1987).

> Annette E. Brenner remembers joking when her oldest son was 4 that she'd approve his marrying outside the family's faith as long as he married a woman. When he "came out" to her and her husband at 17, one of her first reactions was to try to "negotiate" him out of his gayness. She offered him a car, a house, if only he would wait and try marriage. He was at boarding school in Connecticut at the time, and she was convinced it was "just a stage." She remembers thinking, "Sure, this week you're a homosexual. Enjoy the experiment, have fun. Next week you'll be a Hare Krishna." Then she became enraged. "What is this kid doing to me?" she'd ask herself. "What was he doing to his grandparents, his brother and sister?" (Gelman, 1992, p. 50)

Homosexual relationships are often established within a climate of secrecy and social stigma, especially fears about parental rejection. Gay and lesbian couples often perceive less social support from family members and look to other members of the gay or lesbian community to validate and encourage their relationship (Kurdek & Schmitt, 1986).

Lesbian relationships are likely to emerge out of close same-sex friendships. Lesbians are somewhat more likely to be able to establish long-term relationships than gay men. Most lesbians describe their relationships as stable, sexually exclusive, and extremely close. Greater levels of satisfaction in the relationship are associated with greater levels of equality and shared decision-making. Equality in the relationship depends on equal resources and equal commitment to the relationship (Eldridge & Gilbert, 1990). Lesbians are likely to have had sexual relationships with men, and about 25% have been married at one time (Peplau & Amaro, 1982). In comparison with heterosexual wives, women in lesbian relationships are more likely to describe greater satisfaction in their sexual activity and greater dissatisfaction with inequalities in the relationship. Lesbian women place a strong value on companionship and confiding in one another, but they also expect to experience high levels of autonomy within their relationships.

Gay men are also interested in long-term relationships. However, they are less likely than lesbians to be sexually exclusive, and there is less consensus among gay men about the importance of sexual exclusiveness (Hary, 1983). In comparison to lesbian relationships, gay men often find partners in the context of a more active, competitive social scene that involves multiple short-term relationships. Among homosexual couples who are in a long-term relationship, there are few other differences between male and female couples with respect to the values they place on their relationship (Lewis et al., 1981). In a comparison of married couples, gay couples, lesbian couples, and cohabiting heterosexual couples, the cohabiting heterosexual couples had lower relationship satisfaction than the other three types of partners, who did not differ significantly from one another (Kurdek & Schmitt, 1986). In view of the social conflicts that gay men and lesbians are likely to encounter and the lack of social support for their lifestyle, it is remarkable that they are able to establish enduring partnerships that provide the level of intimacy and personal satisfaction evidenced in the research literature.

Adjustment During the Early Years of Marriage

Once the choice has been made and the thrill of courtship has passed, the first few years of marriage involve a process of mutual adaptation. These years may prove to be extremely difficult, particularly because the young married couple does not anticipate the strains that are to come. The partners may be quite distressed to find their "love nest" riddled with the tensions that are part of carving out a life together. In fact, data suggest that the probability of divorce is highest during the first years of marriage and peaks somewhere between two and four years. The median duration of marriage is about seven years. This pattern has been stable since the mid-1970s (U.S. Bureau of the Census, 1992).

There are many sources of tension in a new marriage. If the partners do not have similar religious, educational, or social-class backgrounds, they will have to compromise on many value decisions. Assuming a shared value orientation, certain lifestyle decisions may generate tension. The couple must establish a mutually satisfying sexual relationship. They must work out an agreement about spending and saving money. They must respond to each other's sleep patterns, food preferences, work patterns, and toilet habits. The couple may find the demands of their parents and in-laws to be a source of conflict. Usually it is the number of demands rather than any single one that makes the adjustment process so difficult.

Pablo Picasso, The Two Saltimbanques, *1901. To sustain a marriage, the partners must be able to interact even during periods of conflict. Withdrawal, rejection, and distancing are common reactions to conflict. These strategies may be effective during a brief cooling-off period, but they do not replace direct communication for exploring or resolving differences.*

As part of the adjustment to marriage, the partners must achieve a sense of psychological commitment to each other. The marriage ceremony is intended to make the commitment public and binding. The individuals concerned probably do not fully accept the reality of those marriage vows until they have tested the relationship. There is a period of testing during which each partner is likely to put strain on the relationship just to see how strong it really is. The matter may be posed in this way: "Will you still love me even if I do . . . ?" or "Am I still free to do what I did before we were married?" Every marriage relationship is different. The partners must discover the limits that their particular relationship can tolerate. Both must feel that they still have a degree of freedom. They must also believe that the limits on their freedom are balanced by the love they gain in return. As each test is successfully passed, the partners grow closer. They trust each other more and become increasingly sensitive to each other's feelings. The tests diminish in number as the question of trust is resolved.

Communication and Marital Adjustment

It is reasonable to expect that intimacy and a high level of marital satisfaction will require effective communication and the capacity to cope effectively with conflict. Conflict may be a product of the interaction of two well-developed identities, each with a distinct temperament and a distinct set of values and goals. It may be a product of the uneven distribution of power or resources. It may be a product of the simple day-to-day need to make decisions that the couple has never made before. Finally, conflict may be a product of the failure of a partner or the relationship to meet critical expectations. Whatever the source, marital stability and satisfaction are closely tied to how couples manage conflict (Filsinger & Thoma, 1988).

Two dimensions of conflict seem especially important in differentiating happy and distressed marital relationships. First, the amount of negative communication, especially nonverbal negative expressions and hostile putdowns, are more frequent in distressed than in happy couples. Second, distressed couples show a pattern of *coercive escalation*, a style of interaction in which the probability that a negative remark will be followed by another negative remark increases as the chain of communication gets longer and longer (Gottman & Levenson, 1986). This pattern has been observed, at the behavioral level, by coding the verbal and nonverbal characteristics of an interaction and, at the physiological level, by monitoring heart rate, blood pressure, and release of stress hormones during communication (Markman & Notarius, 1987; Schrof, 1994). As the communication becomes increasingly negative, the partners become so physiologically disorganized that they lose access to their more rational ego functions. Over repeated instances, the couples become sensitive to this physiological state, reaching it sooner. In comparison, happy couples become more effective in soothing one another and in finding ways of preventing conflicts. In a cross-national comparison between German and Australian couples, the German couples had a higher base rate of negative communication in their conversations than the Australian couples, but the differences between the happy and the unhappy couples followed the same pattern in both societies. The happy couples had comparatively fewer negative interactions and were able to interrupt negative interactions before they escalated (Halford, Hahlweg & Dunne, 1990).

In addition to being able to limit the amount of conflictual interaction and to prevent conflict from escalating, happy couples enjoy being together. They value the companionship aspects of their marriage, such as spending time together with friends or having dinner together (Kamo, 1993). In a comparison of American and Japanese couples, the Japanese were significantly less likely to share time together in these ways. However, for both the American and the Japanese couples, those who spent more leisure time together had higher levels of marital satisfaction. The causal nature of this relationship is not fully understood. We might assume that happy couples choose to spend more time together, but it may also be that couples who have opportunities to spend more time together come to feel more positive about their marriage.

Partners who have a high level of marital satisfaction report frequent, pleasurable interaction and a high degree of disclosure (Jorgensen & Gaudy, 1980; Robinson & Price, 1980). Emotional expressiveness, especially among husbands, and a lack of ambivalence about expressing one's feelings are an important element in this communication process, particularly among white middle-class U.S. families (King, 1993). In contrast, a decline in pleasurable interactions and an absence of communication of any kind, even conflicts, are associated with a high probability of divorce (Noller, 1980).

The idea that men and women view the communication process differently is also supported by research. Four types of communication styles have been described: conventional, controlling, speculative, and contactful (Hawkins, Weisberg & Ray, 1980). *Conventional interactions* gloss over issues. They maintain the interaction but do not express much emotional commitment or explore the other person's views. *Controlling interactions* express the person's views quite clearly but do not take the other person's perspective into account. *Speculative interactions* are guarded; they explore the other person's point of view but do not fully reveal the person's own position. *Contactful interactions* are open to the other person's point of view and also clearly express the speaker's own position.

Husbands and wives agreed that the contactful style was most desirable and the controlling style least desirable. However, wives preferred fewer controlling interactions from their husbands than the husbands preferred for themselves.

Wives also preferred more contactful interactions from their husbands than the husbands preferred for themselves. Wives perceived their husbands as being more conventional, more controlling, and less contactful than they themselves were. In other words, wives expressed the view that their husbands were less likely than they were to use the modes of interaction that they preferred. Husbands did not express the same dissatisfaction with the modes of communication used by their wives.

Even among couples who value open, direct, and accepting communication, there are stumbling blocks to intimacy. The socialization of men and women in our culture is still sufficiently distinct to result in differences in expectations and competencies. For example, men tend to be more ambivalent than women about expressing emotions and tend to withdraw to avoid escalating conflict. Women tend to want to "talk things out" so that everyone feels comfortable with the situation. Women are more adequately prepared for an intimate, open relationship than men. They expect and desire a degree of closeness that is often not reciprocated. Men, on the other hand, are quite satisfied with the degree of intimacy that they find in marriage and have fewer expectations of or less desire for greater closeness. These differences make expressing and resolving conflict difficult in marriage. Couples need to learn how to anticipate conflicts and use them as a means to clarify the relationship itself as well as the problem at hand. They need to know how to avert conflict when possible and how to establish some family rules for a "fair fight" when differences arise (Blood & Blood, 1978).

Adjustment in Dual-Earner Marriages

One of the greatest changes in American families in recent years has been the increase in the number of married women who are employed. The percentage of employed married women whose husbands are present rose from 30% in 1960 to 58% in 1991. The number of women with young children who work outside the home has grown substantially. In 1991, 57% of married women with children under 3 years old were in the labor force, compared with 33% in 1975 (U.S. Bureau of the Census, 1992). Rather than drop out of the labor force and return to work after their children are grown, the majority of women now remain in the labor force throughout the early years of parenthood (Piotrkowski, Rapoport & Rapoport, 1987).

There is no question that the involvement of both husband and wife in the labor market requires a redefinition of traditional family roles and the division of labor. Uncertainty about the expectations and behaviors of the husband and wife roles must be worked out between the partners. Sometimes this uncertainty helps to produce greater intimacy by generating interactions that lead to greater self-disclosure by each partner. Very personal preferences and habits must be examined if the partners are to arrive at a successful division of labor that is mutually satisfying. Sometimes this process is threatening. The partners may not really be aware of their expectations of themselves or of the other person until they are married. It is not until some weeks have gone by and no one has done the laundry that it becomes evident that the couple must decide who will do this task or how to share it.

One analysis of the potential conflicts for dual-earner couples focuses on the relative balance of power and demands for household labor for the two partners (Rosenfeld, 1992). In the traditional male-breadwinner, female-homemaker family model, the husband has more power as a result of his access to financial resources and participates little in the low-status household tasks. The wife has little power and the majority of responsibility for the household tasks. As women have entered the labor market, their access to financial resources has increased.

The First Couple is giving new visibility to the challenges that face dual-career couples. Much of the humor that is directed toward this couple reflects the lingering cultural standard for the man to be the "real boss" in a family.

To the extent that their husbands also help in sharing the household tasks, their well-being and mental health improve. For men, especially in families where there is a relatively high family income, as their wives' income matches or surpasses their own and when they have to take on a greater role in domestic tasks, their well-being declines and their mental health suffers. Those men who feel demeaned or threatened by demands to participate in household labor are likely to experience depressive symptoms similar to the reactions that women have when they try to carry the full responsibility of household tasks while also participating in the labor market. Finding the balance of power and of household responsibilities that preserves a comfortable feeling of mutual respect and support is a major challenge in the early years of the marriage and one that has to be fine-tuned and renegotiated throughout the marriage.

It is not only the number of two-worker families that has increased; the number of families in which both partners pursue high-powered professional, technical, or administrative careers has risen steadily. A considerable amount of research has been done on these dual-career marriages. The main variables studied and the major findings about these marriages are summarized in Table 11.3. Given the many sources of pressure on these couples, research has focused on the characteristics of these dual-career couples that are most likely to be associated with high levels of marital satisfaction (Thomas, Albrecht & White, 1984):

- Adequate income, with husbands earning more than their wives
- Couple consensus that husband's career is preeminent
- Husband supports wife's career
- Older children
- Satisfying social life
- Husband empathic to wife's stress
- Good sexual relationship
- Discussion of work-related problems
- Role complementarity and role sharing
- Shared activities and companionship

TABLE 11.3	Major Findings on Dual-Career Marriages

Variable Studied	Findings
Degree of marital satisfaction	Satisfaction related to degree of fit between husband's and wife's attitudes and aspirations. Couples with more traditional sex-role attitudes tend to experience more stress.
Early socialization experiences	Many women in dual-career marriages experienced: 1. Early adjustment to high levels of stress. 2. Little reinforcement for conventional values. 3. A close relationship with parents who supported their career aspirations.
Effects of having husband and wife in the same career field	Wives in the same field as their husbands tend to produce more than those not married to fellow professionals but are less productive and less professionally satisfied than their husbands.
Consequences of status differences between husbands and wives	Degree of stress is related to the extent to which the status difference is congruent with the gender-role identities and expectations of the partners.
Effect of dual careers on family task sharing	Partners tend to do more sharing of traditionally female tasks than do single-career or career/earner couples
Impact of work world on dual-career family	Negative impact of traditional business, which operates on the assumption that career takes precedence over family and that the employee has a full-time support system at home.
Effects of geographic mobility	Mobility has a negative impact on the wife's career; her needs tend not to be the determining factor in the decision to move.
Effect of particular structural variations	Couples who share less than two full-time equivalent positions favor a continuation of the arrangement, devote more time to their work, and are more productive than the average full-time employee; yet employers tend to view such an arrangement with reservation.

Source: Based on Macklin, 1987.

There are indications that highly educated women who are employed in demanding work roles are less inclined to remain in a marriage relationship that is not emotionally satisfying. Economic independence allows women to choose or reject marriage, a freedom that many women of earlier historical periods did not enjoy (Cherlin, 1981). At the same time, the literature confirms the continuation of a traditional, male-dominated career orientation in these successful dual-career marriages where both partners agree to let the husband's career take priority over the wife's so long as the husband also agrees to preserve time for companionate interactions, supports the wife emotionally, and participates at an acceptable level in household and family tasks.

In conclusion, positive adjustment and marital satisfaction in the early years of marriage are a function of the identity status of each partner, the desire for intimacy, open communication, closeness, participation in pleasurable, companionate time together, the resources available to both the husband and the wife and how those resources are shared, the way power is shared or struggled for, the way conflicts are expressed, avoided, or resolved, and the congruence or lack of congruence between the husband's and wife's perceptions of their ideal and actual role enactment.

Childbearing

Sometime during young adulthood, individuals decide whether or not to have children. The median age for entry into motherhood is estimated to be 23.7 and the median age for fatherhood to be about 26 (National Center for Health Statistics, 1990). Usually this decision is made within the context of marriage. A national survey of married men and women who were currently childless but of childbearing age measured their attitudes toward wanting to have children and the considerations associated with wanting or not wanting children (Seccombe, 1991). Men in the sample were more supportive than women of the view that it is better to have a child than to be childless, and a greater percentage of women than men said they did not intend to have children. The results suggest distinct patterns of orientation toward having children for men and women. In the past, men have not had to choose between having a career and having children. It appears that they continue to endorse a view of adulthood in which fatherhood will play an important role. Women, on the other hand, are becoming increasingly sensitive to the difficulties of combining career ambitions and motherhood. Many women perceive that they have to make a choice about whether to have children or to direct their efforts and energy into professional development and career attainment.

In the Seccombe (1991) survey, the benefits the respondents associated with having children included having someone to love; giving their parents grandchildren; having a sibling for another child; having someone to care for them when they were old; and giving them something to do. Women were more likely to endorse the benefit of having someone to care for them when they were old, but for all the other benefits, men and women agreed on their importance. The most important benefit mentioned was having someone to love.

Although the great majority of married couples intend to have children, the timing of their entry into parenthood varies. The notion of the social clock comes into play. Couples who wait a long time to begin their families may be pressured by parents who are eager to become grandparents or by friends who have already experienced the lifestyle changes that accompany the birth of the first child. In recent years, couples have begun to postpone having children until after the first years of their marriage. The decision to postpone childbearing is related to several other aspects of adult life. Couples who have a dual-earner marriage have to think about the effect of children on their family income. They may try to anticipate the best timing for childbearing in relation to job security or career advancement. Some couples set certain material goals for themselves as a prerequisite to having children. For example, they may decide to wait until they can buy a home, purchase some furniture, or travel together before they have children. Given the high divorce rate, couples are likely to want to feel confident that their relationship is strong before deciding to have children.

Delayed entry into parenthood has typically been studied in relation to the characteristics of the woman. It has been found to be related to a woman's level of education, a woman's career commitment, and the family's income. In a study of the timing of entry into fatherhood, men who were characterized as late-entry (30 years old or over) were more involved with their children and had more positive feelings about their children than did the on-time or early fathers (Cooney et al., 1993). Older fathers may feel that they have less conflict between commitments to work and commitments to family. They may feel that they have already demonstrated their ability to succeed in the "breadwinner" role, and therefore they approach parenthood with more confidence and a greater sense of self-efficacy. They may have more emotional resources to bring to their marriage and their parenting relationship.

The Impact of Childbearing on Marriage

In contrast to the elation that usually accompanies the anticipation of and preparation for the newborn, the arrival of the first child often brings a period of stress to the marriage. On the average, the transition to parenthood is associated with lower marital satisfaction and less marital happiness (Glenn & McLanahan, 1982; Belsky & Pensky, 1988). Ratings of marital satisfaction do not usually drop from very satisfied to very unsatisfied. Couples continue to be satisfied with their marriage after their children are born, but the level of satisfaction is somewhat lower.

Looking more closely at this pattern, Belsky and Rovine (1990) found clear evidence of individual differences among couples. In their longitudinal study of 128 families, they observed four patterns of change in the assessment of marital quality. Some couples showed a rapid decline in marital quality after the first baby was born. Some showed a slow, steady decline. A third group showed no significant change, and a fourth group showed slight increases in marital quality. These findings caution us not to overgeneralize group trends to individual cases.

The decline in marital satisfaction that may accompany the transition to parenthood can be accounted for in several ways. For the first months after a child is born, both parents are exhausted by lack of sleep. They are generally unskilled in the care of a newborn baby. They have new responsibilities and a new schedule. Many parents feel inadequate to care for their babies, and they turn to their parents, neighbors, pediatricians, and books for advice on how to do it. This lack of self-confidence creates tension between the marriage partners.

The baby's presence brings out areas of potential conflict between the partners about philosophies of child rearing or beliefs regarding appropriate child-care practices. Feelings of jealousy, competition, and abandonment may arise in the first months after the child is born. The exclusiveness of the husband-wife relationship is interrupted by the repeated demands of the new baby, and there is less time for the couple to be together without the baby. Feelings of resentment may be stronger when a couple's sex-role attitudes conflict with the actual activities they end up carrying out after a child is born (Belsky, Lang & Huston, 1986). For example, those men and women who endorse highly traditional views of sex roles after the transition to parenthood and who end up having to function in a more egalitarian mode, both sharing actively in tasks of child care and household, express lower levels of marital satisfaction (MacDermid, Huston & McHale, 1990).

It is not surprising that one's experiences as a child influence how one reacts to the parent role. It may be a bit more surprising that recollections of one's child-rearing environment are related to the level of marital satisfaction experienced after the birth of the first child. One study reported a more pronounced decline in marital adjustment after the birth of the first child when either the husband or the wife recalled his or her own parents as cold, rejecting, and involved in a conflictual marriage. In addition, negative child-rearing experiences were related to greater discrepancies between husbands' and wives' assessments of the quality of their marriage after their children were born (Belsky & Isabella, 1985). One interpretation of these observations is that memories of negative childhood experiences are reawakened with the child's birth and stimulate increased defensiveness. Another interpretation is that adults whose parents were cold and rejecting

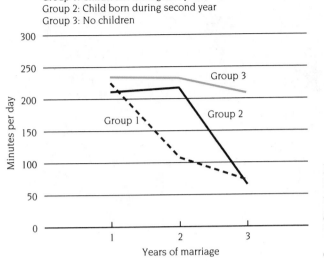

Group 1: Child born during first year
Group 2: Child born during second year
Group 3: No children

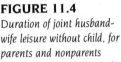

FIGURE 11.4

Duration of joint husband-wife leisure without child, for parents and nonparents
Source: Based on MacDermid, Huston & McHale, 1990.

may not have developed adequate parenting skills. They encounter increased conflict with their spouses when they become parents because they are less competent in this new role.

In an attempt to clarify the effects of many of these factors on marital satisfaction during the transition to parenthood, researchers compared marital activities and evaluations of the marriage by parents and nonparents who had been married the same number of years (MacDermid et al., 1990). They found that, over the first three years of marriage, couples' ratings of love and satisfaction in their marriage declined somewhat. There were no differences in the magnitude of the decline for parents and nonparents. Having children did not account for a greater drop in love or satisfaction than appears to occur as a result of adjusting to marriage in general. This is an important observation that provides new insight into much of the earlier research on marital satisfaction and the transition to parenthood.

However, having children did have a clear impact on marital companionship. The percentage of leisure activities shared by the husband and the wife dropped sharply after the baby was born, but it declined only slightly for the couples without children. During the third year of marriage, parents had a greater number of shared activities per day than nonparents, but very few when the child was not present. Figure 11.4 shows the number of minutes of joint leisure per day without the child for two groups of parents in comparison with joint leisure for nonparents in the first, second, and third years of marriage. After the birth of their child, couples have only about one-third as many minutes together alone as they had when they were childless. The nature of companionship in marriage clearly changes to incorporate a baby and therefore may become less intimate.

Surviving the early months of child rearing may strengthen the bond between the man and the woman. The partners begin to respect each other's competence in caring for their child. They also begin to conceptualize their roles as parents and to view the increasing complexity of their family structure as a challenge rather than a burden. The new child adds a degree of energy to the family through her or his expression of satisfaction, pleasure, and affection.

Once a couple has children, much of their shared leisure time is spent in activities that can include the children. It can be great fun, but it is usually not as intimate as the times before the children were born.

As the roles of mother and father are added to the adults' repertoire of role relationships, their own expectations as well as those of others concerning the raising of a child are aroused. The daily demands that the child places on the parents help them to define their own roles more realistically. Instead of wondering what parents should do, they are preoccupied with the concrete events of parenting. Through this experiential learning, young adults actually formulate their own definitions of parental roles. Assuming that the early experiences are successful and the parents are able to meet the child's needs, they gradually achieve a new level of self-efficacy in the parenting role, gaining new confidence in their ability to provide a nurturing environment for their child.

The process of social attachment and its impact on the infant was discussed in Chapter 5. The theme of mutuality as the central process for the establishment of trust was stressed. Here we can focus on the impact of this mutuality on the parents. Infants actively engage their parents, evoke unique responses, and, through their differential behaviors, begin to shape the adults' parenting behaviors (Brazelton et al., 1979; Bell & Harper, 1977; Lewis & Rosenblum, 1974). Mutuality is important in increasing the parents' capacity to experience intimacy. Successful child care results in the ability to anticipate children's needs, stimulate their interests, and delight their senses. Infants respond through shrieks of delight, elaborate smiles, and the active pursuit of loved ones. Infants are unrestrained in their loving. They mouth, bite, grab, laugh, smile, squeal, and coo in response to pleasure. Through their open demonstrations of affection, they teach adults about the expression of love and increase the adults' ability to demonstrate love.

Parenting is a unique experience of adulthood. There may be some developmental antecedents to parenting, such as baby-sitting, caring for younger siblings, or working with children as a camp counselor or a teacher. However, none of these roles involves the emotional investment and total responsibility of parenthood. As a parent, an adult has an opportunity to discover new aspects of his or her personality. The parent role brings demands that are quite distinct from the role of spouse. One must respond to a person who cannot really reciprocate one's generosity or caring. In this role, one discovers the qualities of nurturance, playfulness, and authoritativeness. As one interacts with one's children, memories of one's own childhood are revived and reviewed. Conflicts in one's relationship with one's parents, feelings of sibling jealousy, and recollections of school days, peer relations, fears, and secret dreams are all reviewed as one strives to respond to and guide one's children. In all of this, there is a new opportunity to put old ghosts to rest, reinterpret past events, and achieve a new sense of adult maturity.

Little has been written about the psychological growth stimulated by the decision to bear children. This is a unique and significant life choice that is made in various ways. Even babies who are unplanned are products of some kind of decision-making, whether it was a decision to have sexual relations knowing that pregnancy was possible, to avoid using effective means of birth control, or not to abort an unplanned pregnancy. During early adulthood, the issue of reproduction is confronted not just once but many times. Adults make choices to delay parenting, to have another child, to wait a while longer before having another child, or to stop having children altogether. In all of these decisions, many powerful themes are reflected. These themes may be linked to one's sense of fulfilling a masculine or feminine life purpose by having children. They may be linked to one's childhood socialization and identification with parental figures. They may be linked to some very intense religious beliefs about sexuality, contraception, or abortion. Reproduction is the means by which the species perpetuates itself. Regardless of the decisions one reaches, this issue cannot help but heighten one's sense of being and one's belief that the decisions of adulthood make a difference.

The Decision Not to Have Children

Not all married couples choose to have children. In 1990, 9.4% of women aged 18–34 expected to have no children during their lifetime. The percentage was lower for African-American (8.4%) and Hispanic (5.9%) women than for white women (9.5%), and it was higher for women with four years or more of college education (12.1%) than for women who had graduated from high school (8.9%) (U.S. Bureau of the Census, 1992). Much like attitudes toward remaining single, attitudes toward a lifestyle in which a couple chooses not to have children are becoming more accepting. This shift is evidenced in part by a change in the sociological jargon from "childlessness" to "voluntarily childfree." The decision not to have children is becoming increasingly common, not only in the United States but in other industrialized nations, especially as women's educational attainment and occupational commitments are reaching new high levels.

Couples who choose not to have children continue to experience social pressures to have children and are aware of negative stereotypes attributed to them by family members. Childless couples may be viewed as selfish, less well adjusted, less nurturant, and likely to have a less fulfilling life than couples with children (Somers, 1993). Resisting social expectations that married women ought to bear children requires a high level of personal autonomy and less need for social support from a wide range of reference groups. Voluntarily childfree men have been described as more independent, less tied to tradition, and more flexible than men who are fathers. Voluntarily childfree women have been described as more self-reliant, assertive, and concerned with personal freedom than women who are mothers (Silka & Kiesler, 1977). In general, couples who decide not to have children have been described as follows: "well educated, live in urban areas, have little or no religious affiliation, and hold nontraditional sex roles" (Somers, 1993, p. 643). They are able to disregard the negative social pressures, and they tend to find support from one another and from a small number of significant family members or close friends (Houseknecht, 1987).

Pablo Picasso, Studio with Plaster Head, 1925. *Picasso gives us a glimpse of the interior of his studio, condensing the tools and images that were important to his artistry at the time.*

Work

Work provides a major structural factor in the establishment of one's lifestyle. One's work is the primary means of accumulating financial resources. In addition, one's work determines in large part the activities, social relationships, challenges, satisfactions, and hassles or frustrations of daily life. The concept of work is complex. The following analysis provides a framework for the consideration of work as a psychological variable, looking at global characteristics of work and their potential impact on one's cognitive, social, and emotional development and sense of self in adulthood. This type of analysis is necessary because the variety of occupational roles in our society is so wide. Each job role places the individual in a somewhat different psychological context and therefore can be seen as exerting unique psychological demands.

The nature of the workplace is changing rapidly as we come to the close of the 20th century. Many factors, including the shift in emphasis from agriculture and manufacturing to service industries, the increasingly global nature of business, the increase in educational standards for entry into many careers, and the rapid evolution and extinction of specific types of work, have introduced new levels of uncertainty into the process of deciding about a career, finding work, and staying employed. There is a broad consensus that American workers need to enhance their efficiency and productivity in order to remain competitive in the global economic environment (Coordinating Committee for the Human Capital Initiative, 1993).

The first important distinction concerning occupations has to do with the training and posttraining periods. Much of the career development research focuses on getting a person ready to enter the labor market (Keller, Pitrowski & McLeod, 1991). The early phases of career decision-making presented in Tiedeman's model in Chapter 10 focus on self-understanding; career exploration; identification of a good match between personal interests, skills, and values and particular careers; and learning as much as possible about the specific job opportunities within a career domain. However, because of the wide variety of possible occupational choices and, within these, the great variety of work settings, one can make only limited progress in preparing to enact a specific occupational role. Even though many employers consider educational attainment a selection criteria, they often use it more as an element in determining one's eligibility for the job rather than as a detailed assessment of whether one has the background and skills to perform the job. In other words, educational attainment is usually viewed as a gross indication of whether one will get into the pool of people who are going to be considered for a position (Miller, 1988). Most jobs require a period of training for the novice employee. The training period may vary from a few weeks in the case of an assembly-line worker to ten years in the case of a physician. For some people, the stage of young adulthood is over before the training experience is completed.

In addition to involving the transmission of information about specific skills, the training period often involves the socialization of the worker. Through this socialization process, the novice learns about the technical skills, interpersonal behaviors, work-related attitudes, and authority relations that are valued by the work group. The training period also acquaints the novice with the specific demands and hazards of the particular occupation. This is the induction phase in Tiedeman's model. During the occupational search and training periods, the individual must evaluate the match between personal characteristics and the four central components of the work situation: (1) technical skills, (2) authority relations, (3) unique demands and hazards, and (4) interpersonal relations with co-workers.

Technical Skills

Most jobs require a certain degree of technical expertise. The amount required varies a great deal from one occupation to another. Individuals must evaluate whether the particular skills that are demanded of them are within their range of competence. They must determine whether they have the potential to improve their skills, and they must evaluate whether they derive pleasure and satisfaction from demonstrating these abilities. The job-training phase involves learning new skills. The success of individuals in this learning determines to some extent whether they will remain in the occupation.

Authority Relations

Each job role specifies status and decision-making relationships among people. One aspect of job training is learning which people evaluate one's work, which criteria they use for evaluation, and what are the limits of one's autonomy in the job. New workers must respond to both the authority structure and the people who occupy positions of authority. With respect to the authority structure, they must assess the channels for decision-making and the ways in which they can influence decisions. With respect to the people who occupy positions of authority, new workers must be able to deal with a variety of personalities in positions of higher and lower status. Having a good relationship with one's supervisor is a key element in job satisfaction.

Demands and Hazards

Each job has unique occupational demands, including norms for self-preservation, productivity, and availability. In some work settings, there are expectations for a very high level of personal commitment. Leisure time, family activities, and political or community roles are all influenced by one's participation in the work role. In other work settings, workers may become quite alienated. Such workers feel little sense of personal contribution to their employers' overall objectives. The norms vary greatly from one occupation to another. It is the task of individuals to assess how well they fit and how strongly they wish to maintain a fit with the unique characteristics of a particular occupational role.

Occupational hazards include a broad range of potential physical and psychological risks associated with the workplace, including exposure to toxins, the risk of work-related injuries, exposure to diseases, exposure to reproductive hazards, and exposure to working conditions such as noise or shift work that have negative psychological consequences (Baker, 1989).

Settings differ in the kinds of pressures or hazards that they inflict on workers. Similarly, individuals differ in their vulnerability to these pressures and hazards, their willingness to risk certain potential dangers, and their evaluation of the payoff for enduring some degree of stress (Gardell, 1977). The individual must ultimately decide whether the particular vulnerabilities are tolerable in light of the rewards.

Interpersonal Relationships with Peers

The final area of learning during the period of occupational search and training involves one's interpersonal relationships with co-workers. The potential for friendship relations in the work setting is usually not advertised as a central component of job satisfaction. Yet such relations are clearly a dominant feature of the decision to be committed to a particular work setting. The need for friends and the need to share with peers the anxieties of learning the new job provide strong motives for seeking comradeship on the job. The presence of congenial co-workers who can relax together and share feelings of accomplishment greatly enhances any work setting. In fact, the spirit of friendship on the job may compensate for many stressful situational demands.

Some work settings stress competition among co-workers. Incentives are arranged to stimulate competition rather than cooperation. In such settings, new workers must shoulder the strains of their new learning independently. They must learn the game of one-upmanship, always taking credit for successes and foisting the blame for failures onto others. The competitive setting may intrigue some individuals, whereas the affiliative setting attracts others. New workers must assess the quality of interpersonal relationships and determine whether or not these meet their social needs.

A number of factors limit the range of occupations open to a given person during the work search phase. Among the most obvious limiting factors are educational attainment, talent, and location. In addition, discrimination on the basis of race and gender continues to operate against the full participation of women and minorities in the work force.

O'Reilly and Caldwell (1980) studied the factors that influence job choice and subsequent job satisfaction. The subjects were graduates of a master's program in business administration. Two groups of factors influenced job choice: intrinsic factors and extrinsic factors. The *intrinsic factors* were interest in the job, personal feelings about the job, responsibility on the job, and opportunities for advancement. The *extrinsic factors* were family or financial pressures, advice of others, job location, and salary. Job satisfaction and commitment to remaining in the job six months after the job was taken were positively related to the strength of the intrinsic factors that influenced job choice. Two extrinsic factors—salary and job location—were also related to job satisfaction and job commitment. Strong pressure to take a job because of family or financial need was associated with lower job satisfaction and less commitment to remain in the job.

Other studies confirm that opportunities to shape the nature of the job during the early years are associated with positive feelings of job satisfaction and involvement. We may think of the new worker as following instructions and trying to fit in or do what he or she is told. However, in many jobs there is a certain amount of ambiguity about how daily tasks should be performed. A supervisor can go a long way in creating a sense of commitment to the job by involving the new employee in solving these problems rather than prescribing every task in great detail. Opportunities for autonomy and self-direction and being asked to shape how meaningful problems are solved are intrinsic rewards that play an important role in a worker's perception of being in a good job (Jencks, Perman & Rainwater, 1988).

In summary, we see the period of early adulthood as the experimental, training phase of work. Through involvement in several work settings, individuals learn to assess the technical requirements, authority relations, job demands, and quality of interpersonal relationships that characterize specific occupational environments. They also begin to project images of themselves moving into the future within a particular work role or work setting. In this context, they begin to assess the potential costs and gains of their occupation.

In an attempt to synthesize career development and individual development, Kathy Kram (1985) proposed a developmental model of career issues (see Table 11.4). Careers are delineated in three phases: early career, middle career, and late career, which correspond roughly to the phases of career exploration, career establishment and advancement, and career maintenance and disengagement (Hall, 1976; Osipow, 1986). In each phase, career development reflects *concerns about self*, including questions of competence and identity; *concerns about the career*, including questions of occupational commitment, advancement, and the quality of relationships in the work setting; and *concerns about family*, especially family role definition and possible conflicts between work and family life. Typical issues facing the person at each phase are suggested in Table 11.4. The issues of greatest concern during the early career phase reflect the need to demonstrate competence and the need to establish a satisfying lifestyle.

Lifestyle

During the course of young adulthood, one experiments with and gradually evolves a lifestyle. Central components of the lifestyle include the tempo or pace of activities, the balance between work and leisure, the focus of time and energy in specific arenas, and the establishment of social relationships at varying degrees of intimacy. One can think of lifestyle as the first enactment of the abstract construction of individual identity that was formed during later adolescence. Through the devotion of time and energy to certain tasks and relationships and the development of certain domains of competence, a young adult transforms values and commitments into actions. Let us consider some of the ways in which intimate relationships, children, and career interact to dictate some characteristics of the lifestyle.

Partners in an intimate relationship must develop a style of life that will reflect the activities and preferences of both. The work setting largely determines the structure of time, including when one goes to work and returns, what one feels energetic enough to do after work, how much time to allot for vacations, and what kinds of preparation must be made during nonworking hours for one's daily occupation (Small & Riley, 1990). Activity level or the pace of life is influenced in part by one's temperament, health, and fitness. To some extent, activity level is also influenced by the climate and the community. In northern climates, for example, there may be fewer social events away from home during the winter, and life may therefore revolve primarily around the home. In the summer, neighborhood

TABLE 11.4   Characteristic Developmental Tasks at Successive Career Stages

	Early Career	Middle Career	Late Career
Concerns about self	*Competence*: Can I be effective in the managerial/professional role? Can I be effective in the role of spouse and/or parent? *Identity*: Who am I as a manager/professional? What are my skills and aspirations?	*Competence*: How do I compare with my peers, with my subordinates, and with my own standards and expectations? *Identity*: Who am I now that I am no longer a novice? What does it mean to be a ``senior'' adult?	*Competence*: Can I be effective in a more consultative and less central role, still having influence as the time to leave the organization gets closer? *Identity*: What will I leave behind of value that will sympoblize my contributions during my career? Who am I apart from a manager/professional and how will it feel to be without that role?
Concerns about career	*Commitment*: How involved and committed to the organization do I want to become? Or do I want to seriously explore other options?	*Commitment*: Do I still want to invest as heavily in my career as I did in previous years? What can I commit myself to if the goal of advancement no longer exists?	*Commitment*: What can I commit myself to outside of my career that will provide meaning and a sense of involvement? How can I let go of my involvement in my work role after so many years?
	Advancement: Do I want to advance? Can I advance without compromising important values?	*Advancement*: Will I have the opportunity to advance? How can I feel productive if I am going to advance no further?	*Advancement*: Given that my next move is likely to be out of the organization, how do I feel about my final level of advancement? Am I satisfied with what I have achieved?
	Relationships: How can I establish effective relationships with peers and supervisors? As I advance, how can I prove my competence and worth to others?	*Relationships*: How can I work effectively with peers with whom I am in direct competition? How can I work effectively with subordinates who may surpass me?	*Relationships*: How can I maintain positive relationships with my boss, peers, and subordinates as I get ready to disengage from this setting? Can I continue to mentor and sponsor as my career comes to an end? What will happen to significant work relationships when I leave?
Concerns about family	*Family role definition*: How can I establish a satisfying personal life? What kind of lifestyle do I want to establish?	*Family role definition*: What is my role in the family now that my children are grown?	*Family role definition*: What will my role in the family be when I am no longer involved in a career? How will my significant relationships with spouse and/or children change?
	Work/family conflict: How can I effectively balance work and family commitments? How can I spend time with my family without jeopardizing my career advancement?	*Work/family conflict*: How can I make up for the time away from my family when I was launching my career as a novice?	*Work/family conflict*: Will family and leisure activities suffice, or will I want to begin a new career?

Source: Kram, 1985.

Pablo Picasso, The Bathers, 1918. *The "Bathers" gives us a glimpse into the leisure side of the notion of lifestyle. For many young adults, spending time with friends on the weekends, relaxing at the beach, enjoying the out-of-doors, or getting away for a brief vacation are important elements that add quality to life.*

activities become a more important stimulus for social life as people emerge from their "caves" and renew their friendships.

The balance of work and leisure is a result of one's disposition toward these two alternatives and the demands of the work setting. For some people, time with the family is more important than time at work. These people value highly the time they have at home with their families and make such time a priority when they choose a career. For other people, advancement in work through the expenditure of large amounts of time supersedes commitments to home and leisure. In these circumstances, the lifestyles of husband and wife may evolve somewhat separately, since the amount of leisure time they share may be limited. Couples who are able to enjoy leisure activities together that provide opportunities for relaxed, open conversation find that these contribute substantially to the strength and satisfaction in their marriage (Holman & Jacquart, 1988).

The more involved one is in the competitive demands of work, the less likely one is to feel comfortable about spending time away from it. The more engrossed one is in a variety of activities away from work, including hobbies and family events, the more time one will find for leisure. In some occupations, the time schedule leaves little room for personal choice. In others, the income from a single job may not suffice to support the family. Time that might be spent in leisure will then be spent in earning additional income through extra work. During later adulthood, following retirement, the balance of work and leisure time has to be revised. Adults who have spent most of their time at work may find themselves poorly prepared for a successful adjustment to the increased leisure of retirement.

During early adulthood, the husband and wife become acquainted with individuals and other couples, forming their social network. They form friendships in the neighborhood and at work. They may become involved in the social life of their religious community. If they have young children, parents of other young children at the day-care center or preschool may become important sources of social support. The orientation of the nuclear family toward outsiders is developed during this stage. An important factor in the establishment of adult friendships is the distance kept from or the degree of intimacy shared with nonfamily members. Some couples have only a few close friends, and others have a large circle of relatively distant acquaintances. This difference in orientation toward friendship determines one's involvement in social activities, one's reputation in the community, and the extent of one's dependence on the family to meet her or his needs for intimacy, approval, and companionship. One source of tension in marriage is a difference between a husband and wife regarding their orientation toward friendships. If one partner seeks intimate friendship with other adults and the other partner prefers only distant acquaintances, they may be in continuing conflict about involvement in social activities.

Another source of tension in early adulthood is the competition of role demands. One part of role learning involves a widening of competencies and relationships. Another part involves balancing the conflicting expectations of simultaneous role responsibilities. Adults struggle with the conflict between the demands of the work setting and the demands for time to build an intimate relationship with one's spouse, and with the tension between the desire to have children and the desire for achievement in work (Voydanoff, 1988; Jones & Butler, 1980). For both men and women, the world of work is likely to provide the most rigorous test of commitment and the greatest pressures for productivity during the early adult years. Pressure in the work setting competes directly with needs for intimacy and with the time and energy needed for parenting.

The contemporary emphasis on health and fitness indicates the importance of lifestyle decisions for illness prevention and longevity. Studies of people who have lived to an old age will be discussed in some detail in Chapters 13 and 14. Much of that research suggests that lifestyle patterns established in early and middle adulthood, including one's diet, activity level, exercise, encounters with challenging and intellectually stimulating tasks, and involvement with cigarette smoking and alcohol, all influence health and vitality in later life.

The Single Lifestyle

In addition to those young adults who are creating lifestyles within a marriage, there are many who remain single during their 20s. In 1991, 47% of males aged 25–29 and 32% of females 25–29 had never married (U.S. Bureau of the Census, 1992). As cited earlier in the chapter, the trend is for young adults to remain single during their 20s, and most young adults view this choice quite positively. Of course, the census data disguise the fact that many of these never-married young adults are actually in some form of committed relationship. Some are gay and lesbian couples who cannot legally marry; others are in a long-term cohabiting relationship. For example, J and L have been living together for five years. He is in law school; she is planning to go to medical school. They are very committed to one another, but they are also supportive of one another's career development. They do not want to impose marriage commitments that might constrain one or the other partner in her or his career development decisions.

TABLE 11.5   Typology of Singlehood

	Voluntary	Involuntary
Temporary	*Ambivalents*: Those not seeking mates but open to the idea of marriage	*Wishfuls*: Those actively seeking mates but currently unsuccessful
Stable	*Resolved*: Those who consciously prefer singlehood or choose it for religious reasons	*Regretfuls*: Those who would rather marry but are resigned to singlehood

Source: Shostak, 1987.

Several stereotypes of the single lifestyle have been examined empirically. One is that singles are very lonely. Another is that singles experience a greater variety of sexual partners and have a more exciting sex life than those who are married. Comparisons of single and married adults suggest that neither of these stereotypes is totally accurate. First, many singles do not live alone; they live with family members, significant partners, or roommates. It is those singles who have already been married and divorced who are most likely to suffer loneliness because of the absence of companions or confidants. The most isolated unmarried people are women who are single parents living with their children. They have the most restricted opportunities for social interaction. Many unmarried adults who live completely alone actually have compensated for their limited contacts at home by having a large number of relationships at work or in the community. Living alone is not associated with lower life satisfaction; in fact, it is often a preferred arrangement (Alwin, 1984). Second, singles who have never been married are not likely to have a great many sexual partners and are somewhat less likely than married couples to experience frequent sexual intercourse—that is, three or more times per week (Cargan, 1981).

The profile of the single lifestyle is rather different for men and women. Highly educated women who value self-determination and career achievement are likely to see distinct advantages in the single lifestyle. Many women choose to remain single while they complete their educational preparation and establish their career. They may view this period of singlehood as a chance to make important identity-related commitments before they are in a relationship in which they may be expected to negotiate or compromise their occupational goals. They may also view this period of becoming established in an occupation as "insurance" against the possibility of having to be fully self-supporting at some later time should their marriage fail or their husband die. Women who remain single experience more rapid advancement in both educational and occupational attainment (Houseknecht, Vaughan & Statham, 1987). Men, on the other hand, have never been subjected to great social pressure to choose between career and marriage. Men who remain single into their 30s are likely to be less well educated, less successful in the world of work, and therefore less desirable as partners.

Relatively little systematic research has been done on the psychosocial development of adults who remain single. Especially critical to this picture is the path along which singlehood is established. As our discussion implies, singles comprise a diverse group (Stein, 1989). It makes sense to see decisions about remaining single as linked to the broader theme of identity development. Table 11.5 suggests a typology of singlehood along two dimensions: stability of the single status and choice of the single status. Within this framework, two groups are single by choice: those who intend to marry but are not ready to marry at present (*ambivalents*) and those who do not intend to marry (*resolved singles*). One would expect the resolved singles to be quite satisfied about the quality of their lifestyle and effective in forming the kinds of relationships that support their choice. In contrast, the *wishful singles* and the *regretful singles* are involuntarily single. They may be more depressed about their situation and more dissatisfied with the quality of their lifestyle. Generalizations about adjustment or well-being among singles often fail to consider these kinds of distinctions (Shostak, 1987; Stein, 1981).

In the past, one of the reasons that young people married was the desire to have children. Today, singlehood and parenthood are more commonly combined. In addition to the large number of adolescents who become parents before marriage, reproductive technologies permit women who are single to bear children, and the courts have been increasingly willing to award custody to single men who want to have a family. Thus, through psychosocial evolution, opportunities for parenting have been separated from the need to have an intimate, adult heterosexual relationship.

Lifestyle is an umbrella concept for the variety of patterns of activities, commitments, and satisfactions that make up adult experience. Lifestyles are enormously diverse. Brothers and sisters may share a household. Adult children may live with their parents. Same-sex adults may live together in an intimate, loving relationship. Individuals may live alone. Couples may cohabit without any plans to marry. In all of these arrangements, a sense of intimacy may flourish, or a feeling of isolation may grow. Nevertheless, the cultural expectations for marriage, childbearing, and work will be confronted, evaluated, and accepted or rejected during these early adult years. In the process of deciding about each of these life tasks, the person begins to crystallize a life pattern that reflects his or her personal response to the array of cultural and social expectations within the context of contemporary resources and opportunities.

The Psychosocial Crisis: Intimacy Versus Isolation

Intimacy

Intimacy is defined as the ability to experience an open, supportive, tender relationship with another person without fear of losing one's own identity in the process. An intimate relationship has both cognitive and affective components. The partners in such a relationship are able to understand each other's point of view. They usually experience a sense of confidence and mutual regard that reflects their respect as well as their affection for each other. Intimacy in a relationship supports independent judgments by each member of the dyad. An intimate relationship permits the disclosure of personal feelings as well as the sharing and developing of ideas and plans. Recent research on the dimensions of love helps clarify the structure of intimate relationships (see Box 11.1).

There is a sense of mutual enrichment in intimate interactions. Each person perceives enhancement of his or her well-being through affectionate or intellectually stimulating interactions with the other (Erikson, 1963, 1980). Coming as it does after the establishment of personal identity, the possibility of establishing intimacy depends on individuals' perceptions of themselves as valuable, competent, and meaningful people.

"In the morning mist, two lovers kissed, and the world stood still."

It is not difficult to understand that a person would be on intimate terms with parents and siblings. The family is clearly the appropriate context for sharing confidences, expressing love, and revealing weaknesses and areas of dependence. The unique task of young adulthood is to establish an intimate relationship with someone who is not a member of one's own family. In fact, two people who eventually establish intimacy may begin as complete strangers who have very few, if any, common cultural bonds. Although an extreme degree of difference is unusual, it represents the greatest challenge that may confront two people.

Although intimacy is generally established within the context of the marriage relationship, marriage itself does not automatically produce intimacy. Our discussion of the early years of marriage indicated several forces potentially disruptive of the establishment of intimacy: (1) the early period of mutual adjustment, (2) the birth of the first child, and (3) the social expectations of members of the extended family.

In addition, differences in interaction styles between men and women suggest that many marriages may survive under conditions of low levels of intimacy. Consistent evidence finds that men interact less intimately than women (Reis, Senchak & Solomon, 1985; Carli, 1989). Men generally demonstrate more competitiveness, less agreement, and lower levels of self-disclosure than women. However, levels of self-disclosure are not related to loneliness for men as they are for women. It appears that men have the same capacity for intimate interaction as women, but they do not choose to exercise it in same-sex interactions. Whereas women consider intimacy appropriate for both same-sex and opposite-sex relationships, men tend to restrict their intimate interactions to women.

When men's and women's intimate relations were compared, men scored lower than women on intimacy, and relationships involving men were described as less intimate than those involving women. Relationships between two women were found to have the highest intimacy scores of the four possible combinations, and relationships between two men had the lowest. This does not mean that the relationships involving men were not intimate, but that they were not as intimate as those involving women (Fischer & Narus, 1981).

For thousands of years the nature of love and the qualities of a loving relationship have been described in songs and stories. Now love has become the focus of social science research (Hendrick & Hendrick, 1989). Robert Sternberg (1988) found that love may be described as a set of feelings, thoughts, and motives that contribute to communication, sharing, and support. According to his theory, almost all types of love may be viewed as a combination of three dimensions: *intimacy*, the emotional investment in a relationship that promotes closeness and connection; *passion*, the expression of physical and psychological needs and desires in the relationship; and *commitment*, the cognitive decision to remain in the relationship. Each of these dimensions is stronger in relationships that are perceived to be exclusive and that have a good chance of enduring than they are in more casual, temporary dating relationships (Whitely, 1993).

Ten components of a loving relationship have been identified:

1. Promoting the welfare of the loved one
2. Experiencing happiness with the loved one
3. High regard for the loved one
4. Being able to count on the loved one in time of need
5. Mutual understanding of the loved one
6. Sharing oneself and one's possessions with the loved one

BOX 11.1

Measuring Love

7. Receiving emotional support from the loved one
8. Giving emotional support to the loved one
9. Intimate communication with the loved one
10. Valuing the loved one in one's own life

These qualities are very close to Erikson's concept of intimacy. They reflect high levels of mutuality and openness as well as a deep commitment.

The nature of love is much the same in our relationships with our parents, siblings, friends, and lovers. The weighting of the ten components, however, may vary. In addition, some love relationships include a dimension of sexual attraction and others do not.

The intensity of love is captured in studies by Keith Davis (1985) on the differences between love and friendship. Lovers describe their relationships as characterized by *fascination*, *exclusiveness*, and *sexual desire*: "I would go to bed thinking about what we would do together, dream about it, and wake up ready to be with him again" (p. 24). They also express more intense caring for their loved ones than for friends. This caring includes giving their utmost, even to the point of self-sacrifice. The intensity of these characteristics accounts for some of the specialness and unsettling euphoria associated with being in love. It may also explain the relative instability of love relationships. Intense emotion is difficult to sustain.

In general, husbands are more likely than wives to be satisfied with the amount of empathy and companionship in their marriages (Scanzoni & Scanzoni, 1981). There are several explanations for this finding. Perhaps men expect less than women in the way of empathic understanding in marriage. Perhaps the socialization of girls really makes women better than men at providing empathy and understanding. The discussion of all-male and all-female friendship groups presented in Chapter 8 suggests that the kinds of interactive skills that girls develop within their friendship groups, including negotiating, supporting, and cooperating, are better suited to the establishment of intimacy in dyadic and family groups than are the interactive skills developed by boys, including bids for dominance, teasing, and roughhousing.

Another common context for the establishment of intimacy is the work setting. Affiliation and close friendship are likely to develop among co-workers. Workers may express devotion to an older leader or teacher. Through conversations, correspondence, conferences, or informal interaction on the golf course or at the bowling alley, co-workers can achieve an affectionate, playful, and enriching relationship. This kind of intimacy can be seen in a conversation reported by Kram (1985):

> ``Alan was very influential. I respected him as being pretty sharp and pretty astute. He had a lot of guts to tackle the problems that existed in the area and that was the union-management business. I was really identifying with him in terms of what and how you run something, how you manage something. You would sit down and talk about or debate how you do certain things, what should we do in this kind of situation. We would be right in line. I think it was the way I came at a problem; it might be similar to the way he would come at a problem.'' (p. 33)

The increased presence of men and women as co-workers in the work setting has introduced new difficulties in the establishment of intimacy among co-workers. Problems with sex discrimination and sexual harassment at work are evidence that many men and women have not developed mature strategies for forming mutually respectful, close relationships with adults of the opposite sex. Often, men and women find it difficult to establish an egalitarian relationship at work. They have a hard time engaging in the kinds of informal interactions that bring a sense of closeness to same-sex co-workers, like going to lunch together, stopping for a drink at the end of the day, or going to the gym to work out. Many men find it difficult to establish a style of interaction with women that is forthright but not sexual in tone. And many women find it difficult to be adequately assertive with men so that their ideas are taken seriously and their views are given full consideration.

Whether they are established in the context of marriage, friendship, or work, intimate relationships are often characterized by an atmosphere of romantic illusions: "Together we can conquer the world." The romance of an intimate relationship is a reflection of the energy and sense of well-being that come from the support and understanding that are shared within it. There may also be a degree of jealousy in the relationship. The devotion and commitment of intimate partners are vulnerable to threats of competing alliances. There is a deep sense that intimate relationships are not replaceable.

Isolation

The negative pole of the crisis of young adulthood is *isolation*. As with the other negative poles, most people experience some periods of this extreme. The more fully developed the ego becomes, the more it is characterized by clear boundaries. A by-product of the cultural values of individuality and independence is a heightened sense of separateness from others.

Loneliness

An estimated 25% of the adult population feel extremely lonely during a given month (Weiss, 1974). Feelings of loneliness may be separated into three categories: transient, situational, and chronic (Meer, 1985). *Transient loneliness* lasts a short time and passes, as when you hear a song or an expression that reminds you of someone you love who is far away. *Situational loneliness* accompanies a sudden loss or a move to a new city. *Chronic loneliness* lasts a long time and cannot be linked to a specific stressor. Chronically lonely people may have an average number of social contacts, but they do not achieve the desired level of intimacy in these

Even though most people desire intimacy, there are many obstacles to its attainment. Lack of social skills, obsessive self-doubts, fears of social rejection, chronic depression, and social conditions that remove one from the sphere of eligible partners can all contribute to a sense of isolation. For some young adults, the strains of poverty and oppression, including the absence of any loving caregiver in their childhood, make it impossible to experience the hopefulness in relationships that is essential for the formation of intimate bonds.

interactions (Berg & Peplau, 1982). Many chronically lonely people are very anxious about all types of social activities. They believe that success in social relationships is very important, but they expect social encounters to be difficult and to end poorly. People who have high levels of social anxiety tend to use interpersonal strategies that place barriers in the way of intimacy. They are likely to be self-deprecating, they are obsessed by the possibilities of negative outcomes of social interactions, and they tend to let others establish the direction and purpose of interpersonal activities (Langston & Cantor, 1989). There appears to be a strong relationship between social skills and loneliness. People who have higher levels of social skill, including friendliness, communication skills, appropriate nonverbal behavior, and appropriate responses to others, have more adequate social support systems and lower levels of loneliness (Sarason et al., 1985).

Depression

For some women, clinical depression appears to be linked to an orientation toward intimacy in which the self is systematically inhibited and devalued (Jack & Dill, 1992). These women have a view of how one ought to be in an intimate relationship that is characterized by four major themes: (1) They judge themselves by external standards, feeling that they never quite measure up to what other people expect of them; (2) they believe that one should build a close relationship with a man by putting his needs ahead of their own, and that to do otherwise is selfish; (3) they try to maintain a relationship by avoiding conflict and inhibiting any expression of their own views if they think those views may lead to disagreement;

and (4) they experience themselves as presenting a false front, one in which they appear happy and satisfied on the outside although they are angry or resentful inside. Over time, women who endorse this outlook on how to preserve an intimate relationship lose contact with their authentic self, and even if the relationship remains stable, they become increasingly depressed.

Fragile Identity

For some people, the possibility of closeness with another person seriously threatens the sense of self. They imagine intimacy to be a blurring of the boundaries of their own identities and thus cannot let themselves engage in intimate relationships. People who experience isolation must continually erect barriers between themselves and others in order to keep their sense of self intact. Their fragile sense of self results from accumulated experiences of childhood that have fostered the development of personal identities that are rigid and brittle or else totally confused. A tenuous sense of identity requires that individuals constantly remind themselves who they are. They may not allow their identities to stand on their own strength while they lose themselves, even momentarily, in others. They are so busy maintaining their identities or struggling to make sense out of confusion that they cannot attain intimacy.

Sexual Disorders

Isolation may be linked to sexual disorders. Two widely cited "desire disorders" are *hypoactive sexual desire*, a decrease or absence of interest in sexual activity, and *compulsive sexual behavior*, a compulsive need to relieve anxiety through sex (Rosellini, 1992). A loss of sexual desire is usually accompanied by physical withdrawal from the partner, as well as feelings of guilt and dread about losing intimacy. At the same time, the unafflicted partner often feels angry and guilty about imposing his or her sexual needs on an unresponsive and uninterested partner:

> At first it was fun: feverish kisses in his red Chevy, giggly nights of passion in the apartment. But then came marriage, two kids, and suddenly her husband's hands on her flesh felt like tentacles, and the sight of him approaching made her body stiffen with revulsion. Then the disagreements began, hurtful scenes ending with each of them lying wedged against opposite sides of the bed, praying for sleep. (p. 62)

In the case of compulsive sexual behavior, sex is disconnected from pleasure or intimacy:

> Gary's pattern was always the same: first, the unbearable anxiety, never feeling good enough to handle the latest stress at his architect's job. Then, the familiar response— a furtive scanning of newspaper ads, a drive to a strip show, two straight Scotches to catch a buzz, and finally a massage parlor. . . . Afterward, he'd sit naked on the edge of the bed, his thought roiling in disgust: "I must be sick . . . I can't change." But a few days later, the anxiety would begin again and he'd pore over the ads. (p. 64)

Some view compulsive sexual behavior as an anxiety-based disorder like other compulsions. Others argue that it is an addiction, like alcoholism. They agree that those who suffer from this disorder are not able to integrate sexual behavior as a meaningful component of an intimate relationship.

Situational Factors

Isolation may result from situational factors. The young man who goes off to war and returns to find that the "eligible" women in his town are married and the young woman who rejects marriage in order to attend medical school may find themselves in situations in which their desires for intimacy cannot be met. Although we may say that the lonely person should try harder to meet new people or develop new social skills, it is possible that the sense of isolation interferes with more active coping strategies (Peplau, Russell & Heim, 1977).

Divergent Spheres of Interest

Isolation may also be a product of diverging spheres of interest and activity. In a traditional marriage, for example, the man and the woman may participate in quite distinct roles and activities. Marriages characterized by such a division of life spheres are sometimes referred to as *his-and-her* marriages (Bernard, 1972). The wife stays home most of the day, interacting with the children and the other wives in the neighborhood. The husband is away from home all day, interacting with his co-workers. When the partners have leisure time, they pursue different interests: The woman likes to play cards and the man likes to hunt. Over the years, the partners have less and less in common. Isolation is reflected in their lack of mutual understanding and lack of support for each other's life goals and needs.

Enmeshment

Although Erikson tended to cast the construct of intimacy in tension with the construct of isolation, some family therapists offer another tension between healthy intimacy and enmeshment (Minuchin, 1978). Within this framework, a family is viewed as a structured system that contains individuals grouped into subsystems linked by patterns of communication, boundaries, alliances, and rules. As individual family members change and grow, the adaptive family experiences transitions that alter the structure. Families are characterized along a continuum from disengaged to enmeshed. The *disengaged* relationships are characterized by infrequent contact and a sense that the members of the family do not really seem to care about one another. This pattern may be viewed as similar to Erikson's concept of isolation within a family group. The *enmeshed* relationships are characterized by overinvolvement in one another to the extent that any change in one family member is met by strong resistance by the others; individuality is viewed as a threat to the relationship. Individuals in an enmeshed relationship may fear isolation to such a degree that they prevent one another from any movement toward autonomy.

The Central Process: Mutuality Among Peers

The central process through which intimacy is acquired is *mutuality* among peers. Intimacy implies the capacity for mutual empathy and mutual regulation of needs. One must be able to give and receive pleasure within the intimate context (Jeffries, 1993). The two young adults must bring equal strengths and resources to the relationship. Their intimacy is built on their ability to meet each other's needs and accept each other's weaknesses. When one partner needs to be dependent, the other is strong and supportive; at another time, the roles may be reversed. Each partner understands that the other is capable of many kinds of relationships. Commitment facilitates the couple's ability to meet each other's needs in different ways over time rather than producing a static, unitary relationship. In fact, mutuality should enhance both partners. In the process of supporting each other, both perform in ways that they might not have adopted had they been alone.

We have used the concept of mutuality to describe the development of a sense of basic trust during infancy. In that context, the distribution of resources, experience, and strength is quite uneven. Mutuality is possible only because the caregiver is committed to the infant's well-being. Through the consistent efforts of caregivers, children eventually learn to regulate their needs to fit the family pattern. However, children at this stage are not expected to be sophisticated enough to assess and meet their caregivers' needs. In young adulthood, the partners are responsible for fulfilling each other's needs. In most cases, there is no benevolent, superordinate caregiver. Just as the infant learns to trust the caregiver's ability to meet personal needs, each adult partner learns to trust the other's ability to anticipate and satisfy his or her needs. By expressing trust and commitment to one another, each partner strengthens the other partner's ability to believe in and invest in the relationship (Avery, 1989). The partners may also realize that they depend on each other to solve certain problems that they face as a couple. Mutuality is strengthened as the two individuals learn to rely on each other and as they discover that their combined efforts are more effective than their individual efforts would be. Mutuality, like attachment, is a characteristic of the dyadic relationship rather than of the individual members of the dyad (Barnhill, 1979). It is formed as two individuals, each of whom has a well-defined identity, discover that they can have open, direct communication; hold each other in high regard; and respond effectively to each other.

The crisis of intimacy versus isolation suggests a new level of ego development in which the individual's personal needs can be met only through the satisfaction of another's needs. Experiences of loving and attachment in the family context are transformed into a new form of affection that combines sexual maturity, cognitive perspective, personal identity, and mature moral thought. The obstacles to attainment of an intimate relationship are many. Some arise from childhood experiences of shame, guilt, inferiority, or alienation, which undermine the achievement of personal identity. Some are the result of incompatibility between partners. The number of adjustments that intimacy requires may overwhelm some young adults. Obstacles to intimacy derive from environmental circumstances that may erode the person's feelings of self-worth or may interfere with the evolution of a sense of mutuality. Finally, obstacles to intimacy may be embedded in the socialization process as children learn distinct gender roles that introduce antagonism between males and females and foster interpersonal styles that stand in the way of forming open, caring interpersonal relationships.

Applied Topic
Divorce

Americans have one of the highest rates of marriage among the modern industrial societies. Almost everyone wants to get married, and does. However, our divorce rate is also extremely high. You may have read that the divorce rate is one out of every three or every two marriages. However, this rate is really not a very accurate measurement of the frequency of divorce. It is based on the number of divorces decreed and the number of marriages performed in a given year. Most divorces are not an outcome of marriages performed in the same year. There are many more marriages that may end in divorce during a single year than there are people planning to marry. The divorce-to-marriage ratio inflates our picture of the frequency of divorce.

A more stable index of the frequency of divorce is the ratio of the total number of divorces to the number of married couples in the population. This ratio is

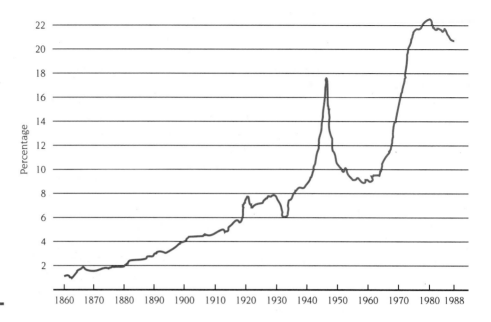

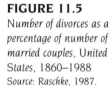

FIGURE 11.5

Number of divorces as a percentage of number of married couples, United States, 1860–1988
Source: Raschke, 1987.

plotted in Figure 11.5 for the 128-year period from 1860 to 1988. The divorce rate peaked rapidly after World War II and then fell, after which it rose from 1965 to 1980 (Raschke, 1987). About 46% of all marriages performed during 1988 involved at least one previously married partner. The slight decrease in the divorce ratio from 1982 to 1988 suggests that the divorce rate may be leveling off (U.S. Bureau of the Census, 1992).

Factors Contributing to Divorce

A large number of variables have been examined as correlates or predictors of divorce. The scope of these analyses encompasses cross-national studies, historical cohort analyses, multicounty comparisons, and cross-sectional comparisons of couples (White, 1990). At the societal level, countries where there are fewer women than men and where women marry at a later age have lower divorce rates. Two other societal factors show a curvilinear relationship: the socioeconomic development of the country and women's participation in the labor force. With respect to both of these variables, the divorce rate is lower in the mid-range than at either extreme (Trent & South, 1989).

In a comparison of divorce rates across more than 3000 counties in the United States, another important construct was identified: *social integration*, or the degree to which "people are tied or connected to one another, shared values being an important element in such integration" (Breault & Kposowa, 1987, p. 556). Characteristics of a community influence this sense of connectedness. Among the most significant of these characteristics are *population change*, the number of people who move in or out of a community each year; *religious integration*, the percentage of the population that belongs to a religious organization; and *urbanity*, the percentage of people within each county who live in an urban area. Divorce rates are significantly linked to each of these characteristics. They are higher in counties with high population change, low religious integration, and high urbanity. These findings suggest that the difficulties individual couples experience in their marriages may be aggravated by the community context. Or on the positive side, marriages may be buffered and supported by a critical sense of community identity and shared destiny.

At the level of couple-to-couple comparisons, four variables have been associated with the likelihood of divorce: age at marriage, socioeconomic level, differences in socioemotional development, and the family's history of divorce. In the United States, the incidence of divorce is especially high for couples who marry under the age of 20. These couples are about twice as likely to divorce as couples who marry in their early or mid-20s. Marital instability is also greater for couples who marry in their late 20s or later, than it is for those who marry in their early to mid-20s (Booth & Edwards, 1985). Such couples may have been single for a long time. Having coped successfully with single life, they may be less willing to remain in an unsatisfying marriage. They may also be more firmly entrenched in behaviors and habits that are not readily modifiable.

Both for couples who marry young and for those who marry at an older age, dissatisfaction with role performance is a significant factor in marital instability. For young couples, dissatisfaction centers on sexual infidelity and jealousy. For older couples, it focuses on interpersonal conflict, a domineering style, and lack of companionship. Age at marriage is associated with different developmental needs and varying threats to marital stability. Of course, age at marriage is not a single explanatory dimension. For those who marry young, there is also a greater incidence of premarital pregnancy, dropping out of school, and lower-paying employment, all of which contribute to the likelihood of divorce.

The concept of *socioeconomic level* is complex. It may be thought of as a combination of education, occupation, and income. Each of these components is uniquely related to the divorce rate (Glenn & Supancic, 1984). Men with more education have lower divorce rates. Women with more education also have lower divorce rates, except that those with five or more years of college are somewhat more likely to divorce than those who have had only four years (that is, have graduated from college). Within this overall pattern, there is also evidence of the *Glick effect*. Both men and women who have dropped out of high school or college have higher divorce rates than those who have completed high school or college. Further, those who have graduated from high school have a lower divorce rate than those who have had one to three years of college. Glick (1957) explained this pattern as evidence of lack of persistence. Those who are not committed to completing a unit of schooling may also lack the commitment to work at resolving the problems they encounter in marriage.

Many people seem to believe that divorce is a privilege of the rich, but the evidence suggests that the opposite is true: The divorce and separation rates are generally higher among couples with minimal education and low incomes (Reiss, 1980). Total family income is related to marital stability in some distinct ways. First, an erratic income and a high level of indebtedness are more strongly associated with marital disruption than a low but steady income. Second, the relationship between income and marital instability is different for men and women. For men, higher income is associated with low divorce rates. For women, there is no clear relationship between income and marital instability. A critical factor appears to be whether a woman is earning more or less than her husband. Divorces are more likely among the former than the latter (Raschke, 1987).

Socioemotional development is reflected in such dimensions as the partners' self-acceptance, autonomy, and expressiveness. Problems in communication are frequently cited by men and women as a major cause of divorce (Cleek & Pearson, 1985; Burns, 1984). In the past, women have experienced more stress and reported more problems in adjusting to marriage than have men (Veroff, Douvan & Kulka, 1981). They tend to be more dissatisfied with the level of intimacy in their marriage than are men. We examined these factors earlier in our discussion of adjustment to marriage. Mutual satisfaction in marriage depends heavily on the husband's qualities. The stability of the husband's masculine identity, the happiness of his parents' marriage, his educational level, his social status, and his ability to be comfortable in the expression of emotions all affect marital happiness. Many husbands, however, come to marriage with a deep need to be nurtured and to continue the pattern of care that they received in childhood. The stability of a marriage depends on both partners' achieving a sense of their own identity. This achievement helps to establish the balance in power and the mutual respect that are so central to emotional and intellectual intimacy.

The family's history of divorce is yet another factor that contributes to marital instability. Children of divorced parents are more likely to get divorced themselves than are children of intact marriages (Glenn & Kramer, 1987; Keith & Finlay, 1988). One interpretation of this finding that has received some empirical support is that children of divorce hold more favorable attitudes toward divorce as a reasonable strategy for resolving marital conflict (Greenberg & Nay, 1982). Another explanation is that children of divorce are likely to marry younger than children of intact marriages (Keith & Finlay, 1988). The available evidence suggests that the attitudes of children of divorced parents toward marriage and family life are as positive as those of children of intact families. As young adults, however, they may have more reservations and ambivalence about getting married, and they may have a less idealized view of marriage than young adults from intact families. As a result, they may enter marriage with strong expectations of a negative outcome. This expectation may stand in the way of achieving the level of commitment and self-disclosure that are characteristic of a mutually intimate relationship (Glenn & Kramer, 1987; Amato, 1988; Wallerstein & Corbin, 1989).

Coping with Divorce

It is an understatement to say that divorce is stressful. Divorce is associated with numerous losses, including the loss of resources, emotional support, one's marital and/or parental role, and social support (Kitson & Morgan, 1990). Studies have highlighted the dramatic income loss associated with divorce. In an analysis of over 2500 court records dating from 1970, Weitzman (1985) found that the divorced woman's standard of living decreased by 73%, while her husband's increased by 42%. The pattern of income loss depends on predivorce income. The incomes of women who were in higher income brackets before divorce (average income of $17,000) dropped to less than 50% of their former income in the first year after divorce. After five years, they were still at 50% of their predivorce income. The incomes of lower-income women (average income of $5,600) dropped to 77% of their predivorce incomes. However, most women in this group depended on public assistance for their continued income (Weiss, 1984). Loss of income may result in other kinds of material loss. For example, a woman and her children may have to move to less expensive housing, sell some of their possessions, and leave the community where they have established a network of friends and social support.

Divorce may bring role loss and social isolation as well as financial loss. Even when a divorce is viewed as a desirable solution, the period from the suggestion of divorce to its conclusion involves a variety of decisions and conflicts that may be very painful (Melichar & Chiriboga, 1985). Many people who experience divorce go through a time of intense self-analysis. They must try to integrate the failure of their marriage with their personal definition of masculinity or femininity, their competence as loving people, and their long-held aspirations to enact the role of husband or wife, father or mother. When children are involved in a divorce, there is the additional challenge of trying to work out the continuity of the parental relationships established before the dissolution.

The stress-related correlates of divorce are seen in the increased health problems of the divorced, the higher incidence of suicide among the divorced, and the overrepresentation of divorced adults in all forms of psychiatric settings (Stack, 1990). More than 40% of divorced adults are in some form of psychotherapy or pastoral counseling (Bloom, Fisher & White, 1978). One analysis of 80 divorced adults who had children identified six specific stressors: contacts with the former spouse, parent-child interactions, interpersonal relations, loneliness, practical problems such as cooking and cleaning, and financial problems. Of these stressors, problems involving interpersonal relations with peers were most closely tied to lower life satisfaction and a depressed, anxious mood (Berman & Turk, 1981).

Evidence of the impact of divorce on adjustment is provided in a comparison of divorced adults with those who are remarried and those who are in first marriages and have never experienced divorce (Weingarten, 1985). Divorced people have lower morale than those who have remarried. They recall the past as having been much happier than the present and are more likely to say they are not very happy at present. However, they do not have lower self-esteem, more anxiety, or more physical symptoms of stress than do remarried adults. In comparison with married people who have never divorced, the divorced have lower feelings of satisfaction, less zest for life, and greater anxiety. Even after remarriage, the experience of divorce has a lingering influence on adjustment. Remarried people say they have experienced a lot of difficult life events, are more likely to have used professional help in dealing with personal problems, and are more likely to suffer from stress-related physical symptoms than married people who have never divorced. The remarried are no different from the never-divorced in personal happiness, self-esteem, or optimism about the future. Reentering the marital state appears to boost morale, but it does not remove the strains of having encountered divorce.

One problem in coping with divorce is that many divorced people retain a strong attachment to their former spouse. Grief in divorce has been compared to bereavement in widowhood. In both cases, there is a loss and a need to adjust to it. Although the loss due to death may be more intense, especially if the death was sudden, the loss due to divorce may be more bitter. If an affectionate bond has been established, there is certain to be ambivalence about losing that bond even when the divorce is desired. Attachment to a former spouse may be positive or negative (one may wish for a reconciliation or blame the spouse) or both.

In a study of over 200 divorced persons, 42% expressed moderate or strong attachment to their former spouse. Some people wondered what their former spouse was doing, spent a lot of time thinking about her or him, expressed disbelief that the divorce had really taken place, and felt that they would never get over it. The attachment was stronger for those who had not initiated the divorce. The lingering feelings of attachment were associated with greater difficulties in adjustment to divorce, especially problems of loneliness and doubt about being able to cope with single life (Kitson, 1982). The stronger the positive or negative postdivorce attachment, the more difficult the adjustment in the years following the divorce (Tschann, Johnston & Wallerstein, 1989).

The fact that divorce is stressful does not mean that it is undesirable. Even among the attached spouses described by Kitson, many said that they felt a sense of relief about the divorce. Many divorced parents report that, despite the difficulties of single parenting, life is more manageable than it was in the midst of the continuing arguments and hostility that preceded the divorce.

Most people who experience divorce are very determined to cope with the stresses it brings. Unfortunately, many adults do not anticipate the specific kinds of stressors that they will encounter. Of course, adults have different coping strategies, some of which may not be effective for the special demands of divorce. Berman and Turk (1981) asked divorced adults to judge the efficacy of 53 strategies for coping with their own stress. Six groups of coping strategies were identified: (1) *social activities*, such as dating or developing new friendships; (2) *learning*, including going back to school or talking to a counselor; (3) *personal understanding*, such as understanding what went wrong; (4) *expressing feelings*; (5) *autonomy*—for example, becoming more independent or taking a job; and (6) *home and family activities*, especially taking care of the house and doing more things with the children. Of these six strategies, social activities, autonomy, and home and family activities were most strongly related to postdivorce life satisfaction. Social activities and autonomy were also linked to few perceived problems in the areas of loneliness and interpersonal relations.

The process of coping with divorce requires strategies devised to deal with the aspects of divorce that are perceived as most troublesome. Further, each of these coping strategies is in an area that lends itself to intervention. It seems quite possible that human service professionals may be very effective in helping adults develop coping skills for resolving some of the stresses of divorce.

Chapter Summary

In early adulthood, individuals begin to apply to themselves all the information they have acquired about adult roles. They may marry or make a commitment to an intimate partner, have children, and choose work roles. Gradually they evolve a style of life. In this process, their commitment to social institutions and to significant others expands. Their worldview becomes more diverse, and their appreciation of the interdependence of systems increases. One of the major sources of stress in this life stage is competition among roles.

The crisis of intimacy versus isolation emphasizes the evolution of adult sexuality into an interpersonal commitment. This crisis requires that needs for personal gratification be subordinated to needs for mutual satisfaction. Success is comparatively difficult to achieve in our culture because of the basic tension between the norm of independence and the desire for closeness. The research on marriage suggests that willingness to make a personal commitment to another adult is no guarantee of success. One of the important elements in a marriage relationship is the ability to engage in and resolve conflict.

The theme of intimacy highlights the management of emotion during adulthood. In our treatment of occupational training, however, we have suggested that many new areas of intellectual awareness are stimulated during the apprenticeship period. Coping with the challenges of early adulthood requires the integration of cognitive capacities, emotional openness, and effective interpersonal relationships. In the process of coping with divorce, we see the very clear need for daily problem solving and emotional expression to manage the grief, loss, and role transitions that accompany this crisis.

References

Adams, B. N. (1986). *The family: A sociological interpretation* (4th ed.). San Diego: Harcourt Brace Jovanovich.

Allport, G. (1961). *Pattern and growth in personality.* New York: Holt, Rinehart & Winston.

Alwin, D. (1984). Living alone. *ISR Newsletter*, 12, 3–4.

Amato, P. R. (1988). Parental divorce and attitudes toward marriage and family. *Journal of Marriage and the Family*, 50, 453–462.

Atchley, R. C. (1975). The life course, age grading, and age-linked demands for decision making. In N. Datan & L. H. Ginsberg (Eds.), *Life-span developmental psychology: Normative life crises.* New York: Academic Press.

Avery, C. S. (1989). How do you build intimacy in an age of divorce? *Psychology Today*, 23(5), 21–31.

Baker, E. L. (1989). Surveillance in occupational health and safety. *American Journal of Public Health*, 79, 9–11.

Barnhill, L. R. (1979). Healthy family systems. *Family Coordinator*, 28, 94–100.

Bell, R. Q. & Harper, L. V. (1977). *Child effects on adults.* Hillsdale, NJ: Erlbaum.

Belsky, J. & Isabella, R. A. (1985). Marital and parent-child relationships in family of origin and marital change following the birth of a baby: A retrospective analysis. *Child Development*, 56, 342–349.

Belsky, J., Lang, M. & Huston, T. L. (1986). Sex typing and division of labor as determinants of marital change across the transition to parenthood. *Journal of Personality and Social Psychology*, 50, 517–522.

Belsky, J. & Pensky, E. (1988). Marital change across the transition to parenthood. *Marriage and the Family Review*, 12, 133–156.

Belsky, J. & Rovine, M. (1990). Patterns of marital change across the transition to parenthood. *Journal of Marriage and the Family*, 52, 5–20.

Berg, J. H. & Peplau, L. A. (1982). Loneliness: The relationship of self-disclosure and androgyny. *Personality and Social Psychology Bulletin*, 8, 624–630.

Berman, W. H. & Turk, D. C. (1981). Adaptation to divorce: Problems and coping strategies. *Journal of Marriage and the Family*, 43, 179–189.

Bernard, J. (1972). *The future of marriage.* New York: World.

Blood, R. O. & Blood, M. (1978). *Marriage.* New York: Free Press.

Bloom, B. L., Fisher, S. J. & White, S. W. (1978). Marital disruption as a stressor: A review and analysis. *Psychological Bulletin*, 85, 867–894.

Booth, A. & Edwards, J. N. (1985). Age at marriage and marital instability. *Journal of Marriage and the Family*, 47, 67–75.

Brazelton, T. B., Yogman, M. W., Als, H. & Tronick, E. (1979). The infant as a focus for family reciprocity. In M. Lewis & L. A. Rosenblum (Eds.), *The child and its family* (pp. 29–45). New York: Plenum.

Breault, K. D. & Kposowa, A. J. (1987). Explaining divorce in the United States, 1980. *Journal of Marriage and the Family*, 49, 549–558.

Brim, O. G., Jr. (1966). Socialization through the life cycle. In O. G. Brim & S. Wheeler (Eds.), *Socialization after childhood: Two essays.* New York: Wiley.

Brim, O. G., Jr. (1968). Adult socialization. In J. Clausen (Ed.), *Socialization and society.* Boston: Little, Brown.

Broman, C. L. (1988). Significance of marriage and parenthood for satisfaction among blacks. *Journal of Marriage and the Family*, 50, 45–51.

Burns, A. (1984). Perceived causes of marriage breakdown and conditions of life. *Journal of Marriage and the Family*, 46, 551–562.

Cargan, L. (1981). Singles: An examination of two stereotypes. *Family Relations*, 30, 377–385.

Carli, L. L. (1989). Gender differences in interaction style and influence. *Journal of Personality and Social Psychology*, 56, 565–576.

Cherlin, A. J. (1981). *Marriage, divorce, remarriage.* Cambridge: Harvard University Press.

Cleek, M. G. & Pearson, T. A. (1985). Perceived causes of divorce: An analysis of interrelationships. *Journal of Marriage and the Family*, 47, 179–183.

Cooney, T. M., Pedersen, F. A., Indelicato, S. & Palkovitz, R. (1993). Timing of fatherhood: Is "on-time" optimal? *Journal of Marriage and the Family*, 55, 205–215.

Coordinating Committee for the Human Capital Initiative. (1993, October). Report of the committee on the changing nature of work. APS *Observer*, pp. 9–24.

Craig-Bray, L., Adams, G. R. & Dobson, W. R. (1988). Identity formation and social relations during late adolescence. *Journal of Youth and Adolescence*, 17, 173–188.

Davis, K. E. (1985, February). Near and dear: Friendship and love compared. *Psychology Today*, 19, 22–30.

DeMaris, A. & Rao, K. V. (1992). Premarital cohabitation and subsequent marital stability in the United States: A reassessment. *Journal of Marriage and the Family*, 54, 178–190.

Elder, G. H. (1975). Age differentiation and the life course. *Annual Review of Sociology*, 1, 165–190.

Elder, G. H. (1985). *Life course dynamics: Trajectories and transitions, 1968–1980.* Ithaca, NY: Cornell University Press.

Elder, G. H. (1986). Military times and turning points in men's lives. *Developmental Psychology*, 22, 233–245.

Elder, G. H., Caspi, A. & van Nguyen, T. (1986). Resourceful and vulnerable children: Family influences in hard times. In R. K. Silbereisen et al. (Eds.), *Development as action in context* (pp. 167–186). Berlin: Springer-Verlag.

Eldridge, N. S. & Gilbert, L. S. (1990). Correlates of relationship satisfaction in lesbian couples. *Psychology of Women Quarterly, 14,* 43–62.

Erikson, E. H. (1963). *Childhood and society* (2nd ed.). New York: Norton.

Erikson, E. H. (1974). *Dimensions of a new identity.* New York: Norton.

Erikson, E. H. (1980). Themes of adulthood in the Freud-Jung correspondence. In N. J. Smelser & E. H. Erikson (Eds.), *Themes of work and love in adulthood* (pp. 43–74). Cambridge: Harvard University Press.

Eshelman, J. R. (1985). One should marry a person of the same religion, race, ethnicity, and social class. In H. Feldman & M. Feldman (Eds.), *Current controversies in marriage and family* (pp. 57–66). Newbury Park, CA: Sage.

Filsinger, E. E. & Thoma, S. J. (1988). Behavioral antecedents of relationship stability and adjustment. *Journal of Marriage and the Family, 50,* 785–795.

Fischer, J. L. & Narus, L. R. (1981). Sex roles and intimacy in same-sex and other-sex relationships. *Psychology of Women Quarterly, 5,* 444–455.

Gardell, B. (1977). Psychosocial aspects of the working environment. *Working Life in Sweden,* 1.

Gelman, D. (1992, February 24). Born or bred: The origins of homosexuality. *Newsweek,* pp. 46–53.

Glenn, N. D. & Kramer, K. B. (1987). Marriages and divorces of children of divorce. *Journal of Marriage and the Family, 49,* 811–826.

Glenn, N. D. & McLanahan, S. (1982). Children and marital happiness: A further specification of the relationship. *Journal of Marriage and the Family, 44,* 63–72.

Glenn, N. D. & Supancic, M. (1984). The social and demographic correlates of divorce and separation in the United States: An update and reconsideration. *Journal of Marriage and the Family, 46,* 563–575.

Glenn, N. D. & Weaver, C. N. (1981). The contribution of marital happiness to global happiness. *Journal of Marriage and the Family, 43,* 161–168.

Glick, P. C. (1957). *American families.* New York: Wiley.

Gottman, J. M. & Levenson, R. W. (1986). Assessing the role of emotion in marriage. *Behavioral Assessment, 8,* 31–48.

Greenberg, E. F. & Nay, W. R. (1982). The intergenerational transmission of marital instability reconsidered. *Journal of Marriage and the Family, 44,* 335–347.

Halford, W. K., Hahlweg, K. & Dunne, M. (1990). The cross-cultural consistency of marital communication associated with marital distress. *Journal of Marriage and the Family, 52,* 487–500.

Hall, D. T. (1976). *Careers in organizations.* Santa Monica, CA: Goodyear.

Hary, J. (1983). Gay male and lesbian relationships. In E. D. Macklin & R. Rubin (Eds.), *Contemporary family forms and alternative lifestyles: Handbook on research and theory.* Newbury Park, CA: Sage.

Hawkins, J. L., Weisberg, C. & Ray, D. W. (1980). Spouse differences in communication style preference, perception, behavior. *Journal of Marriage and the Family, 42,* 585–593.

Hendrick, C. & Hendrick, S. S. (1989). Research on love: Does it measure up? *Journal of Personality and Social Psychology, 56,* 784–794.

Holman, T. B. & Jacquart, M. (1988). Leisure-activity patterns and marital satisfaction. *Journal of Marriage and the Family, 50,* 69–78.

Houseknecht, S. K. (1987). Voluntary childlessness. In M. B. Sussman & S. K. Steinmetz (Eds.), *Handbook of marriage and the family* (pp. 369–396). New York: Plenum.

Houseknecht, S. K., Vaughan, S. & Statham, A. (1987). Singlehood and the careers of professional women. *Journal of Marriage and the Family, 49,* 353–366.

Jack, D. C. & Dill, D. (1992). The silencing the self scale: The schemas of intimacy associated with depression in women. *Psychology of Women Quarterly, 16,* 97–106.

Jeffries, V. (1993). Virtue and attraction: Validation of a measure of love. *Journal of Social and Personal Relationships, 10,* 99–118.

Jencks, C., Perman, L. & Rainwater, L. (1988). What is a good job? A new measure of labor market success. *American Journal of Sociology, 93,* 1322–1357.

Jones, A. P. & Butler, M. C. (1980). A role transition approach to the stresses of organizationally induced family role disruption. *Journal of Marriage and the Family, 42,* 367–376.

Jorgensen, S. R. & Gaudy, J. C. (1980). Self-disclosure and satisfaction in marriage: The relation examined. *Family Relations, 29,* 281–287.

Kacerguis, M. A. & Adams, G. R. (1980). Erikson stage resolution: The relationship between identity and intimacy. *Journal of Youth and Adolescence, 9,* 117–126.

Kalmijn, M. (1991). Shifting boundaries: Trends in religious and educational homogamy. *American Sociological Review, 56,* 786–800.

Kamo, Y. (1993). Determinants of marital satisfaction: A comparison of the United States and Japan. *Journal of Social and Personal Relationships, 10,* 551–568.

Keith, V. M. & Finlay, B. (1988). Parental divorce and children's education, marriage, and divorce. *Journal of Marriage and the Family, 50,* 797–810.

Keller, J. W., Pitrowski, C. & McLeod, C. R. (1991). The development of a career development program. *Education, 112,* 470–473.

King, L. A. (1993). Emotional expression, ambivalence over expression, and marital satisfaction. *Journal of Social and Personal Relationships, 10,* 601–607.

Kitson, G. C. (1982). Attachment to the spouse in divorce: A scale and its application. *Journal of Marriage and the Family, 44,* 379–393.

Kitson, G. C. & Morgan, L. A. (1990). Consequences of divorce. *Journal of Marriage and the Family, 52,* 913–924.

Kram, K. E. (1985). *Mentoring at work: Developmental relationships in organizational life.* Glenview, IL: Scott, Foresman.

Kurdek, L. A. & Schmitt, J. P. (1986). Relationship quality of partners in heterosexual married, heterosexual cohabiting, and gay and lesbian relationships. *Journal of Personality and Social Psychology, 51,* 711–720.

Landale, N. S. & Fennelly, K. S. (1992). Informal unions among mainland Puerto Ricans: Cohabitation or an alternative to legal marriage. *Journal of Marriage and the Family, 54,* 269–280.

Langston, C. A. & Cantor, N. (1989). Social anxiety and social constraint: When making friends is hard. *Journal of Personality and Social Psychology, 56,* 649–661.

Lewis, M. & Rosenblum, L. A. (1974). *The effect of the infant on its caregiver.* New York: Wiley.

Lewis, R. A., Kozac, E. B., Milardo, R. M. & Grosnick, W. A. (1981). Commitment in same-sex love relationships. *Alternative Lifestyles, 4,* 22–42.

MacDermid, S. M., Huston, T. L. & McHale, S. M. (1990). Changes in marriage associated with transition to parenthood. *Journal of Marriage and the Family, 52,* 475–486.

Macklin, E. (1987). Non-traditional family forms. In M. B. Sussman & S. K. Steinmetz (Eds.), *Handbook of marriage and the family* (pp. 317–353). New York: Plenum.

Markman, H. I. & Notarius, C. I. (1987). Coding marital and family interaction: Current status. In T. Jacob (Ed.), *Family interaction and psychopathology* (pp. 329–390). New York: Plenum..

McLaughlin, D. K., Lichter, D. T. & Johnston, G. M. (1993). Some women marry young: Transitions to first marriage in metropolitan and nonmetropolitan areas. *Journal of Marriage and the Family, 55,* 827–838.

Meer, J. (1985, July). Loneliness. *Psychology Today, 19,* 28–33.

Melichar, J. & Chiriboga, D. A. (1985). Timetables in the divorce process. *Journal of Marriage and the Family, 47,* 701–715.

Miller, J. (1988). Jobs and work. In N. J. Smelser (Ed.), *Handbook of sociology* (pp. 327–359). Newbury Park, CA: Sage.

Minuchin, S. (1978). Structural family therapy: Activating alternatives within a therapeutic system. In I. Zwerling (Ed.), *The American family.* Philadelphia: Smith, Kline & French.

National Center for Health Statistics. (1990). *Vital statistics of the United States: 1988: Vol. 1. Natality.* Washington DC: U.S. Government Printing Office.

Neugarten, B. L., Moore, J. W. & Lowe, J. C. (1965). Age norms, age constraints, and adult socialization. *American Journal of Sociology, 70,* 710–717.

Noller, P. (1980). Misunderstandings in marital communication: A study of couples' nonverbal communication. *Journal of Personality and Social Psychology, 39,* 1135–1148.

O'Reilly, C. A. & Caldwell, D. F. (1980). Job choice: The impact of intrinsic and extrinsic factors on subsequent satisfaction and commitment. *Journal of Applied Psychology, 65,* 559–565.

Orlofsky, J. L., Marcia, J. E. & Lesser, I. M. (1973). Ego identity status and intimacy versus isolation crisis of young adulthood. *Journal of Personality and Social Psychology, 27,* 211–219.

Osipow, S. H. (1986). Career issues through the life span. In M. S. Pallak & R. Perloff (Eds.), *Psychology and work: Productivity, change, and employment* (pp. 137–168). Washington, DC: American Psychological Association.

Parsons, T. (1955). Family structure and the socialization of the child. In T. Parsons & R. F. Bales (Eds.), *Family, socialization, and interaction process.* Glencoe, IL: Free Press.

Peplau, L. A. & Amaro, H. (1982). Understanding lesbian relationships. In W. Paul & J. D. Weinrich (Eds.), *Homosexuality.* Newbury Park, CA: Sage.

Peplau, L. A., Russell, D. & Heim, M. (1977). An attributional analysis of loneliness. In I. Frieze, D. Bar-Tal & J. Carroll (Eds.), *Attribution theory: Applications to social problems.* San Francisco: Jossey-Bass.

Piotrkowski, C. S., Rapoport, R. N. & Rapoport, R. (1987). Families and work. In M. B. Sussman & S. K. Steinmetz (Eds.), *Handbook of marriage and the family* (pp. 251–284). New York: Plenum.

Raschke, H. J. (1987): Divorce. In M. B. Sussman & S. K. Steinmetz (Eds.), *Handbook of marriage and the family* (pp. 597–624). New York: Plenum.

Reis, H. T., Senchak, M. & Solomon, B. (1985). Sex differences in the intimacy of social interaction: Further examination of potential explanations. *Journal of Personality and Social Psychology, 48,* 1204–1217.

Reiss, I. L. (1980). *Family systems in America* (3rd ed.). New York: Holt, Rinehart & Winston.

Richardson, L. (1986, February). Another world. *Psychology Today, 20,* 22–27.

Rindfuss, R. R., Swicegood, C. G. & Rosenfeld, R. A. (1987). Disorder in the life course: How common and does it matter? *American Sociological Review, 52,* 785–801.

Rindfuss, R. R. & VandenHeuvel, A. (1990). Cohabitation: Precursor to marriage or alternative to being single? *Population and Development Review, 16,* 703–726.

Robinson, E. A. & Price, M. G. (1980). Pleasurable behavior in marital interaction: An observational study. *Journal of Consulting and Clinical Psychology, 48,* 117–118.

Rosellini, L. (1992, July 6). Sexual desire. U.S. *News & World Report, 113*(1), 60–66.

Rosenfeld, A. & Stark, E. (1987). The prime of our lives. *Psychology Today, 21,* 62–72.

Rosenfeld, S. (1992). The costs of sharing: Wives' employment and husbands' mental health. *Journal of Health and Social Behavior, 33,* 213–225.

Sarason, B. R., Sarason, I. G., Hacker, T. A. & Basham, R. B. (1985). Concomitants of social support: Social skills, physical attractiveness, and gender. *Journal of Personality and Social Psychology*, 49, 469–480.

Scanzoni, L. D. & Scanzoni, J. (1981). *Men, women, and change: A sociology of marriage and family* (2nd ed.). New York: McGraw-Hill.

Schiedel, D. G. & Marcia, J. E. (1985). Ego identity, intimacy, sex role orientation, and gender. *Developmental Psychology*, 21, 149–160.

Schoen, R. (1992). First unions and the stability of first marriages. *Journal of Marriage and the Family*, 54, 281–284.

Schoen, R. & Wooldredge, J. (1989). Marriage choices in North Carolina and Virginia, 1969–71 and 1979–81. *Journal of Marriage and the Family*, 51, 465–482.

Schrof, J. M. (1994). A lens on maternity. U.S. *News & World Report*, 116, 66–69.

Seccombe, K. (1991). Assessing the costs and benefits of children: Gender comparisons among childfree husbands and wives. *Journal of Marriage and the Family*, 53, 191–202.

Shostak, A. B. (1987). Singlehood. In M. B. Sussman & S. K. Steinmetz (Eds.), *Handbook of marriage and the family* (pp. 355–368). New York: Plenum.

Silka, L. & Kiesler, S. (1977). Couples who choose to remain childless. *Family Planning Perspectives*, 9, 16–25.

Small, S. A. & Riley, D. (1990). Assessment of work spillover into family life. *Journal of Marriage and the Family*, 52, 51–62.

Somers, M. D. (1993). A comparison of voluntarily childfree adults and parents. *Journal of Marriage and the Family*, 55, 643–650.

South, S. J. (1993). Racial and ethnic differences in the desire to marry. *Journal of Marriage and the Family*, 55, 357–370.

South, S. J. & Lloyd, K. M. (1992). Marriage opportunities and family formation: Further implications of imbalanced sex ratios. *Journal of Marriage and the Family*, 54, 440–451.

Stack. S. (1990). The impact of divorce on suicide, 1959–1980. *Journal of Marriage and the Family*, 52, 119–128.

Stein, P. J. (1981). Understanding single adulthood. In P. J. Stein (Ed.), *Single life: Unmarried adults in social context*. New York: St. Martin's Press.

Stein, P. J. (1989). The diverse world of the single adult. In J. M. Henslin (Ed.), *Marriage and family in a changing society* (3rd ed.). New York: Free Press.

Stengel, R. S. (1985, September 2). Snapshot of a changing America. *Time*, pp. 16–18.

Sternberg, R. J. (1988). *The triangle of love*. New York: Basic Books.

Stewart, A. J. & Healy, J. M. (1989). Linking individual development and social changes. *American Psychologist*, 44, 30–42.

Tanfer, K. (1987). Premarital cohabitation among never-married women. *Journal of Marriage and the Family*, 49, 483–497.

Taylor, R. J., Chatters, L. M., Tucker, M. B. & Lewis, E. (1990). Black families. *Journal of Marriage and the Family*, 52, 993–1014.

Teachman, J. D., Polonko, K. A. & Scanzoni, J. (1987). Demography of the family. In M. B. Sussman & S. K. Steinmetz (Eds.), *Handbook of marriage and the family* (pp. 3–57). New York: Plenum.

Thoits, P. A. (1986). Multiple identities: Examining gender and marital status differences in distress. *American Sociological Review*, 51, 259–272.

Thomas, S., Albrecht, K. & White, P. (1984). Determinants of marital quality in dual-career couples. *Family Relations*, 33, 513–521.

Thomson, E. & Colella, U. (1992). Cohabitation and marital stability: Quality or commitment? *Journal of Marriage and the Family*, 54, 259–267.

Thornton, A. (1989). Changing attitudes toward family issues in the United States. *Journal of Marriage and the Family*, 51, 873–893.

Trent, K. & South, S. J. (1989). Structural determinants of the divorce rate. *Journal of Marriage and the Family*, 51, 391–404.

Tschann, J. M., Johnston, J. R. & Wallerstein, J. S. (1989). Factors in adults' adjustment after divorce. *Journal of Marriage and the Family*, 51, 1033–1046.

U.S. Bureau of the Census. (1976). *Population profile of the United States*, 1975. Current Population Reports (Ser. P-20, No. 292). Washington, DC: U.S. Government Printing Office.

U.S. Bureau of the Census. (1989). *The black population in the United States, March, 1988*. Current Population Reports (Ser. P-20, No. 442). Washington, DC: U.S. Government Printing Office.

U.S. Bureau of the Census. (1992). *Statistical abstract of the United States, 1992*. Washington, DC: U.S. Government Printing Office.

Veroff, J., Douvan, E. & Kulka, R. A. (1981). *The inner American: A self-portrait from 1957 to 1976*. New York: Basic Books.

Voydanoff, P. (1988). Work roles, family structure, and work/family conflict. *Journal of Marriage and the Family*, 50, 749–762.

Wallerstein, J. S. & Corbin, S. B. (1989). Daughters of divorce: Report from a ten-year follow-up. *American Journal of Orthopsychiatry*, 59, 593–604.

Weingarten, H. R. (1985). Marital status and well-being: A national study comparing first-married, currently divorced, and remarried adults. *Journal of Marriage and the Family*, 47, 653–662.

Weingarten, H. R. & Bryant, F. B. (1987). Marital status and subjective well-being. *Journal of Marriage and the Family*, 49, 883–892.

Weiss, R. S. (1974). The provisions of social relationships. In Z. Rubin, (Ed.), *Doing unto others* (pp. 17–26). Englewood Cliffs, NJ: Prentice-Hall.

Weiss, R. S. (1984). The impact of marital dissolution on income and consumption in single-parent households. *Journal of Marriage and the Family, 46,* 115–127.

Weitzman, L. J. (1985). *The divorce revolution.* New York: Free Press.

White, L. K. (1990). Determinants of divorce: A review of research in the eighties. *Journal of Marriage and the Family, 52,* 904–912.

White, R. W. (1966). *Lives in progress* (2nd ed.). New York: Holt, Rinehart & Winston.

Whitely, B. E., Jr. (1993). Reliability and aspects of the construct validity of Sternberg's triangular love scale. *Journal of Social and Personal Relationships, 10,* 475–480.

Williams, J. D. & Jacoby, A. P. (1989). Effects of premarital sexual experience on desirability. *Journal of Marriage and the Family, 51,* 489–497.

CHAPTER 12

Painted when Picasso was 40, The Three Musicians
is considered one of the great masterpieces of modern art.
It synthesizes much of the exploration and experimentation of Cubism that transformed the way we think about
color, shape, texture, and meaning in art. At the same
time, it is a personal statement of themes that had
preoccupied Picasso's personal development—the masked
Harlequin, Pierrot, and Monk all joining together in
a musical synthesis.

Middle Adulthood (34–60 Years)

Middle adulthood lasts from about age 34 to age 60. From the point of view of psychosocial theory, a new reorganization of personality occurs during middle adulthood that focuses on the achievement of a sense of generativity. This new stage integrates the skills and perspectives of the preceding life stages with a commitment of energy to the future. We find evidence of a greater emphasis on intellectual achievement, a greater openness about oneself, and a greater sense of nurturance during middle adulthood (Haan, 1981), qualities that are expressed in unique ways by each person.

Most people have a value system that guides their priorities and ambitions. People who place a great deal of emphasis on the importance of work and their career base many of the decisions they make in their middle adult years on work values. Others believe that family, work, friendships, and taking care of themselves are equally important, and the decisions they make are guided by this value orientation. Within families, adults bring their values together, sometimes creating a new blend of family values, and sometimes discovering deep and enduring conflicts that do not seem to be readily reconciled. As children mature, they, too, bring their values to the table, introducing new potential conflicts and strains as well as new ideals and goals.

Values give a sense of meaning to one's life. During middle adulthood, one strives to find a balance between one's values and one's actions. Most people discover that this balance is delicate and must be constantly recalibrated. For example, you may feel that you are giving too much time to one domain of life, ignoring an area that you value and seeing it slip into disarray. Or you may come to appreciate a domain of life that you may not have valued as highly earlier and long to give it greater time and attention. Many situations call for decisions where there is no single correct answer. Several alternatives may be possible, and one must rely on one's values to determine which choice is best.

Because middle adulthood covers a relatively long period, there are opportunities to review and revise one's values and goals. We have been impressed by narratives told by many of our students about their fathers, who, in looking back, regret that they did not give more time to their young children and to investing in parenting activities. As a result, these men find ways to modify the demands of work life so that they can spend more time with their family. Others tell of parents who endured several years of long, tedious work hours when they were holding down several jobs in order to achieve some degree of financial security, knowing that they had let their marriage relationship drift. However, in reflection, they say that they realized it was only temporary and that they would live through the tough times knowing they would be there for each other.

Each adult typically engages in each of the developmental tasks discussed below: managing a career, nurturing an intimate relationship, expanding caring relationships, and managing the household. Through their roles in the family, at work, and in the community, middle adults have broad responsibilities for the nurturance, education, and care of children, adolescents, young adults, and older adults. Thus, the emotional well-being of the society as a whole rests largely on the capacity of middle adults to succeed in the developmental tasks of their life stage.

Developmental Tasks

Managing a Career

Work is a major context for adult development. Every person who enters the labor market has an occupational career. This career may not appear to be orderly and progressive. However, one can argue that, as long as a person is involved in an effort to make use of her or his skills and talents, there will be significant transactions between the world of work and the person's individual development.

There is clearly a reciprocity between work experiences and individual growth. We expect that people with certain kinds of experiences, abilities, and values will enter certain kinds of work roles (Holland, 1985). Once those roles have been entered, however, the work environment and the kinds of activities that the person performs also influence the person's intellectual, social, and value orientation. One's lifelong occupational career is a fluid structure of changing activities, ambitions, and sources of satisfaction. As people move through middle adulthood, the management of their occupational career becomes a task of central importance to their sense of personal effectiveness and social integration. Four aspects of the management of a career are discussed for their contribution to adaptation and individual development: achieving new levels of competence; midlife career changes; work and family life; and the impact of joblessness.

Achieving New Levels of Competence in the World of Work

Middle adulthood brings new challenges, a reformulation of ambitions and goals, and new levels of competence. The three areas that are emphasized here relate to the interpersonal and cognitive components of career development: expanding interpersonal skills, understanding and managing authority relationships, and meeting new skill demands by achieving new levels of mastery in critical skill areas.

Interpersonal Relationships   Most occupations place a great deal of emphasis on the development and use of interpersonal skills. Success in career management may require the ability to influence others, appear credible, develop a fluent conversational style, or learn to work effectively in groups or teams. Adults must devote some thought to their social presentation and must work to acquire the interpersonal skills that will increase their value in their work setting.

People use a variety of interpersonal tactics to influence their bosses, coworkers, and subordinates. In one study, subjects were asked to describe the extent to which they used specific interpersonal strategies to influence others in the work setting. Eight dimensions of influence were identified: assertiveness, ingratiation, rationality, sanctions, exchange, upward appeals, blocking, and coalitions. A variety of organizational factors influenced the kinds of strategies employed: the size of the organization, whether workers were unionized, the relationship between the person trying to use influence and the target of influence, and the extent to which the target was resisting influence (Kipnis, Schmidt & Wilkinson, 1980). This analysis emphasized the complexity of interpersonal skills and the need to have a wide repertoire of interpersonal strategies in order to be effective in the workplace. It also suggested that the organizational structure may have a significant impact on the kinds of interpersonal strategies that adults become accustomed to using.

Individuals must also be able to understand the demands that are made on them for interpersonal behavior in their work setting. They must be able to identify and distinguish between a competitive and a cooperative situation. In a highly competitive situation, some of the interpersonal demands may be gamesmanship plays designed to demonstrate one person's weaknesses and promote another person's advantages. In order to succeed in this type of situation, workers must

Interpersonal skills are essential to the development of effective teamwork. The person in charge needs to be able to invite suggestions and opinions and, at the same time, to prevent unproductive arguing. Effective problem solving requires an open interpersonal environment. Differences in gender, race, ethnicity, and age often introduce interpersonal tensions and conflicts that must be resolved.

learn to ignore some of these demands and maintain their productivity. In a highly affiliative situation, workers must be very tactful so as not to appear to be in competition with their peers. They may also find it necessary to comply with certain interpersonal requests even though these demands slow their performance. In most work settings, work norms are developed that enhance or limit the productivity of the entire staff (Katz & Kahn, 1978). Once individuals are accepted into the work setting by virtue of their ability to comply with work norms and to get along with co-workers, they may be able to influence those norms. At that point, they may alter their work environment so as to more fully meet their own needs for stimulation, productivity, and interpersonal relationships.

The interpersonal values held by the leaders in a work group influence the way they shape the work environment. Leaders who place a high priority on task performance tend to have a negative attitude toward workers whom they perceive as interfering with successful task accomplishment. They try to establish an ordered, highly structured work environment in which they can exercise their authority. Leaders who give high priority to interpersonal relationships are more accepting of workers who may interfere with task accomplishment. They try to establish an environment that will foster full participation of the workers. Most work settings require some blend of competitive and cooperative behaviors. The challenge for the worker is to be able to assess interpersonal demands as competitive or cooperative and to respond appropriately. In the process of establishing interpersonal relations, individuals will probably form some temporary alliances, some lasting friendships, and some enduring animosities (Argyle, 1972).

Understanding and Managing Authority Relationships   In addition to interpersonal relationships with colleagues, there are a wide variety of authority relations in the world of work. *Authority relations* encompass all the hierarchical relationships that give one person decision-making authority and supervisory control over another. Initially the individual must identify the authority structure operating in the work setting and must begin to establish a position in that structure. Advancement in a career inevitably involves some increase in responsibility and in the power to make decisions. One cannot hope to advance without assuming some increased authority. Thus, career management eventually involves the ability to assume authority as well as to respond to higher authorities.

Occupations vary in the patterns of advancement they offer. Some careers begin with a long period of subordination, which gradually leads to increased authority. Other careers place new employees in positions of authority quite early and continue to move them up a ladder of authority at a fairly steady pace. Still others initially establish the new worker in a position of authority that never changes much. The adult's task is to identify the authority pattern and to assess which skills will be needed for advancement in the hierarchy.

Some people do not choose to advance beyond a given point in the authority structure. They find a position in which the degrees of responsibility and subordination are comfortable and choose to remain at that level. Others find that if they do not choose to advance, their careers suffer. Still others discover that advancement is not possible and that they have attained some peak in status beyond which they cannot rise.

New competitive pressures on corporations are leading to a more flexible, less hierarchical authority structure (Kanter, 1989). With a reduction in the size of many bureaucracies, companies are asking workers to relate to one another in new ways. Managers are less likely to have ultimate control over chains of communication, work strategies, and project priorities. Managers must learn to facilitate the formation of effective teams of workers and to motivate groups by helping them identify with the importance of their mission within the organization. There are new freedoms to initiate new projects, to make deals, to build partnerships across departments within an organization, and to build alliances with external services and related companies:

> The old bases of managerial authority are eroding, and new tools of leadership are taking their place. Managers whose power derived from hierarchy and who were accustomed to a limited area of personal control are learning to shift their perspectives and widen their horizons. The new managerial work consists of looking outside a defined area of responsibility to sense opportunities and of forming project teams drawn from any relevant sphere to address them. It involves communication and collaboration across functions, across divisions, and across companies whose activities and resources overlap. Thus rank, title, or official charter will be less important factors in success at the new managerial work than having the knowledge, skills, and sensitivity to mobilize people and motivate them to do their best. (Kanter, 1989, p. 92)

Meeting New Skill Demands   The characteristics of the occupation and the work setting determine what kinds of work-related skills will dominate the adult's energies. It makes sense to expect that the actual tasks a person does from day to day will influence his or her intellectual development. The *Dictionary of Occupational Titles* (U.S. Department of Labor, Employment & Training Administration, 1993) uses 44 characteristics to describe the unique blend of aptitudes and temperament required for each type of work. These variables have been condensed to six basic factors: substantive complexity, motor skills, physical demands, management, interpersonal skills, and undesirable working conditions (Cain & Treiman, 1981). Each of these dimensions has the potential to contribute to workers' adaptation to their work life. Further, it is likely that, in the process of adapting to these dimensions, the adult will carry over aspects of work-related competence to family and community roles.

Melvin Kohn (1980; Miller et al., 1979) examined the relationship between occupational demands and psychological development. One of the strongest relationships identified is that between the substantive complexity of the job and intellectual flexibility. *Substantive complexity* means the degree to which the work requires thought, independent judgment, and frequent decision-making. *Intellectual flexibility* refers to the person's ability to handle conflicting information, to take several perspectives on a problem, and to reflect on his or her own values and solutions.

The substantive complexity of a person's job is highly related to his or her intellectual flexibility. This is true even when one takes into account the level of intellectual flexibility that was shown at the time of job entry. In a ten-year longitudinal study, it was found that the level of intellectual flexibility shown ten years earlier was strongly related to the degree of substantive complexity present in the job ten years later. There appears to be a reciprocal effect between these two dimensions. Being in a substantively complex work setting promotes intellectual flexibility. At the same time, a high level of intellectual flexibility appears to lead one to increasingly challenging, complex work.

One of the most significant areas of new skill development in the contemporary labor market is the ever-changing demand for computer skills. A person who filled a secretarial position 15 years ago may have been expected to type, take shorthand or dictation, manage files, make appointments, take telephone messages, and arrange for meetings, travel, or other appointments. Today, a secretary may be expected to perform all these tasks and, in addition, to make use of one or more software programs, usually including word processing, a spread sheet, and list processing. The secretary may be expected to maintain an interactive calendar, posting the calendar to a network of linked associates. The secretary may be required to use electronic mail to communicate with clients at remote locations, to post and retrieve information from electronic bulletin boards, and to keep abreast of software changes to upgrade the office system. In many offices, the secretary is also expected to be familiar with the basic operating principles of high-speed copiers, laser printers, and fax machines, at least in order to serve as the first line of defense when the system fails. Despite these new expectations of technical skill, the position title is likely to remain the same, and the relative salary and status have not changed. Yet the challenge of the work, including the complexity and diversity of tasks, has changed dramatically, and one must adapt to keep one's place.

Midlife Career Changes

Management of a career does not necessarily mean remaining within the same occupational structure throughout adult life. Work activities or work-related goals may change for at least five reasons.

First, some careers end during middle adulthood. One example is the career of the professional athlete, whose strength, speed of reaction time, and endurance decline to the point where he or she can no longer compete.

Second, some adults cannot resolve conflicts between job demands and personal goals. We read about successful business executives who turn to farming or about public relations experts who withdraw to rural areas to sell real estate. During middle adulthood, some workers recognize that the kinds of contributions they thought they could make are simply not possible within their chosen work structure. Others find that they do not have the temperament to be successful in their first career.

A third explanation for midlife career change is the realization that one has succeeded as much as will be possible within a given career. Adults may realize that they will not be promoted further or that changing technology has made their expertise obsolete. They may decide to retrain for new kinds of work or return to school so that they can move in new career directions.

Fourth, some women decide to make a greater commitment to career once their children are in high school or college. Many have chosen to withdraw from the labor market for a time in order to fulfill parenting roles. As they return to work, they may continue to expect to combine responsibilities as homemakers

A midlife career change is more successful for some than for others. Bill Bradley was an all-American basketball player who played professional ball. At the end of his basketball career he turned to politics and, in 1979, was elected to the United States Senate.

with career goals. However, their life course has an anticipated midlife career change built in as they shift their primary involvement from the home to the labor market. Others never worked before marriage, and they face the labor market as novices. These women, sometimes referred to as *displaced homemakers*, may enter the job market as a consequence of divorce or early widowhood, facing extreme economic pressures and competing with much younger workers for entry-level positions.

Fifth, with the restructuring of the work force, some workers are laid off and cannot be rehired in the same field. They have to retrain for a new line of work or for similar work in a new industry.

We must be cautious not to idealize midlife career change (French et al., 1983). Although we know that this type of change is increasingly common as a result of the changing characteristics of the labor market, we suspect that the ease or difficulty of making such a change depends in part on the extent to which workers perceive that they have control over the conditions of the change. Reviewing the reasons cited above for making a midlife career change, for example, the person who has to find a new line of work because the work he or she has been doing—let's say, small family farming—has become economically impossible may face the change with resentment and a sense of futility over reaching a dead end in work that was perceived as challenging and meaningful. The person who is trying a new career direction in order to have more control over her or his time or to deliberately reduce the demands and pressures of a greedy occupation may feel quite rejuvenated about making the change.

Work and Family Life

Almost no person manages a career independently of commitments to spouse, children, parents, other household members, and friends. A decision to assume more authority, work longer hours, accept an offer with another company, quit one's job, or accept a transfer to a new location will touch the lives of other household and family members. For many people, one of the most draining aspects of career management is the effort to meet the conflicting expectations of marital, parental, and work roles.

Family and work life are interconnected whether one or both adults are employed. In the following example, the same work-family conflict is viewed from two points of view:

> *Work*: The atmosphere in the office is somber as three department heads meet to discuss the complaints they have been receiving from one important work team. The focus of the complaints is the employees' travel schedules. Heavy travel during the summer season is a project necessity, but the complaints this year have been particularly bad and the number of sick days and postponed travel schedules have been increasing.
>
> *Family*: In one of the families in which heavy travel was the issue, the wife makes a demand upon her husband. "The teacher told me today it's very important for you to spend more time with our son. She thinks a lot of his disruptive behavior can be traced to wanting more attention from his father, since he told her you're never home." The husband's response is, "But you know I have to finish up this assignment. Things will be better in the fall." (Renshaw, 1976, p. 250)

Conflict between work and family results when the demands of work and family roles make participation in one or both of these sets of roles more difficult or inadequate (Tiedje et al., 1990; Voydanoff, 1988). This conflict is usually a result of competing demands on time or the psychological spillover of one role to another. Some of the characteristics of the work setting that contribute to this conflict are

- Long work hours
- Shift work, especially evenings or weekends
- Role ambiguity or role conflict at work
- Rapid change
- Work overload

Some of the characteristics of family life that contribute to this conflict are

- Number of hours spent in child care and housework
- Number and ages of children
- Perceptions of husband and wife regarding appropriate role enactment

Some factors can buffer or minimize potential conflict. Two of the most critical of these buffers are

- Perceived control over the scheduling of work hours and work demands
- Perceived enhancement or enrichment of work and family roles; a view that multiple roles add to a sense of purpose and personal worth

The degree to which work and family roles conflict depends in part on how the partners view each other's participation in the world of work. Some pairs operate in a traditional value system: The women are heavily invested in their husband's achievements and experience vicarious satisfaction from his successes. For these women, the sense of personal identity is based on contributing in positive ways to their husband's career. These women expect their husbands to provide income and prestige for their families. They are unlikely to have other expectations about their husband's contributions to child-rearing and household tasks (Clark, Nye & Gecas, 1978). Within this traditional value system, the husband may accept some participation by his wife in the labor force as long as it is viewed as clearly supplementary and secondary to his own. He may feel threatened if his wife shows excitement about and involvement in her career at the very time that his own work is beginning to lose its excitement or promise. How a couple copes with these work-family conflicts depends on the husband's success in his work, his income level, and the wife's expectations regarding the kinds of commitments her husband should make to household or child-rearing activities. For example, some men who work long hours also earn high salaries. Thus, their absence from home may be viewed with less resentment than if they were earning less. Increasingly, however, men from this type of structure are reporting that the one thing they regret is not having spent more time with their children.

The conflict between work and family roles is more complex in families in which both husband and wife work in the paid labor force full time and expect one another to work. This structure has been more common in the United States in recent times, in part because of economic factors and in part because of changing values about women's roles. Each partner recognizes the other's psychological need to work in order to satisfy certain ambitions and to achieve a sense of competence. In Chapter 11, the discussion of the dual-earner marriage provided an overview of this increasingly common family structure. Despite the equal involvement of the two partners in the labor force, most couples tend to see child care and certain household maintenance tasks as primarily the wife's domain. This outlook is as common in other countries—Canada, Sweden, and Norway—as it is in the United States (Kalleberg & Rosenfeld, 1990). When both husband and wife are working, the wife may experience considerable strain in trying to meet her work commitments while allowing adequate time for nurturance and recreational activities with her children, intimacy with her husband, and maintenance of the emotional climate and physical environment of the home.

Studies of professional couples carried out in the 1970s found that wives were more likely than husbands to assume greater responsibility for the home and family and to put their spouse's careers ahead of their own (Heckman, Bryson & Bryson, 1977). Research reported in the late 1980s and early 1990s finds the same pattern (Pina & Bengston, 1993). Husbands and wives continue to agree that women have the primary responsibility for making sure that child rearing and household tasks are taken care of. This perception has led to the description of working women as performing a "second shift" (Hochschild, 1989). These women feel that they have demanding work responsibilities at their job, and that when they come home they have additional home-related work responsibilities.

Some women resolve the conflict between career aspirations and family commitment by limiting their competitive, achievement-oriented strivings. For many women, the dual-earner relationship is still a matter of negotiation with their spouse, who is regarded as giving permission for the wife to go to work and who sets the limits on the woman's involvement in work. Other women find that the work setting limits achievement for them through sex-typed assumptions about the woman's commitment to her family role. Women do not tend to be promoted to high-level administrative or managerial positions in which work demands would begin to invade family commitments. As an example, some companies are reluctant to put women in positions in which they may have to be transferred for fear that their husbands will refuse to make the move. In some instances, women who request flexible or part-time work schedules are labeled as not really serious about their career (Rodgers & Rodgers, 1989).

Despite the many difficulties encountered in combining work and family roles, women who enter today's labor market do so in a context of cultural acceptance. Research has been conducted to evaluate the impact of employment status on the self-esteem and personality adjustment of women in middle adulthood. Earlier research found that homemakers—that is, married women who were not in the labor market—had lower self-esteem than career women (Birnbaum, 1975). However, more recent research has shown no differences in self-esteem between homemakers and women who have both family and career roles (Erdwins & Mellinger, 1984). According to these comparisons, homemakers tend to have higher levels of affiliation and responsibility than do career women. Career women perceive that they have greater personal control over their environment than do homemakers. From the available data, it is difficult to determine if these personality differences have contributed to the selection of one life path over the other or if involvement in the two different role configurations has contributed to the variations in personality.

What is the impact of the dual-career arrangement on men? The emphasis in the literature on the difficulties women face in combining work and family life has created a perception that men are singly devoted to the world of work and indifferent to or uninvested in home and family life. This is clearly not the case. Studies consistently find that, for men, happiness in their family roles is a stronger predictor of psychological well-being than adjustment at work (Pleck, 1985). Men find personal meaning and emotional support in their roles as husband and father. For many men, the positive quality of their marital and parental roles helps them cope more effectively with the stresses of work (Barnett, Marshall & Pleck, 1992). In

TABLE 12.1	**Unemployment Rates* by Race, Age, and Sex, 1991**	
	Male (%)	**Female (%)**
White		
35–44	5.0	4.3
45–54	4.4	3.9
Black		
35–44	9.6	7.6
45–54	8.6	6.2
Hispanic		
35–44	8.6	7.6
45–54	7.9	8.1

*According to the U.S. Bureau of the Census, an unemployed person is anyone who "had no employment during the reference week, who made specific efforts to find a job within the previous 4 weeks . . . , and who was available for work during that week" (p. 378).

Source: U.S. Bureau of the Census, 1992.

many instances, specific lessons from home, including the patience and communication necessary to be an effective parent, the willingness to plan and work out alternative strategies for managing daily tasks with his wife, and the admiration he has for his wife in her paid labor-force activities, actually help a man function more effectively at work.

Perhaps because of the centrality of the quality of home life to men's well-being, many men are very sensitive to the possibility that their wife's involvement in the labor force may interfere with the emotional comfort and stability they seek at home (Douvan, 1982; Bell, 1983). A wife's success in the world of work may reduce a husband's sense of power or importance in the marital relationship. Men are especially uncomfortable if their wives are earning more money than they are. Some men find themselves ill prepared to assume the more direct responsibilities of child rearing in order to support their wives' involvement in the labor market.

The picture of adaptation to the dual-career marriage is not a simple one. We cannot say that the women always benefit or that the men always suffer. In fact, there are many dual-career arrangements, each involving the negotiation of roles and responsibilities to meet the convergence of work and family needs. However, a major issue in coping with the dual-career pattern seems to be each partner's capacity to revise some very basic gender-role expectations for their own and their spouse's behavior. This is not a simple task. It touches on very deep emotional commitments to one's view of oneself as a man or a woman, a husband or a wife, and a mother or a father. It touches on the enactment of one's values about work-related accomplishments and achieving a loving, supportive marital relationship. The spouse, parent, and worker roles are not readily integrated. At the same time, the dual-career lifestyle provides new opportunities for extending one's competence across many domains. It also provides opportunities for a new understanding of gender and gender relations within the family system.

The Impact of Joblessness

Some people are alienated from work. They find little satisfaction in the work setting and little opportunity for meaningful labor. In 1991, the unemployment rate was 7.0% for men and 6.3% for women. Table 12.1 summarizes the unemployment rates by race, sex, and age for two age groups in middle adulthood. African-Americans and Hispanics are more likely to be unemployed than whites. Many of these adults experience chronic unemployment. Throughout history, the story of vagrants, "tramps," and homeless men has been linked to the inability of the labor market to absorb all the able-bodied men who want to work (Hopper, 1990). Early in this century, most communities had work for men who were just traveling through, but during the Great Depression, this picture changed dramatically:

> They were called by many names: hoboes, tramps, gandy dancers, knights of the road; only later were "bums" and "derelicts" common epithets. By the time the Great Depression hit in the early 1930s, demand for the special types of work done by homeless men had all but vanished. What had been a vast and variegated pool of casual labor, continually replenished by recruits drawn by the lure of the road and the frontier, was transformed into a stockpile of redundant surplus men. Later winnowed of all able-bodied residents by the domestic war effort, what remained would become the nucleus of "skid row." (Hopper, 1990, pp. 13–14)

Chronically unemployed men have little opportunity to develop competence within the context of work. Because of the cultural emphasis on productive work, these people are likely to experience some guilt about being unable to work. In addition, for men, unemployment disrupts the self-concept of the traditional definition of the adult male role as "breadwinner" for the family. As a result of guilt, shame, and anger, these men may find it hard to direct their energy toward creative solutions to life problems. The inability to work can be expected to become a serious block to the resolution of the psychosocial conflict of generativity versus stagnation.

As a result of the restructuring of the labor market described in Chapter 11, many middle adults who have had a history of steady employment, including increased responsibility and advancement, are being fired or forced into some form of early retirement. Unemployment in middle adulthood has a major psychological impact on the sense of self-worth and hope for the future. The relationship between psychosocial development and the ability to perform meaningful work is illustrated in a study of the experiences of unemployment among white-collar adults (Braginsky & Braginsky, 1975). A group of jobless men who had held managerial or engineering positions were compared with a group of employed men. Most of the jobless men were experiencing their first encounter with unemployment in 20 years of work. They felt unwanted, insignificant, and bitter. They were experiencing a profound reevaluation of long-held values. They expressed feelings that their college years had been wasted, that hard work and skill were less important than "brownnosing the boss," and that their friends had shunned them after they lost their jobs. Because of the importance of their previous work to their sense of worth, these men were left with deep feelings of worthlessness and low self-esteem that persisted even after they were reemployed.

Job loss has been associated with both physical and psychological consequences. In addition to withdrawal and self-doubt, job loss may introduce family strains that lead to new levels of conflict and family violence. In some instances, adjustments that families make to a husband's unemployment result in a further reduction of his sense of importance and accentuate the decline in his self-respect (Piotrkowski, Rapoport & Rapoport, 1987). In a study of 300 unemployed men, social support from among the person's close relationships played two distinct roles (Vinokur, Caplan & Williams, 1987). When a significant person reaffirmed the unemployed person's beliefs that looking for a new job was worthwhile and gave the unemployed person hopeful encouragement, the unemployed person was more likely to engage in active job-seeking efforts. In addition to this specific support for job seeking, social support provided an important global sense of worth and caring that was especially important when job-seeking efforts were not paying off. The authors warn that efforts to encourage intensive job seeking may backfire when a highly motivated person meets with repeated failure. Under these conditions, it is especially important for the person to be embedded in social relationships that provide global, unconditional regard in order to prevent a process of demoralization and self-destructive behavior.

Nurturing the Marriage Relationship

Marriage is a dynamic relationship. It changes as the partners mature, as the family constellation changes, and in response to changing events, including family crises and historical events. It takes focused effort to keep marriages healthy and vital.

What is a vital marriage? Hof and Miller (1981) described it as an intentional, companionship marriage,

> a relationship in which there is a strong commitment to an enduring marital dyad in which each person experiences increases in fulfillment and satisfaction. There is a strong emphasis on developing effective interpersonal relationships and on establishing and maintaining an open communication system. The ability to give and receive affection in an unconditional way, to accept the full range of feelings toward each other, to appreciate common interests and differences and accept and affirm each other's uniqueness, and to see the other as having equal status in the relationship. (p. 9)

A Commitment to Growth

There are at least three requirements for maintaining a vital marriage (Mace, 1982). First, *the partners must be committed to growth both as individuals and as a couple*. This means they must accept the idea that they will change in important ways and that the relationship, too, will change. Holding onto a view of the marriage as it was in the first year or two will not promote vitality. Caring and acceptance of each other must deepen. Each person must also be willing to permit changes in attitudes, needs, and interests in the other (Levinger, 1983; Marks, 1989). In Table 11.2 we summarized the tendencies that Robert White associated with maturity. Looking back to this table, we see that, in addition to the expansion of caring, the freeing of personal relationships, and the deepening of interests, we may expect the partners in a vital marriage to experience the stabilizing of ego identities and the humanizing of values. Within any enduring marriage, each person experiences a dynamic tension between pressures and desires for personal growth, on the one hand, and the pressures and demands of the social context, on the other. Both of these forces have the potential to overwhelm or dominate the sense of mutuality. A vital marriage requires both partners to be open to the needs of the two of them to be themselves (as they continue to discover new things) and an energizing, interpersonal chemistry that is resilient even in the face of the harshest challenges.

One of the most common examples of the need to permit individual growth within a marriage occurs when a woman who has been primarily responsible for child care and household management expresses an interest in joining the paid labor force. Annette, who had worked as a nurse before she married, decided that it was time for her to go back to work. Her three children were in elementary and middle school, and her husband had a full-time job, so that she was by herself for long hours during the day. She began to feel depressed and jealous of everyone else's active lives. So she took a position at a local hospital, working three afternoons and Saturdays. At first, her husband, Gary, fussed and resisted. Why did she need to go to work? They didn't really need the money, and Gary liked to know that she would be at home when he came back from work. He wasn't used to having to take the kids to their activities after school. Plus, Saturday used to be his day to hang out with his friends from work. The kids fussed at being asked to get dinner ready. But Annette insisted that she just had to get back to work, that her mental health and happiness depended on it. The first months were terrible. Annette wondered if she were doing the right thing, and Gary used every trick in the book to lure her back to the house. But there was no denying the value of this new job for Annette's self-confidence, for her renewed feeling of personal identity, and for her ability to return to the home with new energy and enthusiasm for her husband, her children, and her family life. Gary began to get a bit more involved in the children's lives and actually looked forward to the Saturdays they spent together. And the children began to see their mother in a new light, as a professional who took care of other people as well as them. They also felt a new surge of independence in being able to handle the dinner meal on their own. Gary and Annette felt closer to one another as a result of Annette's new independence.

Effective Communication

Second, *the couple must develop an effective communication system*. This means there must be opportunities for interaction. If competing life roles, including work and parenting, dramatically reduce opportunities for interaction, the couple will risk drifting apart. They will have fewer and fewer shared experiences and be less readily influenced by each other's observations and reactions. Studies of the correlates of marital happiness find that there is a reciprocal relationship between interaction and happiness. In a longitudinal study, couples who were happier early in their marriage showed higher levels of interaction in later years (Zuo, 1992). After a number of years of marriage, the two variables were strong predictors of each other: Those who were happy were involved in more frequent interactions, and those who were involved in frequent interactions were happier.

For many couples who do not have an effective communication system, resentments accumulate with no opportunity to resolve them. A common experience is that the wife wants to talk things over, but the husband does not see what good this will do (Rubin, 1976). *Harmonious, satisfied couples* listen to and consider each other's problems. They validate each other's concerns by expressing understanding, even if they cannot offer solutions. *Dissatisfied couples* meet the expression of a problem with either avoidance or counterattack. Instead of validating the concern, the partner raises his or her own complaints and criticisms. Over the years, levels of complaining and negativism escalate, and each partner becomes increasingly disenchanted with the other (McGonagle, Kessler & Gotlib, 1993). In the early years of marriage, it appears that the amount of negativity in the marriage is most disruptive to marital stability. Later in marriage, couples seem to learn how to weather some of the really nasty arguments, but the frequency of disagreements continues to be a strong predictor of marital disruption.

One way of thinking about the differences between harmonious and dissatisfied couples is to see them as differing in their ability to employ positive feedback loops (see the discussion of systems theory in Chapter 3). Harmonious couples

Pablo Picasso, The Kiss, 1969. It is challenging to nurture a vital marriage over the long period of middle and later adulthood. Couples must be committed to individual growth as well as to growth in the marital relationship. They must develop effective communication strategies and arrive at creative approaches to the resolution of conflicts. They must be able to make new adaptations to the changing demands of work and family life.

develop and redevelop the feedback loops needed to maintain communication. Dissatisfied couples may not have had effective feedback loops to begin with, and the interaction pattern tends to be disruptive. The lack of internal feedback loops reduces the capacity of the system to achieve equilibrium and to adjust to changes in the partners or to changing conditions that affect the marriage. Marriages that have effective communication tend to thrive because of the centrality of communication as a mechanism for system development.

Creative Use of Conflict

The third requirement for maintaining a vital marriage is *the couple's ability to make creative use of conflict*. In a vital marriage in which the partners have equal status and appreciate each other's individuality, there are bound to be conflicts. The partners must understand conflict, concur that it is acceptable to disagree, and develop strategies for resolving conflict (Cole & Cole, 1985). Satisfied couples cannot always resolve their conflicts. Many times their disagreements are left at a stalemate (Vuchinich, 1987). However, these couples tend not to escalate negative reactions. If one partner expresses a complaint or acts unpleasantly, the other does not retaliate with another negative action. Rather, such behavior is likely to provoke the partner's sympathy or acceptance (Roberts & Krokoff, 1990; Halford, Hahlweg & Dunne, 1990). When satisfied couples disagree, they try to remain calm during the interaction and to search for a resolution that is satisfactory to both partners. We know that levels of conflict and hostility are greater within the family than they are at work or in the community. Among satisfied couples, however, the impact of anger is minimized, and the goal remains to achieve a mutual level of understanding.

Nurturing vitality in a marriage is a long-term task. Change may be slow. Couples may endure long periods of minimal contact because of work, illness, or education and still preserve the quality of their relationship. It is not surprising that, over 20 or 30 years, a marriage may become predictable, even boring and empty. The challenge is for the partners to create continued interest, nurturance, and appreciation for each other even after they have achieved high levels of security, trust, and empathy, so that the components of a loving relationship (refer to Box 11.1) may be operating continuously in the relationship.

Marital Quality Among African-American Couples

At every income level, African-American couples have a higher rate of marital dissolution than white couples. Given the emphasis in the media and in public policy debates on the decline of African-American families, surprisingly little research has been carried out to determine the factors most closely linked to sustaining marital quality among African-American couples (Broman, 1993). The studies that have looked at marital satisfaction among African-American couples have identified some important factors. A common thread in the prediction of marital quality is the partners' satisfaction with their financial resources. Income per se is not as good a predictor of marital satisfaction among African-American couples as is their satisfaction with or the perceived adequacy of their financial resources (Clark-Nicolas & Gray-Little, 1991). For both husbands and wives, the perception that their family income was adequate to meet their needs and to pay off their debts was positively related to evaluations of the marriage, including global satisfaction and perceptions of reciprocity in the marriage. For African-American wives, perceived economic adequacy was also related to a positive assessment of their husbands' role performance.

However, satisfaction with economic resources does not tell the whole story. Four other variables are especially important:

1. For both men and women, a sense of emotional support from one's spouse is a strong predictor of marital harmony and marital satisfaction.
2. For African-American men, particularly those at the lower income levels, having a smaller number of children is associated with greater marital satisfaction. For African-American women, it is not the number of children but the frequency of problems associated with raising the children that is associated with marital satisfaction. Mothers who are constantly worried about their child's behavior and safety are less satisfied than those who have fewer parenting problems and worries.
3. For African-American men and women, the theme of personal development is interwoven with marital satisfaction. Those who believe that their partner brings out the best in them and that their marriage gives then the opportunity to express their individuality are more satisfied with their marriage than those who feel restricted or constrained by marriage.
4. For African-American women, job satisfaction is a predictor of marital satisfaction, and a sense of value and competence in the world of work is linked to a positive outlook on their family roles as well as a feeling of being supported and encouraged by their husbands.

These findings just begin to clarify how some African-American couples buffer themselves against the effects of race, racism, the exposure to drugs and crime in their neighborhoods, and the strain of trying to "make it" in a predominantly white business environment. They do not illustrate how certain strengths of the African-American community, especially involvement in the church and religious beliefs, the extended-kin network, and the tendency toward greater egalitarian role relationships within families, may contribute to vitality in marriage. More research is needed to understand the dynamics of marital vitality within and between ethnic groups.

Expanding Caring Relationships

As a result of one's sense of responsibility and the interdependence of one's multiple roles, middle adults are under pressure to seek a productive balance among their various interests, relationships, and commitments. Conflicts commonly arise from multiple role commitments—for example, when a person is torn between spending time helping a child to complete a school project and spending time completing a project for work. Internal conflicts may also arise as one wonders if the time and effort being given to a particular role are really worth the effort. Conflict and its resolution or nonresolution play key roles in stimulating individual and group development. In particular, the conflicts of middle adulthood provide the context for the expression of *caring*. How conflicts are handled—whether they are avoided, denied, resolved, escalated, or transformed into opportunities for new learning—determines the extent to which one's intention to function as a caring person has its desired outcome.

Middle adults have opportunities to express caring in many roles. In this section we focus on two: parenting and the care of one's own aging parents. Both domains offer numerous challenges to the intellectual, emotional, and physical resources of the adult caregiver.

Parenting

Being a parent is a difficult and demanding task that requires a great deal of learning. Because children are constantly changing and often unpredictable, the adult must be sensitive and flexible in new situations in order to cope successfully with their demands. Child-rearing experiences are different with each child, and the changing family constellation brings new demands for flexibility and learning. With each successive child, however, there does seem to be less anxiety about parenting skills. Children help adults learn about parenting through their responses to the adults' efforts and their own persistence in following the path of development.

Developmental Stages of the Family   At each stage of a child's life, the demands on parents change. Infants require constant care and attention. Preschoolers require toys and peers. They can spend a great deal of time in independent play, but they require mindful supervision. They also require parental reassurance about their skills, talents, and fears. The early adolescent requires little in the way of physical care but continuing emotional support and guidance, new financial demands, and help in facilitating participation in athletics, after-school activities, and social life.

Several models of family development have been proposed by family researchers. These schemes, especially the ones described by Duvall (1977), Hill (1965), and Spanier, Sauer, and Larzelere (1979), emphasize changes in the family that are tied to changes in the developmental levels of children. The implication is that the changing needs, competence, and social interactions of the children stimulate changing interactions, activities, and values among family members.

There are criticisms of this view of family development. First, the length of the marriage and the ages of the parents are confounded with the ages or stages of the children. It is possible that the parents' ages as much as the children's ages or some combination of the two account for changes in family emphasis (Nock, 1979; Spanier et al., 1979). Second, this view does not help us understand the growth of families that do not have children or families that are a product of remarriage in which the marital relationship has a shorter history than the parental one. Third, from a psychosocial perspective, we regard the influence of parents and children as reciprocal. Changes in the developmental level of children have the potential to influence the quality of their interactions with parents. Changes in the developmental level of parents also have this potential. Further, from a systems perspective, each family member can prompt conflict, change, or growth in every other. The affectional bonds that family members share, as well as the need to protect one another from external threats, contribute to a dynamic interdependence. To some degree, each family member is vulnerable to the influence of every other.

For the purposes of this discussion of parenting, we have chosen to consider the potential influences of phases of family development on adult development. This approach has the advantage of showing the reciprocity of psychosocial themes across the generations. It highlights the processes through which development may prompt new growth among parents. The six periods of family development discussed are

1. The childbearing and postnatal years
2. The years when children are toddlers
3. The years when children are of early and middle school age
4. The years when children are adolescents
5. The years when no children are living at home
6. Grandparenthood

The childbearing and postnatal years. The period before and immediately after birth are often very strenuous for both parents. The family is often anxious about the health of the mother and the infant. These concerns may also be reflected in sympathetic symptoms experienced by the father. After childbirth, parents are likely to be tense and exhausted. Many young adults are discouraged by the inadequacy of their preparation for this major adult role. With the first child, the anxieties about the infant's physical health and the uncertainties about how to handle daily events are at their peak. (That may be why books on child care have had such great success.) With successive children, parents may be more tired but less anxious.

Perhaps the major change for parents during this period is the attachment that forms with each new child. Parents discover their capacity to become deeply—even irrationally—committed to protecting and nurturing their offspring. Mothers often comment that they had no idea how totally absorbing the demands of the mother role would be (Coady, 1982; Newman & Coady, 1982). Fathers as well as mothers are increasingly absorbed by the unique qualities and demands of newborns.

Parents must learn to anticipate an infant's needs on the basis of minimal or undifferentiated cues; to structure the environment so that it will permit safe, stimulating opportunities for exploration; and to convey love through warm, gentle, close handling. A major challenge to adults at this stage is to learn to convey calm reassurance when they are really anxious and uncertain. Parents learn to mask some of their personal concerns in order to foster their children's sense of trust. Of course, not all parents of infants are sensitive and skillful in the way they treat their children, as the incidence of infant abuse attests.

The years when children are toddlers. The parents of toddlers are truly tested with regard to the issue of autonomy. Toddlers, in their efforts to gain control, challenge their parents' limits. Parents, no matter how patient, almost inevitably get pushed too far. In order for parents to be successful during this stage, they must learn a new level of self-control. They rediscover language, fantasy, and the wonders of the natural world. They also learn that they have needs for personal privacy that must be conveyed to children but nevertheless are frequently violated.

During this period, adults also begin to formulate family rules and to employ certain forms of discipline when these rules are violated. The creation of rules, rewards, and punishments is generally the result of some degree of ideology about what is right and wrong and some degree of personal tolerance. Discipline requires full acceptance of the responsibilities of authority that come with parenthood. It also creates a new distance between adults and their children. Parents learn that they will not always be liked for doing what they believe is right.

Parents frequently serve as teachers and tutors for their toddlers, teaching them how to put toys together, how to make things "work," how to solve problems, and how to describe their thoughts and feelings to others. In this process, parents learn to support competent, independent task performance. They modify their teaching strategy to each new level of ability, providing new kinds of information and guidance as the child's performance improves. As their children's teachers and tutors, parents learn to read cues about their child's competence and try to provide interactions that will move the child to a new level of mastery without taking away the child's own sense of satisfaction in discovery (Pratt et al., 1988).

The years when children are of early and middle school age. School-age children tap parents' resources for ideas about things to do, places to go, and friends to meet. Children seek new experiences in order to expand their competence and investigate the larger world outside the home. Parents become active as chauffeurs, secretaries, and buffers between their children and the rest of the community. Parents have many opportunities to function as educators for their children. They actively contribute to their children's academic success through such activities as reading with their children, helping them with homework, praising them for school success, and talking with teachers, visiting school, and participating in school projects. Research on the academic success of African-American children makes it very clear that parents' aspirations for their children, their overall parenting skills, and their involvement in their children's education make a substantial contribution to their children's progress (Jenkins, 1989).

Parenting during this period has the potential for boosting an adult's sense of pride in skills and knowledge already accumulated. Parents are gatekeepers to the resources of the community. They come to see themselves through their children's eyes, as people who know about the world—its rewards, treasures, secrets, and dangers.

During this phase of parenthood, adults are likely to be active in school-related organizations. They find themselves reacting to events that occur in school, planning activities to take place at school, or working with other parents to provide some service, opportunity, or facility for their children that does not currently exist. Through efforts to further their own children's development, parents begin to evolve an attitude toward—even a philosophy of—education that will have implications for a whole community of children. When parents are forced to protect, defend, or reprimand their own children with regard to events that have taken place in school, they develop a stance toward that institution and its function in the community. For some parents, school seems like a hostile place. They did not do well in school themselves and do not have much confidence in their academic abilities. These parents may find it very difficult to retain a sense of self-worth if their children become too involved in school. Out of their own defensiveness, they may even introduce barriers to their children's academic success.

The years when children are adolescents. Parents tend to view the years of their children's adolescence as extremely trying. Adolescents are likely to have a great deal of behavioral independence. They spend most of the day away from home

During a child's early and middle school age years, parents assume new educational roles—teaching their children new skills and opening up new avenues for learning. The scouting organizations depend on the volunteer efforts of adults who find deep satisfaction in building competence and character in children.

and apart from adult supervision. As adolescents gain in physical stature and cognitive skills, they are likely to challenge parental authority.

During this time, the principles that parents have emphasized as important for responsible, moral behavior are frequently tested. Children are exposed to many voices, including the media, popular heroes and heroines, peers, and school adults, suggesting that there may be more than one ideal way to behave and more than one definition of success. On the one hand, parents must allow their children freedom in order to permit them to exercise their judgment. On the other, they must be ready to give support when the children fail to meet adult expectations or when they show poor judgment. Parents must be able to maintain a degree of authority about standards or limits that continue to operate for young adolescents. Parents of adolescents, therefore, attempt to balance freedom, support, and limit setting in the needed proportions so that their children can grow increasingly independent while still being able to rely on an atmosphere of family reassurance (Newman, 1989; Ryan & Lynch, 1989).

Adolescent children are the front line of each new generation. The questions they raise and the choices they make reflect not only what they have learned but also what they are experiencing in the present and what they anticipate in the future. Parents of adolescents are likely to feel persistent pressure to reevaluate their own socialization as well as their effectiveness as parents. Questions are raised about their preparation for their own futures as well as their children's. The ego boost that resulted from being viewed as wise and resourceful is likely to be replaced by doubts as both parents and children face an uncertain future. Parents who can respond to their adolescents in an open, supportive way can benefit by finding an opportunity to clarify their own values. They can begin building new parent-child relationships that will carry them and their emerging adult children into later adulthood.

The years when no children are living at home. Sometime during most parents' 40s or early 50s, children leave home to go to college, join the service, marry, or take jobs and live in their own households. The combination of smaller family size and a longer period of adult life means that many couples will have 15 years or more of family life without the active daily responsibilities of parenting (Glick, 1977, 1979). During this same period, most women enter menopause, bringing a close to their natural childbearing years (see Box 12.1).

BOX 12.1

Menopause

At some time during their late 40s or 50s, most women experience the *climacteric,* or the involution and atrophy of the reproductive organs. Many physiological changes accompany this loss of fertility, including the cessation of menstruation (menopause), gradual diminution in the production of estrogen, atrophy of the breasts and genital tissues, and shrinkage of the uterus (Morokoff, 1988). There is some controversy about whether the menopause affects women at a psychological level because of either its symbolic meaning or the physiological changes it brings. Let us consider the research on menopause—and the entire experience of the climacteric—within the context of its meaning for the woman who is engaged in the task of developing a sense of generativity.

The most commonly reported symptom is a frequent "hot flash," a sudden onset of warmth in the face and neck that lasts several minutes. Sometimes it is accompanied by dizziness, nausea, sweating, or headaches. About 75%–85% of women going through natural menopause report this symptom. Other symptoms are related to the reduction of vaginal fluid and loss of elasticity (Bates, 1981; Hammond & Maxson, 1986). The symptoms appear to be closely related to a drastic drop in the production of estrogen. Postmenopausal women produce only one-sixth as much estrogen as regularly menstruating women do. Several studies on the use of estrogen treatment have found that the administration of this hormone to menopausal women alleviates or even prevents menopausal symptoms.

It is fairly well established, then, that the menopause brings about recognizable physical changes that the adult woman may or may not view as unpleasant. The severity of symptoms is determined in part by the attitude of the culture toward the infertile older woman. In cultures that reward women for reaching the end of the fertile period, menopause is associated with few physiological symptoms. A study describing the reaction of women in India found that menopause was associated with increased social status:

> The absence of menstrual flow signaled an incredible elevation of stature for these women. Women were released from a veiled, secluded life in a compound to talk and socialize (even drink) with menfolk. They then became revered as models of wisdom and experience by the younger generation. (Gillespie, 1989, p. 46)

Similarly, a woman's own attitudes toward aging and her involvement in adult roles influence the ease or difficulty with which she experiences menopause. In our society, for example, a woman who is going through menopause at age 50 may also be experiencing the severe illness or death of her parents and the marriage of her youngest child. Menopausal status is not a good predictor of a woman's health or her psychological well-being. Role strain and prior health are much more accurate predictors (McKinlay, McKinlay & Brambilla, 1987).

A woman's anxiety about menopause depends on her feelings about no longer being able to bear children, on the amount of information she has about the symptoms accompanying menopause, and on the degree of her anxiety about growing old. For example, Neugarten and her colleagues

(continued)

BOX 12.1

(continued)

(1963) found that attitudes toward menopause were more positive among their sample of postmenopausal women 45 and older than among younger women. The older group realized that the menopausal symptoms were temporary and that after menopause would come the potential for feelings of well-being and vigor. In contrast to the younger group, they were aware that menopause may bring an upsurge in sexual impulses and activity.

The younger woman tends to confuse menopause with growing old. Physical beauty may be heavily weighted in her definition of femininity. Further, the younger woman may still be quite invested in her role as mother and fearful of a potential end to her years of childbearing. The older woman, on the other hand, is likely to be glad to have reached the end of the child-bearing years and may eagerly await a future of new roles and freedoms.

Menopause may serve as a significant symbolic event for women in the stage of middle adulthood. For the woman who has failed to develop a sense of generativity, who continues to view her children as a path to self-fulfillment, or who is frightened by the prospect of growing old, menopause may highlight a sense of stagnation. For the woman who has successfully developed a sense of personal achievement in child rearing or other work, menopause signifies the end of the child-rearing years and the beginning of a period in which new energy may be directed to broader, community-oriented tasks. These women are likely to feel more energetic as they uncover new facets of their personality and new avenues for their creative ambitions and goals.

The period during which children leave home has been designated developmentally as the *launching period* (Mattessich & Hill, 1987). For families with only a few children, this period may last only a few years. In larger families, the transition may take 10–15 years. Alternative patterns are clearly evident in current U.S. families. Thirty percent of parents with children in their 20s have one or more of these adult children living at home (Aquilino, 1990). By the time adult children marry, they are almost always ready to leave the parental home.

There is no doubt that roles change during this time. The relationship between the husband and the wife changes as parenting activities diminish. Some couples become closer—closer than they have been since they first fell in love. Divorces also occur when the children are gone. Parents are likely to begin a review and evaluation of their performance as parents as they see the kinds of lives their children establish for themselves. Erikson (Erikson, Erikson & Kivnick, 1986) found that many parents continue to build their identities on the accomplishments of their children. Parents also begin to find new targets for energy and commitment that they had previously directed toward the care of their children.

The transitional period during which children leave home does not seem to be a negative time for adults. A woman who was anticipating her children's leaving home described her feelings this way:

> "From the day the kids are born, if it's not one thing, it's another. After all these years of being responsible for them, you finally get to the point where you want to scream, 'Fall out of the nest already, you guys, will you? It's time.' It's as if I want to take myself back after all these years—to give me back to me, if you know what I mean. Of course, that's providing there's any 'me' left." (Rubin, 1980, p. 313)

There is evidence of greater cohesiveness and affection in the marriage relationship after the children leave home, especially in marriages that had been satisfactory before (Houseknecht & Macke, 1981; Mullan, 1981). Parents are usually pleased as they trace their children's accomplishments. Further, children's independence may permit parents to use their financial resources to enhance their own lifestyle.

Of course, adults maintain certain parental functions during this stage. Many children remain financially dependent on their parents, even after leaving home. If the children are in college or in postgraduate study, the parents may experience greater financial demands than at any earlier period in their parenting history. In many families, parents take on extra labor-market activities and additional loans to meet the financial requirements of their children's college and professional education. Children who have left home may not have resolved decisions about occupation and marriage. Parents remain a source of advice and support as late adolescents and young adults go through periods of identity and intimacy formation and consolidation. Parents begin to feel the pressure of challenges to their value orientation as their children experiment with new roles and new lifestyles. During this stage, parents may serve as sounding boards, as sources of stability, or as jousting partners in young people's attempts to conceptualize their own lifestyle.

Middle adults may begin to feel free to alter their roles and redirect their energies at this point in their lives. However, some parents experience resistance from their children, who expect that their parents will remain the same as they themselves change and grow. Young adult children take many different paths in leaving the parental home, and in many cases they return for intervals when they look for a new job, find a new roommate, recover from a love relationship that has ended, return from military service, or drop out of college (Thornton, Young-DeMarco & Goldscheider, 1993). Throughout these transitions, young adults look to their parents as a source of stability and to their home as a "safe harbor" while they try to establish their own life structure.

One of the major events that occurs during this period is the child's decision to marry. Parents may be expected to accept a new person into their family as their child's husband or wife. Along with this new relationship comes a connection to an entirely new, and often totally unknown, group of in-laws. Parents are usually at the mercy of their child's decision in this matter. They may find themselves associated through marriage with a family that differs significantly from their own or that shares many of their own family's idiosyncrasies.

The first few years of marriage, as discussed in Chapter 11, are somewhat precarious. Parents may have to reintegrate an adult child into the family at this stage if his or her marriage is not successful. It can be assumed that a child who leaves a marriage needs some temporary parental reassurance and support in order to regain confidence in his or her ability to form an intimate relationship. Thus, at times of crisis, middle adults may be called on to practice earlier skills of parenting that they have not used for quite a while and to develop new skills in helping their children deal with new challenges.

Grandparenthood. The time when an adult witnesses the birth of a new generation might be considered the beginning of an additional stage in family development. The transition to grandparenthood is really outside one's own control. Whenever one's children have children of their own, the grandparent becomes alerted to a new sense of ancestry, lineage, and membership in an expanding kinship network. With grandparenthood, adults begin to observe their children as parents. As people reflect on their own roles 20–30 years earlier, they may attribute some of their children's successes to their own parenting techniques and may take responsibility for some of the failures (Erikson et al., 1986). In the next

In Man with Flute and Child (1971), *Picasso suggests the combination of nurturing and teaching that takes place when a grandfather has his grandchild settled securely on his lap.*

chapter, we will consider the role of grandparenthood and its significance to the adult in greater detail. Here, suffice it to say that, as grandparents, adults have the opportunity to relate to small children as an expression of the continuity of their lives into the future. Of course, not all grandparents relate to their grandchildren from this philosophical point of view. However, the attainment of the grandparent role has the potential for bringing with it a new perspective on time, purpose, and the meaning of life that may serve as a source of reassurance during later adulthood.

Adults differ in how they define the role of grandparent. They may see themselves as carriers of the family traditions and wisdom, as needed experts in child care, as convenient and trusted baby-sitters, or as admirers from afar. As grandparents, adults are asked to reinvest energy in small children. The quality of the relationship that develops between grandparents and grandchildren depends not so much on the fact that they are relatives as on the kinds of experiences that the two generations share. Grandparents may also find that the quality of their relationship with their grandchildren is mediated by the child's parents. Especially when the grandchildren are little, the amount of time they spend with their grandparents and the way they view them are filtered through the quality of the adult relationship that their parents have with their grandparents (Brubaker, 1990).

A Psychosocial Analysis of Contributions of Parenting to Adult Development In the process of parenting, adults have an opportunity to review their own development through the experiences they share with their children. They may recall their own thrill at watching a firefly light up or their own trepidation on the night before high school graduation. Parenthood helps adults realize how far they have come in their own efforts at self-definition. At each phase of family development, adults consolidate the gains made in their own growth while learning the skills needed to facilitate the development of their children.

The parent role may stimulate further cognitive and emotional development when adults view the role as positive and desirable (Newman & Newman, 1988). Of course, not all parents do. Some turn against their children or drop to new, low levels of functioning. Yet this important role has growth-promoting possibilities. Given the critical importance of parenting for species survival and for psychosocial evolution, it is highly unlikely that the enactment of the parent role should prove detrimental to most adults. On the contrary, parenting may bring new levels of insight, intellectual flexibility, and social commitment.

The attachment process is central to human relationships. A person's attachment structure may change over the life course. In some respects, the bond that ties children to their parents is the same as the bond that ties parents to their children. But in some ways, the attachment of parents to their children is unique. It is normally characterized by a strong sense of responsibility and an uneven distribution of resources and authority. Evidence suggests that most parents find their attachment to their children deeply satisfying. As a consequence of this deep and enduring attachment, parents are likely to be highly receptive to the new information, new experiences, and new thoughts that are evoked as they observe and interact with their children.

Parents are continually thrown into cognitive disequilibrium. Discrepancies between the competences and expectations an adult has and the realities the adult encounters with each child provide a stimulus for cognitive growth. Parents face numerous discrepancies and are usually highly motivated to resolve them. As a result, parenting may be viewed as having potential influence on at least six aspects of cognitive development during adulthood. First, parenting requires a more probabilistic view of the future and an accompanying contingency approach to planning. Second, parenting promotes the formulation of a philosophy of life in which the rules and limits that parents impose on their children are related to central values and goals.

Third, parenting supports a greater appreciation of individual differences and a more highly differentiated view of individual strengths, weaknesses, and potential. Fourth, parenting requires and promotes the capacity to hold two or more opposing ideas in the mind at the same time. Fifth, the need to protect and nurture children requires the development of greater skill in anticipating the future. Finally, parenting has the potential consequence of expanding the realm of consciousness. One becomes increasingly aware of oneself and others, increasingly capable of conceptualizing past, present, and future, and able to function at varying levels of abstraction in order to be effective with children at different developmental levels.

Parenting contributes to the expansion of caring. Seven aspects of emotional development can be identified as potential consequences of parenting. First, parenting brings a depth of commitment that is tied to the responsibility one feels for the survival of a child. The depth of commitment is strengthened through the reinforcing nature of the child's responses to attempts to meet his or her needs. Second, parenting brings adults into contact with new channels for expressing affection. Third, parenting requires that adults achieve a balance between meeting their own needs and meeting the needs of others. Fourth, parenting enhances an adult's feelings of value and well-being through the significant role the adult plays in the child's life. Fifth, parents achieve a degree of empathy for their child that widens the array of their emotional experiences. Sixth, parents may experience new levels of emotional intensity in reaction to their child's behavior. Seventh, many parents learn to help their children express and understand emotions. By playing a therapeutic role for their children, parents may become more effective in accepting and expressing their own emotions.

We realize that parenting is stressful. It is full of conflicts and challenges, demanding time that the partners might otherwise spend with each other or in pursuit of their own interests and ambitions. We argue, however, that parenting generates the kind of conflict that promises an enormous potential for personal growth. By providing a meaningful, responsive context for children, parents have the opportunity to articulate their own value systems and to see the consequences of their efforts in the continuous development of their children. Psychosocial growth requires a willingness to engage in tasks that may increase stress, uncertainty, and complexity. Growth usually does not mean turning away from or minimizing tension. Frequently it means choosing the challenge that is noticeably difficult or intriguingly complex in hopes of growing while struggling to meet it.

Caring for One's Aging Parents

We tend to think about caring in middle adulthood as a commitment to future generations. Another test of one's capacity for caring, however, comes in the form of commitment to one's aging parents. As one ages from 30 to 50, one's parents may age from 60 to 80. The number of adults over the age of 65 increased from over 25 million in 1980 to over 31 million in 1991. The number of adults over the age of 85 was 3.1 million, an increase of 100% since 1970 (U.S. Bureau of the Census, 1992). It is becoming increasingly likely that middle adults will confront the challenge of meeting the needs of their own aging parents. It is also increasingly possible that their aging parents will survive through a period of vigorous and independent later adulthood into a period of frail and vulnerable old age.

What is the nature of filial obligation as it is viewed from the perspectives of adult children and their aging parents? Who provides what kinds of help? What characterizes optimal parent-child relationships during this phase of life?

What Is Filial Obligation?   What can aging parents expect of their adult children? How do adult children define their responsibilities for their parents? In an analysis of three generations of women, it was clear that each cohort perceived a strong sense of filial obligation. Both sons and daughters endorse a responsibility to care for their aging parents (Brody, Johnsen & Fulcomer, 1984; Roff & Klemmack, 1986). In one study of filial obligation, 144 elderly parents and their adult children were asked to respond to 16 items that could be viewed as elements of filial obligation. The items are listed in Table 12.2, along with the percentage of each group that endorsed them. Parents and adult children clearly agree on the top three items: helping to understand resources, giving emotional support, and talking over matters of importance. They also agree that children ought not to be expected to live near the parent, write weekly, or visit weekly. Items that are starred indicate a significant difference in endorsement by the two groups.

In general, children have a greater sense of obligation than their parents expect of them. Parents do not seem to be comfortable with some forms of help,

TABLE 12.2   Perceptions of Filial Responsibility by Adult Children and Their Parents (Percentages)

Item	Children	Parents
Help understand resources	99.3	97.2
Give emotional support	97.2	95.7
Talk over matters of importance	96.5	98.6
Make room in home in emergency*	94.4	73.0
Sacrifice personal freedom*	93.7	81.0
Care when sick*	92.4	64.3
Be together on special occasions	86.0	86.7
Give financial help*	84.6	41.1
Give parents advice	84.0	88.7
Adjust family schedule to help*	80.6	57.4
Feel responsible for parent**	78.2	66.4
Adjust work schedule to help*	63.2	42.1
Parent should live with child*	60.8	36.7
Visit once a week	51.4	55.6
Live close to parent	32.2	25.7
Write once a week	30.8	39.4

Note: Ranking reflects percentage of respondents who "strongly agreed" or "agreed" with each item.
*Fisher's Exact Test indicated significant differences in proportion of endorsement for children and parents at *$p < .001$ or **$p < .05$.
Source: Harmon & Blieszner, 1990.

such as accepting financial assistance, having their children revise their work schedules in order to provide help, and living in a child's home (Hamon & Blieszner, 1990). In fact, it is more likely that an adult child will live in the household of an older parent than the reverse. And studies of intergenerational economic transfers find that older adults, 65 and over, give more in cash and gifts than they receive from younger generations (Aquilino, 1990).

Who Provides Help?   The evidence suggests that daughters assume much more of the responsibility for their aging parents than sons (Finley, 1989). This involvement is one element of the basic "kinkeeping" tasks that have traditionally been incorporated into women's socialization. Daughters are more likely than sons to provide care for their aging parents even when the women are employed. Daughters are more likely than sons to provide the direct care, such as bathing or dressing a parent, as well as emotional support, such as listening to a parent's concerns or helping the parent feel important and loved. Sons and daughters are about equally likely to assist in some of the tasks involving relations with health and human service organizations, scheduling medical checkups, and reviewing insurance and other financial matters. Aging adults who have three or more children, whether they are sons or daughters, are more likely to end up living with one of them than are adults with fewer than three children. However, for other forms

Pablo Picasso, Woman with a Mirror, *1950. It is not unusual for an adult daughter to have responsibility for the care of her aging, widowed mother. The affection the two held for each other during earlier years influences the quality of their relationship when both are adults.*

of support, such as receiving telephone calls, visiting, and helping in daily tasks, older adults who have one daughter receive more support than those who have one or more sons (Spitze & Logan, 1990).

What Factors Promote an Optimal Relationship Between Adults and Their Aging Parents?   The norms of independence and self-sufficiency are very strong among the current aging population. Many older adults state that they do not need assistance from their adult children. The need for assistance increases as the parents' health fails and their financial resources dwindle. Adult children view themselves as the ones who bear the primary responsibility for meeting their parents' needs. Most, however, do not expect to have to meet a great variety of such needs (Cicirelli, 1981). Some evidence suggests that when obligation to help and need for assistance are both great, older people derive less satisfaction from the parent-child relationship. Morale seems to be highest among older adults who do not need to rely on their children (Wood & Robertson, 1978). There appears to be a strong cultural norm that makes a parent's neediness difficult to express and respond to.

In adulthood, the parent-child relationship is one of choice. Children feel a moral obligation to reciprocate the care and devotion that their parents extended to them when they were young. In addition, a moral obligation to "honor thy father and thy mother" may have been incorporated into the children's religious training. However, the goal of child rearing in this society generally includes the value of promoting the offspring's independence. This means that children are encouraged to leave home, establish residences of their own, and be economically self-sufficient. After children leave home, many adult parents experience a positive sense of role transition. They enjoy focusing their time and attention on each other or on new activities and relationships. The task of reestablishing a close parent-child relationship—one that may involve sharing a household or maintaining frequent contact and interdependence—does not come easily to either the children or the parents. Success in this relationship is closely related to the affection that the children continue to have for their parents during the years in which they have lived relatively independent adult lives (Bengston & Roberts, 1991).

As adult children struggle to work out the nature of their responsibilities to their parents and the means for meeting those obligations effectively, they must weigh them against their commitments to their parental, marital, and work roles. They must also resist tendencies to treat their parents like children. Adult children may have feelings of sadness and loss as they watch a loved parent lose his or her vitality in the last years of life. In some cases, the adult children are not young themselves. They may be experiencing chronic illness, reduced strength or endurance, or diminished financial resources. A woman of 60 who works full time may not have the strength or the financial resources to meet all the needs of her frail 85-year-old mother.

One of the major transitions that evokes requests for help from children is widowhood. Providing help and emotional support to the surviving parent during this period of bereavement gives adult children an avenue for working through their own grief. Helping the widowed parent is a way of identifying with the deceased parent. Spending time with the surviving parent enables adult children to reduce their own sense of loss while meeting the surviving parent's need for comfort (Lopata, 1979; O'Bryant, 1987).

Adult children are often in a position to help their parents by coordinating services and interacting with various agencies. Many adults feel unprepared for this aspect of the caring relationship (Sarason, 1980). They are not comfortable dealing with hospitals, insurance agencies, social service agencies, or residential treatment facilities. However, many aging adults depend on the services of these structured organizations. Middle adults who know their parents' unique needs are among the best people to interpret those needs for service providers. In addition, through such contacts, middle adults have the opportunity to modify agencies in order to make them more effective for future generations of aging adults.

Despite the difficulties in achieving a satisfying adult-child–aging-parent relationship, there are some important possibilities for expressing generativity in this relationship. The manner in which adults respond to their parents provides a model for their own children. By dealing in a sensitive and caring way with their aging parents, adult children provide a pattern of responsiveness that may be a guide to their own children as the latter reach later adulthood.

Caring for aging parents brings middle adults face to face with the eventuality of their own aging and death. For many adults, this may be very anxiety-provoking. Middle adults are generally not ready to die. They are in the midst of complex role demands. Many others depend on their strength and competence. However, through interaction with their aging parents, they can perceive a time in life when they will be more prepared to accept death. By making a commitment to their aging parents, they may have less fear about feeling abandoned or despised in their own later years.

Managing the Household

People tend to live in groups. According to the U.S. Bureau of the Census (1992), all the people who live in a house or other "housing unit," such as an apartment, a single room, or any space designated as separate living quarters, are part of a *household*. In the United States, the Census Bureau records all individuals as living either in households or in group quarters, such as emergency shelters, juvenile detention centers, mental hospitals, prisons, military barracks, or college dormitories. In 1991, there were 94,312,000 households in the United States. Approximately 98% of the population lived in a household. The average household size was 2.63, and two-thirds were defined as *family households* involving two or more individuals related by birth, marriage, or adoption.

Households are much more than a convenient way of counting people. *Household* is a term that describes the entity that is created by people as a style of

People create settings in their household to support their interests. This man clearly has spent years establishing this workroom in his basement to accommodate all the tools, supplies, and shelving needed for his hobby.

living. When we speak of management of the household, we are calling attention to that great universe of thoughts and activities that preoccupy the attention of most adults. We are referring to all the planning, problem solving, and activities adults must engage in in order to take care of themselves and to take care of the others who are entrusted to their care. We are identifying household management, in its broadest connotation, as an area of an individual's psychosocial development that is ready for stimulation.

The household system has the potential for providing an environment that facilitates human growth and mental health. Learning to create such an environment is a task of the middle adult years that requires a great deal of thought and effort. Success in the formation of a positive home environment depends on the adult's ability to anticipate the needs of the people living there and to organize both resources and time so as to meet those needs. Effective household management requires administrative skills, skills related to setting priorities and goals, managing resources, and operationalizing plans (see Table 12.3). The adult's administrative skills affect the nature of the psychological living environment and determine whether it will enhance the growth of each family member. The more scarce the resources, the greater the pressure on the adult to make careful decisions and to find creative solutions to the daily challenges of meeting the household's physical and psychological needs.

Assessing Needs and Abilities

Most family households consist of individuals at different developmental ages. The person who is in the stage of middle adulthood must be able to understand that each member has his or her own needs, preferences, skills, and talents. Differences among family members may be the result of variations in developmental level. The early-school-age child has needs that are quite different from those of the early adolescent. Additional reasons why people's needs differ include sex, temperament, physical abilities, handicapping conditions, intellectual abilities, learning disabilities, demands by the workplace, emotional stability,

	TABLE 12.3 Management Skill Systems and Successful Outcomes	
	Skill System	***Outcomes***
Assessing needs and abilities	Understanding the needs and abilities of people of different ages	Experiencing confidence in contribution to household life
	Understanding individual differences	Creating an environment that will enhance the potential of each family member
	Matching talents and needs of members with opportunities	
	Developing flexibility in solving problems	
Making decisions	Identifying alternatives	Clarifying values
	Evaluating the consequences of various alternatives	Gaining a sense of empowerment
	Selecting and implementing a course of action	Finding satisfaction in fostering well-being of household members
	Accepting responsibility for the outcome of one's decisions	Promoting respect among members of the household
	Developing strategies for group problem-solving and conflict resolution	Teaching decision-making skills to other members of the household
Organizing time	Planning	Developing a psychohistorical perspective
	Coping with unpredictable events	Engaging in probabalistic thinking
	Anticipating changing demands	
Setting goals	Identifying priorities	Finding a new level of commitment to one's life goals
	Developing strategies to attain one's goals	Creating a new conceptualization of the future
	Evaluating progress toward reaching one's goals	
	Revising one's goals following successes and failures	
Establishing relationships with other social structures	Analyzing the interdependence among social systems	Expanding resources
	Protecting the family from unwelcome intrusions	Establishing a sense of community
	Fostering meaningful contacts and building a social network	Establishing a sense of social support
	Managing contacts and boundaries with the extended family	Forming a family identity

birth order, and exposure to stress, to name just a few. What is important for those who are concerned with household management is that they be aware of the differences among the people in their household and be willing to respond to the diverse needs of each. Their behavior is motivated not only by their own needs but by a desire to meet the needs and demands of others.

In addition to fulfilling needs, adults learn to be responsive to the skills and talents of family members. This requires judgment, observation, and a willingness to experiment with the assignment of responsibility. The goal here is to allow each person the opportunity to experience competence in her or his daily contributions to family life. The skill and creativity of the household manager are expressed not only in the assignment of people to tasks but also in the ability to permit the emergence of tasks that will cultivate the skills or talents of particular family members. A family may not need a garden, for example, but if a family member shows some interest and talent in gardening, it may be to everyone's benefit to have one.

Households have the potential for much greater variety and flexibility than most work settings. Beyond a given number of tasks that must be done each day, the members of a household may designate any kind of work as an appropriate task. The adult's challenge is to create an environment that will enhance the potential of each household member and thereby benefit the entire family unit. Two areas of new learning that are stimulated through management of the household during the adult years encompass the understanding of people and the creation of opportunities and environmental conditions that will enhance the members' growth.

Making Decisions

Effective household management requires the ability to make decisions about every aspect of living. Decision-making requires the ability to identify alternatives, to evaluate those possibilities, and to select a course of action. Household decisions range from daily ones, such as what to eat at mealtime or whether to subscribe to a particular magazine, to long-term ones that may have far-reaching consequences, such as whether or not to have a child, to move to another living unit, or to take in a lodger. Areas of household decision-making that most adults have to consider include (1) finances, (2) shelter, (3) education, (4) daily activities, (5) vacations and other recreation, (6) social life, and (7) child-rearing practices.

Many people find it difficult to make decisions. The responsibility for a household places adults in a position in which they cannot avoid exercising their preferences. Adults take actions that will affect all those living in the household. The necessity of making decisions may put some strain on adults, especially when certain decisions are unpopular with other family members. However, the active process of making decisions also serves to clarify one's value orientation and to direct the course of life closer to one's life goals.

Each household evolves a procedure for decision-making. Usually those who have the most control over resources are perceived as having the most power in a family unit. However, power and responsibility may be allocated in many ways. Each pattern has unique implications for the psychosocial development of family members.

We can describe three family decision-making patterns: (1) the single executive (either a male or a female head of household), (2) the adult executive, and (3) the family executive. The term *executive* has been chosen here to differentiate our discussion of family decision-making from a more anthropological treatment of the family power structure in which the word *matriarchy* or *patriarchy* is used. These terms refer more specifically to the line of inheritance and the kinship patterns of the family than to the actual process of household management. Although inheritance or social status may influence which of the adults has more power in the family, we prefer to separate this notion from the discussion of constellations of family decision-making.

The Single Executive   In the male-executive and female-executive patterns, one adult assigns responsibility to all other family members and reserves the right of final approval in most decisions. In this family structure, the *single executive* decides which tasks must be done and who should do them. The single executive is likely to be the primary source of rewards and punishments in the family and therefore the central figure for identification among the children. The single executive also bears the weight of blame when things go wrong.

In the case of marital partners, the role of the other spouse in this pattern depends on the activities that the executive assigns to him or her. For some people, this subordinate role may be quite agreeable, particularly if the single executive is successful in creating an effective home environment. For others, the subordinate role may be experienced as stressful because it results in a limitation or misuse of their talents. If they cannot convince the executive to redefine their roles, they may engage in subtler attempts to challenge the executive's authority or may even leave the household. In the single-executive model, the family may be subjected to some of the executive's idiosyncrasies. If for some reason the executive thinks that six o'clock is the time to eat dinner, dinner will be served at six o'clock no matter what anyone else in the family is doing.

One-parent families. One-parent families provide a special case of the single-executive decision-making pattern. In 1991, about 25% of all family groups with children under the age of 18 were one-parent families (U.S. Bureau of the Census, 1992). Among African-American families, the proportion of female-headed families with children under 18 rose from 31% in 1970 to 54% in 1991. Among white families, the proportion of such families rose from 8% in 1970 to almost 17% in 1987. Among Hispanic families, about 27% were headed by a mother only in 1987. About 4% of families had a male head with no female adult living in the home.

The greatest stress on the single mother is the lack of financial resources. In 1990, 44% of all families comprising single mothers and children had a family income below the poverty level (U.S. Bureau of the Census, 1992). Poverty in these families is a result of a number of factors. Single mothers tend to have a lower earning capacity, they work fewer hours, and, even when they receive some child support, they bear a substantial portion of their children's expenses.

In addition to stresses associated with poverty, single parents may suffer from social isolation, from continuous pressure to meet the needs of their children, and from experiences of overload in trying to combine work, parenting, and household decision-making without a partner (Alwin, 1984; Gongla & Thompson, 1987). Social isolation may result from the need to move to a new residence or to change jobs frequently. Multiple demands on a single parent's time may leave little opportunity for participation in the social network of the community. Single parents also worry that they are placing too many responsibilities on their children and that they are not giving their children the time and attention the children need. Thus, role overload is often combined with emotional strain, which often results in feelings of being chronically on the edge of crisis (McLanahan & Adams, 1987).

Kin support may be an important resource that buffers many single-parent families from negative consequences of poverty and role overload. Data from the National Survey of Black Americans was used to better understand the nature of kin-based support for African-American mothers (Jayakody, Chatters & Taylor, 1993). It is well documented that families in African-American communities benefit from the assistance provided by immediate and extended-family members. Much of this help is in the form of child care, financial help, and emotional

In African-American families, especially those with single parents, grandmothers often provide a critical source of emotional support and contribute significantly to the well-being and optimal development of the mother as well as the grandchild.

support (McAdoo, 1980). In this particular study, special attention was given to differences in the nature of kin support for married, divorced or separated, widowed, and never-married mothers. The majority of these women lived close to their families—in the same city, the same neighborhood, or the same house. They interacted frequently. Over half of the never-married mothers said they interacted with family members nearly every day. And most of the women said they felt very close to their families.

A large majority of the mothers (over 80%) said they received emotional support from their kin network. Emotional support was greatest for the younger mothers and for the widowed mothers. Financial support was greatest for the never-married women (about 24% received financial support from their kin) and least for the married women (16% received support from kin). Mothers living in the South were twice as likely as mothers living in the North to receive financial support from kin. For the never-married mothers, the likelihood of receiving financial support increased the poorer they were and the closer they lived to family members. In contrast, married mothers who lived near their kin and who had relatively more economic resources were less likely to receive financial aid from kin. In fact, they were probably the ones who provided resources to others.

Finally, for married, widowed, and never-married mothers, about 18% received kin support in the form of help with child care. Only 9% of the divorced or separated mothers received this type of help. Mothers in the North were more likely to receive child-care support than mothers in the South. Contrary to expectations, those mothers who received the most help in child care from their families expressed *lower* satisfaction in their family relationships. Perhaps, high levels of kin involvement in child care threaten to erode the mother's authority or reflect an unwanted degree of intrusion into the nuclear mother-child relationship.

The results of this study illustrate several important aspects of the challenges that face single African-American mothers. First, they do appear to be embedded in close, satisfying networks of family relationships. Second, although expressions of satisfaction and closeness to family were high in this group of subjects, actual support to single mothers from their kin varied from 80% who received emotional support, to 25% who received financial support, and slightly less than 20% who received support in the form of child care. Third, patterns of kin support vary according to regional subcultural customs, the age and need of the mother, and the mother's proximity to her kin. Thus, the idea that the difficulties that single African-American mothers face are largely compensated for through kin support appears to be inaccurate.

There appears to be a continuing controversy in the research literature about the quality of parent-child relationships in single-mother families. Some studies emphasize the deficit perspective—for example, identifying factors that place children or adolescents from single-parent families at risk for antisocial behavior and delinquency (Bank et al., 1993). Other studies focus on adaptation and coping within the single-parent structure, addressing factors that help sustain a positive parent-child relationship (Simons et al., 1993). Retrospective studies find that many children who are identified as having psychological problems, especially temper tantrums, bullying, cheating, stealing, and fighting, are from divorced, single-mother families. However, prospective studies, those that look at child-rearing practices and subsequent child outcomes, find that it is poor parenting practices, especially emotional unavailability, ineffective discipline, minimal supervision, and a dominating, hostile style of interaction, that produce these negative child outcomes, in both single-parent and two-parent families (Patterson, 1992). We may readily agree that single-parent families face many problems in addition to those that two-parent families must address. However, it is clearly inaccurate to label all single-parent families as problem families.

The Adult Executive　　In the *adult-executive pattern*, the adults of the household assign responsibility for household tasks. The children are subordinate and are seen as incapable of making decisions. In most cases, the adult executive is really a husband-wife executive. In some households containing grandparents, however, the adult-executive pattern may include more than the two spouses. In either case, assigning responsibilities and allocating resources become group decisions in which adults are involved. Group decisions require discussion, compromise, open conflict, consensus, and mutual respect. The adults come to place more value on the process of joint decision-making than on the feeling of being right every time.

The adult-executive pattern is probably the one most characteristic of the American family pattern (Adams, 1986). An equitable sharing of power and influence is an important component of marital satisfaction. Even in cultures in which the women and the men have traditionally had very distinct spousal roles, as in Puerto Rican families, shared decision-making in marriage is highly valued (Sexton & Perlman, 1989; Rogler & Procidano, 1989).

This "egalitarian" decision-making system is quite a bit more complex than one might assume. First, egalitarian attitudes do not always result in equal sharing of behaviors or responsibilities (Araji, 1977; Nye, 1976). For example, in many families the husband and the wife believe that housework should be equally shared, but in fact the wife does most of it. Similarly, many couples feel that both the husband and the wife should share the responsibility of providing income for the family, but the men tend to be the primary providers.

Second, in many families, decision-making is tied to specific behaviors or activities. Not every decision is shared; rather, actual decisions are divided among the adults in such a way that the wife has her domain and the husband has his. For example, in a study of the household responsibilities of professional women and their husbands, the wives were much more responsible for child-care tasks, especially what might be considered the "unpleasant" aspects of child-care, such as meeting physical needs, waking up with the child in the night, and arranging for alternative care when the regular child-care arrangements fell through. The husbands and wives shared certain duties equally, such as teaching the child new skills or playing with the child. With respect to household chores, the men were most likely to make repairs or arrange for repair services, and the men and women gave about equal time to shopping, but both men and women agreed that the wives had the ultimate responsibility to see that most household tasks, such as laundry, shopping, cooking, paying the bills, and cleaning the house, got done (Biernat & Wortman, 1991). In these couples, husbands and wives had quite equal economic and professional standing in their occupational roles. The husbands did contribute in important ways to child care and household tasks; however, the distribution of responsibility for the home was clearly not equal. Egalitarian values about shared responsibility are difficult to translate into behavior. Many factors, including traditional perceptions of sex-typed behaviors, discrepancies in the resources of the partners, and the number of people who are actually involved in or influenced by the decision, will determine how a decision is reached and who ends up having the primary responsibility for related behaviors (Godwin & Scanzoni, 1989).

The adult-executive pattern is somewhat slower in its functioning than the single-executive pattern. Decisions are likely to be less impulsive and less idiosyncratic. More diverse opinions, suggestions, hypotheses, and courses of action are aired in the process of assigning responsibility. There is opportunity for one of the decision-makers to rest from time to time without fear of the family's malfunctioning. The exclusion of children from the spheres of responsibility may elicit some dissident response from them, including requests for participation. The psychological impact of these demands is shared rather than resting on a single individual.

The Family Executive   In the *family-executive pattern*, all members of the family share, insofar as they are able, in the assignment of responsibility for family tasks. Problems are posed to the entire family—children included—and each person has an opportunity to offer opinions, suggestions, or solutions. When the children are very young, they may be asked to participate in the decisions about which they are likely to have an opinion: where to go to dinner, whom to call as a baby-sitter, and what to do on a Sunday afternoon. Although the adults may initially feel that they are extending executive responsibility to the children at their own discretion, the children quickly come to believe that they should be legitimate participants in all family decisions.

In most modern American families, individuals come into contact with distinct sources of information and ideas depending on each person's participation in varying microsystems: the husband and wife, each in his or her workplace, and the children in their schools, in the neighborhood, and through exposure to television, computer networking, and after-school activities. Rather than looking to the father or to the parents as the primary source of information and expertise, the family executive experiences an influx of ideas and pressures for enacting those ideas from all the members of the family.

> Everybody in the family has his or her own interests, and brings in expertise from far disparate domains. Thus, the father, a computer programmer, may learn about ecology from his 7-year-old son, while the mother, who teaches music, becomes more sensitive to nutrition because of her 11-year-old daughter's study of different food groups in school; next summer, perhaps, the whole family will go to France to take a vacation with the teenage son, who has spent the year as an exchange student in Grenoble. (Gergen, 1991, p. 34)

The family-executive decision-making process is probably the most cumbersome of all the decision-making models because it requires consensus among people at varying levels of cognitive and emotional development and experience. However, such a process provides the family with the benefit of children's unique points of view. Occasionally a child's solution to a family problem is better than any of the adults'. In most cases, the family executive is highly influenced by the adults' opinions, but the presence of the children in the executive group ensures that decisions will be made with maximum attention to everyone's needs. In the family-executive pattern, the adults need a great deal of patience and commitment to the format. The children have the lifelong advantage of learning about issues of decision-making, assigning and accepting responsibility, planning, goal setting, and evaluation.

Each of these decision-making patterns provides the executive with a significant area of learning during the adult years. The single executive learns to make decisions, shoulder the responsibility for them, and feel the personal satisfaction that comes from providing one's family with a good home. The adult-executive pattern requires mutual decision-making and compromise. It makes equal use of the skills of both partners in the marriage. Success in the adult-executive pattern of decision-making strengthens the bond between the marriage partners as they grow more confident in their efforts. Satisfactions and responsibilities are shared in this arrangement. The family-executive pattern requires that the adults learn to be teachers as well as decision-makers. They must learn to think out loud so that the children can begin to appreciate the complexity of the decisions as they are being made. The adults must also be ready for unexpected solutions to problems and must be able to admit when those alternatives are better than their own. The family-executive model probably results in some short-term losses in efficiency, but it also provides the greatest long-term gains in group cooperation and mutual enhancement. Table 12.4 summarizes the advantages and disadvantages of each pattern of decision-making.

Organizing Time

Another characteristic of successful household management is the ability to organize time effectively. In the business world, this skill is usually referred to as *time management*. To some extent, how one's day is organized depends on one's job. Some jobs allow individuals to set their own pace, working when they need to and taking time to be with other household members as they please. Most jobs require that people be away from home between roughly 8 A.M. and 5 P.M. plus the time it takes to commute to and from work. A fair number of other jobs require people to work during the evening or late-night hours, or to bring work home in the evenings. Hospitals, computer centers, and some factories are in operation all night and all day and therefore require workers at all times. Some jobs require

TABLE 12.4   Patterns of Decision-Making in the Family

	Advantages	*Disadvantages*
Single executive	Expediency.	Resentment of the executive's power.
	Clear source of responsibility.	May become easy target for blame.
	Personal sense of competence.	Leadership may be idiosyncratic and impulsive.
		Lack of participation in decision-making by other adults and children.
Adult executive	Decisions reached through discussion may be less idiosyncratic and impulsive.	Slow decision-making.
	Diversity of ideas and opinions.	Lack of children's participation in decision-making.
	Marriage relationship strengthened.	
Family executive	Learning experience for all family members.	Slow and cumbersome decision-making process.
	Diversity of ideas and opinions.	
	Participation in decision-making strengthens family unit.	

people to be on call at all hours, even when they are not actually at work. As children enter adolescence, their involvement in school, work, and extracurricular activities, as well as their own social lives, influences the pattern and pace of a family's time.

Another determinant of how one organizes time is the dependency level of the household members. Adults who are responsible for very young children, for older adults who cannot perform certain tasks of daily living, or for individuals of any age who require assistance or supervision as a result of physical or mental challenges have constraints on their discretionary time, including the time that can be devoted to meeting the needs of other members of the household or to maintaining the household itself.

Effective household management requires that a wide variety of activities, including paying the bills, maintaining the home, grocery shopping, preparing and eating meals, laundry, relaxing, socializing, planning, and playing, be allotted enough time for each to be adequately accomplished. Families differ in how much time they want or need to spend at each of these activities. The apartment dweller may spend far less time in home maintenance than the homeowner. Homeowners themselves differ in the amount of time they invest in activities related to the upkeep of their homes. Some families spend a great deal of time preparing and enjoying group meals, while others rarely eat together. These examples illustrate how the family lifestyle is expressed through the allocation of time to various activities.

In addition to the organization of the day, adults must also be able to think in terms of the week, the month, the year, the stage, and the lifetime. Each of these time periods raises different planning issues that must be confronted and met. Planning for a year, for example, requires the anticipation of cycles of activity, from rather hectic to slow-paced. It requires the anticipation of periods for task activity, social activity, and vacations. Adults learn to anticipate the times when the family will need additional stimulation and times when all members will be exhausted. In most climates, the weather must also be anticipated and prepared

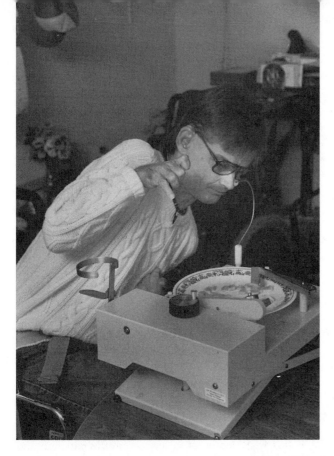

The management of time and the organization of household tasks is guided by the special needs and abilities of family members. Families often devise or seek special household modifications to foster the autonomy of family members who are physically challenged.

for. We do not mean to imply here that adults must plan out every day in great detail (although that may occasionally be necessary), but they must be able to anticipate shifts in the patterns of activity level, opportunities for seasonal activities, and the incorporation of some special occasions, holidays, and rituals into the family's year.

Planning for a life stage requires a *psychotemporal perspective*. This means that adults begin to expect changing needs and resources as they and their children move through each stage of development. As adults anticipate the time when their children will leave home, for example, they may have to consider new demands from them, new needs for themselves, and new patterns of daily activity. They must also anticipate that the event will require some degree of psychological reorientation (see Chapter 13). Planning for this stage, then, may include saving for college expenses, developing interests that can fill spare time when it is available, or just beginning to talk together about the changes in the family that are about to take place. Planning at a life-stage level requires adults to anticipate their parents' needs, their own needs, and the needs of their children and to intervene in order to prepare for future events.

As adults develop skills in organizing and allocating time, they also become aware of the unpredictableness of life (Brim & Ryff, 1980). One of the major realities of middle adulthood is that one is expected to cope with unforeseen events. A parent becomes ill and requires continuous care. A teenage daughter becomes pregnant. An economic recession brings prolonged unemployment. A fire or flood destroys one's home. These are only a few of the unpredictable life events that may fall on the shoulders of middle adults. As middle adults strive to impose order and priorities on their lives, they must also recognize the probabilistic nature of their future.

Setting Goals

The management of a household fosters a conceptualization of future as well as present time. The future is brought into the present through the formation of goals. It is human nature to be driven to new levels of competence and mastery. As one challenge is met, we set a new one for ourselves. Whether the challenge is learning to play the guitar, traveling to a foreign country, saving money for retirement, or starting our own business, we continue to frame the meaning of our daily activities in terms of personal and family goals.

The process of goal setting is complex. Adults identify short-term, intermediate, and long-term goals. This goal setting depends on one's sense of where one would like to be in 2, 5, or 20 years.

As one thinks about goals, one begins to evaluate which things in life are really worth striving for. For some people, the life goal is wealth; for others, fame; for still others, peace of mind. The formulation of life goals during middle adulthood will determine the individual's degree of satisfaction in later adulthood. To some extent, setting realistic life goals for the family unit requires the reevaluation and reconceptualization of life goals that were developed during childhood and adolescence. Individuals may eventually drop some fantasized goals that are still quite attractive but are no longer appropriate to their life situation. They may formulate goals that are quite idiosyncratic and meaningful only in the context of their own personal identity or within the framework of their cultural-ethnic heritage.

> It is a small and beautiful world, the island of Japan revealed in the middle of the Bronx, in a greenhouse of a thousand chrysanthemums. Some are carefully shaped like waterfalls, others like miniature and ancient pine trees, still others like sailboats before the wind. The flowers bloom in ivory and in shades of red, yellow, and purple. . . . Mr. Adachi, who is 36 years old, came here from Tokyo three years ago to bring the traditional Japanese chrysanthemum exhibition to the New York Botanical Garden in the Bronx. At last year's show, his second, many Japanese wept, explaining to startled garden staffers that Mr. Adachi's flowers, so exquisitely true to tradition, made them long for home. (Brim, 1992, p. 13)

As people develop sets of realistic life goals during middle adulthood, they also develop a serious personal commitment to the attainment of those goals. In a sense, they must believe that what they wish to accomplish is worth accomplishing and can, in fact, be attained.

The second phase of goal setting involves a set of operational steps that will lead to the attainment of a goal. If one hopes to have a certain degree of financial independence during later adulthood, one must save money, invest it, and calculate its potential growth in relation to needs anticipated 30–40 years in the future. The same principles apply to the attainment of any long-range goal. The adult must invest resources and anticipate their capacity to change over time. The setting of a goal involves some projection of what one *hopes* things will be like in the future, whereas planning for the attainment of a goal involves some prediction of what things will really be like in the future.

The final stage in the psychological process of goal setting involves the continuous evaluation of the progress being made toward those goals. As people set goals, make plans to attain them, and carry out those plans, they become aware of how well they are progressing toward their goals. They may discover that they can make use of certain skills to reach their goals more quickly. They may find that some goals are far more difficult to attain than they had anticipated and will

The tradition of holding an Easter Sunday family reunion helps this Hispanic family stay in touch with one another and strengthens bonds of kinship within and across generations.

require increased energy. Some goals may be judged to be unattainable, and others may prove to be more easily attainable than had been expected.

Gilbert Brim (1992) has argued that life satisfaction is linked to identifying and working on goals that are within a range of "just manageable difficulty." This idea is very similar to Vygotsky's notion of the zone of proximal development. People who can learn to reframe goals so that they are challenging enough to stimulate new behaviors but not so difficult as to result in repeated failures will find their lives enriched by intermittent experiences of joy in success and a general optimism about reaching out toward the next goal.

Establishing Relationships with Other Social Structures

A final component of household management is the establishment of bonds between the family unit and other social groupings. These other groupings may include (1) individuals, (2) members of the extended family (for example, one's in-laws), (3) other families, (4) business or work-related associations, (5) religious groups, (6) educational groups, and (7) community groups. We introduced this concept briefly in Chapter 3 when describing Bronfenbrenner's (1979) model of the mesosystem. The family is interconnected with other social systems that can expand its resources. Contact with social groups must include the maintenance of goodwill and some evidence of group identification and commitment. Social groups also generate norms that may make demands on the family. The household executive must be able to protect the family from excessive external demands while retaining valuable and satisfying external relationships.

One of the most difficult and subtle kinds of new learning that occurs during middle adulthood is the development of an understanding of how the structures of other organizations affect one's life and the lives of family members. Most of us are not very astute at recognizing how we are influenced by the institutions in which we participate. How do hiring practices at one's workplace influence the kinds of co-workers we are likely to meet? How do hospital policies influence the way we are treated when we are patients or when we seek medical advice for a family member? How do the voting policies of our city or state influence how funds are allocated to schools, social welfare programs, or transportation resources that directly influence the quality of family life? Each of these questions suggests a possible contact between an organizational structure and an adult's efforts to maintain a feeling of control over life events (Sarason, 1980).

Families differ in their investment in relationships outside the family unit. In some households, the nuclear family is more important than any other group. Such households expend very little energy outside the family boundaries. At the other extreme are families who are highly involved in a great many community groups and who incorporate their extended families into frequent family activities. In some families, each person is encouraged to establish his or her own group of close friends. In others, each person's friends are screened or evaluated by the other family members. The adult's task is to define the family's preferred stance toward other social groups and to create opportunities to build desired relationships.

The family's relations with the *extended family* are a most delicate matter. This is the realm of family politics. Courtesies, obligations, insults, and slights within the boundaries of family units are among the most stressful and challenging experiences with which most individuals have to deal. Fischer (1983) described one aspect of family politics in her comparison of the mother-daughter and mother-in-law–daughter-in-law relationship after the birth of the first child. The birth increased the new mother's interactions with both her mother and her mother-in-law. Interactions with the mother tended to become clarified, and there was increased convergence in views within this relationship. However, interactions with the mother-in-law became more strained after the child's birth. Ties with the husband's and wife's kin seem to become less parallel after the birth of the first child. The reason may be that the new mother shares her own mother's child-rearing experiences and therefore feels a new closeness to her. It may be that mothers-in-law are concerned about the well-being of their sons as their daughters-in-law become involved in the new mothering relationship.

Patterns of family interaction between parents and children or between members of the extended kinship group over the life course will influence the quality of these relationships in adulthood. For example, a woman in her 50s recalls with great fondness the relationship she had with her aunt. When the aunt dies, the woman reaches out to her aunt's daughter, her first cousin, and begins to form a closer friendship with this daughter. In another instance, two brothers have been in competition throughout their childhood. When their parents die, they basically drift apart, having little to do with each other from then on. Regardless of the type of kinship relation, feelings of affection are a strong predictor of whether adults will maintain contact with their relatives (Leigh, 1982; Whitbeck, Hoyt & Huck, 1994).

People Who Live Alone

In our discussion of household management, we have assumed that the household consists of two or more people whose lives are intertwined. Questions about decision-making, consensus, and shared responsibilities are all raised in the context of a group of people living together. A large number of people, however, live alone. In 1991, about 25% of households included only one person. These one-person households more frequently consist of men in the younger age groups (under 35) and women in the older age groups (55 and over) (U.S. Bureau of the Census, 1992). Single-person households include people who have never married, those who are divorced or separated, and those who are

The household provides a basic life structure for most people in all cultures. The demands and tasks of household management call forth responses that stimulate cognitive, social, and personal development during adulthood. The household is not only a physical setting, but a shared psychological context for a group of people. In nomadic tribal groups, for example, the continuity of the household is preserved by the group of people and their shared belongings even though the location of the household changes.

The homeless are people who live on the streets or in public shelters. These people have no permanent resting place, no private space (Landers, 1989a, 1989b). In 1990, the census identified roughly 50,000 people who appeared to live on the streets and 190,000 who lived in emergency shelters for the homeless (U.S. Bureau of the Census, 1992). Many of the people who fall into this category are mentally ill persons who have been released from mental institutions. Some are drug and alcohol abusers. Some are runaway youths. The fastest-growing segment of the homeless are families, usually single-parent mothers and their children (Bassuk, 1991).

A combination of the reduction in the buying power of social welfare benefits and shortages in low-income housing have contributed to the increase in the number of families with children who live in the streets or in emergency shelters. Paths toward homelessness for families are diverse. Some of the most common precursors are job loss, domestic violence, substance abuse, mental illness, and divorce (Koblinsky & Anderson, 1993). Although some homeless individuals are in a sudden crisis, many have stumbled from one temporary living situation to the next, and others have never really been able to establish a permanent home. Some of these people are singularly alone and unable to develop minimal social relationships. This is a very unusual phenomenon, as most human beings have some ability to have meaningful social relationships. Among homeless mothers, for example, many have no friends or family. They lack a family social-support system or a sense of social

BOX 12.2

Homelessness

Thousands of mental patients released from New York City's state hospitals became chronically homeless. In cold weather, this homeless man uses the steam from the subway grating to stay warm.

connection, often as a result of some form of victimization earlier in their life. They are commonly suffering from some degree of emotional dysfunction, possibly as a result of an earlier crisis, and often exacerbated by the use of alcohol and drugs (Grigsby et al., 1990; Wright & Devine, 1993).

The number of homeless has grown. Their visibility in every major city in America is presenting a new ethical dilemma to the nation (Gibbs, 1988). In homelessness, we confront the gross failure of the socialization process: the inability of mature adults to meet their basic needs for shelter, food, and clothing. And in the face of the cultural value placed on independence, self-sufficiency, and hard work, we have difficulty making effective societal responses. Policies and programs to assist homeless families have typically focused on short-term emergency intervention with little coordinated effort to address the complex picture of needs, including living arrangements, employment, mental health services, drug or alcohol treatment, the building of a network of support, and gradual integration into a sense of community (Weinreb & Buckner, 1993).

widowed. The reasons for living alone and the backgrounds for this life pattern vary considerably.

We really know little about the differences in psychosocial development between adults who live alone and those who live with others. Some of the aspects of household management, including organizing time, planning for the future, making decisions, and establishing relationships with other social groups still pose challenges to the person living alone. On the other hand, assigning responsibility and establishing a system of group decision-making clearly are not required. People who live alone may not feel the need to engage in elaborate planning and evaluation when they are the only ones who will be immediately affected by their choices. They may be freer to decide spontaneously as each opportunity presents itself.

Most people who live alone compensate for the few contacts they have within their household by maintaining a relatively large number of outside friends. They may spend less time overall in the company of others, but they are more deliberate in identifying confidants who can meet their social needs. Particularly in the area of establishing relationships with other social structures, the situation of living alone appears to promote social integration (Alwin, Converse & Martin, 1985).

In summary, the developmental task of household management is a process of skill building and conceptual learning in five areas: assessing needs and abilities, making decisions, organizing time, setting goals, and establishing relationships with other social groupings. The realm of the household is unique because it allows adults to perform with maximum flexibility, creativity, and adaptability in response to the daily needs and long-term goals of the household members.

The Psychosocial Crisis: Generativity Versus Stagnation

Generativity

A new capacity for directing the course of action in one's own life and in the lives of others emerges during middle adulthood. The psychosocial crisis of *generativity versus stagnation* can be understood as a pressure on the adult to be committed to improving the life conditions of future generations (Erikson, 1963). "Generativity . . . encompasses *procreativity, productivity,* and *creativity,* and thus the generation of new beings, as well as of new products and new ideas, including a kind of self-generation concerned with further identity development" (Erikson, 1982, p. 67). According to Erikson's observations (Erikson et al., 1986), generativity is formed as a result of experiences of maintaining the world, nurturing and being concerned, and caring.

It is worth pausing to consider what it means to *generate.* A basic dictionary definition is "to bring into existence." Through generativity, adults may change the world by introducing new things, new ideas, new beings, or new bonds of relationship, things that have not existed before. During middle adulthood, there appears to be a peak in the desire to produce and create within the framework of one's life structure. This may mean making a success of a remarriage involving children who have been neglected in their early childhood. It may mean trying to provide a better life for one's children than one had growing up. It may mean innovating in the workplace; at the scientist's bench; in poetry, art, music, or literature;

or in creating some splendid form of recreation like Disney World or a refreshing new food like frozen yogurt.

Most people are not physicists, composers, or yogurt inventors. Most people produce generative acts to cope with the challenges of their everyday lives. For example, maintaining networks of family and friends takes energy and time. This activity produces love, support, and encouragement that can be beneficial to the development and health of people in one's circle of close relationships.

The ego strength associated with the achievement of generativity is *care*. Care is a widening commitment *to take care of* the persons, the products, and the ideas one has learned *to care for*. All the strengths arising from earlier developments in the ascending order from infancy to young adulthood (hope and will, purpose and skill, fidelity and love) now prove, on closer study, to be essential to the generative task of cultivating strength in the next generation, for this is indeed the "store of human life" (Erikson, 1982, p. 67).

Generativity is critical to the survival of any society. At some point, adult members of the society must begin to feel an obligation to contribute their resources, skills, and creativity to improving the quality of life for the young. To some degree, this motive is aroused as one recognizes the inevitability of mortality. One will not always be around to direct the course of events. Therefore, one must make contributions to the society, on both personal and public levels, that will stand some chance of continuing after one's death.

The importance of the construct of generativity for understanding the positive, prosocial aspects of adult behavior has led to efforts to create measures of generativity for adult populations. The meaning of generativity is being clarified and elaborated through attempts to operationalize the concept. One line of research provided a cross-sectional comparison of dimensions of generativity among subjects in early (22–27), middle (37–42), and later (67–72) adulthood (McAdams, St. Aubin & Logan, 1993). Four aspects of generativity were measured: generative concern—a sense that one is making a difference in the lives of others; generative commitments—personal strivings or goals that have a generative nature; generative actions—a checklist of actions that the person has performed in the past two months that involved "creating, maintaining, or offering"; and generative narratives—autobiographical recollections coded for generative meaning.

Across all age groups, generative concern was significantly correlated with happiness and life satisfaction. When all four measures of generativity were combined, the middle adults scored higher than the young or older age groups. The measures of generative commitment and generative narration, especially, were higher for the middle adult group. The pattern of responses showed significant differences between the middle adult and the younger adult groups, but the middle adults and the older adults were not significantly different. The implication is that once the generative orientation emerges, it appears to endure in the life goals and activities of a person into later adulthood. We find a similar example in the psychosocial crisis of identity. Once the identity orientation emerges, it, too, appears to endure as a recurring theme to be revised and reworked in later stages.

Peterson and Stewart (1993) measured generativity by scoring certain themes in narrative writing samples: productivity, caring, and general generativity. *Productivity* focuses on "developing or growing through the generation of tangible products or ideas. . . . Feelings of stagnation are also scored . . . whenever a person mentions frustration at not being able to contribute something tangible to society." *Caring* involves all expressions of caring for, taking care of, and doing something for, as well as taking care not to do any thing harmful. *General generativity*

Pablo Picasso, Guernica, 1937. Without a sense of generativity, no society can survive. Guernica is an expression of Picasso's outrage at Franco and fascism. Everything in this painting cries out in pain against the fierce and pointless destruction of life.

is a global expression "about making a lasting contribution, especially to future generations." Peterson and Stewart's sample was made up primarily of people in the stage of early adulthood. Their findings confirm Erikson's prediction that there are foreshadowings of psychosocial themes in earlier life stages. Peterson and Stewart found that expressions of generativity were especially notable among those young adults who had begun parenting.

We want to emphasize how deeply the theme of generativity versus stagnation permeates the psychological dynamics of adult life. In the following section, we discuss the negative pole, stagnation, and its expression in narcissistic self-preoccupation and depression. Since the mid-1980s, the severity of the problems related to depression in adulthood have been documented. Several different patterns of adult depression have been described. Although we read a lot about the negative side of adult life, including people who commit crimes or betray their families, it is important to recognize that the positive forces of generativity are equally dominant in guiding the lives of most adults and that these forces produce acts of creative leadership and caring among even the most humble of humans.

Stagnation

In contrast to generativity, failure to meet the demands of middle adulthood results in stagnation. *Stagnation* suggests a lack of psychological movement or growth. Adults who devote their energy and skills to the sole end of self-aggrandizement and personal satisfaction are likely to have difficulty looking beyond their own needs or experiencing satisfaction in taking care of others. Adults who are unable to cope with the management of a household, the raising of children, or the management of a career are likely to feel psychological stagnation at the end of middle adulthood.

The experience of stagnation may differ for the narcissistic adult and the depressed adult. *Narcissistic people* may expend energy in accumulating wealth and material possessions. They relate to others in terms of how others can serve them. They may exist quite happily until the physical and psychological consequences of aging begin to make their impact. At that point, and continuing toward old age, self-satisfaction is easily undermined by anxieties related to death. It is not uncommon for such persons to undergo some form of "conversion" after a serious illness or an emotional crisis forces them to acknowledge the limitations of a totally self-involved lifestyle.

Chronically depressed people do not feel a sense of accomplishment during middle adulthood. They think of themselves as worthless. They are unable to perceive themselves as having sufficient resources to make any contribution to their society. These people are likely to be very low in self-esteem, very doubtful about any opportunities for future improvement, and therefore unwilling to invest any energy in conceptualizing future progress. Many other types of depression have been documented, which we described in Chapter 9. In our discussion of infancy, we reviewed the results of research that has documented the negative impact of maternal depression on the mother-infant dyad and its potential continuing impact on the formation of interpersonal skill development during childhood. Depression has been linked to alcohol and substance abuse in adulthood, resulting in serious disruptions in the workplace as well as in the household.

In an analysis of men at midlife, Farrell and Rosenberg (1981) provided some insight into stagnation. The case of Tony Williams illustrates how a life of unresolved stresses and disappointments coupled with a defensive denial results in a picture of increasing bankruptcy of personal and interpersonal meaning:

> A number of midlife stresses have hit Tony in the past five years. They began with the death of his mother when Tony was 40. Tony tells of the death with the same apparent stoicism he showed throughout the evening. "When your time is up, you gotta go," he says. But he says that his father went into a prolonged depression, moping around watching television, having no energy for family activities.
>
> Then two friends from childhood died within a year. Tony says, "Better them than me." He doesn't seem to overtly mourn their loss, but he does appear to exaggerate his fatalistic willingness to accept fate as he reports on this period, insisting that he does not fear death.
>
> Over the years Tony had become active in the Knights of Columbus. He helped organize an annual Christmas party for retarded children, and told of how good it felt to stand by as the kids came up to sit on Santa's knee and receive their gifts. But during the past few years he has pulled away from this activity, claiming that younger men coming in are "messing up" what he helped to build. His final break with them came last year, when he ruptured a disc in his back while lifting a heavy barrel at work. He had to spend three weeks in the hospital and none of his friends came to visit him.
>
> This back injury marked a sharp turning point, evoking all the bitterness and depressive symptomatology kept in check after earlier life reversals and his mother's death. His medical treatment required that he stay home a month after returning from the hospital, but that was seven months ago. Tony's doctor tells him he is fine, but Tony has not returned to work because he ostensibly is trying to obtain workman's compensation for the injury and lost work time. His lawyer is still working on the case, and Tony fears that if he goes back to work he'll lose his case. So he stays at home, takes occasional walks, listens to police calls on a police radio, and watches television. His children have grown increasingly annoyed with him. "All he does is pick," says Mary. "He won't let Mom sit down to do a crossword puzzle. He won't let me sew because it interferes with his radio. And if you stay around the house, he starts reading stories out of the newspaper to you. So me and my brother, we leave the house."*

Middle adulthood extends over many years. During this stage, people encounter many complex challenges for which they may not be fully prepared. Promotion to an administrative position, the need to care for an aging parent, and the negotiation of a divorce are examples. Brim (1992) argues that both success and failure bring a person face to face with redefining and reexamining their goals. At many points, adults doubt their ability to move ahead, achieve their goals, or make meaningful contributions. Feelings of stagnation surge temporarily. People may recognize that unless they redefine their situation or take some new risks, the quality of their lives will deteriorate. They face the possibility of feeling outdated by new technology, outmoded by new lifestyles, overburdened by role demands, or alienated from meaningful social contacts. At these moments of crisis, adults may become entangled in a process of self-protection and withdrawal that results in permanent stagnation. However, they may also muster new resources and a new perspective that will permit continuing growth and the expansion of generativity.

The Central Process: Person-Environment Interaction and Creativity

We have identified two aspects of the central process that lead to the development of generativity in middle adulthood. The first is the facilitative interaction between the individual and the social environment. The social environment includes the family, the work setting, the neighborhood, and the larger political community. To a great extent, this environment provides a person's basis of experience. Day-to-day interactions, the expectations for behavior, the available resources, and the social supports that are necessary to the growth of self-confidence are elements of the social environment.

Person-Environment Interaction

Successful personality growth depends on the interaction between a person's needs, skills, and interpersonal style and the demands of the environments in which the person is embedded. The concept of interaction suggests a potential for reciprocal influence between individuals and settings. The structure and demands of settings may alter a person's behavior, values, goals, and sense of self-worth. People also have an impact on the settings in which they participate. Adults do more than maintain or respond to their environment; they shape it (Endler, 1983). People play their roles to allow for the expression of their individual styles. They define their roles for themselves as well as having their roles defined by others. Parents as well as office workers live within structures of expectations. In their own ways of interpreting, denying, or otherwise responding to these expectations, adults present an increasingly independent and authentic "me" if they are moving toward the stabilization of ego identity. If not, they may be more responsive to the expectations of others than is healthy for the continued emergence of a stable identity.

The particular achievement of middle adulthood is to identify those domains in which one has opportunities to influence the quality of the social environment so that it becomes more hospitable, humane, nurturant, or supportive of one's own visions for the future. Caring expands in different domains for different people, but the pressures always lead to having the welfare of people and enduring things (including ideas) deeply at heart. There is an action component to this caring, in that people work to care for what they can. When there is a good fit between personal needs and ways of caring and the environment's demands and the capacity to become more nurturant, a person is able, over the years, to develop a positive resolution to the crisis of generativity versus stagnation.

Most people have some degree of choice about their social environment. They can, for example, decide whom they will marry, whether or not to have children, which occupation they will follow, and where they will live. To the degree that they have a choice in these matters, they are able to influence the kinds of transactions that occur between their personality and their social milieu. Making good decisions about social settings requires that they understand themselves and that they are able to conceptualize the nature of the other people and the social institutions that are part of their social environment.

Most people have trouble conceptualizing how they are shaped by the demands of their social settings. This kind of analysis requires a complex understanding of social settings and some idea of the types of demands that such environments are likely to make. It also requires the ability to speculate about how things may change in the future. It is one thing to fall in love with someone and decide to marry. It is quite another to try to foresee what it would be like to live with that person for 20 or more years.

Although participation in some settings is a matter of choice, many others are the result of chance. Some settings can be abandoned or altered if they do not meet the individual's needs. Other settings are permanent and difficult to alter. If one is in an unsuitable setting, one must be willing to leave it if possible, or to discover some way to influence the setting so that it meets one's needs more adequately. Some people, however, find themselves in social settings that can be neither abandoned nor altered. For example, a group of workers in Michigan were trained for employment in an automotive plant. When the economy slumped, they were laid off. They did not have enough money saved to move to another town; there were no new jobs; and they did not have the resources or the incentive to retrain for other types of employment. When one is forced to remain in social settings that are contrary to one's needs, the possibility of developing generativity is seriously diminished. If one is unable to experience a personal sense of effectiveness in home, work, or community, then one is unlikely to feel capable of contributing to future growth in these spheres.

Fortunately, the social environment is so multifaceted that individuals are likely to experience satisfaction in their participation in at least one special setting even if they feel dissatisfaction in others. Under these conditions, individuals can compensate for their inability to be creative in some settings by placing increased effort and investment in those in which they can more easily attain satisfaction. This may require that individuals reorder their priorities so that frustration in one setting will in fact be less of a thorn in light of accomplishments made in another. If one has little opportunity to find satisfaction in work, for example, one must begin to reevaluate the importance of contributions to one's family, religion, or community.

Creativity

The second part of the central process in the establishment of generativity is personal creativity. Although creativity has been defined in many ways, for our purposes we will consider it the willingness to abandon old forms or patterns of doing things in favor of new ways. This requires the generation, evaluation, and implementation of new ideas. Within this definition, we can include great creative acts that touch the lives of many people as well as a kind of individual creative activity that touches the lives of a few. The importance of a creative response, no matter how small, is that it redefines the world and opens the door to new

Creativity means to see in a fresh light what has been there all along. In his later years, Picasso directed his creative talent to reinterpreting works of the great masters. Luncheon on the Grass (left) was one of a series of 27 paintings and over 100 drawings inspired by Manet's Le Dejeuner sur L'herbe (right), painted about 100 years earlier. Here Picasso focuses on the dialogue between the painter and his model. The painting becomes more personal, revealing a sense of supplication and stiffness on the part of the aging man in the presence of the voluptuous woman.

possibilities (Taylor, 1975; Arieti, 1976). Creativity provides an outlet for caring for something that has not yet been defined or experienced.

Through creative effort, adults impose a new perspective on the organization, expression, or formulation of ideas. Creative adults are not dominated by social forces but are able to direct the course of events themselves. These individuals are at a point in their development at which their own creative responses can become a source of influence on a great many others. Through the process of creative problem solving, adults may plan to reshape the social environment in order to meet both personal and social needs more satisfactorily. Throughout middle adulthood, adults are faced with situations in family, child-rearing, and work settings that provide stimuli for creative problem solving. In their efforts to take into account the requirements of the social setting and to be productive in it, people must develop creative plans. They must also attempt to carry out those plans, a task that itself may require further creativity. The essence of creative problem solving is the formulation of a new plan and the ability to translate it into reality.

Fostering creativity during middle adulthood requires some deliberate attention. Given one's embeddedness in many demanding social roles, it is often difficult to step aside and view one's situation from a fresh perspective. Arieti (1976) recommended nine conditions that foster creativity. They are listed in Table 12.5. In this list you will notice a need to engage in somewhat opposing processes, such as inactivity and alertness. One must strive to be open to the flood of inner and outer experiences and to step away from trying to maintain control over all aspects of the environment. At the same time, one must be alert to insights into the relevance of certain experiences and willing to transform those insights into action.

From the outset, the creative process involves some risk. In order to try new forms, people must give up some old ways of doing things that may have been certain to work. In this process, people must anticipate the possibility that their efforts will fail. For some people, the fear of failure may be so great that creative solutions are never realized. For them, the sense of generativity is blocked by a fear of the unknown or by an inability to violate conventional norms for behavior.

For those who are not inhibited by the fear of failure, the repeated efforts to generate creative solutions eventually result in the formulation of a philosophy of life. This philosophy incorporates the psychological needs of people, the ideals

TABLE 12.5	**Conditions That Foster Creativity**
Aloneness	Being alone allows the person to make contact with the self and to be open to new kinds of inspiration.
Inactivity	Periods of time are needed to focus on inner resources and to be removed from the constraints of routine activities.
Daydreaming	Allows exploration of one's fantasy life and venturing into new avenues of growth.
Free thinking	Allows the mind to wander in any direction without restriction and permits the similarities among remote topics or concepts to emerge.
State of readiness to catch similarities	One must practice recognizing similarities and resemblances across perceptual or cognitive domains.
Gullibility	A willingness to suspend judgment allows one to be open to possibilities without treating them as nonsense.
Remembering and replaying past traumatic conflicts	Conflict may be transformed into more stable creative products.
Alertness	A state of awareness that permits the person to grasp the relevance of seemingly insignificant similarities.
Discipline	A devotion to the techniques, logic, and repetition that permit creative ideas to be realized.

Source: Based on Arieti, 1976.

toward which individuals and groups strive, and the impact of social settings on the functioning of individuals, as well as the direction of human development into the future. Through risk taking, occasional failure, and a predominance of successful creative efforts, adults achieve a sense of what they believe in and what gives meaning to life. With this remarkable integration of experience and information, people enter later adulthood.

There is an old story about three men who were observed laying bricks for the wall of a church. When asked what they were doing, the first man said he was laying bricks, the second said he was building a wall, and the third said he was building a church. During middle adulthood, one must arrive at a philosophy of life that will impart significance to daily activities. One part of generativity lies in the actual attainment of creative goals. The other part lies in the perspective one brings to one's lifework.

Erikson suggests that the outcome of the crisis of generativity versus stagnation has implications for adults at the next life stage in the form of *grand-generativity*:

> The reconciling of generativity and stagnation involves the elder in expressing a "grand-generativity" that is somehow beyond middle age's direct responsibility for maintaining the world. The roles of aging parent, grandparent, old friend, consultant, adviser, and mentor all provide the aging adult with essential social opportunities to experience grand-generativity in current relationships with people of all ages. In these relationships, the individual seeks to integrate outward-looking care for others with inward-looking concern for self. As a complement to caring for others, the elder is also challenged to accept from others that caring which is required, and to do so in a way that is itself caring. In the context of the generational cycle, it is incumbent upon the aged to enhance feelings of generativity in their care givers from the younger generations. (Erikson et al., 1986, pp. 74–75)

Applied Topic
Discrimination in the Workplace

"The U.S.A. is just a horrible place to try to raise a family and have a career. . . . When I was working in the U.S.A., it was a struggle to find decent day care . . . and if I missed a half-day of work [because] my kid had a temperature of 104, I was lectured on how this let down the [department]. In Israel there is 3 months paid maternity leave, day-care centers on every block, and if you *don't* take off from work for your kid's birthday party the department chairman will lecture you on how important these things are to kids and how he never missed one while his kids were little." (Astrophysicist Sara Beck, currently a tenured professor at Tel Aviv University, quoted in Barinaga, 1994, p. 1472)

"A big-city police officer once shared with me his frustration at waiting nineteen years to make detective. In those days before affirmative action, he had watched, one year after another, as less qualified whites were promoted over him. Each year he had swallowed his disappointment, twisted his face into a smile, and congratulated his white friends as he hid his rage—so determined was he to avoid being categorized as a race-obsessed troublemaker. . . . Even though he made detective years ago, and even though, on the side (and on his own time), he managed to become a successful businessman and an exemplary member of the upwardly striving middle class, he says the anger still simmers within him. He worries that someday it will come pouring out, that some luckless white person will tick him off and he will explode, with tragic results." (quoted in Cose, 1993, p. 61)

The United States has been characterized as an "achieving society." As a cultural group, we value individual achievement, usually expressed through accomplishments in the world of work. Thus, in the United States, for men and increasingly for women, the mark of successful adulthood is frequently equated with success in the labor market, and success in the labor market is typically attributed to personal characteristics of ability, intelligence, and motivation. Lack of success in the labor market is similarly attributed to deficiencies in personal characteristics: lack of ability, low intelligence, and poor motivation. Individuals are unlikely to attribute their successes to conditions of the workplace, vagaries in the economy, luck, or conditions of society that give them a special advantage and others an unfair disadvantage. Yet, many Americans face serious and persistent disadvantages in the workplace, disadvantages that are linked to being different from the white, male, Protestant, middle-class norm (Jones, 1988).

The continuation of discrimination in the workplace is an exceedingly costly problem for the society as a whole. Discriminatory practices that lead to the disaffection of individuals from the world of work is costly in economic terms—in lower levels of productivity, high turnover, high levels of irritability and conflict among workers, lawsuits, and less identification with the company and its goals. It is costly in personal terms as well. Feelings of frustration about not being recognized for one's competence or being passed over for promotion by less competent workers interfere with the development of a generative orientation. These experiences may lead to a more self-serving orientation, focusing exclusively on "protecting me and mine," or to a pervasive sense of futility about the future.

Through the 14th Amendment to the U.S. Constitution, "no state shall make or enforce any law which shall abridge the privileges or immunities of citizens of the United States; nor shall any state deprive any person of life, liberty, or property, without due process of law; nor deny any person within its jurisdiction the equal protection of the laws." This commitment to equal rights and equal

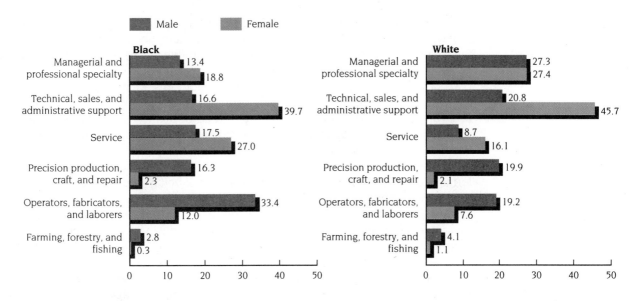

FIGURE 12.1

Occupational distribution of the employed civilian labor force, by sex and race, March 1990 (percentages) Source: U.S. Bureau of the Census, 1991.

protection was guaranteed in 1868. Yet, it was not until 1870 that citizens were guaranteed the right to vote regardless of "race, color, or previous condition of servitude," and it was not until 1920 that women were guaranteed the right to vote. Although the ideals of individual freedom and equality are part of our cultural heritage, so are practices that denied these rights to large groups of individuals. The culture has struggled with the tension between valuing agency, equality, and a system of educational and economic opportunity based on merit, on the one hand, and a persistent tendency to define groups as deviant or deficient, depending on the extent to which they differ from the majority, white European norm. This tension resulted in a surge of civil rights challenges in the 1960s, challenges that brought about the Civil Rights Acts of 1964 and 1968, prohibiting discrimination in public and private employment based on race, religion, sex, or national origin. These laws clearly should have led to an end to open practices of discrimination in the workplace. Yet, discrimination exists.

In 1990, the median income of year-round, full-time workers was $20,849 for white females and $31,186 for white males; $18,518 for African-American females and $21,540 for African-American males; and $16,186 for Hispanic females and $19,314 for Hispanic males. Females with five or more years of college earned $35,827; males with five or more years of college earned $55,831. For persons with incomes below the poverty level, 10.7% were white, 28% were Hispanic, and 32% were African-American. Unemployment patterns for 1990 found African-Americans twice as likely as whites to be unemployed. For teenagers, the unemployment rate for whites was 14%; for African-Americans, 32%. "Blacks constituted 11 percent of the labor force in 1990, but they accounted for 22 percent of the unemployed" (Pinkney, 1993, p. 71).

One explanation for racial, ethnic, and gender differences in salary, rates of poverty, and rates of unemployment is that workers from different groups are distributed unevenly in the occupational structure. Figure 12.1 shows the occupational pattern by race and sex for 1990. One-third of African-American men are operators, fabricators, and laborers, compared to 20% of white men. This group is vulnerable to seasonal layoffs, and to chronic unemployment as the overall direction of the American economy shifts from manufacturing to service industries. Forty percent of African-American women and forty-six percent of white women are in technical, sales, and administrative support positions. These positions vary widely, but many are at the low end of the salary scale, involving clerical, secretarial, and data-entry positions. On the positive side, many state and federal government positions are of this nature, providing more scrutiny against overt practices of discrimination and a greater chance for job stability.

Group differences in occupational position resulting in different salary structures and different risks of layoffs are not in and of themselves evidence of discrimination. Discrimination exists when two people doing the same job are paid substantially different wages. Discrimination occurs when factors other than one's merit prevent a person from being hired, promoted, or rewarded through various forms of compensation or increase a person's risk of being fired. Most specifically, discrimination occurs when a person is evaluated on the basis of group membership rather than on the basis of performance as an individual. In the workplace, this process operates as an in-group–out-group dynamic in which members of the in-group view members of the out-group as deficient and, at some level, possibly threatening to their continued success and well-being.

Employers, supervisors, and others in positions of power establish a normative profile for their employees and judge each new employee against that profile. This profile may include deeply held beliefs and values on the part of men about women. Men may wonder whether women can really perform the same kinds of jobs as men, whether women can effectively assume responsibility to supervise men, whether clients will place their trust in women executives, or whether women will be dedicated to their work when conflicts between work and family arise. This profile may include deeply held beliefs and values on the part of whites about nonwhites, especially beliefs that whites are superior to nonwhites in ability and that the cultural characteristics of nonwhites will be disruptive or damaging to productivity in the workplace (Jones, 1988).

Consider the following situation. At Monsanto, the chemical company, in 1990 an aggressive recruitment effort resulted in 17% minority nonunion new hires and 21% female nonunion new hires. The company was serious about increasing the presence of minorities and women in its chemical subsidiaries and had taken efforts to do so since the 1970s. However, in 1990, of those who quit the company voluntarily, 26% were women and 20% were minorities. Through the use of exit interviews, the company discovered some important discriminatory aspects of the work environment.

> Fully 100% of the minorities who had left said they wanted more job responsibility and that they had experienced difficulty in dealing with their supervisors. Also, 30% more departed minorities than whites felt that Monsanto needs to give employees more help in adjusting to their jobs. Furthermore, they felt treatment by their bosses seemed arbitrary and unfair. . . . Twenty percent more women than men said they were treated unfairly concerning pay and promotion decisions. And of the 40% of the women who had new jobs, a huge 70% said their new employers offered greater opportunities for career advancement. (Ellis, 1991, pp. 60–61)

In general, when we discuss psychosocial development, we look at the outcome for the individual in achieving a positive resolution of the psychosocial crisis. But when considering discrimination in the workplace, we must also look at the consequences for a society. Discrimination in the workplace is one expression of societal stagnation. It is a defensive posture in which those in power try to protect their status, their profits, and their power by preventing members of less powerful groups from gaining a foothold. Rather than treating diversity in the labor force as a factor that will improve the overall flexibility and resources of the work setting, discrimination operates to reduce diversity. Over time, the fate of individuals who have been discriminated against becomes a great cost to the society at large. Some give up and become chronically unemployed or underemployed, and the result is a loss of human capital. Some remain in a discriminatory workplace, trying to "get by," not making trouble, yet operating behind a veil of caution. African-American middle-class adults tell the same stories over and over again about how much effort and energy they spend trying to help white people feel comfortable with them (Whitaker, 1993). Over time, this expenditure is both exhausting and deeply frustrating. One outcome of the various forms of discrimination is the development of an unspoken resentment of work that may be communicated in some form to their children, thus transmitting a cross-generational, cynical outlook on work.

However, the history of our country is also filled with many tales of individuals who succeed against the odds. These are adults who recognize the risks of staying in a setting that does not fit well with their healthy desire to create, to produce, and to care. They may strike out on their own by setting up their own companies, they may challenge unfair practices through the courts, and they may mentor younger workers to help them cope with the conflicts they face in the workplace. And not to place the responsibility for coping with discrimination entirely on the victims, there are also examples of work settings that have taken active steps to challenge their own practices. Companies have been cited for their policies to support the hiring and promotion of women into senior positions, and for their innovations in weaving new levels of understanding about diversity into all aspects of employee development (Konrad, 1990; Gleckman et al., 1991).

The future of the American work force of the 21st century is already before us. Women and ethnic minorities are the fastest-growing groups of new employees. By the year 2000, racial and ethnic minorities will comprise one-third of the school-age children (American Council on Education, 1988). Their preparation for and participation in the labor market will be a determining factor in the quality and productivity of the U.S. economy in the 21st century. The psychosocial approach, which alerts us to the interdependence of the individual and the society, is nowhere more dramatically illustrated than in thinking about the connection between contemporary workplace policies and practices and their implications for the maturation of a sense of industry among school-age children.

Chapter Summary

During the middle adult years, people have an opportunity to make significant contributions to their culture. Through work, home, and child rearing, people express their own value orientations, moral codes, personalities, and talents. They grow more sensitive to the multiple needs of those around them and more skillful in influencing the social environment.

The developmental tasks of middle adulthood are extremely complex and require long-term persistence. During middle adulthood, people gauge their self-worth largely in relation to their contributions to complex social units, especially work, family, and community. Each task calls for a new level of conceptualization of the interaction of the self with immediate and more remote social systems and an increased ability to balance one's individual needs with system goals. Nurturing, managing, caring, and the attainment of new levels of skill are fostered as one engages in the primary tasks of middle adulthood. These competencies provide a foundation for establishing the emotional and social support for oneself and others that is so central to collaborative efforts in the workplace, mentoring younger workers, maintaining and expanding intimate relationships, and preserving optimal functioning for older adults. The well-being of the community as a whole rests largely on the effectiveness of people in middle adulthood to reach new levels of psychosocial maturity.

The psychosocial crisis of the middle adult years is really a moral crisis of commitment to a better way of life. The society must encourage adults to care for others besides themselves. The egocentrism of toddlerhood, early school age, and adolescence must eventually come to an end if the social group is to survive. In the same way that intimacy (giving oneself to another) requires identity, generativity (giving oneself to the next generation) requires love of specific others. The interpersonal sources of satisfaction that exist during middle adulthood are the primary forces propelling people toward a generative approach to society as a whole.

In the applied topic of discrimination in the workplace, we see evidence of societal stagnation. Often it is middle adults in leadership positions who, by deliberate practice or informal example, set a tone that promotes the exclusion of certain workers on the basis of age, gender, racial or ethnic group, or other group characteristics. At the same time, it is others in middle adulthood who suffer from discriminatory policies and are unable to reach the levels of achievement and contribution that their talents merit. Social policies and practices that interfere with a person's ability to perform meaningful work or to achieve recognition and respect for their work pose a hazard to individual psychosocial development and to the future of the social group. These practices, born from the core pathology of rejectivity, act in opposition to the fundamental needs of a society to care about its members and to foster the most optimistic ambitions and goals possible in younger generations.

References

Adams, B. (1986). *The family: A sociological interpretation* (4th ed.). San Diego: Harcourt Brace Jovanovich.

Alwin, D. F. (1984). Living alone. ISR *Newsletter*, 12, 3–4.

Alwin, D. F., Converse, P. E. & Martin, S. S. (1985). Living arrangements and social integration. *Journal of Marriage and the Family*, 47, 319–334.

American Council on Education. (1988). *One-third of a nation*. Washington, DC: Author.

Aquilino, W. S. (1990). Likelihood of parent-adult child coresidence. *Journal of Marriage and the Family*, 52, 405–419.

Araji, S. K. (1977). Husbands' and wives' attitude-behavior congruence on family roles. *Journal of Marriage and the Family*, 39, 309–320.

Argyle, M. (1972). *The social psychology of work*. Harmondsworth: Penguin.

Arieti, S. (1976). *Creativity: The magic synthesis*. New York: Basic Books.

Bank, L., Forgatch, M. S., Patterson, G. R. & Fetrow, R. A. (1993). Parenting practices of single mothers: Mediators of negative contextual factors. *Journal of Marriage and the Family*, 55, 371–384.

Barinaga, M. (1994). Surprise across the cultural divide. *Science*, 263, 1468–1472.

Barnett, R. C., Marshall, N. L. & Pleck, J. H. (1992), Men's multiple roles and their relationship to men's psychological distress. *Journal of Marriage and the Family*, 54, 358–367.

Bassuk, E. L. (1991), Homeless families. *Scientific American*, 265, 66–74.

Bates, G. W. (1981). On the nature of the hot flash. *Clinical Obstetrics and Gynecology*, 24, 231.

Bell, R. R. (1983). *Marriage and family interaction* (6th ed.). Homewood, IL: Dorsey.

Bengtson, V. L. & Roberts, R. E. (1991), Intergenerational solidarity in aging families: An example of formal theory construction. *Journal of Marriage and the Family*, 53, 856–870.

Biernat, M. & Wortman, C. B. (1991), Sharing of home responsibilities between professionally employed women and their husbands. *Journal of Personality and Social Psychology*, 60, 844–860.

Birnbaum, L. A. (1975). Life patterns and self-esteem in gifted family-oriented and career-committed women. In M. T. S. Mednick, S. S. Tangri & L. W. Hoffman (Eds.), *Women and achievement: Social and motivational analyses*. New York: Halsted.

Braginsky, D. D. & Braginsky, B. M. (1975, August). Surplus people: Their lost faith in self and system. *Psychology Today, 9,* 68–72.

Brim, G, (1992). *Ambition: How we manage success and failure throughout our lives.* New York: Basic Books.

Brim, O. G. & Ryff, C. D. (1980). On the properties of life events. In P. B. Baltes & O. G. Brim (Eds.), *Life-span development and behavior* (Vol. 3, pp. 368–388). New York: Academic Press.

Brody, E. M., Johnsen, P. T. & Fulcomer, M. C. (1984). What should adult children do for elderly parents? Opinions and preferences of three generations of women. *Journal of Gerontology, 39,* 736–746.

Broman, C. (1993), Race differences in marital well-being. *Journal of Marriage and the Family, 55,* 724–732.

Bronfenbrenner, U. (1979). *The ecology of human development: Experiments by nature and design.* Cambridge: Harvard University Press.

Brubaker, T. H. (1990). Families in later life: A burgeoning research area. *Journal of Marriage and the Family, 52,* 959–981.

Cain, P. S. & Treiman, D. J. (1981). The DOT as a source of occupational data. *American Sociological Review, 46,* 253–278.

Cicirelli, V. G. (1981). *Helping elderly parents: The role of adult children.* Boston: Auburn House.

Clark, R. A., Nye, F. I. & Gecas, V. (1978). Husbands' work involvement and marital role performance. *Journal of Marriage and the Family, 40,* 9–21.

Clark-Nicolas, P. & Gray-Little, B. (1991), Effect of economic resources on marital quality in black married couples. *Journal of Marriage and the Family, 53,* 645–655.

Coady, S. S. (1982). Correlates of maternal satisfaction among older first time mothers. Ph.D. dissertation, Ohio State University, Columbus.

Cole, C. L. & Cole, A. L. (1985). Husbands and wives should have an equal share in making the marriage work. In H. Feldman & M. Feldman (Eds.), *Current controversies in marriage and family* (pp. 131–141). Newbury Park, CA: Sage

Cose, E. (1993, November 15). Rage of the privileged. *Newsweek,* pp. 56–63.

Douvan, E. (1982, October). Changing roles: Work, marriage, and parenthood. *Michigan Alumnus,* pp. 4–7.

Duvall, E. M. (1977). *Family development* (5th ed.). Philadelphia: Lippincott.

Ellis, J. E. (1991, July 8). Monsanto's new challenge: Keeping minority workers. *Newsweek,* pp. 60–61.

Endler, N. S. (1983). Interactionism: A personality model but not yet a theory. In M. M. Page (Ed.), *Nebraska Symposium on Motivation, 1982* (pp. 155–200). Lincoln: University of Nebraska Press.

Erdwins, C. J. & Mellinger, J. C. (1984). Midlife women: Relation of age and role to personality. *Journal of Personality and Social Psychology, 47,* 390–395.

Erikson, E. H. (1963). *Childhood and society* (2nd ed.). New York: Norton.

Erikson, E. H. (1982). *The life cycle completed.* New York: Norton.

Erikson, E. H., Erikson, J. M. & Kivnick, H. Q. (1986). *Vital involvement in old age.* New York: Norton.

Farrell, M. P. & Rosenberg, S. D. (1981). *Men at midlife.* Boston: Auburn House.

Finley, N. J. (1989). Gender differences in caregiving for elderly parents. *Journal of Marriage and the Family, 51,* 79–86.

Fischer, L. R. (1983). Mothers and mothers-in-law. *Journal of Marriage and the Family, 45,* 187–192.

French, J. P., Doehrman, S. R., Davis-Sacks, M. & Vinokur, A. (1983), *Career change in midlife: Stress, social support and adjustment.* Ann Arbor, MI: Institute for Social Research.

Gergen, K. J. (1991, September/October). The saturated family. *The Family Therapy Networker,* pp. 26–35.

Gibbs, N. R. (1988, September 5). Begging: To give or not to give. *Time,* pp. 68–74.

Gillespie, C. (1989), *Hormones, hot flashes, and mood swings.* New York: Harper & Row.

Gleckman, H., Smart, T., Dwyer, P., Segal, T. & Weber, J. (1991, July 8). Race in the workplace. *Business Week,* pp. 50–62.

Glick, P. C. (1977). Updating the life cycle of the family. *Journal of Marriage and the Family, 39,* 5–13.

Glick, P. C. (1979). Future American families. *Washington COFO Memo, 2,* 2–5.

Godwin, D. D. & Scanzoni, J. (1989). Couple consensus during marital joint decision-making. *Journal of Marriage and the Family, 51,* 943–956.

Gongla, P. A. & Thompson, E. H. (1987). Single-parent families. In M. B. Sussman & S. K. Steinmetz (Eds.), *Handbook of marriage and the family* (pp. 397–418). New York: Plenum.

Grigsby, C., Baumann, D., Gregorich, S. E. & Roberts-Gray, C. (1990). Disaffiliation to entrenchment: A model for understanding homelessness. *Journal of Social Issues, 46,* 141–156.

Haan, N. (1981). Common dimensions of personality development: Early adolescence to mid-life. In D. H. Eichorn, J. A. Clausen, N. Haan, M. P. Hanzik & P. H. Mussen (Eds.), *Present and past in middle life* (pp. 117–151). New York: Academic Press.

Halford, W. K., Hahlweg, K. & Dunne, M. (1990). Cross-cultural study of marital communication and marital distress. *Journal of Marriage and the Family, 52,* 487–500.

Hammond, C. B. & Maxson, W. S. (1986). Estrogen replacement therapy. *Clinical Obstetrics and Gynecology, 29,* 407–430.

Hamon, R. R. & Blieszner, R. (1990). Filial responsibility expectations among adult child–older parent pairs. *Journal of Gerontology: Psychological Sciences, 45,* P110–P112.

Heckman, N. A., Bryson, R. & Bryson, J. B. (1977). Problems of professional couples: A content analysis. *Journal of Marriage and the Family, 39,* 323–330.

Hill, R. (1965). Decision making and the family life cycle. In E. Shanas & G. Streib (Eds.), *Social structure and the family: Generational relations*. Englewood Cliffs, NJ: Prentice-Hall.

Hochschild, A. (1989), *The second shift*. New York: Avon.

Hof, L. & Miller, W. R. (1981). *Marriage enrichment: Philosophy, process, and program*. Bowie, MD: R. J. Brady.

Holland, J. L. (1985). *Making vocational choices* (2nd ed.). Englewood Cliffs, NJ: Prentice-Hall.

Hopper, K. (1990), Public shelter as "a hybrid institution": Homeless men in historical perspective. *Journal of Social Issues, 46*, 13–29.

Houseknecht, S. K. & Macke, A. S. (1981). Combining marriage and career: The marital adjustment of professional women. *Journal of Marriage and the Family, 43*, 651–661.

Jayakody, R., Chatters, L. M. & Taylor, R. J. (1993). Family support to single and married African American mothers: The provision of financial, emotional, and child care assistance. *Journal of Marriage and the Family, 55*, 261–267.

Jenkins, L. E. (1989). The black family and academic achievement. In G. L. Berry & J. K. Asamen (Eds.), *Black students* (pp. 138–152). Newbury Park, CA: Sage.

Jones, J. M. (1988). Racism in black and white: A bicultural model of reaction and evolution. In P. A. Katz & D. A. Taylor (Eds.), *Eliminating racism* (pp. 117–136). New York: Plenum.

Kalleberg, A. L. & Rosenfeld, R. A. (1990). Work in the family and in the labor market. *Journal of Marriage and the Family, 52*, 331–346.

Kanter, R. M. (1989). The new managerial work. *Harvard Business Review, 67*, 85–92.

Katz, D. & Kahn, R. L. (1978). *The social psychology of organizations* (2nd ed.). New York: Wiley.

Kipnis, D., Schmidt, S. M. & Wilkinson, I. (1980). Intraorganizational influence tactics: Explorations in getting one's way. *Journal of Applied Psychology, 65*, 440–452.

Koblinsky, S. A. & Anderson, E. A. (1993, Spring–Summer). Studying homeless children and their families: Issues and challenges. *Division 7 Newsletter*, pp. 1–3.

Kohn, M. L. (1980). Job complexity and adult personality. In N. J. Smelser & E. H. Erikson (Eds.), *Themes of work and love in adulthood* (pp. 193–210). Cambridge: Harvard University Press.

Konrad, P. (1990, August 6). Welcome to the woman-friendly company. *Business Week*, pp. 48–55.

Landers, S. (1989a, December). Homeless children lose childhood. *American Psychological Association Monitor, 20*, 1.

Landers, S. (1989b, April). Homeless mentally ill gain research push. *American Psychological Association Monitor, 20*, 33.

Leigh, G. K. (1982). Kinship interaction over the family life span. *Journal of Marriage and the Family, 44*, 197–208.

Levinger, G. (1983). Development and change. In H. H. Kelley et al. (Eds.), *Close relationships* (pp. 315–359). New York: W. H. Freeman.

Lopata, H. Z. (1979). *Women as widows: Support systems*. New York: Elsevier.

Mace, D. R. (1982). *Close companions*. New York: Continuum.

Marks, S. R. (1989). Toward a systems theory of marital quality. *Journal of Marriage and the Family, 51*, 15–26.

Mattessich, P. & Hill, R. (1987). Life cycle and family development. In M. B. Sussman & S. K. Steinmetz (Eds.), *Handbook of marriage and the family* (pp. 437–469). New York: Plenum.

McAdams, D. P., St. Aubin, E. & Logan, R. L. (1993). Generativity among young, midlife, and older adults. *Psychology and Aging, 8*, 221–230.

McAdoo, H. P. (1980). Black mothers and the extended family support network. In L. F. Rodgers-Rose (Ed.), *The black woman*. Beverly Hills, CA: Sage.

McGonagle, K. A., Kessler, R. C. & Gotlib, I. H. (1993). The effects of marital disagreement style, frequency, and outcome on marital disruption. *Journal of Social and Personal Relationships, 10*, 385–404.

McKinlay, J. B., McKinlay, S. M. & Brambilla, D. J. (1987). Health status and utilization behavior associated with menopause. *American Journal of Epidemiology, 125*, 110–121.

McLanahan, S. & Adams, J. (1987). Parenthood and psychological well-being. In R. Turner & J. Short (Eds.), *Annual review of sociology* (Vol. 13). Palo Alto, CA: Annual Reviews.

Miller, J., Schooler, C., Kohn, M. L. & Miller, K. A. (1979). Women and work: The psychological effects of occupational conditions. *American Journal of Sociology, 85*, 66–94.

Morokoff, P. J. (1988). Sexuality in perimenopausal and postmenopausal women. *Psychology of Women Quarterly, 12*, 489–511.

Mullan, J. (1981). Parental distress and marital happiness: The transition to the empty nest. Ph.D. dissertation, University of Chicago.

Neugarten, B. L., Wood, V., Kraines, R. J. & Loomis, B. (1963). Women's attitudes toward the menopause. *Vita Humana, 6*, 140–151.

Newman, B. M. (1989). The changing nature of the parent-adolescent relationship from early to late adolescence. *Adolescence, 24*, 916–924.

Newman, B. M. & Coady, S. S. (1982). Perceptions of the mother role among first-time mothers of different ages. Paper presented at the annual Michigan Women's Studies Conference, Ann Arbor.

Newman, P. R. & Newman, B. M. (1988). Parenthood and adult development. In R. Palkovitz & M. B. Sussman (Eds.), *Transitions to Parenthood, Marriage and Family Review, 12*, 313–337.

Nock, S. L. (1979). The family life cycle: Empirical or conceptual tool? *Journal of Marriage and the Family, 41*, 15–26.

Nye, I. (1976). *Role structure and analysis of the family*. Newbury Park, CA: Sage.

O'Bryant, S. L. (1987). Attachment to home and support systems of older widows in Columbus, Ohio. In H. Z. Lopata (Ed.), *Widows* (Vol. 2). Durham, NC: Duke University Press.

Patterson, G. R. (1992). Developmental changes in anti-social behavior. In R. D. Peters, R. J. McMahon & V. L. Quignsey (Eds.), *Aggression and violence throughout the lifespan.* Newbury Park, CA: Sage.

Peterson, B. E. & Stewart, A. J. (1993). Generativity and social motives in young adults. *Journal of Personality and Social Psychology, 65,* 186–198.

Pina, D. L. & Bengtson, V. L. (1993). The division of household labor and wives' happiness: Ideology, employment, and perceptions of support. *Journal of Marriage and the Family, 55,* 901–912.

Pinkney, A. (1993), *Black Americans* (4th ed.). Englewood Cliffs, NJ: Prentice-Hall.

Piotrkowski, C. S., Rapoport, R. N. & Rapoport, R. (1987). Families and work. In M. B. Sussman & S. K. Steinmetz (Eds.), *Handbook of marriage and the family* (pp. 251–283). New York: Plenum.

Pleck, J. H. (1985). *Working wives, working husbands.* New York: Sage.

Pratt, M. W., Kerig, P., Cowan, P. A. & Cowan, C. P. (1988). Mothers and fathers teaching 3-year-olds: Authoritative parenting and adult scaffolding of young children's learning. *Developmental Psychology, 24,* 832–838.

Renshaw, J. R. (1976, March). An exploration of the dynamics of the overlapping worlds of work and family. *Family Process, 15,* 143–165

Roberts, L. J. & Krokoff, L. J. (1990). Withdrawal, hostility, and displeasure in marriage. *Journal of Marriage and the Family, 52,* 95–105.

Rodgers, F. A. & Rodgers, C. (1989). Business and the facts of family life. *Harvard Business Review, 67,* 121–129.

Roff, L. L. & Klemmack, D. L. (1986). Norms for employed daughters' and sons' behavior toward frail older parents. *Sex Roles, 14,* 363–368.

Rogler, L. H. & Procidano, M. E. (1989). Heterogamy and marital quality in Puerto Rican families. *Journal of Marriage and the Family, 51,* 363–372.

Rubin, L. B. (1976). *Worlds of pain: Life in the working-class family.* New York: Basic Books.

Rubin, L. B. (1980). The empty nest: Beginning or ending? In L. A. Bond & J. C. Rosen (Eds.), *Competence and coping during adulthood* (pp. 309–331). Hanover, NH: University Press of New England.

Ryan, R. M. & Lynch, J. H. (1989). Emotional autonomy versus detachment: Revisiting the vicissitudes of adolescence and young adulthood. *Child Development, 60,* 340–356.

Sarason, S. B. (1980). Individual psychology: An obstacle to comprehending adulthood. In L. A. Bond & J. C. Rosen (Eds.), *Competence and coping during adulthood* (pp. 6–27). Hanover, NH: University Press of New England.

Sexton, C. S. & Perlman, D. S. (1989). Careers, gender roles, and perceived equity as factors in marital power. *Journal of Marriage and the Family, 51,* 933–941.

Simons, R. L., Beaman, J., Conger, R. D. & Chao, W. (1993). Stress, support and antisocial behavior trait as determinants of emotional well-being and parenting practices among singe mothers. *Journal of Marriage and the Family, 55,* 385–398.

Spanier, G. B., Sauer, W. & Larzelere, R. (1979). An empirical evaluation of the family life cycle. *Journal of Marriage and the Family, 41,* 27–38.

Spitze, G. & Logan, J. (1990). Sons, daughters, and intergenerational social support. *Journal of Marriage and the Family, 52,* 420–430.

Taylor, I. A. (1975). An emerging view of creative actions. In I. A. Taylor & J. W. Getzels (Eds.), *Perspectives in creativity.* Chicago: Aldine-Atherton.

Thornton, A., Young-DeMarco, L. & Goldscheider, F. (1993). Leaving the parental nest: The experience of a young white cohort in the 1980's. *Journal of Marriage and the Family, 55,* 216–229.

Tiedje, L. B., Wortman, C. B., Downey, G., Emmons, C., Biernat, M. & Lang, E. (1990). Role compatibility in women with multiple roles. *Journal of Marriage and the Family, 52,* 63–72.

U.S. Bureau of the Census. (1992). *Statistical abstract of the United States, 1992.* Washington, DC: U.S. Government Printing Office.

U.S. Department of Labor, Employment & Training Administration. (1993). *Selected characteristics of occupations defined in the revised dictionary of occupational titles.* Washington, DC: U.S. Government Printing Office.

Vinokur, A., Caplan, R. D. & Williams, C. C. (1987). Effects of recent and past stress on mental health: Coping with unemployment among Vietnam veterans and non-veterans. *Journal of Applied Social Psychology, 17,* 708–728.

Voydanoff, P. (1988). Work roles, family structure, and work/family conflict. *Journal of Marriage and the Family, 50,* 749–761.

Vuchinich, S. (1987). Starting and stopping spontaneous family conflicts. *Journal of Marriage and the Family, 49,* 591–601.

Weinreb, L. & Buckner, J. C. (1993), Homeless families: Program responses and public policies. *American Journal of Orthopsychiatry, 63,* 400–409.

Whitaker, M. (1993). White and black lies. *Newsweek, 122,* 52–54.

Whitbeck, L., Hoyt, D. R. & Huck, S. M. (1994). Early family relationships, intergenerational solidarity, and support provided to parents by their adult children. *Journal of Gerontology, 49,* S85–S94.

Wood, V. & Robertson, J. F. (1978). Friendship and kinship interaction: Differential effect on the morale of the elderly. *Journal of Marriage and the Family, 40,* 367–375.

Wright, J. D. & Devine, J. A. (1993). Family backgrounds and the substance-abusive homeless: The New Orleans experience. *The Community Psychologist, 26,* 35–37.

Zuo, J. (1992). The reciprocal relationship between marital interaction and marital happiness: A three-wave study. *Journal of Marriage and the Family, 54,* 870–878.

CHAPTER 13

The integrating theme of later adulthood is a search for
personal meaning. The love of peace became an urgent
force in Picasso's personal philosophy during the 1940s.

Later Adulthood (60–75 Years)

For people born in 1990 in the United States, the life expectancy was 72 years for males and 78.8 for females (U.S. Bureau of the Census, 1992). The life expectancy of people born in 1920 was about 54 years. Major improvements in hygiene, nutrition, and medical technology have allowed more people to survive infancy and more to survive the period from 40 to 60. Many more people experience a vigorous later adulthood today than was true 70 years ago.

A discussion of aging in America must acknowledge the changing sex composition of the population at older ages. In 1991, 55% of those 65–69 years old were women; 57% of those 70–75 years old were women; and 72% of those 85 years old and over were women. This gender difference in longevity is observed in virtually all countries of the world, but the differences are accentuated in the developed countries (U.S. Bureau of the Census, 1992). The imbalance in the sex composition is much more noticeable today than it was 50 years ago, when there were just about as many men as women in the over-65 category (U.S. Bureau of the Census, 1983).

The curves in Figure 13.1 show the survival pattern for women born in 1900, 1960, and 1980. You can see that major gains in survival all across the life span were made from 1900 to 1960. As a result, the age to which 50% of females survived (M_{50}) increased from about 57 in the 1900 cohort to an estimated 76 in the 1960 cohort. However, the gains from 1960 to 1980 were primarily in the years after age 60, and the resulting increase for M_{50} was about five years (from about 76 to 81). The three curves also include a life endurance estimate (Ω). This is the age to which one person in 100,000 is expected to survive. Life endurance estimates for women increased from 105 for the cohort born in 1900 to 114 for the cohort born in 1980 (Meyers & Manton, 1984).

As the period of later adulthood becomes increasingly long and healthy, opportunities emerge to experience new relationships, develop new skills, and discover personal potential. We see the years from 60 to 75 as a period of continued

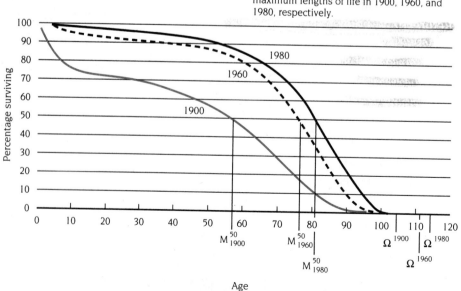

M_{50}^{1900} M_{50}^{1960} and M_{50}^{1980} are the ages to which 50% of females survive, subject to the mortality risks of 1900, 1960, and 1980, respectively.

Ω^{1900}, Ω^{1960}, and Ω^{1980} are estimated maximum lengths of life in 1900, 1960, and 1980, respectively.

FIGURE 13.1

Mortality survival curves for U.S. females in 1900, 1960, and 1980
Source: Myers & Manton, 1984.

psychological growth during which people must adapt to new roles and discover creative outlets for their leisure time as well as prepare themselves for the end of life. We also encounter increasing worries about the costs of longevity. Health costs increase, but in addition to these, one must think about sustaining the quality of daily life for an unknown number of years after retirement.

The integrating theme of this life stage is a search for personal meaning. On entering this stage, adults begin to assert the competence and creativity attained during middle adulthood. As life progresses, motivation for achievement and power may give way to a desire for understanding—reminiscent of the toddler's need to know "why" and the later adolescent's need to challenge and experiment with life roles. The individual is still confronted with essential problems of definition and explanation during later adulthood. At this stage, adults may begin to apply the wealth of their life course experiences, their perspective on time, and their adaptation to life crises to a personally satisfying answer to the question of life's meaning.

For some, the period of later adulthood brings a state of physical or mental deterioration, or both, that impedes further psychological growth. The physical and psychological blows of poverty and hardship may be most damaging. The onset of senescence may result in a dramatic loss of memory, reasoning capacities, and problem-solving abilities, as well as an increase in fantasy activity, physical deterioration, and helplessness. For some, the chronic problems of aging cast a shadow of depression and hopelessness on the years of later adulthood. The chronic problems of aging may cause serious psychological and financial problems for children as they observe their parents' progressive decline. As a result of these changes, older adults may begin to feel alienated from their environment and discouraged about their severe loss of capacities. Because of the extremes in intellectual competence, social involvement, and independence that differentiate the healthy older person from the seriously ill one, it is essential to keep individual differences in physical and mental health in mind in thinking about the pattern of growth in later adulthood.

The life histories of older adults are enormously varied. Depending on life experiences, health, resources, education, family support, and cultural and religious orientation, later adulthood is perceived and enacted differently by each person. The idea of developmental tasks that reflect similar themes for all older adults is bound to miss the vivid and complex reality of each person's experiences. Nevertheless, the tasks discussed here do reflect major themes that are likely to be confronted in the later years. These themes suggest new barriers to adaptation as well as new opportunities. Changes in memory and problem-solving skills may make the accomplishment of daily tasks a greater challenge. Role loss and the death of loved ones introduce needs for new kinds of support and changes in daily lifestyle. Most certainly, they convey a very concrete message that a transition to a new period of the life span is under way.

Developmental Tasks

Promoting Intellectual Vigor

Memory, reasoning, information, problem-solving abilities, and mental rigidity or fluidity all influence the adult's capacity to introspect, to assess his or her personal past history, and to plan for the future. How can we understand cognitive functioning and cognitive change in later life? We need to appreciate several problems in the study of this area in order to interpret the ongoing research.

BOX 13.1

The Introspections of Chester M. Pierce, M.D.

The themes that dominate the life stage of later adulthood—integrity, despair, and introspection—are very abstract. Students may have special difficulty understanding and empathizing with the intense and personally absorbing challenges that face adults during this time of life. In a gesture of generativity, Dr. Chester M. Pierce shared his introspections with us. Dr. Pierce is professor of education and psychiatry at Harvard University. He was founding chairman of Black Psychiatrists of America, and among his many outstanding accomplishments is membership in the National Academy of Sciences. Inspired by an invitation to lecture in honor of Dr. Solomon Carter Fuller, the first African-American psychiatrist in the United States, Dr. Pierce used the occasion to reflect on his own efforts to find meaning and a sense of unity in his life. He set the stage by describing the challenges that faced Dr. Fuller and how the legacy of Dr. Fuller's career helped him to cope with the realities of his own professional development as a psychiatrist:

> No thinking Black person can gaze at the celebrated photo of Freud in his first visit to America, taken at Clark University in Worcester, Massachusetts, without knowing that Solomon Carter Fuller had overcome obstacles and resentments that did not affect the others in the photograph. In addition, one could be certain that unlike the others in the picture, Dr. Fuller, in spite of any achievement, would never be free to pursue his career without the burden of being suspect in the eyes of his peers in terms of ability, effectiveness, or efficiency. Finally, the Black viewer of the picture would know intuitively that throughout his career Dr. Fuller would have had to do more work for less reward and that at each instance of advancement he would have had to demonstrate superior qualifications and credentials than a White colleague aspiring for the same advancement.
>
> In short, the unity that Dr. Fuller sought to bring to American psychiatry was accomplished under inestimable stress and duress. To this day all colored minority psychiatrists are beneficiaries of this legacy. Regrettably, to this day, all colored minority psychiatrists must continue to adapt to the same burdens that afflicted Solomon Carter Fuller.
>
> What will be submitted by this lecture is that being Black in America

(continued)

One problem is the distinction between age differences and age changes (Denney, 1982; Schaie, 1973). Let us say that, in a cross-sectional study conducted in 1985, 70-year-olds performed less well than 40-year-olds. The difference may be clear, but it may not be a result of age alone. The 70-year-olds would have been born in the 1910s and the 40-year-olds in the 1940s. Differences in performance may well be a product of different educational opportunities, varying experiences with standardized tests, or other *cohort* factors rather than of age alone. For example, only 13% of men and 8% of women who were 65 years old or older in 1988 were college graduates. Educational attainment has changed over this century

means being stressed more because you are Black. Being a Black psychiatrist means you are stressed more because you are a Black psychiatrist. In the resolution of the psychological conflicts, all Blacks have a requirement to consolidate, integrate, and make sense of the diversity that being Black, and thereby marginal, brings with it in all interactions with the general society. Therefore there is a need to unify the diversity even as one struggles with the issue of when and how to unite.

Like Solomon Carter Fuller, Black psychiatrists today in their personal and professional lives operate in many circumstances of marginality and fractionation. Coordinating and controlling these operations, all of which are under the aegis of extra stress, may constitute the largest and most difficult developmental task for any Black citizen. Each citizen must order these operations according to his or her own perception of truth. (Pierce, 1989, pp. 297–298)

Later in this chapter, we will return to Dr. Pierce's reflections as a way of clarifying how a person makes sense of a life of stresses, challenges, and achievements to arrive at a point of personal integrity.

so that the younger cohorts are much more likely to have benefited from formal schooling at both the high school and the college levels (U.S. Bureau of the Census, 1989). In any cross-sectional study of cognitive functioning, it is important to recognize the contribution of historical factors as well as possible developmental or aging factors that may contribute to observed differences in performance. Even in longitudinal studies that follow change across time, if only one cohort is sampled, it is impossible to tell whether changes from one period to the next are products of age and development or of particular resources and deficits characterizing that particular generation of subjects.

A second problem is the definition of abilities. *Cognitive functioning* is a very broad term that encompasses such varied abilities as vocabulary, problem solving, and short-term memory. It is very possible that the pattern of change in abilities with age depends on the abilities being tested. Some abilities are frequently used and have been developed to a high level of efficiency. For example, an architect is much more likely to retain abilities in the area of spatial relations and spatial reasoning than is someone whose lifework is not intimately connected with the construction and organization of spatial dimensions.

A third, and related, problem is the level of abstraction and the relevance of the tasks used to measure adult cognitive functioning. The definition of intelligence that is used in the design and application of most intelligence tests refers to capacities that are predictive of school-related success. The criteria for assessing adult intelligence are necessarily more heterogeneous than the ability to succeed in the school curriculum. There are reasons to believe that, as people move through adulthood, their approach to the use of information and problem solving becomes modified by the contexts in which the individuals are most often involved (Labouvie-Vief & Schell, 1982).

Finally, factors associated with health are always intertwined with the functioning of older adults, although these factors are often not directly measured. In a longitudinal study of intelligence, Riegel and Riegel (1972) found that there were clear declines in performance among subjects who were to die before the next testing period. Vocabulary skills, which normally remain high or continue to show increases with age, are especially likely to decline in older subjects who will die within the coming few years (White & Cunningham, 1988). Thus, at each older age, the inclusion of subjects who are approaching death lowers the average performance of the group as a whole.

Productivity in the Work Setting

In attempting to define intelligence in adulthood, several researchers have looked at the pattern of productivity in the work setting (Dennis, 1966; Lehman, 1953; Simonton, 1977). Special attention has been given to the relationship between creative achievement and age. The pattern that has been described is one of a fairly rapid rise to a peak in mid-career, followed by a gradual decline (Simonton, 1988). However, it is clear that opportunities for creative contribution persist throughout the career. What is more, as adults perceive that they may be approaching the end of their career, they may be especially inspired to make a distinctive statement. Thus, last works or career "swan songs" are often marked by a profound simplicity and originality that set them apart from earlier work and illustrate a special facet of the person's creative potential (Simonton, 1989). Lehman reported that productivity of very high quality peaks when people are in their 30s. Work that is rated as "worthy" was observed to peak somewhat later and to decline gradually. In considering total work productivity, Dennis identified the decade of the 40s as the most productive period. He differentiated patterns of productivity among a variety of professions. Among those he studied, the productivity of scholars in the humanities continued at a high level until the 70s, whereas the decline after age 40 was comparatively rapid for persons in the creative arts.

The role of older scholars and scientists is influenced by cultural values. For example, China has a shortage of scientists. Although the retirement age in China is 60, scientists who hold the title of professor can work in their laboratories until age 70. Those who have made unusual contributions may work after age 70,

Albert Einstein lived to be 76 years old. Having revolutionized physics with his special theory of relativity, he was regarded as having one of the greatest human intellects of all time. Throughout his adult life, he worked on a general theory of relativity that he hoped would unite the various laws of physics. He was never satisfied that he could provide the level of mathematical proof needed to support his general theory, but today scientists find substantial merit in his later work.

depending on their health. At the same time, there is an active attempt to advance the 45- to 55-year-old scientists by promoting them to leadership (Guangzhao, 1985). This climate encourages productivity throughout later adulthood.

Memory

Declining competence with age has been identified in a number of areas, including reaction time, visual-motor flexibility (the translation of visual information into new motor responses), and memory. With regard to memory, Botwinick (1984) described a gradual increase in the number of people whose memories decline at each age level. Short-term memory is more seriously affected by aging than long-term memory. Older subjects may find it more difficult than younger subjects to store newly acquired information and then to retrieve it (Fozard & Poon, 1976; Reese, 1976). In studies of long-term memory, older subjects seemed to lose information in the short period right after learning but then to retain a high level of recall for the remaining material for up to 130 weeks (Fozard & Poon, 1976).

Memory functions are especially likely to be disrupted under conditions in which information is presented rapidly and contextual cues are absent. In a memory task involving the recall of five- and eight-word strings, older subjects (65–73) retained fewer words than younger subjects (18–22) when the word strings were presented at high speed and when they were not arranged in a meaningful sentence. Speed of presentation did not significantly reduce recall when the words were arranged in a normal semantic order (Wingfield et al., 1985).

Recent research has focused on individual differences in performance on memory tasks, especially individual differences in intelligence as well as contextual factors. These studies find that age alone continues to be an important predictor of performance on many memory tasks (West, Crook & Barron, 1992). In addition, contemporary intelligence, and especially verbal intelligence, is an equally strong predictor of performance on many tasks. However, several contextual factors, especially satisfaction with social support, education, the personality characteristic of introversion, illness, and intellectual activity, are important predictors of contemporary intelligence (Arbuckle et al., 1992). Normative patterns showing declines in memory do not tell the whole story. The actual pattern of change with age varies, depending on significant contemporary circumstances.

In addition to actual declines in some kinds of memory performance, about 50% of older adults complain of memory problems. It is interesting that, even after participating in programs designed to improve memory performance, these complaints persist (Scogin, Storandt & Lott, 1985). Anxiety and frustration over memory loss nag many older adults, even those whose memory performance has not dramatically declined.

Piagetian Tasks

Some research has focused on the ability of older adults to perform various Piagetian tasks, such as classification, conservation, and formal operational problem solving. In many areas, older adults perform less well than middle or young adults. Older subjects have been described as performing classification and problem-solving tasks in a more egocentric, idiosyncratic way than younger adults (Denney, 1982). They have a particular point of view that may not make sense to others but which they insist in applying since it has worked for them in the past. In the area of conservation, however, the evidence is mixed. Some studies have found that older adults do not handle the conservation-of-volume task as well as younger subjects but do perform other conservation tasks quite well. Other studies report no differences in conservation between younger and older subjects (Selzer & Denney, 1980). In one comparison, academic background rather than age was related to the performance of formal operational problem solving. College-age men and women and college-educated men and women in the age range of 63–75 did equally well on tests of formal thought. However, those who had majored in the natural or physical sciences while in college did better than those with social science and humanities backgrounds (Blackburn, 1984).

Research based on the standard Piagetian tasks has been criticized for its lack of relevance and familiarity to older subjects. In an attempt to control for the relevance of the task, Poon and Fozard (1978) studied the effect of the familiarity and datedness of objects on the time it took to name them. Some objects were clearly dated from the early 1900s. Others were contemporary items used in the 1960s and 1970s. The subjects in the age range of 60–70 named the dated objects faster than did the younger subjects. The younger subjects in the age range of 18–20 named the contemporary objects faster than did the older subjects. The implication of this research is that the performance of older subjects may be partly a product of their familiarity with the materials provided.

Practical Problem Solving

In another approach to problem solving, ten older adults participated in constructing a set of practical problem-solving questions in order to help ensure their relevance to older adults (Denney & Pearce, 1989). One problem they posed was "An elderly woman can drive her car to run errands except in the winter when the weather is bad. What should she do about getting groceries and other necessities

when the weather is bad?" Answers to this and other questions were rated on a scale of 1 to 4, depending on the number of safe and effective solutions offered. Those subjects in their 40s performed best. Subjects in their 50s, 60s, and 70s scored about the same, but slightly less well than those in their 30s and 40s, and about as well as those in their 20s. One could not conclude that problem-solving abilities showed a pattern of deterioration since this was not a longitudinal study. One might conclude that, even when the problems are authentic, older adults are not as likely to try to generate multiple solutions as they are to identify one or two solutions that have a good chance of succeeding.

Patterns of Change in Different Mental Abilities

John Horn (1979) proposed that the course of mental abilities across the life span is not uniform. Some areas are strengthened, and others decline. He made an especially strong case for differentiating *crystallized intelligence* (Gc) and *fluid intelligence* (Gf). Gc is the ability to bring knowledge accumulated through past learning into play in appropriate situations. Gf is the ability to impose organization on information and to generate new hypotheses. Both kinds of intelligence are required for optimal human functioning.

Gc and Gf can be identified as integrated structures in both young and later adulthood (Hayslip & Brookshire, 1985). However, Horn argued that the two kinds of thinking draw on somewhat different neurological and experiential sources. Gc reflects the consequences of life experiences within a society. Socialization in the family, exposure to the media, and participation in school, work, and community settings all emphasize the use and improvement of Gc. Gc increases with age, experience, and physical maturation. It remains at a high level of functioning throughout adulthood. Gf seems to be more characteristic of what we mean when we say that someone has a "good head on his or her shoulders." Finding

Many of the world's political leaders are in the life stage of later adulthood. Their accumulated experience, their knowledge, and their recollection of historical changes give them a rich perspective from which to lead. This photo of Margaret Thatcher, prime minister of Great Britain from 1979 to 1990, was taken when she was 63.

a general relationship and applying it without having been schooled in that problem-solving area is an example of Gf, as is being able to approach new problems logically and systematically. Older adults do not spontaneously impose organization on new information. They are less likely than younger persons to attend to the incidental information or process-level learning that contributes to Gf. Horn also hypothesized that Gf depends more on the specific number of neurons available for its functioning than does Gc. Thus, neurological loss would be more damaging to Gf than to Gc.

Schaie and Hertzog (1983; Hertzog & Schaie, 1988) reported on the results of a 14-year longitudinal and cross-sectional study of adult intellectual development. Five mental abilities were measured: verbal meaning, spatial reasoning, inductive reasoning, number skills, and word fluency. The youngest subjects were in the age range of 25–39; the oldest were 67–81. In general, the longitudinal data showed less decrement with age than the cross-sectional data. The rate of decline in performance was most notable in all five areas after age 60. Decline in some areas, especially spatial and inductive reasoning, was notable during the 50s. The variation among all three groups in the sample remained quite stable. In other words, even though measured intelligence changes over time, the position of one person in relation to another remains about the same. Cohort differences favored the more recently born in the areas of spatial reasoning, inductive reasoning, and verbal meaning.

The Effect of the Environment on Mental Functioning

The quality of thought that is characteristic of older adults may also be a product of their environment. B. F. Skinner (1983) described some possible environmental qualities that fail to reinforce systematic thinking or new ideas in aging people. Many people who live alone, for example, lack the diversity of social interaction that produces cognitive discrepancy and new concepts. Older people may be reinforced for talking about the past. Their recollections of early memories are interesting to students and younger colleagues. However, preoccupation with these reminiscences does not encourage thinking in new directions. Skinner claimed that one is more likely to repeat oneself as one gets older. He suggested that it may be important for older adults to move into new areas of work in order to prevent repetition of old ideas. He believed that it is possible to analyze how the quality of one's thinking is being influenced by the circumstances of aging and also to identify interventions that will prevent the deterioration of cognitive abilities. For Skinner, these interventions included attempts to be sensitive to the signs of fatigue, planning for regular opportunities for stimulating verbal interactions with others, making careful outlines of written work to avoid distraction, and acting on ideas as they come to one's mind rather than counting on remembering them later.

From the variety of evidence, we conclude that the pattern of cognitive functioning in later adulthood is neither unidimensional nor stable. There are wide interindividual differences as well as considerable intraindividual differences, depending on the cognitive domain being evaluated (Hoyer & Rybash, 1994). Thinking back to the model of the developing mind presented in Chapter 8, we recognize that adults experience tremendous growth in domain-specific areas of knowledge. Within these domains, many complex networks of information, strategies, and frameworks of meaning are elaborated that result in high-level, flexible functioning. The overall level of functioning is subject to environmental influences that promote particular specialization and cognitive organization based on the demands of the situation, the stresses and challenges of daily life, and the opportunities for mastery in particular areas of competence. At the same time, certain aspects of the processing base that are dependent on neural functioning may decline with age. The deterioration is not always of a very great magnitude. In some areas, such as information and verbal skills, functioning remains at a high level. It does appear that cognitive functioning in later life is likely to become rather patterned, an outcome that may be accelerated by the predictability and routineness of a low level of daily stimulation.

Factors That Help One to Retain High Levels of Cognitive Functioning

On the basis of extensive longitudinal research, K. Warner Schaie (1989) identified six factors that are associated with retaining a high level of cognitive functioning in later adulthood:

- Absence of cardiovascular and other chronic diseases
- Favorable environment linked to high socioeconomic status
- Involvement in a complex and intellectually stimulating environment
- Flexible personality style at midlife
- High cognitive functioning of spouse
- Maintenance of level of perceptual processing speed

In this list we see evidence of the interplay of the biological and the social systems as they contribute to ego functioning in the later years.

Redirecting Energy to New Roles and Activities

Role transition and role loss are present in every period of the life span. In later adulthood, however, a convergence of role transitions is likely to lead to a revision of major life functions. Roles are lost through widowhood, retirement, and the death of friends. At the same time, new roles—grandparent, senior adviser, community leader, retiree—require the formation of new patterns of behavior and new relationships.

Grandparenthood

Within the course of family development, the role of grandparent may require a renewal of skills that have been stored in the attic along with the bottle sterilizer and the potty chair. Grandparents begin to renew their acquaintance with the delights of childhood, including diapering the baby, telling fairy tales, taking trips to the zoo, and having the pleasure of small helping hands with baking, gardening, or carpentry. A person's skills, patience, and knowledge may be even more in demand in the grandparent role than they were in the parent role (Robertson, 1977).

People differ in the meaning they place on the grandparent role and in the way they enact it. In one of the first empirical studies of grandparenthood, Neugarten and Weinstein (1964) interviewed the grandmother and grandfather in 70 middle-class families. Five grandparenting styles were identified, each expressing a rather distinct interpretation of the grandparent role:

1. *Formal.* These grandparents were interested in their grandchildren but careful not to become involved in parenting them other than by occasional babysitting.
2. *Funseeker.* These grandparents had informal, playful interactions with their grandchildren. They enjoyed mutually self-indulgent fun with them.
3. *Surrogate parent.* This style was especially likely for grandmothers who assumed major child-care responsibilities when the mother worked outside the home.

4. *Reservoir of family wisdom*. This was an authoritarian relationship in which a grandparent, usually the grandfather, dispensed skills and resources. Parents as well as grandchildren were subordinate to this older authority figure.

5. *Distant figure*. This was a grandparent who appeared on birthdays and holidays but generally had little contact with the grandchildren.

It is clear from this list of grandparenting styles that the role prescriptions for the grandparent are ambiguous enough to permit wide differences in their enactment.

In a more recent analysis of grandparent styles, Cherlin and Furstenberg (1986/1992) conducted telephone interviews with a national sample of 510 grandparents. They classified their sample into three groups: remote, companionate, and involved. The *remote grandparents* (29% of the sample) had seen their grandchildren less than once every two or three months in the past year. Most of these grandparents lived far away from their grandchildren, but in some cases, the lack of contact was a result of emotional rather than physical distance.

The *companionate grandparents* (55% of the sample) had seen their grandchildren at least once every two or three months in the past year, but there were low levels of exchange of services or resources with the child's family and very little "parent-like" behavior toward the child. These grandparents were likely to characterize their relationship as one in which they could have fun with their grandchildren and then send them home. They observed a "norm of noninterference" when it came to the conflicts a child was having with his or her parents or any concerns about the child's behavior or the parents' child-rearing strategies.

The *involved grandparents* (16% of the sample) saw their grandchildren at least once every two to three months and showed both high levels of exchanges in services and resources and high levels of "parentlike" behaviors. In fact, most of these involved grandparents had very frequent interactions with their grandchildren, especially while the grandchildren were young. Almost all grandparents noted that they had had less time together with their grandchildren during the teen years because the children had become involved in so many more activities on their own. But the involved grandparents were more likely to take direct action by contacting their adolescent grandchildren and making plans to spend time together.

Most older adults take great satisfaction and pride in their grandchildren. Grandparenthood has a variety of personal meanings that contribute to the grandparent's overall sense of purpose and worth (Kivnick, 1983). Grandchildren symbolize an extension of personal influence that will most assuredly persist well beyond the grandparent's death. To this extent, grandchildren help older adults to feel more comfortable about their own death. Older adults see concrete evidence that some thread of their lives will persist into the future, giving a dimension of immortality to themselves and to the family ancestry that they represent (Mead, 1975).

In an analysis of the sources of vitality in later life, Erikson, Erikson, and Kivnick (1986) found that relationships with grandchildren played a critical role:

> The major involvement that uniformly makes life worth living is the thought of and participation in their relationships with children and grandchildren. Their pride in their own achievement in having brought up their young, through thick and thin, and their satisfaction in the way these young have developed gives them, for the most part, deep gratification. With the arrival of grandchildren, they may identify themselves as ancestors, graduated to venerability. Listen to their voices as they trace their own ancestry and that of their children's traits: "She has her mother's fire, that first girl of ours. She has more energy and more projects than anyone. Come to think of it, my mother had

Grandparents can play a critical role in passing on the skills and traditions of a family's culture to future generations.

that fire, too. And my wife's two grandmothers." "My son is a perfectionist, like me." "The kids are innately smart, like their father." (p. 326)

Grandchildren also stimulate older adults' thoughts about time, the changing of cultural norms across generations, and the patterning of history. In relating to grandchildren as they grow up, grandparents discover elements of the culture that remain stable. Certain stories and songs retain their appeal from generation to generation. Certain toys, games, and preoccupations of children of the current generation are remembered by grandparents from their own childhood. Grandparents may also become aware of changes in the culture that are reflected in new child-rearing practices; new equipment, toys, and games; and new expectations for children's behavior at each life stage. The communication that adults maintain with their grandchildren allows them to keep abreast of the continuities and changes in their culture as these are reflected in the experiences of childhood. Through their grandchildren, adults avoid a sense of alienation from the contemporary world (Kahana & Kahana, 1970). The more involved grandparents are in the daily care and routines of their grandchildren, the more central they become to a young child's sense of security and well-being. This kind of importance is a benefit not only to the child but to the older adult's assessment of his or her personal worth (Tomlin & Passman, 1989).

Some adults interpret the role of grandparent as an opportunity to pass on to grandchildren the wisdom and cultural heritage of their ancestry. In the process of fulfilling this role, older adults must attempt to find meaning in their experiences and to communicate that meaning to their grandchildren in ways that the latter can understand. Grandparents select many avenues to educate their grandchildren. Storytelling, special trips, long walks, attending religious services, and working on special projects are all activities that allow grandparents some moments of intimacy with their grandchildren. During these times, grandparents can influence their grandchildren's thoughts and fantasies. The process of educating one's grandchildren involves a deep sense of investment in those experiences and ideals that one believes to be central to a fruitful life.

The many ways in which grandchildren can contribute to an adult's feelings of well-being have been replicated in studies conducted in European countries (Smith, 1991). A German grandmother addressed the meaning that her grandson gave to her life:

> "Yes, he is the most important thing in my life, because I have nothing else at the moment. They all say I spoil him. I don't know. Mama is a little bit strict, and so I always am careful not to spoil him too much. And it is actually Carsten this and Carsten that; he means so much to me. Since I am a pensioner, I have time for him." (Sticker, 1991, p. 39)

Although the majority of middle-class grandparents claim that they assume a philosophy of noninterference, evidence suggests that grandparents can and do have an impact on their grandchildren's development. This influence may be direct or indirect. *Direct impact* occurs as a result of the quality of interactions. The more frequently grandparents interact with their grandchildren, the more these grandparents are perceived as significant members of the family, and the more the grandparents serve as a source of emotional reassurance and comfort to the grandchild, especially in times of stress (Cherlin & Furstenberg, 1986/1992; Tomlin & Passman, 1989).

The *indirect impact* occurs as grandparents provide emotional support, child-rearing advice, and various resources, including money and skills, to their own child, thereby fostering this adult child's ability to function as an effective parent (Tomlin & Passman, 1991).

Grandparents play an especially important role in supporting the development of their grandchildren during family stress (Werner, 1991). In contemporary American society, one can view grandparents as a potential resource that is called into active duty when certain difficulties arise for the parent generation. In cases of parental divorce, grandparents often assume a more central role in the lives of young children. Some custodial mothers move back home with their parents. Grandmothers often assume more child-care responsibilities during this time. Following divorce, the grandchild's relationships with his or her maternal grandparents are more likely to be enhanced, whereas the relationships with the paternal grandparents are likely to decline. Several studies have shown that having good, ongoing relationships with one's grandparents during the years following one's parents' divorce is associated with a child's ability to cope with school demands, to continue to have positive relationships with peers and teachers, and to have fewer behavior problems (Heatherington, Cox & Cox, 1985; Heatherington, Stanley-Hagan & Anderson, 1989).

Grandparents may also play a key role when their young, unmarried daughters become pregnant. The pattern of unmarried teen mothers living with their own parents is especially common in African-American families. Roughly 30% of African-American children live in an extended family (Tolson & Wilson, 1990). African-American grandmothers are likely to perceive themselves and to be perceived by their daughters as actively involved in child rearing (Werner, 1991). Of course, these grandmothers may be very young themselves, just entering middle adulthood, when they assume the grandparent role.

The presence of grandmothers appears to affect the family atmosphere as well as the child-rearing environment in African-American families. In one study of 64 African-American families, the presence of a grandmother was associated with a high level of moral-religious orientation in the family (Tolson & Wilson, 1990). Having a grandmother in the home allows the mother to be more flexible and to be able to manage daily demands without having to be strict in planning and arranging for daily tasks; thus, there is a reduction in much of the stress that is characteristic of single-parent families.

Maternal employment is a third condition in which grandparents are likely to give direct support. In a national sample of 796 mothers who had children under age 5 and who were employed, 24% said their mother, or the child's grandmother, was the principal child-care provider (Presser, 1989). These grandmothers provided an average of 27 hours per week of child care, and almost 40 hours per week if the mothers were employed full time. Clearly, these grandmothers were intimately involved in the lives of their grandchildren and were directing significant energy, talent, and time to this role.

Widowhood

The most difficult adaptation to a new role occurs when an adult loses a spouse. For many older people, this loss causes severe disruption as well as grief and depression. Although some adults remarry, many others remain unmarried and identify themselves as widows or widowers. Most older widowers remarry, whereas the vast majority of widows live alone (U.S. Bureau of the Census, 1992).

Widows must learn to function socially as well as in their own households without the presence of a marriage partner. Adaptation to this role requires resilience, creative problem solving, and a strong commitment to a belief in one's own personal worth. Since the average woman is widowed at 56 and has a life expectancy of 78, she will be living in a new role status for at least 20 years (Lopata, 1973; O'Leary, 1977).

A number of stressors, in addition to the bereavement itself, may challenge the coping resources of those who have been widowed. Widows are likely to experience a marked decrease in financial resources. Studies of economic changes among widows show that many continue to experience marked fluctuations in their financial resources for years following widowhood (Zick & Smith, 1991; Bound et al., 1991). Women who have never participated in the labor market during their married years may have no marketable skills and feel insecure about entering the labor force. They may be uninformed or uneasy about using social service agencies to meet their needs. For most women, the loss of the husband is most keenly felt as a loss of emotional support: "He is most apt to be mentioned as the person the widow most enjoyed being with, who made her feel important and secure" (Lopata, 1978, p. 221). The transition to widowhood may be especially difficult for those who have been caring for an ill partner, emotionally hoping for recovery yet observing constant decline (Bass & Bowman, 1990).

Despite the extreme pain and prolonged grief that accompany widowhood, most people cope with it successfully. In a study of recent widows between the ages of 60 and 98, a picture emerged of a high degree of self-sufficiency (O'Bryant & Morgan, 1990). The majority of respondents said they performed a variety of daily tasks, including transportation, housekeeping, shopping, preparing meals, personal care and hygiene, financial and other decisions, and providing financial support, without help from others. A large percentage (over 30%) said they managed their own home repairs, yard work, and legal questions without help. Thus, from this study, we see a picture of older, widowed women functioning at a high level of independence and autonomy with assistance from others, especially their children, in specific domains, depending on where help is needed.

Widows are likely to find support from their children and friends. Over time, a widow's siblings, especially her sisters, may become a key source of emotional support as well as direct, instrumental assistance such as home repairs and shopping (O'Bryant, 1988). In an exploratory analysis of the responses of widows in a support group discussion, comments about the positive and negative contributions of their social support network were analyzed (Morgan, 1989). The widows described their nonfamily, reciprocal friendship relationships as somewhat more positive than their family relationships. In many cases, widows found that, as a result of their own sense of family obligation, they were pulled into negative events occurring in their families, especially divorce, illness, and the death of other family members. These negative events added to their distress and prevented them from receiving the support they felt they needed at the time of their own loss. The most positive form of immediate support from family, especially children, was a willingness to accept the widow's feelings of grief and to talk openly about their father. Social support from friends included a similar willingness to allow the widow to take her time in finding a new identity. These women did not want to be forced to "get over it" too quickly or to be told how "strong" they were and how well they were handling their grief: " 'The fact that you're using the strength that you have, just to cope, and to stay alive (another voice: 'to survive') is a big job and they don't recognize that, you know it makes you angry' " (Morgan, 1989, p. 105). They wanted to have their anger, their grief, and the extent to which their lives had been disrupted acknowledged and accepted by their friends. In this way, they felt they could begin to come to terms with their new reality.

If widows do enter the labor force, they may discover a new domain of competence. Widows are likely to become more sensitive to their own needs and feelings and more compassionate toward others. Those widows who can transcend their losses may become more fully aware of the value of life and the need to live each moment to its fullest (Barrett, 1981).

Leisure Activities

Older adults commonly find that, as the role responsibilities of parenthood decrease, they have more time and resources to devote to leisure activities. Different types of leisure activities are available that meet a variety of psychosocial needs. In a study of the benefits of leisure activities, men and women aged 56 and over were asked to describe the sources of satisfaction found in their primary leisure activities (Tinsley et al., 1985). The six clusters of leisure activities and the primary benefits of each are listed in Table 13.1. The table suggests that different clusters of activities meet different needs. It also provides some psychologically equivalent activities for adults who may be unable to continue a given activity or who may be uninterested in one but willing to try another.

One area not included in this list is physical exercise. Physical exercise is becoming a focus of leisure activity for more and more older adults, as its benefits are linked to health, self-esteem, and zest for life. Recent studies suggest a relationship between physical fitness, especially a regular pattern of aerobic exercise, and the improvement of certain visual-spatial cognitive abilities that typically decline with age (Shay & Roth, 1992). In the past, professionals were reluctant to encourage vigorous activity for older adults. They believed that a person who was unaccustomed to active physical exercise might be harmed by physical exertion. However, research on exercise in adulthood suggests quite the opposite interpretation. Not only can adults profit from a program of exercise, but some of the negative consequences of a sedentary lifestyle can be reversed (DeVries, 1975). For example, Hopkins and her associates (1990) described a program in which women aged 57–77 participated in a low-impact aerobic dance class three times a week over 12 weeks. The program included stretching, walking, dance movements,

TABLE 13.1 Leisure Activities and Their Psychological Benefits	
Cluster	**Primary Benefit**

1. Playing cards
   Playing bingo
   Bowling
   Dancing
	Companionship

2. Picnicking	Experiencing something new and unusual

3. Watching sports (not on TV)
   Watching television
	Escape from the pressure of dealing
	   with others

4. Raising houseplants
   Collecting photographs
   Collecting antiques
   Reading
	Solitude and security

5. Knitting or crocheting
   Woodworking
   Ceramics
	Expressiveness and recognition, but in a
	   solitary context

6. Volunteer service
   Volunteer professional activities
   Attending meetings of
     social groups
   Attending meetings of
     religious groups
	Intellectual stimulation, self-expression,
	   and service

Source: Based on Tinsley, Teaff, Colbs & Kaufman, 1985.

large arm movements, and major leg-muscle movement. After 12 weeks, the group showed improvement in cardiorespiratory endurance (walking half a mile as fast as possible), flexibility, muscle strength, body agility, and balance. A comparison group of women who did not participate showed stability or decline in all of these measures of fitness.

A person's exercise program should be developed in response to his or her level of fitness and ability to endure rigorous activity. The goal is a program that raises the heart rate more than 40% of the range from the resting rate to the maximum rate. For men in their 60s and 70s, this means raising their heart rates above 98 and 95, respectively. Rhythmic large-muscle activities, such as walking, jogging, running, and swimming, are the kinds of exercises most likely to lead to improvement in the cardiovascular-respiratory system.

Redirection of energy to new roles in later adulthood requires a degree of flexibility and resilience that often goes unnoticed in observations of older adults. Just imagine what life might be like 30 or 40 years from now. Will you be prepared to embrace the technology, lifestyle, or age-role expectations that you will encounter during your own later adulthood? We are impressed by how readily most people adapt to new roles—especially those of retiree and widow—for which there is little early preparation or social reward.

Accepting One's Life

By later adulthood, evidence about one's successes and failures in the major tasks of middle adulthood—marriage, child rearing, and work—has begun to accumulate. Data by which to judge one's adequacy in these areas are abundant. As

Regular aerobic exercise has been found to be beneficial for improving general health and self-esteem as well as for sustaining certain visual/spatial cognitive abilities that are apt to decline with age.

involvement in the child-rearing role decreases, adults have an opportunity to increase their focus on the degree of harmony in their marriage relationship. They can assess whether they have successfully responded to the changes in their relationship or whether their marriage has deteriorated with the departure of their children. In viewing their own children as mature adults, parents are able to determine whether they have helped them meet the challenges of intimacy, work, and child rearing with creativity and morality. In the work role, older adults can begin to estimate the degree to which their productivity has matched their abilities and the extent to which they have met their private goals for occupational accomplishment.

Individuals are inevitably vulnerable to some degree of discouragement about the limitations of their accomplishments. They must be able to accept the realities that present themselves and to realize that there is a necessary discrepancy between their accomplishments and their goals. The process of accepting one's past life as it has been may be a difficult personal challenge. One must be able to incorporate certain areas of failure, crisis, or disappointment into one's self-image without being overburdened by a sense of inadequacy. One must be able to take pride in areas of achievement even when those accomplishments fall short of one's expectations. At the same time, older adults face the challenge of defining new goals for the future.

There appear to be a variety of responses to the challenge posed by this life task. Some older adults become extremely depressed in thinking about their past and resign themselves to a future of unhappiness. The illnesses, losses, and personal crises of their past become dominant preoccupations. No current experiences can quite compensate for a general feeling of discouragement. Other older

The Vital Elderly

Throughout the United States, thousands of older adults actively participate in weight training, aerobics, jogging, swimming, and tennis—the "new-age" alternatives to shuffleboard and golf. These women are running the 1500-meter women's race in the U.S. Senior Sports Classic in Baton Rouge, Louisiana.

Often the keepers of their culture, many older adults continue to practice highly developed traditional arts. This 78-year-old Canadian Eskimo is doing decorative leather bead work.

A 75-year-old Japanese woman arranges flowers in the traditional, artistic style.

A longtime postcard vendor in Venice, Italy, stays young visiting with tourists from around the world and talking about the magic of her city.

Dressed in traditional style, a Slovakian grandmother and her granddaughter practice a folk dance in the kitchen. Older adults often say that their grandchildren help them stay young.

A comforting hug between grandmother and grandchild seems to have the same wonderful effect in all parts of the world. The smile on the face of this Han Dai woman from the Yunnan province of China speaks for all who delight in such moments of intimacy and affection.

Love and affection play an important role in sustaining emotional well-being at every period of life.

Many older adults share their talents and skills with others, as in this art class for the visually impaired.

When all is said and done, what seems to count is activity, style, and joie de vivre.

adults respond by becoming rigidly self-confident. They see their own lives as examples for younger people and are unable to tolerate any implication of failure. In encountering such adults, one often feels that they have developed a sense of self-righteousness at the expense of compassion. In order to protect their self-image, they reject all doubts and present an impression of total confidence.

Both of these strategies make it impossible for the older person to change during later adulthood. Another type of response is to accept the areas of disappointment or crisis and to put them in perspective with the spheres of personal achievement. For most adults, this approach probably results in an overall balance tending toward pride rather than self-aggrandizement. A more flexible attitude toward one's life history allows one to conceive of new directions for growth, to reframe one's goals and ambitions in the light of changing physical and social realities, and to feel optimistic about the possibility of success in these directions.

Brim (1992) described this adaptive process of matching one's desire for growth and mastery with one's current abilities in his own father's approach to aging. Brim's father, who lived to be 103, had been raised on a farm in Ohio. However, he left the farm to attend Harvard and then Columbia to get his Ph.D. He was a university professor until he retired. Then he and his wife bought a farm, remodeled the farm house, and settled into farming. In the early years of retirement, he cleared and thinned the trees on the hills and mountains of his farm. After a while, he stopped working the hillsides and planted a large vegetable and flower garden. He tilled the garden with a power tiller. When he was 90, he bought a riding tractor. After a while, he could no longer manage the large garden, so he focused on a small border garden and four large window boxes that he planted with flowers. As his eyesight became more impaired, he shifted from reading to listening to "talking books," and when he had to give up actually planting the window boxes, he enjoyed watering them and looking at the flowers. He approached each new challenge of physical decline by investing in a new project and taking pride in his achievements within that domain.

A number of investigators have raised questions about sources of life satisfaction and stress in later adulthood and their relation to perceptions of well-being. One especially intriguing question is whether people in their 60s and 70s feel "old" and just what that means. Most older adults do not perceive themselves as elderly (Kahana, Kahana & McLenigan, 1980). Those who do view themselves as old tend to have more difficulty adjusting to life than those who perceive themselves as middle-aged. Identification with the label *old* is associated with several life stresses, including poor health, reduced activity, widowhood, and reduced income level (Ward, 1977). The fear of growing old is also linked to lower levels of life satisfaction. Those adults over 55 who are quite worried about encountering illness, loneliness, social rejection, and poverty when they are old are also significantly less satisfied with the current quality of their lives (Klemmack & Roff, 1984). They may be chronic worriers.

Although it may not be adaptive for later adults to view themselves as old, it appears that it is also a sign of frustration to view oneself as much younger than one's real age. Montepare and Lachman (1989) asked subjects ranging from the teens to the 80s to describe the age that corresponded to the way they felt and the type of person whose interests and activities were most like theirs. Figure 13.2 shows the subjective age identities (dotted lines) in comparison with the actual ages of the male and female subjects. Younger subjects were likely to have a somewhat *older* subjective age identity. Older subjects were likely to have a *younger*

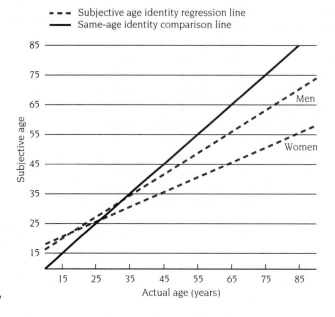

FIGURE 13.2

*Subjective age identities of men
and women across the life span*
Source: *Montepare & Lachman,
1989.*

subjective age identity, and the discrepancy was most noticeable among the old-est women. For younger men and women, having an older subjective age identity was associated with higher life satisfaction. For the oldest men, there was no rela-tionship between subjective age and life satisfaction, but among the oldest women, those with the youngest subjective age had lower life satisfaction. At advanced ages, those with the least discrepancy between their real and their subjective ages had the greatest satisfaction. Although it appears to be common for older adults to identify themselves as younger than they are, a major discrep-ancy between real and subjective age may reflect significant frustration over one's actual age and its constraints. From the open-ended responses of over 3000 subjects, Flanagan (1978, 1980) generated a list of 15 areas of experience that con-tribute to life satisfaction:

1. Material well-being and financial security
2. Health and personal safety
3. Relations with spouse (girlfriend or boyfriend)
4. Having and raising children
5. Relations with parents, siblings, or other relatives
6. Relations with friends
7. Activities related to helping or encouraging other people
8. Activities related to local and national governments
9. Intellectual development
10. Personal understanding and planning
11. Occupational role
12. Creativity and personal expression
13. Socializing
14. Passive and observational recreational activities
15. Active and participatory recreational activities

Three nationally representative groups of subjects aged 30, 50, and 70 were asked to rate each area, telling how important it was for the quality of their lives and how well their needs in each area were being met. Three areas that were described as important by 80% of men and women at every age were health and personal safety, having and raising children, and personal understanding. A spouse or opposite-sex partner was very important to all but the oldest women, 57% of whom were widowed. Areas important to fewer than 70% of the sample at each age level were activities related to government, creativity and personal expression, socializing, and both passive and active recreational activities. Close friends increased in importance more for older women than for older men. Learning was less important for older than for younger subjects. Opportunities to learn were viewed as more adequate at each age, but the importance of learning decreased. In general, 85% of the 50- and 70-year-olds evaluated their overall quality of life as good, very good, or excellent. Flanagan estimated that most Americans felt good about their lives and were satisfied that their relevant needs were being met.

As Flanagan's research suggests, a person's life goals and needs may change over the course of later adulthood, depending on life circumstances. Rather than viewing satisfaction in later adulthood solely in terms of wrapping things up and facing a roleless, undifferentiated future, it makes sense to think that older adults will continue to formulate personal goals and to assess their current life satisfaction in light of how well they are able to achieve those goals. In a study of older adult volunteers, participants were asked to describe the personal goals that were most important to their life satisfaction (Rapkin & Fischer, 1992a, 1992b). The ten groups of life goals identified are listed in Table 13.2. These goals were grouped into five clusters: (1) a high-demand group of people who had many goals that were seen as important or vital to their life satisfaction; (2) an age-prescribed group that was concerned with safety, security, and increased dependence on services, and that showed a preference for disengagement from activities and social relationships; (3) a self-focused group that was especially concerned about having an easy life with little regard for safety, security, or independence; (4) a socially engaged group that had strong concerns about independence and maintaining their social roles and relationships; and (5) a low-demand group that had few goals except for reducing activity and disengaging. In a comparison of these five groups, the socially engaged group had significantly lower scores in depression than the other four. They also had the highest score in self-esteem, whereas the self-focused group had the lowest score.

The most important observation was that each group had its own pattern of predictors of satisfaction. For example, age was not related to satisfaction in the group as a whole, but within the age-prescribed cluster, the older subjects had higher satisfaction than the younger subjects. Gender was also not related to satisfaction in the group as a whole, but women in the high-demand group had higher levels of satisfaction, and men in the socially engaged group had higher satisfaction. One must conclude that an understanding of life satisfaction must be based on the way each person frames his or her contemporary situation and view of the future. Individual differences in satisfaction are due in part to how well people are able to achieve what they perceive as most possible and desirable as they face the challenges of aging.

Demographic variables do not predict perceived life satisfaction adequately. A person's satisfaction with life remains fairly stable over the years despite losses of important roles and some decline in health (Costa et al., 1987). For older women, staying healthy, especially as it relates to being able to remain independent and not become a burden on others, is so central to feelings of well-being that other hopes and concerns seem to be minimized. A 69-year-old woman

TABLE 13.2   Personal Goals of Older Adults

Goal	Definition
Active improvement	To actively improve or increase involvement in many domains of life
Maintenance of social values and relationships	To maintain reciprocal social relationships and community ties, to uphold religious beliefs, and to be financially self-sufficient
Disengagement	To reduce social and community obligations, to increase religious involvement, and to remain independent from social services for the aged
Energetic lifestyle	To be romantically involved and physically attractive, to be energetic and healthy, to get around independently, and to improve one's living situation
Safety and security	To worry about safety and security in the neighborhood and in getting around, avoiding health hazards and financial problems
Stability	To worry about stability in the neighborhood and predictability in the health-care system
Increased reliance on services	Not to be troubled with having to solve problems and wanting to be able to rely on services to meet one's needs
Easy life	To be able to be impulsive, do what one wants, stay independent from family, live in comfort, and have plenty of leisure time
Reduced activity	To reduce volunteer activities because of poor health
Independence in living	To live independently and to have privacy

Source: Based on Rapkin & Fischer, 1992.

described her situation as follows: "God's been good to me. My health is good. I can cut grass, climb ladders, and can paint. If you can do that at 69, that's pretty good, isn't it?" (Bearon, 1989, p. 774).

In an analysis of subjective well-being and life satisfaction among older African-Americans, the most important predictors of well-being in this sample were subjective assessments of health, a low number of stressful life events, a sense of personal efficacy, and self-esteem (Tran, Wright & Chatters, 1991). In addition, marital status and age were both positively associated with well-being. Neither educational level nor income were direct predictors of well-being; however, education and income were linked to factors that did predict well-being. Those with less education tended to have more chronic health conditions, and these were associated with poorer perceived health and a lower sense of well-being. Similarly, lower income was associated with lower feelings of self-esteem, and low self-esteem was linked to lower feelings of well-being.

We all know people who have lived very difficult lives yet appear to be full of zest and enthusiasm. We also know people who appear to have had the benefits of many of life's resources yet are continually complaining about problems. In response to this reality, some researchers have looked to personality factors to predict subjective life satisfaction (Costa & McCrae, 1980; McCrae & Costa, 1983).

Pablo Picasso, La Joie de Vivre, 1946. Adults find value in their life by seeing it as part of a larger, more abstract, infinite order. At age 65, Picasso created this celebration of life, integrating many of his favorite themes including sexuality, fertility, creativity, and mythology.

A personality dimension described as *extroversion* is consistently associated with measures of well-being, happiness, and security. Extroversion includes such qualities as sociability, vigor, sensation seeking, and positive emotions. A personality dimension described as *neuroticism* is consistently associated with discouragement, unhappiness, and hopelessness. Neuroticism includes such qualities as anxiety, hostility, and impulsiveness. The implication is that real-life events are screened and interpreted through the filter of personality. Whether specific events will contribute to feelings of satisfaction or dismay depends on how they are interpreted. Some people are more likely to be grumblers, and others are more likely to be celebrants of life.

Erikson (Erikson et al., 1986) commented on the importance of trust in the acceptance of one's life:

> The life cycle, however, does more than extend itself into the next generation. It curves back on the life of the individual, allowing, as we have indicated, a reexperiencing of earlier stages in a new form. This retracing might be described as a growth toward death, if that did not ring false as a metaphor. Maples and aspens every October bear flamboyant witness to this possibility of a final spurt of growth. Nature unfortunately has not ordained that mortals put on such a fine show.
>
> As aging continues, in fact, human bodies begin to deteriorate and physical and psychosocial capacities diminish in a seeming reversal of the course their development takes. When physical frailty demands assistance, one must accept again an appropriate dependence without the loss of trust and hope. The old, of course, are not endowed with the endearing survival skills of the infant. Old bodies are more difficult to care for, and the task itself is less satisfying to the caretaker than that of caring for infants. Such skills as elders possess have been hard won and are maintained only with determined grace. Only a lifetime of slowly developing trust is adequate to meet this situation, which so naturally elicits despair and disgust at one's own helplessness. Of how many elders could one say, "He surrendered every vestige of his old life with a sort of courteous, half humorous gentleness"? (p. 327)

Developing a Point of View About Death

It is inevitable that during later adulthood serious, frightening, and unhappy questions about death will fill the individual's thoughts. The stage of middle adulthood is the period in which most people lose their parents. During later adulthood, their peers die. These deaths are sources of psychological stress that entail the emotional process of grief and mourning as well as the cognitive strain of trying to accept or understand them.

The development of a perspective on death is a continuous process that begins in childhood and is not fully resolved until later adulthood. The earliest concern with death—during toddlerhood—reflects an inability to conceive of an irreversible state of lifelessness. Toddlers are likely to think that a person may be dead at one moment and "undeaded" the next. By middle school age, children have a rather realistic concept of death but are unlikely to relate that concept to themselves or to others close to them (Anthony, 1972).

People's thoughts about their own death do not become very realistic or focused until sometime during later adolescence. Before then, individuals have not yet established an integrated identity. They are unlikely to project themselves into the distant future or to conceive of their own mortality. In the process of forming a personal identity, individuals ask questions about mortality, the meaning of life, and the possibility of life after death. During this stage, they begin to form a point of view about death. Because older adolescents are deeply preoccupied with their own uniqueness, they may tend to have a heightened sense of their own importance. They also see themselves as being at the very beginning of their adult lives. At this stage, death may be anticipated with great fear. Some adults never overcome this fear of death, which is associated with a deep narcissism and a sense of self-importance.

Young adults form intimate personal bonds that they expect to endure. One's concerns about death at this stage include some anxiety about the possible death of the other person and emerging feelings of responsibility for him or her. One's own death has greater consequences once one's personal fate is linked with that of another. Thus, a point of view about death begins to involve a sense of being able to provide for one's partner or to feel confident that the partner can survive in one's absence. One's view of death broadens from a preoccupation with one's own mortality to an appreciation of one's relationships and interdependencies with other people.

During middle adulthood, people recognize that they have already lived about half of their lives. The issue of death becomes increasingly concrete as parents and older relatives die. At the same time, adults begin to have a larger impact on their families and communities. Increased feelings of effectiveness and vitality lessen the threat of death (Feifel & Branscomb, 1973; Fried-Cassorla, 1977). The degree to which individuals gain satisfaction from their own contributions to future generations determines the extent of their anxiety about death during this stage. Achievement of a sense of generativity should allow adults to feel that their impact will continue to be felt even after death.

Ideally, during later adulthood, ego concerns with respect to death decrease. Individuals come to accept their own lives as they have lived them and begin to see death as a natural part of the life span. Death no longer poses a threat to personal value, to potential for accomplishment, or to the desire to influence the lives of others. As a result of having accepted one's life, one can accept its end without discouragement. This implies not a willingness to die but an acceptance of the fact of death. It takes great courage to face the fact of one's own death and, at the same time, to live out the days of one's life with optimism and enthusiasm. Those older adults who achieve this degree of acceptance of their death appreciate that the usefulness of their contributions does not necessarily depend on their physical presence (Kübler-Ross, 1969, 1972).

The evolution of a point of view about death requires some capacity to absorb the loss of one's close relatives and friends as well as to accept one's own death.

Pablo Picasso, A Self-Portrait, 1972. At age 91, a year before his death, Picasso painted this disturbing self-portrait. He is looking straight ahead, through those famous, piercing eyes, at his dying face.

The former task may be even more difficult than the latter, in that the death of peers begins to destroy the social group of which the adult is a member. Losing one's friends and relatives means a loss of daily companionship, a shared world of memories and plans, and a source of support for values and social norms. The circumstances surrounding the deaths of others may also prove to be very frightening. One sees people suffer through long illnesses, die abruptly in the midst of a thriving and vigorous life, or die in an absurd, meaningless accident. In each instance, the surviving adults must ask themselves about the value of each of these lives and subsequently about the value of their own life. They are also left with a growing set of possibilities in regard to the circumstances of their own death.

Our culture's rituals permit adults to cope with death-related anxiety. The elaborate arrangements for a burial service, the viewing of the body, the selection of a coffin or urn, gravestone, or burial site, and provision for care of the grave allow adults to work through the reality of their own death by focusing on aspects of it over which they can exercise some control. The details of a funeral and burial may not bring adults closer to an emotional acceptance of death, but they do impart some feeling of certainty about the events immediately following their own death. In fact, some people think of their funeral as a last social statement. All of the plans surrounding a death are designed to heighten the perception of the individual's social status and moral virtue. The event of death is a direct contradiction of the cultural values of activity, productivity, and individuality. In order to disguise the view of death as a final failure, individuals may attempt to maintain an illusion of competence by planning the circumstances of their own funeral.

TABLE 13.3	Fear of Death (Percentages)		
		Age	
	20–39	**40–59**	**60+**
Afraid/terrified	40	26	10
Neither afraid nor unafraid	21	20	17
Unafraid/eager	36	52	71
Depends	3	3	2

Source: Based on Kalish & Reynolds, 1976.

Several investigators have considered the sources of personal anxiety about death and the changes in preoccupation with death at various ages. Although older adults seem to think about death more frequently than do young adults, they do not appear to feel more threatened by it. In a survey of over 400 adults in early, middle, and later adulthood, death was a more salient issue for the oldest (over 60) age group (Kalish & Reynolds, 1976). The oldest adults felt that they were more likely to die in the near future. They knew more people who had died and were more likely than younger subjects to have visited a cemetery or attended a funeral. The oldest adults were more likely to have made some specific arrangements related to their death, including purchasing cemetery space, writing a will, and making funeral arrangements. Yet an expressed fear of death was lowest in this oldest age group, and the percentage who said that they were unafraid of death or even eager for it was highest.

Fear of personal death is natural and normal. Death may be feared for a variety of reasons, of which some relate to the actual process of dying and others to the consequences of dying. Concerns about the process of dying include fears of being alone, being in pain, having others see one suffering, or losing control of one's thoughts and body. Concerns about the consequences of dying include fears of the unknown, loss of identity ("People will forget about me"), the grief others will feel, the decomposition of the body, and punishment or pain in the hereafter (Florian & Kravetz, 1983; Conte, Weiner & Plutchik, 1982).

Death does not seem to be as frightening to the old as to the young. Table 13.3 shows the responses of three age groups of adults to the following question: "Some people say they are afraid to die and others say they are not. How do you feel?" Admission of fear decreased with age, and lack of fear or even eagerness to die increased. In another study of over 1200 adults, a similar pattern was observed (Bengston, Cuellar & Ragan, 1977). Expressed fear decreased with age. The group aged 45–49 had the greatest fear of death, and the group aged 70–74 had the lowest.

There are at least three explanations for this finding. First, older people tend to be more religious and may find more comfort in the religious concepts of life after death. Second, older people may feel more accepting of their lives and the decisions they have made than younger people. This view is supported by the responses of subjects in the Kalish and Reynolds study (1976) to the following question: "If you were told that you had a terminal disease and that you had six months to live, how would you want to spend your time?" Older adults were more likely to concentrate on their inner lives or to continue their lives as they were. Young-adult and middle-aged subjects expressed more concern about their

By attending the funerals of family and friends, and by visiting the grave sites of loved ones, older adults begin to be familiar with, and perhaps a bit less terrified of, the reality of their own death.

relationships with loved ones. The youngest subjects were most likely to want new experiences. The idea of death was viewed as less tragic and less disruptive by the old than by the young. A third explanation is that older people are more familiar with death. They have had more opportunities to experience the deaths of others. They have made more preparations for their own deaths. They realistically expect death in the near future. Death is less an uncertainty. Many people who were over 60 in the mid-1970s never anticipated the healthy old age that they were enjoying. The years after 65 were seen as an unexpected bonus that their parents and grand-parents had not enjoyed.

Bereavement and Grief

Adults cope not only with their own illnesses and death but with those of their loved ones. The emotional suffering that follows the death of a loved one is called *bereavement*. It is commonly viewed as a major life stress accompanied by physical symptoms, role loss, and a variety of intense emotions, including anger, sorrow, anxiety, and depression. The stress of bereavement increases the likelihood of illness and even death among survivors.

In the face of bereavement, there is a need to "work through" the reality of the loss as well as the feelings that accompany it. The experience of the bereaved person is not very different from the experience of the person who is coping with his or her own death. Psychiatrist Erich Lindemann (1944) worked with many of the people whose relatives had died in the Coconut Grove fire in Boston. His writings continue to provide a basis of understanding the bereavement process. He described the normal grief reaction as involving three phases. First, the person must achieve "emancipation from bondage to the deceased." This "bondage" may include feelings of guilt about ways he or she had criticized or even harmed the dead person. Second, the person must make an adjustment to all the aspects of the environment from which the deceased is missing. Third, the person must begin to form new relationships. Lindemann found that one big obstacle to working through this grief is a desire to avoid the accompanying emotions and intense physical distress. According to his analysis, the strategy of avoiding grief only prolongs the subject's physical, mental, and emotional preoccupation with the dead person.

The depression and confusion accompanying grieving may decrease the survivors' sensitivity to their own physical health and may pose risks to their mental health as well. Those who are deep in mourning may have feelings of uselessness or emptiness that prevent them from seeking help for their own physical or emotional health problems. Some people try to cope with their grief by increasing their use of medication, alcohol, or tranquilizers, which may threaten their physical health. Loss of appetite and lack of sleep are other symptoms of grief that contribute to the whole pattern of increased vulnerability during this time.

Among people who have lost a spouse, the more intense experiences of depression are felt by those who describe their marriage as very positive and vital. It is clear that this loss strikes at the core of an older adult's sense of attachment, social integration, and personal worth (Futterman et al., 1990). In a comparison study of older widows and widowers with adults who were not experiencing bereavement, the widowed adults showed greater signs of depression, psychopathology, and grief at 2 months after the loss (Thompson et al., 1991). At 12 and 30 months after the loss, the two groups were comparable in levels of depression and psychopathology, but the bereaved group continued to experience higher levels of grief than the nonbereaved group. The research, confirmed by other observations, suggests that, among older adults, one may not expect a full resolution of the grief work associated with the death of a spouse. Rather, older adults come to accept a certain empty place in their hearts for their deceased partner and learn to find appropriate times to experience their profound sense of loss.

A Cultural Comparison

To appreciate how people cope with death, it is helpful to consider the cultural rituals that have emerged for structuring the response to death. Box 13.2, which describes the Amish way of death, illustrates how death is openly incorporated into every aspect of life. The service and ritual are expressions of the belief in a spiritual immortality and a simultaneous recognition of separation. Families customarily care for their aging parents within their own homes. Dying persons are surrounded by their families, who provide reassurance of generational continuity. The bereaved family members receive help and care from community members for at least the first year after a family death. In one study, Amish families found six conditions especially helpful for coping with death:

> (a) The continued presence of the family, both during the course of the illness and at the moment of death; (b) open communication about the process of dying and its impact on the family; (c) the maintenance of a normal life-style by the family during the course of the illness; (d) commitment to as much independence of the dying person as possible; (e) the opportunity to plan and organize one's own death; (f) continued support for the bereaved for at least a year following the funeral, with long-term support given to those who do not remarry. (Bryer, 1979, p. 260)

We are beginning to understand and accept death as a meaningful component of the life course. Scientists are responding more realistically to the needs of the dying, to the process of grieving, and to the need for an ethic that will permit us to encounter death as a natural, dignified element of life. As we experience the deaths of others during adult life, our own lives are clarified. With each death, we reflect on the quality of the relationship we have had with the person, the nature of his or her accomplishments, and the essential value or contribution of that life. The death of each loved or cherished person educates us about the meaning and

BOX 13.2

The Amish Way of Death

The importance that the Amish place on their funeral ceremonies is reflected not only in familiarity with death but also in an intensified awareness of community. As an Amish man reported in a family interview, "The funeral is not for the one who dies, you know; it is for the family." . . .

The Amish community takes care of all aspects of the funeral occasion with the exception of the embalming procedure, the coffin, and the horse-drawn wagon. These matters are taken care of by a non-Amish funeral director who provides the type of service that the Amish desire.

The embalmed body is returned to the home within a day of the death. Family members dress the body in white garments in accordance with the biblical injunction found in Revelation 3:5. For a man, this consists of white trousers, a white shirt, and a white vest. For a woman, the usual clothing is a white cape and apron that she wore at both her baptism and her marriage. At baptism a black dress is worn with the white cape and apron; at marriage a purple or blue dress is worn with the white cape and apron. It is only at her death that an Amish woman wears a white dress, with the cape and apron that she put away for the occasion of her death. This is an example of the lifelong preparation for death as sanctioned by Amish society. The wearing of white clothes signifies the high ceremonial emphasis on the death event as the final rite of passage into a new and better life.

Several Amish women stated that making their parents', husbands', or children's funeral garments was a labor of love that represented the last thing they could do for their loved ones. One Amish woman related that each month her aged grandmother carefully washed, starched, and ironed her own funeral clothing so that it would be in readiness for her death. This act appears to have reinforced for herself and her family her lifelong acceptance of death and to have contributed to laying the foundation for effective grief work for herself and her family. This can be seen as an example of the technique of preventive intervention called *anticipatory guidance* (Caplan, 1964), which focuses on helping individuals to cope with impending loss through open discussion and problem solving before the actual death.

After the body is dressed, it is placed in a plain wooden coffin that is made to specifications handed down through the centuries. The coffin is placed in a room that has been emptied of all furnishings in order to accommodate the several hundred relatives, friends, and neighbors who will begin arriving as soon as the body is prepared for viewing. The coffin is placed in a central position in the house, both for practical considerations of seating and to underscore the importance of the death ceremonial.

The funeral service is held in the barn in the warmer months and in the house during the colder seasons. The service is conducted in German and lasts 1½ hours, with the same order of service as for every funeral. The guests view the body when they arrive and again when they leave to take their places in the single-file procession of the carriages to the burial place.

Source: Bryer, 1979.

value of our own life choices. It is with great admiration that we respond to those who confront their own death openly and with acceptance.

The Psychosocial Crisis: Integrity Versus Despair

Integrity

The attainment of integrity comes only after some considerable thought about the meaning of one's life. *Integrity,* as the term is used in Erikson's theory, refers to an ability to accept the facts of one's life and to face death without great fear. Older adults who have achieved a sense of integrity view their past in an existential light. They appreciate that their lives and their individuality are due to an accumulation of personal satisfactions and crises. They accept this record of events without trying to deny some facts or overemphasize others. Integrity is not so much a quality of honesty and trustworthiness, as we might use the term in daily speech, as it is an ability to integrate one's past history with one's present circumstances and to feel content with the outcome.

Despair

The opposite pole of this crisis is *despair*. It is much more likely that adults will resolve the crisis of integrity versus despair in the negative direction than that infants will resolve the crisis of trust versus mistrust in the negative direction. For infants to experience trust, they must depend on the benevolence of a responsible caregiver who will meet their essential needs. In most cases, this caregiver is present, and the infant learns to rely on him or her. In order to experience integrity, older adults must incorporate into their self-image a lifelong record of conflicts, failures, and disappointments, along with their accomplishments. This in itself is a comparatively difficult process. In addition, older adults must face some degree of devaluation and even hostility from the social community. The negative attitudes expressed by family members, colleagues, and younger people toward the incompetence, dependence, or old-fashioned ways of older people may lead many of them to feel discouraged about their self-worth. The gradual deterioration of certain physical capacities, particularly the loss of hearing, impaired vision, and limited motor agility, feeds into the older person's frustration and discouragement. Older adults observe for themselves that they cannot perform certain tasks as well as they did in the past or that their domains of independent functioning and mastery have diminished. In addition, there is a general cultural sentiment that the death of an older person—in contrast, for example, to that of a child or youth—while sad, is not such a great loss to society since that person has already contributed what she or he is likely to contribute to society. Thus, older adults may perceive that society is already letting go of them, even before they are ready to let go of life (Jecker & Schneiderman, 1994).

All of these factors are likely to create a feeling of regret about one's past and a continuous, haunting desire to be able to do things differently, or of bitterness over how one's life has turned out. People who resolve the crisis of later adulthood in the direction of despair cannot resist speculating about how things might have been or about what actions might have been taken if conditions had only been different. Despair makes calm acceptance of death impossible. These individuals either seek death as a way of ending a miserable existence or desperately fear death because it makes impossible any hope of compensating for past failures.

Depression

The theme of depression has been treated in several sections of this text, especially as a concern in early adolescence, in the mother-infant relationship, and as it is linked with life stressors such as unemployment and divorce. Given the close link between the concept of depression and the concept of despair, it should come as no surprise that depression has been a topic of research in the study of adulthood and aging. A number of cross-sectional studies have documented a U-shaped pattern in the presence of depressive symptoms with age. Depressive symptoms are especially evident in early adulthood, between the ages of 25 and 30; they decline in middle adulthood; and they increase again in those over age

Later adulthood is viewed as a period of wisdom and stability. Through introspection and reminiscence, people begin to discover the meaning and inevitable sense in their life story.

70 (Kessler et al., 1992). The same factors that are known to be associated with depression in younger age groups are associated with depression in older groups as well. Even though the risk of depression increases in later life, we cannot attribute depression to the aging process itself. The negative physiological changes associated with aging, such as high blood pressure, reduced breathing capacity, reduced muscle strength, slowed reaction time, memory loss, and loss of visual or auditory acuity, are not associated with depression (Lewinsohn et al., 1991). Rather, one must assume that depression as a complex affective and cognitive syndrome does not automatically "come with the territory" of aging but occurs in a subset of older adults, especially those who experience a reduced activity level, reduced access to a significant close, confiding relationship, and the accumulation of physical health problems that reduce one's independence and sense of enthusiasm for pleasant activities (Lewinsohn et al., 1991).

The Central Process: Introspection

In order to achieve a sense of integrity, the individual must engage in deliberate self-evaluation and private thought. The final achievement of a sense of integrity requires the ability to *introspect* about the gradual evolution of life events and to appreciate the significance of each event in the formation of the adult personality. This state can be reached only through individual effort. One may even have to isolate oneself temporarily, shutting out the influences of potentially competitive or resentful associates.

As a product of his introspection, Dr. C. M. Pierce began to formulate an analysis of purpose that was embedded in his diverse life experiences, a sense of purpose that transcends the stresses of the many microaggressions to which African-Americans are exposed:

> Meanwhile some other lessons or guidelines about racism have percolated from making analogies during these years. One, following studies on dog sled mushers who raced 1100 miles across Alaska, concerned the need for a clear goal. The mushers, despite organic brain signs at the end of the race, had been able to reach this goal without mishap. This seemed staggering. It suggested that, in spite of obstacles, having a clearly focused goal and informed resolution of conflicts would be valuable for

Blacks' individual and community survival. This means that each Black, in our instance as Black psychiatrists, must do things to help Blacks and ourselves to make such resolutions and goal formulations.

One consideration that seems important for Black professionals to emphasize is service to the international community. Compared to White America we are in short supply of skilled and educated people. Compared to many countries of the world, especially third-world countries, Black America has a superabundance of skilled and educated people. Another opportunity to bring unity out of diversity would be for us to initiate more strong actions to bring our skill and education to other areas, even while we extend our slender resources to alleviate conditions in the U.S.A.

This view can be defended on the basis of historical and humanitarian needs. Also philosophically, due to our acquaintance with oppression, we might, as a group, find more ready congeniality to work on planetary projects. Politically, the model would help Blacks in the U.S.A. and help the country abroad. Psychologically, for those able to do it, it would be an avenue in which to utilize lofty aspirations and our willingness to sacrifice.

As a scouting report, it can be said that for a variety of reasons Black Americans are about to be recruited to wider efforts on a scale never before approached. Here is an instance where we should prepare for unity when our diversity is sought.*

One mode for engaging in self-evaluation is reminiscence. *Reminiscence* has been defined as the recollection of "long-term memories of events in which the reminiscer is either a participant or an observer" (Ross, 1989, p. 341). This process of nostalgic remembering allows adults to recapture some of the memorable events in their life histories. Reminiscence may be a playful recalling of a life adventure or a painful review of some personal or family crisis. The process of simple reminiscence has been described as comprising four elements: the selection of an event or "story" to retell or review; immersion in the details of the story, including the strong emotions linked to the event; withdrawal from the past by distancing oneself from the event or comparing past and present; and bringing closure to the memory by summing up, finding some lesson, or making a general observation (Merriam, 1989). Through this kind of process, a person builds a mental and emotional bridge between the past and the present.

Many accounts have found a positive link between reminiscence and positive adjustment in later life, especially better health, a more positive outlook, and a better ability to cope with the challenges of daily life. However, not all forms of reminiscence are of equal benefit. In particular, reminiscences of the integrative or instrumental type tend to be associated with high levels of well-being, whereas obsessive reminiscences are not. *Integrative reminiscence* involves reviewing one's past in order to find meaning or to reconcile one's current and prior feelings about certain life events. *Instrumental reminiscence* focuses on past accomplishments, past efforts to overcome difficulties, and the use of past experiences to approach current difficulties. *Obsessive reminiscences* suggest an inability to resolve or accept certain past events and a persistent guilt or despair over these events (Wong & Watt, 1991). Contrast the following two narratives:

> "When I was a teenager, my parents broke up and both remarried. I was very resentful because they did not seem to care about my feelings or needs. But as I grow older and look back, I understand that they were really not compatible with each other. They had suffered for many years before their divorce." [Integrative reminiscence]

> "My husband died when I was away for two days visiting my friends in the West. He fell in the bathtub and eventually died because there was no one there to help him. It has been years now, but I still cannot forgive myself for leaving him home alone for two days." [Obsessive reminiscence] (Wong & Watt, 1991, p. 276)

*From Pierce, 1989.

Reminiscence appears to lend continuity to older adults' self-concepts. They can trace the path of their own development through time and identify moments that were of central importance in the crystallization of their personal philosophies. They can revise the meaning of past events by bringing to bear their current wisdom on understanding or accepting what took place in the past. We see reminiscence as an integrating process that has positive value in an eventual attainment of integrity. In excess, however, reminiscence may dominate reality. Some adults tend to dwell on sad events and allow earlier disappointments to preoccupy their current thoughts. In this case, their past lives take precedence over current circumstances. No new events can compete successfully with past memories for their attention. Under these conditions, realistic acceptance of their total life history is not possible.

Of course, the process of introspection is affected by the selectivity of memory, the dominant value orientation, and the general quality of supportiveness or destructiveness in the social milieu. Given these contaminants of purely objective self-assessment, individuals must engage in repeated soul-searching to sort out their lives and come to terms with some of the discordant events that have inevitably been part of their history. They must determine whether the essential nature of their personal identity has survived through time. They must evaluate the quality of their close relationships and determine the degree to which they are able to meet the needs of others. They must identify those contributions that have represented a serious effort to improve the quality of others' lives. Finally, they must determine the extent to which their philosophy of life has been accurately translated into significant actions.

Ryff and Heincke (1983) used a psychosocial model to test the possible changes in personality configurations in later adulthood. Early, middle, and later adults were asked to respond to a variety of statements from three time perspectives: as they applied in the present, in the past during an earlier life stage, and in the future in a later life stage. Generativity was perceived by all age groups as being highest during middle adulthood, regardless of the respondents' ages. Similarly, integrity was perceived as being highest in later adulthood. Older adults rated themselves as being higher in integrity at present than they recalled having been in the past. Young and middle-aged adults expected to be higher in this dimension in the future than they were at present. This research suggests that people not only experience changes in the directions that psychosocial theory would predict but also anticipate changes in those directions at various life stages. These expectations influence how one prepares for future life stages and evaluates them once they arrive.

The attainment of integrity is ultimately a result of the balance of all the psychosocial crises that have come earlier, accompanied by all the ego strengths and core pathologies that have accumulated along the way. The conflict of integrity versus despair is resolved through a dynamic process of life review and self-evaluation. Contemporary factors such as health, family relationships, and role loss or role transition are integrated with an assessment of one's past aspirations and accomplishments. Thoughts of the past may be fleeting or a constant obsession. Memories may be altered to fit contemporary events, or contemporary events may be reinterpreted to fit memories. The achievement of integrity is the culmination of a life of psychosocial growth. Psychologically speaking, it is the peak of the pyramid in that it addresses the ultimate question: How do I find meaning in life given the ultimate reality of death? Achievement of integrity in later adulthood inspires younger age groups to continue to struggle with the challenges of their own life stages.

Applied Topic
Retirement

Retirement usually refers to one's status with respect to the paid labor force. One definition of retirement is that the person works less than full time year round and receives income from a retirement pension earned during earlier periods of employment (Atchley, 1977). Some people define retirement as the time at which people begin to receive social security or other pension benefits. However, retirement also refers to a developmental transition, a predictable, normative change that involves preparation, redefinition of roles and role behaviors, and ongoing psychological adjustment as the structure and significance of paid employment is replaced by other activities (Floyd et al., 1992).

Of course, some people never retire. Some die before they reach retirement age. Some continue to work on a reduced schedule. Some leave their primary job and take on another full-time or part-time job in a related or even a totally different field. Some who are self-employed or whose work involves certain creative skills, such as acting, music, painting, or writing, simply continue to work on into their late adulthood (Herzog, House & Morgan, 1991). In fact, retirement is a relatively new opportunity from a historical perspective. At the turn of the century, almost 70% of men over the age of 65 were in the paid labor force, compared to 16% in 1991 (U.S. Senate, Special Committee on Aging, 1986; U.S. Bureau of the Census, 1992). Men now spend about 20% of their lives in retirement. As the period of healthy later adulthood expands for men, this proportion will increase as well.

Recent cohorts of adults hold more positive views of retirement than did adults who reached retirement age during the 1940s and 1950s. At that time, most adults had not grown up in families in which their parents had retired. They had not expected to have the opportunity to retire when they entered the labor market. Studies of attitudes toward retirement during that period reflected sentiments of dread of having nothing to do or guilt about being paid (in the form of a pension) for doing nothing. Today, most workers see retirement as an appropriate end to their work lives, a transition to which they are entitled. Postretirement perceptions tend to reflect optimism about life and satisfaction with the decision to retire. Many people perceive the decision to retire as one over which they have control and that will lead to positive consequences (Hendrick, Wells & Faletti, 1982).

Adjustment to Retirement

Adjustment during the retirement transition is a very individual process. Studies find that approximately one-third of adults report significant difficulty during this process (Fletcher & Hansson, 1991). Three factors that seem to influence such adjustment include planning for retirement, perceptions of retirement, and the extent of income loss (Newman & Newman, 1983).

Planning for Retirement

Preparation for retirement involves a willingness to anticipate the changes that may occur in finances, family roles, daily activity, and social interactions after retirement, and to take some actions to address these changes. In a national survey of men aged 60–74, fewer than 4% were found to have participated in retirement preparation programs. Those workers who might benefit most from these programs, especially those with lower retirement income, are less likely to learn about or participate in them (Beck, 1984; Ferraro, 1990).

Perceptions of Retirement

Perceptions of retirement involve a person's relief or resentment regarding it. Jahoda (1982) argued that, in addition to the manifest or obvious functions of paid employment, especially income and possibly status, there are a number of latent functions that provide important psychological benefits. She identified these as providing a structure for the use of time; a context for social contact; a content for self-identity; regular, predictable activities; and a sense of participation in a collective effort. Retirement may be perceived as resulting in deprivation in each of these areas and therefore as presenting a threat to psychological well-being.

Fletcher and Hansson (1991) constructed a measure of retirement anxiety that captures some of the apprehensions that adults have as they anticipate retirement. This measure illustrates how people come to rely on work as a primary social structure and highlights the difficulties some people face as they confront the transition to retirement. In particular, Fletcher and Hansson found that, for those who suffer from retirement anxiety, two factors were especially troubling. First, people who had high levels of retirement anxiety worried about the loss of structured social involvement and connection. This concern was linked to worry about losing friendships, being lonely, and having little in common with former co-workers after retirement. Second, people worried about having to be assertive or proactive in finding new relationships and new activities that would meet their needs. This concern was linked to a general difficulty in handling life transitions, a high level of uncertainty about the future, and a general feeling of loss of identity. Although one might think that people who have high levels of retirement anxiety would make use of the services that are available to help people plan for retirement, this was not the case. Those with high anxiety about retirement may try to deny this transition by avoiding planning and counseling sessions.

In addition to worries about being able to meet one's social needs following retirement, some adults find the transition difficult because they feel that the retirement is outside their own control. When people perceive that they are working or not working by their own choice and about as little or as much as they would like, they have higher levels of health and well-being. When they perceive that their involvement or lack of involvement in work is being decided by someone else and they have little say in it, they are also likely to have more difficulty adjusting to retirement, more health problems, and a greater incidence of depressive symptoms (Herzog et al., 1991; Swan, Dame & Carmelli, 1991).

People whose work has brought them little satisfaction and those who are ready to become involved in new directions may feel more effective and independent after they retire (Floyd et al., 1992). They are likely to find new sources of enjoyment, new opportunities to spend time with family and friends, a sense of relief at not having to deal with the stressors of their job, and a new feeling of freedom to develop their interests or to exert more control over their daily life, as the following account makes clear:

> This widowed man lives alone in a cabin in a sparsely populated, rural area. Throughout his working career, he held a variety of low-paying jobs that, in retrospect, neither required nor permitted real discipline or enterprise. He did not particularly like his jobs, and he was never viewed as performing them with particular success. For this man, retirement seems to signify not the loss of valuable structure, but his release from a series of rigid, repetitive demands that in and of themselves precluded

inventiveness and enthusiasm. Retirement presents him with a new opportunity to reexperience the initiative that he now recalls as having characterized him until his midteens.

This man has always enjoyed music. He has always loved listening to the radio and playing records. As an adolescent, he tinkered with radio equipment until the advent of transistors and integrated circuits. Over the years he has accumulated a collection of some two to three thousand 78 rpm records. Recognizing that plastic record disks are likely to warp or break, he has recently begun to copy them onto cassettes. He has removed his tape deck and large loudspeakers from their cabinet and strapped them to a mover's dolly, onto which he has built appropriate shelves. Each day, when he goes to the senior center for lunch, he wheels his movable entertainment center out to his pickup truck and brings his friends their favorite songs. This man has also begun to make his own TV dinners, using the partitioned trays on which his "meals on wheels" are delivered. He cooks large quantities of meat and vegetables and freezes them in these single-meal trays for easy access. The quality of this man's products is far from professional. In fact, his entertainment center looks rather slapdash, and the contents of his frozen meals do not always retain their flavor or texture when reheated. What is striking, instead, is the enthusiasm, the delight, and the pride with which he has devised his various projects. In each case he perceived a problem, combined his own ingenuity with the resources at hand to devise a solution that is satisfactory for his own needs, and created something that is usable, gives him pleasure, and remains a real source of personal pride. (Erikson et al., 1986, pp. 181–182)

Adjustment to retirement is expected to change with time. Atchley (1976) proposed three phases of adjustment: a honeymoon period, which is busy and positive; a letdown phase, in which the meaning and structure of work are really missed; and a reorientation phase, in which a stable life routine is established. In an attempt to assess this model, one study grouped retired men into six 6-month intervals from the date of retirement. Men in the period of 13–18 months after retirement were significantly more dissatisfied with life and had lower levels of physical activity than did those in the first 6 months after retirement. Later periods showed lower levels of satisfaction than the first 6 months but not the marked depression of the 13- to 18-month period (Ekerdt, Bosse & Levkoff, 1985). These findings support the early euphoria idea as well as the notion of a letdown phase. The pattern and degree of recovery are not as clearly described in this research.

Income Loss

Finally, adjustment to retirement is especially difficult when it is associated with a dramatic reduction in income. One can expect about a 25%–30% reduction in income after retirement. Income loss is somewhat greater for those who retire before age 65 (Palmore, Fillenbaum & George, 1984). Although work-related expenses, taxes, and child-care expenses may decrease, health and recreational expenses may increase.

Older householders' annual income is derived from social security (37%), earnings (25%), property (23%), and pensions (13%). About 14% of all retired households receive income from at least three sources: social security, private pensions, and other assets (Kart, Longino & Ullmann, 1989). In 1990, the median income for households headed by someone 65 years old or over was $16,855; about 28% of households headed by someone 65 years old or older had an annual income of less than $10,000 a year. Poverty is greater for older minorities and those who live alone (U.S. Bureau of the Census, 1992). At the other end of the scale, many of the richest Americans are over 65. Among the 14 Americans listed as having wealth worth over $1 billion in 1986, 7 were over 65 years old.

A Look Toward the Future of Retirement

The ongoing dialogue among older workers, retirees, and organizations is likely to result in the formulation of more varied, flexible alternatives to full retirement. More and more businesses are eliminating a mandatory retirement age. At the same time, movements toward reducing the work force seem to include the development of early retirement plans, including phased retirement, part-time work, and reduced or redefined job expectations. Exploration seems to be taking two directions at the same time. One looks at how to retain older workers in meaningful work roles. The other explores ways of permitting more flexible, earlier retirement (Herzog et al., 1991).

Several long-range concerns suggest a need to reexamine the "right-to-retirement" concept. First, prospects for a longer, healthier adulthood mean that a large proportion of the population will be out of the labor force for nearly one-third of their adult lives. With a reduced fertility rate, there may not be enough younger workers available to support this large nonworking population. In addition, it is becoming increasingly difficult to see how one can earn enough during the 40 or so years of employment to pay for the 20 or more years of retirement. Second, many older adults who are well educated and who have enjoyed their work lives want to continue some of the positive experiences of employment through constructive work. They do not really want to retire, and with the lifting of the mandatory retirement age, they do not have to. We are already beginning to sense some of this resistance in the attitudes of professionals in their 50s and 60s. In in-depth interviews with university professors, physicians, lawyers, business professionals, and social service professionals, over 35% were very negative about retiring and another 20% were ambivalent. One of those who was quite negative expressed it this way:

> "I'd probably try to get part-time teaching jobs, writing or editing, or research somewhere until I fall over. I mean really, I just can't imagine [retirement]. . . . This teaching is a rewarding activity. I don't hanker to retire to the sun belt and sit around and contemplate my navel. I just couldn't do that." (Karp, 1989, p. 752)

Third, people who reenter the labor force during midlife or who make major midlife career changes will want to persist in these new activities in order to fulfill both personal and societal expectations of achievement (Horn, 1980; Ragan, 1980). The recent generation of older workers, in their 50s and 60s, have become used to a more fluctuating work history, moving from one company to another or from one type of employer to another. They are more accustomed to taking charge of their occupational career, rather than relying on the built-in career ladder of a single occupation or employer. Thus, just as the past few generations have begun to grow accustomed to retirement, the new generation of older adults is finding ways to prolong their productive work lives and to negotiate new and innovative ways of making transitions in and out of the paid labor force.

Chapter Summary

Variability in the patterns of adjustment during later adulthood results from the interaction between the individual's personality characteristics, coping strategies, and ego strengths and the range of circumstances that may befall him or her. Certain regularities can be anticipated in the termination of old roles and the establishment of new ones. Consolidation of attitudes toward one's own life and toward the reality of one's own death brings about a new perspective on life and leads to a more universalistic moral orientation.

The tasks of later adulthood—promoting intellectual vigor, redirecting energy to new roles and activities, accepting one's life, and developing a point of view about death—require a balance among investments in past, present, and future. There is an expectation that energy will be spent in the evaluative process of reviewing and accepting one's past achievements. However, this focus on the past must be complemented by the enactment of new roles, the resolution of new problems, and efforts to find new and engaging challenges in the present.

The role transitions that accompany retirement illustrate the challenge of later adulthood. Retirement usually results in the giving up of a major life structure, one that provides social status, focus, purpose, and economic resources. The potential loss of daily stimulation poses threats to both cognitive and social functioning. Because so much of one's social status is linked to one's occupational attainment, giving up one's work role is almost like giving up one's social identity. Older adults face numerous demands as they face this and other instances of role loss. They must restructure their lives so that they continue to feel pride in past achievements without dwelling in the past, and so that they seek new and realistic opportunities for making use of their talents in the present.

It is critical to be sensitive to the image that children, adolescents, young and middle-aged adults, and older adults themselves have of later adulthood. We should not underestimate the impact that one's perceptions of later life have on well-being and optimism at every earlier life stage. If the later years hold no promise, all earlier stages will be tinted with a sense of desperation. If the later years can be anticipated with optimism, we will be free at each earlier stage to experience our lives in a more confident and accepting manner.

References

Anthony, S. (1972). *The discovery of death in childhood and after.* New York: Basic Books.

Arbuckle, T. Y., Gold, D. P., Andres, D., Schwartzman, A. & Chaikelson, J. (1992). The role of psychosocial context, age, and intelligence in memory performance of older men. *Psychology and Aging, 7,* 25–36.

Atchley, R. C. (1976). *The sociology of retirement.* New York: Halsted.

Atchley, R. C. (1977). *The social forces of later life.* Belmont, CA: Wadsworth.

Barrett, C. J. (1981). Intimacy in widowhood. *Psychology of Women Quarterly, 5,* 473–487.

Bass, D. M. & Bowman, K. (1990). The transition from caregiving to bereavement: The relationship of care-related strain and adjustment to death. *Gerontologist, 30,* 35–42.

Bearon, L. G. (1989). No great expectations: The underpinnings of life satisfaction for older women. *Gerontologist, 29,* 772–778.

Beck, S. H. (1984). Retirement preparation programs: Differentials in opportunity and use. *Journal of Gerontology, 39,* 596–602.

Bengston, V. L., Cuellar, J. B. & Ragan, P. K. (1977). Stratum contrasts and similarities in attitudes toward death. *Journal of Gerontology, 32,* 76–88.

Blackburn, J. A. (1984). The influence of personality, curriculum, and memory correlates on formal reasoning in young adults and elderly persons. *Journal of Gerontology, 39,* 207–209.

Botwinick, J. (1984). *Aging and behavior* (3rd ed.). New York: Springer.

Bound, J., Duncan, G. J., Laren, D. S. & Oleinick, L. (1991). Poverty dynamics in widowhood. *Journal of Gerontology, 46,* S115–S124.

Brim, G. (1992). *Ambition.* New York: Basic Books.

Bryer, K. B. (1979). The Amish way of death: A study of family support systems. *American Psychologist, 34,* 255–261.

Caplan, G. (1964). *Principles of preventive psychiatry.* New York: Basic Books.

Cherlin, A. J. & Furstenberg, F. F. (1986/1992). *The new American grandparent: A place in the family, a life apart.* Cambridge: Harvard University Press.

Conte, H. R., Weiner, M. B. & Plutchik, R. (1982). Measuring death anxiety: Conceptual, psychometric, and factor-analytic aspects. *Journal of Personality and Social Psychology*, 43, 775–785.

Costa, P. T. & McCrae, R. R. (1980). The influence of extraversion and neuroticism on subjective well-being: Happy and unhappy people. *Journal of Personality and Social Psychology*, 38, 668–678.

Costa, P. T., Zonderman, A. B., McCrae, R. R., Coroni-Huntley, J., Locke, B. Z. & Barbano, H. E. (1987). Longitudinal analyses of psychological well-being in a national sample: Stability of mean levels. *Journal of Gerontology*, 42(1), 50–55.

Denney, N. W. (1982). Aging and cognitive changes. In B. B. Wolman (Ed.), *Handbook of developmental psychology* (pp. 807–827). Englewood Cliffs, NJ: Prentice-Hall.

Denney, N. W. & Pearce, K. A. (1989). A developmental study of practical problem solving in adults. *Psychology and Aging*, 4, 438–442.

Dennis, W. (1966). Creative productivity between the ages of twenty and eighty years. *Journal of Gerontology*, 21, 1–8.

DeVries, H. A. (1975). Physiology of exercise. In D. S. Woodruff & J. E. Birren (Eds.), *Aging: Scientific perspectives and social issues*. New York: Van Nostrand.

Ekerdt, D. J., Bosse, R. & Levkoff, S. (1985). An empirical test for phases of retirement: Findings from the normative aging study. *Journal of Gerontology*, 40, 95–101.

Erikson, E., Erikson, J. & Kivnick, H. (1986). *Vital involvement in old age*. New York: Norton.

Feifel, H. & Branscomb, A. (1973). Who's afraid of death? *Journal of Abnormal Psychology*, 81, 282–288.

Ferraro, K. F. (1990). Cohort analysis of retirement preparation, 1974–1981. *Journal of Gerontology*, 45, S25.

Flanagan, J. C. (1978). A research approach to improving our quality of life. *American Psychologist*, 33, 138–147.

Flanagan, J. C. (1980). Quality of life. In L. A. Bond & J. C. Rosen (Eds.), *Competence and coping during adulthood* (pp. 156–177). Hanover, NH: University Press of New England.

Fletcher, W. L. & Hansson, R. O. (1991). Assessing the social components of retirement anxiety. *Psychology and Aging*, 6, 76–85.

Florian, V. & Kravetz, S. (1983). Fear of personal death: Attribution structure and relation to religious belief. *Journal of Personality and Social Psychology*, 44, 600–607.

Floyd, F. J., Haynes, S. N., Doll, E. R., Winemiller, D., Lemsky, C., Burgy, T. M., Werle, M. & Heilman, N. (1992). Assessing retirement satisfaction and perceptions of retirement experiences. *Psychology and Aging*, 7, 609–621.

Fozard, J. L. & Poon, L. W. (1976). *Research and training activities of the mental performance and aging laboratory* (1973–1976). Technical Report 76-02. Boston: Veterans Administration Outpatient Clinic.

Fried-Cassorla, M. (1977). *Death anxiety and disengagement*. Paper presented at the annual convention of the American Psychological Association, San Francisco.

Futterman, A., Gallagher, D., Thompson, L. W., Lovett, S. & Gilewski, M. (1990). Retrospective assessment of marital adjustment and depression during the first two years of spousal bereavement. *Psychology and Aging*, 5, 277–283.

Guangzhao, Z. (1985). Retirement age for Chinese scientists. *Science*, 230, 738.

Hayslip, B., Jr. & Brookshire, R. G. (1985). Relationships among abilities in elderly adults: A time lag analysis. *Journal of Gerontology*, 40, 748–750.

Heatherington, E. M., Cox, M. & Cox, R. (1985). Long-term effects of divorce and remarriage on the adjustment of children. *Journal of the American Academy of Psychiatry*, 24, 518–530.

Heatherington, E. M., Stanley-Hagan, M. & Anderson, E. R. (1989). Marital transitions: A child's perspective. *American Psychologist*, 44, 303–312.

Hendrick, C., Wells, K. S. & Faletti, M. V. (1982). Social and emotional effects of geographical relocation on elderly retirees. *Journal of Personality and Social Psychology*, 42, 951–962.

Hertzog, D. & Schaie, K. W. (1988). Stability and change in adult intelligence: 2. Simultaneous analysis of longitudinal means and covariance structures. *Psychology and Aging*, 3, 122–130.

Herzog, A. R., House, J. S. & Morgan, J. N. (1991). Relation of work and retirement to health and well-being in older age. *Psychology and Aging*, 6, 202–211.

Hopkins, D. R., Murrah, B., Hoeger, W. W. K. & Rhodes, R. C. (1990). Effect of low-impact aerobic dance on the functional fitness of elderly women. *Gerontologist*, 30, 189–192.

Horn, J. L. (1979). The rise and fall of human abilities. *Journal of Research and Development in Education*, 12, 59–78.

Horn, J. L. (1980). On the future of growing old. Paper presented as a university lecture, University of Denver, CO.

Hoyer, W. J. & Rybash, J. M. (1994). Characterizing adult cognitive development. *Journal of Adult Development*, 1, 7–12.

Jahoda, M. (1982). *Employment and unemployment*. Cambridge, England: Cambridge University Press.

Jecker, N. S. & Schneiderman, L. J. (1994). Is dying young worse than dying old? *Gerontologist*, 34, 66–72.

Kahana, B. & Kahana, E. (1970). Grandparenthood from the perspective of the developing grandchild. *Developmental Psychology*, 3, 98–105.

Kahana, B., Kahana, E. & McLenigan, P. (1980). The adventurous aged: Voluntary relocation in the later years. Paper presented at the meeting of the American Orthopsychiatric Association, Toronto.

Kalish, R. A. & Reynolds, D. K. (1976). *Death and ethnicity: A psychocultural study.* Los Angeles: University of Southern California Press.

Karp, D. A. (1989). The social construction of retirement among professionals 50–60 years old. *Gerontologist, 29,* 750–760.

Kart, C. S., Longino, C. F. & Ullmann, S. G. (1989). Comparing the economically advantaged and the pension elite: 1980 census profiles. *Gerontologist, 29,* 745–749.

Kessler, R. C., Foster, C., Webster, P. S. & House, J. S. (1992). The relationship between age and depressive symptoms in two national surveys. *Psychology and Aging, 7,* 119–126.

Kivnick, H. Q. (1983). Dimensions of grandparenthood meaning: Deductive conceptualization and empirical derivation. *Journal of Personality and Social Psychology, 44,* 1056–1068.

Klemmack, D. L. & Roff, L. L. (1984). Fear of personal aging and subjective well-being in later life. *Journal of Gerontology, 39,* 756–758.

Kübler-Ross, E. (1969). *On death and dying.* New York: Macmillan.

Kübler-Ross, E. (1972, February). On death and dying. *Journal of the American Medical Association, 219,* 10–15

Labouvie-Vief, G. & Schell, D. A. (1982). Learning and memory in later life. In B. B. Wolman (Ed.), *Handbook of developmental psychology* (pp. 828–846). Englewood Cliffs, NJ: Prentice-Hall.

Lehman, H. C. (1953). *Age and achievement.* Princeton, NJ: Princeton University Press.

Lewinsohn, P. H., Rohde, P. & Crozier, L. C. (1991). Age and depression: Unique and shared effects. *Psychology and Aging, 6,* 247–260.

Lindemann, E. (1944). Symptomology and management of acute grief. *American Journal of Psychiatry, 101,* 141–148.

Lopata, H. Z. (1973). *Widowhood in an American city.* Cambridge, MA: Schenkman.

Lopata, H. Z. (1978). Widowhood: Social norms and social integration. In H. Z. Lopata (Ed.), *Family factbook.* Chicago: Marquis Academic Media.

McCrae, R. R. & Costa, P. T. (1983). Psychological maturity and subjective well-being: Toward a new synthesis. *Developmental Psychology, 19,* 243–248.

Mead, M. (1975). On grandparents as educators. In H. J. Leichter (Ed.), *The family as educator.* New York: Teachers College Press.

Merriam, S. B. (1989). The structure of simple reminiscence. *Gerontologist, 29,* 761–767.

Meyers, G. C. & Manton, K. G. (1984). Compression of mortality: Myth or reality? *Gerontologist, 24,* 346–353.

Montepare, J. M. & Lachman, M. E. (1989). "You're only as old as you feel": Self-perceptions of age, fears of aging, and life satisfaction from adolescence to old age. *Psychology and Aging, 4,* 73–78.

Morgan, D. M. (1989). Adjusting to widowhood: Do social networks really make it easier? *Gerontologist, 29,* 101–107.

Neugarten, B. & Weinstein, R. (1964). The changing American grandparent. *Journal of Marriage and the Family, 26,* 199–204.

Newman, B. M. & Newman, P. R. (1983). *Understanding adulthood.* New York: Holt, Rinehart & Winston.

O'Bryant, S. (1988). Sibling support and older widows' well-being. *Journal of Marriage and the Family, 50,* 173–183.

O'Bryant, S. L. & Morgan, L. A. (1990). Recent widows' kin support and orientations to self-sufficiency. *The Gerontologist, 30,* 391–398.

O'Leary, V. E. (1977). The widow as female household head. Paper presented at the annual convention of the American Psychological Association, San Francisco.

Palmore, E. B., Fillenbaum, G. G. & George, L. K. (1984). Consequences of retirement. *Journal of Gerontology, 39,* 109–116.

Pierce, C. M. (1989). Unity in diversity: Thirty-three years of stress. In G. L. Berry & J. K. Asamen (Eds.), *Black students.* Newbury Park, CA: Sage.

Poon, L. W. & Fozard, J. L. (1978). Speed in retrieval from long-term memory in relation to age, familiarity, and datedness of information. *Journal of Gerontology, 33,* 711–717.

Presser, H. B. (1989). Some economic complexities of child care provided by grandmothers. *Journal of Marriage and the Family, 51,* 581–591.

Ragan, P. K. (1980). *Work and retirement: Policy issues.* Los Angeles: University of Southern California Press.

Rapkin, B. D. & Fischer, K. (1992a). Framing the construct of life satisfaction in terms of older adults' personal goals. *Psychology and Aging, 7,* 138–149.

Rapkin, B. D. & Fischer, K. (1992b). Personal goals of older adults: Issues in assessment and prediction. *Psychology and Aging, 7,* 127–137.

Reese, H. W. (1976). The development of memory: Life-span perspectives. In H. W. Reese (Ed.), *Advances in child development and behavior* (Vol. 11). New York: Academic Press.

Riegel, K. F. & Riegel, R. M. (1972). Development, drop, and death. *Developmental Psychology, 6,* 306–319.

Robertson, J. F. (1977). Grandmotherhood: A study of role conceptions. *Journal of Marriage and the Family, 39,* 165–174.

Ross, M. (1989). Relation of implicit theories to the construction of personal histories. *Psychological Review, 96,* 341–357.

Ryff, C. D. & Heincke, S. G. (1983). Subjective organization of personality in adulthood and aging. *Journal of Personality and Social Psychology, 44,* 807–816.

Schaie, K. W. (1973). Methodological problems in descriptive developmental research on adulthood and aging. In J. R. Nesselroade & H. W. Reese (Eds.), *Life-span developmental psychology: Methodological issues.* New York: Academic Press.

Schaie, K. W. (1989). Perceptual speed in adulthood: Cross-sectional and longitudinal studies. *Psychology and Aging*, 4, 443–453.

Schaie, K. W. & Hertzog, C. (1983). Fourteen-year cohort-sequential analyses of adult intellectual development. *Developmental Psychology*, 19, 531–543.

Scogin, F., Storandt, M. & Lott, L. (1985). Memory-skills training, memory complaints, and depression in older adults. *Journal of Gerontology*, 40, 562–568.

Selzer, S. C. & Denney, N. W. (1980). Conservation abilities among middle-aged and elderly adults. *Aging and Human Development*, 11, 135–146.

Shay, K. A. & Roth, D. L. (1992). Association between aerobic fitness and visuospatial performance in healthy older adults. *Psychology and Aging*, 7, 15–24.

Simonton, D. K. (1977). Creative productivity, age, and stress: A biographical time-series analysis of ten classical composers. *Journal of Personality and Social Psychology*, 35, 791–804.

Simonton, D. K. (1988). Age and outstanding achievement: What do we know after a century of research? *Psychological Bulletin*, 104, 251–267.

Simonton, D. K. (1989). The swan-song phenomenon: Last-works effects for 172 classical composers. *Psychology and Aging*, 4, 42–47.

Skinner, B. F. (1983). Intellectual self-management in old age. *American Psychologist*, 38, 239–244.

Smith, P. K. (Ed.). (1991). *The psychology of grandparenthood: An international perspective*. London: Routledge.

Sticker, E. J. (1991). The importance of grandparenthood during the life cycle in Germany. In P. K. Smith (Ed.), *The psychology of grandparenthood: An international perspective* (pp. 32–49). London: Routledge.

Swan, G. E., Dame, A. & Carmelli, D. (1991). Involuntary retirement, type A behavior, and current functioning in elderly men: 27-year follow-up of the Western Collaborative Group study. *Psychology and Aging*, 6, 384–391.

Thompson, L. W., Gallagher-Thompson, D., Futterman, A., Gilewski, M. J. & Peterson, J. (1991). The effects of late-life spousal bereavement over a 30-month interval. *Psychology and Aging*, 6, 434–441.

Tinsley, H. E. A., Teaff, J. D., Colbs, S. L. & Kaufman, N. (1985). System of classifying leisure activities in terms of the psychological benefits of participation reported by older persons. *Journal of Gerontology*, 40, 172–178.

Tolson, T. F. J. & Wilson, M. N. (1990). The impact of two- and three-generational black family structure on perceived family climate. *Child Development*, 61, 416–428.

Tomlin, A. M. & Passman, R. H. (1989). Grandmothers' responsibility in raising two-year-olds facilitates their grandchildren's adaptive behavior: A preliminary intrafamilial investigation of mothers' and maternal grandmothers' effects. *Psychology and Aging*, 4, 119–121.

Tomlin, A. M. & Passman, R. H. (1991). Grandmothers' advice about disciplining grandchildren: Is it accepted by mothers, and does its rejection influence grandmothers' subsequent guidance? *Psychology and Aging*, 6, 182–189.

Tran, T. V., Wright, R. & Chatters, L. (1991). Health, stress, psychological resources, and subjective well-being among older blacks. *Psychology and Aging*, 6, 100–108.

U.S. Bureau of the Census. (1983). *America in transition: An aging society*. Current Population Reports (Ser. P-23, No. 128). Washington, DC: U.S. Government Printing Office.

U.S. Bureau of the Census. (1989). *Population profile of the United States, 1989*. Current Population Reports (Ser. P-23, No. 159). Washington, DC: U.S. Government Printing Office.

U.S. Bureau of the Census. (1992). *Statistical abstract of the United States*. Washington DC: U.S. Government Printing Office.

U.S. Senate, Special Committee on Aging. (1986). *Aging America—Trends and projections*. Washington, DC: U.S. Government Printing Office.

Ward, R. A. (1977). The impact of subjective age and stigma on older persons. *Journal of Gerontology*, 32, 227–232.

Werner, E. E. (1991). Grandparent-grandchild relationships amongst U.S. ethnic groups. In P. K. Smith (Ed.), *The psychology of grandparenthood: An international perspective* (pp. 68–82). London: Routledge.

West, R. L., Crook, T. H. & Barron, K. L. (1992). Everyday memory performance across the life span: Effects of age and noncognitive individual differences. *Psychology and Aging*, 7, 72–82.

White, N. & Cunningham, W. R. (1988). Is terminal drop pervasive or specific? *Journal of Gerontology: Psychological Sciences*, 43, P141–P144.

Wingfield, A., Poon, L. W., Lombardi, L. & Lowe, D. (1985). Speed of processing in normal aging: Effects of speech rate, linguistic structure, and processing time. *Journal of Gerontology*, 40, 579–585.

Wong, P. T. P. & Watt, L. M. (1991). What types of reminiscence are associated with successful aging? *Psychology and Aging*, 6, 272–279.

Zick, C. D. & Smith, K. R. (1991). Patterns of economic change surrounding the death of a spouse. *Journal of Gerontology*, 46, S310–S320.

CHAPTER 14

Father Christmas is a perfect representative of the very old.
He has all the benefits of extreme old age, but he is ever
young in spirit; in fact he is immortal.

Very Old Age
(75 Until Death)

P ablo Picasso, whose works illustrate this book, lived to be 91 years old. When he was 79 he married Jacqueline Roque, with whom he enjoyed 12 years of married life. During the last 20 years of his life, he remained productive and energetic, persistently experimenting with new art forms and ideas.

Here are some other examples of people who achieved major accomplishments after age 80 (Wallechinsky, Wallace & Wallace, 1977; Wallechinsky & Wallace, 1993):

At 100, Grandma Moses was still painting.

At 99, David Eugene Ray of Franklin, Tennessee, started to learn to read.

At 99, twin sisters Kin Narita and Gin Kanie recorded a hit CD single in Japan and starred in a television commercial.

At 94, Bertrand Russell was active in international peace drives.

At 94, George Burns, who won an Oscar at age 80 for his role in the *Sunshine Boys*, performed at Proctor's Theater in Schenectady, New York, 63 years after he had first played there.

At 93, George Bernard Shaw wrote the play *Farfetched Fables*.

At 93, actress Dame Judith Anderson gave a one-hour benefit performance.

At 91, Eamon de Valera served as president of Ireland.

At 91, Adolph Zukor was chairman of Paramount Pictures.

At 91, Hulda Crooks climbed Mount Whitney, the highest mountain in the continental United States.

At 89, Albert Schweitzer headed a hospital in Africa.

At 89, Arthur Rubenstein gave one of his greatest recitals in New York's Carnegie Hall.

At 88, Michelangelo did architectural plans for the Church of Santa Maria degli Angeli.

At 88, Konrad Adenauer was chancellor of Germany.

At 87, Mary Baker Eddy founded the *Christian Science Monitor*.

At 85, Coco Chanel was the head of a fashion design firm.

At 84, W. Somerset Maugham wrote *Points of View*.

At 82, Leo Tolstoy wrote I *Cannot Be Silent*.

At 81, Benjamin Franklin effected the compromise that led to the adoption of the U.S. Constitution.

At 81, Johann Wolfgang von Goethe finished *Faust*.

We are entering a period of human experience in which increasing numbers of people are living into old age. In 1991, 5.3% of the U.S. population was 75 and over. This age group is expected to make up 10% of the population in 50 years. In 1980, over 2 million people were 85 and over; by 1991, this group had grown to 3.1 million. The 85-and-over population is the fastest-growing age group in the United States. This group is expected to triple in size from 1980 to 2020 (U.S. Bureau of the Census, 1989a, 1992; U.S. Senate, Special Committee on Aging, 1986). Every morning on television, Willard Scott wishes happy birthday to men and women who are 100 years old or more.

As more and more people live to be 75 and over, questions continue to be raised regarding the upper limit of the human life span. Meyers and Manton (1984) demonstrated that the most enduring members of each new generation of aging adults appear to be living longer and longer. *Life endurance* is the age to which 1 person in 100,000 can be expected to survive. Between 1900 and 1980, the age of the most enduring adults in the U.S. population increased from 105 to 111 for men and from 105 to 114 for women. Current evidence does not support the view of a fixed upper limit to the human life span.

Frank and Palmina Canovi, both over 100 years old, were born in Italy, married in 1910, and currently live in Seattle, Washington.

As more people reach very old age, tasks and psychosocial competencies emerge that have not yet been systematically delineated. We need to examine and understand the psychosocial competencies and needs of this population in order to maintain the quality of their lives and help younger people form a picture of what they may expect as they get older.

The variations in life experiences and outlook among the very old are great. Chronological age becomes less useful as an indicator of aging. Neugarten (1981) found it useful to distinguish between two groups of the very old: the old-old and the young-old. The old-old have "suffered major physical or mental decrements," which increase their dependence on health and social services. This group will grow as the number of adults over 75 increases. At present, it forms a minority of the very old. The majority of people over 75 can be described as the young-old. They are competent, vigorous, and relatively healthy. They live in their own households and participate in activities in their communities.

Each new cohort of the very old will benefit from the information and technology that have been developed during this century. Those adults who will be over 75 in the year 2000 are quite likely to be high school graduates, to have benefited from many of the educational and health-related innovations of the mid-20th century, and to be even more vigorous than our current older population.

Jewett (1973) described lifestyle characteristics that are common among people whom he called long-living, successful agers, based on observations of 79 individuals between 87 and 103 years of age. Such people are able to maintain social contacts that meet their needs and satisfy their interests. They pursue activities that challenge and intrigue them and that are consistent with their life goals. They are well able to adapt to changing events and life situations, a trait to which Jewett referred as an ability to "roll with the punches." They are religious in the broadest sense of the term. They have a well-developed sense of humor, and they enjoy life.

Guralnik and Kaplan (1989) described the predictive factors of middle adulthood that were linked to healthy aging. Data, collected in 1974, 1982, and 1984, were reported on a sample born between 1895 and 1919. Those who were in the top 20% of healthy functioning in later adulthood had average weight, higher family income, and no symptoms of hypertension, arthritis, or back pain; they did not smoke; and they consumed an average amount of alcohol. Physical activity could not be evaluated as a predictor in this study since physical activity, including any sports, exercise, walking, swimming, vigorous aerobic exercise, or calisthenics or stretching exercise, was included as a selection variable that differentiated the top group of older adults from the others.

In an attempt to learn the secrets of longevity, Jim Heynen (1990) interviewed 100 people who were 100 years or older. He found wide variation in the lifestyles and philosophical perspectives of these centenarians. Here is some of the advice they offer on how to live a long life:

- "Mind your own business, have a good cigar, and take a shot of brandy." —*Brother Adelard Beaudet, Harrisville, Rhode Island*
- "I've lived long because I was so mean."—*Pearl Rombach, Melbourne, Florida*
- "I always walked several miles a day. I'd talk to the flowers."—*Mary Frances Annand, Pasadena, California*
- "Don't smoke before noon. Don't drink or smoke after midnight. The body needs 12 hours of the day to clear itself."—*Harry Wander, Boise, Idaho*
- "I've been a tofu eater all my life; a mild, gentle man, never a worrier."—*Frank Morimitsu, Chicago, Illinois*
- "I picked my ancestors carefully."—*Stella H. Harris, Manhattan, Kansas*
- "Regular hours, taking it easy, smiling, whistling at the women when they walk by."—*John Hilton, Fort Lauderdale, Florida*

The fact that an increasing number of people are reaching advanced years and that they share several characteristics leads us to hypothesize a new stage of psychosocial development that emerges at the upper end of the life span after one has exceeded the life expectancy for one's birth cohort. We call this stage *very old age*. This stage was not specifically identified in Erikson's original formulation of life stages. In his *Vital Involvement in Old Age* (Erikson, Erikson & Kivnick, 1986), however, he began to characterize the dynamics of psychosocial adaptation in this period of life. With the encouragement of many colleagues who teach the human development course and are interested in dealing with this period, we have formulated a psychosocial analysis of development for the very old. We have drawn on research literature, firsthand reports, and personal observations of the very old to describe the developmental tasks, psychosocial crisis, and central process of this stage. We approach this formulation of a new stage realizing full well that, in many domains, especially physical functioning, reaction time, memory, and fluid intelligence, variability increases significantly with age (Morse, 1993). There are many reasons that increasing individual differences may be noted during later life:

> The combined effects of individuals' unique experiences over more years would produce increasing differences among them; genetically based differences would have more time to be expressed and to cause individuals to diverge; and older people, somewhat freer of societal constraints, would be more likely to choose their own courses of action. (Morse, 1993, p. 156)

The concept of reaction range, which was introduced in Chapter 4, seems useful here as a way of understanding the enormous variability in vitality and functioning during very old age. Given one's genetically defined reaction range, the conditions of poverty, discrimination, social alienation, and lack of social support are likely to be linked to lower levels of functioning in relation to one's potential and to greater vulnerability to the restrictive impact of illness in later life. Adequate finances, social integration, social support, and access to appropriate services are likely to be linked to higher levels of functioning in relation to one's potential and to greater resilience in the face of illness.

Our intention is to discuss some of the most salient characteristics of life after 75 and to articulate what appears to be a psychosocial crisis peculiar to this period. We are looking for evidence of common challenges and successful strategies for coping with these challenges amid the great diversity of individual experiences.

Developmental Tasks

Coping with the Physical Changes of Aging

There is no way to avoid the realization that one's body is not what it used to be:

> With aging, as the overall tonus of the body begins to sag and innumerable inner parts call attention to themselves through their malfunction, the aging body is forced into a new sense of invalidness. Some problems may be fairly petty, like the almost inevitable appearance of wrinkles. Others are painful, debilitating, and shaming. Whatever the severity of these ailments, the elder is obliged to turn attention from more interesting aspects of life to the demanding requirements of the body. This can be frustrating and depressing. (Erikson et al., 1986, p. 309)

There is a great deal of variation in fitness among people after age 70 as patterns of activity or inactivity, endurance or frailty, and illness or health take their toll. Most people's strength and capacity for moderate effort are about the same at age 70 as they were at age 40 (Marshall, 1973). However, older people are less resilient after a period of prolonged exertion. Their respiratory and circulatory systems usually degenerate to some extent, so that they are less capable of providing the heart and muscle tissue with oxygenated blood as quickly as they once could. One result is that sudden changes in posture may leave an older person feeling lightheaded. In order to adapt successfully to this kind of bodily change, the older person may find it necessary to move more slowly and to change positions more deliberately. This observable change in the tempo of movement may be incorrectly interpreted as fatigue or weakness; in fact, it is often a purposeful strategy for preventing dizziness.

Slowed metabolism reduces the need for calories, but there is a new risk. Reduction in food intake—particularly the elimination of foods such as milk—may cause essential vitamins and minerals to be missing from an older person's diet. Malnutrition may contribute to feelings of weakness and a lack of resilience. These effects may mistakenly be attributed to the aging process. In order to cope successfully with a diminished appetite, the very old person must become more conscientious in selecting foods that will provide the nutritional elements necessary for healthy functioning.

An increasing number of factors make it difficult to maintain a high level of physical fitness in later life. Figure 14.1 illustrates patterns of the loss of bodily functions associated with age in six areas. For each body area, the level of functioning at age 30 is taken as 100%, and the losses are plotted in comparison with this level. As you can see, maximum breathing capacity suffers the greatest loss, and brain weight changes the least. Most of the bodily changes begin in middle adulthood, but the rate of change appears to increase after age 60. The

Average function remaining (percent age)

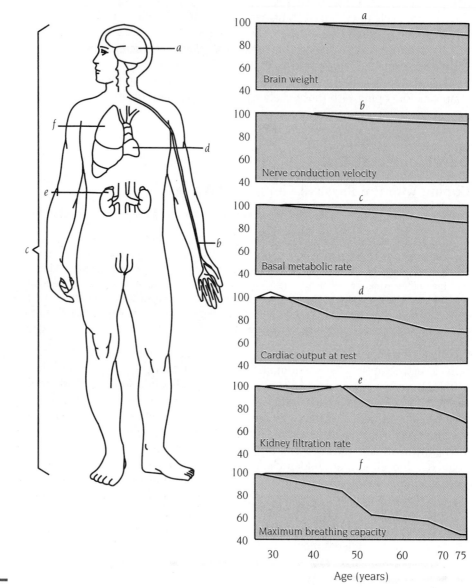

FIGURE 14.1

Loss of bodily functions with increasing age
Source: Leaf, 1973.

consequences of an inactive life, especially obesity and degeneration in muscle strength, contribute to an even greater decline in physical capacity, particularly after age 60.

Being consciously committed to the value of physical fitness is very important for adults. In order to face the later years in the best possible physical condition, adults must keep themselves in shape. Maintenance of optimal physical condition in very old age depends on being active in earlier periods of adulthood. Overweight people, as well as those of normal or below-normal weight, need to commit themselves to a program of physical activity and to realize that it is possible to continue a moderate level of physical activity throughout life.

With advancing age, some people tend to become more sedentary and to lose interest in physical activity. In order to maintain optimal functioning and

Recreational therapy can involve aerobic exercise. Here, very old people with limited mobility enjoy exercising their arms and upper bodies as they work together to keep the ball bouncing and floating.

to retard the degenerative effects of aging, very old adults must continue to have frequent and regular opportunities for physical activity. A regular program of aerobic exercise, for example, may enhance cardiovascular functioning and reverse some of the effects of a sedentary adult lifestyle (Blumenthal et al., 1989). Experimental studies of the effects of exercise on cognitive functioning show that exercise leads to improvements in various central nervous system functions. The benefits of exercise are attributed to higher levels of oxygen, which improve the metabolism of glucose and neurotransmitters in the brain, as well as to increased levels of arousal, which increase response speed (Dustman et al., 1989; Birren & Fisher, 1992).

Behavioral Slowing

One of the most commonly noted markers of aging is a gradual slowing in response to stimuli. Such *behavioral slowing* is observed in motor responses, reaction time, problem-solving abilities, memory skills, and information processing (Salthouse, 1985; Bashore, Osman & Heffley, 1989; Birren & Fisher, 1992). We can think of the speed of behavior as the composite outcome of the time it takes to perceive a stimulus, retrieve related information from memory, integrate it with other relevant stored information, reason as necessary about the required action, and take action, whether that action is simply pressing a button or performing a surgical procedure. Age-related slowing is more readily observable in complex tasks requiring mental processing than in routine tasks. The more complex the task, the greater the processing load—that is, the more domains of information called into play and the more work necessary to select response strategies (Cerella, 1994). Meta-analyses that combine the results of a variety of studies over a wide range of tasks find that the response time for older subjects (60–75 years old) is a linear function of the response time of younger subjects (16–25 years

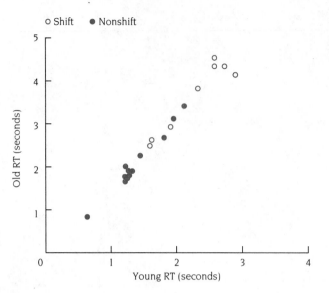

FIGURE 14.2

The relationship of response time of older subjects to that of younger subjects

Notes: *This type of plot, which relates the mean response time for older and younger subjects, was first reported by J. F. Brinley and is now known as a Brinley plot.*

The shift tasks were more complex than the nonshift tasks. In the shift tasks, the subjects had to change their mode of response from one problem to the next.

Source: *Perfect, 1994.*

old). The idea is that the greater the processing load, the longer it takes younger subjects to respond, and that the response time of older subjects increases in a linear relationship to the response time of younger subjects (Perfect, 1994) (see Figure 14.2).

To explain why behavioral slowing occurs, biological, learned, and motivational factors have been suggested. At the biological level of analysis, there is evidence of the slowing of neural firing in certain brain areas, which may result in slower responses. Slowing may also be a product of learned cautiousness. With experience, people learn to respond slowly in order to avoid making mistakes. Finally, slow responses may be a product of a low level of motivation to perform a task. In experimental situations in which reaction time is being tested, adult subjects may be uninterested in the task and unwilling to attempt to achieve a high level of functioning.

The implications of the consequences of behavioral slowing are currently being examined. Some argue that even the slightest reduction in the speed of neural firing may result in reduced sensory and information-processing capacities. Slowness may reduce a person's chances of survival if a situation arises in which a sudden evasive action or an immediate response is required. Others suggest that, if a moment of thought is required before an action is taken, slowness may increase a person's chances of survival.

A more common consequence of slowing is its impact on cognitive functioning. If the nervous system functions at a slowed rate, it takes more time to scan and perceive information, more time to search long-term memory, more time to integrate information from various knowledge domains, and more time to make a response. With increased input each year, it is possible that the time needed for processing information increases. In the face of complex cognitive tasks, information may be lost, or distractions may intervene if the process takes too long (Birren & Fisher, 1992). For example, Hertzog (1989) examined the relationship of age and speed of performance in a variety of mental abilities among subjects ranging in age from 43 to 89. He found that the speed-of-performance measure was a better predictor of mental abilities than was age. Other research looked at crystallized and fluid intelligence (Horn, 1982). You will recall from Chapter 13 that crystallized intelligence tends to increase with age, whereas fluid intelligence declines with age. When the factor of speed of responding was removed from the tests of fluid intelligence, the decline with age was significantly less. These studies support the claim that changes in speed of responding account for much, although probably not all, of the documented evidence about declines in intellectual performance with age. The debate continues, however, about whether this slowing is general, influencing all types of cognitive activity, or if it is specific to certain domains. Further, there is considerable evidence that contemporary circumstances, especially physical fitness and health, as well as the kinds of medications one is taking and the presence of immediate stressors in one's life, influence speed of responding (Willis et al., 1990).

Since slowing occurs gradually, most adults can compensate for it by making their environments more convenient or by changing their lifestyles. Slowing becomes more hazardous in situations that require the older adult to keep pace with a tempo that cannot be modified, as in the problems some older people encounter because of the amount of time given to cross a street at a green light. For many older adults and others with physical impairments, the amount of time the light stays green is insufficient to permit them to get to the other side of the street safely.

As older people recognize some situations in which they have trouble responding quickly, they must review the tempo of their day. The very old need to become more selective in their choice of activities so that they can allocate enough time for the tasks most important to them and perform them to their own satisfaction. This means exercising greater control over their time and being less concerned about whether they are in harmony with the tempo of others.

Sensory Changes

Every sense modality—vision, hearing, taste, touch, and smell—is vulnerable to age-related changes. With age, greater intensity of stimulation is required to make the same impact on the sensory system that was once achieved with lower levels of stimulation. Some changes in the sensory systems of vision, hearing, taste, and smell are seen in Table 14.1. These changes begin in early adulthood, and their effects increase throughout the remainder of life.

Vision   Visual adaptation involves the ability to adapt to changes in the level of illumination. Pupil size decreases with age, so that less light reaches the retina. Older adults need higher levels of illumination to see clearly. It takes them longer to adjust from dark to light and from light to dark. Many older adults find that they are increasingly sensitive to glare. They may draw the shades in their rooms to prevent bright light from striking their eyes. Slower adaptation time and sensitivity to glare also interfere with night driving. Some of the visual problems that are noted by people over 75 are difficulty with tasks that require speed of visual performance, such as reading signs in a moving vehicle; a decline in near vision, which interferes with reading and daily tasks; and difficulties in searching for or tracking visual information (Kosnik et al., 1988).

Several physiological conditions seriously impair vision and may result in partial or total blindness in old age. These conditions include cataracts, which are films covering the lenses, making them less penetrable by light; deterioration or detachment of the retina; and glaucoma, which is an increase in pressure from the fluid in the eyeball. Recent innovations have made cataract surgery much less stressful than it was in the past. In many cases, the hardened lens is removed

TABLE 14.1   Changes in Sensory Systems After Age 20

Age Group	Vision	Hearing	Taste and Smell
20–35	Constant decline in accommodation as lenses begin to harden at about age 20	Pitch discrimination for high-frequency tones begins to decline	No documented changes
35–65	Sharp decline in acuity after 40; delayed adjustment to shifts in light and dark	Continued gradual loss in pitch discrimination to age 50	Loss of taste buds begins
65+	Sensitivity to glare; increased problems with daily visual tasks; increases in diseases of the eye that produce partial or total blindness	Sharp loss in pitch discrimination after 70; sound must be more intense to be heard	Higher thresholds for detecting sour, salt, and bitter tastes; higher threshold for detecting smells, and errors in identifying odors

Source: Based on Newman & Newman, 1983.

and replaced with an artificial lens. In other cases, the person is fitted with contact lenses. Recovery of normal vision is now quite likely as long as the eyes are healthy in other respects (Clayman, 1989).

Loss of vision poses serious challenges to adaptation. It has the effect of separating people from contact with the world. Such impairment is especially linked with feelings of helplessness. Most older adults are not ready to cope with the challenge of learning to function in their daily world without being able to see. Loss of vision reduces activity level, autonomy, and the willingness to leave a familiar setting.

Hearing   Hearing loss increases with age. About 50% of people who are 85 years old or older say they have some hearing impairment (U.S. Bureau of the Census, 1989b). The most common effects of hearing loss are a reduced sensitivity to both high-frequency (high-pitched) and low-intensity (quiet) sounds and a somewhat decreased ability to understand spoken messages. Certain environmental factors, including exposure to loud, unpredictable noise, and life injuries, such as damage to the bones in the middle ear, influence the extent of hearing loss.

Loss of hearing interferes with a basic mode of human connectedness: the ability to participate in conversation. Hearing impairment may be linked to increased feelings of isolation or suspiciousness. When hearing is diminished, a person may hear things imperfectly, miss parts of conversations, or perceive conversations as occurring in whispers rather than in ordinary tones.

The very old adult who is aware of these facts may be able to compensate intellectually for diminished auditory sensitivity. Knowing the people one is with and believing that one is valued in that group can help reassure a person about the nature of conversations and allay suspicions. Self-esteem plays an important part in this process. The older person with high self-esteem is likely to be able to make the intellectual adjustment needed to interpret interactions and to request clarification when necessary. Such requests may even serve to stimulate greater interaction and produce greater clarity in communication. Older people with high self-esteem will insist that those who desire interaction consider their hearing impairment and face them as they speak.

Older people who have low self-esteem are likely to be more vulnerable to suspicions about the behavior of others because they doubt their own worth. They are more likely to perceive inaudible comments as attempts to ridicule or exclude them. These experiences contribute to feelings of rejection. They may produce irritability and social withdrawal.

Taste and Smell   There are wide variations in the density of taste receptors among adult humans. With age, the number of taste buds decreases. Older adults have a higher threshold than young adults for detecting sour, bitter, and salty tastes. Some of this reduced sensitivity may be related to the impact of certain medications or poor oral hygiene. An especially important implication of insensitivity to salt is that older adults may add salt to their food and thereby aggravate hypertension (Spitzer, 1988; Miller, 1988). Older adults also require greater intensity to detect odors and are more likely to misidentify odors (Stevens & Cain, 1987). Changes in the senses of smell and taste may result in a loss of appetite or a disruption of normal eating habits. Loss of appetite (which may accompany illness and new medications), pain due to dental problems, and changes in the digestive system contribute to malnutrition among the elderly.

These patterns of change are trends. They do not occur at the same rate in every person, nor does every person experience all of them. Older adults are much more diverse in their sensory acuity than young adults are.

You probably know older adults who are more vigorous and zestful than you are. You probably also know older adults who are painfully limited in their ability to function because of physical disabilities. Many factors influence the progression of physical changes associated with aging, not the least of which is the level of fitness that was established and maintained during early and middle adulthood.

As a result of the various patterns of aging among this very old group, it is impossible to prescribe an ideal pattern of coping. What one hopes to achieve is a balance between self-sufficiency and a willingness to accept help that preserves as much as possible of the person's dignity and optimizes day-to-day mobility:

> Appropriate dependence can be accommodated and accepted by elders when they realistically appraise their own physical capacities. One of our more practical elders simply states, "Of course, you're still interested in everything. But you don't expect yourself to do everything, the way you used to. Some things you just have to let go." However, inappropriate restriction can be, in its way, insulting and belittling. In describing his current life, one widowed man expresses both his refusal to accept restriction and his willingness to rely on appropriate assistance: "I can stay up here in the woods because I know if I really need help, my son will be here inside of three hours. Now, this deal with fixing my own water pipes, I'd have never tried that without my son so nearby, and I didn't even need him." (Erikson et al., 1986, pp. 309–310)

Illness and Health

Illnesses may be either acute or chronic. *Acute illnesses* usually begin suddenly and last a brief time. Some familiar acute illnesses are colds, measles, and flu. *Chronic illnesses* last a long time. They may be characterized by periods of intense illness followed by periods of remission, or they may grow progressively worse. Arthritis, hypertension, and diabetes are all chronic illnesses.

Pablo Picasso, Portrait of Renoir, *1919. For Renoir, severe arthritis became a major barrier to daily functioning. It is said that he would bind the paintbrush to his hand with twine in order to continue to work.*

Over 80% of people over age 65 have at least one chronic condition, and multiple conditions are common. Table 14.2 shows the rate (persons per 1000 in the age group) of some chronic conditions among persons aged 65–74 and those aged 75 and older (U.S. Bureau of the Census, 1992). About 45% of people aged 85 and older say they cannot perform some major function because of a chronic illness (U.S. Bureau of the Census, 1991).

One consequence of having to cope with chronic diseases is that perceptions of well-being and health change in later life. Rather than judging their health in terms of the absence of symptoms, many older adults are likely to say that they have "good days" and "bad days."

Changes in Functioning with Advanced Age

Do people generally experience rapid general decline after age 65 or 70? A longitudinal study of older adults helps to answer this question (Palmore, Nowlin & Wang, 1985). A group of older men and women who were studied in 1972 were interviewed again between 1980 and 1983. The average age of the group at the time of follow-up was 81. Five areas were evaluated: social functioning, economic stability, mental health, physical health, and the ability to perform the activities of daily living.

The group as a whole experienced no significant decline in social functioning or economic stability over the ten-year period. There were declines in mental and physical health and in the ability to perform the activities of daily living. These declines were moderate. For example, for the activities of daily living, the average

TABLE 14.2 Rate of Chronic Conditions per 1000 Adults 65–74 and 75 Years and Over, 1989		
	Age	
Chronic Condition	**65–74 Yrs.**	**75 Yrs. and Over**
Heart conditions	231.6	353.0
High blood pressure (hypertension)	383.8	375.6
Varicose veins of lower extremities	72.6	86.6
Hemorrhoids	77.4	57.5
Chronic bronchitis	54.2	57.6
Asthma	57.3	42.3
Chronic sinusitis	151.8	155.8
Hay fever, allergic rhinitis without asthma	69.4	65.5
Dermatitis, including eczema	33.5	32.9
Diseases of sebaceous glands[1]	9.3	5.7[2]
Arthritis	437.3	554.5
Trouble with		
Ingrown nails	35.6	64.8
Corns and calluses	41.0	54.3
Dry (itching) skin	23.4	35.5
Diabetes	89.4	85.7
Migraine	28.8	11.8[1]
Diseases of urinary system[3]	57.4	62.2
Visual impairments	69.3	101.7
Cataracts	107.4	234.3
Hearing impairments	239.4	360.3
Tinnitus	76.4	68.9
Deformities or orthopedic impairments	141.4	177.0
Hernia of abdominal cavity	57.3	52.0
Frequent indigestion	34.9	42.8
Frequent constipation	42.2	92.2

[1]Acne and sebaceous skin cyst.
[2]Figure does not meet standards of reliability or precision.
[3]Includes kidney trouble or bladder disorders.
Source: Based on U.S. Bureau of the Census, 1991.

rating on a 6-point scale dropped from 5.1 ("Can perform all the usual instrumental and physical activities but at times this becomes a strain for the person, and he/she would welcome intermittent assistance with some of these") to 4.1 ("Can perform the usual instrumental and physical activities around home under usual circumstances, but requires assistance when additional or extraordinary demands are made such as for long distance travel, major shopping trips, large financial transactions, or during a crisis situation") (Palmore et al., 1985, p. 247).

Organic brain syndromes are a major cause of institutionalization among the aged. These disorders may involve loss of memory for recent as well as past events; confusion or disorientation that renders the person unaware of the day of the week, the season of the year, or the city in which he or she lives; a loss of control over daily functions such as toileting, feeding, and dressing; and an inability to focus attention.

In some acute brain syndromes, the onset of confusion is relatively sudden. Often this pattern is associated with a severe illness, such as heart failure, alcoholism, or extreme malnutrition. In these cases, the symptoms of the brain syndrome can often be reversed if the accompanying illness can be treated. Supportive counseling, attention to diet, and skill training to reestablish control of daily functions may restore the person's previous level of adaptive behavior.

Chronic brain syndrome produces a more gradual loss of memory, reduced intellectual functioning, and an increase of mood disturbances, especially hostility and depression. Whereas a number of conditions may cause the acute brain syndrome, a smaller number of diseases are associated with chronic brain syndrome. Alzheimer's disease is the most common form of this syndrome, accounting for about 50% of the dementias among the elderly (Jarvik & Kumar, 1984). The incidence of this disease increases with age, especially after age 70. The person experiences gradual brain failure over a period of seven to ten years. Symptoms of Alzheimer's disease include severe problems in cognitive functioning, especially increased memory impairment; problems with self-care; and behavioral problems such as wandering, asking the same questions over and over, and becoming suddenly angry or stubborn (O'Leary, Haley & Paul, 1993). At present, there is no treatment that will reverse the disease. Current treatments address specific symptoms, especially mood and memory problems, and attempt to slow its progress.

As the number of older adults who experience Alzheimer's disease and related disorders grows, the plight of their care-

BOX 14.1

Organic Brain Syndromes: Dementia

givers has aroused increasing concern (Weiler, Chiriboga & Black, 1994). Most Alzheimer's patients are cared for at home, often by their adult children. Caregivers often experience high levels of stress and depression as they attempt to cope with their responsibilities and as they assess the effectiveness or ineffectiveness of their efforts. The care of an older person with some form of dementia is fraught with problems and frustrations, but it also provides some opportunities for satisfactions and feelings of encouragement (Haley & Pardo, 1989). The "uplifts" and "hassles" frequently reported by caregivers give us some insight into the typical day-to-day experience of caring for a person who is suffering from this condition (Kinney & Stephens, 1989).

First the uplifts:

Seeing care recipient calm.
Pleasant interactions between care recipient and family. Seeing care recipient responsive.
Care recipient showing affection.
Friends showing understanding about caregiving.
Family showing understanding about caregiving.
Care recipient recognizing familiar people.
Care recipient being cooperative.
Leaving care recipient with others at home.
Care recipient smiling/winking.
Being in care recipient's presence.
Receiving caregiving help from family.
    (p. 404)

Now the hassles:

Care recipient being confused/not making sense.
Care recipient's forgetfulness.
Care recipient's agitation.
Care recipient declining mentally.
Care recipient not cooperating.
Care recipient's bowel/bladder accidents.
Seeing care recipient withdrawn/unresponsive.
Dressing care recipient.
Bathing care recipient.
Assisting with care recipient's toileting.
Care recipient declining physically.
Care recipient not showing interest in things.

(continued)

Going to the market to shop is an example of an instrumental activity of daily life. In very old age, the distance from home to the market is a major factor in retaining independence.

There was also an impressive range in the ability to function among the people in this sample. Some subjects showed marked declines in functioning over the ten-year period, while others actually showed improvements. Some factors assessed in the first period predicted the level of functioning in the second. Women and African-Americans had lower levels of functioning after ten years. Those whose mental health scores were high in 1972 had higher social functioning ten years later. Those who were married maintained higher levels of functioning in most areas.

The very oldest subjects showed the most marked declines in all areas, a finding suggesting that deterioration may accelerate with increasing age. This pattern of rapid decline may be a result of the greater interrelatedness of functioning among those over 80. In those who are very old, when one area of functioning declines, difficulties in many others emerge. For example, loss of a spouse may result in social withdrawal, loss of appetite, sleep disturbance, loss of energy,

---

BOX 14.1

(continued)

Care recipient not sleeping through the night.

Care recipient asking repetitive questions. (p. 403)*

Two of the symptoms most difficult to manage are sleep disturbances and wandering. As cognitive functioning declines, the pattern of sleep deteriorates as well. The Alzheimer's patient sleeps for only short periods at a time, napping on and off during the day and night. Often the napping is accompanied by waking periods at night, during which the person is confused, upset, and likely to wander away. Caregivers must therefore be continuously alert, night and day. When the disease reaches this level, family caregivers are most likely to find it necessary to institutionalize the patient (Wagner, 1984).

*Source: Kinney & Stephens, 1989.

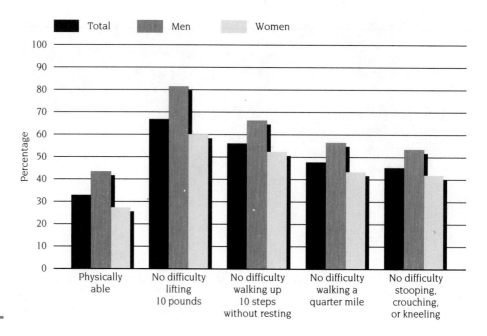

FIGURE 14.3

Physical ability of noninstitutionalized white persons aged 80 and older, 1984

Source: *Harris, Kovar, Suzman, Kleinman & Feldman, 1989.*

unwillingness to take medication, and reductions in physical activity. All of these changes may produce a rapid deterioration of the respiratory, circulatory, and metabolic systems.

Despite our stereotypes of the very old, the level of functioning among adults 80 years old and older is high. Figure 14.3 shows the percentages of men and women in a sample of over 1700 noninstitutionalized white adults 80 years old and over who could perform each of four functional indicators of physical ability. About one-third of the total sample was characterized as physically able in that they reported no difficulty with any of the four tasks. The absence of cardiovascular disease and arthritis was an important predictor of remaining physically able after age 80.

Research of this type must be repeated with various samples and different measures to clarify these patterns. The data indicate that we can expect needs for assistance in daily living and mental or physical health care to change gradually during the 70s and to accelerate during the 80s and after.

Developing a Psychohistorical Perspective

Development in very old age includes gains as well as losses. Through encounters with diverse experiences, decision-making, parenting and other forms of tutoring or mentoring of younger generations, and efforts to formulate a personal philosophy, adults reach new levels of conscious thought. Very old adults are more aware of alternatives. They can look deeply into both the past and the future. They recognize that opposing forces can exist side by side (Riegel, 1973). Through a process of creative coping, very old adults in each generation blend the salient events of their past histories with the demands of current reality. The product of this integration of past, present, and future is the formation of a *psychohistorical perspective*.

Think about what it means to have lived for 75 or more years. Those adults who were 80 years old in 1990 had lived through two world wars and the Great Depression by the time they were 35. They had experienced the political leadership of 16 presidents. They had adapted to dramatic technological innovations in communication, transportation, manufacturing, economics, food production, leisure activities, and health care. They had experienced striking changes in cultural and political values.

One consequence of a long life is the accumulation of experiences. A second consequence is the realization that change is a basic element of all life at the individual and social levels (Clayton & Birren, 1980). Sometimes these changes appear cyclical; sometimes they appear to bring real progress. Within the framework of an extended life, very old adults have opportunities to gain a special perspective on conditions of continuity and change within their culture. In the process of developing a psychohistorical perspective, very old adults develop a personal understanding of stability and change, the effects of history on individual lives, and one's place in the chain of evolution.

We are all part of the process of psychosocial evolution. Each generation adds to the existing knowledge base and reinterprets the norms of society for succeeding generations. The very old are likely to be parents, grandparents, and great-grandparents. Many are seeing their lines of descent continue into the fourth generation, a generation that will dominate the 21st century. The opportunity to see several generations of offspring brings a new degree of continuity to life, linking memories of one's own grandparents to observations of one's great-grandchildren (Wentowski, 1985). We can expect the value of the oral tradition of history and storytelling to take on new meaning as the very old help their great-grandchildren feel connected to the distant past. We may also expect a greater investment in the future as the very old see in their great-grandchildren the concrete extension of their ancestry three generations into the future.

Erikson (Erikson et al., 1986) identified the emergence of these tendencies in the very old:

> The elder has a reservoir of strength in the wellsprings of history and storytelling. As collectors of time and preservers of memory, those healthy elders who have survived into a reasonably fit old age have time on their side—time that is to be dispensed wisely and creatively, usually in the form of stories, to those younger ones who will one day follow in their footsteps. Telling these stories, and telling them well, marks a certain capacity for one generation to entrust itself to the next, by passing on a certain shared and collective identity to the survivors of the next generation: the future. (p. 331)

Wisdom

When people are asked about the positive goals of later life, they frequently mention wisdom. People expect wisdom to emerge in later adulthood and to grow with increasing age (Heckhausen, Dixon & Baltes, 1989; Sternberg, 1990). A psychohistorical perspective is closely linked to emerging definitions of *wisdom*, a cognitive domain that refers to the "fundamental pragmatics of life" (Baltes, Smith & Staudinger, 1992). Wisdom is being conceptualized as a type of expert knowledge, knowledge that reflects sound judgment and good advice about important life issues that usually involve high levels of uncertainty.

Wisdom has been characterized by five basic features (Baltes et al., 1992, p. 272):

1. *Factual knowledge* about fundamental life matters such as general knowledge about the human condition and specific knowledge about life events, the age-related occurrence of such events, and their expected and unexpected course.
2. *Procedural knowledge*, including strategies and ways of approaching the management and interpretation of life matters, including linking past, present, and future.

3. *Life span contextualism*, approaching problems with the realization that events are embedded in a multidimensional context, including age-related, culturally defined, role-related, and sociohistorical frameworks, and that events take their meaning from certain distinct domains, especially family, work, and leisure.

4. *Relativism of values and life goals*, allowing the person to appreciate differences among individuals and societies with respect to the priorities they place on certain values, as well as the ability to preserve a certain core of universal values.

5. *Recognition and management of uncertainty*, incorporating the realization that the future cannot be totally predicted, and that many aspects of the past and present are not fully known, plus an ability to manage and cope with this uncertainty.

Using this approach to defining wisdom, researchers coded the narratives of younger and older adults who were analyzing the life course of a fictitious character. Older adults did indeed have as high levels of wisdom as younger adults—and higher levels than younger adults under some circumstances (Baltes et al., 1992). Of course, not all people who live to a very old age function at a high level of wisdom. We need to carry out more research to determine what factors foster wisdom among the very old. Three dimensions that have been hypothesized to promote wisdom are opportunities to experience a wide variety of life situations and circumstances; encouragement by a mentor or guide to expand one's capacity for thinking about problems from a multidimensional, psychohistorical perspective; and a strong generative orientation, or a desire to continue to gain insight into how people meet the challenges of life (Baltes & Smith, 1990).

Traveling Uncharted Territory: Life Structures of the Very Old

How should very old people behave? What norms exist to guide their social relationships or the structure of their daily lives? What does a healthy 85-year-old woman consider appropriate behavior, and what expectations do others have of her? When we talk about traveling uncharted territory, we are assuming that very old age is a time of life for which there are few age-specific social norms. The very old are creating their own definitions of this life stage (Keith, 1982). You may have heard the expression "Life begins at 80." One interpretation of this adage is that, because there are so few norms for behavior and so few responsibilities when one reaches very old age, one can do whatever one wants.

Consider these class notes from the Bryn Mawr College record of the class of 1929 (these women were in their mid-80s in 1993):

> JBB is a fount of news tho' it had to wait months for use. She's "a stout oak" among sick friends, "healthy as long as home or close to it." Yet she dreamed of a Columbia River trip; favors among elder hostels Alton Collins Retreat, Eagle Rock, OR, near Mt. Hood. She's "still going to school, a habit acquired early," to poetry workshop at the community college, to League of Women Voters, to a political club (California Democratic Council). She recalls meeting Eleanor Roosevelt at a train restroom door: "She greeted me as if she knew me. I found out then that she could look beautiful, contrary to all the photos." J. absorbedly read Blanche Wiesen's biography of E.R.
>
> RMT reports '92 was "fully and busily enjoyed and suffered"; a new son-in-law and "steps"; a successful retrospective exhibition of the work of her first husband, VP; a summer in Vaucluse home, Les Quatres Vents. Two fall months caring for Charles's broken hip; 46-year anniversary celebrated this year; attended Campaign opening at Russian Embassy in Washington. (*Bryn Mawr Alumnae Bulletin*, 1993, p. 32)

FIGURE 14.4
Typical drawings that researchers might use to establish social norms of the very old
Source: *Drawings based on Offenbacher & Poster,* 1985.

In an effort to describe the norms that older adults use to guide their conduct, researchers asked older adults from New York City and Savannah, Georgia, to respond to six pictures similar to the two drawings in Figure 14.4 (Offenbacher & Poster, 1985). The responses to two questions were used to construct a code of conduct: "How do you think that people who know this person, such as family or friends, feel about him/her?" "How do you feel about this person?" Four normative principles were found in the responses:

1. Don't be sorry for yourself.
2. Try to be independent.
3. Don't just sit there; do something.
4. Above all, be sociable.

This code of conduct suggests that older people believe that being sociable, active, and independent constitutes doing a good job of living in later life. Of course, older adults are not the only people who value these qualities. However, these norms are very important as sources of self-esteem for this age group. They promote a sense of vigor and a shield against depression or discouragement.

The themes "Don't be sorry for yourself" and "Don't just sit there" suggest that the very old continue to see their lives as precious resources not to be wasted away in self-pity and passivity. The emphasis on activity as opposed to meditation reflects the Western cultural value of a sense of agency. Thinking is not as highly valued as action. Doing things, having an impact, and receiving the feedback that action stimulates provide the keys to successful living. Although the results of this research cannot be taken as the final word on the norms that govern the behavior of all very old adults, they are an important first step in understanding the structure that very old people impose on their lives.

The fact that older adults must carve out new patterns of adapting to later life is demonstrated in two specific areas of functioning: living arrangements and gender-role definitions.

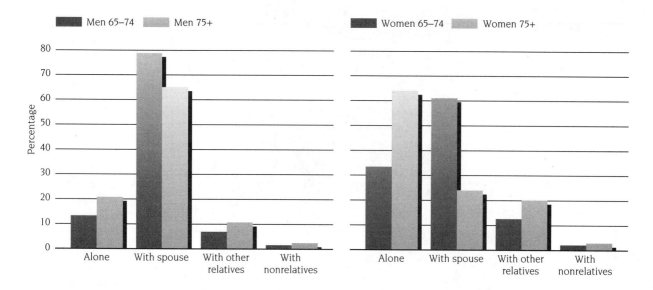

FIGURE 14.5

Living arrangements for older adults by age and sex, 1991 (percentages)

Source: *Based on U.S. Bureau of the Census, 1992.*

Living Arrangements

The pattern of living arrangements for most people changes noticeably after age 75 (see Figure 14.5). Before then, the majority of older adults live in family households, mostly as married couples. Among adults aged 75 and older, only 39% live with a spouse, and 44% live in nonfamily households; that is, they live either alone (41%) or with a nonrelative (3%). The percentage of older women who live alone after age 75 has been increasing steadily, to the point that now they are the norm among elderly women. In 1965, 30% of women over 75 lived alone; in 1991, 53% lived alone (U.S. Bureau of the Census, 1992). Older women are less likely to live with other family members after the death of their spouse than they were in the past. Further, feelings of subjective well-being appear to be high among older widows who live alone (Alwin, 1984).

One implication of these trends in living arrangements is that increasing numbers of very old women are establishing a new single lifestyle in which they function as heads of households. This does not mean that they are not in need of social interaction and support services. However, they are often relieved of the responsibilities of caring for spouses who are ill. Depending on their own health, they may be freer to direct their time and interests toward their friends, grandchildren, hobbies, and activity preferences than they have been at any other time in their lives.

The pattern of elderly women living alone is similar in Canada, the United Kingdom, and the United States, but less than 10% of Japanese women aged 65 and over live alone. Most live with relatives in three-generation households. Among those 85 and over, only 5% or 6% of Japanese women live alone. In most developing countries, families provide housing and care for the very old. Although people may not experience the same degree of longevity in these countries, there is a clear pattern of elderly widows living with their sons or daughters (U.S. Bureau of the Census, 1987).

In the United States, living arrangements for older women differ by race and ethnic group (Choi, 1991). Older unmarried Asian-American women, for example, are much more likely to live with other family members than to live alone, in comparison to white women of similar economic and educational background. Within

Finding a companion in later life can bring a tremendous burst of energy and optimism.

the Asian-American ethnic groups, acculturation appears to increase the likelihood of choosing to live alone. Those who immigrated to the United States before 1965 or were born in the United States are more likely to live alone than the more recent immigrants. And in a comparison among the Asian-American cultures, the older Japanese women were more likely to live alone than the Chinese, Filipino, and Korean women. Consistent with patterns for white women, the more children these Asian-American women had, the less likely they were to be institutionalized (Burr & Mutchler, 1993).

The majority of very old men—about 68%—are married and live with their spouses. Only 24% are widowed. In contrast, 25% of very old women are married and 66% are widowed (U.S. Bureau of the Census, 1992). Widowed men are much more likely to remarry, and they tend to do so quickly. However, remarriage among the very old is still a new frontier. Sexual and social stereotypes inhibit some older people from considering remarriage. In addition, potential financial consequences may make remarriage undesirable. A widow may lose her husband's pension or her social security benefits if she remarries. Some older couples cope with this problem by living together instead of marrying. In 1991, there were 141,000 households consisting of unmarried couples 65 years old and over (U.S. Bureau of the Census, 1992). Those who do remarry usually view the new relationship quite positively. One older woman described her new marriage as follows: "We're like a couple of kids. We fool around—have fun. We go to dances and socialize a lot with our families. We enjoy life together. When you're with someone, you're happy" (Rosenfeld, 1978, p. 56).

Interstate Migration   Although most older adults remain in their home communities, the trend toward interstate migration has increased since the mid-1960s (Flynn et al., 1985). From 1975 to 1980, 1.6 million adults over the age of 60 moved their residence across state lines. We cannot determine how many of these adults were in the very old age group. However, we can infer that many of these older interstate migrants will live out their lives in communities in which they did not grow up, work, or raise their children. They are pioneers, establishing new friendships, community involvements, and lifestyles. Another significantly large group of older adults return to their birth state after they retire. New York,

BOX 14.2

The Impact of Gentrification on the Very Old

Gentrification refers to a pattern of real-estate change in which a higher-income group buys property and develops residential and commercial projects in an area that has previously been serving a lower-income group. Usually the result is that the nearby neighborhoods attract wealthier residents, housing and rental prices increase, and the lower-income residents are often forced to move out. Since older adults tend to remain in their homes for a long time, they are likely to live in neighborhoods that become a target for gentrification, urban areas that may have deteriorated over the years of their residence, but where social supports and services continue to remain available and readily accessible.

Several consequences of gentrification have an impact on the housing options of older adults (Singelakis, 1990). First, apartments are converted to condominiums, and older adults cannot afford to stay there. Second, in areas where there is no rent control, the rent simply rises above the older person's ability to pay. Where there is rent regulation, some landlords use harassment to force the original residents out. Third, properties that have been used as single-room-occupancy hotels are demolished, and new structures are built. Single-room-occupancy hotels provide low-cost housing as well as social support to many older adults who live alone. From 1970 to 1982, over half the single-room-occupancy units in the country were lost to various urban gentrification projects (Hopper & Hamberg, 1986).

In a survey of 115 older adults living on the Upper West Side of Manhattan, 79% had incomes of less than $10,000 in 1989 (Singelakis, 1990). The mean age of this group was 75. Of this group, 99% rented, 68% lived alone, and 74% paid less than $300 per month for rent. In this community, 52% of the single-room units had been removed from availability over the past seven years. These older adults reported that gentrification had resulted in having to walk farther to find affordable shopping. They knew that if they were forced to leave their current apartment because of increased rent, they could not afford to live in this same neighborhood. And if they were forced to leave, 64% did not really know where they could live. Fewer than 8% of the sample felt that they could live with a friend or a family member if their apartment was no longer available.

California, and Florida have an especially strong pull for their native sons and daughters (Rogers, 1990).

About 60% of all older migrants move to ten states. In 1980, more than 25% of all interstate migrants over age 60 moved to Florida. This trend has had a dramatic impact on the housing, health, and social service resources of many Florida communities.

Housing Options   Differences in lifestyle, health, interest, ability to perform daily activities, marital status, and income enter into the very old person's preference for housing arrangements. Housing for the elderly—sometimes referred to as *retirement housing*—has expanded dramatically, and developers have experimented with a great variety of housing configurations that are intended to meet the special needs of particular aging populations. These options range from inner-city hotels for those with minimal incomes to sprawling luxury villages with apartments, medical clinics, and sponsored activities. The majority of older adults live in urban areas, and of these, 31% live in inner-city neighborhoods. As a result, any economic factors that affect the housing options within urban communities have a significant impact on the living arrangements of older adults (see Box 14.2).

Since older adults tend to have a limited income and depend on the quality of community resources and social support for the their well-being, moving may be an especially difficult life event, one that may contribute negatively to their over-all well-being (Singelakis, 1990; Ryff & Essex, 1992).

We know of people who have visited a number of retirement communities and evaluated the options of various housing arrangements before they were really ready to make a housing change. The advice of one of our retired professional col-leagues is to anticipate the move into a retirement setting and to live there before one is seriously restricted by declining health. That way, one becomes more easily integrated into the social network of the residents and is more likely to receive help from neighbors when one needs it. Some older adults maintain two resi-dences, one in a warm climate and one in a cooler climate. There are mobile home parks for older adults who want to spend the winter months in a warm climate but do not want to invest in an expensive second residence. Two of our dearest col-leagues devised a particularly creative arrangement through which they lived in three locations: They spent the summer and autumn at their university-based res-idence, the winter in Mexico, and the spring in Washington, D.C., where they vol-unteered their time to a government agency working on issues related to aging.

Institutional Care   On any given day, about 5% of adults over 65 live in nursing homes and other group-care settings. The rate of institutionalization increases from about 2% of those 65–74 years old to 23% of those 85 and over. These rates, based on one moment in time, underestimate the risk of having to spend some time in a nursing home during one's later life. The lifetime prob-ability of spending some time in a nursing home is estimated to be between 25% and 50%, depending on the technique used to make this projection. About 75% of those in nursing homes do not have spouses. The likelihood of being in a nursing home increases when there is no family member who can help an older person manage his or her daily living needs (U.S. Senate, Special Committee on Aging, 1986).

We tend to think that once people are admitted to a nursing home, they stay there until they die. However, there is actually a high annual turnover among nursing-home residents. Often a person enters a nursing home for a period of convalescence after hospitalization and then returns home. Nursing homes and housing for the very old have adapted to the changing needs of their clients since the mid-1970s. Many nursing homes are part of a *continuing-care retirement community*. These residential settings offer housing and medical, preventive-health, and social services to residents who are well at the time they enter the community. Once admitted, they are guaranteed nursing care if they become ill or disabled (Cohen, Tell & Wallack, 1988). In an analysis of nursing-home use among residents in continuing-care retirement communities, the risk of being transferred to the nursing-home facility appeared to be greater than the rate for older adults in the general community, but the length of stay per admission was shorter (Cohen et al., 1989). The nursing home may be used for recuperative purposes rather than having patients stay in the hospital setting for longer numbers of days. This practice may reduce overall medical costs and provide a better recovery envi-ronment than being discharged to one's home before one can fully manage all the demands of self-care.

In trying to cope with a spouse who had Alzheimer's disease, Mr. G. decided to move to a continuing-care retirement community. He lived in the minimal-care residential part of the community, and his wife lived in a full-service unit. With this arrangement, he could remain close to his wife without having the full responsibility for her care. This solution relieved Mr. G. of many of the financial burdens he had encountered in trying to care for his wife at home. The move also prevented Mr. G. from becoming socially isolated, a concern of many very old adults who are caring for aging parents or spouses.

At present, about half the states are establishing community-based long-term health-care programs to provide medical and social services to those who are chronically ill and are eligible for institutionalization but who nevertheless live in the community. These programs provide relief for family members and friends who are trying to care for the very old, and they bring comfort to the very old clients who prefer to remain in their homes. These programs also offer flexibility by providing needed services and modifying them as a person's condition changes.

Long-term home-health-care programs are experimental. They evolve in response to the patterns of need that emerge in a community and the quality of the services available. As the programs develop, their emphasis tends to shift from providing services to those who would otherwise be institutionalized to preventing institutionalization among a high-risk population (Birnbaum et al., 1984; Branch & Stuart, 1984).

Gender-Role Definitions

Another aspect of traveling uncharted territory is the way in which very old adults view masculinity and femininity. How do the very old define gender roles? How does gender influence behavior? Do very old adults make the same distinctions as college-age populations about the behaviors appropriate or desirable for men and women?

Evaluating the Concept of Sex-Role Convergence   Some researchers have reported a transformation of sex-role orientation during midlife. Men are described as becoming more nurturant and more concerned with social relationships. Women are described as becoming more assertive and concerned with independence and achievement as they get older. Thus, some scholars argue that men and women become more androgynous and, in that sense, become more similar in gender orientation during later life (Gutmann, 1987).

The extent to which men and women do become more similar in outlook and behavior in later adulthood and very old age is a subject of controversy. Unfortunately, few data from longitudinal or cohort sequential studies are available to address this topic. Cross-sectional data collected from men and women across a wide age span from early adulthood to very old age have focused on men's and women's endorsement of affiliative and instrumental values. Men and women appear to be very similar in their *affiliative values*, that is the amount of time they spend and the degree of satisfaction they feel in helping or pleasing others. At each age, men appear to be more invested in *instrumental values* than women— that is, in the amount of time they spend and the degree of satisfaction they feel in doing things that are challenging. However, the youngest age groups appear to value instrumentality more highly and devote more time to it than the oldest age group. Thus, gender differences persist in instrumentality, but the opportunities and centrality of instrumentality become somewhat less prominent for both older men and women, while affiliative behavior is equally important for both men and women and very important at both ages (Fultz & Herzog, 1991).

This 78-year-old grandfather is enjoying the pleasure of opening up birthday presents with his grandsons. Opportunities for meaningful affiliation are very important to men and women as they get older.

The stereotypes that are applied to aging men and women reflect similar patterns. College students and older adults (mean age of 70) were asked to generate characteristics in response to one of four target stimuli: a 35-year-old man, a 35-year-old woman, a 65-year-old man, and a 65-year-old woman (Kite, Deaux & Miele, 1991). Age stereotypes were more prevalent than gender stereotypes. The attributes that were used to characterize older men and women were very similar and were distinct from the attributes used to characterize younger men and women. In general, the older target subjects were evaluated more negatively by the younger subjects, but not as negatively by the older subjects. These negative qualities included unattractive physical qualities as well as irritable and depressed personality qualities. What is more, younger subjects were more likely to characterize both male and female older subjects as lacking in instrumental traits, such as achievement orientation and self-confidence. They did not view older subjects as lacking in affiliative traits, such as caring about others or being kind or generous. One implication is that the gender convergence that has been hypothesized as taking place with advanced age may be more a construction of a younger generation applying its stereotypes to older adults than it is actually a perception of the very old themselves.

Sex-role changes, where they are observed, may be due to changing circumstances rather than to a normative pattern of development in later life. For example, many older women experience a transition from living with their husbands to living alone after age 75. This change is linked to new demands for independence, self-reliance, and agency among these older women. Women who are able to meet these challenges by developing independent living skills, making effective use of social supports and community resources, and initiating new relationships are likely to experience a heightened sense of well-being.

For many older married couples, the physical effects of aging bring new needs for assistance in some of the tasks of daily living. Since men usually marry younger women, they are more likely to require the assistance of their wives in the later years of marriage, thus shifting the balance of power and increasing their sense of dependency. This may be especially true when husbands retire while wives continue to work; when husbands can no longer drive and must depend on their wives for transportation; or when men are restricted from performing the types of household tasks that used to be designated as their domain, such as mowing the grass, shoveling snow, home repair, or other tasks requiring muscle strength and endurance.

Romance and Sexuality   Older men and women tend to be tied to many of the sex-role standards of their historical cohort. For example, older women are likely to believe that the only kinds of relationships that are possible between men and women are romantic or courtship relationships (Adams, 1985). Few very old women have friendships with very old men, partly because few older men are available but also because most older women have no models for independent friendship relationships with men. During their early and middle adult years, their friendships with men were formed while they were part of a couple or were mediated by some other situation, such as a work setting.

Today's very old adults are also likely to be uncomfortable about sexuality and dating. Although most current research on aging confirms that older adults have sexual needs and are able to be sexually active, most older women do not readily integrate sexuality into their single lifestyle. They are members of a generation that did not feel comfortable about open sexuality outside the marriage relationship. Once they are single again, they find it difficult to become involved in a sexual relationship.

Many men among the current cohort of the very old also behave in accordance with the sex-role standards of their young adulthood. Although women far outnumber men at advanced ages, men still seem to prefer to remarry rather than play the field, although they have become a very scarce and valuable commodity. The norm of serial monogamy guides these men's behavior. Many men are probably motivated by a desire to continue to be taken care of as well as to satisfy their sexual needs.

A study of romantic involvement among elderly African-Americans illustrates the differences in outlook of older men and older women (Tucker, Taylor & Mitchell-Kernan, 1993). Among African-Americans, there are only 68 men for every 100 women aged 65 and over. This ratio declines even more dramatically for those 75 and older. Among the sample studied, 52% of the men over 75 years old were married; 9% of the women were married. What is more, among those men over 75 who were not married, 21% said they were romantically involved, and 40% of those not romantically involved said they would like to be. Among the unmarried women over 75, only 2% said they were romantically involved, and only 5% said they would like to be. Among the oldest African-American men, desire for romantic involvement remained strong, but among the women, it declined dramatically. Older African-American women saw the prospect of romantic involvement as very costly. They saw older men as being interested in them because they had money, and because they needed to be taken care of:

> "I wouldn't want a third man. I had two and I'm afraid that the first thing that would come between us is how much money I got. I ain't got none to give them what I work hard for."

> "Men want someone to wait on them, to be a servant, just take care of them." (Tucker et al., 1993, p. S128)

It appears that African-American men continue to seek romantic involvements because they benefit largely from these relationships both financially and in terms of physical and emotional support. African-American women see these relationships as a risk or a burden. They find social support and emotional connection with family members, especially sisters, neighbors, and in-laws.

Sexuality and romance remain very important among older married couples. The majority of couples who have enjoyed a close, sexually active relationship report little change in satisfaction from age 60 to age 85 (Bretschneider & McCoy, 1988). Some couples explore different ways of experiencing sexual pleasure in later life, and some even report a more relaxed, sexually satisfying quality in their recent lovemaking. Most research on the topic confirms that older married adults continue to experience sexual desires and find satisfaction in sexual intimacy (Turner & Rubinson, 1993).

Older adults continue to face negative, ageist social attitudes about sexual activity that may inhibit their sexual behavior. These include assumptions that very old adults do not have sexual desires; that they cannot have intercourse because of sexual dysfunction; that sex may be dangerous to their health; that they are physically and sexually unattractive; and that it is morally wrong or "sick" for older adults to be sexually active (Turner & Rubinson, 1993). Current cohorts of very old adults have little knowledge about sexuality and aging. A number of studies have demonstrated that increasing knowledge through various types of sex-education programs can increase permissive attitudes about sexuality among older adults (Hillman & Stricker, 1994). These interventions have involved the elderly themselves, nursing students, college students, nursing-home staff, and adult children of aging parents. However, increased knowledge does not always result in more permissive attitudes. Especially among health care staff in institutional settings, the institutional regulations, personal moral values, and the practical problems of permitting sexual activity among patients may combine to promote a more negative attitude even with advanced information about sexuality and aging.

Cohort factors may change the current societal attitudes toward sexuality among the very old. Because so many more adult women are in the workplace, they have more experience with male colleagues. Changing sexual norms have already led many more adults to experience nonmarital sexual relationships. Acceptance of new sexual relationships in later life is more likely because many adults will have experienced more sexual relationships in their earlier years of adulthood. The high divorce rate since the mid-1970s means that, in the future, many more older women will have had the experience of developing a single lifestyle that includes a network of both male and female friends. We may expect future groups of older adults to be more comfortable about cross-sex relationships, both those involving romance and those involving friendship.

The Psychosocial Crisis: Immortality Versus Extinction

By the end of later adulthood, most people have developed a point of view about death. Although they may continue to experience anxiety about their impending death, they have found the courage to confront their fears and overcome them. If they have achieved integrity, they believe that life makes sense. The achievement of integrity brings a sense of personal dignity to the choices they have made and the goals they have achieved without despair over the failures, the missed

Pablo Picasso, Aquatint and Etching, *1968. Picasso, the tiny, aged infant, is dwarfed by the abundant imagery of his art. Here he assembles all the forces that were ebbing in his old age—sexuality, movement, heroism, risk, and magic.*

opportunities, or the misfortunes that may have occurred. Thus armed, the very old can accept the end of life and view it as a natural part of the life span. They are capable of distilling wisdom from the events of their lives, including their successes and mistakes.

However, the very old are faced with a new challenge. All of us struggle with a certain disbelief about our own mortality. Even though we know that death is a certainty, an element of human thought prevents us from facing the full realization of death and makes us continue to hope for immortality. This quality may be adaptive in that people who have a sense of hope cope better than those who do not. With advancing age, a conflict builds between the acceptance of death and the intensifying hope for immortality. The very old struggle to find meaning in their survival.

Immortality

We have argued that the very old have a unique appreciation of change. They begin to sense themselves as links in a long, fluid chain of historical and biological growth and change. The positive pole of this crisis is a confidence in the continuity of life, a transcendence of death through the development of a symbolic sense of immortality.

A psychological sense of *immortality* may be achieved and expressed in many ways (Lifton, 1973). Here we explore five possible paths toward immortality. First, one may live on through one's children, sensing a connection and attachment to the future through their lives and those of their offspring. This type of immortality may be extended to include devotion to one's country, to one's social organizations or groups, or to humankind.

Second, one may believe in an afterlife or in a spiritual plane of existence that extends beyond one's biological life. Most religious traditions have a concept that describes a state of harmony with natural forces so that one endures beyond earthly life.

Third, one may achieve a sense of immortality through one's creative achievements and one's impact on others. Many people find great comfort in believing that they are part of a chain of positive influences on the lives of others. This sense of immortality is clearly tied to the achievement of generativity in middle adulthood. Those adults who have made a strong commitment to improving the quality of life for future generations during middle adulthood are likely to see evidence of this effort by the time they reach very old age. In this sense of immortality, the bond between an individual and his or her community makes death less terrible. An African proverb advises that you live as long as someone knows your name. The more embedded you are in your community and the more lives you have touched, the greater your sense of continuity or transcendence.

Fourth, one may develop the notion of participation in the chain of nature. In death, one's body returns to the earth, and one's energy is brought forth in a new form.

Fifth, one may achieve a sense of immortality through what Lifton (1973) described as *experiential transcendence*:

> This state is characterized by extraordinary psychic unity and perceptual intensity. But there also occurs . . . a process of symbolic reordering. . . . Experiential transcendence includes a feeling of . . . "continuous present" that can be equated with eternity or with "mythical time." This continuous present is perceived as not only "here and now" but as inseparable from past and future. (p. 10)

This concept of immortality is independent of religion, offspring, or achievement. It is an insight derived from moments of rapture or ecstasy in which all that one senses is the power of the moment. In these experiences, life and death dissolve, and all that remains is continuous being.

Extinction

The negative pole of this crisis is a sense of being bound by the limits of one's own life history. In place of a belief in continuous existence and transformation, one views the end of life as an end to motion, attachment, and change. In place of a faith in the ideas of connection and continuity, one experiences great fear of *extinction*—a fear that death brings nothingness.

The following quotations from a study of very old men suggest the range in sentiment about immortality and extinction (Rosenfeld, 1978, p. 10). About 28% were described as having low morale and made statements such as the following: "I feel I'm a forgotten man. I don't exist anymore. . . . I don't feel old . . . I'm just living out my life." About 25% were stoic but not very positive about their condition: "You know you're getting old. You have to put your mind to it and take it as it comes. You can't get out of it. Take it gracefully." Almost half found their lives full and rewarding: "I go home with my cup overflowing. There are so many opportunities to do things for people. These are the happiest days of my life."

The Central Process: Social Support

Social support has been defined as those social experiences that lead people to believe that they are cared for and loved, that they are esteemed and valued, and that they belong to a network of communication and mutual obligation (Cobb, 1979). *Social support* is a broad term that includes the quantity and interconnectedness or web of social relationships in which a person is embedded, the strength of those ties, the frequency of contact, and the extent to which the support system is perceived as helpful and caring (Bergeman et al., 1990). For the very old, social support plays a major role in maintaining well-being and fostering the possibility of transcending the physical limitations that accompany aging.

Social support plays a direct role in promoting health and well-being, even when a person is not facing a specific stressful situation. First, because social support involves meaningful social relationships, it reduces isolation. People who have intimate companions in later life have higher levels of life satisfaction. They feel valued and, in turn, valuable. This kind of support is likely to be most appreciated when it comes from friends and neighbors, members of the community who are not bound by familial obligation to care about you but who do care about you anyway. Second, the presence of caring, familiar others provides a flow of affection, information, advice, transportation, assistance with meals and daily activities, finances, and health care—all critical resources (Stephens & Bernstein, 1984). In addition, the presence of a support system tends to reduce the impact of stressors and to protect people from some of the negative consequences of stress, especially serious illnesses and depression (House, 1985; Murrell & Norris, 1991). The support system often serves to encourage an older person to maintain health-care practices and to seek medical attention when it is needed. Members of the immediate family as well as close relatives and friends are the people who provide direct care during times of grave illness or loss and who encourage the older person to cope with difficulties and to remain hopeful (Russell & Cutrona, 1991).

Very old people are likely to experience declines in physical stamina. They may also have limited financial resources. In order for the very old to transcend the limitations of their daily living situations, they must be convinced that they are embedded in a network of social relationships in which they are valued. Their value cannot be based solely on a physical exchange of goods and services. It must be founded on an appreciation of their dignity and a history of reciprocal caring.

The value of reciprocity in both emotional and caregiving support is very strong in our culture. People want and expect to be able to give about the same as or more than they receive. Most older adults continue to see themselves as involved in a reciprocal, supportive relationship with their friends. They may expect to receive more care from their children when they are ill than they will provide. By shifting to a life-span perspective, however, they can retain a sense of balance by seeing the help they receive now as comparable to the help they gave at earlier life stages (Ingersoll-Dayton & Antonucci, 1988). When very old people are highly valued, it is not so important that they reciprocate in the exchange of tangible resources. Wisdom, affection, joie de vivre, and a positive model of surviving into old age are intangible resources that are highly valued by members of the very old person's social support network. Being valued may also mean that the

BOX 14.3

Erikson on Aging

The Eriksons' advice (Erickson et al., 1986) on aging suggests the achievement of a level of experiential transcendence:

> With aging, there are inevitably constant losses—losses of those very close, and friends near and far. Those who have been rich in intimacy also have the most to lose. Recollection is one form of adaptation, but the effort skillfully to form new relationships is adaptive and more rewarding. Old age is necessarily a time of relinquishing—of giving up old friends, old roles, earlier work that was once meaningful, and even possessions that belong to a previous stage of life and are now an impediment to the resiliency and freedom that seem to be requisite for adapting to the unknown challenges that determine the final stage of life.
>
> Trust in interdependence. Give and accept help when it is needed. Old Oedipus well knew that the aged sometimes need three legs; pride can be an asset but not a cane.
>
> When frailty takes over, dependence is appropriate, and one has no choice but to trust in the compassion of others and be consistently surprised at how faithful some caretakers can be.
>
> Much living, however, can teach us only how little is known. Accept that essential "not-knowingness" of childhood and with it also that playful curiosity. Growing old can be an interesting adventure and is certainly full of surprises.
>
> One is reminded here of the image Hindu philosophy uses to describe the final letting go—that of merely being. The mother cat picks up in her mouth the kitten, which completely collapses every tension and hangs limp and infinitely trusting in the maternal benevolence. The kitten responds instinctively. We human beings require at least a whole lifetime of practice to do this. (pp. 332–333)

very old person's advice and conversation are adequate exchange for some of the services and assistance provided by family and friends.

Of course, being an integral part of a social system does not begin in later life. It has its origins in infancy with the formation of a mutual relationship with a caregiver. Social support systems are extended in childhood and early adolescence through identification with a peer group and in early and middle adulthood through marriage, child rearing, and relationships with co-workers and adult friends. In later life, family members are usually the primary sources of social support, especially one's spouse, children, and siblings. The quality of the relationship between an adult child and an aging parent has a long history. Clearly, the nature of the support that an aging parent is able to receive or that an adult child is willing to provide is influenced by the feelings of closeness and connection that were fashioned during the child-rearing process and the child's relationship to the parents during early adulthood years.

For very old people, especially women, the likelihood of living alone is quite high. After the death of a spouse, men and women must realign their social support systems from among relationships that include their adult children, friends, relatives, neighbors, and new acquaintances in order to satisfy their needs for interaction and companionship. Very old adults who are childless and those who have no surviving children or siblings are especially vulnerable to ending their lives in isolation (Hays, 1984).

For many older adults, religious participation provides an additional source of social support. Older adults are more likely than younger adults to describe themselves as religious in their beliefs and their behavior. The place of religion in the lives of the very old is especially significant for African-Americans, who are more likely than whites to attend religious services regularly, even at advanced ages. They are more likely to describe themselves as very religious, a characterization that reflects the frequency of their private prayer, their strong emotional commitment, and their frequent religious reading. Religious involvement among elderly African-Americans is not predicted by income or education (Taylor, 1986). In one study of older African-American residents of an urban area, church membership was significantly related to well-being, particularly as a result of the perceived support these older adults received from other church members (Walls & Zarit, 1991).

Ethnic identity itself may become an important vehicle for social support in later life (Cool, 1987). Ethnic identity may provide a variety of sources of non-familial support, from a loose network of associations to membership in formal clubs and organizations. Members of an ethnic group may feel a strong sense of community as a result of their shared exposure to past discrimination, their realization of common concerns, and their sense of their responsibility to preserve some of the authenticity of their ethnic identity for future generations. Participation in such a support network may be another vehicle for contributing wisdom gained through life experiences to those who will follow. Insofar as members of ethnic groups have felt somewhat marginal to the larger society in the past, their mutual support in later life may protect them from some of the negative stereotypes that the society imposes on the very old.

We view involvement in a social support system as an essential ingredient in the achievement of a sense of immortality by the very old. The social support system confirms the value of very old people, providing direct evidence of their positive impact on others and a sense of embeddedness within their social communities. The social support system of the very old usually includes adult children. Positive interactions with one's children contribute to the sense of living on through one's offspring and their descendants. Interactions with members of the social support system, especially those that are marked by feelings of warmth, caring, and celebration, may be moments of experiential transcendence. These are times at which a very old person feels the fullness and joy of existence that transcend physical and material barriers.

Applied Topic
Meeting the Needs of the Frail Elderly

In thinking about the frail elderly, it is helpful to distinguish between optimal ability level and actual ability (Denney, 1982; Gottesman, Quarterman & Cohn, 1973). *Optimal ability* is what we are capable of doing when we are motivated and well prepared. *Actual ability* is how we usually perform. At every period of life, there is some gap between what we are capable of doing and our actual level of performance. However, there may also be some real limits to the optimal level of performance. For example, we might say that a middle-school-age boy is not as strong as he might be if he exercised more and used his muscles in a more concentrated effort. However, even after exercise and training, his optimal strength would still be less

One of the great challenges in providing residential treatment to the frail elderly is to continue to promote their optimal development. In this nursing home, cooking is a form of recreational therapy. An older adult finds tremendous satisfaction in being able to turn out a batch of homemade cookies with just the right amount of help so that the task is rewarding without becoming overwhelming.

than that of an adolescent who has experienced the increase in muscle mass that accompanies puberty.

We need to ask whether aging itself imposes limits on the optimal performance level of the very old or whether it is the environment and the expectations of others that reduce effective functioning. In tests of hearing, for example, older adults often show reduced sensitivity to high-frequency and low-intensity sounds. However, the hearing tests themselves create a barrier to performance. Older people are cautious about making errors. They tend to say they have heard a tone only if they are absolutely certain that they have. In one study, older subjects were instructed to take a chance and respond even if they were not completely sure about having heard the tone. Their hearing tests showed significant improvement over normal testing conditions (Reese & Botwinick, 1971).

The goal of providing services or community resources to the frail elderly should be to enhance a realistic level of performance. On the one hand, we should not try to get 80-year-olds to live the lives of teenagers or people in their 50s. On the other hand, we should not hold such minimal expectations for the frail elderly that we rob them of their autonomy and undermine their ability to meet challenges or to strive toward achievable goals. One of the current issues that has become a focus of research and policy debate is the extent to which physical frailty in very old age is treatable or preventable, and how to reduce dependency, especially long-term nursing care among the frail elderly (Hadley et al., 1993).

Dependency has been defined in several ways. One common approach is to list difficulties in the activities of daily living (ADLs), including bathing, dressing oneself, transferring from the bed to a chair, using the toilet, and feeding oneself. Sometimes these assessments include walking a short distance, since this degree of motor ability is usually required to function independently. Beyond these very

FIGURE 14.6

Levels of dependency and types of care

Note: Number of persons who receive nursing-home care and informal and formal care in the community according to level of disability. Community-dwelling persons represented in this figure actually receive help for one or more activities of daily living (ADLs) or instrumental activities of daily living (IADLs). ADLs include bathing, dressing, eating, transferring, walking, using the toilet, and continence. IADLs include preparing meals, shopping, managing money, doing light housework, doing heavy housework, and getting outside.

Source: Based on Hing & Bloom, 1990.

Type of care

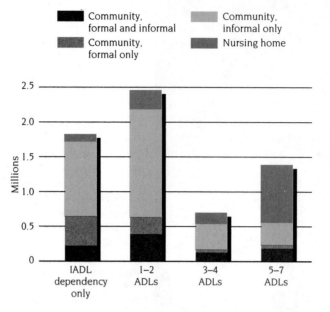

basic types of self-care, an expanded notion of dependency refers to difficulties in managing instrumental activities of daily living (IADLs), such as shopping, preparing meals, doing light housework, using transportation, or using the telephone. These tasks, while clearly more complex than the ADLs, are essential to maintaining one's daily life without dependence on informal or formal community support services (Guralnik & Simonsick, 1993). Figure 14.6 shows the numbers of adults who receive different types of care in relation to the extent of their dependency—that is, the number of activities of daily living with which they need assistance. The largest group requires help with one or two ADLs, and in that group, the vast majority of assistance comes from informal community resources, especially family and friends.

Dependency or difficulty in managing activities of daily living increases markedly after age 85. Many factors combine to produce this dependency. In most postindustrial societies, later adulthood is characterized by a sedentary lifestyle. Estimates suggest that only about 10% of older adults are active enough to sustain appropriate levels of muscle strength and cardiovascular capacity (Fiatarone & Evans, 1993). Weakness resulting from disuse combines with certain biological changes, diseases, medications, and malnutrition to produce muscle atrophy, risk of falling, reduced arousal and cognitive capacity, and a gradual decline in confidence in being able to cope with even moderate types of physical exertion.

Many very old adults resist assistance from human service professionals because they do not understand the purposes of their services. For example, some very old adults will not apply for food stamps even though they may qualify for this form of assistance. They have lived life with an ethic of self-sufficiency, and they simply cannot accept what they perceive to be "welfare" or "something for nothing." Others find that the services require such complicated forms and applications or background information that they cannot manage the paperwork necessary to benefit from the service. In many instances, language barriers or illiteracy makes it difficult for very old adults to request or receive the services they need.

Most community mental health agencies provide counseling services for the elderly. However, this is a service that many older adults do not understand and do not perceive as very important. Consequently, it is one that they infrequently use. The current cohort of older adults has not been socialized to use the assistance of mental health professionals in coping with what we might consider normal life stresses such as grief, isolation, and chronic pain. Programs need to take into account the physical, educational, and attitudinal characteristics of the aging population. Then efforts must be made to educate the very old about the services that are offered.

For many older adults, problems with remaining independent change from time to time. In the winter, when streets are icy and the weather is very cold, a person may need more help because it is difficult to walk outside or wait for the bus. In the event of an acute illness requiring a period of hospitalization, the person may temporarily need support during the posthospital recovery but does not require long-term institutionalization. Full recovery from a week or two of being bedridden may require additional physical therapy, rebuilding muscle tone and endurance, and rebuilding confidence in being able to manage daily tasks. The outcome for the older person depends on the patient, the caregiver, and the health care system, all sharing expectations for recovery and rehabilitation rather than viewing the person as permanently weakened and destined for prolonged dependency (Schulz & Williamson, 1993).

While we do not want to underestimate the limitations of the elderly, neither do we want to overestimate them. We do not want to take away the supports that help very old adults sustain their independence or overreact to their physical or intellectual limitations. We see this tendency in the responses of some adult children to their aging parents. Once the children realize that their parents are not functioning at the same high level of competence that they enjoyed previously, they move toward a role reversal. They may infantilize or dominate their parents. They may insist on taking over all financial matters or attempt to relocate their parents to a more protective housing arrangement. Little by little, they take away all their parents' decision-making responsibilities.

Although children may view such actions as being in the parents' best interests, they may fail to take the parents' own preferences into account. For example, adult children tend to overemphasize the importance of health and financial considerations for their parents and to overlook the significance of familiar housing in preserving the companionship and daily support that are critical to their parents' sense of well-being (Kahana, 1982). Adult children may also fail to realize how important decision-making tasks and responsibility for personal care are to the maintenance of their parents' personality structure. In mutually satisfying relationships between adult daughters and their aging mothers, the daughters make sure that their mothers are consistently involved in decisions that affect their lives, even when the mothers are heavily dependent on their daughters for daily care (Pratt et al., 1989).

In many nursing homes, there is a similar tendency to reduce or eliminate expectations of autonomy by failing to give residents any responsibilities for planning or performing the activities of daily life. Routine chores such as cooking, cleaning, shopping for groceries, doing laundry, planning meals, answering the phone, paying bills, and writing letters all give older adults the sense that life is going along as usual. Replacing these responsibilities with unstructured time may subject very old people to more stress than continuing to expect some forms of regular contribution to daily life. Paid work assignments and structured daily responsibilities are activities that an institutional setting can provide to help maintain a high level of social and intellectual functioning among the residents.

Supporting the optimal functioning of frail elderly people requires an individualized approach. Each person has a unique profile of competencies and limitations. For some, the physical environment presents the greatest barriers to optimal functioning. A person who cannot walk without fear of falling, who cannot see well, or who cannot grasp objects because of arthritis may need to have modifications in the home that will compensate for these limitations. Many creative strategies have been introduced that permit people with serious physical disabilities to retain an optimal level of autonomy in their homes.

For some very old adults, the quality of the neighborhood presents the greatest barrier to optimal functioning. Older people may be afraid of vandalism, theft, or other forms of neighborhood crime. They may need transportation, emergency medical services, and convenient social settings. Table 14.3 summarizes the results of a study of the importance and critical distance of neighborhood services for the very old. The *critical distance* is the limit beyond which a very old person would find the service inaccessible (Newcomer, 1976). Of course, one must keep in mind that the critical distance may vary with the topography. Climbing two blocks up a steep hill may be more difficult for a very old person than doing four blocks of flat walking. Interventions at the community level may be necessary to meet the safety, health, and social needs of some older adults who want to remain in their communities.

For other very old adults, the absence of meaningful interpersonal relationships is the greatest barrier to optimal functioning. The role of the informal social support system cannot be underestimated in meeting the needs of the frail elderly. Children, spouses, other relatives, and neighbors are all important sources of help. Within communities, very old people are themselves likely to provide significant help to age-mates who may be ill, bereaved, or impaired in some way. Older adults prefer not to have to ask for help. However, they are much better off if they have someone to turn to than if they have no one.

In one community intervention in New Haven, Connecticut, LIFE (Learning Informally from the Elderly), community professionals charged with providing services to the frail elderly organized interviews and community meetings with older adults to learn what challenges the elderly were facing in trying to remain as independent as possible in their neighborhood (Pallett-Hehn & Lucas, 1994). The professionals were surprised to find that the older adults brought safety concerns to the fore as a primary issue and that health and service concerns were secondary. In order to preserve and continue the dialogue, the professionals fostered the creation of Elder Forums, neighborhood groups where older adults discuss their mutual concerns and possible solutions. Each month, representatives from the Elder Forums come together in an assembly with professionals and policymakers to raise concerns that had been discussed in the Elder Forum and to identify communitywide resources or changes in policy and procedures for addressing the concern.

Finally, people can do a lot for themselves to promote a fulfilling later life. For example, Thomas Szasz (1982) described the *psychiatric will*, an instrument in which people can declare what kinds of assistance they are and are not willing to accept in their very old age. Both the living will and the designation of someone as having a "durable power of attorney" for health care decisions allow adults who are unable to give reasoned, informed consent to medical treatment a vehicle for

TABLE 14.3	Critical Distances of Neighborhood Services for the Elderly	
Service	**Critical Distance**	**Maximum Recommended Distance**
Bus stop	On site to 3 blocks	1 block
Outdoor area	On site to 3 blocks	3 blocks
Laundromat	On site	On site
Grocery store	1–10 blocks	6 blocks
Supermarket	1–10 blocks	6 blocks
Bank	1–10 blocks	6 blocks
Post office	1–3 blocks	3 blocks
Department store	1–3 blocks	3 blocks
Cleaners	1–11 blocks	6 blocks
Senior center	On site	On site
Beauty shop or barber	On site to 10 blocks	10 blocks
Physician	1–10 blocks	10 blocks
Butcher shop	1–10 blocks	6 blocks
Snack bar	1–10 blocks	10 blocks
Public library	On site to 10 blocks	10 blocks
Dentist	1–10 blocks	10 blocks
Eye doctor	1–10 blocks	10 blocks
Foot doctor	Indeterminate	10 blocks
Center (for all ages)	Used as senior center	On site
Movie	Indeterminate[1]	10 blocks
Church or synagogue	Indeterminate[1]	Indeterminate[1]
Bar	No importance	No importance

[1]Distance indeterminate because of high percentage of persons who do not use and only small number who do use.

Source: Based on Newcomer, 1976.

expressing their preferences about treatment. Through these advance statements, older adults can express their position on receiving psychiatric treatment, on conditions under which they would accept institutionalization, and on various types of life-extending medical interventions. In fact, relatively few adults have formalized their wishes in this way (Zweibel & Cassel, 1989).

Very old adults can alter the structure of their environment to enhance their sense of well-being. They may move to a warmer climate, to homogeneous-age communities, or to more modest homes or apartments that entail fewer maintenance responsibilities. They may participate in exercise classes or other guided physical activity to improve their strength, endurance, and flexibility. They may select some family and friendship relationships that they sustain through frequent interaction, mutual help giving, and shared activities. They may participate in activities in community settings, including churches, senior centers, libraries, and volunteer organizations, in which they will retain a sense of social connectedness. As at earlier ages, very old people make certain choices that direct the course of their lives and influence their overall level of adjustment.

The following case illustrates the importance of psychological attitudes in allowing a person with serious physical problems to play a meaningful role in a social setting for the frail elderly. Mr. Z.'s outlook helps him maintain his vitality and express his love of life:

> Mr. M.L.Z. is an eighty-nine-year-old white male of Eastern European origin. He lives in a midsized nursing home in the Middle West. Many of his daily activities revolve around his circulating among the facility's residents, chatting, playing cards, reading to them, and "fetching things." Most important, Mr. Z. carries his old battered violin about with him and at the drop of a hat will play a tune or break into song in a surprisingly strong, clear, melodic voice. He claims to be able to sing songs in any one of seven languages, and with the least encouragement will try out several for anyone who will listen.
>
> Mr. Z. is small (5'3"), frail-looking, and completely bald. He has facial scars and wears extremely thick-lensed glasses. He seems to be known and well-liked by practically all residents and staff of the facility in which he resides, and by many visitors there as well.
>
> He recalls a colorful history. He "escaped" his homeland at the tender age of fifteen and a half to avoid compulsory military service, and fled to Russia. There he was inducted into the army, and was subsequently sent off to duty in Siberia, where he lived for about six years. After another tour of duty in a border patrol he deserted, made his way across Europe, and eventually came to the United States. Here he took odd jobs, educated himself, and in time "got into show business"; he became a vaudeville prompter. In time his contacts in entertainment took him around the world. Yet time took its toll.
>
> He tells of marrying a woman with whom he lived for "almost forty years." They had no children and she died some fifteen years ago. Following her death, he began to experience a series of physical difficulties. An operation for cataracts left him with the need for very thick glasses. At one time he had a toupee made, which he has not worn for some time. One leg was amputated because of a diabetic condition and he now wears a prosthetic leg. In addition, he wears a hearing aid, false teeth, and, for the last year, a heart pacer. Several years ago he experienced what he calls a "small stroke," which left him "mixed up" for a few days. But he "worked this out," he reports, by "walking a lot," an activity in which he engages frequently.
>
> Mr. Z. says he has never smoked and drinks only on "occasions" or holidays, and then only to a limited degree. He scorns food fads, and eats "mostly" fresh fruits and "lots of vegetables"; he loves fish and drinks lots of tea.
>
> Despite all his troubles, Mr. Z. maintains what is apparently a cheerful, optimistic view of life and circumstances, while he pursues his "hobby" of energetically helping his fellow residents keep their spirits up and their interests high.
>
> He is very highly regarded and seen as filling a very important role in his nursing home as a story-teller and entertainer.*

In summary, the quality of life for the frail elderly depends on three factors: (1) the specific nature and timing of the health-related limitations that accompany aging; (2) the availability of appropriate resources within the home, family, and community to help compensate for or minimize those limitations; and (3) the selective emphasis that the person gives to some life experiences over others as being central to well-being.

---

*From Schwartz, Snyder, & Peterson, 1984.

Chapter Summary

In attempting to describe the psychosocial development of the very old, we are drawn to concepts that have a strong non-Western philosophical flavor. We have introduced such concepts as psychohistorical perspective, experiential transcendence, immortality, and social support—themes that reflect the need to assume a long-range perspective on life and its meaning. The concept of time changes with advanced age so that the continuity of past, present, and future becomes clearer. With the attainment of a deep confidence in being meaningfully integrated into an effective social system, the very old can find pleasure in the natural flow of events without concern about the accumulation of material goods or the need to exercise power.

The actual quality of daily life for the very old is influenced to a great extent by their health. The daily activities of many older adults are restricted by one or more chronic diseases. Nevertheless, the majority of the very old continue to live in their own households and to perform tasks of daily living independently. A key to the ability of the very old to retain their independence lies in whether or not they are integrated into effective social support networks. A support system provides help, resources, meaningful social interaction, and a psychological sense of being valued. Those who are isolated are more likely to face the end of their life bound to the tedium of struggling with physical limitations and resenting their survival. Those who survive within a support system can transcend the real limitations of their health, finding comfort and continuity in their participation in a continuing chain of loving relationships.

References

Adams, R. G. (1985). People would talk: Normative barriers to cross-sex friendships for elderly women. *Gerontologist*, 25, 605–611.

Alwin, D. (1984). Living alone. ISR *Newsletter*, 12, 3–4.

Baltes, P. B. & Smith, J. (1990). The psychology of wisdom and its ontogenesis. In R. J. Sternberg (Ed.), *Wisdom: Its nature, origins and development* (pp. 87–120). New York: Cambridge University Press.

Baltes, P. B., Smith. J. & Staudinger, U. M. (1992). Wisdom and successful aging. In T. B. Sonderegger (Ed.), *Psychology and aging* (pp. 123–168). Lincoln: University of Nebraska Press.

Bashore, T. R., Osman, A. & Heffley, E. F., III. (1989). Mental slowing in elderly persons: A cognitive psychophysiological analysis. *Psychology and Aging*, 4, 235–244.

Bergeman, C. S., Plomin, R., Pedersen, N. L., McClearn, G. E. & Nesselroade, J. R. (1990). Genetic and environmental influences on social support: The Swedish adoption/twin study of aging. *Journal of Gerontology: Psychological Sciences*, 45, 101–106.

Birnbaum, H., Burke, R., Swearingen, C. & Dunlop, B. (1984). Implementing community-based long-term care: Experience of New York's long-term home health care program. *Gerontologist*, 24, 380–386.

Birren, J. E. & Fisher, L. M. (1992). Aging and slowing of behavior: Consequences for cognition and survival. In T. B. Sonderegger (Ed.), *Psychology and aging*. Lincoln: University of Nebraska Press.

Blumenthal, J. A., Emery, C. F., Madden, D. J., George, L. K., Coleman, R. E., Riddle, M. W., McKee, D. C., Reasoner, J. & Williams, R. S. (1989). Cardiovascular and behavioral effects of aerobic exercise training in healthy older men and women. *Journal of Gerontology: Medical Sciences*, 44, M147–M157.

Branch, L. G. & Stuart, N. E. (1984). A five-year history of targeting home care services to prevent institutionalization. *Gerontologist*, 24, 387–392.

Bretschneider, J. G. & McCoy, N. L. (1988). Sexual interest and behavior in healthy 80- to 102-year-olds. *Archives of Sexual Behavior*, 17, 109–129.

Bryn Mawr Alumnae Bulletin. (1993, Fall). Class notes, pp. 31–32.

Burr, J. A. & Mutchler, J. E. (1993). Nativity, acculturation, and economic statues: Explanations of Asian American living arrangements in later life. *The Journals of Gerontology*, 48, S55–S63.

Cerella, J. (1994). Generalized slowing in Brinley Plots. *The Journals of Gerontology*, 49, P65–P71.

Choi, N. G. (1991). Racial differences in the determinants of living arrangements of widowed and divorced elderly women. *Gerontologist*, 4, 496–504.

Clayman, J. L. (1989). *The American Medical Association encyclopedia of medicine.* New York: Random House.

Clayton, V. P. & Birren, J. E. (1980). The development of wisdom across the life span: A reexamination of an ancient topic. In P. B. Baltes & O. G. Brim, Jr. (Eds.), *Life-span development and behavior* (Vol. 3, pp. 104–135). New York: Academic Press.

Cobb, S. (1979). Social support and health through the life course. In M. W. Riley (Ed.), *Aging from birth to death*. Boulder, CO: Westview.

Cohen, M. A., Tell, E. J., Bishop, C. E., Wallack, S. S. & Branch, L. G. (1989). Patterns of nursing home use in a prepaid managed care system: The continuing care retirement community. *Gerontologist*, 29, 74–80.

Cohen, M. A., Tell, E. J. & Wallack, S. S. (1988). The risk factors of nursing home entry among residents of six continuing care retirement communities. *Journal of Gerontology: Social Sciences*, 43, S15–S21.

Cool, L. E. (1987). The effects of social class and ethnicity on the aging process. In P. Silverman (Ed.), *The elderly as modern pioneers*. Bloomington: Indiana University Press.

Denney, N. W. (1982). Aging and cognitive changes. In B. B. Wolman (Ed.), *Handbook of developmental psychology* (pp. 807–827). Englewood Cliffs, NJ: Prentice-Hall.

Dustman, R., Emmerson, R., Ruhling, R., Shearer, D., Steinhaus, L., Johnson, S., Bonekat, H. & Shigeoka, J. (1989). Age and fitness effects on EEG, ERP's, visual sensitivity and cognition. *Neurobiology of Aging*, 10, 2–15.

Erikson, E., Erikson, J. & Kivnick, H. (1986). *Vital involvement in old age*. New York: Norton.

Fiatarone, M. A. & Evans, W. J. (1993). The etiology and reversibility of muscle dysfunctions in the aged. *The Journals of Gerontology*, 48. 77–83.

Flynn, C. B., Longino, C. F., Jr., Wiseman, R. F. & Biggar, J. C. (1985). The redistribution of America's older population: Major national migration patterns for three census decades, 1960–1980. *Gerontologist*, 25, 292–296.

Fultz, N. H. & Herzog, A. R. (1991). Gender differences in affiliation and instrumentality across adulthood. *Psychology and Aging*, 6, 579–586.

Gottesman, L. E., Quarterman, C. E. & Cohn, G. M. (1973). Psychosocial treatment of the aged. In C. Eisdorfer & M. P. Lawton (Eds.), *The psychology of adult development and aging*. Washington, DC: American Psychological Association.

Guralnik, J. M. & Kaplan, G. A. (1989). Predictors of healthy aging: Prospective evidence from the Alameda County study. *American Journal of Public Health*, 79, 703–708.

Guralnik, J. M. & Simonsick, E. M. (1993). Physical disability in older Americans. *The Journals of Gerontology*, 48, 3–10.

Gutmann, D. (1987). *Reclaimed powers: Toward a new psychology of men and women in later life*. New York: Basic Books.

Hadley, E. C., Ory, M. G., Suzman, R. & Weindruch, R. (1993). Forword. *The Journals of Gerontology*, 48, vii–viii.

Haley, W. E. & Pardo, K. M. (1989). Relationship of severity of dementia to caregiving stressors. *Psychology and Aging*, 4, 389–392.

Hays, J. A. (1984). Aging and family resources: Availability and proximity of kin. *Gerontologist*, 24, 149–153.

Heckhausen, J., Dixon, R. A. & Baltes, P. B. (1989). Gains and losses in development throughout adulthood as perceived by different adult age groups. *Developmental Psychology*, 25, 109–121.

Hertzog, C. (1989). Influences of cognitive slowing on age differences in intelligence. *Developmental Psychology*, 25, 636–651.

Heynen, J. (1990). *One hundred over one hundred*. Golden, CO: Fulcrum.

Hillman, J. L. & Stricker, G. (1994). A linkage of knowledge and attitudes toward elderly sexuality: Not necessarily a uniform relationship. *Gerontologist*, 34, 256–260.

Hopper, K. & Hamberg, L. (1986). The making of America's homeless: From skid row to new poor, 1945–1984. In R. Bratt, C. Harman & A. Meyerson (Eds.), *Critical perspectives on housing*. Philadelphia: Temple University Press.

Horn, J. L. (1982). The aging of human abilities. In B. B. Wolman (Ed.), *Handbook of developmental psychology* (pp. 847–870). Englewood Cliffs, NJ: Prentice-Hall.

House, J. S. (1985, Winter). Social support. LSA, 8, 5–8.

Ingersoll-Dayton, B. & Antonucci, T. C. (1988). Reciprocal and nonreciprocal social support: Contrasting sides of intimate relationships. *Gerontology*, 43, S65–S73.

Jarvik, L. F. & Kumar, V. (1984). Update on diagnosis: Update on treatment. *Generations*, pp. 7–11.

Jewett, S. (1973). Longevity and the longevity syndrome. *Gerontologist*, 13, 91–99.

Kahana, B. (1982). Social behavior and aging. In B. B. Wolman (Ed.), *Handbook of developmental psychology* (pp. 871–889). Englewood Cliffs, NJ: Prentice-Hall.

Keith, J. (1982). *Old people as people: Social and cultural influences on aging and old age*. Boston: Little, Brown.

Kinney, J. M. & Stephens, M. A. P. (1989). Hassles and uplifts of giving care to a family member with dementia. *Psychology and Aging*, 4, 402–408.

Kite, M. E., Deaux, K. & Miele, M. (1991). Stereotypes of young and old: Does age outweigh gender? *Psychology and Aging*, 6, 19–27.

Kosnik, W., Winslow, L., Kline, D., Rasinski, K. & Sekuler, R. (1988). Visual changes in daily life throughout adulthood. *Gerontology*, 43, P63–P70.

Lifton, R. J. (1973). The sense of immortality: On death and the continuity of life. *American Journal of Psychoanalysis*, 33, 3–15.

Marshall, W. A. (1973). The body. In R. R. Sears & S. Feldman (Eds.), *The seven ages of man*. Los Altos, CA: William Kaufman.

Meyers, G. C. & Manton, K. G. (1984). Compression of mortality: Myth or reality? *Gerontologist*, 24, 346–353.

Miller, I. J., Jr. (1988). Human taste bud density across adult age groups. *Journal of Gerontology: Biological Sciences*, 43, B26–B30.

Morse, C. K. (1993). Does variability increase with age? An archival study of cognitive measures. *Psychology and Aging*, 8, 156–164.

Murrell, S. A. & Norris, F. H. (1991). Differential social support and life change as contributors to the social class-distress relationship in older adults. *Psychology and Aging*, 6, 223–231.

Neugarten, B. L. (1981). Growing old in 2020. *National Forum*, 61, 28–30.

Newcomer, R. (1976). An evaluation of neighborhood service convenience for elderly housing project residents. In P. Suedfeld & J. Russell (Eds.), *The behavioral basis of design*. New York: McGraw-Hill.

Offenbacher, D. I. & Poster, C. H. (1985). Aging and the baseline code: An alternative to the "normless elderly." *Gerontologist*, 25, 526–531.

O'Leary, P. A., Haley, W. E. & Paul, P. B. (1993). Behavioral assessment in Alzheimer's disease: Use of a 24-hr log. *Psychology and Aging*, 8, 139–143.

Pallett-Hehn, P. & Lucas, M. (1994). LIFE: Learning informally from elders. *Gerontologist*, 34, 267–271.

Palmore, E. B., Nowlin, J. B. & Wang, H. S. (1985). Predictors of function among the old-old: A 10-year follow-up. *Journal of Gerontology*, 40, 244–250.

Perfect, T. J. (1994). What can Brinley Plots tell us about cognitive aging? *The Journals of Gerontology*, 49, P60–P64.

Pratt, C. C., Jones, L. L., Shin, H. & Walker, A. J. (1989). Autonomy and decision making between single older women and their caregiving daughters. *Gerontologist*, 29, 792–797.

Reese, J. N. & Botwinick, J. (1971). Detection and decision factors in auditory behavior of the elderly. *Journal of Gerontology*, 26, 133–136.

Riegel, K. F. (1973). Dialectic operations: The final period of cognitive development. *Human Development*, 16, 346–370.

Rogers, A. (1990). Return migration to region of birth among retirement-age persons in the United States. *Journal of Gerontology: Social Sciences*, 45, S128–S134.

Rosenfeld, A. H. (1978). *New views on older lives*. Rockville, MD: National Institute of Mental Health.

Russell, D. W. & Cutrona, C. E. (1991). Social support, stress, and depressive symptoms among the elderly: Test of a process model. *Psychology and Aging*, 6, 190–201.

Ryff, C. D. & Essex, M. J. (1992). The interpretation of life experiences and well-being: The sample case of relocation. *Psychology and Aging*, 7, 507–517.

Salthouse, T. A. (1985). Speed of behavior and its implications for cognition. In J. W. Birren & K. W. Schaie (Eds.), *Handbook of the psychology of aging* (pp. 400–426). New York: Van Nostrand Reinhold.

Schulz, R. & Willamson, G. M. (1993). Psychosocial and behavioral dimensions of physical frailty. *The Journals of Gerontology*, 48, 39–43.

Schwartz, A. N., Snyder, C. L. & Peterson, J. A. (1984). *Aging and life: An introduction to gerontology* (2nd ed.). New York: Holt, Rinehart & Winston.

Singelakis, A. T. (1990). Real estate market trends and the displacement of the aged: Examination of the linkages in Manhattan. *Gerontologist*, 30, 658–666.

Spitzer, M. E. (1988). Taste acuity in institutionalized and noninstitutionalized elderly men. *Journal of Gerontology: Psychological Sciences*, 43, P71–P74.

Stephens, M. A. P. & Bernstein, M. D. (1984). Social support and well-being among residents of planned housing. *Gerontologist*, 24, 144–148.

Sternberg, R. J. (Ed.). (1990). *Wisdom: Its nature, origins, and development*. New York: Cambridge University Press.

Stevens, J. C. & Cain, W. S. (1987). Old-age deficits in the sense of smell as gauged by thresholds, magnitude matching, and odor identification. *Psychology and Aging*, 2, 36–42.

Szasz, T. S. (1982). The psychiatric will: A new mechanism for protecting persons against "psychosis" and psychiatry. *American Psychologist*, 37, 762–770.

Taylor, R. J. (1986). Religious participation among elderly blacks. *Gerontologist*, 26, 630–636.

Tucker, M. B., Taylor, R. J. & Mitchell-Kernan, C. (1993). Marriage and romantic involvement among aged African Americans. *The Journals of Gerontology*, 48, S123–S132.

Turner, J. S. & Rubinson, L. (1993). *Contemporary human sexuality*. Englewood Cliffs, NJ: Prentice-Hall.

U.S. Bureau of the Census. (1987). *An aging world*. International Population Reports (Ser. P-95, No. 78). Washington, DC: U.S. Government Printing Office.

U.S. Bureau of the Census. (1989a). *Population profile of the United States, 1989*. Current Population Reports (Ser. P-23, No. 159). Washington, DC: U.S. Government Printing Office.

U.S. Bureau of the Census. (1989b). *Statistical abstract of the United States, 1989*. Washington, DC: U.S. Government Printing Office.

U.S. Bureau of the Census. (1991). *Statistical abstract of the United States, 1991*. Washington, DC: U.S. Government Printing Office.

U.S. Bureau of the Census. (1992). *Statistical abstract of the United States, 1992*. Washington, DC: U.S. Government Printing Office.

U.S. Senate, Special Committee on Aging. (1986). *Aging America—trends and projections*. Washington, DC: U.S. Government Printing Office.

Wagner, D. R. (1984, Winter). Sleep. *Generations*, pp. 31–36.

Wallechinsky, D. & Wallace, A. (1993). *The book of lists*. New York: Little, Brown.

Wallechinsky, D., Wallace, I. & Wallace, A. (1977). *The book of lists*. New York: Morrow.

Walls, C. T. & Zarit, S. H. (1991). Informal support from black churches and the well-being of elderly blacks. *Gerontologist*, 31, 490–495.

Weiler, P. G., Chiriboga, D. A. & Black, S. A. (1994). Comparison of mental status tests: Implications for Alzheimer's patients and their caregivers. *The Journals of Gerontology*, 49, S44–51.

Wentowski, G. J. (1985). Older women's perceptions of great-grandmotherhood: A research note. *Gerontologist*, 25, 593–596.

Willis, S., Diehl, M., Gruber-Baldini, A., Marsiske, M. & Haessler, S. (1990, March). Correlates and predictors of intellectual performance and intellectual change in older adults. Paper presented at the Third Cognitive Aging Conference, Atlanta.

Zweibel, N. R. & Cassel, C. K. (1989). Treatment choices at the end of life: A comparison of decisions by older patients and their physician-selected proxies. *Gerontologist, 29,* 615–621.

Appendix: Variations in Life Expectancy

The four tables in this appendix contain information about variations in life expectancy. In Table 1, information about the average remaining lifetime for persons aged 65, 75, and 80 in seven birth cohorts indicates the likelihood of reaching very old age for males and females by race.

In Table 2 we compare the average lifetimes of men and women in the 50 states. Numerous regional factors are associated with longevity, including variations by state in financial and health care resources, education, exposure to environmental hazards, and lifestyle. The data may also reflect genetic patterns in members of regional subgroups.

In Tables 3 and 4 we provide international data on longevity. In Table 3 consistent patterns in gender differences are indicated in 19 developed countries. In Table 4 the impact of economic and educational development on longevity is viewed from a global perspective.

TABLE 1 Average Remaining Lifetime at Various Ages by Sex and Race, 1900 to 1989

Exact Age, Race, and Sex	1989	1978	1968	1954	1939–1941	1929–1931	1900–1902
All Classes							
At birth	75.3	73.3	70.2	69.6	63.6	59.3	49.2
65 years	17.2	16.3	14.6	14.4	12.8	12.3	11.9
75 years	10.9	10.4	9.1	9.0	7.6	7.3	7.1
80 years	8.3	8.1	6.8	6.9	5.7	5.4	5.3
White							
Male:							
At birth	72.2	70.2	67.5	67.4	62.8	59.1	48.2
65 years	15.2	14.0	12.8	13.1	12.1	11.8	11.5
75 years	9.4	8.6	8.1	8.2	7.2	7.0	6.8
80 years	7.1	6.7	6.2	6.3	5.4	5.3	5.1
Female:							
At birth	79.2	77.8	74.9	73.6	67.3	62.7	51.1
65 years	19.0	18.4	16.4	15.7	13.6	12.8	12.2
75 years	11.9	11.5	9.8	9.4	7.9	7.6	7.3
80 years	8.9	8.8	7.0	7.0	5.9	5.6	5.5
Black and Other Races[†]							
Male:							
At birth	64.8	65.0	60.1	61.0	52.3	47.6	32.5
65 years	13.6	14.1	12.1	13.5	12.2	10.9	10.4
75 years	8.8	9.8	9.9	10.4	8.2	7.0	6.6
80 years	6.9	8.8	8.7	9.1	6.6	5.4	5.1
Female:							
At birth	73.5	73.6	67.5	65.8	55.6	49.5	35.0
65 years	17.0	18.0	15.1	15.7	13.9	12.2	11.4
75 years	11.0	12.5	11.5	12.0	9.8	8.6	7.9
80 years	8.5	11.5	9.3	10.1	8.0	6.9	6.5

[†] Black only for 1989, 1929–1931, and 1900–1902.

Source: U.S. Bureau of the Census, 1984, 1992.

TABLE 2 Average Lifetime in Years, by Sex and States: 1979–1981

State	Both Sexes Number	Rank	Male	Female
U.S.	73.88	(x)	70.11	77.62
AL	72.53	45	68.28	76.79
AK	72.24	46	68.71	76.87
AZ	74.30	21	70.46	78.34
AR	73.72	29	69.73	77.83
CA	74.57	20	71.09	78.02
CO	75.30	9	71.78	78.80
CT	75.12	12	71.51	78.57
DE	73.21	40	69.56	76.78
DC	69.20	(x)	64.55	73.70
FL	74.00	¹23	70.08	77.98
GA	72.22	47	68.01	76.35
HI	77.02	1	74.08	80.33
ID	75.19	10	71.52	79.15
IL	73.37	37	69.55	77.13
IN	73.84	¹27	70.16	77.46
IA	75.81	3	72.00	79.60
KS	75.31	8	71.60	78.99
KY	73.06	41	69.14	77.12
LA	71.74	50	67.64	75.89
ME	74.59	19	70.78	78.41
MD	73.32	38	69.71	76.83
MA	75.01	13	71.27	78.46
MI	73.67	¹31	70.07	77.29
MN	76.15	2	72.52	79.82
MS	71.98	48	67.64	76.39
MO	73.84	¹27	69.92	77.72
MT	73.93	25	70.47	77.68
NE	75.49	6	71.73	79.29
NV	72.64	44	69.26	76.48
NH	74.98	15	71.43	78.42
NJ	74.00	¹23	70.48	77.39
NM	74.01	22	69.91	78.34
NY	73.70	30	70.02	77.18
NC	72.96	42	68.60	77.35
ND	75.71	5	72.09	79.68
OH	73.49	35	69.85	77.06
OK	73.67	¹31	69.63	77.81
OR	74.99	14	71.35	78.77
PA	73.58	34	69.90	77.16
RI	74.76	18	70.96	78.33
SC	71.85	49	67.56	76.12
SD	74.97	16	71.03	79.21
TN	73.30	39	69.15	77.47
TX	73.64	33	69.70	77.67
UT	75.76	4	72.38	79.18
VT	74.79	17	71.06	78.49
VA	73.43	36	69.60	77.27
WA	75.13	11	71.74	78.57
WV	72.84	43	68.86	76.93
WI	75.35	7	71.86	78.87
WY	73.85	26	69.95	78.20

(x) Not applicable. ¹Florida and New Jersey share the rank of 23; Indiana and Missouri share the rank of 27; Michigan and Oklahoma share the rank of 31. Therefore, rank numbers 24, 28, and 32 are omitted.

Source: U.S. National Center for Health Statistics, 1985.

TABLE 3   Life Expectancy at Birth and at Age 65, by Sex, for Various Countries: Data Sources from 1981–1988.

	Males		Females	
	At Birth	At Age 65	At Birth	At Age 65
Austria	73.2	14.9	78.2	17.6
Canada	73.3	15.1	80.2	19.6
Czechoslovakia	67.7	11.9	75.3	15.5
Denmark	71.9	14.2	78.0	18.2
England and Wales	72.6	13.9	78.3	17.9
Finland	70.7	13.5	78.9	17.7
France	72.6	15.4	81.1	20.2
Germany*	72.2	14.0	78.9	18.1
Hungary	65.7	12.1	73.9	15.4
Israel	73.4	14.9	77.0	16.0
Italy	72.7	14.3	79.2	18.2
Japan	75.9	16.4	82.1	20.4
Netherlands	73.6	14.4	80.3	19.3
New Zealand	71.0	13.7	77.3	17.6
Norway	72.8	14.4	79.8	18.8
Sweden	74.2	15.1	80.4	19.1
United States	71.5	14.8	78.4	18.7
Soviet Union*	61.5	12.5	73.9	16.2
Yugoslavia	68.5	13.3	74.3	15.6

*This table was compiled before Germany was reunified and the Soviet Union became a commonwealth.

Source: Current Population Reports, 1992.

TABLE 4   Life Expectancy at Birth by Continent or Region: 1994

Continent and Region	1994 Life Expectancy (Years)
World total	**62**
More developed regions	74
Less developed regions	61
Africa	53
Asia, excluding Near East	62
Near East	67
Latin America and the Caribbean	68
North America	76
Europe	76
(Former) Soviet Union	69
Oceania	70

Source: U.S. Bureau of the Census, 1994.

Glossary

abasement A lowering in rank, office, prestige, or esteem.

abdominal cavity The area between the lower border of the ribs and the upper border of the thighs. The abdominal cavity includes organs of both the digestive and urinary systems.

abortion Termination of a pregnancy before the fetus is capable of surviving outside the uterus.

accommodation (a) In Piaget's theory of cognitive development, the process of changing existing schema in order to account for novel elements in the object or the event. (b) In vision, changes in the curvature of the lens in response to the distance of the stimulus.

achievement motivation Internal state of arousal that leads to vigorous, persistent, goal-directed behavior when an individual is asked to perform a task in relation to some standard of excellence and when performance will be evaluated in terms of success and failure.

acoustic Pertaining to the quality of sounds.

acquired immunodeficiency syndrome (AIDS) A deficiency of the immune system due to infection with the human immunodeficiency virus.

acute illness Illness that begins suddenly and lasts a brief time, such as a cold.

adaptation The total process of change in response to environmental conditions.

adaptive self-organization The process by which an open system retains its essential identity when confronted with new and constant environmental conditions. It creates new substructures, revises the relationships among components, and establishes new, higher levels of organization that coordinate existing substructures.

adaptive self-regulation Adjustments made by an operating system in which feedback mechanisms identify and respond to environmental changes in order to maintain and enhance the functioning of the system.

adult executive Family pattern in which all the adults in the household participate in decision making.

advocate A person who pleads another's cause.

affect Emotion, feeling, or mood.

affiliative behavior Actions intended to form positive, affectionate bonds with others.

age-graded expectation An assumption that someone should do something because of how old he or she is.

agency Viewing the self as the originator of action.

aggression Hostile, injurious, or destructive behavior.

alcoholism An addiction to alcohol; excessive and compulsive use of alcohol.

alienation Withdrawal or separation of people or their affections from an object or position of former attachment.

allele The alternate state of a gene at a given locus.

alliances Bonds or connections between families, groups, or individuals.

Alzheimer's disease The most common form of chronic brain syndrome involving gradual brain failure over a period of 7 to 10 years.

ambiguity Uncertainty or confusion of meaning.

ambivalence A state of having simultaneous conflicting feelings about a person, object, or event.

amino acids Organic acids that are the basic building blocks of proteins.

amniocentesis The surgical insertion of a hollow needle through the abdominal wall and into the uterus of a pregnant woman to obtain fluid for the determination of sex or chromosomal abnormality of the fetus.

amniotic sac A thin membrane forming a closed sac around the embryo and containing a fluid in which the embryo is immersed.

anal stage In Freud's psychosexual theory, the second life stage, during which the anus is a primary source of sexual satisfaction. Issues of willfulness and order are central to this stage.

androgeny The capacity to express both masculine and feminine characteristics as the situation demands.

anesthetic A substance that produces loss of sensation with or without loss of consciousness.

animosity Ill will or resentment.

anomaly Irregularity, something that is inconsistent with the normal condition.

anorexia nervosa An emotional disorder in which the person loses the ability to regulate eating behavior; the person is obsessed with a fear of being overweight and avoids food or becomes nauseous after eating.

anoxia A medical term that means complete absence of oxygen within a tissue, such as the brain or a muscle, causing disruption in cell metabolism and cell death unless it is corrected within a few minutes.

antecedent A preceding event, condition, or cause.

antibodies Substances that neutralize toxins and destroy harmful bacteria or viruses in the bloodstream.

anxiety A painful or apprehensive uneasiness of mind, usually over an impending or anticipated problem.

Apgar rating Assessment of the newborn based on heart rate, respiration, muscle tone, response to stimulation, and skin color.

aptitude Potential for learning and future performance of a skill.

arbitrary Selected at random and without logical reason.

artificial insemination Injection of donor sperm into a woman's vagina to promote conception.

aspiration A strong desire to achieve something.

assimilation In Piaget's theory of cognitive development, the process of incorporating objects or events into existing schema.

assumption A fact, statement, or premise that is considered true and that guides the underlying logic of a theory.

attachment The tendency to remain close to a familiar individual who is ready and willing to give care, comfort, and aid in time of need.

attachment behavioral system A complex set of reflexes and signaling behaviors that inspire caregiving and protective responses in adults; these responses shape a baby's expectations and help create an image of the parent in the child's mind.

attachment patterns Three distinct behavior patterns of attachment that are characteristic of infants and seem to lead to different patterns of attachment formation in later relationships. 1. *Secure attachment*: confidence in a caregiver, permitting exploration of the environment with little protest over brief separations; 2. *Anxious-avoidant attachment*: expectation that requests for comfort will be rejected, reflected in considerable distress at separation, and rejection of caregiver's efforts to interact or soothe after separation; 3. *Anxious-resistant attachment*: expectation of unpredictable behavior from caregiver, leading to distress at separation, caution in the presence of strangers, erratic exploratory behavior, and apparent desire for closeness with caregiver combined with anger at caregiver.

attribution The act of ascribing a quality or characteristic to someone else or to oneself.

auditory acuity The ability to recognize sounds of varying pitch and loudness.

auditory system The body parts and neural connections related to hearing.

authoritarian A style of decision making in which the leader assumes total responsibility for making decisions and assigning responsibility. The authoritarian leader or parent expects obedience from everyone in a lower status position.

authority A person who has power and influence and who is seen by others as the legitimate decision maker.

authority structure An influence and decision-making system of relationships in business, government, education, and families.

autonomous morality A more mature moral perspective in which rules are viewed as a product of cooperative agreements.

autonomy The ability to behave independently, to do things on one's own.

autosomal A chromosome other than a sex chromosome.

avoidance conditioning A kind of learning in which specific stimuli are identified as painful or unpleasant and are therefore avoided.

Babinski reflex A response in which toes extend and fan out when the sole of the foot is gently stroked. This reflex is a sign of an immature nervous system. Eventually, a stroke on the sole of the foot makes one's toes curl down.

bar mitzvah In the Jewish religion, a ceremony celebrated at age 13 to mark a boy's entry into adult status (*bas mitzvah* for girls).

basal metabolism Amount of energy used at rest.

behavioral slowing Age-related delay in the speed of response to stimuli.

behavior modification The use of concepts from learning theory, especially reinforcement, repetition, and association, to alter behavior.

bereavement The emotional suffering that follows the death of a loved one.

bilingualism The ability to speak two languages fluently.

biological adaptation A process whereby species evolve that have characteristics most suitable to the conditions of the environment.

birth order The order in which children in a family were born.

breathing capacity Oxygen capacity and efficiency of the lungs.

burn out A feeling of worthlessness brought about through prolonged exposure to work conditions that are frustrating, emotionally draining, and threatening.

cajole To persuade with flattery and humor.

care The commitment to be concerned.

career Occupation(s) or profession(s) followed as a lifework.

case study A research method consisting of an in-depth description and analysis of a single person, family, or group.

categorization The process of arranging, classifying, or describing by labeling or naming.

causal agent A person or object that makes something happen.

causality The relation between a cause and an effect.

cell differentiation A process whereby cells take on specialized structures related to their function.

cell nucleus The part of the cell that contains the material essential to reproduction and protein synthesis.

central process the dominant context or mechanism through which the psychosocial crisis is resolved.

cephalocaudal The direction of development that follows from the head to the feet.

cerebellum A part of the brain located in the back; the area that coordinates muscle activity and equilibrium.

cerebral cortex The layer of gray matter in the brain that serves to coordinate central nervous system functions.

cerebrum The upper part of the brain; the seat of conscious mental processes.

cervix The narrow lower end of the uterus, which forms the beginning of the birth canal.

cesarian delivery Delivering a newborn by lifting it out through an incision in the uterine wall.

chromosome One of the rodlike bodies of a cell nucleus that contain genetic material and that divide when the cell divides. In humans there are 23 pairs of chromosomes.

chronic illness Illness that lasts a long time. It may begin suddenly and recur or become progressively more serious.

chronological Arranged in the order of time.

chronological age The number of years and months since birth.

circular reaction In cognitive development, the infant's use of familiar actions to achieve familiar results.

circumcision Removing the foreskin that covers the glans of the penis.

classical conditioning A form of learning in which a formerly neutral stimulus is repeatedly presented with a stimulus that evokes a specific reflexive response. After repeated pairings, the neutral stimulus elicits a response similar to the reflexive response.

classification The action of grouping objects according to some specific characteristics they have in common, including all objects that show the characteristic and none that do not.

climacteric The period of menopause for women and a parallel period of reduced reproductive competence for men.

clinical studies Research conducted on populations who are or have been treated for a problem, or who are waiting to be treated.

clique A small, exclusive group of people.

condominance A condition in which both genes at a specific allele contribute to the characteristic that is expressed, as in AB blood type.

coercive escalation A style of interaction in which the probability that a negative remark will be followed by another negative remark increases as the chain of communication gets longer and longer.

cognition The capacity for knowing, organizing perceptions, and problem solving.

cognitive behaviorism The study of those cognitive dimensions related to understanding a person's ability to learn and perform tasks.

cognitive differentiation The act of adding additional units of information, which increases the complexity of a concept.

cognitive map An internal mental representation of the environment.

cognitive representation Scheme, mental image.

cognitive style A characteristic way of analyzing problems and organizing events.

cognitive theory An analysis of the quality of thought and changes in thought at various stages of development.

cognitive unconscious The range of mental structures and processes that operate outside awareness but play a significant role in conscious thought and action.

cohabitation A relationship in which a man and woman live together but are not married.

cohort In research design, a group of subjects who are studied during the same time period.

cohort sequential study A research design that combines cross-sectional and longitudinal methods. Cohorts consist of participants in a certain age group. Different cohorts are studied at different times. New cohorts of younger groups are added in successive data collections to replace those who have grown older. This design allows the analysis of age differences, changes over time, and the effects of social and historical factors.

coitus Sexual intercourse.

colloquial Used in familiar or informal conversation.

combinatorial skills The ability to perform mathematical operations, including addition, subtraction, and multiplication. These skills are acquired during the stage of concrete operational thought.

communication skills All those skills involved in accurately expressing one's thoughts to others and in accurately interpreting the meaning of communications from others.

competence The exercise of skill and intelligence in the completion of tasks.

competence (sense of) The sense that one is capable of exercising mastery over one's environment.

competence motivation The desire to exercise mastery by effectively manipulating objects or social interactions.

competition A contest between rivals.

compulsions Repetitive ritualized actions that serve as mechanisms for controlling anxiety.

concrete operational thought In Piaget's theory, a stage of cognitive development in which rules of logic can be applied to observable or manipulatable physical relations.

conditional reward A positive consequence that occurs when a specific condition or standard is met.

conditioned response A response that is evoked by a stimulus as a result of repeated, systematic association.

conditioned stimulus A stimulus that evokes a response as a result of repeated, systematic association.

confidence A conscious trust in oneself and in the meaningfulness of life.

conformity Behavior in accordance with some specified standard or expectation.

congenital Existing from the time of birth.

congruence model A model of sex role identity which suggests that it is most adaptive for males to adopt a strong masculine sex role and for females to adopt a strong feminine sex role.

connotation The images and ideas suggested by a word rather than the specific object or action to which the word refers.

conscious The kind of mental activity of which one is aware.

consensus General agreement.

conservation The concept that physical changes do not alter the mass, weight, number, or volume of matter. This concept is acquired during the concrete operational stage of cognitive development.

consonantal sounds Sounds made by the consonants as opposed to the vowels.

context The set of circumstances or facts that surround a person, event, or situation.

contextual dissonance Discrepancy between a characteristic of the individual and norms related to that characteristic within the community, for example being one of few poor children in a middle-class school.

contextualist A person who argues that behavior takes its meaning from the situation or circumstances in which it occurs.

contextualization of learning Offering instruction in ways that first draw upon a child's existing experiences, knowledge, and concepts and then expand them in new directions.

contingent relationship The effect of a behavior consistently producing a specific outcome.

contingent roles Roles that serve to define the behaviors of adjacent role groups, as parent-child, or student-teacher.

continuing-care retirement community Nursing homes for the elderly that offer housing, medical, and social services to residents who are well when admitted, and that guarantee nursing care to residents who become ill or disabled.

contour The edge or line that encompasses or defines a shape or object.

contraceptive A method of preventing conception or impregnation.

contractions Tightening of the uterine muscles during childbirth.

control group The subjects in an experiment who do not experience the manipulation or treatment and whose responses or reactions are compared with those of subjects who are treated actively to determine the effects of the manipulation.

conventional morality A stage of moral reasoning described by Kohlberg in which right and wrong are closely associated with the rules created by legitimate authorities, including parents, teachers, or political leaders.

cooperation Working or acting together for a common purpose or benefit.

coping Active efforts to respond to stress. Coping includes gathering new information, maintaining control over one's emotions, and preserving freedom of movement.

core pathologies Destructive forces that result from severe, negative resolutions of the psychosocial crises.

corollary Something that follows naturally from a previous statement.

correlation A measure of the strength and direction of the relationship among variables.

creativity The willingness to abandon old forms or patterns of doing things and to think of new ways.

critical period A time of maximum sensitivity to or readiness for the development of a particular skill or behavior pattern.

crossing-over Interchange of genes or chromosome segments.

cross-sectional study A research design in which the behavior of subjects of different ages, social backgrounds, or environmental settings is measured once to acquire information about the effects of these differences.

crowd A large group that is usually recognized by a few predominant characteristics, such as the preppies, the jocks, or the druggies.

crystallized intelligence Skills and information that are acquired through education and socialization.

cultural continuity A smooth transition from the role expectations of childhood through adolescence and adulthood.

cultural determinism The theoretical concept that culture shapes individual experience.

cultural discontinuity Discrete expectations associated with each stage or period of life.

cultural norms Shared expectations held by members of society for one another's behavior.

cultural relativism A premise of cultural anthropology that the meaning of a specific ritual or norm must be interpreted in light of the values and goals of the culture.

culture The concepts, habits, skills, arts, technology, religion, and government of a group of people during a specific period.

cumulative relation In heredity, when the allelic states in a single pair of genes combine to influence a trait.

curriculum The courses offered by an educational institution.

day care A variety of programs and settings designed to care for infants and young children on a daily basis.

decentering Gaining some objectivity over one's own point of view; reducing the dominance of one's subjective perspective in the interpretation of events.

defense mechanism A technique, usually unconscious, that attempts to alleviate the anxiety caused by the conflicting desires of the id and the superego in relation to impulses (e.g., repression, denial, projection).

deference Courteous or respectful regard for the wishes of another.

delay of gratification The ability to postpone receiving a reward or having pleasure until a later time.

dementia Disorders, either acute or chronic, that have various causes and results, some reversible and some irreversible, and that involve serious impairment or loss of intellectual capacities, control of bodily functions, and personality integration.

democratic A style of decision making in which the leader involves all group members in reaching a decision. The democratic leader expects all members to share responsibility for decisions that are made.

dependent variable A factor that is defined by a subject's responses or reactions, and that may or may not be affected by the experimenter's manipulation of the independent variable.

depression A state of feeling sad, often accompanied by feelings of low personal worth and withdrawal from relations with others.

deprivation The state of being without something one needs.

depth perception The ability to recognize and judge depth.

desensitize To provide repeated exposure to a specific stimulus so that it no longer has its original impact, as in desensitization to violence through repeated television viewing.

despair Feeling a loss of all hope and confidence.

developmental stage A period of life dominated by a particular quality of thinking or a particular mode of social relationships. The notion of stages suggests qualitative changes in competence at each phase of development.

developmental tasks Skills and competences that are acquired at each stage of development.

dialect A form of language that differs from the standard in pronunciation, grammar, and word meaning.

diaphragm The dome-shaped sheet of muscle that divides the thorax (chest) from the abdomen. The diaphragm is attached to the spine, ribs, and sternum.

differential responsiveness Responding more intensely or with greater attentiveness to some stimuli than to others.

diffidence The inability to act, due to overwhelming self-doubt.

dilatation Condition of being stretched open beyond normal limits.

discipline A strategy for punishing or changing behavior.

disclosure Revealing confidential information, ideas, feelings, or fantasies.

disdain A feeling of scorn for the weakness and frailty of oneself or others.

disengagement theory A theory describing later adulthood that suggests that psychological adjustment is associated with withdrawal from social roles and social relationships.

dissident Differing in some way.

dissociation Dissolving the ties, no longer associating together.

diuretics Drugs that increase the production of urine.

diversity Variety, differences.

division of labor Splitting the activities needed to accomplish a task between participants.

DNA Deoxyribonucleic acid. DNA molecules are the chemical building blocks of chromosomes found in the cell nucleus.

dominance The personal characteristic of asserting oneself in relation to others and of trying to control others.

dominance hierarchy A social ordering with the most controlling and assertive people at the top and the more submissive people at the bottom.

dominant gene A form of a gene that is always expressed in the phenotype when the gene is present, as in the example of Rr for tongue rolling.

double bind A kind of interaction that carries both an accepting and rejecting message.

doubt A sense of uncertainty about one's abilities and one's worth.

Down syndrome A chromosomal irregularity in which the child has an extra chromosome 21. The condition results in mental retardation.

dramatic role playing Taking on a role in fantasy play.

dual-career marriage A marriage in which both partners have high-powered professional, technical, or administrative careers.

dual-earner marriage A marriage in which both partners work to earn money.

dyadic relationship A two-person relationship.

early adolescence The period of psychosocial development that begins with the onset of puberty and ends around 18 years of age, usually with graduation from high school.

early adulthood The period of psychosocial development that begins in the early twenties and ends in the early thirties.

early school age The period of psychosocial development that begins when the child enters school around the age of five and ends around the age of seven.

effacement The shortening of the cervical canal.

efficacy The power to produce effects.

efficiency The quality of accomplishing what is undertaken with little waste of time or energy.

egalitarian Marked by the treatment of others as peers and equals out of a belief in human equality.

ego In psychoanalytic theory, the mental structure that experiences and interprets reality. The ego includes most cognitive capacities, including perception, memory, reasoning, and problem solving.

egocentric empathy Recognizing distress in another person and responding to it as if it were your own.

egocentrism The perception of oneself at the center of the world; the view that others and events base their behavior on or occur as a result of one's own perceptions.

ego ideal A set of positive standards, ideals, and ambitions that represent the way a person would like to be.

ego processes All those processes necessary for thinking and reasoning; for example, memory.

ego satisfaction Sources of satisfaction that bring a sense of personal accomplishment, pride, or power, or meet other inner motives and goals.

ego strength The soundness of the individual's personality.

Electra conflict In Freud's psychosexual theory, the central conflict of the phallic stage for a girl, when she desires intimacy with her father and expresses hostility toward her mother.

electronic fetal heart rate monitoring Continuous monitoring of fetal heart rate using an electronic amplification device.

embryo The developing human individual from the time of implantation to the end of the eighth week after conception.

embryology A branch of biology that studies the nature and development of embryos.

emotions States of feeling.

empathy The capacity to recognize and experience the emotional state of another person.

empty nest The time when children leave the home.

emulate To try to equal or excel.

enactive attainment Personal experiences of mastery.

endogenous Growing from within.

enhancement Making something more attractive.

enuresis Bed wetting beyond the age when toilet training is usually completed.

enzyme Complex proteins produced by living cells that act as catalysts for biochemical reactions.

epigenetic principle A biological plan for growth such that each function emerges in a systematic sequence until the fully functioning organism has developed.

epinephrine An adrenal hormone.

equilibrium In Piaget's theory, the balance every organism strives to attain in which organized structures (sensory, motor, or cognitive) provide effective ways of interacting with the environment.

equivalence In cognitive theory, the concept that two objects of the same size and shape remain the same in quantity even though the shape of one of them is changed.

estrogen The major female sex hormone.

ethics Principles of conduct founded upon a society's moral code.

ethnic group identity Knowing that one is a member of a certain ethnic group; recognizing that aspects of one's thoughts, feelings, and actions are influenced by ethnic membership; and taking the ethnic group values, outlook, and goals into account when making life choices.

ethnicity Traits, background, allegiance, or association that are associated with an ethnic group.

ethnic subculture The cultural values and behavioral patterns characteristic of a particular group in a society that shares a common ancestry; memories of a shared historical past; and a cultural focus on symbolic elements that distinguish the group from others.

ethology The comparative investigation of the biological bases of behavior from an evolutionary perspective, to determine the proximal causes of behavioral acts, the relative contribution of inheritance and learning to these acts, and the adaptive significance and evolutionary history of different patterns of behavior within and across species.

euphoria A sense of well-being and expansiveness.

Eurocentric Considering Europe and Europeans as focal to world culture, history, economics, philosophy, morality, and so on.

evaluation A determination of the worth of one's skill in a particular behavior.

evolution A theory that accounts for the changes from

one species to another as well as modifications within species over time.

exclusivity　A shutting out of others for elitist reasons.

exhibition　Showing one's talents or skills publicly; attracting attention to oneself.

expansion　Elaborating on a child's expression by adding more words.

expectations　Views held by oneself or by others about what would be appropriate behavior in a given situation or at a given stage of development.

expediency　Most efficient way of achieving the desired end.

experiential transcendence　A way of experiencing immortality through achieving a sense of continuous presence.

experimental group　The subjects who experience the manipulation or treatment in an experiment.

experimentation　A method of research that is conducted under repeatable and highly controlled conditions, in which some variable or group of variables is systematically manipulated while others are held constant; used to assess cause-and-effect relationships.

expressive　Using language to communicate thoughts and feelings.

extended family　The family group that includes family members other than the nucleus of parents and children.

external ear canal　The visible part of the ear, which collects and transmits sound.

extinction　(a) In classical conditioning, the reduction of an association when the unconditioned stimulus is not presented. (b) The negative pole of the psychosocial crisis of very old age in which it is feared that the end of life is the end of all continuity.

extrinsic satisfaction　Sources of job satisfaction including salary, other financial benefits, working conditions, or special privileges.

facilitate　To make easier.

fallopian tube　The tube, extending from the uterus to the ovary, in which fertilization takes place.

false labor　Uterine contractions that do not indicate the start of the birth process.

family constellation　The many variables that describe a family group, including the presence or absence of mother and father, sibling number, spacing, and sex, and the presence or absence of extended family members in the household.

family day care　A child-care arrangement in which a person cares for several children in his or her own home, often along with the person's own children.

family executive　A family pattern in which all people in the household participate in decision making.

family of origin　The family to which one is born.

family of procreation　The family one begins as an adult.

fantasy　A form of symbolic thought that is not restrained by the limits of reality.

fast mapping　Forming a rapid, initial, partial understanding of the meaning of a word by relating it to the known vocabulary and restructuring the known-word storage space and its related conceptual categories.

fear of loss of love　A motive for parental identification in which the child tries to be like the parent in order to preserve a sense of closeness with the loved parent.

feedback　Information about how a particular activity is being carried out that returns to a central control mechanism. Feedback may be automatic information from muscles about a physical activity or evaluative information from a teacher about academic performance.

fertility　The capacity to reproduce.

fertilization　The penetration of an egg by a sperm.

fetal alcohol syndrome　A condition of the fetus involving central nervous system disorders, low birth weight, and malformations of the face; the condition is associated with heavy use of alcohol by mothers, especially during the last trimester of pregnancy.

fetoscopy　Examination of the fetus through the use of a fiberoptic lens.

fetus　The unborn infant. Usually the term *fetus* refers to infants between 8 weeks of gestational age and birth.

fiberoptic lens　A bundle of very thin transparent glass or plastic fibers that transmit light by internal refractions.

fidelity (I)　The ability to freely pledge and sustain loyalties to others.

fidelity (II)　The ability to freely pledge and sustain loyalties to values and ideologies.

filial obligation　The responsibilities of adult children for their aging parents.

fixation　In psychoanalysis, a preoccupation with the issues and tasks of a particular stage of development; an inability to progress to more mature stages.

fixed action pattern　A genetically guided sequence of complex highly patterned behavior, such as nest building or mating, that is characteristic of a particular species and is prompted or triggered by a specific stimulus pattern that signals or releases the innate behavior pattern.

fluid intelligence　The ability to impose organization on information and to generate new hypotheses.

forebrain　The front section of the three primary divisions of the brain in the embryo of a vertebrate; the part of the adult brain derived from this tissue.

formal operations　In Piaget's theory, the final stage of cognitive development characterized by reasoning, hypothesis generating, and hypothesis testing.

frail elderly　Older people who may have delicate health, one or more inactivating chronic conditions, and possibly some form of dementia.

frame of reference　The events or point of view that influence one's judgments.

fraternal twins　Children born at the same time who developed from two different ova.

frustration Dissatisfaction derived from unmet needs.

full-term baby A baby who has developed in utero for the complete gestational period of 9 months or approximately 36 weeks.

functional autonomy of motives In Allport's theory, the notion that behaviors may initially be performed because of specific motives, but may continue because the person enjoys them and/or finds them useful in new ways.

gamete A mature germ cell involved in reproduction.

gender The sex of the person.

gender identity A set of beliefs, attitudes, and values about oneself as a man or woman in many areas of social life including intimate relations, family, work, community, and religion.

gender label Words that identify one's gender, as boy, girl, man, or woman.

gender schema A personal theory about cultural expectations and stereotypes related to gender.

gene The fundamental physical unit of heredity. A gene is a linear sequence of nucleotides along a segment of DNA that carries the coded instructions for synthesis of RNA, which, when translated into protein, leads to hereditary character.

gene pool Genetic information contained in the genes of the population or culture that provides the ancestry for an individual.

generativity The capacity to contribute to the quality of life for future generations. A sense of generativity is attained toward the end of middle adulthood.

genetic anomalies Neurological or physical abnormalities that have a genetic cause.

genetic engineering The development and application of scientific methods, procedures, and technologies that allow direct manipulation of genetic material in order to alter the hereditary traits of a cell, organism, or population.

genetic fingerprinting Study of individual genetic characteristics.

genetics The study of heredity.

gene transfer The insertion of copies of a gene into living cells in order to induce synthesis of the gene's product; the desired gene may be microinjected into the cell directly, or it may be inserted into the core of a virus by gene splicing and the virus allowed to infect the cell to replicate the gene in the cell's DNA.

genitalia The reproductive organs, especially the external ones.

genital stage In Freud's psychosexual theory, the final life stage, during which the genitals are the primary source of sexual satisfaction and in which sexual impulses are directed toward members of the opposite sex.

genome A full set of chromosomes that carries all the inheritable traits of an organism.

genotype The hereditary information contained in the cells. Genotype may or may not be observable in the phenotype (see **phenotype**).

gerontologist A professional who deals with aging and the problems of the aged.

gestation The period from conception to birth.

gestational age The age of the fetus from the time of conception.

Glick effect Statistical evidence of lack of persistence that relates dropping out of high school or college with a high probability of divorce.

global empathy Distress experienced and expressed as a result of witnessing someone else in distress.

grammar Rules for the arrangement of words and phrases in a sentence and for the inflections that convey gender, tense, and number.

grasp reflex An automatic involuntary movement present at birth that disappears as the nervous system matures. Any object placed in the infant's palm will be firmly grasped.

grief Deep sorrow resulting from a loss.

group identity The positive pole of the psychosocial crisis of early adolescence in which the person finds membership in and value convergence with a peer group.

group play An early form of game, such as Ring Around the Rosie or London Bridge, in which winning or losing is not as important as the ritualized behavior.

growth rate The amount of growth that occurs during a given period of time.

guilt An emotion associated with doing something wrong or anticipating doing something wrong.

habituation A form of adaptation in which the child no longer responds to a stimulus that has been repeatedly presented.

hedonic Pertaining to pleasure.

hedonistic behavior Pleasure-seeking behavior.

hemophilia A sex-linked hereditary disease in which blood clots very slowly.

heredity The qualities and potential transmitted genetically from one generation to the next.

heterogeneous Having different qualities.

heteronomous morality A child's moral perspective, in which rules are viewed as fixed and unchangeable.

heterosexual relationships Associations and friendships with members of the opposite sex.

heterozygous Characterized by the presence of different alleles of a particular gene at the same locus.

hindbrain The rearmost section of the three primary divisions of the brain in the embryo of a vertebrate; the part of the adult brain derived from this tissue, including the medulla oblongata, the pons, and the cerebellum.

holophrase A word functioning as a phrase or sentence.

homeostasis A relatively stable state of equilibrium.

Homo erectus An extinct species of early humans, dating from 1.7 million years ago, characterized by upright stature and a well-evolved postcranial skeleton with a smallish brain, low forehead, and protruding face. This species has a differently shaped, larger skull than *Homo habilis* but a smaller brain than *Homo sapiens*. The tools used by Homo erectus were more complex than those used by Homo habilis but less complex than the tools used by Homo sapiens. Homo erectus is the first species known to have controlled fire.

homogeneous Sharing the same qualities.

Homo habilis An extinct species of upright East African hominid, dating from about 1.5 million to more than two million years ago, which had some advanced humanlike characteristics, including the use of some stone tools and the ability to use the hands skillfully.

Homo sapiens The species of bipedal primates to which modern humans belong, characterized by a brain capacity that averages 1400 cubic centimeters (85 cubic inches) and by dependence on language and complex manufactured tools. In the "candelabra" model, we evolved gradually from *Homo erectus* ancestors. In the "Noah's Ark" theory, we evolved separately from Homo erectus and expanded rapidly, whereas Homo erectus underwent rapid extinction.

homozygous Characterized by the presence of matched alleles of a particular gene at the same locus.

hope An enduring belief that one can attain one's essential wishes.

horizontal career movements Changes that represent the same level of attainment at a more personally comfortable work setting.

hormones A group of chemicals, each of which is released into the bloodstream by a particular gland or tissue and has a specific effect on tissues elsewhere in the body.

household All persons who occupy a housing unit, including related family members and all unrelated persons.

hue The property of light by which the color of an object is classified as red, blue, green, or yellow in reference to the spectrum.

human immunodeficiency virus (HIV) The cause of AIDS, it gains access to the body through the bloodstream and attacks the brain, sometimes causing damage and dementia.

hypothesis A tentative proposition that can provide a basis for further inquiry.

hypothetico-deductive reasoning A method of reasoning in which a hypothetical model based on observations is first proposed and then tested by deducing consequences from the model.

id In psychoanalytic theory, the mental structure that expresses impulses and wishes. Much of the content of the id is unconscious.

ideal self A view of the self as one would wish it to be.

identical twins Children born at the same time who developed from the same ovum.

identification A psychological mechanism in which people attempt to enhance their own self-concept by incorporating some of the valued characteristics of important others such as parents into their own behavior.

identification with the aggressor A motive for parental identification in which the child tries to be like the parent in order to prevent injury or rejection from the parent.

identity In cognitive theory, the concept that an object is still the same object even though its shape or location has been changed.

identity achievement Individual identity status in which, after crisis, a sense of commitment to family, work, political, and religious values is established.

identity confusion The negative pole of psychosocial crisis of later adolescence, in which a person is unable to integrate various roles or make commitments.

identity foreclosure Individual identity status in which a commitment to family, work, political, and religious values is established prematurely, without crisis.

idiosyncratic Marked by a characteristic peculiarity of personal habit, temperament, or personality structure.

illusion of incompetence Expressed by children who perform well in academic achievement tests yet perceive themselves as below average in academic ability and behave in accordance with this perception.

imaginary audience The preoccupation with what you believe other people are thinking about you.

imaginary companion A fantasized character created by a child's symbolic capacities.

imitation Repetition of another person's words, gestures, or behaviors.

immortality The positive pole of the psychosocial crisis of very old age, in which the person transcends death through a sense of symbolic continuity.

immunity A state of protection by the immune system against a disease or diseases. Immunity is present from birth and is the first line of defense against the vast majority of infectious agents.

imprinting A process whereby an animal comes to follow a large object, usually its mother, at some point after birth.

impulse Internal psychological drive for certain types of behavior such as aggressive or sexual impulses.

impulse control Control of internal psychological drives for particular types of behavior.

incentive Something that motivates one to act, such as a reward for succeeding.

incest Sexual relations between people so closely related that they are forbidden by law to marry.

independence Self-government; a state of not being subject to the control of others or not relying on others for support.

independent variable A factor that is manipulated in an experiment, and the effects of the manipulation measured.

individual identity The commitment to a personal integration of values, goals, and abilities that occurs as personal choices are made in response to anticipated or actual environmental demands at the end of adolescence.

individuation   The process of becoming a unique and distinct person.

induction   A form of discipline that points out the consequences of a child's actions for others.

industry   A sense of pride and pleasure in acquiring culturally valued competences. The sense of industry is usually acquired by the end of the middle childhood years.

inertia   A paralysis of thought and action that prevents productive work.

infancy   The period of psychosocial development that begins when the child is born and ends when the child is approximately two years old.

infanticide   Killing infants.

inference   (a) The act of moving from one proposition, statement, or judgment considered to be true to another whose truth is believed to follow from the first. (b) The act of moving from statistical sample data to generalizations, usually with calculated degrees of certainty.

inferiority   A sense of incompetence and failure that is built on negative evaluation and lack of skill.

infertility   Inability to conceive or carry a fetus through the gestational period.

inflections   Word endings that indicate tense and number.

in-group   A group of which one is a member; contrasted with out-group.

inhibition   A psychological restraint that prevents freedom of thought, expression, and activity.

initiative   The ability to offer new solutions, to begin new projects, or to seek new social encounters; active investigation of the environment.

innate   Present at birth.

innate behavior   Existing from birth; inborn; hereditary.

inner ear   An extremely intricate series of structures deep within the skull. The front part is concerned with hearing; the rear part is concerned with balance.

inoculation   An injection, usually to prevent disease, that stimulates the production of antibodies.

inordinate   Exceeding reasonable limits.

insight   In Piaget's theory of cognitive development, the last phase of sensorimotor intelligence, in which children solve problems by thinking over the possible solutions and selecting the correct one to try.

instinct   An inherited and largely unalterable tendency of an organism to make a complex specific response to environmental stimuli.

instrumental   Guiding behavior toward solving problems and accomplishing tasks.

instrumental conditioning   A form of associational learning in which the behaving organism emits responses that are shaped into the desired response by reinforcement. Once the desired response occurs it is strengthened by continued reinforcement.

integrity   The ability to accept the facts of one's life and to face death without great fear. The sense of integrity is usually acquired toward the end of later adulthood.

intellectual flexibility   A person's ability to handle conflicting information, to take several perspectives on a problem, and to reflect on personal values in solving ethical problems.

interdependence   (a) Marked by all the elements in a system relying on one another for their continued growth. (b) Systems that depend on each other.

internalization   A process in which the values, beliefs, and norms of the culture become the values, beliefs, and norms of the individual.

intersubjectivity   A shared repertoire of emotions that enables infants and their caregivers to understand each other and create shared meanings; they can engage in reciprocal, rhythmic interactions, appreciate state changes in one another, and modify their actions in response to emotional information about one another.

interview   A research method in which subjects are questioned about various aspects of their lives, including their feelings and thoughts.

intimacy   The ability to experience an open, supportive, tender relationship with another person without fear of losing one's own identity in the process of growing close. The sense of intimacy is usually acquired toward the end of early adulthood.

intonation   Rise and fall in pitch during speech.

intrapsychic   Occurring within the psyche, mind, or personality of an individual.

intravenous (feeding)   Introduction of a substance into a vein.

intrinsic motivation   A drive to behave in a certain way that comes from within the person.

introspection   Deliberate self-evaluation and examination of private thoughts and feelings.

introvert   Focused inward upon the self.

in utero   In the uterus.

in vitro   In an artificial environment.

in vivo   Biological processes occurring or caused to occur within the living body of a plant or animal.

irregular verbs   Verbs that do not conform to the usual pattern of inflection; for example, sell, sold; see, saw.

irritability   The ease with which stimuli cause disruption or pain.

isolation   A crisis resolution in which situational factors or a fragile sense of self leads a person to remain psychologically distant from others.

isolation   The state of being alone.

kibbutz   An Israeli community in which members share the ownership of all property and the profits from production. Children are reared communally.

labor   The period of involuntary contractions of the uterine muscles that occurs prior to giving birth.

lactation   Presence and secretion of milk that automatically occurs in the breasts of the mother of a newborn infant.

laissez-faire   A style of leadership in which the leader permits members to make their own decisions as they see fit.

language perception   The ability to recognize sounds and differentiate among sound combinations before the meanings of these sounds are understood.

latency   The time that elapses between a signal to act and the act itself.

latency stage   In Freud's psychosexual theory, the fourth life stage, during which no significant conflicts or impulses are assumed to rise. Superego development proceeds during this period.

latent learning   Learning about the contextual or background information that surrounds the information or task that is the target of attention.

later adolescence   The period of psychosocial development that begins around the time of graduation from high school and ends in the early twenties.

later adulthood   The period of psychosocial development that begins in the early fifties and ends with death.

launching period   The time in family life during which children leave home.

leading crowd   A group of students identified in James Coleman's research as leaders in the high school who tend to associate with one another and who make up the top group in the social hierarchy of the student culture.

learning   Any relatively permanent change in thought and/or behavior that is the consequence of experience.

learning set   A general strategy for problem solving.

learning theory   A set of principles that account for changes in behavior at every stage of life, usually focusing on ways in which controlled changes in the environment produce predictable changes in behavior.

lexicon   The vocabulary of a language.

life careers   Activities in particular domains that last for a significant amount of time during one's life, such as the parenting career.

life course   Individual life patterns as they are expressed in a social and historical time period.

life crisis   An unusual level of stress and tension that occurs during one's life, including psychosocial crises and events in one's life that cause tension, such as the death of a parent.

life endurancy   The age to which one person in 100,000 can be expected to survive.

life expectancy   The average number of years from birth to death as based on statistical analyses of the length of life for people born in a particular period.

life review   A process of recalling significant life events, accomplishments, and difficulties from earliest memories up to the present.

life span   The length of an individual's existence.

lifestyle   A relatively permanent structure of activity and experience, including the tempo of activity, the balance between work and leisure, and patterns of family and social relationships.

lightening   The stage of pregnancy in which the movements of the fetus are first felt by the pregnant woman.

linguistic system   Combination of vocabulary, grammar, phonetics, and language customs.

literacy   The state of being able to read and write.

loneliness   A feeling of sadness related to being alone; failing to meet one's needs for companionship.

longitudinal study   A research design in which repeated observations of the same subjects are made at different times, in order to examine change over time.

long-term memory   The encoding and storing of events for recall at a much later time.

love   An emotion characterized by a capacity for mutuality that transcends childhood dependency.

love withdrawal   A form of discipline in which parents express disappointment or disapproval and become emotionally cold or distant.

malnutrition   A condition of ill health that results from faulty or inadequate food intake.

mammal   Any vertebrate of the class Mammalia, which nourishes its young with milk from the mammary glands, is more or less covered with hair, and (with the exception of the egg-laying monotremes) gives birth to live young.

masculinity model   A model of sex-role identity that suggests that a masculine sex-role orientation is most adaptive for females as well as for males.

mastery   Competence or skill.

mastery (sense of)   A self-conceptualization that one has acquired certain competence, skill, or control over one's environment.

matched groups sampling   Two or more groups of subjects who are similar on many dimensions are selected as the sample for an experiment. The effects of different treatments or manipulations are determined by comparing the behavior of these groups.

maternal deprivation   Lack of opportunities for interaction with a mother or primary caregiver.

maturation rate   The rate at which certain personal, biological, and behavioral characteristics emerge and develop in an individual through the process of growth.

means-end relationship   A sensorimotor scheme for the causal connection between certain actions and certain consequences.

medulla   A part of the brain just above the spinal cord that controls life-sustaining functions such as breathing, blood pressure, and heart rate.

meiosis   An aspect of cell division resulting in the number of chromosomes in gamete-producing cells being reduced to one half.

memory The power and process of recalling and reproducing what has been learned or experienced. It can be exercised as short-term memory and long-term memory.

menarche The beginning of regular menstrual periods.

menopause The ending of regular menstrual periods.

mental age One's age as measured by an intelligence test. Usually, mental age is determined by the level of difficulty of the questions the person can answer correctly.

mental image A form of representational thought that involves the ability to hold the picture of a person, object, or event in one's mind even in the absence of the stimulus itself.

mental operations A transformation, carried out in thought rather than action, that modifies an object, event, or idea.

mentor A trusted counselor or guide.

metabolism A collective term for all the chemical processes that take place in the body: In some (catabolic), a complex substance is broken down into simpler ones, usually with the release of energy; in others (anabolic), a complex substance is built up from simpler ones, usually with the consumption of energy.

metacognition Thinking about one's own thinking, including what individuals understand about their reasoning capacities and about how information is organized, how knowledge develops, how reality is distinguished from belief or opinion, how to achieve a sense of certainty about what is known, and how to improve understanding.

methodology Particular techniques used to conduct a research investigation.

midbrain The middle of the three primary divisions of the brain in the embryo of a vertebrate, or the part of the adult brain derived from this tissue; also called the mesencephalon, it is the topmost part of the brain stem, situated above the pons.

middle adulthood The period of psychosocial development that begins in the early thirties and ends in the early fifties.

middle school A school containing grades 6 through 8.

middle school age The period of psychosocial development that begins at about age 8 and ends when the child enters puberty.

mistrust A sense of unpredictability in the environment and suspicion about one's own worth. Experiences with mistrust are most critical during infancy.

mitochondrial DNA DNA from mitochondria, rich in proteins, fats, and enzymes, which are found outside the nucleus of a cell and which produce energy for the cell through cellular respiration. The DNA is passed on solely through the mother and can be used to trace genetic lineage.

mobility Ability to engage in movement.

model In social learning theory, the one who is imitated.

modeling Demonstrating behaviors that can be imitated by others.

molecule The smallest part of a substance that retains the properties of the substance.

monozygotic twins Twins who develop from a single fertilized egg. These twins have identical genetic characteristics.

moral judgments Cognitive decisions about right or wrong behavior that involve an underlying rationale.

moral prescriptions Positive rules for valued behavior.

moral prohibitions Rules to suppress negatively valued behavior.

moral script The culture's expectations about valued and devalued behaviors for children of each age and in each social context.

morphological abnormalities Damage to body form and structure.

mortality The quality of life that involves one's eventual death.

mortality (infant) The number of deaths per 100,000 live births.

motherese The simplified, redundant style of speaking used by adults and older children so that they are more likely to be understood by a child who is learning language.

motive Something that causes a person to act.

motor functions Bodily movement of both voluntary and reflexive types.

multiparas A woman who has borne two or more children or who is pregnant for the second time.

muscle tonus A level of moderate contraction that is present in normal muscles.

mutual adaptation Two or more people changing in response to each other.

mutuality Ability of two people to meet each other's needs and share each other's concerns and feelings.

myelination The formation of a soft, white, fatty material called myelin around certain nerve axons, to serve as an electrical insulator that speeds nerve impulses to muscles and other effectors.

narcissistic Extremely self-absorbed and self-loving.

naturalistic observation A research method in which subjects' behavior is observed and described as it occurs in its natural setting without experimental intervention.

natural selection A process whereby those individuals best suited to the characteristics of the immediate environment are most likely to survive and reproduce.

need Physical or psychological requirement for well-being.

negative identity A clearly defined self-image that is completely contrary to the cultural values of the community.

negativism Refusal to comply with others' requests.

neighborhood The physical area and the residents of the area where one lives.

neonatal   Affecting the newborn, especially during the first month of life.

nerve conduction velocity   Speed of neural firing.

neural tube   The tube formed during the early embryonic period that later developed into the brain, spinal cord, nerves, and ganglia.

neurological development   Growth of the nervous system.

neuron   A nerve cell with specialized processes that is the fundamental functional unit of nervous tissue.

nondisjunction   An event occurring during cell division, in which both chromosomes of a pair go to the same new cell. Nondisjunction results in chromosomal irregularities, including Down syndrome.

normative   Conforming to an average pattern.

norms   Collective expectations, or rules for behavior, held by members of a group or society.

nostalgia   A wistful or sentimental yearning for return to some past period.

nuclear family   A household grouping that includes the mother, father, and their children.

nurturance   The tendency to attempt to care for and further the growth and development of another.

obesity   A condition characterized by being excessively fat.

object permanence   A scheme acquired during the sensorimotor stage of development, in which children become aware that an object continues to exist even when it is hidden or moved from place to place.

object relations   The component of ego development that is concerned with the self, self-understanding, and self–other relationships.

observation   A research method in which behavior is watched and recorded.

observational learning   Changes in thought or behavior that result from watching others.

obsessions   Persistent repetitive thoughts that serve as mechanisms for controlling anxiety.

occupational career   The pattern of participation in the labor market.

occupational status   A hierarchy of status among large groups of occupations that reflects their relative power, influence, and respect among members of the society.

Oedipal conflict   In Freud's psychosexual theory, the central conflict of the phallic stage, in which the boy has strong desires for the mother, strong aggressive feelings toward his father, and strong fears of castration by the father.

old-old   Among the very old, those who have suffered major physical or mental decrements.

ontogenesis   The course of development.

operant conditioning   A form of learning in which new responses are strengthened by the presentation of reinforcements.

operational definition   In research, the way an abstract concept is defined in terms of how it will be measured.

optimal ability   The level of performance of which one is capable at the highest levels of motivation and preparation.

oral stage   In Freud's psychosexual theory, the first life stage, during which the mouth is the primary source of sexual satisfaction. Issues of self-concept and personal worth are important at this stage.

organic brain syndromes   Disorders involving memory loss, confusion, loss of ability to manage daily functions, and loss of ability to focus attention.

organ inferiority   In Adler's theory, a strong sense that some organ of one's body is weak and inferior. The person becomes preoccupied with thoughts of this weakness.

outcome variables   Dimensions that are viewed as the consequence of a particular intervention or experimental manipulation.

out-group   A group that competes with one's own group; contrasted with **in-group.**

ovum   An egg; the female germ cell.

palate   The roof of the mouth, separating the mouth from the nasal cavity.

paradox   A statement that may appear to be opposed to common sense, yet is true.

peer   A person belonging to the same group, often on the basis of age or grade.

peer pressure   Expectations and demands to conform to the norms of one's peer group.

perception   The recognition and organization of sensory experiences.

perceptual gestalts   The recognition and integrated organization of sensory experiences in such a way as to perceive a whole.

perineum   The area between the anus and the back of the vagina.

peristalsis   Successive waves of involuntary contraction passing along the walls of the intestine or other hollow muscular structure, forcing the contents onward.

permissive   Marked by a relatively easygoing and tolerant discipline technique that allows the child's desires to be asserted.

personal constructs   In George Kelly's theory, personal points of view about the world through which a person interprets both psychological and social events.

personal fable   An intense investment in one's own thoughts and feelings and a belief that these thoughts are unique.

personal history   The life events that occur during an individual's development.

personality consolidation   The strengthening of personality through a process of self-examination, increasing awareness, crisis, and personal development.

person-environment fit   The fit between the person's needs, skills, and interpersonal style and the characteristics of the environments in which the person participates.

perspective taking   The ability to consider a situation from a point of view other than one's own.

phallic stage   In Freud's psychosexual theory, the third stage of development, during which the Oedipal and Electra conflicts occur.

phenotype   Observable characteristics that result from a particular genotype and a particular environment.

phenylketonuria (PKU)   A genetic disease that restricts intellectual development if it is not treated.

phobia   An intense, irrational fear.

phonetics   The sound system of a language.

phylogeny   The evolutionary chain of species associated with a particular plant or animal.

physical prowess   Physical ability and skill.

physiological   Characteristic of normal physical and chemical functions of the body.

pitch   The range of high to low sounds.

placenta   The vascular organ that connects the fetus to the maternal uterus and mediates metabolic exchanges.

plasticity   The capability of being molded.

pleasure principle   The desire to experience pleasure and avoid pain through the immediate discharge of impulses that guide the functioning of the id.

polygamy   A family organization in which a spouse may have more than one mate.

population   All units for potential observation.

postconventional morality   In Kohlberg's stages of moral reasoning, the most mature form of moral judgments. Moral decisions are based on an appreciation of the social contract that binds members of a social system and on personal values.

postpartum depression   A period of sadness that may be experienced by the mother after giving birth and that appears to be related to hormonal activity.

power assertion   A discipline technique involving physical force, harsh language, or control of resources.

precarious   Characterized by a lack of stability or security.

preconscious   Absent from but capable of being readily brought into consciousness.

preconventional morality   In Kohlberg's stages of moral reasoning, the most immature form of moral judgments. Moral decisions are based on whether the act has positive or negative consequences, or whether it is rewarded or punished.

precursor   Forerunner; the substance from which another organ is formed.

preoperational thought   In Piaget's theory of cognitive development, the stage in which representational skills are acquired.

press   Steady push or demand.

pre-term baby   A baby who is born before the full gestational period.

primal wishes   Very early needs and desires.

primary process   The seemingly unorganized mental activity, characteristic of the id and the unconscious, that occurs in dreams, fantasies, and related processes. Characterized by an absence of negatives, a here-and-now focus, and symbolic flexibility.

primate   Any of various omnivorous mammals of the order Primates, including the three suborders Tarsioidea (tarsiers), Prosimii (lemurs, loris, and their allies), and Anthropoidea (humans, great apes, gibbons, Old World monkeys, and New World monkeys). Distinguished by varied locomotion, use of hands, and flexible, complex behavior involving a high level of cultural adaptability and social interaction.

prime adaptive ego qualities   Mental states that form a basic orientation toward the interpretation of life experiences; new ego qualities emerge in the positive resolution of each psychosocial crisis.

primiparas   A woman who has borne one child or who is pregnant for the first time.

primitive causality   An understanding of cause and effect acquired by infants that is based solely on sensory and motor experience, not symbolic logic.

proactive   Initiating action, as opposed to reactive.

probability   The likelihood that something will happen.

procreation   To give birth to offspring.

progesterone   A hormone related to pregnancy.

projection   The attribution of one's own ideas, feelings, wishes, or attitudes to other people.

projective technique   Method for measuring aspects of personality by asking a person to make responses to ambiguous stimuli.

prompting   Urging a child to say more about an incomplete expression.

prosocial behavior   Positive social behavior such as helping another person.

Protestant ethic   A code of values that emphasizes hard work, achievement, and delay of gratification.

proximity   Close, nearby.

proximodistal   Development in the direction from the center of the body to the extremes.

psychiatric will   A document that explains the kinds of psychiatric treatment a person is or is not willing to accept in very old age.

psychohistorical perspective   An integration of past, present, and future time with respect to personal and societal continuity and change.

psycholinguistics   The study of language as it is affected by psychological factors.

psychosexual theory   Freud's theory of psychological development, which proposes that cognitive, emotional, and social growth are associated with predictable changes in sexual sensitivity during childhood. This theory is sometimes called psychoanalytic theory.

psychosocial crisis   A predictable life tension that arises as people experience some conflict between their own competences and the expectations of their society.

psychosocial environment The influence of culture, values, resources, demands, competences, and motives that are embedded in the structure of the social and physical environment.

psychosocial evolution The contribution of each generation to the knowledge and norms of society.

psychosocial moratorium A period of free experimentation before a final identity is achieved.

psychosocial theory A theory of psychological development that proposes that cognitive, emotional, and social growth are the result of the interaction between social expectations at each life stage and the competences that people bring to each life challenge.

psychotemporal perspective Sense of time as it is affected by psychological factors.

puberty The period of physical development at the onset of adolescence when the reproductive system matures.

punishment A penalty or negative experience imposed on a person for improper behavior.

purpose The ability to imagine and pursue valued goals.

quickening Sensations of fetal movement, usually during the second trimester of fetal growth.

radius of significant relationships The groups of important people in one's life; the breadth and complexity of these groups change over the life span.

random Characteristic of a situation in which each event of a set of events is equally likely to occur.

random sampling A method for choosing the sample for a study in which each member of the population under investigation has an equal chance of being included.

rapport Harmony and understanding in a relationship.

reaction range The range of possible responses to environmental conditions that is established through genetic influences.

reaction time The time that lapses between the signal to make a response and the response itself.

reality principle The motivating force or mechanism by which the ego protects the person by preventing id impulses from being gratified until a socially acceptable form of expression can be found.

receptive language The ability to understand words.

recessive gene A form of a gene that is expressed in the phenotype only when a similar allele is present. In combination with a dominant gene the characteristics associated with the recessive gene are masked.

reciprocal interactions Interactions in which the behavior of each participant influences the responses of the others.

reciprocity A scheme describing the interdependence of related dimensions, such as height and width or time and speed.

redundant Using more words than are necessary to convey meaning.

reference group A group with which an individual identifies and whose values the individual accepts as guiding principles.

reflex An involuntary response to a simple stimulus.

reflexive self-concept Bernstein's concept of the influence of language on shaping a self-concept that is sensitive to social relationships and roles.

reinforcement In operant conditioning, the positive consequence that follows a given behavior.

reinforcement patterns The frequency and timing with which reinforcements are presented.

rejectivity The unwillingness to include certain others or groups of others in one's generative concerns.

releasing stimulus An odor, color, movement, sound, shape, pattern of events, or relationship among any of these that elicits the performance of a fixed action pattern in a particular species.

reliability The consistency of a test in measuring something.

reminiscence Process of thinking and/or telling about past experiences.

repertoire A list of abilities, skills, and full range of performance possible.

representational skill Skills learned in the preoperational stage, including mental imagery, symbolic play, symbolic drawing, imitation, and language, that permit the child to represent experiences or feelings in a symbolic form.

repression A defense mechanism that involves pushing unacceptable anxiety-provoking impulses, memories, thoughts, or feelings into the unconscious.

repudiation Rejection of roles and values that are viewed as alien to oneself.

research design A plan for conducting research that includes the method for gathering data, the sample selected to participate in the study, the frequency with which data are to be gathered, and the statistical techniques that are to be used in analyzing the data.

resilience The capacity to recover from stress.

respiratory distress syndrome An acute lung disease of the newborn. It occurs primarily in premature babies and babies born to sick mothers, and is characterized by rapid breathing, flaring of the nostrils, inelastic lungs, and other physical malformations that may cause serious breathing problems.

response A behavior that follows a particular stimulus event.

response repertoire The range of behaviors that a person or animal is capable of performing.

responsiveness Reacting readily to another's request or need.

retina The light-sensitive membrane lining the back of the eye on which images are cast by the cornea and lens.

retrospective study A research design in which subjects are asked to report on experiences they had earlier in their lives.

reversibility A scheme describing the ability to undo an action and return to the original state.

reward A positive consequence that follows desired behavior.

reward structure The pattern of positive consequences that occurs within an institution, a classroom, or a family group to encourage particular behaviors.

ribs The flat curved bones that form a framework for the chest and a protective cage around the heart, lungs, and other organs.

risk To expose to danger with a possibility of loss or injury.

rite of passage A ritual associated with a crisis or a change of status (for example, marriage for an individual).

ritual A formal and customarily repeated act or series of acts.

RNA Ribonucleic acid; a compound that conveys the information in the DNA strands to the cytoplasm in order to stimulate the production of specific amino acids.

role A set of behaviors that have some socially agreed-upon functions and for which there exists an accepted code of norms, such as the role of teacher, child, or minister.

role compatibility Partners in a relationship approach situations in a manner that works well; their behaviors and responses complement one another.

role diffusion The negative pole of the psychosocial crisis of later adolescence in which the person cannot make a commitment to any unified vision of the self.

role enactment Patterned characteristics of social behavior that one performs as a result of being in a specific role.

role expectations Shared expectations for behavior that are linked to a social role.

role experimentation The central process for the resolution of the psychosocial crisis of later adolescence, which involves participation in a variety of roles before any final commitments are made.

role prescription The specific behaviors and norms associated with a particular role.

role reversal Assuming the behaviors of a person in a reciprocal role, as when a child acts toward his or her parent as a parent.

role strain The conflict and competing demands made by several roles that the person holds simultaneously.

role-taking abilities Skills related to understanding and enacting the roles of others.

rooting An infant reflex in which the baby's head turns toward the direction of the cheek that is stimulated.

saline solution A solution containing salt.

sample The group of people who have been selected to participate as subjects in a research project.

sampling A method of choosing subjects in a study.

sanction A negative consequence that occurs when a standard or rule has been violated.

scaffolding A process through which a child and an adult attempt to arrive at a shared understanding about a communication at which point the adult interacts so as to expand or enrich the child's communicative competence.

schedules of reinforcement The frequency and regularity with which reinforcements are given.

scheme In Piaget's theory, the organization of actions into a unified whole, a mental construct.

school phobia A strong, irrational fear of some aspect of the school situation, interpreted in psychoanalytic theory as an expression of a child's reluctance to leave the mother.

scientific process A process for building a body of knowledge involving observation, theory construction, operationalizing the theory, testing the theory, evaluating and revising the theory.

secondary process The conscious mental activity and logical thinking controlled by the ego and influenced by environmental demands.

secular trend A tendency observed since approximately 1900 for more rapid physical maturation from one generation to the next, probably as a result of favorable nutrition, increased mobility, and greater protection from childhood diseases.

sedentary Sitting still much of the time.

self-concept The characteristics and attributes one applies to oneself.

self-control The ability to control impulses and to achieve intended outcomes.

self-disclosure The ability to communicate personal information and feelings to someone else.

self-efficacy A sense of confidence that one can perform the behaviors that are demanded in a specific situation.

self-encodings Evaluations and concepts related to information about oneself.

self-esteem The evaluative dimension of the self that includes feelings of worthiness, pride, and discouragement.

self-theory An organized set of ideas about the self, the world, and the meaning of interactions between the self and the environment.

semantic contingency The immediate matching of an adult's utterance to the content or topic of a child's verbalization.

semicircular canals The three curved tubular canals in the labyrinth of the inner ear that are concerned with balance.

semiotic thinking The understanding that one thing can stand for another.

senescence The process of becoming old.

sensitive period A span of time during which a particular skill or behavior is most likely to develop.

sensitivity (of caregiver) Attentiveness to an infant's state, accurate interpretation of the infant's signals, and well-timed responses that promote mutually rewarding interactions.

sensorimotor intelligence In Piaget's theory of development, the first stage of cognitive growth during which schema are built on sensory and motor experiences.

sensorimotor play Sensory exploration and motoric manipulation that produce pleasure.

sensory deprivation The relative absence of all forms of stimulation.

sensory functions The responses of the body and nervous system to a variety of stimuli; vision, hearing, taste, smell, and touch.

sensory receptors Millions of microscopic structures throughout the body that collect information about the external environment or the body's internal state. Receptors are attuned to particular stimuli, and fire when excited.

sensory stimulation Events that have an impact on any of the sense receptors, including sounds, sights, tasks, or tactile stimuli.

separation anxiety Feelings of fear or sadness associated with the departure of the object of attachment.

serial monogamy Having one intimate relationship at a time as opposed to having several at once.

sex education An organized curriculum focusing on the biological, psychological, cultural, and interpersonal aspects of love, sexuality, and reproduction.

sex-linked characteristics Characteristics for which the allele is found on the sex chromosomes.

sex-role identification The integration of knowledge about one's gender, awareness of cultural expectations associated with each sex, identification with the like-sex parent, and preference for one's sex role.

sex-role preference A positive value for the expectations and norms held for a specific gender group.

sex-role standards Attributes held by the culture for males and females. These attributes can include both precepts and sanctions.

sex-typed Marked by a trait, characteristic, or behavior that is seen as associated with either men or women by a large number of people.

sexual differentiation Sexual organs take on their unique male and female structure.

shame An intense emotional reaction to being ridiculed or to a negative self-assessment.

shaping In behavior modification, altering behavior by reinforcing progressively closer approximations of the desired behavior.

sibling Brother or sister.

sign Something that represents something else, usually in an abstract, arbitrary way; for example, a word for an object.

single-adult executive Family pattern in which one adult in the household makes the major decisions.

skull plates Making up the bony skeleton of the head, they serve to protect the brain and other organs.

social attachment A strong, affectionate bond that develops between infants and their caregivers.

social clock Expectations for orderly and sequential changes that occur with passage of time as individuals move through life.

social cognition Concepts related to understanding interpersonal behavior and the point of view of others.

social competence The skills involved in making friends, maintaining friendships, and enjoying the benefits of close peer relations.

social convention Socially accepted norms and regulations that guide behavior.

social cooperation Working in a collaborative mode with one or more other people.

social desirability The quality of a person's responding or behaving in ways that are viewed as valuable, acceptable, or proper by others.

social integration Being comfortably involved in meaningful interpersonal associations and friendship relations.

socialization The process of teaching and enforcing group norms and values to the new group members.

social learning theory A theory of learning that emphasizes the ability to learn new responses through observation and imitation of others.

social milieu The environment, especially the people, the norms, and the cultural expectations in one's surroundings.

social perspective taking The capacity to recognize the point of view held by others, especially when it differs from one's own.

social referencing The process by which infants use facial features and verbal expressions as clues to the emotional responses of another person, often the mother, and as information about how to approach an unfamiliar, ambiguous situation.

social role theory The theory that emphasizes participation in varied and more complex roles as a major factor in human development.

social support Information leading people to believe that they are cared for and loved, that they are esteemed and valued, and that they belong to a network of communication and mutual obligation.

societal processes All those processes through which a person becomes integrated into society; for example, cultural rituals.

socioeconomic status One's ranking on a number of social and financial indicators, including years of education, kind of work, and salary.

solicitude Attentive care and protectiveness.

somatic processes All those processes necessary for the functioning of the biological organism; for example, the sensory capacities.

sonar   An apparatus that can detect objects underwater through the use of reflected sound waves.

soothability   The ability to regain a calm state following irritation or pain.

sperm   The male germ cell.

sperm bank   A facility where sperm are donated and frozen for use in artificial insemination.

spontaneous ejaculation   A discharge of semen without deliberate manipulation.

stagnation   A lack of psychological movement or growth during middle adulthood that may result from self-aggrandizement or from the inability to cope with developmental tasks.

status   Relative social prestige or rank.

stethoscope   An instrument for listening to sounds in the body, particularly those made by the heart or lungs.

stimulus   Any change in the energy of the environment that has the potential to influence a perceiver.

stimulus generalization   The capacity for similar stimuli to evoke the same response.

stranger anxiety   Feelings of fear or apprehension in the presence of unfamiliar people, especially during infancy.

strange situation   A standard laboratory procedure designed to describe patterns of attachment behavior. A child is exposed during a 20-minute period to a series of events that are likely to stimulate the attachment system. Child and caregiver enter an unfamiliar laboratory setting; a stranger enters; the caregiver leaves briefly; and the caregiver and infant have opportunities for reunion while researchers observe child, caregiver, and their interactions.

stratified sampling   A method for choosing the sample for a research study in which subjects are selected from a variety of levels or types of people in the population.

subjective age identity   The age one feels oneself to be, based on perceived similarity to people of this age.

subjective reality   The way things appear from the person's point of view.

sublimation   Channeling energy from unconscious wishes into socially acceptable behaviors.

subordinate   Being in a lower, submissive rank.

substantive complexity   The degree to which one's work requires thought, independent judgment, and frequent decision making.

succorance   Giving help or relief.

superego   In psychoanalytic theory, the mental function that embodies moral precepts and moral sanctions. The superego includes the ego ideal, or the goals toward which one strives, as well as the punishing conscience.

surrogate mother   Woman who conceives and bears a child for an infertile couple.

survey   A research method in which carefully worded questions are asked of a large number of respondents, either orally or in writing.

symbol   An object, image, or word that represents something. A symbol can be a word that represents an object, as *chair*, or an object that represents a concept, as a dove.

symbolic drawing   Drawings that represent a specific thought.

symbolic play   Imaginative or pretend activities that express emotions, problems, or roles.

synchronize   To coincide or agree in time.

syntax   The rules for ordering words in a specific language.

system   A combination of things or parts, forming a complex or unitary whole and functioning as a unit.

taboo   Proscribed by society as improper or unacceptable.

tactile stimulation   Any stimuli that evoke a response from the sensory receptors in the skin. Touching, tickling, pinching, and rubbing are examples.

talent   Areas of skill or competence.

teachable moments   The times when a person is maturationally most ready to learn a new skill.

technology   A technical method of achieving a practical purpose.

telegraphic speech   Two-word sentences, used by children, that omit many parts of speech but convey meaning.

temperament   Innate characteristics that determine the person's sensitivity to various sense experiences and his or her responsiveness to patterns of social interaction.

temporal association   Events that occur together or close together in time.

teratogens   Agents that produce malformations during the formation of organs and tissues.

test   Groups of questions or problems that usually indicate and measure abilities, potentials, or psychological characteristics.

testosterone   A hormone that fosters the development of male sex characteristics and growth.

thalamus   An area of the brain near the pituitary gland that integrates sensory information and relays it to the cortex.

theory   A logically interrelated system of concepts and statements that provides a framework for organizing, interpreting, and understanding observations, with the goal of explaining and predicting behavior.

time management   The ability to set goals and use time effectively to achieve those goals.

toddlerhood   The period of psychosocial development that begins around the age of two and ends around the time the child enters kindergarten.

toxemia   The presence of toxins produced by bacteria in the bloodstream.

trauma   An emotional shock that has long-lasting psychological consequences.

trial-and-error learning   A mode of learning in which the solution is discovered by observing the consequences of each response.

trimester A period of three months during the nine months of pregnancy.

trust An emotional sense that both the environment and oneself are reliable and capable of satisfying basic needs.

ultrasound A technique for producing visual images of the fetus in utero through a pattern of deflected sound waves.

unconditioned response A response that is evoked by a stimulus prior to opportunities for learning; sometimes described as a reflexive response.

unconditioned stimulus A stimulus that evokes a response prior to opportunities for learning.

unconscious In Freud's psychosexual theory, a reservoir of wishes, needs, and fantasies that influence behavior but of which we are not normally aware.

underachievement A term describing students who perform below the level of their ability.

uniformitarianism A principle that states that the same laws of nature apply uniformly across time.

uterus In the female reproductive system, the hollow muscular organ in which the fertilized ovum normally becomes embedded and in which the developing embryo and fetus is nourished and grows.

validity The extent to which a test measures what it is supposed to measure.

value A principle or quality that is intrinsically desirable.

variables Dimensions that can have a number of different values.

venereal disease Any infection transmitted primarily but not exclusively by sexual intercourse.

verbal persuasion Encouragement from others.

verbatim Word for word; using the exact words.

vernix caseosa A coating of dead cells and oil that covers the skin during fetal development.

vertical career movements Promotions, the attainment of higher positions, or changes to more prestigious organizations or institutions.

vicarious An experience achieved through the imagined participation in events that happen to another person.

visual acuity The ability to detect visual stimuli under various levels of illumination.

visual tracking Following an object's movement with one's eyes.

vocabulary A list of the words a person uses and understands.

vocalizations Any sounds or utterances a person makes.

voluntary movement Movement that is guided by a person's conscious control.

volunteer sampling In which subjects for a study are selected from volunteers.

will The determination to exercise free choice and self-control.

willfulness Wanting to have your own way.

wisdom The detached yet active concern with life itself in the face of death.

withdrawal Becoming socially and emotionally detached.

work clock Timetable of expectations for the progression of work life.

young-old Among the very old, those who remain healthy, vigorous, and competent.

zone of proximal development The emergent developmental capacity that is just ahead of the level at which the person is currently functioning.

zygote The developing individual formed from two gametes.

Name Index

Subject Index

Credits

Text Photos

Four-Color Photos

Figures, Tables, and Excerpts

Chapter 9: 407: Figure 9.1, From "Development of Self-Body Esteem in Overweight Youngsters," by B. K. Mendelson and D. R. White, 1985, *Developmental Psychology*, 21, p. 92. Copyright © 1985 by the American Psychological Association. Reprinted by permission of the author. 436: Figure 9.2, Adapted from "Parenting Practices and Peer Group Affiliation in Adolescence," by B. Bradford Brown, N. Mounts, S. D. Lamborn & L. Steinberg, 1993, *Child Development*, 64, 467–482. Copyright © 1993 by The Society for Research in Child Development. Adapted by permission. 438: Figure 9.3, From "Initiation of Coitus in Early Adolescence," by J. R. Udry and J. O. Billy, 1987, *American Sociological Review*, 52, 841–855. Copyright © 1987 by the American Sociological Association. Reprinted by permission. 440: Table 9.2, Adapted from "The Transition to First Intercourse Among Racially and Culturally Diverse Youth," by R. D. Day, 1992, *Journal of Marriage and the Family*, 54, 749–763. Copyright © 1992 by the National Council on Family Relations, 3989 Central Ave. N.E., Suite 550, Minneapolis, MN 55421. Adapted by permission. 455: Figure 9.4, From *National Survey Results on Drug Use from Monitoring the Future Study, 1975–1992: Vol. I, Secondary School Students*, p. 79 by L. D. Johnston, P. M. O'Malley & J. G. Bachman, 1993, National Institute on Drug Abuse. 456: Table 9.3, From *Abnormal Psychology and Modern Life*, 5/e by James C. Coleman. Copyright © 1976, 1972, 1964 by Scott, Foresman and Company. Reprinted by permission of HarperCollins College Publishers.

Chapter 10: 476: Excerpt from "Is It Torture or Tradition," by D. A. Kaplan, p. 124. From *Newsweek*, December 20, 1993, Newsweek, Inc. All rights reserved. Reprinted with permission. 482: Figure 10.1, From "A Longitudinal Study of Moral Judgement," by A. Colby, L. Kohlberg, J. Gibbs & M. Lieberman, 1983, *Monographs of the Society for Research in Child Development*, 48 (1, serial no. 200), 46. Copyright © 1983 by The Society for Research in Child Development. Reprinted by permission. 486: Table 10.1, Adapted from "Gender and Developmental Differences in Adolescents' Conception of Moral Reasoning," by K. M. Galotti, S. F. Kozberg & M. C. Farmer, 1991, *Journal of Youth and Adolescence*, 20, Table 2, p. 21. Copyright © 1991 Plenum Publishing Corporation. Adapted by permission. 488: Figure 10.2, From "Research on a Workshop to Reduce the Effects of Sexism and Sex-Role Socialization on Women's Career Planning," by J. M. O'Neil, C. Ohide, C. Barke, B. Prosser-Gelwick & N. Garfield, 1980, *Journal of Counseling Psychology*, 27, 355–363. Reprinted by permission of the author. 489: Table 10.2, Adapted from *Digest of Education Statistics*, 1992, Table 367, p. 391, National Center for Education Statistics. U.S. Government Printing Office. 492: Table 10.3, Statistics from *The Chronicle of Higher Education Almanac*, August 25, 1993, p. 15, provided by the Higher Education Research Institute, UCLA. 508: Figure 10.3, Based on *Career Development: Choice and Adjustment*, by D. V. Tiedeman and P. R. O'Hara, 1963. New York: College Entrance Examination Board.

Chapter 11: 520: Figure 11.1, Adapted from "The Life Course, Age Grading, and Age-Linked Demands for Decision Making," by R. C. Atchley, 1975. In N. Datan and L. H. Ginsberg (eds.), *Lifespan Development Psychology: Normative Life Crisis*, p. 264. Copyright © 1975 by Academic Press, Inc. Adapted by permission. 523: Figure 11.2, Based on data from *Statistical Abstract of the United States*, 1991, p. 45. U.S. Bureau of the Census. United States Printing Office. 528: Figure 11.3, Based on *Marriage and the Family*, by J. Broderick, 1988. Copyright © 1988 Prentice-Hall, Inc. 532: Excerpt from "Born or Bred: The Origins of Homosexuality," by D. Gelman, p. 50. From *Newsweek*, February 24, 1992 Newsweek, Inc. All rights reserved. Reprinted by permission. 538: Table 11.3, Based on "Non-Traditional Family Forms," by E. Macklin. In M. B. Sussman and S. K. Steinmetz (eds.), *Handbook of Marriage and the Family*, pp. 330–331. Copyright © 1987 Plenum Publishing. 541: Figure 11.4, Based on "Changes in Marriage Associated with Transition to Parenthood," by S. M. MacDermid, T. I. Huston & S. M. McHale, 1990, *Journal of Marriage and Family*, 52, 475–486. Copyright © 1990 by the National Council of Family Relations. Minneapolis, MN. 548: Table 11.4, From *Mentoring at Work: Developmental Relationships in Organizational Life*, by E. K. Kram, 1988, p. 72–73. Copyright © 1988 by University Press of America. Reprinted by permission. 551: Table 11.5, From "Singlehood," by A. B. Shostak, 1987. In M. B. Sussman and S. K. Steinmetz (eds.), *Handbook of Marriage and the Family*, p. 357. Copyright © 1987 by Plenum Publishing Corp. Reprinted by permission. 557: Excerpt from "Sexual Desire," by L. Rosellini, 1992, *U.S. News & World Report*, 113, July 6, 1992, pp. 62, 64. Reprinted by permission. 560: Figure 11.5, From "Divorce," by H. J. Raschke, 1987. In M. B. Sussman and S. K. Steinmetz (eds.), *Handbook of Marriage and the Family*, p. 598. Copyright © 1987 by Plenum Publishing Corp. Reprinted by permission. Updated statistics 1985–1988 from U.S. Bureau of the Census, 1992.

Chapter 12: 581: Table 12.1, Adapted from *Statistical Abstract of the United States: 1992*, 112th ed., Table 622, p. 389. U.S. Bureau of the Census. U.S. Government Printing Office. 597: Table 12.2, From "Filial Responsibility Expectations Among Adult Child–Older Parent Pairs," by R. R. Harmon and R. Lieszner, 1990, *Journal of Gerontology: Psychological Sciences*, 45, p. 111. Copyright © 1990 by The Gerontological Society of America. Reprinted by permission. 617: Excerpt from *Men at Midlife*, by Michael P. Farrell and Stanley D. Rosenberg, 1981, Auburn House Publishing Company, an imprint of Greenwood Publishing Group, Inc., pp. 102–103. Reprinted with permission of Greenwood Publishing Group, Inc., Westport, CT. Copyright © 1981 by Auburn House Publishing Company. 621: Table 12.5, Based on *Creativity: The Magic Synthesis*, by S. Arieti, 1976, pp. 372–379. Copyright © 1976 Basic Books. 623: Figure 12.1, From *The Black Population in the United States, March 1990 and 1989*, U.S. Bureau of the Census, Current Population Reports, Series P-20, No. 448. U.S. Government Printing Office. 624: Excerpt from "Monsanto's New Challenge: Keeping Minority Workers," by J. E. Ellis, *Business Week*, July 8, 1991, pp. 60–61. Reproduced by permission.

Chapter 13: 632: Figure 13.1, From "Compression of Mortality: Myth or Reality?," by G. C. Meyers and K. G. Manton, 1984, *Gerontologist*, 24, 374. Copyright © 1984 by The Gerontological Society of America. Reprinted by permission. 634: Excerpt in Box 13.1 and on pp. 661–662: From "Unity in Diversity: Thirty-Three Years of Stress," by C. M. Pierce, 1989. In G. L. Berry and J. K. Asamen (eds.), *Black Students*, pp. 297–298, 304, 305, 309, 310. Copyright © 1989 by Sage Publications, Inc. Reprinted by permission. 647: Table 13.1, Adapted from "System of Classifying Leisure Activities in Terms of the Psychological Benefits of Participation Reported by Older Persons," by H. E. A. Tinsley, J. D. Teaff, S. L. Colbs & N. Kaufman, 1985, *Journal of Gerontology*, 40, 172–178. Copyright © 1985 by The Gerontological Society of America. Adapted by permission. 650: Figure 13.2, From "You're Only as Old as You Feel: Self-Perceptions of Age, Fears of Aging and Life Satisfaction from Adolescence to Old Age," by J. M. Montepare and M. E. Lachman, 1989, *Psychology and Aging*, 4, 75. Copyright © 1989 American Psychological Association. Reprinted by permission of the author. 652: Table 13.2, Adapted from "Personal Goals of Older Adults: Issues in Assessment and Prediction," by B. D. Rapkin and K. Fischer, 1992, *Psychology and Aging*, 7, 132–133. Copyright © 1992 by the American Psychological Association. Adapted by permission of the author. 656: Table 13.3, Based on

To The Owner Of This Book

We hope that you have enjoyed *Development Through Life: A Psychosocial Approach, Sixth Edition* as much as we enjoyed writing it. We would like to know as much about your experience as you would care to offer. Only through your comments and those of others can we learn how to make this a better text for future readers.

School _____ Your instructor's name _____

1. What did you like the most about the book? _____

_____

_____

_____

2. Do you have any recommendations for ways to improve the next edition of this text? _____

_____

_____

_____

3. In the space below or in a separate letter, please write any other comments you have about the book. (For example, were any chapters or concepts particularly difficult?) We'd be delighted to hear from you!

_____

_____

_____

_____

_____

_____

_____

_____

_____

_____

_____

_____

Optional:

Your name: _____ Date: _____

May Brooks/Cole quote you, either in promotion for *Development Through Life: A Psychosocial Approach, Sixth Edition* or in future publishing ventures?

Yes: _____ No: _____

Sincerely,

Barbara and Philip Newman

FOLD HERE

- -

NO POSTAGE
NECESSARY
IF MAILED
IN THE
UNITED STATES

BUSINESS REPLY MAIL

FIRST CLASS   PERMIT NO. 358   PACIFIC GROVE, CA

POSTAGE WILL BE PAID BY ADDRESSEE

ATT: *Barbara and Philip Newman*

**Brooks/Cole Publishing Company
511 Forest Lodge Road
Pacific Grove, California 93950-9968**

- -

FOLD HERE